Oxford
German
Minidictionary

FOURTH EDITION

German–English
English–German

Deutsch–Englisch
Englisch–Deutsch

D1449717

OXFORD
UNIVERSITY PRESS

OXFORD

UNIVERSITY PRESS

Great Clarendon Street, Oxford OX2 6DP

Oxford University Press is a department of the University of Oxford.
It furthers the University's objective of excellence in research, scholarship,
and education by publishing worldwide in

Oxford   New York

Auckland Cape Town Dar es Salaam Hong Kong Karachi Kuala Lumpur
Madrid Melbourne Mexico City Nairobi New Delhi Shanghai Taipei
Toronto

With offices in

Argentina Austria Brazil Chile Czech Republic France Greece
Guatemala Hungary Italy Japan South Korea Poland Portugal
Singapore Switzerland Thailand Turkey Ukraine Vietnam

Oxford is a registered trade mark of Oxford University Press
in the UK and in certain other countries

British Library Cataloguing in Publication Data
Data available

Library of Congress Cataloging in Publication Data
Data available

ISBN 978-0-19-861044-1

10 9 8 7 6 5

Typeset by Interactive Sciences Ltd, Gloucester
Printed and bound in Italy by Legoprint S.p.A.

Contents

Preface

This new edition of the Oxford German Minidictionary provides a handy and up-to-date reference work for tourists, students, and business people. It fully reflects recent changes to the spelling of German.

The dictionary also includes a unique Phrasefinder, which groups together essential phrases you will need for everyday conversation. The section is thematically arranged and covers key topics including: going places, keeping in touch, food and drink, places to stay, shopping and money, sports and leisure, time and dates, and conversion charts.

Proprietary terms

This dictionary includes some words which are, or are asserted to be, proprietary names or trademarks. Their inclusion does not imply that they have acquired for legal purposes a non-proprietary or general significance, nor is any other judgement implied concerning their legal status. In cases where the editor has some evidence that a word is used as a proprietary name or trademark this is indicated by the symbol ®, but no judgement concerning the legal status of such words is made or implied thereby.

Symbols used in this dictionary

familiar	🄵	familiär
slang	🆇	Slang
old spelling	*	alte Schreibung
proprietary term	®	Markenzeichen

List of contributors

Fourth Edition

Editors
Nicholas Rollin
Roswitha Morris
Eva Vennebusch

Data Capture
Susan Wilkin
Anne McConnell

Proof-reading
Katrin Thier
Stephen Curtis

Third Edition

Editors
Gunhild Prowe
Jill Schneider

Second Edition

Editors
Roswitha Morris
Robin Sawers

Supplementary Material
Robin Sawers
Neil and Roswitha Morris
Valerie Grundy
Eva Vennebusch

First Edition

Editors
Gunhild Prowe
Jill Schneider

Introduction

The text of this dictionary reflects changes to the spelling of German ratified in July 1996. The symbol * has been introduced to refer from the old spelling to the new, preferred one:

As* *nt* -ses, -se *s.* Ass
dasein* *vi sep (sein)* da sein, *s.* da
Schiffahrt* *f s.* Schifffahrt

Where both the old and new forms are valid, an equals sign = is used to refer to the preferred form:

aufwändig *adj* = aufwendig
Tunfisch *m* = Thunfisch

When such forms follow each other alphabetically, they are given with commas, with the preferred form in first place:

Panther, Panter *m* -s, - panther

In phrases, od (oder) is used:

...deine(r,s) *poss pron* yours;
die D~en *od* **d~en** *pl* your family *sg*

On the English–German side, only the preferred German form is given.

- A swung dash ~ represents the headword or that part of the headword preceding a vertical bar |. The initial letter of a German headword is given to show whether or not it is a capital.

- The vertical bar | precedes the part of the headword which is not repeated in compounds or derivatives.

- Square brackets [ ] are used for optional material.

- Parentheses are used after a verb translation to indicate the object; before a verb translation to indicate the subject; before an adjective to indicate a typical noun which it qualifies.

- Parentheses are also used for field or style labels (see the inside covers), and for explanatory matter.

- A bold bullet indicates a new part of speech within an entry.

- *od* (oder) and *or* denote that words or portions of a phrase are synonymous. An oblique stroke / is used where there is a difference in usage or meaning.

- ≈ is used where no exact equivalent exists in the other language.

- A dagger † indicates that a German verb is irregular and that the parts can be found in the verb table on pages xxx–xxx. Compound verbs are not listed there as they follow the pattern of the basic verb.

- The stressed vowel is marked in a German headword by _ (long) or . (short). A phonetic transcription is only given for words which do not follow the normal rules of pronunciation. A guide to German pronunciation rules can be found on pages ix–x.

- Phonetics are given for all English headwords. In blocks of compounds, if no stress is shown, it falls on the first element.

- A change in pronunciation or stress within a block of compounds applies only to that particular word (subsequent entries revert to the pronunciation and stress of the headword).

- German headword nouns are followed by the gender and, with the exception of compound nouns, by the genitive and plural. These are only given at compound nouns if they present some difficulty. Otherwise the user should refer to the final element.

- Nouns that decline like adjectives are entered as follows: **-e(r)** *m/f*, **-e(s)** *nt*.

- Adjectives which have no undeclined form are entered in the feminine form with the masculine and neuter in brackets **-e(r,s).**

- The reflexive pronoun sich is accusative unless marked (*dat*).

Phonetic symbols used for German words

a	Hand	hant	ŋ	lang	laŋ
aː	Bahn	baːn	o	Moral	moˈraːl
ɐ	Ober	ˈoːbɐ	oː	Boot	boːt
ɐ̯	Uhr	uːɐ̯	ǫ	loyal	lǫaˈjaːl
ã	Conférencier	kõferãˈsjeː	õ	Konkurs	kõˈkʊrs
ãː	Abonnement	abɔnəˈmãː	õː	Ballon	baˈlõː
ai̯	weit	vai̯t	ɔ	Post	pɔst
au̯	Haut	hau̯t	ø	Ökonom	økoˈnoːm
b	Ball	bal	øː	Öl	øːl
ç	ich	ɪç	œ	göttlich	ˈɡœtliç
d	dann	dan	ɔy̯	heute	ˈhɔy̯tə
dʒ	Gin	dʒɪn	p	Pakt	pakt
e	Metall	meˈtal	r	Rast	rast
eː	Beet	beːt	s	Hast	hast
ɛ	mästen	ˈmɛstən	ʃ	Schal	ʃaːl
ɛː	wählen	ˈvɛːlən	t	Tal	taːl
ɛ̃	Cousin	kuˈzɛ̃ː	ts	Zahl	tsaːl
ə	Nase	ˈnaːzə	tʃ	Couch	kau̯tʃ
f	Faß	fas	u	Kupon	kuˈpõː
ɡ	Gast	ɡast	uː	Hut	huːt
h	haben	ˈhaːbən	y̆	aktuell	akˈty̆ɛl
i	Rivale	riˈvaːlə	ʊ	Pult	pʊlt
iː	viel	fiːl	v	was	vas
i̯	Aktion	akˈtsi̯oːn	x	Bach	bax
ɪ	Birke	ˈbɪrkə	y	Physik	fyˈziːk
j	ja	jaː	yː	Rübe	ˈryːbə
k	kalt	kalt	ỹ	Nuance	ˈnỹãːsə
l	Last	last	ʏ	Fülle	ˈfʏlə
m	Mast	mast	z	Nase	ˈnaːzə
n	Naht	naːt	ʒ	Regime	reˈʒiːm

ˀ Glottal stop, e.g. Koordination /koˀɔrdinaˈtsi̯on/.

ː length sign after a vowel, e.g. Chrom /kroːm/.

ˈ Stress mark before stressed syllable, e.g. Balkon /balˈkõː/.

Guide to German pronunciation

Consonants

Pronounced as in English with the following exceptions:

b	as	p	
d	as	t	at the end of a word or syllable
g	as	k	
ch	as in Scottish lo<u>ch</u>		after a, o, u, au
	like an exaggerated h as in <u>h</u>uge		after i, e, ä, ö, ü, eu, ei
-chs	as	x	(as in bo<u>x</u>)
-ig	as	-ich / ɪç /	when a suffix
j	as	y	(as in <u>y</u>es)
ps			the p is pronounced
pn			
qu	as	k + v	
s	as	z	(as in <u>z</u>ero) at the beginning of a word
	as	s	(as in bu<u>s</u>) at the end of a word or syllable, before a consonant (except p and t), or when doubled
sch	as	sh	
sp	as	shp	at the beginning of a word or syllable
st	as	sht	at the beginning of a word or syllable
v	as	f	(as in <u>f</u>or)
	as	v	(as in <u>v</u>ery) within a word
w	as	v	(as in <u>v</u>ery)
z	as	ts	

....

Vowels

Approximately as follows:

a	short	as	u	(as in b<u>u</u>t)
	long	as	a	(as in c<u>a</u>r)
e	short	as	e	(as in p<u>e</u>n)
	long	as	a	(as in p<u>a</u>per)
i	short	as	i	(as in b<u>i</u>t)
	long	as	ee	(as in qu<u>ee</u>n)
o	short	as	o	(as in h<u>o</u>t)
	long	as	o	(as in p<u>o</u>pe)
u	short	as	oo	(as in f<u>oo</u>t)
	long	as	oo	(as in b<u>oo</u>t)

Vowels are always short before a double consonant, and long when followed by an h or when double

ie	is pronounced	ee	(as in k<u>ee</u>p)

Diphthongs

au	as	ow	(as in h<u>ow</u>)
ei ai	as	y	(as in m<u>y</u>)
eu äu	as	oy	(as in b<u>oy</u>)

Die für das Englische verwendeten Zeichen der Lautschrift

ɑː	barn	bɑːn	l	lot	lɒt
ɑ̃	nuance	'njuːɑ̃s	m	mat	mæt
æ	fat	fæt	n	not	nɒt
æ̃	lingerie	'læ̃ʒərɪ	ŋ	sing	sɪŋ
aɪ	fine	faɪn	ɒ	got	gɒt
aʊ	now	naʊ	ɔː	paw	pɔː
b	bat	bæt	ɔɪ	boil	bɔɪl
d	dog	dɒg	p	pet	pet
dʒ	jam	dʒæm	r	rat	ræt
e	met	met	s	sip	sɪp
eɪ	fate	feɪt	ʃ	ship	ʃɪp
eə	fairy	'feərɪ	t	tip	tɪp
əʊ	goat	gəʊt	tʃ	chin	tʃɪn
ə	ago	ə'gəʊ	θ	thin	θɪn
ɜː	fur	fɜː(r)	ð	the	ðə
f	fat	fæt	uː	boot	buːt
g	good	gʊd	ʊ	book	bʊk
h	hat	hæt	ʊə	tourism	'tʊərɪzm
ɪ	bit, happy	bɪt, 'hæpɪ	ʌ	dug	dʌg
ɪə	near	nɪə(r)	v	van	væn
iː	meet	miːt	w	win	wɪn
j	yet	jet	z	zip	zɪp
k	kit	kɪt	ʒ	vision	'vɪʒn

ː   bezeichnet Länge des vorhergehenden Vokals, z. B. boot /buːt/.

ˈ   Betonung, steht unmittelbar vor einer betonten Silbe, z. B. ago /əˈgəʊ/.

(r) Ein „r" in runden Klammern wird nur gesprochen, wenn im Textzusammenhang ein Vokal unmittelbar folgt, z. B. fire /ˈfaɪə(r)/; fire at /ˈfaɪər æt/.

Pronunciation of the alphabet/
Aussprache des Alphabets

English/Englisch		*German/Deutsch*
eɪ	**a**	a:
biː	**b**	beː
siː	**c**	tseː
diː	**d**	deː
iː	**e**	eː
ef	**f**	ɛf
dʒiː	**g**	geː
eɪtʃ	**h**	haː
aɪ	**i**	iː
dʒeɪ	**j**	jɔt
keɪ	**k**	kaː
el	**l**	ɛl
em	**m**	ɛm
en	**n**	ɛn
əʊ	**o**	oː
piː	**p**	peː
kjuː	**q**	kuː
aː(r)	**r**	ɛr
es	**s**	ɛs
tiː	**t**	teː
juː	**u**	uː
viː	**v**	fau
'dʌbljuː	**w**	veː
eks	**x**	ɪks
waɪ	**y**	'ʏpsilɔn
zed	**z**	tsɛt
eɪ umlaut	**ä**	ɛː
əʊ umlaut	**ö**	øː
juː umlaut	**ü**	yː
es'zed	**ß**	ɛs'tsɛt

Aa

Aal *m* -[e]s,-e eel

Aas *nt* -es carrion; ⊠ swine

ab *prep* (+ *dat*) from ● *adv* off; (*weg*) away; (*auf Fahrplan*) departs; **ab und zu** now and then; **auf und ab** up and down

abändern *vt sep* alter; (*abwandeln*) modify

Abbau *m* dismantling; (*Kohlen-*) mining. **a~en** *vt sep* dismantle; mine (*Kohle*)

abbeißen† *vt sep* bite off

abbeizen *vt sep* strip

abberufen† *vt sep* recall

abbestellen *vt sep* cancel; **jdn a~** put s.o. off

abbiegen† *vi sep* (*sein*) turn off; [nach] links a~ turn left

Abbildung *f* -,-en illustration

abblättern *vi sep* (*sein*) flake off

abblend|en *vt/i sep* (*haben*) [die Scheinwerfer] a~en dip one's headlights. **A~licht** *nt* dipped headlights *pl*

abbrechen† *v sep* ● *vt* break off; (*abreißen*) demolish; (*Computer*) cancel ● *vi* (*sein/haben*) break off

abbrennen† *v sep* ● *vt* burn off; (*niederbrennen*) burn down ● *vi* (*sein*) burn down

abbringen† *vt sep* dissuade (**von** from)

Abbruch *m* demolition; (*Beenden*) breaking off

abbuchen *vt sep* debit

abbürsten *vt sep* brush down; (*entfernen*) brush off

abdanken *vi sep* (*haben*) resign; (*Herrscher:*) abdicate

abdecken *vt sep* uncover; (*abnehmen*) take off; (*zudecken*) cover; **den Tisch a~** clear the table

abdichten *vt sep* seal

abdrehen *vt sep* turn off

Abdruck *m* (*pl* ⸚e) impression. **a~en** *vt sep* print

abdrücken *vt/i sep* (*haben*) fire; **sich a~** leave an impression

Abend *m* -s,-e evening; **am A~** in the evening; **heute A~** this evening, tonight; **gestern A~** yesterday evening, last night. **A~brot** *nt* supper. **A~essen** *nt* dinner; (*einfacher*) supper. **A~mahl** *nt* (*Relig*) [Holy] Communion. **a~s** *adv* in the evening

Abenteuer *nt* -s,- adventure; (*Liebes-*) affair. **a~lich** *adj* fantastic

aber *conj* but; **oder a~** or else ● *adv* (*wirklich*) really

Aber|glaube *m* superstition. **a~gläubisch** *adj* superstitious

abfahr|en† *v sep* ● *vi* (*sein*) leave; (*Auto:*) drive off ● *vt* take away; (*entlangfahren*) drive along; use (*Fahrkarte*); **abgefahrene Reifen** worn tyres. **A~t** *f* departure; (*Talfahrt*) descent; (*Piste*) run; (*Ausfahrt*) exit

Abfall *m* refuse, rubbish; (*auf der Straße*) litter; (*Industrie-*) waste

abfallen† *vi sep* (*sein*) drop, fall; (*übrig bleiben*) be left (**für** for); (*sich neigen*) slope away. **a~d** *adj* sloping

Abfallhaufen *m* rubbish-dump

abfällig *adj* disparaging

abfangen† *vt sep* intercept

abfärben *vi sep* (*haben*) (*Farbe:*)

run; (Stoff:) not be colour-fast

abfassen vt sep draft

abfertigen vt sep attend to; (zoll-amtlich) clear; **jdn kurz a~** 🅃 give s.o. short shrift

abfeuern vt sep fire

abfind|en vt sep pay off; (entschädigen) compensate; **sich a~en mit** come to terms with. **A~ung** f -,-en compensation

abfliegen vi sep (sein) fly off; (Aviat) take off

abfließen† vi sep (sein) drain or run away

Abflug m (Aviat) departure

Abfluss m drainage; (Öffnung) drain. **A~rohr** nt drain-pipe

abfragen vt sep **jdn** od **jdm Vokabeln a~** test s.o. on vocabulary.

Abfuhr f - removal; (fig) rebuff

abführ|en vt sep take or lead away. **A~mittel** nt laxative

abfüllen vt sep **auf** od **in Flaschen a~** bottle

Abgase ntpl exhaust fumes

abgeben† vt sep hand in; (abliefern) deliver; (verkaufen) sell; (zur Aufbewahrung) leave; (Fußball) pass; (ausströmen) give off; (abfeuern) fire; (verlauten lassen) give; cast (Stimme); **jdm etw a~** give s.o. a share of sth

abgehen† vi sep ● vi (sein) leave; (Theat) exit; (sich lösen) come off; (abgezogen werden) be deducted ● vt walk along

abgehetzt adj harassed. **abgelegen** adj remote. **abgeneigt** adj **etw** (dat) **nicht abgeneigt sein** not be averse to sth. **abgenutzt** adj worn. **Abgeordnete(r)** m/f deputy; (Pol) Member of Parliament. **abgepackt** adj pre-packed

abgeschieden adj secluded

abgeschlossen adj (fig) com-

plete; (Wohnung) self-contained.

abgesehen prep apart (from **von**).

abgespannt adj exhausted. **abgestanden** adj stale. **abgestorben** adj dead; (Glied) numb. **abgetragen** adj worn. **abgewetzt** adj threadbare

abgewinnen† vt sep win (**jdm** from s.o.); **etw** (dat) **Geschmack a~** get a taste for sth

abgewöhnen vt sep **jdm/sich das Rauchen a~** cure s.o. of/give up smoking

abgießen† vt sep pour off; drain (Gemüse)

Abgott m idol

abgöttisch adv **a~ lieben** idolize

abgrenz|en vt sep divide off; (fig) define. **A~ung** f - demarcation

Abgrund m abyss; (fig) depths pl

abgucken vt sep 🅃 copy

Abguss m cast

abhacken vt sep chop off

abhaken vt sep tick off

abhalten† vt sep keep off; (hindern) keep, prevent (**von** from); (veranstalten) hold

abhanden adv **a~ kommen** get lost

Abhandlung f treatise

Abhang m slope

abhängen¹ vt sep (reg) take down; (abkuppeln) uncouple

abhängen² vi sep (haben) depend (**von** on). **a~ig** adj dependent (**von** on). **A~igkeit** f - dependence

abhärten vt sep toughen up

abheben† v sep ● vt take off; (vom Konto) withdraw; **sich a~** stand out (**gegen** against) ● vi (haben) (Cards) cut [the cards]; (Aviat) take off; (Rakete:) lift off

abheften vt sep file

Abhilfe f remedy

abholen vt sep collect

abhör|en vt sep listen to; (überwachen) tap; **jdn od jdm Vokabeln a~en** test s.o. on vocabulary. **A~gerät** nt bugging device

Abitur nt -s ≈ A levels pl

>
> **Abitur** The Abitur, or Matura in Austria, is the final exam taken by pupils at a ▷**GYMNASIUM** or comprehensive school. The result is based on continuous assessment during the last two years before the Abitur, plus examinations in four subjects. The Abitur is an obligatory qualification for university entrance.

abkaufen vt sep buy (dat from)

abklingen† vi sep (sein) die away; (nachlassen) subside

abkochen vt sep boil

abkommen† vi sep (sein) **a~ von** stray from; (aufgeben) give up. **A~** nt -s,- agreement

Abkömmling m -s,-e descendant

abkratzen vt sep scrape off

abkühlen vt/i sep (sein) cool; **sich a~** cool [down]

Abkunft f - origin

abkuppeln vt sep uncouple

abkürz|en vt sep shorten; abbreviate (Wort). **A~ung** f short cut; (Wort) abbreviation

abladen† vt sep unload

Ablage f shelf; (für Akten) tray

ablager|n† vt sep deposit. **A~ung** f -,-en deposit

ablassen† vt sep drain [off]; let off (Dampf)

Ablauf m drain; (Verlauf) course; (Ende) end; (einer Frist) expiry. **a~en†** vt sep ● vi (sein) run or drain off; (verlaufen) go off; (enden) ex-

pire; (Zeit:) run out; (Uhrwerk:) run down ● vt walk along; (absuchen) scour (nach for)

ableg|en v sep ● vt put down; discard (Karte); (abheften) file; (ausziehen) take off; sit, take (Prüfung); **abgelegte Kleidung** cast-offs pl ● vi (haben) take off one's coat; (Naut) cast off. **A~er** m -s,- (Bot) cutting; (Schössling) shoot

ablehn|en vt sep refuse; (missbilligen) reject. **A~ung** f -,-en refusal; rejection

ableit|en vt sep divert; **sich a~en** be derived (von/aus from). **A~ung** f derivation; (Wort) derivative

ablenk|en vt sep deflect; divert (Aufmerksamkeit). **A~ung** f -,-en distraction

ablesen† vt sep read

ablicht|en vt sep photocopy. **A~ung** f photocopy

abliefern vt sep deliver

ablös|en vt sep detach; (abwechseln) relieve; **sich a~en** come off; (sich abwechseln) take turns. **A~ung** f relief

abmach|en vt sep remove; (ausmachen) arrange; (vereinbaren) agree. **A~ung** f -,-en agreement

abmager|n vi sep (sein) lose weight. **A~ungskur** f slimming diet

abmelden vt sep cancel; **sich a~** (im Hotel) check out; (Computer) log off

abmessen† vt sep measure

abmühen (sich) vr sep struggle

Abnäher m -s,- dart

abnehm|en† v sep ● vt take off, remove; pick up (Hörer); **jdm etw a~en** take/(kaufen) buy sth from s.o. ● vi (haben) decrease; (nachlassen) decline; (Person:) lose weight; (Mond:) wane. **A~er** m -s,- buyer

a

Abneigung f dislike (**gegen** of)

abnorm adj abnormal

abnutzen vt sep wear out. **A~ung** f - wear [and tear]

Abon|nement /abonə'mã:/ nt -s,-s subscription. **A~nent** m -en, -en subscriber. **a~nieren** vt take out a subscription to

Abordnung f -,-en deputation

abpassen vt sep wait for; **gut a~** time well

abraten† vi sep (haben) **jdm von etw a~** advise s.o. against sth

abräumen vt/i (haben) clear away

abrechn|en v sep ● vt deduct ● vi (haben) settle up. **A~ung** f settlement; (Rechnung) account

Abreise f departure. **a~n** vi sep (sein) leave

abreißen† v sep ● vt tear off; (demolieren) pull down ● vi (sein) come off

abrichten vt sep train

Abriss m demolition; (Übersicht) summary

abrufen† vt sep call away; (Computer) retrieve

abrunden vt sep round off

abrüst|en vt sep (haben) disarm. **A~ung** f disarmament

abrutschen vi sep (sein) slip

Absage f -,-n cancellation; (Ablehnung) refusal. **a~n** v sep ● vt cancel ● vi (haben) **[jdm] a~n** cancel an appointment [with s.o.]; (auf Einladung) refuse [s.o.'s invitation]

Absatz m heel; (Abschnitt) paragraph; (Verkauf) sale

abschaffen† vt sep abolish; get rid of (Auto, Hund)

abschalten vt/i sep (haben) switch off

Abscheu m - revulsion

abscheulich adj revolting

abschicken vt sep send off

Abschied m -[e]s,-e farewell; (Trennung) parting; **A~ nehmen** say goodbye (**von** to)

abschießen† vt sep shoot down; (abfeuern) fire; launch (Rakete)

abschirmen vt sep shield

abschlagen† vt sep knock off; (verweigern) refuse

Abschlepp|dienst m breakdown service. **a~en** vt sep tow away. **A~seil** nt tow-rope

abschließen† v sep ● vt lock; (beenden, abmachen) conclude; make (Wette); balance (Bücher) ● vi (haben) lock up; (enden) end. **a~d** adv in conclusion

Abschluss m conclusion. **A~zeugnis** nt diploma

abschmecken vt sep season

abschmieren vt sep lubricate

abschneiden† v sep ● vt cut off ● vi (haben) **gut/schlecht a~** do well/badly

Abschnitt m section; (Stadium) stage; (Absatz) paragraph

abschöpfen vt sep skim off

abschrauben vt sep unscrew

abschreck|en vt sep deter; (Culin) put in cold water (Ei). **a~end** adj repulsive. **A~ungsmittel** nt deterrent

abschreib|en† v sep ● vt copy; (Comm & fig) write off ● vi (haben) copy. **A~ung** f (Comm) depreciation

Abschrift f copy

Abschuss m shooting down; (Abfeuern) firing; (Raketen-) launch

abschüssig adj sloping; (steil) steep

abschwellen† vi sep (sein) go down

absehbar adj **in a~barer Zeit** in

the foreseeable future. **a~en†** *vt/i sep* (*haben*) copy; (*voraussehen*) foresee; **a~en von** disregard; (*aufgeben*) refrain from

abseits *adv* apart; (*Sport*) offside ● *prep* (+ *gen*) away from. **A~** *nt -* (*Sport*) offside

absend|en† *vt sep* send off. **A~er** *m* sender

absetzen *vt sep* ● *vt* put or set down; (*ablagern*) deposit; (*abnehmen*) take off; (*abbrechen*) stop; (*entlassen*) dismiss; (*verkaufen*) sell; (*abziehen*) deduct ● *vi* (*haben*) pause

Absicht *f -,-en* intention; **mit A~** intentionally, on purpose

absichtlich *adj* intentional

absitzen† *v sep* ● *vi* (*sein*) dismount ● *vt* ⓣ serve (*Strafe*)

absolut *adj* absolute

absolvieren *vt* complete; (*bestehen*) pass

absonder|n *vt sep* separate; (*ausscheiden*) secrete. **A~ung** *f -,-en* secretion

absorbieren *vt* absorb

abspeisen *vt sep* fob off (mit with)

absperr|en *vt sep* cordon off; (*abstellen*) turn off; (*SGer*) lock. **A~ung** *f -,-en* barrier

abspielen *vt sep* play; (*Fußball*) pass; **sich a~** take place

Absprache *f* agreement

absprechen† *vt sep* arrange; **sich a~** agree

abspringen† *vi sep* (*sein*) jump off; (*mit Fallschirm*) parachute; (*abgehen*) come off

Absprung *m* jump

abspülen *vt sep* rinse

abstamm|en *vi sep* (*haben*) be descended (**von** from). **A~ung** *f -*

descent

Abstand *m* distance; (*zeitlich*) interval; **A~ halten** keep one's distance

abstatten *vt sep* **jdm einen Besuch a~** pay s.o. a visit

Abstecher *m -s,-* detour

abstehen† *vi sep* (*haben*) stick out

absteigen† *vi sep* (*sein*) dismount; (*niedersteigen*) descend; (*Fußball*) be relegated

abstell|en *vt sep* put down; (*lagern*) store; (*parken*) park; (*abschalten*) turn off. **A~gleis** *nt* siding. **A~raum** *m* box-room

absterben† *vi sep* (*sein*) die; (*gefühllos werden*) go numb

Abstieg *m -[e]s,-e* descent; (*Fußball*) relegation

abstimm|en *v sep* ● *vi* (*haben*) vote (**über** + *acc* on) ● *vt* coordinate (**auf** + *acc* with). **A~ung** *f* vote

Abstinenzler *m -s, -* teetotaller

abstoßen† *vt sep* knock off; (*verkaufen*) sell; (*fig*: *ekeln*) repel. **a~d** *adj* repulsive

abstreiten† *vt sep* deny

Abstrich *m* (*Med*) smear

abstufen *vt sep* grade

Absturz *m* fall; (*Aviat*) crash

abstürzen *vi sep* (*sein*) fall; (*Aviat*) crash

absuchen *vt sep* search

absurd *adj* absurd

Abszess *m -es,-e* abscess

Abt *m -[e]s,˙e* abbot

abtasten *vt sep* feel; (*Techn*) scan

abtauen *vt/i sep* (*sein*) thaw; (*entfrosten*) defrost

Abtei *f -,-en* abbey

Abteil *nt* compartment

Abteilung *f -,-en* section; (*Admin*, *Comm*) department

abtragen† *vt sep* clear; (*einebnen*)

level; (abnutzen) wear out

abträglich adj detrimental
(dat to)

abtreib|en† vt sep (Naut) drive off
course; **ein Kind a~en lassen** have
an abortion. **A~ung** f -,-en
abortion

abtrennen vt sep detach; (abtei-
len) divide off

Abtreter m -s,- doormat

abtrocknen vt/i sep (haben) dry;
sich a~ dry oneself

abtropfen vi sep (sein) drain

abtun† vt sep (fig) dismiss

abwägen† vt sep (fig) weigh

abwandeln vt sep modify

abwarten v sep ● vt wait for ● vi
(haben) wait [and see]

abwärts adv down[wards]

Abwasch m -[e]s washing-up;
(Geschirr) dirty dishes pl. **a~en**† v
sep ● vt wash; wash up (Geschirr);
(entfernen) wash off ● vi (haben)
wash up. **A~lappen** m dishcloth

Abwasser nt -s,‥ sewage. **A~ka-
nal** m sewer

abwechseln vi/r sep (haben)
[sich] **a~** alternate; (Personen:) take
turns. **a~d** adj alternate

Abwechslung f -,-en change;
zur A~ for a change

abwegig adj absurd

Abwehr f - defence; (Widerstand)
resistance; (Pol) counter-espionage.
a~en vt sep ward off. **A~system**
nt immune system

abweich|en† vi sep (sein) devi-
ate/(von Regel) depart (von from);
(sich unterscheiden) differ (von
from). **a~end** adj divergent; (verschieden) different. **A~ung** f -,-en
deviation

abweis|en† vt sep turn down;
turn away (Person). **a~end** adj un-

friendly. **A~ung** f rejection

abwenden† vt sep turn away;
(verhindern) avert

abwerfen† vt sep throw off;
throw (Reiter); (Aviat) drop; (Kartenspiel) discard; shed (Haut, Blätter);
yield (Gewinn)

abwert|en vt sep devalue.
A~ung f -,-en devaluation

Abwesenheit f - absence; ab-
sent-mindedness

abwickeln vt sep unwind; (erledigen) settle

abwischen vt sep wipe

abzahlen vt sep pay off

abzählen vt sep count

Abzahlung f instalment

Abzeichen nt badge

abzeichnen vt sep copy

Abzieh|bild nt transfer. **a~en**† v
sep ● vt pull off; take off (Laken);
strip (Bett); (häuten) skin; (Phot)
print; run off (Kopien); (zurückziehen) withdraw; (abrechnen) deduct
● vi (sein) go away, (Rauch:) escape

Abzug m withdrawal; (Abrechnung)
deduction; (Phot) print (Korrektur-
proof; (am Gewehr) trigger; (A~söff-
nung) vent; **A~e** pl deductions

abzüglich prep (+ gen) less

Abzugshaube f [cooker] hood

abzweig|en v sep ● vi (sein)
branch off ● vt divert. **A~ung** f
-,-en junction; (Gabelung) fork

ach int oh; **a~ je!** oh dear! **a~ so**
I see

Achse f -,-n axis; (Rad-) axle

Achsel f -,-n shoulder. **A~höhle** f
armpit. **A~zucken** nt -s shrug

acht inv adj eight, **A~**¹ f -,-en eight

Acht f **A~ geben** be careful; **A~
geben auf** (+ acc) look after; **außer
A~ lassen** disregard; **sich in A~
nehmen** be careful

acht|e(r,s) adj eighth. **a~eckig** adj octagonal. **A~el** nt -s,- eighth

achten vt respect ● vi (haben) **a~ auf** (+ acc) pay attention to; (aufpassen) look after

Achterbahn f roller-coaster

achtlos adj careless

achtsam adj careful

Achtung f - respect (**vor** + dat for); **A~!** look out!

acht|zehn inv adj eighteen. **a~zehnte(r,s)** adj eighteenth. **a~zig** a inv eighty. **a~zigste(r,s)** adj eightieth

Acker m -s,ˉ field. **A~bau** m agriculture. **A~land** nt arable land

addieren vt/i (haben) add

Addition /-'tsio:n/ f -,-en addition

ade int goodbye

Adel m -s nobility

Ader f -,-n vein

Adjektiv nt -s,-e adjective

Adler m -s,- eagle

adlig adj noble. **A~e(r)** m nobleman

Administration /-'tsio:n/ f - administration

Admiral m -s,ˉe admiral

adop|tieren vt adopt. **A~tion** f -,-en adoption. **A~tiveltern** pl adoptive parents. **A~tivkind** nt adopted child

Adrenalin nt -s adrenalin

Adres|se f -,-n address. **a~sieren** vt address

Adria f - Adriatic

Adverb nt -s,-ien adverb

Affäre f -,-n affair

Affe m -n,-n monkey; (Menschen-) ape

affektiert adj affected

affig adj affected; (eitel) vain

Afrika nt -s Africa

Afrikan|er(in) m -s,- (f -,-nen) African. **a~isch** adj African

After m -s,- anus

Agen|t(in) m -en,-en (f -,-nen) agent. **A~tur** f -,-en agency

Aggres|sion f -,-en aggression. **a~siv** adj aggressive

Agnostiker m -s,- agnostic

Ägypt|en /ɛ'gʏptən/ nt -s Egypt. **Ä~er(in)** m -s,- (f -,-nen) Egyptian. **ä~isch** adj Egyptian

ähneln vi (haben) (+ dat) resemble; **sich ä~** be alike

ahnen vt have a presentiment of; (vermuten) suspect

Ahnen mpl ancestors. **A~forschung** f genealogy

ähnlich adj similar; **jdm ä~ sehen** resemble s.o. **Ä~keit** f -,-en similarity; resemblance

Ahnung f -,-en premonition; (Vermutung) idea, hunch

Ahorn m -s,-e maple

Ähre f -,-n ear [of corn]

Aids /eɪts/ nt - Aids

Airbag /'ɛːɐ̯bɛk/ m -s, -s (Auto) air bag

Akademie f -,-n academy

Akadem|iker(in) m -s,- (f -,-nen) university graduate. **a~isch** adj academic

akklimatisieren (sich) vr become acclimatized

Akkord m -[e]s,-e (Mus) chord. **A~arbeit** f piecework

Akkordeon nt -s,-s accordion

Akkumulator m -s,-en (Electr) accumulator

Akkusativ m -s,-e accusative. **A~objekt** nt direct object

Akrobat|(in) m -en,-en (f -,-nen) acrobat. **a~isch** adj acrobatic

Akt m -[e]s,-e act; (Kunst) nude

Akte f -,-n file; **A~n** documents.
A~ntasche f briefcase

Aktie /'aktsjə/ f -,-n (*Comm*) share.
A~ngesellschaft f joint-stock
company

Aktion /ak'tsjoːn/ f -,-en action.
A~är m -s,-e shareholder

aktiv adj active

aktuell adj topical; (*gegenwärtig*)
current

Akupunktur f - acupuncture

Akustik f - acoustics pl.

akut adj acute

Akzent m -[e]s,-e accent

akzept|abel adj acceptable.
a~ieren vt accept

Alarm m -s alarm; (*Mil*) alert.
a~ieren vt alert; (*beunruhigen*) alarm

Albdruck m nightmare

albern adj silly ● vi (haben) play
the fool

Albtraum m nightmare

Album nt -s,-ben album

Algebra f - algebra

Algen fpl algae

Algerien /-jən/ nt -s Algeria

Alibi nt -s,-s alibi

Alimente pl maintenance sg

Alkohol m -s alcohol. **a~frei** adj
non-alcoholic

Alkohol|iker(in) m -s,- (f
-,-nen) alcoholic. **a~isch** adj alcoholic

Alkopop nt -(s), -s alcopop

all inv pron all das/mein Geld all
the/my money; **all dies** all this

All nt -s universe

alle pred adj finished

all|e(r,s) pron all; (jeder) every;
a~es everything, all; (alle Leute)
everyone; **a~e** pl all; **a~es Geld** all
the money; **a~e beide** both [of

them/us]; **a~e Tage** every day;
a~e drei Jahre every three years;
ohne a~n Grund without any
reason; **vor a~em** above all; **a~es
in a~em** all in all; **a~es aussteigen!** all change!

Allee f -,-n avenue

allein adv alone; (nur) only; **a~
stehend** single; **a~ der Gedanke**
the mere thought; **von a~[e]** of
its/(*Person*) one's own accord; (*automatisch*) automatically ● conj but.
A~erziehende(r) m/f single parent. **a~ig** adj sole. **A~stehende** pl
single people

allemal adv every time; (*gewiss*)
certainly

allenfalls adv at most; (*eventuell*)
possibly

aller|beste(r,s) adj very best;
am a~besten best of all. **a~dings**
adv indeed; (*zwar*) admittedly.
a~erste(r,s) adj very first

Allergie f -,-n allergy

allergisch adj allergic (gegen) to)

Aller|heiligen nt -s All Saints
Day. **a~höchstens** adv at the very
most. **a~lei** inv adj all sorts of
● pron all sorts of things. **a~letzte(r,s)** adj very last. **a~liebste(r,s)**
adj favourite ● adv am a~liebsten
for preference; **am a~liebsten**
haben like best of all. **a~meiste(r,s)** adj most ● adv am a~meisten most of all. **A~seelen** nt -s
All Souls Day. **a~wenigste(r,s)** adj
very least ● adv am a~wenigsten
least of all

allgemein adj general; **im A~en**
(a~en) in general. **A~heit** f -
community; (*Öffentlichkeit*) general
public

Allianz f -,-en alliance

Alligator m -s,-en alligator

alliiert adj allied; **die A~en** pl

the Allies

all|jährlich *adj* annual. **a~mäh·lich** *adj* gradual

Alltag *m* working day; **der A~** (*fig*) everyday life

alltäglich *adj* daily; (*gewöhnlich*) everyday; (*Mensch*) ordinary

alltags *adv* on weekdays

allzu *adv* [far] too; **a~ oft** all too often; **a~ vorsichtig** over-cautious

Alm *f* -,-en alpine pasture

Almosen *ntpl* alms

Alpdruck* *m* = Albdruck

Alpen *pl* Alps

Alphabet *nt* -[e]s,-e alphabet. **a~isch** *adj* alphabetical

Alptraum* *m* = Albtraum

als *conj* as; (*zeitlich*) when; (*mit Komparativ*) than; **nichts als** nothing but; **als ob** as if or though

also *adv & conj* so; **a~ gut** all right then; **na a~!** there you are!

alt *adj* old; (*gebraucht*) second-hand; (*ehemalig*) former; **alt werden** grow old

Alt *m* -s, -e (*Mus*) contralto

Altar *m* -s, ⁺e altar

Alte(r) *m/f* old man/woman; **die A~en** old people. **A~eisen** *nt* scrap iron. **A~enheim** *nt* old people's home

Alter *nt* -s,- age; (*Bejahrtheit*) old age; **im A~ von** at the age of

älter *adj* older; **mein ä~er Bruder** my elder brother

altern *vi* (*sein*) age

Alternative *f* -,-n alternative

Alters|grenze *f* age limit. **A~heim** *nt* old people's home. **A~rente** *f* old-age pension. **a~schwach** *adj* old and infirm. **A~vorsorge** *f* provision for old age

Alter|tum *nt* -s, ⁺er antiquity.

a~tümlich *adj* old; (*altmodisch*) old-fashioned

altklug *adj* precocious

alt|modisch *adj* old-fashioned. **A~papier** *nt* waste paper. **A~warenhändler** *m* second-hand dealer

Alufolie *f* [aluminium] foil

Aluminium *nt* -s aluminium, (*Amer*) aluminum

am *prep* = an dem; **am Montag** on Monday; **am Morgen** in the morning; **am besten** [the] best

Amateur /-'tø:ɐ/ *m* -s,-e amateur

Ambition /-'tsio:n/ *f* -,-en ambition

Amboss *m* -es,-e anvil

ambulan|t *adj* out-patient ● *adv* **a~t behandeln** treat as an out-patient. **A~z** *f* -,-en out-patients' department

Ameise *f* -,-n ant

amen *int*, **A~** *nt* -s amen

Amerika *nt* -s America

Amerikan|er(in) *m* -s,- (*f* -,-nen) American. **a~isch** *adj* American

Ammoniak *nt* -s ammonia

Amnestie *f* -,-n amnesty

amoralisch *adj* amoral

Ampel *f* -,-n traffic lights *pl*

Amphitheater *nt* amphitheatre

Amputation /-'tsio:n/ *f* -,-en amputation. **a~ieren** *vt* amputate

Amsel *f* -,-n blackbird

Amt *nt* -[e]s, ⁺er office; (*Aufgabe*) task; (*Teleph*) exchange. **a~lich** *adj* official. **A~szeichen** *nt* dialling tone

Amulett *nt* -[e]s,-e [lucky] charm

amüs|ant *adj* amusing. **a~ieren** *vt* amuse; **sich a~ieren** be amused (**über** + *acc* at); (*sich vergnügen*) enjoy oneself

a **an**
● preposition (+ dative)

! Note that **an** plus **dem** can become **am**

····➤ *(räumlich)* on; *(Gebäude, Ort)* at. **an der Wand** on the wall. **Frankfurt an der Oder** Frankfurt on [the] Oder. **an der Ecke** at the corner. **am Bahnhof** at the station. **an vorbei** past. **am 24. Mai** on May 24th

····➤ *(zeitlich)* on. **am Montag** on Monday. **an jedem Sonntag** every Sunday

····➤ *(sonstige Verwendungen)* **arm/reich an Vitaminen** low/rich in vitamins. **jdn an etw erkennen** recognize s.o. by sth. **an etw leiden** suffer from sth. **an einer Krankheit sterben** die of a disease. **an [und für] sich** actually

● preposition (+ accusative)

! Note that **an** plus **das** can become **ans**

····➤ to. **schicke es an deinen Bruder** send it to your brother. **er ging ans Fenster** he went to the window

····➤ *(auf, gegen)* on. **etw an die Wand hängen** to hang sth on the wall. **lehne es an den Baum** lean it on or against the tree

····➤ *(sonstige Verwendungen)* **an etw/jdn glauben** believe in sth/s.o. **an etw denken** think of sth. **sich an etw erinnern** remember sth

● adverb

····➤ *(auf Fahrplan)* **Köln an: 9.15** arriving Cologne 09.15

····➤ *(angeschaltet)* on. **die Waschmaschine/der Fernseher/das Licht/das Gas ist an** the washing machine/television/light/gas is on

····➤ *(ungefähr)* around; about. **an [die] 20000 DM** around or about 20,000 DM

····➤ *(in die Zukunft)* **von heute an** from today (onwards)

analog *adj* analogous; *(Computer)* analog. **A~ie** *f* -,-n analogy

Analphabet *m* -en,-en illiterate person. **a~isch** *adj* -s illiterate

Analy|se *f* -,-n analysis. **a~sieren** *vt* analyse. **A~tiker** *m* -s,- analyst. **a~tisch** *adj* analytical

Anämie *f* - anaemia

Ananas *f* -,-[se] pineapple

Anatomie *f* - anatomy

Anbau *m* cultivation; *(Gebäude)* extension. **a~en** *vt sep* build on; *(anpflanzen)* cultivate, grow

anbei *adv* enclosed

anbeißen† *v sep* ● *vt* take a bite of ● *vi (haben) (Fisch:)* bite

anbeten *vt sep* worship

Anbetracht *m* in **A~** (+ *gen*) in view of

anbieten† *vt sep* offer; **sich a~** offer (**zu** to)

anbinden† *vt sep* tie up

Anblick *m* sight. **a~en** *vt sep* look at

anbrechen† *v sep* ● *vt* start on; break into *(Vorräte)* ● *vi (haben) (Tag:)* break; *(Nacht:)* fall

anbrennen† *v sep* ● *vt* light ● *vi (sein)* burn

anbringen† *vt sep* bring [along]; *(befestigen)* fix

Anbruch *m (fig)* dawn; **bei A~ des Tages/der Nacht** at

11   **Andacht | anfühlen**

daybreak/nightfall

Andacht f -,-en reverence; (Gottesdienst) prayers pl

andächtig adj reverent; (fig) rapt

andauern vi sep (haben) last; (anhalten) continue. **a~d** adj persistent; (ständig) constant

Andenken nt -s,- memory; (Souvenir) souvenir

ander|e(r,s) adj other; (verschie-
den) different; (nächste) next; **ein
a~er, eine a~e** another ● pron
der a~e/die a~en the other/
others; **ein a~er** another [one];
(Person) someone else; **kein a~er**
no one else; **einer nach dem a~en**
one after the other; **alles a~e/
nichts a~e** everything/nothing
else; **unter a~em** among other
things. **a~enfalls** adv otherwise.
a~erseits adv on the other hand.
a~mal adv **ein a~mal** another time

ändern vt alter; (wechseln) change;
sich ä~ change

anders pred adj different; **a~ werden** change ● adv differently; (riechen, schmecken) different; (sonst)
else; **jemand a~** someone else

andersherum adv the other
way round

anderthalb inv adj one and a
half; **a~ Stunden** an hour and
a half

Änderung f -,-en alteration;
(Wechsel) change

andeut|en vt sep indicate; (anspie-
len) hint at. **A~ung** f -,-en indication; hint

Andrang m rush (nach for); (Gedränge) crush

androhen vt sep jdm etw **a~**
threaten s.o. with sth

aneignen vt sep sich (dat) **a~** appropriate; (lernen) learn

aneinander adv & prefix together;
(denken) of one another; **a~ vorbei**
past one another; **a~ geraten**
quarrel

Anekdote f -,-n anecdote

anerkannt adj acknowledged

anerkenn|en† vt sep acknow-
ledge, recognize; (würdigen) appreciate. **a~end** adj approving.
A~ung f - acknowledgement, recognition; appreciation

anfahren† v sep ● vt deliver; (streifen) hit ● vi (sein) start

Anfall m fit, attack. **a~en†** v sep
● vt attack ● vi (sein) arise; (Zinsen:)
accrue

anfällig adj susceptible (für to);
(zart) delicate

Anfang m -s,¨e beginning, start;
zu od **am A~** at the beginning;
(anfangs) at first. **a~en†** vt/i sep
(haben) begin, start; (tun) do

Anfänger(in) m -s,- (f -,-nen)
beginner

anfangs adv at first. **A~buch-
stabe** m initial letter. **A~gehalt** nt
starting salary

anfassen vt sep touch; (behandeln)
treat; tackle (Arbeit); **sich a~**
hold hands

anfechten† vt sep contest

anfertigen vt sep make

anfeuchten vt sep moisten

anflehen vt sep implore, beg

Anflug m (Avia) approach

anforder|n vt sep demand;
(Comm) order. **A~ung** f demand

Anfrage f enquiry. **a~n** vi sep
(haben) enquire, ask

anfreunden (sich) vr sep make
friends (mit with)

anfügen vt sep add

anfühlen vt sep feel; **sich weich
a~** feel soft

a

anführ|en vt sep lead; (zitieren) quote; (angeben) give. **A~er** m leader. **A~ungszeichen** ntpl quotation marks

Angabe f statement; (Anweisung) instruction; (Tennis) service; **nähere A~n** particulars

angeb|en v sep ● vt state; give (Namen, Grund); (anzeigen) indicate; set (Tempo) ● vi (haben) (Tennis) serve; (⊡: protzen) show off. **A~er(in)** m -s,- (f -,-nen) ⊡ show-off. **A~erei** f - ⊡ showing-off

angeblich adj alleged

angeboren adj innate; (Med) congenital

Angebot nt offer; (Auswahl) range; **A~ und Nachfrage** supply and demand

angebracht adj appropriate

angeheiratet adj (Onkel, Tante) by marriage

angeheitert adj ⊡ tipsy

angehen v sep ● vi (sein) begin, start; (Licht, Radio:) come on; (anwachsen) take root; **a~ gegen** fight ● vt attack; (bitten) ask (um for); (betreffen) concern

angehör|en vi sep (haben) (+ dat) belong to. **A~ige(r)** m/f relative

Angeklagte(r) m/f accused

Angel f -,-n fishing-rod; (Tür-) hinge

Angelegenheit f matter

Angel|haken m fish-hook. **a~n** vi (haben) fish (nach for); **a~n gehen** go fishing ● vt (fangen) catch. **A~rute** f fishing-rod

angelsächsisch adj Anglo-Saxon

angemessen adj commensurate (dat with); (passend) appropriate

angenehm adj pleasant; (bei Vorstellung) **a~!** delighted to meet you!

angeregt adj animated

angesehen adj respected; (Firma) reputable

angesichts prep (+ gen) in view of

angespannt adj intent; (Lage) tense

Angestellte(r) m/f employee

angewandt adj applied

angewiesen adj dependent (**auf** + acc on); **auf sich selbst a~** on one's own

angewöhnen vt sep jdm etw **a~** get s.o. used to sth; **sich** (dat) **etw a~** get into the habit of doing sth

Angewohnheit f habit

Angina f - tonsillitis

angleichen vt sep adjust (dat to)

anglikanisch adj Anglican

Anglistik f - English [language and literature]

Angorakatze f Persian cat

angreif|en† vt sep attack; tackle (Arbeit); (schädigen) damage. **A~er** m -s,- attacker; (Pol) aggressor

angrenzen vi sep (haben) adjoin (an etw acc sth). **a~d** adj adjoining

Angriff m attack; **in A~ nehmen** tackle. **a~slustig** adj aggressive

Angst f -,¨e fear; (Psychology) anxiety; (Sorge) worry (um about); **A~ haben** be afraid (vor + dat of); (sich sorgen) be worried (um about); **jdm A~ machen** frighten s.o.

ängstigen vt sep frighten; (Sorge machen) worry; **sich ä~** be frightened; be worried (um about)

ängstlich adj nervous; (scheu) timid; (verängstigt) frightened; scared; (besorgt) anxious

angucken vt sep ⊡ look at

angurten (sich) vr sep fasten one's seat belt

anhaben† vt sep have on; **er/es kann mir nichts a~** (fig) he/it cannot hurt me

anhalt|en† *v sep* ● *vt* stop; hold
(*Atem*); **jdn zur Arbeit a~en** urge
s.o. to work ● *vi* (*haben*) stop; (*andauern*) continue. **a~end** *adj* persistent. **A~e(in)** *m* -s,- (*f* -,-nen)
hitchhiker; **per A~er fahren** hitch-
hike. **A~spunkt** *m* clue

anhand *prep* (+ *gen*) with the
aid of

Anhang *m* appendix

anhängen¹ *vt sep* (*reg*) hang up;
(*befestigen*) attach

anhäng|en²† *vi* (*haben*) be a fol-
lower of. **A~er** *m* -s,- follower;
(*Auto*) trailer; (*Schild*) [tie-on] label;
(*Schmuck*) pendant. **A~erin** *f*
-,-nen follower. **a~lich** *adj* affectionate

anhäufen *vt sep* pile up

Anhieb *m* **auf A~** straight away

Anhöhe *f* hill

anhören *vt sep* listen to; **sich gut
a~** sound good

animieren *vt* encourage (**zu** to)

Anis *m* -es aniseed

Anker *m* -s,- anchor; **vor A~
gehen** drop anchor. **a~n** *vi* (*haben*)
anchor; (*liegen*) be anchored

anketten *vt sep* chain up

Anklage *f* accusation; (*Jur*) charge;
(*Ankläger*) prosecution. **A~bank** *f*
dock. **a~n** *vt sep* accuse (*gen* of);
(*Jur*) charge (*gen* with)

Ankläger *m* accuser; (*Jur*) pros-
ecutor

anklammern *vt sep* clip on; **sich
a~** cling (**an** + *acc* to)

ankleben *vt sep* ● *vt* stick on ● *vi*
(*sein*) stick (**an** + *dat* to)

anklicken *vt sep* click on

anklopfen *vi sep* (*haben*) knock

anknipsen *vt sep* 🔲 switch on

ankommen† *vi sep* (*sein*) arrive;

(*sich nähern*) approach; **gut a~** arrive safely; (*fig*) go down well (**bei**
with); **nicht a~ gegen** (*fig*) be no
match for; **a~ auf** (+ *acc*) depend
on; **das kommt darauf an** it [all]
depends

ankreuzen *vt sep* mark with
a cross

ankündig|en *vt sep* announce.
A~ung *f* announcement

Ankunft *f* - arrival

ankurbeln *vt sep* (*fig*) boost

anlächeln *vt sep* smile at

anlachen *vt sep* smile at

Anlage *f* -,-n installation; (*Indu-
strie-*) plant; (*Komplex*) complex;
(*Geld-*) investment; (*Plan*) layout;
(*Beilage*) enclosure; (*Veranlagung*)
aptitude; (*Neigung*) predisposition;
(*öffentliche*) **A~n** [public] gardens;
als A~ enclosed

Anlass *m* -es,¨e reason; (*Gelegenheit*) occasion; **A~ geben zu** give
cause for

anlass|en† *vt sep* (*Auto*) start; 🔲
leave on (*Licht*); keep on (*Mantel*).
A~er *m* -s,- starter

anlässlich *prep* (+ *gen*) on the occasion of

Anlauf *m* (*Sport*) run-up; (*fig*) attempt. **a~en**† *v sep* ● *vi* (*sein*) start;
(*beschlagen*) mist up; (*Metall:*) tarnish; **rot a~en** blush ● *vt* (*Naut*)
call at

anlegen *v sep* ● *vt* put (**an** + *acc*
against); put on (*Kleidung, Verband*);
lay back (*Ohren*); aim (*Gewehr*); (*investieren*) invest; (*ausgeben*) spend
(**für** on); draw up (*Liste*); **es darauf
a~** (*fig*) aim (**zu** to) ● *vi* (*haben*)
(*Schiff:*) moor; **a~ auf** (+ *acc*)
aim at

anlehnen *vt sep* lean (**an** + *acc*
against); **sich a~** lean (**an** + *acc*
on)

Anleihe *f* -,-n loan

anleit|en *vt sep* instruct. **A~ung** *f* instructions *pl*

anlernen *vt sep* train

Anliegen *nt* -s,- request; (*Wunsch*) desire

anlieg|en† *vi sep* (haben) [eng] **a~en** fit closely; [eng] **a~end** close-fitting. **A~er** *mpl* residents; **'A~er frei'** 'access for residents only'

anlügen† *vt sep* lie to

anmachen *vt sep* 🔲 fix; (*anschalten*) turn on; dress (*Salat*)

anmalen *vt sep* paint

Anmarsch *m* (*Mil*) approach

anmeld|en *vt sep* announce; (*Admin*) register; **sich a~en** say that one is coming; (*Admin*) register; (*Sch*) enrol; (*im Hotel*) check in; (*beim Arzt*) make an appointment; (*Computer*) log on. **A~ung** *f* announcement; (*Admin*) registration; (*Sch*) enrolment; (*Termin*) appointment

anmerk|en *vt sep* mark; **sich** (*dat*) **etw a~en lassen** show sth. **A~ung** *f* -,-en note

Anmut *f* - grace; (*Charme*) charm

anmutig *adj* graceful

annähen *vt sep* sew on

annäher|nd *adj* approximate. **A~ungsversuche** *mpl* advances

Annahme *f* -,-n acceptance; (*Adoption*) adoption; (*Vermutung*) assumption

annehm|bar *adj* acceptable. **a~en†** *vt sep* accept; (*adoptieren*) adopt; acquire (*Gewohnheit*); (*sich zulegen, vermuten*) assume; **angenommen, dass** assuming that. **A~lichkeiten** *fpl* comforts

Anno *adv* **A~** 1920 in the year 1920

Annon|ce /aˈnõːsə/ *f* -,-n advertisement. **a~cieren** *vt/i* (haben) advertise

annullieren *vt* annul; cancel

Anomalie *f* -,-n anomaly

anonym *adj* anonymous

Anorak *m* -s,-s anorak

anordn|en *vt sep* arrange; (*befehlen*) order. **A~ung** *f* arrangement; order

anorganisch *adj* inorganic

anormal *adj* abnormal

anpass|en *vt sep* try on; (*angleichen*) adapt (*dat* to); **sich a~** adapt (*dat* to). **A~ung** *f* - adaptation. **a~ungsfähig** *adj* adaptable. **A~ungsfähigkeit** *f* adaptability

Anpfiff *m* (Sport) kick-off

Anprall *m* -[e]s impact. **a~en** *vi sep* (sein) strike (**an etw** *acc* sth)

anpreisen† *vt sep* commend

Anprob|e *f* fitting. **a~ieren** *vt sep* try on

anrechnen *vt sep* count (**als** as); (*berechnen*) charge for; (*verrechnen*) allow (*Summe*)

Anrecht *nt* right (**auf** + *acc* to)

Anrede *f* [form of] address. **a~n** *vt sep* address; speak to

anreg|en *vt sep* stimulate; (*ermuntern*) encourage (**zu** to); (*vorschlagen*) suggest. **a~end** *adj* stimulating. **A~ung** *f* stimulation; (*Vorschlag*) suggestion

Anreise *f* journey; (*Ankunft*) arrival. **a~n** *vi sep* (sein) arrive

Anreiz *m* incentive

Anrichte *f* -,-n sideboard. **a~n** *vt sep* (*Culin*) prepare; (*garnieren*) garnish (**mit** with); (*verursachen*) cause

anrüchig *adj* disreputable

Anruf *m* call. **A~beantworter** *m* -s,- answering machine. **a~en†** *v sep* ● *vt* call; (*bitten*) call on (**um** for); (*Teleph*) ring ● *vi* (haben) ring (**bei jdm** s.o.)

anrühren vt sep touch; (verrühren) mix

ans prep = **an das**

Ansage f announcement. **a~n** vt sep announce

ansammel|n vt sep collect; (anhäufen) accumulate; **sich a~eln** collect; (sich häufen) accumulate; (Leute:) gather. **A~lung** f collection; (Menschen:) crowd

ansässig adj resident

Ansatz m beginning; (Versuch) attempt

anschaffen vt sep [sich dat] etw **a~en** acquire/(kaufen) buy sth

anschalten vt sep switch on

anschau|en vt sep look at. **a~lich** adj vivid. **A~ung** f -,-en (fig) view

Anschein m appearance. **a~end** adv apparently

anschirren vt sep harness

Anschlag m notice; (Vor-) estimate; (Überfall) attack (auf + acc on); (Mus) touch; (Techn) stop. **a~en†** v sep ● vt put up (Aushang); strike (Note, Taste); cast on (Masche); (beschädigen) chip ● vi (haben) strike/(stoßen) knock (an + acc against); (wirken) be effective ● vi (sein) knock (an + acc against)

anschließen† v sep ● vt connect (an + acc to); (zufügen) add; **sich a~ an** (+ acc) (anstoßen) adjoin; (folgen) follow; (sich anfreunden) become friendly with; **sich jdm a~** join s.o. ● vi (haben) **a~ an** (+ acc) adjoin; (folgen) follow. **a~d** adj adjoining; (zeitlich) following ● adv afterwards

Anschluss m connection; (Kontakt) contact; **A~ finden** make friends; **im A~ an** (+ acc) after

anschmiegsam adj affectionate

anschmieren vt sep smear

anschnallen vt sep strap on; **sich a~** fasten one's seat-belt

anschneiden† vt sep cut into; broach (Thema)

anschreiben† vt sep write (an + acc on); (Comm) put on s.o.'s account; (sich wenden) write to

Anschrift f address

anschuldig|en vt sep accuse. **A~ung** f -,-en accusation

anschwellen† vi sep (sein) swell

ansehen† vt sep look at; (einschätzen) regard (als as); **sich dat** etw **a~** look at sth; (TV) watch sth. **A~** nt -s respect; (Ruf) reputation

ansehnlich adj considerable

ansetzen v sep ● vt join (an + acc to); (veranschlagen) estimate ● vi (haben) (anbrennen) burn; **zum Sprung a~** get ready to jump

Ansicht f view; **meiner A~ nach** in my view; **zur A~** (Comm) on approval. **A~s[post]karte** f picture postcard. **A~ssache** f matter of opinion

ansiedeln (sich) vr sep settle

ansonsten adv apart from that

anspannen vt sep hitch up; (anstrengen) strain; tense (Muskel)

Anspielung f -,-en allusion; hint

Anspitzer m -s,- pencil-sharpener

Ansprache f address

ansprechen† v sep ● vt speak to; (fig) appeal to ● vi (haben) respond (auf + acc to)

anspringen† v sep ● vt jump at ● vi (sein) (Auto) start

Anspruch m claim/(Recht) right (auf + acc on); **A~ haben** be entitled (auf + acc to); **in A~ nehmen** make use of; (erfordern) demand; take up (Zeit); occupy (Person); **hohe A~e stellen** be very demanding. **a~slos** adj undemanding. **a~svoll** adj demanding; (kri-

tisch) discriminating; (*vornehm*) up-market

anstacheln *vt sep* (*fig*) spur on

Anstalt *f -,-en* institution

Anstand *m* decency; (*Benehmen*) [good] manners *pl*

anständig *adj* decent; (*ehrbar*) respectable; (*richtig*) proper

anstandslos *adv* without any trouble

anstarren *vt sep* stare at

anstatt *conj & prep* (+ *gen*) instead of

ansteck|en *v sep* ● *vt* pin (an + *acc* to/on); put on (*Ring*); (*anzünden*) light; (*in Brand stecken*) set fire to; (*Med*) infect; **sich a~en** catch an infection (**bei** from) ● *vi* (*haben*) be infectious. **a~end** *adj* infectious. **A~ung** *f -,-en* infection

anstehen† *vi sep* (*haben*) queue

anstelle *prep* (+ *gen*) instead of

anstell|en *vt sep* put, stand (**an** + *acc* against); (*einstellen*) employ; (*anschalten*) turn on; (*tun*) do; **sich a~en** queue [up]. **A~ung** *f* employment; (*Stelle*) job

Anstieg *m -[e]s,-e* climb; (*fig*) rise

anstift|en *vt sep* cause; (*anzetteln*) instigate

Anstoß *m* (*Anregung*) impetus; (*Stoß*) knock; (*Fußball*) kick-off; **A~ erregen** give offence. **a~en†** *v sep* ● *vt* knock; (*mit dem Ellbogen*) nudge ● *vi* (*sein*) knock (**an** + *acc* against) ● *vi* (*haben*) adjoin (**an etw** *acc* sth); **a~en auf** (+ *acc*) drink to; **mit der Zunge a~en** lisp

anstößig *adj* offensive

anstrahlen *vt sep* floodlight

anstreichen† *vt sep* paint; (*anmerken*) mark

anstreng|en *vt sep* strain; (*ermüden*) tire; **sich a~en** exert oneself; (*sich bemühen*) make an effort (**zu**

to). **a~end** *adj* strenuous; (*ermüdend*) tiring. **A~ung** *f -,-en* strain; (*Mühe*) effort

Anstrich *m* coat [of paint]

Ansturm *m* rush; (*Mil*) assault

Ansuchen *nt -s,-* request

Antarktis *f -* Antarctic

Anteil *m* share; **A~ nehmen** take an interest (**an** + *dat* in). **A~nahme** *f -* interest (**an** + *dat* in); (*Mitgefühl*) sympathy

Antenne *f -,-n* aerial

Anthologie *f -,-n* anthology

Anthrax *m -* anthrax

Anthropologie *f -* anthropology

Anti|alkoholiker *m* teetotaller. **A~biotikum** *nt -s,-ka* antibiotic

antik *adj* antique. **A~e** *f -* [classical] antiquity

Antikörper *m* antibody

Antilope *f -,-n* antelope

Antipathie *f -* antipathy

Antiquariat *nt -[e]s,-e* antiquarian bookshop

Antiquitäten *fpl* antiques. **A~händler** *m* antique dealer

Antrag *m -[e]s,-e* proposal; (*Pol*) motion; (*Gesuch*) application. **A~steller** *m -s,-* applicant

antreffen† *vt sep* find

antreten† *v sep* ● *vt* start; take up (*Amt*) ● *vi* (*sein*) line up

Antrieb *m* urge; (*Techn*) drive; **aus eigenem A~** of one's own accord

Antritt *m* start; **bei A~ eines Amtes** when taking office

antun† *vt sep* jdm **etw a~** do sth to s.o.; **sich** (*dat*) **etwas a~** take one's own life

Antwort *f -,-en* answer, reply (**auf** + *acc* to). **a~en** *vt/i* (*haben*) answer (jdm s.o.)

anvertrauen *vt sep* entrust/(*mitteilen*) confide (**jdm to** s.o.)

Anwalt m -[e]s, :-e, **Anwältin** f -,-nen lawyer; (*vor Gericht*) counsel

Anwandlung f -,-en fit (**von** of)

Anwärter(in) m(f) candidate

anweis|en vt sep assign (*dat* to); (*beauftragen*) instruct. **A~ung** f instruction; (*Geld-*) money order

anwend|en vt sep apply (**auf** + *acc* to); (*gebrauchen*) use. **A~ung** f application; use

anwerben vt sep recruit

Anwesen nt -s,- property

anwesen|d adj present (**bei** at); **die A~den** those present. **A~heit** f - presence

anwidern vt sep disgust

Anwohner mpl residents

Anzahl f number

anzahl|en vt sep pay a deposit on. **A~ung** f deposit

anzapfen vt sep tap

Anzeichen nt sign

Anzeige f -,-n announcement; (*Inserat*) advertisement; **A~ erstatten gegen jdn** report s.o. to the police. **a~n** vt sep announce; (*inserieren*) advertise; (*melden*) report [to the police]; (*angeben*) indicate

anzieh|en vt sep • vt attract; (*festziehen*) tighten; put on (*Kleider, Bremse*); (*ankleiden*) dress; **sich a~en** get dressed. **a~end** adj attractive. **A~ungskraft** f attraction; (*Phys*) gravity

Anzug m suit

anzüglich adj suggestive

anzünden vt sep light; (*in Brand stecken*) set fire to

anzweifeln vt sep question

apart adj striking

Apathie f - apathy

apathisch adj apathetic

Aperitif m -s,-s aperitif

Apfel m -s, :- apple

Apfelsine f -,-n orange

Apostel m -s,- apostle

Apostroph m -s,-e apostrophe

Apotheke f -,-n pharmacy. **A~er(in)** m(f) (f -,-nen) pharmacist, [dispensing] chemist

Apparat m -[e]s,-e device; (*Phot*) camera; (*Radio, TV*) set; (*Teleph*) telephone; **am A~!** speaking!

Appell m -s,-e appeal; (*Mil*) rollcall. **a~ieren** vi (*haben*) appeal (**an** + *acc* to)

Appetit m -s appetite; **guten A~!** enjoy your meal! **a~lich** adj appetizing

Applaus m -es applause

Aprikose f -,-n apricot

April m -[s] April

Aquarell nt -s,-e water-colour

Aquarium nt -s,-ien aquarium

Äquator m -s equator

Ära f - era

Araber(in) m -s,- (f -,-nen) Arab

arabisch adj Arab; (*Geog*) Arabian; (*Ziffer*) Arabic

Arbeit f -,-en work; (*Anstellung*) employment, job; (*Aufgabe*) task; (*Sch*) [written] test; (*Abhandlung*) treatise; (*Qualität*) workmanship; **sich an die A~ machen** set to work; **sich** (*dat*) **viel A~ machen** go to a lot of trouble. **a~en** v sep • vi (*haben*) work (**an** + *dat* on) • vt make. **A~er(in)** m -s,- (f -,-nen) worker; (*Land-, Hilfs-*) labourer. **A~erklasse** f working class

Arbeit|geber m -s,- employer. **A~nehmer** m -s,- employee

Arbeits|amt nt employment exchange. **A~erlaubnis, A~genehmigung** f work permit. **A~kraft** f worker. **a~los** adj unemployed;

a ~los sein be out of work. A~lose(r) m/f unemployed person; die A~losen the unemployed pl. A~losenunterstützung f unemployment benefit. A~losigkeit f - unemployment

arbeitsparend adj labour-saving

Arbeitsplatz m job

Archäologe m -n,-n archaeologist. A~logie f - archaeology

Arche f - die A~ Noah Noah's Ark

Architekt(in) m -en,-en (f -,-nen) architect. a~tonisch adj architectural. A~tur f - architecture

Archiv nt -s,-e archives pl

Arena f -,-nen arena

arg adj bad; (groß) terrible

Argentinien /-jən/ nt -s Argentina. a~isch adj Argentinian

Ärger m -s annoyance; (Unannehmlichkeit) trouble. ä~lich adj annoyed; (leidig) annoying; ä~lich sein be annoyed. ä~n vt annoy; (necken) tease; sich ä~n get annoyed (über jdn/etw with s.o./about sth). Ä~nis nt -ses, -se annoyance; öffentliches Ä~nis public nuisance

Arglist f - malice

arglos adj unsuspecting

Argument nt -[e]s,-e argument. a~ieren vi (haben) argue (dass that)

Arie /'a:rjə/ f -,-n aria

Aristokrat m -en,-en aristocrat. A~kratie f - aristocracy. a~kratisch adj aristocratic

Arktis f - Arctic. a~isch adj Arctic

arm adj poor

Arm m -[e]s,-e arm; jdn auf den Arm nehmen f pull s.o.'s leg

Armaturenbrett nt instrument panel; (Auto) dashboard

Armband nt (pl -bänder) bracelet; (Uhr-) watch-strap. A~uhr f wrist-watch

Arme(r) m/f poor man/woman; die A~en the poor pl

Armee f -,-n army

Ärmel m -s,- sleeve. Ä~kanal m [English] Channel. ä~los adj sleeveless

Armlehne f arm. A~leuchter m candelabra

ärmlich adj poor; (elend) miserable

armselig adj miserable

Armut f - poverty

Arrangement /arãʒəˈmãː/ nt -s,-s arrangement. a~gieren vt arrange

arrogant adj arrogant

Arsch m -[e]s,ːe (vulgar) arse

Arsen nt -s arsenic

Art f -,-en manner; (Weise) way; (Natur) nature; (Sorte) kind; (Biology) species; auf diese Art in this way

Arterie /-jə/ f -,-n artery

Arthritis f - arthritis

artig adj well-behaved

Artikel m -s,- article

Artillerie f - artillery

Artischocke f -,-n artichoke

Arznei f -,-en medicine

Arzt m -[e]s,ːe doctor

Ärztin f -,-nen [woman] doctor. ä~lich adj medical

As* nt -ses,-se = Ass

Asbest m -[e]s asbestos

Asche f - ash. A~nbecher m ashtray. A~rmittwoch m Ash Wednesday

Asiat(in) m -en,-en (f -,-nen) Asian. a~isch adj Asian

Asien /'a:zjən/ nt -s Asia

asozial adj antisocial

Aspekt m -[e]s,-e aspect

Asphalt m -[e]s asphalt. **a~ieren** vt asphalt

Ass nt -es,-e ace

Assistent(in) m -en,-en (f -,-nen) assistant

Ast m -[e]s,ˤe branch

ästhetisch adj aesthetic

Asth|ma nt -s asthma. **a~matisch** adj asthmatic

Astro|loge m -n,-n astrologer. **A~logie** f - astrology. **A~naut** m -en,-en astronaut. **A~nomie** f - astronomy

Asyl nt -s,-e home; (Pol) asylum. **A~bewerber(in)** m -e, -e (f -en, -en) asylum seeker

Atelier /-'lje:/ nt -s,-s studio

Atem m -s breath. **a~los** adj breathless. **A~zug** m breath

Atheist m -en,-en atheist

Äther m -s ether

Äthiopien /-jan/ nt -s Ethiopia

Athlet|(in) m -en,-en (f -,-nen) athlete. **a~isch** adj athletic

Atlant|ik m -s Atlantic. **a~isch** adj Atlantic; **der A~ische Ozean** the Atlantic Ocean

Atlas m -lasses,-lanten atlas

atmen vt/i (haben) breathe

Atmosphäre f -,-n atmosphere

Atmung f - breathing

Atom nt -s,-e atom. **A~bombe** f atom bomb. **A~krieg** m nuclear war

Atten|tat nt -[e]s,-e assassination attempt. **A~täter** m assassin

Attest nt -[e]s,-e certificate

Attrak|tion f -,-en attraction. **a~tiv** adj attractive

Attribut nt -[e]s,-e attribute

ätzen vt corrode; (Med) cauterize; (Kunst) etch. **ä~d** adj corrosive; (Spott) caustic

---

au int ouch; **au fein!** oh good!

Aubergine /ober'ʒi:nə/ f -,-n aubergine

auch adv & conj also, too; (außerdem) what's more; (selbst) even; **a~ wenn** even if; **sie weiß es a~ nicht** she doesn't know either; **wer/wie/was a~ immer** whoever/however/whatever

Audienz f -,-en audience

audiovisuell adj audio-visual

Auditorium nt -s,-ien (Univ) lecture hall

---

auf

● preposition (+ dative)

‣ (nicht unter) on. **auf dem Tisch** on the table. **auf Deck** on deck. **auf der Erde** on earth. **auf der Welt** in the world. **auf der Straße** in the street

‣ (bei Institution, Veranstaltung usw.) at; (bei Gebäude, Zimmer) in. **auf der Schule/Uni** at school/university. **auf einer Party/Hochzeit** at a party/wedding. **Geld auf der Bank haben** have money in the bank. **sie ist auf ihrem Zimmer** she's in her room. **auf einem Lehrgang** on a course. **auf Urlaub** on holiday

● preposition (+ accusative)

‣ (nicht unter) on[to]. **er legte das Buch auf den Tisch** he laid the book on the table. **auf eine Mauer steigen** climb onto a wall. **auf die Straße gehen** go [out] into the street

‣ (bei Institution, Veranstaltung usw.) to. **auf eine Party/die Toilette gehen** go to a party/the toilet. **auf die Schule/Uni gehen** go to school/university. **auf einen Lehrgang/auf Urlaub**

---

a

a

gehen go on a course/on holiday

····▸ (bei Entfernung) auf 10 km [Entfernung] zu sehen/hören visible/audible for [a distance of] 10 km

····▸ (zeitlich) (wie lange) for; (bis) until; (wann) on. auf Jahre [hinaus] for years [to come]. auf ein paar Tage for a few days. etw auf nächsten Mittwoch verschieben postpone sth until next Wednesday. das fällt auf einen Montag it falls on a Monday

····▸ (Art und Weise) in. auf diese [Art und] Weise in this way. auf Deutsch/Englisch in German/English

····▸ (aufgrund) auf Wunsch on request. auf meine Bitte or at my request. auf Befehl on command

····▸ (Proportion) to. ein Teelöffel auf einen Liter Wasser one teaspoon to one litre of water. auf die Sekunde/den Millimeter [genau] [precise] to the nearest second/millimetre

····▸ (Toast) to. auf deine Gesundheit! your health!

● adverb

····▸ (aufgerichtet, aufgestanden) up. auf! (steh auf!) up you get! auf und ab (hin und her) up and down

····▸ (aufsetzen) Helm/Hut/Brille auf! helmet/hat/glasses on!

····▸ (geöffnet, offen) open. Fenster/Mund auf! open the window/your mouth!

aufatmen vi sep (haben) heave a sigh of relief

aufbahren vt sep lay out

Aufbau m construction; (Struktur)

structure. a~en v sep ● vt construct, build; (errichten) erect; (schaffen) build up; (arrangieren) arrange; sich a~en (fig) be based (auf + dat on) ● vi (haben) be based (auf + dat on)

aufbauschen vt sep puff out; (fig) exaggerate

aufbekommen† vt sep get open; (Sch) be given [as homework]

aufbessern vt sep improve; (erhöhen) increase

aufbewahr|en vt sep keep; (lagern) store. A~ung f - safe keeping; storage; (Gepäck-) left-luggage office

aufblas|bar adj inflatable. a~en† vt sep inflate

aufbleiben† vi sep (sein) stay open; (Person:) stay up

aufblenden vt/i sep (haben) (Auto) switch to full beam

aufblühen vi sep (sein) flower

aufbocken vt sep jack up

aufbrauchen vt sep use up

aufbrechen† vt sep ● vt break open ● vi (sein) (Knospe:) open; (sich aufmachen) set out, start

aufbringen† vt sep raise (Geld); find (Kraft)

Aufbruch m start, departure

aufbrühen vt sep make (Tee)

aufbürden vt sep jdm etw a~ (fig) burden s.o. with sth

aufdecken vt sep (auflegen) put on; (abdecken) uncover; (fig) expose

aufdrehen vt sep turn on

aufdringlich adj persistent

aufeinander adv one on top of the other; (schießen) at each other; (warten) for each other; a~ folgend successive; (Tage) consecutive.

Aufenthalt m stay; 10 Minuten A~ haben (Zug:) stop for 10 minutes. A~serlaubnis, A~sgenehmigung f residence permit. A~sraum m recreation room; (im Hotel) lounge

Auferstehung f - resurrection

aufessen† vt sep eat up

auffahr|en† vi sep (sein) drive up; (aufprallen) crash, run (auf + acc into). A~t f drive; (Autobahn-) access road, slip road; (Bergfahrt) ascent

auffallen† vi sep (sein) be conspicuous; **unangenehm a~** make a bad impression

auffällig adj conspicuous

auffangen† vt sep catch; pick up

auffass|en vt sep understand; (deuten) take. A~ung f understanding; (Ansicht) view

aufforder|n vt sep ask; (einladen) invite. A~ung f request; invitation

auffrischen v sep ● vt freshen up; revive (Erinnerung); **seine Englischkenntnisse a~** brush up one's English

aufführ|en vt sep perform; (angeben) list; **sich a~en** behave. A~ung f performance

auffüllen vt sep fill up

Aufgabe f task; (Rechen-) problem; (Verzicht) giving up; A~n (Sch) homework sg

Aufgang m way up; (Treppe) stairs pl; (der Sonne) rise

aufgeb|en† v sep ● vt give up; post (Brief); send (Telegramm); place (Bestellung); register (Gepäck); put in the paper (Annonce); **jdm eine Aufgabe a~** set s.o. a task; **jdm Suppe a~** serve s.o. with soup ● vi (haben) give up

Aufgebot nt contingent (an + dat of); (Relig) banns pl

aufgedunsen adj bloated

aufgehen† vi sep (sein) open; (sich lösen) come undone; (Teig, Sonne:) rise; (Saat:) come up; (Math) come out exactly; **in Flammen a~** go up in flames

aufgelegt adj **gut/schlecht a~ sein** be in a good/bad mood

aufgeregt adj excited; (erregt) agitated

aufgeschlossen adj (fig) open-minded

aufgeweckt adj (fig) bright

aufgießen† vt sep pour on; (aufbrühen) make (Tee)

aufgreifen† vt sep pick up; take up (Vorschlag, Thema)

aufgrund prep (+ gen) on the strength of

Aufguss m infusion

aufhaben† v sep ● vt have on; **den Mund a~** have one's mouth open; **viel a~** (Sch) have a lot of homework ● vi (haben) be open

aufhalten† vt sep hold up; (anhalten) stop; (abhalten) keep; (offenhalten) hold open; hold out (Hand); **sich a~** stay; (sich befassen) spend one's time (**mit** on)

aufhäng|en vt/i sep (haben) hang up; (henken) hang; **sich a~en** hang oneself. A~er m -s,- loop

aufheben† vt sep pick up; (hochheben) raise; (aufbewahren) keep; (beenden) end; (rückgängig machen) lift; (abschaffen) abolish; (Jur) quash (Urteil); repeal (Gesetz); (ausgleichen) cancel out; **gut aufgehoben sein** be well looked after

aufheitern vt sep cheer up; **sich a~** (Wetter:) brighten up

aufhellen vt sep lighten; **sich a~** (Himmel:) brighten

aufhetzen vt sep incite

aufholen v sep ● vt make up ● vi (haben) catch up; (zeitlich) make up time

a

aufhören vi sep (haben) stop

aufklappen vt/i sep (sein) open

aufklär|en vt sep (haben) enlighten s.o.; **sich a~en** be solved; (Wetter:) clear up. **A~ung** f solution; enlightenment; (Mil) reconnaissance; **sexuelle A~ung** sex education

aufkleb|en vt sep stick on. **A~er** m -s,- sticker

aufknöpfen vt sep unbutton

aufkochen v sep ● vt bring to the boil ● vi (sein) come to the boil

aufkommen† vi sep (sein) start; (Wind:) spring up; (Mode:) come in

aufkrempeln vt sep roll up

aufladen† vt sep load; (Electr) charge

Auflage f impression; (Ausgabe) edition; (Zeitungs-) circulation

auflassen† vt sep leave open; leave on (Hut)

Auflauf m crowd; (Culin) ≈ soufflé

auflegen v sep ● vt apply (auf + acc to); put down (Hörer); neu a~ reprint ● vi (haben) ring off

auflehn|en (sich) vr sep (fig) rebel. **A~ung** f - rebellion

auflesen† vt sep pick up

aufleuchten vi sep (haben) light up

auflös|en vt sep dissolve; close (Konto); **sich a~en** dissolve; (Nebel:) clear. **A~ung** f dissolution; (Lösung) solution

aufmach|en v sep ● vt open; (lösen) undo; **sich a~en** set out (nach for) ● vi (haben) open; jdm a~en open the door to s.o. **A~ung** f -,-en get-up

aufmerksam adj attentive; a~ werden auf (+ acc) notice; jdn a~ machen auf (+ acc) draw s.o.'s attention to. **A~keit** f -,-en attention; (Höflichkeit) courtesy

aufmuntern vt sep cheer up

Aufnahme f -,-n acceptance; (Empfang) reception; (in Klub, Krankenhaus) admission; (Einbeziehung) inclusion; (Beginn) start; (Foto) photograph; (Film-) shot; (Mus) recording; (Band-) tape recording. **a~fähig** adj receptive. **A~prüfung** f entrance examination

aufnehmen† vt sep pick up; (absorbieren) absorb; take (Nahrung, Foto); (fassen) hold; (annehmen) accept; (leihen) borrow; (empfangen) receive; (in Klub, Krankenhaus) admit; (beherbergen, geistig erfassen) take in; (einbeziehen) include; (beginnen) take up; (niederschreiben) take down; (filmen) film, shoot; (Mus) record; **auf Band a~** tape[-record]

aufopfer|n vt sep sacrifice; **sich a~n** sacrifice oneself. **A~ung** f self-sacrifice

aufpassen vi sep (haben) pay attention; (sich vorsehen) take care; **a~ auf** (+ acc) look after

Aufprall m -[e]s impact. **a~en** vi sep (sein) **a~en auf** (+ acc) hit

aufpumpen vt sep pump up, inflate

aufputsch|en vt sep incite. **A~mittel** nt stimulant

aufquellen† vi sep (sein) swell

aufraffen vt sep pick up; **sich a~** pick oneself up; (fig) pull oneself together

aufragen vi sep (sein) rise [up]

aufräumen vt/i sep (haben) tidy up; (wegräumen) put away

aufrecht adj & adv upright. **a~erhalten†** vt sep (fig) maintain

aufreg|en vt sep excite; (beunruhigen) upset; (ärgern) annoy; **sich a~en** get excited; (sich erregen) get worked up. **a~end** adj exciting. **A~ung** f excitement

aufreiben† vt sep chafe; (fig) wear down. **a~d** adj trying

aufreißen† v sep ● vt tear open; dig up (Straße); open wide (Augen, Mund) ● vi (sein) split open

aufrichtig adj sincere. **A~keit** f - sincerity

aufrollen vt sep roll up; (entrollen) unroll

aufrücken vi sep (sein) move up; (fig) be promoted

Aufruf m appeal (**an** + dat to); **a~en**† vt sep call out (Namen); **jdn a~en** call s.o.'s name

Aufruhr m -s,-e turmoil; (Empörung) revolt

aufrühr|en vt sep stir up. **A~er** m -s,- rebel. **a~erisch** adj inflammatory; (rebellisch) rebellious

aufrunden vt sep round up

aufrüsten vi sep (haben) arm

aufsagen vt sep recite

aufsässig adj rebellious

Aufsatz m top; (Sch) essay

aufsaugen† vt sep soak up

aufschauen vi sep (haben) look up (**zu** at/(fig) to)

aufschichten vt sep stack up

aufschieben† vt sep slide open; (verschieben) put off, postpone

Aufschlag m impact; (Tennis) service; (Hosen-) turn-up; (Ärmel-) turned cuff; (Revers) lapel; (Comm) surcharge. **a~en**† v sep ● vt open; crack (Ei); (hochschlagen) turn up; (errichten) put up; (erhöhen) increase; cast on (Masche); **sich** (dat) **das Knie a~en** cut [open] one's knee ● vi (haben) hit (**auf etw** acc/ dat sth); (Tennis) serve; (teurer werden) go up

aufschließen† v sep ● vt unlock ● vi (haben) unlock the door

aufschlussreich adj revealing;

(lehrreich) informative

aufschneiden† v sep ● vt cut open; (in Scheiben) slice ● vi (haben) ⊞ exaggerate

Aufschnitt m sliced sausage, cold meat [and cheese]

aufschrauben vt sep screw on; (abschrauben) unscrew

Aufschrei m [sudden] cry

aufschreiben† vt sep write down; **jdn a~** (Polizist:) book s.o.

Aufschrift f inscription; (Etikett) label

Aufschub m delay; (Frist) grace

aufschürfen vt sep **sich** (dat) **das Knie a~** graze one's knee

aufschwingen† (**sich**) vr sep find the energy (**zu** for)

Aufschwung m (fig) upturn

aufsehen† vi sep (haben) look up (**zu** at/(fig) to). **A~** nt -s **A~ erregen** cause a sensation; **A~ erregend** sensational

Aufseher(in) m -s,- (f -,-nen) supervisor; (Gefängnis-) warder

aufsetzen vt sep put on; (verfassen) draw up; (entwerfen) draft; **sich a~** sit up

Aufsicht f supervision; (Person) supervisor. **A~srat** m board of directors

aufsperren vt sep open wide

aufspielen v sep ● vi (haben) play ● vr **sich a~** show off

aufspießen vt sep spear

aufspringen† vi sep (sein) jump up; (aufprallen) bounce; (sich öffnen) burst open

aufspüren vt sep track down

aufstacheln vt sep incite

Aufstand m uprising, rebellion

aufständisch adj rebellious

aufstehen† vi sep (sein) get up; (offen sein) be open; (fig) rise up

aufsteigen† vi sep (sein) get on; (Reiter:) mount; (Bergsteiger:) climb up; (hochsteigen) rise [up]; (fig: befördert werden) rise (zu to); (Sport) be promoted

aufstell|en vt sep put up; (Culin) put on; (postieren) post; (in einer Reihe) line up; (nominieren) nominate; (Sport) select (Mannschaft); make out (Liste); lay down (Regel); make (Behauptung); set up (Rekord). A~ung f nomination; (Liste) list

Aufstieg m -[e]s, -e ascent; (fig) rise; (Sport) promotion

Aufstoßen nt -s burping

aufstrebend adj (fig) ambitious

Aufstrich m [sandwich] spread

aufstützen vt sep rest (auf + acc on); sich a~ lean (auf + acc on)

Auftakt m (fig) start

auftauchen vi sep (sein) emerge; (fig) turn up; (Frage:) crop up

auftauen vt/i sep (sein) thaw

aufteil|en vt sep divide [up]. A~ung f division

auftischen vt sep serve [up]

Auftrag m -[e]s, ⸚e task; (Kunst) commission; (Comm) order; im A~ (+ gen) on behalf of. a~en† vt sep apply; (servieren) serve; (abtragen) wear out; jdm a~en instruct s.o. (zu to). A~geber m -s,- client

auftrennen vt sep unpick, undo

auftreten† vi sep (sein) tread; (sich benehmen) behave, act; (Theat) appear; (die Bühne betreten) enter; (vorkommen) occur

Auftrieb m buoyancy; (fig) boost

Auftritt m (Theat) appearance; (auf die Bühne) entrance; (Szene) scene

aufwachen vi sep (sein) wake up

aufwachsen† vi sep (sein) grow up

Aufwand m -[e]s expenditure; (Luxus) extravagance; (Mühe) trouble; A~ treiben be extravagant

aufwändig adj = aufwendig

aufwärmen vt sep heat up; (fig) rake up; sich a~ warm oneself; (Sport) warm up

Aufwartefrau f cleaner

aufwärts adv upwards; (bergauf) uphill; es geht a~ mit jdm/etw someone/something is improving

Aufwartung f - cleaner

aufwecken vt sep wake up

aufweichen v sep ● vt soften ● vi (sein) become soft

aufweisen† vt sep have, show

aufwend|en† vt sep spend; Mühe a~en take pains. a~ig adj lavish; (teuer) expensive

aufwert|en vt sep revalue. A~ung f revaluation

aufwickeln vt sep roll up; (auswickeln) unwrap

Aufwiegler m -s,- agitator

aufwischen vt sep wipe up; wash (Fußboden). A~lappen m floorcloth

aufwühlen vt sep churn up

aufzähl|en vt sep enumerate, list. A~ung f list

aufzeichn|en vt sep record; (zeichnen) draw. A~ung f recording; A~ungen notes

aufziehen† v sep ● vt pull up; hoist (Segel); (öffnen) open; draw (Vorhang); (großziehen) bring up; rear (Tier); mount (Bild); thread (Perlen); wind up (Uhr); (fam: necken) tease ● vi (sein) approach

Aufzug m hoist; (Fahrstuhl) lift, (Amer) elevator; (Prozession) procession; (Theat) act

Augapfel m eyeball

Auge nt -s,-n eye; (Punkt) spot;

vier A~n werfen throw a four; **gute A~n** good eyesight; **unter vier A~n** in private; **im A~ behalten** keep in sight; (fig) bear in mind

Augenblick m moment; **A~! just a moment! a~lich** adj immediate; (derzeitig) present ● adv immediately; (derzeit) at present

Augen|braue f eyebrow. **A~höhle** f eye socket. **A~licht** nt sight. **A~lid** nt eyelid

August m -[s] August

Auktion /ˈtsjoːn/ f -,-en auction

Aula f -,-len (Sch) [assembly] hall

Au-pair-Mädchen /oˈpɛːr/ nt aupair

aus prep (+ dat) out of; (von) from; (bestehend) [made] of; **aus Angst** from or out of fear; **aus Spaß** for fun ● adv out; (Licht, Radio) off; **aus sein auf** (+ acc) be after; **aus und ein** in and out; **von sich aus** of one's own accord; **von mir aus** as far as I'm concerned

ausarbeiten vt sep work out

ausarten vi sep (sein) degenerate (**in** + acc into)

ausatmen vt/i sep (haben) breathe out

ausbauen vt sep remove; (vergrößern) extend; (fig) expand

ausbedingen† vt sep sich (dat) **a~** insist on; (zur Bedingung machen) stipulate

ausbesser|n vt sep mend, repair. **A~ung** f repair

ausbeulen vt sep remove the dents from; (dehnen) make baggy

ausbild|en vt sep train; (formen) form; (entwickeln) develop; sich **a~en** train (**als/zu** as); (entstehen) develop. **A~ung** f training; (Sch)

ausbitten† vt sep sich (dat) **a~** ask for; (verlangen) insist on

ausblasen† vt sep blow out

ausbleiben† vi sep (sein) fail to appear; (Erfolg:) materialize; (nicht heimkommen) stay out

Ausblick m view

ausbrech|en† vi sep (sein) break out; (Vulkan:) erupt; (fliehen) escape; **in Tränen a~en** burst into tears. **A~er** m runaway

ausbreiten vt sep spread [out]. **A~ung** f spread

Ausbruch m outbreak; (Vulkan-) eruption; (Wut-) outburst; (Flucht) escape, break-out

ausbrüten vt sep hatch

Ausdauer f perseverance; (körperlich) stamina. **a~nd** adj persevering; (unermüdlich) untiring

ausdehnen vt sep stretch; (fig) extend; sich **a~** stretch; (Phys & fig) expand; (dauern) last

ausdenken† vt sep sich (dat) **a~** think up; (sich vorstellen) imagine

Ausdruck m expression; (Fach-) term; (Computer) printout. **a~en** vt sep print

ausdrücken vt sep squeeze out; squeeze (Zitrone); stub out (Zigarette); (äußern) express

ausdrucks|los adj expressionless. **a~voll** adj expressive

auseinander adv apart; (entzwei) in pieces; **a~ falten** unfold; **a~ gehen** part; (Linien, Meinungen:) diverge; (Ehe:) break up; **a~ nehmen** take apart or to pieces; **a~ setzen** explain (jdm to s.o.); **sich a~ setzen** sit apart; (sich aussprechen) have it out (**mit jdm** with s.o.); come to grips (**mit einem Problem** with a problem). **A~setzung** f -,-en discussion; (Streit) argument

auserlesen adj select, choice

Ausfahrt f drive; (Autobahn-)

a *Garagen-)* exit

Ausfall *m* failure; *(Absage)* cancellation; *(Comm)* loss. **a~en†** *vi sep (sein)* fall out; *(versagen)* fail; *(abgesagt werden)* be cancelled; **gut/schlecht a~en** turn out to be good/poor

ausfallend, ausfällig *adj* abusive

ausfertig|en *vt sep* make out. **A~ung** *f* -,-en in doppelter **A~ung** in duplicate

ausfindig *adj* **a~ machen** find

Ausflug *m* excursion, outing

Ausflügler *m* -s,- [day-]tripper

Ausfluss *m* outlet; *(Abfluss)* drain; *(Med)* discharge

ausfragen *vt sep* question

Ausfuhr *f* -,-en *(Comm)* export

ausführ|en *vt sep* take out; *(Comm)* export; *(erklären)* explain. **a~lich** *adj* detailed ● *adv* in detail. **A~ung** *f* execution; *(Comm)* version; *(äußere)* finish; *(Qualität)* workmanship; *(Erklärung)* explanation

Ausgabe *f* issue; *(Buch-)* edition; *(Comm)* version

Ausgang *m* way out, exit; *(Flugsteig)* gate; *(Ende)* end; *(Ergebnis)* outcome. **A~spunkt** *m* starting point. **A~ssperre** *f* curfew

ausgeben† *vt sep* hand out; issue *(Fahrkarten)*; spend *(Geld)*; **sich a~ als** pretend to be

ausgebildet *adj* trained

ausgebucht *adj* fully booked; *(Vorstellung)* sold out

ausgefallen *adj* unusual

ausgefranst *adj* frayed

ausgeglichen *adj* [well-]balanced

ausgeh|en† *vi sep (sein)* go out; *(Haare:)* fall out; *(Vorräte, Geld:)* run out; *(verblassen)* fade; **gut/schlecht a~en** end well/badly; **davon a~en, dass** assume that. **A~ver-**

bot *nt* curfew

ausgelassen *adj* high-spirited

ausgemacht *adj* agreed

ausgenommen *conj* except; **a~ wenn** unless

ausgeprägt *adj* marked

ausgeschlossen *pred adj* out of the question

ausgeschnitten *adj* low-cut

ausgesprochen *adj* marked ● *adv* decidedly

ausgestorben *adj* extinct; [wie] **a~** *(Straße:)* deserted

Ausgestoßene(r) *m/f* outcast

ausgezeichnet *adj* excellent

ausgiebig *adj* extensive; *(ausgedehnt)* long; **a~ Gebrauch machen von** make full use of

ausgießen† *vt sep* pour out

Ausgleich *m* -[e]s balance; *(Entschädigung)* compensation. **a~en†** *v sep* ● *vt* balance; even out *(Höhe)*; *(wettmachen)* compensate for; **sich a~en** balance out ● *vi (haben)* *(Sport)* equalize. **A~streffer** *m* equalizer

ausgrab|en† *vt sep* dig up; *(Archaeology)* excavate. **A~ung** *f* -,-en excavation

Ausguss *m* [kitchen] sink

aushaben† *vt sep* have finished *(Buch)*

aushalten† *vt sep* bear, stand; hold *(Note)*; *(Unterhalt zahlen für)* keep; **nicht auszuhalten, nicht zum A~** unbearable

aushändigen *vt sep* hand over

aushängen¹ *vt sep (reg)* display; take off its hinges *(Tür)*

aushäng|en²† *vi sep (haben)* be displayed. **A~eschild** *nt* sign

ausheben† *vt sep* excavate

aushecken *vt sep (fig)* hatch

aushelfen† *vi sep (haben)*

help out (**jdm** s.o.)

Aushilf|e f [temporary] assistant; **zur A∼e** to help out. **A∼skraft** f temporary worker. **a∼sweise** adv temporarily

aushöhlen vt sep hollow out

auskennen† (**sich**) vr sep know one's way around; **sich mit/in etw** (dat) **a∼** know all about sth

auskommen† vi sep (sein) manage (**mit/ohne** with/without); (**sich vertragen**) get on (**gut** well)

auskugeln vt sep sich (dat) den Arm **a∼** dislocate one's shoulder

auskühlen vt/i sep (sein) cool

auskundschaften vt sep spy out

Auskunft f -,ᵉe information; (**A∼sstelle**) information desk/ (Büro) bureau; (Teleph) enquiries pl; **eine A∼** a piece of information

auslachen vt sep laugh at

Auslage f [window] display; **A∼n** expenses

Ausland nt **im/ins A∼** abroad

Ausländ|er(in) m -s,- (f -,-nen) foreigner. **a∼isch** adj foreign

Auslandsgespräch nt international call

auslass|en† vt sep let out; let down (Saum); (**weglassen**) leave out; (**versäumen**) miss; (Culin) melt; (fig) vent (Ärger) (**an** + acc on). **A∼ungszeichen** nt apostrophe

Auslauf m run. **a∼en†** vi sep (sein) run out; (Farbe:) run; (Naut) put to sea; (Modell:) be discontinued

ausleeren vt sep empty [out]

ausleg|en vt sep lay out; display (Waren); (**auskleiden**) line (**mit** with); (**bezahlen**) pay; (**deuten**) interpret. **A∼ung** f -,-en interpretation

ausleihen† vt sep lend; sich (dat) **a∼** borrow

Auslese f - selection; (fig) pick; (Elite) elite

ausliefer|n vt sep hand over; (Jur) extradite. **A∼ung** f handing over; (Jur) extradition; (Comm) distribution

ausloggen vi sep log off or out

auslosen vt sep draw lots for

auslös|en vt sep set off, trigger; (fig) cause; arouse (Begeisterung); (**einlösen**) redeem; pay a ransom for (Gefangene). **A∼er** m -s,- trigger; (Phot) shutter release

Auslosung f draw

auslüften vt/i sep (haben) air

ausmachen vt sep put out; (**abschalten**) turn off; (**abmachen**) arrange; (**erkennen**) make out; (**betragen**) amount to; (**wichtig sein**) matter

Ausmaß nt extent; **A∼e** dimensions

Ausnahm|e f -,-n exception. **A∼ezustand** m state of emergency. **a∼slos** adv without exception. **a∼sweise** adv as an exception

ausnehmen† vt sep take out; gut (Fisch); sich gut **a∼** look good. **a∼d** adv exceptionally

ausnutz|en, ausnütz|en vt sep exploit. **A∼ung** f exploitation

auspacken vt sep unpack; (**auswickeln**) unwrap

ausplaudern vt sep let out, blab

ausprobieren vt sep try out

Auspuff m -s exhaust [system]. **A∼gase** ntpl exhaust fumes. **A∼rohr** nt exhaust pipe

auspusten vt sep blow out

ausradieren vt sep rub out

ausrauben vt sep rob

ausräuchern vt sep smoke out; fumigate (Zimmer)

ausräumen vt sep clear out

ausrechnen vt sep work out

Ausrede f excuse. **a~n** v sep ● vi (haben) finish speaking ● vt jdm etw **a~n** talk s.o. out of sth

ausreichen vi sep (haben) be enough. **a~d** adj adequate

Ausreise f departure. **a~n** vi sep (sein) leave the country. **A~visum** nt exit visa

ausreißen† vt sep ● vt pull or tear out ● vi (sein) 🔢 run away

ausrenken vt sep dislocate

ausrichten vt sep align; (bestellen) deliver; (erreichen) achieve; jdm **a~** tell s.o. (dass that); **ich soll Ihnen Grüße von X a~** X sends [you] his regards

ausrotten vt sep exterminate; (fig) eradicate

Ausruf m exclamation. **a~en†** vt sep exclaim; call out (Namen); (verkünden) proclaim; jdn **a~en** lassen put out a call for s.o. **A~ezeichen** nt exclamation mark

ausruhen vt/i sep (haben) rest; **sich a~** have a rest

ausrüst|en vt sep equip. **A~ung** f equipment; (Mil) kit

ausrutschen vi sep (sein) slip

Aussage f -,-n statement; (Jur) testimony, evidence; (Gram) predicate. **a~n** vt/i sep (haben) state; (Jur) give evidence, testify

ausschalten vt sep switch off

Ausschank m sale of alcoholic drinks; (Bar) bar

Ausschau f - A~ halten nach look out for

ausscheiden† vi sep (sein) leave; (Sport) drop out; (nicht in Frage kommen) be excluded

ausschenken vt sep pour out

ausscheren vi sep (sein) (Auto) pull out

ausschildern vt sep signpost

ausschimpfen vt sep tell off

ausschlafen† vi/r sep (haben) [sich] **a~** get enough sleep; (morgens) sleep late

Ausschlag m (Med) rash; den **A~ geben** (fig) tip the balance. **a~gebend** adj decisive

ausschließ|en† vt sep lock out; (fig) exclude; (entfernen) expel. **a~lich** adj exclusive

ausschlüpfen vi sep (sein) hatch

Ausschluss m exclusion; expulsion; **unter A~ der Öffentlichkeit** in camera

ausschneiden† vt sep cut out

Ausschnitt m excerpt, extract; (Zeitungs-) cutting; (Hals-) neckline

ausschöpfen vt sep ladle out; (Naut) bail out; exhaust (Möglichkeiten)

ausschreiben† vt sep write out; (ausstellen) make out; (bekanntgeben) announce; put out to tender (Auftrag)

Ausschreitungen fpl riots; (Exzesse) excesses

Ausschuss m committee; (Comm) rejects pl

ausschütten vt sep tip out; (verschütten) spill; (leeren) empty

aussehen† vi sep (haben) look; **wie sieht er/es aus?** what does he/it look like? **A~** nt -s appearance

außen adv [on the] outside; **nach a~** outwards. **A~bordmotor** m outboard motor. **A~handel** m foreign trade. **A~minister** m Foreign Minister. **A~politik** f foreign policy. **A~seite** f outside. **A~seiter** m -s,- outsider; (fig) misfit. **A~stände** mpl outstanding debts

außer prep (+ dat) except [for], apart from; (außerhalb) out of; **a~**

sich (*fig*) beside oneself ● *conj* except; a∼ **wenn** unless. a∼**dem** *adv* in addition, as well ● *conj* moreover

äußer|e(r,s) *adj* external; (*Teil, Schicht*) outer. Ä∼**e(s)** *nt* exterior; (*Aussehen*) appearance

außer|ehelich *adj* extramarital. a∼**gewöhnlich** *adj* exceptional. a∼**halb** *prep* (+ *gen*) outside ● *adv* a∼**halb wohnen** live outside town

äußer|lich *adj* external; (*fig*) outward. ä∼**n** *vt* express; **sich ä∼n** comment; (*sich zeigen*) manifest itself

außerordentlich *adj* extraordinary

äußerst *adv* extremely

äußerste|(r,s) *adj* outermost; (*weiteste*) furthest; (*höchste*) utmost, extreme; (*letzte*) last; (*schlimmste*) worst. Ä∼**(s)** *nt* **das Ä∼** the limit; (*Schlimmste*) the worst; **sein Ä∼s tun** do one's utmost; **aufs Ä∼** extremely

Äußerung *f* -,-en comment; (*Bemerkung*) remark

aussetzen *v sep* ● *vt* expose (*dat* to); abandon (*Kind*); launch (*Boot*); offer (*Belohnung*); **etwas auszusetzen haben an** (+ *dat*) find fault with ● *vi* (*haben*) stop; (*Motor:*) cut out

Aussicht *f* -,-en view/(*fig*) prospect (**auf** + *acc* of); **weitere A∼en** (*Meteorology*) further outlook *sg*. a∼**slos** *adj* hopeless

ausspannen *v sep* ● *vt* spread out; unhitch (*Pferd*) ● *vi* (*haben*) rest

aussperren *vt sep* lock out

ausspielen *v sep* ● *vt* play (*Karte*); (*fig*) play off (*gegen against*) ● *vi* (*haben*) (*Kartenspiel*) lead

Aussprache *f* pronunciation; (*Gespräch*) talk

aussprechen† *vt sep* pronounce; (*äußern*) express; **sich a∼** talk;

come out (**für/gegen** in favour of/against)

Ausspruch *m* saying

ausspucken *v sep* ● *vt* spit out ● *vi* (*haben*) spit

ausspülen *vt sep* rinse out

ausstatt|en *vt sep* equip. A∼**ung** *f* -,-en equipment; (*Innen-*) furnishings *pl*; (*Theat*) scenery and costumes *pl*

ausstehen† *v sep* ● *vt* suffer; **Angst a∼** be frightened; **ich kann sie nicht a∼** I can't stand her ● *vi* (*haben*) be outstanding

aussteigen† *vi sep* (*sein*) get out; (*aus Bus, Zug*) get off; **alles a∼!** all change!

ausstell|en *vt sep* exhibit; (*Comm*) display; (*ausfertigen*) make out; issue (*Pass.*). A∼**ung** *f* exhibition; (*Comm*) display

aussterben† *vi sep* (*sein*) die out; (*Biology*) become extinct

Aussteuer *f* trousseau

Ausstieg *m* -[e]s,-e exit

ausstopfen *vt sep* stuff

ausstoßen† *vt sep* emit; utter (*Fluch*); heave (*Seufzer*); (*ausschließen*) expel

ausstrahl|en *vt/i sep* (*sein*) radiate, emit; (*Radio, TV*) broadcast. A∼**ung** *f* radiation

ausstrecken *vt sep* stretch out; put out (*Hand*)

ausstreichen† *vt sep* cross out

ausströmen *v sep* ● *vi* (*sein*) pour out; (*entweichen*) escape ● *vt* emit; (*ausstrahlen*) radiate

aussuchen *vt sep* pick, choose

Austausch *m* exchange. a∼**bar** *adj* interchangeable. a∼**en** *vt sep* exchange; (*auswechseln*) replace

austeilen *vt sep* distribute

Auster *f* -,-n oyster

austragen† vt sep deliver; hold (*Wettkampf*); play (*Spiel*)

Austral|ien /-jən/ nt -s Australia. A~ier(in) m -s,- (f -,-nen) Australian. **a~isch** adj Australian

austreiben† vt sep drive out; (*Relig*) exorcize

austreten† v sep ● vt stamp out; (*abnutzen*) wear down ● vi (*sein*) come out; (*ausscheiden*) leave (**aus** etw sth); [**mal**] a~ 🚽 go to the loo

austrinken† vt/i sep (haben) drink up; (*leeren*) drain

Austritt m resignation

austrocknen vt/i sep (sein) dry out

ausüben vt sep practise; carry on (*Handwerk*); exercise (*Recht*); exert (*Druck, Einfluss*)

Ausverkauf m [clearance] sale. **a~t** adj sold out

Auswahl f choice, selection; (*Comm*) range; (*Sport*) team

auswählen vt sep choose, select

Auswander|er m emigrant. **a~n** vi sep (sein) emigrate. **A~ung** f emigration

auswärt|ig adj non-local; (*ausländisch*) foreign. **a~s** adv outwards; (*Sport*) away. **A~sspiel** nt away game

auswaschen† vt sep wash out

auswechseln vt sep change; (*ersetzen*) replace; (*Sport*) substitute

Ausweg m (*fig*) way out

ausweichen† vi sep (sein) get out of the way; **jdm/etw a~en** avoid/ (*sich entziehen*) evade someone/ something

Ausweis m -es,-e pass; (*Mitglieds-, Studenten-*) card. **a~en**† vt sep deport; **sich a~en** prove one's identity. **A~papiere** ntpl identification papers. **A~ung** f deportation

auswendig adv by heart

auswerten vt sep evaluate

auswickeln vt sep unwrap

auswirk|en (sich) vr sep have an effect (**auf** + acc on). **A~ung** f effect; (*Folge*) consequence

auswringen vt sep wring out

auszahlen vt sep pay off; (*entlohnen*) pay off; (*abfinden*) buy out; **sich a~** (*fig*) pay off

auszählen vt sep count; (*Boxen*) count out

Auszahlung f payment

auszeichn|en vt sep (Comm) price; (*ehren*) honour; (*mit einem Preis*) award a prize to; (*Mil*) decorate; **sich a~en** distinguish oneself. **A~ung** f honour; (*Preis*) award; (*Mil*) decoration; (*Sch*) distinction

ausziehen† v sep ● vt pull out; (*auskleiden*) undress; take off (*Mantel, Schuhe*) ● vi (*sein*) move out; (*sich aufmachen*) set out

Auszug m departure; (*Umzug*) move; (*Ausschnitt*) extract; (*Bank-*) statement

Auto nt -s,-s car; **A~ fahren** drive; (*mitfahren*) go in the car. **A~bahn** f motorway

Autobiographie f autobiography

Auto|bus m bus. **A~fahrer(in)** m(f) driver, motorist. **A~fahrt** f drive

Autogramm nt -s,-e autograph

Automat m -en,-en automatic device; (*Münz-*) slot-machine; (*Verkaufs-*) vending-machine; (*Fahrkarten-*) machine; (*Techn*) robot. **A~ik** f - automatic mechanism; (*Auto*) automatic transmission

automatisch adj automatic

Autonummer f registration number

Autopsie f -,-n autopsy

Autor m -s,-en author

Auto|reisezug m Motorail. **A~rennen** nt motor race

Autorin f -,-nen author[ess]

Autori|sation /-'tsɪ̯oːn/ f - authorization. **A~tät** f -,-en authority

Auto|schlosser m motor mechanic. **A~skooter** m -s,- dodgem. **A~stopp** m -s per A~stopp fahren hitch-hike. **A~verleih** m car hire [firm]. **A~waschanlage** f car wash

autsch int ouch

Axt f -,ᵉe axe

• •

Bb

• •

B, b /beː/ nt – (Mus) B flat

Baby /'beːbi/ nt -s,-s baby. **B~ausstattung** f layette. **B~sitter** m -s,- babysitter

Bach m -[e]s,ᵉe stream

Backbord nt -[e]s port [side]

Backe f -,-n cheek

backen vt/i† (haben) bake; (braten) fry

Backenzahn m molar

Bäcker m -s,- baker. **B~ei** f -,-en, **B~laden** m baker's shop

Back|obst nt dried fruit. **B~ofen** m oven. **B~pfeife** f 🇦 slap in the face. **B~pflaume** f prune. **B~pulver** nt baking-powder. **B~stein** m brick

Bad nt -[e]s,ᵉer bath; (Zimmer) bathroom; (Schwimm-) pool; (Ort) spa

Bade|anstalt f swimming baths pl. **B~anzug** m swim-suit. **B~hose** f swimming trunks pl. **B~kappe** f

bathing-cap. **B~mantel** m bathrobe. **b~n** vi (haben) have a bath; (im Meer) bathe ● vt bath; (waschen) bathe. **B~ort** m seaside resort. **B~wanne** f bath. **B~zimmer** nt bathroom

Bagger m -s,- excavator; (Nass-) dredger. **B~see** m flooded gravel-pit

Bahn f -,-en path; (Astronomy) orbit; (Sport) track; (einzelne) lane; (Rodel-) run; (Stoff-) width; (Eisen-) railway; (Zug) train; (Straßen-) tram. **b~brechend** adj (fig) pioneering. **B~hof** m [railway] station. **B~steig** m -[e]s,-e platform. **B~übergang** m level crossing

Bahre f -,-n stretcher

Baiser /bɛ'zeː/ nt -s,-s meringue

Bake f -,-n (Naut, Aviat) beacon

Bakterien /-i̯ən/ fpl bacteria

Balanc|e /ba'lãːsə/ f - balance. **b~ieren** vt/i (haben/sein) balance

bald adv soon; (fast) almost

Baldachin /-xiːn/ m -s,-e canopy

bald|ig adj early; (Besserung) speedy. **b~möglichst** adv as soon as possible

Balg nt & m -[e]s,ᵉer 🇦 brat

Balkan m -s Balkans pl

Balken m -s,- beam

Balkon /bal'kõː/ m -s,-s balcony; (Theat) circle

Ball¹ m -[e]s,ᵉe ball

Ball² m -[e]s,ᵉe (Tanz) ball

Ballade f -,-n ballad

Ballast m -[e]s ballast. **B~stoffe** mpl roughage sg

Ballen m -s,- bale; (Anat) ball of the hand/(Fuß-) foot; (Med) bunion

Ballerina f -,-nen ballerina

Ballett nt -s,-e ballet

Ballon /ba'lõː/ m -s,-s balloon

Balsam m -s balm

Balt|ikum nt -s Baltic States pl.
b~isch adj Baltic

Bambus m -ses,-se bamboo

banal adj banal

Banane f -,-n banana

Banause m -n,-n philistine

Band[1] nt -[e]s,ᵉr ribbon; (Naht-, Ton-, Ziel-) tape; **am laufenden B~** 🎞 non-stop

Band[2] m -[e]s,ᵉe volume

Band[3] nt -[e]s,-e (fig) bond

Band[4] /bɛnt/ f -,-s [jazz] band

Bandag|e /ban'da:ʒə/ f -,-n bandage. **b~ieren** vt bandage

Bande f -,-n gang

bändigen vt control, restrain; (zähmen) tame

Bandit m -en,-en bandit

Band|maß nt tape-measure. **B~scheibe** f (Anat) disc. **B~wurm** m tapeworm

Bang|e f **B~e haben** be afraid; **jdm B~e machen** frighten s.o. **b~en** vi (haben) fear (**um** for)

Banjo nt -s,-s banjo

Bank[1] f -,ᵉe bench

Bank[2] f -,-en (Comm) bank. **B~einzug** m direct debit

Bankett nt -s,-e banquet

Bankier /baŋ'kje:/ m -s,-s banker

Bankkonto nt bank account

Bankrott m -s,-s bankruptcy. **b~** adj bankrupt

Bankwesen nt banking

Bann m -[e]s,-e (fig) spell. **b~en** vt exorcize; (abwenden) avert; **[wie] gebannt** spellbound

Banner nt -s,- banner

bar adj (rein) sheer; (Gold) pure; **b~es Geld** cash; **[in] bar bezahlen** pay cash

Bar f -,-s bar

Bär m -en,-en bear

Baracke f -,-n (Mil) hut

Barb|ar m -en,-en barbarian. **b~arisch** adj barbaric

bar|fuß adv barefoot. **B~geld** nt cash

barmherzig adj merciful

barock adj baroque. **B~** nt & m -[s] baroque

Barometer nt -s,- barometer

Baron m -s,-e baron. **B~in** f -,-nen baroness

Barren m -s,- (Gold-) bar, ingot; (Sport) parallel bars pl. **B~gold** nt gold bullion

Barriere f -,-n barrier

Barrikade f -,-n barricade

barsch adj gruff

Barsch m -[e]s,-e (Zool) perch

Bart m -[e]s,ᵉe beard; (der Katze) whiskers pl

bärtig adj bearded

Barzahlung f cash payment

Basar m -s,-e bazaar

Base[1] f -,-n [female] cousin

Base[2] f -,-n (Chemistry) alkali, base

Basel nt -s Basle

basieren vi (haben) be based (**auf** + dat on)

Basilikum nt -s basil

Basis f -,Basen base; (fig) basis

basisch adj (Chemistry) alkaline

Bask|enmütze f beret. **b~isch** adj Basque

Bass m -es,ᵉe bass

Bassin /ba'sɛ̃:/ nt -s,-s pond; (Brunnen-) basin; (Schwimm-) pool

Bassist m -en,-en bass player; (Sänger) bass

Bast m -[e]s raffia

basteln vt make ● vi (haben) do handicrafts

Batterie f -,-n battery

Bau¹ m -[e]s,-e burrow; (Fuchs-) earth

Bau² m -[e]s,-ten construction; (Gebäude) building; (Auf-) structure; (Körper-) build; (B~stelle) building site. **B~arbeiten** fpl building work sg; (Straßen-) roadworks

Bauch m -[e]s, Bäuche abdomen, belly; (Magen) stomach; (Bauchung) bulge. **b~ig** adj bulbous. **B~nabel** m navel. **B~redner** m ventriloquist. **B~schmerzen** mpl stomach-ache sg. **B~speicheldrüse** f pancreas

bauen vt build; (konstruieren) construct • vi (haben) build (**an etw** dat sth); **b~ auf** (+ acc) (fig) rely on

Bauer¹ m -n,-n farmer; (Schach) pawn

Bauer² nt -s,- [bird]cage

bäuerlich adj rustic

Bauern|haus nt farmhouse. **B~hof** m farm

bau|fällig adj dilapidated. **B~genehmigung** f planning permission. **B~gerüst** nt scaffolding. **B~jahr** nt year of construction. **B~kunst** f architecture. **b~lich** adj structural

Baum m -[e]s, Bäume tree

baumeln vi (haben) dangle

bäumen (sich) vr rear [up]

Baum|schule f [tree] nursery. **B~wolle** f cotton

Bausch m -[e]s, Bäusche wad; **in B~ und Bogen** (fig) wholesale. **b~en** vt puff out

Bau|sparkasse f building society. **B~stein** m building brick. **B~stelle** f building site; (Straßen-) roadworks pl. **B~unternehmer** m building contractor

Bayer|(in) m -n,-n (f -,-nen) Bavarian. **B~n** nt -s Bavaria

bay[e]risch adj Bavarian

Bazillus m -,-len bacillus

beabsichtig|en vt intend. **b~t** adj intended; intentional

beacht|en vt take notice of; (einhalten) observe; (folgen) follow; **nicht b~en** ignore. **b~lich** adj considerable. **B~ung** f - observance; **etw** (dat) **keine B~ung schenken** take no notice of sth

Beamte(r) m, **Beamtin** f -,-nen official; (Staats-) civil servant; (Schalter-) clerk

beanspruchen vt claim; (erfordern) demand

beanstand|en vt find fault with; (Comm) make a complaint about. **B~ung** f -,-en complaint

beantragen vt apply for

beantworten vt answer

bearbeiten vt work; (weiter-) process; (behandeln) treat (**mit** with); (Admin) deal with; (redigieren) edit; (Theat) adapt; (Mus) arrange

Beatmungsgerät nt ventilator

beaufsichtig|en vt supervise. **B~ung** f - supervision

beauftragen vt instruct; (Künstler) commission

bebauen vt build on; (bestellen) cultivate

beben vi (haben) tremble

Becher m -s,- beaker; (Henkel-) mug; (Joghurt-, Sahne-) carton

Becken nt -s,- basin; pool; (Mus)

cymbals pl; (Anat) pelvis
bedacht adj careful; **darauf b~**
anxious (**zu** to)
bedächtig adj careful; slow
bedanken (sich) vr thank (**bei
jdm** s.o.)
Bedarf m -s need/(Comm) demand
(**an** + dat for); **bei B~** if required.
B~shaltestelle f request stop
bedauer|lich adj regrettable.
b~licherweise adv unfortunately.
b~n vt regret; (bemitleiden) feel
sorry for; **bedauere!** sorry!
b~nswert adj pitiful; (bedauerlich)
regrettable
bedeckt adj covered; (Himmel)
overcast
bedenken† vt consider; (überlegen) think over. **B~** pl misgivings;
ohne B~ without hesitation
bedenklich adj doubtful; (verdächtig) dubious; (ernst) serious
bedeut|en vi (haben) mean.
b~end adj important; (beträchtlich)
considerable. **B~ung** f -,-en meaning; (Wichtigkeit) importance.
b~ungslos adj meaningless; (unwichtig) unimportant. **b~ungsvoll**
adj significant; (vielsagend) meaningful
bedien|en vt serve; (betätigen) op-
erate; **sich [selbst] b~en** help oneself. **B~ung** f -,-en service; (Betätigung) operation; (Kellner) waiter;
(Kellnerin) f waitress. **B~ungsgeld**
nt service charge
Bedingung f -,-en condition;
B~en conditions; (Comm) terms.
b~slos adj unconditional
bedrohen vt threaten. **b~lich**
adj threatening. **B~ung** f threat
bedrücken vt depress
bedruckt adj printed
bedürf|en† vi (haben) (+ gen)
need. **B~nis** nt -ses,-se need

Beefsteak /'bi:fste:k/ nt -s,-s
steak; **deutsches B~** hamburger
beeilen (sich) vr hurry; hasten
(**zu** to)
beeindrucken vt impress
beeinflussen vt influence
beeinträchtigen vt mar; (schädigen) impair
beengen vt restrict
beerdig|en vt bury. **B~ung** f
-,-en funeral
Beere f -,-n berry
Beet nt -[e]s,-e (Horticulture) bed
Beete f -,-n Rote B~ beetroot
befähig|en vt enable; (qualifizie-
ren) qualify. **B~ung** f - qualifica-
tion; (Fähigkeit) ability
befahrbar adj passable
befallen† vt attack; (Angst:) seize
befangen adj shy; (gehemmt) self-
conscious; (Jur) biased. **B~heit** f -
shyness; self-consciousness; bias
befassen (sich) vr concern one-
self/(behandeln) deal (**mit** with)
Befehl m -[e]s,-e order; (Leitung)
command (**über** + acc of). **b~en †**
vt **jdm etw b~en** order s.o. to do
sth ●vi (haben) give the orders.
B~sform f (Gram) imperative.
B~shaber m -s,- commander
befestigen vt fasten (**an** + dat
to); (Mil) fortify
befeuchten vt moisten
befind|en† (sich) vr be. **B~** nt -s
[state of] health
beflecken vt stain
befolgen vt follow
beförder|n vt transport; (im
Rang) promote. **B~ung** f -,-en
transport; promotion
befragen vt question
befrei|en vt free; (räumen) clear
(**von** of); (freistellen) exempt (**von**
from); **sich b~en** free oneself.

B~er m -s,- liberator. **B~ung** f - liberation; exemption

befreunden (sich) vr make friends; **befreundet sein** be friends

befriedig|en vt satisfy. **b~end** adj satisfying; (zufrieden stellend) satisfactory. **B~ung** f - satisfaction

befrucht|en vt fertilize. **B~ung** f - fertilization; **künstliche B~ung** artificial insemination

Befugnis f -,-se authority

Befund m result

befürcht|en vt fear. **B~ung** f -,-en fear

befürworten vt support

begabt adj gifted. **B~ung** f -,-en gift, talent

begeben† (sich) vr go; **sich in Gefahr b~** expose oneself to danger

begegn|en vi (sein) **jdm/etw b~en** meet someone/something. **B~ung** f -,-en meeting

begehr|en vt desire. **b~t** adj sought-after

begeister|n vt **jdn b~n** arouse someone's enthusiasm. **b~t** adj enthusiastic; (eifrig) keen. **B~ung** f - enthusiasm

Begierde f -,-n desire

Beginn m -s beginning. **b~en†** vt/i (haben) start, begin

beglaubigen vt authenticate

begleichen† vt settle

begleit|en vt accompany. **B~er** m -s,- companion; (Mus) accompanist. **B~ung** f -,-en company; (Mus) accompaniment

beglück|en vt make happy. **b~wünschen** vt congratulate (zu on)

begnadig|en vt (Jur) pardon. **B~ung** f -,-en (Jur) pardon

begraben† vt bury

Begräbnis n -ses,-se burial; (Feier) funeral

begreif|en† vt understand; **nicht zu b~en** incomprehensible. **b~lich** adj understandable

begrenz|en vt form the boundary of; (beschränken) restrict. **b~t** adj limited. **B~ung** f -,-en restriction; (Grenze) boundary

Begriff m -[e]s,-e concept; (Ausdruck) term; (Vorstellung) idea

begründ|en vt give one's reason for. **b~et** adj justified. **B~ung** f -,-en reason

begrüß|en vt greet; (billigen) welcome. **b~enswert** adj welcome. **B~ung** f -,-en greeting; welcome

begünstigen vt favour

begütert adj wealthy

behaart adj hairy

behäbig adj portly

behag|en vi (haben) please (**jdm** s.o.). **B~en** nt -s contentment; (Genuss) enjoyment. **b~lich** adj comfortable. **B~lichkeit** f - comfort

behalten† vt keep; (sich merken) remember

Behälter m -s,- container

behand|eln vt treat; (sich befassen) deal with. **B~lung** f treatment

beharr|en vi (haben) persist (**auf** + dat in). **b~lich** adj persistent

behaupt|en vt maintain; (vorgeben) claim; (sagen) say; (bewahren) retain; **sich b~en** hold one's own. **B~ung** f -,-en assertion; claim; (Äußerung) statement

beheben† vt remedy

behelf|en† (sich) vr make do (**mit** with). **b~smäßig** adj makeshift
● adv provisionally

beherbergen vt put up

beherrsch|en vt rule over; (dominieren) dominate; (meistern, zügeln)

control; (*können*) know. **b∧t** adj
self-controlled. **B∧ung** f - control

beherzigen vt heed

behilflich adj jdm b∼ sein
help s.o.

behinder|n vt hinder; (*blockieren*)
obstruct. **b∧t** adj handicapped;
(*schwer*) disabled. **B∼te(r)** m/f
handicapped/disabled person.
B∼ung f -,-en obstruction; (*Med*)
handicap; disability

Behörde f -,-n [public] authority

behüte|n vt protect. **b∧t** adj
sheltered

behutsam adj careful; (*zart*)
gentle

bei

● *preposition* (+ *dative*)

! Note that **bei** plus **dem** can
   become **beim**

••••➤ (*nahe*) near; (*dicht an,
neben*) by; (*als Begleitung*) with.
wer steht da bei ihm? who is
standing there next to or with
him? **etw bei sich haben** have
sth with or on one. **bleiben Sie
beim Gepäck/bei den Kindern**
stay with the luggage/the
children. **war heute ein Brief
für mich bei der Post?** was
there a letter for me in the
post today?

••••➤ (*an*) by. **jdn bei der Hand
nehmen** take s.o. by the hand

••••➤ (*in der Wohnung von*) at ... 's
home or house/flat. **bei mir
[zu Hause]** at my home or 🏠
place. **bei seinen Eltern leben**
live with one's parents. **wir
sind bei Ulrike eingeladen** we
have been invited to Ulrike's.
bei Schmidt at the Schmidts';

(*Geschäft*) at Schmidts'; (*auf
Briefen*) c/o Schmidt. **bei jdm/
einer Firma arbeiten** work for
s.o./a firm. **bei uns tut man
das nicht** we don't do that
where I come from.

••••➤ (*gegenwärtig*) at; (*verwickelt*)
in. **bei einer Hochzeit/einem
Empfang** at a wedding/recep-
tion. **bei einem Unfall** in an accident

••••➤ (*im Falle von*) in the case of,
with; (*bei Wetter*) in. **wie bei
den Römern** as with the
Romans. **bei Nebel** in fog, if
there is fog. **bei dieser Hitze** in
this heat

••••➤ (*angesichts*) with; (*trotz*) in
spite of. **bei deinen guten
Augen** with your good eyesight.
bei all seinen Bemühungen in
spite of or despite all his efforts

••••➤ (*Zeitpunkt*) at, on. **bei diesen
Worten errötete er** he blushed
at this or on hearing this. **bei
seiner Ankunft** on his arrival.
bei Tag/Nacht by day/night.

••••➤ (*Gleichzeitigkeit, mit Verbalsub-
stantiv*) when ... **en** while or
when ... ing. **beim Spazierenge-
hen im Walde** while walking in
the woods. **beim Überqueren
der Straße** when crossing the
road. **sie war beim Lesen** she
was reading. **wir waren beim
Frühstück** we were having
breakfast

beibehalten† vt sep keep

beibringen† vt sep jdm etw b∼
teach s.o. sth; (*mitteilen*) break sth
to s.o.; (*zufügen*) inflict sth on s.o.

Beicht|e f -,-n confession. **b∼en**
vt/i (*haben*) confess. **B∼stuhl** m
confessional

beide adj & pron both; **b∼s** both;
dreißig b∼ (*Tennis*) thirty all.

b~rseitig adj mutual. **b~rseits** adv & prep (+ gen) on both sides (of)

beieinander adv together

Beifahrer(in) m(f) [front-seat] passenger; (Motorrad) pillion passenger

Beifall m -[e]s applause; (Billigung) approval; **B~ klatschen** applaud

beifügen vt sep add; (beilegen) enclose

beige /bɛːʒ/ inv adj beige

beigeben† vt sep add

Beihilfe f financial aid; (Studien-) grant; (Jur) aiding and abetting

Beil nt -[e]s,-e hatchet, axe

Beilage f supplement; (Gemüse) vegetable

beiläufig adj casual

beilegen vt sep enclose; (schlichten) settle

Beileid nt condolences pl. **B~sbrief** m letter of condolence

beiliegend adj enclosed

beim prep = bei dem; **b~ Militär** in the army; **b~ Frühstück** at breakfast

beimessen† vt sep (fig) attach (dat to)

Bein nt -[e]s,-e leg; **jdm ein B~ stellen** trip s.o. up

beinah[e] adv nearly, almost

Beiname m epithet

beipflichten vi sep (haben) agree (dat with)

Beirat m advisory committee

beisammen adv together; **b~ sein** be together

Beisein nt presence

beiseite adv aside; (abseits) apart; **b~ legen** put aside; (sparen) put by

beisetz|en vt sep bury. **B~ung** f -,-en funeral

Beispiel nt example; **zum B~** for

example. **b~sweise** adv for example

beißen† vt/i (haben) bite; (brennen) sting; **sich b~** (Farben:) clash   **b**

Beistand m -[e]s help. **b~stehen†** vi sep (haben) **jdm b~stehen** help s.o.

beistimmen vi sep (haben) agree

Beistrich m comma

Beitrag m -[e]s,-̈e contribution; (Mitglieds-) subscription; (Versicherungs-) premium; (Zeitungs-) article. **b~en†** vt/i sep (haben) contribute

bei|treten† vi sep (sein) (+ dat) join. **B~tritt** m joining

Beize f -,-n (Holz-) stain

beizeiten adv in good time

beizen vt stain (Holz)

bejahen vt answer in the affirmative; (billigen) approve of

bejahrt adj aged, old

bekämpf|en vt fight. **B~ung** f fight (gen against)

bekannt adj well-known; (vertraut) familiar; **jdn b~ machen** introduce s.o.; **etw b~ machen** od **geben** announce sth; **b~ werden** become known. **B~e(r)** m/f acquaintance; (Freund) friend. **B~gabe** f announcement. **b~lich** adv as is well known. **B~machung** f -,-en announcement; (Anschlag) notice. **B~schaft** f - acquaintance; (Leute) acquaintances pl; (Freunde) friends pl

bekehr|en vt convert. **B~ung** f -,-en conversion

bekenn|en† vt confess, profess (Glauben); **sich [für] schuldig b~en** admit one's guilt. **B~tnis** nt -ses,-se confession; (Konfession) denomination

beklag|en vt lament; (bedauern) deplore; **sich b~en** complain. **b~enswert** adj unfortunate.

B∼te(r) *m/f* (*Jur*) defendant
bekleid|en *vt* hold (*Amt*). B∼ung *f* clothing

Beklemmung *f* -,-en feeling of oppression

bekommen† *vt* get; have (*Baby*); catch (*Erkältung*) ● *vi* (*sein*) jdm gut b∼ do s.o. good; (*Essen:*) agree with s.o.

beköstigen *vt* feed. B∼ung *f* - board; (*Essen*) food

bekräftigen *vt* reaffirm

bekreuzigen (sich) *vr* cross oneself

bekümmert *adj* troubled; (*besorgt*) worried

bekunden *vt* show

Belag *m* -[e]s,-̈e coating; (*Fußboden-*) covering; (*Brot-*) topping; (*Zahn-*) tartar; (*Brems-*) lining

belager|n *vt* besiege. B∼ung *f* -,-en siege

Belang *m* von B∼ of importance; B∼e *pl* interests. b∼los *adj* irrelevant; (*unwichtig*) trivial

belassen† *vt* leave; es dabei b∼ leave it at that

belasten *vt* load; (*fig*) burden; (*beanspruchen*) put a strain on; (*Comm*) debit; (*Jur*) incriminate

belästigen *vt* bother; (*bedrängen*) pester; (*unsittlich*) molest

Belastung *f* -,-en load; (*fig*) strain; (*Comm*) debit. B∼smaterial *nt* incriminating evidence. B∼szeuge *m* prosecution witness

belaufen† (**sich**) *vr* amount (auf + acc to)

belauschen *vt* eavesdrop on

beleb|en *vt* (*fig*) revive; (*lebhaft machen*) enliven. b∼t *adj* lively; (*Straße*) busy

Beleg *m* -[e]s,-e evidence; (*Beispiel*) instance (für of); (*Quittung*) receipt.

b∼en *vt* cover/(*garnieren*) garnish (mit with); (*besetzen*) reserve; (*Univ*) enrol for; (*nachweisen*) provide evidence for; den ersten Platz b∼en (*Sport*) take first place. B∼schaft *f* -,-en workforce. b∼t *adj* occupied; (*Zunge*) coated; (*Stimme*) husky; b∼te Brote open sandwiches

belehren *vt* instruct

beleidig|en *vt* offend; (*absichtlich*) insult. B∼ung *f* -,-en insult

belesen *adj* well-read

beleucht|en *vt* light; (*anleuchten*) illuminate. B∼ung *f* -,-en illumination

Belg|ien *f* -jan/ *nt* -s Belgium. B∼ier(in) *m* -s,- (*f* -,-nen) Belgian. b∼isch *adj* Belgian

belicht|en *vt* (*Phot*) expose. B∼ung *f* - exposure

Belieb|en *nt* -s nach B∼en [just] as one likes. b∼ig *adj* eine b∼ige Zahl any number you like ● *adv* b∼ig oft as often as one likes. b∼t *adj* popular

bellen *vi* (*haben*) bark

belohn|en *vt* reward. B∼ung *f* -,-en reward

belustig|en *vt* amuse. B∼ung *f* -,-en amusement

bemalen *vt* paint

bemängeln *vt* criticize

bemannt *adj* manned

bemerk|bar *adj* sich b∼bar machen attract attention. b∼en *vt* notice; (*äußern*) remark. b∼enswert *adj* remarkable. B∼ung *f* -,-en remark

bemitleiden *vt* pity

bemüh|en *vt* trouble; sich b∼en try (zu to; um etw to get sth); (*sich kümmern*) attend (um to); b∼t sein endeavour (zu to). B∼ung *f* -,-en effort

benachbart *adj* neighbouring

benachrichtig|en vt inform; (amtlich) notify. **B~ung** f -,-en notification

benachteiligen vt discriminate against; (ungerecht sein) treat unfairly

benehmen† (sich) vr behave. **B~** nt -s behaviour

beneiden vt envy (**um etw** sth)

Bengel m -s,- boy; (Rüpel) lout

benötigen vt need

benutz|en, (SGer) **benütz|en** vt use; take (Bahn). **B~ung** f use

Benzin nt -s petrol

beobacht|en vt observe. **B~er** m -s,- observer. **B~ung** f -,-en observation

bequem adj comfortable; (mühelos) easy; (faul) lazy. **b~en** (sich) vr deign (**zu** to). **B~lichkeit** f -,-en comfort; (Faulheit) laziness

berat|en† vt advise; (überlegen) discuss; **sich b~en** confer ● vi (haben) discuss (**über etw** acc sth); (beratschlagen) confer. **B~er(in)** m -s,-. (f -,-nen) adviser. **B~ung** f -,-nen guidance; (Rat) advice; (Besprechung) discussion; (Med, Jur) consultation

berechn|en vt calculate; (anrechnen) charge for; (abfordern) charge. **B~ung** f calculation

berechtig|en vt entitle; (befugen) authorize; (fig) justify. **b~t** adj justified, justifiable. **B~ung** f -,-en authorization; (Recht) right; (Rechtmäßigkeit) justification

bered|en vt talk about; **sich b~en** talk. **B~samkeit** f - eloquence

beredt adj eloquent

Bereich m -[e]s,-e area; (fig) realm; (Fach-) field

bereichern vi enrich

bereit adj ready. **b~en** vt prepare; (verursachen) cause; give (Überraschung). **b~halten†** vt sep have/(ständig) keep ready. **b~legen** vt sep put out [ready]. **b~machen** vt sep get ready. **b~s** adv already

Bereitschaft f -,-en readiness; (Einheit) squad. **B~sdienst** m **B~sdienst haben** (Mil) be on stand-by; (Arzt:) be on call. **B~spolizei** f riot police

bereit|stehen† vi sep (haben) be ready. **b~stellen** vt sep put out ready; (verfügbar machen) make available. **B~ung** f - preparation.

b~willig adj willing

bereuen vt regret

Berg m -[e]s,-e mountain; (Anhöhe) hill; **in den B~en** in the mountains. **b~ab** adv downhill. **B~arbeiter** m miner. **b~auf** adv uphill. **B~bau** m -[e]s mining

bergen† vt recover; (Naut) salvage; (retten) rescue

Berg|führer m mountain guide. **b~ig** adj mountainous. **B~kette** f mountain range. **B~mann** m (pl -leute) miner. **B~steiger(in)** m -s,- (f -,-nen) mountaineer, climber

Bergung f - recovery; (Naut) salvage; (Rettung) rescue

Berg|wacht f mountain rescue service. **B~werk** nt mine

Bericht m -[e]s,-e report; (Reise-) account. **b~en** vt/i (haben) report; (erzählen) tell (**von** of). **B~erstatter(in)** m -s,- (f -,-nen) reporter

berichtigen vt correct

beriesel|n vt irrigate. **B~ungsanlage** f sprinkler system

Berlin nt -s Berlin. **B~er** m -s,- Berliner

Bernhardiner m -s,- St Bernard

Bernstein m amber

berüchtigt adj notorious

berücksichtig|en vt take into

consideration. **B~ung** f - consideration

Beruf m profession; (Tätigkeit) occupation; (Handwerk) trade. **b~en†** vt appoint; **sich b~en** refer (**auf** + acc to); (vorgeben) plead (**auf etw** acc sth); ● adj competent; **b~en sein** be destined (**zu** to). **b~lich** adj professional; (Ausbildung) vocational ● adv professionally; **b~lich tätig sein** work, have a job. **B~sberatung** f vocational guidance. **B~sausbildung** f professional training. **b~smäßig** adv professionally. **B~sschule** f vocational school. **B~ssoldat** m regular soldier. **b~stätig** adj working; **b~stätig sein** work, have a job. **B~stätige(r)** m/f working man/woman. **B~ung** f -,-en appointment; (Bestimmung) vocation; (Jur) appeal. **B~ung einlegen** appeal. **B~ungsgericht** nt appeal court

beruhen vi (haben) be based (**auf** + dat on)

beruhig|en vt calm [down]; (zuversichtlich machen) reassure. **b~end** adj calming; (tröstend) reassuring; (Med) sedative. **B~ung** f - calming; reassurance; (Med) sedation. **B~ungsmittel** nt sedative; (bei Psychosen) tranquillizer

berühmt adj famous. **B~heit** f -,-en fame; (Person) celebrity

berühr|en vt touch; (erwähnen) touch on. **B~ung** f -,-en touch; (Kontakt) contact

besänftigen vt soothe

Besatz m -es, ≈e trimming

Besatzung f -,-en crew; (Mil) occupying force

beschädig|en vt damage. **B~ung** f -,-en damage

beschaffen vt obtain, get ● adj so **b~ sein, dass** be such that. **B~heit** f - consistency

beschäftig|en vt occupy; (Arbeitgeber:) employ; **sich b~en** occupy oneself. **b~t** adj busy; (angestellt) employed (**bei** at). **B~ung** f -,-en occupation; (Anstellung) employment

beschämt adj ashamed; (verlegen) embarrassed

beschatten vt shade; (überwachen) shadow

Bescheid m -[e]s information; **jdm B~ sagen** od **geben** let s.o. know; **B~ wissen** know

bescheiden adj modest. **B~heit** f - modesty

bescheinen† vt shine on; **von der Sonne beschienen** sunlit

bescheinig|en vt certify. **B~ung** f -,-en [written] confirmation; (Schein) certificate

beschenken vt give a present/ presents to

Bescherung f -,-en distribution of Christmas presents

beschildern vt signpost

beschimpf|en vt abuse, swear at. **B~ung** f -,-en abuse

beschirmen vt protect

Beschlag m in **B~ nehmen** monopolize. **b~en†** vt shoe ● vi (sein) steam or mist up ● adj steamed or misted up. **B~nahme** f -,-n confiscation; (Jur) seizure. **b~nahmen** vt confiscate; (Jur) seize

beschleunig|en vt hasten; (schneller machen) speed up (Schritt) ● vi (haben) accelerate. **B~ung** f - acceleration

beschließen† vt decide; (beenden) end ● vi (haben) decide (**über** + acc about)

Beschluss m decision

beschmutzen vt make dirty

beschneid|en† vt trim; (Horticulture) prune; (Relig) circumcise.

B~ung f - circumcision

beschnüffeln vt sniff at

beschönigen vt (fig) gloss over

beschränken vt limit, restrict; **sich b~ auf** (+ acc) confine oneself to

beschrankt adj (Bahnübergang) with barrier[s]

beschränk|t adj limited; (geistig) dull-witted. **B~ung** f -,-en limitation, restriction

beschreib|en† vt describe. **B~ung** f -,-en description

beschuldig|en vt accuse. **B~ung** f -,-en accusation

beschummeln vt 🗓 cheat

Beschuss m (Mil) fire; (Artillerie-) shelling

beschütz|en vt protect. **B~er** m -s,- protector

Beschwerde f -,-n complaint; **B~den** (Med) trouble sg. **b~en** vt weight down; **sich b~en** complain. **b~lich** adj difficult

beschwindeln vt cheat (um out of); (belügen) lie to

beschwipst adj 🗓 tipsy

beseitig|en vt remove. **B~ung** f - removal

Besen m -s,- broom

> ℹ️ **Besenwirtschaft** An inn set up by a local winegrower for a few weeks after the new wine has been made. An inflated pig's bladder is hung up outside the door to show that the new vintage may be sampled there. This is mainly found in Southern Germany. ▷HEURIGE.

---

besessen adj obsessed (von by)

besetz|en vt occupy; fill (Posten); (Theat) cast (Rolle); (verzieren) trim (mit with). **b~t** adj occupied; (Toi-

lette, Leitung) engaged; (Zug, Bus) full up; **der Platz ist b~t** this seat is taken. **B~tzeichen** nt engaged tone. **B~ung** f -,-en occupation; (Theat) cast

besichtig|en vt look round (Stadt); (prüfen) inspect; (besuchen) visit. **B~ung** f -,-en visit; (Prüfung) inspection; (Stadt-) sightseeing

besiedelt adj dünn/dicht b~ sparsely/densely populated

besiegen vt defeat

besinn|en† (sich) vr think, reflect; (sich erinnern) remember (auf jdn/ etw someone/something). **B~ung** f - reflection; (Bewusstsein) consciousness; bei/ohne B~ung conscious/unconscious. **b~ungslos** adj unconscious

Besitz m possession; (Eigentum, Land-) property; (Gut) estate. **b~en**† vt own, possess; (haben) have. **B~er(in)** m -s,- (f -,-nen) owner; (Comm) proprietor

besoffen adj 🗙 drunken; **b~ sein** be drunk

besonder|e(r,s) adj special; (bestimmt) particular; (gesondert) separate. **b~s** adv [e]specially, particularly; (gesondert) separately

besonnen adj calm

besorg|en vt get; (kaufen) buy; (erledigen) attend to; (versorgen) look after. **b~t** adj worried/(bedacht) concerned (um about). **B~ung** f -,-en errand; **B~ungen machen** do shopping

bespitzeln vt spy on

besprech|en† vt discuss; (rezensieren) review. **B~ung** f -,-en discussion; review; (Konferenz) meeting

besser adj & adv better. **b~n** vt improve; **sich b~n** get better. **B~ung** f - improvement; **gute B~ung!** get well soon!

Bestand | beteiligen

42

Bestand m -[e]s, ̈e existence; (*Vorrat*) stock (**an** + dat of)

b **beständig** adj constant; (*Wetter*) settled; **b~ gegen** resistant to

Bestand|aufnahme f stock-taking. **B~teil** m part

bestätig|en vt confirm; acknowledge (*Empfang*); **sich b~en** prove to be true. **B~ung** f -,-en confirmation

bestatt|en vt bury. **B~ung** f -,-en funeral

Bestäubung f - pollination

bestaunen vt gaze at in amazement; (*bewundern*) admire

best|e(r,s) adj best; **b~en Dank!** many thanks! **B~e(r,s)** m/f/nt best; **sein B~es** do one's best

bestech|en vt bribe; (*bezaubern*) captivate. **b~end** adj captivating. **b~lich** adj corruptible. **B~ung** f - bribery. **B~ungsgeld** nt bribe

Besteck nt -[e]s,-e [set of] knife, fork and spoon; (*coll*) cutlery

bestehen† vi (haben) exist; (*fortdauern*) last; (*bei Prüfung*) pass; **~ aus** consist/(*gemacht sein*) be made of; **~ auf** (+ dat) insist on ● vt pass (*Prüfung*)

besteig|en† vt climb; (*aufsteigen*) mount; ascend (*Thron*). **B~ung** f ascent

bestell|en vt order; (*vor-*) book; (*ernennen*) appoint; (*bebauen*) cultivate; (*ausrichten*) tell; **zu sich b~en** send for; **b~t sein** have an appointment; **kann ich etwas b~en?** can I take a message? **B~schein** m order form. **B~ung** f order; (*Botschaft*) message; (*Bebauung*) cultivation

besteuer|n vt tax. **B~ung** f - taxation

Bestie /'bɛstjə/ f -,-n beast

bestimm|en vt fix; (*entscheiden*)

decide; (*vorsehen*) intend; (*ernennen*) appoint; (*ermitteln*) determine; (*definieren*) define; (*Gram*) qualify ● vi (haben) be in charge (**über** + acc of). **~t** adj definite; (*gewiss*) certain; (*fest*) firm. **B~ung** f fixing; (*Vorschrift*) regulation; (*Ermittlung*) determination; (*Definition*) definition; (*Zweck*) purpose; (*Schicksal*) destiny. **B~ungsort** m destination

Bestleistung f (*Sport*) record

bestraf|en vt punish. **B~ung** f -,-en punishment

Bestrahlung f radiotherapy

bestreb|en vt -s endeavour; (*Absicht*) aim. **B~ung** f -,-en effort

bestreiten† vt dispute; (*leugnen*) deny; (*bezahlen*) pay for

bestürz|t adj dismayed; (*erschüttert*) stunned. **B~ung** f - dismay, consternation

Bestzeit f (*Sport*) record [time]

Besuch m -[e]s,-e visit; (*kurz*) call; (*Schul-*) attendance; (*Gast*) visitor; (*Gäste*) visitors pl; **b~ haben** have a visitor/visitors; **bei jdm zu od auf B~ sein** be staying with s.o. **~en** vt visit; (*kurz*) call on; (*teilnehmen*) attend; go to (*Schule, Ausstellung*). **B~er(in)** m -s,- (f -,-nen) visitor; caller. **B~szeit** f visiting hours pl

betagt adj aged, old

betätig|en vt operate; **sich b~en** work (**als** as). **B~ung** f -,-en operation; (*Tätigkeit*) activity

betäub|en vt stun; (*Lärm:*) deafen; (*Med*) anaesthetize; (*lindern*) ease; deaden (*Schmerz*); **wie b~t** dazed. **B~ung** f - daze; (*Med*) anaesthesia. **B~ungsmittel** nt anaesthetic

Bete f -,-n **Rote B~** beetroot

beteilig|en vt give a share to; **sich b~en** take part (**an** + dat at); (*beitragen*) contribute (**an** + dat to). **b~t** adj **b~t sein** take part/(*an Un-*

fall) be involved/(*Comm*) have a share (**an** + *dat* in); **alle B~ten** all those involved. **B~ung** *f* -,-en participation; involvement; (*Anteil*) share

beten *vi* (*haben*) pray

Beton /be'tɔŋ/ *m* -s concrete

betonen *vt* stressed, emphasize

beton|t *adj* stressed; (*fig*) pointed. **B~ung** *f* -,-en stress

Betracht *m* in **B~ ziehen** consider; **außer B~ lassen** disregard; **nicht in B~ kommen** be out of the question. **b~en** *vt* look at; (*fig*) regard (**als** as)

beträchtlich *adj* considerable

Betrachtung *f* -,-en contemplation; (*Überlegung*) reflection

Betrag *m* -[e]s, ⁻e amount. **b~en†** *vt* amount to; **sich b~en** behave. **B~en** *nt* -s behaviour; (*Sch*) conduct

betreff|en† *vt* affect; (*angehen*) concern. **b~end** *adj* relevant. **b~s** *prep* (+ *gen*) concerning

betreiben† *vt* (*leiten*) run; (*ausüben*) carry on

betreten† *vt* step on; (*eintreten*) enter; 'B~ verboten' 'no entry'; (*bei Rasen*) 'keep off [the grass]'

betreuen *vt* look after. **B~er(in)** *m* -s,- (*f* -,-nen) helper; (*Kranken-*) nurse. **B~ung** *f* - care

Betrieb *m* business; (*Firma*) firm; (*Treiben*) activity; (*Verkehr*) traffic; **außer B~** not in use; (*defekt*) out of order

Betriebs|anleitung, B~anweisung *f* operating instructions *pl.* **B~ferien** *f* firm's holiday. **B~leitung** *f* management. **B~rat** *m* works committee. **B~störung** *f* breakdown

betrinken† (sich) *vr* get drunk

betroffen *adj* disconcerted; **b~**

sein be affected (**von** by)

betrüb|en *vt* sadden. **b~t** *adj* sad

Betrug *m* -[e]s deception; (*Jur*) fraud

betrüg|en† *vt* cheat, swindle; (*Jur*) defraud; (*in der Ehe*) be unfaithful to. **B~er(in)** *m* -s,- (*f* -,-nen) swindler. **B~erei** *f* -,-en fraud

betrunken *adj* drunken; **b~ sein** be drunk. **B~e(r)** *m* drunk

Bett *nt* -[e]s,-en bed. **B~couch** *f* sofa-bed. **B~decke** *f* blanket; (*Tages-*) bedspread

Bettel|ei *f* - begging. **b~n** *vi* (*haben*) beg

Bettler(in) *m* -s,- (*f* -,-nen) beggar

Bettpfanne *f* bedpan

Betttuch (Bettuch) *nt* sheet

Bett|wäsche *f* bed linen. **B~zeug** *nt* bedding

betupfen *vt* dab (**mit** with)

beug|en *vt* bend; (*Gram*) decline; conjugate (*Verb*); **sich b~en** bend; (*lehnen*) lean; (*sich fügen*) submit (**dat** to). **B~ung** *f* -,-en (*Gram*) declension; conjugation

Beule *f* -,-n bump; (*Delle*) dent

beunruhig|en *vt* worry; **sich b~en** worry. **B~ung** *f* - worry

beurlauben *vt* give leave to

beurteil|en *vt* judge. **B~ung** *f* -,-en judgement; (*Ansicht*) opinion

Beute *f* - booty, haul; (*Jagd-*) bag; (*eines Raubtiers*) prey

Beutel *m* -s,- bag; (*Tabak- & Zool*) pouch. **B~tier** *nt* marsupial

Bevölkerung *f* -,-en population

bevollmächtigen *vt* authorize

bevor *conj* before; **b~ nicht** until

bevormunden *vt* treat like a child

bevorstehen† *vi sep* (*haben*) approach; (*unmittelbar*) be imminent.

b~d adj approaching, forthcoming; **unmittelbar b~d** imminent

bevorzug|en vt prefer; (begünstigen) favour. **B~t** adj privileged; (Behandlung) preferential

bewachen vt guard

Bewachung f - guard; **unter B~** under guard

bewaffn|en vt arm. **b~et** adj armed. **B~ung** f - armament; (Waffen) arms pl

bewahren vt protect (**vor** + dat from); (behalten) keep; **die Ruhe b~** keep calm

bewähren (sich) vr prove one's/(Ding:) its worth; (erfolgreich sein) prove a success

bewähr|t adj reliable; (erprobt) proven. **B~ung** f - (Jur) probation. **B~ungsfrist** f [period of] probation. **B~ungsprobe** f (fig) test

bewältigen vt cope with; (überwinden) overcome

bewässer|n vt irrigate. **B~ung** f - irrigation

bewegen[1] vt (reg) move; **sich b~** move; (körperlich) take exercise

bewegen[2] vt jdn dazu b~, etw zu tun induce s.o. to do sth

Beweg|grund m motive. **b~lich** adj movable, mobile; (wendig) agile. **B~lichkeit** f - mobility; agility. **B~ung** f -,-en movement; (Phys) motion; (Rührung) emotion; (Gruppe) movement; **körperliche B~ung** physical exercise. **b~ungslos** adj motionless

Beweis m -es,-e proof; (Zeichen) token; **B~e** evidence sg. **b~en[†]** vt prove; (zeigen) show; **sich b~en** prove oneself/(Ding:) itself. **B~material** nt evidence

bewerb|en (sich) vr apply (**um** for; **bei** to). **B~er(in)** m -s,- (f -,-nen) applicant. **B~ung** f -,-en application

bewerten vt value; (einschätzen) rate; (Sch) mark, grade

bewilligen vt grant

bewirken vt cause; (herbeiführen) bring about

bewirt|en vt entertain. **B~ung** f - hospitality

bewohn|bar adj habitable. **b~en** vt inhabit, live in. **B~er(in)** m -s,- (f -,-nen) resident, occupant; (Einwohner) inhabitant

bewölk|en (sich) vr cloud over; **b~t** cloudy. **B~ung** f - clouds pl

bewunder|n vt admire. **b~nswert** adj admirable. **B~ung** f - admiration

bewusst adj conscious (gen of); (absichtlich) deliberate. **b~los** adj unconscious. **B~losigkeit** f - unconsciousness; **B~sein** nt -s consciousness; (Gewissheit) awareness; **bei B~sein** conscious

bezahl|en vt/i (haben) pay; pay for (Ware, Essen). **B~ung** f - payment; (Lohn) pay. **B~fernsehen** nt pay television; pay TV

bezaubern vt enchant

bezeichn|en vt mark; (bedeuten) denote; (beschreiben, nennen) describe (**als** as). **b~end** adj typical. **B~ung** f marking; (Beschreibung) description (**als** as); (Ausdruck) term; (Name) name

bezeugen vt testify to

bezichtigen vt accuse (gen of)

beziehen[†] vt cover; (einziehen) move into; (beschaffen) obtain; (erhalten) get; (in Verbindung bringen) relate (**auf** + acc to); **sich b~en** (bewölken) cloud over; **sich b~en auf** (+ acc) refer to; **das Bett frisch b~en** put clean sheets on the bed. **B~ung** f -,-en relation; (Verhältnis) relationship; (Bezug) respect; **B~un-**

gen haben have connections.
b~ungsweise adv respectively;
(vielmehr) or rather

Bezirk m -[e]s,-e district

Bezug m cover; (Kissen-) case; (Beschaffung) obtaining; (Kauf) purchase; (Zusammenhang) reference;
B~e pl earnings; **B~ nehmen**
(auf + acc to); **in B~ auf** (+ acc) regarding

bezüglich prep (+ gen) regarding
● adj relating (**auf** + acc to)

bezwecken vt (fig) aim at

bezweifeln vt doubt

BH /be:'ha:/ m -[s],-[s] bra

Bibel f -,-n Bible

Biber m -s,- beaver

Biblio|thek f -,-en library.
B~thekar(in) m -s,- (f -,-nen) librarian

biblisch adj biblical

bieg|en vt bend; **sich b~en** bend
● vi (sein) curve (**nach** to); **um die
Ecke b~en** turn the corner.
b~sam adj flexible, supple. **B~ung**
f -,-en bend

Biene f -,-n bee. **B~nstock** m beehive. **B~nwabe** f honey-comb

Bier nt -s,-e beer. **B~deckel** m
beer-mat. **B~krug** m beer-mug

Weizenbier (north-west) and *Weiße*
(Berlin). A *Biergarten* is a rustic open-air pub, or beer garden, which is traditional in Bavaria and Austria.

bieten† vt offer; (bei Auktion) bid

Bifokalbrille f bifocals pl

Bigamie f - bigamy

bigott adj over-pious

Bikini m -s,-s bikini

Bilanz f -,-en balance sheet; (fig)
result; **die B~ ziehen** (fig) draw
conclusions (**aus** from)

Bild nt -[e]s,-er picture;
(Theat) scene

bilden vt form; (sein) be; (erziehen)
educate

Bilderbuch nt picture-book.
B~fläche f screen. **B~hauer** m
-s,- sculptor. **b~lich** adj pictorial;
(figurativ) figurative. **B~nis** nt
-ses,-se portrait. **B~punkt** m pixel.
B~schirm m (TV) screen.
B~schirmgerät nt visual display
unit, VDU. **b~schön** adj very
beautiful

Bildung f - formation; (Erziehung)
education; (Kultur) culture

Billard /'biljart/ nt -s billiards sg.
B~tisch m billiard table

Billett /bil'jɛt/ nt -[e]s,-e & -s
ticket

Billiarde f -,-n thousand million
million

billig adj cheap; (dürftig) poor;
recht und b~ right and proper.
b~en vt approve. **B~flieger** m
low-cost airline. **B~ung** f - approval

Billion /bil'jo:n/ f -,-en million million, billion

Bimsstein m pumice stone

Binde f -,-n band; (Verband) bandage; (Damen-) sanitary towel.
B~hautentzündung f conjunctiv-

itis. **b~n** *vt* tie (**an** + *acc* to); make (*Strauß*) bind (*Buch*); (*fesseln*) tie up; (*Culin*) thicken; **sich b~n** commit oneself. **B~strich** *m* hyphen. **B~wort** *nt* (*pl* **-wörter**) (*Gram*) conjunction

Bind|faden *m* string. **B~ung** *f* -,-en (*fig*) tie; (*Beziehung*) relationship; (*Verpflichtung*) commitment; (*Ski-*) binding; (*Textiles*) weave

binnen *prep* (+ *dat*) within. **B~handel** *m* home trade

Bio- *prefix* organic

Bio|chemie *f* biochemistry. **b~dynamisch** *adj* organic. **B~grafie**, **B~grafie** *f* -,-n biography

Bio|hof *m* organic farm. **B~laden** *m* health-food store

Biolog|e *m* -n,-n biologist. **B~ie** *f* - biology. **b~isch** *adj* biological; **b~ischer Anbau** organic farming; **b~isch angebaut** organically grown

Bioterrorismus *m* bioterrorism

Birke *f* -,-n birch [tree]

Birma|a *nt* -s Burma. **b~anisch** *adj* Burmese

Birn|baum *m* pear-tree. **B~e** *f* -,-n pear; (*Electr*) bulb

bis *prep* (+ *acc*) as far as, [up] to; (*zeitlich*) until, till; (*spätestens*) by; **bis zu** up to; **bis auf** (+ *acc*) (*einschließlich*) [down] to; (*ausgenommen*) except [for]; **drei bis vier Minuten** three to four minutes; **bis morgen!** see you tomorrow! ● *conj* until

Bischof *m* -s,-e bishop

bisher *adv* so far, up to now

Biskuit|rolle /bɪs'kviːt-/ *f* Swiss roll. **B~teig** *m* sponge mixture

Biss *m* -es,-e bite

bisschen *inv pron* **ein b~** a bit, a little; **kein b~** not a bit

Biss|en *m* -s,- bite, mouthful.

b~ig *adj* vicious; (*fig*) caustic

bisweilen *adv* from time to time

bitt|e *adv* please; (*nach Klopfen*) come in; (*als Antwort auf 'danke'*) don't mention it, you're welcome; **wie b~e?** pardon? **B~e** *f* -,-n request/(*dringend*) plea (**um** for). **b~en†** *vt/i* (*haben*) ask/(*dringend*) beg (**um** for); (*einladen*) invite, ask. **b~end** *adj* pleading

bitter *adj* bitter. **B~keit** *f* - bitterness. **b~lich** *adv* bitterly

Bittschrift *f* petition

bizarr *adj* bizarre

blähen *vt* swell; (*Vorhang, Segel*) billow ● *vi* (*haben*) cause flatulence. **B~ungen** *fpl* flatulence *sg*, Ⓘ wind *sg*

Blamage /bla'maːʒə/ *f* -,-n humiliation; (*Schande*) disgrace

blamieren *vt* disgrace; **sich b~** disgrace oneself; (*sich lächerlich machen*) make a fool of oneself

blanchieren /blã'ʃiːrən/ *vt* (*Culin*) blanch

blank *adj* shiny. **B~oscheck** *m* blank cheque

Blase *f* -,-n bubble; (*Med*) blister; (*Anat*) bladder. **b~n†** *vt/i* (*haben*) blow; play (*Flöte*). **B~nentzündung** *f* cystitis

Blas|instrument *nt* wind instrument. **B~kapelle** *f* brass band

blass *adj* pale; (*schwach*) faint

Blässe *f* - pallor

Blatt *nt* -[e]s, -er (*Bot*) leaf; (*Papier*) sheet; (*Zeitung*) paper

Blattlaus *f* greenfly

blau *adj*, **B~** *nt* -s,- blue; **b~er Fleck** bruise; **b~es Auge** black eye; **b~ sein** Ⓘ be tight; **Fahrt ins B~e** mystery tour. **B~beere** *f* bilberry. **B~licht** *nt* blue flashing light

Blech *nt* -[e]s,-e sheet metal; (*Weiß-*) tin; (*Platte*) metal sheet;

(*Back-*) baking sheet; (*Mus*) brass; (▯: *Unsinn*) rubbish. **B∼schaden** *m* (*Auto*) damage to the bodywork

Blei *nt* -[e]s lead

Bleibe *f* - place to stay. **b∼n**† *vi* (*sein*) remain, stay; (*übrig-*) be left; **ruhig b∼n** keep calm; **bei etw b∼n** (*fig*) stick to sth; **b∼n Sie am Apparat** hold the line; **etw b∼n lassen** not do sth. **b∼nd** *adj* permanent; (*anhaltend*) lasting

bleich *adj* pale. **b∼en**† *vi* (*sein*) bleach; (*ver-*) fade ● *vt* (*reg*) bleach. **B∼mittel** *nt* bleach

blei|ern *adj* leaden. **∼frei** *adj* unleaded. **B∼stift** *m* pencil. **B∼stiftabsatz** *m* stiletto heel. **B∼stiftspitzer** *m* -s,- pencil sharpener

Blende *f* -,-n shade, shield; (*Sonnen-*) [sun] visor; (*Phot*) diaphragm; (*Öffnung*) aperture; (*an Kleid*) facing. **b∼n** *vt* dazzle, blind

Blick *m* -[e]s,-e look; (*kurz*) glance; (*Aussicht*) view; **auf den ersten B∼** at first sight. **b∼en** *vi* (*haben*) look/(*kurz*) glance (**auf** + *acc* at). **B∼punkt** *m* (*fig*) point of view

blind *adj* blind; (*trübe*) dull; **b∼er Alarm** false alarm; **b∼er Passagier** stowaway. **B∼darm** *m* appendix. **B∼darmentzündung** *f* appendicitis. **B∼e(r)** *m/f* blind man/woman; **die B∼en** the blind *pl*. **B∼enhund** *m* guidedog. **B∼enschrift** *f* braille. **B∼gänger** *m* -s,- (*Mil*) dud. **B∼heit** *f* - blindness

blink|en *vi* (*haben*) flash; (*funkeln*) gleam; (*Auto*) indicate. **B∼er** *m* -s,- (*Auto*) indicator. **b∼licht** *nt* flashing light

blinzeln *vi* (*haben*) blink

Blitz *m* -es,-e [flash of] lightning; (*Phot*) flash. **B∼ableiter** *m* lightning-conductor. **b∼artig** *adj* lightning ● *adv* like lightning. **b∼en** *vi* (*haben*) flash; (*funkeln*) sparkle; **es**

hat geblitzt there was a flash of lightning. **B∼eis** *nt* sheet ice. **B∼licht** *nt* (*Phot*) flash. **b∼sauber** *adj* spick and span. **b∼schnell** *adj* lightning ● *adv* like lightning

Block *m* -[e]s,⸚e block ● -[e]s,-s & ⸚e pad; (*Häuser-*) block

Blockade *f* -,-n blockade

Blockflöte *f* recorder

blockieren *vt* block; (*Mil*) blockade

Blockschrift *f* block letters *pl*

blöd[e] *adj* feeble-minded; (*dumm*) stupid

Blödsinn *m* -[e]s idiocy; (*Unsinn*) nonsense

blöken *vi* (*haben*) bleat

blond *adj* fair-haired; (*Haar*) fair

bloß *adj* bare; (*alleinig*) mere ● *adv* only, just

bloß|legen *vt sep* uncover. **b∼stellen** *vt sep* compromise

Bluff *m* -s,-s bluff. **b∼en** *vt/i* (*haben*) bluff

blühen *vi* (*haben*) flower; (*fig*) flourish. **b∼d** *adj* flowering; (*fig*) flourishing, thriving

Blume *f* -,-n flower; (*vom Wein*) bouquet. **B∼nbeet** *nt* flower-bed. **B∼ngeschäft** *nt* flower-shop, florist's. **B∼nkohl** *m* cauliflower. **B∼nmuster** *nt* floral design. **B∼nstrauß** *m* bunch of flowers. **B∼ntopf** *m* flowerpot; (*Pflanze*) pot plant. **B∼nzwiebel** *f* bulb

blumig *adj* flowery

Bluse *f* -,-n blouse

Blut *nt* -[e]s blood. **b∼arm** *adj* anaemic. **B∼bahn** *f* blood-stream. **B∼bild** *nt* blood count. **B∼druck** *m* blood pressure. **b∼dürstig** *adj* bloodthirsty

Blüte *f* -,-n flower, bloom; (*vom Baum*) blossom; (*B∼zeit*) flowering period; (*Baum-*) blossom time;

(Höhepunkt) peak, prime
Blut|egel m -s,- leech. **b~en** vi (haben) bleed
Blüten|blatt nt petal. **B~staub** m pollen
Blut|er m -s,- haemophiliac. **B~erguss** m bruise. **B~gefäß** nt blood-vessel. **B~gruppe** f blood group. **b~ig** adj bloody. **B~körperchen** nt -s,- corpuscle. **B~probe** f blood test. **b~rünstig** adj (fig) bloody, gory. **B~schande** f incest. **B~spender** m blood donor. **B~sturz** m haemorrhage. **B~transfusion, B~übertragung** f blood transfusion. **B~ung** f -,-en bleeding; (Med) haemorrhage; (Regel-) period. **b~unterlaufen** adj bruised; (Auge) bloodshot. **B~vergiftung** f blood-poisoning. **B~wurst** f black pudding
Bö f -,-en gust; (Regen-) squall
Bob m -s,-s bob[-sleigh]
Bock m -[e]s,≈e buck; (Ziege) billy goat; (Schaf) ram; (Gestell) support. **b~ig** adj 🔢 stubborn. **B~springen** nt leap-frog
Boden m -s,≈ ground; (Erde) soil; (Fuß-) floor; (Grundfläche) bottom; (Dach-) loft, attic. **B~satz** m sediment. **B~schätze** mpl mineral deposits. **B~see (der)** Lake Constance
Bogen m -s,- & ≈ curve; (Geometry) arc; (beim Skilauf) turn; (Architecture) arch; (Waffe, Geigen-) bow; (Papier) sheet; **einen großen B~ um jdn/etw machen** 🔢 give s.o./ sth a wide berth. **B~schießen** nt archery
Bohle f -,-n [thick] plank
Böhm|en nt -s Bohemia. **b~isch** adj Bohemian
Bohne f -,-n bean; **grüne B~n** French beans
bohner|n vt polish. **B~wachs** nt floor-polish
bohr|en vt/i (haben) drill (nach for); drive (Tunnel); sink (Brunnen); (Insekt:) bore. **B~er** m -s,- drill. **B~insel** f [offshore] drilling rig. **B~turm** m derrick
Boje f -,-n buoy
Böllerschuss m gun salute
Bolzen m -s,- bolt; (Stift) pin
bombardieren vt bomb; (fig) bombard (mit with)
Bombe f -,-n bomb. **B~nangriff** m bombing raid. **B~nerfolg** m huge success
Bon /bɔŋ/ m -s,-s voucher; (Kassen-) receipt
Bonbon /bɔŋˈbɔŋ/ m & nt -s,-s sweet
Bonus m -[ses],-[se] bonus
Boot nt -[e]s,-e boat. **B~ssteg** m landing-stage
Bord¹ nt -[e]s,-e shelf
Bord² m (Naut) **an B~** aboard, on board; **über B~** overboard. **B~buch** nt log[-book]
Bordell nt -s,-e brothel
Bordkarte f boarding-pass
borgen vt borrow; **jdm etw b~** lend s.o. sth
Borke f -,-n bark
Börse f -,-n purse; (Comm) stock exchange. **B~nmakler** m stockbroker
Borst|e f -,-n bristle. **b~ig** adj bristly
Borte f -,-n braid
Böschung f -,-en embankment
böse adj wicked, evil; (unartig) naughty; (schlimm) bad; (zornig) cross; **jdm od auf jdn b~ sein** be cross with s.o.
bos|haft adj malicious, spiteful. **B~heit** f -,-en malice; spite; (Handlung) spiteful act/(Bemerkung)

remark

böswillig adj malicious

Botani|k f - botany. **B~ker(in)** m -s,- (f -,-nen) botanist

Bot|e m -n,-n messenger. **B~engang** m errand. **B~schaft** f -,-en message; (Pol) embassy. **B~schafter** m -s,- ambassador

Bouillon /bul'jɔn/ f -,-s clear soup. **B~würfel** m stock cube

Bowle /'bo:lə/ f -,-n punch

Box f -,-en box; (Pferde-) loose box; (Lautsprecher-) speaker; (Autorennen) pit

box|en vi (haben) box ● vt punch. **B~en** nt -s boxing. **B~enluder** nt pit babe. **B~er** m -s,- boxer. **B~stopp** m pit stop

brachliegen† vi sep (haben) lie fallow

Branche /'brã:ʃə/ f -,-n [line of] business. **B~nverzeichnis** nt (Teleph) classified directory

Brand m -[e]s,ːe fire; (Med) gangrene; (Bot) blight; **in B~** geraten catch fire; **in B~ setzen** or **stecken** set on fire. **B~bombe** f incendiary bomb

Brand|stifter m arsonist. **B~stiftung** f arson

Brandung f - surf

Brand|wunde f burn. **B~zeichen** nt brand

Branntwein m spirit; (coll) spirits pl. **B~brennerei** f distillery

bras|ilianisch adj Brazilian. **B~ilien** nt -s Brazil

Brat|apfel m baked apple. **b~en†** vt/i (haben) roast; (in der Pfanne) fry. **B~en** m -s,- roast; (B~stück) joint. **b~fertig** adj oven-ready. **B~hähnchen** nt roasting chicken. **B~kartoffeln** fpl fried potatoes. **B~pfanne** f frying-pan

Bratsche f -,-n (Mus) viola

Bratspieß m spit

Brauch m -[e]s,Bräuche custom. **b~bar** adj usable; (nützlich) useful. **b~en** vt need; (ge-, verbrauchen) use; take (Zeit); **er b~t es nur zu sagen** he only has to say

Braue f -,-n eyebrow

brau|en vt brew. **B~er** m -s,- brewer. **B~erei** f -,-en brewery

braun adj, m nt -s,- brown; b~ **werden** (Person:) get a tan; b~ [gebrannt] **sein** be [sun-]tanned

Bräune f - [sun-]tan. **b~n** vt/i (haben) brown; (in der Sonne) tan

Braunschweig nt -s Brunswick

Brause f -,-n (Dusche) shower; (an Gießkanne) rose; (B~limonade) fizzy drink

Braut f -,ːe bride; (Verlobte) fiancée

Bräutigam m -s,-e bridegroom; (Verlobter) fiancé

Brautkleid nt wedding dress

Brautpaar nt bridal couple; (Verlobte) engaged couple

brav adj good; (redlich) honest ● adv dutifully; (redlich) honestly

bravo int bravo!

BRD abbr (Bundesrepublik Deutschland) FRG

Brech|eisen nt jemmy; (B~stange) crowbar. **b~en†** vt/i break; (Phys) refract (Licht); (erbrechen) vomit; **sich b~en** (Wellen:) break; (Licht:) be refracted; **sich** (dat) **den Arm b~en** break one's arm ● vi (sein) break ● vi (haben) vomit, be sick. **B~reiz** m nausea. **B~stange** f crowbar

Brei m -[e]s,-e paste; (Culin) purée; (Hafer-) porridge

breit adj wide; (Schultern, Grinsen) broad. **B~band** nt broadband. **B~e** f -,-n width; breadth; (Geog) latitude. **b~en** vt spread (über + acc over). **B~engrad** m [degree of]

latitude. **B~enkreis** m parallel
Bremse¹ f -,-n horsefly
Bremse² f -,-n brake. **b~n** vt
slow down; (fig) restrain ● vi
(haben) brake
Bremslicht nt brake-light
brenn|bar adj combustible; **leicht
b~bar** highly [in]flammable.
b~en† vi (haben) burn; (Licht:) be
on; (Zigarette:) be alight; (weh tun)
smart, sting ● vt burn; (rösten)
roast; (im Brennofen) fire; (destillieren) distil. **b~end** adj burning; (an-
gezündet) lighted; (fig) fervent.
B~er m -s,- burner. **B~erei** f
-,-en distillery
Brennessel† f = Brennnessel
Brenn|holz nt firewood. **B~ofen**
m kiln. **B~nessel** f stinging nettle.
B~punkt m (Phys) focus. **B~spiri-
tus** m methylated spirits. **B~stoff**
m fuel. **B~stoffzelle** f fuel cell
Bretagne /brə'tanjə/ (die) -
Brittany
Brett nt -[e]s,-er board; (im Regal)
shelf; **schwarzes B~** notice board.
B~spiel nt board game
Brezel f -,-n pretzel
Bridge /brɪtʃ/ nt - (Spiel) bridge
Brief m -[e]s,-e letter. **B~be-
schwerer** m -s,- paperweight.
B~freund(in) m(f) pen-friend.
B~kasten m letter-box. **B~kopf** m
letter-head. **b~lich** adj & adv by
letter. **B~marke** f [postage] stamp.
B~öffner m paper-knife. **B~pa-
pier** nt notepaper. **B~tasche** f wal-
let. **B~träger** m postman. **B~um-
schlag** m envelope. **B~wahl** f
postal vote. **B~wechsel** m corres-
pondence
Brikett nt -s,-s briquette
Brillant m -en,-en [cut] diamond
Brille f -,-n glasses pl, spectacles pl;
(Schutz-) goggles pl; (Klosett-) toi-

let seat
bringen† vt bring; (fort-) take;
(ein-) yield; (veröffentlichen) publish;
(im Radio) broadcast; show (Film);
ins Bett b~ put to bed; **jdn nach
Hause b~** take/(begleiten) see s.o.
home; **um etw b~** deprive of sth;
jdn dazu b~, etw zu tun get s.o.
to do sth; **es weit b~** (fig) go far
Brise f -,-n breeze
Brit|e m -n,-n, **B~in** f -,-nen
Briton. **b~isch** adj British
Bröck|chen nt -s,- (Culin) crou-
ton. **b~elig** adj crumbly; (Gestein)
friable. **b~eln** vt/i (haben/sein)
crumble
Brocken m -s,- chunk; (Erde,
Kohle) lump
Brokat m -[e]s,-e brocade
Brokkoli pl broccoli sg
Brombeere f blackberry
Bronchitis f - bronchitis
Bronze /'brõːsə/ f -,-n bronze
Brosch|e f -,-n brooch. **b~iert** adj
paperback. **B~üre** f -,-n brochure;
(Heft) booklet
Brösel mpl (Culin) breadcrumbs
Brot nt -[e]s,-e bread; **ein B~** a
loaf [of bread]; (Scheibe) a slice
of bread
Brötchen nt -s,- [bread] roll
Brotkrümel m breadcrumb
Bruch m -[e]s,ꞋꞋe break; (Brechen)
breaking; (Rohr-) burst; (Med) frac-
ture; (Eingeweide-) rupture, hernia;
(Math) fraction; (fig) breach; (in Be-
ziehung) break-up
brüchig adj brittle
Bruch|landung f crash-landing.
B~rechnung f fractions pl.
B~stück nt fragment. **B~teil** m
fraction
Brücke f -,-n bridge; (Teppich) rug
Bruder m -s,ꞋꞋ brother

brüderlich *adj* brotherly, fraternal

Brügge *nt* -s Bruges

Brüh|e *f* -,-n broth, stock. **B~wür-fel** *m* stock cube

brüllen *vt/i* (haben) roar

brumm|eln *vt/i* (haben) mumble. **b~en** *vi* (haben) (Insekt:) buzz; (Bär:) growl; (Motor:) hum; (murren) grumble. **B~er** *m* -s,- 🗆 blue-bottle. **b~ig** *adj* 🗆 grumpy

brünett *adj* dark-haired

Brunnen *m* -s,- well; (Spring-) fountain; (Heil-) spa water

brüsk *adj* brusque

Brüssel *nt* -s Brussels

Brust *f* -,ⁱe chest; (weibliche, Culin: B~stück) breast. **B~bein** *nt* breastbone

brüsten (sich) *vr* boast

Brust|fellentzündung *f* pleurisy. **B~schwimmen** *nt* breaststroke

Brüstung *f* -,-en parapet

Brustwarze *f* nipple

Brut *f* -,-en incubation

brutal *adj* brutal

brüten *vi* (haben) sit (on eggs); (fig) ponder (über + dat over)

Brutkasten *m* (Med) incubator

brutto *adv*, **B~** prefix gross

BSE *f* - BSE

Bub *m* -en,-en (SGer) boy. **B~e** *m* -n,-n (Karte) jack, knave

Buch *nt* -[e]s, ⁱer book; **B~ führen** keep a record (über + acc of); **die B~ⁱer führen** keep the accounts

Buche *f* -,-n beech

buchen *vt* book; (Comm) enter

Bücher|ei *f* -,-en library. **B~regal** *nt* bookcase, bookshelves *pl*. **B~schrank** *m* bookcase

Buchfink *m* chaffinch

Buch|führung *f* bookkeeping. **B~halter(in)** *m* -s,- (f -,-nen) bookkeeper, accountant. **B~hal-**

tung *f* bookkeeping, accountancy; (Abteilung) accounts department. **B~handlung** *f* bookshop

Büchse *f* -,-n box; (Konserven-) tin, can

Buch|stabe *m* -n,-n letter. **b~stabieren** *vt* spell [out]. **b~stäblich** *adv* literally

Bucht *f* -,-en (Geog) bay

Buchung *f* -,-en booking, reservation; (Comm) entry

Buckel *m* -s,- hump; (Beule) bump; (Hügel) hillock

bücken (sich) *vr* bend down

bucklig *adj* hunchbacked

Bückling *m* -s,-e smoked herring

Buddhis|mus *m* - Buddhism. **B~t(in)** *m* -en,-en (f -,-nen) Buddhist. **b~tisch** *adj* Buddhist

Bude *f* -,-n hut; (Kiosk) kiosk; (Markt-) stall; (🗆: Zimmer) room

Budget /by'dʒe:/ *nt* -s,-s budget

Büfett *nt* -[e]s,-e sideboard; (Theke) bar; **kaltes B~** cold buffet

Büffel *m* -s,- buffalo

Bügel *m* -s,- frame; (Kleider-) coathanger; (Steig-) stirrup; (Brillen-) sidepiece. **B~brett** *nt* ironing-board. **B~eisen** *nt* iron. **B~falte** *f* crease. **b~frei** *adj* non-iron. **b~n** *vt/i* (haben) iron

Bühne *f* -,-n stage. **B~nbild** *nt* set. **B~neingang** *m* stage door

Buhrufe *mpl* boos

Bukett *nt* -[e]s,-e bouquet

Bulgarien /-jan/ *nt* -s Bulgaria

Bull|auge *nt* (Naut) porthole. **B~dogge** *f* bulldog. **B~dozer** *m* -s,- bulldozer. **B~e** *m* -n,-n bull; (sl: Polizist) cop

Bummel *m* -s,- 🗆 stroll. **B~ei** *f* - 🗆 dawdling

bummel|ig *adj* 🗆 slow; (nachläs-

sig) careless. **b~n** *vi* (*sein*) 🚶 stroll ● *vi* (*haben*) 🚶 dawdle. **B~streik** *m* go-slow. **B~zug** *m* 🚋 slow train

Bums *m* -es,-e 🚶 bump, thump

Bund¹ *nt* -[e]s,-e bunch

Bund² *m* -[e]s,ᵉe association; (*Bündnis*) alliance; (*Pol*) federation; (*Rock-, Hosen-*) waistband; **der B~** the Federal Government

Bündel *nt* -s,- bundle. **b~n** *vt* bundle [up]

Bundes|- *prefix* Federal. **B~genosse** *m* ally. **B~kanzler** *m* Federal Chancellor. **B~land** *nt* [federal] state; (*Aust*) province. **B~liga** *f* German national league. **B~rat** *m* Upper House of Parliament. **B~regierung** *f* Federal Government. **B~republik** *f* **die B~republik Deutschland** the Federal Republic of Germany. **B~tag** *m* Lower House of Parliament. **B~wehr** *f* [Federal German] Army

Bundestag The lower house of the German parliament, which is elected every four years. The *Bundestag* is responsible for federal legislation, the federal budget, and electing the *Bundeskanzler*, or Federal Chancellor, (equivalent of prime minister). Half the MPs are elected directly and half by proportional representation. Every citizen has two votes.

Bundeswappen
▷WAPPEN

bünd|ig *adj & adv* **kurz und b~ig** short and to the point. **B~nis** *nt* -ses,-se alliance

Bunker *m* -s,- bunker; (*Luftschutz-*) shelter

bunt *adj* coloured; (*farbenfroh*) colourful; (*grell*) gaudy; (*gemischt*) varied; (*wirr*) confused; **b~e Platte** assorted cold meats. **B~stift** *m* crayon

Bürde *f* -,-n (*fig*) burden

Burg *f* -,-en castle

Bürge *m* -n,-n guarantor. **b~n** *vi* (*haben*) **b~n für** vouch for; (*fig*) guarantee

Bürger|(in) *m* -s,- (*f* -,-nen) citizen. **B~krieg** *m* civil war. **b~lich** *adj* civil; (*Pflicht*) civic; (*mittelständisch*) middle-class. **B~liche(r)** *m/f* commoner. **B~meister** *m* mayor. **B~rechte** *npl* civil rights. **B~steig** *m* -[e]s,-e pavement

Bürgschaft *f* -,-en surety

Burgunder *m* -s,- (*Wein*) Burgundy

Büro *nt* -s,-s office. **B~angestellte(r)** *m/f* office worker. **B~klammer** *f* paper clip. **B~kratie** *f* -,-n bureaucracy. **b~kratisch** *adj* bureaucratic

Bursche *m* -n,-n lad, youth

Bürste *f* -,-n brush. **b~n** *vt* brush. **B~nschnitt** *m* crew cut

Bus *m* -ses,-se bus; (*Reise-*) coach

Busch *m* -[e]s,ᵉe bush

Büschel *nt* -s,- tuft

buschig *adj* bushy

Busen *m* -s,- bosom

Bussard *m* -s,-e buzzard

Buße *f* -,-n penance; (*Jur*) fine

Bußgeld *nt* (*Jur*) fine

Büste *f* -,-n bust; (*Schneider-*) dummy. **B~nhalter** *m* -s,- bra

Butter *f* - butter. **B~blume** *f* buttercup. **B~brot** *nt* slice of bread and butter. **B~milch** *f* buttermilk. **b~n** *vt* butter

b.w. *abbr* (**bitte wenden**) P.T.O.

Cc

ca. *abbr* (*circa*) about

Café /ka'fe:/ *nt* **-s,-s** café

Camcorder /'kamkɔrdɐ/ *m* **-s, -** camcorder

camp|en /'kɛmpən/ *vi* (*haben*) go camping. **C~ing** *nt* **-s** camping. **C~ingplatz** *m* campsite

Caravan /'ka:[l]ravan/ *m* **-s,-s** (*Auto*) caravan; (*Kombi*) estate car

CD /tse:'de:/ *f* **-,-s** compact disc, CD. **CD-ROM** *f* **-,-(s)** CD-ROM

Cell|ist(in) /tʃɛ'lɪst/ *m* **-en,-en** (*f* **-,-nen**) cellist. **C~o** *nt* **-,-los** & **-li** cello

Celsius /'tsɛlzjʊs/ *inv* Celsius, centigrade

Cent/tsɛnt/ *m* **-[s], -[s]** cent

Champagner /ʃam'panjɐ/ *m* **-s** champagne

Champignon /'ʃampɪnjɔn/ *m* **-s,-s** [field] mushroom

Chance /'ʃã:s[ə]/ *f* **-,-n** chance

Chaos /'ka:ɔs/ *nt* **-** chaos

Charakter /ka'raktɐ/ *m* **-s,-e** character. **c~isieren** *vt* characterize. **c~istisch** *adj* characteristic (*für of*)

charm|ant /ʃar'mant/ *adj* charming. **C~e** *m* **-s** charm

Charter|flug /'tʃ-, 'ʃartɐ-/ *m* charter flight. **c~n** *vt* charter

Chassis /ʃa'si:/ *nt* **-,-** chassis

Chauffeur /ʃo'fø:ɐ/ *m* **-s,-e** chauffeur; (*Taxi-*) driver

Chauvinist /ʃovi'nɪst/ *m* **-en,-en** chauvinist

Chef /ʃɛf/ *m* **-s,-s** head; Ⓘ boss

Chemie /çe'mi:/ *f* **-** chemistry

Chem|iker(in) /'çe:-/ *m* **-s,- (***f***

-,-nen) chemist. **c~isch** *adj* chemical; **c~ische Reinigung** dry-cleaning; (*Geschäft*) dry-cleaner's

Chicorée /'ʃikore:/ *m* **-s** chicory

Chiffre /'ʃɪfə, 'ʃɪfrə/ *f* **-,-n** cipher

Chile /'çi:lə/ *nt* **-s** Chile

Chin|a /'çi:na/ *nt* **-s** China. **C~ese** *m* **-n,-n, C~esin** *f* **-,-nen** Chinese. **c~esisch** *adj* Chinese. **C~esisch** *nt* **-[s]** (*Lang*) Chinese

Chip /tʃɪp/ *m* **-s,-s** [micro]chip. **C~s** *pl* crisps

Chirurg /çi'rʊrk/ *m* **-en,-en** surgeon. **C~ie** *f* **-** surgery

Chlor /klo:ɐ/ *nt* **-s** chlorine

Choke /tʃo:k/ *m* **-s,-s** (*Auto*) choke

Cholera /'ko:lera/ *f* **-** cholera

cholerisch /ko'le:rɪʃ/ *adj* irascible

Cholesterin /ço-, kolɛstə'ri:n/ *nt* **-s** cholesterol

Chor /ko:ɐ/ *m* **-[e]s,⁻e** choir

Choreographie, Choreografie /koreogra'fi:/ *f* **-,-n** choreography

Christ /krɪst/ *m* **-en,-en** Christian. **C~baum** *m* Christmas tree. **C~entum** *nt* **-s** Christianity. **C~lich** *adj* Christian

Christus /'krɪstʊs/ *m* **-ti** Christ

Chrom /kro:m/ *nt* **-s** chromium

Chromosom /kromo'zo:m/ *nt* **-s,-en** chromosome

Chronik /'kro:nɪk/ *f* **-,-en** chronicle

chronisch /'kro:nɪʃ/ *adj* chronic

Chrysantheme /kryzan'te:mə/ *f* **-,-n** chrysanthemum

circa /'tsɪrka/ *adv* about

Clique /'klɪkə/ *f* **-,-n** clique

Clou /klu:/ *m* **-s,-s** highlight, Ⓘ high spot

Clown /klaʊn/ *m* **-s,-s** clown

Club /klʊp/ *m* **-s,-s** club

Cocktail /'kɔktel/ *m* **-s,-s** cocktail

Code /'ko:t/ *m* **-s,-s** code

Comic-Heft /'kɔmɪk-/ nt comic

Computer /kɔm'pjuːtɐ/ m -s,-
computer. **c~isieren** vt computer-
ize. **C~spiel** nt computer game

Conférencier /kõferã'sjeː/ m -s,-
compère

Cord /kɔrt/ m -s, **C~samt** m
corduroy

Couch /kaʊtʃ/ f -,-s settee

Cousin /ku'zɛ̃ː/ m -s,-s [male]
cousin. **C~e** f -,-n [female] cousin

Creme /kreːm/ f -s,-s cream;
(Speise) cream dessert

Curry /'kari, 'kœri/ nt & m -s curry
powder ● nt -s,-s (Gericht) curry

Cursor /'køːɐsɐ/ m -s, - cursor

Cyberspace /'saɪbəspeːs/ m -
cyberspace

Dd

da adv there; (hier) here; (zeitlich)
then; (in dem Fall) in that case; **von
da an** from then on; **da sein** be
there/(hier) here; (existieren) exist;
wieder da sein be back ● conj
as, since

dabei (emphatic: **dabei**) adv
nearby; (daran) with it; (eingeschlossen) included; (hinsichtlich) about it;
(währenddem) during this; (gleichzeitig) at the same time; (doch) and
yet; **dicht d~** close by; **d~ sein** be
present; (mitmachen) be involved;
d~ sein, etw zu tun be just
doing sth

Dach nt -[e]s,ˉer roof. **D~boden**
m loft. **D~luke** f skylight.
D~rinne f gutter

Dachs m -es,-e badger

Dachsparren m -s,- rafter

Dackel m -s,- dachshund

dadurch (emphatic: **dadurch**) adv
through it/them; (Ursache) as a
result of it; (deshalb) because of that; **d~, dass**
because

dafür (emphatic: **dafür**) adv for
it/them; (anstatt) instead; (als Ausgleich) but [on the other hand];
d~, dass considering that; **ich
kann nichts dafür** it's not my fault

dagegen (emphatic: **dagegen**) adv
against it/them; (Mittel, Tausch) for
it; (verglichen damit) by comparison;
(jedoch) however; **hast du was
d~?** do you mind?

daheim adv at home

daher (emphatic: **daher**) adv from
there; (deshalb) for that reason; **das
kommt d~, weil** that's because
● conj that's why

dahin (emphatic: **dahin**) adv there;
bis d~ up to there; (bis dann)
until/(Zukunft) by then; **jdn d~
bringen, dass er etw tut** get s.o.
to do sth

dahinten adv back there

dahinter (emphatic: **dahinter**) adv
behind it/them; **d~ kommen** (fig)
get to the bottom of it

Dahlie /-jə/ f -,-n dahlia

dalassen† vt sep leave there

daliegen† vi sep (haben) lie there

damalig adj at that time; **der
d~e Minister** the then minister

damals adv at that time

Damast m -es,-e damask

Dame f -,-n lady; (Karte, Schach)
queen; (D~spiel) draughts sg.
d~nhaft adj ladylike

damit (emphatic: **damit**) adv with
it/them; (dadurch) by it; **hör auf
d~!** stop it! ● conj so that

Damm m -[e]s,ˉe dam

dämmerig adj dim. **D~licht** nt
twilight. **d~n** vi (haben) (Morgen:)

dawn; **es d~t** it is getting
light/(abends) dark. **D~ung** f dawn;
(Abend-) dusk

Dämon m -s,-en demon

Dampf m -es,·-e steam; (Chemistry) vapour. **d~en** vi
(haben) steam

dämpfen vt (Culin) steam; (fig)
muffle (Ton); lower (Stimme)

Dampf|er m -s,- steamer.
D~kochtopf m pressure-cooker.
D~maschine f steam engine.
D~walze f steamroller

danach (emphatic: **danach**) adv
after it/them; (suchen) for it/them;
(riechen) of it; (später) afterwards;
(entsprechend) accordingly; **es sieht
d~ aus** it looks like it

Däne m -n,-n Dane

daneben (emphatic: **daneben**) adv
beside it/them; (außerdem) in addition; (verglichen damit) by comparison

Dän|emark nt -s Denmark. **D~in**
f -,-nen Dane. **d~isch** adj Danish

Dank m -es thanks pl; **vielen D~!**
thank you very much! **d~** prep (+
dat or gen) thanks to. **d~bar** adj
grateful; (erleichtert) thankful; (lohnend) rewarding. **D~barkeit** f -
gratitude. **d~e** adv **d~e [schön od
sehr]!** thank you [very much]!
d~en vi (haben) thank (jdm s.o.);
(ablehnen) decline; **nichts zu d~en!**
don't mention it!

dann adv then; **selbst d~, wenn**
even if

daran (emphatic: **daran**) adv on
it/them; at it/them; (denken) of it;
nahe d~ on the point (etw zu tun
of doing sth). **d~setzen** vt sep
alles d~setzen do one's utmost
(zu to)

darauf (emphatic: **darauf**) adv on
it/them; (warten) for it; (antworten)
to it; (danach) after that; (d~hin) as

a result. **d~hin** adv as a result

daraus (emphatic: **daraus**) adv out
of or from it/them; **er macht sich
nichts d~** he doesn't care for it

darlegen vt sep expound; (erklären) explain

Darlehen nt -s,- loan

Darm m -[e]s,·-e intestine

darstell|en vt sep represent; (bildlich) portray; (Theat) interpret; (spielen) play; (schildern) describe. **D~er**
m -s,- actor. **D~erin** f -,-nen actress. **D~ung** f representation; interpretation; description

darüber (emphatic: **darüber**) adv
over it/them; (höher) above it/them;
(sprechen, lachen, sich freuen) about
it; (mehr) more; (d~hinaus) beyond
[it]; (dazu) on top of that

darum (emphatic: **darum**) adv
round it/them; (bitten, kämpfen) for
it; (deshalb) that is why; **d~, weil**
because

darunter (emphatic: **darunter**) adv
under it/them; (tiefer) below
it/them; (weniger) less; (dazwischen)
among them

das def art & pron s. **der**

dasein* vi sep (sein) = **da sein**, s.
da. D~ nt -s existence

dass conj that

dasselbe pron s. **derselbe**

Daten|sichtgerät nt visual display unit, VDU. **D~verarbeitung** f
data processing

datieren vt/i (haben) date

Dativ m -s,-e dative. **D~objekt** nt
indirect object

Dattel f -,-n date

Datum nt -s,-ten date; **Daten**
dates; (Angaben) data

Dauer f - duration, length; (Jur)
term; **auf die D~** in the long run.
D~auftrag m standing order.
d~haft adj lasting, enduring; (fest)

durable. **D∼karte** f season ticket.
d∼n vi (haben) last; **lange d∼n**
take a long time. **d∼nd** adj lasting;
(ständig) constant. **D∼welle** f perm

Daumen m -s, thumb; **jdm den
D∼ drücken** od **halten** keep one's
fingers crossed for s.o.

Daunen fpl down sg. **D∼decke** f
[down-filled] duvet

davon (emphatic: **davon**) adv from
it/them; (dadurch) by it; (damit)
with it/them; (darüber) about it;
(Menge) of it/them; **das kommt
d∼!** it serves you right! **d∼kom-
men†** vi sep (sein) escape (**mit dem
Leben** with one's life). **d∼laufen†**
vi sep (sein) run away. **d∼machen
(sich)** vr sep 🗓 make off. **d∼tra-
gen†** vt sep carry off; (erleiden) suffer; (gewinnen) win

davor (emphatic: **davor**) adv in
front of it/them; (sich fürchten) of it;
(zeitlich) before it/them

dazu (emphatic: **dazu**) adv to
it/them; (damit) with it/them;
(dafür) for it; **noch d∼** in addition
to that; **jdn d∼ bringen, etwas zu
tun** get s.o. to do sth; **ich kam
nicht d∼** I didn't get round to
[doing] it. **d∼kommen†** vi sep
(sein) arrive [on the scene]; (hinzu-
kommen) be added. **d∼rechnen** vt
sep add to it/them

dazwischen (emphatic: **dazwischen**) adv between them; in between; (darunter) among them.
d∼kommen† vi sep (sein) (fig) crop
up; **wenn nichts d∼kommt** if all
goes well

Debat|te f -,-n debate; **zur D∼te
stehen** be at issue. **d∼tieren** vt/i
(haben) debate

Debüt /de'by:/ nt -s,-s début

Deck nt -[e]s,-s (Naut) deck; **an
D∼** on deck. **D∼bett** nt duvet

Decke f -,-n cover; (Tisch-) table-

cloth; (Bett-) blanket; (Reise-) rug;
(Zimmer-) ceiling; **unter einer D∼
stecken** 🗓 be in league

Deckel m -s,- lid; (Flaschen-) top;
(Buch-) cover

decken vt cover; tile (Dach); lay
(Tisch); (schützen) shield; (Sport)
mark; meet (Bedarf); **jdn d∼** (fig)
cover up for s.o.; **sich d∼** (fig)
cover oneself (**gegen** against);
(übereinstimmen) coincide

Deckname m pseudonym

Deckung f -(Mil) cover; (Sport)
defence; (Mann-) marking; (Boxen)
guard; (Sicherheit) security; **in D∼
gehen** take cover

defin|ieren vt define. **D∼ition** f
-,-en definition

Defizit nt -s,-e deficit

deformiert adj deformed

deftig adj 🗓 (Mahlzeit) hearty;
(Witz) coarse

Degen m -s,- sword; (Fecht-) épée

degeneriert adj (fig) degenerate

degradieren vt (Mil) demote;
(fig) degrade

dehn|bar adj elastic. **d∼en** vt
stretch; lengthen (Vokal); **sich
d∼en** stretch

Deich m -[e]s,-e dike

dein poss pron your. **d∼e(r,s)** poss
pron yours; **die D∼en** od **d∼en** pl
your family sg. **d∼erseits** adv for
your part. **d∼etwegen** adv for
your sake; (wegen dir) because of
you, on your account. **d∼etwillen**
adv **um d∼etwillen** for your sake.
d∼ige poss pron **der/die/das
d∼ige** yours. **d∼s** poss pron yours

Dekan m -s,-e dean

Deklin|ation /-'tsjo:n/ f -,-en de-
clension. **d∼ieren** vt decline

Dekolleté, Dekolletee /dekɔl'te:/
nt -s,-s low neckline

Dekor m & nt -s decoration. **D∼**

ateur m -s,-e interior decorator; (Schaufenster-) window-dresser. **D~ation** f -,-en decoration; (Schaufenster-) window-dressing; (Auslage) display. **d~ativ** adj decorative. **d~ieren** vt decorate; dress (Schaufenster)

Delegation /-'tsi̯o:n/ f -,-en delegation. **D~ierte(r)** m/f delegate

delikat adj delicate; (lecker) delicious; (taktvoll) tactful. **D~essengeschäft** nt delicatessen

Delikt nt -[e]s,-e offence

Delinquent m -en,-en offender

Delle f -,-n dent

Delphin m -s,-e dolphin

Delta nt -s,-s delta

dem def art & pron s. der

dementieren vt deny

dem|entsprechend adj corresponding; (passend) appropriate ● adv accordingly; (passend) appropriately. **d~nächst** adv soon; (in Kürze) shortly

Demokrat m -en,-en democrat. **D~ie** f -,-n democracy. **d~isch** adj democratic

demolieren vt wreck

Demonstr|ant m -en,-en demonstrator. **D~ation** f -,-en demonstration. **d~ieren** vt/i (haben) demonstrate

demontieren vt dismantle

Demoskopie f - opinion research

Demut f - humility

den def art & pron s. der. **d~en** pron s. der

denk|bar adj conceivable. **d~en†** vt/i (haben) think (an + acc of); (sich erinnern) remember (an etw acc sth); **das kann ich mir d~en** I can imagine [that]; **ich d~e nicht daran** I have no intention of doing it. **D~mal** nt memorial; (Monument) monument. **d~würdig**

---

adj memorable

denn conj for; besser/mehr **d~** je better/more than ever ● adv wie/wo **d~**? but how/where? warum **d~** nicht? why ever not? **es sei d~** [, dass] unless

dennoch adv nevertheless

Denunz|iant m -en,-en informer. **d~ieren** vt denounce

Deodorant nt -s,-s deodorant

deplaciert, deplatziert /-'tsi:ɐt/ adj (fig) out of place

Deponie f -,-n dump. **d~ren** vt deposit

deportieren vt deport

Depot /de'po:/ nt -s,-s depot; (Lager) warehouse; (Bank-) safe deposit

Depression f -,-en depression

deprimieren vt depress

---

der, die, das, pl die
● definite article

acc **den**, die, das, pl die; gen **des**, der, des, pl der; dat **dem**, der, dem, pl den

●⋯► the. **der Mensch** the person; (als abstrakter Begriff) man. **die Natur** nature. **das Leben** life. **das Lesen/Tanzen** reading/dancing. **sich** (dat) **das Gesicht/die Hände waschen** wash one's face/hands. **3 Euro das Pfund** 3 euros a pound

● pronoun

acc **den**, die, das, pl die; gen **dessen**, deren, dessen, pl deren; dat **dem**, der, dem, pl denen

● demonstrative pronoun
●⋯► that; (pl) those

derb | Diamant

58

·····► (attributiv) **der** Mann war es it was 'that man

·····► (substantivisch) he, she, it; (pl) they. **der** war es it was 'him. **die da** (person) that woman/girl; (thing) that one

● relative pronoun

·····► (Person) who. **der** Mann, **der/dessen** Sohn hier arbeitet the man who/whose son works here. **die** Frau, **mit der** ich **Tennis spiele** the woman with whom I play tennis, the woman I play tennis with. **das** Mädchen, **das** ich gestern **sah** the girl I saw yesterday

·····► (Ding) which, that. **ich** sah ein Buch, **das** mich interessierte I saw a book that interested me. **die** CD, **die** ich mir anhöre the CD I am listening to. **das** Auto, **mit dem** wir nach **Deutschland** fahren the car we are going to Germany in or in which we are going to Germany

derb adj tough; (kräftig) strong; (grob) coarse; (unsanft) rough

deren pron s. der

dergleichen inv adj such ● pron such a thing/such things

der-/die-/dasselbe, pl **dieselben** pron the same; **ein- und dasselbe** one and the same thing

derzeit adv at present

des def art s. der

Desert|eur /-'tø:ɐ/ m -s,-e deserter. **d~ieren** vi (sein/haben) desert

desgleichen adv likewise ● pron the like

deshalb adv for this reason; (also) therefore

Design nt -s, -s design

Designer(in) /di'zainɐ, -nərin/ m

-s,- (f -,-nen) designer

Desin|fektion /dɛsʔɪnfɛk'tsjoːn/ f disinfecting. **D~fektionsmittel** nt disinfectant. **d~fizieren** vt disinfect

dessen pron s. der

Destill|ation /-tsjoːn/ f - distillation. **d~ieren** vt distil

desto adv je mehr **d~besser** the more the better

deswegen adv = deshalb

Detektiv m -s,-e detective

Deton|ation /-'tsjoːn/ f -,-en explosion. **d~ieren** vi (sein) explode

deut|en vt interpret; predict (Zukunft) ● vi (haben) point (auf + acc at/(fig) to). **d~lich** adj clear; (eindeutig) plain

deutsch adj German. **D~** nt -[s] (Lang) German; **auf D~** in German. **D~e(r)** m/f German. **D~land** nt -s Germany

Deutung f -,-en interpretation

Devise f -,-n motto. **D~n** pl foreign currency or exchange sg

Dezember m -s,- December

dezent adj unobtrusive; (diskret) discreet

Dezernat nt -[e]s,-e department

Dezimalzahl f decimal

d.h. abbr (das heißt) i.e.

Dia nt -s,-s (Phot) slide

Diabet|es m - diabetes. **D~iker** m -s,- diabetic

Diadem nt -s,-e tiara

Diagnose f -,-n diagnosis

diagonal adj diagonal. **D~e** f -,-n diagonal

Diagramm nt -s,-e diagram; (Kurven-) graph

Diakon m -s,-e deacon

Dialekt m -[e]s,-e dialect

Dialog m -[e]s,-e dialogue

Diamant m -en,-en diamond

Diapositiv nt -s,-e (Phot) slide
Diaprojektor m slide projector
Diät f -,-en (Med) diet; **D~ leben** be on a diet
dich pron (acc of **du**) you; (reflexive) yourself
dicht adj dense; (dick) thick; (undurchlässig) airtight; (wasser~) watertight ● adv densely; (nahe) close (**bei** to). **D~e** density. **d~en¹** vt make watertight
dicht|en² vi (haben) write poetry. ● vt write. **D~er(in)** m -s,- (f -,-nen) poet. **d~erisch** adj poetic. **D~ung** f -,-en poetry; (Gedicht) poem
Dichtung² f -,-en seal; (Ring) washer; (Auto) gasket
dick adj thick; (beleibt) fat; (geschwollen) swollen; (fam: eng) close; **d~ machen** be fattening. **d~flüssig** adj thick; (Phys) viscous. **D~kopf** m I stubborn person; **einen D~kopf haben** be stubborn
die def art & pron s. **der**
Dieb|(in) m -[e]s,-e (f -,-nen) thief. **d~isch** adj thieving; (Freude) malicious. **D~stahl** m -[e]s,ˀe theft
Diele f -,-n floorboard; (Flur) hall
dien|en vi (haben) serve. **D~er** m -s,- servant; (Verbeugung) bow. **D~erin** f -,-nen maid, servant
Dienst m -[e]s,-e service; (Arbeit) work; (Amtsausübung) duty; **außer D~** off duty; (pensioniert) retired; **D~ haben** work; (Soldat, Arzt:) be on duty
Dienstag m Tuesday. **d~s** adv on Tuesdays
Dienst|bote m servant. **d~frei** adj **freier Tag** day off; **d~frei haben** have time off; (Soldat, Arzt:) be off duty. **D~grad** m rank. **D~leistung** f service. **d~lich** adj

official ● adv **d~lich verreist** away on business. **D~mädchen** nt maid. **D~reise** f business trip. **D~stelle** f office. **D~stunden** fpl office hours
dies inv pron this. **d~bezüglich** adj relevant ● adv regarding this matter. **d~e(r,s)** pron this; (pl) these; (substantivisch) this [one]; (pl) these; **d~e Nacht** tonight; (letzte) last night
dieselbe pron s. **derselbe**
Dieselkraftstoff m diesel [oil]
diesmal adv this time
Dietrich m -s,-e skeleton key
Diffamation /-'tsjo:n/ f - defamation
Differential /-'tsja:l/ nt -s,-e = **Differenzial**
Differenz f -,-en difference. **D~ial** nt -s,-e differential. **d~ieren** vt/i (haben) differentiate (**zwischen** + dat between)
digital adj digital
Digital- prefix digital. **D~kamera** f digital camera. **D~uhr** f digital clock/watch
digitalisieren vt digitize
Dikt|at nt -[e]s,-e dictation. **D~ator** m -s,-en dictator. **D~atur** f -,-en dictatorship. **d~ieren** vt/i (haben) dictate
Dill m -s dill
Dimension f -,-en dimension
Ding nt -[e]s,-e & I -er thing; **guter D~e sein** be cheerful; **vor allen D~en** above all
Dinosaurier /-iɐ/ m -s,- dinosaur
Diözese f -,-n diocese
Diphtherie f - diphtheria
Diplom nt -s,-e diploma; (Univ) degree
Diplomat m -en,-en diplomat. **d~isch** adj diplomatic
dir pron (dat of **du**) [to] you; (reflexive) yourself; **ein Freund von dir** a

friend of yours

direkt *adj* direct ● *adv* directly; (*wirklich*) really. **D~ion** *f* - management; (*Vorstand*) board of directors. **D~or** *m* -s,-en, **D~orin** *f* -,-nen director; (*Bank-, Theater-*) manager; (*Sch*) head; (*Gefängnis*) governor. **D~übertragung** *f* live transmission

Dirig|ent *m* -en,-en (*Mus*) conductor. **d~ieren** *vt* direct; (*Mus*) conduct

Dirndl *nt* -s,- dirndl [dress]

Discounter *m* -s, - discount supermarket

Diskette *f* -,-n floppy disc

Disko *f* -,-s 🄳 disco. **D~thek** *f* -,-en discothèque

diskret *adj* discreet

Diskus *m* -,-se & Disken discus

Disku|ssion *f* -,-en discussion. **d~tieren** *vt/i* (*haben*) discuss

disponieren *vi* (*haben*) make arrangements; **d~** [**können**] **über** (+ *acc*) have at one's disposal

Disqualifi|kation /-'tsio:n/ *f* disqualification. **d~zieren** *vt* disqualify

Dissertation /-'tsio:n/ *f* -,-en dissertation

Dissident *m* -en,-en dissident

Distanz *f* -,-en distance. **d~ieren (sich)** *vr* dissociate oneself (*von* from). **d~iert** *adj* aloof

Distel *f* -,-n thistle

Disziplin *f* -,-en discipline. **d~arisch** *adj* disciplinary. **d~iert** *adj* disciplined

dito *adv* ditto

diverse *attrib a pl* various

Divid|ende *f* -,-n dividend. **d~ieren** *vt* divide (*durch* by)

Division *f* -,-en division

DJH *abbr* (**Deutsche Jugendherberge**) [German] youth hostel

DM *abbr* (**Deutsche Mark**) DM

doch *conj & adv* but; (*dennoch*) yet; (*trotzdem*) after all; **wenn d~ ...** ! if only ... ! **nicht d~!** I don't!

Docht *m* -[e]s,-e wick

Dock *nt* -s,-s dock. **d~en** *vt/i* (*haben*) dock

Dogge *f* -,-n Great Dane

Dogm|a *nt* -s,-men dogma. **d~atisch** *adj* dogmatic

Dohle *f* -,-n jackdaw

Doktor *m* -s,-en doctor. **D~arbeit** *f* [doctoral] thesis

Dokument *nt* -[e]s,-e document. **D~arbericht** *m* documentary. **D~arfilm** *m* documentary film

Dolch *m* -[e]s,-e dagger

Dollar *m* -s,- dollar

dolmetsch|en *vt/i* (*haben*) interpret. **D~er(in)** *m* -s,- (*f* -,-nen) interpreter

Dom *m* -[e]s,-e cathedral

Domino *nt* -s,-s dominoes *sg.* **D~stein** *m* domino

Dompfaff *m* -en,-en bullfinch

Donau *f* - Danube

Donner *m* -s thunder. **d~n** *vi* (*haben*) thunder

Donnerstag *m* Thursday. **d~s** *adv* on Thursdays

doof *adj* 🄳 stupid

Doppel *nt* -s,- duplicate; (*Tennis*) doubles *pl.* **D~bett** *nt* double bed. **D~decker** *m* -s,- doubledecker [bus]. **d~deutig** *adj* ambiguous.

D~gänger m -s,- double. **D~kinn** nt double chin. **d~klicken** vi (haben) double-click (auf + acc an). **D~name** m double-barrelled name. **D~punkt** m (Gram) colon. **D~stecker** m two-way adaptor. **d~t** adj double; (Boden) false; **in d~ter Ausfertigung** in duplicate; **die d~te Menge** twice the amount ● adv doubly; (zweimal) twice; **d~t so viel** twice as much. **D~zimmer** nt double room

Dorf nt -[e]s,∶er village. **D~bewohner** m villager

dörflich adj rural

Dorn m -[e]s,-en thorn. **d~ig** adj thorny

Dorsch m -[e]s,-e cod

dort adv there. **d~ig** adj local

Dose f -,-n tin, can

dösen vi (haben) doze

Dosen|milch f evaporated milk. **D~öffner** m tin or can opener. **D~pfand** nt deposit (on beer cans etc)

dosieren vt measure out

Dosis f -, Dosen dose

Dotter m & nt -s,- [egg] yolk

Dozent(in) m -en,-en (f -,-nen) (Univ) lecturer

Dr. abbr (Doktor) Dr

Drache m -n,-n dragon. **D~n** m -s,- kite. **D~nfliegen** nt hang-gliding

Draht m -[e]s,∶e wire; **auf D~** 🔢 on the ball. **D~seilbahn** f cable railway

Dram|a nt -s,-men drama. **D~atik** f - drama. **D~atiker** m -s,- dramatist. **d~atisch** adj dramatic

dran adv (fam) = daran; **gut/schlecht d~ sein** be well off/in a bad way; **ich bin d~** = it's my turn

Drang m -[e]s urge; (Druck) pressure

dräng|eln vt/i (haben) push; (bedrängen) pester. **d~en** vt push; (bedrängen) urge; sich **d~en** crowd (um round) ● vi (haben) push; (eilen) be urgent; **d~en auf** (+ acc) press for

dran|halten† (sich) vr sep hurry. **d~kommen†** vi sep (sein) have one's turn

drauf adv 🔢 = darauf; **d~ und dran sein** be on the point (etw zu tun of doing sth). **D~gänger** m -s,- daredevil

draußen adv outside; (im Freien) out of doors

drechseln vt (Techn) turn

Dreck m -s dirt; (Morast) mud

Dreh m -s 🔢 knack; **den D~ heraushaben** have got the hang of it. **D~bank** f lathe. **D~bleistift** m propelling pencil. **D~buch** nt screenplay, script. **d~en** vt turn; (im Kreis) rotate; (verschlingen) twist; roll (Zigarette); shoot (Film); **lauter/leiser d~en** turn up/down; sich **d~en** turn; (im Kreis) rotate; (schnell) spin; (Wind:) change; sich **d~en um** revolve around; (sich handeln) be about ● vi (haben) turn; (Wind:) change; an etw (dat) **d~en** turn sth. **D~stuhl** m swivel chair. **D~tür** f revolving door. **D~ung** f -,-en turn; (im Kreis) rotation. **D~zahl** f number of revolutions

drei inv adj, **D~** f -,-en three; (Sch) ≈ pass. **D~eck** nt -[e]s,-e triangle. **d~eckig** adj triangular. **d~erlei** inv adj three kinds of ● pron three things. **d~fach** adj triple. **d~mal** adv three times. **D~rad** nt tricycle

dreißig inv adj thirty. **d~ste(r,s)** adj thirtieth

dreiviertel* inv adj = **drei viertel**, s. **viertel**. **D~stunde** f three-quarters of an hour

dreizehn inv adj thirteen

d~te(r,s) adj thirteenth

dreschen† vt thresh

dress|ieren vt train. **D~ur** f - training

dribbeln vi (haben) dribble

Drill m -[e]s (Mil) drill. **d~en** vt drill

Drillinge mpl triplets

dringlich adj urgent

Drink m -[s],-s [alcoholic] drink

drinnen adv inside

dritt adv zu **d~** in threes; **wir waren zu d~** there were three of us. **d~e(r,s)** adj third. **D~er** a third person. **d~el** inv adj third. **D~el** nt -s,-. third. **d~ens** adv thirdly. **d~rangig** adj third-rate

Drog|e f -,-n drug. **D~enabhängige(r)** m/f drug addict. **D~erie** f -,-n chemist's shop. **D~ist** m -en, -en chemist

drohen vi (haben) threaten (jdm s.o.)

dröhnen vi (haben) resound; (tönen) boom

Drohung f -,-en threat

drollig adj funny; (seltsam) odd

Drops m -,- [fruit] drop

Drossel f -,-n thrush

drosseln vt (Techn) throttle; (fig) cut back

drüben adv over there

Druck[1] m -[e]s,¨e pressure; **unter D~** setzen (fig) pressurize

Druck[2] m -[e]s,-e printing; (Schrift, Reproduktion) print. **D~buchstabe** m block letter

drucken vt print

drücken vt/i (haben) press; (aus-) squeeze; (Schuh) pinch; (umarmen) hug; **Preise d~** force down prices; (an Tür) **d~** push; **sich d~** 🄳 make oneself scarce; **sich d~ vor** (+ dat) 🄳 shirk. **d~d** adj heavy;

(schwül) oppressive

Drucker m -s,- printer

Druckerei f -,-en printing works

Druck|fehler m misprint. **D~knopf** m press-stud. **D~luft** f compressed air. **D~sache** f printed matter. **D~schrift** f type; (Veröffentlichung) publication; **in D~schrift** in block letters pl

Druckstelle f bruise

Drüse f -,-n (Anat) gland

Dschungel m -s,- jungle

du pron (familiar address) you; **auf Du und Du** on familiar terms

Dübel m -s,- plug

Dudelsack m bagpipes pl

Duell nt -s,-e duel

Duett nt -s,-e [vocal] duet

Duft m -[e]s,¨e fragrance, scent; (Aroma) aroma. **d~en** vi (haben) smell (nach of)

dulden vt tolerate; (erleiden) suffer ● vi (haben) suffer

dumm adj stupid; (unklug) foolish; (🄳: lästig) awkward; **wie d~!**. **d~erweise** adv stupidly; (leider) unfortunately. **D~heit** f -,-en stupidity; (Torheit) foolishness; (Handlung) folly. **D~kopf** m 🄳 fool.

dumpf adj dull

Düne f -,-n dune

Dung m -s manure

Düng|emittel nt fertilizer. **d~en** vt fertilize. **D~er** m -s,- fertilizer

dunk|el adj dark; (vage) vague; (fragwürdig) shady; **d~les Bier** brown ale; **im D~eln** in the dark

Dunkel|heit f - darkness. **D~kammer** f dark-room. **d~n** vi (haben) get dark

dünn adj thin; (Buch) slim; (spärlich) sparse; (schwach) weak

Dunst m -es,¨e mist, haze; (Dampf) vapour

dünsten vt steam

dunstig adj misty, hazy

Duo nt -s,-s [instrumental] duet

Duplikat nt -[e]s,-e duplicate

Dur nt - (Mus) major [key]

durch prep (+ acc) through; (mittels) by; [geteilt] d~ (Math) divided by ● adv **die Nacht d~** throughout the night; **d~ und d~ nass** wet through

durchaus adv absolutely; **d~nicht** by no means

durchblättern vt sep leaf through

durchblicken vi sep (haben) look through; **d~ lassen** (fig) hint at

Durchblutung f circulation

durchbohren vt insep pierce

durchbrechen¹† vt/i sep (haben) break [in two]

durchbrechen²† vt insep break through; break (Schallmauer)

durchbrennen† vi sep (sein) burn through; (Sicherung:) blow

Durchbruch m breakthrough

durchdrehen v sep ● vt mince ● vi (haben/sein) 𝔽 go crazy

durchdringen† vi sep (sein) penetrate; (sich durchsetzen) get one's way. **d~d** adj penetrating; (Schrei) piercing

durcheinander adv in a muddle; (Person) confused; **d~ bringen** muddle [up]; confuse (Person); **d~ geraten** get mixed up; **d~ reden** all talk at once. **D~** nt -s muddle

durchfahren vi sep (sein) drive through; (Zug:) go through

Durchfahrt f journey/drive through; (durch den D~ passing through; **'D~ verboten'** 'no thoroughfare'

Durchfall m diarrhoea. **d~en/vi** sep (sein) fall through; (𝔽: versagen)

flop; (bei Prüfung) fail

Durchfuhr f - (Comm) transit

durchführ|bar adj feasible. **d~en** vt sep carry out

Durchgang m passage; (Sport) round; **'D~ verboten'** 'no entry'. **D~sverkehr** m through traffic

durchgeben† vt sep pass through; (übermitteln) transmit; (Radio, TV) broadcast

durchgebraten adj gut d~ well done

durchgehen† vi sep (sein) go through; (davonlaufen) run away; (Pferd:) bolt; **jdm etw d~ lassen** let s.o. get away with sth. **d~d** adj continuous; **d~d geöffnet** open all day; **d~der Zug** through train

durchgreifen† vi sep (haben) reach through; (vorgehen) take drastic action. **d~d** adj drastic

durchhalte|n|t v sep (fig) ● vi (haben) hold out ● vt keep up. **D~vermögen** nt stamina

durchkommen† vi sep (sein) come through; (gelangen, am Telefon) get through

durchlassen† vt sep let through

durchlässig adj permeable; (undicht) leaky

Durchlauferhitzer m -s,- geyser

durchlesen† vt sep read through

durchleuchten vt insep X-ray

durchlöchert adj riddled with holes

durchmachen vt sep go through; (erleiden) undergo

Durchmesser m -s,- diameter

durchnässt adj wet through

durchnehmen† vt sep (Sch) do

durchnummeriert adj numbered consecutively

durchpausen vt sep trace

durchqueren vt insep cross

Durchreiche f -,-n hatch

Durchreise f journey through; **auf der D~** passing through. **d~n** vi sep (sein) pass through

durchreißen† vt/i sep (sein) tear

Durchsage f -,-n announcement. **d~n** vt sep announce

Durchschlag m carbon copy; (Culin) colander. **d~en†** v sep ● vt (Culin) rub through a sieve; sieve **d~en** (fig) struggle through ● vi (sein) (Sicherung:) blow

durchschlagend adj (fig) effective; (Erfolg) resounding

durchschneiden† vt sep cut

Durchschnitt m average; **im D~** on average. **d~lich** adj average ● adv on average. **D~s-** prefix average

Durchschrift f carbon copy

durchsehen† v sep ● vi (haben) see through ● vt look through

durchseihen vt sep strain

durchsetzen vt sep force through; **sich d~** assert oneself; (Mode:) catch on

Durchsicht f check

durchsichtig adj transparent

durchsickern vi sep (sein) seep through; (Neuigkeit:) leak out

durchstehen† vt sep (fig) come through

durchstreichen† vt sep cross out

durchsuch|en vt insep search. **D~ung** f -,-en search

durchwachsen adj (Speck) streaky; (fig: gemischt) mixed

durchwählen vi sep (haben) (Teleph) dial direct

durchweg adv without exception

durchwühlen vt insep rummage through; ransack (Haus)

Durchzug m through draught

---

dürfen†

● transitive & auxiliary verb

····▸ (Erlaubnis haben zu) be allowed; may, can. **etw [tun] dürfen** be allowed to do sth. **darf ich das tun?** may or can I do that? **nein, das darfst du nicht** no you may not or cannot [do that]. **er sagte mir, ich dürfte sofort gehen** he told me I could go at once. **hier darf man nicht rauchen** smoking is prohibited here. **sie darf/durfte es nicht sehen** she must not/was not allowed to see it.

····▸ (in Höflichkeitsformeln) may. **darf ich rauchen?** may I smoke? **darf/dürfte ich um diesen Tanz bitten?** may/might I have the pleasure of this dance?

····▸ **dürfte** (sollte) should, ought. **jetzt dürften sie dort angekommen sein** they should or ought to be there by now. **das dürfte nicht allzu schwer sein** that should not be too difficult. **ich hätte es nicht tun/sagen dürfen** I ought not to have done/said it

● intransitive verb

····▸ (irgendwohin gehen dürfen) be allowed to go; may go; can go. **darf ich nach Hause?** may or can I go home? **sie durfte nicht ins Theater** she was not allowed to go to the theatre

---

dürftig adj poor; (Mahlzeit) scanty

dürr adj dry; (Boden) arid; (mager) skinny. **D~e** f -,-n drought

Durst m -[e]s thirst; **D~ haben** be thirsty. **d~ig** adj thirsty

Dusche f -,-n shower. **d~n** vi/r (haben) [sich] **d~n** have a shower

Düse f -,-n nozzle. **D~nflugzeug** nt jet

Dutzend nt -s,-e dozen. **d~weise** adv by the dozen

duzen vt jdn d~ call s.o. 'du'

DVD f -,-s DVD

Dynam|ik f - dynamics sg; (fig) dynamism. **d~isch** adj dynamic; (Rente) index-linked

Dynamit nt -es dynamite

Dynamo m -s,-s dynamo

Dynastie f -,-n dynasty

D-Zug /'de:-/ m express [train]

. . . .

Ee

. . . .

Ebbe f -,-n low tide

eben adj level; (glatt) smooth; **zu e~er Erde** on the ground floor ● adv just; (genau) exactly; **e~ noch** only just; (gerade vorhin) just now; **das ist es e~!** that's just it! **E~bild** nt image

Ebene f -,-n (Geog) plain; (Geometry) plane; (fig: Niveau) level

eben|falls adv also; danke, **e~falls** thank you, [the] same to you. **E~holz** nt ebony. **e~so** just the same; (ebenso sehr) just as much; **e~so gut** just as good; just as well; **e~so sehr** just as much; **e~so viel** just as much/ many; **e~so wenig** just as little/ few; (noch) no more

Eber m -s,- boar

ebnen vt level; (fig) smooth

Echo nt -s,-s echo

echt adj genuine, real; authentic ● adv 🅸 really; typically. **E~heit** f - authenticity

Eck|ball m (Sport) corner. **E~e** f -,-n corner; **um die E~e bringen** 🅸 bump off. **e~ig** adj angular; (Klammern) square; (unbeholfen) awkward. **E~zahn** m canine tooth

Ecu, ECU /e'ky:/ m -[s],-[s] ecu

edel adj noble; (wertvoll) precious; (fein) fine. **e~mütig** adj magnanimous. **E~stahl** m stainless steel. **E~stein** m precious stone

Efeu m -s ivy

Effekt m -[e]s,-e effect. **E~en** pl securities. **e~iv** adj actual; (wirksam) effective

EG f - abbr (Europäische Gemeinschaft) EC

egal adj **das ist mir e~** 🅸 it's all the same to me ● adv **e~ wie/wo** no matter how/where

Egge f -,-n harrow

Ego|ismus m - selfishness. **E~ist(in)** m -en,-en (f -,-nen) egoist. **e~istisch** adj selfish

eh adv (Aust, 🅸) anyway

ehe conj before; **ehe nicht** until

Ehe f -,-n marriage. **E~bett** nt double bed. **E~bruch** m adultery. **E~frau** f wife. **e~lich** adj marital; (Recht) conjugal; (Kind) legitimate

ehemalig adj former. **e~s** adv formerly

Ehe|mann m (pl -männer) husband. **E~paar** nt married couple

eher adv earlier, sooner; (lieber, mehr) rather; (mehr) more

Ehering m wedding ring

Ehr|e f -,-n honour. **e~en** vt honour. **e~enamtlich** adj honorary ● adv in an honorary capacity. **E~engast** m guest of honour. **e~enhaft** adj honourable. **E~ensache** f point of honour. **E~enwort** nt word of honour. **e~erbietig** adj deferential. **E~furcht** f reverence; (Scheu) awe. **e~fürchtig** adj reverent. **E~gefühl** nt sense of honour. **E~geiz** m ambition. **e~geizig** adj ambitious. **e~lich** adj honest; **e~lich gesagt** to be honest. **E~lichkeit** f - honesty. **e~los** adj dishonourable. **e~würdig** adj venerable; (als Anrede) Reverend

Ei nt -[e]s,-er egg

Eibe f -,-n yew

Eiche f -,-n oak. **E~l** f -,-n acorn

eichen vt standardize

Eichhörnchen nt -s,- squirrel

Eid m -[e]s,-e oath

Eidechse f -,-n lizard

eidlich adj sworn ● adv on oath

Eidotter m & nt egg yolk

Eier|becher m egg-cup. **E~kuchen** m pancake; (Omelett) omelette. **E~schale** f eggshell. **E~schnee** m beaten egg-white. **E~stock** m ovary

Eifer m -s eagerness. **E~sucht** f jealousy. **e~süchtig** adj jealous

eifrig adj eager

Eigelb nt -[e]s,-e [egg] yolk

eigen adj own; (typisch) characteristic (dat of); (seltsam) odd; (genau) particular. **E~art** f peculiarity. **e~artig** adj peculiar. **e~händig** adj personal; (Unterschrift) own. **E~heit** f -,-en peculiarity. **E~name** m proper name. **e~nützig** adj selfish. **e~s** adv specially. **E~schaft** f -,-en quality; (Phys) property; (Merkmal) characteristic; (Funktion) capacity. **E~schaftswort** nt (pl -wörter) adjective. **E~sinn** m obstinacy. **e~sinnig** adj obstinate

eigentlich adj actual, real; (wahr) true ● adv actually, really; (streng genommen) strictly speaking

Eigen|tor nt own goal. **E~tum** nt -s property. **E~tümer(in)** m -s,- (f -,-nen) owner. **E~tumswohnung** f

freehold flat. **e~willig** adj self-willed; (Stil) highly individual

eignen (sich) vr be suitable

Eil|brief m express letter. **E~e** f - hurry; **E~e haben** be in a hurry; (Sache) be urgent. **e~en** vi (sein) hurry ● (haben) (drängen) be urgent. **e~ig** adj hurried; (dringend) urgent; **es e~ig haben** be in a hurry. **E~zug** m semi-fast train

Eimer m -s,- bucket; (Abfall-) bin

---

ein

● indefinite article

····▸ a, (vor Vokal) an. **ein Kleid/ Apfel/Hotel/Mensch** a dress/an apple/a[n] hotel/a human being. **so ein** such a. **was für ein ...** (Frage) what kind of a ... ? (Ausruf) what a ... !

● adjective

····▸ (Ziffer) one. **eine Minute** one minute. **wir haben nur eine Stunde** we only have an/(betont) one hour. **eines Tages/Abends** one day/evening

····▸ (derselbe) the same. **einer Meinung** sein be of the same opinion. **mit jdm in einem Zimmer schlafen** sleep in the same room as s.o.

---

einander pron one another

Einäscherung f -,-en cremation

einatmen vt/i sep (haben) inhale, breathe in

Einbahnstraße f one-way street

einbalsamieren vt sep embalm

Einband m binding

Einbau m installation; (Montage) fitting. **e~en** vt sep install; (montieren) fit. **E~küche** f fitted kitchen

einbegriffen pred adj included

Einberufung f call-up

Einbettzimmer nt single room

einbeulen vt sep dent

einbeziehen† vt sep [mit] e~ include; (berücksichtigen) take into account

einbiegen† vi sep (sein) turn

einbild|en vt sep sich (dat) etw e~en imagine sth; sich (dat) viel e~en be conceited. **E~ung** f imagination; (Dünkel) conceit. **E~ungskraft** f imagination

einblenden vt sep fade in

Einblick m insight

einbrech|en† vi sep (haben/sein) break in; **bei uns ist eingebrochen worden** we have been burgled. **E~er** m burglar

einbringen† vt sep get in; bring in (Geld)

Einbruch m burglary; **bei E~ der Nacht** at nightfall

einbürger|n vt sep naturalize. **E~ung** f - naturalization

einchecken /-tʃɛkən/ vt/i sep (haben) check in

eindecken (sich) vr sep stock up

eindeutig adj unambiguous; (deutlich) clear

eindicken vt sep (Culin) thicken

eindringen† vi sep (sein) e~en in (+ acc) penetrate into; (mit Gewalt) force one's/(Wasser:) its way into; (Mil) invade

Eindruck m impression

eindrücken vt sep crush

eindrucksvoll adj impressive

ein|e(r,s) pron one; (jemand) someone; (man) one, you

einebnen vt sep level

eineiig adj (Zwillinge) identical

eineinhalb inv adj one and a half; **e~ Stunden** an hour and a half

Einelternfamilie f one-parent family

einengen vt sep restrict

Einer m -s,- (Math) unit. **e~** pron s. **eine(r,s)**. **e~lei** inv adj ● attrib adj one kind of; (eintönig, einheitlich) the same ● pred adj Ⓣ immaterial; **es ist mir e~lei** it's all the same to me. **e~seits** adv on the one hand

einfach adj simple; (Essen) plain; (Faden, Fahrt) single; **e~er Soldat** private. **E~heit** f - simplicity

einfädeln vt sep thread; (fig; arrangieren) arrange

einfahr|en† v sep ● vi (sein) arrive; (Zug:) pull in ● vt (Auto) run in. **E~t** f arrival; (Eingang) entrance, way in; (Auffahrt) drive; (Autobahn-) access road; **keine E~t** no entry

Einfall m idea; (Mil) invasion. **e~en†** vi sep (sein) collapse; (eindringen) invade; **jdm e~en** occur to s.o.; **was fällt ihm ein!** what does he think he is doing!

Einfalt f - naïvety

einfarbig adj of one colour; (Stoff, Kleid) plain

einfass|en vt sep edge; set (Edelstein). **E~ung** f border, edging

einfetten vt sep grease

Einfluss m influence. **e~reich** adj influential

einförmig adj monotonous. **E~keit** f - monotony

einfrieren† vt/i sep (sein) freeze

einfügen vt sep insert; (einschieben) interpolate; **sich e~** fit in

einfühlsam adj sensitive

Einfuhr f -,-en import

einführ|en vt sep introduce; (einstecken) insert; (einweisen) initiate; (Comm) import. **e~end** adj introductory. **E~ung** f introduction; (Einweisung) initiation

Eingabe f petition; (Computer) input

Eingang m entrance, way in; (Ankunft) arrival

eingebaut adj built-in; (Schrank) fitted

eingeben† vt sep hand in; (Computer) feed in

eingebildet adj imaginary; (überheblich) conceited

Eingeborene(r) m/f native

e eingehen† v sep ● vi (sein) come in; (ankommen) arrive; (einlaufen) shrink; (sterben) die; (Zeitung, Firma:) fold; **auf etw** (acc) **e~** go into sth; (annehmen) agree to sth ● vt enter into; contract (Ehe); make (Wette); take (Risiko)

eingemacht adj (Culin) bottled

eingenommen pred adj (fig) taken (von with); prejudiced (gegen against)

eingeschneit adj snowbound

eingeschrieben adj registered

Einge|ständnis† nt admission. **e~stehen†** vt sep admit

eingetragen adj registered

Eingeweide pl bowels, entrails

eingewöhnen (sich) vr sep settle in

eingießen† vt sep pour in; (einschenken) pour

eingleisig adj single-track

eingliedern† vt sep integrate. **E~ung** f integration

eingravieren vt sep engrave

eingreifen† vi sep (haben) intervene. **E~** nt -s intervention

Eingriff m intervention; (Med) operation

einhaken vt/r sep **jdn e~** od **sich bei jdm e~** take someone's arm

einhalten† v sep ● vt keep; (befolgen) observe ● vi (haben) stop

einhändigen vt sep hand in

einhängen vt sep hang; put down (Hörer)

einheimisch adj local; (eines Lan-

des) native; (Comm) homeproduced. **E~e(r)** m/f local, native

Einheit f -,-en unity; (Maß-, Mil) unit. **e~lich** adj uniform. **E~spreis** m standard price; (Fahrpreis) flat fare

einholen vt sep catch up with; (aufholen) make up for; (erbitten) seek; (einkaufen) buy

einhüllen vt sep wrap

einhundert inv adj one hundred

einig adj united; [sich (dat)] e~ sein be in agreement

einig|e(r,s) pron some; (ziemlich viel) quite a lot of; (substantivisch) **e~e** pl some; (mehrere) several; (ziemlich viele) quite a lot; **e~es** sg some things; **vor e~er Zeit** some time ago

einigen vt unite; unify (Land); **sich e~** come to an agreement

einigermaßen adv to some extent; (ziemlich) fairly; (ziemlich gut) fairly well

Einigkeit f - unity; (Übereinstimmung) agreement

einjährig adj one-year-old; **e~e** Pflanze annual

einkalkulieren vt sep take into account

einkassieren vt sep collect

Einkauf m purchase; (Einkaufen) shopping; **Einkäufe machen** do some shopping. **e~en** vt sep buy; **e~en gehen** go shopping. **E~swagen** m shopping trolley

einklammern vt sep bracket

Einklang m harmony; **in E~ stehen** be in accord (**mit** with)

einkleben vt sep stick in

einkleiden vt sep fit out

einklemmen vt sep clamp

einkochen v sep ● vi (sein) boil down ● vt preserve, bottle

Einkommen nt -s income.
E~[s]steuer f income tax

Einkünfte pl income sg; (Einnahmen) revenue sg

einlad|en† vt sep load; (auffordern) invite; (bezahlen für) treat. E~ung f invitation

Einlage f enclosure; (Schuh-) arch support; (Programm-) interlude; (Comm) investment; (Bank-) deposit; Suppe mit E~ soup with noodles/dumplings

Ein|lass m -es admittance. e~lassen† vt sep let in; run (Bad, Wasser); sich auf etw (acc) e~lassen get involved in sth

einleben (sich) vr sep settle in

Einlege|arbeit f inlaid work. e~n vt sep put in; lay in (Vorrat); lodge (Protest); (einfügen) insert; (Auto) engage (Gang); (Culin) pickle; (marinieren) marinade; eine Pause e~n have a break. E~sohle f insole

einleit|en vt sep initiate; (eröffnen) begin. E~ung f introduction

einleuchten vi sep (haben) be clear (dat to). e~d adj convincing

einliefer|n vt sep take (ins Krankenhaus to hospital). E~ung f admission

einlösen vt sep cash (Scheck); redeem (Pfand); (fig) keep

einmachen vt sep preserve

einmal adv once; (eines Tages) one or some day; noch/schon e~ again/before; noch e~ so teuer twice as expensive; auf e~ at the same time; (plötzlich) suddenly; nicht e~ not even. E~eins nt - [multiplication] tables pl. e~ig adj (einzigartig) unique; (①: großartig) fantastic

einmarschieren vi sep (sein) march in

einmisch|en (sich) vr sep interfere. E~ung f interference

Einnahme f -,-n taking; (Mil) capture; E~n pl income sg; (Einkünfte) revenue sg; (Comm) receipts; (eines Ladens) takings

einnehmen† vt sep take; have (Mahlzeit); (Mil) capture; take up (Platz)

einordnen vt sep put in its proper place; (klassifizieren) classify; sich e~ fit in; (Auto) get in lane

einpacken vt sep pack

einparken vt sep park

einpflanzen vt sep plant; implant (Organ)

einplanen vt sep allow for

einprägen vt sep impress (jdm [up]on s.o.); sich (dat) etw e~en memorize sth

einrahmen vt sep frame

einrasten vi sep (sein) engage

einräumen vt sep put away; (zugeben) admit; (zugestehen) grant

einrechnen vt sep include

einreden v sep ● vt jdm/sich (dat) etw e~ persuade s.o./oneself of sth

einreiben† vt sep rub (mit with)

einreichen vt sep submit; die Scheidung e~ file for divorce

Einreihe|r m -s,- single-breasted suit. e~ig adj single-breasted

Einreise f entry. e~n vi sep (sein) enter (nach Irland Ireland)

einrenken vt sep (Med) set

einricht|en vt sep fit out; (möblieren) furnish; (anordnen) arrange; (Med) set (Bruch); (eröffnen) set up; sich e~en furnish one's home; (sich einschränken) economize; (sich vorbereiten) prepare (auf + acc for). E~ung f furnishing; (Möbel) furnishings pl; (Techn) equipment; (Vorrichtung) device; (*Eröffnung*) setting up; (*Institution*) institution; (*Gewohnheit*) practice

einrosten *vi sep* (*sein*) rust; (*fig*) get rusty

eins *inv adj & pron* one; **noch e~** one other thing; **mir ist alles e~** Ⓘ it's all the same to me. **E~** *f* -,-en one; (*Sch*) ≈ A

einsam *adj* lonely; (*allein*) solitary; (*abgelegen*) isolated. **E~keit** *f* - loneliness; solitude; isolation

einsammeln *vt sep* collect

Einsatz *m* use; (*Mil*) mission; (*Wett-*) stake; (*E~teil*) insert; **im E~** in action

einschalten *vt sep* switch on; (*einschieben*) interpolate; (*fig: beteiligen*) call in; **sich e~en** (*fig*) intervene. **E~quote** *f* (*TV*) viewing figures *pl*; ≈ ratings *pl*

einschätzen *vt sep* assess; (*bewerten*) rate

einschenken *vt sep* pour

einscheren *vi sep* (*sein*) pull in

einschicken *vt sep* send in

einschieben† *vt sep* push in; (*einfügen*) insert

einschiff|en (**sich**) *vr sep* embark. **E~ung** *f* - embarkation

einschlafen† *vi sep* (*sein*) go to sleep; (*aufhören*) peter out

einschläfern *vt sep* lull to sleep; (*betäuben*) put out; (*töten*) put to sleep. **e~d** *adj* soporific

Einschlag *m* impact. **e~en†** *v sep* ● *vt* knock in; (*zerschlagen*) smash; (*drehen*) turn; take (*Weg*); take up (*Laufbahn*) ● *vi* (*haben*) hit/(*Blitz:*) strike (**in etw** *acc* sth); (*Erfolg haben*) be a hit

einschleusen *vt sep* infiltrate

einschließ|en† *vt sep* lock in; (*umgeben*) enclose; (*einkreisen*) surround; (*einbeziehen*) include; **sich**

e~en lock oneself in; **Bedienung eingeschlossen** service included. **e~lich** *adv* inclusive ● *prep* (+ *gen*) including

einschneiden† *vt/i sep* (*haben*) [**in**] **etw** *acc* **e~** cut into sth. **e~d** *adj* (*fig*) drastic

Einschnitt *m* cut; (*Med*) incision; (*Lücke*) gap; (*fig*) decisive event

einschränk|en *vt sep* restrict; (*reduzieren*) cut back; **sich e~en** economize. **E~ung** *f* -,-en restriction; (*Reduzierung*) reduction; (*Vorbehalt*) reservation

Einschreib|[e]brief *m* registered letter. **e~en†** *vt sep* enter; register (*Brief*); **sich e~en** put one's name down; (*sich anmelden*) enrol. **E~en** *nt* registered letter/packet; **als** *od* **per E~en** by registered post

einschüchtern *vt sep* intimidate

Einsegnung *f* -,-en confirmation

einsehen† *vt sep* inspect; (*lesen*) consult; (*begreifen*) see

einseitig *adj* one-sided; (*Pol*) unilateral ● *adv* on one side; (*fig*) one-sidedly; (*Pol*) unilaterally

einsenden† *vt sep* send in

einsetzen *v sep* ● *vt* put in; (*einfügen*) insert; (*verwenden*) use; put on (*Zug*); call out (*Truppen*); (*Mil*) deploy; (*ernennen*) appoint; (*wetten*) stake; (*riskieren*) risk ● *vi* begin, start; (*Winter, Regen:*) set in

Einsicht *f* insight; (*Verständnis*) understanding; (*Vernunft*) reason. **e~ig** *adj* understanding

Einsiedler *m* hermit

einsinken† *vi sep* (*sein*) sink in

einspannen *vt sep* harness; **jdn e~** Ⓘ rope s.o. in

einsparen *vt sep* save

einsperren *vt sep* shut/(*im Gefängnis*) lock up

einsprachig adj monolingual

einspritzen vt sep inject

Einspruch m objection; **E~ erheben** object; (Jur) appeal

einspurig adj single-track; (Auto) single-lane

einst adv once; (Zukunft) one day

Einstand m (Tennis) deuce

einstecken vt sep put in; post (Brief); (Electr) plug in; (🔲: behalten) pocket; (🔲: hinnehmen) take; suffer (Niederlage); **etw e~** put sth in one's pocket

einsteigen† vi sep (sein) get in; (in Bus/Zug) get on

einstell|en vt sep put in; (anstellen) employ; (aufhören) stop; (regulieren) adjust, set; (Optik) focus; tune (Motor, Zündung); tune to (Sender); **sich e~en** turn up; (Schwierigkeiten:) arise; **sich e~en auf** (+ acc) adjust to; (sich vorbereiten) prepare for. **E~ung** f employment; (Regulierung) adjustment; (TV, Auto) tuning; (Haltung) attitude

einstig adj former

einstimmig adj unanimous. **E~keit** f - unanimity

einstöckig adj single-storey

einstudieren vt sep rehearse

einstufen vt sep classify

Ein|sturz m collapse. **e~stürzen** vi sep (sein) collapse

einstweilen adv for the time being; (inzwischen) meanwhile

eintasten vt sep key in

eintauchen vt/i sep (sein) dip in

eintauschen vt sep exchange

eintausend inv adj one thousand

einteil|en vt sep divide (in + acc into); (Biology) classify; **sich** (dat) **seine Zeit gut e~en** organize one's time well. **e~ig** adj one-piece. **E~ung** f division

eintönig adj monotonous. **E~keit** f - monotony

Eintopf m, **E~gericht** nt stew

Eintracht f - harmony

Eintrag m -[e]s, ⁓e entry. **e~en†** vt sep enter; (Admin) register; **sich e~en** put one's name down

einträglich adj profitable

Eintragung f -,-en registration

eintreffen† vi sep (sein) arrive; (fig) come true

eintreiben† vt sep drive in; (einziehen) collect

eintreten† v sep • vi (sein) enter; (geschehen) occur; **in einen Klub e~** join a club; **e~ für** (fig) stand up for • vt kick in

Eintritt m entrance; (zu Veranstaltung) admission; (Beitritt) joining; (Beginn) beginning. **E~skarte** f [admission] ticket

einüben vt sep practise

einundachtzig inv adj eighty-one

Einvernehmen nt -s understanding; (Übereinstimmung) agreement

einverstanden adj **e~ sein** agree

Einverständnis nt agreement; (Zustimmung) consent

Einwand m -[e]s, ⁓e objection

Einwander|er m immigrant. **e~n** vi sep (sein) immigrate. **E~ung** f immigration

einwandfrei adj perfect

einwärts adv inwards

einwechseln vt sep change

einwecken vt sep preserve, bottle

Einweg- prefix non-returnable

einweichen vt sep soak

einweih|en vt sep inaugurate; (Relig) consecrate; (einführen) initiate; **in ein Geheimnis e~en** let into a secret. E~ung f -,-en inauguration; consecration; initiation

einweisen† vt sep (einführen) initiate; **ins Krankenhaus e~** send to hospital

einwerfen† vt sep insert; post (Brief); (Sport) throw in

einwickeln vt sep wrap [up]

einwillig|en vi sep (haben) consent, agree (**in** + acc to). E~ung f - consent

Einwohner|(in) m -s,- (f -,-nen) inhabitant. E~zahl f population

Einwurf m interjection; (Einwand) objection; (Sport) throw-in; (Münz-) slot

Einzahl f (Gram) singular

einzahl|en vt sep pay in. E~ung f payment; (Einlage) deposit

einzäunen vt sep fence in

Einzel nt -s,- (Tennis) singles pl. E~bett nt single bed. E~gänger m -s,- loner. E~haft f solitary confinement. E~handel m retail trade. E~händler m retailer. E~haus nt detached house. E~heit f -,-en detail. E~karte f single ticket. E~kind nt only child

einzeln adj single; (individuell) individual; (gesondert) separate; odd (Handschuh, Socken); e~e Fälle some cases. E~e(r,s) pron der/die E~e the individual; E~e pl some; **im E~en** in detail

Einzel|teil nt [component] part. E~zimmer nt single room

einziehen† v sep ● vt pull in; draw in (Atem, Krallen); (Zool, Techn) retract; indent (Zeile); (aus dem Verkehr ziehen) withdraw; (beschlagnahmen) confiscate; (eintreiben) collect; make (Erkundigungen); (Mil) call up ● vi (sein) (umziehen) move in; (eindringen) penetrate

einzig adj only; (einmalig) unique;

eine e~e Frage a a single question ● adv only; e~ **und allein** solely. E~e(r,s) pron der/die/das E~e the only one; **ein/kein E~er** a/not a single one; **das E~e**, **was mich stört** the only thing that bothers me

Eis nt -es ice; (Speise-) ice-cream; **Eis am Stiel** ice lolly; **Eis laufen** skate. E~bahn f ice rink. E~bär m polar bear. E~becher m ice-cream sundae. E~berg m iceberg. E~diele f ice-cream parlour

Eisen nt -s,- iron. E~bahn f railway

eisern adj iron; (fest) resolute; e~er Vorhang (Theat) safety curtain; (Pol) Iron Curtain

Eis|fach nt freezer compartment. e~gekühlt adj chilled. e~ig adj icy. E~kaffee m iced coffee. E~lauf m skating. E~läufer(in) m(f) skater. E~pickel m ice-axe. E~scholle f ice-floe. E~vogel m kingfisher. E~würfel m icecube. E~zapfen m icicle. E~zeit f ice age

eitel adj vain; (rein) pure. E~keit f - vanity

Eiter m -s pus. e~n vi (haben) discharge pus

Eiweiß nt -es,-e egg-white

Ekel m -s disgust; (Widerwille) revulsion. e~haft adj nauseating; (widerlich) repulsive. e~n vt/i (haben) **mich** od **mir e~t [es] davor** it makes me feel sick ● vr **sich e~n vor** (+ dat) find repulsive

eklig adj disgusting, repulsive

Ekzem nt -s,-e eczema

elastisch adj elastic; (federnd) springy; (fig) flexible

Elch m -[e]s,-e elk

Elefant m -en,-en elephant

elegan|t adj elegant.

E~z f - elegance

Elektri|ker m -s,- electrician. **e~sch** adj electric

Elektrizität f - electricity. **E~swerk** nt power station

Elektr|oartikel mpl electrical appliances. **E~ode** f -,-n electrode. **E~onik** f - electronics sg. **e~onisch** adj electronic

Elend nt -s misery; (Armut) poverty. **e~** adj miserable; (krank) poorly; (gemein) contemptible. **E~sviertel** nt slum

elf inv adj. **E~** f -,-en eleven

Elfe f -,-n fairy

Elfenbein nt ivory

Elfmeter m (Fußball) penalty

elfte(r,s) adj eleventh

Ell[en]bogen m elbow

Ellip|se f -,-n ellipse. **e~tisch** adj elliptical

Elsass nt - Alsace

elsässisch adj Alsatian

Elster f -,-n magpie

el|terlich adj parental. **E~n** pl parents. **e~nlos** adj orphaned. **E~nteil** m parent

Email /e'maɪ/ nt -s,-s, **E~le** f -,-n enamel

E-Mail /'i:meɪl/ f -,-s e-mail; e-mail message

Emanzi|pation /-'tsɪoːn/ f - emancipation. **e~piert** adj emancipated

Embargo nt -s,-s embargo

Embryo m -s,-s embryo

Emigr|ant(in) m -en,-en (f -,-nen) emigrant. **E~ation** f - emigration. **e~ieren** vi (sein) emigrate

Empfang m -[e]s,ᵉe reception; (Erhalt) receipt; in **E~ nehmen** receive; (annehmen) accept. **e~en†** vt receive; (Biology) conceive

Empfäng|er m -s,- recipient; (Post-) addressee; (Zahlungs-) payee; (Radio, TV) receiver. **E~nis** f - (Biology) conception

Empfängnisverhütung f contraception. **E~smittel** nt contraceptive

Empfangs|bestätigung f receipt. **E~dame** f receptionist. **E~halle** f [hotel] foyer

empfehl|en† vt recommend. **E~ung** f -,-en recommendation; (Gruß) regards pl

empfind|en† vt feel. **e~lich** adj sensitive (gegen to); (zart) delicate. **E~lichkeit** f - sensitivity; delicacy; tenderness; touchiness. **E~ung** f -,-en sensation; (Regung) feeling

empor adv (literarisch) up[wards]

empören vt incense; sich **e~** be indignant; (sich auflehnen) rebel

Emporkömmling m -s,-e upstart

empör|t adj indignant. **E~ung** f - indignation; (Auflehnung) rebellion

Ende nt -s,-n end; (eines Films, Romans) ending; (🗌: Stück) bit; zu **E~ sein** be finished; etw zu **E~ schreiben** finish writing sth; am **E~** at the end; (schließlich) in the end; (🗌: vielleicht) perhaps; (🗌: erschöpft) at the end of one's tether

end|en vi (haben) end. **e~gültig** adj final; (bestimmt) definite

Endivie /-iǝ/ f -,-n endive

end|lich adv at last, finally; (schließlich) in the end. **e~los** adj endless. **E~station** f terminus. **E~ung** f -,-en (Gram) ending

Energie f - energy

energisch adj resolute; (nachdrücklich) vigorous

eng adj narrow; (beengt) cramped; (anliegend) tight; (nah) close; **e~ anliegend** tight-fitting

Engagement /āgaʒə'mã:/ nt -s,-s
(Theat) engagement; (fig) commitment

Engel m -s,- angel

England nt -s England

Engländer m -s,- Englishman;
(Techn) monkey-wrench; **die E~** the
English pl. **E~in** f -,-nen Englishwoman

englisch adj English. **E~** nt -[s]
(Lang) English; **auf E~** in English

Engpass m (fig) bottleneck

en gros /ã'gro:/ adv wholesale

Enkel m -s,- grandson; **E~** pl
grandchildren. **E~in** f -,-nen granddaughter. **E~kind** nt grandchild.
E~sohn m grandson. **E~tochter** f
granddaughter

Ensemble /ã'sã:bal/ nt -s,-s ensemble; (Theat) company

entart|en vi (sein) degenerate.
e~et adj degenerate

entbehren vt do without; (vermissen) miss

entbind|en† vt release (**von**
from); (Med) deliver (**von** of) ● vi
(haben) give birth. **E~ung** f delivery. **E~ungsstation** f maternity ward

entdeck|en vt discover. **E~er** m
-s,- discoverer; (Forscher) explorer.
E~ung f -,-en discovery

Ente f -,-n duck

entehren vt dishonour

enteignen vt dispossess; expropriate (Eigentum)

enterben vt disinherit

Enterich m -s,-e drake

entfallen† vi (sein) not apply; **auf
jdn e~** be s.o.'s share

entfernen vt remove; **sich e~en**
leave. **e~t** adj distant; (schwach)
vague; **2 Kilometer e~t** 2 kilometres away; **e~t verwandt** dis-
tantly related. **E~ung** f -,-en removal; (Abstand) distance;
(Reichweite) range

entfliehen† vi (sein) escape

entfremden vt alienate

entfrosten vt defrost

entführ|en vt abduct, kidnap; hijack (Flugzeug). **E~er** m abductor,
kidnapper; hijacker. **E~ung** f abduction, kidnapping; hijacking

entgegen adv towards ● prep (+
dat) contrary to. **e~gehen†** vi sep
(sein) (+ dat) go to meet; (fig) be
heading for. **e~gesetzt** adj opposite; (gegensätzlich) opposing.
e~kommen† vi sep (sein) (+ dat)
come to meet; (zukommen auf)
come towards; (fig) oblige.
E~kommen nt -s helpfulness; (Zugeständnis) concession. **e~kommend** adj approaching; (Verkehr)
oncoming; (fig) obliging. **e~nehmen†** vt sep accept. **e~wirken**
vi sep (haben) (+ dat) counteract;
(fig) oppose

entgegn|en vt reply (**auf** + acc
to). **E~ung** f -,-en reply

entgehen† vi sep (sein) (+ dat) escape; **jdm e~** (unbemerkt bleiben)
escape s.o.'s notice; **sich** (dat) **etw
e~ lassen** miss sth

Entgelt nt -[e]s payment; **gegen
E~** for money

entgleis|en vi (sein) be derailed;
(fig) make a gaffe. **E~ung** f -,-en
derailment; (fig) gaffe

entgräten vt fillet, bone

Enthaarungsmittel nt depilatory

enthalt|en† vt contain; **in etw**
(dat) **e~en sein** be contained/ (eingeschlossen) included in sth; **sich
der Stimme e~en** (Pol) abstain.
e~sam adj abstemious. **E~ung** f
(Pol) abstention

enthaupten vt behead

entheben† vt jdn seines Amtes e~ relieve s.o. of his post

Enthüllung f -,-en revelation

Enthusias|mus m - enthusiasm. **E~t** m -en,-en enthusiast

entkernen vt stone; core (Apfel)

entkleiden vt undress; **sich e~en** undress

entkommen† vi (sein) escape

entkorken vt uncork

entladen† vt unload; (Electr) discharge; **sich e~** discharge; (aus der Haft) release. **E~ung** f -,-en dismissal; discharge; release

entlang adv & prep (+ preceding acc or following dat) along; **die Straße e~** along the road; **an etw** (dat) **e~** along sth. **e~fahren**† vi sep (sein) drive along. **e~gehen**† vi sep (sein) walk along

entlarven vt unmask

entlass|en† vt dismiss; (aus Krankenhaus) discharge; (aus der Haft) release. **E~ung** f -,-en dismissal; discharge; release

entlast|en vt relieve the strain on; ease (Gewissen, Verkehr); relieve (von of); (Jur) exonerate. **E~ung** f - relief; exoneration

entlaufen† vi (sein) run away

entleeren vt empty

entlegen adj remote

entlohnen vt pay

entlüft|en vt ventilate. **E~er** m -s,- extractor fan. **E~ung** f ventilation

entmündigen vt declare incapable of managing his own affairs

entmutigen vt discourage

entnehmen† vt take (dat from); (schließen) gather (dat from)

entpuppen (sich) vr (fig) turn out (als etw to be sth)

entrahmt adj skimmed

entrichten vt pay

entrinnen† vi (sein) escape

entrüst|en vt fill with indignation; **sich e~en** be indignant (**über** + acc at). **e~et** adj indignant. **E~ung** f - indignation

entsaft|en vt extract the juice from. **E~er** m -s,- juice extractor

entsagen vi (haben) (+ dat) renounce

entschädig|en vt compensate. **E~ung** f -,-en compensation

entschärfen vt defuse

entscheid|en† vt/i (haben) decide; **sich e~en** decide; (Sache:) be decided. **e~end** adj decisive; (kritisch) crucial. **E~ung** f decision

entschließen† (sich) vr decide, make up one's mind; **sich anders e~** change one's mind

entschlossen adj determined; (energisch) resolute; **kurz e~** without hesitation. **E~heit** f - determination

Entschluss m decision

entschlüsseln vt decode

entschuld|bar adj excusable. **e~igen** vt excuse; **sich e~igen** apologize (**bei** to); **e~igen Sie [bitte]**! sorry! (bei Frage) excuse me. **E~igung** f -,-en apology; (Ausrede) excuse; **um E~igung bitten** apologize

entsetz|en vt horrify. **E~en** nt -s horror. **e~lich** adj horrible; (schrecklich) terrible

Entsorgung f - waste disposal

entspann|en vt relax; **sich e~en** relax; (Lage:) ease. **E~ung** f - relaxation; easing; (Pol) détente

entsprech|en† vi (haben) (+ dat) correspond to; (übereinstimmen) agree with. **e~end** adj corresponding; (angemessen) appropriate; (zuständig) relevant ● adv correspondingly; appropriately; (demgemäß) accordingly ● prep (+ dat) in accordance with

entspringen† vi (sein) (Fluss:) rise; (fig) arise, spring (dat from)

entstammen vi (sein) come from/(abstammen) be descended (dat from)

entsteh|en† vi (sein) come into being; (sich bilden) form; (sich entwickeln) develop; (Brand:) start; (stammen) originate. **E~ung** f - origin; formation; development

entstell|en vt disfigure; (verzerren) distort. **E~ung** f disfigurement; distortion

entstört adj (Electr) suppressed

enttäusch|en vt disappoint. **E~ung** f disappointment

entwaffnen vt disarm

entwässer|n vt drain. **E~ung** f drainage

entweder conj & adv either

entwerfen† vt design; (aufsetzen) draft; (skizzieren) sketch

entwert|en vt devalue; (ungültig machen) cancel. **E~er** m -s,- ticket-cancelling machine. **E~ung** f devaluation; cancelling

entwick|eln vt develop; sich e~eln develop. **E~lung** f -,-en development; (Biology) evolution. **E~lungsland** nt developing country

entwöhnen vt wean (gen from); cure (Süchtige)

entwürdigend adj degrading

Entwurf m design; (Konzept) draft; (Skizze) sketch

entwurzeln vt uproot

entzie|hen† vt take away (dat from); jdm den Führerschein e~hen disqualify s.o. from driving; sich e~hen (+ dat) withdraw from. **E~hungskur** f treatment for drug/alcohol addiction

entziffern vt decipher

Entzug m withdrawal; (Vorenthaltung) deprivation

entzünd|en vt ignite; (anstecken) light; (fig: erregen) inflame; sich e~en ignite; (Med) become inflamed. **e~et** adj (Med) inflamed. **e~lich** adj inflammable. **E~ung** f (Med) inflammation

entzwei adj broken

Enzian m -s,-e gentian

Enzyklo|pädie f -,-en encyclopaedia. **e~pädisch** adj encyclopaedic

Enzym nt -s,-e enzyme

Epidemie f -,-n epidemic

Epi|lepsie f - epilepsy. **E~leptiker(in)** m -s,- (f -,-nen) epileptic. **e~leptisch** adj epileptic

Epilog m -s,-e epilogue

Episode f -,-n episode

Epoche f -,-n epoch

Epos nt -, Epen epic

er pron he; (Ding, Tier) it

erachten vt consider (für nötig necessary). **E~** nt -s meines **E~s** in my opinion

erbarmen (sich) vr have pity/(Gott:) mercy (gen on). **E~** nt -s pity; mercy

erbärmlich adj wretched

erbauen vt build; (fig) edify; **nicht** e~t von 🔲 not pleased about

Erbe¹ m -n,-n heir

Erbe² nt -s inheritance; (fig) heritage. **e~n** vt inherit

erbeuten vt get; (Mil) capture

Erbfolge f (Jur) succession

erbieten† (sich) vr offer (zu to)

Erbin f -,-nen heiress

erbitten† vt ask for

erbittert adj bitter; (heftig) fierce

erblassen vi (sein) turn pale

erblich adj hereditary

erblicken vt catch sight of

erblinden vi (sein) go blind

erbrechen† vt vomit ● vi/r [sich] e∼ vomit. **E∼** nt -s vomiting

Erbschaft f -,-en inheritance

Erbse f -,-n pea

Erb|stück nt heirloom. **E∼teil** nt inheritance

Erd|apfel m (Aust) potato. **E∼beben** nt -s,- earthquake. **E∼beere** f strawberry

Erde f -,-n earth; (Erdboden) ground; (Fußboden) floor. **e∼n** vt (Electr) earth

erdenklich adj imaginable

Erd|gas nt natural gas. **E∼geschoss** nt ground floor. **E∼kugel** f globe. **E∼kunde** f geography. **E∼nuss** f peanut. **E∼öl** nt [mineral] oil

erdrosseln vt strangle

erdrücken vt crush to death

Erd|rutsch m landslide. **E∼teil** m continent

erdulden vt endure

ereignen (sich) vr happen

Ereignis nt -ses,-se event. **e∼los** adj uneventful. **e∼reich** adj eventful

Eremit m -en,-en hermit

erfahr|en† vt learn, hear; (erleben) experience ● adj experienced. **E∼ung** f -,-en experience; **in E∼ung bringen** find out

erfassen vt seize; (begreifen) grasp; (einbeziehen) include; (aufzeichnen) record

erfind|en† vt invent. **E∼er** m -s,- inventor. **e∼erisch** adj inventive. **E∼ung** f -,-en invention

Erfolg m -[e]s,-e success; (Folge) result; **E∼ haben** be successful. **e∼en** vi (sein) take place; (geschehen) happen. **e∼los** adj unsuccessful. **e∼reich** adj successful

erforder|lich adj required, necessary. **e∼n** vt require, demand

erforsch|en vt explore; (untersuchen) investigate. **E∼ung** f exploration; investigation

erfreu|en vt please. **e∼lich** adj pleasing. **e∼licherweise** adv happily. **e∼t** adj pleased

erfrier|en† vi (sein) freeze to death; (Glied:) become frostbitten; (Pflanze:) be killed by the frost. **E∼ung** f -,-en frostbite

erfrisch|en vt refresh. **E∼ung** f -,-en refreshment

erfüll|en vt fill; (nachkommen) fulfil; serve (Zweck); discharge (Pflicht:) **sich e∼en** come true. **E∼ung** f fulfilment

erfunden invented

ergänz|en vt complement; (hinzufügen) add. **E∼ung** f complement; supplement (Zusatz) addition

ergeben† vt produce; (zeigen) show, establish; **sich e∼en** result; (Schwierigkeit:) arise; (kapitulieren) surrender; (sich fügen) submit ● adj devoted; (resigniert) resigned

Ergebnis nt -ses,-se result. **e∼los** adj fruitless

ergiebig adj productive; (fig) rich

ergreifen† vt seize; take (Maßnahme, Gelegenheit); take up (Beruf); (rühren) move; **die Flucht e∼** flee. **e∼d** adj moving

ergriffen adj deeply moved. **E∼heit** f - emotion

ergründen vt (fig) get to the bottom of

erhaben adj raised; (fig) sublime

Erhalt m -[e]s receipt. **e∼en**† vt receive, get; (gewinnen) obtain; (bewahren) preserve, keep; (instand halten) maintain; (unterhalten) support;

am Leben e~en keep alive ● adj gut/schlecht e~en in good/bad condition; e~en bleiben survive

erhältlich adj obtainable

Erhaltung f - preservation; maintenance

erhängen (sich) vr hang oneself

erheb|en† vt raise; levy (Steuer); charge (Gebühr); **Anspruch e~en** lay claim (auf + acc to); **Protest e~en** protest; sich e~en rise; (Frage:) arise. **e~lich** adj considerable. **E~ung** f -,-en elevation; (Anhöhe) rise; (Aufstand) uprising; (Ermittlung) survey

erheiter|n vt amuse. **E~ung** f - amusement

erhitzen vt heat

erhöh|en vt raise; (fig) increase; sich e~en rise, increase. **E~ung** f -,-en increase

erhol|en (sich) vr recover (von from); (nach Krankheit) convalesce; (sich ausruhen) have a rest. **e~sam** adj restful. **E~ung** f - recovery; (Ruhe) rest

erinner|n vt remind (an + acc of); sich e~n remember (an jdn/etw s.o./sth). **E~ung** f -,-en memory; (Andenken) souvenir

erkält|en (sich) vr catch a cold; e~et sein have a cold. **E~ung** f -,-en cold

erkenn|bar adj recognizable; (sichtbar) visible. e~en† vt recognize; (wahrnehmen) distinguish. **E~tnis** f -,-se recognition; realization; (Wissen) knowledge; die neuesten E~tnisse the latest findings

Erker m -s,- bay

erklär|en vt declare; (erläutern) explain; **sich bereit e~en** agree (zu to). e~end adj explanatory. e~lich adj explicable; (verständlich) understandable. **E~licherweise** adv

understandably. **E~ung** f -,-en declaration; explanation; **öffentliche E~ung** public statement

erkrank|en (sein) fall ill; be taken ill (an + dat with). **E~ung** f -,-en illness

erkundig|en (sich) vr enquire (nach jdm/etw after s.o./about sth). **E~ung** f -,-en enquiry

erlangen vt attain, get

Erlass m -es,²e (Admin) decree; (Befreiung) exemption; (Straf-) remission

erlassen† vt (Admin) issue; **jdm etw e~** exempt s.o. from sth; let s.o. off (Strafe)

erlauben vt allow, permit; **ich kann es mir nicht e~** I can't afford it

Erlaubnis f - permission. **E~schein** m permit

erläutern vt explain

Erle f -,-n alder

erleb|en vt experience; (mit-) see; have (Überraschung). **E~nis** nt -ses,-se experience

erledigen vt do; (sich befassen mit) deal with; (beenden) finish; (entscheiden) settle; (töten) kill

erleichter|n vt lighten; (vereinfachen) make easier; (befreien) relieve; (lindern) ease. e~t adj relieved. **E~ung** f - relief

erleiden† vt suffer

erleuchten vt illuminate; **hell** e~et brightly lit

erlogen adj untrue, false

Erlös m -es proceeds pl

erlöschen vi (sein) go out; (vergehen) die; (aussterben) die out; (ungültig werden) expire; **erloschener Vulkan** extinct volcano

erlös|en vt save; (befreien) release (von from); (Relig) redeem. e~t adj relieved. **E~ung** f release; (Erleichterung) relief; (Relig) redemption

ermächtig|en vt authorize.
E~ung f -,-en authorization

Ermahnung f exhortation; admonition

ermäßig|en vt reduce. **E~ung** f -,-en reduction

ermessen† vt judge; (begreifen) appreciate. **E~** nt -s discretion; (Urteil) judgement; **nach eigenem E~** at one's own discretion

ermitt|eln vt establish; (herausfinden) find out ● vi (haben) investigate (**gegen jdn** s.o.). **E~lungen** fpl investigations. **E~lungsverfahren** nt (Jur) preliminary inquiry

ermöglichen vt make possible

ermord|en vt murder. **E~ung** f -,-en murder

ermüd|en vt tire ● vi (sein) get tired. **E~ung** f - tiredness

ermutigen vt encourage. **e~d** adj encouraging

ernähr|en vt feed; (unterhalten) support, keep; **sich e~en von** live/(Tier:) feed on. **E~er** m -s,- breadwinner. **E~ung** f - nourishment; nutrition; (Kost) diet

ernenn|en† vt appoint. **E~ung** f -,-en appointment

erneu|ern vt renew; (auswechseln) replace; change (Verband); (renovieren) renovate. **E~erung** f renewal; replacement; renovation. **e~t** adj renewed; (neu) new ● adv again

ernst adj serious; (ernst zu nehmen take seriously. **E~** m -es seriousness; **im E~** seriously; **mit einer Drohung E~ machen** carry out a threat; **ist das dein E~?** are you serious? **e~haft** adj serious. **e~lich** adj serious

Ernte f -,-n harvest; (Ertrag) crop. **E~dankfest** nt harvest festival. **e~n** vt harvest; (fig) reap, win

ernüchter|n vt sober up; (fig) bring down to earth. **e~nd** adj (fig) sobering

Erober|er m -s,- conqueror. **e~n** vt conquer. **E~ung** f -,-en conquest

eröffn|en vt open; **jdm etw e~en** announce sth to s.o. **E~ung** f opening; (Mitteilung) announcement

erörter|n vt discuss. **E~ung** f -,-en discussion

Erot|ik f - eroticism. **e~isch** adj erotic

Erpel m -s,- drake

erpicht adj **e~ auf** (+ acc) keen on

erpress|en vt extort; blackmail (Person). **E~er** m -s,- blackmailer. **E~ung** f - extortion; blackmail

erprob|en vt test. **e~t** adj proven

erraten† vt guess

erreg|bar adj excitable. **e~en** vt excite; (hervorrufen) arouse; **sich e~en** get worked up. **e~end** adj exciting. **E~er** m -s,- (Med) germ. **e~t** adj agitated; (hitzig) heated. **E~ung** f - excitement

erreich|bar adj within reach; (Ziel) attainable; (Person) available. **e~en** vt reach; catch (Zug); live to (Alter); (durchsetzen) achieve

errichten vt erect

erringen† vt gain, win

erröten vi (sein) blush

Errungenschaft f -,-en achievement; (⊞: Anschaffung) acquisition

Ersatz m -es replacement, substitute; (Entschädigung) compensation. **E~reifen** m spare tyre. **E~teil** nt spare part

erschaffen† vt create

erschein|en vi (sein) appear; (Buch:) be published. **E~ung** f -,-en appearance; (Person) figure; (Phänomen) phenomenon; (Symptom) symptom; (Geist) apparition

erschieß|en† vt shoot [dead].
E~ungskommando nt firing squad

erschlaffen vi (sein) go limp

erschlagen† vt beat to death;
(tödlich treffen) strike dead; **vom
Blitz e~ werden** be killed by
lightning

erschließen† vt develop

erschöpf|en vt exhaust. **e~t** adj
exhausted. **E~ung** f - exhaustion

erschrecken vi (sein) get a
fright ● vt (reg) startle; (beunruhigen) alarm; **du hast mich e~t** you
gave me a fright

erschrocken adj frightened; (er-
schreckt) startled

erschütter|n vt shake; (ergreifen)
upset deeply. **E~ung** f -,-en shock

erschwinglich adj affordable

ersehen† vt (fig) see (aus from)

ersetzen vt replace; make good
(Schaden); refund (Kosten); **jdm etw
e~** compensate s.o. for sth

ersichtlich adj obvious, apparent

erspar|en vt save. **E~nis** f -,-se
saving; **E~nisse** savings

erst adv (zuerst) first; (noch nicht
mehr als) only; (nicht vor) not until;
e~ dann only then; **eben e~**
[only] just

erstarren vi (sein) solidify; (gefrieren) freeze; (steif werden) go stiff;
(vor Schreck) be paralysed

erstatten vt (zurück-) refund; **Bericht e~** report (**jdm** to s.o.)

Erstaufführung f first performance, première

erstaun|en vt amaze, astonish.
E~en nt amazement, astonish-
ment. **e~lich** adj amazing

Erst|ausgabe f first edition.
e~e(r,s) adj first; (beste) best; **e~e
Hilfe** first aid. **E~e(r)** m/f first;
(Beste) best; **fürs E~e** for the time
being; **als E~es** first of all; **er kam**

als E~er he arrived first

erstechen† vt stab to death

ersteigern vt buy at an auction

erst|ens adv firstly, in the first
place. **e~ere(r,s)** adj the former;
der/die/das E~ere the former

ersticken vt suffocate; smother
(Flammen) ● vi (sein) suffocate. **E~**
nt -s suffocation; **zum E~** stifling

erstklassig adj first-class

ersuchen vt ask, request. **E~** nt
-s request

ertappen vt □ catch

erteilen vt give (**jdm** s.o.)

ertönen vi (sein) sound; (erschal-
len) ring out

Ertrag m -[e]s,"e yield. **e~en†**
vt bear

erträglich adj bearable; (leidlich)
tolerable

ertränken vt drown

ertrinken† vi (sein) drown

erübrigen (sich) vr be unnecessary

erwachsen adj grown-up.
E~e(r) m/f adult, grown-up

erwägen† vt consider. **E~ung** f
-,-en consideration; **in E~ung ziehen** consider

erwähn|en vt mention. **E~ung** f
-,-en mention

erwärmen vt warm; **sich e~**
warm up; (fig) warm (**für** to)

erwarten vt expect; (warten auf)
wait for. **E~ung** f -,-en expectation

erweisen† vt prove; (bezeigen) do
(Gefallen, Dienst, Ehre); **sich e~ als**
prove to be

erweitern vt widen; dilate (Pupille); (fig) extend, expand

Erwerb m -[e]s acquisition; (Kauf)
purchase; (Brot-) livelihood; (Verdienst) earnings pl. **e~en†** vt acquire; (kaufen) purchase. **e~slos** adj

unemployed. **e~stätig** adj employed

erwider|n vt reply; return (Besuch, Gruß). **E~ung** f -,-en reply

erwirken vt obtain

erwürgen vt strangle

Erz nt -es,-e ore

erzähl|en vt tell (jdm s.o.) ● vi (haben) talk (von about). **E~er** m -s,- narrator. **E~ung** f -,-en story, tale

Erzbischof m archbishop

erzeug|en vt produce; (Electr) generate. **E~er** m -s,- producer. **E~nis** nt -ses,-se product; landwirtschaftliche **E~nisse** farm produce sg.

erzieh|en† vt bring up; (Sch) educate. **E~er** m -s,- [private] tutor. **E~erin** f -,-nen governess. **E~ung** f - upbringing; education

erzielen vt achieve; score (Tor)

erzogen adj gut/schlecht e~ well/badly brought up

---

es

● pronoun

····▷ (Sache) it; (weibliche Person) she/her; (männliche Person) he/him. **es** bin ich it's me. **wir sind traurig, ihr seid es auch** we are sad, and so are you. **er ist es, der ...** he is the one who ... **es sind Studenten** they are students

····▷ (impers) it. **es hat geklopft** there was a knock. **es klingelt** someone is ringing. **es wird schöner** the weather is improving. **es geht ihm gut/schlecht** he is well/unwell. **es lässt sich aushalten** it is bearable. **es gibt** there is or (pl) are

····▷ (als formales Objekt) **er hat es**

---

gut he has it made; he's well off. **er meinte es gut** he meant well. **ich hoffe/glaube es** I hope/think so

Esche f -,-n ash

Esel m -s,- donkey; (①: Person) ass

Eskimo m -[s],-[s] Eskimo

Eskort|e f -,-n (Mil) escort. **e~ieren** vt escort

essbar adj edible

essen† vt/i (haben) eat; **zu Mittag| Abend e~** have lunch/supper; **e~ gehen** eat out. **E~** nt -s,- food; (Mahl) meal; (festlich) dinner

Esser(in) m -s,- (f -,-nen) eater

Essig m -s vinegar. **E~gurke** f [pickled] gherkin

Esslöffel m ≈ dessertspoon. **Essstäbchen** ntpl chopsticks. **Esstisch** m dining-table. **Esswaren** fpl food sg; (Vorräte) provisions. **Esszimmer** nt dining-room

Estland nt -s Estonia

Estragon m -s tarragon

etablieren (sich) vr establish oneself/(Geschäft:) itself

Etage /eˈtaːʒə/ f -,-n storey. **E~nbett** nt bunk-beds pl. **E~nwohnung** f flat

Etappe f -,-n stage

Etat /eˈtaː/ m -s,-s budget

Eth|ik f - ethic; (Sittenlehre) ethics sg. **e~isch** adj ethical

ethnisch adj ethnic; **e~e Säuberung** ethnic cleansing

Etikett nt -[e]s,-e[n] label; (Preis-) tag. **e~ieren** vt label

Etui /eˈtviː/ nt -s,-s case

etwa adv (ungefähr) about; (zum Beispiel) for instance; (womöglich) perhaps; **nicht e~, dass ...** not that ... ; **denkt nicht e~ ...** don't imagine ...

etwas pron something; (fragend)

verneint) anything; (ein bisschen) some, a little; **sonst noch e~?** anything else? **so e~ Ärgerliches!** what a nuisance! ● adv a bit

Etymologie f - etymology

euch pron (acc of **ihr** pl) you; (dat) [to] you; (reflexive) yourselves; (einander) each other

euer poss pron pl your. **e~e, e~t-s. eure, euret-**

Eule f -,-n owl

Euphorie f - euphoria

eur|e poss pron pl your. **e~e(r,s)** poss pron yours. **e~etwegen** adv for your sake; (wegen euch) because of you, on your account. **e~etwillen** adv um **e~etwillen** for your sake. **e~ige** poss pron **der/die/das e~ige** yours

Euro m -[s],[-s] euro. **E~-** prefix Euro-

Europa nt -s Europe. **E~-** prefix European

Europä|er(in) m -s,- (f -,-nen) European. **e~isch** adj European

Euter nt -s,- udder

evakuier|en vt evacuate. **E~ung** f - evacuation

evan|gelisch adj Protestant. **E~gelium** nt -s,-ien gospel

eventuell adj possible ● adv possibly; (vielleicht) perhaps

Evolution /-ˈtsi̯oːn/ f - evolution

ewig adj eternal; (endlos) neverending; **e~ dauern** 🆃 take ages. **E~keit** f - eternity

Examen nt -s,- & -mina (Sch) examination

Exemplar nt -s,-e specimen; (Buch) copy. **e~isch** adj exemplary

exerzieren vt/i (haben) (Mil) drill; (üben) practise

exhumieren vt exhume

Exil nt -s exile

Existenz f -,-en existence; (Lebensgrundlage) livelihood

existieren vi (haben) exist

exklusiv adj exclusive. **e~e** prep (+ gen) excluding

exkommunizieren vt excommunicate

Exkremente npl excrement sg

Expedition /-ˈtsi̯oːn/ f -,-en expedition

Experiment nt -[e]s,-e experiment. **e~ieren** vi (haben) experiment

Experte m -n,-n expert

explo|dieren vi (sein) explode. **E~sion** f -,-en explosion

Expor|t m -[e]s,-e export. **E~teur** m -s,-e exporter. **e~tieren** vt export

extra adv separately; (zusätzlich) extra; (eigens) specially; (🆃: absichtlich) on purpose

extravagan|t adj flamboyant; (übertrieben) extravagant

extravertiert adj extrovert

extrem adj extreme. **E~ist** m -en,-en extremist

Exzellenz f - (title) Excellency

Exzentr|iker m -s,- eccentric. **e~isch** adj eccentric

Ff

Fabel f -,-n fable. **f~haft** adj 🆃 fantastic

Fabrik f -,-en factory. **F~ant** m -en,-en manufacturer. **F~at** nt -[e]s,-e product; (Marke) make. **F~ation** f - manufacture

Fach nt -[e]s,⁝er compartment;

(Schub-) drawer; (Gebiet) field; (Sch) subject. **F~arbeiter** m skilled worker. **F~arzt** m, **F~ärztin** f specialist. **F~ausdruck** m technical term

Fächer m -s,- fan

Fach|gebiet nt field. **f~kundig** adj expert. **f~lich** adj technical; (beruflich) professional. **F~mann** m (pl -leute) expert. **f~männisch** adj expert. **F~schule** f technical college. **F~werkhaus** nt half-timbered house. **F~wort** nt (pl -wörter) technical term

Fackel f -,-n torch

fade adj insipid; (langweilig) dull

Faden m -s,: thread; (Bohnen-) string; (Naut) fathom

Fagott nt -[e]s,-e bassoon

fähig adj capable (zu/gen of); (tüchtig) able, competent. **F~keit** f -,-en ability; competence

fahl adj pale

fahnd|en vi (haben) search (**nach** for). **F~ung** f -,-en search

Fahne f -,-n flag; (Druck-) galley [proof]; **eine F~ haben** ⊥ reek of alcohol. **F~nflucht** f desertion

Fahr|ausweis m ticket. **F~bahn** f carriageway; (Straße) road. **f~bar** adj mobile

Fähre f -,-n ferry

fahr|en† vi (sein) go, travel; (Fahrer:) drive; (Radfahrer:) ride; (verkehren) run, (ab-) leave; (Schiff:) sail; **mit dem Auto/Zug f~en** go by car/train; **was ist in ihn gefahren?** ⊥ what has got into him? ● vt drive; ride (Fahrrad); take (Kurve). **f~end** adj moving; (f~bar) mobile; (nicht sesshaft) travelling. **F~er** m -s,- driver. **F~erflucht** f failure to stop after an accident. **F~erhaus** nt driver's cab. **F~erin** f -,-nen woman driver. **F~gast** m passen-

ger. **F~geld** nt fare. **F~gestell** nt chassis; (Aviat) undercarriage. **F~karte** f ticket. **F~kartenschalter** m ticket office. **f~lässig** adj negligent. **F~lässigkeit** f - negligence. **F~lehrer** m driving instructor. **F~plan** m timetable. **f~planmäßig** adj scheduled ● adv according to/(pünktlich) on schedule. **F~preis** m fare. **F~prüfung** f driving test. **F~rad** nt bicycle. **F~schein** m ticket. **F~schule** f driving school. **F~schüler(in)** m(f) learner driver. **F~stuhl** m lift

Fahrt f -,-en journey; (Auto) drive; (Ausflug) trip; (Tempo) speed

Fährte f -,-n track; (Witterung) scent

Fahrtkosten pl travelling expenses. **F~werk** nt undercarriage. **F~zeug** nt -[e]s,-e vehicle; (Wasser-) craft, vessel

fair /fɛːɐ/ adj fair

Fakultät f -,-en faculty

Falke m -n,-n falcon

Fall m -[e]s,:-e fall; (Jur, Med, Gram) case; **im F~[e]** in case (gen of); **auf jeden F~** in any case; (bestimmt) definitely; **für alle F~e** just in case; **auf keinen F~** on no account

Falle f -,-n trap

fallen† vi (sein) fall; (sinken) go down; [im Krieg] **f~** be killed in the war; **f~ lassen** drop (etw, fig: Plan, jdn); make (Bemerkung)

fällen vt fell; (fig) pass (Urteil)

fällig adj due; (Wechsel) mature; **längst f~** long overdue. **F~keit** f - (Comm) maturity

falls conj in case; (wenn) if

Fallschirm m parachute. **F~jäger** m paratrooper. **F~springer** m parachutist

Falltür f trapdoor

falsch adj wrong; (nicht echt, unauf-

richtig) false; *(gefälscht)* forged; *(Geld)* counterfeit; *(Schmuck)* fake ● *adv* wrongly; falsely; *(singen)* out of tune; **f~ gehen** *(Uhr:)* be wrong

fälschen *vt* forge, fake

Falschgeld *nt* counterfeit money

fälschlich *adj* wrong; *(irrtümlich)* mistaken

Falsch|meldung *f* false report; *(absichtlich)* hoax report. **F~mün-zer** *m* -s,- counterfeiter

Fälschung *f* -,-en forgery, fake

Falte *f* -,-n fold; *(Rock-)* pleat; *(Knit-ter-)* crease; *(im Gesicht)* line; wrinkle

falten *vt* fold

Falter *m* -s,- butterfly; moth

faltig *adj* creased; *(Gesicht)* lined; wrinkled

familiär *adj* family ; *(vertraut, zu-dringlich)* familiar; *(zwanglos)* in-formal

Familie /-jə/ *f* -,-n family. **F~nfor-schung** *f* genealogy. **F~nname** *m* surname. **F~nplanung** *f* family planning. **F~nstand** *m* marital status

Fan /fɛn/ *m* -s,-s fan

Fana|tiker *m* -s,- fanatic. **f~tisch** *adj* fanatical

Fanfare *f* -,-n trumpet; *(Signal)* fanfare

Fang *m* -[e]s, ⸚e capture; *(Beute)* catch; **F~e** *(Krallen)* talons; *(Zähne)* fangs. **F~arm** *m* tentacle. **f~en†** *vt* catch; *(ein-)* capture; **gefangen nehmen** take prisoner. **F~en** *nt* -s F~en spielen play tag. **F~frage** *f* catch question

Fantasie *f* -,-n = **Phantasie**

Farb|aufnahme *f* colour photo-graph. **F~band** *nt* (*pl* -bänder) typewriter ribbon. **F~e** *f* -,-n colour; *(Maler-)* paint; *(zum Färben)* dye; *(Karten)* suit. **f~echt** *adj* colour-fast

färben *vt* colour; dye *(Textilien, Haare)* ● *vi* (haben) not be colour-fast

farb|enblind *adj* colour-blind. **f~enfroh** *adj* colourful. **F~film** *m* colour film. **f~ig** *adj* coloured ● *adv* in colour. **F~ige(r)** *m/f* coloured man/woman. **F~kasten** *m* box of paints. **f~los** *adj* colourless. **F~stift** *m* crayon. **F~stoff** *m* dye; *(Lebensmittel-)* colouring. **F~ton** *m* shade

Färbung *f* -,-en colouring

Farn *m* -[e]s,-e fern

Färse *f* -,-n heifer

Fasan *m* -[e]s,-e[n] pheasant

Faschierte(s) *nt* (Aust) mince

Fasching *m* -s (SGer) carnival

Fasching, Fastnachtzeit *i*

The carnival season begins at Epiphany and ends on *Aschermittwoch* (Ash Wednesday) for Lent. Depending on the region, it is also called *Karneval* or *Fasnet*, and is celebrated in Germany, Austria and Switzerland. Celebra-tions reach a climax on *Faschings-dienstag*, or *Rosenmontag* in the Rhineland, when there are street processions.

Faschis|mus *m* - fascism. **F~t** *m* -en,-en fascist. **f~tisch** *adj* fascist

Faser *f* -,-n fibre

Fass *nt* -es, ⸚er barrel, cask; **Bier vom F~** draught beer

Fassade *f* -,-n façade

fassbar *adj* comprehensible; *(greif-bar)* tangible

fassen *vt* take [hold of], grasp; *(er-greifen)* seize; *(fangen)* catch; *(ein-)* set; *(enthalten)* hold; *(fig: begreifen)* take in, grasp; conceive *(Plan)*; make *(Entschluss)*; **sich f~** compose oneself; **sich kurz f~** be brief; **nicht zu f~** (fig) unbelievable ● vi (haben) **f~ an** (+ acc) touch

Fassung f -,-en mount; (Edelstein-) setting; (Electr) socket; (Version) version; (Beherrschung) composure; **aus der F~ bringen** disconcert. **f~slos** adj shaken; (entsetzt) flabbergasted. **F~svermögen** nt capacity

fast adv almost, nearly; **f~ nie** hardly ever

fast|en vi (haben) fast. **F~enzeit** f Lent. **F~nacht** f Shrovetide; (Karneval) carnival. **F~nachtsdienstag** m Shrove Tuesday

fatal adj fatal; (peinlich) embarrassing

Fata Morgana f -,- -nen mirage

fauchen vi (haben) spit, hiss ● vt snarl

faul adj lazy; (verdorben) rotten, bad; (Ausrede) lame

faul|en vi (sein) rot; (Zahn-) decay; (verwesen) putrefy. **f~enzen** vi (haben) be lazy. **F~enzer** m -s,- lazy-bones sg. **F~heit** f - laziness

Fäulnis f - decay

Fauna f - fauna

Faust f -,Fäuste fist; **auf eigene F~** (fig) off one's own bat. **F~handschuh** m mitten. **F~schlag** m punch

Fauxpas /fo'pa/ m -,- gaffe

Favorit(in) /favo'ri:t(ɪn)/ m -en, -en (f -,-nen) (Sport) favourite

Fax nt -,-[e] fax. **f~en** vt fax

Faxen fpl 🔲 antics; **F~ machen** fool about

Faxgerät nt fax machine

Februar m -s,-e February

fecht|en† vi (haben) fence. **F~er** m -s,- fencer

Feder f -,-n feather; (Schreib-) pen;

(Spitze) nib; (Techn) spring. **F~ball** m shuttlecock; (Spiel) badminton. **F~busch** m plume. **F~leicht** adj as light as a feather. **f~n** vi (haben) be springy; (nachgeben) give; (hoch-) bounce. **f~nd** adj springy; (elastisch) elastic. **F~ung** f - (Techn) springs pl; (Auto) suspension

Fee f -,-n fairy

Fegefeuer nt purgatory

fegen vt sweep

Fehde f -,-n feud

fehl adj **f~ am Platze** out of place. **F~betrag** m deficit. **f~en** vi (haben) be missing/(Sch) absent; (mangeln) be lacking; **mir f~t die Zeit** I haven't got the time; **was f~t ihm?** what's the matter with him? **das hat uns noch gefehlt!** that's all we need! **f~end** adj missing; (Sch) absent

Fehler m -s,- mistake, error; (Sport & fig) fault; (Makel) flaw. **f~frei** adj faultless. **f~haft** adj faulty. **f~los** adj flawless

Fehl|geburt f miscarriage. **F~griff** m mistake. **F~kalkulation** f miscalculation. **F~schlag** m failure. **f~schlagen†** vi sep (sein) fail. **F~start** m (Sport) false start. **F~zündung** f (Auto) misfire

Feier f -,-n celebration; (Zeremonie) ceremony; (Party) party. **F~abend** m end of the working day; **F~abend machen** stop work. **f~lich** adj solemn; (förmlich) formal. **F~n** vt celebrate; hold (Fest) ● vi (haben) celebrate. **F~tag** m [public] holiday; (kirchlicher) feast-day; **erster/zweiter F~tag** Christmas Day / Boxing Day. **f~tags** adv on public holidays

feige adj cowardly; **f~ sein** be a coward ● adv in a cowardly way

Feige f -,-n fig

Feig|heit f - cowardice. **F~ling** m -s,-e coward

Feile f -,-n file. **F~n** vt/i (haben) file

feilschen vi (haben) haggle

fein adj fine; (zart) delicate; (Strümpfe) sheer; (Unterschied) subtle; (scharf) keen; (vornehm) refined; (prima) great; **sich f~ machen** dress up. **F~arbeit** f precision work

Feind(in) m -es,-e (f -,-nen) enemy. **f~lich** adj enemy; (f~selig) hostile. **F~schaft** f -,-en enmity

fein|fühlig adj sensitive. **F~gefühl** nt sensitivity; (Takt) delicacy. **F~heit** f -,-en fineness; delicacy; subtlety; refinement; **F~heiten** subtleties. **F~kostgeschäft** nt delicatessen [shop]

feist adj fat

Feld nt -[e]s,-er field; (Fläche) ground; (Sport) pitch; (Schach-) square; (auf Formular) box. **F~bett** nt camp-bed. **F~forschung** f fieldwork. **F~herr** m commander. **F~stecher** m -s,- field-glasses pl. **F~webel** m -s,- (Mil) sergeant. **F~zug** m campaign

Felge f -,-n [wheel] rim

Fell nt -[e]s,-e (Zool) coat; (Pelz) fur; (abgezogen) skin, pelt

Fels m -en,-en rock. **F~block** m boulder. **F~en** m -s,- rock

Femininum nt -s,-na (Gram) feminine

Feminist|(in) m -en,-en (f -,-nen) feminist. **f~isch** adj feminist

Fenchel m -s fennel

Fenster nt -s,- window. **F~brett** nt window sill. **F~scheibe** f [window-]pane

Ferien /ˈfeːriən/ pl holidays; (Univ) vacation sg; **F~ haben** be on holiday. **F~ort** m holiday resort

Ferkel nt -s,- piglet

fern adj distant; **der F~e Osten** the Far East; **sich f~ halten** keep away ● adv far away; **von f~** from a distance ● prep (+ dat) far [away] from. **F~bedienung** f remote control. **F~e** f - distance; **in weiter F~e** far away; (zeitlich) in the distant future. **f~er** adj further ● adv (außerdem) furthermore; (in Zukunft) in future. **f~gelenkt** adj remote-controlled; (Rakete) guided. **F~gespräch** nt long-distance call. **F~glas** nt binoculars pl. **F~kurs[us]** m correspondence course. **F~licht** nt (Auto) full beam. **F~meldewesen** nt telecommunications pl. **F~rohr** nt telescope. **F~schreiben** nt telex

Fernseh|apparat m television set. **f~en†** vi sep (haben) watch television. **F~en** nt -s television. **F~er** m -s,- [television] viewer; (Gerät) television set

Fernsprech|amt nt telephone exchange. **F~er** m telephone

Fern|steuerung f remote control. **F~studium** nt distance learning

Ferse f -,-n heel

fertig adj finished; (bereit) ready; (Comm) ready-made; (Gericht) ready-to-serve; **f~ werden mit** finish; (bewältigen) cope with; **f~ sein** have finished; (fig) be through (mit jdm w.s.o.); (ⅰ: erschöpft) be all in/(seelisch) shattered; **etw f~ bringen** manage to do sth; (beenden) finish sth; **etw/jdn f~ machen** finish sth; (bereitmachen) get sth/s.o. ready; (ⅰ: erschöpfen) wear s.o. out; (seelisch) shatter s.o.; **sich f~ machen** get ready; **etw f~ stellen** complete sth ● adv **f~ essen/lesen** finish eating/reading. **F~bau** m (pl -bauten) prefabricated building. **f~en** vt make. **F~gericht**

ready-to-serve meal. **F~haus** nt prefabricated house. **F~keit** f -,-en skill. **F~stellung** f completion. **F~ung** f - manufacture

fesch adj [1] attractive

Fessel f -,-n ankle

fesseln vt tie up; tie (**an** + acc to); (fig) fascinate

fest adj firm; (nicht flüssig) solid; (erstarrt) set; (haltbar) strong; (nicht locker) tight; (feststehend) fixed; (ständig) steady; (Anstellung) permanent; (Schlaf) sound; (Blick, Stimme) steady; f~ **werden** harden; (Gelee:) set; **f~e Nahrung** solids pl ● adv firmly; tightly; steadily; soundly; (kräftig, tüchtig) hard; f~ **schlafen** be fast asleep; f~ **angestellt** permanent

Fest nt -[e]s,-e celebration; (Party) party; (Relig) festival; **frohes F~!** happy Christmas!

fest|binden† vt sep tie (**an** + dat to). **f~bleiben** vi sep (sein) (fig) remain firm. **f~halten**† v sep ● vt hold on to; (aufzeichnen) record; **sich f~halten** hold on ● vi (haben) **f~halten an** (+ dat) (fig) stick to; cling to (Tradition). **f~igen** vt strengthen. **F~iger** m -s,- styling lotion/(Schaum-) mousse. **F~igkeit** f - (s. fest) firmness; solidity; strength; steadiness. **F~land** nt mainland; (Kontinent) continent. **f~legen** vt sep (fig) fix, settle; lay down (Regeln); tie up (Geld); **sich f~legen** commit oneself

festlich adj festive. **F~keiten** fpl festivities

fest|liegen† vi sep (haben) be fixed, settled. **f~machen** v sep ● vt fasten/(Zeichn +dat to); (f~legen) fix, settle ● vi (haben) (Naut) moor. **F~mahl** nt feast. **F~nahme** f -,-n arrest. **f~nehmen**† vt sep arrest. **F~netz** nt land-

line network. **F~platte** f hard disk. **f~setzen** vt sep fix, settle; (inhaftieren) gaol; **sich f~setzen** collect. **f~sitzen**† vi sep (haben) be firm/(Schraube:) tight; (haften) stick; (nicht weiterkommen) be stuck. **F~spiele** npl festival sg. **f~stehen**† vi sep happen be certain. **f~stellen** vt sep fix; (ermitteln) establish; (bemerken) notice; (sagen) state. **F~tag** m special day

Festung f -,-en fortress

Festzug m [grand] procession

Fete /'fe:tə, 'fɛ:tə/ f -,-n party

fett adj fat; fatty; (fettig) greasy; (üppig) rich; (Druck) bold. **F~** nt -[e]s,-e fat; (flüssig) grease. **F~arm** adj low-fat. **f~en** vt grease ● vi (haben) be greasy. **F~fleck** m grease mark. **f~ig** adj greasy

Fetzen m -s,- scrap; (Stoff) rag

feucht adj damp, moist; (Luft) humid. **F~igkeit** f - dampness; (Nässe) moisture; (Luft-) humidity. **F~igkeitscreme** f moisturizer

Feuer nt -s,- fire; (für Zigarette) light; (Begeisterung) passion; **f~machen** light a fire. **F~alarm** m fire alarm. **f~gefährlich** adj [in]flammable. **F~leiter** f fire escape. **F~löscher** m -s,- fire extinguisher. **F~melder** m -s,- fire alarm. **f~n** vi (haben) fire (**auf** + acc on). **F~probe** f (fig) test. **f~rot** adj crimson. **F~stein** m flint. **F~stelle** f hearth. **F~treppe** f fire escape. **F~wache** f fire station. **F~waffe** f firearm. **F~wehr** f -,-en fire brigade. **F~wehrauto** nt fire engine. **F~wehrmann** m (pl -männer u. -leute) fireman. **F~werk** nt firework display, fireworks pl. **F~zeug** nt lighter

feurig adj fiery; (fig) passionate

Fiaker m -s,- (Aust) horse-drawn cab

Fichte f -,-n spruce

Fieber nt -s [raised] temperature; F~ haben have a temperature. f~n vi (haben) be feverish. F~ thermometer nt thermometer

fiebrig adj feverish

Figur f -,-en figure; (Roman-, Film-) character; (Schach-) piece

Filet /fi'le:/ nt -s,-s fillet

Filiale f -,-n (Comm) branch

Filigran nt -s filigree

Film m -[e]s,-e film; (Kino-) film; (Schicht) coating. f~en vt/i (haben) film. F~kamera f cine/(für Kinofilm) film camera

Filter m & (Techn) nt -s, filter; (Zigaretten-) filter-tip. f~ern vt filter. F~erzigarette f filter-tipped cigarette. F~rieren vt filter

Filz m -es felt. f~stift m felt-tipped pen

Fimmel m -s,- 🆒 obsession

Finale nt -s,- (Mus) finale; (Sport) final

Finanz f -,-en finance. F~amt nt tax office. F~iell adj financial. f~ieren vt finance. F~minister m minister of finance

find|en† vt find; (meinen) think; **den Tod f~en** meet one's death; **wie f~est du das?** what do you think of that? **es wird sich f~en** it'll turn up; (fig) it'll be all right ● vi (haben) find one's way. F~er m -s,- finder. F~erlohn m reward. f~ig adj resourceful

Finesse f -,-n (Kniff) trick; F~n (Techn) refinements

Finger m -s,- finger; **die F~ lassen von** 🆒 leave alone. F~abdruck m finger mark; (Admin) fingerprint. F~hut m thimble. F~nagel m fingernail. F~spitze f fingertip. F~zeig m -[e]s,-e hint

Fink m -en,-en finch

Finn|e m -n,-n, F~in f -,-nen Finn. f~isch adj Finnish. F~land nt -s Finland

finster adj dark; (düster) gloomy; (unheildrohend) sinister. F~nis f - darkness; (Astronomy) eclipse

Firm|a f -,-men firm, company

Firmen|wagen m company car. F~zeichen nt trade mark, logo

Firmung f -,-en (Relig) confirmation

Firnis m -ses,-se varnish. f~sen vt varnish

First m -[e]s,-e [roof] ridge

Fisch m -[e]s,-e fish; F~e (Astrology) Pisces. F~dampfer m trawler. f~en vt/i (haben) fish. F~er m -s,- fisherman. F~erei f - fishing. F~händler m fishmonger. F~reiher m heron

Fiskus m - der F~ the Treasury

fit adj fit. **Fitness** f - fitness

fix adj 🆒 quick; (geistig) bright; f~e Idee obsession; fix und fertig all finished; (bereit) all ready; (🆒: erschöpft) shattered. F~er m -s,- 🆒 junkie

fixieren vt stare at; (Phot) fix

Fjord m -[e]s,-e fiord

flach adj flat; (eben) level; (niedrig) low; (nicht tief) shallow

Flachbildschirm m flat screen

Fläche f -,-n area; (Ober-) surface; (Seite) face. F~nmaß nt square measure

Flachs m -es flax. f~blond adj flaxen-haired; (Haar) flaxen

flackern vi (haben) flicker

Flagge f -,-n flag

Flair /flɛːɐ̯/ nt -s air, aura

Flak f -,-[s] anti-aircraft artillery/(Geschütz) gun

flämisch adj Flemish

Flamme f -,-n flame;

(Koch-) burner
Flanell m -s (Textiles) flannel
Flank|e f -,-n flank. **f~ieren**
vt flank
Flasche f -,-n bottle. **F~nbier** nt
bottled beer. **F~nöffner** m bottle-
opener. **F~npfand** nt deposit (on
bottle)
flatter|haft adj fickle. **f~n** vi
(sein/haben) flutter; (Segel:) flap
flau adj (schwach) faint;
(Comm) slack
Flaum m -[e]s down. **f~ig** adj
downy; **f~ig rühren** (Aust
Culin) cream
flauschig adj fleecy; (Spielzeug)
fluffy
Flausen fpl ① silly ideas
Flaute f -,-n (Naut) calm; (Comm)
slack period; (Schwäche) low
fläzen (sich) vr ① sprawl
Flechte f -,-n (Med) eczema; (Bot)
lichen; (Zopf) plait. **f~n†** vt plait;
weave (Korb)
Fleck m -[e]s,-e[n] spot; (größer)
patch; (Schmutz-) stain, mark;
blauer F~ bruise. **f~en** vi (haben)
stain. **f~enlos** adj spotless. **F~ent-**
ferner m -s,- stain remover. **f~ig**
adj stained
Fledermaus f bat
Flegel m -s,- lout. **f~haft** adj
loutish
flehen vi (haben) beg (um for)
Fleisch nt -[e]s flesh; (Culin) meat;
(Frucht-) pulp; **F~ fressend** carniv-
orous. **F~er** m -s,- butcher.
F~fresser m -s,- carnivore. **f~ig**
adj fleshy. **f~lich** adj carnal.
F~wolf m mincer
Fleiß m -es diligence; **mit F~** dili-
gently; (absichtlich) on purpose.
f~ig adj diligent; (arbeitsam) indus-
trious
fletschen vt die Zähne **f~** (Tier:)
bare its teeth
flex|ibel adj flexible; (Einband)
limp. **F~ibilität** f -flexibility
flicken vt mend; (mit Flicken)
patch. **F~** m -s,- patch
Flieder m -s lilac
Fliege f -,-n fly; (Schleife) bow-tie.
f~n† vi (sein) fly; (geworfen werden)
be thrown; (①: fallen) fall; (①: entlassen werden) be fired/(von der
Schule) expelled; **in die Luft f~n**
blow up ● vt fly. **F~nd** adj flying.
F~r m -s,- airman; (Pilot); pilot;
(①: Flugzeug) plane. (Pilot). **F~rangriff** m
air raid
flieh|en† vi (sein) flee (vor + dat
from); (entweichen) escape ● vt
shun. **f~end** adj fleeing; (Kinn,
Stirn) receding
Fliese f -,-n tile
Fließ|band nt assembly line.
f~en† vi (sein) flow; (aus Wasser-
hahn) run. **f~end** adj flowing;
(Wasser) running; (Verkehr) moving;
(geläufig) fluent
flimmern vi (haben) shimmer;
(TV) flicker
flink adj nimble; (schnell) quick
Flinte f -,-n shotgun
Flirt /flœgt/ m -s,-s flirtation. **f~en**
vi (haben) flirt
Flitter m -s sequins pl. **F~wochen**
fpl honeymoon sg
flitzen vi (sein) ① dash
Flock|e f -,-n flake; (Wolle) tuft.
f~ig adj fluffy
Floh m -[e]s,ᵉe flea. **F~spiel** nt
tiddly-winks sg
Flora f - flora
Florett nt -[e]s,-e foil
florieren vi (haben) flourish
Floskel f -,-n [empty] phrase
Floß nt -es,ᵉe raft
Flosse f -,-n fin; (Seehund-, Gum-

mi-) flipper; (*sl: Hand*) paw

Flöt|e *f -,-n* flute; (*Block-*) recorder. **f~en** *vi* (*haben*) play the flute/recorder; (☐: *pfeifen*) whistle ● *vt* play on the flute/recorder. **F~ist(in)** *m -en,-en* (*f -,-nen*) flautist

flott *adj* quick; (*lebhaft*) lively; (*schick*) smart

Flotte *f -,-n* fleet

flottmachen *vt sep wieder f~* (*Naut*) refloat; get going again (*Auto*); put back on its feet (*Unternehmen*)

Flöz *nt -es,-e* [coal] seam

Fluch *m -[e]s,-̈e* curse. **f~en** *vi* (*haben*) curse, swear

Flucht *f* - flight; (*Entweichen*) escape; **die F~ ergreifen** take flight. **f~artig** *adj* hasty

flücht|en *vi* (*sein*) flee (**vor** + *dat* from); (*entweichen*) escape ● *vr* **sich f~en** take refuge. **f~ig** *adj* fugitive; (*kurz*) brief; (*Blick*) fleeting; (*Bekanntschaft*) passing; (*oberflächlich*) cursory; (*nicht sorgfältig*) careless. **f~ig kennen** know slightly. **F~igkeitsfehler** *m* slip. **F~ling** *m -s,-e* fugitive; (*Pol*) refugee

Fluchwort *nt* (*pl -wörter*) swear word

Flug *m -[e]s,-̈e* flight. **F~abwehr** *f* anti-aircraft defence

Flügel *m -s,-* wing; (*Fenster-*) casement; (*Mus*) grand piano

Fluggast *m* [air] passenger

flügge *adj* fully-fledged

Fluggesellschaft *f* airline. **F~hafen** *m* airport. **F~lotse** *m* air-traffic controller. **F~platz** *m* airport; (*klein*) airfield. **F~preis** *m* air fare. **F~schein** *m* air ticket. **F~schneise** *f* flight path. **F~schreiber** *m -s,-* flight recorder. **F~schrift** *f* pamphlet. **F~steig** *m -[e]s,-e* gate. **F~zeug** *nt -[e]s,-e**

aircraft, plane

Flunder *f -,-n* flounder

flunkern *vi* (*haben*) ☐ tell fibs

Flur *m -[e]s,-e* [entrance] hall; (*Gang*) corridor

Fluss *m -es,-̈e* river; (*Fließen*) flow; **im F~** (*fig*) in a state of flux. **f~abwärts** *adv* downstream. **f~aufwärts** *adv* upstream

flüssig *adj* liquid; (*Lava*) molten; (*fließend*) fluent; (*Verkehr*) freely moving. **F~keit** *f -,-en* liquid; (*Anat*) fluid

Flusspferd *nt* hippopotamus

flüstern *vt/i* (*haben*) whisper

Flut *f -,-en* high tide; (*fig*) flood

Föderation /-'tsjo:n/ *f -,-en* federation

Fohlen *nt -s,-* foal

Föhn *m -s* föhn [wind]; (*Haartrockner*) hairdrier. **f~en** *vt* [blow-]dry

Folge *f -,-n* consequence; (*Reihe*) succession; (*Fortsetzung*) instalment; (*Teil*) part. **f~en** *vi* (*sein*) follow (**jdm/etw** s.o./sth); (*zuhören*) listen (*dat* to); **wie f~t** as follows ● (*haben*) (*gehorchen*) obey (**jdm** s.o.). **f~end** *adj* following; **F~endes** the following

folger|n *vt* conclude (**aus** from). **F~ung** *f -,-en* conclusion

folg|lich *adv* consequently. **f~sam** *adj* obedient

Folie /'fo:ljə/ *f -,-n* foil; (*Plastik-*) film

Folklore *f* - folklore

Folter *f -,-n* torture. **f~n** *vt* torture

Fön ® *m -s,-e* hairdrier

Fonds /fõ:/ *m -,-* fund

fönen* *vt* = **föhnen**

Förder|band *nt* (*pl -bänder*) conveyor belt. **f~lich** *adj* beneficial

fordern *vt* demand; (*beanspruchen*) claim; (*zum Kampf*) challenge

fördern vt promote; (*unterstützen*) encourage; (*finanziell*) sponsor; (*gewinnen*) extract

Forderung f -,-en demand; (*Anspruch*) claim

Förderung f - promotion; encouragement; (*Techn*) production

Forelle f -,-n trout

Form f -,-en form; (*Gestalt*) shape; (*Culin, Techn*) mould; (*Back-*) tin; [gut] **in f~** in good form

Formalität f -,-en formality

Format nt -[e]s,-e format; (*Größe*) size; (*fig: Bedeutung*) stature

formatieren vt format

Formel f -,-n formula

formen vt shape, mould; (*bilden*) form; **sich f~** take shape

förmlich adj formal

form|los adj shapeless; (*zwanglos*) informal. **F~sache** f formality

Formular nt -s,-e [printed] form

formulier|en vt formulate, word. **F~ung** f -,-en wording

forsch|en vi (*haben*) search (*nach* for). **f~end** adj searching. **F~er** m -s,- research scientist; (*Reisender*) explorer. **F~ung** f -,-en research

Forst m -[e]s,-e forest

Förster m -s,- forester

Forstwirtschaft f forestry

Fort nt -s,-s (*Mil*) fort

fort adv away; **f~** sein be away; (*gegangen/verschwunden*) have gone; **und so f~** and so on; **in einem f~** continuously. **F~bewegung** f locomotion. **F~bildung** f further education/training. **f~bleiben**† vi sep (sein) stay away. **f~bringen**† vt sep take away. **f~fahren**† vi sep (sein) go away ● (*haben/sein*) continue (**zu** to). **f~fallen**† vi sep (sein) be dropped/(*ausgelassen*) omitted; (*ent-* | *fallen*) no longer apply; (*aufhören*) cease. **f~führen** vt sep continue. **f~gehen**† vi sep (sein) leave, go away; (*ausgehen*) go out; (*andauern*) go on. **f~geschritten** adj advanced; (*spät*) late. **f~geschrittene(r)** m/f advanced student. **f~lassen**† vt sep let go; (*auslassen*) omit. **f~laufen**† vi sep (sein) run away; (*sich f~setzen*) continue. **f~laufend** adj consecutive. **f~pflanzen (sich)** vr sep reproduce; (*Ton, Licht:*) travel. **F~pflanzung** f - reproduction. **F~pflanzungsorgan** nt reproductive organ. **f~schicken** vt sep send away; (*abschicken*) send off. **f~schreiten**† vi sep (sein) continue; (*Fortschritte machen*) progress, advance. **f~schreitend** adj progressive; (*Alter*) advancing. **F~schritt** m progress; **F~schritte machen** make progress. **f~schrittlich** adj progressive. **f~setzen** vt sep continue; take further. **F~setzung** f -,-en continuation; (*Folge*) instalment; **F~setzung folgt** to be continued. **F~setzungsroman** m serialized novel, serial. **f~während** adj constant. **f~ziehen**† v sep ● vt pull away ● vi (sein) move away

Fossil nt -s,-ien fossil

Foto nt -s,-s photo. **F~apparat** m camera. **f~gen** adj photogenic

Fotograf(in) m -en,-en (f -,-nen) photographer. **F~ie** f -,-n photography; (*Bild*) photograph. **f~ieren** vt take a photo[graph] of ● vi (*haben*) take photographs. **f~isch** adj photographic

Fotohandy nt camera phone

Fotokopie f photocopy. **f~ren** vt photocopy. **F~rgerät** nt photocopier

Föt|us m -,-ten foetus

Foul /faul/ nt -s,-s (*Sport*) foul.

f~en vt foul

Fracht f -,-en freight. F~er m -s,- freighter. F~gut nt freight. F~schiff nt cargo boat

Frack m -[e]s,=e & -s tailcoat

Frage f -,-n question; nicht in F~ kommen s. infrage. F~bogen m questionnaire. f~n vt (haben) ask; sich f~n wonder (ob whether).
f~nd adj questioning. F~zeichen nt question mark

frag|lich adj doubtful; (Person, Sache) in question. f~los adv undoubtedly

Fragment nt -[e]s,-e fragment

fragwürdig adj questionable; (verdächtig) dubious

Fraktion /-'tsɪo:n/ f -,-en parliamentary party

Franken[1] m -s,- (Swiss) franc

Franken[2] nt -s Franconia

frankieren vt stamp, frank

Frankreich nt -s France

Fransen fpl fringe sg

Franz|ose m -n,-n Frenchman; die F~osen the French pl. F~ösin f -,-nen Frenchwoman. f~ösisch adj French. F~ösisch nt -[s] (Lang) French

Fraß m -es feed; (pej: Essen) muck

Fratze f -,-n grotesque face; (Grimasse) grimace

Frau f -,-en woman; (Ehe-) wife; F~ Thomas Mrs Thomas; Unsere Liebe F~ (Relig) Our Lady

Frauen|arzt m, F~ärztin f gynaecologist. F~rechtlerin f -,-nen feminist

Fräulein nt -s,- single woman; (jung) young lady; (Anrede) Miss

frech adj cheeky; (unverschämt) impudent. F~heit f -,-en cheekiness; impudence; (Äußerung) impertinence

frei adj free; (freischaffend) freelance; (Künstler) independent; (nicht besetzt) vacant; (offen) open; (bloß) bare; f~er Tag day off; sich (dat) f~ nehmen take time off; f~ machen (räumen) clear; vacate (Platz); (befreien) liberate; f~ lassen leave free; ist dieser Platz f~? is this seat taken? 'Zimmer f~' 'vacancies' ● adv freely; (ohne Notizen) without notes; (umsonst) free

Frei|bad nt open-air swimming pool. f~beruflich adj & adv freelance. F~e nt im F~en in the open air, out of doors. F~gabe f release.
f~geben† v sep ● vt release; (eröffnen) open; jdm einen Tag f~geben give s.o. a day off ● vi (haben) jdm f~geben give s.o. time off.
f~gebig adj generous. F~gebigkeit f - generosity. f~haben† v sep ● vt eine Stunde f~haben have an hour off; (Sch) have a free period ● vi (haben) be off work/(Sch) school; (beurlaubt sein) have time off. f~händig adv without holding on

Freiheit f -,-en freedom, liberty. F~sstrafe f prison sentence

Frei|herr m baron. F~körperkultur f naturism. F~lassung f - release. F~lauf m free-wheel. f~legen vt sep expose. f~lich adv admittedly; (natürlich) of course. F~lichttheater nt open-air theatre. f~machen vt sep (frankieren) frank; (entkleiden) bare; einen Tag f~machen take a day off. F~maurer m Freemason. f~schaffend adj freelance. f~schwimmen† (sich) v sep pass one's swimming test. f~sprechen† vt sep acquit. F~spruch m acquittal. f~stehen† vi sep (haben) stand empty; es steht ihm f~ (fig) he is free (zu to). f~stellen vt sep exempt (von from); jdm etw f~stellen leave sth

up to s.o. **F~stil** m freestyle.
F~stoß m free kick

Freitag m Friday. **f~s** adv on
Fridays

Frei|tod m suicide. **F~umschlag**
m stamped envelope. **f~weg** adv
freely; (offen) openly. **f~willig** adj
voluntary. **F~willige(r)** m/f volunteer. **F~zeichen** nt ringing tone;
(Rufzeichen) dialling tone. **F~zeit** f
free or spare time; (Muße) leisure.
F~zeit- prefix leisure; **F~zeitbekleidung** f casual wear. **F~zügig**
adj unrestricted; (großzügig) liberal

fremd adj foreign; (unbekannt)
strange; (nicht das eigene) other
people's; **ein f~er Mann** a stranger; **f~e Leute** strangers; **unter
f~em Namen** under an assumed
name; **ich bin hier f~** I'm a stranger here. **F~e** f - **in der F~e** away
from home; (im Ausland) in a foreign country. **F~e(r)** m/f stranger;
(Ausländer) foreigner; (Tourist) tourist. **F~enführer** m [tourist] guide.
F~enverkehr m tourism. **F~enzimmer** nt room [to let]; (Gäste-)
guest room. **f~gehen**† vi sep (sein)
🔲 be unfaithful. **F~sprache** f foreign language. **F~wort** nt (pl
-wörter) foreign word

Freske f, **Fresko** nt -s,-ken
fresco

Fresse f,-n 🗙 (Mund) gob; (Gesicht) mug. **f~n**† vt/i (haben) eat.
F~n nt -s feed; (sl: Essen) grub

Fressnapf m feeding bowl

Freud|e f -,-n pleasure; (innere)
joy; **mit F~en** with pleasure; **jdm
eine F~e machen** please s.o. **f~ig**
adj joyful

freuen vt please; **sich f~** be
pleased (über + acc about); **sich f~
auf** (+ acc) look forward to; **es
freut mich** I'm glad (dass that)

Freund m -es,-e friend; (Verehrer)

boyfriend. **F~in** f -,-nen friend;
(Liebste) girlfriend. **f~lich** adj kind;
(umgänglich) friendly; (angenehm)
pleasant. **f~licherweise** adv kindly.
F~lichkeit f -,-en kindness; friendliness; pleasantness

Freundschaft f -,-en friendship;
F~ schließen become friends.
f~lich adj friendly

Frieden m -s peace; **F~ schließen**
make peace; **im F~** in peacetime;
lass mich in F~! leave me alone!
F~svertrag m peace treaty

Fried|hof m cemetery. **f~lich** adj
peaceful

frieren† vi (haben) (Person:) be
cold; impers **es friert/hat gefroren**
it is freezing/there has been a frost;
frierst du? are you cold? ● adv
(gefrieren) freeze

Fries m -es,-e frieze

frisch adj fresh; (sauber) clean;
(leuchtend) bright; (munter) lively;
(rüstig) fit; **sich f~ machen** freshen
up ● adv freshly, newly; **im Bett
f~ beziehen** put clean sheets on a
bed; **f~ gestrichen!** wet paint!
F~e f - freshness; brightness; liveliness; fitness. **F~haltepackung** f
vacuum pack

Fri|seur /fri'zøːɐ/ m -s,-e hairdresser; (Herren-) barber. **F~seursalon** m hairdressing salon.
F~seuse f -,-n hairdresser

frisier|en vt jdn/sich **f~en** do
someone's/one's hair; **die Bilanz /
einen Motor f~en** 🔲 fiddle the accounts/soup up an engine

Frisör m -s,-e = Friseur

Frist f -,-en period; (Termin) deadline; (Aufschub) time; **drei Tage F~**
three days' grace. **f~los** adj instant

Frisur f -,-en hairstyle

frittieren vt deep-fry

frivol /fri'voːl/ adj frivolous

froh | führen

froh adj happy; (freudig) joyful; (erleichtert) glad

fröhlich adj cheerful; (vergnügt) merry. **F~keit** f - cheerfulness; merriment

fromm adj devout; (gutartig) docile

Frömmigkeit f - devoutness

Fronleichnam m Corpus Christi

Front f -,-en front. **f~al** adj frontal; (Zusammenstoß) head-on ● adv from the front; (zusammenstoßen) head-on. **F~alzusammenstoß** m head-on collision

Frosch m -[e]s,⁀e frog. **F~laich** m frog-spawn. **F~mann** m (pl -männer) frogman

Frost m -[e]s,⁀e frost. **F~beule** f chilblain

frösteln vi (haben) shiver

frostig adj frosty. **F~schutzmittel** nt antifreeze

Frottee nt & m -s towelling. **F~[hand]tuch** nt terry towel

frottieren vt rub down

Frucht f -,⁀e fruit; **F~** bear fruit. **f~bar** adj fertile; (fig) fruitful. **F~barkeit** f - fertility

früh adj early ● adv early; (morgens) in the morning; **heute f~** this morning; **von f~ an** od **auf** from an early age. **F~aufsteher** m -s,- early riser. **F~e** f - in aller **F~e** bright and early; **in der F~e** (SGer) in the morning. **F~er** adv earlier; (eher) sooner; (ehemals) formerly; (vor langer Zeit) in the old days; **f~er oder später** sooner or later; **ich wohnte f~er in X** I used to live in X. **f~ere(r,s)** adj earlier; (ehemalig) former; (vorige) previous; **in f~eren Zeiten** in former times. **f~estens** adv at the earliest. **F~geburt** f premature birth/(Kind) baby. **F~jahr** nt spring. **F~ling** m -s,-e spring. **f~morgens** adv early

in the morning. **f~reif** adj precocious

Frühstück nt breakfast. **f~en** vi (haben) have breakfast

frühzeitig adj & adv early; (vorzeitig) premature

Frustr|ation /-ˈtsjoːn/ f -,-en frustration. **f~ieren** vt frustrate

Fuchs m -es,⁀e fox; (Pferd) chestnut. **f~en** vt 🔲 annoy

Füchsin f -,-nen vixen

Fuge¹ f -,-n joint

Fuge² f -,-n (Mus) fugue

füg|en vt fit (in + acc into); (an-) join (an + acc on to); (dazu-) add (zu to); **sich f~en** fit (in + acc into); adjoin/(folgen) follow (an etw acc sth); (fig: gehorchen) submit (dat to). **f~sam** adj obedient.
F~ung f -,-en eine **F~ung** des Schicksals a stroke of fate

fühl|bar adj noticeable. **f~en** vt/i (haben) feel; **sich f~en** feel (krank/einsam** ill/lonely); (🔲: stolz sein) fancy oneself. **F~er** m -s,- feeler. **F~ung** f - contact

Fuhre f -,-n load

führ|en vt lead; guide (Tourist); (geleiten) take; (leiten) run; (befehligen) command; (verkaufen) stock; bear (Namen); keep (Liste, Bücher); **bei od mit sich f~en** carry ● vi (haben) lead; (verlaufen) go, run; **zu etw f~en** lead to sth. **f~end** adj leading. **F~er** m -s,- leader; (Fremden-) guide; (Buch) guide[book]. **F~erhaus** nt driver's cab. **F~erschein** m driving licence; **den F~erschein machen** take one's driving test. **F~erscheinentzug** m disqualification from driving. **F~ung** f -,-en leadership; (Leitung) management; (Mil) command; (Betragen) conduct; (Besichtigung) guided tour; (Vorsprung) lead; **in F~ung gehen** go into the lead

Fuhr|unternehmer m haulage contractor. **F~werk** nt cart

Fülle f -,-n abundance, wealth (**an** + dat of); (Körper-) plumpness. **f~n** vt fill; (Culin) stuff

Füllen nt -s,- foal

Füll|er m -s,-, Ⓘ, **F~federhalter** m fountain pen. **F~ung** f -,-en filling; (Braten-) stuffing

fummeln vi (haben) fumble (**an** + dat with)

Fund m -[e]s,-e find

Fundament nt -[e]s,-e foundations pl. **f~al** adj fundamental

Fundbüro nt lost-property office

fünf inv adj. **F~** f -,-en five; (Sch) ≈ fail mark. **F~linge** mpl quintuplets. **f~te(r,s)** adj fifth. **f~zehn** inv adj fifteen. **f~zehnte(r,s)** adj fifteenth. **f~zig** inv adj fifty. **f~zigste(r,s)** adj fiftieth

fungieren vi (haben) act (**als** as)

Funk m -s radio. **F~e** m -n,-n spark. **f~eln** vi (haben) sparkle; (Stern:) twinkle. **F~en** m -s,- spark. **f~en** vt radio. **F~sprechgerät** nt walkie-talkie. **F~spruch** m radio message. **F~streife** f [police] radio patrol

Funktion /-'tsɪo:n/ f -,-en function; (Stellung) position; (Funktionieren) working; **außer F~** out of action. **F~är** m -s,-e official. **f~ieren** vi (haben) work

für prep (+ acc) for; **Schritt für Schritt** step by step; **was für [ein]** what [a]! (fragend) what sort of [a]? **Für** nt das **Für und Wider** the pros and cons pl

Furche f -,-n furrow

Furcht f - fear (**vor** + dat of); **F~erregend** terrifying. **f~bar** adj terrible

fürcht|en vt/i (haben) fear; **sich f~en** be afraid (**vor** + dat of).

f~erlich adj dreadful

füreinander adv for each other

Furnier nt -s,-e veneer. **f~t** adj veneered

Fürsorg|e f care; (Admin) welfare; (Ⓘ: Geld) ≈ social security. **F~er(in)** m -s,- (f -,-nen) social worker. **f~lich** adj solicitous

Fürst m -en,-en prince. **F~entum** nt -s,ᵉer principality. **F~in** f -,-nen princess

Furt f -,-en ford

Furunkel m -s,- (Med) boil

Fürwort nt (pl -wörter) pronoun

Furz m -es,-e (vulgar) fart

Fusion f -,-en fusion; (Comm) merger

Fuß m -es,ᵉe foot; (Aust: Bein) leg; (Lampen-) base; (von Weinglas) stem; **zu Fuß** on foot; **zu Fuß gehen** walk; **auf freiem Fuß** free. **F~abdruck** m footprint. **F~abtreter** m -s,- doormat. **F~ball** m football. **F~ballspieler** m footballer. **F~balltoto** nt football pools pl. **F~bank** f footstool. **F~boden** m floor

Fussel f -,-n & m -s,-[n] piece of fluff; **f~n** fluff sg. **f~n** vi (haben) shed fluff

fußen vi (haben) be based (**auf** + dat on)

Fußgänger|(in) m -s,- (f -,-nen) pedestrian. **F~brücke** f footbridge. **F~zone** f pedestrian precinct

Fußgeher m -s,- (Aust) = **F~gänger. F~gelenk** nt ankle. **F~hebel** m pedal. **F~nagel** m toenail. **F~note** f footnote. **F~pflege** f chiropody. **F~rücken** m instep. **F~sohle** f sole of the foot. **F~tritt** m kick. **F~weg** m footpath; **eine Stunde F~weg** an hour's walk

futsch pred adj Ⓘ gone

Futter¹ nt -s feed; (Trocken-

fodder
Futter² nt -s,- (Kleider-) lining
Futteral nt -s,-e case
füttern¹ vt feed
füttern² vt line
Futur nt -s (Gram) future

Gabe f -,-n gift; (Dosis) dose
Gabel f -,-n fork. **G~n (sich)** vr
fork. **G~stapler** m -s,- fork-lift
truck. **G~ung** f -,-en fork
gackern vi (haben) cackle
gaffen vi (haben) gape, stare
Gage /'ga:ʒə/ f -,-n (Theat) fee
gähnen vi (haben) yawn
Gala f - ceremonial dress
Galavorstellung f gala performance
Galerie f -,-n gallery
Galgen m -s,- gallows sg. **G~frist**
f ⚰ reprieve
Galionsfigur f figurehead
Galle f - bile; (G~nblase) gall-bladder. **G~nblase** f gall-bladder.
G~nstein m gallstone
Galopp m -s gallop; **im G~** at a
gallop. **g~ieren** vi (sein) gallop
gammeln vi (haben) ⚰ loaf
around. **G~ler(in)** m -s,- (f -,-nen)
drop-out
Gams f -,-en (Aust) chamois
Gämse f -,-n chamois
Gang m -[e]s,-e ⚰ walk; (G~art)
gait; (Boten-) errand; (Funktionieren)
running; (Verlauf, Culin) course;
(Durch-) passage; (Korridor) corridor;
(zwischen Sitzreihen) aisle, gangway;

(Anat) duct; (Auto) gear; **in G~**
bringen get going; **im G~e sein**
be in progress; **Essen mit vier**
G~en four-course meal
gängig adj common; (Comm)
popular
Gangschaltung f gear change
Gangster /'gɛnstɐ/ m -s,-
gangster
Ganove m -n,-n ⚰ crook
Gans f -,-̈e goose
Gänse|blümchen nt -s,- daisy.
G~füßchen ntpl inverted commas.
G~haut f goose-pimples pl.
G~rich m -s,-e gander
ganz adj whole, entire; (vollständig)
complete; (⚰: heil) undamaged, intact; **die g~e Zeit** all the time, the
whole time; **eine g~e Weile/**
Menge quite a while/lot; inv **g~**
Deutschland the whole of Germany; **wieder g~ machen** ⚰
mend; **im Großen und G~en** on
the whole ● adv quite; (völlig) completely, entirely; (sehr) very; **nicht**
g~ not quite; **g~ allein** all on
one's own; **g~ und gar** completely,
totally; **g~ und gar nicht** not at
all. **G~e(s)** nt whole. **g~jährig** adv
all the year round. **g~tägig** adj &
adv full-time; (geöffnet) all day.
g~tags adv all day; (arbeiten)
full-time
gar¹ adj done, cooked
gar² adv **gar nicht/nichts/niemand**
not/nothing/no one at all
Garage /ga'ra:ʒə/ f -,-n garage
Garantie f -,-n guarantee. **g~ren**
vt/i (haben) [für] etw g~ren guarantee sth. **G~schein** m guarantee
Garderobe f -,-n (Kleider) wardrobe; (Ablage) cloakroom; (Künstler-)
dressing-room. **G~nfrau** f cloakroom attendant
Gardine f -,-n curtain

garen vt/i (haben) cook

gären† vi (haben) ferment; (fig)
seethe

Garn nt -[e]s,-e yarn; (Näh-) cotton

Garnele f -,-n shrimp; prawn

garnieren vt decorate; (Culin)
garnish

Garnison f -,-en garrison

Garnitur f -,-en set; (Möbel-) suite

Garten m -s,⸚ garden. **G~arbeit** f
gardening. **G~bau** m horticulture.
G~haus nt, **G~laube** f
summerhouse. **G~schere** f seca-
teurs pl

Gärtner|(in) m -s,- (f -,-nen)
gardener. **G~ei** f -,-en nursery

Gärung f -fermentation

Gas nt -es,-e gas; **Gas geben** 🅰 ac-
celerate. **G~maske** f gas mask.
G~pedal nt (Auto) accelerator

Gasse f -,-n alley; (Aust) street

Gast m -[e]s,⸚e guest; (Hotel-) visitor; (im Lokal) patron; **zum Mittag
G~e haben** have people to lunch;
bei jdm zu G~ sein be staying
with s.o. **G~arbeiter** m foreign
worker. **G~bett** nt spare bed

Gäste|bett nt spare bed. **G~buch**
nt visitors' book. **G~zimmer** nt
[hotel] room; (privat) spare room

gast|freundlich adj hospitable.
G~freundschaft f hospitality.
G~geber m -s,- host. **G~geberin**
f -,-nen hostess. **G~haus** nt,
G~hof m inn, hotel

gastlich adj hospitable

Gastronomie f - gastronomy

Gast|spiel nt guest performance.
G~spielreise f (Theat) tour.
G~stätte f restaurant. **G~wirt** m
landlord. **G~wirtin** f landlady.
G~wirtschaft f restaurant

Gas|werk nt gasworks sg. **G~zäh-
ler** m gas meter

Gatte m -n,-n husband

Gattin f -,-nen wife

Gattung f -,-en kind; (Biology)
genus; (Kunst) genre

Gaudi f - (Aust, 🅳) fun

Gaumen m -s,- palate

Gauner m -s,- crook, swindler.
G~ei f -,-en swindle

Gaze /'ga:zə/ f - gauze

Gazelle f -,-n gazelle

Gebäck nt -s [cakes and] pastries
pl; (Kekse) biscuits pl

Gebälk nt -s timbers pl

geballt adj (Faust) clenched

Gebärde f -,-n gesture

gebär|en† vt give birth to, bear;
geboren werden be born. **G~mut-
ter** f womb, uterus

Gebäude nt -s,- building

Gebeine ntpl [mortal] remains

Gebell nt -s barking

geben† vt give; (tun, bringen) put;
(Karten) deal; (aufführen) perform;
(unterrichten) teach; **etw verloren
g~** give sth up as lost; **viel/wenig
g~ auf** (+ acc) set great/little store
by; **sich g~** (nachlassen) wear off;
(besser werden) get better; (sich verhalten) behave ● impers **es gibt**
there is/are; **was gibt es Neues/
zum Mittag/im Kino?** what's the
news/for lunch/on at the cinema?
es wird Regen g~ it's going to
rain ● vi (haben) (Karten) deal

Gebet nt -[e]s,-e prayer

Gebiet nt -[e]s,-e area; (Hoheits-)
territory; (Sach-) field

gebieten† vt command; (erfordern) demand ● vi (haben) rule

Gebilde nt -s,- structure

gebildet adj educated; (kultiviert)
cultured

Gebirge nt -s,- mountains pl.
g~ig adj mountainous

Gebiss nt -es,-e teeth pl; (künstliches) false teeth pl; dentures pl, (des Zaumes) bit

geblümt adj floral, flowered

gebogen adj curved

geboren adj born; g~er Deutscher German by birth; Frau X, g~e Y Mrs X, née Y

Gebot nt -[e]s,-e rule

gebraten adj fried

Gebrauch m use; (Sprach-) usage; Gebräuche customs; in G~ in use; G~ machen von make use of. g~en vt use; zu nichts zu g~en useless

gebräuchlich adj common; (Wort) in common use

Gebrauch|sanleitung, G~sanweisung f directions pl for use. g~t adj used; (Comm) secondhand. G~twagen m used car

gebrechlich adj frail, infirm

gebrochen adj broken ● adv g~Englisch sprechen speak broken English

Gebrüll nt -s roaring

Gebühr f -,-en charge, fee; über G~ excessively. g~end adj due; (geziemend) proper. g~enfrei adj free ● adv free of charge. g~enpflichtig adj & adv subject to a charge; g~enpflichtige Straße toll road

Geburt f -,-en birth; von G~ by birth. G~enkontrolle, G~enregelung f birth control. G~enziffer f birth rate

gebürtig adj native (aus of); g~er Deutscher German by birth

Geburts|datum nt date of birth. G~helfer m obstetrician. G~hilfe f obstetrics sg. G~ort m place of birth. G~tag m birthday. G~urkunde f birth certificate

Gebüsch nt -[e]s,-e bushes pl

Gedächtnis nt -ses memory; aus dem G~ from memory

Gedanke m -ns,-n thought (an + acc of); (Idee) idea; sich (dat) G~n machen worry (über + acc about). g~nlos adj thoughtless; (zerstreut) absent-minded. G~nstrich m dash

Gedärme ntpl intestines; (Tier-) entrails

Gedeck nt -[e]s,-e place setting; (auf Speisekarte) set meal

gedeihen† vi (sein) thrive, flourish

gedenken† vi (haben) propose (etw zu tun to do sth); jds g~ remember s.o. G~ nt -s memory

Gedenk|feier f commemoration. G~gottesdienst m memorial service

Gedicht nt -[e]s,-e poem

Gedränge|e nt -s crush, crowd. g~t adj (knapp) concise ● adv g~t voll packed

Geduld f - patience; G~ haben be patient. g~en (sich) vr be patient. g~ig adj patient. G~[s]spiel nt puzzle

gedunsen adj bloated

geehrt adj honoured; Sehr g~er Herr X Dear Mr X

geeignet adj suitable; im g~en Moment at the right moment

Gefahr f -,-en danger; in G~ in danger; auf eigene G~ at one's own risk; G~ laufen run the risk (etw zu tun of doing sth)

gefähr|den vt endanger; (fig) jeopardize. g~lich adj dangerous

gefahrlos adj safe

Gefährt nt -[e]s,-e vehicle

Gefährte m -n,-n, **Gefährtin** f -,-nen companion

gefahrvoll adj dangerous, perilous

Gefälle nt -s,- slope

(Straßen-) gradient

gefallen† *vi* (haben) jdm g~ please s.o.; er/es gefällt mir I like him/it; sich (*dat*) etw g~ lassen put up with sth

Gefallen¹ *m* -s,- favour

Gefallen² *nt* -s pleasure (an + *dat* in); dir zu G~ to please you

Gefallene(r) *m* soldier killed in the war

gefällig *adj* pleasing; (*hübsch*) attractive; (*hilfsbereit*) obliging; noch etwas g~? will there be anything else? **G~keit** *f* -,-en favour; (*Freundlichkeit*) kindness

Gefangene|e(r) *m/f* prisoner. **G~nahme** *f* - capture. **g~nehmen*** *vt sep* = **g~ nehmen**, s. **fangen**. **G~schaft** *f* - captivity

Gefängnis *nt* -ses,-se prison; (*Strafe*) imprisonment. **G~strafe** *f* imprisonment; (*Urteil*) prison sentence. **G~wärter** *m* [prison] warder

Gefäß *nt* -es,-e container; (*Blut-*) vessel

gefasst *adj* composed; (*ruhig*) calm; **g~ sein auf** (+ *acc*) be prepared for

gefedert *adj* sprung

gefeiert *adj* celebrated

Gefieder *nt* -s plumage

gefleckt *adj* spotted

Geflügel *nt* -s poultry. **G~klein** *nt* -s giblets *pl.* **g~t** *adj* winged

Geflüster *nt* -s whispering

Gefolge *nt* -s retinue, entourage

gefragt *adj* popular

Gefreite(r) *m* lance corporal

gefrier|en† *vi* (sein) freeze. **G~fach** *nt* freezer compartment. **G~punkt** *m* freezing point. **G~schrank** *m* upright freezer. **G~truhe** *f* chest freezer

gefroren *adj* frozen

gefügig *adj* compliant; (*gehorsam*) obedient

Gefühl *nt* -[e]s,-e feeling; (*Empfindung*) sensation; (*G~sregung*) emotion; im G~ haben know instinctively. **g~los** *adj* insensitive; (*herzlos*) unfeeling; (*taub*) numb. **g~smäßig** *adj* emotional; (*instinktiv*) instinctive. **G~sregung** *f* emotion. **g~voll** *adj* sensitive; (*sentimental*) sentimental

gefüllt *adj* filled; (*voll*) full

gefürchtet *adj* feared, dreaded

gefüttert *adj* lined

gegeben *adj* given; (*bestehend*) present; (*passend*) appropriate. **g~enfalls** *adv* if need be

gegen *prep* (+ *acc*) against; (*Sport*) versus; (*g~über*) to[-wards]; (*Vergleich*) compared with; (*Richtung, Zeit*) towards; (*ungefähr*) around; ein Mittel g~ a remedy for ● *adv* g~ 100 Leute about 100 people. **G~angriff** *m* counter-attack

Gegend *f* -,-en area, region; (*Umgebung*) neighbourhood

gegeneinander *adv* against/(*gegenüber*) towards one another

Gegen|fahrbahn *f* opposite carriageway. **G~gift** *nt* antidote. **G~maßnahme** *f* countermeasure. **G~satz** *m* contrast; (*Widerspruch*) contradiction; (*G~teil*) opposite; im G~satz zu unlike. **g~seitig** *adj* mutual; sich g~seitig hassen hate one another. **G~stand** *m* object; (*Gram, Gesprächs-*) subject. **G~stück** *nt* counterpart; (*G~teil*) opposite. **G~teil** *nt* opposite, contrary; im G~teil on the contrary. **g~teilig** *adj* opposite

gegenüber *prep* (+ *dat*) opposite; (*Vergleich*) compared with; jdm g~ höflich sein be polite to s.o. ● *adv* opposite. **G~** *nt* -s person opposite.

g~**liegend** adj opposite. g~**ste-**
hen† vi sep (haben) (+ dat) face;
feindlich g~stehen (+ dat) be hostile to. **g~stellen** vt sep confront;
(vergleichen) compare

Gegen|verkehr m oncoming
traffic. **G~vorschlag** m counter-
proposal. **G~wart** f - present; (Anwesenheit) presence. **g~wärtig** (adj
present ● adv at present. **G~wehr**
f - resistance. **G~wert** m equivalent. **G~wind** m head wind.
g~zeichnen vt sep countersign

geglückt adj successful
Gegner|(in) m -s,- (f -,-nen) op-
ponent. **g~isch** adj opposing
Gehabe nt -s affected behaviour
Gehackte(s) nt mince
Gehalt m -[e]s,ᵉr salary. **G~s-**
erhöhung f rise
gehässig adj spiteful
gehäuft adj heaped
Gehäuse nt -s,- case; (TV, Radio)
cabinet; (Schnecken-) shell
Gehege nt -s,- enclosure
geheim adj secret; **g~ halten**
keep secret; **im g~en** secretly.
G~dienst m Secret Service. **G~nis**
nt -ses,-se secret. **g~nisvoll** adj
mysterious
gehemmt adj (fig) inhibited

---

gehen†

● intransitive verb (sein)

····▶ (sich irgendwohin begeben) go;
(zu Fuß) walk. **tanzen/schwim-**
men/einkaufen gehen go danc-
ing/swimming/shopping. **schla-**
fen gehen go to bed. **zum Arzt**
gehen go to the doctor's. **in die**
Schule gehen go to school. **auf**
und ab gehen walk up and
down. **über die Straße gehen**
cross the street

····▶ (weggehen; fam: abfahren) go;
leave. **ich muss bald gehen** I
must go soon. **Sie können**
gehen you may go. **der Zug**
geht um zehn Uhr 🔟 the train
leaves or goes at ten o'clock

····▶ (funktionieren) work. **der**
Computer geht wieder/nicht
mehr the computer is working
again/has stopped working.
meine Uhr geht falsch/richtig
my watch is wrong/right

····▶ (möglich sein) be possible. **ja,**
das geht yes, I or we can manage that. **das geht nicht** that
can't be done; (🔟: ist nicht ak-
zeptabel) it's not good enough,
it's not on 🔟. **es geht einfach**
nicht, dass du so spät nach
Hause kommst it simply won't
do for you to come home so
late

····▶ (🔟: gerade noch angehen) **es**
geht [so] it is all right. **Wie war**
die Party? — Es ging so How
was the party? — Not bad or
So-so

····▶ (sich entwickeln) do; go. **der**
Laden geht gut the shop is
doing well. **es geht alles nach**
Wunsch everything is going to
plan

····▶ (impers) **wie geht es Ihnen?**
how are you? **jdm geht es gut/**
schlecht (gesundheitlich) s.o. is
doing well/badly

····▶ (impers; sich um etw handeln)
es geht um it concerns. **worum**
geht es hier? what is this all
about? **es geht ihr nur ums**
Geld she is only interested
in money

Geheul nt -s howling
Gehilfe m -n,-n, **Gehilfin** f -,-nen
trainee; (Helfer) assistant

Gehirn nt -s brain; (Verstand) brains pl **G~erschütterung** f concussion. **G~hautentzündung** f meningitis. **G~wäsche** f brainwashing

gehoben adj (fig) superior

Gehöft nt -[e]s,-e farm

Gehör nt -s hearing

gehorchen vi (haben) (+ dat) obey

gehören vi (haben) belong (dat to); **dazu gehört Mut** that takes courage; **es gehört sich nicht** it isn't done

gehörlos adj deaf

Gehörn nt -s,-e horns pl; (Geweih) antlers pl

gehorsam adj obedient. **G~** m -s obedience

Geh|steig m -[e]s,-e pavement. **G~weg** m = Gehsteig; (Fußweg) footpath

Geier m -s,- vulture

Geig|e f -,-n violin. **g~en** vi (haben) play the violin ● vt play on the violin. **G~er(in)** m -s,- (f -,-nen) violinist

geil adj lecherous; randy; (🔞: toll) great

Geisel f -,-n hostage

Geiß f -,-en (SGer) [nanny-]goat. **G~blatt** nt honeysuckle

Geist m -[e]s,-e mind; (Witz) wit; (Gesinnung) spirit; (Gespenst) ghost; **der Heilige G~** the Holy Ghost or Spirit

geistes|abwesend adj absent-minded. **G~blitz** m brainwave. **g~gegenwärtig** adv with great presence of mind. **g~gestört** adj [mentally] deranged. **g~krank** adj mentally ill. **G~krankheit** f mental illness. **G~wissenschaften** fpl arts. **G~zustand** m mental state

geist|ig adj mental; (intellektuell)

intellectual. **g~lich** adj spiritual; (religiös) religious; (Musik) sacred; (Tracht) clerical. **G~liche(r)** m clergyman. **G~lichkeit** f - clergy. **g~reich** adj clever; (witzig) witty

Geiz m -es meanness. **g~en** vi (haben) be mean (**mit** with). **G~hals** m 🔞 miser. **g~ig** adj mean, miserly. **G~kragen** m 🔞 miser

Gekicher nt -s giggling

geknickt adj 🔞 dejected

gekonnt adj accomplished ● adv expertly

gekränkt adj offended, hurt

Gekritzel nt -s scribble

Gelächter nt -s laughter

geladen adj loaded

gelähmt adj paralysed

Geländer nt -s,- railings pl; (Treppen-) banisters

gelangen vi (sein) reach/(fig) attain (**zu etw/an etw** acc sth)

gelassen adj composed; (ruhig) calm. **G~heit** f - equanimity; (Fassung) composure

Gelatine /ʒelaˈ-/ f - gelatine

geläufig adj common, current; (fließend) fluent; **jdm g~ sein** be familiar to s.o.

gelaunt adj **gut/schlecht g~ sein** be in a good/bad mood

gelb adj yellow; (bei Ampel) amber; **das G~e vom Ei** the yolk of the egg. **G~** nt -s,- yellow. **g~lich** adj yellowish. **G~sucht** f jaundice

Geld nt -es,-er money; **öffentliche G~er** public funds. **G~automat** m cashpoint machine. **G~beutel** m. **G~börse** f purse. **G~geber** m -s,- backer. **g~lich** adj financial. **G~mittel** ntpl funds. **G~schein** m banknote. **G~schrank** m safe. **G~strafe** f fine. **G~stück** nt coin

Gelee /ʒeˈle:/ nt -s,-s jelly

gelegen adj situated; (passend) convenient

Gelegenheit f -,-en opportunity, chance; (Anlass) occasion; (Comm) bargain; **bei G~** some time. **G~sarbeit** f casual work. **G~skauf** m bargain

gelegentlich adj occasional ● adv occasionally; (bei Gelegenheit) some time

Gelehrte(r) m/f scholar

Geleit nt -[e]s escort; freies G~ safe conduct. **g~en** vt escort

Gelenk nt -[e]s,-e joint. **g~ig** adj supple; (Techn) flexible

gelernt adj skilled

Geliebte(r) m/f lover

gelingen vi (sein) succeed, be successful. **G~** nt -s success

gellend adj shrill

geloben vt promise [solemnly]; **das Gelobte Land** the Promised Land

Gelöbnis nt -ses,-se vow

gelöst adj (fig) relaxed

gelten† vi (haben) be valid; (Regel:) apply; **g~ als** be regarded as; **etw nicht g~ lassen** not accept sth; **wenig/viel g~** be worth/(fig) count for little/a lot; **jdm g~** be meant for s.o.; **das gilt nicht** that doesn't count. **g~d** adj valid; (Preise) current; (Meinung) prevailing; **g~d machen** assert (Recht, Forderung); bring to bear (Einfluss)

Geltung f - validity; (Ansehen) prestige; **zur G~ bringen** set off

Gelübde nt -s,- vow

gelungen adj successful

Gelüst nt -[e]s,-e desire

gemächlich adj leisurely ● adv in a leisurely manner

Gemahl m -s,-e husband. **G~in** f -,-nen wife

Gemälde nt -s,- painting. **G~galerie** f picture gallery

gemäß prep (+ dat) in accordance with

gemäßigt adj moderate; (Klima) temperate

gemein adj common; (unanständig) vulgar; (niederträchtig) mean; **g~er Soldat** private

Gemeinde f -,-n [local] community; (Admin) borough; (Pfarr-) parish; (bei Gottesdienst) congregation. **G~rat** m local council/(Person) councillor. **G~wahlen** fpl local elections

gemein|gefährlich adj dangerous. **G~heit** f -,-en commonness; vulgarity; meanness; (Bemerkung, Handlung) mean thing [to say/do]; **so eine G~heit!** how mean! **G~kosten** pl overheads. **g~nützig** adj charitable. **g~sam** adj common ● adv together

Gemeinschaft f -,-en community. **g~lich** adj joint; (Besitz) communal ● adv jointly; (zusammen) together. **G~sarbeit** f team work

Gemenge nt -s,- mixture

Gemisch nt -[e]s,-e mixture. **g~t** adj mixed

Gemme f -,-n engraved gem

Gemse f * -,-n = Gämse

Gemurmel nt -s murmuring

Gemüse nt -s,- vegetable; (coll) vegetables pl. **G~händler** m greengrocer

gemustert adj patterned

Gemüt nt -[e]s,-er nature, disposition; (Gefühl) feelings pl

gemütlich adj cosy; (gemächlich) leisurely; (zwanglos) informal; (Person) genial; **es sich** (dat) **g~ machen** make oneself comfortable. **G~keit** f - cosiness

Gen nt -s,-e gene

genau adj exact, precise; (Waage, Messung) accurate; (sorgfältig) meticulous; (ausführlich) detailed; **nichts G~es wissen** not know any details; **g~ genommen** strictly speaking; **g~!** exactly! **G~igkeit** f – exactitude; precision; accuracy; meticulousness

genauso adv just the same; (g~sehr) just as much; **g~ teuer** just as expensive; **g~ gut** just as good; adv just as well; **g~ sehr** just as much; **g~ viel** just as much/many; **g~ wenig** just as little/few; (noch) no more

Gendarm /ʒã'darm/ m -en,-en (Aust) policeman

Genealogie f – genealogy

genehmig|en vt grant; approve (Plan). **G~ung** f -,-en permission; (Schein) permit

geneigt adj sloping, inclined; (fig) well-disposed (dat towards)

General m -s,-e general. **G~direktor** m managing director. **G~probe** f dress rehearsal. **G~streik** m general strike

Generation /-'tsjo:n/ f -,-en generation

Generator m -s,-en generator

generell adj general

genes|en† vi (sein) recover. **G~ung** f – recovery; (Erholung) convalescence

Genetik f – genetics sg

genetisch adj genetic

Genf nt -s Geneva. **G~er** adj Geneva ; **G~er See** Lake Geneva

genial adj brilliant. **G~ität** f genius

Genick nt -s,-e [back of the] neck; **sich** (dat) **das G~ brechen** break one's neck

Genie /ʒe'ni:/ nt -s,-s genius

genieren /ʒe'ni:rən/ vt embarrass; **sich g~** feel or be embarrassed

genieß|bar adj fit to eat/drink. **g~en†** vt enjoy; (verzehren) eat/drink

Genitiv m -s,-e genitive

genmanipuliert adj genetically modified

Genom nt -s, -e genome

Genosse m -n,-n (Pol) comrade. **G~nschaft** f -,-en cooperative

Gentechnologie f genetic engineering

genug inv adj & adv enough

Genüge f zur G~ sufficiently. **g~n** vi (haben) be enough. **g~nd** inv adj sufficient, enough; (Sch) fair ● adv sufficiently, enough

Genuss m -es,-̈e enjoyment; (Vergnügen) pleasure; (Verzehr) consumption

geöffnet adj open

Geo|graphie, G~grafie f – geography. **g~graphisch, g~grafisch** adj geographical. **G~logie** f – geology. **g~logisch** adj geological. **G~meter** m -s,- surveyor. **G~metrie** f – geometry. **g~metrisch** adj geometric[al]

geordnet adj well-ordered; (stabil) stable; **alphabetisch g~** in alphabetical order

Gepäck nt -s luggage, baggage. **G~ablage** f luggage-rack. **G~aufbewahrung** f left-luggage office. **G~schein** m left-luggage ticket; (Aviat) baggage check. **G~träger** m porter; (Fahrrad-) luggage carrier; (Dach-) roof-rack

Gepard m -s,-e cheetah

gepflegt adj well-kept; (Person) well-groomed; (Hotel) first-class

gepunktet adj spotted

gerade adj straight; (direkt) direct; (aufrecht) upright; (aufrichtig) straightforward; (Zahl) even ● adv straight; directly; (eben) just;

g

(*genau*) exactly; (*besonders*) especially; **g~ sitzen/stehen** sit/stand [up] straight; **g~ erst** only just. **G~ f -,-n** straight line. **g~aus** adv straight ahead/on. **g~heraus** adv (*fig*) straight out. **g~so** adv just the same; **g~so gut** just as good; adv just as well. **g~stehen†** vi sep (*haben*) (*fig*) accept responsibility (**für** for). **g~zu** adv virtually; (*wirklich*) absolutely

Geranie /-jə/ f **-,-n** geranium

Gerät nt **-[e]s,-e** tool; (*Acker-*) implement; (*Küchen-*) utensil; (*Elektro-*) appliance; (*Radio-, Fernseh-*) set; (*Turn-*) piece of apparatus; (*coll*) equipment

geraten† vi (*sein*) get; **in Brand g~** catch fire; **in Wut g~** get angry; **gut g~** turn out well

Geratewohl nt aufs **G~** at random

geräuchert adj smoked

geräumig adj spacious, roomy

Geräusch nt **-[e]s,-e** noise. **g~los** adj noiseless

gerben vt tan

gerecht adj just; (*fair*) fair. **g~fertigt** adj justified. **G~igkeit** f - justice; fairness

Gerede nt **-s** talk

geregelt adj regular

gereizt adj irritable

Geriatrie f - geriatrics sg

Gericht¹ nt **-[e]s,-e** (*Culin*) dish

Gericht² nt **-[e]s,-e** court [of law]; **vor G~** in court; **das Jüngste G~** the Last Judgement. **g~lich** adj judicial; (*Verfahren*) legal ● adv **g~lich vorgehen** take legal action. **G~shof** m court of justice. **G~smedizin** f forensic medicine. **G~ssaal** m court room. **G~svollzieher** m **-s,-** bailiff

gerieben adj grated; (🄁)

schlau) crafty

gering adj small; (*niedrig*) low; (*g~fügig*) slight. **g~fügig** adj slight. **g~schätzig** adj contemptuous; (*Bemerkung*) disparaging. **g~ste(r,s)** adj least; **nicht im G~sten** not in the least

gerinnen† vi (*sein*) curdle; (*Blut:*) clot

Gerippe nt **-s,-** skeleton; (*fig*) framework

gerissen adj 🄁 crafty

Germ m **-[e]s** & (*Aust*) f **-** yeast

German|e m **-n,-n** [ancient] German. **g~isch** adj Germanic. **G~istik** f - German [language and literature]

gern[e] adv gladly; **g~ haben** like; (*lieben*) be fond of; **ich tanze g~** I like dancing; **willst du mit?—g~!** do you want to come?—I'd love to!

Gerste f - barley. **G~nkorn** nt (*Med*) stye

Geruch m **-[e]s,-e** smell (**von**/ **nach** of). **g~los** adj odourless. **G~ssinn** m sense of smell

Gerücht nt **-[e]s,-e** rumour

gerührt adj (*fig*) moved, touched

Gerümpel nt **-s** lumber, junk

Gerüst nt **-[e]s,-e** scaffolding; (*fig*) framework

gesammelt adj collected; (*gefasst*) composed

gesamt adj entire, whole. **G~ausgabe** f complete edition. **G~eindruck** m overall impression. **G~heit** f - whole. **G~schule** f comprehensive school. **G~summe** f total

Gesandte(r) m/f envoy

Gesang m **-[e]s,-e** singing; (*Lied*) song; (*Kirchen-*) hymn. **G~verein** m choral society

Gesäß nt **-es** buttocks pl

Geschäft nt -[e]s,-e business; (*Laden*) shop, store; (*Transaktion*) deal; schmutzige G~e shady dealings; ein gutes G~ machen do very well (mit out of). g~ig adj busy; (*Treiben*) bustling. G~igkeit f - activity. g~lich adj business ● adv on business

Geschäfts|brief m business letter. G~führer m manager; (*Vereins*-) secretary. G~mann m (*pl* -leute) businessman. G~stelle f office; (*Zweigstelle*) branch. g~tüchtig adj g~tüchtig sein be a good businessman/-woman. G~zeiten fpl hours of business

geschehen† vi (sein) happen (dat to); das geschieht dir recht! it serves you right! gern g~! you're welcome! G~ nt -s events pl

gescheit adj clever

Geschenk nt -[e]s,-e present, gift

Geschicht|e f -,-n history; (*Erzählung*) story; (ⓘ: Sache) business. g~lich adj historical

Geschick nt -[e]s fate; (*Talent*) skill. G~lichkeit f - skilfulness, skill. g~t adj skilful; (*klug*) clever

geschieden adj divorced

Geschirr nt -s,-e (coll) crockery; (*Porzellan*) china; (*Service*) service; (*Pferde*-) harness; schmutziges G~ dirty dishes pl. G~spülmaschine f dishwasher. G~tuch nt tea towel

Geschlecht nt -[e]s,-er sex; (*Gram*) gender; (*Generation*) generation. g~lich adj sexual. G~skrankheit f venereal disease. G~steile ntpl genitals. G~sverkehr m sexual intercourse. G~swort nt (pl -wörter) article

geschliffen adj (fig) polished

Geschmack m -[e]s,-̈e taste; (*Aroma*) flavour; (*G~ssinn*) sense of taste; einen guten G~ haben (fig) have good taste. g~los adj taste-

less; g~los sein (fig) be in bad taste. g~voll adj (fig) tasteful

Geschoss nt -es,-e missile; (*Stockwerk*) storey, floor

Geschrei nt -s screaming; (fig) fuss

Geschütz nt -es,-e gun, cannon

geschützt adj protected; (*Stelle*) sheltered

Geschwader nt -s,- squadron

Geschwätz nt -es talk

geschweige conj g~ denn let alone

Geschwindigkeit f -,-en speed; (*Phys*) velocity. G~sbegrenzung, G~sbeschränkung f speed limit

Geschwister pl brother[s] and sister[s]; siblings

geschwollen adj swollen; (fig) pompous

Geschworene(r) m/f juror; die G~n the jury sg

Geschwulst f -,-̈e swelling; (*Tumor*) tumour

geschwungen adj curved

Geschwür nt -s,-e ulcer

gesellig adj sociable; (*Zool*) gregarious; (*unterhaltsam*) convivial; g~er Abend social evening

Gesellschaft f -,-en company; (*Veranstaltung*) party; die G~ society; jdm G~ leisten keep s.o. company. g~lich adj social. G~spiel nt party game

Gesetz nt -es,-e law. G~entwurf m bill. g~gebend adj legislative. G~gebung f - legislation. g~lich adj legal. g~mäßig adj lawful; (*gesetzlich*) legal. g~widrig adj illegal

gesichert adj secure

Gesicht nt -[e]s,-er face; (*Aussehen*) appearance. G~sfarbe f complexion. G~spunkt m point of view. G~szüge mpl features

Gesindel nt -s riff-raff

Gesinnung f -,-en mind; (Einstellung) attitude

gesondert adj separate

Gespann nt -[e]s,-e team; (Wagen) horse and cart/carriage

gespannt adj taut; (fig) tense; (Beziehungen) strained; (neugierig) eager; (erwartungsvoll) expectant; g~ **sein**, ob wonder whether; **auf etw g~ sein** look forward eagerly to sth

Gespenst nt -[e]s,-er ghost. **g~isch** adj ghostly; (unheimlich) eerie

Gespött nt -[e]s mockery; **zum G~ werden** become a laughing stock

Gespräch nt -[e]s-e conversation; (Telefon-) call; **ins G~ kommen** get talking; **im G~ sein** be under discussion. **g~ig** adj talkative **G~sthema** nt topic of conversation

Gestalt f -,-en figure; (Form) shape, form; **G~ annehmen** (fig) take shape. **g~en** vt shape; (organisieren) arrange; (schaffen) create; (entwerfen) design; **sich g~en** turn out

Geständnis nt -ses,-se confession

Gestank m -s stench, [bad] smell

gestatten vt allow, permit; **nicht gestattet** prohibited; g~ **Sie?** may I?

Geste /'gɛ-, 'geːstə/ f -,-n gesture

Gesteck nt -[e]s,-e flower arrangement

gestehen† vt/i (haben) confess; confess to (Verbrechen)

Gestein nt -[e]s,-e rock

Gestell nt -[e]s,-e stand; (Flaschen-) rack; (Rahmen) frame

gesteppt adj quilted

gestern adv yesterday; g~ **Nacht** last night

gestrandet adj stranded

gestreift adj striped

gestrichelt adj (Linie) dotted

gestrichen adj g~er Teelöffel level teaspoon[ful]

gestrig /'gɛstrɪç/ adj yesterday's; **am g~en Tag** yesterday

Gestrüpp nt -s,-e undergrowth

Gestüt nt -[e]s,-e stud [farm]

Gesuch nt -[e]s,-e request; (Admin) application. **g~t** adj sought-after

gesund adj healthy; g~ **sein** be in good health; (Sport, Getränk:) be good for one; **wieder g~ werden** get well again

Gesundheit f - health; **G~!** (bei Niesen) bless you! **g~lich** adj health; **g~licher Zustand** state of health • adv **es geht ihm g~lich gut/ schlecht** he is in good/poor health. **g~sschädlich** adj harmful

getäfelt adj panelled

Getöse nt -s racket, din

Getränk nt -[e]s,-e drink. **G~ekarte** f wine-list

getrauen vt sich (dat) etw g~ dare [to] do sth; **sich g~** dare

Getreide nt -s (coll) grain

getrennt adj separate; g~ **leben** live apart; g~ **schreiben** write as two words

getreu adj faithful • prep (+ dat) true to. **g~lich** adv faithfully

Getriebe nt -s,- bustle; (Techn) gear; (Auto) transmission; (Gehäuse) gearbox

getrost adv with confidence

Getto nt -s,-s ghetto

Getue nt -s 𝔽 fuss

Getümmel nt -s tumult

geübt adj skilled

Gewächs nt -es,-e plant

gewachsen adj jdm g~ sein be

a match for s.o.

Gewächshaus nt greenhouse

gewagt adj daring

gewählt adj refined

gewahr adj g~ werden become aware (acc/gen of)

Gewähr f - guarantee

gewähr|en vt grant; (geben) offer. **g~leisten** vt guarantee

Gewahrsam m -s safekeeping; (Haft) custody

Gewalt f -,-en power; (Kraft) force; (Brutalität) violence; **mit G~** by force. **g~ig** adj powerful; (fig: groß) enormous; (stark) tremendous. **g~sam** adj forcible; (Tod) violent. **g~tätig** adj violent. **G~tätigkeit** f -,-en violence; (Handlung) act of violence

Gewand nt -[e]s,ˉer robe

gewandt adj skilful. **G~heit** f - skill

Gewebe nt -s,- fabric; (Anat) tissue

Gewehr nt -s,-e rifle, gun

Geweih nt -[e]s,-e antlers pl

Gewerb|e nt -s,- trade. **g~lich** adj commercial. **g~smäßig** adj professional

Gewerkschaft f -,-en trade union. **G~ler(in)** m -s,- (f -,-nen) trade unionist

Gewicht nt -[e]s,-e weight; (Bedeutung) importance. **G~heben** nt -s weight lifting

Gewinde nt -s,- [screw] thread

Gewinn m -[e]s,-e profit; (fig) gain, benefit; (beim Spiel) winnings pl; (Preis) prize; (Los) winning ticket. **G~beteiligung** f profit-sharing. **g~en†** vt win; (erlangen) gain; (fördern) extract ● vi (haben) win; **g~en an** (+ dat) gain in. **g~end** adj engaging. **G~er(in)** m -s,- (f -,-nen) winner

Gewächshaus | gießen

Gewirr nt -s,-e tangle; (Straßen-) maze

gewiss adj certain

Gewissen nt -s,- conscience. **g~haft** adj conscientious. **g~los** adj unscrupulous. **G~sbisse** mpl pangs of conscience

gewissermaßen adv to a certain extent; (sozusagen) as it were

Gewissheit f - certainty

Gewitt|er nt -s,- thunderstorm. **g~rig** adj thundery

gewogen adj (fig) well-disposed (dat towards)

gewöhnen vt jdn/sich g~ an (+ acc) get s.o. used to/get used to; [an] jdn/etw gewöhnt sein be used to s.o./sth

Gewohnheit f -,-en habit. **G~srecht** nt common law

gewöhnlich adj ordinary; (üblich) usual; (ordinär) common

gewohnt adj customary; (vertraut) familiar; (üblich) usual; etw (acc) g~ sein be used to sth

Gewölbe nt -s,- vault

Gewühl nt -[e]s crush

gewunden adj winding

Gewürz nt -es,-e spice. **G~nelke** f clove

gezackt adj serrated

gezähnt adj serrated; (Säge) toothed

Gezeiten fpl tides

gezielt adj specific; (Frage) pointed

geziert adj affected

gezwungen adj forced. **g~ermaßen** adv of necessity

Gicht f - gout

Giebel m -s,- gable

Gier f - greed (nach for). **g~ig** adj greedy

gieß|en† vt pour; water (Blumen, Garten); (Techn) cast ● v impers **es**

g~t it is pouring [with rain]. **G~kanne** f watering can

Gift nt -[e]s,-e poison; (Schlangen-) venom; (Med) toxin. **g~ig** adj poisonous; (Schlange) venomous; (Med, Chemistry) toxic; (fig) spiteful. **G~müll** m toxic waste. **G~pilz** m toadstool

Gilde f -,-n guild

Gin /dʒɪn/ m -s gin

Ginster m -s (Bot) broom

Gipfel m -s,- summit, top; (fig) peak. **G~konferenz** f summit conference. **g~n** vi (haben) culminate (in + acc)

Gips m -es plaster. **G~verband** m (Med) plaster cast

Giraffe f -,-n giraffe

Girlande f -,-n garland

Girokonto /ˈʒiːro-/ nt current account

Gischt m -[e]s & f -spray

Gitar|re f -,-n guitar. **G~rist(in)** m -en,-en (f -,-nen) guitarist

Gitter nt -s,- bars pl; (Rost) grating, grid; (Geländer, Zaun) railings pl; (Fenster-) grille; (Draht-) wire screen

Glanz m -es shine; (von Farbe, Papier) gloss; (Seiden-) sheen; (Politur) polish; (fig) brilliance; (Pracht) splendour

glänzen vi (haben) shine. **g~d** adj shining, bright; (Papier) glossy; (fig) brilliant

glanz|los adj dull. **G~stück** nt masterpiece

Glas nt -es,ˁer glass; (Brillen-) lens; (Fern-) binoculars pl; (Marmeladen-) [glass] jar. **G~er** m -s,- glazier

glasieren vt glaze; ice (Kuchen)

glas|ig adj glassy; (durchsichtig) transparent. **G~scheibe** f pane

Glasur f -,-en glaze; (Culin) icing

glatt adj smooth; (eben) even;

(Haar) straight; (rutschig) slippery; (einfach) straightforward; (Absage) flat; **g~ streichen** smooth out; **g~ rasiert** clean-shaven; **g~ gehen** go off smoothly; **das ist g~ gelogen** it's a downright lie

Glätte f -smoothness; (Rutschigkeit) slipperiness

Glatt|eis nt [black] ice. **g~weg** adv ⊞ outright

Glatz|e f -,-n bald patch; (Voll-) bald head; **eine G~e bekommen** go bald. **g~köpfig** adj bald

Glaube m -ns belief (an + acc in); (Relig) faith; **G~n schenken** (+ dat) believe. **g~n** vt/i (haben) believe (an + acc in); (vermuten) think; **jdm g~n** believe s.o.; **nicht zu g~n** unbelievable, incredible. **G~nsbekenntnis** nt creed

gläubig adj religious; (vertrauend) trusting. **G~e(r)** m/f (Relig) believer; **die G~en** the faithful. **G~er** m -s,- (Comm) creditor

glaub|lich adj kaum g~lich scarcely believable. **g~würdig** adj credible; (Person) reliable

gleich adj same; (identisch) identical; (g~wertig) equal; **g~ bleibend** constant; **2 mal 5 [ist] g~ 10** two times 5 equals 10; **das ist mir g~** it's all the same to me; **ganz g~, wo/wer** no matter where/who ● adv equally; (übereinstimmend) identically, the same; (sofort) immediately; (in Kürze) in a minute; (fast) nearly; (direkt) right. **g~altrig** adj [of] the same age. **g~bedeutend** adj synonymous. **g~berechtigt** adj equal. **G~berechtigung** f equality

gleichen† vi (haben) jdm/etw g~ be like or resemble s.o./something

gleich|ermaßen adv equally. **g~falls** adv also, likewise; **danke g~falls** thank you, the same to you. **G~gewicht** nt balance; (Phys & fig) equilibrium. **g~gültig** adj indifferent; (unwichtig) unimportant. **G~gültigkeit** f indifference.

g~machen vt sep make equal; **dem Erdboden g~machen** raze to the ground. **g~mäßig** adj even, regular; (beständig) constant. **G~mäßigkeit** f - regularity

Gleichnis nt -ses,-se parable

Gleich|schritt m **im G~schritt** in step. **g~setzen** vt sep equate/(g~stellen) place on a par (dat/mit with). **g~stellen** vt sep place on a par (dat with). **G~strom** m direct current

Gleichung f -,-en equation

gleichwertig adv adj of equal value. **g~zeitig** adj simultaneous

Gleis nt -es,-e track; (Bahnsteig) platform; **G~ 5** platform 5

gleiten† vi (sein) glide; (rutschen) slide. **g~d** adj sliding; **g~de Arbeitszeit** flexitime

Gleitzeit f flexitime

Gletscher m -s,- glacier

Glied nt -[e]s,-er limb; (Teil) part; (Ketten-) link; (Mitglied) member; (Mil) rank. **g~ern** vt arrange; (einteilen) divide. **G~maßen** fpl limbs

glitschig adj slippery

glitzern vi (haben) glitter

global adj global

globalisier|en vt globalize. **G~ung** f -,-en globalization

Globus m - & -busses,-ben & -busse globe

Glocke f -,-n bell. **G~nturm** m bell tower, belfry

glorreich adj glorious

Glossar nt -s,-e glossary

Glosse f -,-n comment

glotzen vi (haben) stare

Glück nt -[e]s [good] luck; (Zufrie-

denheit) happiness; **G~ bringend** lucky; **G~/kein G~ haben** be lucky/unlucky; **zum G~** luckily, fortunately; **auf gut G~** on the off chance; (wahllos) at random. **g~en** vi (sein) succeed

glücklich adj lucky, fortunate; (zufrieden) happy; (sicher) safe ● adv happily; safely. **g~erweise** adv luckily, fortunately

Glücksspiel nt game of chance; (Spielen) gambling

Glückwunsch m good wishes pl; (Gratulation) congratulations pl; **herzlichen G~!** congratulations! [zum Geburtstag] happy birthday! **G~karte** f greetings card

Glüh|birne f light bulb. **g~en** vi (haben) glow. **G~end** adj glowing; (rot-) red-hot; (Hitze) scorching; (leidenschaftlich) fervent. **G~faden** m filament. **G~wein** m mulled wine. **G~würmchen** nt -s,- glow-worm

Glukose f - glucose

Glut f - embers pl; (Röte) glow; (Hitze) heat; (fig) ardour

Glyzinie /-jə/ f -,-n wisteria

GmbH abbr (Gesellschaft mit beschränkter Haftung) ≈ plc

Gnade f - mercy; (Gunst) favour; (Relig) grace. **G~nfrist** f reprieve

gnädig adj gracious; (mild) lenient; **g~e Frau** Madam

Gnom m -en,-en gnome

Gobelin /gobəˈlɛ̃:/ m -s,-s tapestry

Gold nt -[e]s gold. **g~en** adj gold; (g~farben) golden. **G~fisch** m goldfish. **g~ig** adj sweet, lovely. **G~lack** m wallflower. **G~regen** m laburnum. **G~schmied** m goldsmith

Golf¹ m -[e]s,-e (Geog) gulf

Golf² nt -s gold. **G~platz** m golf course. **G~schläger** m golf club. **G~spieler(in)** m(f) golfer

Gondel f -,-n gondola; (Kabine) cabin

gönnen vt jdm etw g~ not begrudge s.o. sth; jdm etw nicht g~ begrudge s.o. sth

googeln vt/i ® google

Gör nt -s,-en, **Göre** f -,-n 🄣 kid

Gorilla m -s,-s gorilla

Gosse f -,-n gutter

Got|ik f - Gothic. **g~isch** adj Gothic

Gott m -[e]s, ⁻er God; (Myth) god

Götterspeise f jelly

Gottes|dienst m service. **G~lästerung** f blasphemy

Gottheit f -,-en deity

Göttin f -,-nen goddess

göttlich adj divine

gottlos adj ungodly; (atheistisch) godless

Grab nt -[e]s, ⁻er grave

graben† vi (haben) dig

Graben m -s, ⁻ ditch; (Mil) trench

Grab|mal nt tomb. **G~stein** m gravestone, tombstone

Grad m -[e]s,-e degree

Graf m -en,-en count

Grafik f -,-en graphics sg; (Kunst) graphic arts pl; (Druck) print

Gräfin f -,-nen countess

grafisch adj graphic; **g~e Darstellung** f diagram

Grafschaft f -,-en county

Gram m -s grief

grämen (sich) vr grieve

Gramm nt -s,-e gram

Gram|matik f -,-en grammar. **g~matikalisch** adj grammatical

Granat m -[e]s,-e garnet. **G~e** f -,-n shell; (Hand-) grenade

Granit m -s,-e granite

Gras nt -es, ⁻er grass. **g~en** vi (haben) graze. **G~hüpfer** m -s,- grasshopper

grässlich adj dreadful

Grat m -[e]s,-e [mountain] ridge

Gräte f -,-n fishbone

Gratifikation /-'tsjo:n/ f -,-en bonus

gratis adv free [of charge]. **G~probe** f free sample

Gratu|lant(in) m -en,-en (f -,-nen) well-wisher. **G~lation** f -,-en congratulations pl; (Glückwünsche) best wishes pl. **g~lieren** vi (haben) jdm **g~lieren** congratulate s.o. (zu on); (zum Geburtstag) wish s.o. happy birthday

grau adj, **G~** nt -s,- grey

Gräuel m -s,- horror

grauen v impers mir graut [es] davor I dread it. **G~** nt -s dread. **g~haft** adj gruesome; (grässlich) horrible

gräulich adj horrible

grausam adj cruel. **G~keit** f -,-en cruelty

graus|en v impers mir graust davor I dread it. **G~en** nt -s horror, dread. **g~ig** adj gruesome

gravieren vt engrave. **g~d** adj (fig) serious

graziös adj graceful

greifen† vt take hold of; (fangen) catch • vi (haben) reach (nach for); um sich g~ (fig) spread

Greis m -es,-e old man. **G~in** f -,-nen old woman

grell adj glaring; (Farbe) garish; (schrill) shrill

Gremium nt -s,-ien committee

Grenz|e f -,-n border; (Staats-) frontier; (Grundstücks-) boundary; (fig) limit. **g~en** vi (haben) border (an + acc on). **g~enlos** adj boundless; (maßlos) infinite

Griech|e m -n,-n Greek. **G~en-**

land nt -s Greece. **G~in** f -,-nen Greek woman. **g~isch** adj Greek. **G~isch** nt -[s] (Lang) Greek

Grieß m -es semolina

Griff m -[e]s,-e grasp, hold; (Hand-) movement of the hand; (Tür-, Messer-) handle; (Schwert-) hilt. **g~bereit** adj handy

Grill m -s,-s grill; (Garten-) barbecue

Grille f -,-n (Zool) cricket

grill|en vt grill; (im Freien) barbecue ●vi (haben) have a barbecue. **G~fest** nt barbecue

Grimasse f -,-n grimace; **G~n schneiden** pull faces

grimmig adj furious; (Kälte) bitter

grinsen vi (haben) grin

Grippe f -,-n influenza, 𝕋 flu

grob adj coarse; (unsanft, ungefähr) rough; (unhöflich) rude; (schwer) gross; (Fehler) bad; **g~ geschätzt** roughly. **G~ian** m -s,-e brute

Groll m -[e]s resentment. **g~en** vi (haben) be angry (dat with); (Donner:) rumble

Grönland nt -s Greenland

Gros nt -es,- (Maß) gross

Groschen m -s,- (Aust) groschen; 𝕋 ten-pfennig piece

groß adj big; (Anzahl, Summe) large; (bedeutend, stark) great; (g~artig) grand; (Buchstabe) capital; **g~ Ferien** summer holidays; **der größte Teil** the majority or bulk; **g~ werden** (Person:) grow up; **g~ in etw** (dat) **sein** be good at sth; **G~ und Klein** young and old; **im G~en und Ganzen** on the whole ●adv (feiern) in style; (𝕋: viel) much

groß|artig adj magnificent. **G~aufnahme** f close-up. **G~britannien** nt -s Great Britain. **G~buchstabe** m capital letter. **G~e(r)** m/f unser **G~er** our eldest;

die G~en the grown-ups; (fig) great pl

Größe f -,-n size; (Ausmaß) extent; (Körper-) height; (Bedeutsamkeit) greatness; (Math) quantity; (Person) great figure

Großeltern pl grandparents

Groß|handel m wholesale trade. **G~händler** m wholesaler. **G~macht** f superpower. **g~mütig** adj magnanimous. **G~mutter** f grandmother. **G~schreibung** f capitalization. **g~spurig** adj pompous; (überheblich) arrogant. **G~stadt** f [large] city. **g~städtisch** adj city. **G~teil** m large proportion; (Hauptteil) bulk

größtenteils adv for the most part

groß|tun† (sich) vr sep brag. **G~vater** m grandfather. **g~ziehen†** vt sep bring up; rear (Tier). **g~zügig** adj generous. **G~zügigkeit** f - generosity

Grotte f -,-n grotto

Grübchen nt -s,- dimple

Grube f -,-n pit

grübeln vi (haben) brood

Gruft f -,-ᵉe [burial] vault

grün adj green; **im G~en** out in the country; **die G~en** the Greens

Grund m -[e]s,-ᵉe ground; (Boden) bottom; (Hinter-) background; (Ursache) reason; **aus diesem G~e** for this reason; **im G~e** [genommen] basically; **auf G~ laufen** (Naut) run aground; **zu G~e richten/gehen** s. zugrunde. **G~begriffe** mpl basics. **G~besitzer** m landowner

gründ|en vt found, set up; start (Familie), (fig) base (auf + acc on); **sich g~en** be based (auf + acc on). **G~er(in)** m -s,- (f -,-nen) founder

Grund|farbe f primary colour. **G~form** f (Gram) infinitive. **G~**

gesetz nt (Pol) constitution.
G~lage f basis, foundation

>
> **Grundgesetz** The written German constitution, or 'basic law', which came into force in May 1949. It lays down the basic rights of German citizens and the legal framework of the German state.

gründlich adj thorough. **G~keit** f - thoroughness

Gründonnerstag m Maundy Thursday

Grund|regel f basic rule. **G~riss** m ground plan; (fig) outline. **G~satz** m principle. **g~sätzlich** adj fundamental; (im Allgemeinen) in principle; (prinzipiell) on principle. **G~schule** f primary school. **G~stück** nt plot [of land]

Gründung f -,-en foundation

Grün|span m verdigris. **G~streifen** m grass verge; (Mittel-) central reservation

grunzen vi (haben) grunt

Gruppe f -,-n group; (Reise-) party

gruppieren vt group

Gruselgeschichte f horror story. **g~ig** adj creepy

Gruß m -es,ⁿe greeting; (Mil) salute; **einen schönen G~ an X** give my regards to X; **viele/herzliche G~e** regards; **Mit freundlichen G~en** Yours sincerely/faithfully

grüßen vt/i (haben) say hallo (jdn to s.o.); (Mil) salute; **g~ Sie X von mir** give my regards to X; **grüß Gott!** (SGer, Aust) good morning/afternoon/evening!

gucken vi (haben) 🔲 look

Guerilla f -/guer'rɪljɑ/ f - guerrilla warfare. **G~kämpfer** m guerrilla

Gulasch nt & m -[e]s goulash

gültig adj valid

Gummi m & nt -s,-[s] rubber; (Harz) gum. **G~band** nt (pl -bänder) elastic or rubber band

gummiert adj gummed

Gummi|knüppel m truncheon. **G~stiefel** m gumboot, wellington. **G~zug** m elastic

Gunst f - favour

günstig adj favourable; (passend) convenient

Gurgel f -,-n throat. **g~n** vi (haben) gargle

Gurke f -,-n cucumber; (Essig-) gherkin

Gurt m -[e]s,-e strap; (Gürtel) belt; (Auto) safety belt. **G~band** nt (pl -bänder) waistband

Gürtel m -s,- belt. **G~linie** f waistline. **G~rose** f shingles sg

Guss m -es,ⁿe (Techn) casting; (Strom) stream; (Regen-) downpour; (Torten-) icing. **G~eisen** nt cast iron

gut adj good; (Gewissen) clear; (gütig) kind (zu to); **jdm gut sein** be fond of s.o.; **im G~en** amicably; **schon gut** that's all right ● adv well; (schmecken, riechen) good; (leicht) easily; **gut zu sehen** clearly visible; **gut drei Stunden** a good three hours

Gut nt -[e]s,ⁿer possession, property; (Land-) estate; **Gut und Böse** good and evil; **Güter** (Comm) goods

Gutacht|en nt -s,- expert's report. **G~er** m -s,- expert

gutartig adj good-natured; (Med) benign

Gute|(s) nt etwas/nichts **G~s** something/nothing good; **G~s tun** do good; **alles G~!** all the best!

Güte f -,-n goodness, kindness; (Qualität) quality

Güterzug m goods train

gut|gehen vi sep (sein) gut

113 | **gutmachen | Hacke**

gehen, s. **gehen. g~gehend*** adj **gut gehend,** s. **gehen. g~gläubig** adj trusting. **g~haben†** vt sep **fünfzig Euro g~haben** have fifty euros credit (**bei** with). **G~haben** nt **-s,-** [credit] balance; (Kredit) credit

gut|machen vt sep make up for; make good (Schaden). **g~mütig** adj good-natured. **G~mütigkeit** f good nature. **G~schein** m credit note; (Bon) voucher; (Geschenk-) gift token. **g~schreiben†** vt sep credit. **G~schrift** f credit

Guts|haus nt manor house **gut|tun†** vi sep (haben) **gut tun,** s. **tun. g~willig** adj willing

Gymnasium nt **-s,-ien** ≈ grammar school

> **Gymnasium** The secondary school that prepares pupils for the Abitur. After primary school the most academically gifted pupils go to a Gymnasium, or grammar school, for nine years. In their last three years they have some choice as to which subjects they study.

Gymnastik f - [keep-fit] exercises pl; (Turnen) gymnastics sg **Gynäko|loge** m **-n,-n** gynaecologist. **G~logie** f - gynaecology

Hh

H, h /haː/ nt **-,-** (Mus) B, b **Haar** nt **-[e]s,-e** hair; **sich** (dat) **die Haare od das H~ waschen** wash one's hair; **um ein H~** 🔲 very nearly. **H~bürste** f hairbrush.

h~en vi (haben) shed hairs; (Tier:) moult ● **vr sich h~en** moult. **h~ig** adj hairy; 🔲 tricky. **H~klemme** f hair grip. **H~nadelkurve** f hairpin bend. **H~schnitt** m haircut. **H~spange** f slide. **H~waschmittel** nt shampoo

Habe f - possessions pl

> **haben†**
> ● transitive verb
> ⋯▸ have; (im Präsens) have got 🔲. **er hat kein Geld** he has no money or 🔲 he hasn't got any money. **ich habe/hatte die Grippe** I've got flu/had flu. **was haben Sie da?** what have you got there? **wenn ich die Zeit hätte** if I had the time
> ⋯▸ (empfinden) **Angst/Hunger/ Durst haben** be frightened/hungry/thirsty. **was hat er?** what's wrong with him?
> ⋯▸ (+ Adj., es) **es gut/schlecht haben** be well/badly off. **es schwer haben** be having a difficult time
> ⋯▸ (+ zu) (müssen) **du hast zu gehorchen** you must obey
> ● auxiliary verb
> ⋯▸ have. **ich habe/hatte ihn eben gesehen** I have/I've/I had or I'd just seen him. **er hat es gewusst** he knew it. **er hätte ihr geholfen** he would have helped her
> ● reflexive verb
> ⋯▸ (🔲: sich aufregen) make a fuss. **hab dich nicht so!** don't make such a fuss!

Habgier f greed. **h~ig** adj greedy **Habicht** m **-[e]s,-e** hawk **Hachse** f **-,-n** (Culin) knuckle **Hackbraten** m meat loaf **Hacke**¹ f **-,-n** hoe; (Spitz-) pick

Hacke² f -,-n, **Hacken** m -s,- heel
hack|en vt hoe; (schlagen, zerkleinern) chop; (Vogel:) peck. **H~fleisch** nt mince

Hafen m -s,⁼ harbour; (See-) port. **H~arbeiter** m docker. **H~stadt** f port

Hafer m -s oats pl. **H~flocken** fpl [rolled] oats

Haft f - (Jur) custody; (H~strafe) imprisonment. **h~bar** adj (Jur) liable. **H~befehl** m warrant

haften vi (haben) cling; (kleben) stick; (bürgen) vouch/(Jur) be liable (für for)

Häftling m -s,-e detainee

Haftpflicht f (Jur) liability. **H~versicherung** f (Auto) third-party insurance

Haftung f - (Jur) liability

Hagebutte f -,-n rose hip

Hagel m -s hail. **h~n** vi (haben) hail

hager adj gaunt

Hahn m -[e]s,⁼e cock; (Techn) tap

Hähnchen nt -s,- (Culin) chicken

Hai[fisch] m -[e]s,-e shark

Häkchen nt -s,- tick

häkel|n vt/i (haben) crochet. **H~nadel** f crochet hook

Haken m -s,- hook; (Häkchen) tick; (🔲: Schwierigkeit) snag. **h~** vt hook (an + acc to). **H~kreuz** nt swastika

halb adj half; auf **h~em Weg** halfway ● adv half; **h~ drei** half past two; **fünf [Minuten] vor/nach h~ vier** twenty-five [minutes] past three/to four. **H~e(r,s)** f/m/nt half [a litre]

halber prep (+ gen) for the sake of; **Geschäfte h~** on business

Halbfinale nt semifinal

halbieren vt halve, divide in half; (Geometry) bisect

Halb|insel f peninsula. **H~kreis** m semicircle. **H~kugel** f hemisphere. **h~laut** adj low ● adv in an undertone. **H~mast** adv at half-mast. **H~mond** m half moon. **H~pension** f half board. **h~rund** adj semicircular. **H~schuh** m [flat] shoe. **h~tags** adv [for] half a day; **h~tags arbeiten** ≈ work part-time. **H~ton** m semitone. **h~wegs** adv half-way; (ziemlich) more or less. **h~wüchsig** adj adolescent. **H~zeit** f (Sport) half-time; (Spielzeit) half

Halde f -,-n dump, tip

Hälfte f -,-n half; **zur H~** half

Halfter f -,-n & nt -s,- holster

Halle f -,-n hall; (Hotel-) lobby; (Bahnhofs-) station concourse

hallen vi (haben) resound; (wider-) echo

Hallen- prefix indoor

hallo int hallo

Halluzination /-'tsio:n/ f -,-en hallucination

Halm m -[e]s,-e stalk; (Gras-) blade

Hals m -es,⁼e neck; (Kehle) throat; **aus vollem H~e** at the top of one's voice; (lachen) out loud. **H~band** nt (pl -bänder) collar. **H~schmerzen** mpl sore throat sg

halt int stop! (Mil) halt!; 🔲 wait a minute!

Halt m -[e]s,-e hold; (Stütze) support; (innerer) stability; (Anhalten) stop; **H~ machen** stop. **h~bar** adj durable; (Textiles) hard-wearing; (fig) tenable; **h~bar bis** (Comm) use by

halten† vt hold; make (Rede); give (Vortrag); (einhalten, bewahren) keep; [sich (dat)] etw **h~** keep (Hund); take (Zeitung); **h~ für** regard as; **viel h~ von** think highly of; **sich links h~** keep left; **sich**

h~ **an** (+ acc) (fig) keep to ● vi (haben) hold; (haltbar sein, bestehen bleiben) keep; (Freundschaft, Blumen:) last; (Halt machen) stop; **auf sich** (acc) h~ take pride in oneself; **zu jdm** h~ be loyal to s.o.

Halte|stelle f stop. **H~verbot** nt waiting restriction; **'H~verbot'** 'no waiting'

Haltung f -,-en (Körper:) posture; (Verhalten) manner; (Einstellung) attitude; (Fassung) composure; (Halten) keeping

Hammel m -s,- ram; (Culin) mutton. **H~fleisch** nt mutton

Hammer m -s,= hammer

hämmern vt/i (haben) hammer

Hamster m -s,- hamster. **h~n** vt/i 🔲 hoard

Hand f -,=e hand; **jdm die H~ geben** shake hands with s.o.; **rechter/linker H~** on the right/left; **zweiter H~** second-hand; **unter der H~** unofficially; (geheim) secretly; **H~ und Fuß haben** (fig) be sound. **H~arbeit** f manual work; (handwerklich) handicraft; (Nadelarbeit) needlework; (Gegenstand) hand-made article. **H~ball** m [German] handball. **H~bewegung** f gesture. **H~bremse** f handbrake. **H~buch** nt handbook, manual

Händedruck m handshake

Handel m -s trade, commerce; (Unternehmen) business; (Geschäft) deal; **H~ treiben** trade. **h~n** vi (haben) act; (Handel treiben) deal (**mit** in); **von etw od über etw** (acc) **h~n** deal with sth; **sich h~n um** be about, concern. **H~smarine** f merchant navy. **H~sschiff** nt merchant vessel. **H~sschule** f commercial college. **H~sware** f merchandise

Hand|feger m -s,- brush. **H~fläche** f palm. **H~gelenk** nt wrist.

H~gemenge nt -s,- scuffle. **H~gepäck** nt hand luggage. **h~geschrieben** adj hand-written. **h~greiflich** adj tangible; **h~greiflich werden** become violent. **H~griff** m handle

handhaben vt insep (reg) handle

Handikap /'hɛndikæp/ nt -s,-s handicap

Handkuss m kiss on the hand

Händler m -s,- dealer, trader

handlich adj handy

Handlung f -,-en act; (Handeln) action; (Roman:) plot; (Geschäft) shop. **H~sweise** f conduct

Hand|schellen fpl handcuffs. **H~schlag** m handshake. **H~schrift** f handwriting; (Text) manuscript. **H~schuh** m glove. **H~stand** m handstand. **H~tasche** f handbag. **H~tuch** nt towel

Handwerk nt craft, trade. **H~er** m -s,- craftsman; (Arbeiter) workman

Handy /'hɛndi/ nt -s,-s mobile phone, cell phone Amer

Hanf m -[e]s hemp

Hang m -[e]s,=e slope; (fig) inclination

Hänge|brücke f suspension bridge. **H~matte** f hammock

hängen[1] vt (reg) hang

hängen[2]† vi (haben) hang; **h~ an** (+ dat) (fig) be attached to; **h~ lassen** leave

Hannover nt -s Hanover

hänseln vt tease

hantieren vi (haben) busy oneself

Happen m -s,- mouthful; **einen H~ essen** have a bite to eat

Harfe f -,-n harp

Harke f -,-n rake. **h~n** vt/i (haben) rake

harmlos adj harmless;

(*arglos*) innocent

Harmonie f -,-n harmony

Harmonika f -,-s accordion; (*Mund-*) mouth organ

harmonisch adj harmonious

Harn m -[e]s urine. **H~blase** f bladder

Harpune f -,-n harpoon

hart adj hard; (*heftig*) violent; (*streng*) harsh

Härte f -,-n hardness; (*Strenge*) harshness; (*Not*) hardship. **h~n** vt harden

Hart|faserplatte f hardboard. **h~näckig** adj stubborn; (*ausdauernd*) persistent. **H~näckigkeit** f stubbornness; persistence

Harz nt -es,-e resin

Haschee nt -s,-s (*Culin*) hash

Haschisch nt & m -[s] hashish

Hase m -n,-n hare

Hasel f -,-n hazel. **H~maus** f dormouse. **H~nuss** f hazel nut

Hass m -es hatred

hassen vt hate

hässlich adj ugly; (*unfreundlich*) nasty. **H~keit** f - ugliness; nastiness

Hast f - haste. **h~ig** adj hasty, adv -ily, hurried

hast, **hat**, **hatte**, **hätte** s. haben

Haube f -,-n cap; (*Trocken-*) drier; (*Kühler-*) bonnet

Hauch m -[e]s breath; (*Luft-*) breeze; (*Duft*) whiff; (*Spur*) tinge. **h~dünn** adj very thin

Haue f -,-n pick; (□: *Prügel*) beating. **h~n†** vt beat; (*hämmern*) knock; (*meißeln*) hew; **sich h~n** fight; **übers Ohr h~n** 🆃 cheat ● vi (*haben*) bang (**auf** + acc on); **jdm ins Gesicht h~n** hit s.o. in the face

Haufen m -s,- heap, pile; (*Leute*) crowd

häufen vt heap or pile [up]; **sich h~** pile up; (*zunehmen*) increase

häufig adj frequent

Haupt nt -[e]s, Häupter head. **H~bahnhof** m main station. **H~fach** nt main subject. **H~gericht** nt main course

Häuptling m -s,-e chief

Haupt|mahlzeit f main meal. **H~mann** m (pl -leute) captain. **H~post** f main post office. **H~quartier** nt headquarters pl. **H~rolle** f lead; (fig) leading role. **H~sache** f main thing; **in der H~sache** in the main. **h~sächlich** adj main. **H~satz** m main clause. **H~stadt** f capital. **H~verkehrsstraße** f main road. **H~verkehrszeit** f rush hour. **H~wort** nt (pl -wörter) noun

Haus nt -es, Häuser house; (*Gebäude*) building; (*Schnecken-*) shell; **zu H~e** at home; **nach H~e** home. **H~arbeit** f housework; (*Sch*) homework. **H~arzt** m family doctor. **H~aufgaben** fpl homework sg. **H~besetzer** m -s,- squatter

Haus|frau f housewife. **h~gemacht** adj home-made. **H~halt** m -[e]s,-e household; (*Pol*) budget. **h~halten†** vi sep (*haben*) **h~halten mit** manage carefully; conserve (*Kraft*). **H~hälterin** f -,-nen housekeeper. **H~haltsgeld** nt housekeeping [money]. **H~haltsplan** m budget. **H~herr** m head of the household; (*Gastgeber*) host

Hausierer m -s,- hawker

Hauslehrer m [private] tutor. **H~in** f governess

häuslich adj domestic, (*Person*) domesticated

Haus|meister m caretaker. **H~ordnung** f house rules pl.

H~putz m cleaning. **H~rat** m
-[e]s household effects pl.
H~schlüssel m front-door key.
H~schuh m slipper. **H~suchung** f
[police] search. **H~suchungsbe-
fehl** m search warrant. **H~tier** nt
domestic animal; (*Hund, Katze*) pet.
H~tür f front door. **H~wirt** m
landlord. **H~wirtin** f landlady

Haut f -,**Häute** skin; (*Tier-*) hide.
H~arzt m dermatologist

häuten vt skin; **sich h~** moult

haut|eng adj skin-tight. **H~farbe**
f colour; (*Teint*) complexion

Hebamme f -,-n midwife

Hebel m -s,- lever

heben† vt lift; (*hoch-, steigern*)
raise; **sich h~** rise; (*Nebel:*) lift; (*sich
verbessern*) improve

hebräisch adj Hebrew

hecheln vi (*haben*) pant

Hecht m -[e]s,-e pike

Heck nt -s,-s (*Naut*) stern; (*Aviat*)
tail; (*Auto*) rear

Hecke f -,-n hedge

Heck|fenster nt rear window.
H~tür f hatchback

Heer nt -[e]s,-e army

Hefe f - yeast

Heft nt -[e]s,-e booklet; (*Sch*) exercise book; (*Zeitschrift*) issue. **h~en**
vt (*nähen*) tack; (*stecken*) pin/
(*klammern*) clip/(*mit Heftmaschine*)
staple (**an** + *acc* to). **H~er** m
-s,- file

heftig adj fierce, violent; (*Regen*)
heavy; (*Schmerz, Gefühl*) strong

Heft|klammer f staple; (*Büro-*)
paper clip. **H~maschine** f stapler.
H~zwecke f -,-n drawing pin

Heide[1] m -n,-n heathen

Heide[2] f -,-n heath; (*Bot*) heather.
H~kraut nt heather

Heidelbeere f bilberry

Heidin f -,-nen heathen

heikel adj difficult, tricky

heil adj undamaged, intact; (*Person*)
unhurt; **mit h~er Haut** 🛈 unscathed

Heil nt -s salvation

Heiland m -s (*Relig*) Saviour

Heil|anstalt f sanatorium; (*Ner-
ven-*) mental hospital. **H~bad** nt
spa. **h~bar** adj curable

Heilbutt m -[e]s,-e halibut

heilen vt cure; heal (*Wunde*) ● vi
(*sein*) heal

Heilgymnastik f physiotherapy

heilig adj holy; (*geweiht*) sacred;
der **H~e Abend** Christmas Eve; **die
h~e Anna** Saint Anne; (*Feiertag*);
h~ sprechen canonize. **H~abend**
m Christmas Eve. **H~e(r)** m/f saint.
H~enschein m halo. **H~keit** f -
sanctity, holiness. **H~tum** nt -s,**¨er**
shrine

heil|kräftig adj medicinal.
H~kräuter ntpl medicinal herbs.
H~mittel nt remedy. **H~prakti-
ker** m -s,- practitioner of alternative
medicine. **H~sarmee** f Salvation
Army. **H~ung** f - cure

Heim nt -[e]s,-e home; (*Studenten-*)
hostel. **h~** adv home

Heimat f -,-en home; (*Land*) native land. **H~stadt** f home town

heim|begleiten vt sep see
home. **H~computer** m home
computer. **h~fahren†** v sep ● vi
(*sein*) go/drive home ● vt take/drive
home. **H~fahrt** f way home.
h~gehen† vi sep (*sein*) go home

heimisch adj native, indigenous;
(*Pol*) domestic

Heim|kehr f - return [home].
h~kehren vi sep (*sein*) return
home. **h~kommen†** vi sep (*sein*)
come home

heimlich adj secret; **etw h~ tun**

do sth secretly. **H~keit** f -,-en secrecy; **H~keiten** secrets

Heim|reise f journey home. **H~spiel** nt home game. **h~suchen** vt sep afflict. **h~tückisch** adj treacherous; (Krankheit) insidious. **h~wärts** adv home. **H~weg** m way home. **H~weh** nt -s homesickness; **H~weh haben** be homesick. **H~werker** m -s,- handyman. **h~zahlen** vt sep jdm etw **h~zahlen** (fig) pay s.o. back for sth

Heirat f -,-en marriage. **h~en** vt/i (haben) marry. **H~santrag** m proposal; **jdm einen H~santrag machen** propose to s.o.

heiser adj hoarse. **H~keit** f - hoarseness

heiß adj hot; (hitzig) heated; (leidenschaftlich) fervent

heißen† vi (haben) be called; (bedeuten) mean; **ich heiße ...** my name is ...; **wie h~Sie?** what is your name? **wie heißt ... auf Englisch?** what's the English for ...? ● vt call; **jdn etw tun h~** tell s.o. to do sth

heiter adj cheerful; (Wetter) bright; (amüsant) amusing; **aus h~em Himmel** (fig) out of the blue

Heiz|anlage f heating; (Auto) heater. **H~decke** f electric blanket. **h~en** vt heat; light (Ofen) ● vi (haben) put the heating on; (Ofen:) give out heat. **H~gerät** nt heater. **H~kessel** m boiler. **H~körper** m radiator. **H~lüfter** m -s,- fan heater. **H~material** nt fuel. **H~ung** f -,-en heating; (Heizkörper) radiator

Hektar nt & m -s,- hectare

Held m -en,-en hero. **h~enhaft** adj heroic. **H~entum** nt -s heroism. **H~in** f -,-nen heroine

helf|en† vi (haben) help (jdm s.o.);

(nützen) be effective; **sich** (dat) **nicht zu h~en wissen** not know what to do; **es hilft nichts** it's no use. **H~er(in)** m -s,- (f -,-nen) helper, assistant

hell adj light; (Licht ausstrahlend, klug) bright; (Stimme) clear; (🔲: völlig) utter; **h~es Bier** ≈ lager ● adv brightly

Hell|igkeit f - brightness. **H~seher(in)** m -s,- (f -,-nen) clairvoyant

Helm m -[e]s,-e helmet

Hemd nt -[e]s,-en vest; (Ober-) shirt

Hemisphäre f -,-n hemisphere

hemm|en vt check; (verzögern) impede; (fig) inhibit. **H~ung** f -,-en (fig) inhibition; (Skrupel) scruple; **H~ungen haben** be inhibited. **h~ungslos** adj unrestrained

Hendl nt -s,-[n] (Aust) chicken

Hengst m -[e]s,-e stallion

Henkel m -s,- handle

Henne f -,-n hen

her adv here; (zeitlich) ago; **her mit** ... | give me ...! **von Norden/weit her** from the north/far away; **vom Thema her** as far as the subject is concerned; **her sein** come (von from); **es ist schon lange her** it was a long time ago

herab adv down [here]; **von oben h~** from above; (fig) condescending

herablassen† vt sep let down; **sich h~** condescend (zu to)

herab|sehen† vi sep (haben) look down (auf + acc on). **h~setzen** vt sep reduce, cut; (fig) belittle

Heraldik f - heraldry

heran adv near; [bis] **h~ an** (+ acc) up to. **h~kommen** vi sep (sein) approach; **h~kommen an** (+ acc) come up to; (erreichen) get at; (fig) measure up to. **h~machen**

(sich) vr sep **sich h~machen an** (+ acc) approach; get down to (Arbeit). **h~wachsen†** vi sep (sein) grow up. **h~ziehen†** v sep ● vt pull up (**an** + acc to); (züchten) raise; (h~bilden) train; (hinzuziehen) call in ● vi (sein) approach

herauf adv up [here]; **die Treppe h~** up the stairs. **h~setzen** vt sep raise, increase

heraus adv out (**aus** of); **h~ damit** od **mit der Sprache!** out with it! **h~bekommen†** vt sep get out; (ausfindig machen) find out; (lösen) solve; **Geld h~bekommen** get change. **h~finden†** v sep ● vt find out ● vi (haben) find one's way out. **h~fordern†** vt sep provoke; challenge (Person). **H~forderung** f provocation; challenge. **H~gabe** f handing over; (Admin) issue; (Veröffentlichung) publication. **h~geben†** vt sep hand over; (Admin) issue; (veröffentlichen) publish; edit (Zeitschrift); **jdm Geld h~geben** give s.o. change ● vi (haben) give change (**auf** + acc for). **H~geber** m -s,- publisher; editor. **h~halten† (sich)** vr sep (fig) keep out (**aus** of). **h~kommen†** vi sep (sein) come out; (aus Schwierigkeit, Takt) get out; **auf eins** od **dasselbe h~kommen** [T] come to the same thing. **h~lassen†** vt sep let out. **h~nehmen†** vt sep take out; **sich zu viel h~nehmen** (fig) take liberties. **h~reden (sich)** vr sep make excuses. **h~rücken** vt sep move out; (hergeben) hand over ● vi (sein) **h~rücken mit** hand over; (fig: sagen) come out with. **h~schlagen†** vt sep knock out; (fig) gain. **h~stellen** vt sep put out; **sich h~stellen** turn out (**als** to be; **dass** that). **h~ziehen†** vt sep pull out

herb adj sharp; (Wein) dry; (fig) harsh

herbei adv here. **h~führen** vt sep (fig) bring about. **h~schaffen** vt sep get. **h~sehnen** vt sep long for

Herberg|e f -,-n [youth] hostel; (Unterkunft) lodging. **H~svater** m warden

herbestellen vt sep summon

herbitten† vt sep ask to come

herbringen† vt sep bring [here]

Herbst m -[e]s,-e autumn. **h~lich** adj autumnal

Herd m -[e]s,-e stove, cooker

Herde f -,-n herd; (Schaf-) flock

herein adv in [here]; **h~!** come in! **h~bitten†** vt sep ask in. **h~fallen†** vi sep (sein) [T] be taken in (**auf** + acc by). **h~kommen†** vi sep (sein) come in. **h~lassen†** vt sep let in. **h~legen** vt sep [T] take for a ride

Herfahrt f journey/drive here

herfallen† vi sep (sein) ~ **über** (+ acc) attack; fall upon (Essen)

hergeben† vt sep hand over; (fig) give up

hergehen† vi sep (sein) **h~ vor** (+ dat) walk along in front of; **es ging lustig her** [T] there was a lot of merriment

herholen vt sep fetch; **weit hergeholt** (fig) far-fetched

Hering m -s,-e herring; (Zeltpflock) tent peg

her|kommen† vi sep (sein) come here; **wo kommt das her?** where does it come from? **h~kömmlich** adj traditional. **H~kunft** f - origin

herleiten vt sep derive

hermachen vt sep **viel/wenig h~** be impressive/unimpressive; (wichtig nehmen) make a lot of/little fuss (**von** of); **sich h~ über** (+ acc) fall upon; tackle (Arbeit)

Hermelin¹ nt -s,-e (Zool) stoat

Hermelin² m -s,-e (Pelz) ermine

Hernie /ˈhɛrnjə/ f -,-n hernia

Heroin nt -s heroin

heroisch adj heroic

Herr m -n,-en gentleman; (*Gebieter*) master (über + *acc* of); [*Gott,*] der H~ the Lord [God]; H~ Meier Mr Meier; Sehr geehrte H~en Dear Sirs. **H~enhaus** nt manor [house]. **h~enlos** adj ownerless; (*Tier*) stray

Herrgott m der H~ the Lord

herrichten vt sep prepare; **wieder h~** renovate

Herrin f -,-nen mistress

herrlich adj marvellous; (*großartig*) magnificent

Herrschaft f -,-en rule; (*Macht*) power; (*Kontrolle*) control; **meine H~en!** ladies and gentlemen!

herrsch|en vi (*haben*) rule; (*verbreitet sein*) prevail; **es h~te Stille** there was silence. **H~er(in)** m -s,- (f -,-nen) ruler

herrühren vi (*haben*) stem (**von** from)

herstammen vi sep (*haben*) come (**aus/von** from)

herstell|en vt sep establish; (*Comm*) manufacture, make. **H~er** m -s,- manufacturer, maker. **H~ung** f - establishment; manufacture

herüber adv over [here]

herum adv im Kreis h~ [round] in a circle; **falsch h~** the wrong way round; **um ... h~** round ... ; (*ungefähr*) [round] about ; **h~ sein** be over. **h~drehen** vt sep turn round/ (*wenden*) over; turn (*Schlüssel*). **h~gehen†** vi sep (*sein*) walk around; (*Zeit:*) pass; **h~gehen um** go round. **h~kommen†** vi sep (*sein*) get about; **h~kommen um** get round; come round (*Ecke*); **um etw [nicht] h~kommen** (*fig*) [not] get out of sth. **h~sitzen†** vi sep

(*haben*) sit around; **h~sitzen um** sit round. **h~sprechen† (sich)** vr sep (*Gerücht:*) get about. **h~treiben† (sich)** vr sep hang around. **h~ziehen†** vi sep (*sein*) move around; (*ziellos*) wander about

herunter adv down [here]; **die Treppe h~** down the stairs. **h~fallen†** vi fall off. **h~gekommen** adj (*fig*) run-down; (*Gebäude*) dilapidated; (*Person*) down-at-heel. **h~kommen†** vi sep (*sein*) come down; (*fig*) go to rack and ruin; (*Firma, Person:*) go downhill; (*gesundheitlich:*) get run down. **h~laden** vt † download. **h~lassen†** vt sep let down, lower. **h~machen** vt sep ① reprimand; (*herabsetzen*) run down. **h~spielen** vt sep (*fig*) play down

hervor adv out (*aus* of). **h~bringen†** vt sep produce; utter (*Wort*). **h~gehen†** vi sep (*sein*) come/(*sich ergeben*) emerge/(*folgen*) follow (**aus** from). **h~heben†** vt sep (*fig*) stress, emphasize. **h~ragen** vi (*haben*) jut out; (*fig*) stand out. **h~ragend** adj (*fig*) outstanding. **h~rufen†** vt sep (*fig*) cause. **h~stehen†** vi sep (*haben*) protrude. **h~treten†** vi sep (*sein*) protrude, bulge; (*fig*) stand out. **h~tun† (sich)** vr sep (*fig*) distinguish oneself; (*angeben*) show off

Herweg m way here

Herz nt -ens,-en heart; (*Kartenspiel*) hearts pl; **sich** (*dat*) **ein H~ fassen** pluck up courage. **H~anfall** m heart attack

herzhaft adj hearty; (*würzig*) savoury

herziehen† v sep ● vt hinter sich (*dat*) h~ pull along [behind one] ● vi sep **hinter jdm h~** follow along behind s.o.; **über jdn** ① run s.o. down

herz|ig adj sweet, adorable. **H~infarkt** m heart attack. **H~klopfen** nt -s palpitations pl

herzlich adj cordial; (warm) warm; (aufrichtig) sincere; **h~en Dank!** many thanks! **h~e Grüße** kind regards

herzlos adj heartless

Herzog m -s,⁻e duke. **H~in** f -,-nen duchess. **H~tum** nt -s,⁻er duchy

Herzschlag m heartbeat; (Med) heart failure

Hessen nt -s Hesse

heterosexuell adj heterosexual

Hetze f - rush; (Kampagne) virulent campaign (**gegen** against). **h~n** vt chase; **sich h~n** hurry

Heu nt -s hay

Heuchelei f - hypocrisy

heuch|eln vt feign ● vi (haben) pretend. **H~ler(in)** m -s,- / -,-nen) hypocrite. **h~lerisch** adj hypocritical

heuer adv (Aust) this year

heulen vi (haben) howl; (☐: weinen) cry

Heurige This is an Austrian term for both a new wine and an inn with new wine on tap, especially an inn with its own vineyard in the Vienna region. A garland of pine twigs outside the gates of the Heurige shows that the new barrel has been tapped.

i

Heu|schnupfen m hay fever. **H~schober** m -s,- haystack. **H~schrecke** f -,-n grasshopper

heut|e adv today; (heutzutage) nowadays; **h~e früh** od **Morgen** this morning; **von h~e auf morgen** from one day to the next.

h~ig adj today's; (gegenwärtig) present; **der h~ige Tag** today. **h~zutage** adv nowadays

Hexe f -,-n witch. **h~n** vi (haben) work magic. **H~nschuss** m lumbago

Hieb m -[e]s,-e blow; (Peitschen-) lash; **H~e** hiding sg

hier adv here; **h~ sein/bleiben/lassen/behalten** be/stay/leave/keep here; **h~ und da** here and there; (zeitlich) now and again

hier|auf adv on this/these; (antworten) to this; (zeitlich) after this. **h~aus** adv out of or from this/these. **h~durch** adv through this/these; (Ursache) as a result of this. **h~her** adv here. **h~hin** adv here. **h~in** adv in this/these. **h~mit** adv with this/these; (Comm) herewith; (Admin) hereby. **h~nach** adv after this/these; (demgemäß) according to this/these. **h~über** adv over/(höher) above this/these; (sprechen, streiten) about this/these. **h~von** adv from this/these; (h~über) about this/these; (Menge) of this/these. **h~zu** adv to this/these; (h~für) for this/these. **h~zulande** adv here

hiesig adj local. **H~e(r)** m/f local

Hilfe f -,-n help, aid; **um H~e rufen** call for help. **H~los** adj helpless. **H~losigkeit** f - helplessness. **h~reich** adj helpful

Hilfs|arbeiter m unskilled labourer. **h~bedürftig** adj needy; **h~bedürftig sein** be in need of help. **h~bereit** adj helpful. **H~kraft** f helper. **H~mittel** nt aid. **H~verb** nt auxiliary verb

Himbeere f raspberry

Himmel m -s,- sky; (Relig & fig) heaven; (Bett-) canopy; **unter freiem H~** in the open air. **H~bett** nt four-poster [bed].

H~fahrt f Ascension

himmlisch adj heavenly

hin adv there; **hin und her** to and fro; **hin und zurück** there and back; (Rail) return; **hin und wieder** now and again; **an** (+ dat) ... **hin** along; **auf** (+ acc) ... **hin** in reply to (Brief, Anzeige); on (jds Rat); **zu od nach ... hin** towards; **hin sein** 🆃 be gone; **es ist noch lange hin** it's a long time yet

hinauf adv up [there]. **h~gehen**† vi sep (sein) go up. **h~setzen** vt sep raise

hinaus adv out [there]; (nach draußen) outside; **zur Tür h~** out of the door; **auf Jahre h~** for years to come; **über etw** (acc) **h~** be-yond sth; (Menge) [over and] above sth; **über etw** (acc) **h~ sein** (fig) be past sth. **h~gehen**† vi sep (sein) go out; (Zimmer:) face (**nach Norden** north); **h~gehen über** (+ acc) go beyond, exceed. **h~laufen**† vi sep (sein) run out; **h~laufen auf** (+ acc) (fig) amount to. **h~lehnen (sich)** vr sep lean out. **h~schieben**† vt sep push out; (fig) put off. **h~werfen**† vt sep throw out; (🆃: entlassen) fire. **h~wollen** vi sep (haben) want to go out; **h~wollen auf** (+ acc) (fig) aim at. **h~ziehen**† v sep ● vt pull out; (in die Länge ziehen) drag out; (verzögern) delay; **sich h~ziehen** drag on; be delayed ● vi (sein) move out. **h~zögern** vt delay; **sich h~zögern** be delayed

Hinblick m im **H~ auf** (+ acc) in view of; (hinsichtlich) regarding

hinder|lich adj awkward; **jdm h~lich sein** hamper s.o. **h~n** vt hamper; (verhindern) prevent. **H~nis** nt -ses,-se obstacle. **H~nis-rennen** nt steeplechase

Hindu m -s,-s Hindu.

hindurch adv through it/them

hinein adv in [there]; (nach drinnen) inside; **h~ in** (+ acc) into. **h~fallen**† vi sep (sein) fall in. **h~gehen**† vi sep (sein) go in; **h~gehen in** (+ acc) go into. **h~reden** vi sep (haben) jdm **h~reden** interrupt s.o.; (sich einmischen) interfere in s.o.'s affairs. **h~versetzen (sich)** vr sep **sich in jds Lage h~versetzen** put oneself in s.o.'s position. **h~ziehen**† vt sep pull in; **h~ziehen in** (+ acc) pull into; **in etw** (acc) **h~gezogen werden** (fig) become involved in sth

hin|fahren v sep ● vi (sein) go/drive there ● vt take/drive there. **H~fahrt** f journey there/drive there; (Rail) outward journey. **h~fallen**† vi sep (sein) fall. **h~fliegen**† v sep ● vi (sein) fly there; (🆃: fall) ● vt fly there. **H~flug** m flight there; (Aviat) outward flight

Hingeb|ung f - devotion. **h~ungsvoll** adj devoted

hingehen† vi sep (sein) go/(zu Fuß) walk there; (vergehen) pass; **h~ zu** go up to; **wo gehst du hin?** where are you going?

hingerissen adj rapt; **h~ sein** be carried away (**von** by)

hinhalten† vt sep hold out; (warten lassen) keep waiting

hinken vi (haben/sein) limp

hin|knien (sich) vr sep kneel down. **h~kommen**† vi sep (sein) get there; (h~gehören) belong, go; (🆃: auskommen) manage (**mit** with); (🆃: stimmen) be right. **h~laufen**† vi sep (sein) run/(gehen) walk there. **h~legen** vt sep lay or put down; **sich h~legen** lie down. **h~nehmen**† vt sep (fig) accept

hinreichen v sep ● vt hand (dat to) ● vi (haben) extend (**bis** to); (ausreichen) be adequate. **h~d** adj adequate

Hinreise f journey there; (Rail)
outward journey

hinreißen† vt sep (fig) carry
away; **sich h~ lassen** get carried
away. **h~d** adj ravishing

hinricht|en vt sep execute.
H~ung f execution

hinschreiben† vt sep write there;
(aufschreiben) write down

hinsehen† vi sep (haben) look

hinsetzen vt sep put down; **sich
h~** sit down

Hinsicht f - **in dieser H~** in this
respect; **in finanzieller H~** financially. **h~lich** prep (+ gen) regarding

hinstellen vt sep put or set down;
park (Auto)

hinstrecken vt sep hold out; **sich
h~** extend

hinten adv at the back; **dort h~**
back there; **nach/von h~** to the
back/from behind. **h~herum** adv
round the back; ⬛ by devious means

hinter prep (+ dat/acc) behind;
(nach) after; **h~ jdm/etw herlau-
fen** run after s.o./something; **h~
etw** (dat) **stecken** (fig) be behind
sth; **h~ etw** (acc) **kommen** (fig)
get to the bottom of sth; **etw h~
sich** (acc) **bringen** get sth over [and
done] with

Hinterbliebene pl (Admin) sur-
viving dependants; **die H~n** the
bereaved family sg

hintere|(r,s) adj back, rear; **h~s
Ende** far end

hintereinander adv one be-
hind/(zeitlich) after the other; **dreimal h~** three times in succession

Hintergedanke m ulterior
motive

hintergehen† vt deceive

Hinter|grund m background.

H~halt m -[e]s,-e ambush.
h~hältig adj underhand

hinterher adv behind, after; (zeitlich) afterwards

Hinter|hof m back yard. **H~kopf**
m back of the head

hinterlassen† vt leave [behind];
(Jur) leave, bequeath (dat to).
H~schaft f -,-en (Jur) estate

hinterlegen vt deposit

Hinter|leib m (Zool) abdomen.
H~list f deceit. **h~listig** adj de-
ceitful. **H~n** m -s,- ⬛ bottom,
backside. **H~rad** nt rear or back
wheel. **h~rücks** adv from behind.
h~ste(r,s) adj last; **h~ste Reihe**
back row. **H~teil** nt ⬛ behind.
H~treppe f back stairs pl

hinterziehen† vt (Admin) evade

hinüber adv over or across [there];
h~ sein (⬛: unbrauchbar, tot) have
had it. **h~gehen**† vi sep (sein) go
over or across; **h~gehen über** (+
acc) cross

hinunter adv down [there].
h~gehen† vi sep (sein) go down.
h~schlucken vt sep swallow

Hinweg m way there

hinweg adv away, off; **h~ über** (+
acc) over; **über eine Zeit h~** over a
period. **h~kommen**† vi sep (sein)
h~kommen über (+ acc) (fig) get
over. **h~sehen**† vi sep (haben)
h~sehen über (+ acc) see over;
(fig) overlook. **h~setzen** (sich) vr
sep **sich h~setzen über** (+ acc)
ignore

Hinweis m -es,-e reference; (Andeutung) hint; (Anzeichen) indication;
unter H~ auf (+ acc) with reference to. **h~en**† v sep ● vi (haben)
point (**auf** + acc to) ● vt **jdn auf
etw** (acc) **h~en** point sth out
to s.o.

hinwieder adv on the other hand

h

hin|zeigen vi sep (haben) point (auf + acc to). **h~ziehen†** vt sep pull; (fig: in die Länge ziehen) drag out; (verzögern) delay; **sich h~ziehen** drag on

hinzu adv in addition. **h~fügen** vt sep add. **h~kommen** vt sep (sein) be added; (ankommen) arrive [on the scene]; join (**zu jdm** s.o.). **h~ziehen†** vt sep call in

Hiobsbotschaft f bad news sg

Hirn nt -s brain; (Culin) brains pl. **H~hautentzündung** f meningitis

Hirsch m -[e]s,-e deer; (männlich) stag; (Culin) venison

Hirse f - millet

Hirt m -en,-en, **Hirte** m -n,-n shepherd

hissen vt hoist

Histor|iker m -s,- historian. **h~isch** adj historical; (bedeutend) historic

Hitz|e f - heat. **h~ig** adj (fig) heated; (Person) hot-headed; (jähzornig) hot-tempered. **H~schlag** m heat-stroke

H-Milch /'ha:-/ f long-life milk

Hobby nt -s,-s hobby

Hobel m -s,- (Techn) plane; (Culin) slicer. **h~n** vt/i (haben) plane. **H~späne** mpl shavings

hoch adj (attrib hohe(r,s)) high; (Baum, Mast) tall; (Offizier) high-ranking; (Alter) great; (Summe) large; (Strafe) heavy; **hohe Schuhe** ankle boots ● adv high; (sehr) highly; **h~ gewachsen** tall; **h~ begabt** highly gifted; **h~ gestellte Persönlichkeit** important person; **die Treppe h~** up the stairs; **sechs Mann h~** six of us/them. **H~** nt -s,-s cheer; (Meteorology) high

Hoch|achtung f high esteem. **H~achtungsvoll** adv Yours faithfully. **H~betrieb** m great activity;

in den Geschäften herrscht H~betrieb the shops are terribly busy. **H~deutsch** nt High German. **H~druck** m high pressure. **H~ebene** f plateau. **h~fahren†** vi sep (sein) go up; (auffahren) start up; (aufbrausen) flare up. **h~gehen†** vi sep (sein) go up; (explodieren) blow up; (aufbrausen) flare up. **h~gestellt** attrib adj (Zahl) superior; (fig) *h~ gestellt, s. hoch. **H~glanz** m high gloss. **h~gradig** adj extreme. **h~hackig** adj high-heeled. **h~halten†** vt sep hold up; (fig) uphold. **H~haus** nt high-rise building. **h~heben†** vt sep lift up; raise (Hand). **h~kant** adv on end. **h~kommen** vi sep (sein) come up; (aufstehen) get up; (fig) get on [in the world]. **H~konjunktur** f boom. **h~krempeln** vt sep roll up. **h~leben** vi sep (haben) **h~leben lassen** give three cheers for; **H~mut** m pride, arrogance. **h~nä-sig** adj 🔢 snooty. **H~ofen** m blast-furnace. **h~ragen** vi sep rise [up]; (Turm:) soar. **H~ruf** m cheer. **H~saison** f high season. **h~schlagen†** vt sep turn up (Kragen). **H~schule** f university; (Musik-, Kunst-) academy. **H~sommer** m midsummer. **H~spannung** f high/(fig) great tension. **h~spielen** vt sep (fig) magnify. **H~sprung** m high jump

höchst adv extremely, most

Hochstapler m -s,- confidence trickster

höchst|e(r,s) adj highest; (Baum, Turm) tallest; (oberste, größte) top; **es ist h~e Zeit** it is high time. **h~ens** adv at most; (es sei denn) except perhaps. **H~geschwindigkeit** f top or maximum speed. **H~maß** nt maximum. **h~persönlich** adv in person. **H~preis** m top price. **H~temperatur** f maximum temperature

Hoch|verrat m high treason. **H~wasser** nt high tide; (Überschwemmung) floods pl. **H~würden** m -s Reverend; (Anrede) Father

Hochzeit f -,-en wedding. **H~skleid** nt wedding dress. **H~sreise** f honeymoon [trip]. **H~stag** m wedding day/(Jahrestag) anniversary

Hocke f - in der **H~** sitzen squat. **h~n** vi (haben) squat ● vr sich **h~n** squat down

Hocker m -s,- stool

Höcker m -s,- bump; (Kamel-) hump

Hockey /hoki/ nt -s hockey

Hode f -,-n, **Hoden** m -s,- testicle

Hof m -[e]s, ¨e [court]yard; (Bauern-) farm; (Königs-) court; (Schul-) playground; (Astronomy) halo

hoffen vt/i (haben) hope (**auf** + acc for). **h~tlich** adv I hope so, hopefully

Hoffnung f -,-en hope. **h~slos** adj hopeless. **h~svoll** adj hopeful

höflich adj polite. **H~keit** f -,-en politeness, courtesy

hohe(r,s) adj s. hoch

Höhe f -,-n height; (Aviat, Geog) altitude; (Niveau) level; (einer Summe) size; (An-) hill

Hoheit f -,-en (Staats-) sovereignty; (Titel) Highness. **H~sgebiet** nt

[sovereign] territory. **H~szeichen** nt national emblem

Höhe|nlinie f contour line. **H~nsonne** f sun lamp. **H~punkt** m (fig) climax, peak. **h~r** adj & adv higher; **h~re Schule** secondary school

hohl adj hollow; (leer) empty

Höhle f -,-n cave; (Tier-) den; (Hohlraum) cavity; (Augen-) socket

Hohl|maß nt measure of capacity. **H~raum** m cavity

Hohn m -s scorn, derision

höhnen vt deride

holen vt fetch, get; (kaufen) buy; (nehmen) take (**aus** from)

Holland nt -s Holland

Hollände|r m -s,- Dutchman; **die H~r** the Dutch pl. **H~erin** f -,-nen Dutchwoman. **h~isch** adj Dutch

Höll|e f - hell. **h~isch** adj infernal; (schrecklich) terrible

Holunder m -s (Bot) elder

Holz nt -es, ¨er wood; (Nutz-) timber. **H~blasinstrument** nt woodwind instrument

hölzern adj wooden

Holz|hammer m mallet. **~ig** adj woody. **H~kohle** f charcoal. **H~schnitt** m woodcut. **H~wolle** f wood shavings pl

Homöopathie f - homoeopathy

homöopathisch adj homoeopathic

homosexuell adj homosexual. **H~e(r)** m/f homosexual

Honig m -s honey. **H~wabe** f honeycomb

Hono|rar nt -s,-e fee. **h~rieren** vt remunerate; (fig) reward

Hopfen m -s hops pl; (Bot) hop

hopsen vi (sein) jump

horchen vi (haben) listen (**auf** +

acc to); (*heimlich*) eavesdrop

hören vt hear; (*an-*) listen to ● vi (*haben*) hear; (*horchen*) listen; (*gehorchen*) obey; **h~ auf** (+ *acc*) listen to

Hör|er m -s,- listener; (*Teleph*) receiver. **H~funk** m radio. **H~gerät** nt hearing aid

Horizon|t m -[e]s horizon. **h~tal** adj horizontal

Hormon nt -s,-e hormone

Horn nt -s,⁺er horn. **H~haut** f hard skin; (*Augen-*) cornea

Hornisse f -,-n hornet

Horoskop nt -[e]s,-e horoscope

Horrorfilm m horror film

Hör|saal m (*Univ*) lecture hall. **H~spiel** nt radio play

Hort m -[e]s,-e (*Schatz*) hoard; (*fig*) refuge. **h~en** vt hoard

Hortensie /-jə/ f -,-n hydrangea

Hose f -,-n, **Hosen** pl trousers pl. **H~nrock** m culottes pl. **H~nschlitz** m fly, flies pl. **H~nträger** mpl braces

Hostess f -,-ţessen hostess; (*Aviat*) air hostess

Hostie /ˈhɔstjə/ f -,-n (*Relig*) host

Hotel nt -s,-s hotel

hübsch adj pretty; (*nett*) nice

Hubschrauber m -s,- helicopter

Huf m -[e]s,-e hoof. **H~eisen** nt horseshoe

Hüft|e f -,-n hip. **H~gürtel** m -s,- girdle

Hügel m -s,- hill. **h~ig** adj hilly

Huhn nt -s,⁺er chicken; (*Henne*) hen

Hühn|chen nt -s,- chicken. **H~erauge** nt corn **H~erstall** m henhouse

Hülle f -,-n cover; (*Verpackung*) wrapping; (*Platten-*) sleeve. **h~n** vt wrap

Hülse f -,-n (*Bot*) pod; (*Etui*) case. **H~nfrüchte** fpl pulses

human adj humane. **H~ität** f - humanity

Hummel f -,-n bumble bee

Hummer m -s,- lobster

Hum|or m -s humour; **H~or haben** have a sense of humour. **h~orvoll** adj humorous

humpeln vi (*sein/haben*) hobble

Humpen m -s,- tankard

Hund m -[e]s,-e dog; (*Jagd-*) hound. **H~ehütte** f kennel

hundert inv adj one/a hundred. **H~** nt -s,-e hundred; **H~e od h~e von** hundreds of. **H~jahrfeier** f centenary. **h~prozentig** adj & adv one hundred per cent. **h~ste(r,s)** adj hundredth. **H~stel** nt -s,- hundredth

Hündin f -,-nen bitch

Hüne m -n,-n giant

Hunger m -s hunger; **H~ haben** be hungry. **h~n** vi (*haben*) starve. **H~snot** f famine

hungrig adj hungry

Hupe f -,-n (*Auto*) horn. **h~n** vi (*haben*) sound one's horn

hüpfen vi (*sein*) skip; (*Frosch:*) hop; (*Grashüpfer:*) jump

Hürde f -,-n (*Sport & fig*) hurdle; (*Schaf-*) pen, fold

Hure f -,-n whore

hurra int hurray

husten vi (*haben*) cough. **H~** m -s cough. **H~saft** m cough mixture

Hut¹ m -[e]s,⁺e hat; (*Pilz-*) cap

Hut² f - **auf der H~ sein** be on one's guard (**vor** + *dat* against)

hüten vt watch over; tend (*Tiere*); (*aufpassen*) look after; **das Bett h~ müssen** be confined to bed; **sich h~** be on one's guard (**vor** + *dat* against); **sich h~**, **etw zu tun** take care not to do sth

Hütte f -,-n hut; (Hunde-) kennel; (Techn) iron and steel works. **H~nkäse** m cottage cheese. **H~nkunde** f metallurgy

Hyäne f -,-n hyena

hydraulisch adj hydraulic

Hygien|e /hy'gje:nə/ f - hygiene. **h~isch** adj hygienic

Hypno|se f - hypnosis. **h~tisch** adj hypnotic. **H~tiseur** m -s,-e hypnotist. **h~tisieren** vt hypnotize

Hypochonder /hypo'xɔndɐ/ m -s,- hypochondriac

Hypothek f -,-en mortgage

Hypothese f -,-n hypothesis

Hys|terie f - hysteria. **h~terisch** adj hysterical

• •

I i

• •

ich pron I; **ich bins** it's me. **Ich** nt -[s],-[s] self; (Psychology) ego

IC-Zug /iːˈtseː-/ m inter-city train

ideal adj ideal. **I~** nt -s,-e ideal. **I~ismus** m - idealism. **I~ist(in)** m -en,-en (f -,-nen) idealist. **i~istisch** adj idealistic

Idee f -,-n idea; fixe **I~** obsession

identifizieren vt identify

identisch adj identical

Identität f -,-en identity

Ideo|logie f -,-n ideology. **i~logisch** adj ideological

idiomatisch adj idiomatic

Idiot m -en,-en idiot. **i~isch** adj idiotic

idyllisch /iˈdʏlɪʃ/ adj idyllic

Igel m -s,- hedgehog

ihm pron (dat of er, es) [to] him; (Ding, Tier) [to] it

ihn pron (acc of er) him; (Ding, Tier) it. **i~en** pron (dat of sie pl) [to] them. **I~en** pron (dat of Sie) [to] you

ihr pron (2nds pers pl) you ● (dat of sie sg) [to] her; (Ding, Tier) [to] it ● poss pron her; (Ding, Tier) its; (pl) their. **Ihr** poss pron your. **i~e(r,s)** poss pron hers; (pl) theirs. **I~e(r,s)** poss pron yours. **i~erseits** adv for her/(pl) their part. **I~erseits** adv on your part. **i~etwegen** adv for her/(Ding,Tier) its/(pl) their sake; (wegen) because of her/it/them, on her/its/their account. **I~etwegen** adv for your sake; (wegen) because of you, on your account. **i~ige** poss pron der/die/das i~ige hers; (pl) theirs. **I~ige** poss pron der/die/das I~ige yours. **i~s** poss pron hers; (pl) theirs. **I~s** poss pron yours

Ikone f -,-n icon

illegal adj illegal

Illus|ion f -,-en illusion. **i~orisch** adj illusory

Illustr|ation /-ˈtsjoːn/ f -,-en illustration. **i~ieren** vt illustrate. **I~ierte** f -n,-[n] [illustrated] magazine

Iltis m -ses,-se polecat

im prep = in dem

Imbiss m snack. **I~stube** f snack bar

Imit|ation /-ˈtsjoːn/ f -,-en imitation. **i~ieren** vt imitate

Imker m -s,- bee-keeper

Immatrikul|ation /-ˈtsjoːn/ f - (Univ) enrolment. **i~ieren** vt (Univ) enrol; **sich i~ieren** enrol

immer adv always; **für i~** for ever;

(*endgültig*) for good; i∼ **noch still**; i∼ **mehr** more and more; **was** i∼ whatever. i∼**hin** *adv* (*wenigstens*) at least; (*trotzdem*) all the same; (*schließlich*) after all. I∼**zu** *adv* all the time

Immobilien /-jən/ *pl* real estate *sg.* I∼**makler** *m* estate agent

immun *adj* immune (**gegen** to)

Imperialismus *m* - imperialism

impf|en *vt* vaccinate, inoculate. I∼**stoff** *m* vaccine. I∼**ung** *f* -,-en vaccination, inoculation

imponieren *vi* (*haben*) impress (**jdm** s.o.)

Impor|t *m* -[e]s,-e import. I∼**teur** *m* -s,-e importer. i∼**tieren** *vt* import

impoten|t *adj* (*Med*) impotent. I∼**z** *f* - (*Med*) impotence

imprägnieren *vt* waterproof

Impressionismus *m* - impressionism

improvisieren *vt/i* (*haben*) improvise

imstande *pred adj* able (**zu** to); capable (**etw zu tun** of doing sth)

in *prep* (+ *dat*) in; (+ *acc*) into, in; (*bei Bus, Zug*) on; **in der Schule** at school; **in die Schule** to school • *adj* **in sein** be in

Inbegriff *m* embodiment

indem *conj* (*während*) while; (*dadurch*) by (+ -*ing*)

Inder(in) *m* -s, - (*f* -,-nen) Indian

indessen *conj* while • *adv* (*unterdessen*) meanwhile

Indian|er(in) *m* -s,- (*f* -,-nen) (*American*) Indian. i∼**isch** *adj* Indian

Indien /'ɪndjən/ *nt* -s India

indirekt *adj* indirect

indisch *adj* Indian

indiskret *adj* indiscreet

indiskutabel *adj* out of the question

Individu|alist *m* -en,-en individualist. I∼**alität** *f* - individuality. i∼**ell** *adj* individual

Indizienbeweis /ɪn'diːtsjən-/ *m* circumstantial evidence

industr|ialisiert *adj* industrialized. I∼**ie** *f* -,-n industry. i∼**iell** *adj* industrial

ineinander *adv* in/into one another

Infanterie *f* - infantry

Infektion /-'tsjoːn/ *f* -,-en infection. I∼**skrankheit** *f* infectious disease

infizieren *vt* infect; **sich** i∼ become/ (*Person:*) be infected

Inflation /-'tsjoːn/ *f* - inflation. i∼**är** *adj* inflationary

infolge *prep* (+ *gen*) as a result of. i∼**dessen** *adv* consequently

Inform|atik *f* - information science. I∼**ation** *f* -,-en information; I∼**ationen** information *sg.* i∼**ieren** *vt* inform; **sich** i∼**ieren** find out (**über** + *acc* about)

infrage *adv* **etw** i∼ **stellen** question sth; (*ungewiss machen*) make sth doubtful; **nicht** i∼ **kommen** be out of the question

infrarot *adj* infra-red

Ingenieur /ɪnʒe'njoːɐ/ *m* -s,-e engineer

Ingwer *m* -s ginger

Inhaber(in) *m* -s,- (*f* -,-nen) holder; (*Besitzer*) proprietor; (*Scheck-*) bearer

inhaftieren *vt* take into custody

inhalieren *vt/i* (*haben*) inhale

Inhalt *m* -[e]s,-e contents *pl*; (*Bedeutung, Gehalt*) content; (*Ge-*

schichte) story. **I~sangabe** f summary. **I~sverzeichnis** nt list/(in Buch) table of contents

Initiative /initsia'ti:və/ f -,-n initiative

inklusive prep (+ gen) including ● adv inclusive

inkonsequent adj inconsistent

inkorrekt adj incorrect

Inkubationszeit /-'tsjo:ns-/ f (Med) incubation period

Inland nt -[e]s home country; (Binnenland) interior. **I~sgespräch** nt inland call

inmitten prep (+ gen) in the middle of; (unter) amongst

innen adv inside; **nach i~** inwards. **I~architekt(in)** m(f) interior designer. **I~minister** m Minister of the Interior; (in UK) Home Secretary. **I~politik** f domestic policy. **I~stadt** f town centre

inner|e(r,s) adj inner; (Med, Pol) internal. **I~e(s)** nt interior; (Mitte) centre; (fig: Seele) inner being. **I~eien** fpl (Culin) offal sg. **I~halb** prep (+ gen) inside; (zeitlich & fig) within; (während) during ● adv **i~halb von** within. **i~lich** adj internal

innig adj sincere

innovativ adj innovative

Innung f -,-en guild

ins prep = in das

Insasse m -n,-n inmate; (im Auto) occupant; (Passagier) passenger

insbesondere adv especially

Inschrift f inscription

Insekt nt -[e]s,-en insect. **I~envertilgungsmittel** nt insecticide

Insel f -,-n island

Inser|at nt -[e]s,-e [newspaper] advertisement. **I~ieren** vt/i

(haben) advertise

insge|heim adv secretly. **i~samt** adv [all] in all

insofern, insoweit adv in this respect; **i~ als** in as much as

Inspektion /inspɛk'tsjo:n/ f -,-en inspection. **I~ektor** m -en,-en inspector

Install|ateur /ɪnstala'tø:ɐ/ m -s,-e fitter; (Klempner) plumber. **I~ieren** vt install

instand adv **i~ halten** maintain; (pflegen) look after. **I~haltung** f maintenance, upkeep

Instandsetzung f - repair

Instanz /-st-/ f -,-en authority

Instinkt /-st-/ m -[e]s,-e instinct. **i~iv** adj instinctive

Institut /-st-/ nt -[e]s,-e institute

Instrument /-st-/ nt -[e]s,-e instrument. **I~almusik** f instrumental music

Insulin nt -s insulin

inszenier|en vt (Theat) produce. **I~ung** f -,-en production

Integr|ation /-'tsjo:n/ f - integration. **i~ieren** vt integrate; **sich i~ieren** integrate

Intellekt m -[e]s intellect. **i~uell** adj intellectual

intelligen|t adj intelligent. **I~z** f - intelligence

Intendant m -en,-en director

Intensivstation f intensive-care unit

interaktiv adj interactive

inter|essant adj interesting. **I~esse** nt -s,-n interest; **I~esse haben** be interested (an + dat in). **I~essengruppe** f pressure group. **I~essent** m -en,-en interested party; (Käufer) prospective buyer. **I~essieren** vt interest; **sich i~es-**

sieren be interested (**für** in)

Inter|nat nt -[e]s,-e boarding school. **i~national** adj international. **I~nist** m -en,-en specialist in internal diseases. **I~pretation** /-'tsi:ʃo:n/ f -,-en interpretation. **i~pretieren** vt interpret. **I~vall** nt -s,-e interval. **I~vention** /-'tsi:ʃo:n/ f -,-en intervention

Internet nt -s,-s Internet; **im I~** on the Internet

Interview /'ɪntɐvju:/ nt -s,-s interview. **i~en** vt interview

intim adj intimate

intoleran|t adj intolerant. **I~z** f - intolerance

intravenös adj intravenous

Intrige f -,-n intrigue

introvertiert adj introverted

Invalidenrente f disability pension

Invasion f -,-en invasion

Inven|tar nt -s,-e furnishings and fittings pl; (Techn) equipment; (Bestand) stock; (Liste) inventory. **I~tur** f -,-en stock-taking

investieren vt invest

inwie|fern adv in what way. **i~weit** adv how far, to what extent

Inzest m -[e]s incest

inzwischen adv in the meantime

Irak (der) -[s] Iraq. **i~isch** adj Iraqi

Iran (der) -[s] Iran. **i~isch** adj Iranian

irdisch adj earthly

Ire m -n,-n Irishman; **die I~n** the Irish pl

irgend adv somehow **i~ möglich** if at all possible. **i~ein** indefinite article some/any; **i~ein anderer** someone/anyone else. **i~eine(r,s)** pron any one; (jemand) someone/anyone. **i~etwas** pron something;

anything. **i~jemand** pron someone; anyone. **i~wann** pron at some time [or other]/at any time. **i~was** pron 🛈 something [or other]/anything. **i~welche(r,s)** pron any. **i~wer** pron someone/anyone. **i~wie** adv somehow [or other]. **i~wo** adv somewhere

Irin f -,-nen Irishwoman

irisch adj Irish

Irland nt -s Ireland

Ironie f - irony

ironisch adj ironic

irre adj mad, crazy; (🛈: gewaltig) incredible. **I~(r)** m/f lunatic. **i~führen** vt sep (fig) mislead

irre|machen vt sep confuse. **i~n** vi/r (haben) [sich] i~n be mistaken ● vi (sein) wander. **I~nanstalt** f, **I~nhaus** nt lunatic asylum. **i~werden†** vi sep (sein) get confused

Irrgarten m maze

irritieren vt irritate

Irr|sinn m madness, lunacy. **i~sinnig** adj mad; (🛈: gewaltig) incredible. **I~tum** m -s,⁻er mistake

Ischias m & nt - sciatica

Islam (der) -[s] Islam. **islamisch** adj Islamic

Island nt -s Iceland

Isolier|band nt insulating tape. **i~en** vt isolate; (Phys, Electr) insulate; (gegen Schall) soundproof. **I~ung** f - isolation; insulation; soundproofing

Israel /'ɪsrae:l/ nt -s Israel. **I~eli** m -[s],-s & f -,-[s] Israeli. **i~elisch** adj Israeli

ist s. sein; **er ist** he is

Ital|ien /-jən/ nt -s Italy. **I~ien-er(in)** m -s,- (f -,-nen) Italian. **i~ienisch** adj Italian. **I~ienisch** nt -[s] (Lang) Italian

Jj

ja adv, **Ja** nt -[s] yes; **ich glaube ja** I think so; **ja nicht!** not on any account! **da seid ihr ja!** there you are!

Jacht f -,-en yacht

Jacke f -,-n jacket; (Strick-) cardigan

Jackett /ʒaˈkɛt/ nt -s,-s jacket

Jade m -[s] & f - jade

Jagd f -,-en hunt; (Schießen) shoot; (Jagen) hunting; (fig) pursuit (nach of); **auf die J~ gehen** go hunting/shooting. **J~gewehr** nt sporting gun. **J~hund** m gun-dog: (Hetzhund) hound

jagen vt hunt; (schießen) shoot; (verfolgen, wegjagen) chase; (treiben) drive; **sich j~** chase each other; **in die Luft j~** blow up ● vi (haben) hunt, go hunting/shooting; (fig) chase (nach after) ● vi (sein) race, dash

Jäger m -s,- hunter

Jahr nt -[e]s,-e year. **j~elang** adv for years. **J~eszahl** f year. **J~eszeit** f season. **J~gang** m year; (Wein) vintage. **J~hundert** nt century

jährlich adj annual, yearly

Jahr|markt m fair. **J~tausend** nt millennium. **J~zehnt** nt -[e]s,-e decade

Jähzorn m violent temper. **j~ig** adj hot-tempered

Jalousie /ʒaluˈziː/ f -,-n venetian blind

Jammer m -s misery

jämmerlich adj miserable; (Mitleid erregend) pitiful

jammern vi (haben) lament ● vt **jdn j~n** arouse s.o.'s pity

Jänner m -s,- (Aust) January

Januar m -s,-e January

Japan nt -s Japan. **J~aner(in)** m -s,- (f -,-nen) Japanese. **J~anisch** adj Japanese. **J~anisch** nt -[s] (Lang) Japanese

jäten vt/i (haben) weed

jaulen vi (haben) yelp

Jause f -,-n (Aust) snack

jawohl adv yes

Jazz /jats, dʒɛs/ m - jazz

je adv (jemals) ever; (jeweils) each; (pro) per; **je nach** according to; **seit eh und je** always ● conj **je mehr, desto besser** the more the better ● prep (+ acc) per

Jeans /dʒiːns/ pl jeans

jed|e(r,s) pron every; (j~er Einzelne) each; (j~er Beliebige) any; (substantivisch) everyone; each one; anyone; **ohne j~en Grund** without any reason. **j~enfalls** adv in any case; (wenigstens) at least. **J~ermann** pron everyone. **J~erzeit** adv at any time. **j~esmal** adv every time

jedoch adv & conj however

jemals adv ever

jemand pron someone, somebody; (fragend, verneint) anyone, anybody

jen|e(r,s) pron that; (pl) those; (substantivisch) that one; (pl) those. **j~seits** prep (+ gen) [on] the other side of

jetzt adv now

jiddisch adj, **J~** nt -[s] Yiddish

Job /dʒɔp/ m -s,-s job. **J~ben** vi (haben) 🅸 work

Joch nt -[e]s,-e yoke

Jockei, Jockey /ˈdʒɔki/ m -s,-s jockey

Jod nt -[e]s iodine

jodeln vi (haben) yodel

Joga m & nt -[s] yoga

joggen /ˈdʒɔgən/ vi (haben)

sein) jog

Joghurt, Jogurt *m & nt* -[s] yoghurt

Johannisbeere *f* redcurrant

Joker *m* -s,- *(Karte)* joker

Jolle *f* -,-n dinghy

Jongleur /ʒõˈɡløːɐ̯/ *m* -s,-e juggler

Jordanien /-jən/ *nt* -s Jordan

Journalis|mus /ʒʊrnaˈlɪsmʊs/ *m* - journalism. **J~t(in)** *m* -en,-en *(f* -,-nen) journalist

Jubel *m* -s rejoicing, jubilation. **j~n** *vi (haben)* rejoice

Jubiläum *nt* -s,-äen jubilee; *(Jahrestag)* anniversary

jucken *vi (haben)* itch; **sich j~en** scratch; **es j~t mich** I have an itch

Jude *m* -n,-n Jew. **J~ntum** *nt* -s Judaism; *(Juden)* Jewry

Jüd|in *f* -,-nen Jewess. **j~isch** *adj* Jewish

Judo *nt* -[s] judo

Jugend *f* - youth; *(junge Leute)* young people *pl.* **J~herberge** *f* youth hostel. **J~kriminalität** *f* juvenile delinquency. **j~lich** *adj* youthful. **J~liche(r)** *m/f* young man/woman. **J~liche** *pl* young people. **J~stil** *m* art nouveau

Jugoslaw|ien /-jən/ *nt* -s Yugoslavia. **j~isch** *adj* Yugoslav

Juli *m* -[s],-s July

jung *adj* young; *(Wein)* new ● *pron* **J~ und Alt** young and old. **J~e** *m* -n,-n boy. **J~e(s)** *nt* young animal/bird; *(Katzen-)* kitten; *(Bären-)* cub; *(Hunde-)* pup; **die J~en** the young *pl*

Jünger *m* -s,- disciple

Jung|frau *f* virgin; *(Astrology)* Virgo. **J~geselle** *m* bachelor

Jüngling *m* -s,-e youth

jüngst|e(r,s) *adj* youngest; *(neueste)* latest; **in j~er Zeit** recently

Juni *m* -[s],-s June

Jura *pl* law *sg*

Jurist|(in) *m* -en,-en *(f* -,-nen) lawyer. **j~isch** *adj* legal

Jury /ʒyˈriː/ *f* -,-s jury; *(Sport)* judges *pl*

Justiz *f* - **die J~** justice

Juwel *m & nt* -s,-en *& (fig)* -e jewel. **J~ier** *m* -s,-e jeweller

Jux *m* -es,-e joke; **aus Jux** for fun

Kk

Kabarett *nt* -s,-s *& -e* cabaret

Kabel *nt* -s,- cable. **K~fernsehen** *nt* cable television

Kabeljau *m* -s,-e *& -s* cod

Kabine *f* -,-n cabin; *(Umkleide-)* cubicle; *(Telefon-)* booth; *(einer K~nbahn)* car. **K~nbahn** *f* cable-car

Kabinett *nt* -s,-e *(Pol)* Cabinet

Kabriolett *nt* -s,-s convertible

Kachel *f* -,-n tile. **k~n** *vt* tile

Kadenz *f* -,-en *(Mus)* cadence

Käfer *m* -s,- beetle

Kaffee /ˈkafe, kaˈfeː/ *m* -s,-s coffee. **K~kanne** *f* coffee pot. **K~maschine** *f* coffee maker. **K~mühle** *f* coffee grinder

Käfig *m* -s,-e cage

kahl *adj* bare; *(haarlos)* bald; **k~geschoren** shaven

Kahn *m* -s,⁻e boat; *(Last-)* barge

Kai *m* -s,-s quay

Kaiser *m* -s,- emperor. **K~in** *f* -,-nen empress. **k~lich** *adj* imperial. **K~reich** *nt* empire. **K~schnitt**

m Caesarean [section]

Kajüte *f* -,-n (*Naut*) cabin

Kakao /ka'kaʊ/ *m* -s cocoa

Kakerlak *m* -s & -en,-en cockroach

Kaktus *m* -,-teen cactus

Kalb *nt* -[e]s,̈ er calf. **K~fleisch** *nt* veal

Kalender *m* -s,- calendar; (*Termin-*) diary

Kaliber *nt* -s,- calibre; (*Gewehr-*) bore

Kalium *nt* -s potassium

Kalk *m* -[e]s,-e lime; (*Kalzium*) calcium. **k~en** *vt* whitewash. **K~stein** *m* limestone

Kalkulation /-'tsjo:n/ *f* -,-en calculation. **k~ieren** *vt/i* (*haben*) calculate

Kalorie *f* -,-n calorie

kalt *adj* cold; **mir ist k~** I am cold

Kälte *f* - cold; (*Gefühls-*) coldness; **10 Grad K~** 10 degrees below zero

Kalzium *nt* -s calcium

Kamel *nt* -s,-e camel

Kamera *f* -,-s camera

Kamerad(in) *m* -en,-en (*f* -,-nen) companion; (*Freund*) mate; (*Mil, Pol*) comrade

Kameramann *m* (*pl* -männer & -leute) cameraman

Kamille *f* - chamomile

Kamin *m* -s,-e fireplace; (*SGer: Schornstein*) chimney

Kamm *m* -[e]s,̈ e comb; (*Berg-*) ridge; (*Zool, Wellen-*) crest

kämmen *vt* comb; **jdn/sich k~** comb someone's/one's hair

Kammer *f* -,-n small room; (*Techn, Biology, Pol*) chamber. **K~musik** *f* chamber music

Kammgarn *nt* (*Textiles*) worsted

Kampagne /kam'panjə/ *f* -,-n (*Pol, Comm*) campaign

Kampf *m* -es,̈ e fight; (*Schlacht*) battle; (*Wett-*) contest; (*fig*) struggle

kämpf|en *vi* (*haben*) fight; **sich k~en durch** fight one's way through. **K~er(in)** *m* -s,- (*f* -,-nen) fighter

Kampfrichter *m* (*Sport*) judge

Kanada *nt* -s Canada

Kanad|ier(in) /-iɐ, -iɐrɪn/ *m* -s,- (*f* -,-nen) Canadian. **k~isch** *adj* Canadian

Kanal *m* -s,̈ e canal; (*Abfluss-*) drain, sewer; (*Radio, TV*) channel; **der K~** the [English] Channel

Kanalisation /-'tsjo:n/ *f* - sewerage system, drains *pl*

Kanarienvogel /-iən-/ *m* canary

Kanarisch *adj* **K~e Inseln** Canaries

Kandidat(in) *m* -en,-en (*f* -,-nen) candidate

kandiert *adj* candied

Känguru *nt* -s,-s kangaroo

Kaninchen *nt* -s,- rabbit

Kanister *m* -s,- canister; (*Benzin-*) can

Kännchen *nt* -s,- [small] jug; (*Kaffee-*) pot

Kanne *f* -,-n jug; (*Tee-*) pot; (*Öl-*) can; (*große Milch-*) churn

Kannibal|e *m* -n,-n cannibal. **K~ismus** *m* - cannibalism

Kanon *m* -s,-s canon; (*Lied*) round

Kanone *f* -,-n cannon, gun

kanonisieren *vt* canonize

Kantate *f* -,-n cantata

Kante *f* -,-n edge

Kanten *m* -s,- crust [of bread]

Kanter *m* -s,- canter

kantig *adj* angular

Kantine *f* -,-n canteen

Kanton *m* -s,-e (*Swiss*) canton

k

Kanton The name for the individual autonomous states that make up Switzerland. There are 26 cantons, each with its own government and constitution. *i*

Kanu nt -s,-s canoe

Kanzel f -,-n pulpit; (*Aviat*) cockpit

Kanzler m -s,- chancellor

Kap nt -s,-s (*Geog*) cape

Kapazität f -,-en capacity

Kapelle f -,-n chapel; (*Mus*) band

kapern vt (*Naut*) seize

kapieren vt 🗉 understand

Kapital nt -s capital. **K~ismus** m - capitalism. **K~ist** m -en,-en capitalist. **k~istisch** adj capitalist

Kapitän m -s,-e captain

Kapitel nt -s,- chapter

Kaplan m -s,∺e curate

Kappe f -,-n cap

Kapsel f -,-n capsule; (*Flaschen-*) top

kaputt adj 🗉 broken; (*zerrissen*) torn; (*defekt*) out of order; (*ruiniert*) ruined; (*erschöpft*) worn out. **k~gehen†** vi sep (sein) 🗉 break; (*zerreißen*) tear; (*defekt werden*) pack up; (*Ehe, Freundschaft*): break up. **k~lachen (sich)** vr sep 🗉 be in stitches. **k~machen** get to the top

Kapuze f -,-n hood

Kapuzinerkresse f nasturtium

Karaffe f -,-n carafe; (*mit Stöpsel*) decanter

Karamell m -s caramel. **K~bonbon** m & nt -s ≈ toffee

Karat nt -[e]s,-e carat

Karawane f -,-n caravan

Kardinal m -s,∺e cardinal. **K~zahl** f cardinal number

Karfreitag m Good Friday

karg adj meagre; (*frugal*) frugal; (*spärlich*) sparse; (*unfruchtbar*) barren; (*gering*) scant

Karibik f - Caribbean

kariert adj check[ed]; (*Papier*) squared; **schottisch k~** tartan

Karikatur f -,-en caricature; (*Journalismus*) cartoon. **k~ieren** vt caricature

Karneval m -s,-e & -s carnival

Kärnten nt -s Carinthia

Karo nt -s,-s (*Raute*) diamond; (*Viereck*) square; (*Muster*) check (*Kartenspiel*) diamonds pl

Karosserie f -,-n bodywork

Karotte f -,-n carrot

Karpfen m -s,- carp

Karren m -s,- cart; (*Hand-*) barrow. **k~** vt cart

Karriere /ka'rjɛːrə/ f -,-n career; **K~ machen** get to the top

Karte f -,-n card; (*Eintritts-, Fahr-*) ticket; (*Speise-*) menu; (*Land-*) map

Kartei f -,-en card index

Karten|spiel nt card game; (*Spielkarten*) pack of cards. **K~vorverkauf** m advance booking

Kartoffel f -,-n potato. **K~brei** m mashed potatoes

Karton /kar'tɔŋ/ m -s,-s cardboard; (*Schachtel*) carton

Karussell nt -s,-s & -e roundabout

Käse m -s,- cheese

Kaserne f -,-n barracks pl

Kasino nt -s,-s casino

Kasperle nt & m -s,- Punch. **K~theater** nt Punch and Judy show

Kasse f -,-n till; (*Registrier-*) cash register; (*Zahlstelle*) cash desk; (*im Supermarkt*) check out; (*Theater-*)

box office; (*Geld*) pool [of money], 🅃 kitty; (*Kranken-*) health insurance . scheme; **knapp bei K~ sein** 🅃 be short of cash. **K~nwart** *m -[e]s, -e* treasurer. **K~nzettel** *m* receipt

Kasserolle *f -,-n* saucepan

Kassette *f -,-n* cassette; (*Film-, Farbband-*) cartridge. **K~nrekorder** *m -s,-* cassette recorder

kassier|en *vi* (*haben*) collect the money/(*im Bus*) the fares ● *vt* collect. **K~er(in)** *m -s,- (f -,-nen)* cashier

Kastanie /kas'ta:njə/ *f -,-n* [horse] chestnut, 🅃 conker

Kasten *m -s,* box; (*Brot-*) bin; (*Flaschen-*) crate; (*Brief-*) letter box; (*Aust: Schrank*) cupboard

kastrieren *vt* castrate; neuter

Katalog *m -[e]s,-e* catalogue

Katalysator *m -s,-en* catalyst; (*Auto*) catalytic converter

Katapult *nt -[e]s,-e* catapult

Katarrh, Katarr *m -s,-e* catarrh

Katastrophe *f -,-n* catastrophe

Katechismus *m -* catechism

Kategorie *f -,-n* category

Kater *m -s,-* tom cat; (🅃: *Katzenjammer*) hangover

Kathedrale *f -,-n* cathedral

Kath|olik(in) *m -en,-en (f -,-nen)* Catholic. **k~olisch** *adj* Catholic. **K~olizismus** *m -* Catholicism

Kätzchen *nt -s,-* kitten; (*Bot*) catkin

Katze *f -,-n* cat. **K~njammer** *m* 🅃 hangover. **K~nsprung** *m* **ein K~nsprung** 🅃 a stone's throw

Kauderwelsch *nt -[s]* gibberish

kauen *vt/i* (*haben*) chew; bite (*Nägel*)

Kauf *m -[e]s,* Käufe purchase; **guter K~** bargain; **in K~ nehmen**

(*fig*) put up with. **k~en** *vt/i* (*haben*) buy; **k~en bei** shop at

Käufer(in) *m -s,- (f -,-nen)* buyer; (*im Geschäft*) shopper

Kauf|haus *nt* department store. **K~laden** *m* shop

käuflich *adj* saleable; (*bestechlich*) corruptible; **k~ erwerben** buy

Kauf|mann *m (pl -leute)* businessman; (*Händler*) dealer; (*Dialekt*) grocer. **K~preis** *m* purchase price

Kaugummi *m* chewing gum

Kaulquappe *f -,-n* tadpole

kaum *adv* hardly

Kaution /-'tsjo:n/ *f -,-en* surety; (*Jur*) bail; (*Miet-*) deposit

Kautschuk *m -s* rubber

Kauz *m -es,* Käuze owl

Kavalier *m -s,-e* gentleman

Kavallerie *f -* cavalry

Kaviar *m -s* caviare

keck *adj* bold; cheeky

Kegel *m -s,-* skittle; (*Geometry*) cone. **K~bahn** *f* skittle-alley. **k~n** *vi* (*haben*) play skittles

Kehl|e *f -,-n* throat; **aus voller K~e** at the top of one's voice. **K~kopf** *m* larynx. **K~kopfentzündung** *f* laryngitis

Kehr|e *f -,-n* [hairpin] bend. **k~en** *vi* (*haben*) (*fegen*) sweep ● *vt* sweep; (*wenden*) turn; **sich nicht k~en an** (*+ acc*) not care about. **K~icht** *m -s,-e* sweepings *pl*. **K~reim** *m* refrain. **K~seite** *f (fig)* drawback. **K~tmachen** *vi sep* (*haben*) turn back; (*sich umdrehen*) turn round

Keil *m -[e]s,-e* wedge

Keilriemen *m* fan belt

Keim *m -[e]s,-e* (*Bot*) sprout; (*Med*) germ. **k~en** *vi* (*haben*) germinate; (*austreiben*) sprout. **k~frei** *adj* sterile

kein pron no; not a; k~e fünf Minuten less than five minutes.
k~e(r,s) pron no one, nobody; (Ding) none, not one. k~esfalls adv on no account. k~eswegs adv by no means. k~mal adv not once. k~s pron none, not one

Keks m -[es],-[e] biscuit

Kelch m -[e]s,-e goblet, cup; (Relig) chalice; (Bot) calyx

Kelle f -,-n ladle; (Maurer) trowel

Keller m -s,- cellar. K~ei f -,-en winery. K~wohnung f basement flat

Kellner m -s,- waiter. K~in f -,-nen waitress

keltern vt press

keltisch adj Celtic

Kenia nt -s Kenya

kennen† vt know; k~en lernen get to know; (treffen) meet; sich k~en lernen meet; (näher) get to know one another. K~er m -s,-. K~erin f -,-nen connoisseur; (Experte) expert. k~tlich adj recognizable; k~tlich machen mark. K~tnis f -,-se knowledge; zur K~tnis nehmen take note of; in K~tnis setzen inform (von of). K~wort nt (pl -wörter) reference; (geheimes) password. K~zeichen nt distinguishing mark or feature; (Merkmal) characteristic; (Markierung) marking; (Auto) registration. k~zeichnen vt distinguish; (markieren) mark

kentern vi (sein) capsize

Keramik f -,-en pottery

Kerbe f -,-n notch

Kerker m -s,- dungeon; (Gefängnis) prison

Kerl m -s,-e & -s [T] fellow, bloke

Kern m -s,-e pip; (Kirsch-) stone; (Nuss-) kernel; (Techn) core; (Atom-, Zell- & fig) nucleus; (Stadt-) centre;

(einer Sache) heart. K~energie f nuclear energy. K~gehäuse nt core. K~los adj seedless. K~physik f nuclear physics sg

Kerze f -,-n candle. K~nhalter m -s,- candlestick

kess adj pert

Kessel m -s,- kettle

Kette f -,-n chain; (Hals-) necklace. k~n vt (chain an + acc to). K~nladen m chain store

Ketze|r(in) m -s,- (f -,-nen) heretic. K~rei f - heresy

keuchen vi (haben) pant. K~husten m whooping cough

Keule f -,-n club; (Culin) leg; (Hühner-) drumstick

keusch adj chaste

Khaki nt - khaki

kichern vi (haben) giggle

Kiefer¹ f -,-n pine[-tree]

Kiefer² m -s,- jaw

Kiel m -s,-e (Naut) keel

Kiemen fpl gills

Kies m -es gravel. K~el m -s,-. K~elstein m pebble

Kilo nt -s,-[s] kilo. K~gramm nt kilogram. K~hertz nt kilohertz. K~meter m kilometre. K~meterstand m ≈ mileage. K~watt nt kilowatt

Kind nt -es,-er child; von K~ auf from childhood

Kinder|arzt m, K~ärztin f paediatrician. K~bett nt child's cot. K~garten m nursery school. K~geld nt child benefit. K~lähmung f polio. K~leicht adj very easy. K~los adj childless. K~mädchen nt nanny. K~reim m nursery rhyme. K~spiel nt children's game. K~tagesstätte f day nursery. K~teller m children's menu. K~wagen m pram. K~zimmer nt child's/children's room; ((für

Baby) nursery

Kind|heit f - childhood. **k~isch** adj childish. **k~lich** adj childlike

kinetisch adj kinetic

Kinn nt -[e]s,-e chin. **K~lade** f jaw

Kino nt -s,-s cinema

Kiosk m -[e]s,-e kiosk

Kippe f -,-n (*Müll-*) dump; (🗆: *Zigaretten-*) fag end. **k~n** vt tilt; (*schütten*) tip (**in** + acc into) ● vi (*sein*) topple

Kirch|e f -,-n church. **K~enbank** f pew. **K~endiener** m verger. **K~enlied** nt hymn. **K~enschiff** nt nave. **K~hof** m churchyard. **k~lich** adj church ● adv **k~lich getraut werden** be married in church. **K~turm** m church tower, steeple. **K~weih** f -,-en [village] fair

Kirmes f -,-sen = **Kirchweih**

Kirsche f -,-n cherry

Kissen nt -s,- cushion; (*Kopf-*) pillow

Kiste f -,-n crate; (*Zigarren-*) box

Kitsch m -es sentimental rubbish; (*Kunst*) kitsch

Kitt m -s [*adhesive*] cement; (*Fenster-*) putty

Kittel m -s,- overall, smock

Kitz nt -es,-e (*Zool*) kid

Kitz|el m -s,- tickle; (*Nerven-*) thrill. **k~eln** vt/i (*haben*) tickle. **k~lig** adj ticklish

kläffen vi (*haben*) yap

Klage f -,-n lament; (*Beschwerde*) complaint; (*Jur*) action. **k~n** vi (*haben*) lament; (*sich beklagen*) complaint; (*Jur*) sue

Kläger(in) m -s,- (f -,-nen) (*Jur*) plaintiff

klamm adj cold and damp; (*steif*) stiff. **K~** f -,-en (*Geog*) gorge

Klammer f -,-n (*Wäsche-*) peg; (*Büro-*) paper clip; (*Heft-*) staple;

(*Haar-*) grip; (*für Zähne*) brace; (*Techn*) clamp; (*Typography*) bracket. **k~n (sich)** vr cling (**an** + acc to)

Klang m -[e]s,-̈e sound; (*K~farbe*) tone

Klapp|e f -,-n flap; (🗆: *Mund*) trap. **k~en** vt fold; (*hoch-*) tip up ● vi (*haben*) 🗆 work out. **Klapphandy** nt folding mobile phone

Klapper f -,-n rattle. **k~n** vi (*haben*) rattle. **K~schlange** f rattlesnake

klapp|rig adj rickety; (*schwach*) decrepit. **K~stuhl** m folding chair

Klaps m -es,-̈e pat, smack

klar adj clear; **sich** (dat) **k~ werden** make up one's mind; (*erkennen*) realize (**dass** that); **sich** (dat) **k~** sein **über etw** realize (**dass** that) ● adv clearly; (🗆: *natürlich*) of course

klären vt clarify; **sich k~** clear; (*fig: sich lösen*) resolve itself

Klarheit f -,- clarity

Klarinette f -,-n clarinet

klar|machen vt sep make clear (dat to); **sich** (dat) **etw k~machen** understand sth. **k~stellen** vt sep clarify

Klärung f - clarification

Klasse f -,-n class; (*Sch*) class, form; (*Zimmer*) classroom. **k~** inv adj 🗆 super. **K~narbeit** f [written] test. **K~nzimmer** nt classroom

Klass|ik f - classicism; (*Epoche*) classical period. **K~iker** m -s,- classical author/(*Mus*) composer. **k~isch** adj classical; (*typisch*) classic

Klatsch m -[e]s gossip. **K~base** f 🗆 gossip. **k~en** vt slap; *Beifall* **k~en** applaud ● vi (*haben*) make a slapping sound; (*im Wasser*) splash; (*tratschen*) gossip; (*applaudieren*) clap. **k~nass** adj 🗆 soaking wet

klauen vt/i (*haben*) 🗆 steal

Klausel f -,-n clause

Klaustrophobie f - claustrophobia

Klausur f -,-en (Univ) paper

Klavier nt -s,-e piano. **K~spieler(in)** m(f) pianist

kleb|en vt stick/(mit Klebstoff) glue (an + acc to) ● vi (haben) stick (an + dat to). **k~rig** adj sticky. **K~stoff** m adhesive, glue. **K~streifen** m adhesive tape

Klecks m -es,-e stain; (Tinten-) blot; (kleine Menge) dab. **k~en** vi (haben) make a mess

Klee m -s clover

Kleid nt -[e]s,-er dress; **K~er** dresses; (Kleidung) clothes. **k~en** vt dress; (gut stehen) suit. **K~erbügel** m coat hanger. **K~erbürste** f clothes brush. **K~erhaken** m coathook. **K~erschrank** m wardrobe. **k~sam** adj becoming. **K~ung** f - clothes pl, clothing. **K~ungsstück** nt garment

Kleie f - bran

klein adj small, little; (von kleinem Wuchs) short; **k~ schneiden** cut up small. **von k~ auf** from childhood. **K~arbeit** f painstaking work. **K~e(r,s)** m/f/nt little one. **K~geld** nt [small] change. **K~handel** m retail trade. **K~heit** f - smallness; (Wuchs) short stature. **K~holz** nt firewood. **K~igkeit** f -,-en trifle; (Mahl) snack. **K~kind** nt infant. **k~laut** adj subdued. **k~lich** adj petty

klein|schreiben† vt sep write with a small [initial] letter. **K~stadt** f small town. **k~städtisch** adj provincial

Kleister m -s paste. **k~n** vt paste

Klemme f -,-n [hair-]grip. **k~n** vt jam; **sich** (dat) **den Finger k~n** get one's finger caught ● vi (haben)

jam, stick

Klempner m -s,- plumber

Klerus (der) - the clergy

Klette f -,-n burr

kletter|n vi (sein) climb. **K~pflanze** f climber

Klettverschluss m Velcro ® fastening

klicken vi (haben) click

Klient(in) /kliˈɛnt(m)/ m -en,-en (f +,-nen) (Jur) client

Kliff nt -[e]s,-e cliff

Klima m -s climate. **K~anlage** f air conditioning

klimat|isch adj climatic. **k~isiert** adj air-conditioned

klimpern vi (haben) jingle; **k~ auf** (+ dat) tinkle on (Klavier); strum (Gitarre)

Klinge f -,-n blade

Klingel f -,-n bell. **k~n** vi (haben) ring; **es k~t** there's a ring at the door

klingen† vi (haben) sound

Klinik f -,-en clinic

Klinke f -,-n [door] handle

Klippe f -,-n [submerged] rock

Klips m -es,-e clip; (Ohr-) clip-on ear ring

klirren vi (haben) rattle; (Glas:) chink

Klo nt -s,-s ⑤ loo

Klon m -s, -e clone. **k~en** vt clone

klopfen vi (haben) knock; (leicht) tap; (Herz:) pound; **es k~te** there was a knock at the door

Klops m -es,-e meatball

Klosett nt -s,-s lavatory

Kloß m -es,¨e dumpling

Kloster nt -s,¨ monastery; (Nonnen-) convent

klösterlich adj monastic

Klotz m -es,¨e block

Klub m -s,-s club

Kluft f -,⸚e cleft; (fig: Gegensatz) gulf

klug adj intelligent; (schlau) clever. **K~heit** f - cleverness

Klump|en m -s,- lump

knabbern vt/i (haben) nibble

Knabe m -n,-n boy. **k~nhaft** adj boyish

Knäckebrot nt crispbread

knack|en vt/i (haben) crack. **K~s** m -es,-e crack

Knall m -[e]s,-e bang. **k~bonbon** m cracker. **k~en** vi (haben) go bang; (Peitsche:) crack ● vt (𝔉: werfen) chuck; **jdm eine k~en** (𝔉) clout s.o. **k~ig** adj (𝔉) gaudy

knapp adj (gering) scarce; (kurz) short; (mangelnd) scarce; (gerade ausreichend) bare; (eng) tight. **K~heit** f - scarcity

knarren vi (haben) creak

Knast m -[e]s (𝔉) prison

knattern vi (haben) crackle; (Gewehr:) stutter

Knäuel m & nt -s,- ball

Knauf m -[e]s, Knäufe knob

knauserig adj (𝔉) stingy

knautschen vt (𝔉) crumple ● vi (haben) crease

Knebel m -s,- gag. **k~n** vt gag

Knecht m -[e]s,-e farm-hand; (fig) slave

kneif|en† vt pinch ● vi (haben) pinch; (𝔉: sich drücken) chicken out. **K~zange** f pincers pl

Kneipe f -,-n (𝔉) pub

knet|en vt knead; (formen) mould. **K~masse** f Plasticine®

Knick m -[e]s,-e bend; (Kniff) crease. **k~en** vt bend; (kniffen) fold; **geknickt sein** (𝔉) be dejected

Knicks m -es,-e curtsy. **k~en** vi (haben) curtsy

Knie nt -s,- knee

knien /'kni:ən/ vi (haben) kneel ● vr **sich k~** kneel [down]

Kniescheibe f kneecap

Kniff m -[e]s,-e pinch; (Falte) crease; (𝔉: Trick) trick. **k~en** vt fold

knipsen vt (lochen) punch; (Phot) photograph ● vi (haben) take a photograph/photographs

Knirps m -es,-e (𝔉) little chap; ® (Schirm) telescopic umbrella

knirschen vi (haben) grate; (Schnee, Kies:) crunch

knistern vi (haben) crackle; (Papier:) rustle

Knitter|falte f crease. **k~frei** adj crease-resistant. **k~n** vi (haben) crease

knobeln vi (haben) toss (**um** for)

Knoblauch m -s garlic

Knöchel m -s,- ankle; (Finger-) knuckle

Knochen m -s,- bone. **K~mark** nt bone marrow

knochig adj bony

Knödel m -s,- (SGer) dumpling

Knoll|e f -,-n tuber

Knopf m -[e]s,⸚e button; (Griff) knob

knöpfen vt button

Knopfloch nt buttonhole

Knorpel m -s gristle; (Anat) cartilage

Knospe f bud

Knoten m -s,- knot; (Med) lump; (Haar-) bun, chignon. **k~** vt knot. **K~punkt** m junction

knüll|en vt crumple ● vi (haben) crease. **K~er** m -s,- (𝔉) sensation

knüpfen vt knot; (verbinden) attach (**an** + acc to)

Knüppel m -s,- club; (Gummi-) truncheon

knurren vi (haben) growl; (Magen:) rumble

knusprig adj crunchy, crisp

knutschen vi (haben) 🔲 smooch

k.o. /ka'ʔoː/ adj k.o. **schlagen** knock out; **k.o. sein** 🔲 be worn out

Koalition /koali'tsi̯oːn/ f -,-en coalition

Kobold m -[e]s,-e goblin, imp

Koch m -[e]s,-e cook; (im Restaurant) chef. **K~buch** nt cookery book. **k~en** vt cook; (sieden) boil; make (Kaffee, Tee); **hart gekochtes Ei** hard-boiled egg ● vi (haben) cook; (sieden) boil; (Sieden) seethe (vor + dat with). **K~en** nt -s cooking; (Sieden) boiling. **k~end** adj boiling. **K~herd** m cooker, stove

Köchin f -,-nen [woman] cook

Kochlöffel m wooden spoon. **K~nische** f kitchenette. **K~platte** f hotplate. **K~topf** m saucepan

Köder m -s,- bait

Koffein /kɔfe'iːn/ nt -s caffeine. **k~frei** adj decaffeinated

Koffer m -s,- suitcase. **K~kuli** m luggage trolley. **K~raum** m (Auto) boot

Kognak /'kɔnjak/ m -s,-s brandy

Kohl m -[e]s cabbage

Kohle f -,-n coal. **K~[n]hydrat** nt -[e]s,-e carbohydrate. **K~nbergwerk** nt coal mine, colliery. **K~ndioxid** nt carbon dioxide. **K~nsäure** f carbon dioxide. **K~nstoff** m carbon

Koje f -,-n (Naut) bunk

Kokain /koka'iːn/ nt -s cocaine

kokett adj flirtatious. **k~ieren** vi (haben) flirt

Kokon /ko'kõː/ m -s,-s cocoon

Kokosnuss f coconut

Koks m -es coke

Kolben m -s,- (Gewehr:) butt; (Mais-) cob; (Techn) piston; (Chemistry) flask

Kolibri m -s,-s humming bird

Kolik f -,-en colic

Kollaborateur /-'tøːɐ̯/ m -s,-e collaborator

Kolleg nt -s,-s & -ien (Univ) course of lectures

Kollege m -n,-n, **K~in** f -,-nen colleague. **K~ium** nt -s,-ien staff

Kollekte f -,-n (Relig) collection. **K~tion** /-'tsi̯oːn/ f -,-en collection

Köln nt -s Cologne. **K~ischwasser, K~isch Wasser** nt eau-de-Cologne

Kolonie f -,-n colony

Kolonne f -,-n column; (Mil) convoy

Koloss m -es,-e giant

Koma nt -s,-s coma

Kombi m -s,-s = **K~wagen**. **K~nation** /-'tsi̯oːn/ f -,-en combination; (Folgerung) deduction; (Kleidung) co-ordinating outfit. **k~nieren** vt combine; (fig) reason; (folgern) deduce. **K~wagen** m estate car

Kombüse f -,-n (Naut) galley

Komet m -en,-en comet

Komfort /kɔm'foːɐ̯/ m -s comfort; (Luxus) luxury

Komik f - humour. **K~er** m -s,- comic, comedian

komisch adj funny; (Oper) comic; (sonderbar) odd, funny. **k~erweise** adv funnily enough

Komitee nt -s,-s committee

Komma nt -s,-s & -ta comma; (Dezimal-) decimal point; **drei K~ fünf** three point five

Kommando nt -s,-s order; (Befehlsgewalt) command; (Einheit) detachment. **K~brücke** f bridge

kommen† vi (sein) come; (eintref-

fen) arrive; *(gelangen)* get **(nach** to); **k~ lassen** send for; **auf/hinter etw** *(acc)* **k~** think of/find out about sth; **um/zu etw k~** lose/acquire sth; **wieder zu sich k~** come round; **wie kommt das?** why is that? **k~d** *adj* coming; **k~den Montag** next Monday

Kommen|tar *m* -s,-e commentary; *(Bemerkung)* comment. **k~ tieren** *vt* comment on

kommerziell *adj* commercial

Kommissar *m* -s,-e commissioner; *(Polizei-)* superintendent

Kommission *f* -,-en commission; *(Gremium)* committee

Kommode *f* -,-n chest of drawers

Kommunalwahlen *fpl* local elections

Kommunion *f* -,-en [Holy] Communion

Kommun|ismus *m* - Communism. **K~ist(in)** *m* -en,-en *(f* -,-nen) Communist. **k~istisch** *adj* Communist

kommunizieren *vi (haben)* receive [Holy] Communion

Komödie /koˈmøːdjə/ *f* -,-n comedy

Kompagnon /ˈkɔmpanjɔ/ *m* -s,-s *(Comm)* partner

Kompanie *f* -,-n *(Mil)* company

Komparse *m* -n,-n *(Theat)* extra

Kompass *m* -es,-e compass

komplett *adj* complete

Komplex *m* -es,-e complex

Komplikation /-ˈtsjoːn/ *f* -,-en complication

Kompliment *nt* -[e]s,-e compliment

Komplize *m* -n,-n accomplice

komplizier|en *vt* complicate. **k~t** *adj* complicated

Komplott *nt* -[e]s,-e plot

kompo|nieren *vt/i (haben)* compose. **K~nist** *m* -en,-en composer

Kompost *m* -[e]s compost

Kompott *nt* -[e]s,-e stewed fruit

Kompromiss *m* -es,-e compromise; **einen K~ schließen** compromise. **k~los** *adj* uncompromising

Konden|sation /-ˈtsjoːn/ *f* - condensation. **k~sieren** *vt* condense

Kondensmilch *f* evaporated/(gesüßt) condensed milk

Kondition /-ˈtsjoːn/ *f* - *(Sport)* fitness; **in K~** in form

Konditor *m* -s,-en confectioner. **K~ei** *f* -,-en patisserie

Kondo|lenzbrief *m* letter of condolence. **k~lieren** *vi (haben)* express one's condolences

Kondom *nt* & *m* -s,-e condom

Konfekt *nt* -[e]s confectionery; *(Pralinen)* chocolates *pl*

Konfektion /-ˈtsjoːn/ *f* - ready-to-wear clothes *pl*

Konferenz *f* -,-en conference; *(Besprechung)* meeting

Konfession *f* -,-en [religious] denomination. **k~ell** *adj* denominational

Konfetti *nt* -s confetti

Konfirm|and(in) *m* -en,-en *(f* -,-nen) candidate for confirmation. **K~ation** *f* -,-en *(Relig)* confirmation. **k~ieren** *vt (Relig)* confirm

Konfitüre *f* -,-n jam

Konflikt *m* -[e]s,-e conflict

Konföderation /-ˈtsjoːn/ *f* confederation

konfus *adj* confused

Kongress *m* -es,-e congress

König *m* -s,-e king. **K~in** *f* -,-nen queen. **k~lich** *adj* royal; *(hoheitsvoll)* regal; *(großzügig)* handsome. **K~reich** *nt* kingdom

Konjunktiv *m* -s,-e subjunctive

k

Konjunktur f - economic situation; (Hoch-) boom

konkret adj concrete

Konkurren|t(in) m -en,-en (f -,-nen) competitor, rival. **K~z** f - competition; **jdm K~z machen** compete with s.o. **K~zkampf** m competition, rivalry

konkurrieren vi (haben) compete

Konkurs m -es,-e bankruptcy

können†

● auxiliary verb

••••➤ (vermögen) be able to; (Präsens) can; (Vergangenheit, Konditional) could. **ich kann nicht schlafen** I cannot or can't sleep. **kann ich Ihnen helfen?** can I help you? **kann/könnte das explodieren?** can/could it explode? **es kann sein, dass er kommt** he may come

! Distinguish **konnte** and **könnte** (both can be 'could'): **er konnte sie nicht retten** he couldn't or was unable to rescue them. **er konnte sie noch retten** he was able to rescue them. **er könnte sie noch retten, wenn …** he could still rescue them if …

••••➤ (dürfen) can, may. **kann ich gehen?** can or may I go? **können wir mit[kommen]?** can or may we come too?

● transitive verb

••••➤ (beherrschen) know (language); be able to play (game). **können Sie Deutsch?** do you know any German? **sie kann das [gut]** she can do that [well]. **ich kann nichts dafür** I

can't help that, I'm not to blame

● intransitive verb

••••➤ (fähig sein) **ich kann [heute] nicht** I can't [today]. **er kann nicht anders** there's nothing else he can do; (es ist seine Art) he can't help it. **er kann nicht mehr** 🔢 he can't go on; (nicht mehr essen) he can't eat any more

••••➤ (irgendwohin gehen können) be able to go; can go. **ich kann nicht ins Kino** I can't go to the cinema. **er konnte endlich nach Florenz** at last he was able to go to Florence

konsequen|t adj consistent; (logisch) logical. **K~z** f -,-en consequence

konservativ adj conservative

Konserv|en fpl tinned or canned food sg. **K~endose** f tin, can. **K~ierungsmittel** nt preservative

Konsonant m -en,-en consonant

Konstitution /-'tsjo:n/ f -,-en constitution. **k~ell** adj constitutional

konstruieren vt construct; (entwerfen) design

Konstruk|tion /-'tsjo:n/ f -,-en construction; (Entwurf) design. **k~tiv** adj constructive

Konsul m -s,-n consul. **K~at** nt -[e]s,-e consulate

Konsum m -s consumption. **K~güter** npl consumer goods

Kontakt m -[e]s,-e contact. **K~linsen** fpl contact lenses. **K~person** f contact

kontern vt/i (haben) counter

Kontinent /'kɔn-, kɔntɪˈnɛnt/ m -[e]s,-e continent

Konto nt -s,-s account. **K~auszug**

m [bank] statement. **K~nummer** *f* account number. **K~stand** *m* [bank] balance

Kontrabass *m* double bass

Kontroll|abschnitt *m* counterfoil. **K~e** *f* -,-n control; (*Prüfung*) check. **K~eur** *m* -s,-e [ticket] inspector. **k~ieren** *vt* check; inspect (*Fahrkarten*); (*beherrschen*) control

Kontroverse *f* -,-n controversy

Kontur *f* -,-en contour

konventionell *adj* conventional

Konversationslexikon *nt* encyclopaedia

konvert|ieren *vi* (*haben*) (*Relig*) convert. **K~it** *m* -en,-en convert

Konzentration /-'tsjo:n/ *f* -,-en concentration. **K~slager** *nt* concentration camp

konzentrieren *vt* concentrate; **sich k~** concentrate (**auf** + *acc on*)

Konzept *nt* -[e]s,-e [rough] draft; **jdn aus dem K~bringen** put s.o. off his stroke

Konzern *m* -s,-e (*Comm*) group [of companies]

Konzert *nt* -[e]s,-e concert; (*Klavier-*) concerto

Konzession *f* -,-en licence; (*Zugeständnis*) concession

Konzil *nt* -s,-e (*Relig*) council

Kooperation /ko?opera'tsjo:n/ *f* co-operation

Koordin|ation /ko?ordina'tsjo:n/ *f* - co-ordination. **k~ieren** *vt* co-ordinate

Kopf *m* -[e]s,-̈e head; **ein K~ Kohl/Salat** a cabbage/lettuce; **aus dem K~** from memory; (*auswendig*) by heart; **auf dem K~** (*verkehrt*) upside down; **K~ stehen** stand on one's head; **sich** (*dat*) **den K~ waschen** wash one's hair; **sich** (*dat*) **den K~ zerbrechen** rack one's brains. **K~ball** *m* header

köpfen *vt* behead; (*Fußball*) head

Kopf|ende *nt* head. **K~haut** *f* scalp. **K~hörer** *m* headphones *pl*. **K~kissen** *nt* pillow. **k~los** *adj* panic-stricken. **K~rechnen** *nt* mental arithmetic. **K~salat** *m* lettuce. **K~schmerzen** *mpl* headache *sg*. **K~sprung** *m* header, dive. **K~stand** *m* headstand. **K~steinpflaster** *nt* cobblestones *pl*. **K~tuch** *nt* headscarf. **k~über** *adv* head first; (*fig*) headlong. **K~wäsche** *f* shampoo. **K~weh** *nt* headache

Kopie *f* -,-n copy. **k~ren** *vt* copy. **K~rschutz** *m* copy protection

Koppel[1] *f* -,-n enclosure; (*Pferde-*) paddock

Koppel[2] *nt* -s,- (*Mil*) belt. **k~n** *vt* couple

Koralle *f* -,-n coral

Korb *m* -[e]s,-̈e basket; **jdm einen K~ geben** (*fig*) turn s.o. down. **K~ball** *m* [kind of] netball

Kord *m* -s (*Textiles*) corduroy

Kordel *f* -,-n cord

Korinthe *f* -,-n currant

Kork *m* -s,-e cork. **K~en** *m* -s,-cork. **K~enzieher** *m* -s,- corkscrew

Korn[1] *nt* -[e]s,-̈er grain, (*Samen-*) seed; (*am Visier*) front sight

Körn|chen *nt* -s,- granule. **k~ig** *adj* granular

Körper *m* -s,- body; (*Geometry*) solid. **K~bau** *m* build, physique. **k~behindert** *adj* physically disabled. **k~lich** *adj* physical; (*Strafe*) corporal. **K~pflege** *f* personal hygiene. **K~schaft** *f* -,-en corporation, body

korrekt *adj* correct. **K~or** *m* -s,-en proof reader. **K~ur** *f* -,-en correction. **K~urabzug** *m* proof

Korrespon|dent(in) *m* -en,-en (*f* -,-nen) correspondent. **K~denz** *f*

-,-en correspondence

Korridor m -s,-e corridor

korrigieren vt correct

Korrosion f - corrosion

korrup|t adj corrupt. K~tion f - corruption

Korsett nt -[e]s,-e corset

koscher adj kosher

Kosename m pet name

Kosmet|ik f - beauty culture. K~ika ntpl cosmetics. K~ikerin f -,-nen beautician. k~isch adj cosmetic; (Chirurgie) plastic

kosm|isch adj cosmic. K~onaut(in) m -en,-en (f -,-nen) cosmonaut

Kosmos m - cosmos

Kost f - food; (Ernährung) diet; (Verpflegung) board

kostbar adj precious. K~keit f -,-en treasure

kosten¹ vt/i (haben) [von] etw k~ taste sth

kosten² vt cost; (brauchen) take; **wie viel kostet es?** how much is it? K~ pl expense sg, cost sg; (Jur) costs; **auf meine K~** at my expense. K~[vor]anschlag m estimate. k~los adj free ● adv free [of charge]

köstlich adj delicious; (entzückend) delightful

Kostprobe f taste; (fig) sample

Kostüm nt -s,-e (Theat) costume; (Verkleidung) fancy dress; (Schneider-) suit. k~iert adj k~iert sein be in fancy dress

Kot m -[e]s excrement

Kotelett /kɔtˈlɛt/ nt -s,-s chop, cutlet. K~en pl sideburns

Köter m -s,- (pej) dog

Kotflügel m (Auto) wing

kotzen vi (haben) ⊠ throw up

Krabbe f -,-n crab, shrimp

krabbeln vi (sein) crawl

Krach m -[e]s,ᵉe din, racket; (Knall) crash; (⊞: Streit) row; (⊞: Ruin) crash. k~en vi (haben) crash; **es hat gekracht** there was a bang=(⊞: Unfall) a crash ● (sein) break, crack; (auftreffen) crash (gegen into)

krächzen vi (haben) croak

Kraft f -,ᵉe strength; (Gewalt) force; (Arbeits-) worker; **in/außer K~** in/no longer in force. K~fahrer m driver. K~fahrzeug nt motor vehicle. K~fahrzeugbrief m [vehicle] registration document

kräftig adj strong; (gut entwickelt) sturdy; (nahrhaft) nutritious; (heftig) hard

kraft|los adj weak. K~probe f trial of strength. K~stoff m (Auto) fuel. K~wagen m motor car. K~werk nt power station

Kragen m -s,- collar

Krähe f -,-n crow

krähen vi (haben) crow

Kralle f -,-n claw

Kram m -s ⊞ things pl, ⊞ stuff; (Angelegenheiten) business. k~en vi (haben) rummage about (in + dat in; nach for)

Krampf m -[e]s,ᵉe cramp. K~adern fpl varicose veins. k~haft adj convulsive; (verbissen) desperate

Kran m -[e]s,ᵉe (Techn) crane

Kranich m -s,-e (Zool) crane

krank adj sick; (Knie, Herz) bad; k~ sein/werden be/fall ill. K~e(r) m/f sick man/woman, invalid; **die K~en** the sick pl

kränken vt offend, hurt

Kranken|bett nt sick bed. K~geld nt sickness benefit. K~gymnast|in m -en,-en (f -,-nen) physiotherapist. K~gymnastik f physiotherapy. K~haus nt

hospital. **K~kasse** f health insurance scheme/(Amt) office.
K~pflege f nursing. **K~saal** m [hospital] ward. **K~schein** m certificate of entitlement to medical treatment. **K~schwester** f nurse. **K~versicherung** f health insurance. **K~wagen** m ambulance

Krankheit f -,-en illness, disease

kränklich adj sickly

krank|melden vt sep jdn k~melden report s.o. sick; **sich k~melden** report sick

Kranz m -es,⁺e wreath

Krapfen m -s,- doughnut

Krater m -s,- crater

kratzen vt/i (haben) scratch. **K~er** m -s,- scratch

Kraul nt -s (Sport) crawl. **k~en¹** vi (haben/sein) (Sport) do the crawl

kraulen² vt tickle; **sich am Kopf k~** scratch one's head

kraus adj wrinkled; (Haar) frizzy; (verworren) muddled. **K~e** f -,-n frill

kräuseln vt wrinkle; frizz (Haar); gather (Stoff); **sich k~** wrinkle; (sich kringeln) curl; (Haar:) go frizzy

Kraut nt -[e]s, Kräuter herb; (SGer) cabbage; (Sauer-) sauerkraut

Krawall m -s,-e riot; (Lärm) row

Krawatte f -,-n [neck]tie

krea|tiv /krea'ti:f/ adj creative. **K~tur** f -,-en creature

Krebs m -es,-e crayfish; (Med) cancer; (Astrology) Cancer

Kredit m -[e]s,-e credit; (Darlehen) loan; **auf K~** on credit. **K~karte** f credit card

Kreide f - chalk. **k~ig** adj chalky

kreieren /kre'i:rən/ vt create

Kreis m -es,-e circle; (Admin) district

kreischen vt/i (haben) screech; (schreien) shriek

Kreisel m -s,- [spinning] top

kreis|en vi (haben) circle; revolve (um around). **K~förmig** adj circular. **K~lauf** m cycle; (Med) circulation. **K~säge** f circular saw. **K~verkehr** m [traffic] roundabout

Krem f -,-s & m -s cream

Krematorium nt -s,-ien crematorium

Krempe f -,-n [hat] brim

krempeln vt turn (nach oben up)

Krepp m -s,-s & -e crêpe

Krepppapier nt crêpe paper

Kresse f -,-n cress; (Kapuziner-) nasturtium

Kreta nt -s Crete

Kreuz nt -es,-e cross; (Kreuzung) intersection; (Mus) sharp; (Karten-spiel) clubs pl; (Anat) small of the back; **über K~** crosswise; **das K~ schlagen** cross oneself. **k~en** vt cross; **sich k~en** cross; (Straßen:) intersect; (Meinungen:) clash • vi (haben/sein) cruise. **K~fahrt** f (Naut) cruise. **K~gang** m cloister

kreuzig|en vt crucify. **K~ung** f -,-en crucifixion

Kreuz|otter f adder, common viper. **K~ung** f -,-en intersection; (Straßen-) crossroads sg. **K~verhör** nt cross-examination; **k~weise** adv crosswise. **K~worträtsel** nt crossword [puzzle]. **K~zug** m crusade

kribbel|ig adj ① edgy. **k~n** vi (haben) tingle; (kitzeln) tickle

kriech|en vi (sein) crawl; (fig) grovel (vor + dat to). **K~spur** f (Auto) crawler lane. **K~tier** nt reptile

Krieg m -[e]s,-e war

kriegen vt ① get; **ein Kind k~** have a baby

kriegs|beschädigt adj war-disabled. **K~dienstverweigerer** m

-s,- conscientious objector. **K∼ge-fangene(r)** m prisoner of war. **K∼gefangenschaft** f captivity. **K∼gericht** nt court martial. **K∼list** f stratagem. **K∼rat** m council of war. **K∼recht** nt martial law

Krimi m **-s,-s** 🖭 crime story/film. **K∼nalität** f - crime; (*Vorkommen*) crime rate. **K∼nalpolizei** f criminal investigation department. **K∼nalroman** m crime novel. **k∼nell** adj criminal

Krippe f **-,-n** manger; (*Weihnachts-*) crib; (*Kinder-*) crèche. **K∼nspiel** nt Nativity play

Krise f **-,-n** crisis

Kristall m **-s** crystal; (*geschliffen*) cut glass

Kritik f **-,-en** criticism; (*Rezension*) review; **unter aller K∼** 🖭 abysmal

Kriti|ker m **-s,-** critic; (*Rezensent*) reviewer. **k∼sch** adj critical. **k∼sieren** vt criticize; review

kritzeln vt/i (haben) scribble

Krokodil nt **-s,-e** crocodile

Krokus m **-,-[se]** crocus

Krone f **-,-n** crown; (*Baum-*) top

krönen vt crown

Kronleuchter m chandelier

Krönung f **-,-en** coronation; (fig: *Höhepunkt*) crowning event

Kropf m **-[e]s,-e** (Zool) crop; (Med) goitre

Kröte f **-,-n** toad

Krücke f **-,-n** crutch

Krug m **-[e]s,-e** jug; (Bier-) tankard

Krümel m **-s,-** crumb. **k∼ig** adj crumbly. **k∼n** vt crumble ● vi (haben) be crumbly

krumm adj crooked; (gebogen) curved; (verbogen) bent

krümmen vt bend; crook (Finger); **sich k∼** bend; (sich winden) writhe; (vor Lachen) double up

Krümmung f **-,-en** bend, curve

Krüppel m **-s,-** cripple

Kruste f **-,-n** crust; (Schorf) scab

Kruzifix nt **-es,-e** crucifix

Kub|a nt **-s** Cuba. **k∼anisch** adj Cuban

Kübel m **-s,-** tub; (Eimer) bucket; (Techn) skip

Küche f **-,-n** kitchen; (Kochkunst) cooking; **kalte/warme K∼** cold/hot food

Kuchen m **-s,-** cake

Küchen|herd m cooker, stove. **K∼maschine** f food processor, mixer. **K∼schabe** f **-,-n** cockroach

Kuckuck m **-s,-e** cuckoo

Kufe f **-,-n** (sledge) runner

Kugel f **-,-n** ball; (Geometry) sphere; (Gewehr-) bullet; (Sport) shot. **k∼förmig** adj spherical. **K∼lager** nt ball-bearing. **k∼n** vt/i (haben) roll; **sich k∼n** (vor Lachen) fall about. **K∼schreiber** m **-s,-** ballpoint [pen]. **k∼sicher** adj bulletproof. **K∼stoßen** nt **-s** shot-putting

Kuh f **-,-e** cow

kühl adj cool; (kalt) chilly. **K∼box** f **-,-en** cool box. **K∼e** f - coolness; chilliness. **k∼en** vt cool; refrigerate (Lebensmittel); chill (Wein). **K∼er** m **-s,-** (Auto) radiator. **K∼erhaube** f bonnet. **K∼fach** nt frozen-food compartment. **K∼raum** m cold store. **K∼schrank** m refrigerator. **K∼truhe** f freezer. **K∼wasser** nt [radiator] water

kühn adj bold

Kuhstall m cowshed

Küken nt **-s,-** chick; (Enten-) duckling

Kulissen fpl (Theat) scenery sg; (seitlich) wings; **hinter den K∼** (fig) behind the scenes

Kult m **-[e]s,-e** cult

kultivier|en vt cultivate. **k~t** adj cultured

Kultur f -,-en culture. **K~beutel** m toilet bag. **k~ell** adj cultural. **K~film** m documentary film. **K~tourismus** m cultural tourism

Kultusminister m Minister of Education and Arts

Kümmel m -s caraway; (Getränk) kümmel

Kummer m -s sorrow, grief; (Sorge) worry; (Ärger) trouble

kümmer|lich adj puny; (dürftig) meagre; (armselig) wretched. **k~n** vt concern; **sich k~n um** look after; (sich befassen) concern oneself with; (beachten) take notice of

kummervoll adj sorrowful

Kumpel m -s,- 🔲 mate

Kunde m -n,-n customer. **K~ndienst** m [after-sales] service

Kundgebung f -,-en (Pol) rally

kündig|en vt cancel (Vertrag); give notice of withdrawal for (Geld); give notice to quit (Wohnung); **seine Stellung k~en** give [in one's] notice ● vi (haben) give [in one's] notice; **jdm k~en** give s.o. notice. **K~ung** f -,-en cancellation; notice [of withdrawal/dismissal/to quit]; (Entlassung) dismissal. **K~ungsfrist** f period of notice

Kund|in f -,-nen [woman] customer. **K~schaft** f - clientele, customers pl

künftig adj future ● adv in future

Kunst f -,ˆe art; (Können) skill. **K~faser** f synthetic fibre. **K~galerie** f art gallery. **K~geschichte** f history of art. **K~gewerbe** nt arts and crafts pl. **K~griff** m trick

Künstler m -s,- artist; (Könner) master. **K~in** f -,-nen [woman] artist. **k~isch** adj artistic

künstlich adj artificial

Kunst|stoff m plastic. **K~stück** nt trick; (große Leistung) feat. **k~voll** adj artistic; (geschickt) skilful

kunterbunt adj multicoloured; (gemischt) mixed

Kupfer nt -s copper

Kupon /ku'põː/ m -s,-s voucher; (Zins-) coupon; (Stoff-) length

Kuppe f -,-n [rounded] top

Kuppel f -,-n dome

kuppel|n vt couple (an + acc to) ● vi (haben) (Auto) operate the clutch. **K~lung** f -,-en coupling; (Auto) clutch

Kur f -,-en course of treatment, cure

Kur A health cure in a spa town may last up to 6 weeks and usually involves a special diet, exercise programmes, physiotherapy and massage. The cure is intended for people with minor complaints or who are recovering from illness, and it plays an important role in preventative medicine in Germany.

Kür f -,-en (Sport) free exercise; (Eislauf) free programme

Kurbel f -,-n crank. **K~welle** f crankshaft

Kürbis m -ses,-se pumpkin

Kurier m -s,-e courier

kurieren vt cure

kurios adj curious, odd. **K~ität** f -,-en oddness; (Objekt) curiosity

Kurort m health resort; (Badeort) spa

Kurs m -es,-e course; (Aktien-) price. **K~buch** nt timetable

kursieren vi (haben) circulate

kursiv adj italic ● adv in italics. **K~schrift** f italics pl

Kursus m -,Kurse course

Kurswagen m through carriage

Kurtaxe f visitors' tax

Kurve f -,-n curve; (Straßen-) bend

kurz adj short; (knapp) brief; (rasch) quick; (schroff) curt; k~e Hosen shorts; vor k~em a short time ago; seit k~em lately; den Kürzeren ziehen get the worst of it; k~ vor shortly before; sich k~ fassen be brief; k~ und gut in short; zu k~ kommen get less than one's fair share. k~ärmelig adj short-sleeved. k~atmig adj k~atmig sein be short of breath

Kürze f - shortness; (Knappheit) brevity; in K~ shortly. k~n vt shorten; (verringern) cut

kurzfristig adj short-term ● adv at short notice

kürzlich adv recently

Kurz|meldung f newsflash. K~schluss m short circuit. K~schrift f shorthand. k~sichtig adj short-sighted. K~sichtigkeit f short-sightedness. K~streckenrakete f short-range missile

Kürzung f -,-en shortening; (Verringerung) cut (gen in)

Kurz|waren fpl haberdashery sg. K~welle f short wave

kuscheln (sich) vr snuggle (an + acc up to)

Kusine f -,-n [female] cousin

Kuss m -es,ⸯe kiss

küssen vt/i (haben) kiss; sich k~ kiss

Küste f -,-n coast

Küster m -s,- verger

Kutsch|e f -,-n [horse-drawn] carriage/(geschlossen) coach. K~er m -s,- coachman, driver

Kutte f -,-n (Relig) habit

Kutter m -s,- (Naut) cutter

Kuvert /ku've:ɐ̯/ nt -s,-s envelope

LI

Labor nt -s,-s & -e laboratory. L~ant(in) m -en,-en (f -,-nen) laboratory assistant

Labyrinth nt -[e]s,-e maze, labyrinth

Lache f -,-n puddle; (Blut-) pool

lächeln vi (haben) smile. L~ nt -s smile. l~d adj smiling

lachen vi (haben) laugh. L~ nt -s laugh; (Gelächter) laughter

lächerlich adj ridiculous; sich l~ machen make a fool of oneself. L~keit f -,-en ridiculousness; (Kleinigkeit) triviality

Lachs m -es,-e salmon

Lack m -[e]s,-e varnish; (Japan-) lacquer; (Auto) paint. l~en vt varnish. l~ieren vt varnish; (spritzen) spray. L~schuhe mpl patent-leather shoes

laden† vt load; (Electr) charge; (Jur: vor-) summon

Laden m -s,ⸯ shop; (Fenster-) shutter. L~dieb m shoplifter. L~schluss m [shop] closing time. L~tisch m counter

Laderaum m (Naut) hold

lädieren vt damage

Ladung f -,-en load; (Naut, Aviat) cargo; (elektrische) charge

Lage f -,-n position, situation; (Schicht) layer; nicht in der L~ sein not be in a position (zu to)

Lager nt -s,- camp; (L~haus) warehouse; (Vorrat) stock; (Techn) bearing; (Erz-, Ruhe-) bed; (eines Tieres)

lair; **[nicht] auf L~** [not] in stock.
L~haus nt warehouse. **l~n** vt
store; (legen) lay; **sich l~n** settle.
L~raum m store-room. **L~ung** f -
storage

Lagune f -,-n lagoon
lahm adj lame. **l~en** vi (haben)
be lame
lähmen vt paralyse
Lähmung f -,-en paralysis
Laib m -[e]s,-e loaf
Laich m -[e]s (Zool) spawn
Laie m -n,-n layman; (Theat) ama-
teur. **l~nhaft** adj amateurish
Laken nt -s,- sheet
Lakritze f - liquorice
lallen vt/i (haben) mumble; (Baby:)
babble
Lametta nt -s tinsel
Lamm nt -[e]s,ẅer lamb
Lampe f -,-n lamp; (Decken-,
Wand-) light; (Glüh-) bulb. **L~n-
fieber** nt stage fright
Lampion /lamˈpjɔŋ/ m -s,-s
Chinese lantern
Land nt -[e]s,ẅer country; (Fest-)
land; (Bundes-) state, Land; (Aust)
province; **auf dem L~e** in the
country; **an L~ gehen** (Naut) go
ashore. **L~arbeiter** m agricultural
worker. **L~ebahn** f runway. **l~en**
vt/i (sein) land; (🅵: gelangen)
end up

Land Germany is a federal
republic consisting of 16
member states called *Län-
der* or *Bundesländer*. Each *Land* is
responsible for local government,
educational and cultural affairs,
police and the environment.
Austria has 9 *Länder*, while the
Swiss equivalent is the ▸**KANTON**.

Ländereien pl estates

Länderspiel nt international
Landesverrat m treason
Landkarte f map
ländlich adj rural
Land|schaft f -,-en scenery;
(Geog, Kunst) landscape; (Gegend)
country[side]. **l~schaftlich** adj
scenic; (regional) regional. **L~strei-
cher** m -s,- tramp. **L~tag** m
state/(Aust) provincial parliament
Landung f -,-en landing
Land|vermesser m -s,- sur-
veyor. **L~weg** m country lane; **auf
dem L~weg** overland. **L~wirt** m
farmer. **L~wirtschaft** f agriculture;
(Hof) farm. **l~wirtschaftlich** adj
agricultural

lang[1] adv & prep (+ preceding acc or
preceding **an** + dat) along; **den od
am Fluss l~** along the river

lang[2] adj long; (groß) tall; **seit
l~em** for a long time ● adv **eine
Stunde l~** for an hour; **mein
Leben l~** all my life. **l~ärmelig**
adj long-sleeved. **l~atmig** adj long-
winded. **l~e** adv a long time;
(schlafen) late; **schon l~e** [for] a
long time; (zurückliegend) a long
time ago; **l~e nicht** not for a long
time; (bei weitem nicht) nowhere near

Länge f -,-n length; (Geog) longitude; **der L~ nach** lengthways
Längengrad m degree of longitude. **L~e** adv long; (örtlich) (län-
gere Zeit) [for] some time
Langeweile f - boredom; **L~
haben** be bored
lang|fristig adj long-term; (Vor-
hersage) long-range. **l~jährig** adj
long-standing; (Erfahrung) long
länglich adj oblong; **l~ rund** oval
längs adv & prep (+ gen/dat) along;
(der Länge nach) lengthways
lang|sam adj slow. **L~samkeit** f -

slowness

längst adv [schon] l∼ for a long time; (zurückliegend) a long time ago; l∼ nicht nowhere near

Lang|strecken- prefix long-distance; (Mil, Aviat) long-range. l∼weilen vt bore; sich l∼weilen be bored. l∼weilig adj boring

Lanze f -,-n lance

Lappalie /la'pa:liə/ f -,-n trifle

Lappen m -s,- cloth; (Anat) lobe

Laptop m -s,-s laptop

Lärche f -,-n larch

Lärm m -s noise. l∼end adj noisy

Larve /'larfə/ f -,-n larva; (Maske) mask

lasch adj listless; (schlaff) limp

Lasche f -,-n tab, flap

Laser /'le:-, 'la:zɐ/ m -s,- laser

---

lassen†

● transitive verb

····▸ (+ infinitive; veranlassen) **etw tun lassen** have or get sth done. **jdn etw tun lassen** make s.o. do sth; get s.o. to do sth **sich** dat **die Haare schneiden lassen** have or get one's hair cut. **jdn warten lassen** make or let s.o. wait; keep s.o. waiting. **jdn grüßen lassen** send one's regards to s.o. **jdn kommen/rufen lassen** send for s.o.

····▸ (+ infinitive; erlauben) let; allow; (hineinlassen/herauslassen) let or allow (**in** + acc into, **aus** + dat out of). **jdn etw tun lassen** let s.o. do sth; allow s.o. to do sth. **er ließ mich nicht ausreden** he didn't let me finish [what I was saying]

····▸ (belassen, bleiben lassen) leave. **jdn in Frieden lassen** leave s.o. in peace. **etw ungesagt lassen** leave sth unsaid

····▸ (unterlassen) stop. **das Rauchen lassen** stop smoking. **er kann es nicht lassen, sie zu quälen** he can't stop or he is forever tormenting her

····▸ (überlassen) **jdm etw lassen** let s.o. have sth

····▸ (als Aufforderung) **lass/lasst uns gehen/fahren!** let's go!

● reflexive verb

····▸ **das lässt sich machen** that can be done. **das lässt sich nicht beweisen** it can't be proved. **die Tür lässt sich leicht öffnen** the door opens easily

● intransitive verb

····▸ 🔲 **Lass mal. Ich mache das schon** Leave it. I'll do it

---

lässig adj casual. **L∼keit** f - casualness

Lasso nt -s,-s lasso

Last f -,-en load; (Gewicht) weight; (fig) burden; **L∼en** charges; (Steuern) taxes. **L∼auto** nt lorry. **l∼en** vi (haben) weigh heavily/(liegen) rest (**auf** + dat on)

Laster¹ m -s,- 🔲 lorry

Laster² nt -s,- vice

lästern vt blaspheme ● vi (haben) make disparaging remarks (**über** + acc about). **L∼ung** f -,-en blasphemy

lästig adj troublesome; **l∼ sein/werden** be/become a nuisance

Last|kahn m barge. **L∼[kraft]wagen** m lorry

Latein nt -[s] Latin. **L∼amerika** nt Latin America. **l∼isch** adj Latin

Laterne f -,-n lantern; (Straßen-) street lamp. **L∼npfahl** m lamp-post

latschen vi (sein) 🔲 traipse

Latte f -,-n slat; (Tor-, Hochsprung-) bar

Latz m -es,⁓e bib

Lätzchen nt -s,- [baby's] bib

Latzhose f dungarees pl

Laub nt -[e]s leaves pl; (L⁓werk) foliage. **L⁓baum** m deciduous tree

Laube f -,-n summer-house

Laub|säge f fretsaw. **L⁓wald** m deciduous forest

Lauch m -[e]s leeks pl

Lauer f auf der L⁓ liegen lie in wait. **l⁓n** vi (haben) lurk; **l⁓n auf** (+ acc) lie in wait for

Lauf m -[e]s, Läufe run; (Laufen) running; (Verlauf) course; (Wett-) race; (Sport: Durchgang) heat; (Gewehr-) barrel; im L⁓e (+ gen) in the course of. **L⁓bahn** f career. **l⁓en†** vi (sein) run; (zu Fuß gehen) walk; (gelten) be valid; **Ski/Schlittschuh l⁓en** ski/skate. **l⁓end** adj running; (gegenwärtig) current; (regelmäßig) regular; **auf dem L⁓enden sein** be up to date ● adv continually

Läufer m -s,- (Person, Teppich) runner; (Schach) bishop

Lauf|gitter nt play-pen. **L⁓masche** f ladder. **L⁓text** m marquee text. **L⁓zettel** m circular

Lauge f -,-n soapy water

Laun|e f -,-n mood; (Einfall) whim; **guter L⁓e sein, gute L⁓e haben** be in a good mood. **l⁓isch** adj moody

Laus f -,Läuse louse; (Blatt-) greenfly

lauschen vi (haben) listen

laut adj loud; (geräuschvoll) noisy; **l⁓ lesen** read aloud; **l⁓er stellen** turn up ● prep (+ gen/dat) according to. **L⁓** m -[e]s,-e sound

Laute f -,-n (Mus) lute

lauten vi (haben) (Text:) run, read

läuten vt/i (haben) ring

lauter adj pure; (ehrlich) honest; (Wahrheit) plain ● adj inv sheer; (nichts als) nothing but

laut|hals adv at the top of one's voice, (lachen) out loud. **l⁓los** adj silent, (Stille) hushed. **L⁓schrift** f phonetics pl. **L⁓sprecher** m loudspeaker. **L⁓stärke** f volume

lauwarm adj lukewarm

Lava f -,-ven lava

Lavendel m -s lavender

lavieren vi (haben) manœuvre

Lawine f -,-n avalanche

Lazarett nt -[e]s,-e military hospital

leasen /'liːsən/ vt rent

Lebehoch nt cheer

leben vt/i (haben) live (von on); **leb wohl!** farewell! **L⁓** nt -s,- life, (Treiben) bustle; **am L⁓** alive. **l⁓d** adj living

lebendig adj live; (lebhaft) lively; (anschaulich) vivid; **l⁓ sein** be alive. **L⁓keit** f - liveliness/vividness

Lebens|abend m old age. **L⁓alter** nt age. **l⁓fähig** adj viable. **L⁓gefahr** f mortal danger; **in L⁓gefahr** in mortal danger; (Patient) critically ill. **l⁓gefährlich** adj extremely dangerous; (Verletzung) critical. **L⁓haltungskosten** pl cost of living sg. **l⁓länglich** adj life-long ● adv for life. **L⁓lauf** m curriculum vitae. **L⁓mittel** ntpl food sg. **L⁓mittelgeschäft** nt food shop. **L⁓mittelhändler** m grocer. **L⁓retter** m rescuer; (beim Schwimmen) life-guard. **L⁓unterhalt** m livelihood; **seinen L⁓unterhalt verdienen** earn one's living. **L⁓versicherung** f life assurance. **L⁓wandel** m conduct. **L⁓wichtig** adj vital. **L⁓zeit** f auf L⁓zeit for life

Leber f -,-n liver. **L⁓fleck** m mole

Lebe|wesen nt living being.

L~wohl nt -s,-s & -e farewell

leb|haft adj lively; (Farbe) vivid. **L~kuchen** m gingerbread. **L~los** adj lifeless. **L~zeiten** fpl zu jds **L~zeiten** in s.o.'s lifetime

leck adj leaking. **L~** nt -s,-s leak. **l~en[1]** vi (haben) leak

lecken[2] vi (haben) lick

lecker adj tasty. **L~bissen** m delicacy

Leder nt -s,- leather

ledig adj single, unmarried

leer adj empty; (unbesetzt) vacant; **l~ laufen** (sep) vi idle. **l~en** vt empty; **sich l~en** empty. **L~lauf** m (Auto) neutral. **L~ung** f -,-en (Post) collection

legal adj legal. **l~isieren** vt legalize. **L~ität** f - legality

Legasthenie f - dyslexia **L~theniker** m -s,- dyslexic

legen vt put; (hin-, ver-) lay; set (Haare); **sich l~** lie down; (nachlassen) subside

Legende f -,-n legend

leger /le'ʒe:ɐ̯/ adj casual

Legierung f -,-en alloy

Legion f -,-en legion

Legislative f - legislature

legitim adj legitimate. **L~ität** f - legitimacy

Lehm m -s clay

Lehne f -,-n (Rücken-) back; (Arm-) arm. **l~en** vt lean (an + acc against); **sich l~en** lean (an + acc against) ● vi (haben) be leaning (an + acc against)

Lehr|buch nt textbook. **L~e** f -,-n apprenticeship; (Anschauung) doctrine; (Theorie) theory; (Wissenschaft) science; (Erfahrung) lesson. **l~en** vt/i (haben) teach. **L~er** m -s,- teacher; (Fahr-) instructor. **L~erin** f -,-nen teacher. **L~erzim-**

-mer nt staff-room. **L~fach** nt (Sch) subject. **L~gang** m course. **L~kraft** f teacher. **L~ling** m -s,-e apprentice; (Auszubildender) trainee. **L~plan** m syllabus. **l~reich** adj instructive. **L~stelle** f apprenticeship. **L~stuhl** m (Univ) chair. **L~zeit** f apprenticeship

Leib m -es,-er body; (Bauch) belly. **L~eserziehung** f (Sch) physical education. **L~gericht** nt favourite dish. **l~lich** adj physical; (blutsverwandt) real, natural. **L~wächter** m bodyguard

Leiche f -,-n [dead] body; corpse. **L~nbestatter** m -s,- undertaker. **L~nhalle** f mortuary. **L~nwagen** m hearse. **L~nzug** m funeral procession, cortège

Leichnam m -s,-e [dead] body

leicht adj light; (Stoff) lightweight; (gering) slight; (mühelos) easy; **jdm l~ fallen** be easy for s.o.; **etw l~ machen** make sth easy (dat for); **es sich (dat) l~ machen** take the easy way out; **etw l~ nehmen** (fig) take sth lightly. **L~athletik** f [track and field] athletics sg. **L~gewicht** nt (Boxen) lightweight. **l~gläubig** adj gullible. **l~hin** adv casually. **L~igkeit** f - lightness; (Mühelosigkeit) ease; (L~sein) easiness; **mit L~igkeit** with ease. **L~sinn** m carelessness; recklessness; (Frivolität) frivolity. **l~sinnig** adj careless; (unvorsichtig) reckless

Leid nt -[e]s sorrow, grief; (Böses) harm; **es tut mir l~** I am sorry; **er tut mir l~** I feel sorry for him. **l~** adj jdn/etw **l~ sein/werden** be/get tired of s.o./something

Leide|form f passive. **l~n[1]** vt/i (haben) suffer (an + dat from); **jdn/ etw nicht l~n können** dislike s.o./ something. **L~n** nt -s,- suffering; (Med) complaint; (Krankheit) disease. **l~nd** adj suffering. **L~nschaft** f -,-en passion. **l~nschaftlich** adj passionate

leider adv unfortunately; **l~ ja/nicht** I'm afraid so/not

Leier|kasten m barrel-organ. **l~n** vt/i (haben) wind; (herunter-) drone out

Leih|e f -,-n loan. **l~en†** vt lend; **sich** (dat) **etw l~en** borrow sth. **L~gabe** f loan. **L~gebühr** f rental; lending charge. **L~haus** nt pawnshop. **L~wagen** m hire-car. **l~weise** adv on loan

Leim m -s glue. **l~en** vt glue

Leine f -,-n rope; (Wäsche-) line; (Hunde-) lead, leash

Lein|en nt -s linen. **L~wand** f linen; (Kunst) canvas; (Film-) screen

leise adj quiet; (Stimme, Berührung) soft; (schwach) faint; (leicht) light; **l~r stellen** turn down

Leiste f -,-n strip; (Holz-) batten; (Anat) groin

leist|en vt achieve, accomplish; **sich** (dat) **etw l~en** treat oneself to sth; (①: anstellen) get up to sth; **ich kann es mir nicht l~en** I can't afford it. **L~ung** f -,-en achievement; (Sport, Techn) performance; (Produktion) output; (Zahlung) payment

Leit|artikel m leader, editorial. **l~en** vt run, manage; (an-/hinführen) lead; (Mus, Techn, Phys) conduct; (lenken, schicken) direct. **l~end** adj leading; (Posten) executive

Leiter¹ f -,-n ladder

Leit|er² m -s,- director; (Comm) manager; (Führer) leader; (Mus, Phys) conductor. **L~erin** f -,-nen director; manageress; leader. **L~planke** f crash barrier. **L~spruch** m motto. **L~ung** f -,-en

(Führung) direction; (Comm) management; (Aufsicht) control; (Electr: Schnur) lead, flex; (Kabel) cable; (Telefon-) line; (Rohr-) pipe; (Haupt-) main. **L~ungswasser** nt tap water

Lektion /-'tsjo:n/ f -,-en lesson

Lekt|or m -s,-en, **L~orin** f -,-nen (Univ) assistant lecturer; (Verlags-) editor. **L~üre** f -,-n reading matter

Lende f -,-n loin

lenk|en vt guide; (steuern) steer; (regeln) control; **jds Aufmerksamkeit auf sich** (acc) **l~en** attract s.o.'s attention. **L~rad** nt steering-wheel. **L~stange** f handlebars pl. **L~ung** f -,-en steering

Leopard m -en,-en leopard

Lepra f - leprosy

Lerche f -,-n lark

lernen vt/i (haben) learn; (für die Schule) study

Lernkurve f learning curve

Lesb|ierin /'lɛsbjərɪn/ f -,-nen lesbian. **l~isch** adj lesbian

les|en† vt/i (haben) read; (Univ) lecture ●vt pick, gather. **L~en** nt -s reading. **L~er(in)** m -s,- (f -,-nen) reader. **l~erlich** adj legible. **L~ezeichen** nt bookmark

lethargisch adj lethargic

Lettland nt - Latvia

letzt|e(r,s) adj last; (neueste) latest; in **l~er Zeit** recently; **l~en Endes** in the end. **l~ens** adv recently; (zuletzt) lastly. **l~ere(r,s)** adj the latter; **der/die/das L~ere** (**l~ere**) the latter

Leucht|e f -,-n light. **l~en** vi (haben) shine. **l~end** adj shining. **L~er** m -s,- candlestick. **L~feuer** nt beacon. **L~rakete** f flare. **L~reklame** f neon sign. **L~röhre** f fluorescent tube. **L~turm** m lighthouse

leugnen vt deny

Leukämie f - leukaemia

Leumund m -s reputation

Leute pl people; (Mil) men; (Arbeiter) workers

Leutnant m -s,-s second lieutenant

Lexikon nt -s,-ka encyclopaedia; (Wörterbuch) dictionary

Libanon (der) -s Lebanon

Libelle f -,-n dragonfly

liberal adj (Pol) liberal

Libyen nt -s Libya

Licht nt -[e]s,-er light; (Kerze) candle; l~ adj bright; (Med) lucid; (spärlich) sparse. L~bild nt [passport] photograph; (Dia) slide. L~blick m (fig) ray of hope. l~en vt thin out; den Anker l~en (Naut) weigh anchor; sich l~en become less dense; thin. L~hupe f headlight flasher; die L~hupe betätigen flash one's headlights. L~maschine f dynamo. L~ung f -,-en clearing

Lid nt -[e]s,-er [eye]lid. L~schatten m eye-shadow

lieb adj dear; (nett) nice; (artig) good; jdn l~ haben be fond of s.o.; (lieben) love s.o.; es wäre mir l~er I should prefer it (wenn if)

Liebe f -,-n love. l~n vt love; (mögen) like; sich l~n love each other; (körperlich) make love. l~nd adj loving. l~nswert a lovable. L~nswürdig adj kind. L~nswürdigerweise adv very kindly

lieber adv rather; (besser) better; l~ mögen like better; ich trinke l~ Tee I prefer tea

Liebes|brief m love letter. L~dienst m favour. L~kummer m heartache. L~paar nt [pair of] lovers

lieb|evoll adj loving, affectionate. L~haber m -s,- lover; (Sammler) collector. L~haberei f -,-en hobby. L~kosung f -,-en caress. l~lich adj lovely; (sanft) gentle; (süß) sweet. L~ling m darling; (Bevorzugte) favourite. L~lings- prefix favourite. l~los adj loveless; (Eltern) uncaring; (unfreundlich) unkind. L~schaft f -,-en [love] affair.

l~ste(r,s) adj dearest; (bevorzugt) favourite ● adv am l~sten best [of all]; jdn/etw am l~sten mögen like s.o./something best [of all]. L~ste(r) m/f beloved; (Schatz) sweetheart

Lied nt -[e]s,-er song

liederlich adj slovenly; (unordentlich) untidy. L~keit f - slovenliness; untidiness

Lieferant m -en,-en supplier

liefer|bar adj (Comm) available. l~n vt supply; (zustellen) deliver; (hervorbringen) yield. L~ung f -,-en delivery; (Sendung) consignment

Liege f -,-n couch. l~n† vi (haben) lie; (gelegen sein) be situated; l~n bleiben remain lying [there]; (im Bett) stay in bed; (Ding:) be left; (Schnee:) settle; (Arbeit:) remain undone; (zurückgelassen werden) be left behind; l~n lassen leave; (zurücklassen) leave behind; (nicht fortführen) leave undone; l~n an (+ dat) (fig) be due to; (abhängen) depend on; jdm [nicht] l~n [not] suit s.o.; mir liegt viel daran it is very important to me. L~stuhl m deckchair. L~stütz m -es,-e press-up, (Amer) push-up. L~wagen m couchette car

Lift m -[e]s,-e & -s lift

Liga f -,-gen league

Likör m -s,-e liqueur

lila inv adj mauve; (dunkel) purple

Lilie /ˈliːliə/ f -,-n lily

Liliputaner(in) m -s,- (f -,-nen) dwarf

Limo f -,-[s] 🔲, **L~nade** f -,-n
fizzy drink; lemonade

Limousine /limu'zi:nə/ f -,-n
saloon

lind adj mild

Linde f -,-n lime tree

linder|n vt relieve, ease. **L~ung** f
- relief

Lineal nt -s,-e ruler

Linie /-jə/ f -,-n line; (Zweig)
branch; (Bus-) route; **L~** 4 number
4 [bus/tram]; **in erster L~** primarily. **L~nflug** m scheduled flight.
L~nrichter m linesman

lin[i]iert adj lined, ruled

Link|e f -n,-n left side; (Hand) left
hand; (Boxen) left; **die L~e** (Pol)
the left. **l~e(r,s)** adj left; (Pol) left-
wing; **l~e Masche** purl

links adv on the left; (bei Stoff) on
the wrong side; (verkehrt) inside
out; **l~stricken** purl. **L~händer-
(in)** m -s,- (f -,-nen) lefthander.
l~händig adj & adv lefthanded

Linoleum /-leʊm/ nt -s lino, linoleum

Linse f -,-n lens; (Bot) lentil

Lippe f -,-n lip. **L~nstift** m lipstick

Liquid|ation /-'tsjo:n/ f -,-en li-
quidation. **l~ieren** vt liquidate

lispeln vt/i (haben) lisp

List f -,-en trick, ruse

Liste f -,-n list

listig adj cunning, crafty

Litanei f -,-en litany

Litauen nt -s Lithuania

Liter m & nt -s,- litre

Literatur f - literature

Liturgie f -,-n liturgy

Litze f -,-n braid

Lizenz f -,-en licence

Lob nt -[e]s praise

Lobby /'lɔbi/ f - (Pol) lobby

loben vt praise

löblich adj praiseworthy

Lobrede f eulogy

Loch nt -[e]s,-̈er hole. **l~en** vt
punch a hole/holes in; punch (Fahrkarte). **L~er** m -s,- punch

löcherig adj full of holes

Locke f -,-n curl. **l~n¹** vt curl; **sich
l~n** curl

locken² vt lure, entice; (reizen)
tempt. **l~d** adj tempting

Lockenwickler m -s,- curler;
(Rolle) roller

locker adj loose; (Seil) slack; (Erde)
light; (zwanglos) casual; (zu frei) lax.
l~n vt loosen; slacken (Seil); break
up (Boden); relax (Griff); **sich l~n**
become loose; (Seil:) slacken; (sich
entspannen) relax

lockig adj curly

Lockmittel nt bait

Loden m -s (Textiles) loden

Löffel m -s,- spoon; (L~ voll)
spoonful. **l~n** vt spoon up

Logarithmus m -,-men
logarithm

Logbuch nt (Naut) log-book

Loge /'lo:ʒə/ f -,-n lodge;
(Theat) box

Log|ik f - logic. **l~isch** adj logical

Logo nt -s,-s logo

Lohn m -[e]s,-̈e wages pl, pay;
(fig) reward. **L~empfänger** m
wage-earner. **l~en** vi|r (haben)
[sich] l~en be worth it or worth
while ● vt be worth. **l~end** adj
worthwhile; (befriedigend) rewarding. **L~erhöhung** f [pay] rise.
L~steuer f income tax

Lok f -,-s 🔲 = Lokomotive

Lokal nt -s,-e restaurant;
(Trink-) bar

Lokomotiv|e f -,-n engine, loco-
motive. **L~führer** m engine driver

London | Luft 156

London nt -s London. **L~er** adj
London ● m -s,- Londoner

Lorbeer m -s,-en laurel. **L~blatt**
nt (Culin) bay-leaf

Lore f -,-n (Rail) truck

Los nt -es,-e lot; (Lotterie-) ticket;
(Schicksal) fate

los pred adj los sein be loose; **jdn/
etw los sein** be rid of s.o./some-
thing; **was ist [mit ihm] los?**
what's the matter [with him]? ● adv
los! go on! **Achtung, fertig, los!**
ready, steady, go!

lösbar adj soluble

losbinden† vt sep untie

Lösch|blatt nt sheet of blotting-
paper. **l~en** vt put out, extinguish;
quench (Durst); blot (Tinte); (tilgen)
cancel; (streichen) delete

Löschfahrzeug nt fire-engine

lose adj loose

Lösegeld nt ransom

losen vt (haben) draw lots (um for)

lösen vt undo; (lockern) loosen;
(entfernen) detach; (klären) solve;
(auflösen) dissolve; cancel (Vertrag);
break off (Beziehung); (kaufen) buy;
sich l~ come off; (sich trennen) detach oneself/itself; (lose werden)
come undone; (sich klären) resolve
itself; (sich auflösen) dissolve

los|fahren† vi sep (sein) start;
(Auto) drive off; **l~fahren nach** (+
dat) head for. **l~gehen†** vi sep
(sein) set off; (ℤ: anfangen) start;
(Bombe:) go off; **l~gehen nach** (+
dat) head for; (fig: angreifen) go for.
l~kommen† vi sep (sein) get away
(von from). **l~lassen†** vt sep let go
of; (freilassen) release

löslich adj soluble

los|lösen vt sep detach; **sich l~lö-
sen** become detached; (fig) break
away (von from). **l~machen** vt sep
detach; untie. **l~reißen†** vt sep tear

off; **sich l~reißen** break free; (fig)
tear oneself away. **l~schicken** vt
sep send off. **l~sprechen†** vt sep
absolve (von from)

Losung f -,-en (Pol) slogan; (Mil)
password

Lösung f -,-en solution. **L~smit-
tel** nt solvent

loswerden† vt sep get rid of

Lot nt -[e]s,-e perpendicular; (Blei-)
plumb[-bob]. **l~en** vt plumb

löt|en vt solder. **L~lampe** f
blow-lamp

lotrecht adj perpendicular

Lotse m -n,-n (Naut) pilot. **l~n** vt
(Naut) pilot; (fig) guide

Lotterie f -,-n lottery

Lotto nt -s,-s lotto; (Lotterie) lottery

Love Parade A techno
music and dance festival,
which takes place in Berlin
every summer. Originally a celebration of youth culture and very
popular with young people, this
festival has become a major tourist attraction.

Löw|e m -n,-n lion; (Astrology) Leo.
L~enzahn m (Bot) dandelion.
L~in f -,-nen lioness

loyal /loa'ja:l/ adj loyal. **L~ität** f -
loyalty

Luchs m -es,-e lynx

Lücke f -,-n gap. **l~nhaft** adj incomplete; (Wissen) patchy. **l~nlos**
adj complete; (Folge) unbroken

Luder nt -s,- ⚠ (Frau) bitch

Luft f -,ˣe air; **tief l~ holen** take a
deep breath; **in die l~ gehen** explode. **L~aufnahme** f aerial photograph.
L~ballon m balloon. **L~blase** f air
bubble. **L~druck** m atmospheric
pressure

lüften vt air; raise (Hut); reveal (Geheimnis)

Luft|fahrt f aviation. **L~fahrtgesellschaft** f airline. **L~gewehr** nt airgun. **l~ig** adj airy; (Kleid) light. **L~kissenfahrzeug** nt hovercraft. **L~krieg** m aerial warfare. **l~leer** adj **l~leerer Raum** vacuum. **L~linie** f 100 km **L~linie** 100 km as the crow flies. **L~matratze** f airbed, inflatable mattress. **L~pirat** m hijacker. **L~post** f airmail. **L~röhre** f windpipe. **L~schiff** nt airship. **L~schlange** f [paper] streamer. **L~schutzbunker** m air-raid shelter

Lüftung f - ventilation

Luft|veränderung f change of air. **L~waffe** f air force. **L~zug** m draught

Lüg|e f -,-n lie. **l~en†** vt/i (haben) lie. **L~ner(in)** m -s,- (f -,-nen) liar. **l~nerisch** adj untrue; (Person) untruthful

Luke f -,-n hatch; (Dach-) skylight

Lümmel m -s,- lout

Lump m -en,-en scoundrel. **L~en** m -s,- rag; **in L~en** in rags. **L~enpack** nt riff-raff. **L~ensammler** m rag-and-bone man. **L~ig** adj mean, shabby

Lunge f -,-n lungs pl; (L~nflügel) lung. **L~nentzündung** f pneumonia

Lupe f -,-n magnifying glass

Lurch m -[e]s,-e amphibian

Lust f -,⁻e pleasure; (Verlangen) desire; (sinnliche Begierde) lust; **L~ haben** feel like (**auf etw** acc sth); **ich habe keine L~** I don't feel like it; (will nicht) I don't want to

lustig adj jolly; (komisch) funny; **sich l~ machen über** (+ acc) make fun of

Lüstling m -s,-e lecher

lust|los adj listless. **L~mörder** m sex killer. **L~spiel** nt comedy

lutsch|en vt/i (haben) suck. **L~er** m -s,- lollipop

Lüttich nt -s Liège

Luv f & nt - **nach Luv** (Naut) to windward

luxuriös adj luxurious

Luxus m - luxury

Lymph|drüse f /'lymf-/ f, **L~knoten** m lymph gland

lynchen /'lynçən/ vt lynch

Lyr|ik f - lyric poetry. **L~iker** m -s,- lyric poet. **l~isch** adj lyrical

Mm

Machart f style

machen

● transitive verb

···➤ (herstellen, zubereiten) make (money, beds, music, exception, etc). **aus Plastik/Holz gemacht** made of plastic/wood. **sich etw machen lassen** have sth made. **etw aus jdm machen** make s.o. into sth. **jdn zum Präsidenten machen** make s.o. president. **er machte sich** (dat) **viele Freunde/Feinde** he made a lot of friends/enemies. **jdm/ sich** (dat) **[einen] Kaffee machen** make [some] coffee for s.o./oneself. **ein Foto machen** take a photo

···➤ (verursachen) make, cause (difficulties); cause (pain, anxiety). **jdm Arbeit machen** make [extra] work for s.o., cause s.o. extra work. **jdm Mut/Hoffnung machen** give s.o. courage/hope.

das macht Hunger/Durst this makes you hungry/thirsty. **das macht das Wetter** that's [because of] the weather

····> (*ausführen, ordnen*) do (*job, repair, fam: room, washing, etc.*); take (*walk, trip, exam, course*). **sie machte mir die Haare** [!] she did my hair for me. **einen Besuch [bei jdm] machen** pay [s.o.] a visit

····> (*tun*) do (*nothing, everything*). **was machst du [da]?** what are you doing? **so etwas macht man nicht** that [just] isn't done

····> **was macht ... ?** (*wie ist es um bestellt?*) how is ...? **was macht die Gesundheit/Arbeit?** how are you keeping/how is the job [getting on]?

····> (*Math: ergeben*) be. **zwei mal zwei macht vier** two times two is four. **das macht 6 Euro [zusammen]** that's or that comes to six euros [altogether]

····> (*schaden*) **was macht das schon?** what does it matter? **[das] macht nichts!** [!] it doesn't matter

····> **mach's gut!** [!] look after yourself; (*auf Wiedersehen*) so long!

• *reflexive verb*

····> **sich machen** [!] do well

····> **sich an etw** (*acc*) **machen** get down to sth. **sie machte sich an die Arbeit** she got down to work

• *intransitive verb*

····> **das macht hungrig/durstig** it makes you hungry/thirsty. **das macht dick** it's fattening

Macht *f -,⸚e* power. **M~haber** *m -s,-* ruler

mächtig *adj* powerful • *adv* [!]

terribly

machtlos *adj* powerless

Mädchen *nt -s,-* girl; (*Dienst-*) maid. **m~haft** *adj* girlish. **M~name** *m* girl's name; (*vor der Ehe*) maiden name

Made *f -,-n* maggot

madig *adj* maggoty

Madonna *f -,-nen* madonna

Magazin *nt -s,-e* magazine; (*Lager*) warehouse; store-room

Magd *f -,⸚e* maid

Magen *m -s,⸚* stomach. **M~verstimmung** *f* stomach upset

mager *adj* thin; (*Fleisch*) lean; (*Boden*) poor; (*dürftig*) meagre. **M~keit** *f -* thinness; leanness. **M~sucht** *f* anorexia

Magie *f -* magic

Magiler /'ma:gje/ *m -s,-* magician. **m~isch** *adj* magic

Magistrat *m -s,-e* city council

Magnet *m -en & -[e]s,-e* magnet. **m~isch** *adj* magnetic

Mahagoni *nt -s* mahogany

Mäh|drescher *m -s,-* combine harvester. **m~en** *vt/i* (*haben*) mow

Mahl *nt -[e]s,⸚er & -e* meal

mahlen† *vt* grind

Mahlzeit *f* meal; **M~!** enjoy your meal!

Mähne *f -,-n* mane

mahn|en *vt/i* (*haben*) remind (*wegen* about); (*ermahnen*) admonish; (*auffordern*) urge (*zu* to). **M~ung** *f -,-en* reminder; admonition

Mai *m -[e]s,-e* May; **der Erste Mai** May Day. **M~glöckchen** *nt -s,-* lily of the valley

Mailand *nt -s* Milan

Mais *m -es* maize; (*Culin*) sweet corn

Majestät *f -,-en* majesty.

Major | Mansarde

m~isch adj majestic

Major m -s,-e major

Majoran m -s marjoram

makaber adj macabre

Makel m -s,- blemish; (Defekt) flaw

Makkaroni pl macaroni sg

Makler m -s,- (Comm) broker

Makrele f -,-n mackerel

Makrone f -,-n macaroon

mal adv (Math) times; (bei Maßen) by; (🇮🇹: einmal) once; (eines Tages) one day; **nicht mal** not even

Mal nt -[e]s,-e time; **zum ersten/ letzten Mal** for the first/last time; **ein für alle Mal** once and for all; **jedes Mal** every time; **jedes Mal, wenn** whenever

Mal|buch nt colouring book. **m~en** vt/i (haben) paint. **M~er** m -s,- painter. **M~erei** f -,-en painting. **M~erin** f -,-nen painter. **m~erisch** adj picturesque

Mallorca /ma'lɔrka, -'jɔrka/ nt -s Majorca

malnehmen† vt sep multiply (**mit** by)

Malz nt -es malt

Mama /'mama, ma'ma:/ f -s mummy

Mammut nt -s,-e & -s mammoth

mampfen vt 🇮🇹 munch

man pron one, you; (die Leute) people, they; **man sagt** they say, it is said

manch|e(r,s) pron many a; [so] **m~es Mal** many a time; **m~e Leute** some people ● (substantivisch) **m~er/m~e** many a man/ woman; **m~e** pl some (Leute) some people; (viele) many [people]; **m~es** some things; (vieles) many things. **m~erlei** inv adj various ● pron various things

manchmal adv sometimes

Mandant(in) m -en,-en (f -,-nen) (Jur) client

Mandarine f -,-n mandarin

Mandat nt -[e]s,-e mandate; (Jur) brief; (Pol) seat

Mandel f -,-n almond; (Anat) tonsil. **M~entzündung** f tonsillitis

Manege /ma'neːʒə/ f -,-n ring; (Reit-) arena

Mangel[1] m -s,⁼ lack; (Knappheit) shortage; (Med) deficiency; (Fehler) defect

Mangel[2] f -,-n mangle

mangel|haft adj faulty, defective; (Sch) unsatisfactory. **m~n** vi (haben) **es m~t an** (+ dat) there is a lack/(Knappheit) shortage of

mangeln[2] vt put through the mangle

Manie f -,-n mania

Manier f -,-n manner; **M~en** pl manners. **m~lich** adj well-mannered ● adv properly

Manifest nt -[e]s,-e manifesto

Maniküre f -,-n manicure; (Person) manicurist. **m~n** vt manicure

Manko nt -s,-s disadvantage; (Fehlbetrag) deficit

Mann m -[e]s,⁼er man; (Ehe-) husband

Männchen nt -s,- little man; (Zool) male

Mannequin /'manəkɛ̃/ nt -s,-s model

männlich adj male; (Gram & fig) masculine; (mannhaft) manly; (Frau) mannish. **M~keit** f - masculinity; (fig) manhood

Mannschaft f -,-en team; (Naut) crew

Manöv|er nt -s,- manœuvre; (Winkelzug) trick. **m~rieren** vt/i (haben) manœuvre

Mansarde f -,-n attic room;

Manschette | Masse

(*Wohnung*) attic flat

Manschette *f* -,-n cuff.
M~nknopf *m* cuff-link

Mantel *m* -s,⸗ coat; overcoat

Manuskript *nt* -[e]s,-e manuscript

Mappe *f* -,-n folder; (*Akten-*) briefcase; (*Schul-*) bag

Märchen *nt* -s,- fairy-tales

Margarine *f* - margarine

Marienkäfer /ma'riːən-/ *m* lady-bird

Marihuana *nt* -s marijuana

Marine *f* marine; (*Kriegs-*) navy.
m~blau *adj* navy [blue]

marinieren *vt* marinade

Marionette *f* -,-n puppet, marionette

Mark¹ *f* -,- (*alte Währung*) mark;
drei M~ three marks

Mark² *nt* -[e]s (*Knochen-*) marrow
(*Bot*)pith; (*Frucht-*) pulp

markant *adj* striking

Marke *f* -,-n token; (*rund*) disc; (*Erkennungs-*) tag; (*Brief-*) stamp; (*Lebensmittel-*) coupon; (*Spiel-*) counter; (*Markierung*) mark; (*Fabrikat*) make; (*Tabak-*) brand. **M~nartikel** *m* branded article

markieren *vt* mark; (ℝ: *vortäuschen*) fake

Markise *f* -,-n awning

Markstück *nt* one-mark piece

Markt *m* -[e]s,⸗e market;
(*M~platz*) market-place. **M~forschung** *f* market research

Marmelade *f* -,-n jam; (*Orangen-*) marmalade

Marmor *m* -s marble

Marokko *nt* -s Morocco

Marone *f* -,-n [sweet] chestnut

Marsch *m* -[e]s,⸗e march. **m~** *int* (*Mil*) march!

Marschall *m* -s,⸗e marshal

marschieren *vi* (*sein*) march

Marter *f* -,-n torture. **m~n** *vt* torture

Märtyrer(in) *m* -s,- (*f* -,-nen) martyr

Marxismus *m* - Marxism

März *m* -,-e March

Marzipan *nt* -s marzipan

Masche *f* -,-n stitch; (*im Netz*) mesh; (ℝ: *Trick*) dodge. **M~ndraht** *m* wire netting

Maschine *f* -,-n machine; (*Flugzeug*) plane; (*Schreib-*) typewriter; **M~e schreiben** type. **m~egeschrieben** *adj* typewritten, typed. **m~ell** *adj* machine ● *adv* by machine. **M~enbau** *m* mechanical engineering. **M~engewehr** *nt* machine-gun. **M~ist** *m* -en,-en machinist; (*Naut*) engineer

Masern *pl* measles *sg*

Maserung *f* -,-en [wood] grain

Maske *f* -,-n mask; (*Theat*) make-up

maskieren *vt* mask; **sich m~** dress up (**als** as)

maskulin *adj* masculine

Masochist *m* -en,-en masochist

Maß¹ *nt* -es,-e measure; (*Abmessung*) measurement; (*Grad*) degree; (*Mäßigung*) moderation; **in hohem Maße** to a high degree

Maß² *f* -,- (*SGer*) litre [of beer]

Massage /ma'saːʒə/ *f* -,-n massage

Massaker *nt* -s,- massacre

Maßband *nt* (*pl* -bänder) tape-measure

Masse *f* -,-n mass; (*Culin*) mixture; (*Menschen-*) crowd; **eine M~ Arbeit** ℝ masses of work. **m~nhaft** *adv* in huge quantities. **M~nproduktion** *f* mass production. **M~nvernichtungswaffen** *fpl* weapons of mass destruction. **m~nweise** *adv* in huge numbers

Masseu|r /ma'sø:ɐ̯/ *m* **-s,-e** masseur. **M~se** *f* **-,-n** masseuse

maß|gebend *adj* authoritative; (*einflussreich*) influential. **m~geblich** *adj* decisive. **m~geschneidert** *adj* made-to-measure

massieren *vt* massage

massig *adj* massive

mäßig *adj* moderate; (*mittelmäßig*) indifferent. **m~en** *vt* moderate; **sich m~en** moderate; (*sich beherrschen*) restrain oneself. **M~ung** *f* **-** moderation

massiv *adj* solid; (*stark*) heavy

Maß|krug *m* beer mug. **m~los** *adj* excessive; (*grenzenlos*) boundless; (*äußerst*) extreme. **M~nahme** *f* **-,-n** measure

Maßstab *m* scale; (*Norm & fig*) standard. **m~sgerecht, m~sgetreu** *adj* scale ● *adv* to scale

Mast¹ *m* **-[e]s,-en** pole; (*Überland-*) pylon; (*Naut*) mast

Mast² *f* **-** fattening

mästen *vt* fatten

masturbieren *vi* (*haben*) masturbate

Material *nt* **-s,-ien** material; (*coll*) materials *pl*. **M~ismus** *m* **-** materialism. **m~istisch** *adj* materialistic

Mathe *f* **-** 🄳 maths *sg*

Mathe|matik *f* **-** mathematics *sg*. **M~matiker** *m* **-s,-** mathematician. **m~matisch** *adj* mathematical

Matinee *f* **-,-n** (*Theat*) morning performance

Matratze *f* **-,-n** mattress

Matrose *m* **-n,-n** sailor

Matsch *m* **-[e]s** mud; (*Schnee-*) slush

matt *adj* weak; (*gedämpft*) dim; (*glanzlos*) dull; (*Politur, Farbe*) matt.

M~ *nt* **-s** (*Schach*) mate

Matte *f* **-,-n** mat

Mattglas *nt* frosted glass

Matura *f* **-** (*Aust*) ≈ A levels *pl*

Matura ▷ABITUR

Mauer *f* **-,-n** wall. **M~werk** *nt* masonry

Maul *nt* **-[e]s,** Mäuler (*Zool*) mouth; **halts M~!** 🄳 shut up! **M~- und Klauenseuche** *f* footand-mouth disease. **M~korb** *m* muzzle. **M~tier** *nt* mule. **M~wurf** *m* mole

Maurer *m* **-s,-** bricklayer

Maus *f* **-,** Mäuse mouse

Maut *f* **-,-en** (*Aust*) toll. **M~straße** *f* toll road

maximal *adj* maximum

Maximum *nt* **-s,-ma** maximum

Mayonnaise /majo'nɛːzə/ *f* **-,-n** mayonnaise

Mechan|ik /me'çaːnɪk/ *f* - mechanics *sg*; (*Mechanismus*) mechanism. **M~iker** *m* **-s,-** mechanic. **m~isch** *adj* mechanical. **m~isieren** *vt* mechanize. **M~ismus** *m* **-,-men** mechanism

meckern *vi* (*haben*) bleat; (🄳: *nörgeln*) grumble

Medaill|e /me'daljə/ *f* **-,-n** medal. **M~on** *nt* **-s,-s** medallion (*Schmuck*) locket

Medikament *nt* **-[e]s,-e** medicine

Medit|ation /-'tsjoːn/ *f* **-,-en** meditation. **m~ieren** *vi* (*haben*) meditate

Medium *nt* **-s,-ien** medium; **die Medien** the media

Medizin *f* **-,-en** medicine. **M~er** *m* **-s,-** doctor; (*Student*) medical student. **m~isch** *adj* medical;

m

(heilkräftig) medicinal

Meer nt -[e]s,-e sea. **M~busen** m gulf. **M~enge** f strait. **M~esspiegel** m sea-level. **M~jungfrau** f mermaid. **M~rettich** m horseradish. **M~schweinchen** nt -s,- guinea-pig

Mehl nt -[e]s flour. **M~schwitze** f *(Culin)* roux

mehr pron & adv more; **nicht m~** no more; *(zeitlich)* no longer; **nichts m~** no more; *(nichtsweiter)* nothing else; **nie m~** never again. **m~ere** pron several things pl. **m~fach** adj multiple; *(mehrmalig)* repeated ● adv several times. **M~fahrtenkarte** f book of tickets. **M~heit** f -,-en majority. **m~malig** adj repeated. **m~mals** adv several times. **m~sprachig** adj multilingual. **M~wertsteuer** f value-added tax, VAT. **M~zahl** f majority; *(Gram)* plural. **M~zweck-** prefix multipurpose

meiden† vt avoid, shun

Meile f -,-n mile. **m~nweit** adv [for] miles

mein poss pron my. **m~e(r,s)** poss pron mine; **die M~en** od **m~en** pl my family sg

Meineid m perjury

meinen vt mean; *(glauben)* think; *(sagen)* say

mein|erseits adv for my part. **m~etwegen** adv for my sake; *(wegen mir)* because of me; *(🗆: von mir aus)* as far as I'm concerned

Meinung f -,-en opinion; **jdm die M~ sagen** give s.o. a piece of one's mind. **M~sumfrage** f opinion poll

Meise f -,-n *(Zool)* tit

Meißel m -s,- chisel. **m~n** vt/i *(haben)* chisel

meist adv mostly; *(gewöhnlich)*

usually. **m~e** adj der/die/das **m~e** most; **die m~en Leute** most people; **am m~en** [the] most ● pron **das m~e** most [of it]; **die m~en** most. **m~ens** adv mostly; *(gewöhnlich)* usually

Meister m -s,- master craftsman; *(Könner)* master; *(Sport)* champion. **m~n** vt master. **M~schaft** f -,-en mastery; *(Sport)* championship

meld|en vt report; *(anmelden)* register; *(ankündigen)* announce; **sich m~en** report (**bei** to); *(zum Militär)* enlist; *(freiwillig)* volunteer; *(Teleph)* answer; *(Sch)* put up one's hand; *(von sich hören lassen)* get in touch *(bei with)*. **M~ung** f -,-en report; *(Anmeldung)* registration

melken† vt milk

Melodie f -,-n tune, melody

melodisch adj melodic; melodious

Melone f -,-n melon

Memoiren /me'mǫaːrən/ pl memoirs

Menge f -,-n amount, quantity; *(Menschen-)* crowd; *(Math)* set; **eine M~ Geld** a lot of money. **m~n** vt mix

Mensa f -,-sen *(Univ)* refectory

Mensch m -en,-en human being; **der M~** man; **die M~en** people; **jeder/kein M~** everybody/nobody. **M~enaffe** m ape. **m~enfeindlich** adj antisocial. **M~enfresser** m -s,- cannibal; *(Zool)* man-eater. **m~enfreundlich** adj philanthropic. **M~enleben** nt human life; *(Lebenszeit)* lifetime. **m~enleer** adj deserted. **M~enmenge** f crowd. **M~enraub** m kidnapping. **M~enrechte** ntpl human rights. **m~enscheu** adj unsociable. **m~enwürdig** adj humane. **M~heit** f - die **M~heit** mankind, humanity. **m~lich** adj human; *(human)* humane. **M~lichkeit** f - humanity

Menstru|ation /-'tsjo:n/ f - menstruation. **m~ieren** vi (haben) menstruate

Mentalität f -,-en mentality

Menü nt -s,-s menu; (festes M~) set meal

Meridian m -s,-e meridian

merk|bar adj noticeable. **M~blatt** nt [explanatory] leaflet. **m~en** vt notice; **sich** (dat) **etw m~en** remember sth. **M~mal** nt feature

merkwürdig adj odd, strange

Messe[1] f -,-n (Relig) mass; (Comm) [trade] fair

Messe[2] f -,-n (Mil) mess

messen† vt/i (pp gemessen) measure; (ansehen) look at; **[bei jdm] Fieber m~** take s.o.'s temperature; **sich mit jdm m~ können** be a match for s.o.

Messer nt -s,- knife

Messias m - Messiah

Messing nt -s brass

Messung f -,-en measurement

Metabolismus m - metabolism

Metall nt -s,-e metal. **m~isch** adj metallic

Metamorphose f -,-n metamorphosis

metaphorisch adj metaphorical

Meteor m -s,-e meteor. **M~ologie** f - meteorology

Meter m & nt -s,- metre. **M~maß** nt tape-measure

Method|e f -,-n method. **m~isch** adj methodical

Metropole f -,-n metropolis

Metzger m -s,- butcher. **M~ei** f -,-en butcher's shop

Meuterei f -,-en mutiny

meutern vi (haben) mutiny; (🄵: schimpfen) grumble

Mexikan|er(in) m -s,- (f -,-nen) Mexican. **m~isch** adj Mexican

Mexiko nt -s Mexico

miauen vi (haben) mew, miaow

mich pron (acc of **ich**) me; (reflexive) myself

Mieder nt -s,- bodice

Miene f -,-n expression

mies adj 🄵 lousy

Miet|e f -,-n rent; (Mietgebühr) hire charge; **zur M~e wohnen** live in rented accommodation. **m~en** vt rent (Haus, Zimmer); hire (Auto, Boot). **M~er(in)** m -s,- (f -,-nen) tenant. **m~frei** adj & adv rent-free. **M~shaus** nt block of rented flats. **M~vertrag** m lease. **M~wagen** m hire-car. **M~wohnung** f rented flat; (zu vermieten) flat to let

Migräne f -,-n migraine

Mikro|chip m microchip. **M~computer** m microcomputer. **M~film** m microfilm

Mikro|fon, M~phon nt -s,-e microphone. **M~skop** nt -s,-e microscope. **m~skopisch** adj microscopic

Mikrowelle f microwave. **M~nherd** m microwave oven

Milbe f -,-n mite

Milch f - milk. **M~glas** nt opal glass. **m~ig** adj milky. **M~mann** m (pl -männer) milkman. **M~straße** f Milky Way

mild adj mild; (nachsichtig) lenient. **M~e** f - mildness; leniency. **m~ern** vt make milder; (mäßigen) moderate; (lindern) ease; **sich m~ern** become milder; (sich mäßigen) moderate. **m~ernde Umstände** mitigating circumstances

Milieu /mi'ljø:/ nt -s,-s [social] environment

Militär nt -s army; (Soldaten)

troops *pl*; **beim M∼** in the army. **m∼isch** *adj* military

Miliz *f -,-en* militia

Milliarde /mɪˈljardə/ *f -,-n* thousand million, billion

Milli|gramm *nt* milligram. **M∼meter** *m & nt* millimetre. **M∼meterpapier** *nt* graph paper

Million /mɪˈljoːn/ *f -,-en* million. **M∼är** *m -s,-e* millionaire

Milz *f -* (*Anat*) spleen. **∼brand** *m* anthrax

mimen *vt* (🄵: vortäuschen) act

Mimose *f -,-n* mimosa

Minderheit *f -,-en* minority

minderjährig *adj* (*Jur*) underage. **M∼e(r)** *m/f* (*Jur*) minor

mindern *vt* diminish; decrease

minderwertig *adj* inferior. **M∼keit** *f -* inferiority. **M∼keitskomplex** *m* inferiority complex

Mindest- *prefix* minimum. **m∼e** *adj & pron* **der/die/das M∼e** *od* **m∼e** the least; **nicht im M∼en** not in the least. **m∼ens** *adv* at least. **M∼lohn** *m* minimum wage. **M∼maß** *nt* minimum

Mine *f -,-n* mine; (*Bleistift-*) lead; (*Kugelschreiber-*) refill. **M∼nräumboot** *nt* minesweeper

Mineral *nt -s,-e & -ien* mineral. **m∼isch** *adj* mineral. **M∼wasser** *nt* mineral water

Miniatur *f -,-en* miniature

Minigolf *nt* miniature golf

minimal *adj* minimal

Minimum *nt -s,-ma* minimum

Mini|ster *m -s,-* minister. **m∼steriell** *adj* ministerial. **M∼sterium** *nt -s,-ien* ministry

minus *conj, adv & prep* (+ *gen*) minus. **M∼** *nt -* deficit; (*Nachteil*) disadvantage. **M∼zeichen** *nt* minus [sign]

Minute *f -,-n* minute

mir *pron* (*dat of* **ich**) [to] me; (*reflexive*) myself

Misch|ehe *f* mixed marriage. **m∼en** *vt* mix; blend (*Tee, Kaffee*); toss (*Salat*); shuffle (*Karten*); **sich m∼en** mix; (*Person*;) mingle (**unter** + *acc* with); **sich m∼en in** (+ *acc*) join in (*Gespräch*); meddle in (*Angelegenheit*) ● *vi* (*haben*) shuffle the cards. **M∼ung** *f -,-en* mixture; blend

miserabel *adj* abominable

missachten *vt* disregard

Miss|achtung *f* disregard. **M∼bildung** *f* deformity

missbilligen *vt* disapprove of

Miss|billigung *f* disapproval. **M∼brauch** *m* abuse

missbrauchen *vt* abuse; (*vergewaltigen*) rape

Misserfolg *m* failure

Misse|tat *f* misdeed. **M∼täter** *m* 🄵 culprit

missfallen† *vi* (*haben*) displease (**jdm** s.o.)

Miss|fallen *nt -s* displeasure; (*Missbilligung*) disapproval. **M∼geburt** *f* freak; (*fig*) monstrosity. **M∼geschick** *nt* mishap; (*Unglück*) misfortune

miss|glücken *vi* (*sein*) fail. **m∼gönnen** *vt* begrudge

misshandeln *vt* ill-treat

Misshandlung *f* ill-treatment

Mission *f -,-en* mission

Missionar(in) *m -s,-e* (*f -,-nen*) missionary

Missklang *m* discord

misslingen† *vi* (*sein*) fail; **es misslang ihr** she failed. **M∼** *nt -s* failure

Missmut *m* ill humour. **m∼ig** *adj* morose

missraten† *vi* (*sein*) turn

out badly

Miss|stand m abuse; (Zustand) undesirable state of affairs. **M~stimmung** f discord; (Laune) bad mood

misstrauen vi (haben) jdm/etw m~ mistrust s.o./sth; (Argwohn hegen) distrust s.o./sth

Misstrau|en nt -s mistrust; (Argwohn) distrust. **M~ensvotum** nt vote of no confidence. **m~isch** adj distrustful; (argwöhnisch) suspicious

Miss|verständnis nt misunderstanding. **m~verstehen** vt misunderstand. **M~wirtschaft** f mismanagement

Mist m -[e]s manure; ⊞ rubbish

Mistel f -,-n mistletoe

Misthaufen m dungheap

mit prep (+ dat) with; (sprechen) to; (mittels) by; (inklusive) including; (bei) at; **mit Bleistift** in pencil; **mit lauter Stimme** in a loud voice; **mit drei Jahren** at the age of three ● adv (auch) as well; **mit anfassen** (fig) lend a hand

Mitarbeit f collaboration. **m~en** vi sep collaborate (**an** + dat on). **M~er(in)** m(f) collaborator; (Kollege) colleague; employee

Mitbestimmung f co--determination

mitbringen† vt sep bring [along]

miteinander adv with each other

Mitesser m (Med) blackhead

mitfahren† vi sep (sein) go/come along; **mit jdm m~** go with s.o.; (mitgenommen werden) be given a lift by s.o.

mitfühlen vi sep (haben) sympathize

mitgeben† vt sep jdm etw m~ give s.o. sth to take with him

Mitgefühl nt sympathy

mitgehen† vi sep (sein) **mit jdm** m~ go with s.o.

Mitgift f -,-en dowry

Mitglied nt member. **M~schaft** f - membership

mithilfe prep (+ gen) with the aid of

Mithilfe f assistance

mitkommen† vi sep (sein) come [along] too; (fig: folgen können) keep up; (verstehen) follow

Mitlaut m consonant

Mitleid nt pity, compassion; **M~erregend** pitiful. **m~ig** adj pitying; (mitfühlend) compassionate. **m~slos** adj pitiless

mitmachen v sep ● vt take part in; (erleben) go through ● vi (haben) join in

Mitmensch m fellow man

mitnehmen† vt sep take along; (mitfahren lassen) give a lift to; (fig: schädigen) affect badly; (erschöpfen) exhaust; **'zum M~'** 'to take away'

mitreden vi sep (haben) join in [the conversation]; (mit entscheiden) have a say (**bei** in)

mitreißen† vt sep sweep along; (fig: begeistern) carry away; **m~d** rousing

mitsamt prep (+ dat) together with

mitschreiben† vt sep (haben) take down

Mitschuld f partial blame. **m~ig** adj **m~ig sein** be partly to blame

Mitschüler(in) m(f) fellow pupil

mitspielen vi sep (haben) join in; (Theat) be in the cast; (beitragen) play a part

Mittag m midday, noon; (Mahlzeit) lunch; (Pause) lunch-break; **heute/ gestern M~** at lunch-time today/ yesterday; **[zu] M~ essen** have lunch. **M~essen** nt lunch. **m~s** adv at noon; (als Mahlzeit) for lunch; **um 12 Uhr m~s** at noon. **M~spause** f lunch-hour; (Pause) lunch-break. **M~sschlaf** m after-lunch nap

Mittäter|(in) m(f) accomplice. **M~schaft** f - complicity

Mitte f -,-n middle; (Zentrum) centre; **die goldene M~** the golden mean; **M~ Mai** in mid-May; **in unserer M~** in our midst

mitteil|en vt sep jdm etw m~en tell s.o. sth; (amtlich) inform s.o. of sth. **M~ung** f -,-en communication; (Nachricht) piece of news

Mittel nt -s,- means sg; (Heil-) remedy; (Medikament) medicine; (M~wert) mean; (Durchschnitt) average; **M~** pl (Geld-) funds, resources. **m~** pred adj medium; (m~mäßig) middling. **M~alter** nt Middle Ages pl. **m~alterlich** adj medieval. **M~ding** nt (fig) cross. **m~europäisch** adj Central European. **M~finger** m middle finger. **m~los** adj destitute. **m~mäßig** adj middling; [nur] **m~mäßig** mediocre. **M~meer** nt Mediterranean. **M~punkt** m centre; (fig) centre of attention

mittels prep (+ gen) by means of

Mittel|schule f = Realschule. **M~smann** m (pl -männer) intermediary, go-between. **M~stand** m middle class. **m~ste(r,s)** adj middle. **M~streifen** m (Auto) central reservation. **M~stürmer** m centreforward. **M~welle** f medium wave. **M~wort** nt (pl -wörter) participle

mitten adv **m~ in/auf** (dat/acc) in the middle of. **m~durch** adv [right] through the middle

Mitternacht f midnight

mittler|e(r,s) adj middle; (Größe,

Qualität) medium; (durchschnittlich) mean, average. **m~weile** adv meanwhile; (seitdem) by now

Mittwoch m -s,-e Wednesday. **m~s** adv on Wednesdays

mitunter adv now and again

mitwirk|en vi sep (haben) take part; (helfen) contribute. **M~ung** f participation

mix|en vt mix. **M~er** m -s,- (Culin) liquidizer, blender

mobb|en vt bully, harass. **M~ing** nt -s bullying, harassment

Möbel pl furniture sg. **M~stück** nt piece of furniture. **M~wagen** m removal van

Mobiliar nt -s furniture

mobilisier|en vt mobilize. **M~ung** f - mobilization

Mobil|machung f - mobilization. **M~telefon** nt mobile phone

möblier|en vt furnish; **m~tes Zimmer** furnished room

mochte, möchte s. mögen

Mode f -,-n fashion; **M~ sein** be fashionable

Modell nt -s,-e model. **m~ieren** vt model

Modenschau f fashion show

Modera|tor m -s,-en, **M~torin** f -,-nen (TV) presenter

modern adj modern; (modisch) fashionable. **m~isieren** vt modernize

Mode|schmuck m costume jewellery. **M~schöpfer** m fashion designer

modisch adj fashionable

Modistin f -,-nen milliner

modrig adj musty

modulieren vt modulate

Mofa nt -s,-s moped

mogeln vi (haben) ⊞ cheat

mögen†

● *transitive verb*

····▶ like. **sie mag ihn sehr [gern]** she likes him very much. **möchten Sie ein Glas Wein?** would you like a glass of wine? **lieber mögen** prefer. **ich möchte lieber Tee** I would prefer tea

● *auxiliary verb*

····▶ (*wollen*) want to. **sie mochte nicht länger bleiben** she didn't want to stay any longer. **ich möchte ihn [gerne] sprechen** I'd like to speak to him. **möchtest du nach Hause?** do you want to go home? *or* would you like to go home?

····▶ (*Vermutung, Möglichkeit*) may. **ich mag mich irren** I may be wrong. **wer/was mag das sein?** whoever/whatever can it be? **[das] mag sein** that may well be. **mag kommen, was da will** come what may

möglich *adj* possible; **alle m~en** all sorts of; **über alles M~e sprechen** talk about all sorts of things. **m~erweise** *adv* possibly. **M~keit** *f* -,-en possibility. **M~keitsform** *f* subjunctive. **m~st** *adv* if possible; **m~st viel** as much as possible

Mohammedan|er(in) *m* -s,- (*f* -,-nen) Muslim. **m~isch** *adj* Muslim

Mohn *m* -s poppy

Möhre, Mohrrübe *f* -,-n carrot

Mokka *m* -s mocha; (*Geschmack*) coffee

Molch *m* -[e]s,-e newt

Mole *f* -,-n (*Naut*) mole

Molekül *nt* -s,-e molecule

Molkerei *f* -,-en dairy

Moll *nt* - (*Mus*) minor

mollig *adj* cosy; (*warm*) warm; (*rundlich*) plump

Moment *m* -s,-e moment;

M~[mal]! just a moment! **m~an** *adj* momentary; (*gegenwärtig*) at the moment

Monarch *m* -en,-en monarch. **M~ie** *f* -,-n monarchy

Monat *m* -s,-e month. **m~elang** *adv* for months. **m~lich** *adj* & *adv* monthly

Mönch *m* -[e]s,-e monk

Mond *m* -[e]s,-e moon

mondän *adj* fashionable

Mond|finsternis *f* lunar eclipse. **m~hell** *adj* moonlit. **M~sichel** *f* crescent moon. **M~schein** *m* moonlight

monieren *vt* criticize

Monitor *m* -s,-en (*Techn*) monitor

Monogramm *nt* -s,-e monogram

Mono|log *m* -s,-e monologue. **M~pol** *nt* -s,-e monopoly. **m~ton** *adj* monotonous

Monster *nt* -s,- monster

Monstrum *nt* -s,-stren monster

Monsun *m* -s,-e monsoon

Montag *m* Monday

Montage /mɔn'taːʒə/ *f* -,-n fitting; (*Zusammenbau*) assembly; (*Film-*) editing; (*Kunst*) montage

montags *adv* on Mondays

Montanindustrie *f* coal and steel industry

Monteur /mɔn'tøːɐ/ *m* -s,-e fitter. **M~anzug** *m* overalls *pl*

montieren *vt* fit; (*zusammenbauen*) assemble

Monument *nt* -[e]s,-e monument. **m~al** *a* monumental

Moor *nt* -[e]s,-e bog; (*Heide-*) moor

Moos *nt* es,-e moss **m~ig** *adj* mossy

Moped *nt* -s,-s moped

Mopp *m* -s,-s mop

Moral f - morals pl, (Selbstvertrauen) morale; (Lehre) moral.
m~isch adj moral

Mord m -[e]s,-e murder, (Pol) as-
sassination. **M~anschlag** m mur-
der/assassination attempt. **m~en**
vt/i (haben) murder, kill

Mörder m -s,- murderer, (Pol) assassin. **M~in** f -,-nen murderess.
m~isch adj murderous; (□:
schlimm) dreadful

morgen adv tomorrow; **m~**
Abend tomorrow evening

Morgen m -s,- morning; (Maß) ≈
acre; **am M~** in the morning;
heute/Montag M~ this/Monday
morning. **M~dämmerung** f dawn.
M~rock m dressing-gown. **M~rot**
nt red sky in the morning. **m~s** adj
in the morning

morgig adj tomorrow's; **der m~e**
Tag tomorrow

Morphium nt -s morphine

morsch adj rotten

Morsealphabet nt Morse code

Mörtel m -s mortar

Mosaik /moza'i:k/ nt -s,-e[n]
mosaic

Moschee f -,-n mosque

Mosel f - Moselle

Moskau nt -s Moscow

Moskito m -s,-s mosquito

Moslem m -s,-s Muslim

Motiv nt -s,-e motive; (Kunst)
motif

Motor /'mo:tor, mo'to:r/ m -s,-en
engine; (Elektro-) motor. **M~boot**
nt motor boat

motorisieren vt motorize

Motor|rad nt motor cycle.
M~roller m motor scooter

Motte f -,-n moth. **M~nkugel** f
mothball

Motto nt -s,-s motto

Möwe f -,-n gull

Mücke f -,-n gnat; (kleine) midge;
(Stech-) mosquito

müd|e adj tired; **es m~e sein** be
tired (etw zu tun of doing sth).
M~igkeit f - tiredness

muffig adj musty; (□: mürrisch)
grumpy

Mühe f -,-n effort; (Aufwand)
trouble; **sich** (dat) **M~ geben** make
an effort; (sich bemühen) try; nicht
der **M~ wert** not worth while; mit
M~ und Not with great difficulty;
(gerade noch) only just. **m~los** adj
effortless

muhen vi (haben) moo

Mühl|e f -,-n mill; (Kaffee-) grinder.
M~stein m millstone

Müh|sal f -,-e (literarisch) toil;
(Mühe) trouble. **m~sam** adj laborious; (beschwerlich) difficult

Mulde f -,-n hollow

Müll m -s refuse. **M~abfuhr** f refuse collection

Mullbinde f gauze bandage

Mülleimer m waste bin; (Mülltonne) dustbin

Müller m -s,- miller

Müll|halde f [rubbish] dump.
M~schlucker m refuse chute.
M~tonne f dustbin

multi|national adj multinational.
M~plikation f -,-en multiplication.
m~plizieren vt multiply

Mumie /'mu:miə/ f -,-n mummy

Mumm m -s □ energy

Mumps m - mumps

Mund m -[e]s,ᵉer mouth; **ein M~**
voll Suppe a mouthful of soup;
halt den M~! ☒ shut up! **M~art** f
dialect. **m~artlich** adj dialect

Mündel nt & m -s,- (Jur) ward.
m~sicher adj gilt-edged

münden vi (sein) flow/(Straße:)
lead (in + acc into)

Mundharmonika f
mouth-organ

mündig adj m~ sein/werden
(Jur) be/come of age. **M~keit** f -
(Jur) majority

mündlich adj verbal; m~e
Prüfung oral

Mündung f -,-en (Fluss-) mouth;
(Gewehr-) muzzle

Mundwinkel m corner of
the mouth

Munition /-ˈtsjoːn/ f - ammunition

munkeln vt/i (haben) talk (von
of); es wird gemunkelt rumour has
it (dass that)

Münster nt -s,- cathedral

munter adj lively; (heiter) merry;
m~ sein (wach) be wide awake ;
gesund und m~ fit and well

Münz|e f -,-n coin; (M~stätte)
mint. **M~fernsprecher** m
payphone

mürbe adj crumbly; (Obst) mellow;
(Fleisch) tender. **M~teig** m short
pastry

Murmel f -,-n marble

murmeln vt/i (haben) murmur;
(undeutlich) mumble

Murmeltier nt marmot

murren vt/i (haben) grumble

mürrisch adj surly

Mus nt -es purée

Muschel f -,-n mussel; [sea] shell

Museum /muˈzeːʊm/ nt -s,-seen
museum

Musik f - music. **m~alisch** adj
musical

Musiker(in) m -s,- (f -,-nen)
musician

Musik|instrument nt musical
instrument. **M~kapelle** f band.
M~pavillon m bandstand

musisch adj artistic

musizieren vi (haben)
make music

Muskat m -[e]s nutmeg

Muskel m -s,-n muscle. **M~kater**
m stiff and aching muscles pl

muskulös adj muscular

muss s. müssen

Muße f - leisure

müssen†

● auxiliary verb

••••➤ (gezwungen/verpflichtet/not-
wendig sein) have to; must. **er
muss es tun** he must or has to
do it; 🄳 he's got to do it. **ich
musste schnell fahren** I had to
drive fast. **das muss 1968 gewesen sein** it must have been
in 1968. **er muss gleich hier
sein** he must be here at any
moment

••••➤ (in negativen Sätzen; ungezwungen) **sie muss es nicht tun**
she does not have to or 🄳 she
hasn't got to do it. **es musste
nicht so sein** it didn't have to
be like that

••••➤ **es müsste** (sollte) **doch möglich sein** it ought to or should
be possible. **du müsstest es mal
versuchen** you ought to or
should try it

● intransitive verb

••••➤ (irgendwohin gehen müssen)
have to or must go. **ich muss
nach Hause/zum Arzt** I have to
or must go home/to the doctor.
ich musste mal [aufs Klo] I had
to go [to the loo]

müßig adj idle

musste, müsste s. müssen

Muster nt -s,- pattern; (Probe)
sample; (Vorbild) model. **M~bei-
spiel** nt typical example; (Vorbild)
perfect example. **m~gültig,
m~haft** adj exemplary. **m~n** vt
eye; (inspizieren) inspect. **M~ung** f

-,-en inspection; (*Mil*) medical; (*Muster*) pattern

Mut *m* -[e]s courage; **jdm Mut machen** encourage s.o.; **zu M~e sein** feel like it; *s.* zumute

mut|ig *adj* courageous. **m~los** *adj* despondent

mutmaßen *vt* presume; (*Vermutungen anstellen*) speculate

Mutprobe *f* test of courage

Mutter¹ *f* -,¨ mother

Mutter² *f* -,-n (*Techn*) nut

Muttergottes *f* madonna

Mutterland *nt* motherland

mütterlich *adj* maternal; (*fürsorglich*) motherly. **m~erseits** *adv* on one's/the mother's side

Mutter|mal *nt* birthmark; (*dunkel*) mole. **M~schaft** *f* - motherhood. **m~seelenallein** *adj & adv* all alone. **M~sprache** *f* mother tongue. **M~tag** *m* Mother's Day

Mütze *f* -,-n cap; **wollene M~** woolly hat

MwSt. *abbr* (**Mehrwertsteuer**) VAT

mysteriös *adj* mysterious

Mystik /ˈmʏstɪk/ *f* - mysticism

myth|isch *adj* mythical. **M~ologie** *f* - mythology

Nn

na *int* well; **na gut** all right then

Nabel *m* -s,- navel. **N~schnur** *f* umbilical cord

nach

● *preposition* (+ *dative*)

⟶ (*räumlich*) to. **nach London fahren** go to London. **der Zug** **nach München** the train to Munich; (*noch nicht abgefahren*) the train for Munich; **die München Zug** the Munich train. **nach Hause gehen** go home. **nach Osten [zu]** eastwards; towards the east

⟶ (*zeitlich*) after; (*Uhrzeit*) past. **nach fünf Minuten/dem Frühstück** after five minutes/breakfast. **zehn [Minuten] nach zwei** ten [minutes] past two

⟶ (*räumliche und zeitliche Reihenfolge*) after. **nach Ihnen/dir!** after you!

⟶ (*mit bestimmten Verben*) for. **greifen/streben/schicken nach** grasp/strive/send for

⟶ (*gemäß*) according to. **nach der neuesten Mode gekleidet** dressed in [accordance with] the latest fashion. **dem Gesetz nach** in accordance with the law; by law. **nach meiner Ansicht** *od* **Meinung, meiner Ansicht** *od* **Meinung nach** in my view or opinion. **nach etwas schmecken/riechen** taste/smell of sth

● *adverb*

⟶ (*zeitlich*) **nach und nach** little by little; gradually. **nach wie vor** still

nachahm|en *vt sep* imitate. **N~ung** *f* -,-en imitation

Nachbar|(in) *m* -n,-n (*f* -,-nen) neighbour. **N~haus** *nt* house next door. **n~lich** *adj* neighbourly; (*Nachbar-*) neighbouring. **N~schaft** *f* - neighbourhood

nachbestell|en *vt sep* reorder. **N~ung** *f* repeat order

nachbild|en *vt sep* copy, reproduce. **N~ung** *f* copy, reproduction

nachdatieren *vt sep* backdate

nachdem *conj* after; **je n~** it depends

nachdenk|en† vi sep (haben) think (**über** + acc about). **n~lich** adj thoughtful

nachdrücklich adj emphatic

nacheinander adv one after the other

Nachfahre m -n,-n descendant

Nachfolg|e f succession. **N~er(in)** m -s,- (f -,-nen) successor

nachforsch|en vi sep (haben) make enquiries. **N~ung** f enquiry

Nachfrage f (Comm) demand. **n~n** vi sep (haben) enquire

nachfüllen vt sep refill

nachgeben† v sep ● vi (haben) give way; (sich fügen) give in, yield ● vt **jdm Suppe n~** give s.o. more soup

Nachgebühr f surcharge

nachgehen† vi sep (sein) (Uhr:) be slow; **jdm/etw n~** follow s.o./ something; follow up (Spur, Angelegenheit); pursue (Angelegenheit)

Nachgeschmack m after-taste

nachgiebig adj indulgent; (gefällig) compliant. **N~keit** f - indulgence; compliance

nachgrübeln vi sep (haben) ponder (**über** + acc on)

nachhaltig adj lasting

nachhelfen† vi sep (haben) help

nachher adv later; (danach) afterwards; **bis n~!** see you later!

Nachhilfeunterricht m coaching

Nachhinein adv im N~ afterwards

nachhinken vi sep (sein) (fig) lag behind

nachholen vt sep (später holen) fetch later; (mehr holen) get more; (später machen) do later; (aufholen) catch up on

Nachkomme m -n,-n descendant. **n~n**† vi sep (sein) follow [later], come later; **etw** (dat) **n~n** (fig) comply with (Bitte); carry out (Pflicht). **N~nschaft** f - descendants pl, progeny

Nachkriegszeit f post-war period

Nachlass m -es,ⁱe discount; (Jur) [deceased's] estate

nachlassen† v sep ● vi (haben) decrease; (Regen, Hitze:) let up; (Schmerz:) ease; (Sturm:) abate; (Augen, Leistungen:) deteriorate ● vt **etw vom Preis n~** take sth off the price

nachlässig adj careless; (leger) casual; (unordentlich) sloppy. **N~keit** f - carelessness; sloppiness

nachlesen† vt sep look up

nachlöse|n vi sep (haben) pay one's fare on the train or on arrival. **N~schalter** m excess-fare office

nachmachen vt sep (später machen) do later; (imitieren) imitate, copy; (fälschen) forge

Nachmittag m afternoon; **heute/gestern N~** this/yesterday afternoon. **n~s** adv in the afternoon

Nachnahme f etw per N~ schicken send sth cash on delivery or COD

Nachname m surname

Nachporto nt excess postage

nachprüfen vt sep check, verify

Nachricht f -,-en [piece of] news sg; **N~en** news sg; **eine N~** hinterlassen leave a message; **jdm N~ geben** inform s.o. **N~endienst** m (Mil) intelligence service

nachrücken vi sep (sein) move up

Nachruf m obituary

nachsagen vt sep repeat (jdm after s.o.); **jdm Schlechtes/Gutes n~** speak ill/well of s.o.

Nachsaison f late season

nachschicken vt sep (später schi-cken) send later; (hinterher-) send after (jdm s.o.); send on (Post) (jdm to s.o.)

nachschlagen† v sep ● vt look up ● vi (haben) in einem Wörter-buch n~en consult a dictionary; jdm n~en take after s.o.

Nachschrift f transcript; (Nach-satz) postscript

Nachschub m (Mil) supplies pl

nachsehen† v sep ● vt (prüfen) check; (nachschlagen) look up; (hin-wegsehen über) overlook ● vi (haben) have a look; (prüfen) check; im Wörterbuch n~ consult a dic-tionary

nachsenden† vt sep forward (Post) (jdm to s.o.); 'bitte n~' 'please forward'

nachsichtig adj forbearing; leni-ent; indulgent

Nachsilbe f suffix

nachsitzen† vi sep (haben) n~ müssen be kept in [after school]; jdn n~ lassen give s.o. detention. N~ nt -s (Sch) detention

Nachspeise f dessert, sweet

nachsprechen† vt sep repeat (jdm after s.o.)

nachspülen vt sep rinse

nächst /-çst/ prep (+ dat) next to. n~beste(r,s) adj first [available]; (zweitbeste) next best. n~e(r,s) adj next; (nächstgelegene) nearest; (Ver-wandte) closest; in n~er Nähe close by; am n~en sein be nearest or closest ● pron der/die/das N~e (n~e) the next; der N~e (n~e) bitte next please; als N~es (n~es) next; fürs N~e (n~e) for the time being. N~e(r) m fellow man

nachstehend adj following ● adv below

Nächst|enliebe f charity. n~ens adv shortly. n~gelegen adj nearest

nachsuchen vi sep (haben) search; n~ um request

Nacht f -,¨e night; über/bei N~ overnight/at night; morgen N~ to-morrow night; heute N~ tonight; (letzte Nacht) last night; gestern N~ last night; (vorletzte Nacht) the night before last. N~dienst m night duty

Nachteil m disadvantage; zum N~ to the detriment (gen of)

Nacht|falter m moth. N~hemd nt night-dress; (Männer-) night-shirt

Nachtigall f -,-en nightingale

Nachtisch m dessert

Nachtklub m night-club

nächtlich adj nocturnal, night

Nacht|lokal nt night-club. N~mahl nt (Aust) supper

Nachtrag m postscript; (Ergän-zung) supplement. n~ent vt sep add; jdm etw n~en (fig) bear a grudge against s.o. for sth. n~end adj vindictive; n~end sein bear grudges

nachträglich adj subsequent, later; (verspätet) belated ● adv later; (nachher) afterwards; (verspätet) be-latedly

Nacht|ruhe f night's rest; ange-nehme N~ruhe! sleep well! n~s adv at night; 2 Uhr n~s 2 o'clock in the morning. N~schicht f night-shift. N~tisch m bedside table. N~tischlampe f bedside lamp. N~topf m chamber-pot. N~wäch-ter m night-watchman. N~zeit f night-time

Nachuntersuchung f check-up

Nachwahl f by-election

Nachweis m -es,-e proof. n~bar adj demonstrable. n~ent vt sep prove; (aufzeigen) show; (vermitteln)

give details of; **jdm nichts n~en
können** have no proof against s.o.
Nachwelt f posterity
Nachwirkung f after-effect
Nachwuchs m new generation;
(**Ⅱ**: Kinder) offspring. **N~spieler** m
young player

nachzahlen vt/i sep (haben) pay
extra; (später zahlen) pay later;
Steuern n~ pay tax arrears
nachzählen vt/i sep (haben) count
again; (prüfen) check
Nachzahlung f extra/later payment; (Gehalts-) back-payment
nachzeichnen vt sep copy
Nachzügler m -s, - late-comer;
(Zurückgebliebener) straggler

Nacken m -s, - nape or back of
the neck
nackt adj naked; (bloß, kahl) bare;
(Wahrheit) plain. **N~heit** f - naked-
ness, nudity. **N~kultur** f nudism.
N~schnecke f slug

Nadel f -,-n needle; (Häkel-) hook;
(Schmuck-, Hut-) pin. **N~arbeit** f
needlework. **N~baum** m conifer.
N~stich m stitch; (fig) pinprick.
N~wald m coniferous forest

Nagel m -s,: nail. **N~haut** f cut-
icle. **N~lack** m nail varnish. **n~n** vt
nail. **n~neu** adj brand-new

nagen vt/i (haben) gnaw (**an** + dat
at); **n~d** (fig) nagging
Nagetier nt rodent

nah adj, adv & prep = nahe
Näharbeit f sewing
Nahaufnahme f close-up
nahe adj nearby; (zeitlich) imminent; (eng) close; **der N~ Osten**
the Middle East; **in n~r Zukunft** in
the near future; **von n~m** (from)
close to; **n~ sein** be close (dat to)
● adv near, close; (verwandt) closely;
n~ an (+ acc/dat) near [to], close
to; **n~ daran sein, etw zu tun**

nearly do sth; **n~ liegen** be close;
(fig) be highly likely; **n~ legen**
(fig) recommend (dat to); **jdm n~
legen, etw zu tun** urge s.o. to do
sth; **jdm n~ gehen** (fig) affect s.o.
deeply; **jdm zu n~ treten** (fig) offend s.o. ● prep (+ dat) near [to],
close to

Nähe f - nearness, proximity; **aus
der N~** [from] close to; **in der N~**
near or close by

nahe|gehen* vi sep (sein) **n~
gehen**, s. nahe. **n~legen*** vt sep
n~ legen, s. nahe. **n~liegen*** vi
sep (haben) **n~ liegen**, s. nahe

nähen vt/i (haben) sew; (anfertigen)
make; (Med) stitch [up]

näher adj closer; (Weg) shorter;
(Einzelheiten) further ● adv closer;
(genauer) more closely; **n~ kommen** come closer; (fig) get closer
(dat to); **sich n~ erkundigen**
make further enquiries; **n~an** (+
acc/dat) nearer [to], closer to ● prep
(+ dat) nearer [to], closer to.
N~e[s] nt [further] details pl. **n~n
(sich)** vr approach

nahezu adv almost
Nähgarn nt [sewing] cotton
Nahkampf m close combat
Näh|maschine f sewing ma-
chine. **N~nadel** f sewing-needle
nähren vt feed; (fig) nurture
nahrhaft adj nutritious
Nährstoff m nutrient
Nahrung f - food, nourishment.
N~smittel nt food
Nährwert m nutritional value
Naht f -,:e seam; (Med) suture.
n~los adj seamless
Nahverkehr m local service
Nähzeug nt sewing; (Zubehör)
sewing kit
naiv /naˈiːf/ adj naïve. **N~ität** f -
naïvety

Name m -ns,-n name; **im N~n** (+ gen) in the name of; (handeln) on behalf of. **n~nlos** adj nameless; (unbekannt) unknown, anonymous. **N~nstag** m name-day. **N~nvetter** m namesake. **N~nszug** m signature. **n~ntlich** adv by name; (besonders) especially

namhaft adj noted; (ansehnlich) considerable; **n~ machen** name

nämlich adv (und zwar) namely; (denn) because

Nanotechnologie f nanotechnology

nanu int hallo

Napf m -[e]s,⁻e bowl

Narbe f -,-n scar

Narkose f -,-n general anaesthetic. **N~arzt** m anaesthetist. **N~mittel** nt anaesthetic

Narr m -en,-en fool; **zum N~en halten** make a fool of. **n~en** vt fool

Närr|in f -,-nen fool. **n~isch** adj foolish; (⟦️: verrückt⟧) crazy (**auf** + acc about)

Narzisse f -,-n narcissus

naschen vt/i (haben) nibble (**an** + dat at)

Nase f -,-n nose

näseln vi (haben) speak through one's nose; **n~d** nasal

Nasen|bluten nt -s nosebleed. **N~loch** nt nostril

Nashorn nt rhinoceros

nass adj wet

Nässe f - wet; wetness. **n~n** vt wet

Nation /na'tsjoːn/ f -,-en nation. **n~al** adj national. **N~alhymne** f national anthem. **N~alismus** m - nationalism. **N~alität** f -,-en nationality. **N~alspieler** m international

> **Nationalrat** In Austria the *Nationalrat* is the Federal Assembly's lower house, whose 183 members are elected for four years under a system of proportional representation. In Switzerland, the *Nationalrat* is made up of 200 representatives. ⓘ

Natrium nt -s sodium

Natron nt -s doppelkohlensaures **N~** bicarbonate of soda

Natter f -,-n snake; (Gift-) viper

Natur f -,-en nature; **von N~ aus** by nature. **n~alisieren** vt naturalize. **N~alisierung** f -,-en naturalization

Naturell nt -s,-e disposition

Natur|erscheinung f natural phenomenon. **N~forscher** m naturalist. **N~heilkunde** f natural medicine. **N~kunde** f natural history

natürlich adj natural ● adv naturally; (selbstverständlich) of course. **N~keit** f - naturalness

natur|rein adj pure. **N~schutz** m nature conservation; **unter N~schutz stehen** be protected. **N~schutzgebiet** nt nature reserve. **N~wissenschaft** f [natural] science. **N~wissenschaftler** m scientist

nautisch adj nautical

Navigation /-'tsjoːn/ f - navigation

Nazi m -s,-s Nazi

n.Chr. abbr (nach Christus) AD

Nebel m -s,- fog; (leicht) mist

neben prep (+ dat/acc) next to, beside; (+ dat) (außer) apart from. **n~an** adv next door

Neben|anschluss m (Teleph) extension. **N~ausgaben** fpl incidental expenses

nebenbei adv in addition; (beiläufig) casually

Neben|bemerkung f passing remark. **N~beruf** m second job

nebeneinander adv next to each other, side by side

Neben|eingang m side entrance. **N~fach** nt (Univ) subsidiary subject. **N~fluss** m tributary

nebenher adv in addition

nebenhin adv casually

Neben|höhle f sinus. **N~kosten** pl additional costs. **N~produkt** nt by-product. **N~rolle** f supporting role; (Kleine) minor role. **N~sache** f unimportant matter. **n~sächlich** adj unimportant. **N~satz** m subordinate clause. **N~straße** f minor road; (Seiten-) side street. **N~wirkung** f side-effect. **N~zimmer** nt room next door

neblig adj foggy; (leicht) misty

neck|en vt tease. **N~erei** f - teasing. **n~isch** adj teasing

Neffe m -n,-n nephew

negativ adj negative. **N~** nt -s,-e (Phot) negative

Neger m -s,- Negro

nehmen† vt take (dat from); **sich** (dat) **etw n~** take sth; help oneself to (Essen)

Neid m -[e]s envy, jealousy. **n~isch** adj envious, jealous (auf + acc of); **auf jdn n~isch sein** envy s.o.

neig|en vt incline; (zur Seite) tilt; (beugen) bend; **sich n~en** incline; (Boden:) slope; (Person:) bend **über** + acc over) ● vi (haben) **n~en zu** (fig) have a tendency towards; be prone to (Krankheit); incline towards (Ansicht); **dazu n~en, etw zu tun** tend to do sth. **N~ung** f -,-en inclination; (Gefälle) slope; (fig) tendency

nein adv, **N~** nt -s no

Nektar m -s nectar

Nelke f -,-n carnation; (Culin) clove

nenn|en† vt call; (taufen) name; (angeben) give; (erwähnen) mention; **sich n~en** call oneself. **n~enswert** adj significant

Neon nt -s neon. **N~beleuchtung** f fluorescent lighting

Nerv m -s,-en nerve; **die N~en verlieren** lose control of oneself. **n~en** vt **jdn n~en** 🗙 get on s.o.'s nerves. **N~enarzt** m neurologist. **n~enaufreibend** adj nerve-racking. **N~enkitzel** m 🅣 thrill. **N~ensystem** nt nervous system. **N~enzusammenbruch** m nervous breakdown

nervös adj nervy, edgy; (Med) nervous; **n~ sein** be on edge

Nervosität f - nerviness, edginess

Nerz m -es,-e mink

Nessel f -,-n nettle

Nest nt -[e]s,-er nest; (🅣: Ort) small place

nett adj nice; (freundlich) kind

netto adv net

Netz nt -es,-e net; (Einkaufs-) string bag; (Spinnen-) web; (auf Landkarte) grid; (System) network; (Electr) mains pl. **N~haut** f retina. **N~karte** f area season ticket. **N~werk** nt network

neu adj new; (modern) modern; **wie neu** as good as new; **das ist mir neu** it's news to me; **von n~em** all over again ● adv newly; (gerade erst) only just; (erneut) again; **etw neu schreiben** rewrite sth; **neu vermähltes Paar** newly-weds pl. **N~auflage** f new edition; (unverändert) reprint. **N~bau** m (pl -ten) new house/building

Neue(r) m/f new person, newcomer; (Schüler) new boy/girl.

n

N~e(s) nt das N~e the new; etwas N~es something new; (Neuigkeit) a piece of news; **was gibt's N~es?** what's the news?

neuerdings adv [just] recently

neuest|e(r,s) adj newest; (letzte) latest; **seit n~em** just recently. **N~e** nt das N~e the latest thing: (Neuigkeit) the latest news sg

neugeboren adj newborn

Neugier, Neugierde f - curiosity; (Wissbegierde) inquisitiveness

neugierig adj curious (auf + acc about); (wissbegierig) inquisitive

Neuheit f -,-en novelty; newness

Neuigkeit f -,-en piece of news; N~en news sg

Neujahr nt New Year's Day; **über N~** over the New Year

neulich adv the other day

Neumond m new moon

neun inv adj. **N~** f -,-en nine. **n~te(r,s)** adj ninth. **n~zehn** inv adj nineteen. **n~zehnte(r,s)** adj nineteenth. **n~zig** inv adj ninety. **n~zigste(r,s)** adj ninetieth

Neuralgie f -,-n neuralgia

neureich adj nouveau riche

Neurologe m -n,-n neurologist

Neurose f -,-n neurosis

Neuschnee m fresh snow

Neuseeland nt -s New Zealand

neuste(r,s) adj = neueste(r,s)

neutral adj neutral. **N~ität** f - neutrality

Neutrum nt -s,-tra neuter noun

neu|vermählt* adj n~ vermählt, s. neu. **N~zeit** f modern times pl

nicht adv not; **ich kann n~** I cannot or can't; **er ist n~ gekommen** he hasn't come; **bitte n~!** please don't! **n~ berühren!** do not touch! **du kennst ihn doch, n~?** you do

know him, don't you?

Nichte f -,-n niece

Nichtraucher m non-smoker

nichts pron & a nothing; **n~ mehr** no more; **n~ ahnend** unsuspecting; **n~ sagend** meaningless; (uninteressant) nondescript. **N~** nt - nothingness; (Leere) void

Nichtschwimmer m non-swimmer

nichts|nutzig adj good-for-nothing; (📕: unartig) naughty. **n~sagend*** adj n~ sagend, s. nichts. **N~tun** nt -s idleness

Nickel nt -s nickel

nicken vi (haben) nod

Nickerchen nt -s,-, 📕 nap

nie adv never

nieder adj low ● adv down. **n~brennen†** vt/i sep (sein) burn down. **N~deutsch** nt Low German. **N~gang** m (fig) decline. **n~gedrückt** adj (fig) depressed. **n~geschlagen** adj dejected, despondent. **N~kunft** f -,ᵗe confinement. **N~lage** f defeat

Niederlande (die) pl the Netherlands

Niederländ|er m -s,- Dutchman; **die N~er** the Dutch pl. **N~erin** f -,-nen Dutchwoman. **n~isch** adj Dutch

nieder|lassen† vt sep let down; **sich n~lassen** settle; (sich setzen) sit down. **N~lassung** f -,-en settlement; (Zweigstelle) branch. **n~legen** vt sep put or lay down; resign (Amt); **die Arbeit n~legen** go on strike. **n~metzeln** vt sep massacre. **N~sachsen** nt Lower Saxony. **N~schlag** m precipitation; (Regen) rainfall; (radioaktiver) fallout. **n~schlagen†** vt sep knock down; lower (Augen); (unterdrücken) crush. **n~schmettern** vt sep (fig) shatter.

n~setzen vt sep put or set down; **sich n~setzen** sit down. **n~strecken** vt sep fell; (durch Schuss) gun down. **n~trächtig** adj base, vile. **n~walzen** vt sep flatten

niedlich adj pretty; sweet

niedrig adj low; (fig: gemein) base ● adv low

niemals adv never

niemand pron nobody, no one

Niere f -,-n kidney; **künstliche N~** kidney machine

nieseln vi (haben) drizzle. **N~regen** m drizzle

niesen vi (haben) sneeze. **N~** nt -s sneezing; (Nieser) sneeze

Niete¹ f -,-n rivet; (an Jeans) stud

Niete² f -,-n blank; ⊞ failure

nieten vt rivet

Nikotin nt -s nicotine

Nil m -[s] Nile. **N~pferd** nt hippopotamus

nimmer adv (SGer) not any more; **nie und n~** never

nirgend|s, **n~wo** adv nowhere

Nische f -,-n recess, niche

nisten vi (haben) nest

Nitrat nt -[e]s,-e nitrate

Niveau /niˈvoː/ nt -s,-s level; (geistig, künstlerisch) standard

nix adv ⊞ nothing

Nixe f -,-n mermaid

nobel adj noble; (fig: luxuriös) luxurious; (⊞: großzügig) generous

noch adv still; (zusätzlich) as well; (mit Komparativ) even; **n~ nicht** not yet; **gerade n~** only just; **n~ immer** or **immer n~** still; **n~ letzte Woche** only last week; **wer n~?** who else? **n~ etwas** something else; (Frage) anything else? **n~ einmal** again; **n~ ein Bier** another beer; **n~ größer** even bigger; **n~ so sehr** however much

● conj **weder n~ ...** neither nor ...

nochmals adv again

Nomad|e m -n,-n nomad. **n~isch** adj nomadic

nominier|en vt nominate. **N~ung** f -,-en nomination

Nonne f -,-n nun. **N~nkloster** nt convent

Nonstopflug m direct flight

Nord m -[e]s north. **N~amerika** nt North America

Norden m -s north

nordisch adj Nordic

nördlich adj northern; (Richtung) northerly ● adv & prep (+ gen) **n~ [von] der Stadt** [to the] north of the town

Nordosten m north-east

Nord|pol m North Pole. **N~see** f - North Sea. **N~westen** m north-west

Nörgelei f -,-en grumbling

nörgeln vi (haben) grumble

Norm f -,-en norm; (Techn) standard; (Soll) quota

normal adj normal. **n~erweise** adv normally

normen vt standardize

Norwe|gen nt -s Norway. **N~ger(in)** m -s,- (f -,-nen) Norwegian. **n~gisch** adj Norwegian

Nost|algie f - nostalgia. **n~algisch** adj nostalgic

Not f -,⁻e need; (Notwendigkeit) necessity; (Entbehrung) hardship; (seelisch) trouble; **Not leiden** be in need, suffer hardship; **Not leidende Menschen** needy people; **zur Not** if need be; (äußerstenfalls) at a pinch

Notar m -s,-e notary public

Not|arzt m emergency doctor. **N~ausgang** m emergency exit. **N~behelf** m -[e]s,-e makeshift. **N~bremse** f emergency brake.

N~dienst m N~dienst haben be on call
Note f -,-n note; (*Zensur*) mark; **ganze/halbe N~** (*Mus*) semi-breve/ minim; **N~n lesen** read music; **persönliche N~** personal touch. **N~nblatt** nt sheet of music. **N~nschlüssel** m clef
Notfall m emergency; **für den N~** just in case. **N~s** adv if need be
notieren vt note down; (*Comm*) quote; **sich** (dat) **etw n~** make a note of sth
nötig adj necessary; **n~ haben** need; **das N~ste** the essentials pl ● adv urgently. **n~enfalls** adv if need be. **N~ung** f - coercion
Notiz f -,-en note; (*Zeitungs-*) item; [**keine**] **N~ nehmen von** take [no] notice of. **N~buch** nt notebook. **N~kalender** m diary
Not|lage f distress. **n~landen** vi (sein) make a forced landing. **N~landung** f forced landing. **n~leidend*** adj Not leidend, s. Not. **N~lösung** f stopgap
Not|ruf m emergency call; (*Naut, Aviat*) distress call; (*Nummer*) emergency services number. **N~signal** nt distress signal. **N~stand** m state of emergency. **N~unterkunft** f emergency accommodation. **N~wehr** f - (*Jur*) self-defence
notwendig adj necessary; essential ● adv urgently. **N~keit** f -,-en necessity
Notzucht f - (*Jur*) rape
Nougat /'nu:gat/ m & nt -s nougat
Novelle f -,-n novella; (*Pol*) amendment
November m -s,- November
Novize m -n,-n, **Novizin** f -,-nen (*Relig*) novice
Nu m im Nu 🔲 in a flash
nüchtern adj sober; (*sachlich*)

matter-of-fact; (*schmucklos*) bare; (*ohne Würze*) bland; **auf n~en Magen** on an empty stomach
Nudel f -,-n piece of pasta; **N~n** pasta sg; (*Band-*) noodles. **N~holz** nt rolling-pin
Nudist m -en,-en nudist
nuklear adj nuclear
null inv adj zero, nought; (*Teleph*) O; (*Sport*) nil; (*Tennis*) love; **n~ Fehler** no mistakes; **n~ und nichtig** (*Jur*) null and void. **N~** f -,-en nought, zero; (*fig: Person*) nonentity. **N~punkt** m zero
numerieren* vt = nummerieren
Nummer f -,-n number; (*Ausgabe*) issue; (*Darbietung*) item; (*Zirkus-*) act; (*Größe*) size. **n~ieren** vt number. **N~nschild** nt number-plate
nun adv now; (*na*) well; (*halt*) just; **nun gut!** very well then!
nur adv only, just; **wo kann sie nur sein?** wherever can she be? **er soll es nur versuchen!** just let him try!
Nürnberg nt -s Nuremberg
nuscheln vt/i (haben) mumble
Nuss f -,ⁱe nut. **N~knacker** m -s,- nutcrackers pl
Nüstern pl nostrils
Nut f -,-en, **Nute** f -,-n groove
Nutte f -,-n ☒ tart ☒
nutz|bar adj usable; **n~bar machen** utilize; cultivate (*Boden*). **n~bringend** adj profitable
nutzen vt use, utilize; (*aus-*) take advantage of ● vi (haben) = **nützen**. **N~** m -s benefit; (*Comm*) profit; **N~ ziehen aus** benefit from; **von N~ sein** be useful
nützen vi (haben) be useful or of use (dat to); (*Mittel:*) be effective; **nichts n~** be useless or no use; **was nützt mir das?** what good is that to me? ● vt = nutzen
nützlich adj useful. **N~keit** f -

usefulness

nutz|los adj useless; (vergeblich) vain. **N~losigkeit** f - uselessness. **N~ung** f - use, utilization

Nylon /'nailon/ nt -s nylon

Nymphe /'nʏmfə/ f -,-n nymph

....

Oo

....

o int o ja/nein! oh yes/no!

Oase f -,-n oasis

ob conj whether; **ob reich, ob arm** rich or poor; **und ob!** ⊤ you bet!

Obacht f **O~ geben** pay attention; **O~!** look out!

Obdach nt -[e]s shelter. **o~los** adj homeless. **O~lose(r)** m/f homeless person; **die O~losen** the homeless pl

Obduktion /-'tsio:n/ f -,-en post-mortem

O-Beine ntpl ⊤ bow-legs, bandy legs

oben adv at the top; (auf der Oberseite) on top; (eine Treppe hoch) upstairs; (im Text) above; **da o~** up there; **o~ im Norden** up in the north; **siehe o~** see above; **o~ auf** (+ acc/dat) on top of; **nach o~** up[wards]; (die Treppe hinauf) upstairs; **von o~** from above/upstairs; **von o~ bis unten** from top to bottom/(Person) to toe; **jdn von o~ bis unten mustern** look s.o. up and down; **o~ erwähnt** od **genannt** above-mentioned. **o~drein** adv on top of that

Ober m -s,- waiter

Ober|arm m upper arm. **O~arzt** m ≈ senior registrar. **O~deck** nt

upper deck. **o~e(r,s)** adj upper; (höhere) higher. **O~fläche** f surface. **o~flächlich** adj superficial. **O~geschoss** nt upper storey. **o~halb** adv & prep (+ gen) above. **O~haupt** nt (fig) head. **O~haus** nt (Pol) upper house; (in UK) House of Lords. **O~hemd** nt [man's] shirt. **o~irdisch** adj surface ● adv above ground. **O~kiefer** m upper jaw. **O~körper** m upper part of the body. **O~leutnant** m lieutenant. **O~lippe** f upper lip

Obers nt - (Aust) cream

Ober|schenkel m thigh. **O~schule** f grammar school. **O~seite** f upper/(rechte Seite) right side

Oberst m -en & -s,-en colonel

oberste(r,s) adj top; (höchste) highest; (Befehlshaber, Gerichtshof) supreme; (wichtigste) first

Ober|stimme f treble. **O~teil** nt top. **O~weite** f chest/(der Frau) bust size

obgleich conj although

Obhut f - care

obig adj above

Objekt nt -[e]s,-e object; (Haus, Grundstück) property

Objektiv nt -s,-e lens. **o~** adj objective. **O~ität** f - objectivity

Oblate f -,-n (Relig) wafer

Obmann m (pl -männer) [jury] foreman; (Sport) referee

Oboe /o'bo:ə/ f -,-n oboe

Obrigkeit f - authorities pl

obschon conj although

Observatorium nt -s,-ien observatory

obskur adj obscure; dubious

Obst nt -es (coll) fruit. **O~baum** m fruit-tree. **O~garten** m orchard. **O~händler** m fruiterer

n
o

obszön adj obscene

O-Bus m trolley bus

obwohl conj although

Ochse m -n,-n ox

öde adj desolate; (unfruchtbar) barren; (langweilig) dull. **Öde** f - desolation; barrenness; dullness

oder conj or; du kennst ihn doch, o~? you know him, don't you?

Ofen m -s,² stove; (Heiz-) heater; (Back-) oven; (Techn) furnace

offen adj open; (Haar) loose; (Flamme) naked; (o~herzig) frank; (o~ gezeigt) overt; (unentschieden) unsettled; o~e Stelle vacancy; Wein o~ verkaufen sell wine by the glass; o~ bleiben remain open; o~ halten hold open (Tür); keep open (Mund, Augen); o~ lassen leave open; leave vacant (Stelle); o~ stehen be open; (Rechnung:) be outstanding; jdm o~ stehen (fig) be open to s.o.; adv o~ gesagt od gestanden to be honest. **o~bar** adj obvious ● adv apparently. **o~baren** vt reveal. **O~barung** f -,-en revelation. **O~heit** f - frankness, openness. **o~sichtlich** adj obvious

offenstehen* vi sep (haben) offen stehen, s. offen

öffentlich adj public. **Ö~keit** f - public; in aller Ö~keit in public, publicly

Offerte f -,-n (Comm) offer

offiziell adj official

Offizier m -s,-e (Mil) officer

öffn|en vt/i (haben) open; sich ö~en open. **Ö~er** m -s,- opener. **Ö~ung** f -,-en opening. **Ö~ungszeiten** fpl opening hours

oft adv often

öfter adv quite often. **ö~e(r,s)** adj frequent; des Ö~en (ö~en) frequently. **ö~s** adv 🇦 quite often

oh int oh!

ohne prep (+ acc) without; o~ mich! count me out! oben o~ topless ● conj o~ zu überlegen without thinking; o~ dass ich es merkte without my noticing it. o~dies adv anyway. o~gleichen pred adj unparalleled. o~hin adv anyway

Ohn|macht f -,-en faint; (fig) powerlessness; in O~macht fallen faint. **o~mächtig** adj unconscious; (fig) powerless; o~mächtig werden faint

Ohr nt -[e]s,-en ear

Öhr nt -[e]s,-e eye (of needle)

Ohrenschmalz nt ear-wax. **O~schmerzen** mpl earache sg

Ohrfeige f slap in the face. **o~n** vt jdn o~n slap s.o.'s face

Ohr|läppchen nt -s,- ear-lobe. **O~ring** m ear-ring. **O~wurm** m earwig

oje int oh dear!

okay /o'ke:/ adj & adv 🇦 OK

Öko|logie f - ecology. **ö~logisch** adj ecological. **Ö~nomie** f - economy; (Wissenschaft) economics sg. **ö~nomisch** adj economic; (sparsam) economical

Oktave f -,-n octave

Oktober m -s,- October

ökumenisch adj ecumenical

Öl nt -[e]s,-e oil; in Öl malen paint

in oils. **Ölbaum** m olivetree. **ölen** vt oil. **Ölfarbe** f oil-paint. **Ölfeld** nt oilfield. **Ölgemälde** nt oil-painting. **ölig** adj oily

Olive f -,-n olive. **O~enöl** nt olive oil

Ölmessstab m dip-stick. **Ölsardinen** fpl sardines in oil. **Ölstand** m oil-level. **Öltanker** m oil-tanker. **Ölteppich** m oil-slick

Olympiade f -,-n Olympic Games pl, Olympics pl

Olympiasieger(in) /o'lympia-/ m(f) Olympic champion. **o~isch** adj Olympic; **O~ische Spiele** Olympic Games

Ölzeug nt oilskins pl

Oma f -,-s 🔢 granny

Omnibus m bus; (Reise-) coach

onanieren vi (haben) masturbate

Onkel m -s,- uncle

Opa m -s,-s 🔢 grandad

Opal m -s,-e opal

Oper f -,-n opera

Operation /-'tsio:n/ f -,-en operation. **O~ssaal** m operating theatre

Operette f -,-n operetta

operieren vt operate on (Patient, Herz); **sich o~ lassen** have an operation • vi (haben) operate

Opernglas nt opera-glasses pl

Opfer nt -s,- sacrifice; (eines Unglücks) victim; **ein O~ bringen** make a sacrifice; **jdm/etw zum O~ fallen** fall victim to s.o./something. **o~n** vt sacrifice

Opium nt -s opium

Opposition /-'tsio:n/ f - opposition. **O~spartei** f opposition party

Optik f - optics sg, (🔢: Objektiv) lens. **O~er** m -s,- optician

optimal adj optimum

Optimis|mus m - optimism. **O~t** m -en,-en optimist. **o~tisch**

adj optimistic

optisch adj optical; (Eindruck) visual

Orakel nt -s,- oracle

Orange /o'rãːʒə/ f -,-n orange. **o~** inv adj orange. **O~ade** f -,-n orangeade. **O~nmarmelade** f [orange] marmalade

Oratorium nt -s,-ien oratorio

Orchester /ɔr'kɛstɐ/ nt -s,- orchestra

Orchidee /ɔrçi'deːə/ f -,-n orchid

Orden m -s,- (Ritter-, Kloster-) order; (Auszeichnung) medal, decoration

ordentlich adj neat, tidy; (anständig) respectable; (ordnungsgemäß, fam: richtig) proper; (Mitglied, Versammlung) ordinary; (🔢: gut) decent; (🔢: gehörig) good

Order f -,-s & -n order

ordinär adj common

Ordination /-'tsio:n/ f -,-en (Relig) ordination; (Aust) surgery

ordn|en vt put in order; tidy; (an-) arrange. **O~er** m -s,- steward; (Akten-) file

Ordnung f - order; **O~ machen** tidy up; **in O~ bringen** put in order; (aufräumen) tidy; (reparieren) mend; (fig) put right; **in O~ sein** be in order; (ordentlich sein) be tidy; (fig) be all right; **[geht] in O~!** OK! **o~sgemäß** adj proper. **O~sstrafe** f (Jur) fine. **o~swidrig** adj improper

Ordonnanz, Ordonanz f -,-en (Mil) orderly

Organ nt -s,-e organ; voice

Organisation /-'tsio:n/ f -,-en organization

organisch adj organic

organisieren vt organize; (🔢: beschaffen) get [hold of]

Organismus m -,-men organism; (System) system

Organspenderkarte f donor card

Orgasmus m -,-men orgasm

Orgel f -,-n (Mus) organ. **O~pfeife** f organ-pipe

Orgie /ˈɔrgiə/ f -,-n orgy

Orient /ˈoːriɛnt/ m -s Orient. o~**talisch** adj Oriental

orientier|en /oriɛnˈtiːrən/ vt inform (**über** + acc about); **sich o~en** get one's bearings, orientate oneself; (unterrichten) inform oneself (**über** + acc about). **O~ung** f - orientation; **die O~ung verlieren** lose one's bearings

original adj original. **O~** nt -s,-e original. **O~übertragung** f live transmission

originell adj original; (eigenartig) unusual

Orkan m -s,-e hurricane

Ornament nt -[e]s,-e ornament

Ort m -[e]s,-e place; (Ortschaft) [small] town; **am Ort** locally; **am Ort des Verbrechens** at the scene of the crime

ortho|dox adj orthodox. **O~graphie, O~grafie** f - spelling. **O~päde** m -n,-n orthopaedic specialist

örtlich adj local

Ortschaft f -,-en [small] town; (Dorf) village; **geschlossene O~** (Auto) built-up area

Orts|gespräch nt (Teleph) local call. **O~verkehr** m local traffic. **O~zeit** f local time

Öse f -,-n eyelet; (Schlinge) loop; **Haken und Öse** hook and eye

Ost m -[e]s east

Osten m -s east; **nach O~** east

ostentativ adj pointed

Osteopath m -en,-en osteopath

Oster|ei /ˈoːstəʔai̯/ nt Easter egg. **O~fest** nt Easter. **O~glocke** f daffodil. **O~n** nt -,- Easter; **frohe O~n!** happy Easter!

Österreich nt -s Austria. **Ö~er** m, -s,-, **Ö~erin** f -,-nen Austrian. **ö~isch** adj Austrian

östlich adj eastern; (Richtung) easterly ● adv & prep (+ gen) **ö~ [von] der Stadt** [to the] east of the town

Ostsee f Baltic [Sea]

Otter[1] m -s,- otter

Otter[2] f -,-n adder

Ouverture /uvɛrˈtyːrə/ f -,-n overture

oval adj oval. **O~** nt -s,-e oval

Oxid, Oxyd nt -[e]s,-e oxide

Ozean m -s,-e ocean

Ozon nt -s ozone. **O~loch** nt hole in the ozone layer. **O~schicht** f ozone layer

Pp

paar pron inv **ein p~** a few; **ein p~ Mal** a few times; **alle p~ Tage** every few days. **P~** nt -[e]s,-e pair; (Ehe-, Liebes-) couple. **p~en** vt mate; (verbinden) combine; **sich p~en** mate. **P~ung** f -,-en mating. **p~weise** adv in pairs, in twos

Pacht f -,-en lease; (P~summe) rent. **p~en** vt lease

Pächter m -s,- lessee; (eines Hofes) tenant

Pachtvertrag m lease

Päckchen nt -s,- package, small packet

pack|en vt/i (haben) pack; (ergrei-

fen) seize; (fig: fesseln) grip. **P~en**
m -s,- bundle. **p~end** adj (fig)
gripping. **P~papier** nt [strong]
wrapping paper. **P~ung** f -,-en
packet; (Med) pack

Pädagoge m -n,-n educational-
ist; (Lehrer) teacher. **P~ik** f - educational science

Paddel nt -s,- paddle. **P~boot** nt
canoe. **p~n** vt/i (haben/sein) paddle. **P~sport** m canoeing

Page /'pa:ʒə/ m -n,-n page

Paillette /pai'jɛtə/ f -,-n sequin

Paket nt -[e]s,-e packet; (Post-)
parcel

Pakist|an nt -s Pakistan. **P~ane-
r(in)** m -s,- (f -,-nen) Pakistani.
p~anisch adj Pakistani

Palast m -[e]s,ᵉ palace

Paläst|ina nt -s Palestine. **P~i-
nenser(in)** m -s,- (f -,-nen) Palestinian. **p~inensisch** adj Palestinian

Palette f -,-n palette

Palme f -,-n palm[-tree]

Pampelmuse f -,-n grapefruit

Panier|mehl nt (Culin) bread-
crumbs pl. **p~t** adj (Culin) breaded

Panik f - panic

Panne f -,-n breakdown; (Reifen-)
flat tyre; (Missgeschick) mishap

Panter, Panther m -s,- panther

Pantine f -,-n [wooden] clog

Pantoffel m -s,-n slipper; mule

Pantomime¹ f -,-n mime

Pantomime² m -n,-n mime
artist

Panzer m -s,- armour; (Mil) tank;
(Zool) shell. **p~n** vt armourplate.
P~schrank m safe

Papa /'papa, pa'pa:/ m -s,-s daddy

Papagei m -s & -en,-en parrot

Papier nt -[e]s,-e paper. **P~korb**
m waste-paper basket. **P~schlange**
f streamer. **P~waren** fpl

stationery sg

Pappe f - cardboard

Pappel f -,-n poplar

pappig adj 🄓 sticky

Papp|karton m, **P~schachtel** f
cardboard box

Paprika m -s,-[s] [sweet] pepper;
(Gewürz) paprika

Papst m -[e]s,ᵉ pope

päpstlich adj papal

Parade f -,-n parade

Paradies nt -es,-e paradise

Paraffin nt -s paraffin

Paragraf, Paragraph m -en,-en
section

parallel adj & adv parallel. **P~e** f
-,-n parallel

Paranuss f Brazil nut

Parasit m -en,-en parasite

parat adj ready

Parcours /par'ku:ɐ̯/ m -,- /-[s],-s/
(Sport) course

Pardon /par'dõ:/ int sorry!

Parfüm nt -s,-e & -s perfume,
scent. **p~iert** adj perfumed,
scented

parieren vi (haben) 🄓 obey

Park m -s,-s park. **p~en** vt/i
(haben) park. **P~en** nt -s parking;
'P~en verboten' 'no parking'

Parkett nt -[e]s, -e parquet floor;
(Theat) stalls pl

Park|haus nt multi-storey car
park. **P~kralle** f wheel clamp.
P~lücke f parking space. **P~platz**
m car park; parking space.
P~scheibe f parking-disc.
P~schein m car-park ticket.
P~uhr f parking-meter. **P~verbot**
nt parking ban; 'P~verbot' 'no
parking'

Parlament nt -[e]s,-e parliament.
p~arisch adj parliamentary

Parodie f -,-n parody

P

Parole f -,-n slogan; (Mil) password

Partei f -,-en (Pol, Jur) party; (Miet-) tenant; **für jdn P~ ergreifen** take s.o.'s part. **p~isch** adj biased

Parterre /par'tɛr/ nt -s,-s ground floor; (Theat) rear stalls pl

Partie f -,-n part; (Tennis, Schach) game; (Golf) round; (Comm) batch; **eine gute P~ machen** marry well

Partikel nt -s,- particle

Partitur f -,-en (Mus) full score

Partizip nt -s,-ien participle

Partner|(in) m -s,- (f -,-nen) partner. **P~schaft** f -,-en partnership. **P~stadt** f twin town

Party /'pa:ɐti/ f -,-s party

Parzelle f -,-n plot [of ground]

Pass m -es,ᵉe passport; (Geog, Sport) pass

Passage /pa'sa:ʒə/ f -,-n passage; (Einkaufs-) shopping arcade

Passagier /pasa'ʒi:ɐ/ m -s,-e passenger

Passant(in) m -en,-en (f -,-nen) passer-by

Passe f -,-n yoke

passen vi (haben) fit; (geeignet sein) be right (für for); (Sport) pass the ball; (aufgeben) pass; **p~ zu go** [well] with; (übereinstimmen) match; **jdm p~** fit s.o.; (gelegen sein) suit s.o.; **[ich] passe** pass. **p~d** adj suitable; (angemessen) appropriate; (günstig) convenient; (übereinstimmend) matching

passier|en vt pass; cross (Grenze); (Culin) rub through a sieve ● vi (sein) happen (**jdm** to s.o.); **es ist ein Unglück p~t** there has been an accident. **P~schein** m pass

Passiv nt -s,-e (Gram) passive

Passstraße f pass

Paste f -,-n paste

Pastell nt -[e]s,-e pastel

Pastete f -,-n pie; (Gänseleber-) pâté

pasteurisieren /pastøri'zi:rən/ vt pasteurize

Pastor m -s,-en pastor

Pate m -n,-n godfather; (fig) sponsor; **P~n** godparents. **P~nkind** nt godchild

Patent nt -[e]s,-e patent; (Offiziers-) commission. **p~** adj (I) clever; (Person) resourceful. **p~ieren** vt patent

Pater m -s,- (Relig) Father

Patholog|e m -n,-n pathologist. **p~isch** adj pathological

Patience /pa'sjã:s/ f -,-n patience

Patient(in) /pa'tsjɛnt(ɪn)/ m -en,-en (f -,-nen) patient

Patin f -,-nen godmother

Patriot|(in) m -en,-en (f -,-nen) patriot. **p~isch** adj patriotic. **P~ismus** m - patriotism

Patrone f -,-n cartridge

Patrouille /pa'trʊljə/ f -,-n patrol

Patsch|e f in der P~e sitzen (I) be in a jam. **p~nass** adj (I) soaking wet

Patt nt -s stalemate

Patz|er m -s,- (I) slip. **p~ig** adj (I) insolent

Pauk|e f -,-n kettledrum; **auf die P~e hauen** (I) have a good time; (prahlen) boast. **p~en** vt/i (haben) (I) swot

pauschal adj all-inclusive; (einheitlich) flat-rate; (fig) sweeping (Urteil); **p~e Summe** lump sum. **P~e** f -,-n lump sum. **P~reise** f package tour. **P~summe** f lump sum

Pause¹ f -,-n break; (beim Sprechen) pause; (Theat) interval; (im Kino) intermission; (Mus) rest; **P~ machen** have a break

Pause² f -,-n tracing. **p~n** vt trace

pausenlos adj incessant

pausieren vi (haben) have a break; (ausruhen) rest

Pauspapier nt tracing-paper

Pavian m -s,-e baboon

Pavillon /ˈpaviljõ/ m -s,-s pavilion

Pazifik m -s Pacific [Ocean]. **p~sch** adj Pacific

Pazifist m -en,-en pacifist

Pech nt -s pitch; (Unglück) bad luck; **P~ haben** be unlucky

Pedal nt -s,-e pedal

Pedant m -en,-en pedant

Pediküre f -,-n pedicure

Pegel m -s,- level; (Gerät) water-level indicator. **P~stand** m [water] level

peilen vt take a bearing on

peinigen vt torment

peinlich adj embarrassing, awkward; (genau) scrupulous; **es war mir sehr p~** I was very embarrassed

Peitsche f -,-n whip. **p~n** vt whip; (fig) lash ● vi (sein) lash (**an** + acc against). **P~nhieb** m lash

Pelikan m -s,-e pelican

Pelle f -,-n skin. **p~n** vt peel; shell (Ei); **sich p~en** peel

Pelz m -es,-e fur

Pendel nt -s,- pendulum. **p~n** vi (haben) swing ● vi (sein) commute. **P~verkehr** m shuttle-service; (für Pendler) commuter traffic

Pendler m -s,- commuter

penetrant adj penetrating; (fig) obtrusive

Penis m -,-se penis

Penne f -,-n 🔤 school

Pension /pãˈzjoːn/ f -,-en pension; (Hotel) guest-house; **bei voller/halber P~** with full/half board. **P~är(in)** m -s,-e (f -,-nen) pen-

sioner. **P~at** nt -[e]s,-e boarding-school. **p~ieren** vt retire. **P~ierung** f - retirement

Pensum nt -s [allotted] work

Peperoni f -,- chilli

per prep (+ acc) by

Perfekt nt -s (Gram) perfect

Perfektion /-ˈtsjoːn/ f - perfection

perforiert adj perforated

Pergament nt -[e]s,-e parchment. **P~papier** nt grease-proof paper

Period|e f -,-n period. **p~isch** adj periodic

Perl|e f -,-n pearl; (Glas-, Holz-) bead; (Sekt-) bubble. **P~mutt** nt -s mother-of-pearl

Pers|ien /-jən/ nt -s Persia. **p~isch** adj Persian

Person f -,-en person; (Theat) character; **für vier P~en** for four people

Personal nt -s personnel, staff. **P~ausweis** m identity card. **P~chef** m personnel manager. **P~ien** pl personal particulars. **P~mangel** m staff shortage

persönlich adj personal ● adv personally, in person. **P~keit** f -,-en personality

Perücke f -,-n wig

pervers adj [sexually] perverted. **P~ion** f -,-en perversion

Pessimis|mus m - pessimism. **P~t** m -en,-en pessimist. **p~tisch** adj pessimistic

Pest f - plague

Petersilie /-jə/ f - parsley

Petroleum /-leʊm/ nt -s paraffin

Petze f -,-n 🔤 sneak. **p~n** vi (haben) 🔤 sneak

Pfad m -[e]s,-e path. **P~finder** m -s,- [Boy] Scout. **P~finderin** f -,-nen [Girl] Guide

p

Pfahl m -[e]s,¨e stake, post

Pfalz (die) - the Palatinate

Pfand nt -[e]s,¨er pledge; (beim Spiel) forfeit; (Flaschen-) deposit

pfänd|en vt (Jur) seize. **P~erspiel** nt game of forfeits

Pfandleiher m -s,- pawnbroker

Pfändung f -,-en (Jur) seizure

Pfann|e f -,-n (frying-)pan. **P~kuchen** m pancake

Pfarr|er m -s,- vicar, parson; (katholischer) priest. **P~haus** nt vicarage

Pfau m -s,-en peacock

Pfeffer m -s pepper. **P~kuchen** m gingerbread. **P~minze** f (Bot) peppermint. **p~n** vt pepper; (🄳: schmeißen) chuck. **P~streuer** m -s,- pepperpot

Pfeif|e f -,-n whistle; (Tabak-, Orgel-) pipe. **p~en†** vt/i (haben) whistle; (als Signal) blow the whistle

Pfeil m -[e]s,-e arrow

Pfeiler m -s,- pillar; (Brücken-) pier

Pfennig m -s,-e pfennig

Pferch m -[e]s,-e [sheep] pen

Pferd nt -es,-e horse; zu P~e on horseback. **P~erennen** nt horserace; (als Sport) [horse-]racing. **P~eschwanz** m horse's tail; (Frisur) pony-tail. **P~estall** m stable. **P~estärke** f horsepower

Pfiff m -[e]s,-e whistle

Pfifferling m -s,-e chanterelle

pfiffig adj 🄳 smart

Pfingst|en nt -s Whitsun. **P~rose** f peony

Pfirsich m -s,-e peach

Pflanz|e f -,-n plant. **p~en** vt plant. **P~enfett** nt vegetable fat. **p~lich** adj vegetable

Pflaster nt -s,- pavement; (Heft-) plaster. **p~n** vt pave

Pflaume f -,-n plum

Pflege f - care; (Kranken-) nursing; in P~ nehmen look after; (Admin) foster (Kind). **p~bedürftig** adj in need of care. **P~eltern** pl fosterparents. **P~kind** nt foster-child. **p~leicht** adj easy-care. **p~n** vt look after, care for; nurse (Kranke); cultivate (Künste, Freundschaft). **P~r(in)** m -s,- (f -,-nen) nurse; (Tier-) keeper

Pflicht f -,-en duty; (Sport) compulsory exercise/routine. **p~bewusst** adj conscientious. **P~gefühl** nt sense of duty

pflücken vt pick

Pflug m -[e]s,¨e plough

pflügen vt/i (haben) plough

Pforte f -,-n gate

Pförtner m -s,- porter

Pfosten m -s,- post

Pfote f -,-n paw

Pfropfen m -s,- stopper; (Korken-) cork. **p~** vt graft (auf + acc on [to]); (🄳: pressen) cram (in + acc into)

pfui int ugh

Pfund nt -[e]s,-e & - pound

Pfusch|arbeit f 🄳 shoddy work. **p~en** vi (haben) 🄳 botch one's work. **P~erei** f -,-en 🄳 botch-up

Pfütze f -,-n puddle

Phantasie f -,-n imagination; **P~n** fantasies; (Fieber-) hallucinations. **p~los** adj unimaginative. **p~ren** vi (haben) fantasize; (im Fieber) be delirious. **p~voll** adj imaginative

phantastisch adj fantastic

pharma|zeutisch adj pharmaceutical. **P~zie** f - pharmacy

Phase f -,-n phase

Philologie f - [study of] language and literature

Philosoph m -en,-en philosopher.

P~ie f -,-n philosophy
philosophisch adj philosophical
Phobie f -,-n phobia
Phonet|ik f - phonetics sg.
p~isch adj phonetic
Phosphor m -s phosphorus
Photo nt, **Photo-** = Foto, Foto-
Phrase f -,-n empty phrase
Physik f - physics sg. **p~alisch** adj physical
Physiker(in) m -s,- (f -,-nen) physicist
Physiologie f - physiology
physisch adj physical
Pianist(in) m -en,-en (f -,-nen) pianist
Pickel m -s,- pimple, spot; (Spitzhacke) pick. **p~ig** adj spotty
Picknick nt -s,-s picnic
piep[s]|en vi (haben) (Vogel:) cheep; (Maus:) squeak; (Techn) bleep. **P~er** m -s,- bleeper
Pier m -s,-e [harbour] pier
Pietät /pie'tɛːt/ f - reverence. **p~los** adj irreverent
Pigment nt -[e]s,-e pigment. **P~ierung** f - pigmentation
Pik nt -s,-s (Karten) spades pl
pikant adj piquant; (gewagt) racy
piken vt 🔲 prick
pikiert adj offended, hurt
Pilger|(in) m -s,- (f -,-nen) pilgrim. **P~fahrt** f pilgrimage. **p~n** vi (sein) make a pilgrimage
Pille f -,-n pill
Pilot m -en,-en pilot
Pilz m -es,-e fungus; (essbarer) mushroom
pingelig adj 🔲 fussy
Pinguin m -s,-e penguin
Pinie /-iǝ/ f -,-n stone-pine
pinkeln vi (haben) 🔲 pee
Pinsel m -s,- [paint]brush

Pinzette f -,-n tweezers pl
Pionier m -s,-e (Mil) sapper; (fig) pioneer
Pirat m -en,-en pirate
Piste f -,-n (Ski-) run, piste; (Renn-) track; (Aviat) runway
Pistole f -,-n pistol
pitschnass adj 🔲 soaking wet
pittoresk adj picturesque
Pizza f -,-s pizza
Pkw /'peːkaveː/ m -s,-s car
plädieren vi (haben) plead (**für** for); **auf Freispruch p~** (Jur) ask for an acquittal
Plädoyer /plɛdoa'jeː/ nt -s,-s (Jur) closing speech; (fig) plea
Plage f -,-n [hard] labour; (Mühe) trouble; (Belästigung) nuisance. **p~n** vt torment, plague; (bedrängen) pester; **sich p~n** struggle
Plakat nt -[e]s,-e poster
Plakette f -,-n badge
Plan m -[e]s,ˑe plan
Plane f -,-n tarpaulin; (Boden-) groundsheet
planen vt/i (haben) plan
Planet m -en,-en planet
planier|en vt level. **P~raupe** f bulldozer
Planke f -,-n plank
plan|los adj unsystematic. **p~mäßig** adj systematic; (Ankunft) scheduled
Plansch|becken nt paddling pool. **p~en** vi (haben) splash about
Plantage /plan'taːʒə/ f -,-n plantation
Planung f - planning
plappern vi (haben) chatter ● vt talk (Unsinn)
plärren vi (haben) bawl
Plasma nt -s plasma
Plastik[1] f -,-en sculpture

P

Plast|ik² nt -s plastic. **p~isch** adj three-dimensional; (formbar) plastic; (anschaulich) graphic

Plateau /pla'to:/ nt -s,-s plateau

Platin nt -s platinum

platonisch adj platonic

plätschern vi (haben) splash; (Bach:) babble ● vi (sein) (Bach:) babble along

platt adj & adv flat. **P~** nt -[s] (Lang) Low German

Plättbrett nt ironing-board

Platte f -,-n slab; (Druck-) plate; (Metall-, Glas-) sheet; (Fliese) tile; (Koch-) hotplate; (Tisch-) top; (Schall-) record, disc; (zum Servieren) [flat] dish, platter; **kalte P~** assorted cold meats and cheeses pl

Plätt|eisen nt iron. **p~en** vt/i (haben) iron

Plattenspieler m record-player

Platt|form f -,-en platform. **P~füße** mpl flat feet

Platz m -es,ᵉe place; (von Häusern umgeben) square; (Sitz-) seat; (Sport-) ground; (Fußball-) pitch; (Tennis-) court; (Golf-) course; (freier Raum) room, space; **P~ nehmen** take a seat; **P~ machen** make room; **vom P~ stellen** (Sport) send off. **P~anweiserin** f -,-nen usherette

Plätzchen nt -s,- spot; (Culin) biscuit

platzen vi (sein) burst; (auf-) split; (Ⅱ: scheitern) fall through; (Verlobung:) be off

Platz|karte f seat reservation ticket. **P~mangel** m lack of space. **P~patrone** f blank. **P~verweis** m (Sport) sending off. **P~wunde** f laceration

Plauderei f -,-en chat

plaudern vi (haben) chat

plausibel adj plausible

pleite adj Ⅱ **p~ sein** be broke; (Firma:) be bankrupt. **P~** f -,-n Ⅱ bankruptcy; (Misserfolg) flop; **P~ gehen** od **machen** go bankrupt

plissiert adj [finely] pleated

Plomb|e f -,-n seal; (Zahn-) filling. **p~ieren** vt seal; fill (Zahn)

plötzlich adj sudden

plump adj plump; clumsy

plumpsen vi (sein) Ⅱ fall

plündern vt/i (haben) loot

Plünderstück nt Danish pastry

Plural m -s,-e plural

plus adv, conj & prep (+ dat) plus. **P~** nt -,- surplus; (Gewinn) profit (Vorteil) advantage, plus. **P~punkt** m (Sport) point; (fig) plus

Po m -s,-s Ⅱ bottom

Pöbel m -s mob, rabble. **p~haft** adj loutish

pochen vi (haben) knock, (Herz:) pound; **p~ auf** (+ acc) (fig) insist on

pochieren /po'ʃiːrən/ vt poach

Pocken pl smallpox sg

Podest nt -[e]s,-e rostrum

Podium nt -s,-ien platform; (Podest) rostrum

Poesie /poe'ziː/ f - poetry

poetisch adj poetic

Pointe /'poɛ̃:tə/ f -,-n punchline (of a joke)

Pokal m -s,-e goblet; (Sport) cup

pökeln vt (Culin) salt

Poker nt -s poker

Pol m -s,-e pole. **p~ar** adj polar

Polarstern m pole-star

Pole m, -n,-n Pole. **P~n** nt -s Poland

Police /po'liːsə/ f -,-n policy

Polier m -s,-e foreman

polieren vt polish

Polin f -,-nen Pole

~ung f -,-en prophecy
roportion /-'tsio:n/ f -,-en proportion
rosa f - prose
rosit int cheers!
rospekt m -[e]s,-e brochure;
(Comm) prospectus
rost int cheers!
Prostitu|ierte f -n,-n prostitute.
P~tion f - prostitution
Protest m -[e]s,-e protest
Protestant|(in) m -en,-en (f
-,-nen) (Relig) Protestant. **p~isch**
adj (Relig) Protestant
protestieren vi (haben) protest
Prothese f -,-n artificial limb;
(Zahn-) denture
Protokoll nt -s,-e record; (Sit-
zungs-) minutes pl; (diplomatisches)
protocol
protz|en vi (haben) show off (mit
etw sth). **p~ig** adj ostentatious
Proviant m -s provisions pl
Provinz f -,-en province
Provision f -,-en (Comm) commission
provisorisch adj provisional,
temporary
Provokation /-'tsio:n/ f -,-en
provocation
provozieren vt provoke
Prozedur f -,-en [lengthy]
business
Prozent nt -[e]s,-e & - per cent; 5
P~ 5 per cent. **P~satz** m percentage. **p~ual** adj percentage
Prozess m -es,-e process; (Jur)
lawsuit; (Kriminal-) trial
Prozession f -,-en procession
Prozessor m -s,-en processor
prüde adj prudish
prüf|en vt test/(über-) check (auf +
acc for); audit (Bücher); (Sch) examine; **p~ender Blick** searching look.

P~er m -s,- inspector; (Buch-) auditor; (Sch) examiner. **P~ling** m -s,-
examination candidate. **P~ung** f
-,-en examination; (Test) test; (Bü-
cher-) audit; (fig) trial
Prügel m -s,- cudgel; **P~** pl hiding
sg, beating sg. **P~ei** f -,-en brawl,
fight. **p~n** vt beat, thrash
Prunk m -[e]s magnificence,
splendour
Psalm m -s,-en psalm
Pseudonym nt -s,-e pseudonym
pst int shush!
Psychi|ater m -s,- psychiatrist.
P~atrie f - psychiatry. **p~atrisch**
adj psychiatric
psychisch adj psychological
Psycho|analyse f psychoanalysis.
P~loge m -n,-n psychologist.
P~logie f - psychology. **p~logisch**
adj psychological
Pubertät f - puberty
Publi|kum nt -s public; (Zuhörer)
audience; (Zuschauer) spectators pl.
p~zieren vt publish
Pudding m -s,-s blancmange; (im
Wasserbad gekocht) pudding
Pudel m -s,- poodle
Puder m & nt -s,- powder.
P~dose f [powder] compact. **p~n**
vt powder. **P~zucker** m icing sugar
Puff m & nt -s,-s brothel
Puffer m -s,- (Rail) buffer; (Culin)
pancake. **P~zone** f buffer zone
Pull|i m -s,-s jumper. **P~over** m
-s,- jumper; (Herren-) pullover
Puls m -es pulse. **P~ader** f artery
Pult nt -[e]s,-e desk
Pulver nt -s,- powder. **p~ig** adj
powdery
Pulverkaffee m instant coffee
pummelig adj chubby
Pumpe f -,-n pump. **p~n** vt/i
(haben) pump; leihen) lend;

Politesse f -,-n [woman] traffic
warden
Politik f - politics sg; (Vorgehen,
Maßnahme) policy
Polit|iker(in) m -s,- (f, -,-nen)
politician. **p~isch** adj political
Politur f -,-en polish
Polizei f - police pl. **p~lich** adj police ● adv by the police; (sich anmelden) with the police. **P~streife** f
police patrol. **P~stunde** f closing
time. **P~wache** f police station
Polizist m -en,-en policeman.
P~in f -,-nen policewoman
Pollen m -s pollen
polnisch adj Polish
Polster nt -s,- pad; (Kissen) cushion; (Möbel-) upholstery. **p~n** vt
pad; upholster (Möbel). **P~ung** f
padding; upholstery
Polter|abend m eve-of-wedding
party. **P~n** vi (haben) thump bang

Polterabend This is
Germany's equivalent of
pre-wedding stag and hen
nights. The Polterabend is a party
for family and friends of both
bride and groom. It is held a few
days before the wedding, and
guests traditionally smash crockery
to bring good luck to the happy
couple.

Polyäthylen nt -s polythene
Polyester m -s polyester
Polyp m -en,-en polyp. **P~en** ad-
enoids pl
Pommes frites /pɔmˈfriːt/ pl
chips; (dünner) French fries
Pomp m -s pomp
Pompon /pɔ̃ˈpõ/ m -s,-s pompon
pompös adj ostentatious
Pony[1] nt -s,-s pony
Pony[2] m -s,-s fringe

Pop m -[s] pop
Popo m -s,-s bottom
populär adj popular
Pore f -,-n pore
Porno|grafie, Pornographie f -
pornography. **p~grafisch, p~
graphisch** adj pornographic
Porree m -s leeks pl
Portal nt -s,-e portal
Portemonnaie /portmɔˈneː/ nt
-s,-s purse
Portier /porˈtjeː/ m -s,-s doorman,
porter
Portion /-'tsio:n/ f -,-en helping,
portion
Portmonee nt -s,-s = Porte-
monnaie
Porto nt -s postage. **p~frei** adv
post free, post paid
Porträt /porˈtrɛː/ nt -s,-s portrait.
p~tieren vt paint a portrait of
Portugal nt -s Portugal
Portugies|e m -n,-n, **P~in** f
-,-nen Portuguese. **p~isch** adj Por-
tuguese
Portwein m port
Porzellan nt -s china, porcelain
Posaune f -,-n trombone
Position /-'tsio:n/ f -,-en position
positiv adj positive. **P~** nt -s,-e
(Phot) positive
Post f - post office; (Briefe) mail,
post; **mit der P~** by post
postalisch adj postal
Post|amt nt post office. **P~an-
weisung** f postal money order.
P~bote m postman
Posten m -s,- post; (Wache) sen-
try; (Waren-) batch; (Rechnungs-)
item, entry
Poster nt & m -s,- poster
Postfach nt post-office or PO box
Post|karte f postcard. **p~la-
gernd** adv poste restante. **P~leit-**

zahl f postcode. **P~scheckkonto** nt ≈ National Girobank account. **P~stempel** m postmark

postum adj posthumous

post|wendend adv by return of post. **P~wertzeichen** nt [postage] stamp

Potenz f -,-en potency; (Math & fig) power

Pracht f - magnificence, splendour

prächtig adj magnificent; splendid

prachtvoll adj magnificent

Prädikat nt -[e]s,-e rating; (Comm) grade; (Gram) predicate

prägen vt stamp (auf + acc on); emboss (Leder); mint (Münze); coin (Wort); (fig) shape

prägnant adj succinct

prähistorisch adj prehistoric

prahl|en vi (haben) boast, brag (mit about)

Prakti|k f -,-en practice. **P~kant(in)** m -en,-en (f -,-nen) trainee

Prakti|kum nt -s,-ka practical training. **p~sch** adj practical; (nützlich) handy; (tatsächlich) virtual; **p~scher Arzt** general practitioner ● adv practically; virtually; (in der Praxis) in practice. **p~zieren** vt/i (haben) practise; (anwenden) put into practice; (□: bekommen) get

Praline f -,-n chocolate

prall adj bulging; (dick) plump; (Sonne) blazing ● adv **p~ gefüllt** full to bursting. **p~en** vi (sein) **p~ auf** (+ acc)/**gegen** collide with, hit; (Sonne:) blaze down on

Prämie f -/ə/ f -,-n premium; (Preis) award

präm[i]ieren vt award a prize to

Pranger m -s,- pillory

Pranke f -,-n paw

Präparat nt -[e]s,-e preparation

Präsens nt - (Gram) present

präsentieren vt present

Präsenz f - presence

Präservativ nt -s,-e condom

Präsident|(in) m -en,-en (f -,-nen) president. **P~schaft** f - presidency

Präsidium nt -s presidency; (Gremium) executive committee; (Polizei-) headquarters pl

prasseln vi (haben) (Regen:) beat down; (Feuer:) crackle

Prater Vienna's largest amusement park was a private game reserve for the Austrian royal family until 1766. The Prater is famous for its old-fashioned carousels. A Riesenrad, big wheel or Ferris wheel, with a diameter of 67 metres was built there for the World Exhibition of 1897.

Präteritum nt -s imperfect

Praxis f -,-xen practice; (Erfahrung) practical experience; (Arzt-) surgery; **in der P~** in practice

Präzedenzfall m precedent

präzis[e] adj precise

predig|en vt/i (haben) preach. **P~t** f -,-en sermon

Preis m -es,-e price; (Belohnung) prize. **P~ausschreiben** nt competition

Preiselbeere f (Bot) cowberry; (Culin) ≈ cranberry

preisen† vt praise

preisgeben† vt sep abandon (dat to); reveal (Geheimnis)

preis|gekrönt adj award-winning. **p~günstig** adj reasonably priced ● adv at a reasonable price. **P~lage** f price range. **p~lich** adj price ● adv in price. **P~richter** m judge. **P~schild** nt price-tag. **P~träger(in)** m(f) prize-winner.

---

p~wert adj reasonable

Prell|bock m buffers pl. **p~en** vt bounce; (verletzen) bruise; (□: betrügen) cheat. **P~ung** f -,-en bruise

Premiere /prə'mjɛːrə/ f -,-n première

Premierminister(in) /prə'mjeː-/ m(f) Prime Minister

Presse f -,-n press. **p~n** vt press

Pressluftbohrer m pneumatic drill

Preuß|en nt -s Prussia. **p~isch** adj Prussian

prickeln vi (haben) tingle

Priester m -s,- priest

prima inv adj □ first-class, first-rate; (toll) fantastic

primär adj primary

Primel f -,-n primula

primitiv adj primitive

Prinz m -en,-en prince. **P~essin** f -,-nen princess

Prinzip nt -s,-ien principle. **p~iell** adj (Frage) of principle ● adv on principle

Prise f -,-n **P~ Salz** pinch of salt

Prisma nt -s,-men prism

privat adj private, personal. **P~adresse** f home address. **p~isieren** vt privatize

Privileg nt -[e]s,-ien privilege. **p~iert** adj privileged

pro prep (+ dat) per. **Pro** nt - das **Pro und Kontra** the pros and cons pl

Probe f -,-n test, trial; (Menge, Muster) sample; (Theat) rehearsal; **auf die P~ stellen** put to the test; **ein Auto P~ fahren** test-drive a car. **p~n** vt/i (haben) (Theat) rehearse. **p~weise** adv on a trial basis. **P~zeit** f probationary period

probieren vt/i (haben) try; (kosten) taste; (proben) rehearse

---

Problem nt -s,-e prob **tisch** adj problematic

problemlos adj proble ● adv without any proble

Produkt nt -[e]s,-e prod

Produk|tion /-'tsjoːn/ f duction. **p~tiv** adj produ

Produ|zent m -en,-en p **p~zieren** vt produce

Professor m -s,-en profe

Profi m -s,-s (Sport) profes

Profil nt -s,-e profile; (Reife tread; (fig) image

Profit m -[e]s,-e profit. **p~** (haben) profit (von from)

Prognose f -,-n forecast; (M prognosis

Programm nt -s,-e program (Computer-) program; (TV) chan (Comm: Sortiment) range. **p~l** vt/i (haben) (Computer) program **P~ierer(in)** m -s,- (f -,-nen) (c puter) programmer

Projekt nt -[e]s,-e project

Projektor m -s,-en projector

Prolet m -en,-en boor. **P~ariat** -[e]s proletariat

Prolog m -s,-e prologue

Promenade f -,-n promenade

Promille pl □ alcohol level sg in the blood; **zu viel P~ haben** □ be over the limit

Prominenz f - prominent figures pl

Promiskuität f - promiscuity

promovieren vi (haben) obtain one's doctorate

prompt adj prompt

Pronomen nt -s,- pronoun

Propaganda f - propaganda; (Reklame) publicity

Propeller m -s,- propeller

Prophet m -en,-en prophet

prophezei|en vt prophesy.

[sich (dat)] etw p∼n (🗎: borgen) borrow sth

Pumps /pœmps/ pl court shoes
Punkt m -[e]s,-e dot; (Textiles) spot; (Geometry, Sport & fig) point; (Gram) full stop, period; P∼ sechs Uhr at six o'clock sharp
pünktlich adj punctual. **P∼keit** f - punctuality
Pupille f -,-n (Anat) pupil
Puppe f -,-n doll; (Marionette) puppet; (Schaufenster-, Schneider-) dummy; (Zool) chrysalis
pur adj pure; (🗎: bloß) sheer
Püree nt -s,-s purée; (Kartoffel-) mashed potatoes pl
purpurrot adj crimson
Purzel|baum m 🗎 somersault. **p∼n** vi (sein) 🗎 tumble
Puste f - 🗎 breath. **p∼n** vt/i (haben) 🗎 blow
Pute f -,-n turkey
Putsch m -[e]s,-e coup
Putz m -es plaster; (Staat) finery. **p∼en** vt clean; (Aust) dry-clean; (zieren) adorn; **sich p∼en** dress up; **sich** (dat) **die Zähne/Nase p∼en** clean one's teeth/blow one's nose. **P∼frau** f cleaner, charwoman. **p∼ig** adj 🗎 amusing, cute; (seltsam) odd
Puzzlespiel /'pazl-/ nt jigsaw
Pyramide f -,-n pyramid

Qq

Quacksalber m -s,- quack
Quadrat nt -[e]s,-e square. **q∼isch** adj square
quaken vi (haben) quack; (Frosch:) croak

Quäker(in) m -s,- (f -,-nen) Quaker
Qual f -,-en torment; (Schmerz) agony
quälen vt torment; (foltern) torture; (bedrängen) pester; **sich q∼** torment oneself; (leiden) suffer; (sich mühen) struggle
Quälerei f -,-en torture
Qualifi|kation /-'tsjo:n/ f -,-en qualification. **q∼zieren** vt qualify. **q∼ziert** adj qualified; (fähig) competent; (Arbeit) skilled
Qualität f -,-en quality
Qualle f -,-n jellyfish
Qualm m -s [thick] smoke
qualvoll adj agonizing
Quantum nt -s,-ten quantity; (Anteil) share, quota
Quarantäne f - quarantine
Quark m -s quark, ≈ curd cheese
Quartal nt -s,-e quarter
Quartett nt -[e]s,-e quartet
Quartier nt -s,-e accommodation; (Mil) quarters pl
Quarz m -es quartz
quasseln vi (haben) 🗎 jabber
Quaste f -,-n tassel
Quatsch m -[e]s 🗎 nonsense, rubbish; Q∼ machen (Unfug machen) fool around; (etw Dummes machen) do a silly thing. **q∼en** 🗎 vi (haben) talk; (Wasser, Schlamm:) squelch ● vt talk
Quecksilber nt mercury
Quelle f -,-n spring; (Fluss- & fig) source
quengeln vi 🗎 whine
quer adv across, crosswise; (schräg) diagonally; **q∼ gestreift** horizontally striped
Quere f - der Q∼ nach across, crosswise; **jdm in die Q∼ kommen** get in s.o.'s way

p
q

Quer|latte f crossbar. **Q~schiff** nt transept. **Q~schnitt** m cross-section. **q~schnittsgelähmt** adj paraplegic. **Q~straße** f side-street. **Q~verweis** m cross-reference

quetschen vt squash; (drücken) squeeze; (zerdrücken) crush; (Culin) mash; **sich q~** in (+ acc) squeeze into

Queue /køː/ nt -s,-s cue

quieken vi (haben) squeal; (Maus:) squeak

quietschen vi (haben) squeal; (Tür, Dielen:) creak

Quintett nt -[e]s,-e quintet

quirlen vt mix

Quitte f -,-n quince

quittieren vt receipt (Rechnung); sign for (Geldsumme, Sendung); **den Dienst q~** resign

Quittung f -,-en receipt

Quiz /kvɪs/ nt -,- quiz

Quote f -,-n proportion

. . . .

Rr

. . . .

Rabatt m -[e]s,-e discount

Rabatte f -,-n (Horticulture) border

Rabattmarke f trading stamp

Rabbiner m -s,- rabbi

Rabe m -n,-n raven

Rache f - revenge, vengeance

Rachen m -s, pharynx

rächen vt avenge; **sich r~** take revenge (an + dat on); (Fehler:) cost s.o. dear

Rad nt -[e]s,⁻er wheel; (Fahr-) bicycle, 🚲 bike; **Rad fahren** cycle

Radar m & nt -s radar

Radau m -s 🔊 din, racket

radeln vi (sein) 🚲 cycle

Rädelsführer m ringleader

radfahren| vi* vi sep (sein) Rad fahren, s. Rad. **R~er(in)** m(f) -s,- (f -,-nen) cyclist

radier|en vt/i (haben) rub out; (Kunst) etch. **R~gummi** m eraser, rubber. **R~ung** f -,-en etching

Radieschen /-'diːsçən/ nt -s,- radish

radikal adj radical, drastic

Radio nt -s,-s radio

radioaktiv adj radioactive. **R~ität** f - radioactivity

Radius m -,-ien radius

Rad|kappe f hub-cap. **R~ler** m -s,- cyclist; (Getränk) shandy

raffen vt grab; (kräuseln) gather; (kürzen) condense

Raffin|ade f - refined sugar. **R~erie** f -,-n refinery. **R~esse** f -,-n refinement; (Schlauheit) cunning. **r~iert** adj ingenious; (durchtrieben) crafty

ragen vi (haben) rise [up]

Rahm m -s (SGer) cream

rahmen vt frame. **R~** m -s,- frame; (fig) framework; (Grenze) limits pl; (einer Feier) setting

Rakete f -,-n rocket; (Mil) missile

Rallye /'rɛli/ nt -s,-s rally

rammen vt ram

Rampe f -,-n ramp; (Theat) front of the stage

Ramsch m -[e]s junk

ran adv = heran

Rand m -[e]s,⁻er edge; (Teller-, Gläser-, Brillen-) rim; (Zier-) border, edging; (Brief-) margin; (Stadt-) outskirts pl; (Ring) ring

randalieren vi (haben) rampage

Randstreifen m (Auto) hard shoulder

Rang m -[e]s,⁻e rank; (Theat) tier;

erster/zweiter R~ (*Theat*) dress/upper circle; **ersten R~es** first-class

rangieren /raŋ'ʒiːrən/ vt shunt ● vi (*haben*) rank (**vor** + *dat* before)

Rangordnung f order of importance; (*Hierarchie*) hierarchy

Ranke f -,-n tendril; (*Trieb*) shoot

ranken (sich) vr (*Bot*) trail; (*in die Höhe*) climb

Ranzen m -s,- (*Sch*) satchel

ranzig adj rancid

Rappe m -n,-n black horse

Raps m -es (*Bot*) rape

rar adj rare; **er macht sich rar** ⚠ we don't see much of him. **R~ität** f -,-en rarity

rasant adj fast; (*schnittig, schick*) stylish

rasch adj quick

rascheln vi (*haben*) rustle

Rasen m -s,- lawn

rasen vi (*sein*) tear [along]; (*Puls:*) race; (*Zeit:*) fly; **gegen eine Mauer r~** career into a wall ● vi (*haben*) rave; (*Sturm:*) rage. **r~d** adj furious; (*tobend*) raving; (*Sturm, Durst*) raging; (*Schmerz*) excruciating; (*Beifall*) tumultuous

Rasenmäher m lawn-mower

Rasier|apparat m razor. **r~en** vt shave; **sich r~en** shave. **R~klinge** f razor blade. **R~wasser** nt aftershave [lotion]

Raspel f -,-n rasp; (*Culin*) grater. **r~n** vt grate

Rasse f -,-n race. **R~hund** m pedigree dog

Rassel f -,-n rattle. **r~n** vi (*haben*) rattle; (*Schlüssel:*) jangle; (*Kette:*) clank

Rassendiskriminierung f racial discrimination

Rassepferd nt thoroughbred. **rassisch** adj racial

Rassis|mus m - racism. **r~tisch** adj racist

Rast f -,-en rest. **R~platz** m picnic area. **R~stätte** f motorway restaurant [and services]

Rasur f -,-en shave

Rat m -[e]s [piece of] advice; **sich** (*dat*) **keinen Rat wissen** not know what to do; **zu Rat[e] ziehen = zurate ziehen** s. **zurate**

Rate f -,-n instalment

raten † vt guess; (*empfehlen*) advise ● vi (*haben*) guess; **jdm r~** advise s.o.

Ratenzahlung f payment by instalments

Rat|geber m -s,- adviser; (*Buch*) guide. **R~haus** nt town hall

ratifizier|en vt ratify. **R~ung** f -,-en ratification

Ration /ra'tsi̯oːn/ f -,-en ration. **r~ell** adj efficient. **r~ieren** vt ration

rat|los adj helpless; (*unfreundlich*) gruff; (*Klima*) harsh, raw; (*heiser*) husky; (*Hals*) sore

Raub m -[e]s robbery; (*Menschen-*) abduction; (*Beute*) loot, booty. **r~en** vt steal; abduct (*Menschen*)

Räuber m -s,- robber

Raub|mord m robbery with murder. **R~tier** nt predator. **R~vogel** m bird of prey

Rauch m -[e]s smoke. **r~en** vt/i (*haben*) smoke. **R~en** nt -s smok-

Rätsel nt -s,- riddle; (*Kreuzwort-*) puzzle; (*Geheimnis*) mystery. **r~haft** adj puzzling, mysterious. **r~n** vi (*haben*) puzzle

Ratte f -,-n rat

rau adj rough; (*unfreundlich*) gruff; (*Klima*) harsh, raw; (*heiser*) husky; (*Hals*) sore

ing; 'R~en verboten' 'no smoking'.
R~er m -s,-smoker

Räucher|lachs m smoked salmon. r~n vt (Culin) smoke

rauf adv = herauf, hinauf

rauf|en vt pull ● vr/i (haben) [sich]
r~en fight. R~erei f -,-en fight

rauh* adj = rau

Raum m -[e]s, Räume room; (Gebiet) area; (Welt-) space

räumen vt clear; vacate (Wohnung); evacuate (Gebäude, Gebiet,
Mil Stellung); (bringen) put (in/auf
+ acc into/on); (holen) get (aus
out of)

Raum|fahrer m astronaut.
R~fahrt f space travel. R~inhalt
m volume

räumlich adj spatial

Raum|pflegerin f cleaner.
R~schiff nt spaceship

Räumung f - clearing; vacating;
evacuation. R~sverkauf m clearance/closing-down sale

Raupe f -,-n caterpillar

raus adv = heraus, hinaus

Rausch m -[e]s, Räusche intoxication; (fig) exhilaration; einen
R~haben be drunk

rauschen vi (haben) (Wasser,
Wind:) rush; (Bäume Blätter:) rustle
● vi [sein) rush [along]

Rauschgift nt [narcotic] drug;
(coll) drugs pl. R~süchtige(r) m/f
drug addict

räuspern (sich) vr clear one's
throat

rausschmeißen† vt sep [t]
throw out; (entlassen) sack

Raute f -,-n diamond

Razzia f -,-ien [police] raid

Reagenzglas nt test-tube

reagieren vi (haben) react (auf +
acc to)

Reaktion /-'tsjo:n/ f -,-en reaction. r~är adj reactionary

Reaktor m -s,-en reactor

realisieren vt realize

Realis|mus m - realism. R~t m
-en,-en realist. r~tisch adj realistic

Realität f -,-en reality

Realschule f ≈ secondary modern school

Rebe f -,-n vine

Rebell m -en,-en rebel. r~ieren vi
(haben) rebel. R~ion f -,-en rebellion

rebellisch adj rebellious

Rebhuhn nt partridge

Rebstock m vine

Rechen m -s,- rake

Rechen|aufgabe f arithmetical
problem; (Sch) sum. R~maschine f
calculator

recherchieren /reʃɛrˈʃiːrən/ vt/i
(haben) investigate; (Journalism) research

rechnen vi (haben) do arithmetic;
(schätzen) reckon; (zählen) count (zu
among; auf + acc on); r~ mit
reckon with; (erwarten) expect ● vt
calculate, work out; (fig) count (zu
among). R~ nt -s arithmetic

Rechner m -s,- calculator; (Computer) computer

Rechnung f -,-en bill; (Comm) invoice; (Berechnung) calculation; R~
führen über (+ acc) keep account
of. R~sjahr nt financial year.
R~sprüfer m auditor

Recht nt -[e]s,-e law; (Berechtigung) right (auf + acc to); im R~
sein be in the right; R~ haben/behalten be right; R~ bekommen be
proved right; jdm R~ geben agree
with s.o.; mit od zu R~ rightly

recht adj right; (wirklich) real; ich
habe keine r~e Lust I don't really
feel like it; es jdm r~ machen

please s.o.; **jdm r~ sein** be all right with s.o.; **r~ vielen Dank** many thanks

Recht|e f -n,-[n] right side; (Hand) right hand; (Boxen) right; **die R~e** (Pol) the right; **zu meiner R~en** on my right. **r~e(r,s)** adj right; (Pol) right-wing; **r~e Masche** plain stitch. **R~e(r)** m/f der/die R~e the right man/woman; **R~e(s)** nt das R~e the right thing; **etwas R~es lernen** learn something useful; **nach dem R~en sehen** see that everything is all right

Rechteck nt -[e]s,-e rectangle. **r~ig** adj rectangular

rechtfertigen vt justify; **sich r~en** justify oneself

recht|haberisch adj opinionated. **r~lich** adj legal. **r~mäßig** adj legitimate

rechts adv on the right; (bei Stoff) on the right side; **von/nach r~** from/to the right; **zwei r~, zwei links stricken** knit two, purl two. **R~anwalt** m, **R~anwältin** f lawyer

Rechtschreib|programm nt spell checker. **R~ung** f -spelling

Rechts|händer(in) m -s,- (f -,-nen) right-hander. **r~händig** adj & adv right-handed. **r~kräftig** adj legal. **R~streit** m law suit. **R~verkehr** m driving on the right. **r~widrig** adj illegal. **R~wissenschaft** f jurisprudence

rechtzeitig adj & adv in time

Reck nt -[e]s,-e horizontal bar

recken vt stretch

Redakteur /redak'tø:ɐ̯/ m -s,-e editor; (Radio, TV) producer

Redaktion /-'tsjo:n/ f -,-en editing; (Radio, TV) production; (Abteilung) editorial/production department

Rede f -,-n speech; **zur R~stellen** demand an explanation from; **nicht der R~ wert** not worth mentioning

reden vi (haben) talk (von about; mit to); (eine Rede halten) speak ● vt talk; speak (Wahrheit). **R~sart** f saying

Redewendung f idiom

redigieren vt edit

Redner m -s,- speaker

reduzieren vt reduce

Reeder m -s,- shipowner. **R~ei** f -,-en shipping company

Refer|at nt -[e]s,-e report; (Abhandlung) paper; (Abteilung) section. **R~ent(in)** m -en,-en (f -,-nen) speaker; (Sachbearbeiter) expert. **R~enz** f -,-en reference

Reflex m -es,-e reflex; (Widerschein) reflection. **R~ion** f -,-en reflection. **r~iv** adj reflexive

Reform f -,-en reform. **R~ation** f - (Relig) Reformation

Reform|haus nt health-food shop. **r~ieren** vt reform

Refrain /rə'frɛ̃:/ m -s,-s refrain

Regal nt -s,-e [set of] shelves pl

Regatta f -,-ten regatta

rege adj active; (lebhaft) lively; (geistig) alert; (Handel) brisk

Regel f -,-n rule; (Monats-) period. **r~mäßig** adj regular. **r~n** vt regulate; direct (Verkehr); (erledigen) settle. **r~recht** adj real, proper ● adv really. **R~ung** f -,-en regulation; settlement

regen vt move; **sich r~** move; (wach werden) stir

Regen m -s,- rain. **R~bogen** m rainbow. **R~haut** f iris

Regener|ation /-'tsjo:n/ f - regeneration. **r~ieren** vt regenerate

Regen|mantel m raincoat.

R~schirm m umbrella. **R~tag** m rainy day. **R~wetter** nt wet weather. **R~wurm** m earthworm

Regie /reˈʒiː/ f - direction; **R~ führen** direct

regier|en vt/i (haben) govern, rule; (Monarch:) reign [over]; (Gram) take. **R~ung** f -,-en government; (Herrschaft) rule; (eines Monarchen) reign

Regiment nt -[e]s,-er regiment

Region f -,-en region. **r~al** adj regional

Regisseur /reʒɪˈsøːɐ̯/ m -s,-e director

Register nt -s,- register; (Inhaltsverzeichnis) index; (Orgel-) stop

Regler m -s,- regulator

reglos adj & adv motionless

regn|en vi (haben) rain; **es r~et** it is raining. **r~erisch** adj rainy

regul|är adj normal; (rechtmäßig) legitimate. **r~ieren** vt regulate

Regung f -,-en movement; (Gefühls-) emotion. **r~slos** adj & adv motionless

Reh nt -[e]s,-e roe-deer; (Culin) venison

Rehbock m roebuck

reib|en† vt rub; (Culin) grate ● vi (haben) rub. **R~ung** f - friction. **r~ungslos** adj (fig) smooth

reich adj rich (**an** + dat in)

Reich nt -[e]s,-e empire; (König-) kingdom; (Bereich) realm

Reiche(r) m/f rich man/woman; **die R~en** the rich pl

reichen vt hand; (anbieten) offer ● vi (haben) be enough; (in der Länge) be long enough; **r~ bis zu** reach [up to]; (sich erstrecken) extend to; **mit dem Geld r~** have enough money

reich|haltig adj extensive, large (Mahlzeit) substantial. **r~lich** adj

ample; (Vorrat) abundant. **R~tum** m -s,-tümer wealth (**an** + dat of); **R~tümer** riches. **R~weite** f reach; (Techn, Mil) range

Reif m -[e]s [hoar-]frost

reif adj ripe; (fig) mature; **r~ für** ready for. **r~en** vi (sein) ripen; (Wein, Käse & fig) mature

Reifen m -s,- hoop; (Arm-) bangle; (Auto-) tyre. **R~druck** m tyre pressure. **R~panne** f puncture, flat tyre

reiflich adj careful

Reihe f -,-n row; (Anzahl & Math) series; **der R~ nach** in turn; **wer ist an der R~?** whose turn is it? **r~n** (sich) vr **sich r~n an** (+ acc) follow. **R~nfolge** f order. **R~nhaus** nt terraced house

Reiher m -s,- heron

Reim m -[e]s,-e rhyme. **r~en** vt rhyme; **sich r~en** rhyme

rein¹ adj pure; (sauber) clean; (Unsinn, Dummheit) sheer; **ins R~e** (r~e) schreiben make a fair copy of

rein² adv = herein, hinein

Reineclaude /rɛːnəˈkloːdə/ f -,-n greengage

Reinfall m ⚀ let-down; (Misserfolg) flop

Rein|gewinn m net profit. **R~heit** f - purity

reinig|en vt clean; (chemisch) dry-clean. **R~ung** f -,-en cleaning; (*chemische*) dry-cleaning; (*Geschäft*) dry cleaner's

reinlegen vt sep put in; 🄣 dupe; (*betrügen*) take for a ride

reinlich adj clean. **R~keit** f - cleanliness

Reis m -es rice

Reise f -,-n journey; (*See-*) voyage; (*Urlaubs-, Geschäfts-*) trip. **R~andenken** nt souvenir. **R~büro** nt travel agency. **R~bus** m coach. **R~führer** m tourist guide; (*Buch*) guide. **R~gesellschaft** f tourist group. **R~leiter(in)** m(f) courier. **r~n** vi (sein) travel. **R~nde(r)** m/f traveller. **R~pass** m passport. **R~scheck** m traveller's cheque. **R~veranstalter** m -s,- tour operator. **R~ziel** nt destination

Reisig nt -s brushwood

Reißaus m **R~** nehmen 🄣 run away

Reißbrett nt drawing-board

reißen† vt tear; (*weg-*) snatch; (*töten*) kill; Witze r~ crack jokes; **an sich** (*acc*) r~snatch; seize (*Macht*); **sich r~ um** 🄣 fight for ● vi (sein) tear; (*Seil, Faden:*) break ● vi (haben) r~ an (+ *dat*) pull at

Reißer m -s,- 🄣 thriller; (*Erfolg*) big hit

Reiß|nagel m = R~zwecke. **R~verschluss** m zip [fastener]. **R~wolf** m shredder. **R~zwecke** f -,-n drawing-pin

reit|en† vt/i (sein) ride. **R~er(in)** m -s,- (f -,-nen) rider. **R~hose** f riding breeches pl. **R~pferd** nt saddle-horse. **R~weg** m bridle-path

Reiz m -es,-e stimulus; (*Anziehungskraft*) attraction, appeal; (*Charme*) charm. **r~bar** adj irritable. **R~barkeit** f - irritability. **r~en** vt provoke; (*Med*) irritate; (*interessieren,*

locken) appeal to, attract; arouse (*Neugier*); (*beim Kartenspiel*) bid. **R~ung** f -,-en (*Med*) irritation. **r~voll** adj attractive

rekeln (sich) vr 🄣 stretch

Reklamation /-'tsi:o:n/ f -,-en (*Comm*) complaint

Reklam|e f -,-n advertising, publicity; (*Anzeige*) advertisement; (*TV, Radio*) commercial; **R~ machen** advertise (**für etw** sth). **r~ieren** vt complain about; (*fordern*) claim ● vi (haben) complain

Rekord m -[e]s,-e record

Rekrut m -en,-en recruit

Rek|tor m -s,-en (*Sch*) head[master]; (*Univ*) vice-chancellor. **R~torin** f -,-nen head, headmistress; vice-chancellor

Relais /rə'lɛ:/ nt -,- /-s,-s/ (*Electr*) relay

relativ adj relative

Religi|on f -,-en religion; (*Sch*) religious education. **r~ös** adj religious

Reling f -,-s (*Naut*) rail

Reliquie /re'li:kviə/ f -,-n relic

rempeln vt jostle; (*stoßen*) push

Reneklode f -,-n greengage

Rennbahn f race-track; (*Pferde-*) racecourse. **R~boot** nt speed-boat. **r~en**† vi (sein) run; **um die Wette r~en** have a race. **R~en** nt -s,- race. **R~pferd** nt racehorse. **R~sport** m racing. **R~wagen** m racing car

renommiert adj renowned; (*Hotel, Firma*) of repute

renovier|en vt renovate; redecorate (*Zimmer*). **R~ung** f - renovation; redecoration

rentabel adj profitable

Rente f -,-n pension; **in R~ gehen** 🄣 retire. **R~nversicherung** f pension scheme

r

Rentier nt reindeer

rentieren (sich) vr be profitable; (sich lohnen) be worth while

Rentner(in) m -s-, (f -,-nen) [old-age] pensioner

Reparatur f -,-en repair. **R~werkstatt** f repair workshop; (Auto) garage

reparieren vt repair, mend

Reportage /-'ta:ʒə/ f -,-n report

Reporter(in) m -s-, (f -,-nen) reporter

repräsentativ adj representative (für of); (eindrucksvoll) imposing

Reprodu|ktion /-'tsjo:n/ f -,-en reproduction. **r~zieren** vt reproduce

Reptil nt -s,-ien reptile

Republik f -,-en republic. **r~anisch** adj republican

Requisiten pl (Theat) properties, ▣ props

Reservat nt -[e]s,-e reservation

Reserve f -,-n reserve; (Mil, Sport) reserves pl. **R~rad** nt spare wheel

reservier|en vt reserve; **r~en lassen** book. **r~t** adj reserved. **R~ung** f -,-en reservation

Reservoir /rezɛr'voa:ɐ/ nt -s,-s reservoir

Residenz f -,-en residence

Resignation /-'tsjo:n/ f - resignation. **r~ieren** vi (haben) (fig) give up. **r~iert** adj resigned

resolut adj resolute

Resonanz f -,-en resonance

Respekt /-sp-, -ʃp-/ m -[e]s respect (vor + dat for). **r~ieren** vt respect

respektlos adj disrespectful

Ressort /rɛ'so:ɐ/ nt -s,-s department

Rest m -[e]s,-e remainder, rest; **R~e** remains; (Essens-) leftovers

Restaurant /rɛsto'rã:/ nt -s,-s restaurant

Restaur|ation /rɛstaura'tsjo:n/ f - restoration. **r~ieren** vt restore

Rest|betrag m balance. **r~lich** adj remaining

Resultat nt -[e]s,-e result

rett|en vt save (vor + dat from); (aus Gefahr befreien) rescue; **sich r~en** save oneself; (flüchten) escape. **R~er** m -s,- rescuer; (fig) saviour

Rettich m -s,-e white radish

Rettung f -,-en rescue; (fig) salvation; **jds letzte R~** s.o.'s last hope. **R~sboot** nt lifeboat. **R~sdienst** m rescue service. **R~sgürtel** m lifebelt. **r~slos** adv hopelessly. **R~sring** m lifebelt. **R~ssanitäter(in)** m(f) paramedic. **R~swagen** m ambulance

retuschieren vt (Phot) retouch

Reue f - remorse; (Relig) repentance

Revanch|e /re'vã:ʃə/ f -,-n revenge; **R~e fordern** (Sport) ask for a return match. **r~ieren (sich)** vr take revenge; (sich erkenntlich zeigen) reciprocate (mit with)

Revers /re've:ɐ/ nt -,- /-[s],-s/ lapel

Revier nt -s,-e district; (Zool & fig) territory; (Polizei-) [police] station

Revision /-'zjo:n/ f -,-en revision; (Prüfung) check; (Jur) appeal

Revolution /-'tsjo:n/ f -,-en revolution. **r~är** adj revolutionary. **r~ieren** vt revolutionize

Revolver m -s,- revolver

rezen|sieren vt review. **R~sion** f -,-en review

Rezept nt -[e]s,-e prescription; (Culin) recipe

Rezession f -,-en recession

R-Gespräch nt reverse-charge call

Rhabarber m -s rhubarb

Rhein m -s Rhine. **R~land** nt -s

Rhineland. **R~wein** m hock

Rhetorik f - rhetoric

Rheum|a nt -s rheumatism. **r~a-tisch** adj rheumatic. **R~atismus** nt - rheumatism

Rhinozeros nt -[ses],-se rhinoceros

rhyth|misch /'rʏt-/ adj rhythmic[al]. **R~mus** m -,-men rhythm

richten vt direct (**auf** + acc at); address (Frage) (**an** + acc to); aim (Waffe) (**auf** + acc at); (einstellen) set; (vorbereiten) prepare; (reparieren) mend; **in die Höhe r~** raise [up]; **sich r~** be directed (**auf** + acc at; **gegen** against); (Blick:) turn (**auf** + acc on); **sich r~nach** comply with (Vorschrift); fit in with (jds Plänen); (abhängen) depend on ● vi (haben) **r~ über** (+ acc) judge

Richter m -s,- judge

richtig adj right, correct; (wirklich, echt) real; **das R~e** the right thing ● adv correctly; really; **r~ stellen** put right (Uhr); (fig) correct (Irrtum); **die Uhr geht r~** the clock is right

Richtlinien fpl guidelines

Richtung f -,-en direction

riechen† vt/i (haben) smell (**nach** of; **an etw** dat sth)

Riegel m -s,- bolt; (Seife) bar

Riemen m -s,- strap; (Ruder) oar

Riese m -n,-n giant

rieseln vi (sein) trickle; (Schnee:) fall lightly

riesengroß adj huge, enormous

riesig adj huge; (gewaltig) enormous ● adv 🔲 terribly

Riff nt -[e]s,-e reef

Rille f -,-n groove

Rind nt -[e]s,-er ox; (Kuh) cow; (Stier) bull; (R~fleisch) beef; **R~er** cattle pl

Rinde f -,-n bark; (Käse-) rind; (Brot-) crust

Rinder|braten m roast beef. **R~wahnsinn** m 🔲 mad cow disease

Rindfleisch nt beef

Ring m -[e]s,-e ring

ringeln (sich) vr curl

ring|en† vi (haben) wrestle; (fig) struggle (**um/nach** for) ● vt wring (Hände). **R~er** m -s,- wrestler. **R~kampf** m wrestling match; (als Sport) wrestling

ringsherum, **r~um** adv all around

Rinn|e f -,-n channel; (Dach-) gutter. **r~en**† vi (sein) run; (Sand:) trickle. **R~stein** m gutter

Rippe f -,-n rib. **R~nfellentzündung** f pleurisy

Risiko nt -s,-s & -ken risk

risk|ant adj risky. **r~ieren** vt risk

Riss m -es,-e tear; (Mauer-) crack; (fig) rift

rissig adj cracked; (Haut) chapped

Rist m -[e]s,-e instep

Ritt m -[e]s,-e ride

Ritter m -s,- knight

Ritual nt -s,-e ritual

Ritz m -es,-e scratch. **R~e** f -,-n crack; (Fels-) cleft; (zwischen Betten, Vorhängen) gap. **r~en** vt scratch

Rival|e m -n,-n, **R~in** f -,-nen rival. **R~ität** f -,-en rivalry

Robbe f -,-n seal

Robe f -,-n gown; (Talar) robe

Roboter m -s,- robot

robust adj robust

röcheln vi (haben) breathe noisily

Rochen m -s,- (Zool) ray

Rock¹ m -[e]s,ᵉe skirt; (Jacke) jacket

Rock² m -[s] (Mus) rock

rodel|n vi (sein/haben) toboggan. **R~schlitten** m toboggan

roden vt clear (Land); grub up (Stumpf)

Rogen m -s,- [hard] roe

Roggen m -s rye

roh adj rough; (ungekocht) raw; (Holz) bare; (brutal) brutal. **R~bau** m -[e]s,-ten timber shell. **R~kost** f raw [vegetarian] food. **R~ling** m -s,-e brute. **R~öl** nt crude oil

Rohr nt -[e]s,-e pipe; (Geschütz-) barrel; (Bot) reed; (Zucker-, Bambus-) cane

Röhre f -,-n tube; (Radio-) valve; (Back-) oven

Rohstoff m raw material

Rokoko nt -s rococo

Roll|bahn f taxiway; (Start-/Landebahn) runway. **R~balken** m scroll bar

Rolle f -,-n roll; (Garn-) reel; (Draht-) coil; (Techn) roller; (Seil-) pulley; (Lauf-) castor; (Theat) part, role; **das spielt keine R~** (fig) that doesn't matter. **R~n** vt/i (auf-) roll up; (Computer) scroll; **sich r~n** roll ● vi (sein) roll; (Flugzeug:) taxi. **R~r** m -s,- scooter. **R~rblades®** /-ble:ds/ mpl Rollerblades®

Roll|feld nt airfield. **R~kragen** m polo-neck. **R~mops** m rollmop[s] sg

Rollo nt -s,-s (roller) blind

Roll|schuh m roller-skate; **R~schuh laufen** roller-skate. **R~stuhl** m wheelchair. **R~treppe** f escalator

Rom nt -s Rome

Roman m -s,-e novel. **r~isch** adj Romanesque; (Sprache) Romance. **r~isch** adj romantic

Romant|ik f - romanticism. **r~isch** adj romantic

Röm|er(in) m -s,- (f -,-nen) Roman. **r~isch** adj Roman

Rommé, Rommee /'rɔme:/ nt -s rummy

röntgen vt X-ray. **R~aufnahme** f, **R~bild** nt X-ray. **R~strahlen** mpl X-rays

rosa inv adj. **R~** nt -[s],- pink

Rose f -,-n rose. **R~nkohl** m [Brussels] sprouts pl. **R~nkranz** m (Relig) rosary

Rosine f -,-n raisin

Rosmarin m -s rosemary

Ross nt -es,⁻er horse

Rost¹ m -[e]s,-e grating; (Kamin-) grate; (Brat-) grill

Rost² m -[e]s rust. **r~en** vi (haben) rust

rösten vt roast; toast (Brot)

rostfrei adj stainless

rostig adj rusty

rot adj, **Rot** nt -s,- red; **rot werden** turn red; (erröten) go red, blush

Röte f - redness; (Scham-) blush

Röteln pl German measles sg

röten vt redden; **sich r~** turn red

rothaarig adj red-haired

rotieren vi (haben) rotate

Rot|kehlchen nt -s,- robin. **R~kohl** m red cabbage

rötlich adj reddish

Rotwein m red wine

Rou|lade /ru'la:də/ f -,-n beef olive. **R~leau** m -s,-s [roller] blind

Routin|e /ru'ti:nə/ f -,-n routine; (Erfahrung) experience. **r~emäßig** adj routine ● adv routinely. **r~iert** adj experienced

Rowdy /'raudi/ m -s,-s hooligan

Rübe f -,-n beet; **rote R~** beetroot

Rubin m -s,-e ruby

Rubrik f -,-en column

Ruck m -[e]s,-e jerk

ruckartig adj jerky

rück|bezüglich adj (Gram) re-

flexive. **R~blende** f flashback.
R~blick m (fig) review (auf + acc
of). **r~blickend** adv in retrospect.
r~datieren vt (infinitive & pp only)
backdate

Rücken m -s,- back; (Buch-) spine;
(Berg-) ridge. **R~lehne** f back.
R~mark nt spinal cord.
R~schwimmen nt backstroke.
R~wind m following wind; (Aviat)
tail wind

rückerstatten vt (infinitive & pp
only) refund

Rückfahr|karte f return ticket.
R~t f return journey

Rück|fall m relapse. **R~flug** m return flight. **R~frage** f [further]
query. **r~fragen** vi (haben) (infinitive & pp only) check (bei with).
R~gabe f return. **r~gängig** adj
r~gängig machen cancel; break
off (Verlobung). **R~grat** nt -[e]s,-e
spine, backbone. **R~hand** f backhand. **R~kehr** f return. **R~lagen** fpl
reserves. **R~licht** nt rear-light.
R~reise f return journey

Rucksack m rucksack

Rück|schau f review. **R~schlag**
m (Sport) return; (fig) set-back.
r~schrittlich adj retrograde.
R~seite f back; (einer Münze)
reverse

Rücksicht f -,-en consideration.
R~nahme f - consideration.
r~slos adj inconsiderate; (schonungslos) ruthless. **r~svoll** adj considerate

Rück|sitz m back seat; (Sozius) pillion. **R~spiegel** m rear-view mirror.
R~spiel nt return match. **R~stand**
m (Chemistry) residue; (Arbeits-)
backlog; **im R~stand sein** be behind. **r~ständig** adj (fig) backward. **R~stau** m (Auto) tailback.
R~strahler m -s,- reflector.
R~tritt m resignation; (Fahrrad)

back pedalling

rückwärt|ig adj back, rear. **r~s**
adv backwards. **R~sgang** m reverse [gear]

Rückweg m way back

rück|wirkend adj retrospective.
R~wirkung f retrospective force;
mit R~wirkung vom backdated
to. **R~zahlung** f repayment

Rüde m -n,-n [male] dog

Rudel nt -s,- herd; (Wolfs-) pack;
(Löwen-) pride

Ruder nt -s,- oar; (Steuer-) rudder;
am R~ (Naut & fig) at the helm.
R~boot nt rowing boat. **r~n** vt/i
(haben/sein) row

Ruf m -[e]s,-e call; (laut) shout; (Telefon) telephone number; (Ansehen)
reputation. **r~en†** vt/i (haben) call
(nach for); **r~en lassen** have called

Ruf|name m forename by which
one is known. **R~nummer** f telephone number. **R~zeichen** nt dialling tone

Rüge f -,-n reprimand. **r~n** vt reprimand; (kritisieren) criticize

Ruhe f - rest; (Stille) quiet; (Frieden)
peace; (innere) calm; (Gelassenheit)
composure; **R~ [da]!** quiet! **r~los**
adj restless. **r~n** vi (haben) rest
(auf + dat on); (Arbeit, Verkehr:)
have stopped. **R~pause** f rest,
break. **R~stand** m retirement; **im
R~stand** retired. **R~störung** f disturbance of the peace. **R~tag** m
day of rest; 'Montag R~tag'
'closed on Mondays'

ruhig adj quiet; (erholsam) restful;
(friedlich) peaceful; (unbewegt, gelassen) calm; **man kann r~ darüber sprechen** there's no harm in
talking about it

Ruhm m -[e]s fame; (Ehre) glory

rühmen vt praise

ruhmreich adj glorious

Ruhr f - (Med) dysentery

Rühr|ei nt scrambled eggs pl. **r~en** vt move; (Culin) stir; **sich r~en** move ● vi (haben) stir; **r~en an** (+ acc) touch; (fig) touch on. **r~end** adj touching

Rührung f - emotion

Ruin m -s ruin. **R~e** f -,-n ruin; ruins pl (gen of). **r~ieren** vt ruin

rülpsen vi (haben) 🔲 belch

Rum m -s rum

Rumän|ien /-jən/ nt -s Romania. **r~isch** adj Romanian

Rummel m -s 🔲 hustle and bustle; (Jahrmarkt) funfair

Rumpelkammer f junk-room

Rumpf m -[e]s,ᵉe body, trunk; (Schiffs-) hull; (Aviat) fuselage

rund adj round ● adv approximately; **r~ um** [a]round. **R~blick** m panoramic view. **R~brief** m circular [letter]

Runde f -,-n round; (Kreis) circle; (eines Polizisten) beat; (beim Rennen) lap; **eine R~ Bier** a round of beer

Rund|fahrt f tour. **R~frage** f poll

Rundfunk m radio; **im R~** on the radio. **R~gerät** nt radio [set]

Rund|gang m round; (Spaziergang) walk (durch round). **r~heraus** adv straight out. **r~herum** adv all around; (mollig) plump. **R~reise** f [circular] tour. **R~schreiben** nt circular. **r~um** adv all round. **R~ung** f -,-en curve

Runzel f -,-n wrinkle

runzlig adj wrinkled

Rüpel m -s,- 🔲 lout

rupfen vt pull out; pluck (Geflügel)

Rüsche f -,-n frill

Ruß m -es soot

Russe m -n,-n Russian

Rüssel m -s,- (Zool) trunk

Russ|in f -,-nen Russian. **r~isch** adj Russian. **R~isch** nt -[s] (Lang) Russian

Russland nt -s Russia

rüsten vi (haben) prepare (zu/für for) ● vr **sich r~** get ready

rüstig adj sprightly

rustikal adj rustic

Rüstung f -,-en armament; (Harnisch) armour. **R~skontrolle** f arms control

Rute f -,-n twig; (Angel-, Wünschel-) rod; (zur Züchtigung) birch; (Schwanz) tail

Rutsch m -[e]s,-e slide. **R~bahn** f slide. **R~e** f -,-n chute. **r~en** vt slide; (rücken) move ● vi (sein) slide; (aus-, ab-) slip; (Auto) skid. **r~ig** adj slippery

rütteln vt shake ● vi (haben) **r~ an** (+ dat) rattle

Ss

Saal m -[e]s,Säle hall; (Theat) auditorium; (Kranken-) ward

Saat f -,-en seed; (Säen) sowing; (Gesätes) crop

sabbern vi (haben) 🔲 slobber; (Baby): dribble; (reden) patter

Säbel m -s,- sabre

Sabo|tage /zabo'ta:ʒə/ f - sabotage. **S~teur** m -s,-e saboteur. **s~tieren** vt sabotage

Sach|bearbeiter m expert. **S~buch** nt non-fiction book

Sache f -,-n matter, business; (Ding) thing; (fig) cause

Sach|gebiet nt (fig) area, field. **s~kundig** adj expert. **s~lich** adj factual; (*nüchtern*) matter-of-fact

sächlich *adj* (*Gram*) neuter

Sachse *m* -n,-n Saxon. **S~n** *nt* -s Saxony

sächsisch *adj* Saxon

Sach|verhalt *m* -[e]s facts *pl*. **S~verständige(r)** *m/f* expert

Sack *m* -[e]s,⁻e sack

Sack|gasse *f* cul-de-sac; (*fig*) impasse. **S~leinen** *nt* sacking

Sadis|mus *m* - sadism. **S~t** *m* -en,-en sadist

säen *vt/i* (*haben*) sow

Safe /ze:f/ *m* -s,-s safe

Saft *m* -[e]s,⁻e juice; (*Bot*) sap. **s~ig** *adj* juicy

Sage *f* -,-n legend

Säge *f* -,-n saw. **S~mehl** *nt* sawdust

sagen *vt* say; (*mitteilen*) tell; (*bedeuten*) mean

sägen *vt/i* (*haben*) saw

sagenhaft *adj* legendary

Säge|späne *mpl* wood shavings. **S~werk** *nt* sawmill

Sahne *f* - cream. **S~ebonbon** *m* & *nt* ≈ toffee. **s~ig** *adj* creamy

Saison /zɛ'zõ:/ *f* -,-s season

Saite *f* -,-n (*Mus, Sport*) string. **S~ninstrument** *nt* stringed instrument

Sakko *m* & *nt* -s,-s sports jacket

Sakrament *nt* -[e]s,-e sacrament

Sakristei *f* -,-en vestry

Salat *m* -[e]s,-e salad. **S~soße** *f* salad-dressing

Salbe *f* -,-n ointment

Salbei *m* -s & *f* - sage

salben *vt* anoint

Saldo *m* -s,-dos & -den balance

Salon /za'lõ:/ *m* -s,-s salon

salopp *adj* casual; (*Benehmen*) informal

Salto *m* -s,-s somersault

Salut *m* -[e]s,-e salute. **s~ieren** *vi* (*haben*) salute

Salve *f* -,-n volley; (*Geschütz-*) salvo, (*von Gelächter*) burst

Salz *nt* -es,-e salt. **S~en†** *vt* salt. **S~fass** *nt* salt-cellar. **s~ig** *adj* salty. **S~kartoffeln** *fpl* boiled potatoes. **S~säure** *f* hydrochloric acid

---

Salzburger Festspiele   *i*

The Austrian city of Salzburg, the home of Wolfgang Amadeus Mozart (1756-91), hosts this annual festival as a tribute to the great composer. Every summer since 1920, Mozart-lovers have enjoyed his music at the Salzburg Festival.

Samen *m* -s,- seed; (*Anat*) semen, sperm

Sammel|becken *nt* reservoir. **s~n** *vt/i* (*haben*) collect; (*suchen, versammeln*) gather; **sich s~n** collect; (*sich versammeln*) gather; (*sich fassen*) collect oneself. **S~name** *m* collective noun

Sammler(in) *m* -s,- (*f* -,-nen) collector. **S~lung** *f* -,-en collection; (*innere*) composure

Samstag *m* -s Saturday. **s~s** *adv* on Saturdays

samt *prep* (+ *dat*) together with

Samt *m* -[e]s velvet

sämtlich *indefinite pronoun inv* all. **s~e(r,s)** *indefinite pronoun* all the; **s~e Werke** complete works

Sanatorium *nt* -s,-ien sanatorium

Sand *m* -[e]s sand

Sandale *f* -,-n sandal

Sand|bank *f* sandbank. **S~kasten** *m* sand-pit. **S~papier** *nt* sandpaper

sanft *adj* gentle

Sänger(in) *m* -s,-(*f* -,-nen) singer

sanieren *vt* clean up; redevelop (*Gebiet*); (*modernisieren*) modernize; make profitable (*Industrie*, *Firma*); **sich s~** become profitable

sanitär *adj* sanitary

Sanität|er *m* -s,- first-aid man; (*Fahrer*) ambulance man; (*Mil*) medical orderly. **S~swagen** *m* ambulance

Sanktion /zaŋk'tsjoːn/ *f* -,-en sanction. **s~ieren** *vt* sanction

Saphir *m* -s,-e sapphire

Sardelle *f* -,-n anchovy

Sardine *f* -,-n sardine

Sarg *m* -[e]s, ²e coffin

Sarkasmus *m* - sarcasm

Satan *m* -s Satan; (🗆: *Teufel*) devil

Satellit *m* -en,-en satellite. **S~enfernsehen** *nt* satellite television. **S~enschüssel** *f* satellite dish. **S~entelefon** *nt* satphone

Satin /za'tɛ̃/ *m* -s satin

Satire *f* -,-n satire

satt *adj* full; (*Farbe*) rich; **s~ sein** have had enough [to eat]; **etw s~ haben** 🗆 be fed up with sth

Sattel *m* -s, ² saddle. **s~n** *vt* saddle. **S~zug** *m* articulated lorry

sättigen *vt* satisfy; (*Chemistry & fig*) saturate ● *vi* (*haben*) be filling

Satz *m* -es, ²e sentence; (*Teil-*) clause; (*These*) proposition; (*Math*) theorem; (*Mus*) movement; (*Tennis*, *Zusammengehöriges*) set; (*Boden-*) sediment; (*Kaffee-*) grounds *pl*; (*Steuer-*, *Zins-*) rate; (*Druck-*) setting; (*Schrift-*) type; (*Sprung*) leap, bound. **S~aussage** *f* predicate. **S~gegenstand** *m* subject. **S~zeichen** *nt* punctuation mark

Sau *f* -,Säue sow

sauber *adj* clean; (*ordentlich*) neat;

(*anständig*) decent; **s~ machen** clean. **S~keit** *f* - cleanliness; neatness

säuberlich *adj* neat

Sauce /'zoːsə/ *f* -,-n sauce; (*Braten-*) gravy

Saudi-Arabien /-jən/ *nt* -s Saudi Arabia

sauer *adj* sour; (*Chemistry*) acid; (*eingelegt*) pickled; (*schwer*) hard; **saurer Regen** acid rain

Sauerkraut *nt* sauerkraut

säuerlich *adj* slightly sour

Sauerstoff *m* oxygen

saufen† *vt/i* (*haben*) drink; 🗷 booze

Säufer *m* -s,- 🗷 boozer

saugen† *vt/i* (*haben*) suck; (*staub-*) vacuum, hoover; **sich voll Wasser s~** soak up water

säugen *vt* suckle

Säugetier *nt* mammal

saugfähig *adj* absorbent

Säugling *m* -s,-e infant

Säule *f* -,-n column

Saum *m* -[e]s,Säume hem; (*Rand*) edge

säumen *vt* hem; (*fig*) line

Sauna *f* -,-nas & -nen sauna

Säure *f* -,-n acidity; (*Chemistry*) acid

sausen *vi* (*haben*) rush; (*Ohren:*) buzz ● *vi* (*sein*) rush [along]

Saxophon, **Saxofon** *nt* -s,-e saxophone

S-Bahn *f* city and suburban railway

Scanner *m* -s,- scanner

sch *int* shush! (*fort*) shoo!

Schabe *f* -,-n cockroach

schaben *vt/i* (*haben*) scrape

schäbig *adj* shabby

Schablone *f* -,-n stencil; (*Muster*) pattern; (*fig*) stereotype

Schach nt -s chess; S∼! check!
S∼brett nt chessboard

Schachfigur f chess-man

schachmatt adj s∼ setzen
checkmate; s∼! checkmate!

Schachspiel nt game of chess

Schacht m -[e]s,⁼e shaft

Schachtel f -,-n box; (Zigaretten-)
packet

Schachzug m move

schade adj s∼ sein be a pity or
shame: zu s∼ für too good for

Schädel m -s, skull. S∼bruch m
fractured skull

schaden vi (haben) (+ dat) damage; (nachteilig sein) hurt. S∼ m
-s,⁼ damage; (Defekt) defect; (Nachteil) disadvantage. S∼ersatz m
damages pl. S∼freude f malicious
glee. s∼froh adj gloating

schädig|en vt damage, harm.
S∼ung f -,-en damage

schädlich adj harmful

Schädling m -s,-e pest. S∼sbe-
kämpfungsmittel nt pesticide

Schaf nt -[e]s,-e sheep. S∼bock
m ram

Schäfer m -s,- shepherd. S∼hund
m sheepdog; Deutscher S∼hund
alsatian

schaffen¹† vt create; (herstellen)
establish; make (Platz)

schaffen² v (reg) ● vt manage [to
do]; pass (Prüfung); catch (Zug);
(bringen) take

Schaffner m -s,- conductor;
(Zug-) ticket-inspector

Schaffung f - creation

Schaft m -[e]s,⁼e shaft; (Gewehr-)
stock; (Stiefel-) leg

Schal m -s,-s scarf

Schale f -,-n skin; (abgeschält) peel;
(Eier-, Nuss-, Muschel-) shell; (Schüssel) dish

schälen vt peel; sich s∼ peel

Schall m -[e]s sound. S∼dämpfer
m silencer. s∼dicht adj soundproof.
s∼en vi (haben) ring out: (nachhal-
len) resound. S∼mauer f sound
barrier. S∼platte f record, disc

schalt|en vt switch ● vi (haben)
switch/(Ampel:) turn (auf + acc to);
(Auto) change gear; (ℱ: begreifen)
catch on. S∼er m -s,- switch;
(Post-, Bank-) counter; (Fahrkarten-)
ticket window. S∼hebel m (Auto)
gear lever. S∼jahr nt leap
year. S∼ung f -,-en circuit: (Auto)
gear change

Scham f - shame; (Anat) private
parts pl

schämen (sich) vr be ashamed

scham|haft adj modest. s∼los
adj shameless

Schampon nt -s shampoo. S∼ie-
ren vt shampoo

Schande f - disgrace, shame

schändlich adj disgraceful

Schanktisch m bar

Schanze f, -,-n [ski-]jump

Schar f -,-en crowd; (Vogel-) flock

Scharade f -,-n charade

scharen vt um sich s∼ gather
round one; sich s∼ um flock
round. s∼weise adv in droves

scharf adj sharp; (stark) strong;
(stark gewürzt) hot; (Geruch) pun-
gent; (Wind, Augen, Verstand) keen;
(streng) harsh; (Galopp) hard; (Munition) live; (Hund) fierce; s∼ einstellen (Phot) focus; s∼ sein (Phot) be
in focus; s∼ sein auf (+ acc) ℱ be
keen on

Schärfe f sharpness; strength; hot-
ness; pungency; keenness; harshness. s∼n vt sharpen

Scharf|richter m executioner.
S∼schütze m marksman. S∼sinn
m astuteness

Scharlach m -s scarlet fever

Scharlatan m -s,-e charlatan

Scharnier nt -s,-e hinge

Schärpe f -,-n sash

scharren vi (haben) scrape; (Huhn) scratch ● vt scrape

Schaschlik m & nt -s,-s kebab

Schatten m -s,- shadow; (schattige Stelle) shade. **S~riss** m silhouette. **S~seite** f shady side; (fig) disadvantage

schattier|en vt shade. **S~ung** f -,-en shading

schattig adj shady

Schatz m -es,ˉe treasure; (Freund, Freundin) sweetheart

schätzen vt estimate; (taxieren) value; (achten) esteem; (würdigen) appreciate

Schätzung f -,-en estimate; (Taxierung) valuation

Schau f -,-en show. **S~bild** nt diagram

Schauder m -s shiver; (vor Abscheu) shudder. **s~haft** adj dreadful. **s~n** vi (haben) shiver; (vor Abscheu) shudder

schauen vi (haben) (SGer, Aust) look; **s~, dass** make sure that

Schauer m -s,- shower; (Schauder) shiver. **S~geschichte** f horror story. **s~lich** adj ghastly

Schaufel f -,-n shovel; (Kehr-) dustpan. **s~n** vt shovel; (graben) dig

Schaufenster nt shop-window. **S~puppe** f dummy

Schaukel f -,-n swing. **s~n** vt rock ● vi (haben) rock; (auf einer Schaukel) swing; (schwanken) sway. **S~pferd** nt rocking-horse. **S~stuhl** m rocking-chair

Schaum m -[e]s foam; (Seifen-) lather; (auf Bier) froth; (als Frisier-,

Rasiermittel) mousse

schäumen vi (haben) foam, froth; (Seife:) lather

Schaum|gummi m foam rubber. **s~ig** a frothy; **s~ig rühren** (Culin) cream. **S~stoff** m [synthetic] foam. **S~wein** m sparkling wine

Schauplatz m scene

schaurig adj dreadful; (unheimlich) eerie

Schauspiel nt play; (Anblick) spectacle. **S~er** m actor. **S~erin** f actress

Scheck m -s,-s cheque. **S~buch**, **S~heft** nt cheque-book. **S~karte** f cheque card

Scheibe f -,-n disc; (Schieß-) target; (Glas-) pane; (Brot-, Wurst-) slice. **S~nwischer** m -s,- windscreen-wiper

Scheich m -s,-e & -s sheikh

Scheide f -,-n sheath; (Anat) vagina

scheid|en† vt separate; (unterscheiden) distinguish; dissolve (Ehe); **sich s~en lassen** get divorced ● vi (sein) leave; (voneinander) part. **S~ung** f -,-en divorce

Schein m -[e]s,-e light; (Anschein) appearance; (Bescheinigung) certificate; (Geld-) note. **s~bar** adj apparent. **s~en†** vi (haben) shine; (den Anschein haben) seem, appear

scheinheilig adj hypocritical

Scheinwerfer m -s,- floodlight; (Such-) searchlight; (Auto) headlight; (Theat) spotlight

Scheiße f - (vulgar) shit. **s~n†** vi (haben) (vulgar) shit

Scheit nt -[e]s,-e log

Scheitel m -s,- parting

scheitern vi (sein) fail

Schelle f -,-n bell. **s~n** vi (haben) ring

Schellfisch m haddock

Schelm m -s,-e rogue

Schelte f - scolding

Schema nt -s,-mata model, pattern; (Skizze) diagram

Schemel m -s,- stool

Schenke f -,-n tavern

Schenkel m -s,- thigh

schenken vt give [as a present]; jdm Vertrauen s~ trust s.o.

Scherbe f -,-n [broken] piece

Schere f -,-n scissors pl; (Techn) shears pl; (Hummer-) claw. s~n†† vt shear; crop (Haar)

scheren² vt (reg) 🗌 bother; **sich** nicht s~ um not care about

Scherenschnitt m silhouette

Scherereien fpl 🗌 trouble sg

Scherz m -es,-e joke; im/zum S~ as a joke. s~en vi (haben) joke

scheu adj shy; (Tier) timid; s~ werden (Pferd:) shy

scheuchen vt shoo

scheuen vt be afraid of; (meiden) shun; keine Mühe/Kosten s~ spare no effort/expense; sich s~ be afraid (vor + dat of); shrink (etw zu tun from doing sth)

scheuern vt scrub; (reiben) rub; [wund] s~n chafe ● vi (haben) rub, chafe

Scheuklappen fpl blinkers

Scheune f -,-n barn

Scheusal nt -s,-e monster

scheußlich adj horrible

Schi m -s,-er ski; S~ fahren od laufen ski

Schicht f -,-en layer; (Geology) stratum; (Gesellschafts-) class; (Arbeits-) shift. S~arbeit f shift work. s~en vt stack [up]

schick adj stylish; (Frau) chic. S~ m -[e]s style

schicken vt/i (haben) send; s~ nach send for

Schicksal nt -s,-e fate. S~sschlag m misfortune

Schiebe|dach nt (Auto) sun-roof. s~en† vt push; (gleitend) slide; (🗌: handeln mit) traffic in; etw s~en auf (+ acc) (fig) put sth down to; shift (Schuld) on to ● vi (haben) push. S~etür f sliding door. S~ung f -,-en 🗌 illicit deal; (Betrug) rigging, fixing

Schieds|gericht nt panel of judges; (Jur) arbitration tribunal. S~richter m referee; (Tennis) umpire; (Jur) arbitrator

schief adj crooked; (unsymmetrisch) lopsided; (geneigt) slanting, sloping; (nicht senkrecht) leaning; (Winkel) oblique; (fig) false; suspicious ● adv not straight; s~ gehen 🗌 go wrong

Schiefer m -s slate

schielen vi (haben) squint

Schienbein nt shin

Schiene f -,-n rail; (Gleit-) runner; (Med) splint. s~n vt (Med) put in a splint

Schieß|bude f shooting-gallery. s~en† vt shoot; fire (Kugel); score (Tor) ● vi (haben) shoot, fire (auf + acc at). S~scheibe f target. S~stand m shooting-range

Schifahr|en nt skiing. S~er(in) m(f) skier

Schiff nt -[e]s,-e ship; (Kirchen-) nave; (Seiten-) aisle

Schiffahrt * f = Schifffahrt

schiff|bar adj navigable. S~bruch m shipwreck. s~brüchig adj shipwrecked. S~fahrt f shipping

Schikan|e f -,-n harassment; mit allen S~en 🗌 with every refinement. s~ieren vt harass

Schi|laufen nt -s skiing. S~läufer(in) m(f) -s,- (f -,-nen) skier

Schild[1] m -[e]s,-e shield

Schild[2] nt -[e]s,-er sign; (Nummern-) plate; (Mützen-) badge; (Etikett) label

Schilddrüse f thyroid [gland]

schilder|n vt describe. **S~ung** f -,-en description

Schild|kröte f tortoise; (See-) turtle. **S~patt** nt -[e]s tortoiseshell

Schilf nt -[e]s reeds pl

schillern vi (haben) shimmer

Schimmel m -s,- mould; (Pferd) white horse. **s~n** vi (haben/sein) go mouldy

schimmern vi (haben) gleam

Schimpanse m -n,-n chimpanzee

schimpf|en vi (haben) grumble (mit at; über + acc about); scold (mit jdm s.o.) ● vt call. **S~wort** nt (pl -wörter) swear-word

Schinken m -s,- ham. **S~speck** m bacon

Schippe f -,-n shovel. **s~n** vt shovel

Schirm m -[e]s,-e umbrella; (Sonnen-) sunshade; (Lampen-) shade; (Augen-) visor; (Mützen-) peak; (Ofen-, Bild-) screen; (fig: Schutz) shield. **S~herrschaft** f patronage. **S~mütze** f peaked cap

schizophren adj schizophrenic. **S~ie** f - schizophrenia

Schlacht f -,-en battle

schlachten vt slaughter, kill

Schlacht|feld nt battlefield. **S~hof** m abattoir

Schlacke f -,-n slag

Schlaf m -[e]s sleep; im S~ in one's sleep. **S~anzug** m pyjamas pl

Schläfe f -,-n (Anat) temple

schlafen† vi (haben) sleep; s~ gehen go to bed; er schläft noch he is still asleep

schlaff adj limp; (Seil) slack;

(Muskel) flabby

Schlaf|lied nt lullaby. **s~los** adj sleepless. **S~losigkeit** f - insomnia. **S~mittel** nt sleeping drug

schläfrig adj sleepy

Schlaf|saal m dormitory. **S~sack** m sleeping-bag. **S~tablette** f sleeping-pill. **S~wagen** m sleeping-car, sleeper. **S~wandeln** vi (haben/sein) sleep-walk. **S~zimmer** nt bedroom

Schlag m -[e]s,⁝e blow; (Faust-) punch; (Herz-, Puls-, Trommel-) beat; (einer Uhr) chime; (Glocken-, Gong- & Med) stroke; (elektrischer) shock; (Art) type; **S~e bekommen** get a beating; **S~ auf S~** in rapid succession. **S~ader** f artery. **S~anfall** m stroke. **S~baum** m barrier

schlagen† vt hit, strike; (fällen) fell; knock (Loch, Nagel) (in + acc into); (prügeln, besiegen) beat; (Culin) whisk (Eiweiß); whip (Sahne); (legen) throw; (wickeln) wrap; sich s~ fight ● vi (haben) beat; (Tür) bang; (Uhr:) strike; (melodisch) chime; **mit den Flügeln s~** flap its wings ● vi (sein) in etw (acc) s~ (Blitz, Kugel) strike sth; **nach jdm s~** (fig) take after s.o.

Schlager m -s,- popular song; (Erfolg) hit

Schläger m -s,- racket; (Tischtennis-) bat; (Golf-) club; (Hockey-) stick. **S~ei** f -,-en fight, brawl

schlagfertig adj quick-witted. **S~loch** nt pot-hole. **S~sahne** f whipped cream; (ungeschlagen) whipping cream. **S~seite** f (Naut) list. **S~stock** m truncheon. **S~wort** nt (pl -worte) slogan. **S~zeile** f headline. **S~zeug** nt (Mus) percussion. **S~zeuger** m -s,- percussionist; (in Band) drummer

Schlamm m -[e]s mud. **s~ig** adj muddy

Schlampe f -,-n 🔲 slut. **s∼en** vi (haben) 🔲 be sloppy (**bei** in). **s∼ig** adj slovenly; (Arbeit) sloppy

Schlange f -,-n snake; (Menschen-, Auto-) queue; (Schlauch) queue

schlängeln (sich) vr wind; (Person:) weave (**durch** through)

schlank adj slim. **S∼heitskur** f slimming diet

schlapp adj tired; (schlaff) limp

schlau adj clever; (gerissen) crafty; **ich werde nicht s∼ daraus** I can't make head or tail of it

Schlauch m -[e]s,Schläuche tube; (Wasser-) hose[pipe]. **S∼boot** nt rubber dinghy

Schlaufe f -,-n loop

schlecht adj bad; (böse) wicked; (unzulänglich) poor; **s∼ werden** go bad; (Wetter:) turn bad; **mir ist s∼** I feel sick; **s∼ machen** 🔲 run down. **s∼gehen*** vi sep (sein) **s∼ gehen**, s. **gehen**

schlecken vt/i (haben) lick (**an etw** dat sth); (auf-) lap up

Schlegel m -s,- (SGer: Keule) leg; (Hühner-) drumstick

schleichen† vi (sein) creep; (langsam gehen/fahren) crawl ● vr sich **s∼** creep. **s∼d** adj creeping

Schleier m -s,- veil; (fig) haze

Schleife f -,-n bow; (Fliege) bowtie; (Biegung) loop

schleifen¹ v (reg) ● vt drag ● vi (haben) trail, drag

schleifen²† vt grind; (schärfen) sharpen; cut (Edelstein, Glas)

Schleim m -[e]s slime; (Anat) mucus; (Med) phlegm. **s∼ig** adj slimy

schlendern vi (sein) stroll

schlenkern vt/i (haben) swing; **s∼ mit** swing; dangle (Beine)

Schlepp|dampfer m tug. **S∼e** f

-,-n train. **s∼en** vt drag; (tragen) carry; (ziehen) tow; **sich s∼en** drag oneself; (sich hinziehen) drag on; **sich s∼en mit** carry. **S∼er** m -s,- tug; (Traktor) tractor. **S∼kahn** m barge. **S∼lift** m T-bar lift. **S∼tau** nt tow-rope; **jdn ins S∼tau nehmen** take in tow

Schleuder f -,-n catapult; (Wäsche-) spin-drier. **S∼n** vt hurl; spin (Wäsche) ● vi (sein) skid; **ins S∼n geraten** skid. **S∼sitz** m ejector seat

Schleuse f -,-n lock; (Sperre) sluice[-gate]. **s∼n** vt steer

Schliche pl tricks

schlicht adj plain; simple

Schlichtung f - settlement; (Jur) arbitration

schließen f -,-n clasp; buckle

schließen† vt close (ab-) lock; fasten (Kleid, Verschluss); (stilllegen) close down; (beenden, folgern) conclude; enter into (Vertrag); **sich s∼** close; **etw s∼ an** (+ acc) connect sth to; **sich s∼ an** (+ acc) follow ● vi (haben) close, (den Betrieb einstellen) close down; (den Schlüssel drehen) turn the key; (enden, folgern) conclude

Schließ|fach nt locker. **s∼lich** adv finally, in the end; (immerhin) after all. **S∼ung** f -,-en closure

Schliff m -[e]s cut; (Schleifen) cutting; (fig) polish

schlimm adj bad

Schlinge f -,-n loop; (Henkers-) noose; (Med) sling; (Falle) snare

Schlingel m -s,- rascal

schlingen† vt wind, wrap; tie (Knoten) ● vt/i (haben) bolt one's food

Schlips m -es,-e tie

Schlitten m -s,- sledge; (Rodel-) toboggan; (Pferde-) sleigh; **S∼ fahren** toboggan

schlittern vi (haben/ sein) slide

Schlittschuh m skate; **S~** laufen skate. **S~läufer(in)** m(f) -s,- (f -,-nen) skater

Schlitz m -es,-e slit; (für Münze) slot; (Jacken-) vent; (Hosen-) flies pl. **s~en** vt slit

Schloss nt -es,-̈er lock; (Vorhänge-) padlock; (Verschluss) clasp; (Gebäude) castle; palace

Schlosser m -s,- locksmith; (Auto-) mechanic

Schlucht f -,-en ravine, gorge

schluchzen vi (haben) sob

Schluck m -[e]s,-e mouthful; (klein) sip

Schluckauf m -s hiccups pl

schlucken vt/i (haben) swallow

Schlummer m -s slumber

Schlund m -[e]s [back of the] throat; (fig) mouth

schlüpf|en vi (sein) slip; [aus dem Ei] **s~en** hatch. **S~er** m -s,- knickers pl. **s~rig** adj slippery

schlürfen vt/i (haben) slurp

Schluss m -es,̈e end; (S~folgerung) conclusion; **zum S~** finally; **S~** machen stop (mit etw sth); finish (mit jdm with s.o.)

Schlüssel m -s,- key; (Schrauben-) spanner; (Geheim-) code; (Mus) clef. **S~bein** nt collar-bone. **S~bund** m & nt bunch of keys. **S~loch** nt keyhole

Schlussfolgerung f conclusion

schlüssig adj conclusive

Schluss|licht nt rear-light. **S~verkauf** m sale

schmächtig adj slight

schmackhaft adj tasty

schmal adj narrow; (dünn) thin; (schlank) slender; (karg) meagre

schmälern vt diminish; (herabsetzen) belittle

Schmalz¹ nt -es lard; (Ohren-) wax

Schmalz² m -es 🛈 schmaltz

Schmarotzer m -s,- parasite; (Person) sponger

schmatzen vi (haben) eat noisily

schmausen vi (haben) feast

schmecken vi (haben) taste (nach of); [gut] **s~** taste good ● vt taste

Schmeichelei f -,-en flattery; (Kompliment) compliment

schmeichel|haft adj complimentary, flattering. **s~n** vi (haben) (+ dat) flatter

schmeißen† vt/i (haben) **s~** [mit] 🛈 chuck

Schmeißfliege f bluebottle

schmelz|en† vt/i (sein) melt; smelt (Erze). **S~wasser** nt melted snow and ice

Schmerbauch m 🛈 paunch

Schmerz m -es,-en pain; (Kummer) grief; **S~en haben** be in pain. **s~en** vt hurt; (fig) grieve ● vi (haben) hurt, be painful. **S~ensgeld** nt compensation for pain and suffering. **s~haft** adj painful. **s~los** adj painless. **s~stillend** adj pain-killing; **s~stillendes Mittel** analgesic, pain-killer. **S~tablette** f pain-killer

Schmetterball m (Tennis) smash

Schmetterling m -s,-e butterfly

schmettern vt hurl; (Tennis) smash; (singen) sing ● vi (haben) sound

Schmied m -[e]s,-e blacksmith

Schmiede f -,-n forge. **S~eisen** nt wrought iron. **s~n** vt forge

Schmier|e f -,-n grease; (Schmutz) mess. **s~en** vt lubricate; (streichen) spread; (schlecht schreiben) scrawl ● vi (haben) smudge; (schmieren) scrawl. **S~geld** nt 🛈 bribe. **s~ig** adj greasy; (schmutzig) grubby. **S~mittel** nt lubricant

Schminke f -,- make-up. **s~n** vt make up; **sich s~n** put on make-up; **sich** (dat) **die Lippen s~n** put on lipstick

schmirgel|n vt sand down. **S~papier** nt emery-paper

schmollen vi (haben) sulk

schmor|en vt/i (haben) braise. **S~topf** m casserole

Schmuck m -[e]s jewellery; (Verzierung) ornament, decoration

schmücken vt decorate, adorn

schmuck|los adj plain. **S~stück** nt piece of jewellery

Schmuggel m -s smuggling. **s~n** vt smuggle. **S~ware** f contraband

Schmuggler m -s,- smuggler

schmunzeln vi (haben) smile

schmusen vi (haben) cuddle

Schmutz m -es dirt. **s~en** vi (haben) get dirty. **S~ig** adj dirty

Schnabel m -s,⸚ beak, bill; (eines Kruges) lip; (Tülle) spout

Schnalle f -,-n buckle. **s~n** vt strap; (zu-) buckle

schnalzen vi (haben) **mit der Zunge s~** click one's tongue

schnapp|en vi (haben) **nach s~** snap at; gasp for (Luft) ●vt snatch, grab; (🄻: festnehmen) nab. **S~schloss** nt spring lock. **S~schuss** m snapshot

Schnaps m -es,⸚e schnapps

schnarchen vi (haben) snore

schnaufen vi (haben) puff, pant

Schnauze f -,-n muzzle; (eines Kruges) lip; (Tülle) spout

schnäuzen (sich) vr blow one's nose

Schnecke f -,-n snail; (Nackt-) slug; (Spirale) scroll. **S~nhaus** nt snail-shell

Schnee m -s snow; (Eier-) beaten egg-white. **S~besen** m whisk.

S~brille f snow-goggles pl. **S~fall** m snow-fall. **S~flocke** f snowflake. **S~glöckchen** nt -s,- snowdrop. **S~kette** f snow chain. **S~mann** m (pl -männer) snowman. **S~pflug** m snowplough. **S~schläger** m whisk. **S~sturm** m snowstorm, blizzard. **S~wehe** f -,-n snowdrift

Schneide f -,-n [cutting] edge; (Klinge) blade

schneiden† vt cut; (in Scheiben) slice; (kreuzen) cross; (nicht beachten) cut dead; **Gesichter s~** pull faces; **sich s~** cut oneself; (über-) intersect

Schneider m -s,- tailor. **S~in** f -,-nen dressmaker. **s~n** vt make (Anzug, Kostüm)

Schneidezahn m incisor

schneien vi (haben) snow; **es schneit** it is snowing

Schneise f -,-n path

schnell adj quick; (Auto, Tempo) fast ●adv quickly; (in eam Tempo) fast; (bald) soon; **mach s~!** hurry up! **S~igkeit** f - rapidity; (Tempo) speed. **S~kochtopf** m pressure-cooker. **S~stens** adv as quickly as possible. **S~zug** m express [train]

schnetzeln vt cut into thin strips

Schnipsel m & nt -s,- scrap

Schnitt m -[e]s,-e cut; (Film-) cutting; (S~muster) [paper] pattern; **im S~** (durchschnittlich) on average

Schnitte f -,-n slice [of bread]

schnittig adj stylish; (stromlinienförmig) streamlined

Schnitt|lauch m chives pl. **S~muster** nt [paper] pattern. **S~punkt** m [point of] intersection. **S~stelle** f interface. **S~wunde** f cut

Schnitzel nt -s,- scrap; (Culin) escalope. **s~n** vt shred

schnitzen vt/i (haben) carve

schnodderig adj 🔲 brash

Schnorchel m -s,- snorkel

Schnörkel m -s,- flourish; (Kunst) scroll. **s~ig** adj ornate

schnüffeln vi (haben) sniff (an etw dat sth); (🔲: spionieren) snoop [around]

Schnuller m -s,- [baby's] dummy

Schnupf|en m -s,- [head] cold. **s~tabak** m snuff

schnuppern vt/i (haben) sniff (an etw dat sth)

Schnur f -,ⁿe string; (Kordel) cord; (Electr) flex

schnüren vt tie; lace [up] (Schuhe)

Schnurr|bart m moustache. **s~en** vi (haben) hum; (Katze:) purr

Schnürsenkel m [shoe-]lace

Schock m -[e]s,-s shock. **s~en** vt 🔲 shock. **s~ieren** vt shock

Schöffe m -n,-n lay judge

Schokolade f - chocolate

Scholle f -,-n clod [of earth]; (Eis-) [ice-]floe; (Fisch) plaice

schon adv already; (allein) just; (sogar) even; (ohnehin) anyway; **s~ einmal** before; (jemals) ever; **s~ immer/oft/wieder** always/often/again; **s~ deshalb** for that reason alone; **das ist s~ möglich** that's quite possible; **ja s~, aber** well yes, but

schön adj beautiful; (Wetter) fine; (angenehm, nett) nice; (gut) good; (🔲: beträchtlich) pretty; **s~en Dank!** thank you very much!

schonen vt spare; (gut behandeln) look after. **s~d** adj gentle

Schönheit f -,-en beauty. **S~sfehler** m blemish. **S~skonkurrenz** f beauty contest

Schonung f -,-en gentle care; (nach Krankheit) rest; (Baum-) plantation. **s~slos** adj ruthless

Schonzeit f close season

schöpf|en vt scoop [up]; ladle (Suppe); **Mut s~en** take heart. **s~erisch** adj creative. **S~kelle** f. **S~löffel** m ladle. **S~ung** f -,-en creation

Schoppen m -s,- (SGer) ≈ pint

Schorf m -[e]s scab

Schornstein m chimney. **S~feger** m -s,- chimney sweep

Schoß m -es,ⁿe lap; (Frack-) tail

Schössling m -s,-e (Bot) shoot

Schote f -,-n pod; (Erbse) pea

Schotte m -n,-n Scot, Scotsman

Schottin f -nen Scot, Scotswoman

Schotter m -s gravel

schott|isch adj Scottish, Scots. **S~land** nt -s Scotland

schraffieren vt hatch

schräg adj diagonal; (geneigt) sloping; **s~ halten** tilt. **S~strich** m oblique stroke

Schramme f -,-n scratch

Schrank m -[e]s,ⁿe cupboard; (Kleider-) wardrobe; (Akten-, Glas-) cabinet

Schranke f -,-n barrier

Schraube f -,-n screw; (Schiffs-) propeller. **s~n** vt screw; (ab-) unscrew; (drehen) turn. **S~nschlüssel** m spanner. **S~nzieher** m -s,- screwdriver

Schraubstock m vice

Schreck m -[e]s,-e fright. **S~en** m -s,- fright; (Entsetzen) horror

Schreck|gespenst nt spectre. **s~haft** adj easily frightened; (nervös) jumpy. **s~lich** adj terrible.

Schrei m -[e]s,-e cry, shout; (gellend) scream; **der letzte S~** 🔲 the latest thing

schreib|en† vt/i (haben) write; (auf der Maschine) type; **richtig/falsch s~en** spell right/wrong; **sich**

s~en (*Wort:*) be spelt; (*korrespondieren*) correspond. S~en nt -s,- writing; (*Brief*) letter. S~fehler m spelling mistake. S~heft nt exercise book. S~kraft f clerical assistant; (*für Maschineschreiben*) typist. S~maschine f typewriter. S~tisch m desk. S~ung f -,-en spelling. S~waren fpl stationery sg.

schreien† vt/i (haben) cry; (*gellend*) scream; (*rufen, laut sprechen*) shout

Schreiner m -s,- joiner

schreiten† vi (sein) walk

Schrift f -,-en writing; (*Druck-*) type; (*Abhandlung*) paper; die Heilige S~ the Scriptures pl. S~führer m secretary. S~lich adj written ● adv in writing. S~sprache f written language. S~steller(in) m -s,- (f -,-nen) writer. S~stück nt document. S~zeichen nt character

schrill adj shrill

Schritt m -[e]s,e,e step; (*Entfernung*) pace; (*Gangart*) walk; (*der Hose*) crotch. S~macher m -s,- pace-maker. S~weise adv step by step

schroff adj precipitous; (*abweisend*) brusque; (*unvermittelt*) abrupt; (*Gegensatz*) stark

Schrot m & nt -[e]s coarse meal; (*Blei-*) small shot. S~flinte f shotgun

Schrott m -[e]s scrap[-metal]; zu S~ fahren 🔟 write off. S~platz m scrap-yard

schrubben vt/i (haben) scrub

Schrulle f -,-n whim; alte S~e 🔟 old crone. s~ig adj cranky

schrumpfen vi (sein) shrink

schrump[e]lig adj wrinkled

Schub m -[e]s,²e (*Phys*) thrust; (*S~fach*) drawer; (*Menge*) batch. S~fach nt drawer. S~karre f,

S~karren m wheelbarrow. S~lade f drawer

Schubs m -es,-e push, shove s~en vt push, shove

schüchtern adj shy. S~heit f - shyness

Schuft m -[e]s,-e (*pej*) swine

Schuh m -[e]s,-e shoe. S~anzieher m -s,- shoehorn. S~band nt (pl -bänder) shoe-lace. S~creme f shoe-polish. S~löffel m shoehorn. S~macher m -s,- shoemaker

Schul|abgänger m -s,- schoolleaver. S~arbeiten, S~aufgaben fpl homework sg.

Schuld f -,-en guilt; (*Verantwortung*) blame; (*Geld-*) debt; S~en machen get into debt; S~ haben be to blame (an + dat for); jdm S~ geben blame s.o. ● S~ sein be to blame (an + dat for). s~en vt owe

schuldig adj guilty (gen of); (*gebührend*) due; jdm etw s~sein owe s.o. sth. S~keit f - duty

schuld|los adj innocent. S~ner m -s,- debtor. S~spruch m guilty verdict

Schule f -,-n school; in der/die S~ at/to school. s~n vt train

Schüler(in) m -s,- (f -,-nen) pupil

schul|frei adj s~freier Tag day without school; wir haben morgen s~frei there's no school tomorrow. S~hof m [school] playground. S~jahr nt school year; (*Klasse*) form. S~kind nt schoolchild. S~stunde f lesson

Schulter f -,-n shoulder. S~blatt nt shoulder-blade

Schulung f - training

schummeln vi (haben) 🔟 cheat

Schund m -[e]s trash

Schuppe f -,-n scale; S~n pl dandruff sg. s~n (sich) vr flake [off]

Schuppen m -s,- shed

schürf|en vt mine; **sich** (dat) **das Knie s~en** graze one's knee • vi (haben) **s~en nach** prospect for. **S~wunde** f abrasion, graze

Schürhaken m poker

Schurke m -n,-n villain

Schürze f -,-n apron

Schuss m -es, ⸚e shot; (kleine Menge) dash

Schüssel f -,-n bowl; (TV) dish

Schuss|fahrt f (Ski) schuss. **S~waffe** f firearm

Schuster m -s,- = Schuhmacher

Schutt m -[e]s rubble. **S~abladeplatz** m rubbish dump

Schüttel|frost m shivering fit. **s~n** vt shake; **sich s~n** shake oneself/itself; (vor Ekel) shudder; **jdm die Hand s~n** shake s.o.'s hand

schütten vt pour; (kippen) tip; (ver-)spill • vi (haben) **es schüttet** it is pouring [with rain]

Schutz m -es protection; (Zuflucht) shelter; (Techn) guard; **S~ suchen** take refuge. **S~anzug** m protective suit. **S~blech** nt mudguard. **S~brille** goggles pl

Schütze m -n,-n marksman; (Tor-) scorer; (Astrology) Sagittarius

schützen vt protect; (Zuflucht gewähren) shelter (**vor** + dat from) • vi (haben) give protection/shelter (**vor** + dat from)

Schutz|engel m guardian angel. **S~heilige(r)** m/f patron saint

Schützling m -s,-e charge

schutz|los adj defenceless, helpless. **S~mann** m (pl -männer or -leute) policeman. **S~umschlag** m dust-jacket

Schwaben nt -s Swabia

schwäbisch adj Swabian

schwach adj weak; (nicht gut; gering) poor; (leicht) faint

Schwäche f -,-n weakness. **s~n** vt weaken

schwäch|lich adj delicate. **S~ling** m -s,-e weakling

Schwachsinn m mental deficiency. **s~ig** adj mentally deficient; 🄵 idiotic

Schwager m -s, ⸚ brother-in-law

Schwägerin f -,-nen sister-in-law

Schwalbe f -,-n swallow

Schwall m -[e]s torrent

Schwamm m -[e]s, ⸚e sponge; (SGer: Pilz) fungus; (essbar) mushroom. **s~ig** adj spongy

Schwan m -[e]s, ⸚e swan

schwanger adj pregnant

Schwangerschaft f -,-en pregnancy

Schwank m -[e]s, ⸚e (Theat) farce

schwank|en vi (haben) sway; (Boot:) rock; (sich ändern) fluctuate; (unentschieden sein) be undecided • (sein) stagger. **S~ung** f -,-en fluctuation

Schwanz m -es, ⸚e tail

schwänzen vt 🄵 skip; **die Schule s~** play truant

Schwarm m -[e]s, ⸚e swarm; (Fisch-) shoal; (🄵: Liebe) idol

schwärmen vi (haben) swarm; **s~ für** 🄵 adore; (verliebt sein) have a crush on

Schwarte f -,-n (Speck-) rind

schwarz adj black; (🄵: illegal) illegal; **S~er Markt** black market; **s~ gekleidet** dressed in black; **s~ auf weiß** in black and white; **s~ sehen** (fig) be pessimistic; **ins S~e treffen** score a bull's-eye. **S~ m -[e]s,-** black. **S~arbeit** f moonlighting. **s~arbeiten** vi sep (haben) moonlight. **S~e(r)** m/f black

Schwärze f - blackness. **s~n** vt blacken

Schwarz|fahrer m fare-dodger. **S~handel** m black market (mit in). **S~händler** m black marketeer. **S~markt** m black market. **S~wald** m Black Forest. **s~weiß** adj black and white

schwatzen (SGer) **schwätzen** vi (haben) chat; (klatschen) gossip; (Sch) talk [in class] • vt talk

Schwebe f - in der S~ (fig) undecided. **S~bahn** f cable railway. **s~n** vi (haben) float; (fig) be undecided; (Verfahren:) be pending; **in Gefahr s~n** be in danger • (sein) float

Schwed|e m -n,-n Swede. **S~en** nt -s Sweden. **S~in** f -,-nen Swede. **s~isch** adj Swedish

Schwefel m -s sulphur

schweigen† vi (haben) be silent; **ganz zu s~** von let alone. **S~** nt -s silence; **zum S~ bringen** silence

schweigsam adj silent; (wortkarg) taciturn

Schwein nt -[e]s,-e pig; (Culin) pork; ⊠ Schuft) swine; **S~ haben** ⊡ be lucky. **S~ebraten** m roast pork. **S~efleisch** nt pork. **S~erei** f -,-en ⊠ [dirty] mess; (Gemeinheit) dirty trick. **S~estall** m pigsty. **S~sleder** nt pigskin

Schweiß m -es sweat

schweißen vt weld

Schweiz (die) - Switzerland. **S~er** adj & m & pl -s,-, **S~erin** f -,-nen Swiss. **s~erisch** adj Swiss

---

Schweizerische Eidgenossenschaft The Swiss Confederation is the official name for Switzerland. The confederation was established in 1291 when the cantons (▶KANTON) of Uri, Schwyz and Unterwalden swore to defend their traditional rights against the Habsburg Empire. The unified federal state as it is known today was formed in 1848.

Schwelle f -,-n threshold; (Eisenbahn-) sleeper

schwell|en† vi (sein) swell. **S~ung** f -,-en swelling

schwer adj heavy; (schwierig) difficult; (mühsam) hard; (ernst) serious; (schlimm) bad; **3 Pfund s~ sein** weigh 3 pounds • adv heavily; with difficulty; (mühsam) hard; (schlimm, sehr) badly, seriously; **s~ krank/ verletzt** seriously ill/injured; **s~ hören** be hard of hearing; **etw s~ nehmen** take sth seriously; **jdm s~ fallen** be hard for s.o.; **es jdm s~ machen** make it or things difficult for s.o.; **sich s~ tun** have difficulty (mit with); **s~ zu sagen** difficult or hard to say

Schwere f - heaviness; (Gewicht) weight; (Schwierigkeit) difficulty; (Ernst) gravity. **S~losigkeit** f - weightlessness

schwer|fällig adj ponderous, clumsy. **S~gewicht** nt heavyweight. **s~hörig** adj **s~hörig sein** be hard of hearing. **S~kraft** f (Phys) gravity. **s~mütig** adj melancholic. **S~punkt** m centre of gravity; (fig) emphasis

Schwert nt -[e]s,-er sword. **S~lilie** f iris

Schwer|verbrecher m serious offender. **s~wiegend** adj weighty

Schwester f -,-n sister; (Kranken-) nurse. **s~lich** adj sisterly

Schwieger|eltern pl parents-in-law. **S~mutter** f mother-in-law. **S~sohn** m son-in-law. **S~tochter** f daughter-in-law. **S~vater** m father-in-law

schwierig adj difficult. **S~keit** f

-,-en difficulty

Schwimm|bad nt swimming-baths pl. **S~becken** nt swimming-pool. **s~en†** vt/i (sein/haben) swim; (auf dem Wasser treiben) float. **S~weste** f life-jacket

Schwindel m -s dizziness, vertigo; (🎯: Betrug) fraud; (Lüge) lie. **S~anfall** m dizzy spell. **s~frei** adj **s~frei sein** have a good head for heights. **s~n** vi (haben) lie

Schwindl|er m -s,- liar; (Betrüger) fraud, con-man. **s~ig** adj dizzy; **mir ist** od **wird s~ig** I feel dizzy

schwing|en† vi (haben) swing; (Phys) oscillate; (vibrieren) vibrate ● vt swing; wave (Fahne); (drohend) brandish. **S~ung** f -,-en oscillation; vibration

Schwips m -es,-e **einen S~ haben** 🎯 be tipsy

schwitzen vi (haben) sweat; **ich s~e** I am hot

schwören† vt/i (haben) swear (auf + acc by)

schwul adj (🎯: homosexuell) gay

schwül adj close. **S~e** f - closeness

Schwung m -[e]s,ᵉe swing; (Bogen) sweep; (Schnelligkeit) momentum; (Kraft) vigour. **s~los** adj dull. **s~voll** adj vigorous; (Bogen, Linie) sweeping; (mitreißend) spirited

Schwur m -[e]s,ᵉe vow; (Eid) oath. **S~gericht** nt jury (court)

sechs inv adj six, **S~** f -,-en six; (Sch) ≈ fail mark. **s~eckig** adj hexagonal. **s~te(r,s)** adj sixth

sech|zehn inv adj sixteen. **s~ze-hnte(r,s)** adj sixteenth. **s~zig** inv adj sixty. **s~zigste(r,s)** adj sixtieth

See¹ m -s,-n lake

See² f - sea; **an die/der See** to/at the seaside; **auf See** at sea. **S~fahrt** f [sea] voyage; (Schifffahrt)

navigation. **S~gang** m schwerer **S~gang** rough sea. **S~hund** m seal. **s~krank** adj seasick

Seele f -,-n soul

seelisch adj psychological; (geistig) mental

See|macht f maritime power. **S~mann** m (pl -leute) seaman, sailor. **S~not** f in **S~not** in distress. **S~räuber** m pirate. **S~reise** f [sea] voyage. **S~rose** f water-lily. **S~sack** m kitbag. **S~stern** m starfish. **S~tang** m seaweed. **S~tüch-tig** adj seaworthy. **S~zunge** f sole

Segel nt -s,- sail. **S~boot** nt sailing-boat. **S~flugzeug** nt glider. **s~n** vt/i (sein/haben) sail. **S~schiff** nt sailing-ship. **S~sport** m sailing. **S~tuch** nt canvas

Segen m -s blessing

Segler m -s,- yachtsman

segnen vt bless

sehen† vt see; watch (Fernsehsendung); **jdn/etw wieder s~** see s.o./sth again; **sich s~ lassen** show oneself ● vi (haben) see; (blicken) look (auf + acc at); (ragen) show (aus above); **gut/schlecht s~** have good/bad eyesight; **vom S~ kennen** know by sight; **s~ nach** keep an eye on; (betreuen) look after; (suchen) look for. **s~swert, s~swür-dig** adj worth seeing. **S~swürdig-keit** f -,-en sight

Sehne f -,-n tendon; (eines Bogens) string

sehnen (sich) vr long (nach for)

Sehn|sucht f - longing (nach for). **s~süchtig** adj longing; (Wunsch) dearest

sehr adv very; (mit Verb) very much; **so s~**, **dass** so much that

seicht adj shallow

seid s. **sein¹**

Seide f -,-n silk

Seidel *nt* -s,- beer-mug

seiden *adj* silk **S~papier** *nt* tissue paper. **S~raupe** *f* silk-worm

seidig *adj* silky

Seife *f* -,-n soap. **S~npulver** *nt* soap powder. **S~nschaum** *m* lather

Seil *nt* -[e]s,-e rope; (Draht-) cable. **S~bahn** *f* cable railway. **s~springen†** *vi* (sein) (infinitive & pp only) skip. **S~tänzer(in)** *m(f)* tightrope walker

---

sein†¹

● *intransitive verb* (sein)

····▸ be. **ich bin glücklich** I am happy. **er ist Lehrer/Schwede** he is a teacher/Swedish. **bist du es?** is that you? **sei still!** be quiet! **sie waren in Paris** they were in Paris. **morgen bin ich zu Hause** I shall be at home tomorrow. **er ist aus Berlin** he is or comes from Berlin

····▸ (impers + dat) **mir ist kalt/ besser** I am cold/better. **ihr ist schlecht** she feels sick

····▸ (existieren) be. **es ist/sind ...** there is/are .... **es ist keine Hoffnung mehr** there is no more hope. **es sind vier davon** there are four of them. **es war einmal ein Prinz** once upon a time there was a prince

● *auxiliary verb*

····▸ (zur Perfektumschreibung) have. **er ist gestorben** he has died. **sie sind angekommen** they have arrived. **sie war dort gewesen** she had been there. **ich wäre gefallen** I would have fallen

····▸ (zur Bildung des Passivs) be. **wir sind gerettet worden/ waren gerettet** we were saved

····▸ (+ zu + Infinitiv) be to be. **es**

---

war niemand zu sehen there was no one to be seen. **das war zu erwarten** that was to be expected. **er ist zu bemit- leiden** he is to be pitied. **die Richtlinien sind strengstens zu beachten** the guidelines are to be strictly followed

sein² *poss pron* his; (Ding, Tier) its; (nach man) one's; **sein Glück ver- suchen** try one's luck. **s~e(r,s)** *poss pron* his; (nach man) one's own; **das S~e tun** do one's share. **s~erseits** *adv* for his part. **s~er- zeit** *adv* in those days. **s~et- wegen** *adv* for his sake; (wegen ihm) be- cause of him, on his account. **s~ige** *poss pron* **der/die/das s~ige** his

seins *poss pron* his; (nach man) one's own

seit *conj & prep* (+ dat) since; **s~ ei- niger Zeit** for some time [past]; **ich wohne s~ zehn Jahren hier** I've lived here for ten years. **s~dem** *conj* since ● *adv* since then

Seite *f* -,-n side; (Buch-) page; **zur S~ treten** step aside; **auf der einen/anderen S~** (fig) on the one/other hand

seitens *prep* (+ gen) on the part of

Seiten|schiff *nt* [side] aisle. **S~sprung** *m* infidelity. **S~stechen** *nt* -s (Med) stitch. **S~straße** *f* side- street. **S~streifen** *m* verge; (Auto- bahn-) hard shoulder

seither *adv* since then

seit|lich *adj* side ● *adv* at/on the side; **s~lich von** to one side of ● *prep* (+ gen) to one side of. **s~wärts** *adv* on/to one side; (zur Seite) sideways

Sekret|är *m* -s,-e secretary; (Schrank) bureau. **S~ariat** *nt* -[e]s,- e secretary's office. **S~ärin** *f* -,-nen secretary

Sekt *m* -[e]s [German] sparkling wine

Sekte *f* -,-n sect

Sektor *m* -s,-en sector

Sekunde *f* -,-n second

Sekundenschlaf *m* microsleep

selber *pron* 🔲 = **selbst**

selbst *pron* oneself; **ich/du/er/sie s~** I myself you yourself/ he himself/she herself; **wir/ihr/sie s~** we ourselves/you yourselves/they themselves; **ich schneide mein Haar s~** I cut my own hair; **von s~** of one's own accord; *(automatisch)* automatically; **s~ gemacht** home-made ● *adv* even

selbständig *adj* = **selbstständig**. **S~keit** *f* - = **Selbstständigkeit**

Selbst|bedienung *f* self-service. **S~befriedigung** *f* masturbation. **s~bewusst** *adj* self-confident. **S~bewusstsein** *nt* self-confidence. **S~bildnis** *nt* self-portrait. **S~erhaltung** *f* self-preservation. **s~gemacht*** *adj* = **s~ gemacht**. *siehe* **selbst**. **s~haftend** *adj* self-adhesive. **S~hilfe** *f* self-help. **s~klebend** *adj* self-adhesive. **S~kostenpreis** *m* cost price. **S~laut** *m* vowel. **s~los** *adj* selfless. **S~mord** *m* suicide. **S~mordattentat** *nt* suicide attack. **S~mörder(in)** *m(f)* suicide. **s~mörderisch** *adj* suicidal. **S~porträt** *nt* self-portrait. **s~sicher** *adj* self-assured. **s~ständig** *adj* independent; self-employed *(Handwerker)*; **sich s~ständig machen** set up on one's own. **S~ständigkeit** *f* - independence. **s~süchtig** *adj* selfish. **S~tanken** *nt* self-service (*for petrol*). **s~tätig** *adj* automatic. **S~versorgung** *f* self-catering. **s~verständlich** *adj* natural; **etw für s~ halten** take sth for granted; **das ist s~** that goes

without saying; **s~!** of course! **S~verteidigung** *f* self-defence. **S~vertrauen** *nt* self-confidence. **S~verwaltung** *f* self-government

selig *adj* blissfully happy; *(Relig)* blessed; *(verstorben)* late. **S~keit** *f* - bliss

Sellerie *m* -s,-s & *f* -,- celeriac; *(Stangen-)* celery

selten *adj* rare ● *adv* rarely, seldom; *(besonders)* exceptionally. **S~heit** *f* -,-en rarity

seltsam *adj* odd, strange. **s~erweise** *adv* oddly

Semester *nt* -s,- *(Univ)* semester

Semikolon *nt* -s,-s semicolon

Seminar *nt* -s,-e seminar; *(Institut)* department; *(Priester-)* seminary

Semmel *f* -,-n *(Aust, SGer)* [bread] roll. **S~brösel** *pl* breadcrumbs

Senat *m* -[e]s,-e senate. **S~or** *m* -s,-en senator

senden¹† *vt* send

sende|n² *vt (reg)* broadcast; *(über Funk)* transmit, send. **S~r** *m* -s,- [broadcasting] station; *(Anlage)* transmitter. **S~reihe** *f* series

Sendung *f* -,-en consignment, shipment; *(TV)* programme

Senf *m* -s mustard

senil *adj* senile. **S~ität** *f* - senility

Senior *m* -s,-en senior; **S~en** senior citizens. **S~enheim** *nt* old people's home

senken *vt* lower; bring down *(Fieber, Preise)*; bow *(Kopf)*; **sich s~** come down, fall; *(absinken)* subside

senkrecht *adj* vertical. **S~e** *f* -n,-n perpendicular

Sensation /-'tsjo:n/ *f* -,-en sensation. **s~ell** *adj* sensational

Sense *f* -,-n scythe

sensibel *adj* sensitive

sentimental *adj* sentimental

September *m* **-s,-** September

Serie /'ze:rjə/ *f* **-,-n** series; (*Briefmarken*) set; (*Comm*) range. **S~nnummer** *f* serial number

seriös *adj* respectable; (*zuverlässig*) reliable

Serpentine *f* **-,-n** winding road; (*Kehre*) hairpin bend

Serum *nt* **-s,Sera** serum

Server *m* **-s,-** server

Service[1] /'zœrvɪs/ *nt* **-[s],-** service, set

Service[2] /'zø:gvɪs/ *m* & *nt* **-s** (*Comm, Tennis*) service

servier|en *vt/i* (haben) serve. **S~erin** *f* **-,-nen** waitress

Serviette *f* **-,-n** napkin, serviette

Servus *int* (*Aust*) cheerio; (*Begrüßung*) hallo

Sessel *m* **-s,-** armchair. **S~bahn** *f* **S~lift** *m* chairlift

sesshaft *adj* settled

Set /zɛt/ *nt* & *m* **-[s],-s** set; (*Deckchen*) place-mat

setz|en *vt* put; (abstellen) set down; (hin-) sit down (Kind); move (Spielstein); (pflanzen) plant; (schreiben, wetten) put; **sich s~en** sit down; (sinken) settle ● *vi* (sein) leap ● *vi* (haben) **s~en auf** (+ acc) back

Seuche *f* **-,-n** epidemic

seufz|en *vi* (haben) sigh. **S~er** *m* **-s,-** sigh

Sex /zɛks/ *m* **-[es]** sex

Sexualität *f* **-** sexuality. **s~ell** *adj* sexual

sezieren *vt* dissect

Shampoo /ʃam'pu:/, **Shampoon** /ʃam'po:n/ *nt* **-s** shampoo

siamesisch *adj* Siamese

sich *reflexive pron* oneself; (mit er/sie/es) himself/herself/itself; (mit sie pl) themselves; (mit Sie) yourself; (pl) yourselves; (einander) each other; **s~ kennen** know oneself/(einander) each other; **s~ waschen** have a wash; **s~** (dat) **die Haare kämmen** comb one's hair; **s~ wundern** be surprised; **s~ gut verkaufen** sell well; **von s~ aus** of one's own accord

Sichel *f* **-,-n** sickle

sicher *adj* safe; (gesichert) secure; (gewiss) certain; (zuverlässig) reliable; sure (Urteil); steady (Hand); (selbstbewusst) self-confident; **bist du s~?** are you sure? ● *adv* safely; securely; certainly; reliably; self-confidently; (wahrscheinlich) most probably; **s~!** certainly! **s~gehen†** *vi sep* (sein) (fig) be sure

Sicherheit *f* **-** safety; (Pol, Psych, Comm) security; (Gewissheit) certainty; (Zuverlässigkeit) reliability; (des Urteils) surety; (Selbstbewusstsein) self-confidence. **S~sgurt** *m* safety belt; (Auto) seat belt. **S~snadel** *f* safety pin

sicherlich *adv* certainly; (wahrscheinlich) most probably

sicher|n *vt* secure; (garantieren) safeguard; (schützen) protect; put the safety catch on (Pistole). **S~ung** *f* **-,-en** safeguard, protection; (Gewehr-) safety catch; (Electr) fuse

Sicht *f* **-** view; (S~weite) visibility; **auf lange S~** in the long term. **s~bar** *adj* visible. **S~vermerk** *m* visa. **S~weite** *f* visibility; **außer S~weite** out of sight

sie *pron* (nom) (sg) she; (Ding, Tier) it; (pl) they; (acc) (sg) her; (Ding, Tier) it; (pl) them

Sie *pron* you; **gehen/warten Sie!** go/wait!

Sieb *nt* **-[e]s,-e** sieve; (Tee-) strainer. **s~en**[1] *vt* sieve, sift

sieben[2] *inv adj*, **S~** *f* **-,-en** seven. **S~sachen** *fpl* 🔢 belongings.

s~te(r,s) adj seventh. **s~zehn**
inv adj seventeen. **s~zehnte(r,s)**
adj seventeenth. **s~zig** inv adj seventy. **s~zigste(r,s)** adj seventieth

siede|n† vt/i (haben) boil.
S~punkt m boiling point

Siedlung f -,-en [housing] estate;
(Niederlassung) settlement

Sieg m -[e]s,-e victory

Siegel nt -s,- seal. **S~ring** m signet-ring

sieg|en vi (haben) win. **S~er(in)** m
-s,- (f -,-nen) winner. **s~reich** adj
victorious

siezen vt jdn s~ call s.o. 'Sie'

Signal nt -s,-e signal

Silbe f -,-n syllable

Silber nt -s silver. **s~n** adj silver

Silhouette /zɪ'lvɛtə/ f -,-n silhouette

Silizium nt -s silicon

Silo m & nt -s,-s silo

Silvester nt -s New Year's Eve

Sims m & nt -es,-e ledge

simsen vt/i text, send a text
message

simultan adj simultaneous

sind s. **sein¹**

Sinfonie f -,-n symphony

singen† vt/i (haben) sing

Singvogel m songbird

sinken† vi (sein) sink; (nieder-)
drop; (niedriger werden) go down,
fall; **den Mut s~ lassen** lose
courage

Sinn m -[e]s,-e sense; (Denken)
mind; (Zweck) point; **in gewissem
S~e** in a sense; **es hat keinen S~**
it is pointless. **S~bild** nt symbol

sinnlich adj sensory; (sexuell) sensual; (Genüsse) sensuous. **S~keit** f -
sensuality; sensuousness

sinn|los adj senseless; (zwecklos)

pointless. **s~voll** adj meaningful;
(vernünftig) sensible

Sintflut f flood

Siphon /'zi:fõ/ m -s,-s siphon

Sippe f -,-n clan

Sirene f -,-n siren

Sirup m -s,-e syrup; treacle

Sitte f -,-n custom; **S~n** manners

sittlich adj moral. **S~keit** f - morality. **S~keitsverbrecher** m sex offender

sittsam adj well-behaved; (züchtig)
demure

Situation /-'tsjo:n/ f -,-en situation. **s~iert** adj **gut/schlecht
s~iert** well/badly off

Sitz m -es,-e seat; (Passform) fit

sitzen† vi (haben) sit; (sich befinden) be; (passen) fit; (⊤: treffen) hit
home; **[im Gefängnis] s~** ⊤ be in
jail; **s~ bleiben** remain seated; (Sch) stay or be kept down; (nicht
heiraten) be left on the shelf; **s~
bleiben auf** (+ dat) be left with

Sitz|gelegenheit f seat.
S~platz m seat. **S~ung** f -,-en
session

Sizilien /-jən/ nt -s Sicily

Skala f -,-len scale; (Reihe) range

Skalpell nt -s,-e scalpel

skalpieren vt scalp

Skandal m -s,-e scandal. **s~ös** adj
scandalous

Skandinav|ien /-jən/ nt -s Scandinavia. **s~isch** adj Scandinavian

Skat m -s skat

Skateboard /'ske:tbo:gt/ nt -s, -s
skateboard

Skelett nt -[e]s,-e skeleton

Skep|sis f - scepticism. **s~tisch**
adj sceptical

Ski /ʃi:/ m -s,-er ski; **Ski fahren** od
laufen ski. **S~fahrer(in), S~läufer(in)** m(f) -s,- (f -,-nen) skier.

S∼sport m skiing
Skizz|e f -,-n sketch. **s∼ieren** vt sketch
Sklav|e m -n,-n slave. **S∼erei** f - slavery. **S∼in** f -,-nen slave
Skorpion m -s,-e scorpion; (Astrology) Scorpio
Skrupel m -s,- scruple. **s∼los** adj unscrupulous
Skulptur f -,-en sculpture
Slalom m -s,-s slalom
Slaw|e m -n,-n, **S∼in** f -,-nen Slav. **s∼isch** adj Slav; (Lang) Slavonic
Slip m -s,-s briefs pl
Smaragd m -[e]s,-e emerald
Smoking m -s,-s dinner jacket
SMS-Nachricht f text message
Snob m -s,-s snob. **S∼ismus** m - snobbery **s∼istisch** adj snobbish
so adv so; (so sehr) so much; (auf diese Weise) like this/that; (solch) such; (🗖: sowieso) anyway; (🗖: umsonst) free; (🗖: ungefähr) about; **so viel** so much; **so gut/bald wie** as good/soon as; **so ein Zufall!** what a coincidence! **mir ist so, als ob** I feel as if; **so oder so** in any case; **so um zehn Euro** 🗖 about ten euros; **so?** really? ● conj (also) so; (dann) then; **so dass** = **sodass**
sobald conj as soon as
Söckchen nt -s,- [ankle] sock
Socke f -,-n sock
Sockel m -s,- plinth, pedestal
Socken m -s,- sock
sodass conj so that
Sodawasser nt soda water
Sodbrennen nt -s heartburn
soeben adv just [now]
Sofa nt -s,-s settee, sofa
sofern adv provided [that]
sofort adv at once, immediately; (auf der Stelle) instantly

Software /'zɔftvɛːɐ/ f - software
sogar adv even
sogenannt adj so-called
sogleich adv at once
Sohle f -,-n sole; (Tal-) bottom
Sohn m -[e]s,-̈e son
Sojabohne f soya bean
solange conj as long as
solch inv pron such; **s∼ ein(e)** such a; **s∼ einer/eine/eins** one/(Person) someone like that. **s∼e(r,s)** pron such ● (substantivisch) **ein s∼er/eine s∼e/ein s∼es** one/(Person) someone like that; (Leute) **s∼e** pl those; (Leute) people like that
Soldat m -en,-en soldier
Söldner m -s,- mercenary
Solidarität f - solidarity
solide adj solid; (haltbar) sturdy; (sicher) sound; (anständig) respectable
Solist(in) m -en,-en (f -,-nen) soloist
Soll nt -s (Comm) debit; (Produktions-) quota

---

sollen†

● *auxiliary verb*

····▸ (Verpflichtung) be [supposed or meant] to. **er soll morgen zum Arzt gehen** he is [supposed] to go to the doctor tomorrow. **die beiden Flächen sollen fluchten** the two surfaces are meant to be or should be in alignment. **du solltest ihn anrufen** you were meant to phone him or should have phoned him

····▸ (Befehl) **du sollst sofort damit aufhören** you're to stop that at once. **er soll hereinkommen** he is to come in; (sagen Sie es ihm) tell him to come in

····▸ **sollte** (subjunctive) should;

ought to. **wir sollten früher aufstehen** we ought to or should get up earlier. **das hätte er nicht tun/sagen sollen** he shouldn't have done/ said that

····▸ *(Zukunft, Geplantes)* be to. **ich soll die Abteilung übernehmen** I am to take over the department. **du sollst das Geld zurückbekommen** you are to or shall get your money back. **es soll nicht wieder vorkommen** it won't happen again. **sie sollten ihr Reiseziel nie erreichen** they were never to reach their destination

····▸ *(Ratlosigkeit)* be to; shall. **was soll man nur machen?** what is one to do?; what shall I/we do? **ich weiß nicht, was ich machen soll** I don't know what I should do or what to do

····▸ *(nach Bericht)* be supposed to. **er soll sehr reich sein** he is supposed or is said to be very rich. **sie soll geheiratet haben** they say or I gather she has got married

····▸ *(Absicht)* be meant or supposed to. **was soll dieses Bild darstellen?** what is this picture supposed to represent? **das sollte ein Witz sein** that was meant or supposed to be a joke

····▸ *(in Bedingungssätzen)* should. **sollte er anrufen, falls od wenn er anrufen sollte** should he or if he should telephone

● *intransitive verb*

····▸ *(irgendwohin gehen sollen)* be [supposed] to go. **er soll morgen zum Arzt/nach Berlin** he is [supposed] to go to the doctor/ to Berlin tomorrow. **ich sollte ins Theater** I was supposed to

go to the theatre

····▸ *(sonstige Wendungen)* **soll er doch!** let him! **was soll das?** what's that in aid of? Ⓣ

Solo *nt* -s,-los & -li solo
somit *adv* therefore, so
Sommer *m* -s,- summer. **s~lich** *adj* summery; *(Sommer-)* summer ● *adv* **s~lich warm** as warm as summer. **S~sprossen** *fpl* freckles
Sonate *f* -,-n sonata
Sonde *f* -,-n probe
Sonder|angebot *nt* special offer. **s~bar** *adj* odd. **S~fahrt** *f* special excursion. **S~fall** *m* special case. **s~gleichen** *adv* **eine Gemeinheit s~gleichen** unparalleled meanness. **S~ling** *m* -s,-e crank. **S~marke** *f* special stamp
sondern *conj* but; **nicht nur ... s~ auch** not only ... but also
Sonder|preis *m* special price. **S~schule** *f* special school
Sonett *nt* -[e]s,-e sonnet
Sonnabend *m* -s,-e Saturday. **s~s** *adv* on Saturdays
Sonne *f* -,-n sun. **s~n (sich)** *vr* sun oneself
Sonnen|aufgang *m* sunrise. **s~baden** *vi* (haben) sunbathe. **S~bank** *f* sun-bed. **S~blume** *f* sunflower. **S~brand** *m* sunburn. **S~brille** *f* sunglasses *pl.* **S~energie** *f* solar energy. **S~finsternis** *f* solar eclipse. **S~milch** *f* sun-tan lotion. **S~öl** *nt* sun-tan oil. **S~schein** *m* sunshine. **S~schirm** *m* sunshade. **S~stich** *m* sunstroke. **S~uhr** *f* sundial. **S~untergang** *m* sunset. **S~wende** *f* solstice
sonnig *adj* sunny
Sonntag *m* -s,-e Sunday. **s~s** *adv* on Sundays
sonst *adv* *(gewöhnlich)* usually; *(im*

Übrigen apart from that; (*andernfalls*) otherwise, or [else]; **wer/was/wie/wo s~?** who/what/how/where else? **s~ niemand** no one else; **s~ noch etwas?** anything else? **s~ noch Fragen?** any more questions? **s~ jemand od wer** someone else/(*fragend, verneint*) anyone else; (*irgendjemand*) [just] anyone; **s~ wo** somewhere/(*fragend, verneint*) anywhere else; (*irgendwo*) [just] anywhere. **s~ig** adj other

soost conj whenever

Sopran m -s,-e soprano

Sorge f -,-n worry (um about); (*Fürsorge*) care; **sich** (dat) **S~n machen** worry. **s~n** vi (haben) **s~n für** look after, care for; (*vorsorgen*) provide for; (*sich kümmern*) see to; **dafür s~n, dass** see or make sure that ● vr **sich s~n** worry. **s~frei** adj carefree. **s~nvoll** adj worried. **S~recht** nt (Jur) custody

Sorg|falt f - care. **s~fältig** adj careful

Sorte f -,-n kind, sort; (*Comm*) brand

sort|ieren vt sort [out]; (*Comm*) grade. **S~iment** nt -[e]s,-e range

sosehr conj however much

Soße f -,-n sauce; (*Braten-*) gravy; (*Salat-*) dressing

Souvenir /zuvə'niːɐ̯/ nt -s,-s souvenir

souverän /zuvə'rɛːn/ adj sovereign

soviel conj however much; **s~ ich weiß** as far as I know ● adv *so viel, s. viel

soweit conj as far as; (*insoweit*) [in] so far as ● adv* so weit, s. weit

sowenig conj however little ● adv *so wenig, s. wenig

sowie conj as well as; (*sobald*) as soon as

sowieso adv anyway, in any case

sowjet|isch adj Soviet. **S~union** f - Soviet Union

sowohl adv **s~ ... als** od **wie auch** as well as ...

sozial adj social; (*Einstellung, Beruf*) caring. **S~arbeit** f social work. **S~demokrat** m social democrat. **S~hilfe** f social security

Sozialis|mus m - socialism. **S~t** m -en,-en socialist

Sozial|versicherung f National Insurance. **S~wohnung** f ≈ council flat

Soziologie f - sociology

Sozius m -,-se (*Comm*) partner; (*Beifahrersitz*) pillion

Spachtel m -s,- & f -,-n spatula

Spagat m -[e]s,-e (*Aust*) string; **s~ machen** do the splits pl

Spaghetti, Spagetti pl spaghetti sg

Spalier nt -s,-e trellis

Spalt|e f -,-n crack; (*Gletscher-*) crevasse; (*Druck-*) column; (*Orangen-*) segment. **s~en†** vt split. **S~ung** f -,-en splitting; (*Kluft*) split; (*Phys*) fission

Span m -[e]s, ̈e [wood] chip

Spange f -,-n clasp; (*Haar-*) slide; (*Zahn-*) brace

Span|ien /-jən/ nt -s Spain. **S~ier** m -s,-, **S~ierin** f -,-nen Spaniard. **s~isch** adj Spanish. **S~isch** nt -[s] (*Lang*) Spanish

Spann m -[e]s instep

Spanne f -,-n span; (*Zeit-*) space; (*Comm*) margin

spann|en vt stretch; put up (*Leine*); (*straffen*) tighten; (*an-*) harness (an + acc to); **sich s~en** tighten ● vi (haben) be too tight. **s~end** adj exciting. **S~ung** f -,-en tension; (*Erwartung*) suspense; (*Electr*) voltage

Spar|buch nt savings book.
S~büchse f money-box. **s~en** vt/i
(haben) save; (sparsam sein) economize (**mit/an** + dat on). **S~er** m
-s,- saver

Spargel m -s,- asparagus

Spar|kasse f savings bank.
S~konto nt deposit account

sparsam adj economical; (Person)
thrifty. **S~keit** f - economy; thrift

Sparschwein nt piggy bank

Sparte f -,-n branch; (Zeitungs-)
section; (Rubrik) column

Spaß m -es,⸚e fun; (Scherz) joke;
im/aus/zum S~ for fun; **S~ machen** be fun; (Person:) be joking;
viel S~! I have a good time! **s~en**
vi (haben) joke. **S~vogel** m joker

Spastiker m -s,- spastic

spät adj & adv late; **wie s~ ist es?**
what time is it? **zu s~ kommen**
be late

Spaten m -s,- spade

später adj later; (zukünftig) future
● adv later

spätestens adv at the latest

Spatz m -en,-en sparrow

Spätzle pl (Culin) noodles

spazieren vi (sein) stroll; **s~
gehen** go for a walk

Spazier|gang m walk; **einen
S~gang machen** go for a walk.
S~gänger(in) m -s,- (f -,-nen)
walker. **S~stock** m walking-stick

Specht m -[e]s,-e woodpecker

Speck m -s bacon. **s~ig** adj greasy

Spedi|teur /ʃpediˈtøːɐ/ m -s,-e
haulage/(für Umzüge) removals con-
tractor. **S~tion** f -,-en carriage,
haulage; (Firma) haulage/(für Umzüge) removals firm

Speer m -[e]s,-e spear; (Sport)
javelin

Speiche f -,-n spoke

Speichel m -s saliva

Speicher m -s,- warehouse; (Dialekt: Dachboden) attic; (Computer)
memory. **s~n** vt store

Speise f -,-n food; (Gericht) dish;
(Pudding) blancmange. **S~eis** nt
ice-cream. **S~kammer** f larder.
S~karte f menu. **s~n** vi (haben)
eat ● vt feed. **S~röhre** f oesopha-
gus. **S~saal** m dining room.
S~wagen m dining car

Spektrum nt -s,-tra spectrum

Spekul|ant m -en,-en speculator.
s~ieren vi (haben) speculate;
s~ieren auf (+ acc) 🅸 hope to get

Spelze f -,-n husk

spendabel adj generous

Spende f -,-n donation. **s~n** vt
donate; give (Blut, Schatten); **Beifall
s~n** applaud. **S~r** m -s,- donor;
(Behälter) dispenser

spendieren vt pay for

Sperling m -s,-e sparrow

Sperre f -,-n barrier; (Verbot) ban;
(Comm) embargo. **s~n** vt close;
(ver-) block; (verbieten) ban; cut off
(Strom, Telefon); stop (Scheck, Kredit); **s~n in** (+ acc) put in (Gefängnis, Käfig)

Sperr|holz nt plywood. **S~müll**
m bulky refuse. **S~stunde** f closing time

Spesen pl expenses

spezial|isieren (sich) vr special-
ize (**auf** + acc in). **S~ist** m -en,-en
specialist. **S~ität** f -,-en speciality

spicken vt (Culin) lard; **gespickt
mit** (fig) full of ● vi (haben) 🅸 crib
(**bei** from)

Spiegel m -s,- mirror; (Wasser-, Al-
kohol-) level. **S~bild** nt reflection.
S~ei nt fried egg. **s~n** vt reflect;
sich s~n be reflected ● vi (haben)
reflect [the light]; (glänzen) gleam.
S~ung f -,-en reflection

Spiel nt -[e]s,-e game; (Spielen) playing; (Glücks-) gambling; (Schau-) play; (Satz) set; **auf dem S~ stehen** be at stake; **aufs S~ setzen** risk. **S~automat** m fruit machine. **S~bank** f casino. **S~dose** f musical box. **s~en** vt/i (haben) play; (im Glücksspiel) gamble; (vortäuschen) act; (Roman:) be set (**in** + dat in); **s~en mit** (fig) toy with

Spieler(in) m -s,- (f -,-nen) player; (Glücks-) gambler

Spiel|feld nt field, pitch. **S~marke** f chip. **S~plan** m programme. **S~platz** m playground. **S~raum** m (fig) scope; (Techn) clearance. **S~regeln** fpl rules [of the game]. **S~sachen** fpl toys. **S~verderber** m -s,- spoilsport. **S~waren** fpl toys. **S~warengeschäft** nt toyshop. **S~zeug** nt toy; (S~sachen) toys pl

Spieß m -es,-e spear; (Brat-) spit; skewer; (Fleisch-) kebab. **S~er** m -s,- [petit] bourgeois. **s~ig** adj bourgeois

Spike[s]reifen /ˈʃpaɪk[s]-/ m studded tyre

Spinat m -s spinach

Spindel f -,-n spindle

Spinne f -,-n spider

spinn|en vt/i (haben) spin; **er spinnt** 🔟 he's crazy. **S~[en]gewebe** nt, **S~webe** f -,-n cobweb

Spion m -s spy

Spionage /ʃpioˈnaːʒə/ f - espionage, spying. **S~abwehr** f counterespionage

spionieren vi (haben) spy

Spionin f -,-nen [woman] spy

Spirale f -,-n spiral. **s~ig** adj spiral

Spirituosen pl spirits

Spiritus m - alcohol; (Brenn-) methylated spirits pl. **S~kocher** m

spirit stove

spitz adj pointed; (scharf) sharp; (schrill) shrill; (Winkel) acute. **S~bube** m scoundrel

Spitze f -,-n point; (oberer Teil) top; (vorderer Teil) front; (Pfeil-, Finger-, Nasen-) tip; (Schuh-, Strumpf-) toe; (Zigarren-, Zigaretten-) holder; (Höchstleistung) maximum; (Textiles) lace; (🔟: Anspielung) dig; **an der S~ liegen** be in the lead

Spitzel m -s,- informer

spitzen vt sharpen; purse (Lippen); prick up (Ohren). **S~geschwindigkeit** f top speed

Spitzname m nickname

Spleen /ʃpliːn/ m -s,-e obsession

Splitter m -s,- splinter. **s~n** vi (sein) shatter

sponsern vt sponsor

Spore f -,-n (Biology) spore

Sporn m -[e]s, Sporen spur

Sport m -[e]s sport; (Hobby) hobby. **S~art** f sport. **S~ler** m -s,- sportsman. **S~lerin** f -,-nen sportswoman. **s~lich** adj sports; (fair) sporting; (schlank) sporty. **S~platz** m sports ground. **S~verein** m sports club. **S~wagen** m sports car; (Kinder-) push-chair, (Amer) stroller

Spott m -[e]s mockery

spotten vi (haben) mock; **s~ über** (+ acc) make fun of; (höhnend) ridicule

spöttisch adj mocking

Sprach|e f -,-n language; (Sprechfähigkeit) speech; **zur S~e bringen** bring up. **S~fehler** m speech defect. **S~labor** nt language laboratory. **s~lich** adj linguistic. **s~los** adj speechless

Spray /ʃpreː/ nt & m -s,-s spray. **S~dose** f aerosol [can]

Sprechanlage f intercom

s

sprechen† vi (haben) speak/(sich unterhalten) talk (**über** + acc/**von** about/of); **Deutsch s~** speak German ● vt speak; (sagen) say; pronounce (Urteil); **schuldig s~** find guilty; **Herr X ist nicht zu s~** Mr X is not available

Sprecher(in) m -s,- (f -,-nen) speaker; (Radio, TV) announcer; (Wortführer) spokesman, f spokeswoman

Sprechstunde f consulting hours pl; (Med) surgery. **S~nhilfe** f (Med) receptionist

Sprechzimmer nt consulting room

spreizen vt spread

spreng|en vt blow up; blast (Felsen); (fig) burst; (begießen) water; (mit Sprenger) sprinkle; dampen (Wäsche). **S~er** m -s,- sprinkler. **S~kopf** m warhead. **S~körper** m explosive device. **S~stoff** m explosive

Spreu f - chaff

Sprich|wort nt (pl -wörter) proverb. **s~wörtlich** adj proverbial

Springbrunnen m fountain

spring|en† vi (sein) jump; (Schwimmsport) dive; (Ball:) bounce; (spritzen) spurt; (zer-) break; (rissig werden) crack; (SGer: laufen) run. **S~er** m -s,- jumper; (Kunst-) diver; (Schach) knight. **S~reiten** nt show-jumping

Sprint m -s,-s sprint

Spritze f -,-n syringe; (Injektion) injection; (Feuer-) hose. **s~n** vt spray; (be-, ver-) splash; (Culin) pipe; (Med) inject ● vi (haben) splash; (Fett:) spit ● vi (sein) splash; (hervor-) spurt. **S~er** m -s,- splash; (Schuss) dash

spröde adj brittle; (trocken) dry

Sprosse f -,-n rung

Sprotte f -,-n sprat

Spruch m -[e]s,ːe saying; (Denk-) motto; (Zitat) quotation. **S~band** nt (pl -bänder) banner

Sprudel m -s,- sparkling mineral water. **s~n** vi (haben/sein) bubble

Sprüh|dose f aerosol [can]. **s~en** vt spray ● vi (sein) (Funken:) fly; (fig) sparkle

Sprung m -[e]s,ːe jump, leap; (Schwimmsport) dive; (❑: Katzen-) stone's throw; (Riss) crack. **S~brett** nt springboard. **S~schanze** f skijump. **S~seil** nt skipping rope

Spucke f - spit. **s~n** vt/i (haben) spit; (sich übergeben) be sick

Spuk m -[e]s,-e [ghostly] apparition. **s~en** vi (haben) (Geist:) walk; **in diesem Haus s~t es** this house is haunted

Spülbecken nt sink

Spule f -,-n spool

Spüle f -,-n sink

spulen vt spool

spül|en vt rinse; (schwemmen) wash; **Geschirr s~en** wash up ● vi (haben) flush [the toilet]. **S~kasten** m cistern. **S~mittel** nt washing-up liquid

Spur f -,-en track; (Fahr-) lane; (Fährte) trail; (Anzeichen) trace; (Hinweis) lead

spürbar adj noticeable

spür|en vt feel; (seelisch) sense. **S~hund** m tracker dog

spurlos adv without trace

spurten vi (sein) put on a spurt

sputen (sich) vr hurry

Staat m -[e]s,-en state; (Land) country; (Putz) finery. **s~lich** adj state ● adv by the state

Staatsangehörige(r) m/f national. **S~keit** f - nationality

Staats|anwalt m state prosecutor. **S~beamte(r)** m civil servant. **S~besuch** m state visit. **S~bürger(in)** m(f) national. **S~mann** m (pl **-männer**) statesman. **S~streich** m coup

Stab m -[e]s,ˉe rod; (Gitter-) bar (Sport) baton; (Mil) staff

Stäbchen ntpl chopsticks

Stabhochsprung m pole-vault

stabil adj stable; (gesund) robust; (solide) sturdy

Stachel m -s,- spine; (Gift-) sting; (Spitze) spike. **S~beere** f gooseberry. **S~draht** m barbed wire. **S~schwein** nt porcupine

Stadion nt -s,-ien stadium

Stadium nt -s,-ien stage

Stadt f -,ˉe town; (Groß-) city

städtisch adj urban; (kommunal) municipal

Stadt|mitte f town centre. **S~plan** m street map. **S~teil** m district

Staffel f -,-n team; (S~lauf) relay; (Mil) squadron

Staffelei f -,-en easel

Staffel|lauf m relay race. **s~n** vt stagger; (abstufen) grade

Stahl m -s steel. **S~beton** m reinforced concrete

Stall m -[e]s,ˉe stable; (Kuh-) shed; (Schweine-) sty; (Hühner-) coop; (Kaninchen-) hutch

Stamm m -[e]s,ˉe trunk; (Sippe) tribe; (Wort-) stem. **S~baum** m family tree; (eines Tieres) pedigree

stammeln vt/i (haben) stammer

stammen vi (haben) come/(zeitlich) date (von/aus from)

stämmig adj sturdy

Stamm|kundschaft f regulars pl. **S~lokal** nt favourite pub

Stammtisch A large table reserved for regulars in most German Kneipen (pubs). The word is also used to refer to the group of people who meet around this table for a drink and lively discussion. *i*

stampfen vi (haben) stamp; (Maschine:) pound ● vi (sein) tramp ● vt pound; mash (Kartoffeln)

Stand m -[e]s,ˉe standing position; (Zustand) state; (Spiel-) score; (Höhe) level; (gesellschaftlich) class; (Verkaufs-) stall; (Messe-) stand; (Taxi-) rank; **auf den neuesten S~ bringen** update

Standard m -s,-s standard

Standbild nt statue

Ständer m -s,- stand; (Geschirr-) rack; (Kerzen-) holder

Standesamt nt registry office. **S~beamte(r)** m registrar

standhaft adj steadfast

ständig adj constant; (fest) permanent

Stand|licht nt sidelights pl. **S~ort** m position; (Firmen-) location; (Mil) garrison. **S~punkt** m point of view. **S~uhr** f grandfather clock

Stange f -,-n bar; (Holz-) pole; (Gardinen-) rail; (Hühner-) perch; (Zimt-) stick; **von der S~** 🄃 off the peg

Stängel m -s,- stalk, stem

Stangenbohne f runner bean

Stanniol nt -s tin foil. **S~papier** nt silver paper

stanzen vt stamp; punch (Loch)

Stapel m -s,- stack, pile. **S~lauf** m launch[ing]. **s~n** vt stack or pile up

Star¹ m -[e]s,-e starling

Star² m -[e]s (Med) [grauer] S~ cataract; **grüner S~** glaucoma

Star³ m -s,-s (*Theat, Sport*) star

stark *adj* strong; (*Motor*) powerful; (*Verkehr, Regen*) heavy; (*Hitze, Kälte*) severe; (*groß*) big; (*schlimm*) bad; (*dick*) thick; (*korpulent*) stout ● *adv* (*sehr*) very much

Stärk|e f -,-n strength; power; thickness; stoutness; (*Größe*) size; (*Mais-, Wäsche-*) starch. **S~emehl** nt cornflour. **s~en** strengthen; starch (*Wäsche*); **sich s~en** fortify oneself. **S~ung** f -,-en strengthening; (*Erfrischung*) refreshment

starr *adj* rigid; (*steif*) stiff

starren vi (*haben*) stare

Starr|sinn m obstinacy. **s~sinnig** *adj* obstinate

Start m -s,-s start; (*Aviat*) take-off. **S~bahn** f runway. **s~en** vi (*sein*) start; (*Aviat*) take off ● vt start; (*fig*) launch

Station /-'tsjo:n/ f -,-en station; (*Haltestelle*) stop; (*Abschnitt*) stage; (*Med*) ward; **S~ machen** break one's journey. **s~är** *adv* as an in-patient. **s~ieren** vt station

statisch *adj* static

Statist(in) m -en,-en (f -,-nen) (*Theat*) extra

Statisti|k f -,-en statistics *sg*; (*Aufstellung*) statistics *pl*. **s~sch** *adj* statistical

Stativ nt -s,-e (*Phot*) tripod

statt *prep* (+ *gen*) instead of; **an seiner s~** in his place; **an Kindes s~ annehmen** adopt ● *conj* s~ **etw zu tun** instead of doing sth. **s~dessen** *adv* instead

statt|finden vi *sep* (*haben*) take place. **s~haft** *adj* permitted

Statue /'ʃta:tuǝ/ f -,-n statue

Statur f - build, stature

Status m⁻ status. **S~symbol** nt status symbol

Statut nt -[e]s,-en statute

Stau m -[e]s,-s congestion; (*Auto*) [traffic] jam; (*Rück-*) tailback

Staub m -[e]s dust; **S~ wischen** dust; **S~ saugen** vacuum, hoover

Staubecken nt reservoir

staub|ig *adj* dusty. **s~saugen** vt/i (*haben*) vacuum, hoover. **S~sauger** m vacuum cleaner, Hoover®

Staudamm m dam

stauen vt dam up; **sich s~** accumulate; (*Autos:*) form a tailback

staunen vi (*haben*) be amazed or astonished

Stau|see m reservoir. **S~ung** f -,-en congestion; (*Auto*) [traffic] jam

Steak /ʃte:k, ste:k/ nt -s,-s steak

stechen† vt stick (**in** + *acc* in); (*verletzen*) prick; (*mit Messer*) stab; (*Insekt:*) sting; (*Mücke:*) bite ● vi (*haben*) prick; (*Insekt:*) sting; (*Mücke:*) bite; (*mit Stechuhr*) clock in/out; **in See s~** put to sea

Stech|ginster m gorse. **S~kahn** m punt. **S~palme** f holly. **S~uhr** f time clock

Steck|brief m 'wanted' poster. **S~dose** f socket. **s~en** vt put; (*mit Nadel, Reißzwecke*) pin; (*pflanzen*) plant ● vi (*haben*) be; (*fest-*) be stuck; **s~en bleiben** get stuck; **den Schlüssel s~en lassen** leave the key in the lock

Steckenpferd nt hobby-horse

Steck|er m -s,- (*Electr*) plug. **S~nadel** f pin

Steg m -[e]s,-e foot-bridge; (*Boots-*) landing-stage; (*Brillen-*) bridge

stehen† vi (*haben*) stand; (*sich befinden*) be; (*still-*) be stationary; (*Maschine, Uhr:*) have stopped; **s~ bleiben** remain standing; (*gebäude:*) be left standing; (*anhalten*) stop; (*Motor:*) stall; (*Zeit:*) stand still; **vor dem Ruin s~** face ruin; **zu jdm/etw s~** (*fig*) stand by s.o./sth

jdm [gut] s~ suit s.o.; **sich gut** s~ be on good terms; **es steht 3 zu 1** the score is 3–1. **s~d** *adj* standing; (*sich nicht bewegend*) stationary; (*Gewässer*) stagnant

Stehlampe *f* standard lamp

stehlen† *vt/i* (*haben*) steal; **sich** s~ steal, creep

Steh|platz *m* standing place. **S~vermögen** *nt* stamina, staying-power

steif *adj* stiff

Steig|bügel *m* stirrup. **S~eisen** *nt* crampon

steigen† *vi* (*sein*) climb; (*hochgehen*) rise, go up; (*Schulden, Spannung*:) mount; s~ **auf** (+ *acc*) climb on [to] (*Stuhl*); climb (*Berg, Leiter*); get on (*Pferd, Fahrrad*); s~ **in** (+ *acc*) climb into; get in (*Auto*); get on (*Bus, Zug*); s~ **aus** climb out of; get out of (*Bett, Auto*); get off (*Bus, Zug*); s~**de Preise** rising prices

steiger|n *vt* increase; **sich** s~**n** increase; (*sich verbessern*) improve. **S~ung** *f* -,-en increase; improvement; (*Gram*) comparison

steil *adj* steep. **S~küste** *f* cliffs *pl*

Stein *m* -[e]s,-e stone; (*Ziegel-*) brick; (*Spiel-*) piece. s~ **alt** *adj* ancient. **S~bock** *m* ibex; (*Astrology*) Capricorn. **S~bruch** *m* quarry. **S~garten** *m* rockery. **S~gut** *nt* earthenware. s~**ig** *adj* stony. s~**igen** *vt* stone. **S~kohle** *f* [hard] coal. **S~schlag** *m* rock fall

Stelle *f* -,-n place; (*Fleck*) spot; (*Abschnitt*) passage; (*Stellung*) job, post; (*Behörde*) authority; **auf der** S~ immediately

stellen *vt* put; (*aufrecht*) stand; set (*Wecker, Aufgabe*); ask (*Frage*); make (*Antrag, Forderung, Diagnose*); **zur Verfügung** ~ provide; **lauter/leiser** s~ turn up/down; **kalt/warm** s~ chill/keep hot; **sich** s~ [go and]

stand; give oneself up (**der Polizei** to the police); **sich tot** ~ pretend to be dead; **gut gestellt sein** be well off

Stellen|anzeige *f* job advertisement. **S~vermittlung** *f* employment agency. s~**weise** *adv* in places

Stellung *f* -,-en position; (*Arbeit*) job; **S~nehmen** make a statement (**zu** on). **S~suche** *f* job-hunting

Stellvertreter *m* deputy

Stelzen *fpl* stilts. s~ *vi* (*sein*) stalk

stemmen *vt* press; lift (*Gewicht*)

Stempel *m* -s,- stamp; (*Post-*) post-mark; (*Präge-*) die; (*Feingehalts-*) hallmark. s~**n** *vt* stamp; hallmark (*Silber*); cancel (*Marke*)

Stengel *m* -s,- * **Stängel**

Steno *f* - 🛈 shorthand

Steno|gramm *nt* -[e]s,-e shorthand text. **S~grafie** *f* - shorthand. s~**grafieren** *vt* take down in shorthand ● *vi* (*haben*) do shorthand

Steppdecke *f* quilt

Steppe *f* -,-n steppe

Stepptanz *m* tap-dance

sterben† *vi* (*sein*) die (**an** + *dat* of); **im** S~ **liegen** be dying

sterblich *adj* mortal. **S~keit** *f* - mortality

stereo *adv* in stereo. **S~anlage** *f* stereo [system]

steril *adj* sterile. **S~isieren** *vt* sterilize. **S~ität** *f* - sterility

Stern *m* -[e]s,-e star. **S~bild** *nt* constellation. **S~chen** *nt* -s,- asterisk. **S~kunde** *f* astronomy. **S~schnuppe** *f* -,-n shooting star. **S~warte** *f* -,-n observatory

stets *adv* always

Steuer[1] *nt* -s,- steering-wheel; (*Naut*) helm; **am** S~ at the wheel

Steuer[2] *f* -,-n tax

Steuer|bord nt -[e]s starboard [side]. **s~erklärung** f tax return. **s~frei** adj & adv tax-free. **S~mann** m (pl -leute) helmsman; (beim Rudern) cox. **s~n** vt steer; (Aviat) pilot; (Techn) control ● vi (haben) be at the wheel/(Naut) helm. **s~pflichtig** adj taxable. **S~rad** nt steering-wheel. **S~ruder** nt helm. **S~ung** f -,-en steering; (Techn) controls pl. **S~zahler** m -s,- taxpayer

Stewardess /ˈstjuːˈɛdɛs/ f -,-en air hostess, stewardess

Stich m -[e]s,-e prick; (Messer-) stab; (S~wunde) stab wound; (Bienen-) sting; (Mücken-) bite; (Schmerz) stabbing pain; (Näh-) stitch; (Kupfer-) engraving; (Kartenspiel) trick

stick|en vt/i (haben) embroider. **S~erei** f - embroidery

Stickstoff m nitrogen

Stiefel m -s,- boot

Stief|kind nt stepchild. **S~mutter** f stepmother. **S~mütterchen** nt -s,- pansy. **S~sohn** m stepson. **S~tochter** f stepdaughter. **S~vater** m stepfather

Stiege f -,-n stairs pl

Stiel m -[e]s,-e handle; (Blumen-, Gläser-) stem; (Blatt-) stalk

Stier m -[e]s,-e bull; (Astrology) Taurus

Stierkampf m bullfight

Stift[1] m -[e]s,-e pin; (Nagel) tack; (Blei-) pencil; (Farb-) crayon

Stift[2] nt -[e]s,-e [endowed] foundation. **s~en** vt endow; (spenden) donate; create (Unheil, Verwirrung); bring about (Frieden). **S~ung** f -,-en foundation; (Spende) donation

Stil m -[e]s,-e style

still adj quiet; (reglos, ohne Kohlensäure) still; (heimlich) secret; **der S~e Ozean** the Pacific; **im S~en**

secretly. **S~e** f - quiet; (Schweigen) silence

Stilleben[*] nt = Stillleben

stillen vt satisfy; quench (Durst); stop (Schmerzen, Blutung); breastfeed (Kind)

still|halten† vi sep (haben) keep still. **S~leben** nt still life. **s~legen** vt sep close down. **S~schweigen** nt silence. **S~stand** m standstill; **zum S~stand bringen/kommen** stop. **s~stehen**† vi sep (haben) stand still; (anhalten) stop; (Verkehr:) be at a standstill

Stimm|bänder ntpl vocal cords. **s~berechtigt** adj entitled to vote. **S~bruch** m er ist im S~bruch his voice is breaking

Stimme f -,-n voice; (Wahl-) vote

stimmen vi (haben) be right; (wählen) vote ● vt tune

Stimmung f -,-en mood; (Atmosphäre) atmosphere

Stimmzettel m ballot-paper

stink|en† vi (haben) smell/(stark) stink (nach of). **S~tier** nt skunk

Stipendium nt -s,-ien scholarship; (Beihilfe) grant

Stirn f -,-en forehead

stochern vi (haben) s~ **in** (+ dat) poke (Feuer); pick at (Essen)

Stock[1] m -[e]s,ˁe stick; (Ski-) pole; (Bienen-) hive; (Rosen-) bush; (Reb-) vine

Stock[2] m -[e]s,-e storey, floor. **S~bett** nt bunk-beds pl.

stock|en vi (haben) stop; (Verkehr:) come to a standstill; (Person:) falter. **S~ung** f -,-en hold-up

Stockwerk nt storey, floor

Stoff m -[e]s,-e substance; (Textiles) fabric, material; (Thema) subject [matter]; (Gesprächs-) topic. **S~wechsel** m metabolism

stöhnen vi (haben) groan, moan

Stola f -,-len stole

Stollen m -s,- gallery; (Kuchen) stollen

stolpern vi (sein) stumble; s~ über (+ acc) trip over

stolz adj proud (auf + acc of). S~ m -es pride

stopfen vt stuff; (stecken) put; (ausbessern) darn ● vi (haben) be constipating

Stopp m -s,-s stop. s~ int stop!

stoppelig adj stubbly

stopp|en vt stop; (Sport) time ● vi (haben) stop. S~uhr f stop-watch

Stöpsel m -s,- plug; (Flaschen-) stopper

Storch m -[e]s,⸚e stork

Store /ʃtoːɐ/ m -s,-s net curtain

stören vt disturb; disrupt (Rede); jam (Sender); (missfallen) bother ● vi (haben) be a nuisance

stornieren vt cancel

störrisch adj stubborn

Störung f -,-en disturbance; disruption; (Med) trouble; (Radio) interference; technische S~ technical fault

Stoß m -es,⸚e push, knock; (mit Ellbogen) dig; (Hörner-) butt; (mit Waffe) thrust; (Schwimm-) stroke; (Ruck) jolt; (Erd-) shock; (Stapel) stack, pile. S~dämpfer m -s,- shock absorber

stoßen† vt push, knock; (mit Füßen) kick; (mit Kopf) butt; (an-) poke, nudge; (treiben) thrust; sich s~ knock oneself; sich (dat) den Kopf s~ hit one's head ● vi (haben) push; s~ an (+ acc) knock against; (angrenzen) adjoin ● vi (sein) s~ gegen knock against; bump into (Tür); s~ auf (+ acc) bump into; (entdecken) come across; strike (Öl)

Stoß|stange f bumper. S~verkehr m rush-hour traffic. S~zahn

m tusk. S~zeit f rush-hour

stottern vt/i (haben) stutter, stammer

Str. abbr (Straße) St

Strafanstalt f prison

Strafe f -,-n punishment; (Jur & fig) penalty; (Geld-) fine; (Freiheits-) sentence. s~n vt punish

straff adj tight, taut. s~en vt tighten

Strafgesetz nt criminal law

sträf|lich adj criminal. S~ling m -s,-e prisoner

Straf|mandat nt (Auto) [parking/speeding] ticket. S~porto nt excess postage. S~raum m penalty area. S~stoß m penalty. S~tat f crime

Strahl m -[e]s,-en ray; (einer Taschenlampe) beam; (Wasser-) jet. s~en vi (haben) shine; (funkeln) sparkle; (lächeln) beam. S~enbehandlung f radiotherapy. S~ung f - radiation

Strähne f -,-n strand

stramm adj tight

Strampel|höschen /-sç-/ nt -s,- rompers pl. s~n vi (haben) (Baby:) kick

Strand m -[e]s,⸚e beach. s~en vi (sein) run aground

Strang m -[e]s,⸚e rope

Strapaze f -,-n strain. s~ieren vt be hard on; tax (Nerven)

Strass m - & -es paste

Straße f -,-n road; (in der Stadt auch) street; (Meeres-) strait. S~nbahn f tram. S~nkarte f road-map. S~nsperre f road-block

Strat|egie f -,-n strategy. s~egisch adj strategic

Strauch m -[e]s, Sträucher bush

Strauß¹ m -es, Sträuße bunch [of flowers]; (Bukett) bouquet

Strauß² m -es,-e ostrich

streben vi (haben) strive (**nach** for) ● vi (sein) head (**nach/zu** for)

Streber m -s,- pushy person

Strecke f -,-n stretch, section; (Entfernung) distance; (Rail) line; (Route) route

strecken vt stretch; (aus-) stretch out; (gerade machen) straighten; (Culin) thin down; **den Kopf aus dem Fenster s~** put one's head out of the window

Streich m -[e]s,-e prank, trick

streicheln vt stroke

streichen† vt spread; (weg-) smooth; (an-) paint; (aus-) delete; (kürzen) cut ● vi (haben) s~ **über** (+ acc) stroke

Streichholz nt match

Streich|instrument nt stringed instrument. **S~käse** m cheese spread. **S~orchester** nt string orchestra. **S~ung** f -,-en deletion; (Kürzung) cut

Streife f -,-n patrol

streifen vt brush against; (berühren) touch; (verletzen) graze; (fig) touch on (Thema)

Streifen m -s,- stripe; (Licht-) streak; (auf der Fahrbahn) line; (schmales Stück) strip

Streifenwagen m patrol car

Streik m -s,-s strike; **in den S~ treten** go on strike. **S~brecher** m strike-breaker, (pej) scab. **s~en** vi (haben) strike; 🄸 refuse; (versagen) pack up

Streit m -[e]s,-e quarrel; (Auseinandersetzung) dispute. **s~en†** vr/i (haben) [sich] s~en quarrel. **S~igkeiten** fpl quarrels. **S~kräfte** fpl armed forces

streng adj strict; (Blick, Ton) stern; (rau, nüchtern) severe; (Geschmack) sharp; **s~ genommen** strictly

speaking. **S~e** f - strictness; sternness; severity

Stress m -es,-e stress

stressig adj stressful

streuen vt spread; (ver-) scatter; sprinkle (Zucker, Salz); **die Straßen s~** grit the roads

streunen vi (sein) roam

Strich m -[e]s,-e line; (Feder-, Pinsel-) stroke; (Morse-, Gedanken-) dash. **S~kode** m bar code. **S~punkt** m semicolon

Strick m -[e]s,-e cord; (Seil) rope

strick|en vt/i (haben) knit. **S~jacke** f cardigan. **S~leiter** f rope ladder. **S~nadel** f knitting-needle. **S~waren** fpl knitwear sg. **S~zeug** nt knitting

striegeln vt groom

strittig adj contentious

Stroh nt -[e]s straw. **S~blumen** fpl everlasting flowers. **S~dach** nt thatched roof. **S~halm** m straw

Strolch m -[e]s,-e 🄸 rascal

Strom m -[e]s,-̈e river; (Menschen-, Auto-, Blut-) stream; (Tränen-) flood; (Schwall) torrent; (Electr) current, power; **gegen den S~** (fig) against the tide. **s~abwärts** adv downstream. **s~aufwärts** adv upstream

strömen vi (sein) flow; (Menschen, Blut:) stream, pour

Strom|kreis m circuit. **s~linienförmig** adj streamlined. **S~sperre** f power cut

Strömung f -,-en current

Strophe f -,-n verse

Strudel m -s,- whirlpool; (SGer Culin) strudel

Strumpf m -[e]s,-̈e stocking; (Knie-) sock. **S~band** nt (pl -bänder) suspender. **S~hose** f tights pl

Strunk m -[e]s,-̈e stalk

struppig adj shaggy

Stube f -,-n room. **s~nrein** adj house-trained

Stuck m -s stucco

Stück nt -[e]s,-e piece; (Zucker-) lump; (Seife) tablet; (Theater-) play; (Gegenstand) item; (Exemplar) specimen; **ein S~** (Entfernung) some way. **S~chen** nt -s,- [little] bit. **s~weise** adv bit by bit; (einzeln) singly

Student|(in) m -en,-en (f -,-nen) student. **s~isch** adj student

Studie /-iə/ f -,-n study

studieren vt/i (haben) study

Studio nt -s,-s studio

Studium nt -s,-ien studies pl

Stufe f -,-n step; (Treppen-) stair; (Raketen-) stage; (Niveau) level. **s~n** vt terrace; (staffeln) grade

Stuhl m -[e]s,¨e chair; (Med) stools pl. **S~gang** m bowel movement

stülpen vt put (über + acc over)

stumm adj dumb; (schweigsam) silent

Stummel m -s,- stump; (Zigaretten-) butt; (Bleistift-) stub

Stümper m -s,- bungler

stumpf adj blunt; (Winkel) obtuse; (glanzlos) dull; (fig) apathetic. **S~** m -[e]s,¨e stump

Stumpfsinn m apathy; tedium

Stunde f -,-n hour; (Sch) lesson

stunden vt jdm eine Schuld s~ give s.o. time to pay a debt

Stunden|kilometer mpl kilometres per hour. **s~lang** adj for hours. **S~lohn** m hourly rate. **S~plan** m timetable. **s~weise** adv by the hour

stündlich adj & adv hourly

stur adj pigheaded

Sturm m -[e]s,¨e gale; storm; (Mil) assault

stürmen vi (haben) (Wind:) blow

hard ● vi (sein) rush ● vt storm; (bedrängen) besiege. **S~er** m -s,- forward. **s~isch** adj stormy; (Überfahrt) rough

Sturz m -es,¨e [heavy] fall; (Preis-) sharp drop; (Pol) overthrow

stürzen vi (sein) fall [heavily]; (in die Tiefe) plunge; (Preise:) drop sharply; (Regierung:) fall; (eilen) rush ● vt throw; (umkippen) turn upside down; turn out (Speise, Kuchen); (Pol) overthrow, topple; sich s~ throw oneself (aus/in + acc out of/into)

Sturzhelm m crash-helmet

Stute f -,-n mare

Stütze f -,-n support

stützen vt support; (auf-) rest; sich s~ auf (+ acc) lean on

stutzig adj puzzled; (misstrauisch) suspicious

Stützpunkt m (Mil) base

Substantiv nt -s,-e noun

Substanz f -,-en substance

Subvention /-'tsjo:n/ f -,-en subsidy. **s~ieren** vt subsidize

Such|e f - search; **auf der S~e nach** looking for. **s~en** vt look for; (intensiv) search for; seek (Hilfe, Rat); 'Zimmer gesucht' 'room wanted' ● vi (haben) look, search (nach for). **S~er** m -s,- (Phot) viewfinder. **S~maschine** f search engine

Sucht f -,¨e addiction; (fig) mania

süchtig adj addicted. **S~e(r)** m/f addict

Süd m -[e]s south. **S~afrika** nt South Africa. **S~amerika** nt South America. **s~deutsch** adj South German

Süden m -s south; nach S~ south

Südfrucht f tropical fruit. **s~lich** adj southern; (Richtung) southerly ● adv & prep (+ gen) s~lich der Stadt south of the town. **S~pol** m

s

South Pole. **s~wärts** *adv* southwards

Sühne *f* -,-n atonement; (*Strafe*) penalty. **s~n** *vt* atone for

Sultanine *f* -,-n sultana

Sülze *f* -,-n [meat] jelly

Summe *f* -,-n sum

summen *vi* (haben) hum; (*Biene:*) buzz ● *vt* hum

summieren (sich) *vr* add up

Sumpf *m* -[e]s,ˉe marsh, swamp

Sünd|e *f* -,-n sin. **S~enbock** *m* scapegoat. **S~er(in)** *m* -s,- (*f* -,-nen) sinner. **s~igen** *vi* (haben) sin

super *inv adj* 🅃 great. **S~markt** *m* supermarket

Suppe *f* -,-n soup. **S~nlöffel** *m* soup-spoon. **S~nteller** *m* soup plate. **S~nwürfel** *m* stock cube

Surf|brett /'sœːɐ̯f-/ *nt* surfboard. **s~en** *vi* (haben) surf. **S~en** *nt* -s surfing

surren *vi* (haben) whirr

süß *adj* sweet. **S~e** *f* - sweetness. **s~en** *vt* sweeten. **S~igkeit** *f* -,-en sweet. **s~lich** *adj* sweetish; (*fig*) sugary. **S~speise** *f* sweet. **S~stoff** *m* sweetener. **S~waren** *fpl* confectionery *sg*, sweets *pl*. **S~wasser**- *prefix* freshwater

Sylvester *nt* -s = Silvester

Symbol *nt* -s,-e symbol. **S~ik** *f* - symbolism. **s~isch** *adj* symbolic

Sym|metrie *f* - symmetry. **s~metrisch** *adj* symmetrical

Sympathie *f* -,-n sympathy

sympathisch *adj* agreeable; (*Person*) likeable

Symptom *nt* -s,-e symptom. **s~atisch** *adj* symptomatic

Synagoge *f* -,-n synagogue

synchronisieren /zynkroni'ziːrən/ *vt* synchronize; dub (*Film*)

Syndikat *nt* -[e]s,-e syndicate

Syndrom *nt* -s,-e syndrome

synonym *adj* synonymous

Synthese *f* -,-n synthesis

Syrien /-jən/ *nt* -s Syria

System *nt* -s,-e system. **s~atisch** *adj* systematic

Szene *f* -,-n scene

- -

Tt

- -

Tabak *m* -s,-e tobacco

Tabelle *f* -,-n table; (*Sport*) league table

Tablett *nt* -[e]s,-s tray

Tablette *f* -,-n tablet

tabu *adj* taboo. **T~** *nt* -s,-s taboo

Tacho *m* -s,-s, **Tachometer** *m & nt* speedometer

Tadel *m* -s,- reprimand; (*Kritik*) censure; (*Sch*) black mark. **t~los** *adj* impeccable. **t~n** *vt* reprimand; censure

Tafel *f* -,-n (*Tisch, Tabelle*) table; (*Platte*) slab; (*Anschlag-, Hinweis-*) board; (*Gedenk-*) plaque; (*Schiefer-*) slate; (*Wand-*) blackboard; (*Bild-*) plate; (*Schokolade*) bar

Täfelung *f* - panelling

Tag *m* -[e]s,-e day; **unter T~e** underground; **es wird Tag** it is getting light; **guten Tag!** good morning/afternoon!

Tage|buch *nt* diary. **t~lang** *adv* for days

Tages|anbruch *m* daybreak. **T~ausflug** *m* day trip. **T~decke** *f* bedspread. **T~karte** *f* day ticket; (*Speise-*) menu of the day. **T~licht** *nt* daylight. **T~mutter** *f* child-

minder. **T~ordnung** f agenda.
T~rückfahrkarte f day return
[ticket]. **T~zeit** f time of the day.
T~zeitung f daily [news]paper

täglich adj & adv daily; **zweimal
t~** twice a day

tags adv by day; **t~ zuvor/darauf**
the day before/after

tagsüber adv during the day

tag|täglich adj daily ● adv every
single day. **T~ung** f -,-en meeting;
conference

Taill|e /'taljə/ f -,-n waist. **t~iert**
adj fitted

Takt m -[e]s,-e tact; (Mus) bar;
(Tempo) time; (Rhythmus) rhythm;
im T~ in time

Taktik f - tactics pl.

takt|los adj tactless. **T~losigkeit**
f - tactlessness. **T~stock** m baton.
t~voll adj tactful

Tal nt -[e]s,⸚er valley

Talar m -s,-e robe; (Univ) gown

Talent nt -[e]s,-e talent. **t~iert**
adj talented

Talg m -s tallow; (Culin) suet

Talsperre f dam

Tampon /tam'põ:/ m -s,-s tampon

Tank m -s,-s tank. **t~en** vt fill up
with (Benzin) ● vi (haben) fill up
with petrol; (Aviat) refuel. **T~er** m
-s,- tanker. **T~stelle** f petrol station. **T~wart** m -[e]s,-e petrol-
pump attendant

Tanne f -,-n fir [tree]. **T~nbaum**
m fir tree; (Weihnachtsbaum) Christmas tree. **T~nzapfen** m fir cone

Tante f -,-n aunt

Tantiemen /tan'tje:mən/ pl roy-
alties

Tanz m -es,⸚e dance. **t~en** vt/i
(haben) dance

Tänzer(in) m -s,- (f -,-nen)
dancer

Tapete f -,-n wallpaper

tapezieren vt paper

tapfer adj brave. **T~keit** f -
bravery

Tarif m -s,-e rate; (Verzeichnis) tariff

tarn|en vt disguise; (Mil) camou-
flage. **T~ung** f - disguise; camouflage

Tasche f -,-n bag; (Hosen-, Mantel-)
pocket. **T~nbuch** nt paperback.
T~ndieb m pickpocket. **T~ngeld**
nt pocket-money. **T~nlampe** f
torch. **T~nmesser** nt penknife.
T~ntuch nt handkerchief

Tasse f -,-n cup

Tastatur f -,-en keyboard

Tast|e f -,-n key; (Druck-) push but-
ton. **t~en** vi (haben) feel, grope
(nach for) ● vt key in (Daten); **sich
t~en** feel one's way (zu to)

Tat f -,-en action; (Helden-) deed;
(Straf-) crime; **auf frischer Tat er-
tappt** caught in the act

Täter(in) m -s,- (f -,-nen) culprit;
(Jur) offender

tätig adj active; **t~ sein** work.
T~keit f -,-en activity; (Arbeit)
work, job

Tatkraft f energy

Tatort m scene of the crime

tätowier|en vt tattoo. **T~ung** f
-,-en tattooing; (Bild) tattoo

Tatsache f fact. **T~nbericht** m
documentary

tatsächlich adj actual

Tatze f -,-n paw

Tau¹ m -[e]s dew

Tau² nt -[e]s,-e rope

taub adj deaf; (gefühllos) numb

Taube f -,-n pigeon; dove.
T~nschlag m pigeon loft

Taub|heit f - deafness. **t~stumm**
adj deaf and dumb

tauch|en vt dip, plunge; (unter-)

duck ● vi (haben/sein) dive/(ein-)plunge (**in** + acc into); (auf-) appear (**aus** out of). T~er m -s,- diver. T~eranzug m diving-suit

tauen vi (sein) melt, thaw ● impers es taut it is thawing

Tauf|becken nt font. T~e f -,-n christening, baptism. t~en vt christen, baptize. T~pate m godfather

taugen vi (haben) **etwas/nichts t~** be good/no good

tauglich adj suitable; (Mil) fit

Tausch m -[e]s,-e exchange, ⊞ swap. t~en vt exchange/(handeln) barter (**gegen** for) ● vi (handeln) swap (**mit etw** sth; **mit jdm** with s.o.)

täuschen vt deceive, fool; betray (Vertrauen); **sich t~** delude oneself; (sich irren) be mistaken ● vi (haben) be deceptive. t~d adj deceptive; (Ähnlichkeit) striking

Täuschung f -,-en deception; (Irrtum) mistake; (Illusion) delusion

tausend inv adj one/a thousand. T~ nt -s,-e thousand. T~füßler m -s,- centipede. t~ste(r, s) adj thousandth. T~stel nt -s,- thousandth

Tau|tropfen m dewdrop. T~wetter nt thaw

Taxe f -,-n charge; (Kur-) tax; (Taxi) taxi

Taxi nt -s,-s taxi, cab

Taxi|fahrer m taxi driver. T~stand m taxi rank

Teakholz /'tiːk-/ nt teak

Team /tiːm/ nt -s,-s team

Techni|k f -,-en technology; (Methode) technique. T~ker m -s,- technician. t~sch adj technical; (technologisch) technological; T~sche Hochschule Technical University

Techno|logie f -,-n technology. t~logisch adj technological

Teddybär m teddy bear

Tee m -s,-s tea. T~beutel m tea-bag. T~kanne f teapot. T~löffel m teaspoon

Teer m -s tar. t~en vt tar

Tee|sieb nt tea strainer. T~wagen m [tea] trolley

Teich m -[e]s,-e pond

Teig m -[e]s,-e pastry; (Knet-) dough; (Rühr-) mixture; (Pfannkuchen-) batter. T~rolle f rolling-pin. T~waren fpl pasta sg

Teil m -[e]s,-e part; (Bestand-) component; (Jur) party; **zum T~** partly; **zum großen/größten T~** for the most part ● m & nt -[e]s inheritance share; **ich für mein[en] T~** for my part ● nt -[e]s,-e part; (Ersatz-) spare part; (Anbau-) unit

teil|bar adj divisible. T~chen nt -s,- particle. t~en vt divide; (auf-) share out; (gemeinsam haben) share; (Pol) partition (Land); **sich** (dat) **etw t~en** share sth; **sich t~en** divide; (sich gabeln) fork; (Meinungen:) differ ● vi (haben) share

Teilhaber m -s,- (Comm) partner

Teilnahme f - participation; (innere) interest; (Mitgefühl) sympathy

teilnehm|en† vi sep (haben) t~en an (+ dat) take part in; (mitfühlen) share [in]. T~er(in) m -s,- (f -,-nen) participant; (an Wettbewerb) competitor

teil|s adv partly. T~ung f -,-en division; (Pol) partition. t~weise adj partial ● adv partially, partly. T~zahlung f part payment; (Rate) instalment. T~zeitbeschäftigung f part-time job

Teint /tɛ̃ː/ m -s,-s complexion

Telearbeit f teleworking

Telefax nt fax

Telefon nt -s,-e [tele]phone. T~anruf m, T~at nt -[e]s,-e

[tele]phone call. T~**buch** nt [tele-]phone book. t~**ieren** vi (haben) [tele]phone

telefon|isch adj [tele]phone ● adv by [tele]phone. T~**ist(in)** m -en,-en (f -,-nen) telephonist. T~**karte** f phone card. T~**nummer** f [tele]phone number. T~**zelle** f [telephone box

Telegraf m -en,-en telegraph. T~**enmast** m telegraph pole. t~**ieren** vi (haben) send a telegram. t~**isch** adj telegraphic ● adv by telegram

Telegramm nt -s,-e telegram

Teleobjektiv nt telephoto lens

Telepathie f - telepathy

Teleskop nt -s,-e telescope

Telex nt -,-[e] telex. t~**en** vt telex

Teller m -s,- plate

Tempel m -s,- temple

Temperament nt -s,-e temperament; (Lebhaftigkeit) vivacity

Temperatur f -,-en temperature

Tempo nt -s,-s speed; T~ [T~]! hurry up!

Tendenz f -,-en trend; (Neigung) tendency

Tennis nt - tennis. T~**platz** m tennis-court. T~**schläger** m tennis-racket

Teppich m -s,-e carpet. T~**boden** m fitted carpet

Termin m -s,-e date; (Arzt-) appointment. T~**kalender** m [appointments] diary

Terpentin nt -s turpentine

Terrasse f -,-n terrace

Terrier /ˈtɛrjɐ/ m -s,- terrier

Terrine f -,-n tureen

Territorium nt -s,-ien territory

Terror m -s terror. t~**isieren** vt terrorize. T~**ismus** m - terrorism. T~**ist** m -en,-en terrorist

Tesafilm® m ≈ Sellotape®

Test m -[e]s,-s & -e test

Testament nt -[e]s,-e will; Altes/Neues T~ Old/New Testament. T~**svollstrecker** m -s,- executor

testen vt test

Tetanus m - tetanus

teuer adj expensive; (lieb) dear; wie t~? how much?

Teufel m -s,- devil. T~**skreis** m vicious circle

teuflisch adj fiendish

Text m -[e]s,-e text; (Passage) passage; (Bild-) caption; (Lied-) lyrics pl. T~**er** m -s,- copywriter; (Schlager-) lyricist

Textilien /-jən/ pl textiles; (Textilwaren) textile goods

Text|nachricht f text message. T~**verarbeitungssystem** nt word processor

Theater nt -s,- theatre; (fig: Getue) fuss. T~**kasse** f box-office. T~**stück** nt play

Theke f -,-n bar; (Ladentisch) counter

Thema nt -s,-men subject

Themse f - Thames

Theolo|ge m -n,-n theologian. T~**gie** f - theology

theor|etisch adj theoretical. T~**ie** f -,-n theory

Therapeut(in) m -en,-en (f -,-nen) therapist

Therapie f -,-n therapy

Thermalbad nt thermal bath

Thermometer nt -s,- thermometer

Thermosflasche® f Thermos flask®

Thermostat m -[e]s,-e thermostat

These f -,-n thesis

Thrombose f -,-n thrombosis

t

Thron m -[e]s,-e throne. **t~en** vi
(haben) sit [in state]. **T~folge** f
succession. **T~folger** m -s,- heir to
the throne

Thunfisch m tuna

Thymian m -s thyme

ticken vi (haben) tick

tief adj deep; (t~ liegend, niedrig)
low; (t~gründig) profound; **t~er**
Teller soup-plate ● adv deep; low;
(sehr) deeply, profoundly; (schlafen)
soundly. **T~** nt -s,-s (Meteorology)
depression. **T~bau** m civil engineering. **T~e** f -,-n depth. **T~ga-
rage** f underground car park.
t~gekühlt adj [deep-]frozen

Tiefkühl|fach nt freezer compart-
ment. **T~kost** f frozen food.
T~truhe f deep-freeze

Tiefsttemperatur f minimum
temperature

Tier nt -[e]s,-e animal. **T~arzt** m,
T~ärztin f vet, veterinary surgeon.
T~garten m zoo. **T~kreis** m zodiac. **T~kunde** f zoology. **T~quä-
lerei** f cruelty to animals

Tiger m -s,- tiger

tilgen vt pay off (Schuld); (streichen) delete; (fig: auslöschen)
wipe out

Tinte f -,-n ink. **T~nfisch** m squid

Tipp (Tip) m -s,-s 🔲 tip

tipp|en vi/t (haben) (be-
rühren) touch (auf/an etw acc sth);
(🔲: Maschine schreiben) type; **t~en
auf** (+ acc) (🔲: wetten) bet on.
T~schein m pools/lottery coupon

tipptopp adj 🔲 immaculate

Tirol nt -s [the] Tyrol

Tisch m -[e]s,-e table; (Schreib-)
desk; nach **T~** after the meal.
T~decke f table-cloth. **T~gebet** nt
grace. **T~ler** m -s,- joiner; (Möbel-)
cabinet-maker. **T~rede** f after-din-
ner speech. **T~tennis** nt

table tennis

Titel m -s,- title

Toast /to:st/ m -[e]s,-e toast;
(Scheibe) piece of toast. **T~er** m
-s,- toaster

toben vi (haben) rave; (Sturm:)
rage; (Kinder:) play boisterously

Tochter f -,-⁐ daughter. **T~gesell-
schaft** f subsidiary

Tod m -es death

Todes|angst f mortal fear. **T~an-
zeige** f death announcement; (Zei-
tungs-) obituary. **T~fall** m death.
T~opfer nt fatality, casualty.
T~strafe f death penalty. **T~urteil**
nt death sentence

todkrank adj dangerously ill

tödlich adj fatal; (Gefahr) mortal

Toilette /tŏa'lεta/ f -,-n toilet.
T~npapier nt toilet paper

toler|ant adj tolerant. **T~anz** f -
tolerance. **t~ieren** vt tolerate

toll adj crazy, mad; (🔲: prima) fantastic; (schlimm) awful ● adv (sehr)
very; (schlimm) badly. **t~kühn** adj
foolhardy. **T~wut** f rabies. **t~wü-
tig** adj rabid

Tölpel m -s,- fool

Tomate f -,-n tomato. **T~nmark**
nt tomato purée

Tombola f -,-s raffle

Ton¹ m -[e]s clay

Ton² m -[e]s,-⁐e tone; (Klang)
sound; (Note) note; (Betonung)
stress; (Farb-) shade; **der gute Ton**
(fig) good form. **T~abnehmer** m
-s,- pick-up. **T~angebend** adj (fig)
leading. **T~art** f tone [of voice];
(Mus) key. **T~band** nt (pl -bänder)
tape. **T~bandgerät** nt tape recorder

tönen vi (haben) sound ● vt tint

Tonleiter f scale

Tonne f -,-n barrel, cask; (Müll-)

bin; (Maß) tonne, metric ton

Topf m -[e]s, ⸚e pot; (Koch-) pan

Topfen m -s (Aust) ≈ curd cheese

Töpferei f -,-en pottery

Topf|lappen m oven-cloth.
T~pflanze f potted plant

Tor nt -[e]s,-e gate; (Einfahrt) gateway; (Sport) goal

Torf m -s peat

torkeln vi (sein/habe) stagger

Tornister m -s,- knapsack; (Sch) satchel

Torpedo m -s,-s torpedo

Torpfosten m goal-post

Torte f -,-n gateau; (Obst-) flan

Tortur f -,-en torture

Torwart m -s,-e goalkeeper

tot adj dead; **tot geboren** stillborn;
sich tot stellen pretend to be dead

total adj total. **T~schaden** m ≈
write-off

Tote|(r) m/f dead man/woman;
(Todesopfer) fatality; **die T~n** the
dead pl

töten vt kill

Toten|gräber m -s,- grave-digger. **T~kopf** m skull. **T~schein** m
death certificate

totfahren† vt sep run over and kill

Toto nt & m -s football pools pl.
T~schein m pools coupon

tot|schießen† vt sep shoot dead.
T~schlag m (Jur) manslaughter.
t~schlagen† vt sep kill

Tötung f -,-en killing; **fahrlässige
T~** (Jur) manslaughter

Toupet /tu'pe:/ nt -s,-s toupee.
t~ieren vt back-comb

Tour /tu:ɐ/ f -,-en tour; (Ausflug)
trip; (Auto-) drive; (Rad-) ride; (Strecke) distance; (Techn) revolution;
(🄸: Weise) way

Touris|mus /tu'rɪsmʊs/ m - tourism. **T~t** m -en,-en tourist

Tournee /tʊr'ne:/ f -,-n tour

Trab m -[e]s trot

Trabant m -en,-en satellite

traben vi (haben/sein) trot

Tracht f -,-en [national] costume

Tradition /-'tsio:n/ f -,-en tradition. **t~ell** adj traditional

Trag|bahre f stretcher. **t~bar** adj
portable; (Kleidung) wearable

tragen† vt carry; (an-/ aufhaben)
wear; (fig) bear ● vi (haben) carry;
gut t~ (Baum:) produce a
good crop

Träger m -s,- porter; (Inhaber)
bearer; (eines Ordens) holder; (Bau-)
beam; (Stahl-) girder; (Achsel-)
[shoulder] strap. **T~kleid** nt pinafore dress

Trag|etasche f carrier bag.
T~flächenboot, **T~flügelboot** nt
hydrofoil

Trägheit f - sluggishness; (Faulheit)
laziness; (Phys) inertia

Trag|ik f - tragedy. **t~isch** adj
tragic

Tragödie /-jə/ f -,-n tragedy

Train|er /'trɛːnɐ/ m -s,- trainer;
(Tennis-) coach. **t~ieren** vt/i
(haben) train

Training /'trɛːnɪŋ/ nt -s training.
T~sanzug m tracksuit. **T~s-
schuhe** mpl trainers

Traktor m -s tractor

trampeln vi (haben) stamp one's
feet ● vi (sein) trample (**auf** + acc
on) ● vt trample

trampen /'trɛmpən/ vi (sein) 🄸
hitch-hike

Tranchiermesser /trã'ʃiːɐ-/ nt
carving knife

Träne f -,-n tear. **t~n** vi (haben)
water. **T~ngas** nt tear-gas

Tränke f -,-n watering place; (Trog)
drinking trough. **t~n** vt water

(*Pferd*); (*nässen*) soak (mit with)

Trans|formator *m* -s,-en transformer. **T~fusion** *f* -,-en [blood] transfusion

Transit /tran'zi:t/ *m* -s transit

Transparent *nt* -[e]s,-e banner; (*Bild*) transparency

transpirieren *vi* (*haben*) perspire

Transport *m* -[e]s,-e transport; (*Güter-*) consignment. **t~ieren** *vt* transport

Trapez *nt* -es,-e trapeze

Tratte *f* -,-n (*Comm*) draft

Traube *f* -,-n bunch of grapes; (*Beere*) grape; (*fig*) cluster. **T~nzucker** *m* glucose

trauen *vi* (*haben*) (+ *dat*) trust ● *vt* marry; **sich t~** dare (*etw zu tun* [to] do sth); venture (**in** + *acc*/**aus** into/out of)

Trauer *f* - mourning; (*Schmerz*) grief (**um** for); **T~ tragen** be [dressed] in mourning. **T~fall** *m* bereavement. **T~feier** *f* funeral service. **t~n** *vi* (*haben*) grieve; **t~n um** mourn [for]. **T~spiel** *nt* tragedy. **T~weide** *f* weeping willow

Traum *m* -[e]s,-e, Träume dream

Trauma *nt* -s,-men trauma

träumen *vt/i* (*haben*) dream

traumhaft *adj* dreamlike; (*schön*) fabulous

traurig *adj* sad; (*erbärmlich*) sorry. **T~keit** *f* - sadness

Trau|ring *m* wedding-ring. **T~schein** *m* marriage certificate. **T~ung** *f* -,-en wedding [ceremony]

Treff *nt* -s,-s (*Karten*) spades *pl*

treffen† *vt* hit; (*Blitz:*) strike; (*fig: verletzen*) hurt; (*zusammenkommen mit*) meet; take (*Maßnahme*); **sich t~en** meet (**mit jdm** s.o.); **sich gut t~en** be convenient; **es gut/ schlecht t~en** be lucky/unlucky ● *vi* (*haben*) hit the target; **t~en**

auf (+ *acc*) meet; (*fig*) meet with. **T~en** *nt* -s,- meeting. **T~er** *m* -s,- hit; (*Los*) winner. **T~punkt** *m* meeting-place

treiben† *vt* drive; (*sich befassen mit*) do; carry on (*Gewerbe*); indulge in (*Luxus*); get up to (*Unfug*); **Handel t~** trade ● *vi* (*sein*) drift; (*schwimmen*) float ● *vi* (*haben*) (*Bot*) sprout. **T~** *nt* -s activity

Treib|haus *nt* hothouse. **T~haus- effekt** *m* greenhouse effect. **T~holz** *nt* driftwood. **T~riemen** *m* transmission belt. **T~sand** *m* quicksand. **T~stoff** *m* fuel

trenn|bar *adj* separable. **t~en** *vt* separate/(*abmachen*) detach (*von* from); divide, split (*Wort*); **sich t~en** separate; (*auseinander gehen*) part; **sich t~en von** leave; (*fortgeben*) part with. **T~ung** *f* -,-en separation; (*Silben-*) division. **T~ungs- strich** *m* hyphen. **T~wand** *f* partition

trepp|ab *adv* downstairs. **t~auf** *adv* upstairs

Treppe *f* -,-n stairs *pl*; (*Außen-*) steps *pl*. **T~ngeländer** *nt* banisters *pl*

Tresor *m* -s,-e safe

Tresse *f* -,-n braid

Treteimer *m* pedal bin

treten† *vi* (*sein/haben*) step; (*versehentlich*) tread; (*ausschlagen*) kick (**nach** at); **in Verbindung t~** get in touch ● *vt* tread; (*mit Füßen*) kick

treu *adj* faithful; (*fest*) loyal. **T~e** *f* - faithfulness; loyalty; (*eheliche*) fidelity. **T~ekarte** *f* loyalty card. **T~händer** *m* -s,- trustee. **T~los** *adj* disloyal; (*untreu*) unfaithful

Tribüne *f* -,-n platform; (*Zuschauer-*) stand

Trichter *m* -s,- funnel; (*Bomben-*) crater

Trick m -s,-s trick. **T~film** m cartoon. **T~reich** adj clever

Trieb m -[e]s,-e drive, urge; (*Instinkt*) instinct; (*Bot*) shoot. **T~verbrecher** m sex offender. **T~werk** nt (*Aviat*) engine; (*Uhr-*) mechanism

triefen† vi (haben) drip; (*nass sein*) be dripping (**von/vor** + dat with)

Trigonometrie f - trigonometry

Trikot[1] /triˈkoː/ m -s (*Textiles*) jersey

Trikot[2] nt -s,-s (*Sport*) jersey; (*Fußball-*) shirt

Trimester nt -s,- term

Trimm-dich nt -s keep-fit

trimmen vt trim; tune (*Motor*); **sich t~** keep fit

trink|en† vt/i (haben) drink. **T~er(in)** m -s,- (f -,-nen) alcoholic. **T~geld** nt tip. **T~spruch** m toast

trist adj dreary

Tritt m -[e]s,-e step; (*Fuß-*) kick. **T~brett** nt step

Triumph m -s,-e triumph. **t~ieren** vi (haben) rejoice

trocken adj dry. **T~haube** f drier. **T~heit** f -,-en dryness; (*Dürre*) drought. **t~legen** vt sep change (*Baby*); drain (*Sumpf*). **T~milch** f powdered milk

trockn|en vt/i (sein) dry. **T~er** m -s,- drier

Trödel m -s 🔲 junk. **t~n** vi (haben) dawdle

Trödler m -s,- 🔲 slowcoach; (*Händler*) junk-dealer

Trog m -[e]s,ᵉe trough

Trommel f -,-n drum. **T~fell** nt ear-drum. **t~n** vi (haben) drum

Trommler m -s,- drummer

Trompete f -,-n trumpet. **T~r** m -s,- trumpeter

Tropen pl tropics

Tropf m -[e]s,-e (*Med*) drip

tröpfeln vt/i (sein/haben) drip

tropfen vt/i (sein/haben) drip. **T~** m -s,- drop; (*fallend*) drip. **t~weise** adv drop by drop

Trophäe /troˈfɛːə/ f -,-n trophy

tropisch adj tropical

Trost m -[e]s consolation, comfort

tröst|en vt console, comfort; **sich t~en** console oneself. **t~lich** adj comforting

trost|los adj desolate; (*elend*) wretched; (*reizlos*) dreary. **T~preis** m consolation prize

Trott m -s amble; (*fig*) routine

Trottel m -s,- 🔲 idiot

Trottoir /trɔˈto̯aːɐ̯/ nt -s,-s pavement

trotz prep (+ gen) despite, in spite of. **T~** m -es defiance. **t~dem** adv nevertheless; (*dennoch*). **t~ig** adj defiant; stubborn

trübe adj dull; (*Licht*) dim; (*Flüssigkeit*) cloudy; (*fig*) gloomy

Trubel m -s bustle

trüben vt dull; make cloudy (*Flüssigkeit*); (*fig*) spoil; strain (*Verhältnis*); **sich t~** (*Flüssigkeit*): become cloudy; (*Himmel*): cloud over; (*Augen*:) dim

Trüb|sal f - misery. **T~sinn** m melancholy. **t~sinnig** adj melancholy

trügen† vt deceive ● vi (haben) be deceptive

Trugschluss m fallacy

Truhe f -,-n chest

Trümmer pl rubble sg; (*T~teile*) wreckage sg, (*fig*) ruins

Trumpf m -[e]s,ᵉe trump [card]. **t~en** vi (haben) play trumps

Trunk m -[e]s drink. **T~enheit** f -

drunkenness; T~enheit am Steuer drink-driving

Trupp m -s,-s group; (Mil) squad. **T~e** f -,-n (Mil) unit; (Theat) troupe; T~en troops

Truthahn m turkey

Tschech|e m -n,-n, **T~in** f -,-nen Czech. **t~isch** adj Czech. **T~oslowakei** (die) - Czechoslovakia

tschüs, **tschüss** int bye, cheerio

Tuba f -,-ben (Mus) tuba

Tube f -,-n tube

Tuberkulose f - tuberculosis

Tuch nt -[e]s,¨er cloth; (Hals-, Kopf-) scarf; (Schulter-) shawl

tüchtig adj competent; (reichlich, beträchtlich) good; (groß) big ● adv competently; (ausreichend) well

Tück|e f -,-n malice. **t~isch** adj malicious; (gefährlich) treacherous

Tugend f -,en virtue. **t~haft** adj virtuous

Tülle f -,-n spout

Tulpe f -,-n tulip

Tümmler m -s,- porpoise

Tumor m -s,-en tumour

Tümpel m -[e]s,- pond

Tumult m -[e]s,-e commotion; (Aufruhr) riot

tun† vt do; take (Schritt, Blick); work (Wunder); (bringen) put (in + acc into); sich tun happen; **jdm etwas tun** hurt s.o.; **das tut nichts** it doesn't matter ● vi (haben) act (**als ob** as if); **er tut nur so** he's just pretending; **jdm/etw gut tun** do s.o./sth good; **zu tun haben** have things/work to do; **[es] zu tun haben mit** have to deal with. **Tun** nt -s actions pl

Tünche f -,-n whitewash; (fig) veneer. **t~n** vt whitewash

Tunesien /-jən/ nt -s Tunisia

Tunfisch m Thunfisch

Tunnel m -s,- tunnel

tupf|en vt dab ● vi (haben) t~en an/auf (+ acc) touch. **T~en** m -s,- spot. **T~er** m -s,- spot; (Med) swab

Tür f -,-en door

Turban m -s,-e turban

Turbine f -,-n turbine

Türk|e m -n,-n Turk. **T~ei** (die) - Turkey. **T~in** f -,-nen Turk

türkis inv adj turquoise

türkisch adj Turkish

Turm m -[e]s,¨e tower; (Schach) rook, castle

Türm|chen nt -s,- turret. **t~en** vt pile [up]; **sich t~en** pile up

Turmspitze f spire

turn|en vi (haben) do gymnastics. **T~en** nt -s gymnastics sg; (Sch) physical education. **T~er(in)** m -s,- (f -,-nen) gymnast. **T~halle** f gymnasium

Turnier nt -s,-e tournament; (Reit-) show

Turnschuhe mpl gym shoes; trainers

Türschwelle f doorstep, threshold

Tusche f -,-n [drawing] ink

tuscheln vt/i (haben) whisper

Tüte f -,-n bag; (Comm) packet; (Eis-) cornet; **in die T~ blasen** 𝕋 be breathalysed

TÜV m - ≈ MOT [test]

Typ m -s,-en type; (𝕋: Kerl) bloke. **T~e** f -,-n type

Typhus m - typhoid

typisch adj typical (für of)

Typus m -, Typen type

Tyrann m -en,-en tyrant. **T~ei** f - tyranny. **t~isch** adj tyrannical. **t~isieren** vt tyrannize

Uu

U-Bahn f underground

übel adj bad; (hässlich) nasty; **mir ist ü~** I feel sick; **jdm etw ü~ nehmen** hold sth against s.o. **Ü~keit** f - nausea

üben vt/i (haben) practise

über prep (+ dat/acc) over; (höher als) above; (betreffend) about; (Buch, Vortrag) on; (Scheck, Rechnung) for; (quer ü~) across; **über Köln fahren** go via Cologne; **ü~ Ostern** over Easter; **die Woche ü~** during the week; **Fehler ü~ Fehler** mistake after mistake ● adv **ü~ und ü~** all over; **jdm ü~ sein** be better/(stärker) stronger than s.o. ● adj 🔢 **ü~ sein** be left over; **etw ü~ sein** be fed up with sth

überall adv everywhere

überanstrengen vt insep overtax; strain (Augen)

überarbeiten vt insep revise; **sich ü~en** overwork

überbieten† vt insep outbid; (übertreffen) surpass

Überblick m overall view; (Abriss) summary

überblicken vt insep overlook; (abschätzen) assess

überbringen† vt insep deliver

überbrücken vt insep (fig) bridge

überbuchen vt insep overbook

überdies adv moreover

überdimensional adj oversized

Überdosis f overdose

überdrüssig adj **ü~ sein/werden** be/grow tired (gen of)

übereignen vt insep transfer

übereilt adj over-hasty

übereinander adv one on top of/above the other; (sprechen) about each other

überein|kommen† vi sep (sein) agree. **Ü~kunft** f - agreement. **ü~stimmen** vi sep (haben) agree; (Zahlen:) tally; (Ansichten:) coincide; (Farben:) match. **Ü~stimmung** f agreement

überfahren† vt insep run over

Überfahrt f crossing

Überfall m attack; (Bank-) raid

überfallen† vt insep attack; raid (Bank); (bestürmen) bombard (mit with)

Überfluss m abundance; (Wohlstand) affluence

überflüssig adj superfluous

überfordern vt insep overtax

überführ|en vt insep transfer; (Jur) convict (gen of). **Ü~ung** f transfer; (Straße) flyover; (Fußgänger-) foot-bridge

überfüllt adj overcrowded

Übergabe f handing over; transfer

Übergang m crossing; (Wechsel) transition

übergeben† vt insep hand over; (übereignen) transfer; **sich ü~** be sick

übergehen† vt insep (fig) pass over; (nicht beachten) ignore; (auslassen) leave out

Übergewicht nt excess weight; (fig) predominance; **Ü~ haben** be overweight

über|greifen vi sep (haben) spread (**auf** + acc to). **Ü~griff** m infringement

über|groß adj outsize; (übertrieben) exaggerated. **Ü~größe** f outsize

überhand adv **ü~ nehmen**

increase alarmingly

überhäufen vt insep inundate (mit with)

überhaupt adv (im Allgemeinen) altogether; (eigentlich) anyway; (überdies) besides; ü~ nicht/nichts not/nothing at all

überheblich adj arrogant. Ü~keit f - arrogance

überhol|en vt insep overtake; (reparieren) overhaul. ü~t adj outdated. Ü~ung f -,-en overhaul. Ü~verbot nt 'Ü~verbot' 'no overtaking'

überhören vt insep fail to hear; (nicht beachten) ignore

überirdisch adj supernatural

überkochen vi sep (sein) boil over

überlassen† vt insep jdm etw ü~ leave sth to s.o.; (geben) let s.o. have sth; sich (dat) selbst ü~ sein be left to one's own devices

Überlauf m overflow

überlaufen† vi sep (sein) overflow; (Mil, Pol) defect

Überläufer m defector

überleben vt/i insep (haben) survive. Ü~de(r) m/f survivor

überlegen¹ vt sep put over

überlegen² v insep ● vt [sich dat] ü~ think over, consider; es sich (dat) anders ü~ change one's mind ● vi (haben) think, reflect

überlegen³ adj superior. Ü~heit f - superiority

Überlegung f -,-en reflection

überliefer|n vt insep hand down. Ü~ung f tradition

überlisten vt insep outwit

Übermacht f superiority

übermäßig adj excessive

Übermensch m superman. ü~lich adj superhuman

übermitteln vt insep convey; (senden) transmit

übermorgen adv the day after tomorrow

übermüdet adj overtired

Über|mut m high spirits pl. ü~mütig adj high-spirited

übernächst|e(r,s) adj next but one; ü~es Jahr the year after next

übernacht|en vi insep (haben) stay overnight. Ü~ung f -,-en overnight stay; Ü~ung und Frühstück bed and breakfast

Übernahme f - taking over; (Comm) take-over

übernatürlich adj supernatural

übernehmen† vt insep take over; (annehmen) accept; sich ü~ overdo things; (finanziell) overreach oneself

überqueren vt insep cross

überrasch|en vt insep surprise. ü~end adj surprising; (unerwartet) unexpected. Ü~ung f -,-en surprise

überreden vt insep persuade

Überreste mpl remains

Überschall- prefix supersonic

überschätzen vt insep overestimate

Überschlag m rough estimate; (Sport) somersault

überschlagen¹† vt sep cross (Beine)

überschlagen²† vt insep estimate roughly; (auslassen) skip; sich ü~ somersault; (Ereignisse:) happen fast ● adj tepid

überschneiden† (sich) vr insep intersect, cross; (zusammenfallen) overlap

überschreiten† vt insep cross; (fig) exceed

Überschrift f heading; (Zeitungs-)

u

Über|schuss m surplus.
ü~schüssig adj surplus

überschwemm|en vt insep
flood; (fig) inundate. Ü~ung f
-,-en flood

Übersee in/nach Ü~ overseas;
aus/von Ü~ from overseas.
Ü~dampfer m ocean liner. ü~isch
adj overseas

übersehen† vt insep look out
over; (abschätzen) assess; (nicht
sehen) overlook, miss; (ignorieren)
ignore

übersenden† vt insep send

übersetzen¹ vi sep (haben/sein)
cross [over]

übersetz|en² vt insep translate.
Ü~er(in) m -s,- (f -,-nen) transla-
tor. Ü~ung f -,-en translation

Übersicht f overall view; (Abriss)
summary; (Tabelle) table. ü~lich
adj clear

Übersiedlung f move

überspielen vt insep (fig) cover
up; auf Band ü~ tape

überstehen† vt insep come
through; get over (Krankheit); (überleben) survive

übersteigen† vt insep climb
[over]; (fig) exceed

überstimmen vt insep outvote

Überstunden fpl overtime sg;
Ü~ machen work overtime

überstürz|en vt insep rush; sich
ü~en (Ereignisse:) happen fast. Ü~t
adj hasty

übertrag|bar adj transferable;
(Med) infectious. ü~en† vt insep
transfer; (übergeben) assign (dat to);
(Techn, Med) transmit; (Radio, TV)
broadcast; (übersetzen) translate;
(anwenden) apply (auf + acc to)
● adj transferred, figurative.
Ü~ung f -,-en transfer; transmis-

sion; broadcast; translation, application

übertreffen† vt insep surpass;
(übersteigen) exceed; sich selbst ü~
excel oneself

übertreib|en† vt insep exagger-
ate; (zu weit treiben) overdo.
Ü~ung f -,-en exaggeration

übertreten¹† vi sep (sein) step
over the line; (Pol) go over/(Relig)
convert (zu to)

übertret|en²† vt insep infringe;
break (Gesetz). Ü~ung f -,-en infringement; breach

übertrieben adj exaggerated

übervölkert adj overpopulated

überwachen vt insep supervise;
(kontrollieren) monitor; (bespitzeln)
keep under surveillance

überwältigen vt insep over-
power; (fig) overwhelm

überweis|en† vt insep transfer;
refer (Patienten). Ü~ung f transfer;
(ärztliche) referral

überwiegen† v insep ●vi (haben)
predominate. ●vt outweigh

überwind|en† vt insep overcome;
sich ü~en force oneself. Ü~ung f
effort

Über|zahl f majority. ü~zählig
adj spare

überzeug|en vt insep convince;
sich [selbst] ü~en satisfy oneself.
ü~end adj convincing. Ü~ung f
-,-en conviction

überziehen¹† vt sep put on

überziehen²† vt insep cover;
overdraw (Konto)

Überzug m cover; (Schicht)
coating

üblich adj usual; (gebräuchlich) customary

U-Boot nt submarine

übrig adj remaining; (andere) other;

u

alles Ü~e [all] the rest; **im Ü~en** besides; (*ansonsten*) apart from that; **ü~ sein** *od* **bleiben** be left [over]; **etw ü~ lassen** leave sth [over]; **uns blieb nichts anderes ü~** we had no choice

Übung f -,-en exercise; (*Üben*) practice; **außer** *od* **aus der Ü~** out of practice

Ufer nt -s,- shore; (*Fluss-*) bank

Uhr f -,-en clock; (*Armband-*) watch; (*Zähler*) meter; **um ein U~** at one o'clock; **wie viel U~ ist es?** what's the time? **U~macher** m -s,- watch and clockmaker. **U~werk** nt clock/watch mechanism. **U~zeiger** m [clock-/watch-]hand. **U~zeit** f time

Uhu m -s,-s eagle owl

UKW abbr (*Ultrakurzwelle*) VHF

ulkig adj funny; (*seltsam*) odd

Ulme f -,-n elm

Ultimatum nt -s,-ten ultimatum

Ultra|kurzwelle f very high frequency. **Ü~leichtflugzeug** nt microlight [aircraft]

Ultraschall m ultrasound

ultraviolett adj ultraviolet

um prep (+ acc) [a]round; (*Uhrzeit*) at; (*bitten*) for; (*streiten*) over; (*sich sorgen*) about; (*betrügen*) out of; (*bei Angabe einer Differenz*) by; **um [... herum]** around, [round] about; **Tag um Tag** day after day; **um seinetwillen** for his sake ● adv (*ungefähr*) around, about; (*vorbei*) over; (*Zeit*) be up ● conj **um zu** to; (*Absicht*) [in order] to; **zu müde, um zu ...** too tired to ...

umarm|en vt insep embrace, hug. **U~ung** f -,-en embrace, hug

Umbau m rebuilding; conversion (**zu** into). **u~en** vt sep rebuild; convert (**zu** into)

Umbildung f reorganization; (*Pol*) reshuffle

umbinden† vt sep put on

umblättern v sep ● vt turn [over] ● vi (*haben*) turn the page

umbringen† vt sep kill; **sich u~** kill oneself

umbuchen v sep ● vt change; (*Comm*) transfer ● vi (*haben*) change one's booking

umdrehen v sep ● vt turn round/(*wenden*) over; turn (*Schlüssel*); (*umkrempeln*) turn inside out; **sich u~** turn round; (*im Liegen*) turn over ● vi (*haben/sein*) turn back

Umdrehung f turn; (*Motor-*) revolution

umeinander adv around each other; **sich u~ sorgen** worry about each other

umfahren†[1] vt sep run over

umfahren†[2] vt insep go round; bypass (*Ort*)

umfallen† vi sep (*sein*) fall over; (*Person:*) fall down

Umfang m girth; (*Geometry*) circumference; (*Größe*) size

umfangreich adj extensive; (*dick*) big

umfassen vt insep consist of, comprise; (*umgeben*) surround. **u~d** adj comprehensive

Umfrage f survey, poll

umfüllen vt sep transfer

umfunktionieren vt sep convert

Umgang m [social] contact; (*Umgehen*) dealing (**mit** with)

Umgangssprache f colloquial language

umgeb|en† vt/i insep (*haben*) surround ● adj **u~en von** surrounded by. **U~ung** f -,-en surroundings pl

umgehen† vt insep avoid; (*nicht beachten*) evade; (*Straße:*) bypass

umgehend adj immediate

unbegründet *adj* unfounded

Unbehagen *nt* unease; *(körperlich)* discomfort

unbekannt *adj* unknown; *(nicht vertraut)* unfamiliar. **U~e(r)** *m/f* stranger

unbekümmert *adj* unconcerned; *(unbeschwert)* carefree

unbeliebt *adj* unpopular. **U~heit** *f* unpopularity

unbemannt *adj* unmanned

unbemerkt *adj & adv* unnoticed

unbenutzt *adj* unused

unbequem *adj* uncomfortable; *(lästig)* awkward

unberechenbar *adj* unpredictable

unberechtigt *adj* unjustified; *(unbefugt)* unauthorized

unberührt *adj* untouched; *(fig)* virgin; *(Landschaft)* unspoilt

unbescheiden *adj* presumptuous

unbeschrankt *adj* unguarded

unbeschränkt *adj* unlimited
● *adv* without limit

unbeschwert *adj* carefree

unbesiegt *adj* undefeated

unbespielt *adj* blank

unbeständig *adj* inconsistent; *(Wetter)* unsettled

unbestechlich *adj* incorruptible

unbestimmt *adj* indefinite; *(Alter)* indeterminate; *(ungewiss)* uncertain; *(unklar)* vague

unbestritten *adj* undisputed
● *adv* indisputably

unbeteiligt *adj* indifferent; **u~ an** (+ *dat*) not involved in

unbetont *adj* unstressed

unbewacht *adj* unguarded

unbewaffnet *adj* unarmed

unbeweglich *adj & adv* motionless, still

unbewohnt *adj* uninhabited

unbewusst *adj* unconscious

unbezahlbar *adj* priceless

unbrauchbar *adj* useless

und *conj* and; **und so weiter** and so on; **nach und nach** bit by bit

Undank *m* ingratitude. **u~bar** *adj* *(ungrateful)* thankless. **U~barkeit** *f* ingratitude

undeutlich *adj* indistinct; vague

undicht *adj* leaking; **u~e Stelle** leak

Unding *nt* absurdity

undiplomatisch *adj* undiplomatic

unduldsam *adj* intolerant

undurch|dringlich *adj* impenetrable; *(Miene)* inscrutable. **u~führbar** *adj* impracticable

undurch|lässig *adj* impermeable. **u~sichtig** *adj* opaque; *(fig)* doubtful

uneben *adj* uneven. **U~heit** *f* -,-en unevenness; *(Buckel)* bump

unecht *adj* false; **u~er Schmuck** imitation jewellery

unehelich *adj* illegitimate

uneinig *adj* *(fig)* divided; [**sich** *(dat)*] **u~ sein** disagree

uneins *adj* ~ **sein** be at odds

unempfindlich *adj* insensitive *(gegen* to); *(widerstandsfähig)* tough; *(Med)* immune

unendlich *adj* infinite; *(endlos)* endless. **U~keit** *f* - infinity

unentbehrlich *adj* indispensable

unentgeltlich *adj* free, *(Arbeit)* unpaid ● *adv* free of charge

unentschieden *adj* undecided; *(Sport)* drawn; **u~ spielen** draw. **U~** *nt* -s,- draw

unentschlossen *adj* indecisive; *(unentschieden)* undecided

unentwegt *adj* persistent; *(unauf-*

u

hörlich) incessant

unerfahren *adj* inexperienced.
U~heit *f* - inexperience

unerfreulich *adj* unpleasant

unerhört *adj* enormous; *(empörend)* outrageous

unerklärlich *adj* inexplicable

unerlässlich *adj* essential

unerlaubt *adj* unauthorized ● *adv* without permission

unerschwinglich *adj* prohibitive

unersetzlich *adj* irreplaceable; *(Verlust)* irreparable

unerträglich *adj* unbearable

unerwartet *adj* unexpected

unerwünscht *adj* unwanted; *(Besuch)* unwelcome

unfähig *adj* incompetent; **u~,** etw zu tun incapable of doing sth; *(nicht in der Lage)* unable to do sth. **U~keit** *f* incompetence; inability *(zu* to)

unfair *adj* unfair

Unfall *m* accident. **U~flucht** *f* failure to stop after an accident. **U~station** *f* casualty department

unfassbar *adj* incomprehensible

Unfehlbarkeit *f* - infallibility

unfolgsam *adj* disobedient

unförmig *adj* shapeless

unfreiwillig *adj* involuntary; *(unbeabsichtigt)* unintentional

unfreundlich *adj* unfriendly; *(unangenehm)* unpleasant. **U~keit** *f* unfriendliness; unpleasantness

Unfriede[n] *m* discord

unfruchtbar *adj* infertile; *(fig)* unproductive. **U~keit** *f* infertility

Unfug *m* -s mischief; *(Unsinn)* nonsense

Ungar|(in) *m* -n,-n *(f* -,-nen) Hungarian. **u~isch** *adj* Hungarian. **U~n** *nt* -s Hungary

ungeachtet *prep* (+ *gen*) in spite of; **dessen u~** notwithstanding [this]. **ungebraucht** *adj* unused.

ungedeckt *adj* uncovered; *(Sport)* unmarked; *(Tisch)* unlaid

Ungeduld *f* impatience. **u~ig** *adj* impatient

ungeeignet *adj* unsuitable

ungefähr *adj* approximate, rough

ungefährlich *adj* harmless

ungeheuer *adj* enormous. **U~** *nt* -s,- monster

ungehorsam *adj* disobedient. **U~** *m* disobedience

ungeklärt *adj* unsolved; *(Frage)* unsettled; *(Ursache)* unknown

ungelegen *adj* inconvenient

ungelernt *adj* unskilled

ungemütlich *adj* uncomfortable; *(unangenehm)* unpleasant

ungenau *adj* inaccurate; vague. **U~igkeit** *f* -,-en inaccuracy

ungeniert /ˈʊnʒeniːɡt/ *adj* uninhibited ● *adv* openly

ungenießbar *adj* inedible; *(Getränk)* undrinkable. **ungenügend** *adj* inadequate; *(Sch)* unsatisfactory.

ungepflegt *adj* neglected; *(Person)* unkempt. **ungerade** *adj* *(Zahl)* odd

ungerecht *adj* unjust. **U~igkeit** *f* -,-en injustice

ungern *adv* reluctantly

ungesalzen *adj* unsalted

Ungeschick|lichkeit *f* clumsiness. **u~t** *adj* clumsy

ungeschminkt *adj* without make-up; *(Wahrheit)* unvarnished.

ungesetzlich *adj* illegal. **ungestört** *adj* undisturbed. **ungesund** *adj* unhealthy. **ungesüßt** *adj* unsweetened. **ungetrübt** *adj* perfect

Ungetüm *nt* -s,-e monster

ungewiss *adj* uncertain; **im Ungewissen sein/lassen** be/leave in the dark. **U~heit** f uncertainty

ungewöhnlich adj unusual. **ungewohnt** adj unaccustomed; (nicht vertraut) unfamiliar

Ungeziefer nt -s vermin

ungezogen adj naughty

ungezwungen adj informal; (natürlich) natural

ungläubig adj incredulous

unglaublich adj incredible, unbelievable

ungleich adj unequal; (verschieden) different. **U~heit** f - inequality. **u~mäßig** adj uneven

Unglück nt -s,-e misfortune; (Pech) bad luck; (Missgeschick) mishap; (Unfall) accident. **u~lich** adj unhappy; (ungünstig) unfortunate. **u~licherweise** adv unfortunately

ungültig adj invalid; (Jur) void

ungünstig adj unfavourable; (unpassend) inconvenient

Unheil nt -s disaster; **U~ anrichten** cause havoc

unheilbar adj incurable

unheimlich adj eerie; (gruselig) creepy; (🄘: groß) terrific ● adv eerily; (🄘: sehr) terribly

unhöflich adj rude. **U~keit** f rudeness

unhygienisch adj unhygienic

Uni f -,-s 🄘 university

uni /y'ni:/ inv adj plain

Uniform f -,-en uniform

uninteressant adj uninteresting

Union f -,-en union

universell adj universal

Universität f -,-en university

Universum nt -s universe

unkenntlich adj unrecognizable

unklar adj unclear; (ungewiss) uncertain; (vage) vague; **im U~en (u~en) sein** be in the dark

unkompliziert adj un-

complicated

Unkosten pl expenses

Unkraut nt weed; (coll) weeds pl; **U~ jäten** weed. **U~vertilgungsmittel** nt weed-killer

unlängst adv recently

unlauter adj dishonest; (unfair) unfair

unleserlich adj illegible

unleugbar adj undeniable

unlogisch adj illogical

Unmenge f enormous amount/(Anzahl) number

Unmensch m 🄘 brute. **u~lich** adj inhuman

unmerklich adj imperceptible

unmittelbar adj immediate; (direkt) direct

unmöbliert adj unfurnished

unmodern adj old-fashioned

unmöglich adj impossible. **U~keit** f - impossibility

Unmoral f immorality. **u~isch** adj immoral

unmündig adj under-age

Unmut m displeasure

unnatürlich adj unnatural

unnormal adj abnormal

unnötig adj unnecessary

unordentlich adj untidy; (nachlässig) sloppy. **U~nung** f disorder; (Durcheinander) muddle

unorthodox adj unorthodox ● adv in an unorthodox manner

unparteiisch adj impartial

unpassend adj inappropriate; (Moment) inopportune

unpersönlich adj impersonal

unpraktisch adj impractical

unpünktlich adj unpunctual ● adv late

unrealistisch adj unrealistic

unrecht adj wrong ● n jdm u~

tun do s.o. an injustice. **U~** *nt* wrong; **zu U~** wrongly; **U~ haben** be wrong; **jdm U~ geben** disagree with s.o. **u~mäßig** *adj* unlawful

unregelmäßig *adj* irregular

unreif *adj* unripe; (*fig*) immature

unrein *adj* impure; (*Luft*) polluted; (*Haut*) bad; **ins U~e schreiben** make a rough draft of

unrentabel *adj* unprofitable

Unruh|e *f -,-n* restlessness; (*Erregung*) agitation; (*Besorgnis*) anxiety; **U~en** (*Pol*) unrest *sg.* **u~ig** *adj* restless; (*laut*) noisy; (*besorgt*) anxious

uns *pron* (*acc/dat of* **wir**) us; (*reflexive*) ourselves; (*einander*) each other

unsauber *adj* dirty; (*nachlässig*) sloppy

unschädlich *adj* harmless

unscharf *adj* blurred

unschätzbar *adj* inestimable

unscheinbar *adj* inconspicuous

unschlagbar *adj* unbeatable

unschlüssig *adj* undecided

Unschuld *f -* innocence; (*Jungfräulichkeit*) virginity. **u~ig** *adj* innocent

unselbständig,
unselbständig *adj* dependent
● *adv* **u~ denken** not think for oneself

unser *poss pron* our. **u~e(r,s)** *poss pron* ours. **u~erseits** *adv* for our part. **u~twegen** *adv* for our sake; (*wegen uns*) because of us, on our account

unsicher *adj* unsafe; (*ungewiss*) uncertain; (*nicht zuverlässig*) unreliable; (*Schritte, Hand*) unsteady; (*Person*) insecure ● *adv* unsteadily. **U~heit** *f* uncertainty; unreliability; insecurity

unsichtbar *adj* invisible

Unsinn *m* nonsense. **u~ig** *adj* nonsensical, absurd

Unsitt|e *f* bad habit. **u~lich** *adj* indecent

unsportlich *adj* not sporty; (*unfair*) unsporting

uns|re(r,s) *poss pron* = **unsere(r,s)**. **u~rige** *poss pron* **der/die/das u~rige** ours

unsterblich *adj* immortal. **U~keit** *f* immortality

Unsumme *f* vast sum

unsympathisch *adj* unpleasant; **er ist mir u~** I don't like him

untätig *adj* idle

untauglich *adj* unsuitable; (*Mil*) unfit

unten *adv* at the bottom; (*auf der Unterseite*) underneath; (*eine Treppe tiefer*) downstairs; (*im Text*) below; **hier/da u~** down here/there; **nach u~** down[wards]; (*die Treppe hinunter*) downstairs; **siehe u~** see below

unter *prep* (+ *dat/acc*) under; (*niedriger als*) below; (*inmitten, zwischen*) among; **u~ anderem** among other things; **u~ der Woche** during the week; **u~ sich** by themselves

Unter|arm *m* forearm. **U~bewusstsein** *nt* subconscious

unterbieten† *vt insep* undercut; beat (*Rekord*)

unterbinden† *vt insep* stop

unterbrech|en† *vt insep* interrupt; break (*Reise*). **U~ung** *f -,-en* interruption, break

unterbringen† *vt sep* put; (*beherbergen*) put up

unterdessen *adv* in the meantime

Unterdrückung *f -* suppression; oppression

untere(r,s) *adj* lower

untereinander adv one below the other; (miteinander) among ourselves/yourselves/themselves

unterernähr|t adj undernourished. **U∼ung** f malnutrition

Unterführung f underpass; (Fußgänger-) subway

Untergang m (der Sonne) setting; (Naut) sinking; (Zugrundegehen) disappearance; (der Welt) end

Untergebene(r) m/f subordinate

untergehen† vi sep (sein) (Astronomy) set; (versinken) go under; (Schiff:) go down, sink; (zugrunde gehen) disappear; (Welt:) come to an end

Untergeschoss nt basement

Untergrund m foundation; (Hintergrund) background. **U∼bahn** f underground [railway]

unterhaken vt sep jdn u∼ take s.o.'s arm; **untergehakt** arm in arm

unterhalb adv & prep (+ gen) below

Unterhalt m maintenance

unterhalt|en† vt insep maintain; (ernähren) support; (betreiben) run; (erheitern) entertain; **sich u∼en** talk; (sich vergnügen) enjoy oneself. **U∼ung** f -,-en maintenance; (Gespräch) conversation; (Zeitvertreib) entertainment

Unter|haus nt (Pol) lower house; (in UK) House of Commons. **U∼hemd** nt vest. **U∼hose** f underpants pl. **u∼irdisch** adj & adv underground

Unterkiefer m lower jaw

unterkommen† vi sep (sein) find accommodation; (eine Stellung finden) get a job

Unterkunft f -,-künfte accommodation

Unterlage f pad; **U∼n** papers

Unterlass m ohne U∼ incessantly

Unterlassung f -,-en omission

unterlegen adj inferior; (Sport) losing; **zahlenmäßig u∼** out-numbered (dat by). **U∼e(r)** m/f loser

Unterleib m abdomen

unterliegen† vi insep (sein) lose (dat to); (unterworfen sein) be subject (dat to)

Unterlippe f lower lip

Untermiete f zur U∼ wohnen be a lodger. **U∼r(in)** m(f) lodger

unternehm|en† vt insep undertake; take (Schritte); **etw/nichts u∼en** do sth/nothing. **U∼en** nt -s,- undertaking, enterprise; (Betrieb) concern. **U∼er** m -s,- employer; (Bau-) contractor; (Industrieller) industrialist. **u∼ungslustig** adj enterprising

Unteroffizier m non-commissioned officer

unterordnen vt sep subordinate

Unterredung f -,-en talk

Unterricht m -[e]s teaching; (Privat-) tuition; (U∼sstunden) lessons pl

unterrichten vt/i insep (haben) teach; (informieren) inform; **sich u∼** inform oneself

Unterrock m slip

untersagen vt insep forbid

Untersatz m mat; (mit Füßen) stand; (Gläser-) coaster

unterscheid|en† vt/i insep (haben) distinguish; (auseinander halten) tell apart; **sich u∼en** differ. **U∼ung** f -,-en distinction

Unterschied m -[e]s,-e difference; (Unterscheidung) distinction; **im U∼ zu ihm** unlike him. **u∼lich** adj different; (wechselnd) varying

unterschlag|en† vt insep embezzle; (verheimlichen) suppress. **U∼ung** f -,-en embezzlement;

suppression

Unterschlupf *m* -[e]s shelter; (*Versteck*) hiding-place

unterschreiben† *vt/i insep* (*haben*) sign

Unter|schrift *f* signature; (*Bild-*) caption. **U~seeboot** *nt* submarine

Unterstand *m* shelter

unterste(r,s) *adj* lowest, bottom

unterstehen† *v insep* ● *vi* (*haben*) be answerable (*dat* to); (*unterliegen*) be subject (*dat* to)

unterstellen¹ *vt sep* put underneath; (*abstellen*) store; **sich u~** shelter

unterstellen² *vt insep* place under the control (*dat* of); (*annehmen*) assume; (*fälschlich zuschreiben*) impute (*dat* to)

unterstreichen† *vt insep* underline

unterstütz|en *vt insep* support; (*helfen*) aid. **U~ung** *f* -,-en support; (*finanziell*) aid; (*regelmäßiger Betrag*) allowance; (*Arbeitslosen-*) benefit

untersuch|en *vt insep* examine; (*Jur*) investigate; (*prüfen*) test; (*überprüfen*) check; (*durchsuchen*) search. **U~ung** *f* -,-en examination; investigation; test; check; search. **U~ungshaft** *f* detention on remand

Untertan *m* -s & -en,-en subject

Untertasse *f* saucer

Unterteil *nt* bottom (part)

Untertitel *m* subtitle

untervermieten *vt/i insep* (*haben*) sublet

Unterwäsche *f* underwear

unterwegs *adv* on the way; (*außer Haus*) out; (*unterwegs*) away

Unterwelt *f* underworld

unterzeichnen *vt insep* sign

unterziehen† *vt insep* **etw einer**

Untersuchung/Überprüfung u~ examine/ check sth; **sich einer Operation/Prüfung u~** have an operation/take a test

Untier *nt* monster

untragbar *adj* intolerable

untrennbar *adj* inseparable

untreu *adj* disloyal; (*in der Ehe*) unfaithful. **U~e** *f* disloyalty; infidelity

untröstlich *adj* inconsolable

unübersehbar *adj* obvious; (*groß*) immense

ununterbrochen *adj* incessant

unveränderlich *adj* invariable; (*gleichbleibend*) unchanging

unverändert *adj* unchanged

unverantwortlich *adj* irresponsible

unverbesserlich *adj* incorrigible

unverbindlich *adj* non-committal; (*Comm*) not binding ● *adv* without obligation

unverdaulich *adj* indigestible

unver|gesslich *adj* unforgettable. **u~gleichlich** *adj* incomparable. **u~heiratet** *adj* unmarried. **u~käuflich** *adj* not for sale; (*Muster*) free

unverkennbar *adj* unmistakable

unverletzt *adj* unhurt

unvermeidlich *adj* inevitable

unver|mindert *adj* & *adv* undiminished. **u~mutet** *adj* unexpected

Unvernunft *f* folly. **u~nünftig** *adj* foolish

unverschämt *adj* insolent; (🗉: *ungeheuer*) outrageous. **U~heit** *f* -,-en insolence

unver|sehens *adv* suddenly. **u~sehrt** *adj* unhurt; (*unbeschädigt*) intact

unverständlich *adj* incomprehensible; (*undeutlich*) indistinct

unverträglich adj incompatible; (Person) quarrelsome; (unbekömmlich) indigestible

unver|wundbar adj invulnerable. **u~wüstlich** adj indestructible; (Person, Humor) irrepressible; (Gesundheit) robust. **u~zeihlich** adj unforgivable

unverzüglich adj immediate

unvollendet adj unfinished

unvollkommen adj imperfect; (unvollständig) incomplete

unvollständig adj incomplete

unvor|bereitet adj unprepared. **u~hergesehen** adj unforeseen

unvorsichtig adj careless

unvorstellbar adj unimaginable

unvorteilhaft adj unfavourable; (nicht hübsch) unattractive

unwahr adj untrue. **U~heit** f -,-en untruth. **u~scheinlich** adj unlikely; (unglaublich) improbable; (**E**: groß) incredible

unweit adv & prep (+ gen) not far

unwesentlich adj unimportant

Unwetter nt -s,- storm

unwichtig adj unimportant

unwider|legbar adj irrefutable. **u~stehlich** adj irresistible

Unwille|e m displeasure. **u~ig** adj angry; (widerwillig) reluctant

unwirklich adj unreal

unwirksam adj ineffective

unwirtschaftlich adj uneconomic

unwissen|d adj ignorant. **U~heit** f - ignorance

unwohl adj unwell; (unbehaglich) uneasy

unwürdig adj unworthy (gen of)

Unzahl f vast number. **unzählig** adj innumerable, countless

unzerbrechlich adj unbreakable

unzerstörbar adj indestructible

unzertrennlich adj inseparable

Unzucht f sexual offence; **gewerbsmäßige U~** prostitution

unzüchtig adj indecent; (Schriften) obscene

unzufrieden adj dissatisfied; (innerlich) discontented. **U~heit** f dissatisfaction

unzulässig adj inadmissible

unzurechnungsfähig adj insane. **U~keit** f insanity

unzusammenhängend adj incoherent

unzutreffend adj inapplicable; (falsch) incorrect

unzuverlässig adj unreliable

unzweifelhaft adj undoubted

üppig adj luxuriant; (überreichlich) lavish

uralt adj ancient

Uran nt -s uranium

Uraufführung f first performance

Urenkel m great-grandson; (pl) great-grandchildren

Urgroß|mutter f great-grandmother. **U~vater** m great-grandfather

Urheber m -s,- originator; (Verfasser) author. **U~recht** nt copyright

Urin m -s urine

Urkunde f -,-n certificate; (Dokument) document

Urlaub m -s holiday; (Mil, Admin) leave; **auf U~** on holiday/leave; **U~ haben** be on holiday/leave. **U~er(in)** m -s,- (f -,-nen) holidaymaker. **U~sort** m holiday resort

Urne f -,-n urn; (Wahl-) ballot-box

Ursache f cause; (Grund) reason; **keine U~!** don't mention it!

Ursprung m origin

ursprünglich adj original; (anfänglich) initial; (natürlich) natural

Urteil nt -s,-e judgement; (Meinung) opinion; (U~sspruch) verdict; (Strafe) sentence. **u~en** vi (haben) judge

Urwald m primeval forest; (tropischer) jungle

Urzeit f primeval times pl

USA pl USA sg

usw. abbr (und so weiter) etc.

utopisch adj Utopian

Vv

Vakuum /'va:kuɔm/ nt -s vacuum. **v~verpackt** adj vacuum-packed

Vanille /va'nɪljə/ f - vanilla

variieren vt/i (haben) vary

Vase /'va:zə/ f -,-n vase

Vater m -s,⁼ father. **V~land** nt fatherland

väterlich adj paternal; (fürsorglich) fatherly. **v~erseits** adv on one's/ the father's side

Vater|schaft f - fatherhood; (Jur) paternity. **V~unser** nt -s,- Lord's Prayer

v. Chr. abbr (vor Christus) BC

Vegetar|ier(in) /vege'ta:riɐ, -jərɪn/ m(f) -s,- (f~,-nen) vegetarian. **v~isch** adj vegetarian

Veilchen nt -s,-n violet

Vene /'ve:nə/ f -,-n vein

Venedig /ve'ne:dɪç/ nt -s Venice

Ventil /vɛn'ti:l/ nt -s,-e valve. **V~ator** m -s,-en fan

verabred|en vt arrange; **sich [mit jdm] v~en** arrange to meet [s.o.]. **V~ung** f -,-en arrangement; (Treffen) appointment

verabschieden vt say goodbye to; (aus dem Dienst) retire; pass (Gesetz); **sich v~** say goodbye

verachten vt despise

Verachtung f - contempt

verallgemeinern vt/i (haben) generalize

veränder|lich adj changeable; (Math) variable. **v~n** vt change; **sich v~n** change; (beruflich) change one's job. **V~ung** f change

verängstigt adj frightened, scared

verankern vt anchor

veranlag|t adj künstlerisch/musikalisch **v~t sein** have an artistic/a musical bent; **praktisch v~t** practically minded. **V~ung** f -,-en disposition; (Neigung) tendency; (künstlerisch) bent

veranlassen vt (reg) arrange for; (einleiten) institute; **jdn v~** prompt s.o. (**zu** to)

veranschlagen vt (reg) estimate

veranstalt|en vt organize; hold, give (Party); make (Lärm). **V~er** m -s,- organizer. **V~ung** f -,-en event

verantwort|lich adj responsible; **v~lich machen** hold responsible. **V~ung** f - responsibility. **v~ungsbewusst** adj responsible. **v~ungslos** adj irresponsible. **v~ungsvoll** adj responsible

verarbeiten vt use; (Techn) process; (verdauen & fig) digest

verärgern vt annoy

verausgaben (sich) vr spend all one's money (or) strength

veräußern vt sell

Verb /vɛrp/ nt -s,-en verb

Verband m -[e]s,⁼e association; (Mil) unit; (Med) bandage; (Wund-) dressing. **V~szeug** nt first-aid kit

verbann|en vt exile; (fig) banish. **V~ung** f - exile

verbergen† vt hide; **sich v~** hide

verbesser|n vt improve; (berichtigen) correct. **V~ung** f -,-en improvement; correction

verbeug|en (sich) vr bow. **V~ung** f bow

verbeulen vt dent

verbiegen† vt bend

verbieten† vt forbid; (Admin) prohibit, ban

verbillig|en vt reduce [in price]. **v~t** adj reduced

verbinden† vt connect (mit to); (zusammenfügen) join; (verknüpfen) combine; (in Verbindung bringen) associate; (Med) bandage; dress (Wunde); **jdm verbunden sein** (fig) be obliged to s.o.

verbindlich adj friendly; (bindend) binding

Verbindung f connection; (Verknüpfung) combination; (Kontakt) contact; (Vereinigung) association; **chemische V~** chemical compound; **in V~ stehen/sich in V~ setzen** be/get in touch

verbissen adj grim

verbitter|n vt make bitter. **v~t** adj bitter. **V~ung** f - bitterness

verblassen vi (sein) fade

Verbleib m -s whereabouts pl

verbleit adj (Benzin) leaded

verblüff|en vt amaze, astound. **V~ung** f - amazement

verblühen vi (sein) wither, fade

verbluten vi (sein) bleed to death

verborgen vt lend

Verbot nt -[e]s,-e ban. **v~en** adj forbidden; (Admin) prohibited

Verbrauch m -[e]s consumption. **v~en** vt use; consume (Lebensmittel); (erschöpfen) use up. **V~er** m -s,- consumer

Verbrechen† nt -s,- crime

Verbrecher m -s,- criminal

verbreiten vt spread. **v~et** adj widespread. **V~ung** f - spread; (Verbreiten) spreading

verbrenn|en† vt/i (sein) burn; cremate (Leiche). **V~ung** f -,-en burning; cremation; (Wunde) burn

verbringen† vt spend

verbrühen vt scald

verbuchen vt enter

verbünd|en (sich) vr form an alliance. **V~ete(r)** m/f ally

verbürgen vt guarantee; **sich v~ für** vouch for

Verdacht m -[e]s suspicion; **in** or **im V~ haben** suspect

verdächtig adj suspicious. **v~en** vt suspect (gen of). **V~te(r)** m/f suspect

verdamm|en vt condemn; (Relig) damn. **v~t** adj & adv 🗙 damned; **v~t!** damn!

verdampfen vt/i (sein) evaporate

verdanken vt owe (dat to)

verdau|en vt digest. **v~lich** adj digestible. **V~ung** f - digestion

Verdeck nt -[e]s,-e hood; (Oberdeck) top deck

verderb|en† vi (sein) spoil; (Lebensmittel:) go bad ● vt spoil; **ich habe mir den Magen verdorben** I have an upset stomach. **V~en** nt -s ruin. **v~lich** adj perishable; (schädlich) pernicious

verdien|en vt/i (haben) earn; (fig) deserve. **V~er** m -s,- wage-earner

Verdienst¹ m -[e]s earnings pl

Verdienst² nt -[e]s,-e merit

verdient adj well-deserved

verdoppeln vt double

verdorben adj spoilt, ruined; (Magen) upset; (moralisch) corrupt; (verkommen) depraved

verdreh|en vt twist; roll (Augen);

(*fig*) distort. **v~t** *adj* Ⅱ crazy

verdreifachen *vt* treble, triple

verdrücken *vt* crumple; (Ⅱ: *essen*) polish off; **sich v~** Ⅱ slip away

Verdruss *m* -es annoyance

verdünnen *vt* dilute; **sich v~** taper off

verdunst|en *vi* (*sein*) evaporate. **V~ung** *f* - evaporation

verdursten *vi* (*sein*) die of thirst

veredeln *vt* refine; (*Horticulture*) graft

verehr|en *vt* revere; (*Relig*) worship; (*bewundern*) admire; (*schenken*) give. **V~er(in)** *m* -s,- (*f* -,-nen) admirer. **V~ung** *f* - veneration; worship; admiration

vereidigen *vt* swear in

Verein *m* -s,-e society; (*Sport*:) club

vereinbar *adj* compatible. **v~en** *vt* arrange. **V~ung** *f* -,-en agreement

vereinfachen *vt* simplify

vereinheitlichen *vt* standardize

vereinig|en *vt* unite; merge (*Firmen*); **wieder v~en** reunite; reunify (*Land*); **sich v~en** unite; **V~te Staaten [von Amerika]** United States *sg* (*of America*). **V~ung** *f* -,-en union; (*Organisation*) organization

vereinzelt *adj* isolated ● *adv* occasionally

vereist *adj* frozen; (*Straße*) icy

vereitert *adj* septic

verenden *vi* (*sein*) die

verengen *vt* restrict; **sich v~** narrow; (*Pupille*:) contract

vererb|en *vt* leave (*dat* to); (*Biology & fig*) pass on (*dat* to). **V~ung** *f* - heredity

verfahren† *vi* (*sein*) proceed; **v~**

mit deal with ● *vr* **sich v~** lose one's way ● *adj* muddled. **V~** *nt* -s,- procedure; (*Techn*) process; (*Jur*) proceedings *pl*

Verfall *m* decay; (*eines Gebäudes*) dilapidation; (*körperlich & fig*) decline; (*Ablauf*) expiry. **v~en†** *vi* (*sein*) decay; (*Person, Sitten*:) decline; (*ablaufen*) expire; **v~en in** (+ *acc*) lapse into; **v~en auf** (+ *acc*) hit on (*Idee*)

verfärben (sich) *vr* change colour; (*Stoff*:) discolour

verfass|en *vt* write; (*Jur*) draw up; (*entwerfen*) draft. **V~er** *m* -s,- author. **V~ung** *f* (*Pol*) constitution; (*Zustand*) state

verfaulen *vi* (*sein*) rot, decay

verfechten† *vt* advocate

verfehlen *vt* miss

verfeinde|n (sich) *vr* become enemies; **v~t** sein be enemies

verfeinern *vt* refine; (*verbessern*) improve

verfilmen *vt* film

verfluch|en *vt* curse. **v~t** *adj* & *adv* Ⅱ damned; **v~t!** damn!

verfolg|en *vt* pursue; (*folgen*) follow; (*bedrängen*) pester; (*Pol*) persecute; **strafrechtlich v~en** prosecute. **V~er** *m* -s,- pursuer. **V~ung** *f* - pursuit; persecution

verfrüht *adj* premature

verfügbar *adj* available

verfüg|en *vt* order; (*Jur*) decree ● *vi* (*haben*) **v~en über** (+ *acc*) have at one's disposal. **V~ung** *f* -,-en order; (*Jur*) decree; **jdm zur V~ung stehen** be at s.o.'s disposal

verführ|en *vt* seduce; tempt. **V~ung** *f* seduction; temptation

vergangen *adj* past; (*letzte*) last. **V~heit** *f* - past; (*Gram*) past tense

vergänglich *adj* transitory

vergas|en *vt* gas. **V~er** *m* -s,-

carburettor

vergeb|en† vt award (**an** + dat to); (weggeben) give away; (verzeihen) forgive. **v~lich** adj futile, vain ● adv in vain. **V~ung** f - forgiveness

vergehen† vi (sein) pass; **sich v~** violate (**gegen etw** sth). **V~** nt -s,- offence

vergelt|en† vt repay. **V~ung** f - retaliation; (Rache) revenge

vergessen† vt forget; (liegen lassen) leave behind

vergesslich adj forgetful. **V~keit** f - forgetfulness

vergeuden vt waste, squander

vergewaltig|en vt rape. **V~ung** f -,-en rape

vergießen† vt spill; shed (Tränen, Blut)

vergift|en vt poison. **V~ung** f -,-en poisoning

Vergissmeinnicht nt -[e]s,-[e] forget-me-not

vergittert adj barred

verglasen vt glaze

Vergleich m -[e]s,-e comparison; (Jur) settlement. **v~bar** adj comparable. **v~en**† vt compare (**mit** with/to)

vergnüg|en (sich) vr enjoy oneself. **V~en** nt -s,- pleasure; (Spaß) fun; **viel V~en!** have a good time! **v~t** adj cheerful; (zufrieden) happy. **V~ungen** fpl entertainments

vergolden vt gild; (plattieren) gold-plate

vergraben† vt bury

vergriffen adj out of print

vergrößer|n vt enlarge; (Linse:) magnify; (vermehren) increase; (erweitern) extend; expand (Geschäft); **sich v~n** grow bigger; (Firma:) expand; (zunehmen) increase. **V~ung** f -,-en magnification; increase; ex-

pansion; (Phot) enlargement. **V~ungsglas** nt magnifying glass

vergüt|en vt pay for; **jdm etw v~en** reimburse s.o. for sth. **V~ung** f -,-en remuneration; (Erstattung) reimbursement

verhaft|en vt arrest. **V~ung** f -,-en arrest

verhalten† (**sich**) vr behave; (handeln) act; (beschaffen sein) be. **V~** nt -s behaviour, conduct

Verhältnis nt -ses,-se relationship; (Liebes-) affair; (Math) ratio; **V~se** circumstances; conditions. **v~mäßig** adv comparatively, relatively

verhand|eln vt discuss; (Jur) try ● vi (haben) negotiate. (Jur) **V~lung** f (Jur) trial; **V~lungen** negotiations

Verhängnis nt -ses fate, doom

verhärten vt/i (sein) harden

verhasst adj hated

verhätscheln vt spoil

verhauen† vt ① beat; make a mess of (Prüfung)

verheilen vi (sein) heal

verheimlichen vt keep secret

verheirat|en (sich) vr get married (**mit** to); **sich wieder v~en** remarry. **v~et** adj married

verhelfen† vi (haben) **jdm zu etw v~** help s.o. get sth

verherrlichen vt glorify

verhexen vt bewitch

verhindern vt prevent; **v~t sein** be unable to come

Verhör nt -s,-e interrogation; **ins V~ nehmen** interrogate. **v~en** vt interrogate; **sich v~en** mishear

verhungern vi (sein) starve

verhüt|en vt prevent. **V~ung** f - prevention. **V~ungsmittel** nt contraceptive

verirren (sich) vr get lost

v

verjagen vt chase away

verjüngen vt rejuvenate

verkalkt adj ① senile

verkalkulieren (sich) vr miscalculate

Verkauf m sale; **zum V~** for sale. **v~en** vt sell; **zu v~en** for sale

Verkäufer(in) m(f) seller; (im Geschäft) shop assistant

Verkehr m -s traffic; (Kontakt) contact; (Geschlechts-) intercourse; **aus dem V~ ziehen** take out of circulation. **v~en** vi (haben) operate; (Bus, Zug:) run; (Umgang haben) associate, mix (**mit** with); (Gast sein) visit (**bei jdm** s.o.)

Verkehrs|ampel f traffic lights pl. **V~unfall** m road accident. **V~verein** m tourist office. **V~zeichen** nt traffic sign

verkehrt adj wrong; **v~ herum** adv the wrong way round; (links) inside out

verklagen vt sue (**auf** + acc for)

verkleid|en vt disguise; (Techn) line; **sich v~en** disguise oneself; (für Kostümfest) dress up. **V~ung** f -,-en disguise; (Kostüm) fancy dress; (Techn) lining

verkleiner|n vt reduce [in size]. **V~ung** f - reduction

verknittern vt/i (sein) crumple

verknüpfen vt knot together

verkommen† vi (sein) be neglected; (sittlich) go to the bad; (verfallen) decay; (Haus:) fall into disrepair; (Gegend:) become run-down; (Lebensmittel:) go bad ● adj neglected; (sittlich) depraved; (Haus) dilapidated; (Gegend) run-down

verkörpern vt embody, personify

verkraften vt cope with

verkrampft adj (fig) tense

verkriechen† (sich) vr hide

verkrümmt adj crooked, bent

verkrüppelt adj crippled; (Glied) deformed

verkühl|en (sich) vr catch a chill. **V~ung** f -,-en chill

verkümmern vi (sein) waste/(Pflanze:) wither away

verkünden vt announce; pronounce (Urteil)

verkürzen vt shorten; (verringern) reduce; (abbrechen) cut short; while away (Zeit)

Verlag m -[e]s,-e publishing firm

verlangen vt ask for; (fordern) demand; (berechnen) charge. **V~** nt -s desire; (Bitte) request

verlänger|n vt extend; lengthen (Kleid); (zeitlich) prolong; renew (Pass, Vertrag); (Culin) thin down. **V~ung** f -,-en extension; renewal. **V~ungsschnur** f extension cable

verlassen† vt leave; (im Stich lassen) desert; **sich v~ auf** (+ acc) rely or depend on ● adj deserted. **V~heit** f - desolation

verlässlich adj reliable

Verlauf m course; **im V~** (+ gen) in the course of. **v~en†** vi (sein) run; (ablaufen) go; **gut v~en** go [off] well ● vr **sich v~en** lose one's way

verlegen vt move; (verschieben) postpone; (nach vorn) bring forward; (verlieren) mislay; (versperren) block; (legen) lay (Teppich, Rohre); (veröffentlichen) publish; **sich v~ auf** (+ acc) take up (Beruf); resort to (Bitten) ● adj embarrassed. **V~heit** f - embarrassment

Verleger m -s,- publisher

verleihen† vt lend; (gegen Gebühr) hire out; (überreichen) award, confer; (fig) give

verlernen vt forget

verletz|en vt injure; (kränken)

hurt; (*verstoßen gegen*) infringe; violate (*Grenze*). **v~end** *adj* hurtful, wounding. **V~te(r)** *m/f* injured person; (*bei Unfall*) casualty. **V~ung** *f -,-en* (*Verstoß*) infringement; violation

verleugnen *vt* deny; disown (*Freund*)

verleumd|en *vt* slander; (*schriftlich*) libel. **v~erisch** *adj* slanderous; libellous. **V~ung** *f -,-en* slander; (*schriftlich*) libel

verlieben (sich) *vr* fall in love (**in** + *acc* with); **verliebt sein** be in love (**in** + *acc* with)

verlier|en† *vt* lose; shed (*Laub*) ● *vi* (haben) lose (**an etw** *dat* sth). **V~er** *m -s,-* loser

verlob|en (sich) *vr* get engaged (**mit** to); **v~t sein** be engaged. **V~te** *f* fiancée. **V~te(r)** *m* fiancé. **V~ung** *f -,-en* engagement

verlock|en *vt* tempt. **V~ung** *f -,-en* temptation

verloren *adj* lost; **v~ gehen** get lost

verlos|en *vt* raffle. **V~ung** *f -,-en* raffle; (*Ziehung*) draw

Verlust *m -[e]s,-e* loss

vermachen *vt* leave, bequeath

Vermächtnis *nt -ses,-se* legacy

vermähl|en (sich) *vr* marry. **V~ung** *f -,-en* marriage

vermehren *vt* increase; propagate (*Pflanzen*); **sich v~** increase; (*sich fortpflanzen*) breed

vermeiden† *vt* avoid

Vermerk *m -[e]s,-e* note. **v~en** note [down]

vermessen† *vt* measure; survey (*Gelände*) ● *adj* presumptuous

vermiet|en *vt* let, rent [out]; hire out (*Boot, Auto*); **zu v~en** to let (*Boot*); for hire. **V~er** *m* landlord. **V~erin** *f* landlady

vermindern *vt* reduce

vermischen *vt* mix

vermissen *vt* miss

vermisst *adj* missing

vermitteln *vi* (haben) mediate
● *vt* arrange; (*beschaffen*) find; place (*Arbeitskräfte*)

Vermittl|er *m -s,-* agent; (*Schlichter*) mediator. **V~ung** *f -,-en* arrangement; (*Agentur*) agency; (*Teleph*) exchange; (*Schlichtung*) mediation

Vermögen *nt -s,-* fortune. **v~d** *adj* wealthy

vermut|en *vt* suspect; (*glauben*) presume. **v~lich** *adj* probable ● *adv* presumably. **V~ung** *f -,-e* supposition; (*Verdacht*) suspicion

vernachlässigen *vt* neglect

vernehm|en† *vt* hear; (*verh* question; (*Jur*) examine. **V~** *-,-en* questioning

verneigen *vr* bow

vernein|en *vt* answer in t tive; (*ablehnen*) reject. **v~e** negative. **V~ung** *f -,-en** n answer

vernicht|en *vt* destroy; (*ten*) exterminate. **V~ung** struction; extermination

Vernunft *f -* reason

vernünftig *adj* reasonab sensible

veröffentlich|en *vt* pu **V~ung** *f -,-en* publication

verordn|en *vt* prescribe **V~ung** *f -,-en* prescriptio *gung*) decree

verpachten *vt* lease [ou

verpack|en *vt* pack; (*ei n*) wrap. **V~ung** *f* packaging wrapping

verpassen *vt* miss; (**⬚** geben) give

verpfänden vt pawn

verpflanzen vt transplant

verpfleg|en vt feed: **sich selbst v~en** cater for oneself. **V~ung** f - board; (Essen) food; **Unterkunft und V~ung** board and lodging

verpflicht|en vt oblige; (einstellen) engage; (Sport) sign; **sich v~en** undertake/(versprechen) promise (**zu** to); (vertraglich) sign a contract. **V~ung** f -,-en obligation, commitment

verprügeln vt beat up, thrash

Verputz m -es plaster. **v~en** vt plaster

Verrat m -[e]s betrayal, treachery. **v~en†** vt betray; give away (Geheimnis)

Verräter m -s,- traitor

verrech|nen vt settle; clear (Scheck); **sich v~nen** make a mistake; (fig) miscalculate. **V~nungsscheck** m crossed cheque

verreisen vi (sein) go away; **verreist sein** be away

verrenken vt dislocate

verrichten vt perform, do

verriegeln vt bolt

verringer|n vt reduce; **sich v~n** ~crease. **V~ung** f - reduction; de~ease

~rost|en vi (sein) rust. **v~et** ~ rusty

~rückt adj crazy, mad. **V~e(r)** ~lunatic, **V~heit** f -,-en madness; (Torheit) folly

~ühren vt mix

~unzelt adj wrinkled

~utschen vi (sein) slip

~fers/ m -es,-e verse

~gl~en vi (haben) fail ● vt sich **v~en** deny oneself sth. **V~en** nt ~ failure. **V~er** m -s,- failure

~salzen† vt put too much salt

in/on; (fig) spoil

versamm|eln vt assemble. **V~lung** f assembly, meeting

Versand m -[e]s dispatch. **V~haus** nt mail-order firm

versäumen vt miss; lose (Zeit); (unterlassen) neglect; **[es] v~en, etw zu tun** fail to do sth

verschärfen vt intensify; tighten (Kontrolle); increase (Tempo); aggravate (Lage); **sich v~** intensify; increase; (Lage:) worsen

verschätzen (sich) vr **sich v~ in** (+ dat) misjudge

verschenken vt give away

verscheuchen vt shoo/(jagen) chase away

verschicken vt send; (Comm) dispatch

verschieb|en† vt move; (aufschieben) put off, postpone; **sich v~en** move, shift; (verrutschen) slip; (zeitlich) be postponed. **V~ung** f shift; postponement

verschieden adj different; **v~e** pl different; (mehrere) various; **V~es** some things; (dieses und jenes) various things; **das ist v~** it varies ● adv differently; **v~ groß** of different sizes. **v~artig** adj diverse

verschimmeln vi (sein) go mouldy. **v~t** adj mouldy

verschlafen† vi (haben) oversleep ● vt sleep through (Tag); **sich v~** oversleep ● adj sleepy

verschlagen† vt lose (Seite); **jdm die Sprache/den Atem v~** leave s.o. speechless/take s.o.'s breath away ● adj sly

verschlechter|n vt make worse; **sich v~n** get worse, deteriorate. **V~ung** f -,-en deterioration

Verschleiß m -es wear and tear

verschleppen vt carry off; (entführen) abduct; spread (Seuche);

neglect (*Krankheit*); (*hinausziehen*) delay

verschleudern *vt* sell at a loss

verschließen† *vt* close; (*abschließen*) lock; (*einschließen*) lock up

verschlimmer|n *vt* make worse; aggravate (*Lage*); **sich v~n** get worse, deteriorate. **V~ung** *f* -,-en deterioration

verschlossen *adj* reserved. **V~heit** *f* - reserve

verschlucken *vt* swallow; **sich v~** choke (**an** + *dat* on)

Verschluss *m* -es,⁻e fastener, clasp; (*Koffer-*) catch; (*Flaschen-*) top; (*luftdicht*) seal; (*Phot*) shutter

verschlüsselt *adj* coded

verschmelzen† *vt/i* (*sein*) fuse

verschmerzen *vt* get over

verschmutz|en *vt* soil; pollute (*Luft*) ● *vi* (*sein*) get dirty. **V~ung** *f* - pollution

verschneit *adj* snow-covered

verschnörkelt *adj* ornate

verschnüren *vt* tie up

verschollen *adj* missing

verschonen *vt* spare

verschossen *adj* faded

verschränken *vt* cross

verschreiben† *vt* prescribe; **sich v~** make a slip of the pen

verschulden *vt* be to blame for. **V~** *nt* -s fault

verschuldet *adj* **v~ sein** be in debt

verschütten *vt* spill; (*begraben*) bury

verschweigen† *vt* conceal, hide

verschwend|en *vt* waste. **V~ung** *f* - extravagance; (*Vergeudung*) waste

verschwiegen *adj* discreet

verschwinden† *vi* (*sein*) disappear; (*mal*) **v~** Ⓘ spend a penny

verschwommen *adj* blurred

verschwör|en† (**sich**) *vr* conspire. **V~ung** *f* -,-en conspiracy

versehen† *vt* perform; hold (*Posten*); keep (*Haushalt*); **v~ mit** provide with; **sich v~** make a mistake. **V~** *nt* -s,- oversight; (*Fehler*) slip; **aus V~** by mistake. **v~tlich** *adv* by mistake

Versehrte(r) *m* disabled person

versengen *vt* singe; (*stärker*) scorch

versenken *vt* sink

versessen *adj* keen (**auf** + *acc* on)

versetz|en *vt* move; transfer (*Person*); (*Sch*) move up; (*verpfänden*) pawn; (*verkaufen*) sell; (*vermischen*) blend; (*jdn* Ⓘ: *warten lassen*) stand s.o. up; **jdm in Angst/Erstaunen v~** frighten/astonish s.o.; **sich in jds Lage v~** put oneself in s.o.'s place. **V~ung** *f* -,-en move; transfer; (*Sch*) move to a higher class

verseuchen *vt* contaminate

versicher|n *vt* insure; (*bekräftigen*) affirm; **jdm v~n** assure s.o. (**dass** that). **V~ung** *f* -,-en insurance; assurance

versiegeln *vt* seal

versiert /vɛrˈziːɐt/ *adj* experienced

versilbert *adj* silver-plated

Versmaß /ˈfɛrs-/ *nt* metre

versöhn|en *vt* reconcile; **sich v~en** become reconciled. **V~ung** *f* -,-en reconciliation

versorg|en *vt* provide, supply (**mit** with); provide for (*Familie*); (*betreuen*) look after. **V~ung** *f* - provision, supply; (*Betreuung*) care

verspät|en (**sich**) *vr* be late. **v~et** *adj* late; (*Zug*) delayed; (*Dank*) belated. **V~ung** *f* - lateness; **V~ung haben** be late

versperren *vt* block; bar (*Weg*)

verspiel|en vt gamble away. **v~t** adj playful

verspotten vt mock, ridicule

versprech|en† vt promise; **sich v~en** make a slip of the tongue; **sich** (dat) **viel v~en von** have high hopes of; **ein viel v~ender Anfang** a promising start. **V~en** nt **-s,-** promise. **V~ungen** fpl promises

verstaatlich|en vt nationalize. **V~ung** f - nationalization

Verstand m **-[e]s** mind; (Vernunft) reason; **den V~ verlieren** go out of one's mind

verständig adj sensible; (klug) intelligent. **v~en** vt notify, inform; **sich v~en** communicate; (sich verständlich machen) make oneself understood. **V~ung** f - notification; communication; (Einigung) agreement

verständlich adj comprehensible; (deutlich) clear; (begreiflich) understandable; **sich v~ machen** make oneself understood. **v~erweise** adv understandably

Verständnis nt **-ses** understanding

verstärk|en vt strengthen, reinforce; (steigern) intensify, increase; amplify (Ton). **V~er** m **-s,-** amplifier. **V~ung** f reinforcement; increase; amplification; (Truppen) reinforcements pl

verstaubt adj dusty

verstauchen vt sprain

Versteck nt **-[e]s,-e** hiding-place; **V~ spielen** play hide-and-seek. **v~en** vt hide; **sich v~en** hide

verstehen† vt understand; (können) know; **falsch v~** misunderstand; **sich v~** understand one another; (auskommen) get on

versteiger|n vt auction. **V~ung** f auction

versteinert adj fossilized

verstell|en vt adjust; (versperren) block; (verändern) disguise; **sich v~en** pretend. **V~ung** f - pretence

versteuern vt pay tax on

verstimm|t adj disgruntled; (Magen) upset; (Mus) out of tune. **V~ung** f - ill humour; (Magen-) upset

verstockt adj stubborn

verstopf|en vt plug; (versperren) block; **v~t** blocked; (Person) constipated. **V~ung** f **-,-en** blockage; (Med) constipation

verstorben adj late, deceased. **V~e(r)** m/f deceased

verstört adj bewildered

Verstoß m infringement. **v~en†** vt disown • vi (haben) **v~en gegen** contravene, infringe

verstreuen vt scatter

verstümmeln vt mutilate; garble (Text)

Versuch m **-[e]s,-e** attempt; (Experiment) experiment. **v~en** vt (haben) try; **v~t sein** be tempted (zu to). **V~ung** f **-,-en** temptation

vertagen vt adjourn; (aufschieben) postpone; **sich v~** adjourn

vertauschen vt exchange; (verwechseln) mix up

verteidig|en vt defend. **V~er** m **-s,-** defender; (Jur) defence counsel. **V~ung** f **-,-en** defence

verteil|en vt distribute; (zuteilen) allocate; (ausgeben) hand out; (verstreichen) spread. **V~ung** f - distribution; allocation

vertief|en vt deepen; **v~t sein in** (+ acc) be engrossed in. **V~ung** f **-,-en** hollow, depression

vertikal /vɛrtiˈkaːl/ adj vertical

vertilgen vt exterminate; kill [off] (Unkraut)

vertippen (sich) vr make a typing mistake

vertonen vt set to music

Vertrag m -[e]s, ⁼e contract; (Pol) treaty

vertragen† vt tolerate, stand; take (Kritik, Spaß); **sich v~** get on

vertraglich adj contractual

verträglich adj good-natured; (bekömmlich) digestible

vertrauen vi (haben) trust (jdm/ etw s.o./sth; auf + acc in). **V~** nt -s trust, confidence (zu in); **im V~** in confidence. **v~swürdig** adj trustworthy

vertraulich adj confidential; (intim) familiar

vertraut adj intimate; (bekannt) familiar. **V~heit** f - intimacy, familiarity

vertreiben† vt drive away; drive out (Feind); (Comm) sell; **sich (dat) die Zeit v~en** pass the time. **V~ung** f -,-en expulsion

vertreten† vt represent; (einspringen für) stand in or deputize for; (verfechten) support; hold (Meinung); **sich (dat) den Fuß v~en** twist one's ankle. **V~er** m -s,- representative; deputy; (Arzt-) locum; (Verfechter) supporter. **V~ung** f -,-en representation; (Person) deputy; (eines Arztes) locum; (Handels-) agency

Vertrieb m -[e]s (Comm) sale

vertrocknen vi (sein) dry up

verüben vt commit

verunglücken vi (sein) be involved in an accident; (🄸: missglücken) go wrong; **tödlich v~** be killed in an accident

verunreinigen vt pollute; (verseuchen) contaminate

verursachen vt cause

verurteilen vt condemn; (Jur)

convict (wegen of); sentence (zum Tode to death). **V~ung** f - condemnation; (Jur) conviction

vervielfachen vt multiply

vervielfältigen vt duplicate

vervollständigen vt complete

verwählen (sich) vr misdial

verwahren vt keep; (verstauen) put away

verwahrlost adj neglected; (Haus) dilapidated

Verwahrung f - keeping; **in V~ nehmen** take into safe keeping

verwaist adj orphaned

verwalt|en vt administer; (leiten) manage; govern (Land). **V~er** m -s,- administrator; manager. **V~ung** f -,-en administration; management; government

verwand|eln vt transform, change (in + acc into); **sich v~eln** change, turn (in + acc into). **V~lung** f transformation

verwandt adj related (mit to). **V~e(r)** m/f relative. **V~schaft** f - relationship; (Menschen) relatives pl

verwarn|en vt warn, caution. **V~ung** f warning, caution

verwechs|eln vt mix up, confuse; (halten für) mistake (mit for). **V~lung** f -,-en mix-up

verweiger|n vt/i (haben) refuse (jdm etw s.o. sth). **V~ung** f refusal

Verweis m -es,-e reference (auf + acc to); (Tadel) reprimand; **v~en†** vt refer (auf/an + acc to); (tadeln) reprimand; **von der Schule v~en** expel

verwelken vi (sein) wilt

verwend|en† vt use; spend (Zeit, Mühe). **V~ung** f use

verwerten vt utilize, use

verwesen vi (sein) decompose

verwick|eln *vt* involve (**in** + *acc* in); **sich v~eln** get tangled up. **v~elt** *adj* complicated
verwildert *adj* wild; (*Garten*) overgrown; (*Aussehen*) unkempt
verwinden† *vt* (*fig*) get over
verwirklichen *vt* realize
verwirr|en *vt* tangle up; (*fig*) confuse; **sich v~en** get tangled; (*fig*) become confused. **v~t** *adj* confused. **V~ung** *f* - confusion
verwischen *vt* smudge
verwittert *adj* weathered
verwitwet *adj* widowed
verwöhn|en *vt* spoil. **v~t** *adj* spoilt
verworren *adj* confused
verwund|bar *adj* vulnerable. **v~en** *vt* wound
verwunder|lich *adj* surprising. **v~n** *vt* surprise; **sich v~n** be surprised. **V~ung** *f* - surprise
Verwund|ete(r) *m* wounded soldier; **die V~eten** the wounded *pl*. **V~ung** *f* -,-en wound
verwüst|en *vt* devastate, ravage. **V~ung** *f* -,-en devastation
verzählen (sich) *vr* miscount
verzaubern *vt* bewitch; (*fig*) enchant; **v~ in** (+ *acc*) turn into
Verzehr *m* -s consumption. **v~en** *vt* eat
verzeih|en† *vt* forgive; **v~en Sie!** excuse me! **V~ung** *f* - forgiveness; **um V~ung bitten** apologize; **V~ung!** sorry! (*bei Frage*) excuse me!
Verzicht *m* -[e]s renunciation (**auf** + *acc* of). **v~en** *vi* (*haben*) do without; **v~en auf** (+ *acc*) give up; renounce (*Recht, Erbe*)
verziehen† *vt* pull out of shape; (*verwöhnen*) spoil; **sich v~** lose shape; (*Holz:*) warp; (*Gesicht:*) twist; (*verschwinden*) disappear; (*Nebel:*) disperse; (*Gewitter:*) pass ● *vi* (*sein*) move [away]
verzier|en *vt* decorate. **V~ung** *f* -,-en decoration
verzinsen *vt* pay interest on
verzöger|n *vt* delay; (*verlangsamen*) slow down. **V~ung** *f* -,-en delay
verzollen *vt* pay duty on; **haben Sie etwas zu v~?** have you anything to declare?
verzweif|eln *vi* (*sein*) despair. **v~elt** *adj* desperate. **V~lung** *f* - despair; (*Ratlosigkeit*) desperation
verzweigen (sich) *vr* branch [out]
Veto /ˈveːto/ *nt* -s,-s veto
Vetter *m* -s,-n cousin
vgl. *abbr* (**vergleiche**) cf.
Viadukt /vi̯aˈdʊkt/ *nt* -[e]s,-e viaduct
Video /ˈviːdeo/ *nt* -s,-s video. **V~handy** *nt* vision phone. **V~kassette** *f* video cassette. **V~recorder** *m* -s,- video recorder
Vieh *nt* -[e]s livestock; (*Rinder*) cattle *pl*; (**!**: *Tier*) creature
viel *pron* a great deal/**!** a lot of; (*pl*) many, **!** a lot of; (*substantivisch*) **v~[es]** much, **!** a lot; **nicht/so/wie/zu v~** not/so/how/too much/ (*pl*) many; **v~e** *pl* many; **das v~e Geld** all that money ● *adv* much, **!** a lot; **v~ mehr/weniger** much more/less; **v~zu groß/klein** much *or* far too big/small; **so v~ wie möglich** as much as possible; **so/zu v~ arbeiten** work so/too much
viel|deutig *adj* ambiguous. **v~fach** *adj* multiple ● *adv* many times; (**!**: *oft*) frequently. **V~falt** *f* - diversity, [great] variety
vielleicht *adv* perhaps, maybe;

(**I**: *wirklich*) really

vielmals *adv* very much

vielmehr *adv* rather; (*im Gegenteil*) on the contrary

vielseitig *adj* varied; (*Person*) versatile. **V~keit** *f* - versatility

vielversprechend* *adj* **viel versprechend**, *s.* **sprechen**

vier *inv adj*, **V~** *f* -,-**en** four; (*Sch*) ≈ fair. **V~eck** *nt* -[e]s,-**e** oblong, rectangle; (*Quadrat*) square. **v~eckig** *adj* oblong, rectangular; square. **V~linge** *mpl* quadruplets

viertel /'fɪrtəl/ *inv adj* quarter; um **v~** neun at [a] quarter past eight; um drei **v~** neun at [a] quarter to nine. **V~** *nt* -s,- quarter; (*Wein*) quarter litre; **v~** vor/nach sechs [a] quarter to/past six. **V~finale** *nt* quarter-final. **V~jahr** *nt* three months *pl*; (*Comm*) quarter. **v~jährlich** *adj* & *adv* quarterly. **V~stunde** *f* quarter of an hour

vier|zehn /'fɪr-/ *inv adj* fourteen. **v~zehnte(r,s)** *adj* fourteenth. **v~zig** *inv adj* forty. **v~zigste(r,s)** *adj* fortieth

Villa /'vɪla/ *f* -,-**len** villa

violett /vjo'lɛt/ *adj* violet

Vio|line /vjo'liːnə/ *f* -,-**n** violin. **V~linschlüssel** *m* treble clef

Virus /'viːrʊs/ *nt* -,-**ren** virus

Visier /vi'ziːɐ̯/ *nt* -s,-**e** visor

Visite /vi'ziːtə/ *f* -,-**n** round; **V~** machen do one's round

Visum /'viːzʊm/ *nt* -s,-**sa** visa

Vitamin /vita'miːn/ *nt* -s,-**e** vitamin

Vitrine /vi'triːnə/ *f* -,-**n** display cabinet/(*im Museum*) case

Vizepräsident /'fiːtsə-/ *m* vice president

Vogel *m* -s,⁑ bird; einen **V~** haben **I** have a screw loose. **V~scheuche** *f* -,-**n** scarecrow

Vokabeln /vo'kaːbəln/ *fpl* vocabulary *sg*

Vokal /vo'kaːl/ *m* -s,-**e** vowel

Volant /vo'lãː/ *m* -s,-**s** flounce

Volk *nt* -[e]s,⁑er people *sg*; (*Bevölkerung*) people *pl*

Völker|kunde *f* ethnology. **V~mord** *m* genocide. **V~recht** *nt* international law

Volks|abstimmung *f* plebiscite. **V~fest** *nt* public festival. **V~hochschule** *f* adult education classes *pl*/(*Gebäude*) centre. **V~lied** *nt* folksong. **V~tanz** *m* folk-dance. **v~tümlich** *adj* popular. **V~wirt** *m* economist. **V~wirtschaft** *f* economics *sg*. **V~zählung** *f* [national] census

voll *adj* full (**von** *o dat* of); (*Haar*) thick; (*Erfolg, Ernst*) complete; (*Wahrheit*) whole; **v~ machen** fill up; **v~ tanken** fill up with petrol ● *adv* (*ganz*) completely; (*arbeiten*) full-time; (*auszahlen*) in full; **v~ und ganz** completely

Vollblut *nt* thoroughbred

vollende|n *vt insep* complete. **v~t** *adj* perfect

Vollendung *f* completion; (*Vollkommenheit*) perfection

voller *inv adj* full of

Volleyball /'vɔli-/ *m* volleyball

vollführen *vt insep* perform

vollfüllen *vt sep* fill up

Vollgas *nt* **V~** geben put one's foot down; **mit V~** flat out

völlig *adj* complete

volljährig *adj* **v~ sein** (*Jur*) be of age. **V~keit** *f* (*Jur*) majority

Vollkaskoversicherung *f* fully comprehensive insurance

vollkommen *adj* perfect; (*völlig*) complete

Voll|kornbrot *nt* wholemeal

bread. **V~macht** f -,-en authority;
(Jur) power of attorney. **V~mond**
m full moon. **V~pension** f
full board

vollständig adj complete

vollstrecken vt insep execute;
carry out (Urteil)

volltanken* vi sep (haben) voll
tanken, s. voll

Volltreffer m direct hit

vollzählig adj complete

vollziehen* vt insep carry out;
perform (Handlung); consummate
(Ehe); **sich v~** take place

Volt /vɔlt/ nt -[s],- volt

Volumen /vo'luːmən/ nt -s,-
volume

vom prep = von dem

---

von

● preposition (+ dative)

! Note that von dem can become vom

····▶ (räumlich) from; (nach Richtungen) of. **von hier an** from
here on[ward]. **von Wien aus**
[starting] from Vienna. **nörd-
lich/südlich von Mannheim**
[to the] north/south of Mannheim. **rechts/links von mir** to
the right/left of me; on my
right/left

····▶ (zeitlich) from. **von jetzt an**
from now on. **von heute/mor-
gen an** [as] from today/to-
morrow; starting today/to-
morrow

····▶ (zur Angabe des Urhebers, der
Ursache; nach Passiv) by. **der
Roman ist von Fontane** the
novel is by Fontane. **sie hat ein
Kind von ihm.** she has a child

by him. **er ist vom Blitz er-
schlagen worden** he was killed
by lightning

····▶ (anstelle eines Genitivs; Hinge-
hören, Beschaffenheit, Menge etc.)
of. **ein Stück von dem Kuchen**
a piece of the cake. **einer von
euch** one of you. **eine Fahrt
von drei Stunden** a drive of
three hours; a three-hour drive.
das Brot von gestern yesterday's bread. **ein Tal von er-
staunlicher Schönheit** a valley
of extraordinary beauty

····▶ (betreffend) about. **handeln/
wissen/erzählen** od **reden von
...** be/know/talk about .... **eine
Geschichte von zwei Elefanten**
a story about or of two ele-
phants

voneinander adv from each
other; (abhängig) on each other

vonseiten prep (+ gen) on the
part of

vonstatten adv **v~ gehen**
take place

vor prep (+ dat/acc) in front of;
(zeitlich, Reihenfolge) before; (+ dat)
(bei Uhrzeit) to; (warnen, sich fürchten) of; (schützen, davonlaufen)
from; (Respekt haben) for; **vor Angst
zittern** tremble with fear; **vor drei
Tagen** three days ago; **vor allen
Dingen** ● adv forward; **vor und zurück** backwards and
forwards

Vorabend m eve

voran adv at the front; (voraus)
ahead; (vorwärts) forward. **v~ge-
hen†** vi sep (sein) lead the way;
(Fortschritte machen) make progress.
v~kommen† vi sep (sein) make
progress; (fig) get on

Voranschlag m estimate.
V~anzeige f advance notice.
V~arbeiter m foreman

voraus adv ahead (dat of); (vorn) at the front; (vorwärts) forward ● im Voraus in advance. **v~bezahlen** vt sep pay in advance. **v~gehen**† vi sep (sein) go on ahead; jdm/etw **v~gehen** precede s.o./ sth. **v~sage** f -,-en prediction. **v~sagen** vt sep predict

voraussetz|en vt sep take for granted; (erfordern) require; **vorausgesetzt, dass** provided that. **V~ung** f -,-en assumption; (Erfordernis) prerequisite

voraussichtlich adj anticipated, expected ● adv probably

Vorbehalt m -[e]s,-e reservation

vorbei adv past (an jdm/etw s.o./ sth); (zu Ende) over. **v~fahren** vi sep (sein) drive/go past. **v~gehen**† vi sep (sein) go past; (verfehlen) miss; (vergehen) pass; (🔲: besuchen) drop in (**bei** on)

vorbereit|en vt sep prepare; prepare for (Reise); **sich v~en** prepare [oneself] (**auf** + acc for). **V~ung** f -,-en preparation

vorbestellen vt sep order/(im Theater, Hotel) book in advance

vorbestraft adj **v~ sein** have a [criminal] record

Vorbeugung f - prevention

Vorbild nt model. **v~lich** adj exemplary, model ● adv in an exemplary manner

vorbringen† vt sep put forward; offer (Entschuldigung)

vordatieren vt sep post-date

Vorder|bein nt foreleg. **v~e(r,s)** adj front. **V~grund** m foreground. **V~rad** nt front wheel. **V~seite** f front; (einer Münze) obverse. **V~ste(r,s)** adj front, first. **V~teil** nt front

vor|drängeln (sich) vr sep 🔲 jump the queue. **v~drängen**

(sich) vr sep push forward. **v~drängen**† vi sep (sein) advance

voreilig adj rash

voreingenommen adj biased, prejudiced. **V~heit** f - bias

vorenthalten† vt sep withhold

vorerst adv for the time being

Vorfahr m -en,-en ancestor

Vorfahrt f right of way; '**V~ beachten**' 'give way'. **V~sstraße** f ≈ major road

Vorfall m incident. **v~en**† vi sep (sein) happen

vorfinden† vt sep find

Vorfreude f [happy] anticipation

vorführ|en vt sep present, show; (demonstrieren) demonstrate; (aufführen) perform. **V~ung** f presentation; demonstration; performance

Vor|gabe f (Sport) handicap. **V~gang** m occurrence; (Techn) process. **V~gänger(in)** m -s,- (f -,-nen) predecessor

vorgehen† vi sep (sein) go forward; (voraus-) go on ahead; (Uhr:) be fast; (wichtig sein) take precedence; (verfahren) act, proceed; (geschehen) happen, go on. **V~** nt -s action

vor|geschichtlich adj prehistoric. **V~geschmack** m foretaste. **V~gesetzte(r)** m/f superior. **v~gestern** adv the day before yesterday; **v~gestern Abend** the evening before last

vorhaben† vt sep propose, intend (**zu** to); **etw v~** have sth planned. **V~** nt -s,- plan

Vorhand f (Sport) forehand

vorhanden adj existing; **v~ sein** exist; be available

Vorhang m curtain

Vorhängeschloss nt padlock

vorher adv before[hand]

vorhergehend adj previous

vorherrschend adj predominant

Vorher|sage f -,-n prediction: (Wetter-) forecast. **v~sagen** vt sep predict; forecast (Wetter). **v~sehen†** vt sep foresee

vorhin adv just now

vorige(r,s) adj last, previous

Vor|kehrungen fpl precautions. **V~kenntnisse** fpl previous knowledge sg

vorkommen† vi sep (sein) happen; (vorhanden sein) occur; (nach vorn kommen) come forward; (hervorkommen) come out; (zu sehen sein) show; **jdm bekannt v~** seem familiar to s.o.

Vorkriegszeit f pre-war period

vorlad|en† vt sep (Jur) summons. **V~ung** f summons

Vorlage f model; (Muster) pattern; (Gesetzes-) bill

vorlassen† vt sep admit; **jdn v~** Ⓣ let s.o. pass; (den Vortritt lassen) let s.o. go first

Vor|lauf m (Sport) heat. **V~läufer** m forerunner. **v~läufig** adj provisional; (zunächst) for the time being. **V~laut** adj forward. **V~leben** nt past

vorleg|en vt sep put on (Kette); (unterbreiten) present; (vorzeigen) show. **V~er** m -s,- mat; (Bett-) rug

vorles|en† vt sep read [out]; **jdm v~en** read to s.o. **V~ung** f lecture

vorletzt|e(r,s) adj last ... but one; **v~es Jahr** the year before last

Vorliebe f preference

vorliegen† vi sep (haben) be present/(verfügbar) available; (bestehen) exist, be

vorlügen† vt sep lie (dat to)

vormachen vt sep put up; put on (Kette); push (Riegel); (zeigen) demonstrate; **jdm etwas v~** (Ⓣ:

täuschen) kid s.o.

Vormacht f supremacy

vormals adv formerly

vormerken vt sep make a note of; (reservieren) reserve

Vormittag m morning; **gestern/heute V~** yesterday/this morning. **v~s** adv in the morning

Vormund m -[e]s,-munde & -münder guardian

vorn adv at the front; **nach v~** to the front; **von v~** from the front/(vom Anfang) beginning; **von v~ anfangen** start afresh

Vorname m first name

vorne adv = vorn

vornehm adj distinguished; smart

vornehmen† vt sep carry out; **sich** (dat), **etw zu tun v~** plan to do sth

vornherein adv von v~herein from the start

Vor|ort m suburb. **V~rang** m priority, precedence (vor + dat over). **V~rat** m -[e]s,-e supply, stock (an + dat of). **v~rätig** adj available; **v~rätig haben** have in stock. **V~ratskammer** f larder. **V~recht** nt privilege. **V~richtung** f device

Vorrunde f qualifying round

vorsagen vt/i sep (haben) recite; **jdm v~** tell s.o. the answer

Vor|satz m resolution. **v~sätzlich** adj deliberate; (Jur) premeditated

Vorschau f preview; (Film-) trailer

Vorschein m zum V~kommen appear

Vorschlag m suggestion, proposal. **v~en†** vt sep suggest, propose

vorschnell adj rash

vorschreiben† vt sep lay down; dictate (dat to); **vorgeschriebene Dosis** prescribed dose

Vorschrift f regulation; (*Anweisung*) instruction; **jdm V~en machen** tell s.o. what to do. **v~smäßig** adj correct

Vorschule f nursery school

Vorschuss m advance

vorseh|en† v sep ● vt intend (**für/als** for/as); (*planen*) plan; **sich v~en** be careful (**vor** + dat of) ● vi (*haben*) peep out. **V~ung** f - providence

Vorsicht f - care; (*bei Gefahr*) caution; **V~!** carefull (*auf Schild*) 'caution'. **v~ig** adj careful; cautious. **V~smaßnahme** f precaution

Vorsilbe f prefix

Vorsitz m chairmanship; **den V~ führen** be in the chair. **V~ende(r)** m/f chairman

Vorsorge f V~ treffen take precautions; make provisions (**für** for). **v~n** vi sep (*haben*) provide (**für** for)

Vorspeise f starter

Vorspiel nt prelude. **v~en** v sep ● vt perform/ (*Mus*) play (*dat* for) ● vi (*haben*) audition

vorsprechen† v sep ● vt recite; (*zum Nachsagen*) say (*dat* to) ● vi (*haben*) (*Theat*) audition; **bei jdm v~** call on s.o.

Vor|sprung m projection; (*Fels-*) ledge; (*Vorteil*) lead (**vor** + dat over). **V~stadt** f suburb. **V~stand** m board (*of directors*); (*Vereins-*) committee; (*Partei-*) executive

vorsteh|en† vi sep (*haben*) project, protrude; **einer Abteilung v~en** be in charge of a department. **V~er** m -s,- head

vorstell|en† vt sep put forward (*Bein, Uhr*); (*darstellen*) represent; (*bekanntmachen*) introduce; **sich v~en** introduce oneself; (*als Bewerber*) go for an interview; **sich** (*dat*) **etw v~en** imagine sth. **V~ung** f

introduction; (*bei Bewerbung*) interview; (*Aufführung*) performance; (*Idee*) idea; (*Phantasie*) imagination. **V~ungsgespräch** nt interview

Vorstoß m advance

Vorstrafe f previous conviction

Vortag m day before

vortäuschen vt sep feign, fake

Vorteil m advantage. **v~haft** adj advantageous; flattering

Vortrag m -[e]s,ːe talk; (*wissenschaftlich*) lecture. **v~en**† vt sep perform; (*aufsagen*) recite; (*singen*) sing; (*darlegen*) present (*dat* to)

vortrefflich adj excellent

Vortritt m precedence; **jdm den V~ lassen** let s.o. go first

vorüber adv **v~ sein** be over; **an etw** (*dat*) **v~** past sth. **v~gehend** adj temporary

Vor|urteil nt prejudice. **V~verkauf** m advance booking

vorverlegen vt sep bring forward

Vor|wahl[nummer] f dialling code. **V~wand** m -[e]s,ːe pretext; (*Ausrede*) excuse

vorwärts adv forward[s]; **v~kommen** make progress; (*fig*) get on or ahead

vorwegnehmen† vt sep anticipate

vorweisen† vt sep show

vorwiegend adv predominantly

Vorwort nt (*pl* -worte) preface

Vorwurf m reproach; **jdm Vorwürfe machen** reproach s.o. **v~svoll** adj reproachful

Vorzeichen nt sign; (*fig*) omen

vorzeigen vt sep show

vorzeitig adj premature

vorziehen† vt sep pull forward; draw (*Vorhang*); (*lieber mögen*) prefer; favour

Vor|zimmer nt anteroom; (*Büro*)

outer office. **V~zug** m preference;
(*gute Eigenschaft*) merit, virtue;
(*Vorteil*) advantage

vorzüglich adj excellent

vulgär /vʊlˈgɛːɐ̯/ adj vulgar ● adv
in a vulgar way

Vulkan /vʊlˈkaːn/ m -s,-e volcano

Ww

Waage f -,-n scales pl; (*Astrology*)
Libra. **w~recht** adj horizontal

Wabe f -,-n honeycomb

wach adj awake; (*aufgeweckt*) alert;
w~ werden wake up

Wache f -,-n guard; (*Posten*) sentry; (*Dienst*) guard duty; (*Naut*)
watch; (*Polizei-*) station; **W~e halten** keep watch. **W~hund** m
guard-dog

Wacholder m -s juniper

Wachposten m sentry

Wachs nt -es wax

wachsam adj vigilant. **W~keit**
f - vigilance

wachsen† vi (*sein*) grow

wachsen² vt (*reg*) wax. **W~fi-
gur** f waxwork

Wachstum nt -s growth

Wächter m -s,- guard; (*Park-*)
keeper; (*Parkplatz-*) attendant

Wacht|meister m [police] con-
stable. **W~posten** m sentry

wackel|ig adj wobbly; (*Stuhl*) rick-
ety; (*Person*) shaky. **W~kontakt** m
loose connection. **w~n** vi (*haben*)
wobble; (*zittern*) shake

Wade f -,-n (*Anat*) calf

Waffe f -,-n weapon; **W~n** arms

Waffel f -,-n waffle; (*Eis-*) wafer

Waffen|ruhe f cease-fire.
W~schein m firearms licence.
W~stillstand m armistice

Wagemut m daring

wagen vt risk; **es w~**, etw zu tun
dare [to] do sth; **sich w~** (*gehen*)
venture

Wagen m -s,- cart; (*Eisenbahn-*)
carriage, coach; (*Güter-*) wagon;
(*Kinder-*) pram; (*Auto*) car. **W~he-
ber** m -s,- jack

Waggon /vaˈgõː/ m -s,-s wagon

Wahl f -,-en choice; (*Pol, Admin*)
election; (*geheime*) ballot; **zweite
W~** (*Comm*) seconds pl

wähl|en vt/i (*haben*) choose; (*Pol,
Admin*) elect; (*stimmen*) vote; (*Teleph*) dial. **W~er(in)** m -s,- (f
-,-nen) voter. **w~erisch** adj
choosy, fussy

Wahl|fach nt optional subject.
w~frei adj optional. **W~kampf** m
election campaign. **W~kreis** m
constituency. **W~lokal** nt polling-
station. **w~los** adj indiscriminate

Wahl|spruch m motto.
W~urne f ballot-box

Wahn m -[e]s delusion;
(*Manie*) mania

Wahnsinn m madness. **w~ig** adj
mad, insane; (fam: *unsinnig*) crazy;
(fam: *groß*) terrible; **w~ig werden**
go mad ● adv fam terribly.
W~ige(r) m/f maniac

wahr adj true; (*echt*) real; **du
kommst doch, nicht w~?** you are
coming, aren't you?

während prep (+ gen) during
● conj while; (*wohingegen*) whereas

Wahrheit f -,-en truth.
w~sgemäß adj truthful

wahrnehm|en† vt sep notice;
(*nutzen*) take advantage of; exploit
(*Vorteil*); look after (*Interessen*)

W∼ung f -,-en perception

Wahrsagerin f -,-nen fortune teller

wahrscheinlich adj probable. **W∼keit** f - probability

Währung f -,-en currency

Wahrzeichen nt symbol

Waise f -,-n orphan. **W∼nhaus** nt orphanage. **W∼nkind** nt orphan

Wal m -[e]s,-e whale

Wald m -[e]s,¨er wood; (groß) forest. **w∼ig** adj wooded

Waldorfschule An increasingly popular type of private school originally inspired by the Austrian educationist Rudolf Steiner (1861-1925) in the 1920s. The main aim of Waldorf schools is to develop pupils' creative and cognitive abilities through music, art and crafts.

Waliser m -s,- Welshman

Waliserin f -,-nen Welshwoman

w∼isch adj Welsh

Wall m -[e]s,¨e mound

Wallfahr|er(in) m(f) pilgrim. **W∼t** f pilgrimage

Walnuss f walnut

Walze f -,-n roller. **w∼n** vt roll

Walzer m -s,- waltz

Wand f -,¨e wall; (Trenn-) partition; (Seite) side; (Fels-) face

Wandel m -s change

Wander|er m -s,-, **W∼in** f -,-nen hiker, rambler. **w∼n** vi (sein) hike, ramble; (ziehen) travel; (gemächlich gehen) wander; (ziellos) roam. **W∼schaft** f - travels pl. **W∼ung** f -,-en hike, ramble. **W∼weg** m footpath

Wandlung f -,-en change, transformation

Wand|malerei f mural. **W∼ta-**

fel f blackboard. **W∼teppich** m tapestry

Wange f -,-n cheek

wann adv when

Wanne f -,-n tub

Wanze f -,-n bug

Wappen nt -s,- coat of arms. **W∼kunde** f heraldry

Bundeswappen The federal coat of arms features a heraldic eagle, which was originally the emblem of Roman emperors. It was incorporated into the coat of arms of the German Empire when it was founded in 1871. In 1950 it was revived as the official coat of arms of the Federal Republic of Germany.

war, wäre s. sein[1]

Ware f -,-n article; (Comm) commodity; (coll) merchandise. **W∼n** goods. **W∼nhaus** nt department store. **W∼nprobe** f sample. **W∼nzeichen** nt trademark

warm adj warm; (Mahlzeit) hot; **w∼ machen** heat ● adv warmly; **w∼ essen** have a hot meal

Wärm|e f - warmth; (Phys) heat; **10 Grad W∼e** 10 degrees above zero. **w∼en** vt warm; heat (Essen, Wasser). **W∼flasche** f hot-water bottle

Warn|blinkanlage f hazard [warning] lights pl. **w∼en** vt/i (haben) warn (vor + dat of). **W∼ung** f -,-en warning

Warteliste f waiting list

warten vi (haben) wait (auf + acc for) ● vt service

Wärter(in) m -s,- (f -,-nen) keeper; (Museums-) attendant; (Gefängnis-) warder; (Kranken-) orderly

Warte|raum, W∼saal m wait-

w

ing-room. **W~zimmer** nt (Med)
waiting-room

Wartung f - (Techn) service

warum adv why

Warze f -,-n wart

was pron what ● rel pron that;
alles, was ich brauche all [that] I
need ● indefinite pronoun (□:
etwas) something; (fragend, verneint) anything; **so was Ärgerliches!** what a nuisance! ● adv □
(warum) why; (wie) how

wasch|bar adj washable. **W~
becken** nt wash-basin

Wäsche f - washing; (Unter-)
underwear

waschecht adj colour-fast

Wäscheklammer f clothes-peg

waschen† vt wash; **sich w~** have
a wash; **w~ und Legen** shampoo
and set ● vi (haben) do the washing

Wäscherei f -,-en laundry

Wäsche|schleuder f spin-drier.
W~trockner m tumble-drier

Wasch|küche f laundry-room.
W~lappen m face-flannel.
W~maschine f washing machine.
W~mittel nt detergent. **W~pul-
ver** nt washing-powder. **W~salon**
m launderette. **W~zettel** m blurb

Wasser nt -s water. **W~ball** m
beach-ball; (Spiel) water polo.
w~dicht adj watertight; (Kleidung)
waterproof. **W~fall** m waterfall.
W~farbe f water-colour. **W~hahn**
m tap. **W~kraft** f water-power.
W~kraftwerk nt hydroelectric
power-station. **W~leitung** f water-
main; **aus der W~leitung** from the
tap. **W~mann** m (Astrology)
Aquarius

wässern vt soak; (begießen) water
● vi (haben) water

Wasser|ski nt -s water-skiing.
W~stoff m hydrogen. **W~straße**

f waterway. **W~waage** f spirit-level

wässrig adj watery

watscheln vi (sein) waddle

Watt nt -s,- (Phys) watt

Watt|e f - cotton wool. **w~iert**
adj padded; (gesteppt) quilted

WC /ve'tse:/ nt -s,-s WC

Web|cam f -,-s web camera.
W~design nt web design

web|en vt/i (haben) weave. **W~er**
m -s,- weaver

Web|seite /'vep-/ f web page.
W~site f -,-s website

Wechsel m -s,- change; (Tausch)
exchange; (Comm) bill of exchange.
W~geld nt change. **w~haft** adj
changeable. **W~jahre** npl menopause sg. **W~kurs** m exchange
rate. **W~n** vt change; (tauschen) exchange ● vi (haben) change; vary.
w~nd adj changing; varying.
W~strom m alternating current.
W~stube f bureau de change

weck|en vt wake [up]; (fig)
awaken ● vi (haben) (Wecker:) go
off. **W~er** m -s,- alarm [clock]

wedeln vi (haben) wave; **mit dem
Schwanz w~** wag its tail

weder conj **w~ ... noch** neither
... nor

Weg m -[e]s,-e way; (Fuß-) path;
(Fahr-) track; (Gang) errand; **sich
auf den Weg machen** set off

weg adv away, off; (verschwunden)
gone; **weg sein** be away; (gegan-
gen/verschwunden) have gone;
Hände weg! hands off!

wegen prep (+ gen) because of;
(um ... willen) for the sake of; (bezüglich) about

weg|fahren† vi sep (sein) go
away; (abfahren) leave. **W~fahr-
sperre** f immobilizer. **w~fallen†** vi
sep (sein) be dropped/(ausgelassen)
omitted; (entfallen) no longer apply.

w

w~geben† vt sep give away.
w~gehen† vi sep (sein) leave, go away; (ausgehen) go out. w~kommen† vi sep (sein) get away; (verloren gehen) disappear; **schlecht** w~kommen Ⅰ get a raw deal. w~lassen† vt sep let go; (auslassen) omit. w~laufen† vi sep (sein) run away. w~räumen vt sep put away; (entfernen) clear away. w~schicken vt sep send away; (abschicken) send off. w~tun† vt sep put away; (wegwerfen) throw away

Wegweiser m -s,- signpost

weg|werfen† vt sep throw away. w~ziehen† v sep ● vt pull away ● vi (sein) move away

weh adj sore; **weh tun** hurt; (Kopf, Rücken:) ache; **jdm weh tun** hurt s.o.

wehe int alas; w~ **[dir/euch]!** (drohend) don't you dare!

wehen vi (haben) blow; (flattern) flutter ● vt blow

Wehen fpl contractions

Wehr[1] nt -[e]s,-e weir

Wehr[2] f sich zur W~ setzen resist. W~dienst m military service. W~dienstverweigerer m -s,- conscientious objector

wehren (sich) vr resist; (gegen Anschuldigung) protest; (sich sträuben) refuse

wehr|los adj defenceless. W~macht f armed forces pl. W~pflicht f conscription

Weib nt -[e]s,-er woman; (Ehe-) wife. W~chen nt -s,- (Zool) female. w~lich adj feminine; (Biology) female

weich adj soft; (gar) done

Weiche f -,-n (Rail) points pl

Weich|heit f - softness. w~lich adj soft; (Charakter) weak. W~spüler m -s,- (Textiles) conditioner

W~tier nt mollusc

Weide[1] f -,-n (Bot) willow

Weide[2] f -,-n pasture. w~n vt/i (haben) graze

weiger|n (sich) vr refuse. W~ung f -,-en refusal

Weihe f -,-n consecration; (Priester-) ordination. w~n vt consecrate; (zum Priester) ordain

Weiher m -s,- pond

Weihnacht|en nt -s & pl Christmas. w~lich adj Christmassy. W~sbaum m Christmas tree. W~slied nt Christmas carol. W~smann m (pl -männer) Father Christmas. W~stag m erster/zweiter W~stag Christmas Day/Boxing Day

>
> **Weihnachtsmarkt** During the weeks of Advent, Christmas markets are held in most German towns. Visitors can buy Christmas decorations, handmade toys and crib figures, traditional Christmas biscuits, and mulled wine to sustain them while they shop.

Weih|rauch m incense. W~wasser nt holy water

weil conj because; (da) since

Weile f - while

Wein m -[e]s,-e wine; (Bot) vines pl; (Trauben) grapes pl. W~bau m winegrowing. W~berg m vineyard. W~brand m -[e]s brandy

weinen vt/i (haben) cry, weep

Wein|glas nt wine glass. W~karte f wine list. W~lese f grape harvest. W~liste f wine list. W~probe f wine tasting. W~rebe f, W~stock m vine. W~stube f wine bar. W~traube f bunch of grapes; (W~beere) grape

weise adj wise

W

Weise f -,-n way; (Melodie) tune

Weisheit f -,-en wisdom.
W~szahn m wisdom tooth

weiß adj, W~ nt -,- white

weissag|en vt/i insep (haben)
prophesy. W~ung f -,-en prophecy

Weiß|brot nt white bread.
W~e(r) m/f white man/woman.
w~en vt whitewash. W~wein m
white wine

Weisung f -,-en instruction; (Befehl) order

weit adj wide; (ausgedehnt) extensive; (lang) long ● adv widely;
(offen, öffnen) wide; (lang) far; von
w~em from a distance; bei
w~em by far; w~ und breit far
and wide; ist es noch w~? is it
much further? so w~ wie möglich
as far as possible; ich bin so w~
I'm ready; w~ verbreitet widespread; w~ reichende Folgen far-
reaching consequences

Weite f -,-n expanse; (Entfernung)
distance; (Größe) width. w~n vt
widen; stretch (Schuhe)

weiter adj further ● adv further;
(außerdem) in addition; (anschließend) then; etw w~ tun go
on doing sth; w~ nichts/niemand
nothing/no one else; und so w~
and so on

weiter|e(r,s) adj further; ohne
w~es just like that; (leicht) easily

weiter|erzählen vt sep go on
with; (w~sagen) repeat. w~fah-
rent vi sep (sein) go on. w~geben†
vt sep pass on. w~hin adv (immer
noch) still; (in Zukunft) in future;
(außerdem) furthermore; etw
w~hin tun go on doing sth.
w~machen vi sep (haben) carry on

weit|gehend adj extensive ● adv
to a large extent. w~sichtig adj
long-sighted; (fig) far-sighted.
W~sprung m long jump. w~ver-

breitet adj = w~ verbreitet,
s. weit

Weizen m -s wheat

welch inv pron what; w~ ein(e)
what a. w~e(r,s) pron which; um
w~e Zeit? at what time? ● rel pron
which; (Person) who ● indefinite pronoun some; (fragend) any; was für
w~e? what sort of?

Wellblech nt corrugated iron

Well|e f -,-n wave; (Techn) shaft.
W~enlänge f wavelength. W~en-
linie f wavy line. W~enreiten nt
surfing. W~ensittich m -s,-e
budgerigar. w~ig adj wavy.

Wellness f - mental and physical
wellbeing

Welt f -,-en world; auf der W~ in
the world; auf die od zur W~
kommen be born. W~all nt universe. w~berühmt adj world-fam-
ous. w~fremd adj unworldly.
W~kugel f globe. w~lich adj
worldly; (nicht geistlich) secular

Weltmeister|(in) m(f) world
champion. W~schaft f world
championship

Weltraum m space. W~fahrer
m astronaut

Weltrekord m world record

wem pron (dat of wer) to whom

wen pron (acc of wer) whom

Wende f -,-n change. W~kreis m
(Geog) tropic

Wendeltreppe f spiral staircase

wenden¹ vt (reg) turn ● vi (haben)
turn [round]

wenden²† (& reg) vt turn; sich
w~ turn; sich an jdn w~
turn/(schriftlich) write to s.o.

Wend|epunkt m (fig) turning-
point. W~ung f -,-en turn; (Biegung) bend; (Veränderung) change

wenig pron little; (pl) few; so/zu
w~ so/too little/(pl) few; w~e pl

few ● *adv* little; (*kaum*) not much; **so w~ wie möglich** as little as possible. **w~er** *pron* less; (*pl*) fewer; **immer w~er** less and less ● *adv & conj* less. **w~ste(r,s)** least; **am w~sten** least [of all]. **w~stens** *adv* at least

wenn *conj* if; (*sobald*) when; **immer w~** whenever; **w~ nicht** *od* **außer w~** unless; **w~ auch** even though

wer *pron* who; (□: *jemand*) someone; (*fragend*) anyone

Werbe|agentur *f* advertising agency. **w~n†** *vt* recruit; (*Kunden, Besucher*) ● *vi* (*haben*) **w~n für** advertise; canvass for (*Partei*). **W~spot** *m* -s,-s commercial

Werbung *f* - advertising

---

werden†

● *intransitive verb* (*sein*)
••••▶ (+ *adjective*) become; get; (*allmählich*) grow. **müde/alt/länger werden** become or get/ grow tired/old/longer. **taub/ blind/wahnsinnig werden** go deaf/blind/mad. **blass werden** become or turn pale. **krank werden** become or fall ill. **es wird warm/dunkel** it is getting warm/dark. **mir wurde schlecht/schwindlig** I began to feel sick/dizzy

••••▶ (+ *noun*) become. **Arzt/Lehrer/Mutter werden** become a doctor/teacher/mother. **er will Lehrer werden** he wants to be a teacher. **was ist aus ihm geworden?** what has become of him?

••••▶ **werden zu** become; turn into. **das Erlebnis wurde zu einem Albtraum** the experience

became or turned into a nightmare. **zu Eis werden** turn into ice

● *auxiliary verb*
••••▶ (*Zukunft*) will; shall. **er wird bald hier sein** he will or he'll soon be here. **wir werden sehen** we shall see. **es wird bald regnen** it's going to rain soon

••••▶ (*Konjunktiv*) **würde(n)** would. **ich würde es kaufen, wenn ...** I would buy it if .... **würden Sie so nett sein?** would you be so kind?

••••▶ (*beim Passiv; pp* **worden**) be. **geliebt/geboren werden** be loved/born. **du wirst gerufen** you are being called. **er wurde gebeten** he was asked. **es wurde gemunkelt** it was rumoured. **mir wurde gesagt, dass ...** I was told that .... **das Haus ist soeben/1995 renoviert worden** the house has just been renovated/was renovated in 1995

---

werfen† *vt* throw; cast (*Blick, Schatten*); **sich w~** (*Holz:*) warp

Werft *f* -,-en shipyard

Werk *nt* -[e]s,-e work; (*Fabrik*) works *sg*, factory; (*Trieb-*) mechanism. **W~en** *nt* -s (*Sch*) handicraft. **W~statt** *f* -,^:en workshop; (*Auto-*) garage. **W~tag** *m* weekday. **w~tags** *adv* on weekdays. **w~tätig** *adj* working

Werkzeug *nt* tool; (*coll*) tools *pl*. **W~leiste** *f* toolbar

Wermut *m* -s vermouth

wert *adj* **viel w~** worth a lot; **nichts w~ sein** be worthless; **jds Liebe w~ sein** be worthy of s.o. **W~** *m* -[e]s,-e value; (*Nenn-*) denomination; **im W~ von** worth. **w~en**

W

vt rate

Wert|gegenstand *m* object of value. **w~los** *adj* worthless. **W~minderung** *f* depreciation. **W~papier** *nt* (*Comm*) security. **W~sachen** *fpl* valuables. **w~voll** *adj* valuable

Wesen *nt* -s,- nature; (*Lebe-*) being; (*Mensch*) creature

wesentlich *adj* essential; (*grundlegend*) fundamental ● *adv* considerably, much

weshalb *adv* why

Wespe *f* -,-n wasp

wessen *pron* (*gen of* **wer**) whose

westdeutsch *adj* West German

Weste *f* -,-n waistcoat

Westen *m* -s west

Western *m* -[s],- western

Westfalen *nt* -s Westphalia

Westindien *nt* West Indies *pl*

west|lich *adj* western; (*Richtung*) westerly ● *adv & prep* (+ *gen*) **w~lich [von] der Stadt** [to the] west of the town. **w~wärts** *adv* westwards

weswegen *adv* why

Wettbewerb *m* -s,-e competition

Wette *f* -,-n bet; **um die W~ laufen race (mit jdm** s.o.)

wetten *vt/i* (*haben*) bet (**auf** + *acc* on); **mit jdm** have a bet with s.o.

Wetter *nt* -s,- weather; (*Un-*) storm. **W~bericht** *m* weather report. **W~vorhersage** *f* weather forecast. **W~warte** *f* -,-n meteorological station

Wett|kampf *m* contest. **W~kämpfer(in)** *m*(*f*) competitor. **W~lauf** *m* race. **W~rennen** *nt* race. **W~streit** *m* contest

Whisky *m* -s whisky

wichtig *adj* important; **w~ nehmen** take seriously. **W~keit** *f* - importance

Wicke *f* -,-n sweet pea

Wickel *m* -s,- compress

wickeln *vt* wind; (*ein-*) wrap; (*bandagieren*) bandage; **ein Kind frisch w~** change a baby

Widder *m* -s,- ram; (*Astrology*) Aries

wider *prep* (+ *acc*) against; (*entgegen*) contrary to; **w~ Willen** against one's will

widerlegen *vt insep* refute

wider|lich *adj* repulsive. **W~rede** *f* contradiction; **keine W~redel** don't argue!

widerrufen† *vt/i insep* (*haben*) retract; revoke (*Befehl*)

Widersacher *m* -s,- adversary

widersetzen (sich) *vr insep* resist (**jdm/etw** s.o./sth)

widerspiegeln *vt sep* reflect

widersprechen† *vi insep* (*haben*) contradict (**jdm/etw** s.o./something)

Wider|spruch *m* contradiction; (*Protest*) protest. **w~sprüchlich** *adj* contradictory. **w~spruchslos** *adj* without protest

Widerstand *m* resistance; **W~ leisten** resist. **w~sfähig** *adj* resistant; (*Bot*) hardy

widerstehen† *vi insep* (*haben*) resist (**jdm/etw** s.o./sth); (*anwidern*) be repugnant (**jdm** to s.o.)

Widerstreben *nt* -s reluctance

widerwärtig *adj* disagreeable

Wider|will *m* aversion, repugnance. **w~ig** *adj* reluctant

widm|en *vt* dedicate (*dat* to); (*verwenden*) devote (*dat* to); **sich w~en** (+ *dat*) devote oneself to. **W~ung** *f* -,-en dedication

w

wie adv how; **wie viel** how much/(pl) many; **um wie viel Uhr?** at what time? **wie viele?** how many? **wie ist Ihr Name?** what is your name? **wie ist das Wetter?** what is the weather like? ● conj as; (gleich wie) like; (sowie) as well as; (als) when, as; **so gut wie** as good as; **nichts wie** nothing but

wieder adv again; **jdn/etw w~erkennen** recognize s.o./something; **etw w~ verwenden/verwerten** reuse/recycle sth; **etw w~ gutmachen** make up for (Schaden); redress (Unrecht); (bezahlen) pay for sth

Wiederaufbau m reconstruction

wieder|bekommen† vt sep get back. **W~belebung** f - resuscitation. **w~bringen†** vt sep bring back. **w~erkennen†** vt sep * **w~erkennen**, s. wieder. **w~geben†** vt sep give back, return; (darstellen) portray; (ausdrücken, übersetzen) render; (zitieren) quote. **W~geburt** f reincarnation

Wiedergutmachung f - reparation; (Entschädigung) compensation

wiederherstellen† vt sep reestablish, restore (Gebäude); restore to health (Kranke)

wiederhol|en† vt insep repeat; (Sch) revise; **sich w~en** recur; (Person:) repeat oneself. **w~t** adj repeated. **W~ung** f -,-en repetition; (Sch) revision

Wieder|hören nt auf W~hören! goodbye! **W~käuer** m -s,- ruminant. **W~kehr** f - return; (W~holung) recurrence. **w~kommen†** vi sep (sein) come back

wiedersehen† vt sep wieder sehen, s. sehen. **W~** nt -s,- reunion; **auf W~!** goodbye!

wiedervereinig|en† vt sep wieder vereinigen, s. vereinigen.

W~ung f reunification

wieder|verwenden† vt sep* **w~ verwenden**, s. wieder. **w~verwerten†** vt sep **w~verwerten**, s. wieder

Wiege f -,-n cradle

wiegen¹† vt/i (haben) weigh

wiegen² vt (reg) rock. **W~lied** nt lullaby

wiehern vi (haben) neigh

Wien nt -s Vienna. **W~er** adj Viennese ● m -s,- Viennese ● f -,- ≈ frankfurter. **w~erisch** adj Viennese

Wiese f -,-n meadow

Wiesel nt -s,- weasel

wieso adv why

wieviel* pron wie viel, s. wie. **w~te(r,s)** adj which; **der W~te ist heute?** what is the date today?

wieweit adv how far

wild adj wild; (Stamm) savage; **w~er Streik** wildcat strike; **w~ wachsen** grow wild ● nt -[e]s game; (Rot-) deer; (Culin) venison. **W~e(r)** m/f savage

Wilder|er m -s,- poacher. **w~n** vt/i (haben) poach

Wild|heger m -s,- gamekeeper. **W~leder** nt suede. **W~nis** f - wilderness. **W~schwein** nt wild boar. **W~westfilm** m western

Wille m -ns will

w

Willenskraft f will-power

willig adj willing

willkommen adj welcome; **w~ heißen** welcome. **W~** nt -s welcome

wimmeln vi (haben) swarm

wimmern vi (haben) whimper

Wimpel m -s,- pennant

Wimper f -,-n [eye]lash; **W~n- tusche** f mascara

Wind m -[e]s,-e wind

Winde f -,-n (Techn) winch

Windel f -,-n nappy

winden† vt wind; make (Kranz); **in die Höhe w~** winch up; **sich w~** wind (um round); (sich krümmen) writhe

Wind|hund m greyhound. **w~ig** adj windy. **W~mühle** f windmill. **W~park** m wind farm. **W~po- cken** fpl chickenpox sg. **W~schutzscheibe** f windscreen. **W~stille** f calm. **W~stoß** m gust of wind. **W~surfen** nt windsurfing

Windung f -,-n bend; (Spirale) spiral

Winkel m -s,- angle; (Ecke) corner. **W~messer** m -s,- protractor

winken vi (haben) wave

Winter m -s,- winter. **w~lich** adj wintry; (Winter-) winter **W~schlaf** m hibernation. **W~sport** m winter sports pl

Winzer m -s,- winegrower

winzig adj tiny, minute

Wipfel m -s,- [tree]top

Wippe f -,-n see-saw

wir pron we; **wir sind es** it's us

Wirbel m -s,- eddy; (Drehung) whirl; (Trommel-) roll; (Anat) verte- bra; (Haar-) crown; (Aufsehen) fuss. **w~n** vt/i (sein/haben) whirl. **W~säule** f spine. **W~sturm** m cyclone. **W~tier** nt vertebrate.

W~wind m whirlwind

wird s. werden

wirken vi (haben) have an effect (auf + acc on); (zur Geltung kom- men) be effective; (tätig sein) work; (scheinen) seem ● vt (Textiles) knit

wirklich adj real. **W~keit** f -,-en reality

wirksam adj effective

Wirkung f -,-en effect. **w~slos** adj ineffective. **w~svoll** adj ef- fective

wirr adj tangled; (Haar) tousled; (verwirrt, verworren) confused

Wirt m -[e]s,-e landlord. **W~in** f -,-nen landlady

Wirtschaft f -,-en economy; (Gast-) restaurant; (Kneipe) pub. **w~en** vi (haben) manage one's fi- nances. **w~lich** adj economic; (sparsam) economical. **W~sflücht- ling** m economic refugee. **W~sgeld** nt housekeeping [money]. **W~sprüfer** m auditor

Wirtshaus nt inn; (Kneipe) pub

wischen vt/i (haben) wipe; wash (Fußboden)

wissen† vt/i (haben) know; **weißt du noch?** do you remember? **nichts w~ wollen** von not want anything to do with. **W~** nt -s knowledge; **meines W~s** to my knowledge

Wissenschaft f -,-en science. **W~ler** m -s,- academic; (Natur-) scientist. **w~lich** adj academic; scientific

wissenswert adj worth knowing

witter|n vt scent; (ahnen) sense. **W~ung** f - scent; (Wetter) weather

Witwe f -,-n widow. **W~r** m -s,- widower

Witz m -es,-e joke; (Geist) wit. **W~bold** m -[e]s,-e joker. **w~ig** adj funny; witty

w

wo adv where; (als) when; (irgendwo) somewhere; **wo immer** wherever ● conj seeing that; (obwohl) although; (wenn) if

woanders adv somewhere else

wobei adv how; (relativ) during the course of which

Woche f -,-n week. **W~nende** nt weekend. **W~nkarte** f weekly ticket. **w~nlang** adv for weeks. **W~ntag** m day of the week; (Werktag) weekday. **w~tags** adv on weekdays

wöchentlich adj & adv weekly

Wodka m -s vodka

wofür adv what ... for; (relativ) for which

Woge f -,-n wave

woher adv where from; **woher weißt du das?** how do you know that? **wohin** adv where [to]; **wohin gehst du?** where are you going?

wohl adv well; (vermutlich) probably; (etwa) about; (zwar) perhaps; **w~ kaum** hardly; **sich w~ fühlen** feel well/(behaglich) comfortable; **jdm w~ tun** do s.o. good. **W~** nt -[e]s welfare, well-being; **zum W~** (+ gen) for the good of; **zum W~!** cheers!

Wohl|befinden nt well-being. **W~behagen** nt feeling of wellbeing. **W~ergehen** nt -s welfare. ● **w~erzogen** adj well brought-up

Wohlfahrt f - welfare. **W~sstaat** m Welfare State

wohl|habend adj prosperous, well-to-do. **w~ig** adj comfortable. **w~schmeckend** adj tasty

Wohlstand m prosperity. **W~sgesellschaft** f affluent society

Wohltat f [act of] kindness; (Annehmlichkeit) treat; (Genuss) bliss

Wohltät|er m benefactor. **w~ig** adj charitable

wohl|tuend adj agreeable. **w~tun*** vi sep (haben) **w~ tun**, s. **wohl**

Wohlwollen nt -s goodwill; (Gunst) favour. **w~d** adj benevolent

Wohn|block m block of flats. **w~en** vi (haben) live; (vorübergehend) stay. **w~gegend** f residential area. **w~haft** adj resident. **W~haus** nt house. **W~heim** nt hostel; (Alten-) home. **W~lich** adj comfortable. **W~mobil** nt -s,-e camper. **W~ort** m place of residence. **W~sitz** m place of residence

Wohnung f -,-en flat; (Unterkunft) accommodation. **W~snot** f housing shortage

Wohn|wagen m caravan. **W~zimmer** nt living-room

wölb|en vt curve; arch (Rücken). **W~ung** f -,-en curve; (Architecture) vault

Wolf m -[e]s,̈-e wolf; (Fleisch-) mincer; (Reiß-) shredder

Wolk|e f -,-n cloud. **W~enbruch** m cloudburst. **W~enkratzer** m skyscraper. **w~enlos** adj cloudless. **w~ig** adj cloudy

Woll|decke f blanket. **W~e** f -,-n wool

---

wollen¹

● auxiliary verb

····▶ (den Wunsch haben) want to. **ich will nach Hause gehen** I want to go home. **ich wollte Sie fragen, ob ...** I wanted to ask you if ...

····▶ (im Begriff sein) be about to. **wir wollten gerade gehen** we were just about to go

····▶ (sich in der gewünschten Weise verhalten) will. **nicht wollen** refuses to.

w

der Motor will nicht anspringen the engine won't start

● *intransitive verb*

····▶ want to. ob du willst oder nicht whether you want to or not. ganz wie du willst just as you like

····▶ (II: *irgendwohin zu gehen wünschen*) ich will nach Hause I want to go home. zu wem wollen Sie? who[m] do you want to see?

····▶ (II: *funktionieren*) will nicht won't go. meine Beine wollen nicht mehr my legs are giving up (II)

● *transitive verb*

····▶ want; (*beabsichtigen*) intend. er will nicht, dass du ihm hilfst he does not want you to help him. das habe ich nicht gewollt I never intended or meant that to happen

Wollsachen *fpl* woollens

womit *adv* what ... with; (*relativ*) with which. **wonach** *adv* what ... after/(*suchen*) for/(*riechen*) of; (*relativ*) after/for/of which

woran *adv* what ... on/(*denken, sterben*) of; (*relativ*) on/of which; **woran hast du ihn erkannt?** how did you recognize him? **worauf** *adv* what on .../(*warten*) for; (*relativ*) on/for which; (*woraufhin*) whereupon. **woraus** *adv* what ... from; (*relativ*) from which

Wort *nt* -[e]s, ≈er & -e *word*. **jdm ins W~ fallen** interrupt s.o. **Wörterbuch** *nt* dictionary **Wort|führer** *m* spokesman. **w~getreu** *adj & adv* word-for-word. **W~karg** *adj* taciturn. **W~laut** *m* wording **wörtlich** *adj* literal; (*wortgetreu*) word-for-word

wort|los *adj* silent ● *adv* without a word. **W~schatz** *m* vocabulary. **W~spiel** *nt* pun, play on words

worüber *adv* what ... over/(*lachen, sprechen*) about; (*relativ*) over/about which. **worum** *adv* what ... round/(*bitten, kämpfen*) for; (*relativ*) round/for which; **worum geht es?** what is it about? **wovon** *adv* what ... from/(*sprechen*) about; (*relativ*) from/about which. **wovor** *adv* what ... in front of; (*sich fürchten*) of; (*relativ*) in front of which; of which. **wozu** *adv* what ... to/(*brauchen, benutzen*) for; (*relativ*) to/for which; **wozu?** what for?

Wrack *nt* -s,-s wreck

wringen† *vt* wring

Wucher|preis *m* extortionate price. **W~ung** *f* -,-en growth

Wuchs *m* -es growth; (*Gestalt*) stature

Wucht *f* - force

wühlen *vi* (*haben*) rummage; (*in der Erde*) burrow ● *vt* dig

Wulst *m* -[e]s,≈e bulge; (*Fett-*) roll

wund *adj* sore; **w~ reiben** chafe; **sich w~ liegen** get bedsores. **W~brand** *m* gangrene

Wunde *f* -,-n wound

Wunder *nt* -s,- wonder, marvel; (*übernatürliches*) miracle; **kein W~!** no wonder! **w~bar** *adj* miraculous; (*herrlich*) wonderful. **W~kind** *nt* infant prodigy. **w~n** *vt* surprise; **sich w~n** be surprised (**über** + *acc* at). **w~schön** *adj* beautiful

Wundstarrkrampf *m* tetanus

Wunsch *m* -[e]s,≈e wish (*Verlangen*) desire; (*Bitte*) request

wünschen *vt* want; **sich** (*dat*) **etw w~** want sth; (*bitten um*) ask for sth; **jdm Glück/gute Nacht w~** wish s.o. luck/good night; **Sie w~?** can I help you? **w~swert** *adj*

desirable

Wunschkonzert *nt* musical request programme

wurde, würde s. werden

Würde *f* -,-n dignity; (*Ehrenrang*) honour. **w~los** *adj* undignified. **W~nträger** *m* dignitary. **w~voll** *adj* dignified ● *adv* with dignity

würdig *adj* dignified; (*wert*) worthy

Wurf *m* -[e]s,ˉe throw; (*Junge*) litter

Würfel *m* -s,- cube; (*Spiel-*) dice; (*Zucker-*) lump. **w~n** *vi* (*haben*) throw the dice; (*um etw*) play dice for ● *vt* throw; (*in Würfel schneiden*) dice. **W~zucker** *m* cube sugar

würgen *vt* choke ● *vi* (*haben*) retch; choke (**an** + *dat* on)

Wurm *m* -[e]s,ˉer worm; (*Made*) maggot. **w~en** *vi* (*haben*) jdn **w~en** ① rankle [with s.o.]

Wurst *f* -,ˉe sausage; **das ist mir W~** ① I couldn't care less

Würze *f* -,-n spice; (*Aroma*) aroma

Wurzel *f* -,-n root; **W~n schlagen** take root. **w~n** *vi* (*haben*) root

würz|en *vt* season. **w~ig** *adj* tasty; (*aromatisch*) aromatic; (*pikant*) spicy

wüst *adj* chaotic; (*wirr*) tangled; (*öde*) desolate; (*wild*) wild; (*schlimm*) terrible

Wüste *f* -,-n desert

Wut *f* - rage, fury. **W~anfall** *m* fit of rage

wüten *vi* (*haben*) rage. **w~d** *adj* furious; **w~d machen** infuriate

Xx

x /ɪks/ *inv adj* (*Math*) x; ① umpteen. **X-Beine** *ntpl* knock-knees. **x-beinig, X-beinig** *adj* knock-kneed. **x-beliebig** *adj* ① any. **x-mal** *adv* ① umpteen times

Yy

Yoga /ˈjoːɡa/ *m & nt* -[s] yoga

Zz

Zack|e *f* -,-n point; (*Berg-*) peak; (*Gabel-*) prong. **z~ig** *adj* jagged; (*gezackt*) serrated

zaghaft *adj* timid; (*zögernd*) tentative

zäh *adj* tough; (*hartnäckig*) tenacious. **z~flüssig** *adj* viscous; (*Verkehr*) slow-moving. **Z~igkeit** *f* - toughness; tenacity

Zahl *f* -,-en number; (*Ziffer, Betrag*) figure

zahlen *vt/i* (*haben*) pay; (*bezahlen*) pay for; **bitte z~!** the bill please!

zählen *vi* (*haben*) count; **z~ zu** (*fig*) be one/(*pl*) some of ● *vt* count; **z~ zu** add to; (*fig*) count among

zahlenmäßig *adj* numerical

w
x
y
z

Zähler m -s,- meter

Zahl|grenze f fare-stage.
Z~karte f paying-in slip. **Z~los** adj
countless. **Z~reich** adj numerous;
(Anzahl, Gruppe) large ● adv in large
numbers. **Z~ung** f -,-en payment;
in Z~ung nehmen take in part-ex-
change

Zählung f -,-en count

Zahlwort nt (pl -wörter) numeral

zahm adj tame

zähmen vt tame; (fig) restrain

Zahn m -[e]s, ̈e tooth; (am Zahn-
rad) cog. **Z~arzt** m, **Z~ärztin** f
dentist. **Z~belag** m plaque.
Z~bürste f toothbrush. **Z~fleisch**
nt gums pl. **Z~los** adj toothless.
Z~pasta f -,- toothpaste.
Z~rad nt cog-wheel. **Z~schmelz**
m enamel. **Z~schmerzen** mpl
toothache sg. **Z~spange** f brace.
Z~stein m tartar. **Z~stocher** m
-s,- toothpick

Zange f -,-n pliers pl; (Kneif-) pincers pl; (Kohlen-, Zucker-) tongs pl;
(Geburts-) forceps pl

Zank m -[e]s squabble. **Z~en** vr
sich z~en squabble

Zäpfchen nt -s,- (Anat) uvula;
(Med) suppository

zapfen vt tap, draw. **Z~streich** m
(Mil) tattoo

Zapf|hahn m tap. **Z~säule** f pet-
rol-pump

zappeln vi (haben) wriggle; (Kind)
fidget

zart adj delicate; (weich, zärtlich)
tender; (sanft) gentle. **Z~gefühl**
nt tact

zärtlich adj tender; (liebevoll) loving. **Z~keit** f -,-en tenderness;
(Liebkosung) caress

Zauber m -s magic; (Bann) spell.
Z~er m -s,- magician. **z~haft** adj
enchanting. **Z~künstler** m con-

juror. **z~n** vi (haben) do magic;
(Zaubertricks ausführen) do conjuring tricks ● vt produce as if by
magic. **Z~stab** m magic wand.
Z~trick m conjuring trick

Zaum m -[e]s,Zäume bridle

Zaun m -[e]s,Zäune fence

z.B. abbr (zum Beispiel) e.g.

Zebra nt -s,-s zebra. **Z~streifen** m
zebra crossing

Zeche f -,-n bill; (Bergwerk) pit

zechen vi (haben) Ⓣ drink

Zeder f -,-n cedar

Zeh m -[e]s,-en toe. **Z~e** f -,-n toe;
(Knoblauch-) clove

zehn inv adj. **Z~** f -,-en ten.
z~te(r,s) adj tenth. **Z~tel** nt
-s,- tenth

Zeichen nt -s,- sign; (Signal) signal. **Z~setzung** f- punctuation.
Z~trickfilm m cartoon

zeichn|en vt/i (haben) draw;
(kenn-) mark; (unter-) sign. **Z~ung** f
-,-en drawing

Zeige|finger m index finger. **z~n**
vt show; **sich z~n** appear; (sich herausstellen) become clear ● vi (haben)
point (auf + acc to). **Z~r** m -s,-
pointer; (Uhr-) hand

Zeile f -,-n line; (Reihe) row

Zeit f -,-en time; (Gram) tense; **sich (dat) Z~ lassen** take one's time; **es hat Z~**
there's no hurry; **mit der Z~** in
time; **in nächster Z~** in the near
future; **zur Z~** (rechtzeitig) in time;
*(derzeit) s. **zurzeit** (in time);* **eine Z~ lang**
for a time or while

Zeit|alter nt age, era. **z~gemäß**
adj modern, up-to-date. **Z~ge-
nosse** m, **Z~genossin** f contemporary. **z~genössisch** adj contemporary. **z~ig** adj & adv early

zeitlich adj (Dauer) in time; (Folge)
chronological. ● adv **z~ begrenzt**
for a limited time

zeit|los adj timeless. **Z~lupe** f slow motion. **Z~punkt** m time. **z~raubend** adj time-consuming. **Z~raum** m period. **Z~schrift** f magazine, periodical

Zeitung f -,-en newspaper. **Z~spapier** nt newspaper

Zeit|verschwendung f waste of time. **Z~vertreib** m pastime. **z~weise** adv at times. **Z~wort** nt (pl -wörter) verb. **Z~zünder** m time fuse

Zelle f -,-n cell; (Telefon-) box

Zelt nt -[e]s,-e tent; (Fest-) marquee. **z~en** vi (haben) camp. **Z~en** nt -s camping. **Z~plane** f tarpaulin. **Z~platz** m campsite

Zement m -[e]s cement

zen|sieren vt (Sch) mark; censor (Presse, Film). **Z~sur** f -,-en (Sch) mark; (Presse-) censorship

Zentimeter m & nt centimetre. **Z~maß** nt tape-measure

Zentner m -s,- [metric] hundred-weight (50 kg)

zentral adj central. **Z~e** f -,-n central office; (Partei-) headquarters pl; (Teleph) exchange. **Z~heizung** f central heating

Zentrum nt -s,-tren centre

zerbrech|en vt/i (haben) break. **z~lich** adj fragile

zerdrücken vt crush

Zeremonie f -,-n ceremony

Zerfall m disintegration; (Verfall) decay. **z~en†** vi (sein) disintegrate; (verfallen) decay

zergehen† vi (sein) melt; (sich auflösen) dissolve

zerkleinern vt chop/(schneiden) cut up; (mahlen) grind

zerknüllen vt crumple [up]

zerkratzen vt scratch

zerlassen† vt melt

zerlegen vt take to pieces, dismantle; (zerschneiden) cut up; (tranchieren) carve

zerlumpt adj ragged

zermalmen vt crush

zermürben vt (fig) wear down

zerplatzen vi (sein) burst

zerquetschen vt squash; crush

Zerrbild nt caricature

zerreißen† vt tear; (in Stücke) tear up; break (Faden, Seil) ● vi (sein) tear; break

zerren vt drag; pull (Muskel) ● vi (haben) pull (an + dat at)

zerrissen adj torn

zerrütten vt ruin, wreck; shatter (Nerven)

zerschlagen† vt smash; smash up (Möbel); **sich z~** (fig) fall through; (Hoffnung:) be dashed

zerschmettern vt/i (sein) smash

zerschneiden† vt cut; (in Stücke) cut up

zersplittern vi (sein) splinter; (Glas:) shatter ● vt shatter

zerspringen† vi (sein) shatter; (bersten) burst

Zerstäuber m -s,- atomizer

zerstör|en vt destroy; (zunichte machen) wreck. **Z~er** m -s,- destroyer. **Z~ung** f destruction

zerstreu|en vt scatter; disperse (Menge); dispel (Zweifel); **sich z~en** disperse; (sich unterhalten) amuse oneself. **z~t** adj absent-minded

Zertifikat nt -[e]s,-e certificate

zertrümmern vt smash [up]; wreck (Gebäude, Stadt)

Zettel m -s,- piece of paper; (Notiz) note; (Bekanntmachung) notice

Zeug nt -s 🔢 stuff; (Sachen) things pl; (Ausrüstung) gear; **dummes Z~** nonsense

Zeuge m -n,-n witness. **z~n** vi

z

(*haben*) testify; **z~n von** (*fig*) show ● *vt* father. **Z~naussage** *f* testimony. **Z~nstand** *m* witness box

Zeugin *f* -,-nen witness

Zeugnis *nt* -ses,-se certificate; (*Sch*) report; (*Referenz*) reference; (*fig: Beweis*) evidence

Zickzack *m* -[e]s,-e zigzag

Ziege *f* -,-n goat

Ziegel *m* -s,- brick; (*Dach-*) tile. **Z~stein** *m* brick

ziehen† *vt* pull; (*sanfter: zücken; zeichnen*) draw; (*heraus-*) pull out; extract (*Zahn*); raise (*Hut*); put on (*Bremse*); move (*Schachfigur*); (*dehnen*) stretch; make (*Grimasse, Scheitel*); (*züchten*) breed; grow (*Rosen*); **nach sich z~** (*fig*) entail ● *vr* **sich z~** (*sich erstrecken*) run; (*sich verziehen*) warp ● *vi* (*haben*) pull (**an** + *dat* on/at); (*Tee, Ofen:*) draw; (*Culin*) simmer; **es zieht** there is a draught; **solche Filme z~ nicht mehr** films like that are no longer popular ● *vi* (*sein*) (*um-*) move (**nach** to); (*Menge:*) march; (*Vögel:*) migrate; (*Wolken, Nebel:*) drift

Ziehharmonika *f* accordion

Ziehung *f* -,-en draw

Ziel *nt* -[e]s,-e destination; (*Sport*) finish; (*Z~scheibe & Mil*) target; (*Zweck*) aim, goal. **z~bewusst** *adj* purposeful. **z~en** *vi* (*haben*) aim (**auf** + *acc* at). **z~los** *adj* aimless. **Z~scheibe** *f* target

ziemlich *adj* Ⅰ fair ● *adv* rather, fairly

Zier|de *f* -,-n ornament. **z~en** *vt* adorn

zierlich *adj* dainty

Ziffer *f* -,-n figure, digit; (*Zahlzeichen*) numeral. **Z~blatt** *nt* dial

Zigarette *f* -,-n cigarette

Zigarre *f* -,-n cigar

Zigeuner(in) *m* -s,-

(*f* -,-nen) gypsy

Zimmer *nt* -s,- room. **Z~mädchen** *nt* chambermaid. **Z~mann** *m* (*pl* -leute) carpenter. **Z~nachweis** *m* accommodation bureau. **Z~pflanze** *f* house plant

Zimt *m* -[e]s cinnamon

Zink *nt* -s zinc

Zinn *nt* -s tin; (*Gefäße*) pewter

Zins|en *mpl* interest *sg*; **Z~en tragen** earn interest. **Z~eszins** *m* -es,-en compound interest. **Z~fuß, Z~satz** *m* interest rate

Zipfel *m* -s,- corner; (*Spitze*) point

zirka *adv* about

Zirkel *m* -s,- [pair of] compasses *pl*; (*Gruppe*) circle

Zirkul|ation /-'tsjo:n/ *f* - circulation. **z~ieren** *vi* (*sein*) circulate

Zirkus *m* -,-se circus

zirpen *vi* (*haben*) chirp

zischen *vi* (*haben*) hiss; (*Fett:*) sizzle ● *vt* hiss

Zit|at *nt* -[e]s,-e quotation. **z~ieren** *vt/i* (*haben*) quote

Zitr|onat *nt* -[e]s candied lemonpeel. **Z~one** *f* -,-n lemon

zittern *vi* (*haben*) tremble; (*vor Kälte*) shiver; (*beben*) shake

zittrig *adj* shaky

Zitze *f* -,-n teat

zivil *adj* civilian; (*Ehe, Recht*) civil. **Z~** *nt* -s civilian clothes *pl*. **Z~dienst** *m* community service

Zivili|sation /-'tsjo:n/ *f* -,-en civilization. **z~sieren** *vt* civilize. **z~siert** *adj* civilized ● *adv* in a civilized manner

Zivilist *m* -en,-en civilian

zögern *vi* (*haben*) hesitate. **Z~** *nt* -s hesitation. **z~d** *adj* hesitant

Zoll¹ *m* -[e]s,- inch

Zoll² *m* -[e]s,⁻e [customs] duty; (*Behörde*) customs *pl*. **Z~abferti-**

gung f customs clearance. **Z~beamte(r)** m customs officer. **z~frei** adj & adv duty-free. **Z~kontrolle** f customs check

Zone f -,-n zone

Zoo m -s,-s zoo

zoologisch adj zoological

Zopf m -[e]s, ⸚e plait

Zorn m -[e]s anger. **z~ig** adj angry

---

zu

● *preposition* (+ *dative*)

! Note that **zu dem** can become **zum** and **zu der, zur**

····▶ (*Richtung*) to; (*bei Beruf*) into. **wir gehen zur Schule** we are going to school. **ich muss zum Arzt** I must go to the doctor's. **zu ... hin** towards. **er geht zum Theater/Militär** he is going into the theatre/army

····▶ (*zusammen mit*) with. **zu dem Käse gab es Wein** there was wine with the cheese. **zu etw passen** go with sth

····▶ (*räumlich; zeitlich*) at. **zu Hause** at home. **zu ihren Füßen** at her feet. **zu Ostern** at Easter. **zur Zeit** (+ *gen*) at the time of

····▶ (*preislich*) at; for. **zum halben Preis** at half price. **das Stück zu zwei Euro** at or for two euros each. **eine Marke zu 60 Cent** a 60-cent stamp

····▶ (*Zweck, Anlass*) for. **zu diesem Zweck** for this purpose. **zum Spaß** for fun. **zum Lesen** for reading. **zum Geburtstag bekam ich ...** for my birthday I got ... **zum ersten Mal** for the first time

····▶ (*Art und Weise*) **zu meinem**

Erstaunen/Entsetzen to my surprise/horror. **zu Fuß/Pferde** on foot/horseback. **zu Dutzenden** by the dozen. **wir waren zu dritt/viert** there were three/four of us

····▶ (*Zahlenverhältnis*) to. **es steht 5 zu 3** the score is 5–3

····▶ (*Ziel, Ergebnis*) into. **zu etw werden** turn into sth

····▶ (*gegenüber*) to; towards. **freundlich/hässlich zu jdm sein** be friendly/nasty to s.o.

····▶ (*über*) on; about. **sich zu etw äußern** to comment on sth

● *adverb*

····▶ (*allzu*) too. **zu groß/viel/weit** too big/much/far

····▶ (*Richtung*) towards. **nach dem Fluss zu** towards the river

····▶ (*geschlossen*) closed; (*an Schalter, Hahn*) off. **Augen zu!** close your eyes! **Tür zu!** shut the door!

● *conjunction*

····▶ to. **etwas zu essen** something to eat. **nicht zu glauben** unbelievable. **zu erörternde Probleme** problems to be discussed

zuallererst adv first of all. **z~letzt** adv last of all

Zubehör nt -s accessories pl

zubereit|en vt sep prepare. **Z~ung** f - preparation; (*in Rezept*) method

zubinden† vt sep tie [up]

zubring|en† vt sep spend. **Z~er** m -s,- access road; (*Bus*) shuttle

Zucchini /tsuˈkiːniː/ pl courgettes

Zucht f -,-en breeding; (*Pflanzen-*) cultivation; (*Art, Rasse*) breed; (*von Pflanzen*) strain; (*Z~farm*) farm; (*Pferde-*) stud

z

zücht|en vt breed; cultivate, grow (Rosen). **Z~er** m -s,- breeder; grower

Zuchthaus nt prison

Züchtung f -,-en breeding; (Pflanzen-) cultivation; (Art, Rasse) breed; (von Pflanzen) strain

zucken vi (haben) twitch; (sich z~d bewegen) jerk; (Blitz:) flash; (Flamme:) flicker ● vt **die Achseln z~** shrug one's shoulders

Zucker m -s sugar. **Z~dose** f sugar basin. **Z~guss** m icing. **z~krank** adj diabetic. **Z~krankheit** f diabetes. **z~n** vt sugar. **Z~rohr** nt sugar cane. **Z~rübe** f sugar beet. **Z~watte** f candyfloss

zudecken vt sep cover up; (im Bett) tuck up; cover (Topf)

zudem adv moreover

zudrehen vt sep turn off

zueinander adv to one another; **z~ passen** go together; **z~ halten** (fig) stick together

zuerkennen† vt sep award (dat to)

zuerst adv first; (anfangs) at first

zufahr|en† vi sep (sein) **z~en auf** (+ acc) drive towards. **Z~t** f access; (Einfahrt) drive

Zufall m chance; (Zusammentreffen) coincidence; **durch Z~** by chance/coincidence. **z~en†** vi sep (sein) close, shut; **jdm z~en** (Aufgabe:) fall/(Erbe:) go to s.o.

zufällig adj chance, accidental ● adv by chance

Zuflucht f refuge; (Schutz) shelter

zufolge prep (+ dat) according to

zufrieden adj contented; (befriedigt) satisfied; **sich z~ geben** be satisfied; **jdn z~ lassen** leave s.o. in peace; **jdn z~ stellen** satisfy s.o.; **z~ stellend** satisfactory. **Z~heit** f - contentment;

satisfaction

zufrieren† vi sep (sein) freeze over

zufügen vt sep inflict (dat on); do (Unrecht) (dat to)

Zufuhr f - supply

Zug m -[e]s, ¨e train; (Kolonne) column; (Um-) procession; (Mil) platoon; (Vogelschar) flock; (Ziehen, Zugkraft) pull; (Wandern, Ziehen) migration; (Schluck, Luft-) draught; (Atem-) breath; (beim Rauchen) puff; (Schach-) move; (beim Schwimmen, Rudern) stroke; (Gesichts-) feature; (Wesens-) trait

Zugabe f (Geschenk) [free] gift; (Mus) encore

Zugang m access

zugänglich adj accessible; (Mensch:) approachable

Zugbrücke f drawbridge

zugeben† vt sep add; (gestehen) admit; (erlauben) allow

zugehen† vi sep (sein) close; **jdm z~** be sent to s.o.; **z~ auf** (+ acc) go towards; **dem Ende z~** draw to a close; (Vorräte:) run low; **auf der Party ging es lebhaft zu** the party was pretty lively

Zugehörigkeit f - membership

Zügel m -s,- rein

zugelassen adj registered

zügel|los adj unrestrained. **z~n** vt rein in; (fig) curb

Zuge|ständnis nt concession. **z~stehen†** vt sep grant

zügig adj quick

Zugkraft f pull; (fig) attraction

zugleich adv at the same time

Zugluft f draught

zugreifen† vi sep (haben) grab it/them; (bei Tisch) help oneself; (bei Angebot) jump at it; (helfen) lend a hand

zugrunde adv **z~ richten** destroy; **z~ gehen** be destroyed; (*sterben*) die; **z~ liegen** form the basis (*dat* of)

zugunsten *prep* (+ *gen*) in favour of; (*Sammlung*) in aid of

zugute *adv* **jdm/etw z~ kommen** benefit s.o./something

Zugvogel *m* migratory bird

zuhalten† *v sep* ● *vt* keep closed; (*bedecken*) cover; **sich** (*dat*) **die Nase z~** hold one's nose

Zuhälter *m* -s,- pimp

zuhause *adv* = **zu Hause**, s. **Haus**. **Z~** *nt* -s,- home

zuhör|en *vi sep* (*haben*) listen (*dat* to). **Z~er(in)** *m(f)* listener

zujubeln *vi sep* (*haben*) **jdm z~** cheer s.o.

zukleben *vt sep* seal

zuknöpfen *vt sep* button up

zukommen† *vi sep* (*sein*) **z~ auf** (+ *acc*) come towards; (*sich nähern*) approach; **z~ lassen** send (**jdm** s.o.); devote (*Pflege*) (*dat* to); **jdm z~** be s.o.'s right

Zukunft *f* -. future. **zukünftig** *adj* future ● *adv* in future

zulächeln *vi sep* (*haben*) smile (*dat* at)

zulangen *vi sep* (*haben*) help oneself

zulassen† *vt sep* allow, permit; (*teilnehmen lassen*) admit; (*Admin*) license, register; (*geschlossen lassen*) leave closed; leave unopened (*Brief*)

zulässig *adj* permissible

Zulassung *f* -,-en admission; registration; (*Lizenz*) licence

zuleide *adv* **jdm etwas z~ tun** hurt s.o.

zuletzt *adv* last; (*schließlich*) in the end

zuliebe *adv* **jdm/etw z~** for the sake of someone/something

zum *prep* = **zu dem**; **zum Spaß** for fun; **etw zum Lesen** sth to read

zumachen *v sep* ● *vt* close, shut; do up (*Jacke*); seal (*Umschlag*); turn off (*Hahn*); (*stillegen*) close down ● *vi* (*haben*) close, shut; (*stillgelegt werden*) close down

zumal *adv* especially ● *conj* especially since

zumindest *adv* at least

zumutbar *adj* reasonable

zumute *adv* **mir ist nicht danach z~** I don't feel like it

zumut|en *vt sep* **jdm etw z~en** ask or expect sth of s.o.; **sich** (*dat*) **zu viel z~en** overdo things. **Z~ung** *f* - imposition

zunächst *adv* first [of all]; (*anfangs*) at first; (*vorläufig*) for the moment ● *prep* (+ *dat*) nearest to

Zunahme *f* -,-n increase

Zuname *m* surname

zünd|en *vt/i* (*haben*) ignite. **Z~er** *m* -s,- detonator, fuse. **Z~holz** *nt* match. **Z~kerze** *f* sparking-plug. **Z~schlüssel** *m* ignition key. **Z~schnur** *f* fuse. **Z~ung** *f* -,-en ignition

zunehmen† *vi sep* (*haben*) increase (**an** + *dat* in); (*Mond:*) wax; (*an Gewicht*) put on weight. **z~d** *adj* increasing

Zuneigung *f* - affection

Zunft *f* -,²e guild

Zunge *f* -,-n tongue. **Z~nbrecher** *m* tongue-twister

zunutze *adj* **sich** (*dat*) **etw z~ machen** make use of sth; (*ausnutzen*) take advantage of sth

zuoberst *adv* right at the top

zuordnen *vt sep* assign (*dat* to)

zupfen *vt/i* (*haben*) pluck (**an** + *dat* at); pull out (*Unkraut*)

zur *prep* = **zu der**; **zur Schule** to

school; **zur Zeit** at present
zur<u>a</u>te *adv* z~ **ziehen** consult

> **Zürcher Festspiele** The
> Zurich festival in Switzer-
> land is an annual celebra-
> tion of classical music, opera,
> dance and art, with special per-
> formances held throughout the
> city. The festival concludes with a
> brilliant Midsummer Night's Ball in
> central Zurich.

zurechnungsfähig *adj* of
sound mind
zurecht|finden† (**sich**) *vr sep*
find one's way. z~**kommen†** *vi sep*
(*sein*) cope (**mit** with); (*rechtzeitig
kommen*) be in time. z~**legen** *vt
sep* put out ready; **sich** (*dat*) **eine
Ausrede** z~**legen** have an excuse
all ready. z~**machen** *vt sep* get
ready. **Z~weisung** *f* reprimand
zureden *vi sep* (*haben*) **jdm** z~
try to persuade s.o.
zurichten *vt sep* prepare; (*beschädigen*) damage; (*verletzen*) injure
zuriegeln *vt sep* bolt
zur<u>ü</u>ck *adv* back; **Berlin, hin und
z~** return to Berlin. z~**bekom-
men†** *vt sep* get back. z~**bleiben†**
vi sep (*sein*) stay behind; (*nicht mit-
halten*) lag behind. z~**bringen†**
vt sep bring back; (*wieder hinbringen*)
take back. z~**erstatten** *vt sep* refund. z~**fahren†** *v sep* ● *vt* drive
back ● *vi* (*sein*) return, go back; (*im
Auto*) drive back; (*z~weichen*) recoil. z~**finden†** *vi sep* (*haben*) find
one's way back. z~**führen** *v sep*
● *vt* take back; (*fig*) attribute (**auf** +
acc) ● *vi* (*haben*) lead back. z~**ge-
ben†** *vt sep* give back, return.
z~**geblieben** *adj* retarded. z~**ge-
hen†** *vi sep* (*sein*) go back, return;
(*abnehmen*) go down; z~**gehen auf**

(+ *acc*) (*fig*) go back to
zurückgezogen *adj* secluded.
Z~heit *f* - seclusion
zurückhalt|en† *vt sep* hold back;
(*abhalten*) stop; **sich** z~**en** restrain
oneself. z~**end** *adj* reserved.
Z~ung *f* - reserve
zurück|kehren *vi sep* (*sein*) re-
turn. z~**kommen** *vi sep* (*sein*)
come back, return; (*ankommen*) get
back. z~**lassen†** *vt sep* leave behind; (*z~kehren lassen*) allow back.
z~**legen** *vt sep* put back; (*reservieren*) keep; (*sparen*) put by; cover
(*Strecke*). z~**liegen†** *vi sep* (*haben*)
be in the past; (*Sport*) be behind;
das liegt lange zurück that was
long ago. z~**melden** (**sich**) *vr sep*
report back. z~**schicken** *vt sep*
send back. z~**schlagen†** *v sep* ● *vi*
(*haben*) hit back ● *vt* hit back; (*umschlagen*) turn back. z~**schrecken**
vi sep (*sein*) shrink back, recoil; (*fig*)
shrink (**vor** + *dat* from). z~**stellen**
vt sep put back; (*reservieren*) keep;
(*fig*) put aside; (*aufschieben*) postpone. z~**stoßen†** *v sep* ● *vt* push
back ● *vi* (*sein*) reverse, back up.
z~**treten†** *vi sep* (*sein*) step back;
(*vom Amt*) resign; (*verzichten*) withdraw. z~**weisen†** *vt sep* turn away;
(*fig*) reject. z~**zahlen** *vt sep* pay
back. z~**ziehen†** *vt sep* draw back;
(*fig*) withdraw; **sich** z~**ziehen** withdraw; (*vom Beruf*) retire
Zuruf *m* shout. z~**en†** *vt sep* shout
(*dat* to)
zurz<u>ei</u>t *adv* at present
Zusage *f* -,-**n** acceptance; (*Versprechen*) promise. z~**n** *v sep* ● *vt*
promise ● *vi* (*haben*) accept
zusammen *adv* together; (*insgesamt*) altogether; z~ **sein** be
together. **Z~arbeit** *f* co-operation.
z~**arbeiten** *vi sep* (*haben*) co-oper-
ate. z~**bauen** *vt sep* assemble.

z~bleiben† vi sep (sein) stay together. **z~brechen†** vi sep (sein) collapse. **Z~bruch** m collapse; (Nerven- & fig) breakdown. **z~fallen†** vi sep (sein) collapse; (zeitlich) coincide. **z~fassen** vt sep summarize, sum up. **Z~fassung** f summary. **z~fügen** vt sep fit together. **z~gehören** vi sep (haben) belong together; (z~passen) go together. **z~gesetzt** adj (Gram) compound. **z~halten†** v sep ● vt hold together; (beisammenhalten) keep together ● vi (haben) (fig) stick together. **Z~hang** m connection; (Kontext) context. **z~hanglos** adj incoherent. **z~klappen** v sep ● vt fold up ● vi (sein) collapse. **z~kommen†** vi sep (sein) meet; (sich sammeln) accumulate. **Z~kunft** f -,ᵉe meeting. **z~laufen†** vi sep (sein) gather; (Flüssigkeit:) collect; (Linien:) converge. **z~leben** vi sep (haben) live together. **z~legen** v sep ● vt put together; (z~falten) fold up; (vereinigen) amalgamate; pool (Geld) ● vi (haben) club together. **z~nehmen†** vt sep gather up; summon up (Mut); collect (Gedanken); **sich z~nehmen** pull oneself together. **z~passen** vi sep (haben) go together, match. **Z~prall** m collision. **z~rechnen** vt sep add up. **z~schlagen†** vt sep smash up; (prügeln) beat up. **z~schließen†** (sich) vr sep join together; (Firmen:) merge. **Z~schluss** m union; (Comm) merger

Zusammensein nt -s get-together

zusammensetz|en vt sep put together; (Techn) assemble; **sich z~en** sit [down] together; (bestehen) be made up (aus from). **Z~ung** f -,-en composition; (Techn) assembly; (Wort) compound

zusammen|stellen vt sep put

together; (gestalten) compile. **Z~stoß** m collision; (fig) clash. **z~treffen†** vi sep (sein) meet; (zeitlich) coincide. **Z~treffen** nt add up. **z~zählen** vt sep add up. **z~ziehen†** v sep ● vt draw together; (addieren) add up; (konzentrieren) mass; **sich z~ziehen** contract; (Gewitter:) gather ● vi (sein) move in together; move in (mit with)

Zusatz m addition; (Jur) rider; (Lebensmittel-) additive. **zusätzlich** adj additional ● adv in addition

zuschauen vi sep (haben) watch. **Z~er(in)** m -s,- (f -,-nen) spectator; (TV) viewer

Zuschlag m surcharge; (Zug) supplement. **z~pflichtig** adj (Zug) for which a supplement is payable

zuschließen† v sep ● vt lock ● vi (haben) lock up

zuschneiden† vt sep cut out; cut to size (Holz)

zuschreiben† vt sep attribute (dat to); **jdm die Schuld z~** blame s.o.

Zuschrift f letter; (auf Annonce) reply

zuschulden adv sich (dat) etwas z~ kommen lassen do wrong

Zuschuss m contribution; (staatlich) subsidy

zusehends adv visibly

zusein* vi sep (sein) zu sein, s. zu

zusenden† vt sep send

zusetzen v sep ● vt add; (einbüßen) lose

zusicher|n vt sep promise. **Z~ung** f promise.

zuspielen vt sep (Sport) pass

zuspitzen (sich) vr sep (fig) become critical

Zustand m condition, state

zustande adv z~ bringen/kommen bring/come about

zuständig adj competent; (verant-wortlich) responsible

zustehen† vi sep (haben) jdm z~ be s.o.'s right; (Urlaub:) be due to s.o.

zusteigen† vi sep (sein) get on; **noch jemand zugestiegen?** ≈ tickets please; (im Bus) ≈ any more fares please?

zustell|en vt sep block; (bringen) deliver. **Z~ung** f delivery

zusteuern v sep • vi (sein) head (auf + acc for) • vt contribute

zustimm|en vi sep (haben) agree; (billigen) approve (dat of). **Z~ung** f consent; approval

zustoßen† vi sep (sein) happen (dat to)

Zustrom m influx

Zutat f (Culin) ingredient

zuteil|en vt sep allocate; assign (Aufgabe). **Z~ung** f allocation

zutiefst adv deeply

zutragen† vt sep carry/(fig) report (dat to); **sich z~** happen

zutrau|en vt sep jdm etw z~ believe s.o. capable of sth. **Z~en** nt -s confidence

zutreffen† vi sep (haben) be correct; **z~ auf** (+ acc) apply to

Zutritt m admittance

zuunterst adv right at the bottom

zuverlässig adj reliable. **Z~keit** f - reliability

Zuversicht f - confidence. **z~lich** adj confident

zuviel* pron & adv zu viel, s. viel

zuvor adv before; (erst) first

zuvorkommen† vi sep (sein) (+ dat) anticipate. **z~d** adj obliging

Zuwachs m -es increase

Zuwanderung f immigration

zuwege adv z~ bringen achieve

zuweilen adv now and then

zuweisen† vt sep assign

Zuwendung f donation; (Für-sorge) care

zuwenig* pron & adv zu wenig, s. wenig

zuwerfen† vt sep slam (Tür); jdm etw z~ throw s.o. sth

zuwider adv jdm z~ sein be re-pugnant to s.o. • prep (+ dat) con-trary to

zuzahlen vt sep pay extra

zuziehen† v sep • vt pull tight; draw (Vorhänge); (hinzu-) call in; **sich** (dat) **etw z~** contract (Krank-heit); sustain (Verletzung); incur (Zorn) • vi (sein) move into the area

zuzüglich prep (+ gen) plus

Zwang m -[e]s,⁻e compulsion; (Gewalt) force; (Verpflichtung) obli-gation

zwängen vt squeeze

zwanglos adj informal. **Z~igkeit** f - informality

Zwangsjacke f straitjacket

zwanzig inv adj twenty. **z~ste(r,s)** adj twentieth

zwar adv admittedly

Zweck m -[e]s,-e purpose; (Sinn) point. **z~los** adj pointless. **z~mäßig** adj suitable; (praktisch) functional

zwei inv adj, **Z~** f -,-en two; (Sch) ≈ B. **Z~bettzimmer** nt twin-bed-ded room

zweideutig adj ambiguous

zwei|erlei inv adj two kinds of • pron two things. **z~fach** adj double

Zweifel m -s,- doubt. **z~haft** adj doubtful; (fragwürdig) dubious. **z~los** adv undoubtedly. **z~n** vi (haben) doubt (an etw dat sth)

Zweig m -[e]s,-e branch. **Z~stelle** f branch [office]

Zwei|kampf m duel. **z~mal** adv twice. **z~reihig** adj (Anzug) double-breasted. **z~sprachig** adj bilingual

zweit adv zu **z~** in twos; **wir waren zu z~** there were two of us. **z~beste(r,s)** adj second-best. **z~e(r,s)** adj second

zweitens adv secondly

Zwerchfell nt diaphragm

Zwerg m -[e]s,-e dwarf

Zwickel m -s,- gusset

zwicken vt/i (haben) pinch

Zwieback m -[e]s,⁻e rusk

Zwiebel f -,-n onion; (Blumen-)bulb

Zwielicht nt half-light; (Dämmerlicht) twilight. **z~ig** adj shady

Zwiespalt m conflict

Zwilling m -s,-e twin; **Z~e** (Astrology) Gemini

zwingen† vt force; **sich z~** force oneself. **z~d** adj compelling

Zwinger m -s,- run; (Zucht-)

kennels pl

zwinkern vi (haben) blink; (als Zeichen) wink

Zwirn m -[e]s button thread

zwischen prep (+ dat/acc) between; (unter) among[st]. **Z~bemerkung** f interjection. **z~durch** adv in between; (in der Z~zeit) in the meantime. **Z~fall** m incident. **Z~landung** f stopover. **Z~raum** m gap, space. **Z~wand** f partition. **Z~zeit** f **in der Z~zeit** in the meantime

Zwist m -[e]s,-e discord; (Streit) feud

zwitschern vi (haben) chirp

zwo inv adj two

zwölf inv adj twelve. **z~te(r,s)** adj twelfth

Zylind|er m -s,- cylinder; (Hut) top hat. **z~risch** adj cylindrical

Zyn|iker m -s,- cynic. **z~isch** adj cynical. **Z~ismus** m - cynicism

Zypern nt -s Cyprus

Zypresse f -,-n cypress

Zyste /ˈtsʏstə/ f -,-n cyst

Phrasefinder

Key phrases

Nützliche Redewendungen

yes, please
no, thank you
sorry!
you're welcome
I don't understand

ja bitte
nein danke
Entschuldigung!
nichts zu danken
ich verstehe das nicht

Meeting people
hello/goodbye
how are you?
fine, thank you
see you later!

Wir lernen uns kennen
hallo!/auf Wiedersehen!
wie geht es Ihnen?/wie geht's?
danke, gut
bis nachher!

Asking questions
do you speak English/German?

what's your name?
where are you from?

how much is it?
how far is it?

Fragen
sprechen Sie/sprichst du Englisch/
    Deutsch?
wie heißen Sie?/wie heißt du?
woher kommen Sie?/woher kommst
    du?
wie viel kostet das?
wie weit ist es?

Statements about yourself
my name is...
I'm English
I don't speak German/English
    very well
I'm here on holiday
I live near Manchester/Hamburg

Alles über mich
ich heiße...
ich bin Engländer/Engländerin
ich kann nicht gut Deutsch/
    Englisch sprechen
ich bin im Urlaub hier
ich wohne in der Nähe von
    Manchester/Hamburg

Emergencies
can you help me, please?
I'm lost
call an ambulance
get the police/a doctor
watch out!

Im Notfall
können Sie mir bitte helfen?
ich habe mich verlaufen
rufen Sie einen Krankenwagen
holen Sie die Polizei/einen Arzt
Vorsicht!, Achtung!

❶ Going Places

On the road	Auf der Straße
where's the nearest garage (for repairs)/petrol station (*Amer* filling station)?	wo ist die nächste Werkstatt/ Tankstelle?
what's the best way to get there?	wie komme ich am besten dorthin?
I've got a puncture	ich habe eine Reifenpanne
I'd like to hire a bike/car	ich möchte ein Rad/Auto mieten
where can I park around here?	wo kann man hier parken?
there's been an accident	es ist ein Unfall passiert
my car's broken down	mein Auto hat eine Panne
the car won't start	der Wagen springt nicht an

By rail	Mit der Bahn
where can I buy a ticket?	wo kann ich eine Fahrkarte kaufen?
what time is the next train to York/Berlin?	wann geht der nächste Zug nach York/Berlin?
do I have to change?	muss ich umsteigen?
can I take my bike on the train?	kann ich mein Rad im Zug mitnehmen?
which platform for the train to Bath/Cologne?	von welchem Bahnsteig fährt der Zug nach Bath/Köln ab?
the train is arriving on platform 2	der Zug fährt auf Gleis 2 ein
there's a train to London at 10 o'clock	es gibt einen Zug nach London um zehn Uhr
a single/return to Birmingham/ Frankfurt, please	einmal einfach/eine Rückfahrkarte nach Birmingham/Frankfurt, bitte
I'd like a cheap day return/an all-day ticket	ich möchte eine Tagesrückfahrkarte/ Tageskarte
I'd like to reserve a seat	ich möchte einen Platz reservieren

At the airport

when's the next flight to Paris/Rome?

what time do I have to check in?

where do I check in?

I'd like to confirm/cancel my flight

can I change my booking?

I'd like a window seat/an aisle seat

Am Flughafen

wann geht der nächste Flug nach Paris/Rom?

um wie viel Uhr muss ich einchecken?

wo checkt man ein?

ich möchte meinen Flug bestätigen/stornieren

kann ich umbuchen?

ich möchte einen Fensterplatz/Platz am Gang

Asking how to get there

could you tell me the way to the castle?

how long will it take me to walk there?

how far is it from here?

which bus do I take for the cathedral?

where does this bus go?

where do I get the bus for...?

does this bus/train go to...?

which bus goes to...?

where do I get off?

how much is the fare to the town centre (Amer center)?

what time is the last bus?

how do I get to the airport?

where's the nearest underground (Amer subway) station?

is this the turning for...?

take the first turning right

Nach dem Weg fragen

können Sie mir bitte sagen, wie ich zum Schloss komme?

wie lange braucht man zu Fuß?

wie weit ist das von hier?

mit welchem Bus komme ich zum Dom?

wohin fährt dieser Bus?

wo fährt der Bus nach... ab?

fährt dieser Bus/Zug nach...?

welcher Bus fährt nach...?

wo muss ich aussteigen?

was kostet es ins Stadtzentrum?

wann fährt der letzte Bus?

wie komme ich zum Flughafen?

wo ist die nächste U-Bahn-Station?

ist das die Abzweigung nach...?

nehmen Sie die erste Straße rechts

❷ Keeping in touch

On the phone	Am Telefon
where can I buy a phone card?	wo kann man Telefonkarten kaufen?
may I use your phone?	darf ich Ihr Telefon benutzen?
do you have a mobile (Amer cell phone)?	haben Sie ein Handy?
what is the code for Leipzig/Sheffield?	wie ist die Vorwahl von Leipzig/Sheffield?
I'd like to make a phone call	ich möchte gern telefonieren
I'd like to reverse the charges (Amer call collect)	ich möchte ein R-Gespräch anmelden
the line's engaged/busy	es ist besetzt
there's no answer	es meldet sich niemand
hello, this is Natalie	hallo, hier spricht Natalie
can I speak to Simon, please?	kann ich bitte Simon sprechen?
who's calling?	wer ist am Apparat?
sorry, I must have the wrong number	Entschuldigung, ich habe mich verwählt
just a moment, please	einen Augenblick bitte
please hold the line	bleiben sie bitte am Apparat
please tell him/her I called	richten Sie ihm/ihr bitte aus, dass ich angerufen habe
can I leave a message for Eva?	kann ich eine Nachricht für Eva hinterlassen?
I'll try again later	Ich versuche es später noch einmal
please tell her that Danielle called	sagen Sie ihr bitte, dass Danielle angerufen hat
can he/she ring me back?	kann er/sie mich zurückrufen?
my home number is...	meine Privatnummer ist...
my office number is...	meine Nummer im Büro ist...
my fax number is...	meine Faxnummer ist...
can I send a fax from here?	kann ich von hier faxen?
we were cut off	wir sind unterbrochen worden

In Verbindung bleiben ❷

Writing

can you give me your address?

where is the nearest post office?

two one-euro stamps

I'd like a stamp for a letter to Germany/Italy

can I have stamps for two postcards to England/ the USA, please?

I'd like to send a parcel/a telegram

Schreiben

können Sie mir Ihre/kannst du mir deine Adresse geben?

wo ist die nächste Post?

zwei Briefmarken zu einem Euro

ich hätte gern eine Briefmarke für einen Brief nach Deutschland/Italien

kann ich bitte Briefmarken für zwei Postkarten nach England/in die USA haben?

ich möchte ein Paket abschicken/ein Telegramm aufgeben

On line

are you on the Internet?

what's your e-mail address?

we could send it by e-mail

I'll e-mail it to you on Thursday

I've looked for it on the Internet

he found the information surfing the net

Online

hast du Zugang zum Internet?

was ist deine E-Mail-Adresse?

wir könnten es per E-Mail schicken

ich schicke es Ihnen am Donnerstag per E-Mail

ich habe es im Internet gesucht

er hat die Information beim Surfen im Internet gefunden

Meeting up

what shall we do this evening?

where shall we meet?

see you outside the cinema at 6 o'clock

do you fancy joining in?

I can't today, I'm busy

Verabredungen

was machen wir heute Abend?

wo treffen wir uns?

ich treffe dich um sechs Uhr vor dem Kino

hast du Lust mitzumachen?

ich kann heute nicht, ich habe keine Zeit

❸ Food and Drink

Booking a table in a restaurant

can you recommend a good restaurant?

I'd like to reserve a table for four

I booked a table for two

Vorbestellungen

können Sie uns/mir ein gutes Restaurant empfehlen?

ich möchte einen Tisch für vier Personen bestellen

ich habe einen Tisch für zwei Personen bestellt

Ordering

could we see the menu/wine list, please?

do you have a vegetarian/children's menu?

could we have some more bread?

what would you recommend?

I'd like a white/black coffee

... an espresso

... a decaffeinated coffee

... a liqueur

could I have the bill, (Amer) check, please?

Wir möchten bestellen

können wir bitte die Speisekarte/ Weinkarte haben?

haben Sie vegetarianische Gerichte/ Kinderportionen?

noch etwas Brot, bitte

was würden Sie mir/uns empfehlen?

ich möchte einen Kaffee mit Milch/einen Kaffee ohne Milch

... einen Espresso

... einen entkoffeinierten Kaffee

... einen Likör

... die Rechnung, bitte

You will hear

hätten Sie gern einen Aperitif?

haben Sie schon bestellt?

möchten Sie eine Vorspeise?

was nehmen Sie als Hauptgericht?

möchten Sie eine Nachspeise?

möchten Sie einen Kaffee?/einen Likör?

haben Sie noch einen Wunsch?

guten Appetit!

die Bedienung ist (nicht) inbegriffen

Sie hören

would you like an aperitif?

are you ready to order?

would you like a starter?

what will you have for the main course?

would you like a dessert?

would you like some coffee?/a liqueur?

anything else?

enjoy your meal!

service is (not) included

The menu		Die Speisekarte	
starters	**Vorspeisen**	**Vorspeisen**	**starters**
canapés	Häppchen	Häppchen	canapés
hors d'oeuvres	Horsd'oeuvres, Vorspeisen	Horsd'oeuvres, Vorspeisen	hors d'oeuvres
omelette	Omelett	Omelett	omelette
soup	Suppe	Suppe	soup
fish	**Fisch**	**Fisch**	**fish**
bass	Barsch	Aal	eel
cod	Kabeljau	Austern	oysters
eel	Aal	Barsch	bass
haddock	Schellfisch	Calamares	squid
hake	Seehecht	Forelle	trout
herring	Hering	Garnelen	prawns
monkfish	Anglerfisch	Hering	herring
mullet	Meeräsche	Kabeljau	cod
mussels	Muscheln	Krabben	shrimps
oysters	Austern	Lachs	salmon
plaice	Scholle	Meeräsche	mullet
prawns	Garnelen	Muscheln	mussels
red mullet	Meerbarbe	Sardinen	sardines
salmon	Lachs	Schellfisch	haddock
sardines	Sardinen	Scholle	plaice
shrimps	Krabben	Seehecht	hake
sole	Seezunge	Seezunge	sole
squid	Calamares	Steinbutt	turbot
trout	Forelle	Thunfisch	tuna
tuna	Thunfisch		
turbot	Steinbutt	**Fleisch**	**meat**
		Ente	duck
meat	**Fleisch**	Gans	goose
chicken	Hühnchen	Hase	hare
duck	Ente	Hühnchen	chicken
goose	Gans	Kalbfleisch	veal
guinea fowl	Perlhuhn	Kaninchen	rabbit
hare	Hase	Lammfleisch	lamb
kidneys	Nieren	Leber	liver
lamb	Lammfleisch	Nieren	kidneys
liver	Leber	Sauerbraten	braised beef

❸ Food and Drink

pork	Schweinefleisch	Schweinefleisch	pork
rabbit	Kaninchen	Steak	steak
steak	Steak	Wiener Schnitzel	breaded escalope
veal	Kalbfleisch	Wildschwein	wild boar
wild boar	Wildschwein		

vegetables	**Gemüse**	**Gemüse**	**vegetables**
artichokes	Artischocken	Artischocken	artichokes
asparagus	Spargel	Aubergine	aubergine
aubergine	Aubergine	Blaukraut (*Aust.*)	red cabbage
beans	Bohnen	Blumenkohl	cauliflower
cabbage	Kohl	Bohnen	beans
carrots	Möhren, Karotten	Endivie	endive
cauliflower	Blumenkohl	Erbsen	peas
celery	Sellerie	Kartoffeln	potatoes
endive	Endivie	Kohl	cabbage
mushrooms	Pilze	Möhren, Karotten	carrots
onions	Zwiebeln	Paprikaschoten	peppers
peas	Erbsen	Pilze	mushrooms
peppers	Paprikaschoten	Rotkohl	red cabbage
potatoes	Kartoffeln	Sellerie	celeriac
red cabbage	Rotkohl,	Spargel	asparagus
	Blaukraut (*Aust.*)	Zwiebeln	onions

the way it's cooked/ **wie es zubereitet wird**		**wie es zubereitet wird/** **the way it's cooked**	
boiled	gekocht	englisch gebraten	rare
fried	gebraten, in der	gebraten, geröstet	roast
	Pfanne gebraten	gebraten, in der	fried
grilled	gegrillt	Pfanne gebraten	
medium	halb	gegrillt	grilled
	durchgebraten	geschmort	stewed
puréed	püriert	durch	well done
rare	englisch	halb	medium
	gebraten,	durchgebraten	
	schwach	püriert	puréed
	gebraten	schwach gebraten	rare
roast	gebraten,	**Nachspeisen**	**desserts**
	geröstet	Eis	ice cream
stewed	geschmort	Käse	cheese
well done	durch	Käseplatte	cheeseboard

desserts	Nachspeisen
cheese	Käse
cheeseboard	Käseplatte
chocolate gateau	Schokoladentorte
fruit	Obst
fruit tart	Obsttorte
ice cream	Eis
pie	Obstkuchen

Nachspeisen	desserts
Kaiserschmarren (*Aust.*)	pancake strips sprinkled with sugar and raisins
Kompott	stewed fruit
Kuchen	cake
Nockerln (*Aust.*)	sweet dumplings
rote Grütze	red-berry compote

side dishes/condiments	Beilagen/Gewürze
bread	Brot
butter	Butter
herbs	Gewürzkräuter
mayonnaise	Majonäse
mustard	Senf
olive oil	Olivenöl
pepper	Pfeffer
rolls	Brötchen, Semmeln (*Aust.*)
salt	Salz
sauce	Soße
seasoning	Gewürze
vinegar	Essig

Beilagen/Gewürze side dishes/condiments	
Brot	bread
Brötchen	rolls
Butter	butter
Essig	vinegar
Gewürze	seasoning
Gewürzkräuter	herbs
Majonäse	mayonnaise
Olivenöl	olive oil
Pfeffer	pepper
Salz	salt
Semmeln (*Aust.*)	rolls
Senf	mustard
Soße	sauce

drinks	Getränke
beer	Bier
bottle	Flasche
carbonated	mit Kohlensäure
draught beer	Bier vom Fass
half-bottle	eine halbe Flasche
liqueur	Likör
red wine	Rotwein
rosé	Rosé
soft drink	alkoholfreies Getränk
spritzer	Schorle
still	ohne Kohlensäure
table wine	Tafelwein
white wine	Weißwein
wine	Wein

Getränke	drinks
alkoholfreies Getränk	soft drink
Bier	beer
Bier vom Fass	draught beer
Flasche	bottle
Likör	liqueur
mit Kohlensäure	carbonated
ohne Kohlensäure	still
Rosé	rosé
Rotwein	red wine
Schoppenwein	wine by the glass
Schorle	spritzer
Tafelwein	table wine
Wein	wine
Weißwein	white wine

❹ Places to stay

Camping

we're looking for a campsite

this is a list of local campsites

can we pitch our tent here?

can we park our caravan here?

do you have space for a caravan/tent?

are there shopping facilities?

how much is it per night?

we go on a camping holiday every year

Camping

wir suchen einen Campingplatz

in diesem Campingführer stehen alle hiesigen Campingplätze

können wir hier zelten?

können wir unseren Wohnwagen hier parken?

haben Sie Platz für einen Wohnwagen/ein Zelt?

gibt es Einkaufsmöglichkeiten?

was kostet es pro Nacht?

wir machen jedes Jahr Campingurlaub

At the hotel

I'd like a double/single room with bath

we have a reservation in the name of Milnes

I reserved two rooms

for three nights, from Friday to Sunday

how much does the room cost?

I'd like to see the room first, please

what time is breakfast?

can I leave this in the safe?

bed and breakfast

we'd like to stay another night

please call me at 7:30

are there any messages for me?

Im Hotel

ich möchte ein Doppelzimmer/ Einzelzimmer mit Bad

wir haben auf den Namen Milnes reservieren lassen

ich habe zwei Zimmer reservieren lassen

für drei Nächte, von Freitag bis Sonntag

was kostet das Zimmer?

ich möchte das Zimmer erst sehen, bitte

wann gibt es Frühstück?

kann ich das im Safe lassen?

Zimmer mit Frühstück

wir möchten noch eine Nacht bleiben

bitte wecken Sie mich um 7:30

hat jemand eine Nachricht für mich hinterlassen?

Übernachtungsmöglichkeiten ❹

Hostels

could you tell me where the youth hostel is?

what time does the hostel close?

I spent the night in a youth hostel

the hostel we're staying in is great value

I'm staying in a youth hostel

I know a really good youth hostel in Dublin

I'd like to go backpacking in Australia

Heime und Jugendherbergen

können Sie mir sagen, wo die Jugendherberge ist?

um wie viel Uhr macht das Heim zu?

ich habe in einer Jugendherberge übernachtet

unsere Herberge ist sehr preiswert

ich wohne in einer Jugendherberge

ich kenne eine sehr gute Jugendherberge in Dublin

ich würde gern in Australien mit dem Rucksack herum reisen

Rooms to let

I'm looking for a room with a reasonable rent

I'd like to rent an apartment for three weeks

where do I find out about rooms to let?

what's the weekly rent for the apartment?

I'm staying with friends at the moment

I rent an apartment on the outskirts of town

the room's fine—I'll take it

Zimmer zu vermieten

ich suche ein preiswertes Zimmer

ich möchte eine Wohnung für drei Wochen mieten

wo kann man sich nach Fremdenzimmern erkundigen?

was kostet die Wohnung pro Woche?

ich wohne zur Zeit bei Freunden

ich habe eine Wohnung am Stadtrand gemietet

das Zimmer ist gut—ich nehme es

....

❺ Shopping and money

At the bank	In der Bank
I'd like to change some money	ich möchte gern Geld wechseln
I want to change 100 euros into pounds	ich möchte 100 Euro[s] in Pfund wechseln
do you take Eurocheques?	nehmen Sie Eurochecks?
what's the exchange rate today?	wie steht der Wechselkurs heute?
I prefer traveller's cheques (Amer traveler's checks) to cash	mir sind Reiseschecks lieber als Bargeld
I'd like to transfer some money from my account	ich möchte Geld von meinem Konto überweisen
I'll get some money from the cash machine/ATM	ich hole mir Geld vom Automaten
a £50 cheque (Amer check)	ein Scheck über 50 Pfund
can I cash this cheque (Amer check) here?	kann ich diesen Scheck hier einlösen?
can I get some cash with my credit card?	kann ich auf meine Kreditkarte Bargeld bekommen?

Finding the right shop	Das richtige Geschäft finden
where's the main shopping district?	wo ist das Haupteinkaufsviertel?
is the shopping centre (Amer mall) far from here?	ist das Einkaufszentrum weit von hier?
where's a good place to buy sunglasses/shoes?	wo kauft man am besten Schuhe/eine Sonnenbrille?
where can I buy batteries/postcards?	wo kann ich Batterien/Postkarten kaufen?
where's the nearest pharmacy (Amer drugstore)?	wo ist die nächste Drogerie?
what time do the shops open/close?	um wie viel Uhr machen die Läden auf/zu?
where did you get those?	wo hast du die her?
I'm looking for a present for my mother	ich suche ein Geschenk für meine Mutter

Einkaufen und Geld ❺

Are you being served?

how much does that cost?

can I try it on?

can you keep it for me?

could you gift-wrap it for me, please?

please wrap it up well

can I pay by credit card/cheque (*Amer* check)?

do you have this in another colour?

I'm just looking

a receipt, please

I need a bigger size

I take a size...

it doesn't suit me

Werden Sie schon bedient?

was kostet das?

kann ich es anprobieren?

können Sie es mir zurücklegen?

können Sie es bitte als Geschenk einpacken?

verpacken Sie es bitte gut

kann ich mit Kreditkarte/Scheck zahlen?

haben Sie das in einer anderen Farbe?

ich sehe mich nur um

eine Quittung bitte

ich brauche die nächste Größe

ich habe Größe...

das steht mir nicht

Changing things

can I have a refund?

can you mend it for me?

can I speak to the manager?

it doesn't work

I'd like to change the dress

I bought this here yesterday

Umtauschen

kann ich mein Geld zurückbekommen?

können Sie es mir reparieren?

kann ich den Geschäftsführer/ die Geschäftsführerin sprechen?

es funktioniert nicht

ich möchte das Kleid umtauschen

ich habe das gestern hier gekauft

⑥ Sport and leisure

Keeping fit	Wir halten uns fit
where can we play football/squash?	wo kann man Fußball/Squash spielen?
is there a local sports centre (*Amer* center)?	gibt es hier ein Sportzentrum?
what's the charge per day?	was kostet das pro Tag?
is there a reduction for children/a student discount?	gibt es eine Ermäßigung für Kinder/Studenten?
where can we go swimming/play tennis?	wo kann man schwimmen gehen/Tennis spielen?
do you have to be a member?	muss man Mitglied sein?
I play tennis on Mondays	ich spiele jeden Montag Tennis
I would like to go fishing/riding	ich würde gern angeln gehen/reiten
I want to do aerobics	ich möchte Aerobic machen
I love swimming/playing baseball	ich schwimme gern/spiele gern Baseball
we want to hire skis/snowboards	wir möchten Skier/Snowboards mieten

Watching sport	Zuschauen
is there a football match on Saturday?	gibt es am Samstag ein Fußballspiel?
who's playing?	wer spielt?
which teams are playing?	welche Mannschaften spielen?
where can I get tickets?	wo kann man Karten bekommen?
can you get me a ticket?	kannst du mir eine Karte besorgen?
I'd like to see a rugby/football match	ich würde gern ein Rugbyspiel/Fußballspiel sehen
my favourite (*Amer* favorite) team is Bayern	ich bin ein Bayern-Fan
let's watch the match on TV	sehen wir uns das Spiel im Fernsehen an

Going to the cinema/theatre/club	Wir gehen ins Kino/Theater/in einen Club
what's on at the cinema/at the movies?	was läuft im Kino?
what's on at the theatre?	was wird im Theater gespielt?
how long is the performance?	wie lange dauert die Vorstellung?
when does the box office open/close?	wann macht die Kasse auf/zu?
what time does the performance start?	um wie viel Uhr fängt die Aufführung an?
when does the film/movie finish?	wann ist der Film zu Ende?
are there any tickets left?	gibt es noch Karten?
how much are the tickets?	was kosten die Karten?
where can I get a programme (*Amer* program)?	wo kann man ein Programm kaufen?
I want to book tickets for tonight	ich möchte für heute Abend Karten bestellen
I'd rather have seats in the stalls	Plätze im Parkett wären mir lieber
we'd like to go to a club	wir wollen in einen Club gehen
I go clubbing every weekend	ich gehe am Wochenende immer in Clubs

Hobbies	Hobbys
do you have any hobbies?	hast du irgendwelche Hobbys?
what do you do at the weekend?	was macht ihr am Wochenende?
I like yoga/listening to music	ich mache gern Yoga/höre gern Musik
I spend a lot of time surfing the Net	ich surfe viel im Internet
I read a lot	ich lese viel
I collect comics	ich sammle Comichefte/Comics

❼ Good timing

Telling the time	Uhrzeit
could you tell me the time?	können Sie mir sagen, wie spät es ist?
what time is it?	wie viel Uhr ist es?
it's 2 o'clock	es ist zwei Uhr
at about 8 o'clock	gegen acht Uhr
at 9 o'clock tomorrow	morgen um neun Uhr
from 10 o'clock onwards	ab zehn Uhr
the meeting starts at 8 p.m.	die Besprechung fängt um zwanzig Uhr an/um acht Uhr abends
at 5 o'clock in the morning/afternoon	um fünf Uhr morgens/um fünf Uhr nachmittags (um siebzehn Uhr)
at exactly 1 o'clock	um Punkt eins
it's five past.../quarter past...	es ist fünf nach.../Viertel nach...
it's half past one	es ist halb zwei
it's twenty-five to one	es ist fünf nach halb eins
it's quarter to/five to one	es ist Viertel vor/fünf vor eins
a quarter of an hour	eine Viertelstunde
three quarters of an hour	eine Dreiviertelstunde

Days and date	Wochentage und Datum
Sunday, Monday, Tuesday, Wednesday, Thursday, Friday, Saturday	Sonntag, Montag, Dienstag, Mittwoch, Donnerstag, Freitag, Samstag/Sonnabend
January, February, March, April, May, June, July, August, September, October, November, December	Januar, Februar, März, April, Mai, Juni, Juli, August, September, Oktober, November, Dezember
what's the date?	der Wievielte ist heute?
it's the second of June	heute ist der zweite Juni
we meet up every Monday	wir treffen uns jeden Montag

she comes on Tuesdays	sie kommt immer dienstags
we're going away in August	wir verreisen im August
I forgot it was the first of April today	ich habe ganz vergessen, dass heute der erste April ist
on November 8th	am achten November
about the 8th of June	um den 8. Juni

Public holidays and special days	**Feste und Feiertage**
Bank holiday	gesetzlicher Feiertag
New Year's Day (Jan 1)	Neujahr
Epiphany (Jan 6)	Heilige Drei Könige
St Valentine's Day (Feb 14)	Valentinstag
Shrove Tuesday	Fastnachtsdienstag/ Faschingsdienstag
Ash Wednesday	Aschermittwoch
Mothering Sunday/Mother's Day	Muttertag
Palm Sunday	Palmsonntag
Maundy Thursday	Gründonnerstag
Good Friday	Karfreitag
Easter Day	Ostersonntag
Easter Monday	Ostermontag
May Day (May 1)	der Erste Mai, Maifeiertag
Father's Day	Vatertag
Day of German Unity (Oct 3)	Tag der Deutschen Einheit
First Sunday in Advent	erster Advent
St Nicholas' Day (Dec 6)	Nikolaus
Christmas Eve	Heiligabend
Christmas Day (Dec 25)	erster Weihnachtstag
Boxing Day (Dec 26)	zweiter Weihnachtstag
New Year's Eve (Dec 31)	Silvester

❽ Weights & measures/Maße u. Gewichte

Length/Längenmaße

inches/Zoll	0.39	3.9	7.8	11.7	15.6	19.7	39
cm/Zentimeter	1	10	20	30	40	50	100

Distance/Entfernungen

miles/Meilen	0.62	6.2	12.4	18.6	24.9	31	62
km/Kilometer	1	10	20	30	40	50	100

Weight/Gewichte

pounds/Pfund	2.2	22	44	66	88	110	220
kg/Kilogramm	1	10	20	30	40	50	100

Capacity/Hohlmaße

gallons/Gallonen	0.22	2.2	4.4	6.6	8.8	11	22
litres/Liter	1	10	20	30	40	50	100

Temperature/Temperatur

°C	0	5	10	15	20	25	30	37	38	40
°F	32	41	50	59	68	77	86	98.4	100	104

Clothing and shoe sizes/Kleider- und Schuhgrößen

Women's clothing sizes/Damengrößen

UK	8	10	12	14	16	18
US	6	8	10	12	14	16
Continent	36	38	40	42	44	46

Men's clothing sizes/Herrengrößen

UK/US	36	38	40	42	44	46
Continent	46	48	50	52	54	56

Men's and women's shoes/Schuhgrößen

UK women	4	5	6	7	7.5	8				
UK men				6	7	8	9	10	11	
US	6.5	7.5	8.5	9.5	10.5	11.5	12.5	13.5	14.5	
Continent	37	38	39	40	41	42	43	44	45	

Aa

a /ə/, betont /eɪ/

vor einem Vokal **an**

● *indefinite article*

····▸ ein (*m*), eine (*f*), ein (*nt*). **a problem** ein Problem. **an apple** ein Apfel. **a cat** eine Katze. **have you got a pencil?** hast du einen Bleistift? **I gave it to a beggar** ich gab es einem Bettler

! There are some cases where a is not translated, such as when talking about people's professions or nationalities: **she is a lawyer** sie ist Rechtsanwältin. **he's an Italian** er ist Italiener

····▸ (*with 'not'*) kein (*m*), keine (*f*), kein (*nt*), keine (*pl*). **that's not a problem/not a good idea** das ist kein Problem/keine gute Idee. **there was not a chance that ...** es bestand keine Möglichkeit, dass .... **she did not say a word** sie sagte kein Wort. **I didn't tell a soul** ich habe es keinem Menschen gesagt

····▸ (*per; each*) pro. **£300 a week** 300 Pfund pro Woche. **30 miles an hour** 30 Meilen pro Stunde. (*in prices*) **it costs 90p a pound** es kostet 90 Pence das Pfund.

aback /ə'bæk/ *adv* **be taken** ∼ verblüfft sein

abandon /ə'bændən/ *vt* verlassen;

(*give up*) aufgeben

abate /ə'beɪt/ *vi* nachlassen

abattoir /'æbətwɑ:(r)/ *n* Schlachthof *m*

abb|ey /'æbɪ/ *n* Abtei *f.* ∼**ot** *n* Abt *m*

abbreviat|e /ə'bri:vɪeɪt/ *vt* abkürzen. ∼**ion** *n* Abkürzung *f*

abdicat|e /'æbdɪkeɪt/ *vi* abdanken. ∼**ion** *n* Abdankung *f*

abdom|en /'æbdəmən/ *n* Unterleib *m.* ∼**inal** *adj* Unterleibs-

abduct /əb'dʌkt/ *vt* entführen. ∼**ion** *n* Entführung *f*

aberration /æbə'reɪʃn/ *n* Abweichung *f*; (*mental*) Verwirrung *f*

abeyance /ə'beɪəns/ *n* **in** ∼ [zeitweilig] außer Kraft

abhor /əb'hɔ:(r)/ *vt* (*pt/pp* **abhorred**) verabscheuen. ∼**rent** *adj* abscheulich

abide /ə'baɪd/ *vt* (*pt/pp* **abided**) (*tolerate*) aushalten; **aus**stehen (*person*)

ability /ə'bɪlətɪ/ *n* Fähigkeit *f*; (*talent*) Begabung *f*

abject /'æbdʒekt/ *adj* erbärmlich; (*humble*) demütig

ablaze /ə'bleɪz/ *adj* in Flammen

able /'eɪbl/ *adj* (**-r, -st**) fähig; **be** ∼ **to do sth** etw tun können. ∼**-'bodied** *adj* körperlich gesund

ably /'eɪblɪ/ *adv* gekonnt

abnormal /æb'nɔ:ml/ *adj* anormal; (*Med*) abnorm. ∼**ity** *n* Abnormität *f.* ∼**ly** *adv* ungewöhnlich

aboard /ə'bɔ:d/ *adv & prep* an Bord (+ *gen*)

abolish /ə'bɒlɪʃ/ *vt* abschaffen.

a

~ition n Abschaffung f
abominable /əˈbɒmɪnəbl/ adj,
-**bly** adv abscheulich
aborigines /æbəˈrɪdʒəniːz/ npl Ureinwohner pl
abort /əˈbɔːt/ vt abtreiben. ~**ion** n
Abtreibung f. ~**ive** adj (attempt)
vergeblich
about /əˈbaʊt/ adv umher, herum;
(approximately) ungefähr; **be ~** (in
circulation) umgehen; (in existence)
vorhanden sein; **be ~ to do** sth im
Begriff sein, etw zu tun; **there was
no one ~** es war kein Mensch da;
run/play ~ herumlaufen/-spielen
● prep um (+ acc) [... herum]; (concerning) über (+ acc); **what is it ~?**
worum geht es? (book:) wovon handelt es? **I know nothing ~ it** ich
weiß nichts davon; **talk/know ~**
reden/wissen von
about: ~'**face** n, -'**turn** n Kehrtwendung f
above /əˈbʌv/ adv oben ● prep
über (+ dat/acc); ~ **all** vor allem
above: ~'**board** adj legal.
~-**mentioned** adj oben erwähnt
abrasive /əˈbreɪsɪv/ adj Scheuer-;
(remark) verletzend ● n Scheuermittel nt; (Techn) Schleifmittel nt
abreast /əˈbrest/ adv nebeneinander; **keep ~ of** Schritt halten mit
abridge /əˈbrɪdʒ/ vt kürzen
abroad /əˈbrɔːd/ adv im Ausland;
go ~ ins Ausland fahren
abrupt /əˈbrʌpt/ adj abrupt; (sudden) plötzlich; (curt) schroff
abscess /ˈæbsɪs/ n Abszess m
absence /ˈæbsəns/ n Abwesenheit f
absent /ˈæbsənt/ adj abwesend; **be
~** fehlen
absentee /æbsənˈtiː/ n Abwesende(r) m/f
absent-minded /æbsənt

'maɪndɪd/ adj geistesabwesend;
(forgetful) zerstreut
absolute /ˈæbsəluːt/ adj absolut
absorb /əbˈsɔːb/ vt absorbieren,
aufsaugen; ~**ed in** vertieft in (+
acc). ~**ent** adj saugfähig
absorption /əbˈsɔːpʃn/ n Absorption f
abstain /əbˈsteɪn/ vi sich enthalten
(**from** gen)
abstemious /əbˈstiːmɪəs/ adj enthaltsam
abstention /əbˈstenʃn/ n (Pol)
[Stimm]enthaltung f
abstract /ˈæbstrækt/ adj abstrakt
● n (summary) Abriss m
absurd /əbˈsɜːd/ adj absurd. ~**ity**
n Absurdität f
abundan|ce /əˈbʌndəns/ n Fülle f
(**of** an + dat). ~**t** adj reichlich
abuse[1] /əˈbjuːz/ vt missbrauchen;
(insult) beschimpfen
abus|e[2] /əˈbjuːs/ n Missbrauch m;
(insults) Beschimpfungen pl. ~**ive**
adj ausfallend
abysmal /əˈbɪzml/ adj 🆒 katastrophal
abyss /əˈbɪs/ n Abgrund m
academic /ækəˈdemɪk/ adj, -**ally**
adv akademisch
academy /əˈkædəmɪ/ n Akademie f
accelerat|e /əkˈseləreɪt/ vt/i beschleunigen. ~**ion** n Beschleunigung f. ~**or** n (Auto) Gaspedal nt
accent /ˈæksənt/ n Akzent m
accept /əkˈsept/ vt annehmen;
(fig) akzeptieren ● vi zusagen.
~**able** adj annehmbar. ~**ance** n
Annahme f; (of invitation) Zusage f
access /ˈækses/ n Zugang m.
~**ible** adj zugänglich
accessor|y /əkˈsesərɪ/ n (Jur) Mitschuldige(r) m/f; ~**ies** pl (fashion)

Accessoires pl; (Techn) Zubehör nt

accident /ˈæksɪdənt/ n Unfall m; (chance) Zufall m; **by** ~ zufällig; (unintentionally) versehentlich. ~**al** adj zufällig; (unintentional) versehentlich

acclaim /əˈkleɪm/ vt feiern (**as** als)

acclimatize /əˈklaɪmətaɪz/ vt **become** ~**d** sich akklimatisieren

accommodat|e /əˈkɒmədeɪt/ vt unterbringen. ~**ing** adj entgegenkommend. ~**ion** (rooms) Unterkunft f

accompan|iment /əˈkʌmpəni mənt/ n Begleitung f. ~**ist** n (Mus) Begleiter(in) m(f)

accompany /əˈkʌmpəni/ vt (pt/ pp -ied) begleiten

accomplice /əˈkʌmplɪs/ n Komplize/-zin m/f

accomplish /əˈkʌmplɪʃ/ vt erfüllen (task); (achieve) erreichen. ~**ed** adj fähig. ~**ment** n Fertigkeit f; (achievement) Leistung f

accord /əˈkɔːd/ n of one's own ~ aus eigenem Antrieb. ~**ance** n in ~**ance with** entsprechend (+ dat)

according /əˈkɔːdɪŋ/ adv ~ **to** nach (+ dat). ~**ly** adv entsprechend

accordion /əˈkɔːdɪən/ n Akkordeon nt

account /əˈkaʊnt/ n Konto nt; (bill) Rechnung f; (description) Darstellung f; (report) Bericht m; ~**s** pl (Comm) Bücher pl; **on** ~ **of** wegen (+ gen); **on no** ~ auf keinen Fall; **take into** ~ in Betracht ziehen, berücksichtigen ● vi ~ **for** Rechenschaft ablegen für; (explain) erklären

accountant /əˈkaʊntənt/ n Buchhalter(in) m(f); (chartered) Wirtschaftsprüfer m

accumulat|e /əˈkjuːmjʊleɪt/ vt ansammeln, anhäufen ● vi sich ansammeln, sich anhäufen. ~**ion** n

Ansammlung f, Anhäufung f

accura|cy /ˈækʊrəsɪ/ n Genauigkeit f. ~**te** adj genau

accusation /ækjuːˈzeɪʃn/ n Anklage f

accusative /əˈkjuːzətɪv/ adj & n ~ **[case]** (Gram) Akkusativ m

accuse /əˈkjuːz/ vt (Jur) anklagen (**of** gen); ~ **s.o. of doing sth** jdn beschuldigen, etw getan zu haben

accustom /əˈkʌstəm/ vt gewöhnen (**to** an + dat); **grow** or **get** ~**ed to** sich gewöhnen an (+ acc). ~**ed** adj gewohnt

ace /eɪs/ n (Cards, Sport) Ass nt

ache /eɪk/ n Schmerzen m pl ● vi weh tun, schmerzen

achieve /əˈtʃiːv/ vt leisten; (gain) erzielen; (reach) erreichen. ~**ment** n (feat) Leistung f

acid /ˈæsɪd/ adj sauer; (fig) beißend ● n Säure f. ~**ity** n Säure f. ~'**rain** n saurer Regen m

acknowledge /əkˈnɒlɪdʒ/ vt anerkennen; (admit) zugeben; erwidern (greeting); ~ **receipt of** den Empfang bestätigen (+ gen). ~**ment** n Anerkennung f; (of letter) Empfangsbestätigung f

acne /ˈæknɪ/ n Akne f

acorn /ˈeɪkɔːn/ n Eichel f

acoustic /əˈkuːstɪk/ adj, -**ally** adv akustisch. ~**s** npl Akustik f

acquaint /əˈkweɪnt/ vt **be** ~**ed with** kennen; vertraut sein mit (fact). ~**ance** n (person) Bekannte(r) m/f; **make s.o.'s** ~**ance** jdn kennen lernen

acquire /əˈkwaɪə(r)/ vt erwerben

acquisit|ion /ækwɪˈzɪʃn/ n Erwerb m; (thing) Erwerbung f. ~**ive** adj habgierig

acquit /əˈkwɪt/ vt (pt/pp acquitted) freisprechen

acre /ˈeɪkə(r)/ n ≈ Morgen m

a

acrimon|ious /ˈækrɪˈməʊnɪəs/ adj bitter

acrobat /ˈækrəbæt/ n Akrobat(in) m(f). **~ic** adj akrobatisch

across /əˈkrɒs/ adv hinüber/herüber; (wide) breit; (not lengthwise) quer; (in crossword) waagerecht; **come ~ sth** auf etw (acc) stoßen; **go ~** hinübergehen; **bring ~** herüberbringen ● prep über (+ acc); (on the other side of) auf der anderen Seite (+ gen)

act /ækt/ n Tat f; (action) Handlung f; (law) Gesetz nt; (Theat) Akt m; (item) Nummer f ● vi handeln; (behave) sich verhalten; (Theat) spielen; (pretend) sich verstellen; **~ as** fungieren als ● vt spielen (role). **~ing** adj (deputy) stellvertretend ● n (Theat) Schauspielerei f

action /ˈækʃn/ n Handlung f; (deed) Tat f; (Mil) Einsatz m; (Jur) Klage f; (effect) Wirkung f; (Techn) Mechanismus m; **out of ~** (machine:) außer Betrieb; **take ~** handeln; **killed in ~** gefallen

activate /ˈæktɪveɪt/ vt betätigen

active /ˈæktɪv/ adj aktiv; **on ~e service** im Einsatz. **~ity** n Aktivität f

act|or /ˈæktə(r)/ n Schauspieler m. **~ress** n Schauspielerin f

actual /ˈæktʃʊəl/ adj eigentlich; (real) tatsächlich. **~ly** adv sehr

acupuncture /ˈækjʊ-/ n Akupunktur f

acute /əˈkjuːt/ adj scharf; (angle) spitz; (illness:) akut. **~ly** adv sehr

ad /æd/ n 🔟 = advertisement

AD abbr (Anno Domini) n.Chr.

adamant /ˈædəmənt/ adj **be ~ that** darauf bestehen, dass

adapt /əˈdæpt/ vt anpassen; bearbeiten (play) ● vi sich anpassen. **~able** adj anpassungsfähig

adaptation /ædæpˈteɪʃn/ n (Theat) Bearbeitung f

add /æd/ vt hinzufügen; (Math) addieren ● vi zusammenzählen, addieren; **~ to** hinzufügen zu; (fig: increase) steigern; (compound) verschlimmern. **~ up** vt zusammenzählen (figures) ● vi zusammenzählen, addieren

adder /ˈædə(r)/ n Kreuzotter f

addict /ˈædɪkt/ n Süchtige(r) m/f

addict|ed /əˈdɪktɪd/ adj süchtig; **~ed to drugs** drogensüchtig. **~ion** n Sucht f

addition /əˈdɪʃn/ n Hinzufügung f; (Math) Addition f; (thing added) Ergänzung f; **in ~** zusätzlich. **~al** adj zusätzlich

additive /ˈædɪtɪv/ n Zusatz m

address /əˈdres/ n Adresse f, Anschrift f; (speech) Ansprache f ● vt adressieren (**to** an + acc); (speak to) anreden (person); sprechen vor (+ dat) (meeting). **~ee** n Empfänger m

adequate /ˈædɪkwət/ adj ausreichend

adhere /ædˈhɪə(r)/ vi kleben/(fig) festhalten (**to** an + dat)

adhesive /ædˈhiːsɪv/ adj klebend ● n Klebstoff m

adjacent /əˈdʒeɪsnt/ adj angrenzend

adjective /ˈædʒɪktɪv/ n Adjektiv nt

adjoin /əˈdʒɔɪn/ vt angrenzen an (+ acc). **~ing** adj angrenzend

adjourn /əˈdʒɜːn/ vt vertagen (**until** auf + acc) ● vi sich vertagen. **~ment** n Vertagung f

adjudicate /əˈdʒuːdɪkeɪt/ vi (in competition) Preisrichter sein

adjust /əˈdʒʌst/ vt einstellen; (alter) verstellen ● vi sich anpassen (**to** dat). **~able** adj verstellbar. **~ment** n Einstellung f; Anpassung f

ad lib /ædˈlɪb/ adv aus dem Stegreif ● *vi* (*pt/pp* **ad libbed**) 🗓 improvisieren

administer /əd'mɪnɪstə(r)/ *vt* verwalten; verabreichen (*medicine*)

administration /ədmɪnɪ'streɪʃn/ *n* Verwaltung *f*; (*Pol*) Regierung *f*

admirable /'ædmərəbl/ *adj* bewundernswert

admiral /'ædmərəl/ *n* Admiral *m*

admiration /ædmə'reɪʃn/ *n* Bewunderung *f*

admire /əd'maɪə(r)/ *vt* bewundern. **~r** *n* Verehrer(in) *m(f)*

admission /əd'mɪʃn/ *n* Eingeständnis *nt*; (*entry*) Eintritt *m*

admit /əd'mɪt/ *vt* (*pt/pp* **admitted**) (*let in*) hereinlassen; (*acknowledge*) zugeben; **~ to sth** etw zugeben. **~tance** *n* Eintritt *m*. **~tedly** *adv* zugegebenermaßen

admonish /əd'mɒnɪʃ/ *vt* ermahnen

adolescen|ce /ædə'lesns/ *n* Jugend *f*, Pubertät *f*. **~t** *adj* Jugend-; (*boy, girl*) halbwüchsig ● *n* Jugendliche(r) *m/f*

adopt /ə'dɒpt/ *vt* adoptieren; ergreifen (*measure*); (*Pol*) annehmen (*candidate*). **~ion** *n* Adoption *f*

ador|able /ə'dɔːrəbl/ *adj* bezaubernd. **~ation** *n* Anbetung *f*

adore /ə'dɔː(r)/ *vt* (*worship*) anbeten; (🗓: *like*) lieben

adorn /ə'dɔːn/ *vt* schmücken. **~ment** *n* Schmuck *m*

Adriatic /eɪdrɪ'ætɪk/ *adj* & *n* **~ [Sea]** Adria *f*

adrift /ə'drɪft/ *adj* **be ~** treiben

adroit /ə'drɔɪt/ *adj* gewandt, geschickt

adulation /ædjʊ'leɪʃn/ *n* Schwärmerei *f*

adult /'ædʌlt/ *n* Erwachsene(r) *m/f*

adulterate /ə'dʌltəreɪt/ *vt* verfäl-

schen; panschen (*wine*)

adultery /ə'dʌltərɪ/ *n* Ehebruch *m*

advance /əd'vɑːns/ *n* Fortschritt *m*; (*Mil*) Vorrücken *nt*; (*payment*) Vorschuss *m*; **in ~** im Voraus ● *vi* vorankommen; (*Mil*) vorrücken; (*make progress*) Fortschritte machen ● *vt* fördern (*cause*); vorbringen (*idea*); vorschießen (*money*). **~d** *adj* fortgeschritten; (*progressive*) fortschrittlich. **~ment** *n* Förderung *f*; (*promotion*) Beförderung *f*

advantage /əd'vɑːntɪdʒ/ *n* Vorteil *m*; **take ~ of** ausnutzen. **~ous** *adj* vorteilhaft

adventur|e /əd'ventʃə(r)/ *n* Abenteuer *nt*. **~er** *n* Abenteurer *m*. **~ous** *adj* abenteuerlich; (*person*) abenteuerlustig

adverb /'ædvɜːb/ *n* Adverb *nt*

adverse /'ædvɜːs/ *adj* ungünstig

advert /'ædvɜːt/ *n* 🗓 = advertisement

advertise /'ædvətaɪz/ *vt* Reklame machen für; (*by small ad*) inserieren ● *vi* Reklame machen; inserieren

advertisement /əd'vɜːtɪsmənt/ *n* Anzeige *f*; (*publicity*) Reklame *f*; (*small ad*) Inserat *nt*

advertis|er /'ædvətaɪzə(r)/ *n* Inserent *m*. **~ing** *n* Werbung *f*

advice /əd'vaɪs/ *n* Rat *m*

advisable /əd'vaɪzəbl/ *adj* ratsam

advis|e /əd'vaɪz/ *vt* raten (**s.o.** jdm); (*counsel*) beraten; (*inform*) benachrichtigen; **~e s.o. against sth** jdm von etw abraten ● *vi* raten. **~er** *n* Berater(in) *m(f)*. **~ory** *adj* beratend

advocate[1] /'ædvəkət/ *n* (*supporter*) Befürworter *m*

advocate[2] /'ædvəkeɪt/ *vt* befürworten

aerial /'eərɪəl/ *adj* Luft- ● *n*

a Antenne f

aerobics /eə'rəʊbɪks/ n Aerobic nt

aero|drome /'eərədrəʊm/ n Flugplatz m. **~plane** n Flugzeug nt

aerosol /'eərəsɒl/ n Spraydose f

aesthetic /iːs'θetɪk/ adj ästhetisch

affair /ə'feə(r)/ n Angelegenheit f, Sache f; (scandal) Affäre f; [love-]~ [Liebes]verhältnis nt

affect /ə'fekt/ vt sich auswirken auf (+ acc); (concern) betreffen; (move) rühren; (pretend) vortäuschen. **~ation** n Affektiertheit f. **~ed** adj affektiert

affection /ə'fekʃn/ n Liebe f. **~ate** adj liebevoll

affirm /ə'fɜːm/ vt behaupten

affirmative /ə'fɜːmətɪv/ adj bejahend ●n Bejahung f

afflict /ə'flɪkt/ vt be ~ed with behaftet sein mit. **~ion** n Leiden nt

afflluen|ce /'æfluəns/ n Reichtum m. **~t** adj wohlhabend. **~t society** n Wohlstandsgesellschaft f

afford /ə'fɔːd/ vt be able to ~ sth sich (dat) etw leisten können. **~able** adj erschwinglich

affront /ə'frʌnt/ n Beleidigung f ●vt beleidigen

afloat /ə'fləʊt/ adj be ~ (ship:) flott sein; keep ~ (person:) sich über Wasser halten

afraid /ə'freɪd/ adj be ~ Angst haben (of vor + dat); I'm ~ not leider nicht; I'm ~ so [ja] leider

Africa /'æfrɪkə/ n Afrika nt. **~n** adj afrikanisch ●n Afrikaner(in) m(f)

after /'ɑːftə(r)/ adv danach ●prep nach (+ dat); ~ that danach; ~ all schließlich; the day ~ tomorrow übermorgen; be ~ aus sein auf (+ acc) ●conj nachdem

after: **~-effect** n Nachwirkung f. **~math** /-mɑːθ/ n Auswirkungen pl. **~'noon** n Nachmittag m; good

~noon! guten Tag! **~-sales service** n Kundendienst m. **~shave** n Rasierwasser nt. **~thought** n nachträglicher Einfall m. **~wards** adv nachher

again /ə'gen/ adv wieder; (once more) noch einmal; ~ and ~ immer wieder

against /ə'genst/ prep gegen (+ acc)

age /eɪdʒ/ n Alter nt; (era) Zeitalter nt; **~s** ☐ ewig; under ~ minderjährig; of ~ volljährig; two years of ~ zwei Jahre alt ●v (pres p ageing) ●vt älter machen ●vi altern; (mature) reifen

aged¹ /eɪdʒd/ adj ~ two zwei Jahre alt

aged² /'eɪdʒɪd/ adj betagt ●n the ~ pl die Alten

ageless /'eɪdʒlɪs/ adj ewig jung

agency /'eɪdʒənsɪ/ n Agentur f; (office) Büro nt

agenda /ə'dʒendə/ n Tagesordnung f

agent /'eɪdʒənt/ n Agent(in) m(f); (Comm) Vertreter(in) m(f); (substance) Mittel nt

aggravat|e /'ægrəveɪt/ vt verschlimmern; (☐: annoy) ärgern. **~ion** n ☐ Ärger m

aggregate /'ægrɪgət/ adj gesamt ●n Gesamtzahl f; (sum) Gesamtsumme f

aggress|ion /ə'greʃn/ n Aggression f. **~ive** adj aggressiv. **~or** n Angreifer(in) m(f)

aggro /'ægrəʊ/ n ☐ Ärger m

aghast /ə'gɑːst/ adj entsetzt

agil|e /'ædʒaɪl/ adj flink, behände; (mind) wendig. **~ity** n Flinkheit f, Behändigkeit f

agitat|e /'ædʒɪteɪt/ vt bewegen; (shake) schütteln ●vi (fig) for ~ agitieren für. **~ed** adj erregt. **~ion**

n Erregung f; (Pol) Agitation f

ago /əˈɡəʊ/ adv vor (+ dat); **a long time ~** vor langer Zeit; **how long ~ is it?** wie lange ist es her?

agony /ˈæɡənɪ/ n Qual f; **be in ~** furchtbare Schmerzen haben

agree /əˈɡriː/ vt vereinbaren; (admit) zugeben; **~ to do sth** sich bereit erklären, etw zu tun ● vi (people, figures:) übereinstimmen; (reach agreement) sich einigen; (get on) gut miteinander auskommen; (consent) einwilligen (**to** in + acc); **~ with s.o.** jdm zustimmen; (food:) jdm bekommen; **~ with sth** (approve of) mit etw einverstanden sein

agreeable /əˈɡriːəbl/ adj angenehm

agreed /əˈɡriːd/ adj vereinbart

agreement /əˈɡriːmənt/ n Übereinstimmung f; (consent) Einwilligung f; (contract) Abkommen nt; **reach ~** sich einigen

agricultural /æɡrɪˈkʌltʃərəl/ adj landwirtschaftlich. **~e** n Landwirtschaft f

aground /əˈɡraʊnd/ adj gestrandet; **run ~** (ship:) stranden

ahead /əˈhed/ adv **straight ~** geradeaus; **be ~ of s.o./sth** vor jdm/ etw sein; (fig) voraus sein; **go on ~** vorgehen; (fig) vorankommen; **go ~!** 🔲 bitte! **look/plan ~** vorausblicken/-planen

aid /eɪd/ n Hilfe f; (financial) Unterstützung f; **in ~ of** zugunsten (+ gen) ● vt helfen (+ dat)

Aids /eɪdz/ n Aids nt

aim /eɪm/ n Ziel nt; **take ~** zielen ● vt richten (**at** auf + acc) ● vi zielen (**at** auf + acc); **~ to do sth** beabsichtigen, etw zu tun. **~less** adj ziellos

air /eə(r)/ n Luft f; (expression)

Miene f; (appearance) Anschein m; **be on the ~** (programme:) gesendet werden; (person:) auf Sendung sein; **by ~** auf dem Luftweg; (airmail) mit Luftpost ● vt lüften; vorbringen (views)

air: ~ bag n (Auto) Airbag m. **~-conditioned** adj klimatisiert. **~-conditioning** n Klimaanlage f. **~craft** n Flugzeug nt. **~field** n Flugplatz m. **~ force** n Luftwaffe f. **~ freshener** n Raumspray nt. **~gun** n Luftgewehr nt. **~ hostess** n Stewardess f. **~ letter** n Aerogramm nt. **~line** n Fluggesellschaft f. **~mail** n Luftpost f. **~man** n Flieger m. **~plane** n (Amer) Flugzeug nt. **~port** n Flughafen m. **~-raid** n Luftangriff m. **~-raid shelter** n Luftschutzbunker m. **~ship** n Luftschiff nt. **~ ticket** n Flugschein m. **~tight** adj luftdicht. **~-traffic controller** n Fluglotse m

airy /ˈeərɪ/ adj luftig; (manner) nonchalant

aisle /aɪl/ n Gang m

ajar /əˈdʒɑː(r)/ adj angelehnt

alarm /əˈlɑːm/ n Alarm m; (device) Alarmanlage f; (clock) Wecker m; (fear) Unruhe f ● vt erschrecken

alas /əˈlæs/ int ach!

album /ˈælbəm/ n Album nt

alcohol /ˈælkəhɒl/ n Alkohol m. **~ic** adj alkoholisch ● n Alkoholiker(in) m(f). **~ism** n Alkoholismus m

alert /əˈlɜːt/ adj aufmerksam ● n Alarm m

algebra /ˈældʒɪbrə/ n Algebra f

Algeria /ælˈdʒɪərɪə/ n Algerien nt

alias /ˈeɪlɪəs/ n Deckname m ● adv alias

alibi /ˈælɪbaɪ/ n Alibi nt

alien /ˈeɪlɪən/ adj fremd ● n Ausländer(in) m(f)

alienate /ˈeɪlɪəneɪt/ vt entfremden

a

alight¹ /ə'laɪt/ vi aussteigen (**from** aus)

alight² adj be ~ brennen; **set ~** anzünden

align /ə'laɪn/ vt ausrichten. **~ment** n Ausrichtung f

alike /ə'laɪk/ adj & adv ähnlich; (same) gleich; **look ~** sich (dat) ähnlich sehen

alive /ə'laɪv/ adj lebendig; **be ~** leben; **be ~ with** wimmeln von

all /ɔːl/

● adjective

····▸ (plural) alle. **all [the] children** alle Kinder. **all our children** alle unsere Kinder. **all the books** alle Bücher. **all the others** alle anderen

····▸ (singular = whole) ganz. **all the wine** der ganze Wein. **all the town** die ganze Stadt. **all my money** mein ganzes Geld; all mein Geld. **all day** den ganzen Tag. **all Germany** ganz Deutschland

● pronoun

····▸ (plural = all persons/things) alle. **all are welcome** alle sind willkommen. **they all came** sie sind alle gekommen. **are we all here?** sind wir alle da? **the best pupils of all** die besten Schüler (von allen). **the most beautiful of all** der/die/das schönste von allen

····▸ (singular = everything) alles. **that is all** das ist alles. **all that I possess** alles, was ich besitze

····▸ (in phrases) **all of** ganz; (with plural) alle. **all of the money** das ganze Geld. **all of the paintings** alle Gemälde. **all of you/them** Sie/ sie alle

····▸ (in phrases) **all in all** alles in

allem. **in all** insgesamt. **most of all** am meisten. **once and for all** ein für alle Mal. **not at all** gar nicht

● adverb

····▸ (completely) ganz. **she was all alone** sie war ganz allein. **I was all dirty** ich war ganz schmutzig

····▸ (in scores) **four all** vier zu vier

····▸ (in phrases) **all right** (things) in Ordnung. **is everything all right?** ist alles in Ordnung? **is that all right for you?** passt das Ihnen? **I'm all right** mir geht es gut. **did you get home all right?** sind Sie gut nach Hause gekommen? **is it all right to go in?** kann ich reingehen? **yes, all right** ja, gut. **work out all right** gut gehen; klappen 🔟

····▸ (in phrases) **all but** (almost) fast. **all at once** auf einmal. **all the better** umso besser. **all the same** (nevertheless) trotzdem

allege /ə'ledʒ/ vt behaupten. **~d** adj angeblich

allegiance /ə'liːdʒəns/ n Treue f

allerg|ic /ə'lɜːdʒɪk/ adj allergisch (**to** gegen). **~y** n Allergie f

alleviate /ə'liːvɪeɪt/ vt lindern

alley /'ælɪ/ n Gasse f; (for bowling) Bahn f

alliance /ə'laɪəns/ n Verbindung f; (Pol) Bündnis nt

allied /'ælaɪd/ adj alliiert

alligator /'ælɪɡeɪtə(r)/ n Alligator m

allocat|e /'æləkeɪt/ vt zuteilen; (share out) verteilen. **~ion** n Zuteilung f

allot /ə'lɒt/ vt (pt/pp allotted) zuteilen (s.o. jdm)

allow /ə'laʊ/ vt erlauben; (give)

geben; (*grant*) gewähren; (*reckon*) rechnen; (*agree, admit*) zugeben; ~ **for** berücksichtigen; ~ **s.o. to do sth** jdm erlauben, etw zu tun; **be ~ed to do sth** etw tun dürfen

allowance /ə'lauəns/ *n* [finanzielle] Unterstützung *f*; **make ~s for** berücksichtigen

alloy /'ælɔɪ/ *n* Legierung *f*

allude /ə'luːd/ *vi* anspielen (**to** auf + *acc*)

allusion /ə'luːʒn/ *n* Anspielung *f*

ally¹ /'ælaɪ/ *n* Verbündete(r) *m/f*; **the Allies** *pl* die Alliierten

ally² /ə'laɪ/ *vt* (*pt/pp* **-ied**) verbinden; ~ **oneself with** sich verbünden mit

almighty /ɔːl'maɪtɪ/ *adj* allmächtig; (🔲: *big*) Riesen-. ● *n* **the A~** der Allmächtige

almond /'ɑːmənd/ *n* (*Bot*) Mandel *f*

almost /'ɔːlməʊst/ *adv* fast, beinahe

alone /ə'ləʊn/ *adj & adv* allein; **leave me ~** lass mich in Ruhe; **leave that ~** lass die Finger davon! **let ~** ganz zu schweigen von

along /ə'lɒŋ/ *prep* entlang (+ *acc*); ~ **the river** den Fluss entlang ● *adv* ~ **with** zusammen mit; **all** ~ die ganze Zeit; **come** ~ komm doch; **I'll bring it** ~ ich bringe es mit

along|side *adv* daneben ● *prep* neben (+ *dat*)

aloud /ə'laʊd/ *adv* laut

alphabet /'ælfəbet/ *n* Alphabet *nt*. ~**ical** *adj* alphabetisch

alpine /'ælpaɪn/ *adj* alpin; **A~** Alpen-

Alps /ælps/ *npl* Alpen *pl*

already /ɔːl'redɪ/ *adv* schon

Alsace /'ælsæs/ *n* Elsass *nt*

Alsatian /æl'seɪʃn/ *n* (*dog*) [deut-

scher] Schäferhund *m*

also /'ɔːlsəʊ/ *adv* auch

altar /'ɔːltə(r)/ *n* Altar *m*

alter /'ɔːltə(r)/ *vt* ändern ● *vi* sich verändern. ~**ation** *n* Änderung *f*

alternate¹ /'ɔːltəneɪt/ *vi* [sich] abwechseln ● *vt* abwechseln

alternate² /ɔːl'tɜːnət/ *adj* abwechselnd; **on ~ days** jeden zweiten Tag

alternative /ɔːl'tɜːnətɪv/ *adj* andere(r,s); ~ **medicine** Alternativmedizin *f* ● *n* Alternative *f*. ~**ly** *adv* oder aber

although /ɔːl'ðəʊ/ *conj* obgleich, obwohl

altitude /'æltɪtjuːd/ *n* Höhe *f*

altogether /ɔːltə'geðə(r)/ *adv* insgesamt; (*on the whole*) alles in allem

aluminium /æljʊ'mɪnɪəm/ *n*, (*Amer*) **aluminum** *n* Aluminium *nt*

always /'ɔːlweɪz/ *adv* immer

am /æm/ *see* **be**

a.m. *abbr* (**ante meridiem**) vormittags

amass /ə'mæs/ *vt* anhäufen

amateur /'æmətə(r)/ *n* Amateur *m* ● *attrib* Amateur-; (*Theat*) Laien-. ~**ish** *adj* laienhaft

amaze /ə'meɪz/ *vt* erstaunen. ~**d** *adj* erstaunt. ~**ment** *n* Erstaunen *nt*

amazing /ə'meɪzɪŋ/ *adj* erstaunlich

ambassador /æm'bæsədə(r)/ *n* Botschafter *m*

amber /'æmbə(r)/ *n* Bernstein *m* ● *adj* (*colour*) gelb

ambigu|ity /æmbɪ'gjuːətɪ/ *n* Zweideutigkeit *f*. ~**ous** *adj* **-ly** *adv* zweideutig

ambiti|on /æm'bɪʃn/ *n* Ehrgeiz *m*; (*aim*) Ambition *f*. ~**ous** *adj* ehrgeizig

amble /'æmbl/ vi schlendern

ambulance /'æmbjʊləns/ n Krankenwagen m. **~ man** n Sanitäter m

ambush /'æmbʊʃ/ n Hinterhalt m • vt aus dem Hinterhalt überfallen

amen /ɑː'men/ int amen

amend /ə'mend/ vt ändern. **~ment** n Änderung f

amenities /ə'miːnətɪz/ npl Einrichtungen pl

America /ə'merɪkə/ n Amerika nt. **~n** adj amerikanisch • n Amerikaner(in) m(f). **~nism** n Amerikanismus m

American dream Der Glaube, dass Amerika das Land unbegrenzter Möglichkeiten ist, in dem jeder sein Leben erfolgreich gestalten kann. Für Minderheiten und Einwanderer bedeutet der Traum weitgehende Toleranz und Anspruch auf eine freie Lebensgestaltung. Der American dream verkörpert eine optimistische allgemeine Grundhaltung mit auf Erfolg gerichtetem Denken und Handeln.

amiable /'eɪmɪəbl/ adj nett

amicable /'æmɪkəbl/ adj, **-bly** adv freundschaftlich; (agreement) gütlich

amid[st] /ə'mɪd[st]/ prep inmitten (+ gen)

ammonia /ə'məʊnɪə/ n Ammoniak nt

ammunition /æmjʊ'nɪʃn/ n Munition f

amnesty /'æmnəstɪ/ n Amnestie f

among[st] /ə'mʌŋ[st]/ prep unter (+ dat/acc); **~ yourselves** untereinander

amoral /eɪ'mɒrəl/ adj amoralisch

amorous /'æmərəs/ adj zärtlich

amount /ə'maʊnt/ n Menge f; (sum of money) Betrag m; (total) Gesamtsumme f • vi **~ to** sich belaufen auf (+ acc); (fig) hinauslaufen auf (+ acc)

amphibi|an /æm'fɪbɪən/ n Amphibie f. **~ous** adj amphibisch

amphitheatre /'æmfɪ-/ n Amphitheater nt

ample /'æmpl/ adj (-r, -st) reichlich; (large) füllig

amplif|ier /'æmplɪfaɪə(r)/ n Verstärker m. **~y** vt (pt/pp -ied) weiter ausführen; verstärken (sound)

amputat|e /'æmpjʊteɪt/ vt amputieren. **~ion** n Amputation f

amuse /ə'mjuːz/ vt amüsieren, belustigen; (entertain) unterhalten. **~ment** n Belustigung f; Unterhaltung f

amusing /ə'mjuːzɪŋ/ adj amüsant

an /ən/, betont /æn/ see **a**

anaem|ia /ə'niːmɪə/ n Blutarmut f, Anämie f. **~ic** adj blutarm

anaesthetic /ænəs'θetɪk/ n Narkosemittel nt, Betäubungsmittel nt; **under [an] ~** in Narkose

anaesthetist /ə'niːsθətɪst/ n Narkosearzt m

analogy /ə'nælədʒɪ/ n Analogie f

analyse /'ænəlaɪz/ vt analysieren

analysis /ə'næləsɪs/ n Analyse f

analyst /'ænəlɪst/ n Chemiker(in) m(f); (psychologist) Analytiker m

analytical /ænə'lɪtɪkl/ adj analytisch

anarch|ist /'ænəkɪst/ n Anarchist m. **~y** n Anarchie f

anatom|ical /ænə'tɒmɪkl/ adj anatomisch. **~y** n Anatomie f

ancest|or /'ænsestə(r)/ n Vorfahr m. **~ry** n Abstammung f

anchor /'æŋkə(r)/ n Anker m • vi ankern • vt verankern

ancient /'eɪnʃənt/ adj alt

and /ənd/, betont /ænd/ conj und;
~ **so on** und so weiter; **six hundred ~ two** sechshundertzwei;
more ~ more immer mehr; **nice
~ warm** schön warm

anecdote /ˈænɪkdəʊt/ n Anekdote f

angel /ˈeɪndʒl/ n Engel m. ~**ic** adj
engelhaft

anger /ˈæŋgə(r)/ n Zorn m ● vt
zornig machen

angle /ˈæŋgl/ n Winkel m; (fig)
Standpunkt m; **at an** ~ schräg

angler /ˈæŋglə(r)/ n Angler m

Anglican /ˈæŋglɪkən/ adj anglikanisch ● n Anglikaner(in) m(f)

Anglo-Saxon /æŋgləʊˈsæksn/
adj angelsächsisch ● n (Lang) Angelsächsisch nt

angry /ˈæŋgrɪ/ adj, **-ily** adv zornig;
be ~ with jdm böse sein auf (+ acc)

anguish /ˈæŋgwɪʃ/ n Qual f

angular /ˈæŋgjʊlə(r)/ adj eckig;
(features) kantig

animal /ˈænɪml/ n Tier nt ● adj
tierisch

animat|e /ˈænɪmeɪt/ vt beleben.
~**ed** adj lebhaft

animosity /ænɪˈmɒsətɪ/ n Feind-
seligkeit f

ankle /ˈæŋkl/ n [Fuß]knöchel m

annex[e] /ˈæneks/ n Nebengebäude nt; (extension) Anbau m

annihilate /əˈnaɪəleɪt/ vt vernichten

anniversary /ænɪˈvɜːsərɪ/ n Jahrestag m

annotate /ˈænəteɪt/ vt kommentieren

announce /əˈnaʊns/ vt bekannt
geben; (over loudspeaker) durchsa-
gen; (at reception) ankündigen;
(Radio, TV) ansagen; (in newspaper)
anzeigen. ~**ment** n Bekanntgabe f,

Bekanntmachung f; Durchsage f;
Ansage f; Anzeige f. ~**r** n Ansage-
r(in) m(f)

annoy /əˈnɔɪ/ vt ärgern; (pester)
belästigen; **get ~ed** sich ärgern.
~**ance** n Ärger m. ~**ing** adj ärgerlich

annual /ˈænjʊəl/ adj jährlich ● n
(book) Jahresalbum nt

anonymous /əˈnɒnɪməs/ adj
anonym

anorak /ˈænəræk/ n Anorak m

anorexi|a /ænəˈreksɪə/ n Mager-
sucht f; **be ~c** n Magersucht
leiden

another /əˈnʌðə(r)/ adj & pron ein
anderer/eine andere/ein anderes;
(additional) noch eine(r); ~ **[one]**
noch einer/eine/eins; ~ **time**
andermal; **one ~** einander

answer /ˈɑːnsə(r)/ n Antwort f;
(solution) Lösung f ● vt antworten
(s.o. jdm); beantworten (question,
letter); ~ **the door/telephone** an
die Tür/ans Telefon gehen ● vi antworten; (Teleph) sich melden; ~
back eine freche Antwort geben.
~**ing machine** n (Teleph) Anruf-
beantworter m

ant /ænt/ n Ameise f

antagonis|m /ænˈtægənɪzm/ n
Antagonismus m. ~**tic** adj
feindselig

Antarctic /ænˈtɑːktɪk/ n Antarktis f

antelope /ˈæntɪləʊp/ n Antilope f

antenatal /æntɪˈneɪtl/ adj ~ **care**
Schwangerschaftsfürsorge f

antenna /ænˈtenə/ n Fühler m;
(Amer: aerial) Antenne f

anthem /ˈænθəm/ n Hymne f

anthology /ænˈθɒlədʒɪ/ n Anthologie f

anthrax /ˈænθræks/ n Milzbrand
m, Anthrax m

a

anthropology /æneθrə'pɒlədʒɪ/ n
Anthropologie f

antibiotic /æntɪbaɪ'ɒtɪk/ n Anti-
biotikum nt

anticipat|e /æn'tɪsɪpeɪt/ vt vor-
hersehen; (*forestall*) zuvorkommen
(+ *dat*); (*expect*) erwarten. **~ion** n
Erwartung f

anti'climax n Enttäuschung f

anti'clockwise adj & adv gegen
den Uhrzeigersinn

antics /'æntɪks/ npl Mätzchen pl

antidote /'æntɪdəʊt/ n Gegen-
gift nt

'antifreeze n Frostschutzmittel nt

antipathy /æn'tɪpəθɪ/ n Abneigung f, Antipathie f

antiquated /'æntɪkweɪtɪd/ adj
veraltet

antique /æn'ti:k/ adj antik ● n An-
tiquität f. **~ dealer** n Antiquitäten-
händler m

antiquity /æn'tɪkwətɪ/ n Al-
tertum nt

anti'septic adj antiseptisch ● n
Antiseptikum nt

anti'social adj asozial; 🗌 ungesellig

antlers /'æntləz/ npl Geweih nt

anus /'eɪnəs/ n After m

anvil /'ænvɪl/ n Amboss m

anxiety /æŋ'zaɪətɪ/ n Sorge f

anxious /'æŋkʃəs/ adj ängstlich;
(*worried*) besorgt; **be ~ to do sth**
etw gerne machen wollen

any /'enɪ/ adj irgendein(e); pl ir-
gendwelche; (*every*) jede(r,s); pl alle;
(*after negative*) kein(e); pl keine; **~
colour/number you like** eine belie-
bige Farbe/Zahl; **have you ~ wine/
apples?** haben Sie Wein/Äpfel?
● pron [irgend]einer/eine/eins; pl [ir-
gend]welche; (*some*) welche(r,s); pl
welche; (*all*) alle pl; (*negative*) kei-

ner/keine/keins; pl keine; **I don't
want ~ of it** ich will nichts davon;
there aren't ~ es gibt keine ● adv
noch; **~ quicker/slower** noch
schneller/langsamer; **is it ~ better?**
geht es etwas besser? **would you
like ~ more?** möchten Sie noch
[etwas]? **I can't eat ~ more** ich
kann nichts mehr essen

'anybody pron [irgend]jemand;
(*after negative*) niemand; **~ can do
that** das kann jeder

'anyhow adv jedenfalls; (*nevertheless*) trotzdem; (*badly*) irgendwie

'anyone pron = anybody

'anything pron [irgend]etwas;
(*after negative*) nichts; (*everything*) alles

'anyway adv jedenfalls; (*in any
case*) sowieso

'anywhere adv irgendwo; (*after
negative*) nirgendwo; (*be, live*) überall; (*go*) überallhin

apart /ə'pɑ:t/ adv auseinander; **live
~** getrennt leben; **~ from** abgesehen von

apartment /ə'pɑ:tmənt/ n Zimmer nt; (*flat*) Wohnung f

ape /eɪp/ n [Menschen]affe m ● vt
nachäffen

aperitif /ə'perətɪf/ n Aperitif m

apologetic /əpɒlə'dʒetɪk/ adj,
-ally adv entschuldigend; **be ~** sich
entschuldigen

apologize /ə'pɒlədʒaɪz/ vi sich
entschuldigen (**to** bei)

apology /ə'pɒlədʒɪ/ n Entschuldigung f

apostle /ə'pɒsl/ n Apostel m

apostrophe /ə'pɒstrəfɪ/ n Apostroph m

appal /ə'pɔ:l/ vt (pt/pp appalled)
entsetzen. **~ling** adj entsetzlich

apparatus /æpə'reɪtəs/ n Appara-
tur f; (*Sport*) Geräte pl; (*single piece*)

Gerät *nt*

apparent /əˈpærənt/ *adj* offenbar; (*seeming*) scheinbar. **~ly** *adv* offenbar, anscheinend

appeal /əˈpiːl/ *n* Appell *m*, Aufruf *m*; (*request*) Bitte *f*; (*attraction*) Reiz *m*; (*Jur*) Berufung *f* ● *vi* appellieren (**to** an + *acc*); (*ask*) bitten (**for** um); (*be attractive*) zusagen (**to** dat); (*Jur*) Berufung einlegen. **~ing** *adj* ansprechend

appear /əˈpɪə(r)/ *vi* erscheinen; (*seem*) scheinen; (*Theat*) auftreten. **~ance** *n* Erscheinen *nt*; (*look*) Aussehen *nt*; **to all ~ances** allem Anschein nach

appendicitis /əpendɪˈsaɪtɪs/ *n* Blinddarmentzündung *f*

appendix /əˈpendɪks/ *n* (*pl* **-ices** /-ɪsiːz/) (*of book*) Anhang *m* ● (*pl* **-es**) (*Anat*) Blinddarm *m*

appetite /ˈæpɪtaɪt/ *n* Appetit *m*

appetizing /ˈæpɪtaɪzɪŋ/ *adj* appetitlich

applau|d /əˈplɔːd/ *vt/i* Beifall klatschen (+ *dat*). **~se** *n* Beifall *m*

apple /ˈæpl/ *n* Apfel *m*

appliance /əˈplaɪəns/ *n* Gerät *nt*

applicable /ˈæplɪkəbl/ *adj* anwendbar (**to** auf + *acc*); (*on form*) **not ~** nicht zutreffend

applicant /ˈæplɪkənt/ *n* Bewerber(in) *m(f)*

application /æplɪˈkeɪʃn/ *n* Anwendung *f*; (*request*) Antrag *m*; (*for job*) Bewerbung *f*; (*diligence*) Fleiß *m*

applied /əˈplaɪd/ *adj* angewandt

apply /əˈplaɪ/ *vt* (*pt/pp* **-ied**) auftragen (*paint*); anwenden (*force, rule*) ● *vi* zutreffen (**to** auf + *acc*); **~ for** beantragen; sich bewerben um (*job*)

appoint /əˈpɔɪnt/ *vt* ernennen; (*fix*) festlegen. **~ment** *n* Ernennung *f*; (*meeting*) Verabredung *f*; (*at*

doctor's, hairdresser's) Termin *m*; (*job*) Posten *m*; **make an ~ment** sich anmelden

appreciable /əˈpriːʃəbl/ *adj* merklich; (*considerable*) beträchtlich

appreciat|e /əˈpriːʃeɪt/ *vt* zu schätzen wissen; (*be grateful for*) dankbar sein für; (*enjoy*) schätzen; (*understand*) verstehen ● *vi* (*increase in value*) im Wert steigen. **~ion** *n* (*gratitude*) Dankbarkeit *f*. **~ive** *adj* dankbar

apprehens|ion /æprɪˈhenʃn/ *n* Festnahme *f*; (*fear*) Angst *f*. **~ive** *adj* ängstlich

apprentice /əˈprentɪs/ *n* Lehrling *m*. **~ship** *n* Lehre *f*

approach /əˈprəʊtʃ/ *n* Näherkommen *nt*; (*of time*) Nahen *nt*; (*access*) Zugang *m*; (*road*) Zufahrt *f* ● *vi* sich nähern; (*time:*) nahen ● *vt* sich nähern (+ *dat*); (*with request*) herantreten an (+ *acc*); (*set about*) sich heranmachen an (+ *acc*). **~able** *adj* zugänglich

appropriate /əˈprəʊprɪət/ *adj* angebracht, angemessen

approval /əˈpruːvl/ *n* Billigung *f*; **on ~** zur Ansicht

approv|e /əˈpruːv/ *vt* billigen ● *vi* **~e of sth/s.o.** mit etw/jdm einverstanden sein. **~ing** *adj* anerkennend

approximate /əˈprɒksɪmət/ *adj*, **-ly** *adv* ungefähr

approximation /əprɒksɪˈmeɪʃn/ *n* Schätzung *f*

apricot /ˈeɪprɪkɒt/ *n* Aprikose *f*

April /ˈeɪprəl/ *n* April *m*; **make an ~ fool of** in den April schicken

apron /ˈeɪprən/ *n* Schürze *f*

apt /æpt/ *adj* passend; **be ~ to do sth** dazu neigen, etw zu tun

aqualung /ˈækwəlʌŋ/ *n* Tauchgerät *nt*

aquarium /ə'kweərɪəm/ n Aquarium nt

aquatic /ə'kwætɪk/ adj Wasser-

Arab /'ærəb/ adj arabisch ● n Araber(in) m(f). **~ian** adj arabisch

Arabic /'ærəbɪk/ adj arabisch

arbitrary /'ɑ:bɪtrəri/ adj, **-ily** adv willkürlich

arbitrat|e /'ɑ:bɪtreɪt/ vi schlichten. **~ion** n Schlichtung f

arc /ɑ:k/ n Bogen m

arcade /ɑ:'keɪd/ n Laubengang m; (shops) Einkaufspassage f

arch /ɑ:tʃ/ n Bogen m; (of foot) Gewölbe nt ● vt ~ its back (cat:) einen Buckel machen

archaeological /ɑ:kɪə'lɒdʒɪkl/ adj archäologisch

archaeolog|ist /ɑ:kɪ'ɒlədʒɪst/ n Archäologe m/-login f. **~y** n Archäologie f

archaic /ɑ:'keɪɪk/ adj veraltet

arch'bishop /ɑ:tʃ-/ n Erzbischof m

archer /'ɑ:tʃə(r)/ n Bogenschütze m. **~y** n Bogenschießen nt

architect /'ɑ:kɪtekt/ n Architekt(in) m(f). **~ural** adj architektonisch

architecture /'ɑ:kɪtektʃə(r)/ n Architektur f

archives /'ɑ:kaɪvz/ npl Archiv nt

archway /'ɑ:tʃweɪ/ n Torbogen m

Arctic /'ɑ:ktɪk/ adj arktisch ● n the ~ die Arktis

ardent /'ɑ:dənt/ adj leidenschaftlich

ardour /'ɑ:də(r)/ n Leidenschaft f

arduous /'ɑ:djʊəs/ adj mühsam

are /ɑ:(r)/ see be

area /'eərɪə/ n (surface) Fläche f; (Geometry) Flächeninhalt m; (region) Gegend f; (fig) Gebiet nt

arena /ə'ri:nə/ n Arena f

Argentina /ɑ:dʒən'ti:nə/ n Argentinien nt

Argentin|e /'ɑ:dʒəntaɪn/, **~ian** /-'tɪnɪən/ adj argentinisch

argue /'ɑ:gju:/ vi streiten (about über + acc); (two people:) sich streiten; (debate) diskutieren; **don't ~!** keine Widerrede! ● vt (debate) diskutieren; (reason) ~ **that** argumentieren, dass

argument /'ɑ:gjʊmənt/ n Streit m, Auseinandersetzung f; (reasoning) Argument nt; **have an ~** sich streiten. **~ative** adj streitlustig

aria /'ɑ:rɪə/ n Arie f

arise /ə'raɪz/ vi (pt arose, pp arisen) sich ergeben (from aus)

aristocracy /ærɪ'stɒkrəsi/ n Aristokratie f

aristocrat /'ærɪstəkræt/ n Aristokrat(in) m(f). **~ic** adj aristokratisch

arithmetic /ə'rɪθmətɪk/ n Rechnen nt

arm /ɑ:m/ n Arm m; (of chair) Armlehne f; **~s** pl (weapons) Waffen pl; (Heraldry) Wappen nt ● vt bewaffnen

armament /'ɑ:məmənt/ n Bewaffnung f; **~s** pl Waffen pl

'armchair n Sessel m

armed /ɑ:md/ adj bewaffnet; **~ forces** Streitkräfte pl

armour /'ɑ:mə(r)/ n Rüstung f. **~ed** adj Panzer-

'armpit n Achselhöhle f

army /'ɑ:mi/ n Heer nt; (specific) Armee f; **join the ~** zum Militär gehen

aroma /ə'rəʊmə/ n Aroma nt, Duft m. **~tic** adj aromatisch

arose /ə'rəʊz/ see arise

around /ə'raʊnd/ adv [all] ~ rings herum; **he's not ~** er ist nicht da; **travel ~** herumreisen ● prep um (+ acc) ... herum; (approximately) nearly) gegen

arouse /ə'raʊz/ vt aufwecken; (*excite*) erregen

arrange /ə'reɪndʒ/ vt arrangieren; anordnen (*furniture, books*); (*settle*) abmachen. **~ment** n Anordnung f; (*agreement*) Vereinbarung f; (*of flowers*) Gesteck nt; **make ~ments** Vorkehrungen treffen

arrest /ə'rest/ n Verhaftung f; **under ~** verhaftet ● vt verhaften

arrival /ə'raɪvl/ n Ankunft f; **new ~s** pl Neuankömmlinge pl

arrive /ə'raɪv/ vi ankommen; **~ at** (*fig*) gelangen zu

arrogan|ce /'ærəgəns/ n Arroganz f. **~t** adj arrogant

arrow /'ærəʊ/ n Pfeil m

arse /ɑːs/ n (*vulgar*) Arsch m

arson /'ɑːsn/ n Brandstiftung f. **~ist** n Brandstifter m

art /ɑːt/ n Kunst f; **work of ~** Kunstwerk nt; **~s and crafts** pl Kunstgewerbe nt; **A~s** pl (*Univ*) Geisteswissenschaften pl

artery /'ɑːtəri/ n Schlagader f, Arterie f

'art gallery n Kunstgalerie f

arthritis /ɑː'θraɪtɪs/ n Arthritis f

artichoke /'ɑːtɪtʃəʊk/ n Artischocke f

article /'ɑːtɪkl/ n Artikel m; (*object*) Gegenstand m; **~ of clothing** Kleidungsstück nt

artificial /ɑːtɪ'fɪʃl/ adj künstlich

artillery /ɑː'tɪləri/ n Artillerie f

artist /'ɑːtɪst/ n Künstler(in) m(f)

artiste /ɑː'tiːst/ n (*Theat*) Artist(in) m(f)

artistic /ɑː'tɪstɪk/ adj, **-ally** adv künstlerisch

as /æz/ conj (*because*) da; (*when*) als; (*while*) während ● prep als; **as a child/foreigner** als Kind/Ausländer

● adv as well auch; **as soon as** sobald; **as much as** so viel wie; **as quick as** so schnell wie du; **as you know** wie Sie wissen; **as far as I'm concerned** was mich betrifft

asbestos /æz'bestɒs/ n Asbest m

ascend /ə'send/ vi [auf]steigen ● vt besteigen (*throne*)

ascent /ə'sent/ n Aufstieg m

ascertain /æsə'teɪn/ vt ermitteln

ash¹ /æʃ/ n (*tree*) Esche f

ash² n Asche f

ashamed /ə'feɪmd/ adj beschämt; **be ~** sich schämen (**of** über + acc)

ashore /ə'ʃɔː(r)/ adv an Land

'ashtray n Aschenbecher m

Asia /'eɪʃə/ n Asien nt. **~n** adj asiatisch ● n Asiat(in) m(f). **~tic** adj asiatisch

aside /ə'saɪd/ adv beiseite

ask /ɑːsk/ vt/i fragen; stellen (*question*); (*invite*) einladen; **~ for** bitten um; verlangen (*s.o.*); **~ after** sich erkundigen nach; **~ s.o. in** jdn hereinbitten; **~ s.o. to do sth** jdn bitten, etw zu tun

asleep /ə'sliːp/ adj **be ~** schlafen; **fall ~** einschlafen

asparagus /ə'spærəgəs/ n Spargel m

aspect /'æspekt/ n Aspekt m

asphalt /'æsfælt/ n Asphalt m

aspire /ə'spaɪə(r)/ vi **~ to** streben nach

ass /æs/ n Esel m

assail /ə'seɪl/ vt bestürmen. **~ant** n Angreifer(in) m(f)

assassin /ə'sæsɪn/ n Mörder(in) m(f). **~ate** vt ermorden. **~ation** n [politischer] Mord m

assault /ə'sɔːlt/ n (*Mil*) Angriff m; (*Jur*) Körperverletzung f ● vt [tätlich] angreifen

assemble /ə'sembl/ vi sich vera sammeln ● *vt* versammeln; (*Techn*) montieren

assembly /əˈsemblɪ/ *n* Versammlung *f*; (*Sch*) Andacht *f*; (*Techn*) Montage *f*. ~ **line** *n* Fließband *nt*

assent /əˈsent/ *n* Zustimmung *f*

assert /əˈsɜːt/ *vt* behaupten; ~ **oneself** sich durchsetzen. ~**ion** *n* Behauptung *f*

assess /əˈses/ *vt* bewerten; (*fig & for tax purposes*) einschätzen: schätzen (*value*). ~**ment** *n* Einschätzung *f*; (*of tax*) Steuerbescheid *m*

asset /ˈæset/ *n* Vorteil *m*; ~s *pl* (*money*) Vermögen *nt*; (*Comm*) Aktiva *pl*

assign /əˈsaɪn/ *vt* zuweisen (**to** *dat*). ~**ment** *n* (*task*) Aufgabe *f*

assist /əˈsɪst/ *vt/i* helfen (+ *dat*). ~**ance** *n* Hilfe *f*. ~**ant** *adj* Hilfs- ● *n* Assistent(in) *m(f)*; (*in shop*) Verkäufer(in) *m(f)*

associat|e[1] /əˈsəʊʃɪeɪt/ *vt* verbinden; (*Psychology*) assoziieren ● *vi* ~ **with** verkehren mit. ~**ion** *n* Verband *m*

associate[2] /əˈsəʊʃɪət/ *adj* assoziiert ● *n* Kollege *m*-*gin*

assort|ed /əˈsɔːtɪd/ *adj* gemischt. ~**ment** *n* Mischung *f*

assum|e /əˈsjuːm/ *vt* annehmen; übernehmen (*office*); ~**ing that** angenommen, dass

assumption /əˈsʌmpʃn/ *n* Annahme *f*; **on the** ~ in der Annahme (**that** dass)

assurance /əˈʃʊərəns/ *n* Versicherung *f*; (*confidence*) Selbstsicherheit *f*

assure /əˈʃʊə(r)/ *vt* versichern (**s.o.** jdm); **I** ~ **you [of that]** das versichere ich Ihnen. ~**d** *adj* sicher

asterisk /ˈæstərɪsk/ *n* Sternchen *nt*

asthma /ˈæsmə/ *n* Asthma *nt*

astonish /əˈstɒnɪʃ/ *vt* erstaunen. ~**ing** *adj* erstaunlich. ~**ment** *n* Erstaunen *nt*

astray /əˈstreɪ/ *adv* **go** ~ verloren gehen; (*person:*) sich verlaufen

astride /əˈstraɪd/ *adv* rittlings ● *prep* rittlings auf (+ *dat/acc*)

astrolog|er /əˈstrɒlədʒə(r)/ *n* Astrologe *m*/-*gin f*. ~**y** *n* Astrologie *f*

astronaut /ˈæstrənɔːt/ *n* Astronaut(in) *m(f)*

astronom|er /əˈstrɒnəmə(r)/ *n* Astronom *m*. ~**ical** *adj* astronomisch. ~**y** *n* Astronomie *f*

astute /əˈstjuːt/ *adj* scharfsinnig

asylum /əˈsaɪləm/ *n* Asyl *nt*; **[lunatic]** ~ Irrenanstalt *f*. ~**seeker** *n* Asylbewerber(in) *m(f)*

---

at /æt/, *unbetont* /ət/

● *preposition*

····▸ (*expressing place*) an (+ *dat*). **at the station** am Bahnhof. **at the end** am Ende. **at the corner** an der Ecke. **at the same place** an der gleichen Stelle

····▸ (*at s.o.'s house or shop*) bei (+ *dat*). **at Lisa's** bei Lisa. **at my uncle's** bei meinem Onkel. **at the baker's/butcher's** beim Bäcker/Fleischer

····▸ (*inside a building*) in (+ *dat*). **at the theatre/supermarket** im Theater/Supermarkt. **we spent the night at a hotel** wir übernachteten in einem Hotel. **he is still at the office** er ist noch im Büro

····▸ (*expressing time*) (*with clock time*) um; (*with main festivals*) zu. **at six o'clock** um sechs Uhr. **at midnight** um Mitternacht. **at midday** um zwölf Uhr mittags. **at Christmas/Easter** zu

Weihnachten/Ostern

····▸ (expressing age) mit. **at [the age of] forty** mit vierzig; im Alter von vierzig

····▸ (expressing price) zu. **at £2.50 [each]** zu je [je] 2,50 Pfund

····▸ (expressing speed) mit. **at 30 m.p.h.** mit dreißig Meilen pro Stunde

····▸ (in phrases) **good/bad at languages** gut/schlecht in Sprachen. **two at a time** zwei auf einmal. **at that** (at that point) dabei; (at that provocation) daraufhin; (moreover) noch dazu

ate /et/ see eat

atheist /'eɪθɪɪst/ n Atheist(in) m(f)

athlet|e /'æθliːt/ n Athlet(in) m(f). **∼ic** adj sportlich. **∼ics** n Leichtathletik f

Atlantic /ət'læntɪk/ adj & n the ∼ [Ocean] der Atlantik

atlas /'ætləs/ n Atlas m

atmosphere /'ætməsfɪə(r)/ n Atmosphäre f

atom /'ætəm/ n Atom nt. ∼ **bomb** n Atombombe f

atomic /ə'tɒmɪk/ adj Atom-

atrocious /ə'trəʊʃəs/ adj abscheulich

atrocity /ə'trɒsətɪ/ n Gräueltat f

attach /ə'tætʃ/ vt befestigen (**to an** + dat); beimessen (importance) (**to** dat); **be ∼ed to** (fig) hängen an (+ dat)

attack /ə'tæk/ n Angriff m; (Med) Anfall m ● vt/i angreifen. **∼er** n Angreifer m

attain /ə'teɪn/ vt erreichen. **∼able** adj erreichbar

attempt /ə'tempt/ n Versuch m ● vt versuchen

attend /ə'tend/ vt anwesend sein bei; (go regularly to) besuchen; (take

part in) teilnehmen an (+ dat); (accompany) begleiten; (doctor:) behandeln ● vi anwesend sein; (pay attention) aufpassen; ∼ **to** sich kümmern um; (in shop) bedienen. **∼ance** n Anwesenheit f; (number) Besucherzahl f. **∼ant** n Wärter(in) m(f); (in car park) Wächter m

attention /ə'tenʃn/ n Aufmerksamkeit f; ∼! (Mil) stillgestanden! **pay** ∼ aufpassen; **pay** ∼ **to** beachten, achten auf (+ acc)

attentive /ə'tentɪv/ adj aufmerksam

attic /'ætɪk/ n Dachboden m

attitude /'ætɪtjuːd/ n Haltung f

attorney /ə'tɜːnɪ/ n (Amer: lawyer) Rechtsanwalt m; **power of** ∼ Vollmacht f

attract /ə'trækt/ vt anziehen; erregen (attention); **s.o.'s attention** jds Aufmerksamkeit auf sich (acc) lenken. **∼ion** n Anziehungskraft f; (charm) Reiz m; (thing) Attraktion f. **∼ive** adj, **-ly** adv attraktiv

attribute /ə'trɪbjuːt/ vt zuschreiben (**to** dat)

aubergine /'əʊbəʒiːn/ n Aubergine f

auburn /'ɔːbən/ adj kastanienbraun

auction /'ɔːkʃn/ n Auktion f Versteigerung f ● vt versteigern. **∼eer** n Auktionator m

audaci|ous /ɔː'deɪʃəs/ adj verwegen. **∼ty** n Verwegenheit f; (impudence) Dreistigkeit f

audible /'ɔːdəbl/ adj, **-bly** adv hörbar

audience /'ɔːdɪəns/ n Publikum nt; (Theat, TV) Zuschauer pl; (Radio) Zuhörer pl; (meeting) Audienz f

audit /'ɔːdɪt/ n Bücherrevision f ● vt (Comm) prüfen

audition /ɔː'dɪʃn/ n (Theat) Vorsprechen nt; (Mus) Vorspielen nt

(for singer) Vorsingen nt ● vi vorsprechen; vorspielen; vorsingen

auditor /ˈɔːdɪtə(r)/ n Buchprüfer m

auditorium /ɔːdɪˈtɔːrɪəm/ n Zuschauerraum m

August /ˈɔːɡəst/ n August m

aunt /ɑːnt/ n Tante f

au pair /əʊˈpeə(r)/ n **~ [girl]** Au-pair-Mädchen nt

aura /ˈɔːrə/ n Fluidum nt

auspicious /ɔːˈspɪʃəs/ adj günstig; (occasion) freudig

auster|e /ɒˈstɪə(r)/ adj streng; (simple) nüchtern. **~ity** n Strenge f; (hardship) Entbehrung f

Australia /ɒˈstreɪlɪə/ n Australien nt. **~n** adj australisch ● n Australier(in) m(f)

Austria /ˈɒstrɪə/ n Österreich nt **~n** adj österreichisch ● n Österreicher(in) m(f)

authentic /ɔːˈθentɪk/ adj echt, authentisch. **~ate** vt beglaubigen. **~ity** n Echtheit f

author /ˈɔːθə(r)/ n Schriftsteller m, Autor m; (of document) Verfasser m

authoritarian /ɔːθʊrɪˈteərɪən/ adj autoritär

authoritative /ɔːˈθʊrɪtətɪv/ adj maßgebend

authority /ɔːˈθɒrɪtɪ/ n Autorität f; (public) Behörde f; **in ~** verantwortlich

authorization /ɔːθəraɪˈzeɪʃn/ n Ermächtigung f

authorize /ˈɔːθəraɪz/ vt ermächtigen (s.o.); genehmigen (sth)

autobi'ography /ɔːtə-/ n Autobiographie f

autograph /ˈɔːtə-/ n Autogramm nt

automatic /ɔːtəˈmætɪk/ adj, **-ally** adv automatisch

automation /ɔːtəˈmeɪʃn/ n Auto-

mation f

automobile /ˈɔːtəməbiːl/ n Auto nt

autonom|ous /ɔːˈtɒnəməs/ adj autonom. **~y** n Autonomie f

autumn /ˈɔːtəm/ n Herbst m. **~al** adj herbstlich

auxiliary /ɔːɡˈzɪlɪərɪ/ adj Hilfs- ● n Helfer(in) m(f), Hilfskraft f

avail /əˈveɪl/ n **to no ~** vergeblich

available /əˈveɪləbl/ adj verfügbar; (obtainable) erhältlich

avalanche /ˈævəlɑːnʃ/ n Lawine f

avenge /əˈvendʒ/ vt rächen

avenue /ˈævənjuː/ n Allee f

average /ˈævərɪdʒ/ adj Durchschnitts-, durchschnittlich ● n Durchschnitt m; **on ~** im Durchschnitt, durchschnittlich ● vt durchschnittlich schaffen

averse /əˈvɜːs/ adj **not be ~e to** sth etw (dat) nicht abgeneigt sein

avert /əˈvɜːt/ vt abwenden

aviary /ˈeɪvɪərɪ/ n Vogelhaus nt

aviation /eɪvɪˈeɪʃn/ n Luftfahrt f

avocado /ævəˈkɑːdəʊ/ n Avocado f

avoid /əˈvɔɪd/ vt vermeiden; **~ s.o.** jdm aus dem Weg gehen. **~able** adj vermeidbar. **~ance** n Vermeidung f

await /əˈweɪt/ vt warten auf (+ acc)

awake /əˈweɪk/ adj wach; **wide ~** hellwach ● vi (pt **awoke**, pp **awoken**) erwachen

awaken /əˈweɪkn/ vt wecken ● vi erwachen. **~ing** n Erwachen nt

award /əˈwɔːd/ n Auszeichnung f; (prize) Preis m ● vt zuerkennen (**to** s.o. dat); verleihen (prize)

aware /əˈweə(r)/ adj **become ~** gewahr werden (of gen); **be ~ that** wissen, dass. **~ness** n Bewusstsein nt

away /ə'weɪ/ adv weg, fort; (absent) abwesend; **four kilometres ~** vier Kilometer entfernt; **play ~** (Sport) auswärts spielen. **~ game** n Auswärtsspiel nt

awful /'ɔ:fl/ adj furchtbar

awkward /'ɔ:kwəd/ adj schwierig; (clumsy) ungeschickt; (embarrassing) peinlich; (inconvenient) ungünstig. **~ly** adv ungeschickt; (embarrassedly) verlegen

awning /'ɔ:nɪŋ/ n Markise f

awoke(n) /ə'wəʊk(n)/ see **awake**

axe /æks/ n Axt f ● vt (pres p **axing**) streichen

axle /'æksl/ n (Techn) Achse f

Bb

B /bi:/ n (Mus) H nt

baboon /bə'bu:n/ n Pavian m

baby /'beɪbɪ/ n Baby nt; (Amer, [I]) Schätzchen nt

baby: **~ish** adj kindisch. **~-sit** vi babysitten. **~-sitter** n Babysitter m

bachelor /'bætʃələ(r)/ n Junggeselle m

back /bæk/ n Rücken m; (reverse) Rückseite f; (of chair) Rückenlehne f; (Sport) Verteidiger m; **at/(Auto) in the ~** hinten; **on the ~** auf der Rückseite; **~ to front** verkehrt ● adj Hinter- ● adv zurück; **~ here/there** hier/da hinten; **~ at home** zu Hause; **go ~** zurückgehen/-zahlen ● vt (support) unterstützen; (with money) finanzieren; (Auto) zurücksetzen; (Betting) [Geld] setzen auf (+ acc); (cover the back of) mit einer Verstärkung versehen ● vi (Auto) zurücksetzen. **~ down** vi

klein beigeben. **~ in** vi rückwärts hineinfahren. **~ out** vi rückwärts hinaus-/herausfahren; (fig) aussteigen (of aus). **~ up** vt unterstützen; (confirm) bestätigen ● vi (Auto) zurücksetzen

back: **~ache** n Rückenschmerzen pl. **~biting** n gehässiges Gerede nt. **~bone** n Rückgrat nt. **~date** vt rückdatieren; **~dated to** rückwirkend von. **~'door** n Hintertür f

backer /'bækə(r)/ n Geldgeber m

back: **~'fire** vi (Auto) fehlzünden; (fig) fehlschlagen. **~ground** n Hintergrund m; **family ~ground** Familienverhältnisse pl. **~hand** n (Sport) Rückhand f. **~'handed** adj (compliment) zweifelhaft

backing /'bækɪŋ/ n (support) Unterstützung f; (material) Verstärkung f

back: **~lash** n (fig) Gegenschlag m. **~log** n Rückstand m (**of** an + dat). **~pack** n Rucksack m. **~'seat** n Rücksitz m. **~side** n [I] Hintern m. **~stroke** n Rückenschwimmen nt. **~-up** n Unterstützung f; (Amer: traffic jam) Stau m

backward /'bækwəd/ adj zurückgeblieben; (country) rückständig ● adv rückwärts. **~s** rückwärts; **~s and forwards** hin und her

back'yard n Hinterhof m; **not in my ~yard** [I] nicht vor meiner Haustür

bacon /'beɪkn/ n [Schinken]speck m

bacteria /bæk'tɪərɪə/ npl Bakterien pl

bad /bæd/ adj (**worse, worst**) schlecht; (serious) schwer, schlimm; (naughty) unartig. **~ language** gemeine Ausdrucksweise f; **feel ~** sich schlecht fühlen; (feel guilty) ein schlechtes Gewissen haben

badge /bædʒ/ n Abzeichen nt

badger /'bædʒə(r)/ n Dachs m • vt plagen

badly /'bædlɪ/ adv schlecht; (*seriously*) schwer; ~ **off** schlecht gestellt; ~ **behaved** unerzogen; **want** ~ sich (*dat*) sehnsüchtig wünschen; **need** ~ dringend brauchen

bad-'mannered adj mit schlechten Manieren

badminton /'bædmɪntən/ n Federball m

bad-'tempered adj schlecht gelaunt

baffle /'bæfl/ vt verblüffen

bag /bæg/ n Tasche f; (*of paper*) Tüte f; (*pouch*) Beutel m; ~**s of** 🄳 jede Menge • vt (🄳: *reserve*) in Beschlag nehmen

baggage /'bægɪdʒ/ n [Reise]gepäck nt

baggy /'bægɪ/ adj (*clothes*) ausgebeult

'bagpipes npl Dudelsack m

bail /beɪl/ n Kaution f; **on** ~ gegen Kaution • vt ~ **s.o. out** jdn gegen Kaution freibekommen; (*fig*) jdm aus der Patsche helfen

bait /beɪt/ n Köder m • vt mit einem Köder versehen; (*fig: torment*) reizen

bake /beɪk/ vt/i backen

baker /'beɪkə(r)/ n Bäcker m; ~**'s** [**shop**] Bäckerei f. ~**y** n Bäckerei f

baking /'beɪkɪŋ/ n Backen nt. ~**-powder** n Backpulver nt

balance /'bæləns/ n (*equilibrium*) Gleichgewicht nt, Balance f; (*scales*) Waage f; (*Comm*) Saldo m; (*outstanding sum*) Restbetrag m; [**bank**] ~ Kontostand m; **in the** ~ (*fig*) in der Schwebe • vt balancieren; (*equalize*) ausgleichen; (*Comm*) abschließen (*books*) • vi balancieren;

(*fig & Comm*) sich ausgleichen. ~**d** adj ausgewogen

balcony /'bælkənɪ/ n Balkon m

bald /bɔːld/ adj (**-er**, **-est**) kahl; (*person*) kahlköpfig

bald|ly adv unverblümt. ~**ness** n Kahlköpfigkeit f

ball[1] /bɔːl/ n Ball m; (*Billiards, Croquet*) Kugel f; (*of yarn*) Knäuel m & nt; **on the** ~ 🄳 auf Draht

ball[2] n (*dance*) Ball m

ball-'bearing n Kugellager nt

ballerina /bælə'riːnə/ n Ballerina f

ballet /'bæleɪ/ n Ballett nt. ~ **dancer** n Balletttänzer(in) m(f)

balloon /bə'luːn/ n Luftballon m; (*Aviat*) Ballon m

ballot /'bælət/ n [geheime] Wahl f; (*on issue*) Abstimmung f. ~**-box** n Wahlurne f. ~**-paper** n Stimmzettel m

ball: ~**point** ['pen] n Kugelschreiber m. ~**room** n Ballsaal m

balm /bɑːm/ n Balsam m

balmy /'bɑːmɪ/ adj sanft

Baltic /'bɔːltɪk/ adj & n **the** ~ [**Sea**] die Ostsee

bamboo /bæm'buː/ n Bambus m

ban /bæn/ n Verbot nt • vt (*pt/pp* **banned**) verbieten

banal /bə'nɑːl/ adj banal. ~**ity** n Banalität f

banana /bə'nɑːnə/ n Banane f

band /bænd/ n Band nt; (*stripe*) Streifen m; (*group*) Schar f; (*Mus*) Kapelle f

bandage /'bændɪdʒ/ n Verband m; (*for support*) Bandage f • vt verbinden; bandagieren (*limb*)

b. & b. abbr bed and breakfast

bandit /'bændɪt/ n Bandit m

band: ~**stand** n Musikpavillon m. ~**wagon** n **jump on the** ~**wagon**

(*fig*) sich einer erfolgreichen Sache anschließen

bang /bæŋ/ n (*noise*) Knall m; (*blow*) Schlag m ● *adv* go ~ knallen ● *int* bums! peng! ● *vt* knallen; (*shut noisily*) zuknallen; (*strike*) schlagen auf (+ *acc*) ● ~ **one's head** sich (*dat*) den Kopf stoßen (**on** an + *acc*) ● *vi* schlagen; (*door:*) zuknallen

banger /ˈbæŋə(r)/ n (*firework*) Knallfrosch m; (**[**𝕋**]**: *sausage*) Wurst f; **old** ~ (**[**𝕋**]**: *car*) Klapperkiste f

bangle /ˈbæŋɡl/ n Armreifen m

banish /ˈbænɪʃ/ *vt* verbannen

banisters /ˈbænɪstəz/ *npl* [Treppen]geländer nt

banjo /ˈbændʒəʊ/ n Banjo nt

bank[1] /bæŋk/ n (*of river*) Ufer nt; (*slope*) Hang m ● *vi* (*Aviat*) in die Kurve gehen

bank[2] n Bank f ● ~ **on** *vt* sich verlassen auf (+ *acc*)

'**bank account** n Bankkonto nt

banker /ˈbæŋkə(r)/ n Bankier m

bank: ~ '**holiday** n gesetzlicher Feiertag m. ~**ing** n Bankwesen nt. ~**note** n Banknote f

bankrupt /ˈbæŋkrʌpt/ adj bankrott; **go** ~ Bankrott machen ● n Bankrotteur m ● *vt* Bankrott machen. ~**cy** n Bankrott m

banner /ˈbænə(r)/ n Banner nt; (*carried by demonstrators*) Transparent nt, Spruchband nt

banquet /ˈbæŋkwɪt/ n Bankett nt

baptism /ˈbæptɪzm/ n Taufe f

baptize /bæpˈtaɪz/ *vt* taufen

bar /bɑː(r)/ n Stange f, (*of cage*) [Gitter]stab m; (*of gold*) Barren m; (*of chocolate*) Tafel f; (*of soap*) Stück nt; (*long*) Riegel m; (*café*) Bar f; (*Mus*) Takt m; (*fig:* *obstacle*) Hindernis nt; **parallel** ~**s** (*Sport*) Barren m; **behind** ~**s [**𝕋**]** hin-

ter Gittern ● *vt* (*pt/pp* **barred**) versperren (*way, door*); ausschließen (*person*)

barbar|ic /bɑːˈbærɪk/ adj barbarisch. ~**ity** n Barbarei f. ~**ous** adj barbarisch

barbecue /ˈbɑːbɪkjuː/ n Grill m; (*party*) Grillfest nt ● *vt* [im Freien] grillen

barbed /bɑːbd/ adj ~ **wire** Stacheldraht m

barber /ˈbɑːbə(r)/ n [Herren]friseur m

'**bar code** n Strichkode m

bare /beə(r)/ adj (**-r, -st**) nackt, bloß; (*tree*) kahl; (*empty*) leer; (*mere*) bloß

bare: ~**back** adv ohne Sattel. ~**faced** adj schamlos. ~**foot** adv barfuß. ~**headed** adj mit unbedecktem Kopf

barely /ˈbeəlɪ/ adv kaum

bargain /ˈbɑːɡɪn/ n (*agreement*) Geschäft nt; (*good buy*) Gelegenheitskauf m; **into the** ~ noch dazu; **make a** ~ sich einigen ● *vi* handeln; (*haggle*) feilschen; ~ **for** (*expect*) rechnen mit

barge /bɑːdʒ/ n Lastkahn m, (*towed*) Schleppkahn m ● *vi* ~ **in [**𝕋**]** hereinplatzen

baritone /ˈbærɪtəʊn/ n Bariton m

bark[1] /bɑːk/ n (*of tree*) Rinde f

bark[2] n Bellen nt ● *vi* bellen

barley /ˈbɑːlɪ/ n Gerste f

bar: ~**maid** n Schankmädchen nt. ~**man** Barmann m

barmy /ˈbɑːmɪ/ adj **[**𝕋**]** verrückt

barn /bɑːn/ n Scheune f

barometer /bəˈrɒmɪtə(r)/ n Barometer nt

baron /ˈbærn/ n Baron m. ~**ess** n Baronin f

barracks /'bærəks/ npl Kaserne f

barrage /'bærɑ:ʒ/ n (in river) Wehr nt; (Mil) Sperrfeuer nt; (fig) Hagel m

barrel /'bærl/ n Fass nt; (of gun) Lauf m; (of cannon) Rohr nt. **~-organ** n Drehorgel f

barren /'bærn/ adj unfruchtbar; (landscape) öde

barricade /bærɪ'keɪd/ n Barrikade f ● vt verbarrikadieren

barrier /'bærɪə(r)/ n Barriere f; (across road) Schranke f; (Rail) Sperre f; (fig) Hindernis nt

barrow /'bærəʊ/ n Karre f, Karren m

base /beɪs/ n Fuß m; (fig) Basis f; (Mil) Stützpunkt m ● vt stützen (on auf + acc); **be ~d on** basieren auf (+ dat)

base: **~ball** n Baseball m. **~less** adj unbegründet. **~ment** n Kellergeschoss nt

bash /bæʃ/ n Schlag m; **have a ~!** probier es mal! ● vt hauen

basic /'beɪsɪk/ adj Grund-; (fundamental) grundlegend; (essential) wesentlich; (unadorned) einfach; **the ~s** das Wesentliche. **~ally** adv grundsätzlich

basin /'beɪsn/ n Becken nt; (for washing) Waschbecken nt; (for food) Schüssel f

basis /'beɪsɪs/ n (pl **-ses** /-si:z/) Basis f

bask /bɑ:sk/ vi sich sonnen

basket /'bɑ:skɪt/ n Korb m. **~ball** n Basketball m

Basle /bɑ:l/ n Basel nt

bass /beɪs/ adj Bass-; **~ voice** Bassstimme f ● n Bass m; (person) Bassist m

bassoon /bə'su:n/ n Fagott nt

bastard /'bɑ:stəd/ n ⚠ Schuft m

bat¹ /bæt/ n Schläger m; **off one's own ~** 🗨 auf eigene Faust ● vt (pt/pp batted) schlagen; **not ~ an eyelid** (fig) nicht mit der Wimper zucken

bat² n (Zool) Fledermaus f

batch /bætʃ/ n (of people) Gruppe f; (of papers) Stoß m; (of goods) Sendung f; (of bread) Schub m

bath /bɑ:θ/ n (pl **~s** /bɑ:ðz/) Bad nt; (tub) Badewanne f; **~s** pl Badeanstalt f; **have a ~** baden

bathe /beɪð/ n Bad nt ● vt/i baden. **~r** n Badende(r) m/f

bathing /'beɪðɪŋ/ n Baden nt. **~-cap** n Bademütze f. **~-costume** n Badeanzug m

bath: **~-mat** n Bademitte f. **~-room** n Badezimmer nt. **~-towel** n Badetuch nt

battalion /bə'tælɪən/ n Bataillon nt

batter /'bætə(r)/ n (Culin) flüssiger Teig m ● vt schlagen; **~ed** adj (car) verbeult; (wife) misshandelt

battery /'bætərɪ/ n Batterie f

battle /'bætl/ n Schlacht f; (fig) Kampf m ● vi (fig) kämpfen (for um)

battle: **~field** n Schlachtfeld nt. **~ship** n Schlachtschiff nt

batty /'bætɪ/ adj 🗨 verrückt

Bavaria /bə'veərɪə/ n Bayern nt. **~n** adj bayrisch ● n Bayer(in) m(f)

bawl /bɔ:l/ vt/i brüllen

bay¹ /beɪ/ n (Geog) Bucht f; (in room) Erker m

bay² n (Bot) [echter] Lorbeer m. **~-leaf** n Lorbeerblatt nt

bayonet /'beɪənɛt/ n Bajonett nt

bay 'window n Erkerfenster nt

bazaar /bə'zɑ:(r)/ n Basar m

BC abbr (before Christ) v.Chr.

be /biː/

(*pres* **am, are, is**, *pl* **are**; *pt* **was**, *pl* **were**; *pp* **been**)

● *intransitive verb*

····▸ (*expressing identity, nature, state, age etc.*) sein. **he is a teacher** er ist Lehrer. **she is French** sie ist Französin. **he is very nice** er ist sehr nett. **I am tall** ich bin groß. **you are thirty** du bist dreißig. **it was very cold** es war sehr kalt

····▸ (*expressing general position*) sein; (*lie*) liegen; (*stand*) stehen. **where is the bank?** wo ist die Bank? **the book is on the table** das Buch liegt auf dem Tisch. **the vase is on the shelf** die Vase steht auf dem Brett

····▸ (*feel*) **I am cold/hot** mir ist kalt/heiß. **I am ill** ich bin krank. **I am well** mir geht es gut. **how are you?** wie geht es ihnen?

····▸ (*date*) **it is the 5th today** heute haben wir den Fünften

····▸ (*go, come, stay*) sein. **I have been to Vienna** ich bin in Wien gewesen. **have you ever been to London?** bist du schon einmal in London gewesen? **has the postman been?** war der Briefträger schon da? **I've been here for an hour** ich bin seit einer Stunde hier

····▸ (*origin*) **where are you from?** woher stammen *od* kommen Sie? **she is from Australia** sie stammt *od* ist aus Australien

····▸ (*cost*) kosten. **how much are the eggs?** was kosten die Eier?

····▸ (*in calculations*) **two threes are six** zweimal drei ist *od* sind sechs

····▸ (*exist*) **there is/are** es gibt (+ *acc*). **there's no fish left** es gibt keinen Fisch mehr

● *auxiliary verb*

····▸ (*forming continuous tenses: not translated*) **I'm working** ich arbeite. **I'm leaving tomorrow** ich reise morgen [ab]. **they were singing** sie sangen. **they will be coming on Tuesday** sie kommen am Dienstag

····▸ (*forming passive*) werden. **the child was found** das Kind wurde gefunden. **German is spoken here** hier wird Deutsch gesprochen; hier spricht man Deutsch

····▸ (*expressing arrangement, obligation, destiny*) sollen. **I am to go/inform you** ich soll gehen/Sie unterrichten. **they were to fly today** sie sollten heute fliegen. **you are to do that immediately** das sollst du sofort machen. **you are not to ...** (*prohibition*) du darfst nicht .... **they were never to meet again** (*destiny*) sie sollten sich nie wieder treffen

····▸ (*in short answers*) **Are you disappointed? — Yes I am** Bist du enttäuscht? — Ja. (*negating previous statement*) **Aren't you coming? — Yes I am!** Kommst du nicht? — Doch!

····▸ (*in tag questions*) **isn't it? wasn't she? aren't they?** *etc.* nicht wahr. **it's a beautiful house, isn't it?** das Haus ist sehr schön, nicht wahr?

beach /biːtʃ/ *n* Strand *m*

bead /biːd/ *n* Perle *f*

beak /biːk/ *n* Schnabel *m*

beam /biːm/ n Balken m; (of light) Strahl m ● vi strahlen. **~ing** adj [freude]strahlend

bean /biːn/ n Bohne f

bear¹ /beə(r)/ n Bär m

bear² vt/i (pt bore, pp borne) tragen; (endure) ertragen; gebären (child); **~ right** sich rechts halten. **~able** adj erträglich

beard /bɪəd/ n Bart m. **~ed** adj bärtig

bearer /ˈbeərə(r)/ n Träger m; (of news, cheque) Überbringer m; (of passport) Inhaber(in) m(f)

bearing /ˈbeərɪŋ/ n Haltung f; (Techn) Lager nt; **get one's ~s** sich orientieren

beast /biːst/ n Tier nt; (🗆: person) Biest nt

beastly /ˈbiːstlɪ/ adj 🗓 scheußlich; (person) gemein

beat /biːt/ n Schlag m; (of policeman) Runde f; (rhythm) Takt m ● vt/i (pt beat, pp beaten) schlagen; (thrash) verprügeln; klopfen (carpet); (hammer) hämmern (on an + acc); **~ it!** 🗓 hau ab! **it ~s me** 🗓 das begreife ich nicht. **~ up** vt zusammenschlagen

beaten /ˈbiːtn/ adj **off the ~en track** abseits. **~ing** n Prügel pl

beauti|ful /ˈbjuːtɪfl/ adj schön. **~fy** vt (pt/pp -ied) verschönern

beauty /ˈbjuːtɪ/ n Schönheit f. **~ parlour** n Kosmetiksalon m. **~ spot** n Schönheitsfleck m; (place) landschaftlich besonders reizvolles Fleckchen m

beaver /ˈbiːvə(r)/ n Biber m

became /brˈkeɪm/ see become

because /brˈkɒz/ conj weil ● adv **~ of** wegen (+ gen)

become /brˈkʌm/ vt/i (pt became, pp become) werden. **~ing** adj (clothes) kleidsam

bed /bed/ n Bett nt; (layer) Schicht f; (of flowers) Beet nt; **in ~** im Bett; **go to ~** ins od zu Bett gehen; **~ and breakfast** Zimmer mit Frühstück. **~clothes** npl, **~ding** n Bettzeug nt. **~room** n Schlafzimmer nt

---

bed and breakfast Überall in Großbritannien sieht man Schilder mit der Aufschrift Bed & Breakfast oder B & B. Sie weisen auf Privathäuser hin, die preisgünstige Unterkunft anbieten, wobei im Zimmerpreis das Frühstück schon eingeschlossen ist. Zum traditionellen Frühstück gehört vor allem, Cornflakes, bacon and eggs (Spiegeleier mit Speck), Toast und Orangenmarmelade und Tee.

'bedside n **at his ~** an seinem Bett. **~ 'lamp** n Nachttischlampe f. **~ 'table** n Nachttisch m

bed: **~sitter** n, **~'sitting-room** n Wohnschlafzimmer nt. **~spread** n Tagesdecke f. **~time** n **at ~time** vor dem Schlafengehen

bee /biː/ n Biene f

beech /biːtʃ/ n Buche f

beef /biːf/ n Rindfleisch nt. **~burger** n Hamburger m

bee: **~hive** n Bienenstock m. **~line** n **make a ~line for** 🗓 zusteuern auf (+ acc)

been /biːn/ see be

beer /bɪə(r)/ n Bier nt

beet /biːt/ n (Amer: beetroot) rote Bete f; [sugar] ~ Zuckerrübe f

beetle /ˈbiːtl/ n Käfer m

'beetroot n rote Bete f

before /brˈfɔː(r)/ prep vor (+ dat/acc); **the day ~ yesterday** vorgestern; **~ long** bald ● adv vorher; (already) schon; **never ~** noch nie; **~ that** davor ● conj (time) ehe,

b

bevor. **~hand** adv vorher, im Voraus

beg /beg/ v (pt/pp **begged**) ● vi betteln ● vt (entreat) anflehen; (ask) bitten (**for** um)

began /bɪˈgæn/ see **begin**

beggar /ˈbegə(r)/ n Bettler(in) m(f); ⚠ Kerl m

begin /bɪˈgɪn/ vt/i (pt **began**, pp **begun**, pres p **beginning**) anfangen, beginnen; **to ~** with anfangs. **~ner** n Anfänger(in) m(f). **~ning** n Anfang m, Beginn m

begun /bɪˈgʌn/ see **begin**

behalf /bɪˈhɑːf/ n **on ~** of im Namen von; **on my ~** meinetwegen

behave /bɪˈheɪv/ vi sich verhalten; **~ oneself** sich benehmen

behaviour /bɪˈheɪvjə(r)/ n Verhalten nt; **good/bad ~** gutes/schlechtes Benehmen nt

behind /bɪˈhaɪnd/ prep hinter (+ dat/acc); **be ~ sth** hinter etw (dat) stecken ● adv hinten; (late) im Rückstand; **a long way ~** weit zurück ● n ⚠ Hintern m. **~hand** adv im Rückstand

beige /beɪʒ/ adj beige

being /ˈbiːɪŋ/ n Dasein nt; **living ~** Lebewesen nt; **come into ~** entstehen

belated /bɪˈleɪtɪd/ adj verspätet

belfry /ˈbelfrɪ/ n Glockenstube f; (tower) Glockenturm m

Belgian /ˈbeldʒən/ adj belgisch ● n Belgier(in) m(f)

Belgium /ˈbeldʒəm/ n Belgien nt

belief /bɪˈliːf/ n Glaube m

believable /bɪˈliːvəbl/ adj glaubhaft

believe /bɪˈliːv/ vt/i glauben (s.o. jdm; **in** an + acc). **~r** n (Relig) Gläubige(r) m/f

belittle /bɪˈlɪtl/ vt herabsetzen

bell /bel/ n Glocke f; (on door) Klingel f

bellow /ˈbeləʊ/ vt/i brüllen

belly /ˈbelɪ/ n Bauch m

belong /bɪˈlɒŋ/ vi gehören (**to** dat); (be member) angehören (**to** dat). **~ings** npl Sachen pl

beloved /bɪˈlʌvɪd/ adj geliebt ● n Geliebte(r) m/f

below /bɪˈləʊ/ prep unter (+ dat/ acc) ● adv unten; (Naut) unter Deck

belt /belt/ n Gürtel m; (area) Zone f; (Techn) [Treib]riemen m ● vi (⚠: rush) rasen ● vt (⚠: hit) hauen

bench /bentʃ/ n Bank f; (work-) Werkbank f

bend /bend/ n Biegung f; (in road) Kurve f; **round the ~** ⚠ verrückt ● v (pt/pp **bent**) ● vt biegen; beugen (arm, leg) ● vi sich biegen; (thing): sich biegen; (road:) eine Biegung machen. **~ down** vi sich bücken. **~ over** vi sich vornüberbeugen

beneath /bɪˈniːθ/ prep unter (+ dat/acc); **~ him** (fig) unter seiner Würde ● adv darunter

benefactor /ˈbenɪfæktə(r)/ n Wohltäter(in) m(f)

beneficial /benɪˈfɪʃl/ adj nützlich

benefit /ˈbenɪfɪt/ n Vorteil m; (allowance) Unterstützung f; (insurance) Leistung f; **sickness ~** Krankengeld nt ● v (pt/pp **-fited**, pres p **-fiting**) ● vt nützen (+ dat) ● vi profitieren (**from** von)

benevolen|ce /bɪˈnevələns/ n Wohlwollen nt. **~t** adj wohlwollend

bent /bent/ see **bend** ● adj (person) gebeugt; (distorted) verbogen; (⚠: dishonest) korrupt; **be ~ on doing sth** darauf erpicht sein, etw zu tun ● n Hang m, Neigung f (**for** zu); **artistic ~** künstlerische Ader f

bequeath /bɪˈkwiːð/ vt vermachen (**to** dat)

bereave|d /bɪˈriːvd/ n the ~**d** pl die Hinterbliebenen

beret /ˈbereɪ/ n Baskenmütze f

Berne /bɜːn/ n Bern nt

berry /ˈberɪ/ n Beere f

berth /bɜːθ/ n (on ship) [Schlaf]koje f; (ship's anchorage) Liegeplatz m; **give a wide ~ to** 🔲 einen großen Bogen machen um

beside /bɪˈsaɪd/ prep neben (+ dat/ acc); ~ **oneself** außer sich (dat)

besides /bɪˈsaɪdz/ prep außer (+ dat) ● adv außerdem

besiege /bɪˈsiːdʒ/ vt belagern

best /best/ adj & n beste(r,s); the ~ der/die/das Beste; **at** ~ bestenfalls; **all the ~** alles Gute! **do one's ~** sein Bestes tun; **the ~ part of a year** fast ein Jahr; **to the ~ of my knowledge** so viel ich weiß; **make the ~ of it** das Beste daraus machen ● adv am besten; **as I could** so gut ich konnte. **~ 'man** n ≈ Trauzeuge m. **~'seller** n Bestseller m

bet /bet/ n Wette f ● v (pt/pp **bet** or **betted**) ● vt wetten; **£5** ~ um £5 wetten ● vi wetten; ~ **on** [Geld] setzen auf (+ acc)

betray /bɪˈtreɪ/ vt verraten. **~al** n Verrat m

better /ˈbetə(r)/ adj besser; **get ~** sich bessern; (after illness) sich erholen ● adv besser; ~ **off** besser dran; ~ **not** lieber nicht; **all the ~** umso besser; **the sooner the ~** je eher, desto besser; **think ~ of sth** sich eines Besseren besinnen; **you'd ~ stay** du bleibst am besten hier ● vt verbessern; (do better than) übertreffen; ~ **oneself** sich verbessern

between /bɪˈtwiːn/ prep zwischen (+ dat/acc); ~ **you and me** unter

uns; ~ **us** (together) zusammen ● adv [in] ~ dazwischen

beware /bɪˈweə(r)/ vi sich in Acht nehmen (**of** vor + dat); ~ **of the dog!** Vorsicht, bissiger Hund!

bewilder /bɪˈwɪldə(r)/ vt verwirren. **~ment** n Verwirrung f

bewitch /bɪˈwɪtʃ/ vt verzaubern; (fig) bezaubern

beyond /bɪˈjɒnd/ prep über (+ acc) ... hinaus; (further) weiter als; ~ **reach** außer Reichweite; ~ **doubt** ohne jeden Zweifel; **it's ~ me** 🔲 das geht über meinen Horizont ● adv darüber hinaus

bias /ˈbaɪəs/ n Voreingenommenheit f; (preference) Vorliebe f; (Jur) Befangenheit f ● vt (pt/pp **biased**) (influence) beeinflussen. **~ed** adj voreingenommen; (Jur) befangen

bib /bɪb/ n Lätzchen nt

Bible /ˈbaɪbl/ n Bibel f

biblical /ˈbɪblɪkl/ adj biblisch

bibliography /bɪblɪˈɒɡrəfɪ/ n Bibliographie f

bicycle /ˈbaɪsɪkl/ n Fahrrad nt ● vi mit dem Rad fahren

bid /bɪd/ n Gebot nt; (attempt) Versuch m ● vt/i (pt/pp **bid**, pres p **bidding**) bieten (**for** auf + acc); (Cards) reizen

bidder /ˈbɪdə(r)/ n Bieter(in) m(f)

bide /baɪd/ vt ~ **one's time** den richtigen Moment abwarten

big /bɪɡ/ adj (**bigger, biggest**) groß ● adv **talk** ~ 🔲 angeben

bigam|ist /ˈbɪɡəmɪst/ n Bigamist m. **~y** n Bigamie f

big-'headed adj 🔲 eingebildet

bigot /ˈbɪɡət/ n Eiferer m. **~ed** adj engstirnig

'bigwig n 🔲 hohes Tier m

bike /baɪk/ n 🔲 [Fahr]rad nt

bikini /bɪˈkiːnɪ/ n Bikini m

bile /baɪl/ n Galle f

bilingual /baɪˈlɪŋgwəl/ adj zweisprachig

bilious /ˈbɪlɪəs/ adj (Med) ~ attack verdorbener Magen m

bill¹ /bɪl/ n Rechnung f; (poster) Plakat nt; (Pol) Gesetzentwurf m; (Amer: note) Banknote f. ~ of exchange Wechsel m ● vt eine Rechnung schicken (+ dat)

bill² n (beak) Schnabel m

'billfold n (Amer) Brieftasche f

billiards /ˈbɪljədz/ n Billard nt

billion /ˈbɪljən/ n (thousand million) Milliarde f; (million million) Billion f

bin /bɪn/ n Mülleimer m; (for bread) Kasten m

bind /baɪnd/ vt (pt/pp bound) binden (to an + acc); (bandage) verbinden; (Jur) verpflichten; (cover the edge of) einfassen. ~ing adj verbindlich ● n Einband nt; (braid) Borte f; (on ski) Bindung f

binge /bɪndʒ/ n 🔟 go on the ~ eine Sauftour machen

binoculars /bɪˈnɒkjʊləz/ npl [pair of] ~ Fernglas nt

bioˈ**chemistry** /baɪəʊ-/ n Biochemie f. ~**degradable** adj biologisch abbaubar

biograph|er /baɪˈɒgrəfə(r)/ n Biograph(in) m(f). ~**y** n Biographie f

biological /baɪəˈlɒdʒɪkl/ adj biologisch

biolog|ist /baɪˈɒlədʒɪst/ n Biologe m. ~**y** n Biologie f

bioˈ**terrorism** /baɪəʊ-/ n Bioterrorismus m

birch /bɜːtʃ/ n Birke f; (whip) Rute f

bird /bɜːd/ n Vogel m; (🔟: girl) Mädchen nt; **kill two ~s with one stone** zwei Fliegen mit einer Klappe schlagen

Biro ® /ˈbaɪrəʊ/ n Kugel-

schreiber m

birth /bɜːθ/ n Geburt f

birth: ~ **certificate** n Geburtsurkunde f. ~**control** n Geburtenregelung f. ~**day** n Geburtstag m. ~**-rate** n Geburtenziffer f

biscuit /ˈbɪskɪt/ n Keks m

bishop /ˈbɪʃəp/ n Bischof m

bit¹ /bɪt/ n Stückchen nt; (for horse) Gebiss nt; (Techn) Bohreinsatz m; **a ~ in bisschen; ~ by ~ nach und nach; a ~ of bread** ein bisschen Brot; **do one's ~** sein Teil tun

bit² see **bite**

bitch /bɪtʃ/ n Hündin f; 🗙 Luder nt. ~**y** adj gehässig

bit|e /baɪt/ n Biss m; [insect] ~ Stich m; (mouthful) Bissen m ● vt/i (pt bit, pp bitten) beißen; (insect:) stechen; kauen (one's nails). ~**ing** adj beißend

bitten /ˈbɪtn/ see **bite**

bitter /ˈbɪtə(r)/ adj bitter; ~**ly cold** bitterkalt ● n bitteres Bier nt. ~**ness** n Bitterkeit f

bitty /ˈbɪtɪ/ adj zusammengestoppelt

bizarre /bɪˈzɑː(r)/ adj bizarr

black /blæk/ adj (-er, -est) schwarz; **be ~and blue** grün und blau sein ● n Schwarz nt; (person) Schwarze(r) m/f ● vt schwärzen; boykottieren (goods)

black: ~**berry** n Brombeere f. ~**bird** n Amsel f. ~**board** n (Sch) [Wand]tafel f. ~**currant** n schwarze Johannisbeere f

blacken vt/i schwärzen

black: ~ '**eye** n blaues Auge nt. **B** ~ '**Forest** n Schwarzwald m. ~ '**Ice** n Glatteis nt. ~ **list** vt auf die schwarze Liste setzen. ~**mail** n Erpressung f ● vt erpressen. ~**mailer** n Erpresser(in) m(f). ~ '**market** n schwarzer Markt m. ~**-out** n have a ~-out (*Med*) das Bewusstsein verlieren. ~ 'pudding *n* Blutwurst *f*

b **bladder** /'blædə(r)/ *n* (*Anat*) Blase *f*

blade /bleɪd/ *n* Klinge *f*; (*of grass*) Halm *m*

blame /bleɪm/ *n* Schuld *f* ● *vt* die Schuld geben (+ *dat*); **no one is to ~** keiner ist schuld daran. **~less** *adj* schuldlos

bland /blænd/ *adj* (**-er, -est**) mild

blank /blæŋk/ *adj* leer; (*look*) ausdruckslos ● *n* Lücke *f*; (*cartridge*) Platzpatrone *f*. ~ **'cheque** *n* Blankoscheck *m*

blanket /'blæŋkɪt/ *n* Decke *f*; **wet** ~ 🔳 Spielverderber(in) *m(f)*

blare /bleə(r)/ *vt/i* schmettern

blasé /'blɑːzeɪ/ *adj* blasiert

blast /blɑːst/ *n* (*gust*) Luftstoß *m*; (*sound*) Schmettern *nt*; (*of horn*) Tuten *nt* ● *vt* sprengen ● *int* 🔳 verdammt. **~ed** *adj* 🔳 verdammt

'blast-off *n* (*of missile*) Start *m*

blatant /'bleɪtənt/ *adj* offensichtlich

blaze /bleɪz/ *n* Feuer *nt* ● *vi* brennen

blazer /'bleɪzə(r)/ *n* Blazer *m*

bleach /bliːtʃ/ *n* Bleichmittel *nt* ● *vt/i* bleichen

bleak /bliːk/ *adj* (**-er, -est**) öde; (*fig*) trostlos

bleary-eyed /'blɪərɪ-/ *adj* mit trüben/(*on waking up*) verschlafenen Augen

bleat /bliːt/ *vi* blöken

bleed /bliːd/ *v* (*pt/pp* **bled**) ● *vi* bluten ● *vt* entlüften (*radiator*)

bleep /bliːp/ *n* Piepton *m* ● *vi* piepsen ● *vt* mit dem Piepser rufen. **~er** *n* Piepser *m*

blemish /'blemɪʃ/ *n* Makel *m*

blend /blend/ *n* Mischung *f* ● *vt*

mischen ● *vi* sich vermischen

bless /bles/ *vt* segnen. **~ed** *adj* heilig; 🔳 verflixt. **~ing** *n* Segen *m*

blew /bluː/ *see* **blow**[1]

blight /blaɪt/ *n* (*Bot*) Brand *m*

blind /blaɪnd/ *adj* blind; (*corner*) unübersichtlich; ~ **man/woman** Blinde(r) *m/f* ● *n* [**roller**] ~ Rouleau *nt* ● *vt* blenden

blind: ~ **'alley** *n* Sackgasse *f*. **~fold** *adj* & *adv* mit verbundenen Augen ● *n* Augenbinde *f* ● *vt* die Augen verbinden (+ *dat*). **~ly** *adv* blindlings. **~ness** *n* Blindheit *f*

blink /blɪŋk/ *vi* blinzeln; (*light:*) blinken

bliss /blɪs/ *n* Glückseligkeit *f*. **~ful** *adj* glücklich

blister /'blɪstə(r)/ *n* (*Med*) Blase *f*

blitz /blɪts/ *n* 🔳 Großaktion *f*

blizzard /'blɪzəd/ *n* Schneesturm *m*

bloated /'bləʊtɪd/ *adj* aufgedunsen

blob /blɒb/ *n* Klecks *m*

block /blɒk/ *n* Block *m*; (*of wood*) Klotz *m*; (*of flats*) [Wohn]block *m* ● *vt* blockieren. ~ **up** *vt* zustopfen

blockade /blɒ'keɪd/ *n* Blockade *f* ● *vt* blockieren

blockage /'blɒkɪdʒ/ *n* Verstopfung *f*

block: **~head** *n* 🔳 Dummkopf *m*. ~ **'letters** *npl* Blockschrift *f*

bloke /bləʊk/ *n* 🔳 Kerl *m*

blonde /blɒnd/ *adj* blond ● *n* Blondine *f*

blood /blʌd/ *n* Blut *nt*

blood: **~-curdling** *adj* markerschütternd. ~ **donor** *n* Blutspender *m*. ~ **group** *n* Blutgruppe *f*. **~hound** *n* Bluthund *m*. **~poisoning** *n* Blutvergiftung *f*. ~ **pressure** *n* Blutdruck *m*. **~shed** *n* Blutvergießen *nt*. **~shot** *adj* blutunterlaufen. **~ sports** npl Jagdsport m. **~-stained** adj blutbefleckt. **~ test** n Blutprobe f. **~thirsty** adj blutdürstig. **~-vessel** n Blutgefäß nt

bloody /'blʌdɪ/ adj blutig; 🅇 verdammt. **~-minded** adj 🅇 stur

bloom /bluːm/ n Blüte f ● vi blühen

blossom /'blɒsəm/ n Blüte f ● vi blühen

blot /blɒt/ n [Tinten]klecks m; (fig) Fleck m ● **~ out** vt (fig) auslöschen

blotch /blɒtʃ/ n Fleck m. **~y** adj fleckig

'blotting-paper n Löschpapier nt

blouse /blaʊz/ n Bluse f

blow¹ /bləʊ/ n Schlag m

blow² v (pt blew, pp blown) ● vt blasen; (fam; squander) verpulvern; **~ one's nose** sich (dat) die Nase putzen ● vi blasen; (fuse:) durchbrennen. **~ away** vt wegblasen ● vi wegfliegen. **~ down** vt umwehen ● vi umfallen. **~ out** vt (extinguish) ausblasen. **~ over** vi umfallen; (fig: die down) vorübergehen. **~ up** vt (inflate) aufblasen; (enlarge) vergrößern; (shatter by explosion) sprengen ● vi explodieren

'blowlamp n Lötlampe f

blown /bləʊn/ see **blow²**

'blowtorch n (Amer) Lötlampe f

blowy /'bləʊɪ/ adj windig

blue /bluː/ adj (-r, -st) blau; **feel ~** deprimiert sein ● n Blau nt; **have the ~s** deprimiert sein; **out of the ~** aus heiterem Himmel

blue: **~bell** n Sternhyazinthe f. **~berry** n Heidelbeere f. **~bottle** n Schmeißfliege f. **~ film** n Pornofilm m. **~print** n (fig) Entwurf m

bluff /blʌf/ n Bluff m ● vi bluffen

blunder /'blʌndə(r)/ n Schnitzer m

● vi einen Schnitzer machen

blunt /blʌnt/ adj stumpf; (person) geradeheraus. **~ly** adv unverblümt, geradeheraus

blur /blɜː(r)/ n **it's all a ~** alles ist verschwommen ● vt (pt/pp blurred) verschwommen machen; **~red** verschwommen

blush /blʌʃ/ n Erröten nt ● vi erröten

bluster /'blʌstə(r)/ n Großtuerei f. **~y** adj windig

boar /bɔː(r)/ n Eber m

board /bɔːd/ n Brett nt; (for notices) schwarzes Brett nt; (committee) Ausschuss m; (of directors) Vorstand m; **on ~** an Bord; **full ~** Vollpension f; **~ and lodging** Unterkunft und Verpflegung pl ● vt einsteigen in (+ acc); (Naut, Aviat) besteigen ● vi an Bord gehen. **~ up** vt mit Brettern verschlagen

boarder /'bɔːdə(r)/ n Pensionsgast m; (Sch) Internatsschüler(in) m(f)

board: **~-game** n Brettspiel nt. **~ing-house** n Pension f. **~ing-school** n Internat nt

boast /bəʊst/ vt sich rühmen (+ gen) ● vi prahlen (about mit). **~ful** adj prahlerisch

boat /bəʊt/ n Boot nt; (ship) Schiff nt

Boat Race ℹ Seit 1829 findet jährlich (meist am Samstag vor Ostern) ein Ruderrennen auf der Themse in London statt. Das Achterrennen wird von den Rudermannschaften der Universitäten Oxford und Cambridge ausgetragen. Im Gegensatz zu anderen sportlichen Universitätswettbewerben wird dieses Ruderrennen landesweit im Fernsehen übertragen.

bob /bɒb/ vi (pt/pp **bobbed**) ∼ **up and down** sich auf und ab bewegen

'bob-sleigh n Bob m

bodily /'bɒdɪlɪ/ adj körperlich ● adv (forcibly) mit Gewalt

body /'bɒdɪ/ n Körper m; (corpse) Leiche f; (corporation) Körperschaft f. ∼**guard** n Leibwächter m. ∼ **part** n Leichenteil nt. ∼**work** n (Auto) Karosserie f

bog /bɒg/ n Sumpf m

bogus /'bəʊgəs/ adj falsch

boil¹ n Furunkel m

boil² n bring/come to the ∼ zum Kochen bringen/kommen ● vt/i kochen; ∼**ed potatoes** Salzkartoffeln pl. ∼ **down** vi (fig) hinauslaufen (**to** auf + acc). ∼ **over** vi überkochen

boiler /'bɔɪlə(r)/ n Heizkessel m

'boiling point n Siedepunkt m

boisterous /'bɔɪstərəs/ adj übermütig

bold /bəʊld/ adj (**-er, -est**) kühn; (Printing) fett. ∼**ness** n Kühnheit f

bolster /'bəʊlstə(r)/ n Nackenrolle f ● vt ∼ **up** Mut machen (+ dat)

bolt /bəʊlt/ n Riegel m; (Techn) Bolzen m ● vt schrauben (**to** an + acc); verriegeln (door); hinunterschlingen (food) ● vi abhauen; (horse:) durchgehen

bomb /bɒm/ n Bombe f ● vt bombardieren

bombard /bɒm'bɑːd/ vt beschießen; (fig) bombardieren

bombastic /bɒm'bæstɪk/ adj bombastisch

bomber /'bɒmə(r)/ n (Aviat) Bomber m; (person) Bombenleger(in) m(f)

bond /bɒnd/ n (fig) Band nt; (Comm) Obligation f

bone /bəʊn/ n Knochen m; (of fish) Gräte f ● vt von den Knochen lösen (meat); entgräten (fish). ∼-**'dry** adj knochentrocken

bonfire /'bɒn-/ n Gartenfeuer nt; (celebratory) Freudenfeuer nt

bonus /'bəʊnəs/ n Prämie f; (gratuity) Gratifikation f; (fig) Plus nt

bony /'bəʊnɪ/ adj knochig; (fish) grätig

boo /buː/ int buh! ● vt ausbuhen ● vi buhen

boob /buːb/ n (🄘: mistake) Schnitzer m

book /bʊk/ n Buch nt; (of tickets) Heft nt; **keep the** ∼**s** (Comm) die Bücher führen ● vt/i buchen; (reserve) [vor]bestellen; (for offence) aufschreiben

book: ∼**case** n Bücherregal nt. ∼-**ends** npl Buchstützen pl. ∼**ing-office** n Fahrkartenschalter m. ∼**keeping** n Buchführung f. ∼**let** n Broschüre f. ∼**maker** n Buchmacher m. ∼**mark** n Lesezeichen nt. ∼**seller** n Buchhändler(in) m(f). ∼**shop** n Buchhandlung f. ∼**stall** n Bücherstand m

boom /buːm/ n (Comm) Hochkonjunktur f; (upturn) Aufschwung m ● vi dröhnen; (fig) blühen

boon /buːn/ n Segen m

boost /buːst/ n Auftrieb m ● vt Auftrieb geben (+ dat)

boot /buːt/ n Stiefel m; (Auto) Kofferraum m

booth /buːð/ n Bude f; (cubicle) Kabine f

booty /'buːtɪ/ n Beute f

booze /buːz/ n 🄘 Alkohol m ● vi 🄘 saufen

border /'bɔːdə(r)/ n Rand m; (frontier) Grenze f; (in garden) Rabatte f ● vi ∼ **on** grenzen an (+ acc). ∼**line case** n Grenzfall m

bore¹ /bɔː(r)/ *see* bear²

bor|e² *n* (*of gun*) Kaliber *nt*; (*person*) langweiliger Mensch *m*; (*thing*) langweilige Sache *f* ● *vt* langweilen; **be ~ed** sich langweilen. **~edom** *n* Langeweile *f*. **~ing** *adj* langweilig

born /bɔːn/ *pp* **be ~** geboren werden ● *adj* geboren

borne /bɔːn/ *see* bear²

borrow /ˈbɒrəʊ/ *vt* [sich (*dat*)] borgen *od* leihen (**from** von)

bosom /ˈbʊzm/ *n* Busen *m*

boss /bɒs/ *n* ① Chef *m* ● *vt* herumkommandieren. **~y** *adj* herrschsüchtig

botanical /bəˈtænɪkl/ *adj* botanisch

botan|ist /ˈbɒtənɪst/ *n* Botaniker(in) *m* (*f*). **~y** *n* Botanik *f*

both /bəʊθ/ *adj & pron* beide; **~[of] the children** beide Kinder; **~ of them** beide [von ihnen] ● *adv* **~ men and women** sowohl Männer als auch Frauen

bother /ˈbɒðə(r)/ *n* Mühe *f*; (*minor trouble*) Ärger *m* ● *int* ① verflixt! ● *vt* belästigen; (*disturb*) stören ● *vi* sich kümmern (**about** um)

bottle /ˈbɒtl/ *n* Flasche *f* ● *vt* auf Flaschen abfüllen; (*preserve*) einmachen

bottle: ~-neck *n* (*fig*) Engpass *m*. **~-opener** *n* Flaschenöffner *m*

bottom /ˈbɒtəm/ *adj* unterste(r,s) ● *n* (*of container*) Boden *m*; (*of river*) Grund *m*; (*of page, hill*) Fuß *m*; (*buttocks*) Hintern *m*; **at the ~** unten; **get to the ~ of sth** (*fig*) hinter etw (*acc*) kommen

bought /bɔːt/ *see* buy

bounce /baʊns/ *vi* [auf]springen; (*cheque*) ① nicht gedeckt sein ● *vt* aufspringen lassen (*ball*)

bouncer /ˈbaʊnsə(r)/ *n* ① Rausschmeißer *m*

bound¹ /baʊnd/ *n* Sprung *m* ● *vi* springen

bound² *see* bind ● *adj* **~ for** (*ship*) mit Kurs auf (+ *acc*); **be ~ to do sth** etw bestimmt machen; (*obliged*) verpflichtet sein, etw zu machen

boundary /ˈbaʊndərɪ/ *n* Grenze *f*

bounds /baʊndz/ *npl* (*fig*) Grenzen *pl*; **out of ~** verboten

bouquet /bʊˈkeɪ/ *n* [Blumen-]strauß *m*; (*of wine*) Bukett *nt*

bourgeois /ˈbʊəʒwɑː/ *adj* (*pej*) spießbürgerlich

bout /baʊt/ *n* (*Med*) Anfall *m*; (*Sport*) Kampf *m*

bow¹ /bəʊ/ *n* (*weapon & Mus*) Bogen *m*; (*knot*) Schleife *f*

bow² /baʊ/ *n* Verbeugung *f* ● *vi* sich verbeugen ● *vt* neigen (*head*)

bow³ /baʊ/ *n* (*Naut*) Bug *m*

bowel /ˈbaʊəl/ *n* Darm *m*. **~s** *pl* Eingeweide *pl*

bowl¹ /bəʊl/ *n* Schüssel *f*; (*shallow*) Schale *f*

bowl² *n* (*ball*) Kugel *f* ● *vt/i* werfen. **~ over** *vt* umwerfen

bowler /ˈbəʊlə(r)/ *n* (*Sport*) Werfer *m*

bowling /ˈbəʊlɪŋ/ *n* Kegeln *nt*. **~-alley** *n* Kegelbahn *f*

bowls /bəʊlz/ *n* Bowlsspiel *nt*

bow-'tie /baʊ-/ *n* Fliege *f*

box¹ /bɒks/ *n* Schachtel *f*; (*wooden*) Kiste *f*; (*cardboard*) Karton *m*; (*Theat*) Loge *f*

box² *vt/i* (*Sport*) boxen

box|er /ˈbɒksə(r)/ *n* Boxer *m*. **~ing** *n* Boxen *nt*. **B~ing Day** *n* zweiter Weihnachtstag *m*

box: ~-office *n* (*Theat*) Kasse *f*. **~-room** *n* Abstellraum *m*

boy /bɔɪ/ *n* Junge *m*. **~ band** *n* Jungenband *f*

boycott /'bɔɪkɒt/ n Boykott m • vt boykottieren

boy: ~**friend** n Freund m. ~**ish** adj jungenhaft

bra /brɑː/ n BH m

brace /breɪs/ n Strebe f, Stütze f; (dental) Zahnspange f; ~**s** npl Hosenträger mpl

bracelet /'breɪslɪt/ n Armband nt

bracing /'breɪsɪŋ/ adj stärkend

bracket /'brækɪt/ n Konsole f; (group) Gruppe f; (Printing) **round**-**square** ~**s** runde/eckige Klammern • vt einklammern

brag /bræg/ vi (pt/pp bragged) prahlen (about mit)

braille /breɪl/ n Blindenschrift f

brain /breɪn/ n Gehirn nt; ~**s** (fig) Intelligenz f

brain: ~**less** adj dumm. ~**wash** vt einer Gehirnwäsche unterziehen. ~**wave** n Geistesblitz m

brainy /'breɪnɪ/ adj klug

brake /breɪk/ n Bremse f • vt/i bremsen. ~**light** n Bremslicht nt

bramble /'bræmbl/ n Brombeerstrauch m

branch /brɑːntʃ/ n Ast m; (fig) Zweig m; (Comm) Zweigstelle f, (shop) Filiale f • vi sich gabeln

brand /brænd/ n Marke f • vt (fig) brandmarken als

brandish /'brændɪʃ/ vt schwingen

brand-'new adj nagelneu

brandy /'brændɪ/ n Weinbrand m

brash /bræʃ/ adj nassforsch

brass /brɑːs/ n Messing nt; (Mus) Blech nt; **top** ~ □ hohe Tiere pl. ~ **band** n Blaskapelle f

brassy /'brɑːsɪ/ adj □ ordinär

brat /bræt/ n (pej) Balg nt

bravado /brə'vɑːdəʊ/ n Forschheit f

brave /breɪv/ adj (-r, -st) tapfer

• vt die Stirn bieten (+ dat). ~**ry** n Tapferkeit f

bravo /brɑː'vəʊ/ int bravo!

brawl /brɔːl/ n Schlägerei f

brawn /brɔːn/ n (Culin) Sülze f

brawny /'brɔːnɪ/ adj muskulös

bray /breɪ/ vi iahen

brazen /'breɪzn/ adj unverschämt

Brazil /brə'zɪl/ n Brasilien nt. ~**ian** adj brasilianisch. ~ **nut** n Paranuss f

breach /briːtʃ/ n Bruch m; (Mil & fig) Bresche f. ~ **of contract** Vertragsbruch m

bread /bred/ n Brot nt; **slice of** ~ **and butter** Butterbrot nt. ~**crumbs** npl Brotkrümel pl; (Culin) Paniermehl nt

breadth /bredθ/ n Breite f

break /breɪk/ n Bruch m; (interval) Pause f; (interruption) Unterbrechung f; (□: chance) Chance f • v (pt broke, pp broken) • vt brechen; (smash) zerbrechen; (damage) kaputtmachen □; (interrupt) unterbrechen; ~ **one's arm** sich (dat) den Arm brechen • vi brechen; (day:) anbrechen; (storm:) losbrechen; (thing:) kaputtgehen □; (rope, thread:) reißen; (news:) bekannt werden; **his voice is** ~**ing** er ist im Stimmbruch. ~ **away** vi sich losreißen/(fig) sich absetzen (from von). ~ **down** vi zusammenbrechen; (Techn) eine Panne haben; (negotiations:) scheitern • vt aufbrechen (door); aufgliedern (figures). ~ **in** vi einbrechen. ~ **off** vt/i abbrechen; lösen (engagement). ~ **out** vi ausbrechen. ~ **up** vt zerbrechen • vi (crowd:) sich zerstreuen; (marriage, couple:) auseinander gehen; (Sch) Ferien bekommen

break|able /'breɪkəbl/ adj zerbrechlich. ~**age** n Bruch m. ~**down** n (Techn) Panne f; (Med)

Zusammenbruch m; (of figures) Aufgliederung f. **~er** n (wave) Brecher m

breakfast /'brekfəst/ n Frühstück nt

break: **~through** n Durchbruch m. **~water** n Buhne f

breast /brest/ n Brust f. **~bone** n Brustbein nt. **~feed** vt stillen. **~stroke** n Brustschwimmen nt

breath /breθ/ n Atem m; **out of ~** außer Atem; **under one's ~** vor sich (acc) hin

breathe /bri:ð/ vt/i atmen. **~ in** vt/i einatmen. **~ out** vt/i ausatmen

breathing n Atmen nt

breath: **~less** adj atemlos. **~taking** adj atemberaubend

bred /bred/ see **breed**

breed /bri:d/ n Rasse f ● v (pt/pp **bred**) ● vt züchten; (give rise to) erzeugen ● vi sich vermehren. **~er** n Züchter m. **~ing** n Zucht f; (fig) [gute] Lebensart f

breez|e /bri:z/ n Lüftchen nt; (Naut) Brise f. **~y** adj windig

brevity /'brevətɪ/ n Kürze f

brew /bru:/ n Gebräu nt ● vt brauen; kochen (tea). **~er** n Brauer m. **~ery** n Brauerei f

bribe /braɪb/ n (money) Bestechungsgeld nt ● vt bestechen. **~ry** n Bestechung f

brick /brɪk/ n Ziegelstein m, Backstein m

'bricklayer n Maurer m

bridal /'braɪdl/ adj Braut-

bride /braɪd/ n Braut f. **~groom** n Bräutigam m. **~smaid** n Brautjungfer f

bridge¹ /brɪdʒ/ n Brücke f; (of nose) Nasenrücken m; (of spectacles) Steg m

bridge² n (Cards) Bridge nt

bridle /'braɪdl/ n Zaum m

brief /bri:f/ adj (-er, -est) kurz; **be ~** (person:) sich kurz fassen

brief² n Instruktionen pl; (Jur: case) Mandat nt. **~case** n Aktentasche f

brief|ing /'bri:fɪŋ/ n Informationsgespräch nt. **~ly** adv kurz. **~ness** n Kürze f

briefs /bri:fs/ npl Slip m

brigade /brɪ'geɪd/ n Brigade f

bright /braɪt/ adj (-er, -est) hell; (day) heiter; **~ red** hellrot

bright|en /'braɪtn/ v **~en [up]** ● vt aufheitern ● vi sich aufheitern. **~ness** n Helligkeit f

brilliance /'brɪljəns/ n Glanz m; (of person) Genialität f

brilliant /'brɪljənt/ adj glänzend; (person) genial

brim /brɪm/ n Rand m; (of hat) Krempe f

bring /brɪŋ/ vt (pt/pp **brought**) bringen; **~ them with you** bring sie mit; **I can't ~ myself to do it** ich bringe es nicht fertig. **~ about** vt verursachen. **~ along** vt mitbringen. **~ back** vt zurückbringen. **~ down** vt herunterbringen; senken (price). **~ off** vt vollbringen. **~ on** vt (cause) verursachen. **~ out** vt herausbringen. **~ round** vt vorbeibringen; (persuade) überreden; wieder zum Bewusstsein bringen (unconscious person). **~ up** vt heraufbringen; (vomit) erbrechen; aufziehen (children); erwähnen (question)

brink /brɪŋk/ n Rand m

brisk /brɪsk/ adj (-er, -est,) **-ly** adv lebhaft; (quick) schnell

bristle /'brɪsl/ n Borste f.

Brit|ain /'brɪtn/ n Großbritannien nt. **~ish** adj britisch; **the ~ish** die Briten pl. **~on** n Brite m/Britin f

Brittany /'brɪtənɪ/ n die Bretagne

brittle /'brɪtl/ adj brüchig, spröde

broad /brɔːd/ adj (-er, -est) breit; (hint) deutlich; **in ~ daylight** am helllichten Tag. **~ beans** npl dicke Bohnen pl

broadband /'brɔːdbænd/ n Breitband nt

'broadcast n Sendung f ● vt/i (pt/ pp -cast) senden. **~er** n Rundfunk- und Fernsehpersönlichkeit f. **~ing** n Funk und Fernsehen pl

broaden /'brɔːdn/ vt verbreitern; (fig) erweitern ● vi sich verbreitern

broadly /'brɔːdlɪ/ adv breit; **~ speaking** allgemein gesagt

broad'minded adj tolerant

broccoli /'brɒkəlɪ/ n inv Brokkoli pl

brochure /'brəʊʃə(r)/ n Broschüre f

broke /brəʊk/ see **break** ● adj 🄵 pleite

broken /'brəʊkn/ see **break** ● adj zerbrochen; 🄵 kaputt. **~-hearted** adj untröstlich

broker /'brəʊkə(r)/ n Makler m

brolly /'brɒlɪ/ n 🄵 Schirm m

bronchitis /brɒŋ'kaɪtɪs/ n Bronchitis f

bronze /brɒnz/ n Bronze f

brooch /brəʊtʃ/ n Brosche f

brood /bruːd/ vi (fig) grübeln

broom /bruːm/ n Besen m; (Bot) Ginster m

broth /brɒθ/ n Brühe f

brothel /'brɒθl/ n Bordell nt

brother /'brʌðə(r)/ n Bruder m

brother: ~-in-law n (pl -s-in- law) Schwager m. **~ly** adj brüderlich

brought /brɔːt/ see **bring**

brow /braʊ/ n Augenbraue f; (fore- head) Stirn f; (of hill) [Berg]kuppe f

brown /braʊn/ adj (-er, -est)

braun; **~ 'paper** Packpapier nt ● n Braun nt ● vt bräunen ● vi braun werden

browse /braʊz/ vi (read) schmökern; (in shop) sich umsehen. **~r** n (Computing) Browser m

bruise /bruːz/ n blauer Fleck m ● vt beschädigen (fruit); **~ one's arm** sich (dat) den Arm quetschen

brunette /bruː'net/ n Brünette f

brush /brʌʃ/ n Bürste f; (with han- dle) Handfeger m; (for paint, pastry) Pinsel m; (bushes) Unterholz nt; (fig: conflict) Zusammenstoß m ● vt bür- sten; putzen (teeth); **~ against** streifen [gegen]; **~ aside** (fig) abtun. **~ off** vt abbürsten. **~ up** vt/i (fig) **~ up [on]** auffrischen

brusque /brʊsk/ adj brüsk

Brussels /'brʌslz/ n Brüssel nt. **~ sprouts** npl Rosenkohl m

brutal /'bruːtl/ adj brutal. **~ity** n Brutalität f

brute /bruːt/ n Unmensch m. **~ force** n rohe Gewalt f

BSE abbr (bovine spongiform en- cephalopathy) BSE f

bubble /'bʌbl/ n [Luft]blase f ● vi sprudeln

buck[1] /bʌk/ n (deer & Gym) Bock m; (rabbit) Rammler m ● vi (horse): bocken

buck[2] /bʌk/ n (Amer 🄵) Dollar m

buck[3] n **pass the ~** die Verant- wortung abschieben

bucket /'bʌkɪt/ n Eimer m

buckle /'bʌkl/ n Schnalle f ● vt zu- schnallen ● vi sich verbiegen

bud /bʌd/ n Knospe f

buddy /'bʌdɪ/ n 🄵 Freund m

budge /bʌdʒ/ vt bewegen ● vi sich [von der Stelle] rühren

budget /'bʌdʒɪt/ n Budget nt; (Pol) Haushaltsplan m; (money available)

Etat m ● vi (pt/pp budgeted) ~ for sth etw einkalkulieren

buff /bʌf/ adj (colour) sandfarben ● n Sandfarbe f. [i] Fan m ● vt polieren

buffalo /'bʌfələʊ/ n (inv or pl -es) Büffel m

buffer /'bʌfə(r)/ n (Rail) Puffer m

buffet[1] /'bʊfeɪ/ n Büfett nt; (on station) Imbissstube f

buffet[2] /'bʌfɪt/ vt (pt/pp buffeted) hin und her werfen

bug /bʌɡ/ n Wanze f; ([i]: virus) Bazillus m; ([i]: device) Abhörgerät m, [i] Wanze f ● vt (pt/pp bugged) [i] verwanzen (room); abhören (telephone); (Amer: annoy) ärgern

bugle /'bjuːɡl/ n Signalhorn

build /bɪld/ n (of person) Körperbau m ● vt/i (pt/pp built) bauen. ~ **on** vt anbauen (to an + acc). ~ **up** vt aufbauen ● vi zunehmen

builder /'bɪldə(r)/ n Bauunternehmer m

building /'bɪldɪŋ/ n Gebäude nt. ~ **site** n Baustelle f. ~ **society** n Bausparkasse f

built /bɪlt/ see build. ~-**in** adj eingebaut. ~-**in 'cupboard** n Einbauschrank m. ~-**up area** n bebautes Gebiet nt; (Auto) geschlossene Ortschaft f

bulb /bʌlb/ n [Blumen]zwiebel f; (Electr) [Glüh]birne f

bulbous /'bʌlbəs/ adj bauchig

Bulgaria /bʌl'ɡeərɪə/ n Bulgarien nt

bulge /bʌldʒ/ n Ausbauchung f ● vi sich ausbauchen. ~**ing** adj prall; (eyes) hervorquellend

bulk /bʌlk/ n Masse f; (greater part) Hauptteil m. ~**y** adj sperrig; (large) massig

bull /bʊl/ n Bulle m, Stier m

'bulldog n Bulldogge f

bulldozer /'bʊldəʊzə(r)/ n Planierraupe f

bullet /'bʊlɪt/ n Kugel f

bulletin /'bʊlɪtɪn/ n Bulletin nt

'bullet-proof adj kugelsicher

'bullfight n Stierkampf m. ~**er** n Stierkämpfer m

'bullfinch n Dompfaff m

bullock /'bʊlək/ n Ochse m

bull: ~**ring** n Stierkampfarena f. ~**'s-eye** n score a ~'s-eye ins Schwarze treffen

bully /'bʊlɪ/ n Tyrann m ● vt tyrannisieren

bum /bʌm/ n [x] Hintern m

bumble-bee /'bʌmbl-/ n Hummel f

bump /bʌmp/ n Bums m; (swelling) Beule f; (in road) holperige Stelle f ● vt stoßen; ~ **into** stoßen gegen; (meet) zufällig treffen. ~ **off** vt [i] um die Ecke bringen

bumper /'bʌmpə(r)/ adj Rekord- ● n (Auto) Stoßstange f

bumpy /'bʌmpɪ/ adj holperig

bun /bʌn/ n Milchbrötchen nt; (hair) [Haar]knoten m

bunch /bʌntʃ/ n (of flowers) Strauß m; (of radishes, keys) Bund m; (of people) Gruppe f; ~ **of grapes** [ganze] Weintraube f

bundle /'bʌndl/ n Bündel nt ● vt ~ **[up]** bündeln

bungalow /'bʌŋɡələʊ/ n Bungalow m

bungle /'bʌŋɡl/ vt verpfuschen

bunk /bʌŋk/ n [Schlaf]koje f. ~-**beds** npl Etagenbett nt

bunker /'bʌŋkə(r)/ n Bunker m

bunny /'bʌnɪ/ n [i] Kaninchen nt

buoy /bɔɪ/ n Boje f

buoyan|cy /'bɔɪənsɪ/ n Auftrieb m. ~**t** adj be ~**t** schwimmen

burden /'bɜːdn/ n Last f

bureau /ˈbjʊəˈrəʊ/ n (pl **-x** or **~s**) (desk) Sekretär m; (office) Büro nt

b **bureaucracy** /bjʊəˈrɒkrəsɪ/ n Bürokratie f

bureaucratic /bjʊərəˈkrætɪk/ adj bürokratisch

burger /ˈbɜːgə(r)/ n Hamburger m

burglar /ˈbɜːglə(r)/ n Einbrecher m. **~ alarm** n Alarmanlage f

burglary /ˈbɜːglərɪ/ n Einbruch m

burgle /ˈbɜːgl/ vt einbrechen in (+ acc); **they have been ~d** bei ihnen ist eingebrochen worden

burial /ˈberɪəl/ n Begräbnis nt

burly /ˈbɜːlɪ/ adj stämmig

Burm|a /ˈbɜːmə/ n Birma nt. **~ese** adj birmanisch

burn /bɜːn/ n Verbrennung f; (on skin) Brandwunde f; (on material) Brandstelle f ● v (pt/pp **burnt** or **burned**) ● vt verbrennen ● vi brennen; (food:) anbrennen. **~ down** vt/i niederbrennen

burner /ˈbɜːnə(r)/ n Brenner m

burnt /bɜːnt/ see **burn**

burp /bɜːp/ vi 🆃 aufstoßen

burrow /ˈbʌrəʊ/ n Bau m ● vi wühlen

burst /bɜːst/ n Bruch m; (surge) Ausbruch m ● v (pt/pp **burst**) ● vt platzen machen ● vi platzen; (bud:) aufgehen; **~ into tears** in Tränen ausbrechen

bury /ˈberɪ/ vt (pt/pp **-ied**) begraben; (hide) vergraben

bus /bʌs/ n [Auto]bus m

bush /bʊʃ/ n Strauch m; (land) Busch m. **~y** adj buschig

busily /ˈbɪzɪlɪ/ adv eifrig

business /ˈbɪznɪs/ n Angelegenheit f; (Comm) Geschäft nt; **on ~** geschäftlich; **he has no ~** er hat kein Recht (**to** zu); **mind one's own ~** sich um seine eigenen Angele-

genheiten kümmern; **that's none of your ~** das geht Sie nichts an. **~-like** adj geschäftsmäßig. **~man** n Geschäftsmann m

'bus-stop n Bushaltestelle f

bust¹ /bʌst/ n Büste f

bust² adj 🆃 kaputt; **go ~** Pleite gehen ● v (pt/pp **busted** or **bust**) 🆃 vt kaputtmachen ● vi kaputtgehen

busy /ˈbɪzɪ/ adj beschäftigt; (day) voll; (street) belebt; (with traffic) stark befahren; (Amer Teleph) besetzt; **be ~** zu tun haben ● vt **~ oneself** sich beschäftigen (**with** mit)

but /bʌt/, unbetont /bət/ conj aber; (after negative) sondern ● prep außer (+ dat); **~ for** (without) ohne (+ acc); **the last ~ one** der/die/das vorletzte; **the next ~ one** der/die/ das übernächste ● adv nur

butcher /ˈbʊtʃə(r)/ n Fleischer m, Metzger m; **~'s [shop]** Fleischerei f, Metzgerei f ● vt [ab]schlachten

butler /ˈbʌtlə(r)/ n Butler m

butt /bʌt/ n (of gun) [Gewehr]kolben m; (fig: target) Zielscheibe f; (of cigarette) Stummel m; (for water) Regentonne f ● vi **~ in** unterbrechen

butter /ˈbʌtə(r)/ n Butter f ● vt mit Butter bestreichen. **~ up** vt 🆃 schmeicheln (+ dat)

butter: **~cup** adj Butterblume f, Hahnenfuß m. **~fly** n Schmetterling m

buttocks /ˈbʌtəks/ npl Gesäß nt

button /ˈbʌtn/ n Knopf m ● vt **~ [up]** zuknöpfen. **~hole** n Knopfloch nt

buy /baɪ/ n Kauf m ● vt (pt/pp **bought**) kaufen. **~er** n Käufer(in) m(f)

buzz /bʌz/ n Summen nt ● vi

summen

buzzer /'bʌzə(r)/ n Summer m

by /baɪ/ prep (close to) bei (+ dat);
(next to) neben (+ dat/acc); (past)
an (+ dat) ... vorbei; (to the extent
of) um (+ acc); (at the latest) bis;
(by means of) durch; **by Mozart/
Dickens** von Mozart/Dickens;
~ oneself allein; **~ the sea** am Meer;
~ car/bus mit dem Auto/Bus; **~
sea** mit dem Schiff; **~ day/night**
bei Tag/Nacht; **~ the hour** pro
Stunde; **~ the metre** meterweise;
six metres ~ four sechs mal vier
Meter; **win ~ a length** mit einer
Länge Vorsprung gewinnen; **miss
the train ~ a minute** den Zug um
eine Minute verpassen ● adv **~ and
large** im Großen und Ganzen; **put
~** beiseite legen; **go/pass ~** vorbeigehen

bye /baɪ/ int 🅸 tschüs

by: **~-election** n Nachwahl f.
~-pass n Umgehungsstraße f; (Med)
Bypass m ● vt umfahren. **~-pro-
duct** n Nebenprodukt m. **~-stander**
n Zuschauer(in) m(f)

Cc

cab /kæb/ n Taxi nt; (of lorry, train)
Führerhaus nt

cabaret /'kæbəreɪ/ n Kabarett nt

cabbage /'kæbɪdʒ/ n Kohl m

cabin /'kæbɪn/ n Kabine f; (hut)
Hütte f

cabinet /'kæbɪnɪt/ n Schrank m;
[display] ~ Vitrine f; **C~** (Pol) Kabinett nt

cable /'keɪbl/ n Kabel nt; (rope) Tau
nt. **~ 'railway** n Seilbahn f. **~**

'**television** n Kabelfernsehen nt

cackle /'kækl/ vi gackern

cactus /'kæktəs/ n (pl **-ti** or
-tuses) Kaktus m

cadet /kə'det/ n Kadett m

cadge /kædʒ/ vt/i 🅸 schnorren

Caesarean /sɪ'zeərɪən/ adj & n **~
[section]** Kaiserschnitt m

café /'kæfeɪ/ n Café nt

cafeteria /kæfə'tɪərɪə/ n Selbstbe-
dienungsrestaurant nt

cage /keɪdʒ/ n Käfig m

cagey /'keɪdʒɪ/ adj 🅸 **be ~** mit
der Sprache nicht herauswollen

cake /keɪk/ n Kuchen m; (of soap)
Stück m. **~d** adj verkrustet
(**with** mit)

calamity /kə'læmɪtɪ/ n Katastrophe f

calculat|e /'kælkjʊleɪt/ vt berech-
nen; (estimate) kalkulieren. **~ing**
adj (fig) berechnend. **~ion** n Rechnung f, Kalkulation f. **~or** n Rechner m

calendar /'kælɪndə(r)/ n Kalender m

calf[1] /kɑːf/ n (pl **calves**) Kalb nt

calf[2] n (pl **calves**) (Anat) Wade f

calibre /'kælɪbə(r)/ n Kaliber nt

call /kɔːl/ n Ruf m; (Teleph) Anruf m;
(visit) Besuch m ● vt rufen; (Teleph)
anrufen; (wake) wecken; (Teleph)
anrufen; (strike) (name) nennen; **be ~ed**
heißen **~ [in or round]**
vorbeikommen. **~ back** vt zurückrufen ● vi noch einmal vorbeikommen. **~ for** vt rufen nach; (demand) verlangen; (fetch) abholen.
~ off vt zurückrufen (dog); (cancel)
absagen. **~ on** vt bitten (**for** um);
(appeal to) appellieren an (+ acc);
(visit) besuchen. **~ out** vt rufen;
aufrufen (names) ● vi rufen. **~ up**
vt (Mil) einberufen; (Teleph) anrufen

call: **~-box** n Telefonzelle f. **~**

centre n Callcenter nt. **~er** n Besucher m; (Teleph) Anrufer m. **~ing** n Berufung f. **~-up** n (Mil) Einberufung f

calm /kɑːm/ adj (-er, -est) ruhig ● n Ruhe f ● vt ~ **[down]** beruhigen ● vi ~ **down** sich beruhigen. **~ness** n Ruhe f; (of sea) Stille f

calorie /'kælərɪ/ n Kalorie f

calves /kɑːvz/ npl see **calf**[1] & [2]

camcorder /'kæmkɔːdə(r)/ n Camcorder m

came /keɪm/ see **come**

camel /'kæml/ n Kamel nt

camera /'kæmərə/ n Kamera f

camouflage /'kæməflɑːʒ/ n Tarnung f ● vt tarnen

camp /kæmp/ n Lager nt ● vi campen; (Mil) kampieren

campaign /kæm'peɪn/ n Feldzug m; (Comm, Pol) Kampagne f ● vi (Pol) im Wahlkampf arbeiten

camp: **~-bed** n Feldbett nt. **~er** n Camper m; (Auto) Wohnmobil nt. **~ing** n Camping nt. **~site** n Campingplatz m

can[1] /kæn/ n (for petrol) Kanister m; (tin) Dose f, Büchse f; a ~ **of beer** eine Dose Bier

can[2] /kæn/, unbetont /kən/

pres **can**, *pt* **could**

● *modal verb*

••••▶ (be able to) können. I **can't** or **cannot go** ich kann nicht gehen. he **couldn't** or **could not go** (was unable to) sie konnte nicht gehen; (would not be able to) sie könnte nicht gehen. he **could go if he had time** er könnte gehen, wenn er Zeit hätte. **if I could go** wenn ich gehen könnte. **that cannot**

be true das kann nicht stimmen

••••▶ (know how to) können. **can you swim?** können Sie schwimmen? **she can drive** sie kann Auto fahren

••••▶ (be allowed to) dürfen. **you can't smoke here** hier dürfen Sie nicht rauchen. **can I go?** kann ich gehen?

••••▶ (in requests) können. **can I have a glass of water, please?** kann ich ein Glas Wasser haben, bitte? **could you ring me tomorrow?** könnten Sie mich morgen anrufen?

••••▶ **could** (expressing possibility) könnte. **that could be so** das könnte od kann sein. I **could have killed him** ich hätte ihn umbringen können

Canad|a /'kænədə/ n Kanada nt. **~ian** adj kanadisch ● n Kanadier(in) m(f)

canal /kə'næl/ n Kanal m

canary /kə'neərɪ/ n Kanarienvogel m

cancel /'kænsl/ vt/i (pt/pp **cancelled**) absagen; abbestellen (newspaper); (Computing) abbrechen; **be ~led** ausfallen. **~lation** n Absage f

cancer /'kænsə(r)/ n (also Astrology) C~ Krebs m. **~ous** adj krebsig

candid /'kændɪd/ adj offen

candidate /'kændɪdət/ n Kandidat(in) m(f)

candle /'kændl/ n Kerze f. **~stick** n Kerzenständer m, Leuchter m

candy /'kændɪ/ n (Amer) Süßigkeiten pl; [piece of] ~ Bonbon m

cane /keɪn/ n Rohr nt; (stick) Stock m ● vt mit dem Stock züchtigen

canine /'keɪnaɪn/ adj Hunde-. ~ **tooth** n Eckzahn m

cannabis /ˈkænəbɪs/ n Haschisch nt

canned /kænd/ adj Dosen-, Büchsen-

cannibal /ˈkænɪbl/ n Kannibale m. **~ism** n Kannibalismus m

cannon /ˈkænən/ n inv Kanone f

cannot /ˈkænɒt/ see can²

canoe /kəˈnuː/ n Paddelboot nt; (Sport) Kanu nt

'can-opener n Dosenöffner m

can't /kɑːnt/ = cannot. See can²

canteen /kænˈtiːn/ n Kantine f; **~ of cutlery** Besteckkasten m

canter /ˈkæntə(r)/ n Kanter m ● vi kantern

canvas /ˈkænvəs/ n Segeltuch nt; (Art) Leinwand f; (painting) Gemälde nt

canvass /ˈkænvəs/ vi um Stimmen werben

canyon /ˈkænjən/ n Cañon m

cap /kæp/ n Kappe f, Mütze f; (nurse's) Haube f; (top, lid) Verschluss m

capability /keɪpəˈbɪlətɪ/ n Fähigkeit f

capable /ˈkeɪpəbl/ adj, **-bly** adv fähig; **be ~ of doing sth** fähig sein, etw zu tun

capacity /kəˈpæsətɪ/ n Fassungsvermögen nt; (ability) Fähigkeit f; **in my ~ as** in meiner Eigenschaft als

cape¹ /keɪp/ n (cloak) Cape nt

cape² n (Geog) Kap nt

capital /ˈkæpɪtl/ adj (letter) groß ● n (town) Hauptstadt f; (money) Kapital nt; (letter) Großbuchstabe m

capital|ism /ˈkæpɪtəlɪzm/ n Kapitalismus m. **~ist** adj kapitalistisch ● n Kapitalist m. **~ letter** n Großbuchstabe m. **~ 'punishment** n Todesstrafe f

Capitol Der Sitz des amerikanischen ▶**CONGRESS** auf dem Capitol Hill in Washington D.C. *i*

c

capsize /kæpˈsaɪz/ vi kentern ● vt zum Kentern bringen

captain /ˈkæptɪn/ n Kapitän m; (Mil) Hauptmann m ● vt anführen (team)

caption /ˈkæpʃn/ n Überschrift f; (of illustration) Bildtext m

captivate /ˈkæptɪveɪt/ vt bezaubern

captive /ˈkæptɪv/ adj **hold/take ~e** gefangen halten/nehmen ● n Gefangene(r) m/f. **~ity** n Gefangenschaft f

capture /ˈkæptʃə(r)/ n Gefangennahme f ● vt gefangen nehmen; [ein]fangen (animal); (Mil) einnehmen (town)

car /kɑː(r)/ n Auto nt, Wagen m; **by ~** mit dem Auto od Wagen

caramel /ˈkærəmel/ n Karamell m

carat /ˈkærət/ n Karat nt

caravan /ˈkærəvæn/ n Wohnwagen m; (procession) Karawane f

carbon /ˈkɑːbən/ n Kohlenstoff m; (paper) Kohlepapier nt; (copy) Durchschlag m

carbon: ~ copy n Durchschlag m. **~ paper** n Kohlepapier nt

carburettor /kɑːbjʊˈretə(r)/ n Vergaser m

carcass /ˈkɑːkəs/ n Kadaver m

card /kɑːd/ n Karte f

'cardboard n Pappe f, Karton m. **~ 'box** n Pappschachtel f; (large) [Papp]karton m

'card-game n Kartenspiel nt

cardigan /ˈkɑːdɪgən/ n Strickjacke f

cardinal /ˈkɑːdɪnl/ adj Kardinal-

● *n* (*Relig*) Kardinal *m*
card 'index *n* Kartei *f*
care /keə(r)/ *n* Sorgfalt *f*; (*caution*) Vorsicht *f*; (*protection*) Obhut *f*; (*looking after*) Pflege *f*; (*worry*) Sorge *f*; ~ **of** (*on letter abbr* **c/o**) bei; **take** ~ vorsichtig sein; **take into** ~ in Pflege nehmen; **take** ~ **of** sich kümmern um ● *vi* ~ **for** (*like*) mögen; (*look after*) betreuen; **I don't** ~ das ist mir gleich
career /kə'rɪə(r)/ *n* Laufbahn *f*; (*profession*) Beruf *m* ● *vi* rasen
care: ~**free** *adj* sorglos. ~**ful** *adj* sorgfältig; (*cautious*) vorsichtig. ~**less** *adj* nachlässig. ~**lessness** *n* Nachlässigkeit *f*. ~**r** *n* Pflegende(r) *m/f*
'caretaker *n* Hausmeister *m*
'car ferry *n* Autofähre *f*
cargo /'kɑ:gəʊ/ *n* (*pl* **-es**) Ladung *f*
Caribbean /kærɪ'bi:ən/ *n* the ~ die Karibik
caricature /'kærɪkətjʊə(r)/ *n* Karikatur *f* ● *vt* karikieren
caring /'keərɪŋ/ *adj* (*parent*) liebevoll; (*profession, attitude*) sozial
carnation /kɑ:'neɪʃn/ *n* Nelke *f*
carnival /'kɑ:nɪvl/ *n* Karneval *m*
carol /'kærl/ *n* [*Christmas*] ~ Weihnachtslied *nt*
carp¹ /kɑ:p/ *n inv* Karpfen *m*
carp² *vi* nörgeln
'car park *n* Parkplatz *m*; (*multi-storey*) Parkhaus *nt*; (*underground*) Tiefgarage *f*
carpent|er /'kɑ:pɪntə(r)/ *n* Zimmermann *m*; (*joiner*) Tischler *m*. ~**ry** *n* Tischlerei *f*
carpet /'kɑ:pɪt/ *n* Teppich *m*
carriage /'kærɪdʒ/ *n* Kutsche *f*; (*Rail*) Wagen *m*; (*of goods*) Beförderung *f*; (*cost*) Frachtkosten *pl*; (*bearing*) Haltung *f*

carrier /'kærɪə(r)/ *n* Träger(in) *m(f)*; (*Comm*) Spediteur *m*; ~ [-**bag**] Tragetasche *f*
carrot /'kærət/ *n* Möhre *f*, Karotte *f*
carry /'kærɪ/ *vt/i* (*pt/pp* **-ied**) tragen; **be carried away** ⊞ hingerissen sein. ~ **off** *vt* wegtragen; gewinnen (*prize*). ~ **on** *vi* weitermachen; ~ **on with** ⊞ eine Affäre haben mit ● *vt* führen; (*continue*) fortführen. ~ **out** *vt* hinaustragen; (*perform*) ausführen
cart /kɑ:t/ *n* Karren *m*; **put the** ~ **before the horse** das Pferd beim Schwanz aufzäumen ● *vt* karren; (⊞: *carry*) schleppen
carton /'kɑ:tn/ *n* [Papp]karton *m*, (*for drink*) Tüte *f*; (*of cream, yoghurt*) Becher *m*
cartoon /kɑ:'tu:n/ *n* Karikatur *f*; (*joke*) Witzzeichnung *f*; (*strip*) Comic Strips *pl*; (*film*) Zeichentrickfilm *m*. ~**ist** *n* Karikaturist *m*
cartridge /'kɑ:trɪdʒ/ *n* Patrone *f*; (*for film*) Kassette *f*
carve /kɑ:v/ *vt* schnitzen; (*in stone*) hauen; (*Culin*) aufschneiden
carving /'kɑ:vɪŋ/ *n* Schnitzerei *f*. ~**knife** *n* Tranchiermesser *nt*
'car wash *n* Autowäsche *f*; (*place*) Autowaschanlage *f*
case¹ /keɪs/ *n* Fall *m*; **in any** ~ auf jeden Fall; **just in** ~ für alle Fälle; **in** ~ **he comes** falls er kommt
case² *n* Kasten *m*; (*crate*) Kiste *f*; (*for spectacles*) Etui *nt*; (*suitcase*) Koffer *m*; (*for display*) Vitrine *f*
cash /kæʃ/ *n* Bargeld *nt*; **pay [in]** ~ [**in**] bar bezahlen; ~ **on delivery** per Nachnahme ● *vt* einlösen (*cheque*). ~ **desk** *n* Kasse *f*
cashier /kæ'ʃɪə(r)/ *n* Kassierer(in) *m(f)*
cash: ~**point [machine]** *n* Geld-

automat m. ~ **register** n Registrierkasse f

cassette /kə'set/ n Kassette f. ~ **recorder** n Kassettenrecorder m

cast /kɑːst/ n (mould) Form f; (model) Abguss m; (Theat) Besetzung f; (plaster) ~ (Med) Gipsverband m ● vt (pt/pp **cast**) (throw) werfen; (shed) abwerfen; abgeben (vote); gießen (metal); (Theat) besetzen (role). ~ **off** vi (Naut) ablegen

castle /'kɑːsl/ n Schloss nt; (fortified) Burg f; (Chess) Turm m

'**cast-offs** npl abgelegte Kleidung f

castor /'kɑːstə(r)/ n (wheel) [Lauf]rolle f

'**castor sugar** n Streuzucker m

casual /'kæʒʊəl/ adj (chance) zufällig; (offhand) lässig; (informal) zwanglos; (not permanent) Gelegenheits-; ~ **wear** Freizeitbekleidung f

casualty /'kæʒʊəltɪ/ n [Todes]opfer nt; (injured person) Verletzte(r) m/f; ~ [**department**] Unfallstation f

cat /kæt/ n Katze f

catalogue /'kætəlɒg/ n Katalog m ● vt katalogisieren

catapult /'kætəpʌlt/ n Katapult nt ● vt katapultieren

cataract /'kætərækt/ n (Med) grauer Star m

catarrh /kə'tɑː(r)/ n Katarrh m

catastroph|e /kə'tæstrəfi/ n Katastrophe f. ~**ic** adj katastrophal

catch /kætʃ/ n (of fish) Fang m; (fastener) Verschluss m; (on door) Klinke f; (fig: snag) Haken m ☐ ● v (pt/pp **caught**) ● vt fangen; (be in time for) erreichen; (travel by) fahren mit; bekommen (illness); ~ **a cold** sich erkälten; ~ **sight of** erblicken; ~ **s.o. stealing** jdn beim Stehlen erwischen; ~ **one's finger in the**

door sich (dat) den Finger in der Tür [ein]klemmen ● vi (burn) anbrennen; (get stuck) klemmen. ~ **on** vi ☐ (understand) kapieren; (become popular) sich durchsetzen. ~ **up** vt einholen ● vi aufholen; ~ **up with** einholen (s.o.); nachholen (work)

catching /'kætʃɪŋ/ adj ansteckend

catch: ~-**phrase** n, ~**word** n Schlagwort nt

catchy /'kætʃɪ/ adj einprägsam

categor|ical /kætɪ'gɒrɪkl/ adj kategorisch. ~**y** n Kategorie f

cater /'keɪtə(r)/ vi ~ **for** beköstigen; (firm): das Essen liefern für (party); (fig) eingestellt sein auf (+ acc). ~**ing** n (trade) Gaststättengewerbe nt

caterpillar /'kætəpɪlə(r)/ n Raupe f

cathedral /kə'θiːdrl/ n Dom m, Kathedrale f

Catholic /'kæθəlɪk/ adj katholisch ● n Katholik(in) m(f). **C** ~**ism** n Katholizismus m

cattle /'kætl/ npl Vieh nt

catty /'kætɪ/ adj boshaft

caught /kɔːt/ see **catch**

cauliflower /'kɒlɪ-/ n Blumenkohl m

cause /kɔːz/ n Ursache f; (reason) Grund m; **good** ~ gute Sache f ● vt verursachen; ~ **s.o. to do sth** jdn veranlassen, etw zu tun

caution /'kɔːʃn/ n Vorsicht f; (warning) Verwarnung f ● vt (Jur) verwarnen

cautious /'kɔːʃəs/ adj vorsichtig

cavalry /'kævəlrɪ/ n Kavallerie f

cave /keɪv/ n Höhle f ● vi ~ **in** einstürzen

cavern /'kævən/ n Höhle f

caviare /'kævɪɑː(r)/ n Kaviar m

cavity /'kævətɪ/ n Hohlraum m; (in tooth) Loch nt

CCTV abbr (closed-circuit television) CCTV nt; (surveillance) Videoüberwachung f

CD abbr (compact disc) CD f; **~-ROM** CD-ROM f

cease /siːs/ vt/i aufhören. **~-fire** n Waffenruhe f. **~less** adj unaufhörlich

cedar /'siːdə(r)/ n Zeder f

ceiling /'siːlɪŋ/ n [Zimmer]decke f; (fig) oberste Grenze f

celebrat|e /'selɪbreɪt/ vt/i feiern. **~ed** adj berühmt (for wegen). **~ion** n Feier f

celebrity /sɪ'lebrətɪ/ n Berühmtheit f

celery /'selərɪ/ n [Stangen]sellerie m & f

cell /sel/ n Zelle f

cellar /'selə(r)/ n Keller m

cellist /'tʃelɪst/ n Cellist(in) m(f)

cello /'tʃeləʊ/ n Cello nt

cellphone /'selfəʊn/ n Handy nt

Celsius /'selsɪəs/ adj Celsius

Celt /kelt/ n Kelte m/ Keltin f. **~ic** adj keltisch

cement /sɪ'ment/ n Zement m; (adhesive) Kitt m

cemetery /'semətrɪ/ n Friedhof m

censor /'sensə(r)/ n Zensor m ● vt zensieren. **~ship** n Zensur f

census /'sensəs/ n Volkszählung f

cent /sent/ n Cent m

centenary /sen'tiːnərɪ/ n, (Amer) **centennial** n Hundertjahrfeier f

center /'sentə(r)/ n (Amer) = centre

centi|grade /'sentɪ-/ adj Celsius. **~metre** n Zentimeter m & nt

central /'sentrəl/ adj zentral. **~ 'heating** n Zentralheizung f. **~ize** vt zentralisieren

centre /'sentə(r)/ n Zentrum nt; (middle) Mitte f ● v (pt/pp centred) ● vt zentrieren. **~-'forward** n Mittelstürmer m

century /'sentʃərɪ/ n Jahrhundert nt

ceramic /sɪ'ræmɪk/ adj Keramik-

cereal /'sɪərɪəl/ n Getreide nt; (breakfast food) Frühstücksflocken pl

ceremon|ial /serɪ'məʊnɪəl/ adj zeremoniell, feierlich ● n Zeremoniell nt. **~ious** adj formell

ceremony /'serɪmənɪ/ n Zeremonie f, Feier f

certain /'sɜːtn/ adj sicher; (not named) gewiss; **for ~** mit Bestimmtheit; **make ~** (check) sich vergewissern (that dass); (ensure) dafür sorgen (that dass); **he is ~ to win** er wird ganz bestimmt siegen. **~ly** adv bestimmt, sicher; **~ly not!** auf keinen Fall! **~ty** n Sicherheit f, Gewissheit f; **it's a ~ty** es ist sicher

certificate /sə'tɪfɪkət/ n Bescheinigung f; (Jur) Urkunde f; (Sch) Zeugnis nt

certify /'sɜːtɪfaɪ/ vt (pt/pp -ied) bescheinigen; (declare insane) für geisteskrank erklären

cf. abbr (compare) vgl.

chafe /tʃeɪf/ vt wund reiben

chaffinch /'tʃæfɪntʃ/ n Buchfink m

chain /tʃeɪn/ n Kette f ● vt ketten (to an + acc). **~ up** vt anketten

chain: **~ re'action** n Kettenreaktion f. **~-smoker** n Kettenraucher m. **~ store** n Kettenladen m

chair /tʃeə(r)/ n Stuhl m; (Univ) Lehrstuhl m; (Adm) Vorsitzende(r) m/f. **~-lift** n Sessellift m. **~man** n Vorsitzende(r) m/f

chalet /'ʃæleɪ/ n Chalet nt

chalk /tʃɔːk/ n Kreide f

challeng|e /'tʃælɪndʒ/ n Herausforderung f; (Mil) Anruf m ● vt herausfordern; (Mil) anrufen; (fig) anfechten (statement). **~er** n Herausforderer m. **~ing** adj herausfordernd; (demanding) anspruchsvoll

chamber /'tʃeɪmbə(r)/ n Kammer f; **C~ of Commerce** Handelskammer f. **~ music** n Kammermusik f

chamois /'ʃæmɪ/ n **~[-leather]** Ledertuch nt

champagne /ʃæm'peɪn/ n Champagner m

champion /'tʃæmpɪən/ n (Sport) Meister(in) m(f); (of cause) Verfechter m ● vt sich einsetzen für. **~ship** n (Sport) Meisterschaft f

chance /tʃɑːns/ n Zufall m; (prospect) Chancen pl; (likelihood) Aussicht f; (opportunity) Gelegenheit f; **by ~** zufällig; **take a ~** ein Risiko eingehen; **give s.o. a ~** jdm eine Chance geben ● attrib zufällig ● vt **~ it** es riskieren

chancellor /'tʃɑːnsələ(r)/ n Kanzler m; (Univ) Rektor m

chancy /'tʃɑːnsɪ/ adj riskant

change /tʃeɪndʒ/ n Veränderung f; (alteration) Änderung f; (money) Wechselgeld nt; **for a ~** zur Abwechslung ● vt wechseln; (alter) ändern; (exchange) umtauschen (for gegen); (transform) verwandeln; trocken legen (baby); **~ one's clothes** sich umziehen; (~ trains) umsteigen ● vi sich verändern; (~ clothes) sich umziehen; (~ trains) umsteigen; **all ~!** alles aussteigen!

changeable /'tʃeɪndʒəbl/ adj wechselhaft

'changing-room n Umkleideraum m

channel /'tʃænl/ n Rinne f; (Radio, TV) Kanal m; (fig) Weg m; **the [English] C~** der Ärmelkanal; **the C~ Islands** die Kanalinseln

chant /tʃɑːnt/ vt singen; (demonstrators:) skandieren

chaos /'keɪɒs/ n Chaos nt. **~tic** adj chaotisch

chap /tʃæp/ n 🔟 Kerl m

chapel /'tʃæpl/ n Kapelle f

chaplain /'tʃæplɪn/ n Geistliche(r) m

chapped /tʃæpt/ adj (skin) aufgesprungen

chapter /'tʃæptə(r)/ n Kapitel nt

character /'kærɪktə(r)/ n Charakter m; (in novel, play) Gestalt f; (Printing) Schriftzeichen nt; **out of ~** uncharakteristisch; **quite a ~** 🔟 ein Original

characteristic /kærɪktə'rɪstɪk/ adj, **-ally** adv charakteristisch (of für) ● n Merkmal nt

characterize /'kærɪktəraɪz/ vt charakterisieren

charge /tʃɑːdʒ/ n (price) Gebühr f; (Electr) Ladung f; (attack) Angriff m; (Jur) Anklage f; **free of ~** kostenlos; **be in ~** verantwortlich sein (of für); **take ~** die Aufsicht übernehmen (of über + acc) ● vt berechnen (fee); (Electr) laden; (attack) angreifen; (Jur) anklagen (**with** gen); **~ s.o. for sth** jdm etw berechnen

charitable /'tʃærɪtəbl/ adj wohltätig; (kind) wohlwollend

charity /'tʃærətɪ/ n Nächstenliebe f; (organization) wohltätige Einrichtung f; **for ~** für Wohltätigkeitszwecke

charm /tʃɑːm/ n Reiz m; (of person) Charme m; (object) Amulett nt ● vt bezaubern. **~ing** adj reizend; (person, smile) charmant

chart /tʃɑːt/ n Karte f; (table) Tabelle f

charter /'tʃɑːtə(r)/ n **~ [flight]** Charterflug m ● vt chartern; **~ed accountant** Wirtschaftsprüfer m

Wirtschaftsprüferin m(f)

chase /tʃeɪs/ n Verfolgungsjagd f
● vt jagen, verfolgen. ~ **away** or
off vt wegjagen

chassis /'ʃæsɪ/ n (pl **chassis**)
Chassis nt

chaste /tʃeɪst/ adj keusch

chat /tʃæt/ n Plauderei f; **have a** ~
with plaudern mit ● vi (pt/pp **chat-
ted**) plaudern. ~ **show** n
Talkshow f

chatter /'tʃætə(r)/ n Geschwätz nt
● vi schwatzen; (child:) plappern;
(teeth:) klappern. ~**box** n 🔲 Plap-
permaul nt

chatty /'tʃætɪ/ adj geschwätzig

chauffeur /'ʃəʊfə(r)/ n
Chauffeur m

cheap /tʃiːp/ adj & adv (-er, -est)
billig. ~**en** vt entwürdigen

cheat /tʃiːt/ n Betrüger(in) m(f);
(at games) Mogler m ● vt betrügen
● vi (at games) mogeln 🔲

check¹ /tʃek/ adj (squared) kariert
● n Karo nt

check² n Überprüfung f; (inspection) Kontrolle f; (Chess) Schach nt;
(Amer: bill) Rechnung f; (Amer:
cheque) Scheck m; (Amer: tick)
Haken m; **keep a** ~ **on** kontrollieren ● vt [über]prüfen; (inspect)
kontrollieren; (restrain) hemmen; (stop)
aufhalten ● vi [**go and**] ~ nachsehen. ~ **in** vi sich anmelden; (Aviat)
einchecken ● vt abfertigen; einchecken. ~ **out** vi sich abmelden. ~
up vi prüfen, kontrollieren; ~ **up**
on überprüfen

checked /tʃekt/ adj kariert

check: ~**out** n Kasse f. ~**room** n
(Amer) Garderobe f. ~**up** n (Med)
[Kontroll]untersuchung f

cheek /tʃiːk/ n Backe f; (impudence) Frechheit f. ~**y** adj, **-ily**
adv frech

cheer /tʃɪə(r)/ n Beifallsruf m;
three ~**s** ein dreifaches Hoch (**for**
auf + acc); ~**s!** prost! (goodbye)
tschüs! ● vt zujubeln (+ dat) ● vi ju-
beln. ~ **up** vt aufmuntern; aufheitern ● vi munterer werden. ~**ful**
adj fröhlich. ~**fulness** n Fröhlichkeit f

cheerio /tʃɪərɪ'əʊ/ int 🔲 tschüs!

cheese /tʃiːz/ n Käse m. ~**cake**
n Käsekuchen m

chef /ʃef/ n Koch m

chemical /'kemɪkl/ adj chemisch
● n Chemikalie f

chemist /'kemɪst/ n (pharmacist)
Apotheker(in) m(f); (scientist) Che-
miker(in) m(f); ~**'s [shop]** Drogerie f; (dispensing) Apotheke f. ~**ry** n
Chemie f

cheque /tʃek/ n Scheck m.
~**book** n Scheckbuch nt. ~ **card**
n Scheckkarte f

cherish /'tʃerɪʃ/ vt lieben;
(fig) hegen

cherry /'tʃerɪ/ n Kirsche f ● attrib
Kirsch-

chess /tʃes/ n Schach nt

chess: ~**board** n Schachbrett nt.
~**man** n Schachfigur f

chest /tʃest/ n Brust f; (box) Truhe f

chestnut /'tʃesnʌt/ n Esskastanie
f, Marone f; (horse-) [Ross]kastanie
f; (Ross) kastanien f

chest of 'drawers n
Kommode f

chew /tʃuː/ vt kauen. ~**ing-gum** n
Kaugummi m

chick /tʃɪk/ n Küken nt

chicken /'tʃɪkɪn/ n Huhn nt
● attrib Hühner- ● adj 🔲 feige

chief /tʃiːf/ adj Haupt- ● n Chef m;
(of tribe) Häuptling m. ~**ly** adv
hauptsächlich

child /tʃaɪld/ n (pl ~**ren**) Kind nt

child: ~**birth** n Geburt f. ~**hood**

n Kindheit *f*. **~ish** *adj* kindisch. **~less** *adj* kinderlos. **~like** *adj* kindlich. **~-minder** *n* Tagesmutter *f*

children /'tʃɪldrən/ *npl see* child

Chile /'tʃɪlɪ/ *n* Chile *nt*

chill /tʃɪl/ *n* Kälte *f*; (*illness*) Erkältung *f* ● *vt* kühlen

chilly /'tʃɪlɪ/ *adj* kühl; **I felt ~** mich fröstelte [es]

chime /tʃaɪm/ *vi* läuten; (*clock:*) schlagen

chimney /'tʃɪmnɪ/ *n* Schornstein *m*. **~-pot** *n* Schornsteinaufsatz *m*. **~-sweep** *n* Schornsteinfeger *m*

chin /tʃɪn/ *n* Kinn *nt*

china /'tʃaɪnə/ *n* Porzellan *nt*

China|a *n* China *nt*. **~ese** *adj* chinesisch ● *n* (*Lang*) Chinesisch *nt*; **the ~ese** *pl die* Chinesen

chink[1] /tʃɪŋk/ *n* (*slit*) Ritze *f*

chink[2] *n* Geklirr *nt* ● *vi* klirren; (*coins:*) klimpern

chip /tʃɪp/ *n* (*fragment*) Span *m*; (*in china, paintwork*) angeschlagene Stelle *f*; (*Computing, Gambling*) Chip *m*; **~s** *pl* (*Culin*) Pommes frites *pl*; (*Amer: crisps*) Chips *pl* ● *vt* (*pt/pp* chipped) (*damage*) anschlagen. **~ped** *adj* angeschlagen

chirp /tʃɜːp/ *vi* zwitschern; (*cricket:*) zirpen. **~y** *adj* munter

chit /tʃɪt/ *n* Zettel *m*

chocolate /'tʃɒkəlat/ *n* Schokolade *f*; (*sweet*) Praline *f*

choice /tʃɔɪs/ *n* Wahl *f*; (*variety*) Auswahl *f* ● *adj* auserlesen

choir /'kwaɪə(r)/ *n* Chor *m*. **~boy** *n* Chorknabe *m*

choke /tʃəʊk/ *n* (*Auto*) Choke *m* ● *vt* würgen; (*to death*) erwürgen ● *vi* sich verschlucken; **~ on** [fast] ersticken an (+ *dat*)

choose /tʃuːz/ *vt/i* (*pt* chose, *pp* chosen) wählen; (*select*) sich (*dat*)

aussuchen; **~ to do/go** [freiwillig] tun/gehen; **as you ~** wie Sie wollen

choos[e]y /'tʃuːzɪ/ *adj* 🔲 wählerisch

chop /tʃɒp/ *n* (*blow*) Hieb *m*; (*Culin*) Kotelett *nt* ● *vt* (*pt/pp* chopped) hacken. **~ down** *vt* abhacken; fällen (*tree*). **~ off** *vt* abhacken

chop|per /'tʃɒpə(r)/ *n* Beil *nt*; 🔲 Hubschrauber *m*. **~py** *adj* kabbelig

'chopsticks *npl* Essstäbchen *pl*

choral /'kɔːrəl/ *adj* Chor-

chord /kɔːd/ *n* (*Mus*) Akkord *m*

chore /tʃɔː(r)/ *n* lästige Pflicht *f*; [**household**] **~s** Hausarbeit *f*

chorus /'kɔːrəs/ *n* Chor *m*; (*of song*) Refrain *m*

chose, chosen *see* choose

Christ /kraɪst/ *n* Christus *m*

christen /'krɪsn/ *vt* taufen

Christian /'krɪstʃən/ *adj* christlich ● *n* Christ(in) *m(f)*. **~ity** *n* Christentum *nt*. **~ name** *nt* Vorname *m*

Christmas /'krɪsməs/ *n* Weihnachten *nt*. **~ card** *n* Weihnachtskarte *f*. **~ 'Day** *n* erster Weihnachtstag *m*. **~ 'Eve** *n* Heiligabend *m*. **~ tree** *n* Weihnachtsbaum *m*

chrome /krəʊm/ *n*, **chromium** /'krəʊmɪəm/ *n* Chrom *nt*

chronic /'krɒnɪk/ *adj* chronisch

chronicle /'krɒnɪkl/ *n* Chronik *f*

chrysanthemum /krɪ 'sænθəməm/ *n* Chrysantheme *f*

chubby /'tʃʌbɪ/ *adj* mollig

chuck /tʃʌk/ *vt* 🔲 schmeißen. **~ out** *vt* 🔲 rausschmeißen

chuckle /'tʃʌkl/ *vi* in sich (*acc*) hineinlachen

chum /tʃʌm/ *n* Freund(in) *m(f)*

chunk /tʃʌŋk/ *n* Stück *nt*

church /tʃɜːtʃ/ *n* Kirche *f*. **~yard** *n* Friedhof *m*

churn /tʃɜːn/ vt ~ out am laufenden Band produzieren

cider /'saɪdə(r)/ n ≈ Apfelwein m

cigar /sɪ'gɑː(r)/ n Zigarre f

cigarette /sɪgə'ret/ n Zigarette f

cine-camera /'sɪnɪ-/ n Filmkamera f

cinema /'sɪnɪmə/ n Kino nt

cinnamon /'sɪnəmən/ n Zimt m

circle /'sɜːkl/ n Kreis m; (Theat) Rang m ● vt umkreisen ● vi kreisen

circuit /'sɜːkɪt/ n Runde f; (racetrack) Rennbahn f; (Electr) Stromkreis m. ~ous adj ~ route Umweg m

circular /'sɜːkjʊlə(r)/ adj kreisförmig ● n Rundschreiben nt. ~'saw n Kreissäge f. ~'tour n Rundfahrt f

circulat|e /'sɜːkjʊleɪt/ vt in Umlauf setzen ● vi zirkulieren. ~ion n Kreislauf m; (of newspaper) Auflage f

circumference /sə'kʌmfərəns/ n Umfang m

circumstance /'sɜːkəmstəns/ n Umstand m; ~s pl Umstände pl; (financial) Verhältnisse pl

circus /'sɜːkəs/ n Zirkus m

cistern /'sɪstən/ n (tank) Wasserbehälter m; (of WC) Spülkasten m

cite /saɪt/ vt zitieren

citizen /'sɪtɪzn/ n Bürger(in) m(f). ~ship n Staatsangehörigkeit f

citrus /'sɪtrəs/ n ~ **[fruit]** Zitrusfrucht f

city /'sɪtɪ/ n [Groß]stadt f

---

i

City The City of London ist das Gebiet innerhalb der alten Stadtgrenzen von London. Heute ist es das Geschäfts- und Finanzzentrum Londons und viele Banken und andere Geldinstitute haben dort ihre Hauptstellen. Wenn Leute über die City sprechen, beziehen sie sich oft auf diese Institutionen und nicht auf den Ort.

---

civic /'sɪvɪk/ adj Bürger-

civil /'sɪvl/ adj bürgerlich; (aviation, defence) zivil; (polite) höflich. ~ en-gi'neering n Hoch- und Tiefbau m

civilian /sɪ'vɪljən/ adj Zivil-; in ~ clothes in Zivil ● n Zivilist m

civiliz|ation /sɪvəlaɪ'zeɪʃn/ n Zivilisation f. ~e vt zivilisieren

civil: ~'servant n Beamte(r) m/Beamtin f. C~ 'Service n Staatsdienst m

claim /kleɪm/ n Anspruch m; (application) Antrag m; (demand) Forderung f; (assertion) Behauptung f ● vt beanspruchen; (apply for) beantragen; (demand) fordern; (assert) behaupten; (collect) abholen

clam /klæm/ n Klaffmuschel f

clamber /'klæmbə(r)/ vi klettern

clammy /'klæmɪ/ adj feucht

clamour /'klæmə(r)/ n Geschrei nt ● vi ~ for schreien nach

clamp /klæmp/ n Klammer f; [wheel] ~ Parkkralle f ● vt [ein]spannen ● vt ① ~ **down on** vorgehen gegen

clan /klæn/ n Clan m

clang /klæŋ/ n Schmettern nt. ~er n ① Schnitzer m

clank /klæŋk/ vi klirren

clap /klæp/ n **give s.o. a** ~ jdm Beifall klatschen; ~ **of thunder** Donnerschlag m ● vt/i (pt/pp clapped) Beifall klatschen (+ dat); ~ **one's hands** in die Hände klatschen

clari|fication /klærɪfɪ'keɪʃn/ n Klärung f. ~fy vt/i (pt/pp -ied) klären

clarinet /klærɪ'net/ n Klarinette f

clarity /'klærətɪ/ n Klarheit f

clash | clinic

clash /klæʃ/ n Geklirr nt; (fig) Konflikt m ● vi klirren; (colours:) sich beißen; (events:) ungünstig zusammenfallen

clasp /klɑːsp/ n Verschluss m ● vt ergreifen; (hold) halten

class /klɑːs/ n Klasse f; **travel first/second ~** erster/zweiter Klasse reisen ● vt einordnen

classic /ˈklæsɪk/ adj klassisch ● n Klassiker m. **~al** adj klassisch

classi|fication /klæsɪfɪˈkeɪʃn/ n Klassifikation f. **~fy** vt (pt/pp -ied) klassifizieren

'classroom n Klassenzimmer nt

classy /ˈklɑːsɪ/ adj 🔢 schick

clatter /ˈklætə(r)/ n Geklapper nt ● vi klappern

clause /klɔːz/ n Klausel f; (Gram) Satzteil m

claw /klɔː/ n Kralle f; (of bird of prey & Techn) Klaue f; (of crab, lobster) Schere f ● vt kratzen

clay /kleɪ/ n Lehm m; (pottery) Ton m

clean /kliːn/ adj (-er, -est) sauber ● adv glatt ● vt sauber machen; putzen (shoes, windows); **~ one's teeth** sich (dat) die Zähne putzen; **have sth ~ed** etw reinigen lassen. **~ up** vt sauber machen

cleaner /ˈkliːnə(r)/ n Putzfrau f; (substance) Reinigungsmittel nt; [dry] **~'s** chemische Reinigung f

cleanliness /ˈklenlɪnɪs/ n Sauberkeit f

cleanse /klenz/ vt reinigen

clear /klɪə(r)/ adj (-er, -est) klar; (obvious) eindeutig; (distinct) deutlich; (conscience) rein; (without obstacles) frei; **make sth ~** etw klarmachen (to an + dat) ● adv **stand ~** zurücktreten; **keep ~ of** aus dem Wege gehen (+ dat) ● vt räumen; abräumen (table); (acquit) freispre-

chen; (authorize) genehmigen; (jump over) überspringen; **~ one's throat** sich räuspern ● vi (fog:) sich auflösen. **~ away** vt wegräumen. **~ off** vi 🔢 abhauen. **~ out** vt ausräumen ● vi 🔢 abhauen. **~ up** vt (tidy) aufräumen; (solve) aufklären ● vi (weather): sich aufklären

clearance /ˈklɪərəns/ n Räumung f; (authorization) Genehmigung f; (customs) [Zoll]abfertigung f; (Techn) Spielraum m. **~ sale** n Räumungsverkauf m

clench /klentʃ/ vt **~ one's fist** die Faust ballen; **~ one's teeth** die Zähne zusammenbeißen

clergy /ˈklɜːdʒɪ/ npl Geistlichkeit f. **~man** n Geistliche(r) m

clerk /klɑːk, Amer: klɜːk/ n Büroangestellte(r) m/f; (Amer: shop assistant) Verkäufer(in) m(f)

clever /ˈklevə(r)/ adj (-er, -est), -ly adv klug; (skilful) geschickt

cliché /ˈkliːʃeɪ/ n Klischee nt

click /klɪk/ vi klicken

client /ˈklaɪənt/ n Kunde m/ Kundin f; (Jur) Klient(in) m(f)

cliff /klɪf/ n Kliff nt

climat|e /ˈklaɪmət/ n Klima nt

climax /ˈklaɪmæks/ n Höhepunkt m

climb /klaɪm/ n Aufstieg m ● vt besteigen (mountain); steigen auf (+ acc) (ladder, tree) ● vi klettern; (rise) steigen (road:) ansteigen. **~ down** vi hinunter-/herunterklettern; (from ladder, tree) heruntersteigen; 🔢 nachgeben

climber /ˈklaɪmə(r)/ n Bergsteiger m; (plant) Kletterpflanze f

cling /klɪŋ/ vi (pt/pp clung) sich klammern (to an + acc); (stick) haften (to an + dat). **~ film** n Sichtfolie f mit Hafteffekt

clinic /ˈklɪnɪk/ n Klinik f. **~al** adj

klinisch

clink /klɪŋk/ vi klirren

clip¹ /klɪp/ n Klammer f; (jewellery) Klipp m ● vt (pt/pp clipped) anklammern (to an + acc)

clip² n (extract) Ausschnitt m ● vt schneiden; knipsen (ticket). ~ping n (extract) Ausschnitt m

cloak /kləʊk/ n Umhang m. ~room n Garderobe f; (toilet) Toilette f

clobber /'klɒbə(r)/ n 🗉 Zeug nt ● vt (🗉: hit, defeat:) schlagen

clock /klɒk/ n Uhr f; (🗉: speedometer) Tacho m ● vi ~ in/out stechen

clock: ~wise adj & adv im Uhrzeigersinn. ~work n Uhrwerk nt; (of toy) Aufziehmechanismus m; like ~work 🗉 wie am Schnürchen

clod /klɒd/ n Klumpen m

clog /klɒg/ vt/i (pt/pp clogged) ~ [up] verstopfen

cloister /'klɔɪstə(r)/ n Kreuzgang m

clone /kləʊn/ n Klon m ● vt klonen

close¹ /kləʊs/ adj (-r, -st) nah[e] (to dat); (friend) eng; (weather) schwül; **have a ~ shave** 🗉 mit knapper Not davonkommen ● adv nahe an (street) Sackgasse f

close² /kləʊz/ n Ende nt; **draw to a ~** sich dem Ende nähern ● vt zumachen, schließen; (bring to an end) beenden; sperren (road) ● vi sich schließen; (shop:) schließen, zumachen; (end) enden. ~ **down** vt schließen; stilllegen (factory) ● vi schließen; (factory:) stillgelegt werden

closely /'kləʊslɪ/ adv eng, nah[e]; (with attention) genau

closet /'klɒzɪt/ n (Amer) Schrank m

close-up /'kləʊs-/ n Nahaufnahme f

closure /'kləʊʒə(r)/ n Schließung f; (of factory) Stilllegung f; (of road) Sperrung f

clot /klɒt/ n [Blut]gerinnsel nt; (🗉: idiot) Trottel m

cloth /klɒθ/ n Tuch nt

clothe /kləʊð/ vt kleiden

clothes /kləʊðz/ npl Kleider pl. ~-line n Wäscheleine f

clothing /'kləʊðɪŋ/ n Kleidung f

cloud /klaʊd/ n Wolke f ● vi ~ over sich bewölken

cloudy /'klaʊdɪ/ adj wolkig, bewölkt; (liquid) trübe

clout /klaʊt/ n 🗉 Schlag m; (influence) Einfluss m

clove /kləʊv/ n [Gewürz]nelke f; ~ **of garlic** Knoblauchzehe f

clover /'kləʊvə(r)/ n Klee m. ~ leaf n Kleeblatt nt

clown /klaʊn/ n Clown m ● vi ~ [about] herumalbern

club /klʌb/ n Klub m; (weapon) Keule f; (Sport) Schläger m; ~s pl (Cards) Kreuz nt, Treff nt

clue /kluː/ n Anhaltspunkt m; (in crossword) Frage f; **I haven't a ~** 🗉 ich habe keine Ahnung

clump /klʌmp/ n Gruppe f

clumsiness /'klʌmzɪnɪs/ n Ungeschicklichkeit f

clumsy /'klʌmzɪ/ adj, -ily adv ungeschickt; (unwieldy) unförmig

clung /klʌŋ/ see cling

clutch /klʌtʃ/ n Griff m; (Auto) Kupplung f; **be in s.o.'s ~es** 🗉 in jds Klauen sein ● vt festhalten; (grab) ergreifen ● vi ~ **at** greifen nach

clutter /'klʌtə(r)/ n Kram m ● vt ~ [up] vollstopfen

c/o abbr (care of) bei

coach /kəʊtʃ/ n [Reise]bus m; (Rail) Wagen m; (horse-drawn) Kutsche f;

(*Sport*) Trainer *m* ● *vt* Nachhilfestunden geben (+ *dat*); (*Sport*) trainieren

coal /kəʊl/ *n* Kohle *f*

coalition /kəʊə'lɪʃn/ *n* Koalition *f*

'coal-mine *n* Kohlenbergwerk *nt*

coarse /kɔːs/ *adj* (**-r, -st**) grob

coast /kəʊst/ *n* Küste *f* ● *vi* (*freewheel*) im Freilauf fahren; (*Auto*) im Leerlauf fahren. **~er** *n* (*mat*) Untersatz *m*

coast: **~guard** *n* Küstenwache *f*. **~line** *n* Küste *f*

coat /kəʊt/ *n* Mantel *m*; (*of animal*) Fell *nt*; (*of paint*) Anstrich *m*; **~ of arms** Wappen *m* ● *vt* überziehen; (*with paint*) streichen. **~-hanger** *n* Kleiderbügel *m*. **~-hook** *n* Kleiderhaken *m*

coating /'kəʊtɪŋ/ *n* Überzug *m*, Schicht *f*; (*of paint*) Anstrich *m*

coax /kəʊks/ *vt* gut zureden (+ *dat*)

cobble¹ /'kɒbl/ *n* Kopfstein *m*; **~s** *pl* Kopfsteinpflaster *nt*

cobble² *vt* flicken. **~r** *n* Schuster *m*

cobweb /'kɒb-/ *n* Spinnengewebe *nt*

cock /kɒk/ *n* Hahn *m*; (*any male bird*) Männchen *nt* ● *vt* (*animal*): **~ its ears** die Ohren spitzen; **~ the gun** den Hahn spannen

cockerel /'kɒkərəl/ *n* [junger] Hahn *m*

cockney /'kɒknɪ/ *n* (*dialect*) Cockney *nt*; (*person*) Cockney *m*

cock: **~pit** *n* (*Aviat*) Cockpit *nt*. **~roach** /-rəʊtʃ/ *n* Küchenschabe *f*. **~tail** *n* Cocktail *m*. **~-up** *n* 🗙 **make a ~-up** Mist bauen (*of* bei)

cocky /'kɒkɪ/ *adj* 🎓 eingebildet

cocoa /'kəʊkəʊ/ *n* Kakao *m*

coconut /'kəʊkənʌt/ *n* Kokosnuß *f*

cod /kɒd/ *n inv* Kabeljau *m*

COD *abbr* (**cash on delivery**) per

Nachnahme

coddle /'kɒdl/ *vt* verhätscheln

code /kəʊd/ *n* Kode *m*; (*Computing*) Code *m*; (*set of rules*) Kodex *m*. **~d** *adj* verschlüsselt

coerc|e /kəʊ'ɜːs/ *vt* zwingen. **~ion** *n* Zwang *m*

coffee /'kɒfɪ/ *n* Kaffee *m*

coffee: **~-grinder** *n* Kaffeemühle *f*. **~-pot** *n* Kaffeekanne *f*. **~-table** *n* Couchtisch *m*

coffin /'kɒfɪn/ *n* Sarg *m*

cogent /'kəʊdʒənt/ *adj* überzeugend

coherent /kəʊ'hɪərənt/ *adj* zusammenhängend; (*comprehensible*) verständlich

coil /kɔɪl/ *n* Rolle *f*; (*Electr*) Spule *f*; (*one ring*) Windung *f* ● *vt* **~[up]** zusammenrollen

coin /kɔɪn/ *n* Münze *f* ● *vt* prägen

coincide /kəʊɪn'saɪd/ *vi* zusammenfallen; (*agree*) übereinstimmen

coinciden|ce /kəʊ'ɪnsɪdəns/ *n* Zufall *m*. **~tal** *adj* zufällig

coke /kəʊk/ *n* Koks *m*

Coke (**R**) /kəʊk/ *n* (*drink*) Cola *f*

cold /kəʊld/ *adj* (**-er, -est**) kalt; **I am** *or* **feel ~** mir ist kalt ● *n* Kälte *f*; (*Med*) Erkältung *f*

cold: **~-blooded** *adj* kaltblütig. **~-hearted** *adj* kaltherzig. **~ly** *adv* (*fig*) kalt, kühl. **~ness** *n* Kälte *f*

collaborat|e /kə'læbəreɪt/ *vi* zusammenarbeiten (**with** mit); **~e on sth** mitarbeiten bei etw. **~ion** *n* Zusammenarbeit *f*, Mitarbeit *f*; (*with enemy*) Kollaboration *f*. **~or** *n* Mitarbeiter(in) *m(f)*; Kollaborateur *m*

collaps|e /kə'læps/ *n* Zusammenbruch *m*; Einsturz *m* ● *vi* zusammenbrechen; (*roof, building*) einstürzen. **~ible** *adj* zusammenklappbar

collar /'kɒlə(r)/ *n* Kragen *m*; (*for

animal) Halsband nt. **~-bone** n Schlüsselbein nt

colleague /'kɒliːg/ n Kollege m/Kollegin f

collect /kə'lekt/ vt sammeln; (*fetch*) abholen; einsammeln (*tickets*); einziehen (*taxes*) ● vi sich [an]sammeln ● adv **call ~** (*Amer*) ein R-Gespräch führen

collection /kə'lekʃn/ n Sammlung f; (*in church*) Kollekte f; (*of post*) Leerung f; (*designer's*) Kollektion f

collector /kə'lektə(r)/ n Sammler(in) m(f)

college /'kɒlɪdʒ/ n College nt

collide /kə'laɪd/ vi zusammenstoßen

colliery /'kɒlɪərɪ/ n Kohlengrube f

collision /kə'lɪʒn/ n Zusammenstoß m

colloquial /kə'ləʊkwɪəl/ adj umgangssprachlich

Cologne /kə'ləʊn/ n Köln nt

colon /'kəʊlən/ n Doppelpunkt m

colonel /'kɜːnl/ n Oberst m

colonial /kə'ləʊnɪəl/ adj Kolonial-

colony /'kɒlənɪ/ n Kolonie f

colossal /kə'lɒsl/ adj riesig

colour /'kʌlə(r)/ n Farbe f; (*complexion*) Gesichtsfarbe f; (*race*) Hautfarbe f; **off ~** 🛈 nicht ganz auf der Höhe ● vt färben; **~ [in]** ausmalen

colour: ~-blind adj farbenblind. **~ed** adj farbig ● n (*person*) Farbige(r) m/f. **~-fast** adj farbecht. **~ film** n Farbfilm m. **~ful** adj farbenfroh. **~less** adj farblos. **~ photo-[graph]** n Farbaufnahme f. **~ television** n Farbfernsehen nt

column /'kɒləm/ n Säule f; (*of soldiers, figures*) Kolonne f; (*Printing*) Spalte f; (*newspaper*) Kolumne f

comb /kəʊm/ n Kamm m ● vt kämmen; (*search*) absuchen; **~**

one's hair sich (*dat*) [die Haare] kämmen

combat /'kɒmbæt/ n Kampf m

combination /kɒmbɪ'neɪʃn/ n Kombination f

combine¹ /kəm'baɪn/ vt verbinden ● vi sich verbinden; (*people:*) sich zusammenschließen

combine² /'kɒmbaɪn/ n (*Comm*) Konzern m

combustion /kəm'bʌstʃn/ n Verbrennung f

come /kʌm/ vi (*pt* came, *pp* come) kommen; (*reach*) reichen (**to** an + *acc*); **that ~s to £10** das macht £10; **~ into money** zu Geld kommen; **~ true** wahr werden; **~ in two sizes** in zwei Größen erhältlich sein; **the years to ~** die kommenden Jahre; **how ~?** 🛈 wie das? **~ about** vi geschehen. **~ across** vi herüberkommen; 🛈 klar werden ● vt stoßen auf (+ *acc*). **~ apart** vi sich auseinander nehmen lassen; (*accidentally*) auseinander gehen. **~ away** vi weggehen; (*thing:*) abgehen. **~ back** vi zurückkommen. **~ by** vi vorbeikommen ● vt (*obtain*) bekommen. **~ in** vi hereinkommen. **~ off** vi abgehen; (*take place*) stattfinden; (*succeed*) klappen 🛈. **~ out** vi herauskommen; (*book:*) erscheinen; (*stain:*) herausgehen. **~ round** vi vorbeikommen; (*after fainting*) [wieder] zu sich kommen; (*change one's mind*) sich umstimmen lassen. **~ to** vi [wieder] zu sich kommen. **~ up** vi heraufkommen; (*plant:*) aufgehen; (*reach*) reichen (**to** bis); **~ up with** sich (*dat*) einfallen lassen

'come-back n Comeback nt

comedian /kə'miːdɪən/ n Komiker m

'come-down n Rückschritt m

comedy /'kɒmədɪ/ n Komödie f

comet /'kɒmɪt/ n Komet m

comfort /'kʌmfət/ n Bequemlichkeit f; (consolation) Trost m ● vt trösten

comfortable /'kʌmfətəbl/ adj, **-bly** adv bequem

'comfort station n (Amer) öffentliche Toilette f

comfy /'kʌmfɪ/ adj 🆃 bequem

comic /'kɒmɪk/ adj komisch ● n Komiker m; (periodical) Comic-Heft nt

coming /'kʌmɪŋ/ adj kommend ● n Kommen nt

comma /'kɒmə/ n Komma nt

command /kə'mɑːnd/ n Befehl m; (Mil) Kommando nt; (mastery) Beherrschung f ● vt befehlen (+ dat); kommandieren (+ acc)

command|er /kə'mɑːndə(r)/ n Befehlshaber m. **~ing officer** n Befehlshaber m

commemorat|e /kə'meməreɪt/ vt gedenken (+ gen). **~ion** n Gedenken nt

commence /kə'mens/ vt/i anfangen, beginnen

commend /kə'mend/ vt loben; (recommend) empfehlen (to dat)

comment /'kɒment/ n Bemerkung f; **no ~!** kein Kommentar! ● vi sich äußern (on zu); **~ on** (an event) kommentieren

commentary /'kɒməntrɪ/ n Kommentar m; **[running] ~** (Radio, TV) Reportage f

commentator /'kɒmənteɪtə(r)/ n Kommentator m; (Sport) Reporter m

commerce /'kɒmɜːs/ n Handel m

commercial /kə'mɜːʃl/ adj kommerziell ● n (Radio, TV) Werbespot m

commission /kə'mɪʃn/ n (order for work) Auftrag m; (body of

people) Kommission f; (payment) Provision f; (Mil) [Offiziers]patent nt; **out of ~** außer Betrieb ● vt beauftragen (s.o.); in Auftrag geben (thing); (Mil) zum Offizier ernennen

commit /kə'mɪt/ vt (pt/pp committed) begehen; (entrust) anvertrauen (to dat); (consign) einweisen (to in + acc); **~ oneself** sich festlegen; (involve oneself) sich engagieren. **~ment** n Verpflichtung f; (involvement) Engagement nt. **~ted** adj engagiert

committee /kə'mɪtɪ/ n Ausschuss m, Komitee nt

common /'kɒmən/ adj (-er, -est) gemeinsam; (frequent) häufig; (ordinary) gewöhnlich; (vulgar) ordinär ● n Gemeindeland nt; **have in ~** gemeinsam haben; **House of C~s** Unterhaus nt

common: ~ly adv allgemein. **C~ 'Market** n Gemeinsamer Markt m. **~place** adj häufig. **~-room** n Aufenthaltsraum m. **~ 'sense** n gesunder Menschenverstand m

---

🛈 **Commonwealth** Seit 1931 ist das Commonwealth die Gemeinschaft der 53 unabhängigen Staaten des ehemaligen britischen Weltreichs. Die Mitgliedstaaten, die jetzt bildungs- und kulturpolitisch miteinander verbunden sind, nehmen alle zwei Jahre an den Commonwealth-Konferenzen teil. Alle vier Jahre finden die Commonwealth-Spiele statt. In den USA ist Commonwealth die offizielle Bezeichnung der vier US-Staaten: Kentucky, Massachusetts, Pennsylvania und Virginia.

---

commotion /kə'məʊʃn/ n Tumult m

communal /ˈkɒmjʊnl/ adj gemeinschaftlich

communicate /kəˈmjuːnɪkeɪt/ vt mitteilen (**to** dat); übertragen (disease) ● vi sich verständigen

communication /kəmjuːnɪˈkeɪʃn/ n Verständigung f; (contact) Verbindung f; (message) Mitteilung f; ~s pl (technology) Nachrichtenwesen nt

communicative /kəˈmjuːnɪkətɪv/ adj mitteilsam

Communion /kəˈmjuːnɪən/ n [Holy] ~ das [heilige] Abendmahl; (Roman Catholic) die [heilige] Kommunion

communis|m /ˈkɒmjʊnɪzm/ n Kommunismus m. ~t adj kommunistisch ● n Kommunist(in) m(f)

community /kəˈmjuːnəti/ n Gemeinschaft f; local ~ Gemeinde f

commute /kəˈmjuːt/ vi pendeln. ~r n Pendler(in) m(f)

compact /kəmˈpækt/ adj kompakt

companion /kəmˈpænjən/ n Begleiter(in) m(f). ~ship n Gesellschaft f

company /ˈkʌmpəni/ n Gesellschaft f; (firm) Firma f; (Mil) Kompanie f; (▣: guests) Besuch m. ~ car n Firmenwagen m

comparable /ˈkɒmpərəbl/ adj vergleichbar

comparative /kəmˈpærətɪv/ adj vergleichend; (relative) relativ ● n (Gram) Komparativ m. ~ly adv verhältnismäßig

compare /kəmˈpeə(r)/ vt vergleichen (**with/to** mit) ● vi sich vergleichen lassen

comparison /kəmˈpærɪsn/ n Vergleich m

compartment /kəmˈpɑːtmənt/ n Fach nt; (Rail) Abteil nt

compass /ˈkʌmpəs/ n Kompass m

compassion /kəmˈpæʃn/ n Mitleid nt. ~ate adj mitfühlend

compatible /kəmˈpætəbl/ adj vereinbar; (drugs) verträglich; (Techn) kompatibel; **be** ~ (people:) [gut] zueinander passen

compatriot /kəmˈpætrɪət/ n Landsmann m /-männin f

compel /kəmˈpel/ vt (pt/pp compelled) zwingen

compensat|e /ˈkɒmpənseɪt/ vt entschädigen. ~ion n Entschädigung f; (fig) Ausgleich m

compete /kəmˈpiːt/ vi konkurrieren; (take part) teilnehmen (**in** an + dat)

competen|ce /ˈkɒmpətəns/ n Fähigkeit f. ~t adj fähig

competition /kɒmpəˈtɪʃn/ n Konkurrenz f; (contest) Wettbewerb m; (in newspaper) Preisausschreiben nt

competitive /kəmˈpetətɪv/ adj (Comm) konkurrenzfähig

competitor /kəmˈpetɪtə(r)/ n Teilnehmer m; (Comm) Konkurrent m

compile /kəmˈpaɪl/ vt zusammenstellen

complacen|cy /kəmˈpleɪsənsi/ n Selbstzufriedenheit f. ~t adj selbstzufrieden

complain /kəmˈpleɪn/ vi klagen (**about/of** über + acc); (formally) sich beschweren. ~t n Klage f; (formal) Beschwerde f; (Med) Leiden nt

complement¹ /ˈkɒmplɪmənt/ n Ergänzung f; **full** ~ volle Anzahl f

complement² /ˈkɒmplɪment/ vt ergänzen

complete /kəmˈpliːt/ adj vollständig; (finished) fertig; (utter) völlig ● vt vervollständigen; (finish) abschließen; (fill in) ausfüllen. ~ly adv völlig

completion /kəmˈpliːʃn/ n Vervollständigung f; (end) Abschluss m

complex /ˈkɒmpleks/ adj komplex ● n Komplex m

complexion /kəmˈplekʃn/ n Teint m; (colour) Gesichtsfarbe f

complexity /kəmˈpleksəti/ n Komplexität f

complicat|e /ˈkɒmplɪkeɪt/ vt komplizieren. **~ed** adj kompliziert. **~ion** n Komplikation f

compliment /ˈkɒmplɪmənt/ n Kompliment nt; **~s** pl Grüße pl ● vt ein Kompliment machen (+ dat). **~ary** adj schmeichelhaft; (given free) Frei-

comply /kəmˈplaɪ/ vi (pt/pp -ied) **~ with** nachkommen (+ dat)

compose /kəmˈpəʊz/ vt verfassen; (Mus) komponieren; **be ~d of** sich zusammensetzen aus. **~r** n Komponist m

composition /kɒmpəˈzɪʃn/ n Komposition f; (essay) Aufsatz m

compost /ˈkɒmpɒst/ n Kompost m

composure /kəmˈpəʊzə(r)/ n Fassung f

compound /ˈkɒmpaʊnd/ adj zusammengesetzt; (fracture) kompliziert ● n (Chemistry) Verbindung f; (Gram) Kompositum nt

comprehen|d /kɒmprɪˈhend/ vt begreifen, verstehen. **~sible** adj, **-bly** adv verständlich. **~sion** n Verständnis nt

comprehensive /kɒmprɪˈhensɪv/ adj & n umfassend; **[school]** Gesamtschule f. **~ insurance** n (Auto) Vollkaskoversicherung f

compress /kəmˈpres/ vt zusammenpressen; **~ed air** Druckluft f

comprise /kəmˈpraɪz/ vt umfassen, bestehen aus

compromise /ˈkɒmprəmaɪz/ n Kompromiss m ● vt kompromittie-

ren (person) ● vi einen Kompromiss schließen

compuls|ion /kəmˈpʌlʃn/ n Zwang m. **~ive** adj zwanghaft. **~ory** adj obligatorisch

comput|e /kəmˈpjuːt/ vb berechnen. **~er** Computer m. **~er game** n Computerspiel. **~erize** vt computerisieren (data); auf Computer umstellen (firm). **~-literate** adj mit Computern vertraut. **~ing** n Computertechnik f

comrade /ˈkɒmreɪd/ n Kamerad m; (Pol) Genosse m/Genossin f

con[1] /kɒn/ see **pro**

con[2] /kɒn/ [I] Schwindel m ● vt (pt/pp **conned**) [I] beschwindeln

concave /ˈkɒŋkeɪv/ adj konkav

conceal /kənˈsiːl/ vt verstecken; (keep secret) verheimlichen

concede /kənˈsiːd/ vt zugeben; (give up) aufgeben

conceit /kənˈsiːt/ n Einbildung f. **~ed** adj eingebildet

conceivable /kənˈsiːvəbl/ adj denkbar

conceive /kənˈsiːv/ vt (child) empfangen; (fig) sich (dat) ausdenken ● vi schwanger werden

concentrat|e /ˈkɒnsəntreɪt/ vt konzentrieren ● vi sich konzentrieren. **~ion** n Konzentration f

concern /kənˈsɜːn/ n Angelegenheit f; (worry) Sorge f; (Comm) Unternehmen nt ● vt (be about, affect) betreffen; (worry) kümmern; **be ~ed about** besorgt sein um; **~ oneself with** sich beschäftigen mit; **as far as I am ~ed** was mich angeht od betrifft. **~ing** prep bezüglich (+ gen)

concert /ˈkɒnsət/ n Konzert nt

concerto /kənˈtʃeətəʊ/ n Konzert nt

concession /kənˈseʃn/ n Zugeständnis *nt;* (*Comm*) Konzession *f;* (*reduction*) Ermäßigung *f*

concise /kənˈsaɪs/ *adj* kurz
conclude /kənˈkluːd/ *vt/i* schließen
conclusion /kənˈkluːʒn/ *n* Schluss *m;* in ∼ abschließend, zum Schluss
conclusive /kənˈkluːsɪv/ *adj* schlüssig
concoct /kənˈkɒkt/ *vt* zusammenstellen; (*fig*) fabrizieren. ∼**ion** *n* Zusammenstellung *f;* (*drink*) Gebräu *nt*
concrete /ˈkɒnkriːt/ *adj* konkret ● *n* Beton *m* ● *vt* betonieren
concurrently /kənˈkʌrəntlɪ/ *adv* gleichzeitig
concussion /kənˈkʌʃn/ *n* Gehirnerschütterung *f*
condemn /kənˈdem/ *vt* verurteilen; (*declare unfit*) für untauglich erklären. ∼**ation** *n* Verurteilung *f*
condensation /kɒndenˈseɪʃn/ *n* Kondensation *f*
condense /kənˈdens/ *vt* zusammenfassen
condescend /kɒndɪˈsend/ *vi* sich herablassen (**to** zu). ∼**ing** *adj* herablassend
condition /kənˈdɪʃn/ *n* Bedingung *f;* (*state*) Zustand *m;* ∼**s** *pl* Verhältnisse *pl;* **on** ∼ **that** unter der Bedingung, dass ● *vt* (*mentally*) konditionieren. ∼**al** *adj* bedingt ● *n* (*Gram*) Konditional *m.* ∼**er** *n* Pflegespülung *f;* (*for fabrics*) Weichspüler *m*
condolences /kənˈdəʊlənsɪz/ *npl* Beileid *nt*
condom /ˈkɒndəm/ *n* Kondom *nt*
condominium /kɒndəˈmɪnɪəm/ *n* (*Amer*) ≈ Eigentumswohnung *f*
conduct[1] /ˈkɒndʌkt/ *n* Verhalten *nt;* (*Sch*) Betragen *nt*
conduct[2] /kənˈdʌkt/ *vt* führen; (*Phys*) leiten; (*Mus*) dirigieren. ∼**or** *n* Dirigent *m;* (*of bus*) Schaffner *m;*

(*Phys*) Leiter *m*
cone /kəʊn/ Kegel *m;* (*Bot*) Zapfen *m;* (*for ice-cream*) [Eis]tüte *f;* (*Auto*) Leitkegel *m*
confectioner /kənˈfekʃənə(r)/ *n* Konditor *m.* ∼**y** *n* Süßwaren *pl*
conference /ˈkɒnfərəns/ *n* Konferenz *f*
confess /kənˈfes/ *vt/i* gestehen; (*Relig*) beichten. ∼**ion** *n* Geständnis *nt;* (*Relig*) Beichte *f*
confetti /kənˈfetɪ/ *n* Konfetti *nt*
confide /kənˈfaɪd/ *vt* anvertrauen ● *vi* ∼ **in s.o.** sich jdm anvertrauen
confidence /ˈkɒnfɪdəns/ *n* (*trust*) Vertrauen *nt;* (*self-assurance*) Selbstvertrauen *nt;* (*secret*) Geheimnis *nt;* **in** ∼ im Vertrauen. ∼ **trick** *n* Schwindel *m*
confident /ˈkɒnfɪdənt/ *adj* zuversichtlich; (*self-assured*) selbstsicher
confidential /kɒnfɪˈdenʃl/ *adj* vertraulich
configuration /kənfɪgəˈreɪʃn/ *n* Anordnung *f,* Konfiguration *f*
confine /kənˈfaɪn/ *vt* beschränken (**to** auf + *acc*). ∼**d** *adj* (*narrow*) eng
confirm /kənˈfɜːm/ *vt* bestätigen; (*Relig*) konfirmieren; (*Roman Catholic*) firmen. ∼**ation** *n* Bestätigung *f,* Konfirmation *f,* Firmung *f*
confiscat|e /ˈkɒnfɪskeɪt/ *vt* beschlagnahmen. ∼**ion** *n* Beschlagnahme *f*
conflict[1] /ˈkɒnflɪkt/ *n* Konflikt *m*
conflict[2] /kənˈflɪkt/ *vi* im Widerspruch stehen (**with** zu). ∼**ing** *adj* widersprüchlich
conform /kənˈfɔːm/ *vi* (*person:*) sich anpassen; (*thing:*) entsprechen (**to** *dat*). ∼**ist** *n* Konformist *m*
confounded /kənˈfaʊndɪd/ *adj* 🄳 verflixt
confront /kənˈfrʌnt/ *vt* konfrontieren. ∼**ation** *n* Konfrontation *f*

confus|e /kənˈfjuːz/ vt verwirren; (*mistake for*) verwechseln (**with** mit). **~ing** adj verwirrend. **~ion** n Verwirrung f; (*muddle*) Durcheinander nt

congenial /kənˈdʒiːnɪəl/ adj angenehm

congest|ed /kənˈdʒestɪd/ adj verstopft; (*with people*) überfüllt. **~ion** n Verstopfung f; Überfüllung f

congratulat|e /kənˈgrætjʊleɪt/ vt gratulieren (+ dat) (**on** zu). **~ions** npl Glückwünsche pl; **~ions!** [ich] gratuliere!

congregation /kɒŋgrɪˈgeɪʃn/ n (*Relig*) Gemeinde f

congress /ˈkɒŋgres/ n Kongress m. **~man** n Kongressabgeordnete(r) m

Congress Die nationale gesetzgebende Versammlung in den Vereinigten Staaten. Der Kongress tritt im ▶CAPITOL zusammen und besteht aus zwei Kammern, dem Senat und dem Repräsentantenhaus. Der Kongress erlässt Gesetze, die von beiden Kammern angenommen und anschließend vom Präsidenten verabschiedet werden.

conical /ˈkɒnɪkl/ adj kegelförmig

conifer /ˈkɒnɪfə(r)/ n Nadelbaum m

conjecture /kənˈdʒektʃə(r)/ n Mutmaßung f

conjunction /kənˈdʒʌŋkʃn/ n Konjunktion f; **in ~ with** zusammen mit

conjur|e /ˈkʌndʒə(r)/ vi zaubern ● vt **~e up** heraufbeschwören. **~or** n Zauberkünstler m

conk /kɒŋk/ vi **~ out** 🗆 (*machine:*) kaputtgehen

conker /ˈkɒŋkə(r)/ n 🗆 Kastanie f

'con-man n 🗆 Schwindler m

connect /kəˈnekt/ vt verbinden (**to** mit); (*Electr*) anschließen (**to** an + acc) ● vi verbinden sein; (*train:*) Anschluss haben (**with** an + acc); **be ~ed with** zu tun haben mit; (*be related to*) verwandt sein mit

connection /kəˈnekʃn/ n Verbindung f; (*Rail, Electr*) Anschluss m; **in ~ with** in Zusammenhang mit. **~s** npl Beziehungen pl

connoisseur /kɒnəˈsɜː(r)/ n Kenner m

conquer /ˈkɒŋkə(r)/ vt erobern; (*fig*) besiegen. **~or** n Eroberer m

conquest /ˈkɒŋkwest/ n Eroberung f

conscience /ˈkɒnʃəns/ n Gewissen nt

conscientious /kɒnʃɪˈenʃəs/ adj gewissenhaft

conscious /ˈkɒnʃəs/ adj bewusst; [**fully**] **~** bei [vollem] Bewusstsein; **be/become ~ of** sich (dat) etw (gen) bewusst sein/werden. **~ness** n Bewusstsein nt

conscript /ˈkɒnskrɪpt/ n Einberufene(r) m

consecrat|e /ˈkɒnsɪkreɪt/ vt weihen; einweihen (*church*). **~ion** n Weihe f; Einweihung f

consecutive /kənˈsekjʊtɪv/ adj aufeinanderfolgend. **-ly** adv fortlaufend

consent /kənˈsent/ n Einwilligung f, Zustimmung f ● vi einwilligen (**to** in + acc), zustimmen (**to** dat)

consequen|ce /ˈkɒnsɪkwəns/ n Folge f. **~t** adj daraus folgend. **~tly** adv folglich

conservation /kɒnsəˈveɪʃn/ n Erhaltung f, Bewahrung f. **~ist** n Umweltschützer m

conservative /kənˈsɜːvətɪv/ adj konservativ; (*estimate:*) vorsichtig.

C~ (Pol) adj konservativ ● n Konservative(r) m/f

conservatory /kən'sɜːvətrɪ/ n Wintergarten m

conserve /kən'sɜːv/ vt erhalten, bewahren; sparen (energy)

consider /kən'sɪdə(r)/ vt erwägen; (think over) sich (dat) überlegen; (take into account) berücksichtigen; (regard as) betrachten als; ~ **doing sth** erwägen, etw zu tun. ~**able** adj, **-ably** adv erheblich

consider|ate /kən'sɪdərət/ adj rücksichtsvoll. ~**ation** n Erwägung f; (thoughtfulness) Rücksicht f; (payment) Entgelt nt; **take into** ~**ation** berücksichtigen. ~**ing** prep wenn man bedenkt (that dass)

consist /kən'sɪst/ vi ~ **of** bestehen aus

consisten|cy /kən'sɪstənsɪ/ n Konsequenz f; (density) Konsistenz f. ~**t** adj konsequent; (unchanging) gleichbleibend. ~**tly** adv konsequent; (constantly) ständig

consolation /kɒnsə'leɪʃn/ n Trost m. ~ **prize** n Trostpreis m

console /kən'səʊl/ vt trösten

consonant /'kɒnsənənt/ n Konsonant m

conspicuous /kən'spɪkjʊəs/ adj auffällig

conspiracy /kən'spɪrəsɪ/ n Verschwörung f

constable /'kʌnstəbl/ n Polizist m

constant /'kɒnstənt/ adj beständig; (continuous) ständig

constipat|ed /'kɒnstɪpeɪtɪd/ adj verstopft. ~**ion** n Verstopfung f

constituency /kən'stɪtjʊənsɪ/ n Wahlkreis m

constitut|e /'kɒnstɪtjuːt/ vt bilden. ~**ion** n (Pol) Verfassung f; (of person) Konstitution f

constraint /kən'streɪnt/ n Zwang

m; (restriction) Beschränkung f; (strained manner) Gezwungenheit f

construct /kən'strʌkt/ vt bauen. ~**ion** n Bau m; (Gram) Konstruktion f; (interpretation) Deutung f; **under** ~**ion** im Bau

consul /'kɒnsl/ n Konsul m. ~**ate** n Konsulat nt

consult /kən'sʌlt/ vt [um Rat] fragen, konsultieren (doctor); nachschlagen in (+ dat) (book). ~**ant** n Berater m; (Med) Chefarzt m. ~**ation** n Beratung f; (Med) Konsultation f

consume /kən'sjuːm/ vt verzehren; (use) verbrauchen. ~**r** n Verbraucher m

consumption /kən'sʌmpʃn/ n Konsum m; (use) Verbrauch m

contact /'kɒntækt/ n Kontakt m; (person) Kontaktperson f ● vt sich in Verbindung setzen mit. ~ **'lenses** npl Kontaktlinsen pl

contagious /kən'teɪdʒəs/ adj direkt übertragbar

contain /kən'teɪn/ vt enthalten; (control) beherrschen. ~**er** n Behälter m; (Comm) Container m

contaminat|e /kən'tæmɪneɪt/ vt verseuchen. ~**ion** n Verseuchung f

contemplat|e /'kɒntəmpleɪt/ vt betrachten; (meditate) nachdenken über (+ acc). ~**ion** n Betrachtung f; Nachdenken n

contemporary /kən'tempərərɪ/ adj zeitgenössisch ● n Zeitgenosse m/ -genossin f

contempt /kən'tempt/ n Verachtung f; **beneath** ~ verabscheuungswürdig. ~**ible** adj verachtenswert. ~**uous** adj verächtlich

content[1] /'kɒntent/ n (also **contents** pl) Inhalt m

content[2] /kən'tent/ adj zufrieden ● n **to one's heart's** ~ nach Her-

zenslust ● *vt* ~ oneself sich begnü-
gen (with mit). ~ed *adj* zufrieden
contentment /kən'tentmənt/ *n*
Zufriedenheit *f*
contest /'kɒntest/ *n* Kampf *m*;
(*competition*) Wettbewerb *m*. ~ant
n Teilnehmer *m*
context /'kɒntekst/ *n* Zusammenhang *m*
continent /'kɒntɪnənt/ *n* Kontinent *m*
continental /kɒntɪ'nentl/ *adj*
Kontinental-. ~ **breakfast** *n* kleines
Frühstück *nt*. ~ **quilt** *n* Daunendecke *f*
continual /kən'tɪnjʊəl/ *adj*
dauernd
continuation /kən'tɪnjʊ'eɪʃn/ *n*
Fortsetzung *f*
continue /kən'tɪnjuː/ *vt* fortset-
zen; ~ **doing** *or* **to do sth** fortfahren, etw zu tun; **to be ~d** Fortsetzung folgt ● *vi* weitergehen; (*doing
sth*) weitermachen; (*speaking*) fortfahren; (*weather:*) anhalten
continuity /kɒntɪ'njuːəti/ *n* Konti-
nuität *f*
continuous /kən'tɪnjʊəs/ *adj* anhaltend, ununterbrochen
contort /kən'tɔːt/ *vt* verzerren.
~ion *n* Verzerrung *f*
contour /'kɒntʊə(r)/ *n* Kontur *f*;
(*line*) Höhenlinie *f*
contracep|tion /kɒntrə'sepʃn/ *n*
Empfängnisverhütung *f*. ~tive *n*
Empfängnisverhütungsmittel *nt*
contract[1] /'kɒntrækt/ *n*
Vertrag *m*
contract[2] /kən'trækt/ *vi* sich zusammenziehen. ~or *n* Unterneh-
mer *m*
contradict /kɒntrə'dɪkt/ *vt* wider-
sprechen (+ *dat*). ~ion *n* Widerspruch *m*. ~ory *adj* widersprüchlich
contralto /kən'træltəʊ/ *n* Alt *m*;

(*singer*) Altistin *f*
contraption /kən'træpʃn/ *n*[🔲] Apparat *m*
contrary[1] /'kɒntrəri/ *adj & adv*
entgegengesetzt; ~ **to** entgegen (+
dat) ● *n* Gegenteil *nt*; **on the** ~ im
Gegenteil
contrast[1] /'kɒntrɑːst/ *n* Kontrast *m*
contrast[2] /kən'trɑːst/ *vt* gegen-
überstellen (with *dat*) ● *vi* einen
Kontrast bilden (with zu). ~ing
adj gegensätzlich; (*colour*) Kontrast-
contribut|e /kən'trɪbjuːt/ *vt/i* bei-
tragen; beisteuern (*money*); (*donate*)
spenden. ● ~ion *n* Beitrag *m*; (*donation*) Spende *f*. ~or *n* Beitragen-
de(r) *m/f*
contrivance /kən'traɪvəns/ *n*
Vorrichtung *f*
control /kən'trəʊl/ *n* Kontrolle *f*;
(*mastery*) Beherrschung *f*; (*Techn*)
Regler *m*; ~s *pl* (*of car, plane*)
Steuerung *f*; **get out of** ~ außer
Kontrolle geraten ● *vt* (*pt/pp* con-
trolled) kontrollieren; (*restrain*)
unter Kontrolle halten; ~ oneself
sich beherrschen
controvers|ial /kɒntrə'vɜːʃl/ *adj*
umstritten. ~y *n* Kontroverse *f*
convalesce /kɒnvə'les/ *vi* sich erholen. ~nce *n* Erholung *f*
convalescent /kɒnvə'lesnt/ *adj*
~ **home** *n* Erholungsheim *nt*
convenience /kən'viːnɪəns/ *n* Bequemlichkeit *f*; [**public**] – öffentliche Toilette *f*; **with all modern** ~s
mit allem Komfort
convenient /kən'viːnɪənt/ *adj*
günstig; **be** ~ **for s.o.** jdm gelegen
sein *od* jdm passen; **if it is** ~ **[for
you]** wenn es Ihnen passt
convent /'kɒnvənt/ *n* [Nonnen]-
kloster *nt*
convention /kən'venʃn/ *n* (*cus-*

tom) Brauch m, Sitte f. **~al** adj konventionell

converge /kən'vɜ:dʒ/ vi zusammenlaufen

conversation /kɒnvə'seɪʃn/ n Gespräch nt; (Sch) Konversation f

conversion /kən'vɜ:ʃn/ n Umbau m; (Relig) Bekehrung f; (calculation) Umrechnung f

convert¹ /'kɒnvɜ:t/ n Bekehrte(r) m/f, Konvertit m

convert² /kən'vɜ:t/ vt bekehren (person); (change) umwandeln (into in + acc); umbauen (building); (calculate) umrechnen; (Techn) umstellen. **~ible** a verwandelbar ● n (Auto) Kabrio[lett] nt

convex /kɒnveks/ adj konvex

convey /kən'veɪ/ vt befördern; vermitteln (idea, message). **~or belt** n Förderband nt

convict¹ /'kɒnvɪkt/ n Sträfling m

convict² /kən'vɪkt/ vt verurteilen (of wegen). **~ion** n Verurteilung f; (belief) Überzeugung f; previous **~ion** Vorstrafe f

convinc|e /kən'vɪns/ vt überzeugen. **~ing** adj überzeugend

convoy /'kɒnvɔɪ/ n Konvoi m

convulse /kən'vʌls/ vt be **~ed** sich krümmen (with vor + dat)

coo /ku:/ vi gurren

cook /kʊk/ n Koch m/ Köchin f ● vt/i kochen; **is it ~ed?** ist es gar? **~ the books** 𝔽 die Bilanz frisieren. **~book** n Kochbuch nt

cooker /'kʊkə(r)/ n [Koch]herd m; (apple) Kochapfel m. **~y** n Kochen nt. **~y book** n Kochbuch nt

cookie /'kʊkɪ/ n (Amer) Keks m

cool /ku:l/ adj (-er, -est) kühl ● n Kühle f ● vt kühlen ● vi abkühlen. **~-box** n Kühlbox f. **~ness** n Kühle f

coop /ku:p/ vt ~ **up** einsperren

co-operat|e /kəʊ'ɒpəreɪt/ vi zusammenarbeiten. **~ion** n Kooperation f

co-operative /kəʊ'ɒpərətɪv/ adj hilfsbereit ● n Genossenschaft f

cop /kɒp/ n 𝔽 Polizist m

cope /kəʊp/ vi 𝔽 zurechtkommen; **~ with** fertig werden mit

copious /'kəʊpɪəs/ adj reichlich

copper¹ /'kɒpə(r)/ n Kupfer nt ● adj kupfern

copper² /'kɒpə(r)/ n 𝔽 Polizist m

copper 'beech n Blutbuche f

coppice /'kɒpɪs/ n, **copse** n Gehölz nt

copy /'kɒpɪ/ n Kopie f; (book) Exemplar nt ● vt (pt/pp **-ied**) kopieren; (imitate) nachahmen; (Sch) abschreiben

copy: ~right n Copyright nt. **~-writer** n Texter m

coral /'kɒrl/ n Koralle f

cord /kɔ:d/ n Schnur f; (fabric) Cordsamt m; **~s** pl Cordhose f

cordial /'kɔ:dɪəl/ adj herzlich ● n Fruchtsirup m

cordon /'kɔ:dn/ n Kordon m ● vt **~ off** absperren

corduroy /'kɔ:dərɔɪ/ n Cordsamt m

core /kɔ:(r)/ n Kern m; (of apple, pear) Kerngehäuse nt

cork /kɔ:k/ n Kork m; (for bottle) Korken m. **~screw** n Korkenzieher m

corn¹ /kɔ:n/ n Korn nt; (Amer: maize) Mais m

corn² n (Med) Hühnerauge nt

corned beef /kɔ:nd'bi:f/ n Cornedbeef nt

corner /'kɔ:nə(r)/ n Ecke f; (bend) Kurve f; (football) Eckball m ● vt (fig) in die Enge treiben; (Comm) monopolisieren (market). **~-stone**

n Eckstein m

cornet /'kɔ:nɪt/ n (Mus) Kornett nt; (for ice-cream) [Eis]tüte f

corn: ~**flour** n, (Amer) ~**starch** n Stärkemehl nt

corny /'kɔ:nɪ/ adj 🔢 abgedroschen

coronation /kʊrə'neɪʃn/ n Krönung f

coroner /'kʊrənə(r)/ n Beamte(r) m, der verdächtige Todesfälle untersucht

corporal /'kɔ:pərəl/ n (Mil) Stabsunteroffizier m

corps /kɔ:(r)/ n (pl **corps** /kɔ:z/) Korps nt

corpse /kɔ:ps/ n Leiche f

correct /kə'rekt/ adj richtig; (proper) korrekt ● vt verbessern; (text, school work) korrigieren. ~**ion** n Verbesserung f; (Typ) Korrektur f

correspond /kʊrɪ'spɒnd/ vi entsprechen (**to** dat); (two things:) sich entsprechen; (write) korrespondieren. ~**ence** n Briefwechsel m; (Comm) Korrespondenz f. ~**ent** n Korrespondent(in) m(f). ~**ing** adj entsprechend

corridor /'kʊrɪdɔ:(r)/ n Gang m; (Pol, Aviat) Korridor m

corro|de /kə'rəʊd/ vt zerfressen ● vi rosten. ~**sion** n Korrosion f

corrugated /'kʊrəgeɪtɪd/ adj gewellt. ~ **iron** n Wellblech nt

corrupt /kə'rʌpt/ adj korrupt ● vt korrumpieren; (spoil) verderben. ~**ion** n Korruption f

corset /'kɔ:sɪt/ n Korsett nt

Corsica /'kɔ:sɪkə/ n Korsika nt

cosh /kɒʃ/ n Totschläger m

cosmetic /kʊz'metɪk/ adj kosmetisch ● n ~**s** pl Kosmetika pl

cosset /'kʊsɪt/ vt verhätscheln

cost /kʊst/ n Kosten pl; ~**s** pl (Jur) Kosten; **at all** ~**s** um jeden Preis

● vt (pt/pp **cost**) kosten; **it** ~ **me £20** es hat mich £20 gekostet ● vt (pt/pp **costed**) ~ **[out]** die Kosten kalkulieren für

costly /'kʊstlɪ/ adj teuer

cost: ~ **of 'living** n Lebenshaltungskosten pl. ~ **price** n Selbstkostenpreis m

costume /'kʊstjuːm/ n Kostüm nt; (national) Tracht f. ~ **jewellery** n Modeschmuck m

cosy /'kəʊzɪ/ adj gemütlich ● n (tea-, egg-) Wärmer m

cot /kʊt/ n Kinderbett nt; (Amer: camp bed) Feldbett nt

cottage /'kʊtɪdʒ/ n Häuschen nt. ~ **'cheese** n Hüttenkäse m

cotton /'kʊtn/ n Baumwolle f; (thread) Nähgarn nt ● adj baumwollen ● vi ~ **on** 🔢 kapieren

cotton 'wool n Watte f

couch /kaʊtʃ/ n Liege f

couchette /kuː'ʃet/ n (Rail) Liegeplatz m

cough /kɒf/ n Husten m ● vi husten. ~ **up** vt/i husten; (🔢: pay) blechen

'cough mixture n Hustensaft m

could /kʊd/, unbetont /kəd/ see can[2]

council /'kaʊnsl/ n Rat m; (Admin) Stadtverwaltung f; (rural) Gemeindeverwaltung f. ~ **house** n ≈ Sozialwohnung f

councillor /'kaʊnsələ(r)/ n Ratsmitglied nt

'council tax n Gemeindesteuer f

count[1] /kaʊnt/ n Graf m

count[2] /kaʊnt/ n Zählung f; **keep** ~ zählen ● vt/i zählen. ~ **on** vt rechnen auf (+ acc)

counter[1] /'kaʊntə(r)/ n (in shop) Ladentisch m; (in bank) Schalter m; (in café) Theke f; (Games)

Spielmarke f

counter² adj Gegen- ● vt/i kontern

counter'act vt entgegenwirken (+ dat)

'counterfeit /-fɪt/ adj gefälscht

'counterfoil n Kontrollabschnitt m

'counterpart n Gegenstück nt

counter-pro'ductive adj be ~ das Gegenteil bewirken

'countersign vt gegenzeichnen

countess /'kaʊntɪs/ n Gräfin f

countless /'kaʊntlɪs/ adj unzählig

country /'kʌntrɪ/ n Land nt; (native land) Heimat f; (countryside) Landschaft f; **in the** ~ auf dem Lande. ~**man** n [fellow] ~**man** Landsmann m. ~**side** n Landschaft f

county /'kaʊntɪ/ n Grafschaft f

coup /kuː/ n (Pol) Staatsstreich m

couple /'kʌpl/ n Paar nt; **a** ~ **of** (two) zwei ● vt verbinden

coupon /'kuːpɒn/ n Kupon m; (voucher) Gutschein m; (entry form) Schein m

courage /'kʌrɪdʒ/ n Mut m. ~**ous** adj mutig

courgettes /kʊə'ʒets/ npl Zucchini pl

courier /'kʊrɪə(r)/ n Bote m; (diplomatic) Kurier m; (for tourists) Reiseleiter(in) m(f)

course /kɔːs/ n (Naut, Sch) Kurs m; (Culin) Gang m; (for golf) Platz m; ~ **of treatment** (Med) Kur f; **of** ~ natürlich, selbstverständlich; **in the** ~ **of** im Lauf[e] (+ gen)

court /kɔːt/ n Hof m; (Sport) Platz m; (Jur) Gericht nt

courteous /'kɜːtɪəs/ adj höflich

courtesy /'kɜːtəsɪ/ n Höflichkeit f

court: ~ **'martial** n (pl ~s mar-

tial) Militärgericht nt. ~**yard** n Hof m

cousin /'kʌzn/ n Vetter m, Cousin m; (female) Kusine f

cove /kəʊv/ n kleine Bucht f

cover /'kʌvə(r)/ n Decke f; (of cushion) Bezug m; (of umbrella) Hülle f; (of typewriter) Haube f; (of book, lid) Deckel m; (of magazine) Umschlag m; (protection) Deckung f, Schutz m; **take** ~ Deckung nehmen; **under separate** ~ mit getrennter Post ● vt bedecken; beziehen (cushion); decken (costs, needs); zurücklegen (distance); berichten über (+ acc) event; (insure) versichern. ~ **up** vt zudecken; (fig) vertuschen

coverage /'kʌvərɪdʒ/ n (Journalism) Berichterstattung f (**of** über + acc)

cover: ~**ing** n Decke f; (for floor) Belag m. ~**-up** n Vertuschung f

cow /kaʊ/ n Kuh f

coward /'kaʊəd/ n Feigling m. ~**ice** n Feigheit f. ~**ly** adj feige

'cowboy n Cowboy m; 🄳 unsolider Handwerker m

cower /'kaʊə(r)/ vi sich [ängstlich] ducken

'cowshed n Kuhstall m

cox /kɒks/ n, **coxswain** n Steuermann m

coy /kɔɪ/ adj (-er, -est) gespielt schüchtern

crab /kræb/ n Krabbe f

crack /kræk/ n Riss m; (in china, glass) Sprung m; (noise) Knall m; (🄳: joke) Witz m; (🄳: attempt) Versuch m ● adj 🄳 erstklassig ● vt knacken (nut, code); einen Sprung machen in (+ acc) (china, glass); 🄳 reißen (joke); 🄳 lösen (problem) ● vi (china, glass:) springen; (whip:) knallen. ~ **down** vi 🄳 durchgreifen

cracked /krækt/ adj gesprungen; (*rib*) angebrochen; (🆒: *crazy*) verrückt

cracker /'krækə(r)/ n (*biscuit*) Kräcker m; (*firework*) Knallkörper m; **[Christmas]** ~ Knallbonbon m. ~**s** adj be ~**s** 🆒 einen Knacks haben

crackle /'krækl/ vi knistern

cradle /'kreɪdl/ n Wiege f

craft n Handwerk nt; (*technique*) Fertigkeit f. ~**sman** n Handwerker m

crafty /'krɑːftɪ/ adj , -ily adv gerissen

crag /kræg/ n Felszacken m

cram /kræm/ v (*pt/pp* crammed) ● vt hineinstopfen (**into** in + acc); vollstopfen (**with** mit) ● vi (*for exams*) pauken

cramp /kræmp/ n Krampf m. ~**ed** adj eng

cranberry /'krænbərɪ/ n (*Culin*) Preiselbeere f

crane /kreɪn/ n Kran m; (*bird*) Kranich m

crank /kræŋk/ n 🆒 Exzentriker m

'crankshaft n Kurbelwelle f

crash /kræʃ/ n (*noise*) Krach m; (*Auto*) Zusammenstoß m; (*Aviat*) Absturz m ● vi krachen (**into** gegen); (*cars:*) zusammenstoßen; (*plane:*) abstürzen ● vt einen Unfall haben mit (*car*)

crash: ~**helmet** n Sturzhelm m. ~**landing** n Bruchlandung f

crate /kreɪt/ n Kiste f

crater /'kreɪtə(r)/ n Krater m

crawl /krɔːl/ n (*Swimming*) Kraul nt; **do the** ~ kraulen; **at a** ~ im Kriechtempo ● vi kriechen; (*baby:*) krabbeln; ~ **with** wimmeln von

crayon /'kreɪən/ n Wachsstift m; (*pencil*) Buntstift m

craze /kreɪz/ n Mode f

crazy /'kreɪzɪ/ adj verrückt; **be** ~ **about** verrückt sein nach

creak /kriːk/ vi knarren

cream /kriːm/ n Sahne f; (*Cosmetic, Med, Culin*) Creme f ● adj (*colour*) cremefarben ● vt (*Culin*) cremig rühren. ~**y** adj sahnig; (*smooth*) cremig

crease /kriːs/ n Falte f; (*unwanted*) Knitterfalte f ● vt falten; (*accidentally*) zerknittern ● vi knittern

creat|e /kriː'eɪt/ vt schaffen. ~**ion** n Schöpfung f. ~**ive** adj schöpferisch. ~**or** n Schöpfer m

creature /'kriːtʃə(r)/ n Geschöpf nt

crèche /kreʃ/ n Kinderkrippe f

credibility /kredə'bɪlətɪ/ n Glaubwürdigkeit f

credible /'kredəbl/ adj glaubwürdig

credit /'kredɪt/ n Kredit m; (*honour*) Ehre f ● vt glauben; ~ **s.o. with sth** (*Comm*) jdm etw gutschreiben; (*fig*) jdm etw zuschreiben. ~**able** adj lobenswert

credit: ~ **card** n Kreditkarte f. ~**or** n Gläubiger m

creep /kriːp/ vi (*pt/pp* crept) schleichen ● n 🆒 fieser Kerl m; **it gives me the** ~**s** es ist mir unheimlich. ~**er** n Kletterpflanze f. ~**y** adj gruselig

cremat|e /krɪ'meɪt/ vt einäschern. ~**ion** n Einäscherung f

crêpe /kreɪp/ n Krepp m. ~ **paper** n Kreppapier nt

crept /krept/ *see* creep

crescent /'kresənt/ n Halbmond m

cress /kres/ n Kresse f

crest /krest/ n Kamm m; (*coat of arms*) Wappen nt

crew /kruː/ n Besatzung f; (*gang*) Bande f. ~ **cut** n Bürstenschnitt m

crib¹ /krɪb/ n Krippe f

crib² vt/i (pt/pp **cribbed**) 🔲 abschreiben

cricket /'krɪkɪt/ n Kricket nt. **~er** n Kricketspieler m

crime /kraɪm/ n Verbrechen nt; (rate) Kriminalität f

criminal /'krɪmɪnl/ adj kriminell, verbrecherisch; (law, court) Straf-● n Verbrecher m

crimson /'krɪmzn/ adj purpurrot

crinkle /'krɪŋkl/ vt/i knittern

cripple /'krɪpl/ n Krüppel m ● vt zum Krüppel machen; (fig) lahmlegen. **~d** adj verkrüppelt

crisis /'kraɪsɪs/ n (pl **-ses** /-si:z/) Krise f

crisp /krɪsp/ adj (-er, -est) knusprig. **~bread** n Knäckebrot nt. **~s** npl Chips pl

criss-cross /'krɪs-/ adj schräg gekreuzt

criterion /kraɪ'tɪərɪən/ n (pl **-ria** /-rɪə/) Kriterium nt

critic /'krɪtɪk/ n Kritiker m. **~al** adj kritisch. **~ally** adv kritisch; **~ally ill** schwer krank

criticism /'krɪtɪsɪzm/ n Kritik f

criticize /'krɪtɪsaɪz/ vt kritisieren

croak /krəʊk/ vi krächzen; (frog:) quaken

crockery /'krɒkərɪ/ n Geschirr nt

crocodile /'krɒkədaɪl/ n Krokodil nt

crocus /'krəʊkəs/ n (pl **-es**) Krokus m

crony /'krəʊnɪ/ n Kumpel m

crook /krʊk/ n (stick) Stab m; (🔲: criminal) Schwindler m, Gauner m

crooked /'krʊkɪd/ adj schief; (bent) krumm; (🔲: dishonest) unehrlich

crop /krɒp/ n Feldfrucht f; (harvest) Ernte f ● v (pt/pp **cropped**) ● vt

stutzen ● vi **~ up** 🔲 zur Sprache kommen; (occur) dazwischenkommen

croquet /'krəʊkeɪ/ n Krocket nt

cross /krɒs/ adj (annoyed) böse (**with** auf + acc); **talk at ~ purposes** aneinander vorbeireden ● n Kreuz nt; (Bot, Zool) Kreuzung f ● vt kreuzen (cheque, animals); überqueren (road); **~ oneself** sich bekreuzigen; **~ one's arms** die Arme verschränken; **~ one's legs** die Beine übereinander schlagen; **keep one's fingers ~ed for s.o.** jdm die Daumen drücken; **it ~ed my mind** es fiel mir ein ● vi (go across) hinübergehen/-fahren; (lines:) sich kreuzen. **~ out** vt durchstreichen

cross: ~-country n (Sport) Crosslauf m. **~'eyed** adj schielend; **be ~-eyed** schielen. **~fire** n Kreuzfeuer nt. **~ing** n Übergang m; (sea journey) Überfahrt f. **~roads** n [Straßen]kreuzung f. **~-'section** n Querschnitt m. **~wise** adv quer. **~word** n **~word [puzzle]** Kreuzworträtsel nt

crotchety /'krɒtʃɪtɪ/ adj griesgrämig

crouch /krautʃ/ vi kauern

crow /krəʊ/ n Krähe f; **as the ~ flies** Luftlinie

crowd /kraud/ n [Menschen]menge f ● vi sich drängen. **~ed** adj [gedrängt] voll

crown /kraun/ n Krone f ● vt krönen; überkronen (tooth)

crucial /'kru:ʃl/ adj höchst wichtig; (decisive) entscheidend (**to** für)

crude /kru:d/ adj (-r, -st) primitiv; (raw) roh

cruel /krʊəl/ adj (crueller, cruellest) grausam (**to** gegen). **~ty** n Grausamkeit f

cruis|e /kru:z/ n Kreuzfahrt f ● vi

359

crumb | current

kreuzen; (car:) fahren. **~er** n (Mil) Kreuzer m; (motor boat) Kajütboot nt

crumb /krʌm/ n Krümel m

crumb|le /'krʌmbl/ vt/i krümeln; (collapse) einstürzen

crumple /'krʌmpl/ vt zerknittern ● vi knittern

crunch /krʌntʃ/ n ⚊ when it comes to the ~ wenn es [wirklich] drauf ankommt ● vt mampfen ● vi knirschen

crusade /kru:'seɪd/ n Kreuzzug m; (fig) Kampagne f. **~r** n Kreuzfahrer m; (fig) Kämpfer m

crush /krʌʃ/ n (crowd) Gedränge nt ● vt zerquetschen; zerknittern (clothes); (fig: subdue) niederschlagen

crust /krʌst/ n Kruste f

crutch /krʌtʃ/ n Krücke f

cry /kraɪ/ n Ruf m; (shout) Schrei m; **a far ~ from** (fig) weit entfernt von ● vi (pt/pp cried) (weep) weinen; (baby:) schreien; (call) rufen

crypt /krɪpt/ n Krypta f. **~ic** adj rätselhaft

crystal /'krɪstl/ n Kristall m; (glass) Kristall m

cub /kʌb/ n (Zool) Junge(s) nt

Cuba /'kju:bə/ n Kuba nt

cubby-hole /'kʌbɪ-/ n Fach nt

cub|e /kju:b/ n Würfel m. **~ic** adj Kubik-

cubicle /'kju:bɪkl/ n Kabine f

cuckoo /'kʊku:/ n Kuckuck m. **~ clock** n Kuckucksuhr f

cucumber /'kju:kʌmbə(r)/ n Gurke f

cuddl|e /'kʌdl/ vt herzen ● vi **~e up to** sich kuscheln an (+ acc). **~y** adj kuschelig

cue¹ /kju:/ n Stichwort nt

cue² n (Billiards) Queue nt

cuff /kʌf/ n Manschette f; (Amer: turn-up) [Hosen]aufschlag m; (blow) Klaps m. **off the ~** ⚊ aus dem Stegreif. **~-link** n Manschettenknopf m

cul-de-sac /'kʌldəsæk/ n Sackgasse f

culinary /'kʌlɪnəri/ adj kulinarisch

culprit /'kʌlprɪt/ n Täter m

cult /kʌlt/ n Kult m

cultivate /'kʌltɪveɪt/ vt anbauen (crop); bebauen (land)

cultural /'kʌltʃərəl/ adj kulturell

culture /'kʌltʃə(r)/ n Kultur f. **~d** adj kultiviert

cumbersome /'kʌmbəsəm/ adj hinderlich; (unwieldy) unhandlich

cunning /'kʌnɪŋ/ adj listig ● n List f

cup /kʌp/ n Tasse f; (prize) Pokal m

cupboard /'kʌbəd/ n Schrank m

Cup 'Final n Pokalendspiel nt

curable /'kjʊərəbl/ adj heilbar

curate /'kjʊərət/ n Vikar m; (Roman Catholic) Kaplan m

curb /kɜ:b/ vt zügeln

curdle /'kɜ:dl/ vi gerinnen

cure /kjʊə(r)/ n [Heil]mittel nt ● vt heilen; (salt) pökeln; (smoke) räuchern; gerben (skin)

curiosity /kjʊərɪ'ɒsɪti/ n Neugier f; (object) Kuriosität f

curious /'kjʊərɪəs/ adj neugierig; (strange) merkwürdig, seltsam

curl /kɜ:l/ n Locke f ● vt locken ● vi sich locken

curly /'kɜ:lɪ/ adj lockig

currant /'kʌrənt/ n (dried) Korinthe f

currency /'kʌrənsi/ n Geläufigkeit f; (money) Währung f. **foreign ~** Devisen pl

current /'kʌrənt/ adj augenblicklich, gegenwärtig; (in general use) geläufig, gebräuchlich ●*n* Strömung *f*; (*Electr*) Strom *m*. ~ **affairs** *or* **events** *npl* Aktuelle(s) *nt*. ~**ly** *adv* zurzeit

curriculum /kə'rɪkjʊləm/ *n* Lehrplan *m*. ~ **vitae** *n* Lebenslauf *m*

curry /'kʌrɪ/ *n* Curry *nt & m*; (*meal*) Currygericht *nt*

curse /kɜːs/ *n* Fluch *m* ●*vt* verfluchen ●*vi* fluchen

cursor /'kɜːsə(r)/ *n* Cursor *m*

cursory /'kɜːsərɪ/ *adj* flüchtig

curt /kɜːt/ *adj* barsch

curtain /'kɜːtn/ *n* Vorhang *m*

curtsy /'kɜːtsɪ/ *n* Knicks *m* ●*vi* (*pt/pp* **-ied**) knicksen

curve /kɜːv/ *n* Kurve *f* ●*vi* einen Bogen machen; ~ **to the right/left** nach rechts/links biegen. ~**d** *adj* gebogen

cushion /'kʊʃn/ *n* Kissen *nt* ●*vt* dämpfen; (*protect*) beschützen

cushy /'kʊʃɪ/ *adj* 🔢 bequem

custard /'kʌstəd/ *n* Vanillesoße *f*

custom /'kʌstəm/ *n* Brauch *m*; (*habit*) Gewohnheit *f*; (*Comm*) Kundschaft *f*. ~**ary** *adj* üblich; (*habitual*) gewohnt. ~**er** *n* Kunde *m*/Kundin *f*

customs /'kʌstəmz/ *npl* Zoll *m*. ~ **officer** *n* Zollbeamte(r) *m*

cut /kʌt/ *n* Schnitt *m*; (*Med*) Schnittwunde *f*; (*reduction*) Kürzung *f*; (*in price*) Senkung *f*; ~ **[of meat]** [Fleisch]stück *nt* ●*vt/i* (*pt/pp* **cut**, *pres p* **cutting**) schneiden; (*mow*) mähen; abheben (*cards*); (*reduce*) kürzen; senken (*price*); ~ **one's finger** sich in den Finger schneiden; ~ **s.o.'s hair** jdm die Haare schneiden; ~ **short** abkürzen. ~ **back** *vt* zurückschneiden; (*fig*) einschränken, kürzen. ~ **down** *vt* fällen; (*fig*) einschränken. ~ **off** *vt* abschneiden; (*disconnect*) abstellen; **be ~ off** (*Teleph*) unterbrochen werden. ~

out *vt* ausschneiden; (*delete*) streichen; **be ~ out for** 🔢 geeignet sein zu. ~ **up** *vt* zerschneiden; (*slice*) aufschneiden

'cut-back *n* Kürzung *f*

cute /kjuːt/ *adj* (**-r, -st**) 🔢 niedlich

cut 'glass *n* Kristall *nt*

cutlery /'kʌtlərɪ/ *n* Besteck *nt*

cutlet /'kʌtlɪt/ *n* Kotelett *nt*

'cut-price *adj* verbilligt

cutting /'kʌtɪŋ/ *adj* (*remark*) bissig ●*n* (*from newspaper*) Ausschnitt *m*; (*of plant*) Ableger *m*

CV *abbr* curriculum vitae

cyberspace /'saɪbəspeɪs/ *n* Cyberspace *m*

cycl|e /'saɪkl/ *n* Zyklus *m*; (*bicycle*) [Fahr]rad *nt* ●*vi* mit dem Rad fahren. ~**ing** *n* Radfahren *nt*. ~**ist** *n* Radfahrer(in) *m(f)*

cylind|er /'sɪlɪndə(r)/ *n* Zylinder *m*. ~**rical** *adj* zylindrisch

cynic /'sɪnɪk/ *n* Zyniker *m*. ~**al** *adj* zynisch. ~**ism** *n* Zynismus *m*

Cyprus /'saɪprəs/ *n* Zypern *nt*

Czech /tʃek/ *adj* tschechisch; ~ **Republic** Tschechische Republik *f* ●*n* Tscheche *m*/ Tschechin *f*

Dd

dab /dæb/ *n* Tupfer *m*; (*of butter*) Klecks *m*

dabble /'dæbl/ *vi* ~ **in sth** (*fig*) sich nebenbei mit etw befassen

dachshund /'dækshʊnd/ *n* Dackel *m*

dad[dy] /'dæd[ɪ]/ *n* 🔢 Vati *m*

daddy-'long-legs *n* [Kohl]-schnake *f*; (*Amer: spider*) Weberknecht m

daffodil /'dæfədɪl/ n Osterglocke f, gelbe Narzisse f

daft /dɑːft/ adj (-er, -est) dumm

dagger /'dægə(r)/ n Dolch m

dahlia /'deɪlɪə/ n Dahlie f

Dáil Éireann Das Repräsentantenhaus, der *Dáil Éireann* (ausgesprochen dɑːl'ern) ist das Unterhaus und gesetzgebende Organ des irischen Parlaments in der Republik Irland. Es setzt sich aus 166 Abgeordneten zusammen, die für fünf Jahre durch allgemeine Wahlen (Verhältniswahlsystem) bestimmt werden. Die Verfassung sorgt dafür, dass ein Abgeordneter je 20- bis 30 000 Einwohner vertritt.

---

daily /'deɪlɪ/ adj & adv täglich

dainty /'deɪntɪ/ adj zierlich

dairy /'deərɪ/ n Molkerei f; (shop) Milchgeschäft nt. ~ **products** pl Milchprodukte pl

daisy /'deɪzɪ/ n Gänseblümchen nt

dam /dæm/ n [Stau]damm m ● vt (pt/pp dammed) eindämmen

damage /'dæmɪdʒ/ n Schaden m (**to** an + dat); **~es** pl (Jur) Schadenersatz m ● vt beschädigen; (fig) beeinträchtigen

damn /dæm/ adj, int & adv Ⓘ verdammt ● n **I don't care** or **give a ~** Ⓘ ich schere mich einen Dreck darum ● vt verdammen. **~ation** n Verdammnis f

damp /dæmp/ adj (-er, -est) feucht ● n Feuchtigkeit f

damp|en /'dæmpn/ vt anfeuchten; (fig) dämpfen. **~ness** n Feuchtigkeit f

dance /dɑːns/ n Tanz m; (function) Tanzveranstaltung f ● vt/i tanzen. ~ **music** n Tanzmusik f

dancer /'dɑːnsə(r)/ n Tänzer(in) m(f)

dandelion /'dændɪlaɪən/ n Löwenzahn m

dandruff /'dændrʌf/ n Schuppen pl

Dane /deɪn/ n Däne m/Dänin f

danger /'deɪndʒə(r)/ n Gefahr f; **in/out of ~** in/außer Gefahr. **~ous** adj gefährlich; **~ously ill** schwer erkrankt

dangle /'dæŋgl/ vi baumeln ● vt baumeln lassen

Danish /'deɪnɪʃ/ adj dänisch. ~ **'pastry** n Hefeteilchen nt

Danube /'dænjuːb/ n Donau f

dare /deə(r)/ vt/i (challenge) herausfordern (**to** zu); ~ **[to] do sth** [es] wagen, etw zu tun. **~devil** n Draufgänger m

daring /'deərɪŋ/ adj verwegen ● n Verwegenheit f

dark /dɑːk/ adj (-er, -est) dunkel; ~ **blue/brown** dunkelblau/ -braun; ~ **horse** (fig) stilles Wasser nt ● n Dunkelheit f; **after ~** nach Einbruch der Dunkelheit; **in the ~** im Dunkeln

dark|en /'dɑːkn/ vt verdunkeln ● vi dunkler werden. **~ness** n Dunkelheit f

'dark-room n Dunkelkammer f

darling /'dɑːlɪŋ/ adj allerliebst ● n Liebling m

darn /dɑːn/ vt stopfen

dart /dɑːt/ n Pfeil m; **~s** sg (game) [Wurf]pfeil m ● vi flitzen

dash /dæʃ/ n (Printing) Gedankenstrich m; **a ~ of milk** ein Schuss Milch ● vi stürzen ● vt schleudern. ~ **off** vi losstürzen ● vt (write quickly) hinwerfen

'dashboard n Armaturenbrett nt

data /'deɪtə/ npl & sg Daten pl. ~ **processing** n Datenverarbeitung f

date¹ /deɪt/ n (*fruit*) Dattel f

date² /deɪt/ n Datum nt; ⓣ Verabredung f; **to ~** bis heute; **out of ~** überholt; (*expired*) ungültig; **be up to ~** auf dem Laufenden sein ● vt/i datieren; (*Amer, fam: go out with*) ausgehen mit

dated /'deɪtɪd/ adj altmodisch

dative /'deɪtɪv/ adj & n (*Gram*) ~ [case] Dativ m

daub /dɔːb/ vt beschmieren (**with** mit); schmieren (*paint*)

daughter /'dɔːtə(r)/ n Tochter f. **~-in-law** n (pl **~s-in-law**) Schwiegertochter f

dawdle /'dɔːdl/ vi trödeln

dawn /dɔːn/ n Morgendämmerung f; **at ~** bei Tagesanbruch ● vi anbrechen; **it ~ed on me** (*fig*) es ging mir auf

day /deɪ/ n Tag m; **~ by ~** Tag für Tag; **~ after ~** Tag um Tag; **these ~s** heutzutage; **in those ~s** zu der Zeit

day: ~-dream n Tagtraum m ● vi [mit offenen Augen] träumen. **~light** n Tageslicht nt. **~time** n **in the ~time** am Tage

daze /deɪz/ n **in a ~** wie benommen. **~d** adj benommen.

dazzle /'dæzl/ vt blenden

dead /ded/ adj tot; (*flower*) verwelkt; (*numb*) taub; **~ body** Leiche f; **~ centre** genau in der Mitte ● adv **~ tired** todmüde; **~ slow** sehr langsam ● n **the ~** pl die Toten; **in the ~ of night** mitten in der Nacht

deaden /'dedn/ vt dämpfen (*sound*); betäuben (*pain*)

dead: ~ 'end n Sackgasse f. **~ 'heat** n totes Rennen nt. **~line** n [letzter] Termin m

deadly /'dedlɪ/ adj tödlich; (ⓣ: *dreary*) sterbenslangweilig

deaf /def/ adj (**-er, -est**) taub; **~ and dumb** taubstumm

deaf|en /'defn/ vt betäuben; (*permanently*) taub machen. **~ening** adj ohrenbetäubend. **~ness** n Taubheit f

deal /diːl/ n (*transaction*) Geschäft nt; **whose ~?** (*Cards*) wer gibt? **a good** or **great ~** eine Menge; **get a raw ~** ⓣ schlecht wegkommen ● v (pt/pp **dealt** /delt/) ● vt (*Cards*) geben; **~ out** austeilen ● vi **~ in** handeln mit; **~ with** zu tun haben mit; (*handle*) sich befassen mit; (*cope with*) fertig werden mit; (*be about*) handeln von; **that's been dealt with** das ist schon erledigt

deal|er /'diːlə(r)/ n Händler m

dean /diːn/ n Dekan m

dear /dɪə(r)/ adj (**-er, -est**) lieb; (*expensive*) teuer; (*in letter*) liebe(r,s); (*formal*) sehr geehrte(r,s) ● n Liebe(r) m/f ● int **oh ~!** oje! **~ly** adv (*love*) sehr; (*pay*) teuer

death /deθ/ n Tod m; **three ~s** drei Todesfälle. **~ certificate** n Sterbeurkunde f

deathly /'deθlɪ/ adj **~ silence** Totenstille f ● adv **~ pale** totenblass

death: ~ penalty n Todesstrafe f. **~-trap** n Todesfalle f

debatable /dɪ'beɪtəbl/ adj strittig

debate /dɪ'beɪt/ n Debatte f ● vt/i debattieren

debauchery /dɪ'bɔːtʃərɪ/ n Ausschweifung f

debit /'debɪt/ n [side] Soll nt ● vt (pt/pp **debited**) belasten; abbuchen (*sum*)

debris /'debriː/ n Trümmer pl

debt /det/ n Schuld f; **in ~** verschuldet. **~ or** n Schuldner m

début /'deɪbuː/ n Debüt nt

decade /'dekeɪd/ n Jahrzehnt nt

decadence /'dekədəns/ n Deka-

363

denz f. ~t adj dekadent

decaffeinated /dɪˈkæfɪneɪtɪd/ adj koffeinfrei

decay /dɪˈkeɪ/ n Verfall m; (rot) Verwesung f; (of tooth) Zahnfäule f • vi verfallen; (rot) verwesen; (tooth:) schlecht werden

deceased /dɪˈsiːsd/ adj verstorben • n the ~d der/die Verstorbene

deceit /dɪˈsiːt/ n Täuschung f. ~ful adj unaufrichtig

deceive /dɪˈsiːv/ vt täuschen; (be unfaithful to) betrügen

December /dɪˈsembə(r)/ n Dezember m

decency /ˈdiːsənsɪ/ n Anstand m

decent /ˈdiːsənt/ adj anständig

decept|ion /dɪˈsepʃn/ n Täuschung f; (fraud) Betrug m. ~ive adj täuschend

decide /dɪˈsaɪd/ vt entscheiden • vi sich entscheiden (on für)

decided /dɪˈsaɪdɪd/ adj entschieden

decimal /ˈdesɪml/ adj Dezimal- • n Dezimalzahl f. ~ '**point** n Komma nt

decipher /dɪˈsaɪfə(r)/ vt entziffern

decision /dɪˈsɪʒn/ n Entscheidung f; (firmness) Entschlossenheit f

decisive /dɪˈsaɪsɪv/ adj ausschlaggebend; (firm) entschlossen

deck[1] /dek/ vt schmücken

deck[2] n (Naut) Deck nt; **on** ~ an Deck; ~ **of cards** (Amer) [Karten]-spiel m. ~**chair** n Liegestuhl m

declaration /dekləˈreɪʃn/ n Erklärung f

declare /dɪˈkleə(r)/ vt erklären; angeben (goods); **anything to** ~? etwas zu verzollen?

decline /dɪˈklaɪn/ n Rückgang m; (in health) Verfall m • vt ablehnen; (Gram) deklinieren • vi ablehnen;

decaffeinated | default

(fall) sinken; (decrease) nachlassen

decommission /diːkəˈmɪʃn/ vt stilllegen; außer Dienst stellen (Schiff)

décor /ˈdeɪkɔː/ n Ausstattung f

decorat|e /ˈdekəreɪt/ vt (adorn) schmücken; verzieren (cake); (paint) streichen; (wallpaper) tapezieren; (award medal to) einen Orden verleihen (+ dat). ~**ion** n Verzierung f; (medal) Orden m; ~**ions** pl Schmuck m. ~**ive** adj dekorativ. ~**or** n painter and ~**or** Maler und Tapezierer m

decoy /ˈdiːkɔɪ/ n Lockvogel m

decrease[1] /ˈdiːkriːs/ n Verringerung f; (in number) Rückgang m

decrease[2] /dɪˈkriːs/ vt verringern; herabsetzen (price) • vi sich verringern; (price:) sinken

decrepit /dɪˈkrepɪt/ adj altersschwach

dedicat|e /ˈdedɪkeɪt/ vt widmen; (Relig) weihen. ~**ed** adj hingebungsvoll; (person) aufopfernd. ~**ion** n Hingabe f; (in book) Widmung f

deduce /dɪˈdjuːs/ vt folgern (from aus)

deduct /dɪˈdʌkt/ vt abziehen

deduction /dɪˈdʌkʃn/ n Abzug m; (conclusion) Folgerung f

deed /diːd/ n Tat f; (Jur) Urkunde f

deep /diːp/ adj (-er, -est) tief; **go off the** ~ **end** 🔲 auf die Palme gehen • adv tief

deepen /ˈdiːpn/ vt vertiefen

deep-'freeze n Gefriertruhe f; (upright) Gefrierschrank m

deer /dɪə(r)/ n inv Hirsch m; (roe) Reh nt

deface /dɪˈfeɪs/ vt beschädigen

default /dɪˈfɔːlt/ n **win by** ~ (Sport) kampflos gewinnen

defeat /dɪˈfiːt/ n Niederlage f; (*defeating*) Besiegung f; (*rejection*) Ablehnung f ● vt besiegen; ablehnen; (*frustrate*) vereiteln

defect /ˈdiːfekt/ n Fehler m; (*Techn*) Defekt m. **~ive** adj fehlerhaft; (*Techn*) defekt

defence /dɪˈfens/ n Verteidigung f. **~less** adj wehrlos

defend /dɪˈfend/ vt verteidigen; (*justify*) rechtfertigen. **~ant** n (*Jur*) Beklagte(r) m/f; (*in criminal court*) Angeklagte(r) m/f

defensive /dɪˈfensɪv/ adj defensiv

defer /dɪˈfɜː(r)/ vt (*pt/pp* deferred) (*postpone*) aufschieben

deferen|ce /ˈdefərəns/ n Ehrerbietung f. **~tial** adj ehrerbietig

defian|ce /dɪˈfaɪəns/ n Trotz m; in **~ce** of zum Trotz (+ *dat*). **~t** adj aufsässig

deficien|cy /dɪˈfɪʃənsɪ/ n Mangel m. **~t** adj mangelhaft

deficit /ˈdefɪsɪt/ n Defizit nt

define /dɪˈfaɪn/ vt bestimmen; definieren (*word*)

definite /ˈdefɪnɪt/ adj bestimmt; (*certain*) sicher

definition /defɪˈnɪʃn/ n Definition f; (*Phot, TV*) Schärfe f

definitive /dɪˈfɪnətɪv/ adj endgültig; (*authoritative*) maßgeblich

deflat|e /dɪˈfleɪt/ vt die Luft auslassen aus. **~ion** n (*Comm*) Deflation f

deflect /dɪˈflekt/ vt ablenken

deform|ed /dɪˈfɔːmd/ adj missgebildet. **~ity** n Missbildung f

defraud /dɪˈfrɔːd/ vt betrügen (*of* um)

defray /dɪˈfreɪ/ vt bestreiten

defrost /diːˈfrɒst/ vt entfrosten; abtauen (*fridge*); auftauen (*food*)

deft /deft/ adj (*-er, -est*) geschickt. **~ness** n Geschicklichkeit f

defuse /diːˈfjuːz/ vt entschärfen

defy /dɪˈfaɪ/ vt (*pt/pp -ied*) trotzen (+ *dat*); widerstehen (+ *dat*) (*attempt*)

degrading /dɪˈɡreɪdɪŋ/ adj entwürdigend

degree /dɪˈɡriː/ n Grad m; (*Univ*) akademischer Grad m; **20 ~s** 20 Grad

de-ice /diːˈaɪs/ vt enteisen

deity /ˈdiːɪtɪ/ n Gottheit f

dejected /dɪˈdʒektɪd/ adj niedergeschlagen

delay /dɪˈleɪ/ n Verzögerung f; (*of train, aircraft*) Verspätung f; **without ~** unverzüglich ● vt aufhalten; (*postpone*) aufschieben ● vi zögern

delegate[1] /ˈdelɪɡət/ n Delegierte(r) m/f

delegat|e[2] /ˈdelɪɡeɪt/ vt delegieren. **~ion** n Delegation f

delete /dɪˈliːt/ vt streichen. **~ion** n Streichung f

deliberate /dɪˈlɪbərət/ adj absichtlich; (*slow*) bedächtig

delicacy /ˈdelɪkəsɪ/ n Feinheit f; Zartheit f; (*food*) Delikatesse f

delicate /ˈdelɪkət/ adj fein; (*fabric, health*) zart; (*situation*) heikel; (*mechanism*) empfindlich

delicatessen /delɪkəˈtesn/ n Delikatessengeschäft nt

delicious /dɪˈlɪʃəs/ adj köstlich

delight /dɪˈlaɪt/ n Freude f ● vt entzücken ● vi **~** in sich erfreuen an (+ *dat*). **~ed** adj hocherfreut; be **~ed** sich sehr freuen. **~ful** adj reizend

delinquent /dɪˈlɪŋkwənt/ adj straffällig ● n Straffällige(r) m/f

deli|rious /dɪˈlɪrɪəs/ adj be **~rious** im Delirium sein. **~rium** n Delirium nt

deliver /dɪˈlɪvə(r)/ vt liefern; zustellen (*post, newspaper*); halten (*speech*); überbringen (*message*); versetzen (*blow*); (*set free*) befreien; **~ a baby** ein Kind zur Welt bringen. **~y** n Lieferung f. (*of post*) Zustellung f; (*Med*) Entbindung f; **cash on ~y** per Nachnahme

delta /'deltə/ n Delta nt

deluge /'deljuːdʒ/ n Flut f; (*heavy rain*) schwerer Guss m

delusion /dɪ'luːʒn/ n Täuschung f

de luxe /də'lʌks/ adj Luxus-

demand /dɪ'mɑːnd/ n Forderung f; (*Comm*) Nachfrage f; **in ~** gefragt; **on ~** auf Verlangen ● vt verlangen, fordern (**of**/**from** von). **~ing** adj anspruchsvoll

demented /dɪ'mentɪd/ adj verrückt

demister /diː'mɪstə(r)/ n (*Auto*) Defroster m

demo /'deməʊ/ n (pl **~s**) 🗓 Demonstration f

democracy /dɪ'mɒkrəsɪ/ n Demokratie f

democrat /'deməkræt/ n Demokrat m. **~ic** adj, **~ally** adv demokratisch

demo|lish /dɪ'mɒlɪʃ/ vt abbrechen; (*destroy*) zerstören. **~lition** n Abbruch m

demon /'diːmən/ n Dämon m

demonstrat|e /'demənstreɪt/ vt beweisen; vorführen (*appliance*) ● vi (*Pol*) demonstrieren. **~ion** n Vorführung f; (*Pol*) Demonstration f

demonstrator /'demənstreɪtə(r)/ n Vorführer m; (*Pol*) Demonstrant m

demoralize /dɪ'mɒrəlaɪz/ vt demoralisieren

demote /dɪ'məʊt/ vt degradieren

demure /dɪ'mjʊə(r)/ adj sittsam

den /den/ n Höhle f; (*room*) Bude f

denial /dɪ'naɪəl/ n Leugnen nt; official **~** Dementi nt

denim /'denɪm/ n Jeansstoff m; **~s** pl Jeans pl

Denmark /'denmɑːk/ n Dänemark nt

denounce /dɪ'naʊns/ vt denunzieren; (*condemn*) verurteilen

dens|e /dens/ adj (-**r**, -**st**) dicht; (🗓 *stupid*) blöd[e]. **~ity** n Dichte f

dent /dent/ n Delle f, Beule f ● vt einbeulen; **~ed** verbeult

dental /'dentl/ adj Zahn-; (*treatment*) zahnärztlich. **~ floss** n Zahnseide f. **~ surgeon** n Zahnarzt m

dentist /'dentɪst/ n Zahnarzt m/-ärztin f. **~ry** n Zahnmedizin f

denture /'dentʃə(r)/ n Zahnprothese f; **~s** pl künstliches Gebiss nt

deny /dɪ'naɪ/ vt (pt/pp -**ied**) leugnen; (*officially*) dementieren; **~ s.o. sth** jdm etw verweigern

deodorant /diː'əʊdərənt/ n Deodorant nt

depart /dɪ'pɑːt/ vi abfahren; (*Aviat*) abfliegen; (*go away*) weggehen/-fahren; (*deviate*) abweichen (**from** von)

department /dɪ'pɑːtmənt/ n Abteilung f; (*Pol*) Ministerium nt. **~ store** n Kaufhaus nt

departure /dɪ'pɑːtʃə(r)/ n Abfahrt f; (*Aviat*) Abflug m; (*from rule*) Abweichung f

depend /dɪ'pend/ vi abhängen (**on** von); (*rely*) sich verlassen (**on** auf + acc); **it all ~s** das kommt darauf an. **~able** adj zuverlässig. **~ant** n Abhängige(r) m/f. **~ence** n Abhängigkeit f. **~ent** adj abhängig (**on** von)

depict /dɪ'pɪkt/ vt darstellen

deplor|able /dɪ'plɔːrəbl/ adj bedauerlich. **~e** vt bedauern

deploy /dɪ'plɔɪ/ vt (*Mil*) einsetzen

depopulate /diːˈpɒpjʊleɪt/ vt entvölkern

deport /dɪˈpɔːt/ vt deportieren, ausweisen. **~ation** n Ausweisung f

depose /dɪˈpəʊz/ vt absetzen

deposit /dɪˈpɒzɪt/ n Anzahlung f; (against damage) Kaution f; (on bottle) Pfand nt; (sediment) Bodensatz m; (Geology) Ablagerung f ● vt (pt/pp **deposited**) legen; (for safety) deponieren; (Geology) ablagern. **~ account** n Sparkonto nt

depot /ˈdepəʊ/ n Depot nt; (Amer: railway station) Bahnhof m

deprave /dɪˈpreɪv/ vt verderben. **~ed** adj verkommen

depreciat|e /dɪˈpriːʃɪeɪt/ vi an Wert verlieren. **~ion** n Wertminderung f; (Comm) Abschreibung f

depress /dɪˈpres/ vt deprimieren; (press down) herunterdrücken. **~ed** adj deprimiert. **~ing** adj deprimierend. **~ion** n Vertiefung f; (Med) Depression f; (weather) Tiefdruckgebiet nt

deprivation /deprɪˈveɪʃn/ n Entbehrung f

deprive /dɪˈpraɪv/ vt **~ s.o. of sth** jdm etw entziehen. **~d** adj benachteiligt

depth /depθ/ n Tiefe f; **in ~** gründlich; **in the ~s of winter** im tiefsten Winter

deputize /ˈdepjʊtaɪz/ vi **~ for** vertreten

deputy /ˈdepjʊti/ n Stellvertreter m ● attrib stellvertretend

derail /dɪˈreɪl/ vt **be ~ed** entgleisen. **~ment** n Entgleisung f

derelict /ˈderəlɪkt/ adj verfallen; (abandoned) verlassen

derisory /dɪˈraɪsəri/ adj höhnisch; (offer) lächerlich

derivation /derɪˈveɪʃn/ n Ableitung f

derivative /dɪˈrɪvətɪv/ adj abgeleitet ● n Ableitung f

derive /dɪˈraɪv/ vt/i (obtain) gewinnen (from aus); **be ~d from** (word:) hergeleitet sein aus

derogatory /dɪˈrɒgətrɪ/ adj abfällig

derv /dɜːv/ n Diesel[kraftstoff] m

descend /dɪˈsend/ vt/i hinunter-/heruntergehen; (vehicle, lift:) hinunter-/herunterfahren; **be ~ed from** abstammen von. **~ant** n Nachkomme m

descent /dɪˈsent/ n Abstieg m; (lineage) Abstammung f

describe /dɪˈskraɪb/ vt beschreiben

descrip|tion /dɪˈskrɪpʃn/ n Beschreibung f; (sort) Art f. **~tive** adj beschreibend; (vivid) anschaulich

desecrate /ˈdesɪkreɪt/ vt entweihen

desert[1] /ˈdezət/ n Wüste f. **~ island** verlassene Insel f

desert[2] /dɪˈzɜːt/ vt verlassen ● vt desertieren. **~ed** adj verlassen. **~er** n (Mil) Deserteur m. **~ion** n Fahnenflucht f

deserv|e /dɪˈzɜːv/ vt verdienen. **~edly** adv verdientermaßen. **~ing** adj verdienstvoll

design /dɪˈzaɪn/ n Entwurf m; (pattern) Muster nt; (construction) Konstruktion f; (aim) Absicht f ● vt entwerfen; (construct) konstruieren; **be ~ed for** bestimmt sein für

designer /dɪˈzaɪnə(r)/ n Designer m; (Techn) Konstrukteur m; (Theat) Bühnenbildner m

desirable /dɪˈzaɪərəbl/ adj wünschenswert; (sexually) begehrenswert

desire /dɪˈzaɪə(r)/ n Wunsch m; (longing) Verlangen nt (for nach); (sexual) Begierde f ● vt [sich (dat)] wünschen; (*sexually*) begehren

desk /desk/ n Schreibtisch m; (*Sch*) Pult nt

desolat|e /'desələt/ adj trostlos. **~ion** n Trostlosigkeit f

despair /dɪ'speə(r)/ n Verzweiflung f; **in ~** verzweifelt ● vi verzweifeln

desperat|e /'despərət/ adj verzweifelt; (*urgent*) dringend; **be ~e for** dringend brauchen. **~ion** n Verzweiflung f

despicable /dɪ'spɪkəbl/ adj verachtenswert

despise /dɪ'spaɪz/ vt verachten

despite /dɪ'spaɪt/ prep trotz (+ gen)

despondent /dɪ'spɒndənt/ adj niedergeschlagen

dessert /dɪ'zɜ:t/ n Dessert nt, Nachtisch m. **~ spoon** n Dessertlöffel m

destination /destɪ'neɪʃn/ n [Reise]ziel nt; (*of goods*) Bestimmungsort m

destiny /'destɪnɪ/ n Schicksal nt

destitute /'destɪtju:t/ adj völlig mittellos

destroy /dɪ'strɔɪ/ vt zerstören; (*totally*) vernichten. **~er** n (*Naut*) Zerstörer m

destruc|tion /dɪ'strʌkʃn/ n Zerstörung f; Vernichtung f. **-tive** adj zerstörerisch; (*fig*) destruktiv

detach /dɪ'tætʃ/ vt abnehmen; (*tear off*) abtrennen. **~able** adj abnehmbar. **~ed** adj **~ed house** Einzelhaus nt

detail /'di:teɪl/ n Einzelheit f, Detail nt; **in ~** ausführlich ● vt einzeln aufführen. **~ed** adj ausführlich

detain /dɪ'teɪn/ vt aufhalten; (*police:*) in Haft behalten; (*take into custody*) in Haft nehmen

detect /dɪ'tekt/ vt entdecken; (*perceive*) wahrnehmen. **~ion** n Ent-

deckung f

detective /dɪ'tektɪv/ n Detektiv m. **~ story** n Detektivroman m

detention /dɪ'tenʃn/ n Haft f; (*Sch*) Nachsitzen nt

deter /dɪ'tɜ:(r)/ vt (pt/pp deterred) abschrecken; (*prevent*) abhalten

detergent /dɪ'tɜ:dʒənt/ n Waschmittel nt

deteriorat|e /dɪ'tɪərɪəreɪt/ vi sich verschlechtern. **~ion** n Verschlechterung f

determination /dɪtɜ:mɪ'neɪʃn/ n Entschlossenheit f

determine /dɪ'tɜ:mɪn/ vt bestimmen. **~d** adj entschlossen

deterrent /dɪ'terənt/ n Abschreckungsmittel nt

detest /dɪ'test/ vt verabscheuen. **~able** adj abscheulich

detonate /'detəneɪt/ vt zünden

detour /'di:tʊə(r)/ n Umweg m

detract /dɪ'trækt/ vi **~ from** beeinträchtigen

detriment /'detrɪmənt/ n **to the ~ (of)** zum Schaden (+ gen). **~al** adj schädlich (**to** dat)

deuce /dju:s/ n (*Tennis*) Einstand m

devaluation /di:væljʊ'eɪʃn/ n Abwertung f

de'value vt abwerten (*currency*)

devastat|e /'devəsteɪt/ vt verwüsten. **~ing** adj verheerend. **~ion** n Verwüstung f

develop /dɪ'veləp/ vt entwickeln; bekommen (*illness*); erschließen (*area*) ● vi sich entwickeln (**into** zu). **~er** n [**property**] **~er** Bodenspekulant m

development /dɪ'veləpmənt/ n Entwicklung f

deviat|e /'di:vɪeɪt/ vi abweichen. **~ion** n Abweichung f

device /dɪ'vaɪs/ n Gerät nt; (*fig*)

Mittel nt

devil /ˈdɛvl/ n Teufel m. ~ish adj teuflisch

devious /ˈdiːvɪəs/ adj verschlagen

devise /dɪˈvaɪz/ vt sich (dat) ausdenken

devot|e /dɪˈvəʊt/ vt widmen (**to** dat). ~**ed** adj ergeben; (care) liebevoll; **be** ~**ed to** s.o. sehr an jdm hängen

devotion /dɪˈvəʊʃn/ n Hingabe f

devour /dɪˈvaʊə(r)/ vt verschlingen

devout /dɪˈvaʊt/ adj fromm

dew /djuː/ n Tau m

dexterity /dɛkˈstɛrətɪ/ n Geschicklichkeit f

diabet|es /daɪəˈbiːtiːz/ n Zuckerkrankheit f. ~**ic** n Diabetiker(in) m(f)

diabolical /daɪəˈbɒlɪkl/ adj teuflisch

diagnose /daɪəgˈnəʊz/ vt diagnostizieren

diagnosis /daɪəgˈnəʊsɪs/ n (pl -oses /-siːz/) Diagnose f

diagonal /daɪˈægənl/ adj diagonal ● n Diagonale f

diagram /ˈdaɪəgræm/ n Diagramm nt

dial /ˈdaɪəl/ n (of clock) Zifferblatt nt; (Techn) Skala f; (Teleph) Wählscheibe f ● vt/i (pt/pp dialled) (Teleph) wählen; ~ **direct** durchwählen

dialect /ˈdaɪəlɛkt/ n Dialekt m

dialling: ~ **code** n Vorwahlnummer f. ~ **tone** n Amtszeichen nt

dialogue /ˈdaɪəlɒg/ n Dialog m

diameter /daɪˈæmɪtə(r)/ n Durchmesser m

diamond /ˈdaɪəmənd/ n Diamant m; (cut) Brillant m; (shape) Raute f; ~**s** pl (Cards) Karo nt

diaper /ˈdaɪəpə(r)/ n (Amer)

Windel f

diarrhoea /daɪəˈrɪə/ n Durchfall m

diary /ˈdaɪərɪ/ n Tagebuch nt; (for appointments) [Termin]kalender m

dice /daɪs/ n inv Würfel m.

dictat|e /dɪkˈteɪt/ vt/i diktieren. ~**ion** n Diktat nt

dictator /dɪkˈteɪtə(r)/ n Diktator m. ~**ial** adj diktatorisch. ~**ship** n Diktatur f

dictionary /ˈdɪkʃənrɪ/ n Wörterbuch nt

did /dɪd/ see **do**

didn't /ˈdɪdnt/ = **did not**

die[1] /daɪ/ n (Techn) Prägestempel m; (metal mould) Gussform f

die[2] /daɪ/ vi (pres p **dying**) sterben (**of** an + dat); (plant, animal:) eingehen; (flower:) verwelken; **be dying to do sth** [T] darauf brennen, etw zu tun; **be dying for sth** [T] sich nach etw sehnen. ~ **down** vi nachlassen; (fire:) herunterbrennen. ~ **out** vi aussterben

diesel /ˈdiːzl/ n Diesel m. ~ **engine** n Dieselmotor m

diet /ˈdaɪət/ n Kost f; (restricted) Diät f; (for slimming) Schlankheitskur f; **be on a** ~ Diät leben; eine Schlankheitskur machen ● vi Diät leben; eine Schlankheitskur machen

differ /ˈdɪfə(r)/ vi sich unterscheiden; (disagree) verschiedener Meinung sein

differen|ce /ˈdɪfrəns/ n Unterschied m; (disagreement) Meinungsverschiedenheit f. ~**t** adj andere(r,s); (various) verschiedene; **be** ~**t** anders sein (**from** als)

differential /dɪfəˈrɛnʃl/ adj Differenzial- ● n Unterschied m; (Techn) Differenzial nt

differentiate /dɪfəˈrɛnʃɪeɪt/ vt/i unterscheiden (**between**

differently | director

zwischen + *dat*)

differently /'dɪfrəntlɪ/ *adv* anders

difficult /'dɪfɪkəlt/ *adj* schwierig, schwer. **~y** *n* Schwierigkeit *f*

diffiden|ce /'dɪfɪdəns/ *n* Zaghaftigkeit *f*. **~t** *adj* zaghaft

dig /dɪg/ *n* (*poke*) Stoß *m*; (*remark*) spitze Bemerkung *f*; (*archaeological*) Ausgrabung *f* ● *vt/i* (*pt/pp* dug, *pres p* digging) graben; umgraben (*garden*). **~ out** *vt* ausgraben. **~ up** *vt* ausgraben; umgraben (*garden*); aufreißen (*street*)

digest /dɪ'dʒest/ *vt* verdauen. **~ible** *adj* verdaulich. **~ion** *n* Verdauung *f*

digit /'dɪdʒɪt/ *n* Ziffer *f*; (*finger*) Finger *m*; (*toe*) Zehe *f*. **~ize** *vt* digitalisieren

digital /'dɪdʒɪtl/ *adj* Digital-; **~ camera** Digitalkamera *f*; **~ television** Digitalfernsehen *nt*

dignified /'dɪgnɪfaɪd/ *adj* würdevoll

dignity /'dɪgnɪtɪ/ *n* Würde *f*

dilapidated /dɪ'læpɪdeɪtɪd/ *adj* baufällig

dilatory /'dɪlətərɪ/ *adj* langsam

dilemma /dɪ'lemə/ *n* Dilemma *nt*

dilettante /dɪlɪ'tæntɪ/ *n* Dilettant(in) *m(f)*

dilute /daɪ'luːt/ *vt* verdünnen

dim /dɪm/ *adj* (dimmer, dimmest). **-ly** *adv* (*weak*) schwach; (*dark*) trüb[e]; (*indistinct*) undeutlich; (🄸: *stupid*) dumm, 🄸 doof ● *vt* (*pt/pp* dimmed) *vt* dämpfen

dime /daɪm/ *n* (*Amer*) Zehncentstück *nt*

dimension /daɪ'menʃn/ *n* Dimension *f*; **~s** *pl* Maße *pl*

diminutive /dɪ'mɪnjʊtɪv/ *adj* winzig ● *n* Verkleinerungsform *f*

dimple /'dɪmpl/ *n* Grübchen *nt*

din /dɪn/ *n* Krach *m*, Getöse *nt*

dine /daɪn/ *vi* speisen. **~r** *n* Speisende(r) *m/f*; (*Amer: restaurant*) Esslokal *nt*

dinghy /'dɪŋgɪ/ *n* Dinghi *nt*; (*inflatable*) Schlauchboot *nt*

dingy /'dɪndʒɪ/ *adj* trübe

dining /'daɪnɪŋ/: **~-car** *n* Speisewagen *m*. **~-room** *n* Esszimmer *nt*. **~-table** *n* Esstisch *m*

dinner /'dɪnə(r)/ *n* Abendessen *nt*; (*at midday*) Mittagessen *nt*; (*formal*) Essen *nt*. **~-jacket** *n* Smoking *m*

dinosaur /'daɪnəsɔː(r)/ *n* Dinosaurier *m*

diocese /'daɪəsɪs/ *n* Diözese *f*

dip /dɪp/ *n* (*in ground*) Senke *f*; (*Culin*) Dip *m* ● *v* (*pt/pp* dipped) *vt* [ein]tauchen; **~ one's headlights** (*Auto*) [die Scheinwerfer] abblenden ● *vi* sich senken

diploma /dɪ'pləʊmə/ *n* Diplom *nt*

diplomacy /dɪ'pləʊməsɪ/ *n* Diplomatie *f*

diplomat /'dɪpləmæt/ *n* Diplomat *m*. **~ic** *adj*, **-ally** *adv* diplomatisch

'dip-stick *n* (*Auto*) Ölmessstab *m*

dire /daɪə(r)/ *adj* (-r, -st) bitter; (*consequences*) furchtbar

direct /dɪ'rekt/ *adj & adv* direkt ● *vt* (*aim*) richten (**at** auf / (*fig*) an + *acc*); (*control*) leiten; (*order*) anweisen; **~ a film/play** bei einem Film/Theaterstück Regie führen

direction /dɪ'rekʃn/ *n* Richtung *f*; (*control*) Leitung *f*; (*of play, film*) Regie *f*; **~s** *pl* Anweisungen *pl*; **~s for use** Gebrauchsanweisung *f*

directly /dɪ'rektlɪ/ *adv* direkt; (*at once*) sofort

director /dɪ'rektə(r)/ *n* (*Comm*) Direktor *m*; (*of play, film*) Regisseur *m*, Regisseurin *f*

directory /dɪˈrektərɪ/ *n* Verzeichnis *nt*; (*Teleph*) Telefonbuch *nt*

dirt /dɜːt/ *n* Schmutz *m*; (*soil*) Erde *f*; **~ cheap** 🔲 spottbillig

dirty /ˈdɜːtɪ/ *adj* schmutzig

dis|a'bility /dɪs-/ *n* Behinderung *f*. **~abled** /adj* [körper]behindert

disad'vantage *n* Nachteil *m*; **at a ~** im Nachteil. **~d** *adj* benachteiligt

disa'gree *vi* nicht übereinstimmen (with mit); **I ~** ich bin anderer Meinung; **oysters ~ with me** Austern bekommen mir nicht

disa'greeable *adj* unangenehm

disa'greement *n* Meinungsverschiedenheit *f*

disap'pear *vi* verschwinden. **~ance** *n* Verschwinden *nt*

disap'point *vt* enttäuschen. **~ment** *n* Enttäuschung *f*

disap'proval *n* Missbilligung *f*

disap'prove *vi* dagegen sein; **~ of** missbilligen

dis'arm *vt* entwaffnen ● *vi* (*Mil*) abrüsten. **~ament** *n* Abrüstung *f*. **~ing** *adj* entwaffnend

disast|er /dɪˈzɑːstə(r)/ *n* Katastrophe *f*; (*accident*) Unglück *nt*. **~rous** *adj* katastrophal

disbe'lief *n* Ungläubigkeit *f*; **in ~** ungläubig

disc /dɪsk/ *n* Scheibe *f*; (*record*) [Schall]platte *f*; (*CD*) CD *f*

discard /dɪˈskɑːd/ *vt* ablegen; (*throw away*) wegwerfen

discerning /dɪˈsɜːnɪŋ/ *adj* anspruchsvoll

'discharge[1] *n* Ausstoßen *nt*; (*Naut, Electr*) Entladung *f*; (*dismissal*) Entlassung *f*; (*Jur*) Freispruch *m*; (*Med*) Ausfluss *m*

dis'charge[2] *vt* ausstoßen; (*Naut,*

Electr) entladen; (*dismiss*) entlassen; (*Jur*) freisprechen (*accused*)

disciplinary /ˈdɪsɪplɪnərɪ/ *adj* disziplinarisch

discipline /ˈdɪsɪplɪn/ *n* Disziplin *f* ● *vt* Disziplin beibringen (+ *dat*); (*punish*) bestrafen

'disc jockey *n* Diskjockey *m*

dis'claim *vt* abstreiten. **~er** *n* Verzichterklärung *f*

dis'clos|e *vt* enthüllen. **~ure** *n* Enthüllung *f*

disco /ˈdɪskəʊ/ *n* 🔲 Disko *f*

dis'colour *vt* verfärben ● *vi* sich verfärben

dis'comfort *n* Beschwerden *pl*; (*fig*) Unbehagen *nt*

discon'nect *vt* trennen; (*Electr*) ausschalten; (*cut supply*) abstellen

discon'tent *n* Unzufriedenheit *f*. **~ed** *adj* unzufrieden

discon'tinue *vt* einstellen; (*Comm*) nicht mehr herstellen

'discord *n* Zwietracht *f*; (*Mus & fig*) Missklang *m*

discothèque /ˈdɪskətek/ *n* Diskothek *f*

'discount *n* Rabatt *m*

dis'courage *vt* entmutigen; (*dissuade*) abraten (+ *dat*)

dis'courteous *adj* unhöflich

discover /dɪˈskʌvə(r)/ *vt* entdecken. **~y** *n* Entdeckung *f*

discreet /dɪˈskriːt/ *adj* diskret

discretion /dɪˈskreʃn/ *n* Diskretion *f*; (*judgement*) Ermessen *nt*

discriminat|e /dɪˈskrɪmɪneɪt/ *vi* unterscheiden (**between** zwischen + *dat*); **~e against** diskriminieren. **~ing** *adj* anspruchsvoll. **~ion** *n* Diskriminierung *f*

discus /ˈdɪskəs/ *n* Diskus *m*

discuss /dɪˈskʌs/ *vt* besprechen; (*examine critically*) diskutieren.

~**ion** n Besprechung f; Diskussion f

disdain /dɪsˈdeɪn/ n Verachtung f

disease /dɪˈziːz/ n Krankheit f

disem'bark vi an Land gehen

disen'chant vt ernüchtern

disen'gage vt losmachen

disen'tangle vt entwirren

dis'figure vt entstellen

dis'grace n Schande f; **in ~** in Ungnade ● vt Schande machen (+ dat). **~ful** adj schändlich

disgruntled /dɪsˈgrʌntld/ adj verstimmt

disguise /dɪsˈgaɪz/ n Verkleidung f; **in ~** verkleidet ● vt verkleiden; verstellen (voice)

disgust /dɪsˈgʌst/ n Ekel m; **in ~** empört ● vt anekeln; (appal) empören. **~ing** adj eklig; (appalling) abscheulich

dish /dɪʃ/ n Schüssel f; (shallow) Schale f; (small) Schälchen nt; (food) Gericht nt. **~ out** vt austeilen. **~ up** vt auftragen

'dishcloth n Spültuch nt

dis'hearten vt entmutigen

dis'honest adj **-ly** adv unehrlich. **~y** n Unehrlichkeit f

dis'honour n Schande f. **~able** adj, **-bly** adv unehrenhaft

'dishwasher n Geschirrspülmaschine f

disil'lusion vt ernüchtern. **~ment** n Ernüchterung f

disin'fect vt desinfizieren. **~ant** n Desinfektionsmittel nt

disin'herit vt enterben

dis'integrate vi zerfallen

dis'jointed adj unzusammenhängend

disk /dɪsk/ n = disc

dis'like n Abneigung f ● vt nicht mögen

dislocate /ˈdɪsləkeɪt/ vt ausrenken

dis'lodge vt entfernen

dis'loyal adj illoyal. **~ty** n Illoyalität f

dismal /ˈdɪzməl/ adj trüb[e]; (person) trübselig

dismantle /dɪsˈmæntl/ vt auseinander nehmen; (take down) abbauen

dis'may n Bestürzung f. **~ed** adj bestürzt

dis'miss vt entlassen; (reject) zurückweisen. **~al** n Entlassung f; Zurückweisung f

diso'bedien|ce n Ungehorsam m. **~t** adj ungehorsam

diso'bey vt/i nicht gehorchen (+ dat); nicht befolgen (rule)

dis'order n Unordnung f; (Med) Störung f. **~ly** adj unordentlich

dis'organized adj unorganisiert

dis'own vt verleugnen

disparaging /dɪsˈpærɪdʒɪŋ/ adj abschätzig

dispassionate /dɪsˈpæʃənət/ adj gelassen; (impartial) unparteiisch

dispatch /dɪsˈpætʃ/ n (Comm) Versand m; (Mil) Nachricht f; (report) Bericht m ● vt [ab]senden; (kill) töten

dispel /dɪsˈpel/ vt (pt/pp dispelled) vertreiben

dispensary /dɪsˈpensərɪ/ n Apotheke f

dispense /dɪsˈpens/ vt austeilen. **~ with** verzichten auf (+ acc). **~r** n (device) Automat m

disperse /dɪsˈpɜːs/ vt zerstreuen ● vi sich zerstreuen

dispirited /dɪsˈpɪrɪtɪd/ adj entmutigt

display /dɪsˈpleɪ/ n Ausstellung f; (Comm) Auslage f; (performance) Vorführung f ● vt zeigen; ausstellen (goods)

dis'please vt missfallen (+ dat)

dis'pleasure n Missfallen nt

disposable /dɪ'spəʊzəbl/ adj
Wegwerf-; (income) verfügbar

disposal /dɪ'spəʊzl/ n Beseitigung
f; **be at s.o.'s ~** jdm zur Verfügung
stehen

dispose /dɪ'spəʊz/ vi **~ of** beseitigen; (deal with) erledigen

disposition /dɪspə'zɪʃn/ n Veranlagung f; (nature) Wesensart f

disproportionate /dɪsprə'pɔː-
ʃənət/ adj unverhältnismäßig

dis'prove vt widerlegen

dispute /dɪ'spjuːt/ n Disput m;
(quarrel) Streit m ● vt bestreiten

disqualifi'cation n Disqualifikation f

dis'qualify vt disqualifizieren; **~
s.o. from driving** jdm den Führerschein entziehen

disre'gard vt nicht beachten

disre'pair n **fall into ~** verfallen

dis'reputable adj verrufen

disre'pute n Verruf m

disre'spect n Respektlosigkeit f.
~ful adj respektlos

disrupt /dɪs'rʌpt/ vt stören. **~ion**
n Störung f

dissatis'faction n Unzufriedenheit f

dis'satisfied adj unzufrieden

dissect /dɪ'sekt/ vt zergliedern;
(Med) sezieren. **~ion** n Zergliederung f; (Med) Sektion f

dissent /dɪ'sent/ n Nichtübereinstimmung f ● vi nicht übereinstimmen

dissident /'dɪsɪdənt/ n Dissident m

dis'similar adj unähnlich (to dat)

dissociate /dɪ'səʊʃɪeɪt/ vt **~ oneself** sich distanzieren (from von)

dissolute /'dɪsəluːt/ adj zügellos;

(life) ausschweifend

dissolve /dɪ'zɒlv/ vt auflösen ● vi
sich auflösen

dissuade /dɪ'sweɪd/ vt abbringen
(from von)

distance /'dɪstəns/ n Entfernung f;
long/short ~ lange/kurze Strecke f;
in the/from a ~ in/aus der Ferne

distant /'dɪstənt/ adj fern; (aloof)
kühl; (relative) entfernt

dis'tasteful adj unangenehm

distil /dɪ'stɪl/ vt (pt/pp distilled)
brennen; (Chemistry) destillieren.
~lery n Brennerei f

distinct /dɪ'stɪŋkt/ adj deutlich;
(different) verschieden. **~ion** n Unterschied m; (Sch) Auszeichnung f.
~ive adj kennzeichnend; (unmistak-
able) unverwechselbar. **~ly** adv
deutlich

distinguish /dɪ'stɪŋgwɪʃ/ vt/i unterscheiden; (make out) erkennen;
~ oneself sich auszeichnen. **~ed**
adj angesehen; (appearance) distinguiert

distort /dɪ'stɔːt/ vt verzerren; (fig)
verdrehen. **~ion** n Verzerrung f;
(fig) Verdrehung f

distract /dɪ'strækt/ vt ablenken.
~ion n Ablenkung f; (despair) Verzweiflung f

distraught /dɪ'strɔːt/ adj [völlig]
aufgelöst

distress /dɪ'stres/ n Kummer m;
(pain) Schmerz m; (poverty, danger)
Not f ● vt Kummer/Schmerz bereiten (+ dat); (sadden) bekümmern;
(shock) erschüttern. **~ing** adj
schmerzlich; (shocking) erschütternd

distribut|e /dɪ'strɪbjuːt/ vt verteilen; (Comm) vertreiben. **~ion** n
Verteilung f; Vertrieb m. **~or** n Verteiler m

district /'dɪstrɪkt/ n Gegend f;
(Admin) Bezirk m

dis'trust n Misstrauen nt ● vt misstrauen (+ dat). **~ful** adj misstrauisch

disturb /dɪ'stɜ:b/ vt stören; (perturb) beunruhigen; (touch) anrühren. **~ance** n Unruhe f; (interruption) Störung f. **~ed** adj beunruhigt; [mentally] **~ed** geistig gestört. **~ing** adj beunruhigend

dis'used adj stillgelegt; (empty) leer

ditch /dɪtʃ/ n Graben m ● vt (⊞: abandon) fallen lassen (plan)

dither /'dɪðə(r)/ vi zaudern

ditto /'dɪtəʊ/ n dito; (⊞) ebenfalls

dive /daɪv/ n [Kopf]sprung m; (Aviat) Sturzflug m; (⊞: place) Spelunke f ● vi einen Kopfsprung machen; (when in water) tauchen; (Aviat) einen Sturzflug machen; (⊞: rush) stürzen

diver /'daɪvə(r)/ n Taucher m; (Sport) [Kunst]springer m

diverse /daɪ'vɜ:s/ adj verschieden

diversify /daɪ'vɜ:sɪfaɪ/ vt/i (pt/pp -ied) variieren (Comm) diversifizieren

diversion /daɪ'vɜ:ʃn/ n Umleitung f; (distraction) Ablenkung f

diversity /daɪ'vɜ:sətɪ/ n Vielfalt f

divert /daɪ'vɜ:t/ vt umleiten; ablenken (attention); (entertain) unterhalten

divide /dɪ'vaɪd/ vt teilen; (separate) trennen; (Math) dividieren (by durch) ● vi sich teilen

dividend /'dɪvɪdend/ n Dividende f

divine /dɪ'vaɪn/ adj göttlich

diving /'daɪvɪŋ/ n (Sport) Kunstspringen nt. **~-board** n Sprungbrett nt

divinity /dɪ'vɪnətɪ/ n Göttlichkeit f; (subject) Theologie f

division /dɪ'vɪʒn/ n Teilung f; (sep-

aration) Trennung f; (Math, Mil) Division f; (Parl) Hammelsprung m; (line) Trennlinie f; (group) Abteilung f

divorce /dɪ'vɔ:s/ n Scheidung f ● vt sich scheiden lassen von. **~d** adj geschieden; **get ~d** sich scheiden lassen

DIY abbr do-it-yourself

dizziness /'dɪzɪnəs/ n Schwindel m

dizzy /'dɪzɪ/ adj schwindlig; **I feel ~** mir ist schwindlig

do /du:/, unbetont /də/

3 sg pres tense **does**; pt **did**; pp **done**

● transitive verb

••••▸ (perform) machen (homework, favour, exam, handstand etc); tun (duty, favour, something, nothing); vorführen (trick, dance); durchführen (test). **what are you doing?** was tust od machst du? **what can I do for you?** was kann ich für Sie tun? **do something!** tu doch etwas! **have you nothing better to do?** hast du nichts Besseres zu tun? **do the washing-up** /**cleaning** abwaschen/sauber machen

••••▸ (as job) **what does your father do?** was macht dein Vater?; was ist dein Vater von Beruf?

••••▸ (clean) putzen; (arrange) [zu-recht]machen (hair)

••••▸ (cook) kochen; (roast, fry) braten. **well done** (meat) durch[gebraten]. **the potatoes aren't done yet** die Kartoffeln sind noch nicht richtig durch

••••▸ (solve) lösen (problem, riddle); machen (puzzle)

····▶ (□: *swindle*) reinlegen. **do s.o. out of sth** jdn um etw bringen

● *intransitive verb*

····▶ (*with as or adverb*) es tun; es machen. **do as they do** mach es wie sie. **he can do as he likes** er kann tun od machen, was er will. **you did well** du hast es gut gemacht

····▶ (*get on*) vorankommen; (*in exams*) abschneiden. **do well/ badly at school** gut/schlecht in der Schule sein. **how are you doing?** wie geht's dir? **how do you do?** (*formal*) guten Tag!

····▶ **will do** (*serve purpose*) es tun; (*suffice*) [aus]reichen; (*be suitable*) gehen. **that won't do** das geht nicht. **that will do!** jetzt aber genug!

● *auxiliary verb*

····▶ (*in questions*) **do you know him?** kennst du ihn? **what does he want?** was will er?

····▶ (*in negation*) **I don't** od **do not wish to take part** ich will nicht teilnehmen. **don't be so noisy!** seid [doch] nicht so laut!

····▶ (*as verb substitute*) **you mustn't act as he does** du darfst nicht so wie er handeln. **come in, do!** komm doch herein!

····▶ (*in tag questions*) **don't you, doesn't he** *etc.* nicht wahr. **you went to Paris, didn't you?** du warst in Paris, nicht wahr?

····▶ (*in short questions*) **Does he live in London? — Yes, he does** Wohnt er in London? — Ja, stimmt

····▶ (*for special emphasis*) **I do love Greece** Griechenland gefällt mir wirklich gut

····▶ (*for inversion*) **little did he know that …** er hatte keine Ahnung, dass …

● *noun*

pl **do's** *or* **dos** /duːz/

····▶ (□: *celebration*) Feier *f*

● *phrasal verbs*

● **do away with** *vt* abschaffen. ● **do for** *vt* □: do for s.o. jdn fertig machen □; **be done for** erledigt sein. ● **do in** *vt* (*sl: kill*) kaltmachen 🗵. ● **do up** *vt* (*fasten*) zumachen; binden (*shoe-lace, bow-tie*); (*wrap*) einpacken; (*renovate*) renovieren.

● **do with** *vt*: **I could do with … ich** brauche … ● **do without** *vt*: **do without sth** auf etw (*acc*) verzichten; *vi* darauf verzichten

docile /ˈdəʊsaɪl/ *adj* fügsam

dock¹ /dɒk/ *n* (*Jur*) Anklagebank *f*

dock² *n* Dock *nt* ● *vi* anlegen. **~er** *n* Hafenarbeiter *m*. **~yard** *n* Werft *f*

doctor /ˈdɒktə(r)/ *n* Arzt *m*/ Ärztin *f*; (*Univ*) Doktor *m* ● *vt* kastrieren; (*spay*) sterilisieren

doctrine /ˈdɒktrɪn/ *n* Lehre *f*

document /ˈdɒkjʊmənt/ *n* Dokument. *nt*. **~ary** *adj* Dokumentar- ● *n* Dokumentarbericht *m*; (*film*) Dokumentarfilm *m*

dodge /dɒdʒ/ *n* □ Trick *m*, Kniff *m* ● *vt/i* ausweichen (+ *dat*)

dodgy /ˈdɒdʒɪ/ *adj* □ (*awkward*) knifflig; (*dubious*) zweifelhaft

doe /dəʊ/ *n* Ricke *f*; (*rabbit*) [Kaninchen]weibchen *nt*

does /dʌz/ *see* **do**

doesn't /ˈdʌznt/ = **does not**

dog /dɒg/ *n* Hund *m*

dog: **~-biscuit** *n* Hundekuchen *m*.

~-**collar** n Hundehalsband nt; (Relig, ⚐) Kragen m eines Geistlichen. ~-**eared** adj be ~-eared Eselsohren haben

dogged /'dɒɡɪd/ adj beharrlich

dogma /'dɒɡmə/ n Dogma nt. ~**tic** adj dogmatisch

do-it-yourself /'du:ɪtjə'self/ n Heimwerken nt. ~ **shop** n Heimwerkerladen m

doldrums /'dɒldrəmz/ npl be in the ~ niedergeschlagen sein; (business:) daniederliegen

dole /dəʊl/ n ⚐ Stempelgeld nt; be on the ~ arbeitslos sein ● vt ~ out austeilen

doll /dɒl/ n Puppe f ● vt ⚐ ~ one-self up sich herausputzen

dollar /'dɒlə(r)/ n Dollar m

dolphin /'dɒlfɪn/ n Delphin m

domain /də'meɪn/ n Gebiet nt

dome /dəʊm/ n Kuppel m

domestic /də'mestɪk/ adj häuslich; (Pol) Innen-; (Comm) Binnen-. ~ **animal** n Haustier nt. ~ **flight** n Inlandflug m

domestic flight n Inlandflug m

dominant /'dɒmɪnənt/ adj vorherrschend

dominat|e /'dɒmɪneɪt/ vt beherrschen ● vi dominieren. ~**ion** n Vorherrschaft f

domineering /dɒmɪ'nɪə(r)ɪŋ/ adj herrschsüchtig

domino /'dɒmɪnəʊ/ n (pl -es) Dominostein m; ~**es** sg (game) Domino nt

donat|e /dəʊ'neɪt/ vt spenden. ~**ion** n Spende f

done /dʌn/ see **do**

donkey /'dɒŋkɪ/ n Esel m; ~**'s years** ⚐ eine Ewigkeit. ~-**work** n Routinearbeit f

donor /'dəʊnə(r)/ n Spender m,

Spenderin f

don't /dəʊnt/ = **do not**

doom /du:m/ n Schicksal nt; (ruin) Verhängnis nt

door /dɔ:(r)/ n Tür f; out of ~s im Freien

door: ~**man** n Portier m. ~**mat** n [Fuß]abtreter m. ~**step** n Türschwelle f; on the ~**step** vor der Tür. ~**way** n Türöffnung f

dope /dəʊp/ n ⚐ Drogen pl; (⚐: information) Informationen pl; (⚐: idiot) Trottel m ● vt betäuben; (Sport) dopen

dormant /'dɔ:mənt/ adj ruhend

dormitory /'dɔ:mɪtərɪ/ n Schlafsaal m

dormouse /'dɔ:-/ n Haselmaus f

dosage /'dəʊsɪdʒ/ n Dosierung f

dose /dəʊs/ n Dosis f

dot /dɒt/ n Punkt m; on the ~ pünktlich

dote /dəʊt/ vi ~ **on** vernarrt sein in (+ acc)

dotted /'dɒtɪd/ adj ~ **line** punktierte Linie f; be ~ **with** bestreut sein mit

dotty /'dɒtɪ/ adj ⚐ verdreht

double /'dʌbl/ adj & adv doppelt; (bed, chin) Doppel-; (flower) gefüllt ● n das Doppelte; (person) Doppelgänger m; ~**s** pl (Tennis) Doppel nt; ● vt verdoppeln; (fold) falten ● vi sich verdoppeln. ~ **up** vi sich krümmen (with vor + dat)

double: ~'**bass** n Kontrabass m. ~-**breasted** adj zweireihig. ~-**click** vt/i doppelklicken (on auf). ~-'**cross** vt ein Doppelspiel treiben mit. ~-'**decker** n Doppeldecker m. ~ '**glazing** n Doppelverglasung f. ~ '**room** n Doppelzimmer nt

doubly /'dʌblɪ/ adv doppelt

doubt /daʊt/ n Zweifel m ● vt bezweifeln. ~**ful** adj zweifelhaft; (dis-

believing) skeptisch. **~less** *adv* zweifellos

dough /dəʊ/ *n* (fester) Teig *m*; (Ⅱ: *money*) Pinke *f*. **~nut** *n* Berliner [Pfannkuchen] *m*

dove /dʌv/ *n* Taube *f*

dowdy /'daʊdɪ/ *adj* unschick

down[1] /daʊn/ *n* (*feathers*) Daunen *pl*

down[2] *adv* unten; (*with movement*) nach unten; **go ~** hinuntergehen; **come ~** herunterkommen; **~ there** *a* da unten; **£50 ~ £50** Anzahlung; **~!** (*to dog*) Platz! **~ with ...!** nieder mit ...! ● *prep* **~ the road/stairs** die Straße/Treppe hinunter; **~ the river** den Fluss abwärts **● vt** ⅡⅡ (*drink*) runterkippen; **~ tools** die Arbeit niederlegen

down: **~cast** *adj* niedergeschlagen. **~fall** *n* Sturz *m*; (*ruin*) Ruin *m*. **~-'hearted** *adj* entmutigt. **~'hill** *adv* bergab. **~load** *vt* herunterladen. **~ payment** *n* Anzahlung *f*. **~pour** *n* Platzregen *m*. **~right** *adj & adv* ausgesprochen. **~size** *vt* verschlanken ● *vi* abspecken. **~'stairs** *adv* unten; (*go*) nach unten ● *adj* im Erdgeschoss. **~stream** *adv* stromabwärts. **~-to-'earth** *adj* sachlich. **~town** *adv* (*Amer*) im Stadtzentrum. **~ward** *adj* nach unten; (*slope*) abfallend ● *adv* **~[s]** abwärts, nach unten

doze /dəʊz/ *n* Nickerchen *nt* ● *vi* dösen. **~ off** *vi* einnicken

dozen /'dʌzn/ *n* Dutzend *nt*

Dr *abbr* doctor

draft[1] /drɑːft/ *n* Entwurf *m*; (*Comm*) Tratte *f*; (*Amer Mil*) Einberufung *f* ● *vt* entwerfen; (*Amer Mil*) einberufen

draft[2] *n* (*Amer*) = **draught**

drag /dræg/ *n* **in ~** ⅡⅠ (*man*) als Frau gekleidet ● *vt* (*pt/pp* **dragged**) schleppen; absuchen (*river*). **~ on** *vi* sich in die Länge ziehen

dragon /'drægən/ *n* Drache *m*. **~-fly** *n* Libelle *f*

drain /dreɪn/ *n* Abfluss *m*; (*underground*) Kanal *m*; **the ~s** die Kanalisation *f vt* entwässern (*land*); ablassen (*liquid*); das Wasser ablassen aus (*tank*); abgießen (*vegetables*); austrinken (*glass*) ● *vi* **~ [away]** ablaufen

drain|age /'dreɪnɪdʒ/ *n* Kanalisation *f*; (*of land*) Dränage *f*. **~ing board** *n* Abtropfbrett *nt*. **~pipe** *n* Abflussrohr *nt*

drake /dreɪk/ *n* Enterich *m*

drama /'drɑːmə/ *n* Drama *m*

dramatic /drə'mætɪk/ *adj*, **-ally** *adv* dramatisch

dramat|ist /'dræmətɪst/ *n* Dramatiker *m*. **~ize** *vt* für die Bühne bearbeiten; (*fig*) dramatisieren

drank /dræŋk/ *see* **drink**

drape /dreɪp/ *n* (*Amer*) Vorhang *m* ● *vt* drapieren

drastic /'dræstɪk/ *adj*, **-ally** *adv* drastisch

draught /drɑːft/ *n* [Luft]zug *m*; **~s** *sg* (*game*) Damespiel *nt*; **there is a ~** es zieht

draught beer *n* Bier *nt* vom Fass

draughty /'drɑːftɪ/ *adj* zugig

draw /drɔː/ *n* Attraktion *f*; (*Sport*)

Unentschieden nt; (in lottery) Ziehung f ● vt (pt **drew**, pp **drawn**) ● vt ziehen; (attract) anziehen; zeichnen (picture); abheben (money); ～ the curtains die Vorhänge zuziehen/ (back) aufziehen ● vi (Sport) unentschieden spielen. ～ **back** vt zurückziehen ● vi (recoil) zurückweichen. ～ **in** vt einziehen ● vi einfahren. ～ **out** vt herausziehen; abheben (money) ● vi ausfahren. ～ **up** vt aufsetzen (document); herrücken (chair) ● vi [an]halten

draw: ～**back** n Nachteil m. ～**bridge** n Zugbrücke f

drawer /drɔː(r)/ n Schublade f

drawing /'drɔːɪŋ/ n Zeichnung f

drawing: ～**board** n Reißbrett nt. ～**pin** n Reißzwecke f. ～**room** n Wohnzimmer nt

drawl /drɔːl/ n schleppende Aussprache f

drawn /drɔːn/ see **draw**

dread /dred/ n Furcht f (of vor + dat) ● vt fürchten. ～**ful** adj, **-fully** adv fürchterlich

dream /driːm/ n Traum m ● vt/i (pt/pp **dreamt** or **dreamed**) träumen (**about/of** von)

dreary /'drɪərɪ/ adj trüb[e]; (boring) langweilig

dregs /dregz/ npl Bodensatz m

drench /drentʃ/ vt durchnässen

dress /dres/ n Kleid nt; (clothing) Kleidung f ● vt anziehen; (Med) verbinden; ～ **oneself, get** ～**ed** sich anziehen ● vi sich anziehen. ～ **up** vi sich schön anziehen; (in disguise) sich verkleiden (**as** als)

dress: ～ **circle** n (Theat) erster Rang m. ～**er** n (furniture) Anrichte f; (Amer: dressing-table) Frisiertisch m

dressing n (Culin) Soße f; (Med) Verband m

dressing: ～**-gown** n Morgenmantel m. ～**-room** n Ankleidezimmer nt; (Theat) [Künstler]garderobe f. ～**-table** n Frisiertisch m

dress: ～**maker** n Schneiderin f. ～ **rehearsal** n Generalprobe f

drew /druː/ see **draw**

dried /draɪd/ adj getrocknet; ～ **fruit** Dörrobst nt

drier /'draɪə(r)/ n Trockner m

drift /drɪft/ n Abtrift f; (of snow) Schneewehe f; (meaning) Sinn m ● vi treiben; (off course) abtreiben; (snow:) Wehen bilden; (fig) (person:) sich treiben lassen

drill /drɪl/ n Bohrer m; (Mil) Drill m ● vt/i bohren (**for** nach); (Mil) drillen

drily /'draɪlɪ/ adv trocken

drink /drɪŋk/ n Getränk nt; (alcoholic) Drink m; (alcohol) Alkohol m ● vt/i (pt **drank**, pp **drunk**) trinken. ～ **up** vt/i austrinken

drink|able /'drɪŋkəbl/ adj trinkbar. ～**er** n Trinker m

'drinking-water n Trinkwasser nt

drip /drɪp/ n Tropfen nt; (drop) Tropfen m; (Med) Tropf m; (🔢: person) Niete f ● vi (pt/pp **dripped**) tropfen

drive /draɪv/ n [Auto]fahrt f; (entrance) Einfahrt f; (energy) Elan m; (Psychology) Trieb m; (Pol) Aktion f; (Sport) Treibschlag m; (Techn) Antrieb m ● v (pt **drove**, pp **driven**) ● vt treiben; fahren (car); (Sport: hit) schlagen; (Techn) antreiben; ～ **s.o. mad** 🔢 jdn verrückt machen; **what are you driving at?** 🔢 worauf willst du hinaus? ● vi fahren. ～ **away** vt vertreiben ● vi abfahren. ～ **off** vt vertreiben ● vi abfahren. ～ **on** vi weiterfahren. ～ **up** vi vorfahren

drivel /'drɪvl/ n 🔲 Quatsch m

driven /'drɪvn/ see drive

driver /'draɪvə(r)/ n Fahrer(in) m(f); (of train) Lokführer m

driving: ~ **lesson** n Fahrstunde f. ~ **licence** n Führerschein m. ~ **school** n Fahrschule f. ~ **test** Fahrprüfung f

drizzle /'drɪzl/ n Nieselregen m • vi nieseln

drone /drəʊn/ n (sound) Brummen nt

droop /druːp/ vi herabhängen

drop /drɒp/ n Tropfen m; (fall) Fall m; (in price, temperature) Rückgang m • v t (pt/pp **dropped**) • vt fallen lassen; abwerfen (bomb); (omit) auslassen; (give up) aufgeben • vi fallen; (fall lower) sinken; (wind:) nachlassen. ~ **in** vi vorbeikommen. ~ **off** vt absetzen (person) • vi abfallen; (fall asleep) einschlafen. ~ **out** vi herausfallen; (give up) aufgeben

drought /draʊt/ n Dürre f

drove /drəʊv/ see drive

drown /draʊn/ vi ertrinken • vt ertränken; übertönen (noise); **be** ~**ed** ertrinken

drowsy /'draʊzɪ/ adj schläfrig

drudgery /'drʌdʒərɪ/ n Plackerei f

drug /drʌg/ n Droge f • vt (pt/pp **drugged**) betäuben

drug: ~ **addict** n Drogenabhängige(r) m/f. ~**store** n (Amer) Drogerie f; (dispensing) Apotheke f

drum /drʌm/ n Trommel f; (for oil) Tonne f • v (pt/pp **drummed**) • vi trommeln • vt ~ **sth into s.o.** 🔲 jdm etw einbläuen. ~**mer** n Trommler m; (in pop-group) Schlagzeuger m. ~**stick** n Trommelschlegel m; (Culin) Keule f

drunk /drʌŋk/ see drink • adj betrunken; **get** ~ sich betrinken • n Betrunkene(r) m

drunk|ard /'drʌŋkəd/ n Trinker m. ~**en** adj betrunken

dry /draɪ/ adj (drier, driest) trocken • vt/i trocknen. ~ **up** vt/i austrocknen

dry: ~'**clean** vt chemisch reinigen. ~'**cleaner's** n (shop) chemische Reinigung f. ~**ness** n Trockenheit f

dual /'djuːəl/ adj doppelt

dual 'carriageway n ≈ Schnellstraße f

dubious /'djuːbɪəs/ adj zweifelhaft

duchess /'dʌtʃɪs/ n Herzogin f

duck /dʌk/ n Ente f • vt (in water) untertauchen • vi sich ducken

duct /dʌkt/ n Rohr nt; (Anat) Gang m

dud /dʌd/ adj 🔲 nutzlos; (coin) falsch; (cheque) ungedeckt; (forged) gefälscht

due /djuː/ adj angemessen; **be** ~ fällig sein; (baby:) erwartet werden; (train:) planmäßig ankommen; ~ **to** (owing to) wegen (+ gen); **be** ~ **to** zurückzuführen sein auf (+ acc) • adv ~ **west** genau westlich

duel /'djuːəl/ n Duell nt

duet /dju'et/ n Duo nt; (vocal) Duett nt

dug /dʌg/ see dig

duke /djuːk/ n Herzog m

dull /dʌl/ adj (-er, -est) (overcast, not bright) trüb[e]; (not shiny) matt; (sound) dumpf; (boring) langweilig; (stupid) schwerfällig

duly /'djuːlɪ/ adv ordnungsgemäß

dumb /dʌm/ adj (-er, -est) stumm. ~ **down** vt/i verflachen

dummy /'dʌmɪ/ n (tailor's) [Schneider]puppe f; (for baby) Schnuller m; (Comm) Attrappe f

dump /dʌmp/ n Abfallhaufen m, (for refuse) Müllhalde f, Deponie f; (🔲: town) Kaff nt; **be down in the**

dumpling | earnings

~s 🔲 deprimiert sein ● vt abladen

dumpling /'dʌmplɪŋ/ n Kloß m

dunce /dʌns/ n Dummkopf m

dune /djuːn/ n Düne f

dung /dʌŋ/ n Mist m

dungarees /dʌŋgə'riːz/ npl Latzhose f

dungeon /'dʌndʒən/ n Verlies nt

dunk /dʌŋk/ vt eintunken

duo /'djuːəʊ/ n Paar nt; (Mus) Duo nt

dupe /djuːp/ n Betrogene(r) m/f ● vt betrügen

duplicate¹ /'djuːplɪkət/ n Doppel nt; **in** ~ in doppelter Ausfertigung f

duplicate² /'djuːplɪkeɪt/ vt kopieren; (do twice) zweimal machen

durable /'djʊərəbl/ adj haltbar

duration /djʊə'reɪʃn/ n Dauer f

during /'djʊərɪŋ/ prep während (+ gen)

dusk /dʌsk/ n [Abend]dämmerung f

dust /dʌst/ n Staub m ● vt abstauben; (sprinkle) bestäuben (with mit) ● vi Staub wischen

dust: ~**bin** n Mülltonne f. ~**cart** n Müllwagen m. ~**er** n Staubtuch nt. ~**jacket** n Schutzumschlag m. ~**man** n Müllmann m. ~**pan** n Kehrschaufel f

dusty /'dʌstɪ/ adj staubig

Dutch /dʌtʃ/ adj holländisch ● n (Lang) Holländisch nt; **the** ~ pl die Holländer. ~**man** n Holländer m

dutiful /'djuːtɪfl/ adj pflichtbewusst

duty /'djuːtɪ/ n Pflicht f; (task) Aufgabe f; (tax) Zoll m; **be on** ~ Dienst haben. ~**-free** adj zollfrei

duvet /'duːveɪ/ n Steppdecke f

DVD abbr (digital versatile disc) DVD f

dwarf /dwɔːf/ n (pl -s or dwarves) Zwerg m

dwell /dwel/ vi (pt/pp dwelt); ~ **on** (fig) verweilen bei. ~**ing** n Wohnung f

dwindle /'dwɪndl/ vi abnehmen, schwinden

dye /daɪ/ n Farbstoff m ● vt (pres p dyeing) färben

dying /'daɪɪŋ/ see die²

dynamic /daɪ'næmɪk/ adj dynamisch

dynamite /'daɪnəmaɪt/ n Dynamit nt

dyslex|ia /dɪs'leksɪə/ n Legasthenie f. ~**ic** adj legasthenisch; **be** ~**ic** Legastheniker sein

d
e

Ee

each /iːtʃ/ adj & pron jede(r,s); (per) je; ~ **other** einander; **£1** ~ £1 pro Person; (for thing) pro Stück

eager /'iːgə(r)/ adj eifrig; **be** ~ **to** do sth etw gerne machen wollen. ~**ness** n Eifer m

eagle /'iːgl/ n Adler m

ear n Ohr nt. ~**ache** n Ohrenschmerzen pl. ~**drum** n Trommelfell nt

earl /ɜːl/ n Graf m

early /'ɜːlɪ/ adj & adv (-ier, -iest) früh; (reply) baldig; **be** ~ früh dran sein

earn /ɜːn/ vt verdienen

earnest /'ɜːnɪst/ adj ernsthaft ● n **in** ~ im Ernst

earnings /'ɜːnɪŋz/ npl Verdienst m

ear: ~**phones** npl Kopfhörer pl. ~**-ring** n Ohrring m; (clip-on) Ohrklips m. ~**shot** n **within/out of** ~**shot** in/außer Hörweite

earth /ɜ:θ/ n Erde f; (of fox) Bau m
● vt (Electr) erden

earthenware /'ɜ:θn-/ n Tonwaren pl

earthly /'ɜ:θlɪ/ adj irdisch; **be no
~ use** [!] völlig nutzlos sein

'earthquake n Erdbeben nt

earthy /'ɜ:θɪ/ adj erdig;
(coarse) derb

ease /i:z/ n Leichtigkeit f ● vt erleichtern; lindern (pain) ● vi (pain:)
nachlassen; (situation:) sich entspannen

easily /'i:zɪlɪ/ adv leicht, mit Leichtigkeit

east /i:st/ n Osten m; **to the ~ of**
östlich von ● adj Ost-, ost- ● adv
nach Osten

Easter /'i:stə(r)/ n Ostern nt
● attrib Oster-. **~ egg** n Osterei nt

east|erly /'i:stəlɪ/ adj östlich.
~ern adj östlich. **~ward[s]** adv
nach Osten

easy /'i:zɪ/ adj leicht; **take it ~** [!]
sich schonen; **go ~ with** [!] sparsam umgehen mit

easy: **~ chair** n Sessel m.
~'going adj gelassen

eat /i:t/ vt/i (pt ate, pp eaten)
essen; (animal:) fressen. **~ up** vt
aufessen

eatable /'i:təbl/ adj genießbar

eau-de-Cologne /əʊdəkə'ləʊn/
n Kölnisch Wasser nt

eaves /i:vz/ npl Dachüberhang m.
~drop vi (pt/pp ~ dropped)
[heimlich] lauschen

ebb /eb/ n (tide) Ebbe f ● vi zurückgehen; (fig) verebben

ebony /'ebənɪ/ n Ebenholz nt

EC abbr (European Community)
EG f

eccentric /ɪk'sentrɪk/ adj exzentrisch ● n Exzentriker m

ecclesiastical /ɪkli:zɪ'æstɪkl/ adj
kirchlich

echo /'ekəʊ/ n (pl -es) Echo nt, Widerhall m ● v (pt/pp echoed, pres p
echoing) ● vi widerhallen
(with von)

eclipse /ɪ'klɪps/ n (Astronomy) Finsternis f

ecolog|ical /i:kə'lɒdʒɪkl/ adj ökologisch. **~y** n Ökologie f

e-commerce /i:'kɒmɜ:s/ n
E-Commerce m

economic /i:kə'nɒmɪk/ adj wirtschaftlich. **~al** adj sparsam. **~ally**
adv wirtschaftlich; (thriftily) sparsam. **~ refugee** n Wirtschaftsflüchtling m. **~s** n Volkswirtschaft f

economist /ɪ'kɒnəmɪst/ n Volkswirt m; (Univ) Wirtschaftswissenschaftler m

economize /ɪ'kɒnəmaɪz/ vi sparen (**on** an + dat)

economy /ɪ'kɒnəmɪ/ n Wirtschaft
f; (thrift) Sparsamkeit f

ecstasy /'ekstəsɪ/ n Ekstase f

ecstatic /ɪk'stætɪk/ adj, **-ally** adv
ekstatisch

eczema /'eksɪmə/ n Ekzem nt

eddy /'edɪ/ n Wirbel m

edge /edʒ/ n Rand m; (of table,
lawn) Kante f; (of knife) Schneide f;
on ~ [!] nervös ● vt einfassen. **~
forward** vi sich nach vorn schieben

edgy /'edʒɪ/ adj [!] nervös

edible /'edɪbl/ adj essbar

edifice /'edɪfɪs/ n [großes] Gebäude nt

Edinburgh Festival *i*
Großbritanniens berühmtestes Kunst- und Theaterfestival findet seit 1947 jedes Jahr
im August in der schottischen
Hauptstadt statt. Die Festspiele

ziehen Besucher aus aller Welt an. Ergänzt wird das Programm durch das gleichzeitig stattfindende *Edinburgh Festival Fringe*, das ein Forum für unbekannte Künstler, experimentelle Kunst und alternative Veranstaltungen ist.

edit /ˈedɪt/ vt (pt/pp **edited**) redigieren; herausgeben (*anthology, dictionary*); schneiden (*film, tape*)

edition /ɪˈdɪʃn/ n Ausgabe f; (*impression*) Auflage f

editor /ˈedɪtə(r)/ n Redakteur m; (*of anthology, dictionary*) Herausgeber m; (*of newspaper*) Chefredakteur m; (*of film*) Cutter(in) m(f)

editorial /edɪˈtɔːrɪəl/ adj redaktionell, Redaktions- ● n (*in newspaper*) Leitartikel m

educate /ˈedjʊkeɪt/ vt erziehen. ~**d** adj gebildet

education /edjʊˈkeɪʃn/ n Erziehung f; (*culture*) Bildung f. ~**al** adj pädagogisch; (*visit*) kulturell

eel /iːl/ n Aal m

eerie /ˈɪərɪ/ adj unheimlich

effect /ɪˈfekt/ n Wirkung f, Effekt m; **take** ~ in Kraft treten

effective /ɪˈfektɪv/ adj wirksam, effektiv; (*striking*) wirkungsvoll, effektvoll; (*actual*) tatsächlich. ~**ness** n Wirksamkeit f

effeminate /ɪˈfemɪnət/ adj unmännlich

effervescent /efəˈvesnt/ adj sprudelnd

efficiency /ɪˈfɪʃənsɪ/ n Tüchtigkeit f; (*of machine, organization*) Leistungsfähigkeit f

efficient /ɪˈfɪʃənt/ adj tüchtig; (*machine, organization*) leistungsfähig; (*method*) rationell. ~**ly** adv gut; (*function*) rationell

effort /ˈefət/ n Anstrengung f;

make an ~ sich (dat) Mühe geben. ~**less** adj mühelos

e.g. abbr (**exempli gratia**) z.B.

egalitarian /ɪɡælɪˈteərɪən/ adj egalitär

egg n Ei nt. ~**-cup** n Eierbecher m. ~**shell** n Eierschale f

ego /ˈiːɡəʊ/ n Ich nt. ~**ism** n Egoismus m. ~**ist** n Egoist m. ~**tism** n Ichbezogenheit f. ~**tist** n ichbezogener Mensch m

Egypt /ˈiːdʒɪpt/ n Ägypten nt. ~**ian** adj ägyptisch ● n Ägypter(in) m(f)

eiderdown /ˈaɪdə-/ n (*quilt*) Daunendecke f

eigh|t /eɪt/ adj acht ● n Acht f; (*boat*) Achter m. ~**teen** adj achtzehn. ~**'teenth** adj achtzehnte(r,s)

eighth /eɪtθ/ adj achte(r,s) ● n Achtel m

eightieth /ˈeɪtɪɪθ/ adj achtzigste(r,s)

eighty /ˈeɪtɪ/ adj achtzig

either /ˈaɪðə(r)/ adj & pron ~ [of them] einer (von [den] beiden; (both) beide; on ~ side auf beiden Seiten ● adv I don't ~ ich auch nicht ● conj ~ ... or entweder ... oder

eject /ɪˈdʒekt/ vt hinauswerfen

elaborate /ɪˈlæbərət/ adj kunstvoll; (*fig*) kompliziert

elapse /ɪˈlæps/ vi vergehen

elastic /ɪˈlæstɪk/ adj elastisch. ~ **'band** n Gummiband nt

elasticity /ɪlæsˈtɪsətɪ/ n Elastizität f

elated /ɪˈleɪtɪd/ adj überglücklich

elbow /ˈelbəʊ/ n Ellbogen m

elder¹ /ˈeldə(r)/ n Holunder m

eld|er² /ˈeldə(r)/ adj ältere(r,s) ● n the ~**er** der/die Ältere. ~**erly** adj alt. ~**est** adj älteste(r,s) ● n the ~**est**

der/die Älteste

elect /ɪˈlekt/ vt wählen. ~**ion** n Wahl f

elector /ɪˈlektə(r)/ n Wähler(in) m(f). ~ **ate** n Wählerschaft f

electric /ɪˈlektrɪk/ adj, **-ally** adv elektrisch

electrical /ɪˈlektrɪkl/ adj elektrisch; ~ **engineering** Elektrotechnik f

electric: ~ '**blanket** n Heizdecke f. ~ '**fire** n elektrischer Heizofen m

electrician /ɪlekˈtrɪʃn/ n Elektriker m

electricity /ɪlekˈtrɪsɪti/ n Elektrizität f; (supply) Strom m

electrify /ɪˈlektrɪfaɪ/ vt (pt/pp -ied) elektrifizieren. ~**ing** adj (fig) elektrisierend

electrocute /ɪˈlektrəkjuːt/ vt durch einen elektrischen Schlag töten

electrode /ɪˈlektrəʊd/ n Elektrode f

electronic /ɪlekˈtrɒnɪk/ adj elektronisch. ~**s** n Elektronik f

elegance /ˈelɪɡəns/ n Eleganz f

elegant /ˈelɪɡənt/ adj elegant

elegy /ˈelɪdʒi/ n Elegie f

element /ˈelɪmənt/ n Element nt. ~**ary** adj elementar

elephant /ˈelɪfənt/ n Elefant m

elevat|e /ˈelɪveɪt/ vt heben; (fig) erheben. ~**ion** n Erhebung f

elevator /ˈelɪveɪtə(r)/ n (Amer) Aufzug m, Fahrstuhl m

eleven /ɪˈlevn/ adj elf ● n Elf f. ~**th** adj elfte(r,s); **at the ~th hour** 🄳 in letzter Minute

eligible /ˈelɪdʒəbl/ adj berechtigt

eliminate /ɪˈlɪmɪneɪt/ vt ausschalten

élite /eɪˈliːt/ n Elite f

elm /elm/ n Ulme f

elocution /eləˈkjuːʃn/ n Sprecherziehung f

elope /ɪˈləʊp/ vi durchbrennen 🄳

eloquen|ce /ˈeləkwəns/ n Beredsamkeit f. ~**t** adj, ~**ly** adv beredt

else /els/ adv sonst; **nothing** ~ sonst nichts; **or** ~ oder; (otherwise) sonst; **someone/somewhere** ~ jemand/irgendwo anders; **anyone** ~ jeder andere; (as question) sonst noch jemand? **anything** ~ alles andere; (as question) sonst noch etwas? ~**where** adv woanders

elucidate /ɪˈluːsɪdeɪt/ vt erläutern

elusive /ɪˈluːsɪv/ adj **be** ~ schwer zu fassen sein

emaciated /ɪˈmeɪsieɪtɪd/ adj abgezehrt

e-mail /ˈiːmeɪl/ n E-Mail f ● vt per E-Mail übermitteln (Ergebnisse, Datei usw.); ~ **s.o.** jdm eine E-Mail schicken. ~ **address** n E-Mail-Adresse f. ~ **message** n E-Mail f

emancipat|ed /ɪˈmænsɪpeɪtɪd/ adj emanzipiert. ~**ion** n Emanzipation f; (of slaves) Freilassung f

embankment /ɪmˈbæŋkmənt/ n Böschung f; (of railway) Bahndamm m

embark /ɪmˈbɑːk/ vi sich einschiffen. ~**ation** n Einschiffung f

embarrass /ɪmˈbærəs/ vt in Verlegenheit bringen. ~**ed** adj verlegen. ~**ing** adj peinlich. ~**ment** n Verlegenheit f

embassy /ˈembəsi/ n Botschaft f

embellish /ɪmˈbelɪʃ/ vt verzieren; (fig) ausschmücken

embezzle /ɪmˈbezl/ vt unterschlagen. ~**ment** n Unterschlagung f

emblem /ˈembləm/ n Emblem nt

embodiment /ɪmˈbɒdɪmənt/ n Verkörperung f

embody /ɪmˈbɒdɪ/ vt (pt/pp -ied) verkörpern; (include) enthalten

embrace /ɪmˈbreɪs/ n Umarmung f • vt umarmen; (fig) umfassen • vi sich umarmen

embroider /ɪmˈbrɔɪdə(r)/ vt besticken; sticken (design) • vi sticken. **~y** n Stickerei f

embryo /ˈembrɪəʊ/ n Embryo m

emerald /ˈemərəld/ n Smaragd m

emer|ge /ɪˈmɜːdʒ/ vi auftauchen (from aus); (become known) sich herausstellen; (come into being) entstehen. **~gence** n Auftauchen nt; Entstehung f

emergency /ɪˈmɜːdʒənsɪ/ n Notfall m. **~ exit** n Notausgang m

emigrant /ˈemɪɡrənt/ n Auswanderer m

emigrat|e /ˈemɪɡreɪt/ vi auswandern. **~ion** n Auswanderung f

eminent /ˈemɪnənt/ adj eminent

emission /ɪˈmɪʃn/ n Ausstrahlung f; (of pollutant) Emission f

emit /ɪˈmɪt/ vt (pt/pp emitted) ausstrahlen (light, heat); ausstoßen (smoke, fumes, cry)

emotion /ɪˈməʊʃn/ n Gefühl nt. **~al** adj emotional; **become ~al** sich erregen

empathy /ˈempəθɪ/ n Einfühlungsvermögen nt

emperor /ˈempərə(r)/ n Kaiser m

emphasis /ˈemfəsɪs/ n Betonung f

emphasize /ˈemfəsaɪz/ vt betonen

emphatic /ɪmˈfætɪk/ adj, **-ally** adv nachdrücklich

empire /ˈempaɪə(r)/ n Reich nt

employ /ɪmˈplɔɪ/ vt beschäftigen; (appoint) einstellen; (fig) anwenden. **~ee** n Beschäftigte(r) m/f; (in contrast to employer) Arbeitnehmer m. **~er** n Arbeitgeber m. **~ment** n Beschäftigung f; (work) Arbeit f. **~ment agency** n Stellenvermittlung f

empress /ˈemprɪs/ n Kaiserin f

emptiness /ˈemptɪnɪs/ n Leere f

empty /ˈemptɪ/ adj leer • vt leeren; ausleeren (container) • vi sich leeren

emulsion /ɪˈmʌlʃn/ n Emulsion f

enable /ɪˈneɪbl/ vt **~ s.o. to** es jdm möglich machen, zu

enact /ɪˈnækt/ vt (Theat) aufführen

enamel /ɪˈnæml/ n Email nt; (on teeth) Zahnschmelz m; (paint) Lack m

enchant /ɪnˈtʃɑːnt/ vt bezaubern. **~ing** adj bezaubernd. **~ment** n Zauber m

encircle /ɪnˈsɜːkl/ vt einkreisen

enclos|e /ɪnˈkləʊz/ vt einschließen; (in letter) beilegen (with dat). **~ure** n (at zoo) Gehege nt; (in letter) Anlage f

encore /ˈɒŋkɔː(r)/ n Zugabe f • int bravo!

encounter /ɪnˈkaʊntə(r)/ n Begegnung f • vt begegnen (+ dat); (fig) stoßen auf (+ acc)

encourag|e /ɪnˈkʌrɪdʒ/ vt ermutigen; (promote) fördern. **~ement** n Ermutigung f. **~ing** adj ermutigend

encroach /ɪnˈkrəʊtʃ/ vi **~ on** eindringen in (+ acc) (land)

encyclopaed|ia /ɪnsaɪkləˈpiːdɪə/ n Enzyklopädie f, Lexikon nt. **~ic** adj enzyklopädisch

end /end/ n Ende nt; (purpose) Zweck m; **in the ~** schließlich; **at the ~** of May Ende Mai; **on ~** hochkant; **for days on ~** tagelang; **make ~s meet** 🔲 [gerade] auskommen; **no ~ of** 🔲 unheimlich viel(e) • vt beenden • vi enden; **~ up in** (🔲: arrive at) landen in (+ dat)

endanger /ɪnˈdeɪndʒə(r)/ vt gefährden

endeavour /ɪnˈdevə(r)/ n Bemühung f • vi sich bemühen (to zu)

ending | ensue

ending /'endɪŋ/ n Schluss m, Ende nt; (Gram) Endung f

endless /'endlɪs/ adj endlos

endorse /ɛn'dɔːs/ vt (Comm) indossieren; (confirm) bestätigen. **~ment** n (Comm) Indossament nt; (fig) Bestätigung f; (on driving licence) Strafvermerk m

endow /ɪn'daʊ/ vt stiften; **be ~ed with** (fig) haben

endurance /ɪn'djʊərəns/ n Durchhaltevermögen nt; **beyond ~** unerträglich

endure /ɪn'djʊə(r)/ vt ertragen

enemy /'enəmɪ/ n Feind m ● attrib feindlich

energetic /enə'dʒetɪk/ adj tatkräftig; **be ~** voller Energie sein

energy /'enədʒɪ/ n Energie f

enforce /ɪn'fɔːs/ vt durchsetzen. **~d** adj unfreiwillig

engage /ɪn'ɡeɪdʒ/ vt einstellen (staff); (Theat) engagieren; (Auto) einlegen (gear) ● vi sich beteiligen (**in** an + dat); (Techn) ineinandergreifen. **~d** adj besetzt; (person) beschäftigt; (to be married) verlobt; **get ~d** sich verloben (**to** mit). **~ment** n Verlobung f; (appointment) Verabredung f; (Mil) Gefecht nt

engaging /ɪn'ɡeɪdʒɪŋ/ adj einnehmend

engine /'endʒɪn/ n Motor m; (Naut) Maschine f; (Rail) Lokomotive f; (of jet plane) Triebwerk nt. **~-driver** n Lokomotivführer m

engineer /endʒɪ'nɪə(r)/ n Ingenieur m; (service, installation) Techniker m; (Naut) Maschinist m; (Amer) Lokomotivführer m. **~ing** n [mechanical] **~ing** Maschinenbau m

England /'ɪŋɡlənd/ n England nt

English /'ɪŋɡlɪʃ/ adj englisch; **the ~ Channel** der Ärmelkanal ● n

(Lang) Englisch nt; **in ~** auf Englisch; **into ~** ins Englische; **the ~** pl die Engländer. **~man** n Engländer m. **~woman** n Engländerin f

engrave /ɪn'ɡreɪv/ vt eingravieren. **~ing** n Stich m

enhance /ɪn'hɑːns/ vt verschönern; (fig) steigern

enigma /ɪ'nɪɡmə/ n Rätsel nt. **~tic** adj rätselhaft

enjoy /ɪn'dʒɔɪ/ vt genießen; **~ oneself** sich amüsieren; **~ cooking** gern kochen; **I ~ed it** es hat mir gut gefallen; (food:) geschmeckt. **~able** adj angenehm, nett. **~ment** n Vergnügen nt

enlarge /ɪn'lɑːdʒ/ vt vergrößern. **~ment** n Vergrößerung f

enlist /ɪn'lɪst/ vt (Mil) einziehen; **~ s.o.'s help** jdn zur Hilfe heranziehen ● vi (Mil) sich melden

enliven /ɪn'laɪvn/ vt beleben

enmity /'enmətɪ/ n Feindschaft f

enormity /ɪ'nɔːmətɪ/ n Ungeheuerlichkeit f

enormous /ɪ'nɔːməs/ adj riesig

enough /ɪ'nʌf/ a, adv & n genug; **be ~** reichen; **funnily ~** komischerweise

enquir|e /ɪn'kwaɪə(r)/ vi sich erkundigen (**about** nach). **~y** n Erkundigung f; (investigation) Untersuchung f

enrage /ɪn'reɪdʒ/ vt wütend machen

enrich /ɪn'rɪtʃ/ vt bereichern

enrol /ɪn'rəʊl/ v (pt/pp **-rolled**) ● vt einschreiben ● vi sich einschreiben

ensemble /ɒn'sɒmbl/ n (clothing & Mus) Ensemble nt

enslave /ɪn'sleɪv/ vt versklaven

ensue /ɪn'sjuː/ vi folgen; (result) sich ergeben (**from** aus)

ensure /ɪnˈʃʊə(r)/ vt sicherstellen; ~ **that** dafür sorgen, dass

entail /ɪnˈteɪl/ vt erforderlich machen; **what does it** ~? was ist damit verbunden?

entangle /ɪnˈtæŋgl/ vt **get** ~**d** sich verfangen (**in** in + dat)

enter /ˈentə(r)/ vt eintreten; (vehicle:) einfahren in (+ acc); einreisen in (+ acc) (country); (register) eintragen; sich anmelden zu (competition) ●vi eintreten; (vehicle:) einfahren; (Theat) auftreten; (register as competitor) sich anmelden; (take part) sich beteiligen (**in** an + dat)

enterpris|**e** /ˈentəpraɪz/ n Unternehmen nt; (quality) Unternehmungsgeist m. ~**ing** adj unternehmend

entertain /entəˈteɪn/ vt unterhalten; (invite) einladen; (to meal) bewirten (guest) ●vi unterhalten; (have guests) Gäste haben. ~**er** n Unterhalter m. ~**ment** n Unterhaltung f

enthral /ɪnˈθrɔːl/ vt (pt/pp **enthralled**) **be** ~**led** gefesselt sein (**by** von)

enthuse /ɪnˈθjuːz/ vi ~ **over** schwärmen von

enthusias|**m** /ɪnˈθjuːzɪæzm/ n Begeisterung f. ~**t** n Enthusiast m. ~**tic** adj, **-ally** adv begeistert

entice /ɪnˈtaɪs/ vt locken. ~**ment** n Anreiz m

entire /ɪnˈtaɪə(r)/ adj ganz. ~**ly** adv ganz, völlig. ~**ty** n **in its** ~**ty** in seiner Gesamtheit

entitle /ɪnˈtaɪtl/ vt berechtigen; ~**d** ... mit dem Titel ...; **be** ~**d to sth** das Recht auf etw (acc) haben. ~**ment** n Berechtigung f; (claim) Anspruch m (**to** auf + acc)

entrance[1] /ˈentrəns/ n Eintritt m; (Theat) Auftritt m; (way in) Eingang

m; (for vehicle) Einfahrt f. ~ **fee** n Eintrittsgebühr f

entrant /ˈentrənt/ n Teilnehmer(in) m(f)

entreat /ɪnˈtriːt/ vt anflehen (**for** um)

entrust /ɪnˈtrʌst/ vt ~ **s.o. with sth,** ~ **sth to s.o.** jdm etw anvertrauen

entry /ˈentrɪ/ n Eintritt m; (into country) Einreise f; (on list) Eintrag m; **no** ~ Zutritt/ (Auto) Einfahrt verboten

envelop /ɪnˈveləp/ vt (pt/pp **enveloped**) einhüllen

envelope /ˈenvələʊp/ n [Brief]umschlag m

enviable /ˈenvɪəbl/ adj beneidenswert

envious /ˈenvɪəs/ adj neidisch (**of** auf + acc)

environment /ɪnˈvaɪərənmənt/ n Umwelt f

environmental /ɪnvaɪərən'mentl/ adj Umwelt-. ~**ist** n Umweltschützer m. ~**ly** adv ~**ly friendly** umweltfreundlich

envisage /ɪnˈvɪzɪdʒ/ vt sich (dat) vorstellen

envoy /ˈenvɔɪ/ n Gesandte(r) m

envy /ˈenvɪ/ n Neid m ●vt (pt/pp **-ied**) ~ **s.o. sth** jdn um etw beneiden

epic /ˈepɪk/ adj episch ●n Epos nt

epidemic /epɪˈdemɪk/ n Epidemie f

epilep|**sy** /ˈepɪlepsɪ/ n Epilepsie f. ~**tic** adj epileptisch ●n Epileptiker(in) m(f)

epilogue /ˈepɪlɒg/ n Epilog m

episode /ˈepɪsəʊd/ n Episode f; (instalment) Folge f

epitome /ɪˈpɪtəmɪ/ n Inbegriff m

epoch /ˈiːpɒk/ n Epoche f. ~**-mak-**

ing adj epochemachend

equal /'iːkwl/ adj gleich (**to** dat); **be ~ to a task** einer Aufgabe gewachsen sein ● n Gleichgestellte(r) m/f ● vt (pt/pp **equalled**) gleichen (+ dat); (fig) gleichkommen (+ dat). **~ity** n Gleichheit f

equalize /'iːkwəlaɪz/ vt/i ausgleichen

equally /'iːkwəlɪ/ adv gleich; (divide) gleichmäßig; (just as) genauso

equate /ɪ'kweɪt/ vt gleichsetzen (**with** mit). **~ion** n (Math) Gleichung f

equator /ɪ'kweɪtə(r)/ n Äquator m

equestrian /ɪ'kwestrɪən/ adj Reit-

equilibrium /iːkwɪ'lɪbrɪəm/ n Gleichgewicht nt

equinox /'iːkwɪnɒks/ n Tagundnachtgleiche f

equip /ɪ'kwɪp/ vt (pt/pp **equipped**) ausrüsten; (furnish) ausstatten. **~ment** n Ausrüstung f; Ausstattung f

equity /'ekwətɪ/ n Gerechtigkeit f

equivalent /ɪ'kwɪvələnt/ adj gleichwertig; (corresponding) entsprechend ● n Äquivalent nt; (value) Gegenwert m; (counterpart) Gegenstück nt

era /'ɪərə/ n Ära f, Zeitalter nt

eradicate /ɪ'rædɪkeɪt/ vt ausrotten

erase /ɪ'reɪz/ vt ausradieren; (from tape) löschen

erect /ɪ'rekt/ adj aufrecht ● vt errichten. **~ion** n Errichtung f; (building) Bau m; (Physiology) Erektion f

erode /ɪ'rəʊd/ vt (water:) auswaschen; (acid:) angreifen. **~sion** n Erosion f

erotic /ɪ'rɒtɪk/ adj erotisch

errand /'erənd/ n Botengang m

erratic /ɪ'rætɪk/ adj unregelmäßig;

(person) unberechenbar

erroneous /ɪ'rəʊnɪəs/ adj falsch; (belief, assumption) irrig

error /'erə(r)/ n Irrtum m; (mistake) Fehler m; **in ~** irrtümlicherweise

erupt /ɪ'rʌpt/ vi ausbrechen. **~ion** n Ausbruch m

escalat|e /'eskəleɪt/ vt/i eskalieren. **~or** n Rolltreppe f

escape /ɪ'skeɪp/ n Flucht f; (from prison) Ausbruch m; **have a narrow ~** gerade noch davonkommen ● vi flüchten; (prisoner:) ausbrechen; entkommen (**from** aus; **from s.o.** jdm); (gas:) entweichen ● vt **the name ~s me** der Name entfällt mir

escapism /ɪ'skeɪpɪzm/ n Eskapismus m

escort¹ /'eskɔːt/ n (of person) Begleiter m; (Mil) Eskorte f

escort² /ɪ'skɔːt/ vt begleiten; (Mil) eskortieren

Eskimo /'eskɪməʊ/ n Eskimo m

esoteric /esə'terɪk/ adj esoterisch

especially /ɪ'speʃəlɪ/ adv besonders

espionage /'espɪənɑːʒ/ n Spionage f

essay /'eseɪ/ n Aufsatz m

essence /'esns/ n Wesen nt; (Chemistry, Culin) Essenz f

essential /ɪ'senʃl/ adj wesentlich; (indispensable) unentbehrlich ● n **the ~s** das Wesentliche; (items) das Nötigste. **~ly** adv im Wesentlichen

establish /ɪ'stæblɪʃ/ vt gründen; (form) bilden; (prove) beweisen

estate /ɪ'steɪt/ n Gut nt; (possessions) Besitz m; (after death) Nachlass m; (housing) [Wohn]siedlung f. **~ agent** n Immobilienmakler m. **~ car** n Kombi[wagen] m

esteem /ɪ'stiːm/ n Achtung f ● vt hochschätzen

estimate[1] /'estɪmət/ n Schätzung f; (Comm) [Kosten]voranschlag m; **at a rough ~** grob geschätzt

estimat|e[2] /'estɪmeɪt/ vt schätzen. **~ion** n Einschätzung f

estuary /'estjʊərɪ/ n Mündung f

etc. /et'setərə/ abbr (et cetera) und so weiter, usw.

eternal /ɪ'tɜːnl/ adj ewig

eternity /ɪ'tɜːnətɪ/ n Ewigkeit f

ethical /'eθɪkl/ adj ethisch; (morally correct) moralisch einwandfrei. **~s** n Ethik f

Ethiopia /iːθɪ'əʊpɪə/ n Äthiopien nt

ethnic /'eθnɪk/ adj ethnisch. **~ cleansing** n ethnische Säuberung

etiquette /'etɪket/ n Etikette f

EU abbr (European Union) EU f

eulogy /'juːlədʒɪ/ n Lobrede f

euphemis|m /'juːfəmɪzm/ n Euphemismus m. **~tic** adj, **-ally** adv verhüllend

euro /'jʊərəʊ/ n Euro m. **E~cheque** n Euroscheck m. **E~land** n Euroland nt

Europe /'jʊərəp/ n Europa nt

European /jʊərə'piːən/ adj europäisch; **~ Union** Europäische Union f ● n Europäer(in) m(f)

eurosceptic /'jʊərəʊskeptɪk/ n Euroskeptiker(in) m(f)

evacuat|e /ɪ'vækjʊeɪt/ vt evakuieren; räumen (building, area). **~ion** n Evakuierung f, Räumung f

evade /ɪ'veɪd/ vt sich entziehen (+ dat); hinterziehen (taxes)

evaluat|e /ɪvæljʊ'eɪt/ vt einschätzen. **~ion** n Beurteilung f, Einschätzung f

evange|lical /iːvæn'dʒelɪkl/ adj evangelisch. **~list** n Evangelist m

evaporat|e /ɪ'væpəreɪt/ vi verdunsten. **~ion** n Verdampfung f

evasion /ɪ'veɪʒn/ n Ausweichen nt; **tax ~** Steuerhinterziehung f

evasive /ɪ'veɪsɪv/ adj ausweichend; **be ~** ausweichen

even /'iːvn/ adj (level) eben; (same, equal) gleich; (regular) gleichmäßig; (number) gerade; **get ~ with** ⊞ sich an jdm heimzahlen ● adv sogar, selbst; **~ so** trotzdem; **not ~** nicht einmal ● vt **~ the score** ausgleichen

evening /'iːvnɪŋ/ n Abend m; **this ~** heute Abend; **in the ~** abends, am Abend. **~ class** n Abendkurs m

evenly /'iːvnlɪ/ adv gleichmäßig

event /ɪ'vent/ n Ereignis nt; (function) Veranstaltung f; (Sport) Wettbewerb m. **~ful** adj ereignisreich

eventual /ɪ'ventjʊəl/ adj his ~ **success** der Erfolg, der ihm schließlich zuteil wurde. **~ly** adv schließlich

ever /'evə(r)/ adv je[mals]; **not ~** nie; **for ~** für immer; **hardly ~** fast nie; **~ since** seitdem

'evergreen n immergrüner Strauch m/ (tree) Baum m

ever'lasting adj ewig

every /'evrɪ/ adj jede(r,s); **~ one** jede(r,s) Einzelne; **~ other day** jeden zweiten Tag

every: ~body pron jeder[mann]; alle pl. **~day** adj alltäglich. **~ one** pron jeder[mann]; alle pl. **~thing** pron alles. **~where** adv überall

evict /ɪ'vɪkt/ vt [aus der Wohnung] hinausweisen. **~ion** n Ausweisung f

eviden|ce /'evɪdəns/ n Beweise pl; (Jur) Beweismaterial nt; (testimony) Aussage f; **give ~ce** aussagen. **~t** adj offensichtlich

evil /'iːvl/ adj böse ● n Böse nt

evoke /ɪ'vəʊk/ vt heraufbeschwören

evolution /iːvə'luːʃn/ n Evolution f

evolve /ɪ'vɒlv/ vt entwickeln ● vi sich entwickeln

ewe /juː/ n Schaf nt

exact /ɪg'zækt/ adj genau; **not ~ly** nicht gerade. **~ness** n Genauigkeit f

exaggerat|e /ɪg'zædʒəreɪt/ vt/i übertreiben. **~ion** n Übertreibung f

exam /ɪg'zæm/ n 🄵 Prüfung f

examination /ɪgzæmɪ'neɪʃn/ n Untersuchung f; (Sch) Prüfung f

examine /ɪg'zæmɪn/ vt untersuchen; (Sch) prüfen

example /ɪg'zɑːmpl/ n Beispiel n (**of** für); **for ~** zum Beispiel; **make an ~ of** ein Exempel statuieren an (+ dat)

exasperat|e /ɪg'zæspəreɪt/ vt zur Verzweiflung treiben. **~ion** n Verzweiflung f

excavat|e /'ekskəveɪt/ vt ausschachten; ausgraben (site). **~ion** n Ausgrabung f

exceed /ɪk'siːd/ vt übersteigen. **~ingly** adv äußerst

excel /ɪk'sel/ v (pt/pp **excelled**) vi sich auszeichnen ● vt **~ oneself** sich selbst übertreffen

excellen|ce /'eksələns/ n Vorzüglichkeit f. **~t** adj ausgezeichnet, vorzüglich

except /ɪk'sept/ prep außer (+ dat); **~ for** abgesehen von ● vt ausnehmen

exception /ɪk'sepʃn/ n Ausnahme f. **~al** adj außergewöhnlich

excerpt /'eksɜːpt/ n Auszug m

excess /ɪk'ses/ n Übermaß nt (**of** an + dat); (surplus) Überschuss m; **~es** pl Exzesse pl

excessive /ɪk'sesɪv/ adj übermäßig

exchange /ɪks'tʃeɪndʒ/ n Austausch m; (Teleph) Fernsprechamt nt; (Comm) [Geld]wechsel m; **in ~**

dafür ● vt austauschen (**for** gegen); tauschen (places). **~ rate** n Wechselkurs m

excitable /ɪk'saɪtəbl/ adj [leicht] erregbar

excit|e /ɪk'saɪt/ vt aufregen; (cause) erregen. **~ed** adj aufgeregt; **get ~ed** sich aufregen. **~ement** n Aufregung f; Erregung f. **~ing** adj aufregend; (story) spannend

exclaim /ɪk'skleɪm/ vt/i ausrufen

exclamation /eksklə'meɪʃn/ n Ausruf m. **~ mark** n, (Amer) **~ point** n Ausrufezeichen nt

exclu|de /ɪk'skluːd/ vt ausschließen. **~ding** prep ausschließlich (+ gen). **~sion** n Ausschluss m

exclusive /ɪk'skluːsɪv/ adj ausschließlich; (select) exklusiv

excrement /'ekskrɪmənt/ n Kot m

excrete /ɪk'skriːt/ vt ausscheiden

excruciating /ɪk'skruːʃieɪtɪŋ/ adj grässlich

excursion /ɪk'skɜːʃn/ n Ausflug m

excusable /ɪk'skjuːzəbl/ adj entschuldbar

excuse¹ /ɪk'skjuːs/ n Entschuldigung f; (pretext) Ausrede f

excuse² /ɪk'skjuːz/ vt entschuldigen; **~ me!** Entschuldigung!

ex-di'rectory adj **be ~** nicht im Telefonbuch stehen

execute /'eksɪkjuːt/ vt ausführen; (put to death) hinrichten

execution /eksɪ'kjuːʃn/ n Ausführung f; Hinrichtung f

executive /ɪg'zekjʊtɪv/ adj leitend ● n leitende(r) Angestellte(r) m/f; (Pol) Exekutive f

exemplary /ɪg'zemplərɪ/ adj beispielhaft

exemplify /ɪg'zemplɪfaɪ/ vt (pt/pp **-ied**) veranschaulichen

exempt /ɪg'zempt/ adj befreit ● vt befreien (**from** von). **~ion** n Befreiung f

exercise /'eksəsaɪz/ n Übung f; **physical ~** körperliche Bewegung f ● vt (use) ausüben; bewegen (horse) ● vi sich bewegen. **~ book** n [Schul]heft nt

exert /ɪg'zɜ:t/ vt ausüben; **~ one-self** sich anstrengen. **~ion** n Anstrengung f

exhale /eks'heɪl/ vt/i ausatmen

exhaust /ɪg'zɔ:st/ n (Auto) Auspuff m; (fumes) Abgase pl ● vt erschöpfen. **~ed** adj erschöpft. **~ing** adj anstrengend. **~ion** n Erschöpfung f. **~ive** adj (fig) erschöpfend

exhibit /ɪg'zɪbɪt/ n Ausstellungsstück nt; (Jur) Beweisstück nt ● vt ausstellen

exhibition /eksɪ'bɪʃn/ n Ausstellung f; (Univ) Stipendium nt. **~ist** n Exhibitionist(in) m(f)

exhibitor /ɪg'zɪbɪtə(r)/ n Aussteller m

exhilarat|ing /ɪg'zɪləreɪtɪŋ/ adj berauschend. **~ion** n Hochgefühl nt

exhume /ɪg'zju:m/ vt exhumieren

exile /'eksaɪl/ n Exil nt; (person) im Exil Lebende(r) m/f ● vt ins Exil schicken

exist /ɪg'zɪst/ vi bestehen, existieren. **~ence** n Existenz f; **be in ~ence** existieren

exit /'eksɪt/ n Ausgang m; (Auto) Ausfahrt f; (Theat) Abgang m

exorbitant /ɪg'zɔ:bɪtənt/ adj übermäßig hoch

exotic /ɪg'zɒtɪk/ adj exotisch

expand /ɪk'spænd/ vt ausdehnen; (explain better) weiter ausführen ● vi sich ausdehnen; (Comm) expandieren

expans|e /ɪk'spæns/ n Weite f.

~ion n Ausdehnung f; (Techn, Pol, Comm) Expansion f

expect /ɪk'spekt/ vt erwarten; (suppose) annehmen; **I ~ so** wahrscheinlich

expectan|cy /ɪk'spektənsɪ/ n Erwartung f. **~t** adj erwartungsvoll; **~t mother** werdende Mutter f

expectation /ekspek'teɪʃn/ n Erwartung f

expedient /ɪk'spi:dɪənt/ adj zweckdienlich

expedite /'ekspɪdaɪt/ vt beschleunigen

expedition /ekspɪ'dɪʃn/ n Expedition f

expel /ɪk'spel/ vt (pt/pp expelled) ausweisen (from aus); (from school) von der Schule verweisen

expenditure /ɪk'spendɪtʃə(r)/ n Ausgaben pl

expense /ɪk'spens/ n Kosten pl; **business ~s** pl Spesen pl; **at my ~** auf meine Kosten

expensive /ɪk'spensɪv/ adj teuer

experience /ɪk'spɪərɪəns/ n Erfahrung f; (event) Erlebnis nt ● vt erleben. **~d** adj erfahren

experiment /ɪk'sperɪmənt/ n Versuch m, Experiment nt ● /-ment/ vi experimentieren. **~al** adj experimentell

expert /'ekspɜ:t/ adj fachmännisch ● n Fachmann m, Experte m

expertise /ekspɜ:'ti:z/ n Sachkenntnis f

expire /ɪk'spaɪə(r)/ vi ablaufen

expiry /ɪk'spaɪərɪ/ n Ablauf m

explain /ɪk'spleɪn/ vt erklären

explana|tion /ekspla'neɪʃn/ n Erklärung f. **~tory** adj erklärend

explicit /ɪk'splɪsɪt/ adj deutlich

explode /ɪk'spləʊd/ vi explodieren ● vt zur Explosion bringen

e

exploit[1] /'eksplɔɪt/ n [Helden]tat f

exploit[2] /ɪk'splɔɪt/ vt ausbeuten. **~ation** f Ausbeutung f

exploration /eksplə'reɪʃn/ n Erforschung f

explore /ɪk'splɔː(r)/ vt erforschen. **~r** n Forschungsreisende(r) m

explos|ion /ɪk'spləʊʒn/ n Explosion f. **~ive** adj explosiv ● n Sprengstoff m

export[1] /'ekspɔːt/ n Export m, Ausfuhr f

export[2] /ɪk'spɔːt/ vt exportieren, ausführen. **~er** n Exporteur m

expos|e /ɪk'spəʊz/ vt freilegen; (to danger) aussetzen (**to** dat); (reveal) aufdecken; (Phot) belichten. **~ure** n Aussetzung f; (Med) Unterkühlung f; (Phot) Belichtung f; **24 ~ures** 24 Aufnahmen

express /ɪk'spres/ adv (send) per Eilpost ● n (train) Schnellzug m ● vt ausdrücken; **~ oneself** sich ausdrücken. **~ion** n Ausdruck m. **~ive** adj ausdrucksvoll. **~ly** adv ausdrücklich

expulsion /ɪk'spʌlʃn/ n Ausweisung f; (Sch) Verweisung f von der Schule

exquisite /ek'skwɪzɪt/ adj erlesen

extend /ɪk'stend/ vt verlängern; (stretch out) ausstrecken; (enlarge) vergrößern ● vi sich ausdehnen; (table:) sich ausziehen lassen

extension /ɪk'stenʃn/ n Verlängerung f; (to house) Anbau m; (Teleph) Nebenanschluss m

extensive /ɪk'stensɪv/ adj weit; (fig) umfassend. **~ly** adv viel

extent /ɪk'stent/ n Ausdehnung f; (scope) Ausmaß nt, Umfang m; **to a certain ~** in gewissem Maße

exterior /ɪk'stɪərɪə(r)/ adj äußere(r,s) ● n the **~** das Äußere

exterminat|e /ɪk'stɜːmɪneɪt/ vt

ausrotten. **~ion** n Ausrottung f

external /ɪk'stɜːnl/ adj äußere(r,s); **for ~ use only** (Med) nur äußerlich. **~ly** adv äußerlich

extinct /ɪk'stɪŋkt/ adj ausgestorben; (volcano) erloschen. **~ion** n Aussterben nt

extinguish /ɪk'stɪŋgwɪʃ/ vt löschen. **~er** n Feuerlöscher m

extort /ɪk'stɔːt/ vt erpressen. **~ion** n Erpressung f

extortionate /ɪk'stɔːʃənət/ adj übermäßig hoch

extra /'ekstrə/ adj zusätzlich ● adv extra; (especially) besonders ● n (Theat) Statist(in) m(f); **~s** pl Nebenkosten pl; (Auto) Extras pl

extract[1] /'ekstrækt/ n Auszug m

extract[2] /ɪk'strækt/ vt herausziehen; ziehen (tooth)

extraordinary /ɪk'strɔːdɪnərɪ/ adj, **-ily** adv außerordentlich; (strange) seltsam

extravagan|ce /ɪk'strævəgəns/ n Verschwendung f; **an ~ce** ein Luxus m. **~t** adj verschwenderisch

extrem|e /ɪk'striːm/ adj äußerste(r,s); (fig) extrem ● n Extrem nt; **in the ~e** im höchsten Grade. **~ely** adv äußerst. **~ist** n Extremist m

extricate /'ekstrɪkeɪt/ vt befreien

extrovert /'ekstrəvɜːt/ n extravertierter Mensch m

exuberant /ɪg'zjuːbərənt/ adj überglücklich

exude /ɪg'zjuːd/ vt absondern; (fig) ausstrahlen

exult /ɪg'zʌlt/ vi frohlocken

eye /aɪ/ n Auge nt; (of needle) Öhr nt; (for hook) Öse f; **keep an ~ on** aufpassen auf (+ acc) ● vt (pt/pp **eyed**, pres p **ey[e]ing**) ansehen

eye: ~ brow n Augenbraue f. **~lash** n Wimper f. **~lid** n Augenlid

nt. ~-**shadow** n Lidschatten m.
~**sight** n Sehkraft f. ~**sore** n 🔢
Schandfleck m. ~**witness** n Augen-
zeuge m

Ff

fable /'feɪbl/ n Fabel f
fabric /'fæbrɪk/ n Stoff m
fabrication /fæbrɪ'keɪʃn/ n Erfindung f
fabulous /'fæbjʊləs/ adj 🔢 phantastisch
façade /fə'sɑːd/ n Fassade f
face /feɪs/ n Gesicht nt; (surface)
Fläche f; (of clock) Zifferblatt nt; pull
~s Gesichter schneiden; **in the** ~
of angesichts (+ gen); **on the** ~ **of**
it allem Anschein nach ● vt/i gegen-
überstehen (+ dat); ~ **north**
(house:) nach Norden liegen; ~ **the**
fact that sich damit abfinden, dass
face: ~-**flannel** n Waschlappen m.
~**less** adj anonym. ~-**lift** n Ge-
sichtsstraffung f

facet /'fæsɪt/ n Facette f; (fig)
Aspekt m
facetious /fə'siːʃəs/ adj spöttisch
facial /'feɪʃl/ adj Gesichts-
facile /'fæsaɪl/ adj oberflächlich
facilitate /fə'sɪlɪteɪt/ vt erleichtern
facility /fə'sɪlətɪ/ n Leichtigkeit f;
(skill) Gewandtheit f; ~**ies** pl Einrichtungen pl
facsimile /fæk'sɪməlɪ/ n Faksi-
mile nt
fact /fækt/ n Tatsache f; **in** ~ tatsächlich; (actually) eigentlich
faction /'fækʃn/ n Gruppe f
factor /'fæktə(r)/ n Faktor m

factory /'fæktərɪ/ n Fabrik f
factual /'fæktʃʊəl/ adj sachlich
faculty /'fækəltɪ/ n Fähigkeit f;
(Univ) Fakultät f
fad /fæd/ n Fimmel m
fade /feɪd/ vi verblassen; (material:)
verbleichen; (sound:) abklingen;
(flower:) verwelken
fag /fæg/ n (chore) Plage f; (🔢: cigarette) Zigarette f
fail /feɪl/ n **without** ~ unbedingt
● vi (attempt:) scheitern; (grow
weak) nachlassen; (break down) versagen; (in exam) durchfallen; ~ **to**
do sth etw nicht tun ● vt nicht bestehen (exam); durchfallen lassen
(candidate); (disappoint) enttäuschen
failing /'feɪlɪŋ/ n Fehler m
failure /'feɪljə(r)/ n Misserfolg m;
(breakdown) Versagen nt; (person)
Versager m
faint /feɪnt/ adj (-er, -est) schwach;
I feel~ mir ist schwach ● n Ohn-
macht f ● vi ohnmächtig werden.
~**ness** n Schwäche f
fair¹ /feə(r)/ n Jahrmarkt m;
(Comm) Messe f
fair² /feə(r)/ adj (-er, -est) (hair) blond;
(skin) hell; (weather) heiter; (just)
gerecht, fair; (quite good) ziemlich
gut; (Sch) genügend; **a** ~ **amount**
ziemlich viel ● adv play ~ fair sein.
~**ly** adv gerecht; (rather) ziemlich.
~**ness** n Blondheit f; Helle f; Gerechtigkeit f; (Sport) Fairness f
fairy /'feərɪ/ n Elfe f; **good/wicked**
~ gute/böse Fee f. ~ **story**,
~-**tale** n Märchen nt
faith /feɪθ/ n Glaube m; (trust) Vertrauen nt (in zu)
faithful /'feɪθfl/ adj treu; (exact)
genau; **Yours** ~**ly** Hochachtungs-
voll. ~**ness** n Treue f; Genauigkeit f
fake /feɪk/ adj falsch ● n Fälschung
f; (person) Schwindler m ● vt fäl-

schen; (*pretend*) vortäuschen

falcon /ˈfɔːlkən/ n Falke m

fall /fɔːl/ n Fall m; (*heavy*) Sturz m; (*in prices*) Fallen nt; (*Amer: autumn*) Herbst m; **have a ~** fallen ● vi (*pt* **fell**, *pp* **fallen**) fallen; (*heavily*) stürzen; (*night:*) anbrechen; **~ in love** sich verlieben; **~ back on** zurückgreifen auf (+ *acc*); **~ for s.o.** ⚠ sich in jdn verlieben; **~ for sth** ⚠ auf etw (*acc*) hereinfallen; **~ about** vi (*with laughter*) sich [vor Lachen] kringeln; **~ down** vi umfallen; (*thing:*) herunterfallen; (*building:*) einstürzen; **~ in** vi hineinfallen; (*collapse*) einfallen; (*Mil*) antreten; **~ in with** sich anschließen (+ *dat*). **~ off** vi herunterfallen; (*diminish*) abnehmen. **~ out** vi herausfallen; (*hair:*) ausfallen; (*quarrel*) sich überwerfen. **~ over** vi hinfallen. **~ through** vi durchfallen; (*plan:*) ins Wasser fallen

fallacy /ˈfæləsɪ/ n Irrtum m

fallible /ˈfæləbl/ adj fehlbar

'fall-out n [radioaktiver] Niederschlag m

false /fɔːls/ adj falsch; (*artificial*) künstlich. **~hood** n Unwahrheit f. **~ly** adv falsch

false 'teeth npl [künstliches] Gebiss nt

falsify /ˈfɔːlsɪfaɪ/ vt (*pt/pp* **-ied**) fälschen

falter /ˈfɔːltə(r)/ vi zögern

fame /feɪm/ n Ruhm m.

familiar /fəˈmɪljə(r)/ adj vertraut; (*known*) bekannt; **too ~** familiär. **~ity** n Vertrautheit f. **~ize** vt vertraut machen (**with** mit)

family /ˈfæmɪlɪ/ n Familie f

family: **~ 'doctor** n Hausarzt m. **~ 'life** n Familienleben nt. **~ 'planning** n Familienplanung f. **~ 'tree** n Stammbaum m

famine /ˈfæmɪn/ n Hungersnot f

famished /ˈfæmɪʃt/ adj sehr hungrig

famous /ˈfeɪməs/ adj berühmt

fan¹ /fæn/ n Fächer m; (*Techn*) Ventilator m

fan² n (*admirer*) Fan m

fanatic /fəˈnætɪk/ n Fanatiker m. **~al** adj fanatisch. **~ism** n Fanatismus m

fanciful /ˈfænsɪfl/ adj phantastisch; (*imaginative*) phantasiereich

fancy /ˈfænsɪ/ n Phantasie f; **I have taken a real ~ to him** er hat es mir angetan ● adj ausgefallen ● vt (*believe*) meinen; (*imagine*) sich (*dat*) einbilden; (⚠: *want*) Lust haben auf (+ *acc*); **~ that!** stell dir vor! (*really*) tatsächlich! **~ 'dress** n Kostüm nt

fanfare /ˈfænfeə(r)/ n Fanfare f

fang /fæŋ/ n Fangzahn m

'fan heater n Heizlüfter m

fantasize /ˈfæntəsaɪz/ vi phantasieren. **~tic** adj phantastisch. **~y** n Phantasie f

far /fɑː(r)/ adv weit; (*much*) viel; **by ~** bei weitem; **~ away** weit weg; **as ~ as I know** soviel ich weiß; **as ~ as the church** bis zur Kirche ● adj at the ~ end am anderen Ende; **the F~ East** der Ferne Osten

farce /fɑːs/ n Farce f. **~ical** adj lächerlich

fare /feə(r)/ n Fahrpreis m; (*money*) Fahrgeld nt; (*food*) Kost f. **air ~** Flugpreis m

farewell /feəˈwel/ int (*literary*) lebe wohl! ● n Lebewohl nt

far-'fetched adj weit hergeholt

farm /fɑːm/ n Bauernhof m ● vi Landwirtschaft betreiben ● vt bewirtschaften (*land*). **~er** n Landwirt m

farm: **~house** n Bauernhaus nt. **~ing** n Landwirtschaft f.

~yard n Hof m

far: ~-'reaching adj weit reichend.
~-'sighted adj (fig) umsichtig;
(Amer: long-sighted) weitsichtig

farther /'fɑːðə(r)/ adv weiter; ~
off weiter entfernt

fascinat|e /'fæsɪneɪt/ vt faszinieren. ~ing adj faszinierend. ~ion n
Faszination f

fascis|m /'fæʃɪzm/ n Faschismus
m. ~t n Faschist m ● adj faschistisch

fashion /'fæʃn/ n Mode f; (manner) Art f. ~able adj, -bly adv
modisch

fast /fɑːst/ adj & adv (-er, -est)
schnell; (firm) fest; (colour) waschecht; be ~ (clock:) vorgehen; be ~
asleep fest schlafen

fasten /'fɑːsn/ vt zumachen; (fix)
befestigen (to an + dat). ~er n,
~ing n Verschluss m

fastidious /fə'stɪdɪəs/ adj wählerisch; (particular) penibel

fat /fæt/ adj (fatter, fattest) dick;
(meat) fett ● n Fett nt

fatal /'feɪtl/ adj tödlich; (error) verhängnisvoll. ~ity n Todesopfer nt.
~ly adv tödlich

fate /feɪt/ n Schicksal nt. ~ful adj
verhängnisvoll

'fat-head n 🔢 Dummkopf m

father /'fɑːðə(r)/ n Vater m; F ~
Christmas der Weihnachtsmann
● vt zeugen

father: ~hood n Vaterschaft f.
~-in-law n (pl ~s-in-law) Schwiegervater m. ~ly adj väterlich

fathom /'fæðəm/ n (Naut) Faden m
● vt verstehen

fatigue /fə'tiːg/ n Ermüdung f

fatten /'fætn/ vt mästen (animal)

fatty /'fætɪ/ adj fett; (foods) fetthaltig

fatuous /'fætjʊəs/ adj albern

fault /fɔːlt/ n Fehler m; (Techn) Defekt m; (Geology) Verwerfung f; at
~ im Unrecht; find ~ with etwas
auszusetzen haben an (+ dat); it's
your ~ du bist schuld. ~less adj
fehlerfrei

faulty /'fɔːltɪ/ adj fehlerhaft

favour /'feɪvə(r)/ n Gunst f; I am
in ~ ich bin dafür; do s.o. a ~ jdm
einen Gefallen tun ● vt begünstigen; (prefer) bevorzugen. ~able
adj, -bly adv günstig; (reply) positiv

favourit|e /'feɪvərɪt/ adj Lieblings-
● n Liebling m, (Sport) Favorit(in)
m(f). ~ism n Bevorzugung f

fawn /fɔːn/ adj rehbraun ● n
Hirschkalb nt

fax /fæks/ n Fax nt ● vt faxen (s.o.
jdm). ~ machine n Faxgerät nt

fear /fɪə(r)/ n Furcht f, Angst f (of
vor + dat) ● vt/i fürchten

fear|ful /'fɪəfl/ adj besorgt; (awful)
furchtbar. ~less adj furchtlos

feas|ibility /fiːzə'bɪlətɪ/ n Durchführbarkeit f. ~ible adj durchführbar; (possible) möglich

feast /fiːst/ n Festmahl nt; (Relig)
Fest nt ● vi ~ [on] schmausen

feat /fiːt/ n Leistung f

feather /'feðə(r)/ n Feder f

feature /'fiːtʃə(r)/ n Gesichtszug
m; (quality) Merkmal nt, (article)
Feature nt ● vt darstellen

February /'febrʊərɪ/ n Februar m

fed /fed/ see feed ● adj be ~ up 🔢
die Nase voll haben (with von)

federal /'fedərəl/ adj Bundes-

federation /fedə'reɪʃn/ n Föderation f

fee /fiː/ n Gebühr f; (professional)
Honorar nt

feeble /'fiːbl/ adj (-r, -st), -bly adv
schwach

feed /fiːd/ n Futter nt; (for baby)
Essen nt ● v (pt/pp fed) ● vt füttern; (support) ernähren; (into machine) eingeben; speisen (computer)
● vi sich ernähren (on von)

'feedback n Feedback nt

feel /fiːl/ v (pt/pp felt) ● vt fühlen;
(experience) empfinden; (think) meinen ● vi sich fühlen; ∼ soft/hard
sich weich/hart anfühlen; I ∼ hot/ill
mir ist heiß/schlecht; ∼ing n Gefühl nt; no hard ∼ings nichts
für ungut

feet /fiːt/ see foot

feline /ˈfiːlaɪn/ adj Katzen-; (catlike)
katzenartig

fell[1] /fel/ vt fällen

fell[2] see fall

fellow /ˈfeləʊ/ n (fam: man) Kerl m

fellow: ∼'countryman n Landsmann m. ∼ men pl Mitmenschen pl

felt[1] /felt/ see feel

felt[2] n Filz m. ∼[-tipped] 'pen n
Filzstift m

female /ˈfiːmeɪl/ adj weiblich ● nt
Weibchen nt; (pej: woman) Weib nt

femin|ine /ˈfemmɪn/ adj weiblich
● n (Gram) Femininum nt. ∼inity n
Weiblichkeit f. ∼ist adj feministisch
● n Feminist(in) m(f)

fenc|e /fens/ n Zaun m; (fam: per-
son) Hehler m ● vi (Sport) fechten
● vt ∼e in einzäunen. ∼er n Fech-
ter m. ∼ing n Zaun m; (Sport)
Fechten nt

fender /ˈfendə(r)/ n Kaminvorset-
zer m; (Naut) Fender m; (Amer:
wing) Kotflügel m

ferment /fəˈment/ vi gären ● vt
gären lassen

fern /fɜːn/ n Farn m

feroc|ious /fəˈrəʊʃəs/ adj wild.
∼ity n Wildheit f

ferry /ˈferɪ/ n Fähre f

fertil|e /ˈfɜːtaɪl/ adj fruchtbar. ∼ity
n Fruchtbarkeit f

fertilize /ˈfɜːtəlaɪz/ vt befruchten;
düngen (land). ∼r n Dünger m

fervent /ˈfɜːvənt/ adj leidenschaftlich

fervour /ˈfɜːvə(r)/ n Leidenschaft f

festival /ˈfestɪvl/ n Fest nt; (Mus,
Theat) Festspiele pl

festiv|e /ˈfestɪv/ adj festlich.
∼ities npl Feierlichkeiten pl

festoon /feˈstuːn/ vt behängen
(with mit)

fetch /fetʃ/ vt holen; (collect) abholen; (be sold for) einbringen

fetching /ˈfetʃɪŋ/ adj anziehend

fête /feɪt/ n Fest nt ● vt feiern

feud /fjuːd/ n Fehde f

feudal /ˈfjuːdl/ adj Feudal-

fever /ˈfiːvə(r)/ n Fieber nt. ∼ish
adj fiebrig; (fig) fieberhaft

few /fjuː/ adj (-er, -est) wenige;
every ∼ days alle paar Tage ● n a
∼ ein paar; quite a ∼ ziemlich viele

fiancé /frˈɒnseɪ/ n Verlobte(r) m. **fiancée** n Verlobte f

fiasco /frˈæskəʊ/ n Fiasko nt

fib /fɪb/ n kleine Lüge

fibre /ˈfaɪbə(r)/ n Faser f

fiction /ˈfɪkʃn/ n Erfindung f;
[works of] ∼ Erzählungsliteratur f.
∼al adj erfunden

fictitious /fɪkˈtɪʃəs/ adj [frei] erfunden

fiddle /ˈfɪdl/ n (fam) Geige f; (cheat-
ing) Schwindel m ● vi herumspielen
(with mit) ● vt (fam) frisieren (accounts)

fiddly /ˈfɪdlɪ/ adj knifflig

fidelity /frˈdelətɪ/ n Treue f

fidget /ˈfɪdʒɪt/ vi zappeln. ∼y adj
zappelig

field /fiːld/ n Feld nt; (meadow)

Wiese f; (subject) Gebiet nt

field: ~ **events** npl Sprung- und Wurfdisziplinen pl. **F**~ **'Marshal** n Feldmarschall m

fiendish /'fiːndɪʃ/ adj teuflisch

fierce /fɪəs/ adj (-r, -st) wild; (fig) heftig. ~**ness** n Wildheit f; (fig) Heftigkeit f

fiery /'faɪərɪ/ adj feurig

fifteen /fɪf'tiːn/ adj fünfzehn ● n Fünfzehn f. ~**th** adj fünfzehnte(r,s)

fifth /fɪfθ/ adj fünfte(r,s)

fiftieth /'fɪftɪɪθ/ adj fünfzigste(r,s)

fifty /'fɪftɪ/ adj fünfzig

fig /fɪg/ n Feige f

fight /faɪt/ n Kampf m; (brawl) Schlägerei f; (between children, dogs) Rauferei f ● v (pt/pp **fought**) ● vt kämpfen gegen; (fig) bekämpfen ● vi kämpfen; (brawl) sich schlagen; (children, dogs:) sich raufen. ~**er** n Kämpfer m; (Aviat) Jagdflugzeug nt. ~**ing** n Kampf m

figurative /'fɪgjərətɪv/ adj bildlich, übertragen

figure /'fɪgə(r)/ n (digit) Ziffer f; (number) Zahl f; (sum) Summe f; (carving, sculpture, woman's) Figur f; (form) Gestalt f; (illustration) Abbildung f; **good at** ~**s** gut im Rechnen ● vi (appear) erscheinen ● vt (Amer: think) glauben

filch /fɪltʃ/ vt 🔲 klauen

file[1] /faɪl/ n Akte f; (for documents) [Akten]ordner m ● vt ablegen (documents); (Jur) einreichen

file[2] n (line) Reihe f; **in single** ~ im Gänsemarsch

file[3] n (Techn) Feile f ● vt feilen

fill /fɪl/ n **eat one's** ~ sich satt essen ● vt füllen; plombieren (tooth) ● vi sich füllen. ~ **in** vt auffüllen; ausfüllen (form). ~ **out** vt ausfüllen (form). ~ **up** vi sich füllen ● vt vollfüllen; (Auto) volltanken; ausfüllen

(questionnaire)

fillet /'fɪlɪt/ n Filet nt ● vt (pt/pp **filleted**) entgräten

filling /'fɪlɪŋ/ n Füllung f; (of tooth) Plombe f. ~ **station** n Tankstelle f

filly /'fɪlɪ/ n junge Stute f

film /fɪlm/ n Film m ● vt/i filmen; verfilmen (book). ~ **star** n Filmstar m

filter /'fɪltə(r)/ n Filter m ● vt filtern

filth /fɪlθ/ n Dreck m. ~**y** adj dreckig

fin /fɪn/ n Flosse f

final /'faɪnl/ adj letzte(r,s); (conclusive) endgültig ● n (Sport) Endspiel nt; ~**s** pl (Univ) Abschlussprüfung f

finale /fɪ'nɑːlɪ/ n Finale nt

final|ist /'faɪnəlɪst/ n Finalist(in) m(f)

final|ize /'faɪnəlaɪz/ vt endgültig festlegen. ~**ly** adv schließlich

finance /faɪ'næns/ n Finanz f ● vt finanzieren

financial /faɪ'nænʃl/ adj finanziell

find /faɪnd/ n Fund m ● vt (pt/pp **found**) finden; (establish) feststellen; **go and** ~ holen; **try to** ~ suchen. ~ **out** vt herausfinden; (learn) erfahren ● vi (enquire) sich erkundigen

fine[1] /faɪn/ n Geldstrafe f ● vt zu einer Geldstrafe verurteilen

fine[2] adj (-r, -st., -ly adv fein; (weather) schön; **he's** ~ es geht ihm gut ● adv gut; **cut it** ~ 🔲 sich (dat) wenig Zeit lassen

finesse /fɪ'nes/ n Gewandtheit f

finger /'fɪŋgə(r)/ n Finger m ● vt anfassen

finger: ~**nail** n Fingernagel m. ~**print** n Fingerabdruck m. ~**tip** n Fingerspitze f

finicky /'fɪnɪkɪ/ adj knifflig; (choosy) wählerisch

finish /'fɪnɪʃ/ n Schluss m; (Sport)

Finish nt; (line) Ziel nt; (of product) Ausführung f ● vt beenden; (use up) aufbrauchen; ~ **one's drink** austrinken; ~ **reading** zu Ende lesen ● vi fertig werden; (performance:) zu Ende sein; (runner:) durchs Ziel gehen

Finland /'fɪnlənd/ n Finnland nt

Finn /fɪn/ n Finne m/ Finnin f. ~**ish** adj finnisch

fir /fɜː(r)/ n Tanne f

fire /'faɪə(r)/ n Feuer nt; (forest, house) Brand m; **be on** ~ brennen; **catch** ~ Feuer fangen; **set** ~ **to** anzünden; (arsonist:) in Brand stecken; **under** ~ unter Beschuss ● vt brennen (pottery); abfeuern (shot); schießen mit (gun); (🗆: dismiss) feuern ● vi schießen (**at** auf + acc); (engine:) anspringen

fire: ~ **alarm** n Feuermelder m. ~ **brigade** n Feuerwehr f. ~**engine** n Löschfahrzeug nt. ~**extinguisher** n Feuerlöscher m. ~**man** n Feuerwehrmann m. ~**place** n Kamin m. ~**side** n **by** or **at the** ~**side am Kamin. ~ **station** n Feuerwache f. ~**wood** n Brennholz nt. ~**work** n Feuerwerkskörper m; ~**works** pl (display) Feuerwerk nt

firm[1] /fɜːm/ n Firma f

firm[2] /fɜːm/ adj (-er, -est) fest; (resolute) entschlossen; (strict) streng

first /fɜːst/ adj & n erste(r,s); **at** ~ zuerst; **at** ~ **sight** auf den ersten Blick; **from the** ~ von Anfang an ● adv zuerst; (firstly) erstens

first: ~ **aid** n erste Hilfe. ~-**'aid kit** n Verbandkasten m. ~-**class** adj erstklassig; (Rail) erster Klasse. ~ /-'-/ adv (travel) erster Klasse. ~ **'floor** n erster Stock; (Amer: ground floor) Erdgeschoss nt. ~**ly** adv erstens. ~**name** n Vorname m. ~-**rate** adj erstklassig

fish /fɪʃ/ n Fisch m ● vt/i fischen;

(with rod) angeln

fish: ~**bone** n Gräte f. ~**erman** n Fischer m. ~ **'finger** n Fischstäbchen nt

fishing /'fɪʃɪŋ/ n Fischerei f. ~ **boat** n Fischerboot nt. ~-**rod** n Angel[rute] f

fish: ~**monger** /-mʌŋgə(r)/ n Fischhändler m. ~**y** adj Fisch-; (🗆: suspicious) verdächtig

fission /'fɪʃn/ n (Phys) Spaltung f

fist /fɪst/ n Faust f

fit[1] /fɪt/ n (attack) Anfall m

fit[2] adj (fitter, fittest) (suitable) geeignet; (healthy) gesund; (Sport) fit; ~ **to eat** essbar

fit[3] n (of clothes) Sitz m; **be a good** ~ gut passen ● v (pt/pp fitted) ● vi (be the right size) passen ● vt anbringen (**to** an + dat); (install) einbauen; ~ **with** versehen mit. ~ **in** vi hineinpassen; (adapt) sich einfügen (**with** + acc) ● vt (accommodate) unterbringen

fit|ness n Eignung f; [**physical**] ~**ness** Gesundheit f; (Sport) Fitness f. ~ **ted** adj eingebaut; (garment) tailliert

fitted: ~ **'carpet** n Teppichboden m. ~ **'kitchen** n Einbauküche f. ~ **'sheet** n Spannlaken f

fitting /'fɪtɪŋ/ adj passend ● n (of clothes) Anprobe f; (of shoes) Weite f; (Techn) Zubehörteil nt; ~**s** pl Zubehör nt

five /faɪv/ adj fünf ● n Fünf f. ~**r** n Fünfpfundschein m

fix /fɪks/ n (sl: drugs) Fix m; **be in a** ~ 🗆 in der Klemme sitzen ● vt befestigen (**to** an + dat); (arrange) festlegen; (repair) reparieren; (Phot) fixieren; ~ **a meal** Essen machen

fixed /'fɪkst/ adj fest

fixture /'fɪkstʃə(r)/ n (Sport) Veranstaltung f; ~**s and fittings** zu einer Wohnung gehörende Einrichtungen *pl*

fizz /fɪz/ *vi* sprudeln

fizzle /'fɪzl/ *vi* ~ **out** verpuffen

fizzy /'fɪzɪ/ *adj* sprudelnd. ~ **drink** *n* Brause[limonade] *f*

flabbergasted /'flæbəgɑːstɪd/ *adj* **be** ~ platt sein 🔲

flabby /'flæbɪ/ *adj* schlaff

flag /flæg/ *n* Fahne *f*; (*Naut*) Flagge *f*

'flag-pole *n* Fahnenstange *f*

flagrant /'fleɪgrənt/ *adj* flagrant

'flagstone *n* [Pflaster]platte *f*

flair /fleə(r)/ *n* Begabung *f*

flake /fleɪk/ *n* Flocke *f* ● *vi* ~**[off]** abblättern

flamboyant /flæm'bɔɪənt/ *adj* extravagant

flame /fleɪm/ *n* Flamme *f*

flan /flæn/ *n* **[fruit]** ~ Obsttorte *f*

flank /flæŋk/ *n* Flanke *f*

flannel /'flænl/ *n* Flanell *m*; (*for washing*) Waschlappen *m*

flap /flæp/ *n* Klappe *f*; **in a** ~ 🔲 aufgeregt ● *v* (*pt/pp* **flapped**) *vi* flattern; 🔲 sich aufregen ● *vt* ~ **its wings** mit den Flügeln schlagen

flare /fleə(r)/ *n* Leuchtsignal *nt*. ● *vi* ~ **up** auflodern; (🔲: *get angry*) aufbrausen

flash /flæʃ/ *n* Blitz *m*; **in a** ~ 🔲 im Nu ● *vi* blitzen; (*repeatedly*) blinken; ~ **past** vorbeirasen

flash: ~**back** *n* Rückblende *f*. ~**er** *n* (*Auto*) Blinker *m*. ~**light** *n* (*Phot*) Blitzlicht *nt*; (*Amer: torch*) Taschenlampe *f*. ~**y** *adj* auffällig

flask /flɑːsk/ *n* Flasche *f*

flat /flæt/ *adj* (**flatter, flattest**) flach; (*surface*) eben; (*refusal*) glatt; (*beer*) schal; (*battery*) verbraucht; (*Auto*) leer; (*tyre*) platt; (*Mus*) **A** ~ As *nt*; **B** ~ B *nt* ● *n* Wohnung *f*;

(🔲: *puncture*) Reifenpanne *f*

flat: ~**ly** *adv* (*refuse*) glatt. ~ **rate** *n* Einheitspreis *m*

flatten /'flætn/ *vt* platt drücken

flatter /'flætə(r)/ *vt* schmeicheln (+ *dat*). ~**y** *n* Schmeichelei *f*

flat 'tyre *n* Reifenpanne *f*

flaunt /flɔːnt/ *vt* prunken mit

flautist /'flɔːtɪst/ *n* Flötist(in) *m*(*f*)

flavour /'fleɪvə(r)/ *n* Geschmack *m* ● *vt* abschmecken. ~**ing** *n* Aroma *nt*

flaw /flɔː/ *n* Fehler *m*. ~**less** *adj* tadellos; (*complexion*) makellos

flea /fliː/ *n* Floh *m*

fleck /flek/ *n* Tupfen *m*

fled /fled/ *see* **flee**

flee /fliː/ *v* (*pt/pp* **fled**) ● *vi* fliehen (**from** *vor* + *dat*) ● *vt* flüchten aus

fleece /fliːs/ *n* Vlies *nt* ● *vt* 🔲 schröpfen

fleet /fliːt/ *n* Flotte *f*; (*of cars*) Wagenpark *m*

fleeting /'fliːtɪŋ/ *adj* flüchtig

Flemish /'flemɪʃ/ *adj* flämisch

flesh /fleʃ/ *n* Fleisch *nt*

flew /fluː/ *see* **fly**[2]

flex[1] /fleks/ *vt* anspannen (*muscle*)

flex[2] *n* (*Electr*) Schnur *f*

flexibility /fleksə'bɪlətɪ/ *n* Biegsamkeit *f*; (*fig*) Flexibilität *f*. ~**le** *adj* biegsam; (*fig*) flexibel

flick /flɪk/ *vt* schnippen

flicker /'flɪkə(r)/ *vi* flackern

flier /'flaɪə(r)/ *n* = **flyer**

flight[1] /flaɪt/ *n* (*fleeing*) Flucht *f*

flight[2] *n* (*flying*) Flug *m*; ~ **of stairs** Treppe *f*

'flight recorder *n* Flugschreiber *m*

flimsy /'flɪmzɪ/ *adj* dünn; (*excuse*) fadenscheinig

flinch /flɪntʃ/ *vi* zurückzucken

fling /flɪŋ/ vt (pt/pp flung) schleudern

flint /flɪnt/ n Feuerstein m

flip /flɪp/ vt/i schnippen; ~ **through** durchblättern

flippant /ˈflɪpənt/ adj leichtfertig

flirt /flɜːt/ n kokette Frau f ● vi flirten

flirtat|ion /flɜːˈteɪʃn/ n Flirt m. ~**ious** adj kokett

flit /flɪt/ vi (pt/pp flitted) flattern

float /fləʊt/ n Schwimmer m; (in procession) Festwagen m; (money) Wechselgeld nt ● vi (thing:) schwimmen; (person:) sich treiben lassen; (in air) schweben

flock /flɒk/ n Herde f; (of birds) Schwarm m ● vi strömen

flog /flɒg/ vt (pt/pp flogged) auspeitschen; (🆒: sell) verkloppen

flood /flʌd/ n Überschwemmung f; (fig) Flut f ● vt überschwemmen

'floodlight n Flutlicht nt ● vt (pt/pp floodlit) anstrahlen

floor /flɔː(r)/ n Fußboden m; (storey) Stock m

floor: ~ **board** n Dielenbrett nt. ~**polish** n Bohnerwachs nt. ~ **show** n Kabarettvorstellung f

flop /flɒp/ n 🆒 (failure) Reinfall m; (Theat) Durchfall m ● vi (pt/pp flopped) 🆒 (fail) durchfallen

floppy /ˈflɒpɪ/ adj schlapp. ~ '**disc** n Diskette f

floral /ˈflɔːrl/ adj Blumen-

florid /ˈflɒrɪd/ adj (complexion) gerötet; (style) blumig

florist /ˈflɒrɪst/ n Blumenhändler(in) m(f)

flounder /ˈflaʊndə(r)/ vi zappeln

flour /ˈflaʊə/ n Mehl nt

flourish /ˈflʌrɪʃ/ n große Geste f; (scroll) Schnörkel m ● vi gedeihen; (fig) blühen ● vt schwenken

flout /flaʊt/ vt missachten

flow /fləʊ/ n Fluss m; (of traffic, blood) Strom m ● vi fließen

flower /ˈflaʊə(r)/ n Blume f ● vi blühen

flower: ~**bed** n Blumenbeet nt. ~**pot** n Blumentopf m. ~**y** adj blumig

flown /fləʊn/ see **fly**²

flu /fluː/ n 🆒 Grippe f

fluctuat|e /ˈflʌktjʊeɪt/ vi schwanken. ~**ion** n Schwankung f

fluent /ˈfluːənt/ adj fließend

fluff /flʌf/ n Fusseln pl; (down) Flaum m. ~**y** adj flauschig

fluid /ˈfluːɪd/ adj flüssig; (fig) veränderlich ● n Flüssigkeit f

fluke /fluːk/ n [glücklicher] Zufall m

flung /flʌŋ/ see **fling**

fluorescent /flʊəˈresnt/ adj fluoreszierend

fluoride /ˈflʊəraɪd/ n Fluor nt

flush /flʌʃ/ n (blush) Erröten nt ● vi rot werden ● vt spülen ● adj in einer Ebene (with mit); (🆒: affluent) gut bei Kasse

flustered /ˈflʌstəd/ adj nervös

flute /fluːt/ n Flöte f

flutter /ˈflʌtə(r)/ n Flattern nt ● vi flattern

fly¹ /flaɪ/ n 🆒 (fly:) Fliege f

fly² v (pt flew, pp flown) ● vi fliegen; (flag:) wehen; (rush) sausen ● vt fliegen; führen (flag)

fly³ n & **flies** pl (on trousers) Hosenschlitz m

flyer /ˈflaɪə(r)/ n Flieger(in) m(f); (leaflet) Flugblatt nt

foal /fəʊl/ n Fohlen nt

foam /fəʊm/ n Schaum m; (synthetic) Schaumstoff m ● vi schäumen

fob /fɒb/ vt (pt/pp fobbed) ~ **sth off** etw andrehen (on s.o. jdm); ~

s.o. off jdn abspeisen (**with** mit)
focal /ˈfəʊkl/ n Brenn-
focus /ˈfəʊkəs/ n Brennpunkt m; in
~ **scharf eingestellt** ● v (pt/pp fo-
cused or focussed) ● vt einstellen
(**on** auf + acc) ● vi (fig) sich konzentrieren (**on** auf + acc)
fog /fɒg/ n Nebel m
foggy /ˈfɒgɪ/ adj (foggier, foggi-
est) neblig
'**fog-horn** n Nebelhorn nt
foible /ˈfɔɪbl/ n Eigenart f
foil[1] /fɔɪl/ n Folie f; (Culin) Alufolie f
foil[2] vt (thwart) vereiteln
foil[3] n (Fencing) Florett nt
fold n Falte f; (in paper) Kniff m ● vt
falten; ~ **one's arms** die Arme verschränken ● vi sich falten lassen;
(fail) eingehen. ~ **up** vt zusam-
menfalten; zusammenklappen
(chair) ● vi sich zusammenfalten/-
klappen lassen; ⌧ (business:)
eingehen
fold|er /ˈfəʊldə(r)/ n Mappe f.
~**ing** adj Klapp-
foliage /ˈfəʊlɪɪdʒ/ n Blätter pl; (of
tree) Laub nt
folk /fəʊk/ npl Leute pl
folk: ~-**dance** n Volkstanz m.
~-**song** n Volkslied nt
follow /ˈfɒləʊ/ vt/i folgen (+ dat);
(pursue) verfolgen; (in vehicle) nach-
fahren (+ dat). ~ **up** vt nachgehen
(+ dat)
follow|er /ˈfɒləʊə(r)/ n Anhänge-
r(in) m(f). ~**ing** adj folgend ● n
Folgende(s) nt; (supporters) Anhän-
gerschaft f ● prep im Anschluss an
(+ acc)
folly /ˈfɒlɪ/ n Torheit f
fond /fɒnd/ adj (-er, -est) liebevoll;
be ~ **of** gern haben; gern essen
(food)
fondle /ˈfɒndl/ vt liebkosen
fondness /ˈfɒndnɪs/ n Liebe f

(**for** zu)
food /fuːd/ n Essen nt; (for animals)
Futter nt; (groceries) Lebensmittel
pl. ~ **poisoning** n Lebensmittelver-
giftung f
food poisoning n Lebensmittel-
vergiftung f
fool[1] /fuːl/ n (Culin) Fruchtcreme f
fool[2] n Narr m; **make a** ~ **of oneself** sich lächerlich machen ● vt hereinlegen ● vi ~ **around** herumalbern
'**fool|hardy** adj tollkühn. ~**ish** adj
dumm. ~**ishness** n Dummheit f.
~**proof** adj narrensicher
foot /fʊt/ n (pl feet) Fuß m; (measure) Fuß m (30,48 cm); (of bed)
Fußende nt; **on** ~ zu Fuß; **on one's
feet** auf den Beinen; **put one's** ~
in it ⌧ ins Fettnäpfchen treten
foot: ~-**and-'mouth [disease]** n
Maul- und Klauenseuche f. ~**ball** n
Fußball m. ~**baller** n Fußballspieler
m. ~**ball pools** npl Fußballtoto nt.
~-**bridge** n Fußgängerbrücke f.
~**hills** npl Vorgebirge nt. ~**hold** n
Halt m. ~**ing** n Halt m. ~**lights**
npl Rampenlicht nt. ~**note** n Fuß-
note f. ~**path** n Fußweg m.
~**print** n Fußabdruck m. ~**step** n
Schritt m; **follow in s.o.'s** ~**steps**
(fig) in jds Fußstapfen treten.
~**wear** n Schuhwerk nt

---

for /fɔː(r)/, unstressed /fə(r)/
● preposition
⋯▸ (on behalf of; in place of; in favour of) für (+ acc). **I did it for
you** ich habe es für dich gemacht. **I work for a
bank** ich arbeite für ihn/für eine
Bank. **be for doing sth** dafür
sein, etw zu tun. **cheque/bill for
£5** Scheck/Rechnung über 5
Pfund. **for nothing** umsonst.

what have you got for a cold? was haben Sie gegen Erkältung?

••••➤ (expressing reason) wegen (+ gen); (with emotion) aus. **famous for these wines** berühmt wegen dieser Weine od für diese Weine. **he was sentenced to death for murder** er wurde wegen Mordes zum Tode verurteilt. **were it not for you/your help** ohne dich/deine Hilfe. **for fear/love of** aus Angst vor (+ dat)/aus Liebe zu (+ dat)

••••➤ (expressing purpose) (with action, meal) zu (+ dat); (with object) für (+ acc). **it's for washing the car** es ist zum Autowaschen. **we met for a discussion** wir trafen uns zu einer Besprechung. **for pleasure** zum Vergnügen. **meat for lunch** Fleisch zum Mittagessen. **what is that for?** wofür od wozu ist das? **a dish for nuts** eine Schale für Nüsse

••••➤ (expressing direction) nach (+ dat); (less precise) in Richtung. **the train for Oxford** der Zug nach Oxford. **they were heading** or **making for London** sie fuhren in Richtung London

••••➤ (expressing time) (completed process) ... lang; (continuing process) seit (+ dat). **I lived here for two years** ich habe zwei Jahre [lang] hier gewohnt. **I have been living here for two years** ich wohne hier seit zwei Jahren. **we are staying for a week** wir werden eine Woche bleiben

••••➤ (expressing difficulty, impossibility, embarrassment etc.) + dat. **it's impossible/inconvenient for her** es ist ihr unmöglich/ungelegen. **it was embarrassing**

for our teacher unserem Lehrer war es peinlich

● conjunction

••••➤ denn. **he's not coming for he has no money** er kommt nicht mit, denn er hat kein Geld

forbade /fə'bæd/ see forbid

forbid /fə'bɪd/ vt (pt forbade, pp forbidden) verbieten (s.o. jdm). **~ding** adj bedrohlich; (stern) streng

force /fɔːs/ n Kraft f; (of blow) Wucht f; (violence) Gewalt f; **in ~** gültig; (in large numbers) in großer Zahl; **come into ~** in Kraft treten; **the ~s** pl die Streitkräfte pl ● vt zwingen; (break open) aufbrechen

forced /fɔːst/ adj gezwungen; **~ landing** Notlandung f

force: ~-'feed vt (pt/pp -fed) zwangsernähren. **~ful** adj energisch

forceps /'fɔːseps/ n inv Zange f.

forcible /'fɔːsəbl/ adj gewaltsam

ford /fɔːd/ n Furt f ● vt durchwaten; (in vehicle) durchfahren

fore /fɔː(r)/ adj vordere(r,s)

fore: ~arm n Unterarm m. **~cast** n Voraussage f; (for weather) Vorhersage f ● vt (pt/pp ~cast) voraussagen, vorhersagen. **~finger** n Zeigefinger m. **~gone** adj **be a ~gone conclusion** von vornherein feststehen. **~ground** n Vordergrund m. **~head** /'fɒrɪd/ n Stirn f. **~hand** n Vorhand f

foreign /'fɒrən/ adj ausländisch; (country) fremd; **he is ~** er ist Ausländer. **~ currency** n Devisen pl. **~er** n Ausländer(in) m(f). **~ language** n Fremdsprache f

Foreign: ~ Office n ≈ Außenministerium m ≈. **'Secretary** n ≈ Außenminister m

fore: ~leg n Vorderbein nt. **~man**

n Vorarbeiter m. **∼most** a führend
● **odv first and ∼most** zuallererst.
∼name n Vorname m. **∼runner** n
Vorläufer m

fore'see vt (pt **-saw**, pp **-seen**)
voraussehen, vorhersehen. **∼able**
adj in the **∼able future** in absehbarer Zeit

'foresight n Weitblick m

forest /'fɒrɪst/ n Wald m. **∼er** n
Förster m

forestry /'fɒrɪstrɪ/ n Forstwirtschaft f

'foretaste n Vorgeschmack m

forever /fə'revə(r)/ adv für immer

fore'warn vt vorher warnen

foreword /'fɔːwɜːd/ n Vorwort nt

forfeit /'fɔːfɪt/ n (in game) Pfand nt
● vt verwirken

forgave /fə'geɪv/ see **forgive**

forge /fɔːdʒ/ n Schmiede f ● vt
schmieden; (counterfeit) fälschen.
∼r n Fälscher m. **∼ry** n Fälschung f

forget /fə'get/ vt/i (pt **-got**, pp
-gotten) vergessen; verlernen (language, skill). **∼ful** adj vergesslich.
∼fulness n Vergesslichkeit f.
∼-me-not n Vergissmeinnicht nt

forgive /fə'gɪv/ vt (pt **-gave**, pp
-given) ∼ s.o. for sth jdm etw vergeben od verzeihen

forgot(ten) /fə'gɒt(n)/ see **forget**

fork /fɔːk/ n Gabel f; (in road) Gabelung f ● vi (road:) sich gabeln; ∼
right rechts abzweigen

fork-lift 'truck n Gabelstapler m

forlorn /fə'lɔːn/ adj verlassen;
(hope) schwach

form /fɔːm/ n Form f; (document)
Formular nt; (bench) Bank f; (Sch)
Klasse f ● vt (into zu); (create)
bilden ● vi sich bilden; (idea:)
Gestalt annehmen

formal /'fɔːml/ adj formell, förm-

lich. **∼ity** n Förmlichkeit f; (requirement) Formalität f

format /'fɔːmæt/ n Format nt ● vt
formatieren

formation /fɔː'meɪʃn/ n Formation f

former /'fɔːmə(r)/ adj ehemalig;
the ∼ der/die/das Erstere. **∼ly** adv
früher

formidable /'fɔːmɪdəbl/ adj gewaltig

formula /'fɔːmjʊlə/ n (pl **-ae** or **-s**)
Formel f

formulate /'fɔːmjʊleɪt/ vt formulieren

forsake /fə'seɪk/ vt (pt **-sook**
/-sʊk/, pp **-saken**) verlassen

fort /fɔːt/ n (Mil) Fort nt

forth /fɔːθ/ adv back and ∼ hin
und her; and so ∼ und so weiter

forth: **∼'coming** adj bevorstehend; (⚏: communicative) mitteilsam. **∼right** adj direkt

fortieth /'fɔːtɪθ/ adj vierzigste(r,s)

fortification /fɔːtɪfɪ'keɪʃn/ n Befestigung f

fortify /'fɔːtɪfaɪ/ vt (pt/pp **-ied**) befestigen; (fig) stärken

fortnight /'fɔːt-/ n vierzehn Tage
pl. **∼ly** adj vierzehntäglich ● adv
alle vierzehn Tage

fortress /'fɔːtrɪs/ n Festung f

fortunate /'fɔːtʃʊnət/ adj glücklich; **be** ∼ Glück haben. **∼ly** adv
glücklicherweise

fortune /'fɔːtʃuːn/ n Glück nt;
(money) Vermögen nt. **∼-teller** n
Wahrsagerin f

forty /'fɔːtɪ/ adj vierzig

forward /'fɔːwəd/ adv vorwärts;
(to the front) nach vorn ● adj Vorwärts-; (presumptuous) anmaßend
● n (Sport) Stürmer m ● vt nachsenden (letter). **∼s** adv vorwärts

fossil /'fɒsl/ n Fossil nt

foster /'fɒstə(r)/ vt fördern; in Pflege nehmen (child). **~-child** n Pflegekind nt. **~-mother** n Pflegemutter f

fought /fɔːt/ see fight

foul /faul/ adj (-er, -est) widerlich; (language) unflätig; **~ play** (Jur) Mord m • n (Sport) Foul nt • vt verschmutzen; (obstruct) blockieren; (Sport) foulen

found¹ /faund/ see find

found² vt gründen

foundation /faun'deɪʃn/ n (basis) Grundlage f; (charitable) Stiftung f; **~s** pl Fundament nt

founder /'faundə(r)/ n Gründer(in) m(f)

foundry /'faundrɪ/ n Gießerei f

fountain /'fauntɪn/ n Brunnen m

four /fɔː(r)/ adj vier • n Vier f

four: ~teen adj vierzehn • n Vierzehn f. **~'teenth** adj vierzehnte(r,s)

fourth /fɔːθ/ adj vierte(r,s)

fowl /faul/ n Geflügel nt

fox /fɒks/ n Fuchs m • vt (puzzle) verblüffen

foyer /'fɔɪeɪ/ n Foyer nt; (in hotel) Empfangshalle f

fraction /'frækʃn/ n Bruchteil m; (Math) Bruch m

fracture /'fræktʃə(r)/ n Bruch m • vt/i brechen

fragile /'frædʒaɪl/ adj zerbrechlich

fragment /'frægmənt/ n Bruchstück m, Fragment nt

fragran|ce /'freigrəns/ n Duft m. **~t** adj duftend

frail /freɪl/ adj (-er, -est) gebrechlich

frame /freɪm/ n Rahmen m; (of spectacles) Gestell nt; (Anat) Körperbau m • vt einrahmen; (fig) formulieren; ⊠ ein Verbrechen anhängen

(+ dat). **~work** n Gerüst nt; (fig) Gerippe nt

franc /fræŋk/ n (French, Belgian) Franc m; (Swiss) Franken m

France /frɑːns/ n Frankreich nt

franchise /'fræntʃaɪz/ n (Pol) Wahlrecht nt; (Comm) Franchise nt

frank /fræŋk/ adj offen

frankfurter /'fræŋkfɜːtə(r)/ n Frankfurter f

frantic /'fræntɪk/ adj, **-ally** adv verzweifelt; außer sich (dat) (with vor)

fraternal /frə'tɜːnl/ adj brüderlich

fraud /frɔːd/ n Betrug m; (person) Betrüger(in) m(f)

fray /freɪ/ vi ausfransen

freak /friːk/ n Missbildung f; (person) Missgeburt f • adj anormal

freckle /'frekl/ n Sommersprosse f

free /friː/ adj (freer, freest) frei; (ticket, copy, time) Frei-; (lavish) freigebig; **~ [of charge]** kostenlos; **set ~** freilassen; (rescue) befreien • vt (pt/pp freed) freilassen; (rescue) befreien; (disentangle) freibekommen

free: ~dom n Freiheit f. **~hold** n [freier] Grundbesitz m. **~lance** adj & adv freiberuflich. **~ly** adv frei; (voluntarily) freiwillig; (generously) großzügig. **F~mason** n Freimaurer m. **~-range** adj **~-range eggs** Landeier pl. **~'sample** n Gratisprobe f. **~style** n Freistil m. **~way** n (Amer) Autobahn f

freez|e /friːz/ vt (pt froze, pp frozen) einfrieren; stoppen (wages) • vi **it's ~ing** es friert.

freez|er /'friːzə(r)/ n Gefriertruhe f; (upright) Gefrierschrank m.

freezing adj eiskalt • n **five degrees below ~ing** fünf Grad unter Null

freight /freɪt/ n Fracht f. **~er** n Frachter m. **~ train** n Güterzug m

French /frentʃ/ adj französisch ● n (Lang) Französisch nt; **the ~** pl die Franzosen

French: ~ beans npl grüne Bohnen pl. **~ bread** n Stangenbrot nt. **~' fries** npl Pommes frites pl. **~man** n Franzose m. **~'window** n Terrassentür f. **~woman** n Französin f

frenzy /'frenzɪ/ n Raserei f

frequency /'friːkwənsɪ/ n Häufigkeit f; (Phys) Frequenz f

frequent¹ /'friːkwənt/ adj häufig

frequent² /frɪ'kwent/ vt regelmäßig besuchen

fresh /freʃ/ adj (-er, -est) frisch; (new) neu; (cheeky) frech

freshness /'freʃnɪs/ n Frische f

'freshwater adj Süßwasser-

fret /fret/ vi (pt/pp fretted) sich grämen. **~ful** adj weinerlich

'fretsaw n Laubsäge f

friction /'frɪkʃn/ n Reibung f; (fig) Reibereien pl

Friday /'fraɪdeɪ/ n Freitag m

fridge /frɪdʒ/ n Kühlschrank m

fried /fraɪd/ see **fry³** ● adj gebraten; **~ egg** Spiegelei nt

friend /frend/ n Freund(in) m(f). **~liness** n Freundlichkeit f. **~ly** adj freundlich; **~ly with** befreundet mit. **~ship** n Freundschaft f

fright /fraɪt/ n Schreck m

frighten /'fraɪtn/ vt Angst machen (+ dat); (startle) erschrecken; **be ~ed** Angst haben (of vor + dat). **~ing** adj Angst erregend

frightful /'fraɪtfl/ adj schrecklich

frigid /'frɪdʒɪd/ adj frostig; (sexually) frigide. **~ity** n Frostigkeit f; Frigidität f

frill /frɪl/ n Rüsche f; (paper) Man-

schette f. **~y** adj rüschenbesetzt

fringe /frɪndʒ/ n Fransen pl; (of hair) Pony m; (fig: edge) Rand m

frisk /frɪsk/ vi herumspringen ● vt (search) durchsuchen

frisky /'frɪskɪ/ adj lebhaft

fritter /'frɪtə(r)/ vt **~ [away]** verplempern 🔟

frivol|ity /frɪ'vɒlətɪ/ n Frivolität f. **~ous** adj frivol, leichtfertig

fro /frəʊ/ see **to**

frock /frɒk/ n Kleid nt

frog /frɒg/ n Frosch m. **~man** n Froschmann m

frolic /'frɒlɪk/ vi (pt/pp frolicked) herumtollen

from /frɒm/ prep von (+ dat); (out of) aus (+ dat); (according to) nach (+ dat); **~ Monday** ab Montag; **~ that day** seit dem Tag

front /frʌnt/ n Vorderseite f; (fig) Fassade f; (of garment) Vorderteil nt; (sea~) Strandpromenade f; (Mil, Pol, Meteorol) Front f; **in ~ of** vor; **in** or **at the ~** vorne; **to the ~** nach vorne ● adj vordere(r,s); (page, row) erste(r,s); (tooth, wheel) Vorder-

front: ~ 'door n Haustür f. **~ 'garden** n Vorgarten m

frontier /'frʌntɪə(r)/ n Grenze f

frost /frɒst/ n Frost m; (hoar~) Raureif m; **ten degrees of ~** zehn Grad Kälte. **~bite** n Erfrierung f. **~bitten** adj erfroren

frost|ed /'frɒstɪd/ adj **~ed glass** Mattglas nt. **~ing** n (Amer Culin) Zuckerguss m. **~y** adj, **-ily** adv frostig

froth /frɒθ/ n Schaum m ● vi schäumen. **~y** adj schaumig

frown /fraʊn/ n Stirnrunzeln nt ● vi die Stirn runzeln

froze /frəʊz/ see **freeze**

frozen /'frəʊzn/ see **freeze** ● adj

gefroren; (*Culin*) tiefgekühlt; **I'm ~** 🔲 mir ist eiskalt. **~ food** *n* Tiefkühlkost *f*

frugal /'fru:gl/ *adj* sparsam; (*meal*) frugal

fruit /fru:t/ *n* Frucht *f*; (*collectively*) Obst *nt*. **~ cake** *n* englischer [Tee-]kuchen *m*

fruitful *adj* fruchtbar

fruit: ~ juice *n* Obstsaft *m*. **~less** *adj* fruchtlos. **~ salad** *n* Obstsalat *m*

fruity /'fru:tɪ/ *adj* fruchtig

frustrat|e /frʌ'streɪt/ *vt* vereiteln; (*Psychology*) frustrieren. **~ion** *n* Frustration *f*

fry /fraɪ/ *vt/i* (*pt/pp* **fried**) [in der Pfanne] braten. **~ing-pan** *n* Bratpfanne *f*

fuel /'fju:əl/ *n* Brennstoff *m*; (*for car*) Kraftstoff *m*; (*for aircraft*) Treibstoff *m*

fugitive /'fju:dʒətɪv/ *n* Flüchtling *m*

fulfil /fʊl'fɪl/ *vt* (*pt/pp* **-filled**) erfüllen. **~ment** *n* Erfüllung *f*

full /fʊl/ *adj & adv* (**-er, -est**) voll; (*detailed*) ausführlich; (*skirt*) weit; **~ of** voll von (+ *dat*), voller (+ *gen*); **at ~ speed** in voller Fahrt ● **in ~** vollständig

full: ~ 'moon *n* Vollmond *m*. **~-scale** *adj* (*model*) in Originalgröße; (*rescue, alert*) großangelegt. **~ 'stop** *n* Punkt *m*. **~-time** *adj* ganztägig ● *adv* ganztags

fully /'fʊlɪ/ *adv* völlig; (*in detail*) ausführlich

fumble /'fʌmbl/ *vi* herumfummeln (**with** an + *dat*)

fume /fju:m/ *vi* vor Wut schäumen

fumes /fju:mz/ *npl* Dämpfe *pl*; (*from car*) Abgase *pl*

fun /fʌn/ *n* Spaß *m*; **for ~** aus *od* zum Spaß; **make ~ of** sich lustig

machen über (+ *acc*); **have ~!** viel Spaß!

function /'fʌŋkʃn/ *n* Funktion *f*; (*event*) Veranstaltung *f* ● *vi* funktionieren; (*serve*) dienen (**as** als). **~al** *adj* zweckmäßig

fund /fʌnd/ *n* Fonds *m*; (*fig*) Vorrat *m*; **~s** *pl* Geldmittel *pl* ● *vt* finanzieren

fundamental /fʌndə'mentl/ *adj* grundlegend; (*essential*) wesentlich

funeral /'fju:nərəl/ *n* Beerdigung *f*; (*cremation*) Feuerbestattung *f*

funeral: ~ march *n* Trauermarsch *m*. **~ service** *n* Trauergottesdienst *m*

'funfair *n* Jahrmarkt *m*

fungus /'fʌŋgəs/ *n* (*pl* **-gi** /-gaɪ/) Pilz *m*

funnel /'fʌnl/ *n* Trichter *m*; (*on ship, train*) Schornstein *m*

funnily /'fʌnɪlɪ/ *adv* komisch; **~ enough** komischerweise

funny /'fʌnɪ/ *adj* komisch

fur /fɜ:(r)/ *n* Fell *nt*; (*for clothing*) Pelz *m*; (*in kettle*) Kesselstein *m*. **~ 'coat** *n* Pelzmantel *m*

furious /'fjʊərɪəs/ *adj* wütend (**with** auf + *acc*)

furnace /'fɜ:nɪs/ *n* (*Techn*) Ofen *m*

furnish /'fɜ:nɪʃ/ *vt* einrichten; (*supply*) liefern. **~ed** *adj* **~ed room** möbliertes Zimmer *nt*. **~ings** *npl* Einrichtungsgegenstände *pl*

furniture /'fɜ:nɪtʃə(r)/ *n* Möbel *pl*

further /'fɜ:ðə(r)/ *adj* weitere(r,s); **at the ~ end** am anderen Ende; **until ~ notice** bis auf weiteres ● *adv* weiter; **~ off** weiter entfernt ● *vt* fördern

furthermore /fɜ:ðə'mɔ:(r)/ *adv* außerdem

furthest /'fɜ:ðɪst/ *adj* am weitesten entfernt ● *adv* am weitesten

fury /'fjʊərɪ/ n Wut f

fuse¹ /fjuːz/ n (of bomb) Zünder m; (cord) Zündschnur f

fuse² n (Electr) Sicherung f • vt/i verschmelzen; **the lights have ~d** die Sicherung [für das Licht] ist durchgebrannt. **~-box** n Sicherungskasten m

fuselage /'fjuːzəlɑːʒ/ n (Aviat) Rumpf m

fuss /fʌs/ n Getue nt; **make a ~ of** verwöhnen; (caress) liebkosen • vi Umstände machen

fussy /'fʌsɪ/ adj wählerisch; (particular) penibel

futil|e /'fjuːtaɪl/ adj zwecklos. **~ity** n Zwecklosigkeit f

future /'fjuːtʃə(r)/ adj zukünftig • n Zukunft f; (Gram) [erstes] Futur nt

futuristic /fjuːtʃə'rɪstɪk/ adj futuristisch

fuzzy /'fʌzɪ/ adj (hair) kraus; (blurred) verschwommen

Gg

gabble /'gæbl/ vi schnell reden

gable /'geɪbl/ n Giebel m

gadget /'gædʒɪt/ n [kleines] Gerät nt

Gaelic /'geɪlɪk/ n Gälisch nt

gag /gæg/ n Knebel m; (joke) Witz m; (Theat) Gag m • vt (pt/pp gagged) knebeln

gaiety /'geɪətɪ/ n Fröhlichkeit f

gaily /'geɪlɪ/ adv fröhlich

gain /geɪn/ n Gewinn m; (increase) Zunahme f • vt gewinnen; (obtain) erlangen; **~ weight** zunehmen • vi

(clock:) vorgehen

gait /geɪt/ n Gang m

gala /'gɑːlə/ n Fest nt • attrib Gala-

galaxy /'gæləksɪ/ n Galaxie f; **the G~** die Milchstraße

gale /geɪl/ n Sturm m

gallant /'gælənt/ adj tapfer; (chivalrous) galant. **~ry** n Tapferkeit f

'gall-bladder n Gallenblase f

gallery /'gælərɪ/ n Galerie f

galley /'gælɪ/ n (ship's kitchen) Kombüse f; **~ [proof]** [Druck-]fahne f

gallon /'gælən/ n Gallone f (= 4,5 l; Amer = 3,785 l)

gallop /'gæləp/ n Galopp m • vi galoppieren

gallows /'gæləʊz/ n Galgen m

galore /gə'lɔː(r)/ adv in Hülle und Fülle

gamble /'gæmbl/ n (risk) Risiko nt • vi [um Geld] spielen; **~ on** (rely) sich verlassen auf (+ acc). **~r** n Spieler(in) m(f)

game /geɪm/ n Spiel nt; (animals, birds) Wild nt; **~s** (Sch) Sport m • adj (brave) tapfer; (willing) bereit (for zu). **~keeper** n Wildhüter m

gammon /'gæmən/ n [geräucherter] Schinken m

gang /gæŋ/ n Bande f; (of workmen) Kolonne f

gangling /'gæŋglɪŋ/ adj schlaksig

gangmaster /'gæŋmɑːstə(r)/ n Aufseher(in) m(f) von (meist illegalen) Gelegenheitsarbeitern

gangrene /'gæŋgriːn/ n Wundbrand m

gangster /'gæŋstə(r)/ n Gangster m

gangway /'gæŋweɪ/ n Gang m; (Naut, Aviat) Gangway f

gaol /dʒeɪl/ n Gefängnis nt • vt ins Gefängnis sperren. **~er** n

Gefängniswärter m

gap /gæp/ n Lücke f; (interval) Pause f; (difference) Unterschied m

gaple /geɪp/ vi gaffen; **~e at** anstarren. **~ing** adj klaffend

gap year Britische Schulabsolventen legen vor Universitätsbeginn oft eine einjährige Pause ein. In diesem gap year jobben sie, um Arbeitserfahrung zu erwerben oder Geld für ihr Studium zu verdienen. Viele reisen um die Welt, lernen die Kultur anderer Länder kennen, sammeln Auslandserfahrungen, belegen Sprachkurse oder arbeiten ehrenamtlich in Entwicklungsländern.

garage /'gærɑːʒ/ n Garage f; (for repairs) Werkstatt f; (for petrol) Tankstelle f

garbage /'gɑːbɪdʒ/ n Müll m. **~ can** n (Amer) Mülleimer m

garbled /'gɑːbld/ adj verworren

garden /'gɑːdn/ n Garten m; [public] **~s** pl [öffentliche] Anlagen pl ● vi im Garten arbeiten. **~er** n Gärtner(in) m(f). **~ing** n Gartenarbeit f

gargle /'gɑːgl/ n (liquid) Gurgelwasser nt ● vi gurgeln

garish /'geərɪʃ/ adj grell

garland /'gɑːlənd/ n Girlande f

garlic /'gɑːlɪk/ n Knoblauch m

garment /'gɑːmənt/ n Kleidungsstück n

garnet /'gɑːnɪt/ n Granat m

garnish /'gɑːnɪʃ/ n Garnierung f ● vt garnieren

garrison /'gærɪsn/ n Garnison f

garrulous /'gærʊləs/ adj geschwätzig

garter /'gɑːtə(r)/ n Strumpfband nt; (Amer: suspender) Strumpf-

halter m

gas /gæs/ n Gas nt; (Amer, fam: petrol) Benzin nt ● v (pt/pp gassed) ● vt vergasen ● vi i schwatzen. **~cooker** n Gasherd m. **~'fire** n Gasofen m

gash /gæʃ/ n Schnitt m; (wound) klaffende Wunde f

gasket /'gæskɪt/ n (Techn) Dichtung f

gas: ~ mask n Gasmaske f. **~-meter** n Gaszähler m

gasoline /'gæsəliːn/ n (Amer) Benzin nt

gasp /gɑːsp/ vi keuchen; (in surprise) hörbar die Luft einziehen

'gas station n (Amer) Tankstelle f

gastric /'gæstrɪk/ adj Magen-

gastronomy /gæ'strɒnəmɪ/ n Gastronomie f

gate /geɪt/ n Tor nt; (to field) Gatter nt; (barrier) Schranke f; (at airport) Flugsteig m

gate: ~crasher n ungeladener Gast m. **~way** n Tor nt

gather /'gæðə(r)/ vt sammeln; (pick) pflücken; (conclude) folgern (from aus) ● vi sich versammeln; (storm:) sich zusammenziehen. **~ing family ~ing** Familientreffen nt

gaudy /'gɔːdɪ/ adj knallig

gauge /geɪdʒ/ n Stärke f; (Rail) Spurweite f; (device) Messinstrument nt

gaunt /gɔːnt/ adj hager

gauze /gɔːz/ n Gaze f

gave /geɪv/ see give

gawky /'gɔːkɪ/ adj schlaksig

gay /geɪ/ adj (-er, -est) fröhlich; (homosexual) homosexuell

gaze /geɪz/ n [langer] Blick m ● vi sehen; **~ at** ansehen

GB abbr Great Britain

gear /gɪə(r)/ n Ausrüstung f; (Techn) Getriebe nt; (Auto) Gang m; **change ~** schalten

gear: ~box n (Auto) Getriebe nt. **~lever** n, (Amer) **~shift** n Schalthebel m

geese /giːs/ see **goose**

gel /dʒel/ n Gel nt

gelatine /ˈdʒelətiːn/ n Gelatine f

gem /dʒem/ n Juwel nt

gender /ˈdʒendə(r)/ n (Gram) Geschlecht nt

gene /dʒiːn/ n Gen nt

genealogy /dʒiːnɪˈælədʒɪ/ n Genealogie f

general /ˈdʒenrəl/ adj allgemein ●n General m; **in ~** im Allgemeinen. **~ e'lection** n allgemeine Wahlen pl

generaliz|ation /dʒenrəlaɪˈzeɪʃn/ n Verallgemeinerung f. **~e** vi verallgemeinern

generally /ˈdʒenrəlɪ/ adv im Allgemeinen

general prac'titioner n praktischer Arzt m

generate /ˈdʒenəreɪt/ vt erzeugen

generation /dʒenəˈreɪʃn/ n Generation f

generator /ˈdʒenəreɪtə(r)/ n Generator m

generosity /dʒenəˈrɒsɪtɪ/ n Großzügigkeit f

generous /ˈdʒenərəs/ adj großzügig

genetic /dʒəˈnetɪk/ adj, **-ally** adv genetisch. **~ally modified** gentechnisch verändert; genmanipuliert. **~ engineering** n Gentechnologie f

Geneva /dʒɪˈniːvə/ n Genf nt

genial /ˈdʒiːnɪəl/ adj freundlich

genitals /ˈdʒenɪtlz/ pl [äußere] Geschlechtsteile pl

genitive /ˈdʒenɪtɪv/ adj & n ~

[case] Genitiv m

genius /ˈdʒiːnɪəs/ n (pl **-uses**) Genie m; (quality) Genialität f

genome /ˈdʒiːnəʊm/ n Genom nt

genre /ˈʒɑːrə/ n Gattung f, Genre nt

gent /dʒent/ n 1 Herr m; **the ~s** sg die Herrentoilette f

genteel /dʒenˈtiːl/ adj vornehm

gentle /ˈdʒentl/ adj (**-r, -st**) sanft

gentleman /ˈdʒentlmən/ n Herr m; (well-mannered) Gentleman m

gent|leness /ˈdʒentlnɪs/ n Sanftheit f. **~ly** adv sanft

genuine /ˈdʒenjʊɪn/ adj echt; (sincere) aufrichtig. **~ly** adv (honestly) ehrlich

geograph|ical /dʒɪəˈgræfɪkl/ adj geographisch. **~y** n Geographie f, Erdkunde f

geological /dʒɪəˈlɒdʒɪkl/ adj geologisch

geolog|ist /dʒɪˈɒlədʒɪst/ n Geologe m/-gin f. **~y** n Geologie f

geometr|ic(al) /dʒɪəˈmetrɪk(l)/ adj geometrisch. **~y** n Geometrie f

geranium /dʒəˈreɪnɪəm/ n Geranie f

geriatric /dʒerɪˈætrɪk/ adj geriatrisch ●n geriatrischer Patient m

germ /dʒɜːm/ n Keim m; **~s** pl 1 Bazillen pl

German /ˈdʒɜːmən/ adj deutsch ●n (person) Deutsche(r) m/f; (Lang) Deutsch nt; **in ~** auf Deutsch; **into ~** ins Deutsche

Germanic /dʒəˈmænɪk/ adj germanisch

Germany /ˈdʒɜːmənɪ/ n Deutschland nt

germinate /ˈdʒɜːmɪneɪt/ vi keimen

gesticulate /dʒeˈstɪkjʊleɪt/ vi gestikulieren

gesture /ˈdʒestʃə(r)/ n Geste f

g

get /get/ v

pt **got**, pp **got** (Amer also **gotten**), pres p **getting**

● *transitive verb*

····▶ (*obtain, receive*) bekommen; 🛈 kriegen; (*procure*) besorgen; (*buy*) kaufen; (*fetch*) holen. **get a job/taxi for s.o.** jdm einen Job verschaffen/ein Taxi besorgen. **I must get some bread** ich muss Brot holen. **get permission** die Erlaubnis erhalten. **I couldn't get her on the phone** ich konnte sie nicht telefonisch erreichen

····▶ (*prepare*) machen (*meal*). **he got the breakfast** er machte das Frühstück

····▶ (*cause*) **get s.o. to do sth** jdn dazu bringen, etw zu tun. **get one's hair cut** sich (*dat*) die Haare schneiden lassen. **get one's hands dirty** sich (*dat*) die Hände schmutzig machen

····▶ **get the bus/train**. (*travel by*) den Bus/Zug nehmen; (*be in time for, catch*) den Bus/Zug erreichen

····▶ **have got** (🛈: *have*) haben. **I've got a cold** ich habe eine Erkältung

····▶ **have got to do sth** etw tun müssen. **I've got to hurry** ich muss mich beeilen

····▶ (🛈: *understand*) kapieren 🛈. **I don't get it** ich kapiere nicht

● *intransitive verb*

····▶ (*become*) werden. **get older** älter werden. **the weather got worse** das Wetter wurde schlechter. **get to** kommen zu /nach (*town*); (*reach*)

erreichen. **get dressed** sich anziehen. **get married** heiraten.

● *phrasal verbs*

● **get about** vi (*move*) sich bewegen; (*travel*) herumkommen; (*spread*) sich verbreiten. ● **get at** vt (*have access*) herankommen an (+ *acc*); (🛈: *criticize*) anmachen 🛈. (*mean*) **what are you getting at?** worauf willst du hinaus? ● **get away** vi (*leave*) wegkommen; (*escape*) entkommen. ● **get back** vi zurückkommen; vt (*recover*) zurückbekommen; **get one's own back** sich revanchieren. ● **get by** vi vorbeikommen; (*manage*) sein Auskommen haben. ● **get down** vi heruntersteigen; vt (*depress*) deprimieren; **get down to** sich [heran]machen an (+ *acc*). ● **get in** vi (*into bus*) einsteigen; vt (*fetch*) hereinholen. ● **get off** vi (*dismount*) absteigen; (*from bus*) aussteigen; (*leave*) wegkommen; (*Jur*) freigesprochen werden; vt (*remove*) abbekommen. ● **get on** vi (*mount*) aufsteigen; (*to bus*) einsteigen; (*be on good terms*) gut auskommen (**with** mit + *dat*); (*make progress*) Fortschritte machen; **how are you getting on?** wie geht's? ● **get out** vi herauskommen; (*of car*) aussteigen; **get out of** (*avoid doing*) sich drücken um; vt (*take out*) herausholen; herausbekommen (*cork, stain*). ● **get over** vi hinübersteigen; vt (*fig*) hinwegkommen über (+ *acc*). ● **get round** vi herumkommen; **I never get round to it** ich komme nie dazu; vt herumkriegen; (*avoid*) umgehen. ● **get through** vi durchkommen. ● **get up** vi aufstehen

get: ~**away** n Flucht f. ~**-up** n Aufmachung f

ghastly /'gɑːstlɪ/ adj grässlich; (pale) blass

gherkin /'gɜːkɪn/ n Essiggurke f

ghost /ɡəʊst/ n Geist m, Gespenst nt. ~**ly** adj geisterhaft

ghoulish /'ɡuːlɪʃ/ adj makaber

giant /'dʒaɪənt/ n Riese m ● adj riesig

gibberish /'dʒɪbərɪʃ/ n Kauderwelsch nt

giblets /'dʒɪblɪts/ npl Geflügelklein nt

giddiness /'ɡɪdɪnɪs/ n Schwindel m

giddy /'ɡɪdɪ/ adj schwindlig

gift /ɡɪft/ n Geschenk nt; (to charity) Gabe f; (talent) Begabung f. ~**ed** adj begabt

gigantic /dʒaɪˈɡæntɪk/ adj riesig, riesengroß

giggle /'ɡɪɡl/ n Kichern nt ● vi kichern

gild /ɡɪld/ vt vergolden

gilt /ɡɪlt/ adj vergoldet ● n Vergoldung f. ~**-edged** adj (Comm) mündelsicher

gimmick /'ɡɪmɪk/ n Trick m

gin /dʒɪn/ n Gin m

ginger /'dʒɪndʒə(r)/ adj rotblond; (cat) rot ● n Ingwer m. ~**bread** n Pfefferkuchen m

gingerly /'dʒɪndʒəlɪ/ adv vorsichtig

gipsy /'dʒɪpsɪ/ n = gypsy

giraffe /dʒɪˈrɑːf/ n Giraffe f

girder /'ɡɜːdə(r)/ n (Techn) Träger m

girl /ɡɜːl/ n Mädchen nt; (young woman) junge Frau f. ~ **band** n Mädchenband f. ~**friend** n Freundin f. ~**ish** adj mädchenhaft

gist /dʒɪst/ n **the** ~ das

Wesentliche

give /ɡɪv/ n Elastizität f ● vt (pt gave, pp given) ● vt geben/(as present) schenken (to dat); (donate) spenden; (lecture) halten; (one's name) angeben ● vi geben; (yield) nachgeben. ~ **away** vt verschenken; (betray) verraten; (distribute) verteilen. ~ **back** vt zurückgeben. ~ **in** vt einreichen ● vi (yield) nachgeben. ~ **off** vt abgeben. ~ **up** vt/i aufgeben; ● vi nachgeben sich stellen. ~ **way** vi nachgeben; (Auto) die Vorfahrt beachten

glacier /'ɡlæsɪə(r)/ n Gletscher m

glad /ɡlæd/ adj froh (of über + acc)

gladly /'ɡlædlɪ/ adv gern[e]

glamorous /'ɡlæmərəs/ adj glanzvoll; (film star) glamourös

glamour /'ɡlæmə(r)/ n [betörender] Glanz m

glance /ɡlɑːns/ n [flüchtiger] Blick m ● vi ~ **at** einen Blick werfen auf (+ acc). ~ **up** vi aufblicken

gland /ɡlænd/ n Drüse f

glare /ɡleə(r)/ n grelles Licht nt; (look) ärgerlicher Blick m ● vi ~ **at** böse ansehen

glaring /'ɡleərɪŋ/ adj grell; (mistake) krass

glass /ɡlɑːs/ n Glas nt; (mirror) Spiegel m; ~**es** pl (spectacles) Brille f. ~**y** adj glasig

glaze /ɡleɪz/ n Glasur f

gleam /ɡliːm/ n Schein m ● vi glänzen

glib /ɡlɪb/ adj (pej) gewandt

glid|e /ɡlaɪd/ vi gleiten; (through the air) schweben. ~**er** n Segelflugzeug nt. ~**ing** n Segelfliegen nt

glimmer /'ɡlɪmə(r)/ n Glimmen nt ● vi glimmen

glimpse /ɡlɪmps/ vt flüchtig sehen

glint /ɡlɪnt/ n Blitzen nt ● vi blitzen

glisten /ˈglɪsn/ vi glitzern

glitter /ˈglɪtə(r)/ vi glitzern

global /ˈgləʊbl/ adj global

globaliz|e /ˈgləʊbəlaɪz/ vt globalisieren. **~ation** n Globalisierung f

globe /gləʊb/ n Kugel f; (map) Globus m

gloom /gluːm/ n Düsterkeit f; (fig) Pessimismus m

gloomy /ˈgluːmɪ/ adj, **-ily** adv düster; (fig) pessimistisch

glorif|y /ˈglɔːrɪfaɪ/ vt (pt/pp -ied) verherrlichen

glorious /ˈglɔːrɪəs/ adj herrlich; (deed, hero) glorreich

glory /ˈglɔːrɪ/ n Ruhm m; (splendour) Pracht f ● vi ~ in genießen

gloss /glɒs/ n Glanz m ● adj Glanz- ● vi ~ over beschönigen

glossary /ˈglɒsərɪ/ n Glossar nt

glossy /ˈglɒsɪ/ adj glänzend

glove /glʌv/ n Handschuh m

glow /gləʊ/ n Glut f; (of candle) Schein m ● vi glühen; (candle:) scheinen. **~ing** adj glühend; (account) begeistert

glucose /ˈgluːkəʊs/ n Traubenzucker m, Glukose f

glue /gluː/ n Klebstoff m ● vt (pres p gluing) kleben (**to** an + acc)

glum /glʌm/ adj (glummer, glummest) niedergeschlagen

glut /glʌt/ n Überfluss m (**of** an + dat)

glutton /ˈglʌtən/ n Vielfraß m

GM abbr (genetically modified); ~ crops/food gentechnisch veränderte Feldfrüchte/Nahrungsmittel

gnash /næʃ/ vt ~ one's teeth mit den Zähnen knirschen

gnat /næt/ n Mücke f

gnaw /nɔː/ vt/i nagen (**at** an + dat)

---

go /gəʊ/

3 sg pres tense **goes**; pt **went**; pp **gone**

● *intransitive verb*

····▸ gehen; (in vehicle) fahren. **go by air** fliegen. **where are you going?** wo gehst du hin? **I'm going to France** ich fahre nach Frankreich. **go to the doctor's/dentist's** zum Arzt/Zahnarzt gehen. **go to the theatre/cinema** ins Theater/Kino gehen. **I must go to Paris/to the doctor's** ich muss nach Paris/zum Arzt. **go shopping** einkaufen gehen. **go swimming** schwimmen gehen. **go to see s.o.** jdn besuchen [gehen]

····▸ (leave) weggehen; (on journey) abfahren. **I must go now** ich muss jetzt gehen. **we're going on Friday** wir fahren am Freitag

····▸ (work, function) (engine, clock) gehen

····▸ (become) werden. **go deaf** taub werden. **go mad** verrückt werden. **he went red** er wurde rot

····▸ (pass) (time) vergehen

····▸ (disappear) weggehen; (coat, hat, stain) verschwinden. **my headache/my coat/the stain has gone** mein Kopfweh/mein Mantel/der Fleck ist weg

····▸ (turn out, progress) gehen; verlaufen. **everything's going very well** alles geht od verläuft sehr gut. **how did the party go?** wie war die Party? **go smoothly/according to plan** reibungslos/planmäßig verlaufen

....➤ (*match*) zusammenpassen. **the two colours don't go [together]** die beiden Farben passen nicht zusammen

....➤ (*cease to function*) kaputtgehen; (*fuse*) durchbrennen. **his memory is going** sein Gedächtnis lässt nach

● auxiliary verb

....➤ **be going to** werden + *inf.* **it's going to rain** es wird regnen. **I'm not going to** ich werde es nicht tun

● noun

pl **goes**

....➤ (*turn*) **it's your go** du bist jetzt an der Reihe *od* dran

....➤ (*attempt*) Versuch. **have a go at doing sth** versuchen, etw zu tun. **have another go!** versuch's noch mal!

....➤ (*energy, drive*) Energie

....➤ (*in phrases*) **on the go** auf Trab. **make a go of sth** das Beste aus etw machen

● phrasal verbs

● **go across** *vi* hinübergehen/-fahren; *vt* überqueren. ● **go after** *vt* (*pursue*) jagen. ● **go away** *vi* weggehen/-fahren; (*on holiday or business*) verreisen. ● **go back** *vi* zurückgehen/-fahren. ● **go back on** *vt* nicht [ein]halten (*promise*). ● **go by** *vi* vorbeigehen/-fahren; (*time*) vergehen. ● **go down** *vi* hinuntergehen/-fahren; (*sun, ship*) untergehen; (*prices*) fallen; (*temperature, swelling*) zurückgehen. ● **go for** *vt* holen; (𝕀: *attack*) losgehen auf (+ *acc*). ● **go in** *vi* hineingehen/-fahren; ● **go in for** teilnehmen an (+ *dat*) (*competition*); (*take up*)

sich verlegen auf (+ *acc*). ● **go off** *vi* weggehen/-fahren; (*alarm clock*) klingeln; (*alarm, gun, bomb*) losgehen; (*light*) ausgehen; (*go bad*) schlecht werden; *vt*: **go off sth** von etw abkommen. ● **go off well** gut verlaufen. ● **go on** *vi* weitergehen/-fahren; (*light*) angehen; (*continue*) weitermachen; (*talking*) fortfahren; (*happen*) vorgehen. ● **go on at** 𝕀 herumnörgeln an (+ *dat*). ● **go out** *vi* (*from home*) ausgehen; (*leave*) hinausgehen/-fahren; (*fire, light*) ausgehen; **go out to work/for a meal** arbeiten/essen gehen; **go out with s.o.** (𝕀: *date s.o.*) mit jdm gehen 𝕀. ● **go over** *vi* hinübergehen/-fahren; *vt* (*rehearse*) durchgehen. ● **go round** *vi* herumgehen/-fahren; (*visit*) vorbeigehen; (*turn*) sich drehen; (*be enough*) reichen. ● **go through** *vi* durchgehen/-fahren; *vt* (*suffer*) durchmachen; (*rehearse*) durchgehen; (*bags*) durchsuchen. ● **go through with** *vt* zu Ende machen. ● **go under** *vi* untergehen/-fahren; (*fail*) scheitern. ● **go up** *vi* hinaufgehen/-fahren; (*lift*) hochfahren; (*prices*) steigen. ● **go without** *vt*: **go without sth** auf etw (*acc*) verzichten; *vi* darauf verzichten

'**go-ahead** *adj* fortschrittlich; (*enterprising*) unternehmend ● *n* (*fig*) grünes Licht *nt*

goal /gəʊl/ *n* Ziel *nt*; (*sport*) Tor *nt*. **~keeper** *n* Torwart *m*. **~post** *n* Torpfosten *m*

goat /gəʊt/ *n* Ziege *f*

gobble /'gɒbl/ *vt* hinunterschlingen

God, god /gɒd/ *n* Gott *m*

god: ~**child** n Patenkind nt.
~**-daughter** n Patentochter f.
~**dess** n Göttin f. ~**father** n Pate
m. ~**mother** n Patin f. ~**parents**
npl Paten pl. ~**send** n Segen m.
~**son** n Patensohn m

goggles /'gɒglz/ npl Schutzbrille f

going /'gəʊɪŋ/ adj (price, rate) gängig; (concern) gut gehend ● n **it is
hard** ~ es ist schwierig

gold /gəʊld/ n Gold nt ● adj golden

golden /'gəʊldn/ adj golden. ~
'**wedding** n goldene Hochzeit f

gold: ~**fish** n inv Goldfisch m.
~**mine** n Goldgrube f. ~**-plated**
adj vergoldet. ~**smith** n Gold-
schmied m

golf /gɒlf/ n Golf nt

golf: ~**club** n Golfklub m; (implement) Golfschläger m. ~**course** n
Golfplatz m. ~**er** n Golfspiele-
r(in) m(f)

gone /gɒn/ see **go**

good /gʊd/ adj (better, best) gut;
(well-behaved) brav, artig; ~ **at**
in (+ dat); **a** ~ **deal** ziemlich viel; ~
morning/evening guten Morgen/
Abend ● **n for** ~ für immer; **do** ~
Gutes tun; **do s.o.** ~ jdm gut tun;
it's no ~ es ist nutzlos; (hopeless)
da ist nichts zu machen

goodbye /gʊd'baɪ/ int Auf Wiedersehen; (Teleph, Radio) auf Wie-
derhören

good: **G**~ '**Friday** n Karfreitag m.
~**-looking** adj gut aussehend.
~**-natured** adj gutmütig

goodness /'gʊdnɪs/ n Güte f;
thank ~! Gott sei Dank!

goods /gʊdz/ npl Waren pl. ~
train n Güterzug m

good'will n Wohlwollen nt;
(Comm) Goodwill m

gooey /'guːɪ/ adj 🗉 klebrig

google /'guːgl/ ® vt, vi googeln

goose /guːs/ n (pl geese) Gans f

gooseberry /'gʊzbərɪ/ n Stachel-
beere f

goose: /guːs/ ~**flesh** n, ~**-pimp-
les** npl Gänsehaut f

gorge /gɔːdʒ/ n (Geog) Schlucht f
● vt ~ **oneself** sich vollessen

gorgeous /'gɔːdʒəs/ adj prachtvoll; 🗉 herrlich

gorilla /gə'rɪlə/ n Gorilla m

gormless /'gɔːmlɪs/ adj 🗉 doof

gorse /gɔːs/ n inv Stechginster m

gory /'gɔːrɪ/ adj blutig; (story) blut-
rünstig

gosh /gɒʃ/ int 🗉 Mensch!

gospel /'gɒspl/ n Evangelium nt

gossip /'gɒsɪp/ n Klatsch m; (person) Klatschbase f ● vi klatschen

got /gɒt/ see **get**; **have** ~ haben;
have ~ **to** müssen; **have** ~ **to do**
sth etw tun müssen

Gothic /'gɒθɪk/ adj gotisch

gotten /'gɒtn/ see **get**

goulash /'guːlæʃ/ n Gulasch nt

gourmet /'gʊəmeɪ/ n Feinschme-
cker m

govern /'gʌvn/ vt/i regieren; (determine) bestimmen

government /'gʌvnmənt/ n Regierung f

governor /'gʌvənə(r)/ n Gouver-
neur m; (on board) Vorstandsmit-
glied nt; (of prison) Direktor m; (🗉:
boss) Chef m

gown /gaʊn/ n [elegantes] Kleid
nt; (Univ, Jur) Talar m

GP abbr general practitioner

GPS abbr (Global Positioning System) GPS nt

grab /græb/ vt (pt/pp grabbed) ergreifen; ~ [**hold of**] packen

grace /greɪs/ n Anmut f; (before
meal) Tischgebet nt; **three days'**
~ drei Tage Frist. ~**ful** adj anmutig

gracious /'greɪʃəs/ adj gnädig; (*elegant*) vornehm

grade /greɪd/ n Stufe f; (*Comm*) Güteklasse f; (*Sch*) Note f; (*Amer, Sch: class*) Klasse f; (*Amer*) = **gradient** ● vt einstufen; (*Comm*) sortieren. ~ **crossing** n (*Amer*) Bahnübergang m

gradient /'greɪdɪənt/ n Steigung f; (*downward*) Gefälle nt

gradual /'grædʒʊəl/ adj allmählich

graduate /'grædʒʊət/ n Akademiker(in) m(f)

graffiti /grə'fiːtɪ/ npl Graffiti pl

graft /graːft/ n (*Bot*) Pfropfreis nt; (*Med*) Transplantat nt; (*hard work*) Plackerei f

grain /greɪn/ n (*sand, salt, rice*) Korn nt; (*cereals*) Getreide nt; (*in wood*) Maserung f

gram /græm/ n Gramm nt

grammar /'græmə(r)/ n Grammatik f. ~ **school** n ≈ Gymnasium nt

grammatical /grə'mætɪkl/ adj grammatisch

grand /grænd/ adj (**-er, -est**) großartig

grandad /'grændæd/ n 🔘 Opa m

grandchild n Enkelkind nt

granddaughter n Enkelin f

grandeur /'grændʒə(r)/ n Pracht f

grandfather n Großvater m. ~ **clock** n Standuhr f

grandiose /'grændɪəʊs/ adj grandios

grand: ~**mother** n Großmutter f. ~**parents** npl Großeltern pl. ~ **pi'ano** n Flügel m. ~**son** n Enkel m. ~**stand** n Tribüne f

granite /'grænɪt/ n Granit m

granny /'grænɪ/ n 🔘 Oma f

grant /graːnt/ n Subvention f; (*Univ*) Studienbeihilfe f ● vt gewähren; (*admit*) zugeben; **take sth for**

~**ed** etw als selbstverständlich hinnehmen

grape /greɪp/ n [Wein]traube f; **bunch of** ~**s** [ganze] Weintraube f

grapefruit /'greɪp-/ n invar Grapefruit f

graph /graːf/ n grafische Darstellung f

graphic /'græfɪk/ adj, **-ally** adv grafisch; (*vivid*) anschaulich

'graph paper n Millimeterpapier nt

grapple /'græpl/ vi ringen

grasp /graːsp/ n Griff m ● vt ergreifen; (*understand*) begreifen. ~**ing** adj habgierig

grass /graːs/ n Gras nt; (*lawn*) Rasen m. ~**hopper** n Heuschrecke f

grassy /'graːsɪ/ adj grasig

grate¹ /greɪt/ n Feuerrost m; (*hearth*) Kamin m

grate² vt (*Culin*) reiben

grateful /'greɪtfl/ adj dankbar (**to** dat)

grater /'greɪtə(r)/ n (*Culin*) Reibe f

gratify /'grætɪfaɪ/ vt (pt/pp **-ied**) befriedigen. ~**ing** adj erfreulich

gratis /'graːtɪs/ adv gratis

gratitude /'grætɪtjuːd/ n Dankbarkeit f

gratuitous /grə'tjuːɪtəs/ adj (*uncalled for*) überflüssig

grave¹ /greɪv/ adj (**-r, -st**) ernst; ~**ly ill** schwer krank

grave² /greɪv/ n Grab nt. ~**digger** n Totengräber m

gravel /'grævl/ n Kies m

grave: ~**stone** n Grabstein m. ~**yard** n Friedhof m

gravity /'grævətɪ/ n Ernst m; (*force*) Schwerkraft f

gravy /'greɪvɪ/ n [Braten]soße f

gray /greɪ/ adj (*Amer*) = **grey**

g

graze[1] /greɪz/ vi (animal:) weiden

graze[2] n Schürfwunde f ● vt (car) streifen; (knee) aufschürfen

grease /griːs/ n Fett nt; (lubricant) Schmierfett nt ● vt einfetten; (lubricate) schmieren

greasy /ˈgriːsɪ/ adj fettig

great /greɪt/ adj (-er, -est) groß; (fig: marvellous) großartig

great: ~'**aunt** n Großtante f. **G~** '**Britain** n Großbritannien nt. ~'**grandchildren** npl Urenkel pl. ~'**grandfather** n Urgroßvater m. ~'**grandmother** n Urgroßmutter f

great|ly /ˈgreɪtlɪ/ adv sehr. ~**ness** n Größe f

great-'uncle n Großonkel m

Greece /griːs/ n Griechenland nt

greed /griːd/ n [Hab]gier f

greedy /ˈgriːdɪ/ adj , **-ily** adv gierig

Greek /griːk/ adj griechisch ● n Grieche m/Griechin f; (Lang) Griechisch nt

green /griːn/ adj (-er, -est) grün; (fig) unerfahren ● n Grün nt; (grass) Wiese f; ~**s** pl Kohl m; **the G~s** pl (Pol) die Grünen f

---

green card Ein offizielles Dokument, das nichtamerikanische Bürger zur Erwerbstätigkeit in den USA berechtigt. Die green card braucht jeder, der beabsichtigt, eine feste Stelle in den USA anzutreten. In Europa ist die grüne Karte ein vom Versicherungsverband ausgestellter grüner Ausweis, mit dem ein Kraftfahrer beim Grenzübertritt nachweist, dass er haftpflichtversichert ist.

---

greenery /ˈgriːnərɪ/ n Grün nt

green: ~**fly** n Blattlaus f. ~**grocer** n Obst- und Gemüsehändler m. ~**house** n Gewächshaus nt

Greenland /ˈgriːnlənd/ n Grönland nt

greet /griːt/ vt grüßen; (welcome) begrüßen. ~**ing** n Gruß m; (welcome) Begrüßung f

grew /gruː/ see **grow**

grey /greɪ/ adj (-er, -est) grau ● n Grau nt ● vi grau werden. ~**hound** n Windhund m

grid /grɪd/ n Gitter nt

grief /griːf/ n Trauer f

grievance /ˈgriːvəns/ n Beschwerde f

grieve /griːv/ vi trauern (for um)

grill /grɪl/ n Gitter nt; (Culin) Grill m; **mixed** ~ Gemischtes vom Grill ● vt/i grillen; (interrogate) [streng] verhören

grille /grɪl/ n Gitter nt

grim /grɪm/ adj (grimmer, grimmest) ernst; (determination) verbissen

grimace /grɪˈmeɪs/ n Grimasse f ● vi Grimassen schneiden

grime /graɪm/ n Schmutz m

grimy /ˈgraɪmɪ/ adj schmutzig

grin /grɪn/ n Grinsen n ● vi (pt/pp grinned) grinsen

grind /graɪnd/ n (fam: hard work) Plackerei f ● vt (pt/pp ground) mahlen; (smooth, sharpen) schleifen; (Amer: mince) durchdrehen

grip /grɪp/ n Griff m; (bag) Reisetasche f ● vt (pt/pp gripped) ergreifen; (hold) festhalten

gripping /ˈgrɪpɪŋ/ adj fesselnd

grisly /ˈgrɪzlɪ/ adj grausig

gristle /ˈgrɪsl/ n Knorpel m

grit /grɪt/ n [grober] Sand m; (for roads) Streugut nt; (courage) Mut m ● vt (pt/pp gritted) streuen (road)

groan /grəʊn/ n Stöhnen nt ● vi stöhnen

grocer /ˈgrəʊsə(r)/ n Lebensmittelhändler m; **~'s [shop]** Lebensmittelgeschäft nt. **~ies** npl Lebensmittel pl

groin /grɔɪn/ n (Anat) Leiste f

groom /gruːm/ n Bräutigam m; (for horse) Pferdepfleger(in) m(f) ● vt striegeln (horse)

groove /gruːv/ n Rille f

grope /grəʊp/ vi tasten (**for** nach)

gross /grəʊs/ adj (-**er**, -**est**) fett; (coarse) derb; (glaring) grob; (Comm) brutto; (salary, weight) Brutto-. **~ly** adv (very) sehr

grotesque /grəʊˈtesk/ adj grotesk

ground[1] /graʊnd/ see **grind**

ground[2] n Boden m; (terrain) Gelände nt; (reason) Grund m; (Amer, Electr) Erde f. **~s** pl (park) Anlagen pl; (of coffee) Satz m

ground: **~ floor** n Erdgeschoss nt. **~ing** n Grundlage f. **~less** adj grundlos. **~sheet** n Bodenplane f. **~work** n Vorarbeiten pl

group /gruːp/ n Gruppe f ● vt gruppieren ● vi sich gruppieren

grouse[1] vi 🔲 meckern

grovel /ˈgrɒvl/ vi (pt/pp grovelled) kriechen

grow /grəʊ/ v (pt grew, pp grown) ● vi wachsen; (become) werden; (increase) zunehmen ● vt anbauen. **~ up** vi aufwachsen; (town:) entstehen

growl /graʊl/ n Knurren nt ● vi knurren

grown /grəʊn/ see **grow**. **~-up** adj erwachsen ● n Erwachsene(r) m/f

growth /grəʊθ/ n Wachstum nt; (increase) Zunahme f; (Med) Gewächs nt

grub /grʌb/ n (larva) Made f; (🔲: food) Essen nt

grubby /ˈgrʌbɪ/ adj schmuddelig

grudge /grʌdʒ/ n Groll m ● vt **~e s.o. sth** jdm etw missgönnen. **~ing** adj widerwillig

gruelling /ˈgruːəlɪŋ/ adj strapaziös

gruesome /ˈgruːsəm/ adj grausig

gruff /grʌf/ adj barsch

grumble /ˈgrʌmbl/ vi schimpfen (**at** mit)

grumpy /ˈgrʌmpɪ/ adj griesgrämig

grunt /grʌnt/ n Grunzen nt ● vi grunzen

guarantee /gærənˈtiː/ n Garantie f; (document) Garantieschein m ● vt garantieren; garantieren für (quality, success)

guard /gɑːd/ n Wache f; (security) Wächter m; (on train) ≈ Zugführer m; (Techn) Schutz m; **be on ~** Wache stehen; **on one's ~** auf der Hut ● vt bewachen; (protect) schützen ● vi **~ against** sich hüten vor (+ dat). **~-dog** n Wachhund m

guarded /ˈgɑːdɪd/ adj vorsichtig

guardian /ˈgɑːdɪən/ n Vormund m

guess /ges/ n Vermutung f ● vt erraten ● vi raten; (Amer: believe) glauben. **~work** n Vermutung f

guest /gest/ n Gast m. **~-house** n Pension f

guidance /ˈgaɪdəns/ n Führung f, Leitung f; (advice) Beratung f

guide /gaɪd/ n Führer(in) m(f); (book) Führer m; **[Girl] G~** Pfadfinderin f ● vt führen, leiten. **~book** n Führer m

guided /ˈgaɪdɪd/ adj **~ tour** Führung f

guide: **~-dog** n Blindenhund m. **~lines** npl Richtlinien pl

guilt /gɪlt/ n Schuld f. **~ily** adv schuldbewusst

guilty /ˈgɪltɪ/ adj schuldig (**of** gen); (look) schuldbewusst; (conscience) schlecht

guinea-pig /'gɪnɪ-/ n Meerschweinchen nt; (person) Versuchskaninchen nt

guitar /gɪ'tɑ:(r)/ n Gitarre f. **~ist** n Gitarrist(in) m (f)

gulf /gʌlf/ n (Geog) Golf m; (fig) Kluft f

gull /gʌl/ n Möwe f

gullible /'gʌlɪbl/ adj leichtgläubig

gully /'gʌlɪ/ n Schlucht f; (drain) Rinne f

gulp /gʌlp/ n Schluck m ● vi schlucken ● vt ~ **down** hinunterschlucken

gum¹ /gʌm/ n (also pl **-s**) (Anat) Zahnfleisch nt

gum² n Gummi[harz] nt; (glue) Klebstoff m; (chewing gum) Kaugummi m

gummed /gʌmd/ ● adj (label) gummiert

gun /gʌn/ n Schusswaffe f; (pistol) Pistole f; (rifle) Gewehr nt; (cannon) Geschütz nt

gun: **~fire** n Geschützfeuer nt. **~man** bewaffneter Bandit m

gunner /'gʌnə(r)/ n Artillerist m

gunpowder n Schießpulver nt

gurgle /'gɜ:gl/ vi gluckern; (of baby) glucksen

gush /gʌʃ/ vi strömen; (enthuse) schwärmen (over von)

gust /gʌst/ n (of wind) Windstoß m; (Naut) Bö f

gusto /'gʌstəʊ/ n with ~ mit Schwung

gusty /'gʌstɪ/ adj böig

gut /gʌt/ n Darm m; **~s** pl Eingeweide pl; (: courage) Schneid m ● vt (pt/pp gutted) (Culin) ausnehmen; **~ted by fire** ausgebrannt

gutter /'gʌtə(r)/ n Rinnstein m; (fig) Gosse f; (on roof) Dachrinne f

guy /gaɪ/ n Kerl m

guzzle /'gʌzl/ vt/i schlingen; (drink) schlürfen

gym /dʒɪm/ n 🔲 Turnhalle f; (gymnastics) Turnen nt

gymnasium /dʒɪm'neɪzɪəm/ n Turnhalle f

gymnast /'dʒɪmnæst/ n Turner(in) m (f). **~ics** n Turnen nt

gym shoes pl Turnschuhe pl

gynaecolog|ist /gaɪnɪ'kɒlədʒɪst/ n Frauenarzt m /-ärztin f. **~y** n Gynäkologie f

gypsy /'dʒɪpsɪ/ n Zigeuner(in) m (f)

Hh

habit /'hæbɪt/ n Gewohnheit f; (Relig: costume) Ordenstracht f; **be in the ~** die Angewohnheit haben (of zu)

habitat /'hæbɪtæt/ n Habitat nt

habitation /hæbɪ'teɪʃn/ n unfit for human ~ für Wohnzwecke ungeeignet

habitual /hə'bɪtjʊəl/ adj gewohnt; (inveterate) gewohnheitsmäßig. **~ly** adv gewohnheitsmäßig; (constantly) ständig

hack¹ /hæk/ n (writer) Schreiberling m; (hired horse) Mietpferd nt

hack² vt hacken; **~ to pieces** zerhacken

hackneyed /'hæknɪd/ adj abgedroschen

'hacksaw n Metallsäge f

had /hæd/ see have

haddock /'hædək/ n inv Schellfisch m

haggard /'hægəd/ adj abgehärmt

haggle /'hægl/ vi feilschen

(over um)

hail¹ /heɪl/ vt begrüßen; herbeirufen (taxi) ● vi ~ from kommen aus

hail² n Hagel m ● vi hageln. **~stone** n Hagelkorn nt

hair /heə(r)/ n Haar nt; **wash one's** ~ sich (dat) die Haare waschen

hair: **~brush** n Haarbürste f. **~cut** n Haarschnitt m; **have a ~cut** sich (dat) die Haare schneiden lassen. **~do** n Ⓣ Frisur f. **~dresser** n Friseur m/Friseuse f. **~drier** n Haartrockner m; (hand-held) Föhn m. **~pin** n Haarnadel f. **~pin 'bend** n Haarnadelkurve f. **~raising** adj haarsträubend. **~style** n Frisur f

hairy /'heəri/ adj behaart; (excessively) haarig; (Ⓣ frightening) brenzlig

hake /heɪk/ n inv Seehecht m

half /hɑːf/ n (pl **halves**) Hälfte f; **cut in** ~ halbieren; **one and a** ~ eineinhalb, anderthalb; ~ **a dozen** ein halbes Dutzend; ~ **an hour** eine halbe Stunde ● adj & adv halb; ~ **past two** halb drei; [at] ~ **price** zum halben Preis

half: **~-hearted** adj lustlos. **~-term** n schulfreie Tage nach dem halben Trimester. **~-timbered** adj Fachwerk-. **~-time** n (Sport) Halbzeit f. **~-'way** adj the **~-way mark/stage** die Hälfte ● adv auf halbem Weg

halibut /'hælɪbət/ n inv Heilbutt m

hall /hɔːl/ n Halle f; (room) Saal m; (Sch) Aula f; (entrance) Flur m; (mansion) Gutshaus nt; ~ **of residence** (Univ) Studentenheim nt

'hallmark n [Feingehalts]stempel m; (fig) Kennzeichen nt (of für)

hallo /hə'ləʊ/ int [guten] Tag! Ⓣ hallo!

hallucination /həluːsɪ'neɪʃn/ n Halluzination f

halo /'heɪləʊ/ n (pl **-es**) Heiligenschein m; (Astronomy) Hof m

halt /hɔːlt/ n Halt m; **come to a** ~ stehen bleiben; (traffic:) zum Stillstand kommen ● vi Halt machen; ~! **halt!** ● **~ing** adj, adv **-ly** zögernd

halve /hɑːv/ vt halbieren; (reduce) um die Hälfte reduzieren

ham /hæm/ n Schinken m

hamburger /'hæmbɜːgə(r)/ n Hamburger m

hammer /'hæmə(r)/ n Hammer m ● vt/i hämmern (**at** an + acc)

hammock /'hæmək/ n Hängematte f

hamper vt behindern

hamster /'hæmstə(r)/ n Hamster m

hand /hænd/ n Hand f; (of clock) Zeiger m; (writing) Handschrift f; (worker) Arbeiter/in m(f); (Cards) Blatt nt; **on the one/other** ~ einer-/andererseits; **out of** ~ außer Kontrolle; (summarily) kurzerhand; **in** ~ unter Kontrolle; (available) verfügbar; **give s.o. a** ~ jdm behilflich sein ● vt reichen (**to** dat). ~ **in** vt abgeben. ~ **out** vt austeilen. ~ **over** vt überreichen

hand: **~bag** n Handtasche f. **~book** n Handbuch nt. **~brake** n Handbremse f. **~cuffs** npl Handschellen pl. **~ful** n Handvoll f; **be [quite] a ~ful** Ⓣ nicht leicht zu haben sein

handicap /'hændɪkæp/ n Behinderung f; (Sport & fig) Handikap nt. **~ped** adj **mentally/physically ~ped** geistig/körperlich behindert

handkerchief /'hæŋkətʃɪf/ n (pl ~**s** & **-chieves**) Taschentuch nt

handle /'hændl/ n Griff m; (of door) Klinke f; (of cup) Henkel m; (of broom) Stiel m ● vt handhaben; (treat) umgehen mit; (touch) anfassen. ~**bars** *npl* Lenkstange *f*

hand: ~**made** *adj* handgemacht.
~**shake** *n* Händerdruck *m*

handsome /'hænsəm/ *adj* gut
aussehend; (*generous*) großzügig;
(*large*) beträchtlich

hand: ~**writing** *n* Handschrift *f*.
~-**'written** *adj* handgeschrieben

handy /'hændɪ/ *adj* handlich; (*person*) geschickt; **have/keep** ~ griff-
bereit haben/halten

hang /hæŋ/ *vt/i* (*pt/pp* hung) hängen; ~ **wallpaper** tapezieren ● *vt*
(*pt/pp* hanged) hängen (*criminal*)
● **n get the** ~ **of it** 🇬🇧 den Dreh
herauskriegen. ~ **about** *vi* sich her-
umdrücken. ~ **on** *vi* sich festhalten
(**to** an + *dat*); (🇬🇧: *wait*) warten. ~
out *vi* heraushängen; (🇬🇧: *live*) wohnen ● *vt* draußen aufhängen (*washing*). ~ **up** *vt/i* aufhängen

hangar /'hæŋə(r)/ *n* Flugzeug-
halle *f*

hanger /'hæŋə(r)/ *n* [Kleider]-
bügel *m*

hang: ~-**glider** *n* Drachenflieger
m. ~-**gliding** *n* Drachenfliegen *nt*.
~**man** *n* Henker *m*. ~**over** *n* 🇬🇧
Kater *m* 🇬🇧. ~-**up** *n* 🇬🇧 Komplex *m*

hanker /'hæŋkə(r)/ *vi* ~ **after sth**
sich (*dat*) etw wünschen

hanky /'hæŋkɪ/ *n* 🇬🇧 Taschentuch *nt*

haphazard /hæp'hæzəd/ *adj*
planlos

happen /'hæpn/ *vi* geschehen,
passieren; **I** ~**ed to be there** ich
war zufällig da; **what has** ~**ed to
him?** was ist mit ihm los? (*become
of*) was ist aus ihm geworden?
~**ing** *n* Ereignis *nt*

happily /'hæpɪlɪ/ *adv* glücklich;
(*fortunately*) glücklicherweise.
~**ness** *n* Glück *nt*

happy /'hæpɪ/ *adj* glücklich.

~-**go-'lucky** *adj* sorglos

harass /'hærəs/ *vt* schikanieren.
~**ed** *adj* abgehetzt. ~**ment** *n* Schi-
kane *f*; (*sexual*) Belästigung *f*

harbour /'hɑːbə(r)/ *n* Hafen *m*

hard /hɑːd/ *adj* (**-er, -est**) hart; (*difficult*) schwer; ~ **of hearing**
schwerhörig ● *adv* hart; (*work*)
schwer; (*pull*) kräftig; (*rain, snow*)
stark; **be** ~ **up** 🇬🇧 knapp bei
Kasse sein

hard: ~**back** *n* gebundene Ausgabe *f*. ~**board** *n* Hartfaserplatte *f*.
~-**boiled** *adj* hart gekocht ~**disk**
n Festplatte *f*

harden /'hɑːdn/ *vi* hart werden

hard-'hearted *adj* hartherzig

hard|ly /'hɑːdlɪ/ *adv* kaum; ~**ly
ever** kaum [jemals]. ~**ness** *n* Härte
f. ~**ship** *n* Not *f*

hard: ~ '**shoulder** *n* (*Auto*) Randstreifen *m*. ~**ware** *n* Haushaltswa-
ren *pl*; (*Computing*) Hardware *f*.
~-'**wearing** *adj* strapazierfähig.
~'**working** *adj* fleißig

hardy /'hɑːdɪ/ *adj* abgehärtet;
(*plant*) winterhart

hare /heə(r)/ *n* Hase *m*

harm /hɑːm/ *n* Schaden *m*; **it
won't do any** ~ es kann nichts
schaden ● *vt* ~ **s.o.** jdm etwas
antun. ~**ful** *adj* schädlich. ~**less**
adj harmlos

harmonious /hɑː'məʊnɪəs/ *adj*
harmonisch

harmon|ize /'hɑːmənaɪz/ *vi* (*fig*)
harmonieren. ~**y** *n* Harmonie *f*

harness /'hɑːnɪs/ *n* Geschirr *nt*; (*of
parachute*) Gurtwerk *nt* ● *vt* anschirren (*horse*); (*use*) nutzbar machen

harp /hɑːp/ *n* Harfe *f*. ~**ist** *n* Har-
fenist(in) *m*(*f*)

harpsichord /'hɑːpsɪkɔːd/ *n*
Cembalo *nt*

harrowing /'hærəʊɪŋ/ *adj*

grauenhaft

harsh /hɑːʃ/ *adj* (**-er, -est**) hart; (*voice*) rau; (*light*) grell. **∼ness** *n* Härte *f*; Rauheit *f*

harvest /ˈhɑːvɪst/ *n* Ernte *f* ● *vt* ernten

has /hæz/ *see* **have**

hassle /ˈhæsl/ *n* **①** Ärger *m* ● *vt* schikanieren

haste /heɪst/ *n* Eile *f*

hasten /ˈheɪsn/ *vi* sich beeilen (**to** zu); (*go quickly*) eilen ● *vt* beschleunigen

hasty /ˈheɪstɪ/ *adj* , **-ily** *adv* hastig; (*decision*) voreilig

hat /hæt/ *n* Hut *m*; (*knitted*) Mütze *f*

hatch¹ /hætʃ/ *n* (*for food*) Durchreiche *f*; (*Naut*) Luke *f*

hatch² *vi* **∼[out]** ausschlüpfen ● *vt* ausbrüten

'hatchback *n* (*Auto*) Modell *nt* mit Hecktür

hate /heɪt/ *n* Hass *m* ● *vt* hassen. **∼ful** *adj* abscheulich

hatred /ˈheɪtrɪd/ *n* Hass *m*

haughty /ˈhɔːtɪ/ *adj* , **-ily** *adv* hochmütig

haul /hɔːl/ *n* (*loot*) Beute *f* ● *vt/i* ziehen (**on** an + *dat*)

haunt /hɔːnt/ *n* Lieblingsaufenthalt *m* ● *vt* umgehen in (+ *dat*); **this house is ∼ed** in diesem Haus spukt es

---

hat einen Bruder. **we have [got] five minutes** wir haben fünf Minuten

••••➤ (*eat*) essen; (*drink*) trinken; (*smoke*) rauchen. **have a cup of tea** eine Tasse Tee trinken. **have a pizza** eine Pizza essen. **have a cigarette** eine Zigarette rauchen. **have breakfast/dinner/ lunch** frühstücken/zu Abend essen/zu Mittag essen

••••➤ (*take esp. in shop, restaurant*) nehmen. **I'll have the soup/the red dress** ich nehme die Suppe/ das rote Kleid. **have a cigarette!** nehmen Sie eine Zigarette!

••••➤ (*get, receive*) bekommen. **I had a letter from her** ich bekam einen Brief von ihr. **have a baby** ein Baby bekommen

••••➤ (*suffer*) haben (*illness, pain, disappointment*); erleiden (*shock*)

••••➤ (*organize*) **have a party** eine Party veranstalten. **they had a meeting** sie hielten eine Versammlung ab

••••➤ (*take part in*) **have a game of football** Fußball spielen. **have a swim** schwimmen

••••➤ (*as guest*) **have s.o. to stay** jdn zu Besuch haben

••••➤ **have had it** **①** (*thing*) ausgedient haben; (*person*) geliefert sein. **you've had it now** jetzt ist es aus

••••➤ **have sth done** etw machen lassen. **we had the house painted** wir haben das Haus malen lassen. **have a dress made** sich (*dat*) ein Kleid machen lassen. **have a tooth out** sich (*dat*) einen Zahn ziehen lassen. **have one's hair cut** sich (*dat*) die Haare schneiden lassen

••••➤ **have to do sth** etw tun

---

have /hæv/, *unbetont* /həv/, /əv/

3 sg pres tense **has**; *pt and pp* **had**

● *transitive verb*

••••➤ (*possess*) haben. **he has [got] a car** er hat ein Auto. **she has [got] a brother** sie

müssen. **I have to go now** ich muss jetzt gehen

● *auxiliary verb*

••••▷ (*forming perfect and past perfect tenses*) haben; (*with verbs of motion and some others*) sein. **I have seen him** ich habe ihn gesehen. **he has never been there** er ist nie da gewesen. **I had gone** ich war gegangen. **if I had known** ... wenn ich gewusst hätte ...

••••▷ (*in tag questions*) nicht wahr. **you've met her, haven't you?** du kennst sie, nicht wahr?

••••▷ (*in short answers*) **Have you seen the film? — Yes, I have** Hast du den Film gesehen? — Ja [, stimmt]

● **have on** vt (*be wearing*) anhaben; (*dupe*) anführen

havoc /'hævǝk/ n Verwüstung f

hawk /hɔːk/ n Falke m

hawthorn /'hɔː-/ n Hagedorn m

hay /heɪ/ n Heu nt. ~ **fever** n Heuschnupfen m. ~**stack** n Heuschober m

hazard /'hæzǝd/ n Gefahr f; (*risk*) Risiko nt ● vt riskieren. ~**ous** adj gefährlich; (*risky*) riskant

haze /heɪz/ n Dunst m

hazel /'heɪzl/ n Haselbusch m. ~**nut** n Haselnuss f

hazy /'heɪzɪ/ adj dunstig; (*fig*) unklar

he /hiː/ pron er

head /hed/ n Kopf m; (*chief*) Oberhaupt nt; (*of firm*) Chef(in) m(f); (*of school*) Schulleiter(in) m(f); (*on beer*) Schaumkrone f; Kopfende nt; ~ **first** kopfüber ● vt anführen; (*Sport*) köpfen (*ball*) ● vi ~ **for** zusteuern auf (+ *acc*). ~**ache** n Kopfschmerzen pl

head|er /'hedǝ(r)/ n Kopfball m; (*dive*) Kopfsprung m. ~**ing** n Überschrift f

head: ~**lamp**, ~**light** n (*Auto*) Scheinwerfer m. ~**line** n Schlagzeile f. ~**long** adv kopfüber. ~**master** n Schulleiter m. ~**mistress** n Schulleiterin f. ~**-on** adj & adv frontal. ~**phones** npl Kopfhörer m. ~**quarters** npl Hauptquartier nt; (*Pol*) Zentrale f. ~**rest** n Kopfstütze f. ~**room** n lichte Höhe f. ~**scarf** n Kopftuch m. ~**strong** adj eigenwillig. ~**way** n make ~**way** Fortschritte machen. ~**word** n Stichwort nt

heady /'hedɪ/ adj berauschend

heal /hiːl/ vt/i heilen

health /helθ/ n Gesundheit f

health: ~ **farm** n Schönheitsfarm f. ~ **foods** npl Reformkost f. ~**-food shop** n Reformhaus nt. ~ **insurance** n Krankenversicherung f

healthy /'helθɪ/ adj , **-ily** adv gesund

heap /hiːp/ n Haufen m; ~**s** 🔢 jede Menge ● vt ~ **[up]** häufen

hear /hɪǝ(r)/ vt/i (pt/pp **heard**) hören; ~,~**!** hört, hört! **he would not** ~ **of it** er ließ es nicht zu

hearing /'hɪǝrɪŋ/ n Gehör nt; (Jur) Verhandlung f. ~**-aid** n Hörgerät nt

hearse /hɜːs/ n Leichenwagen m

heart /hɑːt/ n Herz nt; (*courage*) Mut m; ~**s** pl (Cards) Herz nt; **by** ~ auswendig

heart: ~**ache** n Kummer m. ~**attack** n Herzanfall m. ~**beat** n Herzschlag m. ~**breaking** adj herzzerreißend. ~**broken** adj untröstlich. ~**burn** n Sodbrennen nt. ~**en** vt ermutigen. ~**felt** adj herzlich[st]

hearth /hɑːθ/ n Herd m; (fireplace) Kamin m

heart|ily /'hɑːtɪlɪ/ adv herzlich;

(*eat*) viel. **~less** *adj* herzlos. **~y** *adj* herzlich; (*meal*) groß; (*person*) burschikos

heat /hi:t/ *n* Hitze *f*; (*Sport*) Vorlauf *m* • *vt* heiß machen; heizen (*room*). **~ed** *adj* geheizt; (*swimming pool*) beheizt; (*discussion*) hitzig. **~er** *n* Heizgerät *nt*; (*Auto*) Heizanlage *f*

heath /hi:θ/ *n* Heide *f*

heathen /'hi:ðn/ *adj* heidnisch • *n* Heide *m*/Heidin *f*

heather /'heðə(r)/ *n* Heidekraut *nt*

heating /'hi:tɪŋ/ *n* Heizung *f*

heat wave *n* Hitzewelle *f*

heave /hi:v/ *vt/i* ziehen; (*lift*) heben; (🔲: *throw*) schmeißen

heaven /'hevn/ *n* Himmel *m*. **~ly** *adj* himmlisch

heavy /'hevɪ/ *adj* , **-ily** *adv* schwer; (*traffic, rain*) stark. **~weight** *n* Schwergewicht *nt*

heckle /'hekl/ *vt* [durch Zwischenrufe] unterbrechen. **~r** *n* Zwischenrufer *m*

hectic /'hektɪk/ *adj* hektisch

hedge /hedʒ/ *n* Hecke *f*. **~hog** *n* Igel *m*

heed /hi:d/ *vt* beachten

heel¹ /hi:l/ *n* Ferse *f*; (*of shoe*) Absatz *m*; **down at ~** heruntergekommen

heel² *vi* **~ over** (*Naut*) sich auf die Seite legen

hefty /'heftɪ/ *adj* kräftig; (*heavy*) schwer

height /haɪt/ *n* Höhe *f*; (*of person*) Größe *f*. **~en** *vt* (*fig*) steigern

heir /eə(r)/ *n* Erbe *m*. **~ess** *n* Erbin *f*. **~loom** *n* Erbstück *nt*

held /held/ *see* **hold²**

helicopter /'helɪkɒptə(r)/ *n* Hubschrauber *m*

hell /hel/ *n* Hölle *f*; **go to ~!** 🔲 geh zum Teufel! • *int* verdammt!

hello /hə'ləʊ/ *int* [guten] Tag! 🔲 hallo!

helm /helm/ [Steuer]ruder *nt*

helmet /'helmɪt/ *n* Helm *m*

help /help/ *n* Hilfe *f*; (*employees*) Hilfskräfte *pl*; **that's no ~** das nützt nichts • *vt/i* helfen (**s.o.** jdm); **~ oneself** *vr* sich (*dat*) etw nehmen; **~ yourself** (*at table*) greif zu; **I could not ~ laughing** ich musste lachen; **it cannot be ~ed** es lässt sich nicht ändern; **I can't ~ it** ich kann nichts dafür

help|er /'helpə(r)/ *n* Helfer(in) *m(f)*. **~ful** *adj*, **-ly** *adv* hilfsbereit; (*advice*) nützlich. **~ing** *n* Portion *f*. **~less** *adj* hilflos

hem /hem/ *n* Saum *m* • *vt* (*pt/pp* hemmed) säumen; **~ in** umzingeln

hemisphere /'hemɪ-/ *n* Hemisphäre *f*

'**hem-line** *n* Rocklänge *f*

hen /hen/ *n* Henne *f*; (*any female bird*) Weibchen *nt*

hence /hens/ *adv* daher; **five years ~** in fünf Jahren. **~forth** *adv* von nun an

'**henpecked** *adj* **~ husband** Pantoffelheld *m*

her /hɜ:(r)/ *adj* ihr • *pron* (*acc*) sie; (*dat*) ihr

herald /'herəld/ *vt* verkünden. **~ry** *n* Wappenkunde *f*

herb /hɜ:b/ *n* Kraut *nt*

herbaceous /hɜ:'beɪʃəs/ *adj* **~ border** Staudenrabatte *f*

herd /hɜ:d/ *n* Herde *f*. **~ together** *vt* zusammentreiben

here /hɪə(r)/ *adv* hier; (*to this place*) hierher; **in ~** hier drinnen; **come/ bring ~** herkommen/herbringen

hereditary /hə'redɪtərɪ/ *adj* erblich

here|sy /'herəsɪ/ *n* Ketzerei *f*. **~tic** *n* Ketzer(in) *m(f)*

here'with adv (Comm) beiliegend

heritage /ˈherɪtɪdʒ/ n Erbe nt. ∼ **tourism** n Kulturtourismus m

hero /ˈhɪərəʊ/ n (pl -es) Held m

heroic /hɪˈrəʊɪk/ adj, **-ally** adv heldenhaft

heroin /ˈherəʊɪn/ n Heroin nt

hero|ine /ˈherəʊɪn/ n Heldin f. ∼ **ism** n Heldentum nt

heron /ˈhern/ n Reiher m

herring /ˈherɪŋ/ n Hering m

hers /hɜːz/ poss pron ihre(r), ihrs; **a friend of** ∼ ein Freund von ihr; **that is** ∼ das gehört ihr

her'self pron selbst; (reflexive) sich; **by** ∼ allein

hesitant /ˈhezɪtənt/ adj zögernd

hesitat|e /ˈhezɪteɪt/ vi zögern. ∼ **ion** n Zögern nt; **without** ∼ **ion** ohne zu zögern

hexagonal /hekˈsægənl/ adj sechseckig

heyday /ˈheɪ-/ n Glanzzeit f

hi /haɪ/ int he! (hallo) Tag!

hiatus /haɪˈeɪtəs/ n (pl -tuses) Lücke f

hibernat|e /ˈhaɪbəneɪt/ vi Winterschlaf halten. ∼ **ion** n Winterschlaf m

hiccup /ˈhɪkʌp/ n Hick m; (🔢: hitch) Panne f; **have the** ∼ **s** den Schluckauf haben ● vi hick machen

hid /hɪd/, **hidden** see hide²

hide v (pt hid, pp hidden) ● vt verstecken; (keep secret) verheimlichen ● vi sich verstecken

hideous /ˈhɪdɪəs/ adj hässlich; (horrible) grässlich

'hide-out n Versteck nt

hiding¹ /ˈhaɪdɪŋ/ n 🔢 **give s.o. a** ∼ jdn verdreschen

hiding² n **go into** ∼ untertauchen

hierarchy /ˈhaɪərɑːkɪ/ n Hierarchie f

high /haɪ/ adj (-er, -est) hoch; attrib hohe(r,s); (meat) angegangen; (wind) stark; (on drugs) high; **it's** ∼ **time** es ist höchste Zeit ● adv hoch; ∼ **and low** überall ● n Hoch nt; (temperature) Höchsttemperatur f

high: ∼ **brow** adj intellektuell. ∼ **chair** n Kinderhochstuhl m. ∼ **'-handed** adj selbstherrlich. ∼ **'-heeled** adj hochhackig. ∼ **jump** n Hochsprung m

'highlight n (fig) Höhepunkt m; ∼ **s** pl (in hair) helle Strähnen pl ● vt (emphasize) hervorheben

highly /ˈhaɪlɪ/ adv hoch; **speak** ∼ **of** loben; **think** ∼ **of** sehr schätzen. ∼ **'-strung** adj nervös

Highness /ˈhaɪnɪs/ n Hoheit f

---

high school Eine weiterführende Schule in den USA, normalerweise für Schüler von vierzehn bis achtzehn Jahren. Schüler erwerben einen Highschoolabschluss durch Nachweis von credits (Punkten) in bestimmten Pflicht- und Wahlkursen. Der Abschluss ist Voraussetzung zum Besuch einer Hochschule. Auch in Großbritannien werden einige weiterführende Schulen als high schools bezeichnet.

---

high: ∼ **season** n Hochsaison f. ∼ **street** n Hauptstraße f. ∼ **'tide** n Hochwasser nt. ∼ **way** n public ∼ **way** öffentliche Straße f

hijack /ˈhaɪdʒæk/ vt entführen. ∼ **er** n Entführer m

hike /haɪk/ n Wanderung f ● vi wandern. ∼ **r** n Wanderer m

hilarious /hɪˈleərɪəs/ adj sehr komisch

hill /hɪl/ n Berg m; (mound) Hügel m; (slope) Hang m

hill: ∼ **side** n Hang m. ∼ **y** adj

hügelig

him /hɪm/ pron (acc) ihn; (dat) ihm. **~'self** pron selbst; (reflexive) sich; **by ~self** allein

hind /haɪnd/ adj Hinter-

hind|er /'hɪndə(r)/ vt hindern. **~rance** n Hindernis nt

hindsight /'haɪnd-/ n **with ~** rückblickend

Hindu /'hɪndu:/ n Hindu m ● adj Hindu-. **~ism** n Hinduismus m

hinge /hɪndʒ/ n Scharnier nt; (on door) Angel f

hint /hɪnt/ n Wink m, Andeutung f; (advice) Hinweis m; (trace) Spur f ● vi **~ at** anspielen auf (+ acc)

hip /hɪp/ n Hüfte f

hip 'pocket n Gesäßtasche f

hippopotamus /hɪpə'pɒtəməs/ n (pl -muses or -mi /-maɪ/) Nilpferd nt

hire /'haɪə(r)/ vt mieten (car); leihen (suit); einstellen (person); **~[out]** vermieten; verleihen

his /hɪz/ adj sein ● poss pron seine(r), seins; **a friend of ~** ein Freund von ihm; **that is ~** das gehört ihm

hiss /hɪs/ n Zischen nt ● vt/i zischen

historian /hɪ'stɔ:rɪən/ n Historiker(in) m(f)

historic /hɪ'stɒrɪk/ adj historisch. **~al** adj geschichtlich, historisch

history /'hɪstərɪ/ n Geschichte f

hit /hɪt/ n (blow) Schlag m; (success) Erfolg m; (direct ~) Volltreffer m ● vt/i (pt/pp hit, pres p hitting) schlagen; (knock against, collide with, affect) treffen; **~ the target** das Ziel treffen; **~ on** (fig) kommen auf (+ acc); **~ it off** gut auskommen (with mit); **~ one's head on sth** sich (dat) den Kopf an etw (dat) stoßen

hitch /hɪtʃ/ n Problem nt; tech-

nical **~ Panne** f ● vt festmachen (to an + dat); **~ up** hochziehen. **~-hike** vi 🛈 trampen. **~-hiker** n Anhalter(in) m(f)

hive /haɪv/ n Bienenstock m

hoard /hɔ:d/ n Hort m ● vt horten, hamstern

hoarding /'hɔ:dɪŋ/ n Bauzaun m; (with advertisements) Reklamewand f

hoar-frost /'hɔ:-/ n Raureif m

hoarse /hɔ:s/ adj (-r, -st) heiser. **~ness** n Heiserkeit f

hoax /həʊks/ n übler Scherz m; (false alarm) blinder Alarm m

hobble /'hɒbl/ vi humpeln

hobby /'hɒbɪ/ n Hobby nt. **~-horse** n (fig) Lieblingsthema nt

hockey /'hɒkɪ/ n Hockey nt

hoe /həʊ/ n Hacke f ● vt (pres p hoeing) hacken

hog /hɒg/ vt (pt/pp hogged) 🛈 mit Beschlag belegen

hoist /hɔɪst/ n Lastenaufzug m ● vt hochziehen; hissen (flag)

hold¹ /həʊld/ n (Naut) Laderaum m

hold² n Halt m; (Sport) Griff m; (fig: influence) Einfluss m; **get ~ of** fassen; (☎: contact) erreichen ● v (pt/pp held) vt halten; (container:) fassen; (believe) meinen; (possess) haben; anhalten (breath) ● vi (rope:) halten; (weather:) sich halten. **~ back** vt zurückhalten ● vi zögern. **~ on** vi (wait) warten; (on telephone) am Apparat bleiben; **~ on to** (keep) behalten; (cling to) sich festhalten an (+ dat). **~ out** vt hinhalten ● vi (resist) aushalten. **~ up** vt hochhalten; (delay) aufhalten; (rob) überfallen

'hold|all n Reisetasche f. **~er** n Inhaber(in) m(f); (container) Halter m. **~up** n Verzögerung f; (attack) Überfall m

hole /həʊl/ n Loch nt

holiday | hopeful

holiday /ˈhɒlədeɪ/ n Urlaub m; (Sch) Ferien pl; (public) Feiertag m; (day off) freier Tag m; **go on ~** in Urlaub fahren

holiness /ˈhəʊlɪnɪs/ n Heiligkeit f

Holland /ˈhɒlənd/ n Holland nt

hollow /ˈhɒləʊ/ adj hohl; (promise) leer ● n Vertiefung f; (in ground) Mulde f. **~ out** vt aushöhlen

holly /ˈhɒlɪ/ n Stechpalme f

holster /ˈhəʊlstə(r)/ n Pistolentasche f

holy /ˈhəʊlɪ/ adj (-ier, -est) heilig. **H~ Ghost** or **Spirit** n Heiliger Geist m

homage /ˈhɒmɪdʒ/ n Huldigung f; **pay ~ to** huldigen (+ dat)

home /həʊm/ n Zuhause nt; (institution) Heim nt; (native land) Heimat f ● adv at ~ zu Hause; **come/go ~** nach Hause kommen/gehen

home: **~ ad'dress** n Heimatanschrift f. **~ game** n Heimspiel nt. **~ help** n Haushaltshilfe f. **~land** n Heimatland nt. **~land security** n innere Sicherheit f. **~less** adj obdachlos

homely /ˈhəʊmlɪ/ adj adj gemütlich; (Amer: ugly) unscheinbar

home: **~'made** adj selbst gemacht. **H~ Office** n Innenministerium nt. **~ page** n Homepage f. **H~ 'Secretary** n Innenminister m. **~sick** adj **be ~sick** Heimweh haben (for nach). **~sickness** n Heimweh nt. **~ 'town** n Heimatstadt f. **~work** n (Sch) Hausaufgaben pl

homo'sexual adj homosexuell ● n Homosexuelle(r) m/f

honest /ˈɒnɪst/ adj ehrlich. **~y** n Ehrlichkeit f

honey /ˈhʌnɪ/ n Honig m (🔢: darling) Schatz m

honey: **~comb** n Honigwabe f. **~moon** n Flitterwochen pl; (journey) Hochzeitsreise f

honorary /ˈɒnərərɪ/ adj ehrenamtlich; (member, doctorate) Ehren-

honour /ˈɒnə(r)/ n Ehre f ● vt ehren; honorieren (cheque). **~able** adj, **~bly** adv ehrenhaft

hood /hʊd/ n Kapuze f; (of car, pram) [Klapp]verdeck nt; (over cooker) Abzugshaube f; (Auto, Amer) Kühlerhaube f

hoof /huːf/ n (pl ~s or hooves) Huf m

hook /hʊk/ n Haken m ● vt festhaken (**to** an + acc)

hook|ed /hʊkt/ adj **~ed nose** Hakennase f. **~ed on** 🔢 abhängig von; (keen on) besessen von. **~er** n (Amer, 🔲) Nutte f

hookey /ˈhʊkɪ/ n **play ~** (Amer, 🔢) schwänzen

hooligan /ˈhuːlɪgən/ n Rowdy m. **~ism** n Rowdytum nt

hooray /hʊˈreɪ/ int & n = **hurrah**

hoot /huːt/ n Ruf m; **~s of laughter** schallendes Gelächter nt ● vi (owl:) rufen; (car:) hupen; (jeer) johlen. **~er** n (of factory) Sirene f; (Auto) Hupe f

hoover /ˈhuːvə(r)/ n **H~** ® Staubsauger m ● vt/i [staub]saugen

hop[1] /hɒp/ n, & **~s** pl Hopfen m

hop[2] vi (pt/pp hopped) hüpfen; **~ it!** 🔢 hau ab!

hope /həʊp/ n Hoffnung f; (prospect) Aussicht f (**of** auf + acc) ● vt/i hoffen (**for** auf + acc); **I ~ so** hoffentlich

hope|ful /ˈhəʊpfl/ adj hoffnungsvoll; **be ~ful that** hoffen, dass. **~fully** adv hoffnungsvoll; (it is hoped) hoffentlich. **~less** adj hoffnungslos; (useless) nutzlos; (incompetent) untauglich

horde /hɔːd/ n Horde f

horizon /həˈraɪzn/ n Horizont m

horizontal /hɒrɪˈzɒntl/ adj horizontal. ~ **bar** n Reck nt

horn /hɔːn/ n Horn nt; (Auto) Hupe f

hornet /ˈhɔːnɪt/ n Hornisse f

horoscope /ˈhɒrəskəʊp/ n Horoskop nt

horrible /ˈhɒrɪbl/ adj, **-bly** adv schrecklich

horrid /ˈhɒrɪd/ adj grässlich

horrific /həˈrɪfɪk/ adj entsetzlich

horrify /ˈhɒrɪfaɪ/ vt (pt/pp **-ied**) entsetzen

horror /ˈhɒrə(r)/ n Entsetzen nt

hors-d'œuvre /ɔːˈdɜːvr/ n Vorspeise f

horse /hɔːs/ n Pferd nt

horse: ~**back** n on ~**back** zu Pferde. ~**man** n Reiter m. ~**power** n Pferdestärke f. ~**-racing** n Pferderennen nt. ~**radish** n Meerrettich m. ~**shoe** n Hufeisen nt

'**horticulture** n Gartenbau m

hose /həʊz/ n (pipe) Schlauch m ● vt ~ **down** abspritzen

hosiery /ˈhəʊzɪərɪ/ n Strumpfwaren pl

hospitable /hɒˈspɪtəbl/ adj, **-bly** adv gastfreundlich

hospital /ˈhɒspɪtl/ n Krankenhaus nt

hospitality /hɒspɪˈtælətɪ/ n Gastfreundschaft f

host[1] /həʊst/ n Gastgeber m

hostage /ˈhɒstɪdʒ/ n Geisel f

hostel /ˈhɒstl/ n [Wohn]heim nt

hostess /ˈhəʊstɪs/ n Gastgeberin f

hostile /ˈhɒstaɪl/ adj feindlich; (unfriendly) feindselig

hostilit|y /hɒˈstɪlətɪ/ n Feindschaft f; **~ies** Feindseligkeiten pl

hot /hɒt/ adj (**hotter, hottest**) heiß; (meal) warm; (spicy) scharf; **I am** or **feel ~** mir ist heiß

hotel /həʊˈtel/ n Hotel nt

hot: ~**head** n Hitzkopf m. ~**house** n Treibhaus nt. ~**ly** adv (fig) heiß, heftig. ~**plate** n Tellerwärmer m; (of cooker) Kochplatte f. ~ **tap** n Warmwasserhahn m. ~**-tempered** adj jähzornig. ~**-'waterbottle** n Wärmflasche f

hound /haʊnd/ n Jagdhund m ● vt (fig) verfolgen

hour /ˈaʊə(r)/ n Stunde f. ~**ly** adj & adv stündlich

house[1] /haʊs/ n Haus nt; **at my ~** bei mir

house[2] /haʊz/ vt unterbringen

house: ~**breaking** n Einbruch m. ~**hold** n Haushalt m. ~**holder** n Hausinhaber(in) m(f). ~**keeper** n Haushälterin f. ~**keeping** n Hauswirtschaft f; (money) Haushaltsgeld nt. ~**plant** n Zimmerpflanze f. ~**-trained** adj stubenrein. ~**-warming** n have a ~**-warming party** Einstand feiern. ~**wife** n Hausfrau f. ~**work** n Hausarbeit f

housing /ˈhaʊzɪŋ/ n Wohnungen pl; (Techn) Gehäuse nt

hovel /ˈhɒvl/ n elende Hütte f

hover /ˈhɒvə(r)/ vi schweben. ~**craft** n Luftkissenfahrzeug nt

how /haʊ/ adv wie; ~ **do you do?** guten Tag!; **and ~!** und ob!

how'ever adv (in question) wie; (nevertheless) jedoch, aber; ~ **small** wie klein es auch sein mag

howl /haʊl/ n Heulen nt ● vi heulen; (baby:) brüllen

hub /hʌb/ n Nabe f

huddle /ˈhʌdl/ vi ~ **together** sich zusammendrängen

huff /hʌf/ n **in a ~** beleidigt

hug /hʌg/ n Umarmung f ● vt (pt/

pp hugged) umarmen

huge /hjuːdʒ/ *adj* riesig

hull /hʌl/ *n* (*Naut*) Rumpf *m*

hullo /həˈləʊ/ *int* = hallo

hum /hʌm/ *n* Summen *nt*; Brummen *nt* ●*vt/i* (*pt/pp* hummed) summen; (*motor:*) brummen

human /ˈhjuːmən/ *adj* menschlich ●*n* Mensch *m*. ~ **'being** *n* Mensch *m*

humane /hjuːˈmeɪn/ *adj* human

humanitarian /hjuːmænɪˈteərɪən/ *adj* humanitär

humanity /hjuːˈmænətɪ/ *n* Menschheit *f*

humble /ˈhʌmbl/ *adj* (-r, -st), -bly *adv* demütig ●*vt* demütigen

'humdrum *adj* eintönig

humid /ˈhjuːmɪd/ *adj* feucht. ~ity *n* Feuchtigkeit *f*

humiliat|e /hjuːˈmɪlɪeɪt/ *vt* demütigen. ~ion *n* Demütigung *f*

humility /hjuːˈmɪlətɪ/ *n* Demut *f*

humorous /ˈhjuːmərəs/ *adj* humorvoll; (*story*) humoristisch

humour /ˈhjuːmə(r)/ *n* Humor *m*; (*mood*) Laune *f*; **have a sense of** ~ Humor haben

hump /hʌmp/ *n* Buckel *m*; (*of camel*) Höcker *m* ●*vt* schleppen

hunch /hʌntʃ/ *n* (*idea*) Ahnung *f*

'hunch|back *n* Bucklige(r) *m/f*

hundred /ˈhʌndrəd/ *adj* one/a ~ [ein]hundert ●*n* Hundert *nt*; (*written figure*) Hundert *f*. ~th *adj* hundertste(r,s) ●*n* Hundertstel *nt*. ~weight *n* ≈ Zentner *m*

hung /hʌŋ/ *see* hang

Hungarian /hʌŋˈɡeərɪən/ *adj* ungarisch ●*n* Ungar(in) *m(f)*

Hungary /ˈhʌŋɡərɪ/ *n* Ungarn *nt*

hunger /ˈhʌŋɡə(r)/ *n* Hunger *m*. ~-strike *n* Hungerstreik *m*

hungry /ˈhʌŋɡrɪ/ *adj*, -ily *adv*

hungrig; **be** ~ Hunger haben

hunt /hʌnt/ *n* Jagd *f*; (*for criminal*) Fahndung *f* ●*vt/i* jagen; fahnden nach (*criminal*); ~ **for** suchen. ~er *n* Jäger *m*; (*horse*) Jagdpferd *nt*. ~ing *n* Jagd *f*

hurdle /ˈhɜːdl/ *n* (*Sport & fig*) Hürde *f*

hurl /hɜːl/ *vt* schleudern

hurrah /hʊˈrɑː/, **hurray** /hʊˈreɪ/ *int* hurra! ●*n* Hurra *nt*

hurricane /ˈhʌrɪkən/ *n* Orkan *m*

hurried /ˈhʌrɪd/ *adj* eilig; (*superficial*) flüchtig

hurry /ˈhʌrɪ/ *n* Eile *f*; **be in a** ~ es eilig haben ●*vi* (*pt/pp* -ied) sich beeilen; (*go quickly*) eilen. ~ **up** *vi* sich beeilen ●*vt* antreiben

hurt /hɜːt/ *vt/i* (*pt/pp* hurt) weh tun (+ *dat*); (*injure*) verletzen; (*offend*) kränken

hurtle /ˈhɜːtl/ *vi* ~ **along** rasen

husband /ˈhʌzbənd/ *n* [Ehe]mann *m*

hush /hʌʃ/ *n* Stille *f* ●*vt* ~ **up** vertuschen. ~ed *adj* gedämpft

husky /ˈhʌskɪ/ *adj* heiser; (*burly*) stämmig

hustle /ˈhʌsl/ *vt* drängen ●*n* Gedränge *nt*

hut /hʌt/ *n* Hütte *f*

hutch /hʌtʃ/ *n* [Kaninchen]stall *m*

hybrid /ˈhaɪbrɪd/ *adj* hybrid ●*n* Hybride *f*

hydraulic /haɪˈdrɔːlɪk/ *adj*, -ally *adv* hydraulisch

hydroe'lectric /haɪdrəʊ-/ *adj* hydroelektrisch

hydrogen /ˈhaɪdrədʒən/ *n* Wasserstoff *m*

hygiene /ˈhaɪdʒiːn/ *n* Hygiene *f*. ~ic *adj*, -ally *adv* hygienisch

hymn /hɪm/ *n* Kirchenlied *nt*. ~-book *n* Gesangbuch *nt*

hyphen /'haɪfn/ n Bindestrich m. **~ate** vt mit Bindestrich schreiben

hypno|sis /hɪp'nəʊsɪs/ n Hypnose f. **~tic** adj hypnotisch

hypno|tism /'hɪpnətɪzm/ n Hypnotik f. **~tist** n Hypnotiseur m. **~tize** vt hypnotisieren

hypochondriac /haɪpə-'kɒndriæk/ n Hypochonder m

hypocrisy /hɪ'pɒkrəsɪ/ n Heuchelei f

hypocrit|e /'hɪpəkrɪt/ n Heuchler(in) m(f)

hypodermic /haɪpə'dɜːmɪk/ adj & n **~ [syringe]** Injektionsspritze f

hypothe|sis /haɪ'pɒθəsɪs/ n Hypothese f. **~tical** adj hypothetisch

hyster|ia /hɪ'stɪərɪə/ n Hysterie f. **~ical** adj hysterisch. **~ics** npl hysterischer Anfall m

I

I /aɪ/ pron ich

ice /aɪs/ n Eis nt ● vt mit Zuckerguss überziehen (cake)

ice: **~berg** /-bɜːg/ n Eisberg m. **~box** n (Amer) Kühlschrank m. **~'cream** n [Speise]eis nt. **~cube** n Eiswürfel m

Iceland /'aɪslənd/ n Island nt

ice: **~lolly** n Eis nt am Stiel. **~rink** n Eisbahn f

icicle /'aɪsɪkl/ n Eiszapfen m

icing /'aɪsɪŋ/ n Zuckerguss m. **~sugar** n Puderzucker m

icon /'aɪkɒn/ n Ikone f

icy /'aɪsɪ/ adj , **-ily** adv eisig; (road) vereist

idea /aɪ'dɪə/ n Idee f; (conception)

Vorstellung f; **I have no ~!** ich habe keine Ahnung!

ideal /aɪ'dɪəl/ adj ideal ● n Ideal nt. **~ism** n Idealismus m. **~ist** n Idealist(in) m(f). **~istic** adj idealistisch. **~ize** vt idealisieren. **~ly** adv ideal; (in ideal circumstances) idealerweise

identical /aɪ'dentɪkl/ adj identisch; (twins) eineiig

identi|fication /aɪdentɪfɪ'keɪʃn/ n Identifizierung f; (proof of identity) Ausweispapiere pl. **~fy** vt (pt/pp -ied) identifizieren

identity /aɪ'dentəti/ n Identität f. **~ card** n [Personal]ausweis m. **~ theft** Identitätsdiebstahl m

idiom /'ɪdɪəm/ n [feste] Redewendung f. **~atic** adj, **-ally** adv idiomatisch

idiosyncrasy /ɪdɪə'sɪŋkrəsɪ/ n Eigenart f

idiot /'ɪdɪət/ n Idiot m. **~ic** adj idiotisch

idle /'aɪdl/ adj (-r, -st) untätig; (lazy) faul; (empty) leer; (machine) nicht in Betrieb ● vi faulenzen; (engine:) leer laufen. **~ness** n Untätigkeit f; Faulheit f

idol /'aɪdl/ n Idol m. **~ize** vt vergöttern

idyllic /ɪ'dɪlɪk/ adj idyllisch

i.e. abbr (id est) d.h.

if /ɪf/ conj wenn; (whether) ob; **as if** als ob

ignition /ɪg'nɪʃn/ n (Auto) Zündung f. **~ key** n Zündschlüssel m

ignoramus /ɪgnə'reɪməs/ n Ignorant m

ignoran|ce /'ɪgnərəns/ n Unwissenheit f. **~t** adj unwissend

ignore /ɪg'nɔː(r)/ vt ignorieren

ill /ɪl/ adj krank; (bad) schlecht; **feel ~ at ease** sich unbehaglich fühlen ● adv schlecht

illegal /ɪ'liːgl/ adj illegal

illegible /ɪˈledʒəbl/ *adj*, **-bly** *adv* unleserlich

illegitimate /ɪlɪˈdʒɪtɪmət/ *adj* unehelich; *(claim)* unberechtigt

illicit /ɪˈlɪsɪt/ *adj* illegal

illiterate /ɪˈlɪtərət/ *adj* nicht lesen und schreiben können

illness /ˈɪlnɪs/ *n* Krankheit *f*

illogical /ɪˈlɒdʒɪkl/ *adj* unlogisch

ill-treat /ɪlˈtriːt/ *vt* misshandeln. **~ment** *n* Misshandlung *f*

illuminat|e /ɪˈluːmɪneɪt/ *vt* beleuchten. **~ion** *n* Beleuchtung *f*

illusion /ɪˈluːʒn/ *n* Illusion *f*; **be under the ~ that** sich *(dat)* einbilden, dass

illustrat|e /ˈɪləstreɪt/ *vt* illustrieren. **~ion** *n* Illustration *f*

illustrious /ɪˈlʌstrɪəs/ *adj* berühmt

image /ˈɪmɪdʒ/ *n* Bild *nt*; *(statue)* Standbild *nt*; *(exact likeness)* Ebenbild *nt*; **[public]** ~ Image *nt*

imagin|able /ɪˈmædʒɪnəbl/ *adj* vorstellbar. **~ary** *adj* eingebildet

imaginat|ion /ɪmædʒɪˈneɪʃn/ *n* Phantasie *f*; *(fancy)* Einbildung *f*. **~ive** *adj* phantasievoll; *(full of ideas)* einfallsreich

imagine /ɪˈmædʒɪn/ *vt* sich *(dat)* vorstellen; *(wrongly)* sich *(dat)* einbilden

im'balance *n* Unausgeglichenheit *f*

imbecile /ˈɪmbəsiːl/ *n* Schwachsinnige(r) *m/f*; *(pej)* Idiot *m*

imitat|e /ˈɪmɪteɪt/ *vt* nachahmen, imitieren. **~ion** *n* Nachahmung *f*, Imitation *f*

immaculate /ɪˈmækjʊlət/ *adj* tadellos; *(Relig)* unbefleckt

imma'ture *adj* unreif

immediate /ɪˈmiːdɪət/ *adj* sofortig; *(nearest)* nächste(r,s). **~ly** *adv*

sofort; **~ly next to** unmittelbar neben ● *conj* sobald

immemorial /ɪməˈmɔːrɪəl/ *adj* **from time ~** seit Urzeiten

immense /ɪˈmens/ *adj* riesig; 𝔼 enorm

immerse /ɪˈmɜːs/ *vt* untertauchen

immigrant /ˈɪmɪɡrənt/ *n* Einwanderer *m*

immigration /ɪmɪˈɡreɪʃn/ *n* Einwanderung *f*

imminent /ˈɪmɪnənt/ *adj* **be ~** unmittelbar bevorstehen

immobil|e /ɪˈməʊbaɪl/ *adj* unbeweglich. **~ize** *vt* *(fig)* lähmen; *(Med)* ruhig stellen. **~izer** *n* *(Auto)* Wegfahrsperre *f*

immodest /ɪˈmɒdɪst/ *adj* unbescheiden

immoral /ɪˈmɒrəl/ *adj* unmoralisch. **~ity** *n* Unmoral *f*

immortal /ɪˈmɔːtl/ *adj* unsterblich. **~ity** *n* Unsterblichkeit *f*. **~ize** *vt* verewigen

immune /ɪˈmjuːn/ *adj* immun *(to/from* gegen)

immunity /ɪˈmjuːnəti/ *n* Immunität *f*

imp /ɪmp/ *n* Kobold *m*

impact /ˈɪmpækt/ *n* Aufprall *m*; *(collision)* Zusammenprall *m*; *(of bomb)* Einschlag *m*; *(fig)* Auswirkung *f*

impair /ɪmˈpeə(r)/ *vt* beeinträchtigen

impart /ɪmˈpɑːt/ *vt* übermitteln *(to* dat); vermitteln *(knowledge)*

im'parti|al *adj* unparteiisch. **~ality** *n* Unparteilichkeit *f*

im'passable *adj* unpassierbar

impassioned /ɪmˈpæʃnd/ *adj* leidenschaftlich

im'passive *adj* unbeweglich

im'patien|ce *n* Ungeduld *f*. **~t**

adj ungeduldig

impeccable /ɪmˈpekəbl/ *adj*, **-bly** *adv* tadellos

impede /ɪmˈpiːd/ *vt* behindern

impediment /ɪmˈpedɪmənt/ *n* Hindernis *nt*; (*in speech*) Sprachfehler *m*

impel /ɪmˈpel/ *vt* (*pt/pp* **impelled**) treiben

impending /ɪmˈpendɪŋ/ *adj* bevorstehend

impenetrable /ɪmˈpenɪtrəbl/ *adj* undurchdringlich

imperative /ɪmˈperətɪv/ *adj* **be** ∼ dringend notwendig sein ● *n* (*Gram*) Imperativ *m*

imper'ceptible *adj* nicht wahrnehmbar

im'perfect *adj* unvollkommen; (*faulty*) fehlerhaft ● *n* (*Gram*) Imperfekt *nt*. ∼**ion** *n* Unvollkommenheit *f*; (*fault*) Fehler *m*

imperial /ɪmˈpɪərɪəl/ *adj* kaiserlich. ∼**ism** *n* Imperialismus *m*

im'personal *adj* unpersönlich

impersonat|e /ɪmˈpɜːsəneɪt/ *vt* sich ausgeben als; (*Theat*) nachahmen, imitieren. ∼**or** *n* Imitator *m*

impertinen|ce /ɪmˈpɜːtɪnəns/ *n* Frechheit *f*. ∼**t** *adj* frech

imperturbable /ɪmpəˈtɜːbəbl/ *adj* unerschütterlich

impetuous /ɪmˈpetjʊəs/ *adj* ungestüm

impetus /ˈɪmpɪtəs/ *n* Schwung *m*

implacable /ɪmˈplækəbl/ *adj* unerbittlich

im'plant *vt* einpflanzen

implement[1] /ˈɪmplɪmənt/ *n* Gerät *nt*

implement[2] /ˈɪmplɪment/ *vt* ausführen. ∼**ation** *n* Ausführung *f*, Durchführung *f*

implication /ɪmplɪˈkeɪʃn/ *n* Ver-

wicklung *f*; ∼**s** *pl* Auswirkungen *pl*; **by** ∼ implizit

implicit /ɪmˈplɪsɪt/ *adj* unausgesprochen; (*absolute*) unbedingt

implore /ɪmˈplɔː(r)/ *vt* anflehen

imply /ɪmˈplaɪ/ *vt* (*pt/pp* **-ied**) andeuten; **what are you** ∼**ing?** was wollen Sie damit sagen?

impo'lite *adj* unhöflich

import[1] /ˈɪmpɔːt/ *n* Import *m*, Einfuhr *f*

import[2] /ɪmˈpɔːt/ *vt* importieren, einführen

importan|ce /ɪmˈpɔːtns/ *n* Wichtigkeit *f*. ∼**t** *adj* wichtig

importer /ɪmˈpɔːtə(r)/ *n* Importeur *m*

impose /ɪmˈpəʊz/ *vt* auferlegen (**on** *dat*) ● *vi* sich aufdrängen (**on** *dat*). ∼**ing** *adj* eindrucksvoll

impossi'bility *n* Unmöglichkeit *f*

im'possible *adj*, **-bly** *adv* unmöglich

impostor /ɪmˈpɒstə(r)/ *n* Betrüger(in) *m(f)*

impoten|ce /ˈɪmpətəns/ *n* Machtlosigkeit *f*; (*Med*) Impotenz *f*. ∼**t** *adj* machtlos; (*Med*) impotent

impoverished /ɪmˈpɒvərɪʃt/ *adj* verarmt

im'practicable *adj* undurchführbar

im'practical *adj* unpraktisch

impre'cise *adj* ungenau

im'press *vt* beeindrucken; ∼ **sth** [**up**]**on s.o.** jdm etw einprägen

impression /ɪmˈpreʃn/ *n* Eindruck *m*; (*imitation*) Nachahmung *f*; (*edition*) Auflage *f*. ∼**ism** *n* Impressionismus *m*

impressive /ɪmˈpresɪv/ *adj* eindrucksvoll

im'prison *vt* gefangen halten; (*put in prison*) ins Gefängnis sperren

i

im'probable adj unwahrscheinlich

impromptu /ɪm'prɒmptjuː/ adj improvisiert ● adv aus dem Stegreif

im'proper adj inkorrekt; (indecent) unanständig

impro'priety n Unkorrektheit f

improve /ɪm'pruːv/ vt verbessern; verschönern (appearance) ● vi sich bessern; ~ [up]on übertreffen. ~ment n Verbesserung f; (in health) Besserung f

improvise /ɪmprəvaɪz/ vt/i improvisieren

im'prudent adj unklug

impuden|ce /ɪmpjʊdəns/ n Frechheit f. ~t adj frech

impulse /ɪmpʌls/ n Impuls m; on [an] ~e impulsiv. ~ive adj impulsiv

im'pure adj unrein. ~ity n Unreinheit f

in /ɪn/ prep in (+ dat/(into) + acc); sit **in** the garden im Garten sitzen; go **in** the garden in den Garten gehen; **in** May im Mai; **in** 1992 [im Jahre] 1992; **in** this heat bei dieser Hitze; **in** the evening am Abend; **in** the sky am Himmel; **in** the world auf der Welt; **in** the street auf der Straße; deaf **in** one ear auf einem Ohr taub; **in** the army beim Militär; **in** English/German auf Englisch/Deutsch; **in** ink/pencil mit Tinte/Bleistift; **in** a soft/loud voice mit leiser/lauter Stimme; **in** doing this, he ... indem er das tut/tat, ... er ● adv (at home) zu Hause; (indoors) drinnen; he's not **in** yet er ist noch nicht da; all **in** alles inbegriffen; (🆇: exhausted) kaputt; day **in**, day out tagaus, tagein; have it **in** for s.o. 🆇 es auf jdn abgesehen haben; send/go **in** hineinschicken/-gehen; come/bring **in** hereinkommen/-bringen ● adj (🆇: in fashion) in ● n

the ins and outs alle Einzelheiten pl

ina'bility n Unfähigkeit f

inac'cessible adj unzugänglich

in'accura|cy n Ungenauigkeit f. ~te adj ungenau

in'ac|tive adj untätig. ~'tivity n Untätigkeit f

in'adequate adj unzulänglich

inad'missable adj unzulässig

inadvertently /ɪnəd'vɜːtəntlɪ/ adv versehentlich

inad'visable adj nicht ratsam

inane /ɪ'neɪn/ adj albern

in'animate adj unbelebt

in'applicable adj nicht zutreffend

inap'propriate adj unangebracht

inar'ticulate adj undeutlich; be ~ sich nicht gut ausdrücken können

inat'tentive adj unaufmerksam

in'audible adj, **-bly** adv unhörbar

inaugural /ɪ'nɔːgjʊrl/ adj Antritts-

inau'spicious adj ungünstig

inborn /'ɪnbɔːn/ adj angeboren

inbred /ɪn'bred/ adj angeboren

incalculable /ɪn'kælkjʊləbl/ adj nicht berechenbar; (fig) unabsehbar

in'capable adj unfähig; be ~ of doing sth nicht fähig sein, etw zu tun

incapacitate /ɪnkə'pæsɪteɪt/ vt unfähig machen

incarnation /ɪnkɑː'neɪʃn/ n Inkarnation f

incendiary /ɪn'sendɪərɪ/ adj & n ~ [bomb] Brandbombe f

incense¹ /'ɪnsens/ n Weihrauch m

incense² /ɪn'sens/ vt wütend machen

incentive /ɪn'sentɪv/ n Anreiz m

incessant /ɪn'sesnt/ adj unaufhörlich

incest /'ɪnsest/ n Inzest m,

Blutschande f

inch /ɪntʃ/ n Zoll m ● vi ~ **forward** sich ganz langsam vorwärts schieben

incident /'ɪnsɪdənt/ n Zwischenfall m

incidental /ɪnsɪ'dentl/ adj nebensächlich; (remark) beiläufig; (expenses) Neben-. ~**ly** adv übrigens

incinerat|e /ɪn'sɪnəreɪt/ vt verbrennen

incision /ɪn'sɪʒn/ n Einschnitt m

incisive /ɪn'saɪsɪv/ adj scharfsinnig

incite /ɪn'saɪt/ vt aufhetzen. ~**ment** n Aufhetzung f

in'clement adj rau

inclination /ɪnklɪ'neɪʃn/ n Neigung f

incline /ɪn'klaɪn/ vt neigen; **be ~d to do sth** dazu neigen, etw zu tun ● vi sich neigen

inclu|de /ɪn'kluːd/ vt einschließen; (contain) enthalten; (incorporate) aufnehmen (**in** + acc). ~**ding** prep einschließlich (+ gen). ~**sion** n Aufnahme f

inclusive /ɪn'kluːsɪv/ adj Inklusiv-; ~ **of** einschließlich (+ gen)

incognito /ɪnkɒg'niːtəʊ/ adv inkognito

inco'herent adj zusammenhanglos; (incomprehensible) unverständlich

income /'ɪnkəm/ n Einkommen nt. ~ **tax** n Einkommensteuer f

'incoming adj ankommend; (mail, call) eingehend

in'comparable adj unvergleichlich

incom'patible adj unvereinbar; **be ~** (people:) nicht zueinander passen

in'competen|ce n Unfähigkeit f. ~**t** adj unfähig

incom'plete adj unvollständig

incompre'hensible adj unverständlich

incon'ceivable adj undenkbar

incon'clusive adj nicht schlüssig

incongruous /ɪn'kɒŋgrʊəs/ adj unpassend

incon'siderate adj rücksichtslos

incon'sistent adj widersprüchlich; (illogical) inkonsequent; **be ~** nicht übereinstimmen

inconsolable /ɪnkən'səʊləbl/ adj untröstlich

incon'spicuous adj unauffällig

incontinen|ce /ɪn'kɒntɪnəns/ n Inkontinenz f. ~**t** adj inkontinent

incon'venien|ce n Unannehmlichkeit f; (drawback) Nachteil m. ~**t** adj ungünstig; **be ~t for s.o.** jdm nicht passen

incorporate /ɪn'kɔːpəreɪt/ vt aufnehmen; (contain) enthalten

incor'rect adj inkorrekt

incorrigible /ɪn'kɒrɪdʒəbl/ adj unverbesserlich

incorruptible /ɪnkə'rʌptəbl/ adj unbestechlich

increase¹ /'ɪnkriːs/ n Zunahme f; (rise) Erhöhung f. **be on the ~** zunehmen

increas|e² /ɪn'kriːs/ vt vergrößern; (raise) erhöhen ● vi zunehmen; (rise) sich erhöhen. ~**ing** adj zunehmend

in'credi|ble adj, **-bly** adv unglaublich

incredulous /ɪn'kredjʊləs/ adj ungläubig

incriminate /ɪn'krɪmɪneɪt/ vt (Jur) belasten

incur /ɪn'kɜː(r)/ vt (pt/pp incurred) sich (dat) zuziehen; (make debts) machen (debts)

in'cura|ble adj, **-bly** adv unheilbar

indebted /ɪn'detɪd/ adj verpflichtet (**to** dat)

indecent | inebriated

in'decent adj unanständig

inde'cision n Unentschlossenheit f

inde'cisive adj ergebnislos; (person) unentschlossen

indeed /ɪnˈdiːd/ adv in der Tat, tatsächlich; **very much ~** sehr

indefatigable /ɪndɪˈfætɪɡəbl/ adj unermüdlich

in'definite adj unbestimmt. **~ly** adv unbegrenzt; (postpone) auf unbestimmte Zeit

indent /ɪnˈdent/ vt (Printing) einrücken. **~ation** n Einrückung f; (notch) Kerbe f

inde'penden|ce n Unabhängigkeit f; (self-reliance) Selbstständigkeit f. **~t** adj unabhängig; selbstständig

indescriba|ble /ɪndɪˈskraɪbəbl/ adj. **-bly** adv unbeschreiblich

indestructible /ɪndɪˈstrʌktəbl/ adj unzerstörbar

indeterminate /ɪndɪˈtɜːmɪnət/ adj unbestimmt

index /ˈɪndeks/ n Register nt

index: ~ card n Karteikarte f. **~ finger** n Zeigefinger m. **~-linked** adj (pension) dynamisch

India /ˈɪndɪə/ n Indien nt. **~n** adj indisch; (American) indianisch ● n Inder(in) m(f); (American) Indianer(in) m(f)

Indian 'summer n Nachsommer m

indicat|e /ˈɪndɪkeɪt/ vt zeigen; (point at) zeigen auf (+ acc); (hint) andeuten; (register) anzeigen ● vi (Auto) blinken. **~ion** n Anzeichen nt

indicative /ɪnˈdɪkətɪv/ n (Gram) Indikativ m

indicator /ˈɪndɪkeɪtə(r)/ n (Auto) Blinker m

in'differen|ce n Gleichgültigkeit f. **~t** adj gleichgültig; (not good) mittelmäßig

indi'gest|ible adj unverdaulich; (difficult to digest) schwer verdaulich. **~ion** n Magenverstimmung f

indigna|nt /ɪnˈdɪɡnənt/ adj entrüstet, empört. **~tion** n Entrüstung f, Empörung f

in'dignity n Demütigung f

indi'rect adj indirekt

indi'screet adj indiskret

indis'cretion n Indiskretion f

indis'pensable adj unentbehrlich

indisposed /ɪndɪˈspəʊzd/ adj indisponiert

indisputable /ɪndɪˈspjuːtəbl/ adj. **-bly** adv unbestreitbar

indi'stinct adj undeutlich

indistinguishable /ɪndɪˈstɪŋɡwɪʃəbl/ adj **be ~** nicht zu unterscheiden sein

individual /ɪndɪˈvɪdjʊəl/ adj individuell; (single) einzeln ● n Individuum nt. **~ity** n Individualität f

indi'visible adj unteilbar

indoctrinate /ɪnˈdɒktrɪneɪt/ vt indoktrinieren

indolen|ce /ˈɪndələns/ n Faulheit f. **~t** adj faul

indomitable /ɪnˈdɒmɪtəbl/ adj unbeugsam

indoor /ˈɪndɔː(r)/ adj Innen-; (clothes) Haus-; (plant) Zimmer-; (Sport) Hallen-. **~s** adv im Haus, drinnen; **go ~s** ins Haus gehen

indulge /ɪnˈdʌldʒ/ vt frönen (+ dat); verwöhnen (child) ● vi **~ in** frönen (+ dat). **~nce** n Nachgiebigkeit f; (leniency) Nachsicht f. **~nt** adj [zu] nachgiebig; nachsichtig

industrial /ɪnˈdʌstrɪəl/ adj Industrie-. **~ist** n Industrielle(r) m

industr|ious /ɪnˈdʌstrɪəs/ adj fleißig. **~y** n Industrie f; (zeal) Fleiß m

inebriated /ɪˈniːbrɪeɪtɪd/ adj

betrunken

in'edible adj nicht essbar

inef'fective adj unwirksam; (*person*) untauglich

inef'ficient adj unfähig; (*organization*) nicht leistungsfähig; (*method*) nicht rationell

in'eligible adj nicht berechtigt

inept /ɪ'nept/ adj ungeschickt

ine'quality n Ungleichheit f

inertia /ɪ'nɜːʃə/ n Trägheit f

inescapable /ɪnɪ'skeɪpəbl/ adj unvermeidlich

inestimable /ɪn'estɪməbl/ adj unschätzbar

inevitab|le /ɪn'evɪtəbl/ adj unvermeidlich. ~**ly** adv zwangsläufig

ine'xact adj ungenau

inex'cusable adj unverzeihlich

inexhaustible /ɪnɪg'zɔːstəbl/ adj unerschöpflich

inex'pensive adj preiswert

inex'perience n Unerfahrenheit f. ~**d** adj unerfahren

inexplicable /ɪnɪk'splɪkəbl/ adj unerklärlich

in'fallible adj unfehlbar

infamous /'ɪnfəməs/ adj niederträchtig; (*notorious*) berüchtigt

infan|cy /'ɪnfənsɪ/ n frühe Kindheit f; (*fig*) Anfangsstadium nt. ~**t** n Kleinkind nt. ~**tile** adj kindisch

infantry /'ɪnfəntrɪ/ n Infanterie f

infatuated /ɪn'fætjʊeɪtɪd/ adj vernarrt (**with** in + acc)

infect /ɪn'fekt/ vt anstecken, infizieren; **become** ~**ed** (*wound:*) sich infizieren. ~**ion** n Infektion f. ~**ious** adj ansteckend

inferior /ɪn'fɪərɪə(r)/ adj minderwertig; (*in rank*) untergeordnet ● n Untergebene(r) m/f

inferiority /ɪnfɪərɪ'ɒrətɪ/ n Minderwertigkeit f. ~ **complex** n Min-

derwertigkeitskomplex m

infern|al /ɪn'fɜːnl/ adj höllisch. ~**o** n flammendes Inferno nt

in'fertile adj unfruchtbar

infest /ɪn'fest/ vt **be** ~**ed with** befallen sein von; (*place*) verseucht sein mit

infi'delity n Untreue f

infighting /'ɪnfaɪtɪŋ/ n (*fig*) interne Machtkämpfe pl

infinite /'ɪnfɪnət/ adj unendlich

infinitive /ɪn'fɪnətɪv/ n (*Gram*) Infinitiv m

infinity /ɪn'fɪnətɪ/ n Unendlichkeit f

inflame /ɪn'fleɪm/ vt entzünden. ~**d** adj entzündet

in'flammable adj feuergefährlich

inflammation /ɪnflə'meɪʃn/ n Entzündung f

inflammatory /ɪn'flæmətrɪ/ adj aufrührerisch

inflat|e /ɪn'fleɪt/ vt aufblasen; (*with pump*) aufpumpen. ~**ion** n Inflation f. ~**ionary** adj inflationär

in'flexible adj starr; (*person*) unbeugsam

inflict /ɪn'flɪkt/ vt zufügen (**on** dat); versetzen (*blow*) (**on** dat)

influen|ce /'ɪnfluəns/ n Einfluss m ● vt beeinflussen. ~**tial** adj einflussreich

influenza /ɪnflu'enzə/ n Grippe f

inform /ɪn'fɔːm/ vt benachrichtigen; (*officially*) informieren; ~ **s.o. of sth** jdm etw mitteilen; **keep s.o.** ~**ed** jdn auf dem Laufenden halten ● vi ~ **against** denunzieren

in'for|mal adj zwanglos; (*unofficial*) inoffiziell. ~'**mality** n Zwanglosigkeit f

informant /ɪn'fɔːmənt/ n Gewährsmann m

informat|ion /ɪnfə'meɪʃn/ n Auskunft f; **a piece of ~ion** eine Auskunft. **~ive** adj aufschlussreich; (*instructive*) lehrreich

informer /ɪnˈfɔːmə(r)/ n Spitzel m; (*Pol*) Denunziant m

infra-'red /ɪnfrə-/ adj infrarot

in'frequent adj selten

infringe /ɪnˈfrɪndʒ/ vt/i ~ **[on]** verstoßen gegen. **~ment** n Verstoß m

infuriat|e /ɪnˈfjʊərɪeɪt/ vt wütend machen. **~ing** adj ärgerlich

ingenious /ɪnˈdʒiːnɪəs/ adj erfinderisch; (*thing*) raffiniert

ingenuity /ɪndʒɪˈnjuːətɪ/ n Geschicklichkeit f

ingrained /ɪnˈgreɪnd/ adj eingefleischt; **be ~** (*dirt:*) tief sitzen

ingratiate /ɪnˈgreɪʃɪeɪt/ vt ~ **oneself** sich einschmeicheln (**with** bei)

in'gratitude n Undankbarkeit f

ingredient /ɪnˈgriːdɪənt/ n (*Culin*) Zutat f

ingrowing /ˈɪngrəʊɪŋ/ adj (*nail*) eingewachsen

inhabit /ɪnˈhæbɪt/ vt bewohnen. **~ant** n Einwohner(in) m(f)

inhale /ɪnˈheɪl/ vt/i einatmen; (*Med & when smoking*) inhalieren

inherent /ɪnˈhɪərənt/ adj natürlich

inherit /ɪnˈherɪt/ vt erben. **~ance** n Erbschaft f, Erbe nt

inhibit|ed /ɪnˈhɪbɪtɪd/ adj gehemmt. **~ion** n Hemmung f

inho'spitable adj ungastlich

in'human adj unmenschlich

inimitable /ɪˈnɪmɪtəbl/ adj unnachahmlich

initial /ɪˈnɪʃl/ adj anfänglich, Anfangs- • n Anfangsbuchstabe m; **my ~s** meine Initialen. **~ly** adv anfangs, am Anfang

initiat|e /ɪˈnɪʃɪeɪt/ vt einführen.

~ion n Einführung f

initiative /ɪˈnɪʃɪətɪv/ n Initiative f

inject /ɪnˈdʒekt/ vt einspritzen, injizieren. **~ion** n Spritze f, Injektion f

injur|e /ˈɪndʒə(r)/ vt verletzen. **~y** n Verletzung f

in'justice n Ungerechtigkeit f; **do s.o. an ~** jdm unrecht tun

ink /ɪŋk/ n Tinte f

inlaid /ɪnˈleɪd/ adj eingelegt

inland /ˈɪnlənd/ adj Binnen- • adv landeinwärts. **I~ Revenue** (*UK*) ≈ Finanzamt nt

in-laws /ˈɪnlɔːz/ npl 🔲 Schwiegereltern pl

inlay /ˈɪnleɪ/ n Einlegearbeit f

inlet /ˈɪnlet/ n schmale Bucht f; (*Techn*) Zuleitung f

inmate /ˈɪnmeɪt/ n Insasse m

inn /ɪn/ n Gasthaus nt

innate /ɪˈneɪt/ adj angeboren

inner /ˈɪnə(r)/ adj innere(r,s). **~most** adj innerste(r,s)

innocen|ce /ˈɪnəsəns/ n Unschuld f. **~t** adj unschuldig. **~tly** adv in aller Unschuld

innocuous /ɪˈnɒkjʊəs/ adj harmlos

innovat|ion /ɪnəˈveɪʃn/ n Neuerung f. **~ive** adj innovativ. **~or** n Neuerer m

innumerable /ɪˈnjuːmərəbl/ adj unzählig

inoculat|e /ɪˈnɒkjʊleɪt/ vt impfen. **~ion** n Impfung f

inof'fensive adj harmlos

in'operable adj nicht operierbar

in'opportune adj unpassend

inor'ganic adj anorganisch

'in-patient n [stationär behandelter] Krankenhauspatient m

input /ˈɪnpʊt/ n Input m & nt

inquest /ˈɪnkwest/ n gerichtliche Untersuchung f der Todesursache

inquir|e /ɪnˈkwaɪə(r)/ *vi* sich erkundigen (**about** nach); **~e into** untersuchen ● *vt* sich erkundigen nach. **~y** n Erkundigung f; (*investigation*) Untersuchung f

inquisitive /ɪnˈkwɪzətɪv/ *adj* neugierig

in'sane *adj* geisteskrank; (*fig*) wahnsinnig

in'sanitary *adj* unhygienisch

in'sanity n Geisteskrankheit f

insatiable /ɪnˈseɪʃəbl/ *adj* unersättlich

inscription /ɪnˈskrɪpʃn/ n Inschrift f

inscrutable /ɪnˈskruːtəbl/ *adj* unergründlich; (*expression*) undurchdringlich

insect /ˈɪnsekt/ n Insekt nt. **~icide** n Insektenvertilgungsmittel nt

inse'cur|e *adj* nicht sicher; (*fig*) unsicher. **~ity** n Unsicherheit f

in'sensitive *adj* gefühllos; **~ to** unempfindlich gegen

in'separable *adj* untrennbar; (*people*) unzertrennlich

insert¹ /ˈɪnsɜːt/ n Einsatz m

insert² /ɪnˈsɜːt/ *vt* einfügen, einsetzen; einstecken (*key*); einwerfen (*coin*). **~ion** n (*insert*) Einsatz m; (*in text*) Einfügung f

inside /ɪnˈsaɪd/ n Innenseite f; (*of house*) Innere(s) nt ● *attrib* Innen- ● *adv* innen; (*indoors*) drinnen; **go ~** hineingehen; **come ~** hereinkommen; **~ out** links [herum]; **know sth ~** out etw in- und auswendig kennen ● *prep* **~** [**of**] in + *dat*/(*into*) + acc)

insight /ˈɪnsaɪt/ n Einblick m (**into** in + acc); (*understanding*) Einsicht f

insig'nificant *adj* unbedeutend

insin'cere *adj* unaufrichtig

insinuat|e /ɪnˈsɪnjʊeɪt/ *vt* andeuten. **~ion** n Andeutung f

insipid /ɪnˈsɪpɪd/ *adj* fade

insist /ɪnˈsɪst/ *vi* darauf bestehen; **~ on** bestehen auf (+ *dat*) ● *vt* **~ that** darauf bestehen, dass. **~ence** n Bestehen nt. **~ent** *adj* beharrlich; **be ~ent** darauf bestehen

'insole n Einlegesohle f

insolen|ce /ˈɪnsələns/ n Unverschämtheit f. **~t** *adj* unverschämt

in'soluble *adj* unlöslich; (*fig*) unlösbar

in'solvent *adj* zahlungsunfähig

insomnia /ɪnˈsɒmnɪə/ n Schlaflosigkeit f

inspect /ɪnˈspekt/ *vt* inspizieren; (*test*) prüfen; kontrollieren (*ticket*). **~ion** n Inspektion f. **~or** n Inspektor m; (*of tickets*) Kontrolleur m

inspiration /ɪnspəˈreɪʃn/ n Inspiration f

inspire /ɪnˈspaɪə(r)/ *vt* inspirieren

insta'bility n Unbeständigkeit f; (*of person*) Labilität f

install /ɪnˈstɔːl/ *vt* installieren. **~ation** n Installation f

instalment /ɪnˈstɔːlmənt/ n (*Comm*) Rate f; (*of serial*) Fortsetzung f; (*Radio, TV*) Folge f

instance /ˈɪnstəns/ n Fall m; (*example*) Beispiel nt; **in the first ~** zunächst; **for ~** zum Beispiel

instant /ˈɪnstənt/ *adj* sofortig; (*Culin*) Instant- ● n Augenblick m, Moment m. **~aneous** *adj* unverzüglich, unmittelbar

instant 'coffee n Pulverkaffee m

instantly /ˈɪnstəntlɪ/ *adv* sofort

instead /ɪnˈsted/ *adv* statt dessen; **~ of** statt (+ *gen*), anstelle von; **~ of me** an meiner Stelle; **~ of going** anstatt zu gehen

'instep n Spann m, Rist m

instigat|e /ˈɪnstɪɡeɪt/ *vt* anstiften; einleiten (*proceedings*). **~ion** n Anstiftung f; **at his ~ion** auf seine

Veranlassung

instil /ɪnˈstɪl/ vt (pt/pp **instilled**) einprägen (**into** s.o. jdm)

instinct /ˈɪnstɪŋkt/ n Instinkt m. **~ive** adj instinktiv

institut|e /ˈɪnstɪtjuːt/ n Institut nt. **~ion** n Institution f; (home) Anstalt f

instruct /ɪnˈstrʌkt/ vt unterrichten; (order) anweisen. **~ion** n Unterricht m; Anweisung f. **~ions** pl **for use** Gebrauchsanweisung f. **~ive** adj lehrreich. **~or** n Lehrer(in) m(f); (Mil) Ausbilder m

instrument /ˈɪnstrʊmənt/ n Instrument nt. **~al** adj Instrumental-

insu'bordi|nate adj ungehorsam. **~nation** n Ungehorsam m; (Mil) Insubordination f

insuf'ficient adj nicht genügend

insulat|e /ˈɪnsjʊleɪt/ vt isolieren. **~ing tape** n Isolierband nt. **~ion** n Isolierung f

insult[1] /ˈɪnsʌlt/ n Beleidigung f

insult[2] /ɪnˈsʌlt/ vt beleidigen

insur|ance /ɪnˈʃʊərəns/ n Versicherung f. **~e** vt versichern

intact /ɪnˈtækt/ adj unbeschädigt; (complete) vollständig

'intake n Aufnahme f

in'tangible adj nicht greifbar

integral /ˈɪntɪgrl/ adj wesentlich

integrat|e /ˈɪntɪgreɪt/ vt integrieren. **~e** vi sich integrieren. **~ion** n Integration f

integrity /ɪnˈtegrəti/ n Integrität f

intellect /ˈɪntəlekt/ n Intellekt m. **~ual** adj intellektuell

intelligen|ce /ɪnˈtelɪdʒəns/ n Intelligenz f; (Mil) Nachrichtendienst m; (information) Meldungen pl. **~t** adj intelligent

intelligible /ɪnˈtelɪdʒəbl/ adj verständlich

intend /ɪnˈtend/ vt beabsichtigen;

be **~ed for** bestimmt sein für

intense /ɪnˈtens/ adj intensiv; (pain) stark. **~ly** adv äußerst; (study) intensiv

intensify /ɪnˈtensɪfaɪ/ v (pt/pp -ied) • vt intensivieren • vi zunehmen

intensity /ɪnˈtensəti/ n Intensität f

intensive /ɪnˈtensɪv/ adj intensiv; be **in ~ care** auf der Intensivstation sein

intent /ɪnˈtent/ adj aufmerksam; **~ on** (absorbed in) vertieft in (+ acc) • n Absicht f

intention /ɪnˈtenʃn/ n Absicht f. **~al** adj absichtlich

inter'acti|on n Wechselwirkung f. **~ve** adj interactiv

intercede /ɪntəˈsiːd/ vi Fürsprache einlegen (**on behalf of** für)

intercept /ɪntəˈsept/ vt abfangen

'interchange n Austausch m; (Auto) Autobahnkreuz nt

intercom /ˈɪntəkɒm/ n [Gegen]sprechanlage f

'intercourse n (sexual) Geschlechtsverkehr m

interest /ˈɪntrəst/ n Interesse nt; (Comm) Zinsen pl • vt interessieren; be **~ed** sich interessieren (**in** für). **~ing** adj interessant. **~ rate** n Zinssatz m

interface /ˈɪntəfeɪs/ n Schnittstelle f

interfere /ɪntəˈfɪə(r)/ vi sich einmischen. **~nce** n Einmischung f; (Radio, TV) Störung f

interim /ˈɪntərɪm/ adj Zwischen-; (temporary) vorläufig

interior /ɪnˈtɪərɪə(r)/ adj inner(e,r,s), Innen- • n Innere(s) nt

interject /ɪntəˈdʒekt/ vt einwerfen. **~ion** n Interjektion f; (remark) Einwurf m

interlude /ˈɪntəluːd/ n Pause f;

(*performance*) Zwischenspiel nt

inter'marry vi untereinander heiraten; (*different groups:*) Mischehen schließen

intermediary /ɪntəˈmiːdɪərɪ/ n Vermittler(in) m(f)

intermediate /ɪntəˈmiːdɪət/ adj Zwischen-

interminable /ɪnˈtɜːmɪnəbl/ adj endlos [lang]

intermittent /ɪntəˈmɪtənt/ adj in Abständen auftretend

internal /ɪnˈtɜːnl/ adj innere(r,s); (*matter, dispute*) intern. **I~ Revenue** (USA) ≈ Finanzamt nt. **~ly** adv innerlich; (*deal with*) intern

inter'national adj international ● n Länderspiel nt; (*player*) Nationalspieler(in) m(f)

'Internet n Internet nt; **on the ~** im Internet

internment /ɪnˈtɜːnmənt/ n Internierung f

'interplay n Wechselspiel nt

interpolate /ɪnˈtɜːpəleɪt/ vt einwerfen

interpret /ɪnˈtɜːprɪt/ vt interpretieren; auslegen (*text*); deuten (*dream*); (*translate*) dolmetschen ● vi dolmetschen. **~ation** n Interpretation f. **~er** n Dolmetscher(in) m(f)

interrogat|e /ɪnˈterəgeɪt/ vt verhören. **~ion** n Verhör nt

interrogative /ɪntəˈrɒgətɪv/ adj & n ~ **[pronoun]** Interrogativpronomen nt

interrupt /ɪntəˈrʌpt/ vt/i unterbrechen; **don't ~!** red nicht dazwischen! **~ion** n Unterbrechung f

intersect /ɪntəˈsekt/ vi sich kreuzen; (*of lines*) sich schneiden. **~ion** n Kreuzung f

interspersed /ɪntəˈspɜːst/ adj ~ with durchsetzt mit

inter'twine vi sich ineinanderschlingen

interval /ˈɪntəvl/ n Abstand m; (*Theat*) Pause f; (*Mus*) Intervall nt; **at hourly ~s** alle Stunde; **bright ~s** pl Aufheiterungen pl

interven|e /ɪntəˈviːn/ vi eingreifen; (*occur*) dazwischenkommen. **~tion** n Eingreifen nt; (*Mil, Pol*) Intervention f

interview /ˈɪntəvjuː/ n (*in media*) Interview nt; (*for job*) Vorstellungsgespräch n ● vt interviewen; ein Vorstellungsgespräch führen mit. **~er** n Interviewer(in) m(f)

intimacy /ˈɪntɪməsɪ/ n Vertrautheit f; (*sexual*) Intimität f

intimate /ˈɪntɪmət/ adj vertraut; (*friend*) eng; (*sexually*) intim

intimidat|e /ɪnˈtɪmɪdeɪt/ vt einschüchtern. **~ion** n Einschüchterung f

into /ˈɪntə/, vor einem Vokal /ˈɪntʊ/ prep in (+ acc); **be ~** ⓘ sich auskennen mit; **7 ~ 21** 21 [geteilt] durch 7

in'tolerable adj unerträglich

in'toleran|ce n Intoleranz f. **~t** adj intolerant

intonation /ɪntəˈneɪʃn/ n Tonfall m

intoxicat|ed /ɪnˈtɒksɪkeɪtɪd/ adj betrunken; (*fig*) berauscht. **~ion** n Rausch m

intransigent /ɪnˈtrænsɪdʒənt/ adj unnachgiebig

in'transitive adj intransitiv

intrepid /ɪnˈtrepɪd/ adj kühn, unerschrocken

intricate /ˈɪntrɪkət/ adj kompliziert

intrigu|e /ɪnˈtriːg/ n Intrige f ● vt faszinieren. **~ing** adj faszinierend

intrinsic /ɪnˈtrɪnsɪk/ adj ~ **value** Eigenwert m

introduce /ɪntrə'dju:s/ vt vorstellen; (bring in, insert) einführen

introduct|ion /ɪntrə'dʌkʃn/ n Einführung f; (to person) Vorstellung f; (to book) Einleitung f. **~ory** adj einleitend

introvert /'ɪntrəvɜːt/ n introvertierter Mensch m

intru|de /ɪn'tru:d/ vi stören. **~der** n Eindringling m. **~sion** n Störung f

intuit|ion /ɪntju:'ɪʃn/ n Intuition f. **~ive** adj intuitiv

inundate /'ɪnʌndeɪt/ vt überschwemmen

invade /ɪn'veɪd/ vt einfallen in (+ acc). **~r** n Angreifer m

invalid[1] /'ɪnvəlɪd/ n Kranke(r) m/f

invalid[2] /ɪn'vælɪd/ adj ungültig

in'valuable adj unschätzbar; (person) unersetzlich

in'variab|le adj unveränderlich. **~ly** adv immer

invasion /ɪn'veɪʒn/ n Invasion f

invent /ɪn'vent/ vt erfinden. **~ion** n Erfindung f. **~ive** adj erfinderisch. **~or** n Erfinder m

inventory /'ɪnvəntrɪ/ n Bestandsliste f

invert /ɪn'vɜːt/ vt umkehren. **~ed commas** npl Anführungszeichen pl

invest /ɪn'vest/ vt investieren, anlegen; **~ in** (I: buy) sich (dat) zulegen

investigat|e /ɪn'vestɪgeɪt/ vt untersuchen. **~ion** n Untersuchung f

invest|ment /ɪn'vestmənt/ n Anlage f; **be a good ~ment** (fig) sich bezahlt machen. **~or** n Kapitalanleger m

invidious /ɪn'vɪdɪəs/ adj unerfreulich; (unfair) ungerecht

invincible /ɪn'vɪnsəbl/ adj unbesiegbar

inviolable /ɪn'vaɪələbl/ adj unantastbar

in'visible adj unsichtbar

invitation /ɪnvɪ'teɪʃn/ n Einladung f

invit|e /ɪn'vaɪt/ vt einladen. **~ing** adj einladend

invoice /'ɪnvɔɪs/ n Rechnung f ● vt **~ s.o.** jdm eine Rechnung schicken

in'voluntary adj, **-ily** adv unwillkürlich

involve /ɪn'vɒlv/ vt beteiligen; (affect) betreffen; (implicate) verwickeln; (entail) mit sich bringen; (mean) bedeuten; **be ~d in** beteiligt sein an (+ dat); (implicated) verwickelt sein in (+ acc); **get ~d with s.o.** sich mit jdm einlassen. **~d** adj kompliziert. **~ment** n Verbindung f

in'vulnerable adj unverwundbar; (position) unangreifbar

inward /'ɪnwəd/ adj innere(r,s). **~s** adv nach innen

iodine /'aɪədiːn/ n Jod nt

IOU abbr Schuldschein m

Iran /ɪ'rɑːn/ n der Iran

Iraq /ɪ'rɑːk/ n der Irak

irascible /ɪ'ræsəbl/ adj aufbrausend

irate /aɪ'reɪt/ adj wütend

Ireland /'aɪələnd/ n Irland nt

iris /'aɪərɪs/ n (Anat) Regenbogenhaut f, Iris f; (Bot) Schwertlilie f

Irish /'aɪərɪʃ/ adj irisch ● n **the ~** pl die Iren. **~man** n Ire m. **~woman** n Irin f

iron /'aɪən/ adj Eisen-; (fig) eisern ● n Eisen nt; (appliance) Bügeleisen nt ● vt/i bügeln

ironic[al] /aɪ'rɒnɪk[l]/ adj ironisch

ironing /'aɪənɪŋ/ n Bügeln nt; (articles) Bügelwäsche f. **~-board** n Bügelbrett nt

ironmonger /'aɪənmʌŋgə(r)/ n **~'s** [shop] Haushaltswarengeschäft n

irony /ˈaɪərənɪ/ n Ironie f

irrational /ɪˈræʃənl/ adj irrational

irreconcilable /ɪˈrekənsaɪləbl/ adj unversöhnlich

irrefutable /ɪrɪˈfjuːtəbl/ adj unwiderlegbar

irregular /ɪˈreɡjʊlə(r)/ adj unregelmäßig; (against rules) regelwidrig. **~ity** n Unregelmäßigkeit f; Regelwidrigkeit f

irrelevant /ɪˈreləvənt/ adj irrelevant

irreparable /ɪˈrepərəbl/ adj nicht wieder gutzumachen

irreplaceable /ɪrɪˈpleɪsəbl/ adj unersetzlich

irrepressible /ɪrɪˈpresəbl/ adj unverwüstlich; **be ~** (person:) nicht unterzukriegen sein

irresistible /ɪrɪˈzɪstəbl/ adj unwiderstehlich

irresolute /ɪˈrezəluːt/ adj unentschlossen

irrespective /ɪrɪˈspektɪv/ adj **~ of** ungeachtet (+ gen)

irresponsible /ɪrɪˈspɒnsəbl/ adj, **-bly** adv unverantwortlich; (person) verantwortungslos

irreverent /ɪˈrevərənt/ adj respektlos

irrevocable /ɪˈrevəkəbl/ adj, **-bly** adv unwiderruflich

irrigat|e /ˈɪrɪɡeɪt/ vt bewässern. **~ion** n Bewässerung f

irritable /ˈɪrɪtəbl/ adj reizbar

irritant /ˈɪrɪtənt/ n Reizstoff m

irritat|e /ˈɪrɪteɪt/ vt irritieren; (Med) reizen. **~ion** n Ärger m; (Med) Reizung f

is /ɪz/ see **be**

Islam /ˈɪzlɑːm/ n der Islam. **~ic** adj islamisch

island /ˈaɪlənd/ n Insel f. **~er** n Inselbewohner(in) m(f)

isolat|e /ˈaɪsəleɪt/ vt isolieren.

~ed adj (remote) abgelegen; (single) einzeln. **~ion** n Isoliertheit f; (Med) Isolierung f

Israel /ˈɪzreɪl/ n Israel nt. **~i** adj israelisch ● n Israeli m/f

issue /ˈɪʃuː/ n Frage f; (outcome) Ergebnis nt; (of magazine, stamps) Ausgabe f; (offspring) Nachkommen pl ● vt ausgeben; ausstellen (passport); erteilen (order); herausgeben (book); **be ~d with** sth etw erhalten

---

it /ɪt/

● pronoun

••••▸ (as subject) er (m), sie (f), es (nt); (in impersonal sentence) es. **where is the spoon? It's on the table** wo ist der Löffel? Er liegt auf dem Tisch. **it was very kind of you** es war sehr nett von Ihnen. **it's five o'clock** es ist fünf Uhr

••••▸ (as direct object) ihn (m), sie (f), es (nt). **that's my pencil — give it to me** das ist mein Bleistift — gib ihn mir.

••••▸ (as dative object) ihm (m), ihr (f), ihm (nt). **he found a track and followed it** er fand eine Spur und folgte ihr.

••••▸ (after prepositions)

! Combinations such as with it, from it, to it are translated by the prepositions with the prefix **da-** (damit, davon, dazu). Prepositions beginning with a vowel insert an 'r' (daran, darauf, darüber). **I can't do anything with it** ich kann nichts damit anfangen. **don't lean on it!** lehn dich nicht daran!

••••▸ (the person in question) es.

it's me ich bin's. **is it you,
Dad?** bist du es, Vater? **who is
it?** wer ist da?

Italian /ɪˈtæljən/ adj italienisch ● n
Italiener(in) m(f); (Lang) Italienisch nt

italics /ɪˈtælɪks/ npl Kursivschrift f;
in ~s kursiv

Italy /ˈɪtəlɪ/ n Italien nt

itch /ɪtʃ/ n Juckreiz m; **I have an ~**
es juckt mich ● vi jucken; **I'm ~ing**
🛈 es juckt mich (**to** zu). **~y** adj **be
~y** jucken

item /ˈaɪtəm/ n Gegenstand m;
(Comm) Artikel m; (on agenda)
Punkt m; (on invoice) Posten m;
(act) Nummer f

itinerary /aɪˈtɪnərərɪ/ n [Reise]-
route f

its /ɪts/ poss pron sein; (f) ihr

it's = it is, it has

itself /ɪtˈself/ pron selbst; (reflexive)
sich; **by ~** von selbst; (alone) allein

ivory /ˈaɪvərɪ/ n Elfenbein nt
● attrib Elfenbein-

ivy /ˈaɪvɪ/ n Efeu m

> *i* **Ivy League** Amerikanische
> Universitäten sind in
> Gruppen von Institutio-
> nen aufgeteilt, die untereinander
> sportliche Veranstaltungen durch-
> führen. Die exklusivste Gruppe ist
> die Ivy League im Nordosten der
> USA. (Efeuliga, nach den mit Efeu
> bewachsenen, alten Universitäts-
> bäuden.) Harvard und Yale haben
> den besten akademischen Ruf der
> acht Eliteuniversitäten. Viele ame-
> rikanische Politiker haben an einer
> Ivy-League Universität studiert.

Jj

jab /dʒæb/ n Stoß m; (🛈: injection)
Spritze f ● vt (pt/pp jabbed) stoßen

jabber /ˈdʒæbə(r)/ vi plappern

jack /dʒæk/ n (Auto) Wagenheber
m; (Cards) Bube m ● vt **~ up** (Auto)
aufbocken

jacket /ˈdʒækɪt/ n Jacke f; (of book)
Schutzumschlag m

'jackpot n **hit the ~** das große
Los ziehen

jade /dʒeɪd/ n Jade m

jagged /ˈdʒæɡɪd/ adj zackig

jail /dʒeɪl/ = gaol

jam¹ /dʒæm/ n Marmelade f

jam² /dʒæm/ n Gedränge nt; (Auto) Stau m;
(fam. difficulty) Klemme f ● v (pt/pp
jammed) ● vt klemmen (**in in** +
acc); stören (broadcast) ● vi
klemmen

Jamaica /dʒəˈmeɪkə/ n Jamaika nt

jangle /ˈdʒæŋɡl/ vi klimpern ● vt
klimpern mit

January /ˈdʒænjʊərɪ/ n Januar m

Japan /dʒəˈpæn/ n Japan nt. **~ese**
adj japanisch ● n Japaner(in) m(f);
(Lang) Japanisch nt

jar /dʒɑː(r)/ n Glas nt; (earthenware)
Topf m

jargon /ˈdʒɑːɡən/ n Jargon m

jaunt /dʒɔːnt/ n Ausflug m

jaunt|y /ˈdʒɔːntɪ/ adj **-ily** adv keck

javelin /ˈdʒævlɪn/ n Speer m

jaw /dʒɔː/ n Kiefer m

jazz /dʒæz/ n Jazz m. **~y** adj knallig

jealous /ˈdʒeləs/ adj eifersüchtig
(**of** auf + acc). **~y** n Eifersucht f

jeans /dʒiːnz/ npl Jeans pl

jeer /dʒɪə(r)/ vi johlen; **~ at**

verhöhnen

jelly /'dʒelɪ/ n Gelee nt; (dessert) Götterspeise f. **~fish** n Qualle f

jeopar|dize /'dʒepədaɪz/ vt gefährden. **~dy** n in **~dy** gefährdet

jerk /dʒɜ:k/ n Ruck m ● vt stoßen; (pull) reißen ● vi rucken; (limb, muscle:) zucken. **~ily** adv ruckweise. **~y** adj ruckartig

jersey /'dʒɜ:zɪ/ n Pullover m; (Sport) Trikot nt; (fabric) Jersey m

jest /dʒest/ n in **~** im Spaß

jet n (of water) [Wasser]strahl m; (nozzle) Düse f; (plane) Düsenflugzeug nt

jet: ~-'black adj pechschwarz. **~-pro'pelled** adj mit Düsenantrieb

jetty /'dʒetɪ/ n Landesteg m; (breakwater) Buhne f

Jew /dʒu:/ n Jude m /Jüdin f

jewel /'dʒu:əl/ n Edelstein m; (fig) Juwel nt. **~ler** n Juwelier m; **~ler's [shop]** Juweliergeschäft nt. **~lery** n Schmuck m

Jew|ess /'dʒu:ɪs/ n Jüdin f. **~ish** adj jüdisch

jib /dʒɪb/ vi (pt/pp jibbed) (fig) sich sträuben (at gegen)

jigsaw /'dʒɪgsɔ:/ n **~ [puzzle]** Puzzlespiel nt

jilt /dʒɪlt/ vt sitzen lassen

jingle /'dʒɪŋgl/ n (rhyme) Versehen nt ● vi klimpern

jinx /dʒɪŋks/ n 🔲 **it's got a ~ on it** es ist verhext

jittery /'dʒɪtərɪ/ adj 🔲 nervös

job /dʒɒb/ n Aufgabe f; (post) Stelle f, 🔲 Job m; **be a ~** 🔲 nicht leicht sein; **it's a good ~ that** es ist [nur] gut, dass. **~less** adj arbeitslos

jockey /'dʒɒkɪ/ n Jockei m

jocular /'dʒɒkjʊlə(r)/ adj spaßhaft

jog /dʒɒg/ n Stoß m ● v (pt/pp jogged) ● vt anstoßen; **~ s.o.'s**

memory jds Gedächtnis nachhelfen ● vi (Sport) joggen. **~ging** n Jogging nt

john /dʒɒn/ n (Amer, 🔲) Klo nt

join /dʒɔɪn/ n Nahtstelle f ● vt verbinden (to mit); sich anschließen (+ dat) (person); (become member of) beitreten (+ dat); eintreten in (+ acc) (firm) ● vi (roads:) sich treffen. **~ in** vi mitmachen. **~ up** vi (Mil) Soldat werden ● vt zusammenfügen

joint /dʒɔɪnt/ adj gemeinsam ● n Gelenk nt; (in wood, brickwork) Fuge f; (Culin) Braten m; (🔲: bar) Lokal nt

jok|e /dʒəʊk/ n Scherz m; (funny story) Witz m; (trick) Streich m ● vi scherzen. **~er** n Witzbold m; (Cards) Joker m. **~ing** n **~ing apart** Spaß beiseite. **~ingly** adv im Spaß

jolly /'dʒɒlɪ/ adj lustig ● adv 🔲 sehr

jolt /dʒəʊlt/ n Ruck m ● vt einen Ruck versetzen (+ dat) ● vi holpern

Jordan /'dʒɔ:dn/ n Jordanien nt

jostle /'dʒɒsl/ vt anrempeln

jot /dʒɒt/ vt (pt/pp jotted) **~ [down]** sich (dat) notieren

journal /'dʒɜ:nl/ n Zeitschrift f; (diary) Tagebuch nt. **~ese** n Zeitungsjargon m. **~ism** n Journalismus m. **~ist** n Journalist(in) m(f)

journey /'dʒɜ:nɪ/ n Reise f

jovial /'dʒəʊvɪəl/ adj lustig

joy /dʒɔɪ/ n Freude f. **~ful** adj freudig, froh. **~ride** n 🔲 Spritztour f [im gestohlenen Auto]

jubil|ant /'dʒu:bɪlənt/ adj überglücklich. **~ation** n Jubel m

jubilee /'dʒu:bɪli:/ n Jubiläum nt

judder /'dʒʌdə(r)/ vi rucken

judge /dʒʌdʒ/ n Richter m; (of competition) Preisrichter m ● vt beurteilen; (estimate) [ein]schätzen ● vi urteilen (by nach). **~ment** n Beurteilung f; (Jur) Urteil nt; (fig)

Urteilsvermögen nt

judic|ial /dʒu:'dɪʃl/ adj gerichtlich. **~ious** adj klug

jug /dʒʌg/ n Kanne f; (small) Kännchen nt; (for water, wine) Krug m

juggle /'dʒʌgl/ vi jonglieren. **~r** n Jongleur m

juice /dʒu:s/ n Saft m

juicy /'dʒu:sɪ/ adj saftig; 🅵 (story) pikant

juke-box /'dʒu:k-/ n Musikbox f

July /dʒu'laɪ/ n Juli m

jumble /'dʒʌmbl/ n Durcheinander nt ● vt ~ [up] durcheinander bringen. **~ sale** n [Wohltätigkeits] basar m

jump /dʒʌmp/ n Sprung m; (in prices) Anstieg m; (in horse racing) Hindernis nt ● vi springen; (start) zusammenzucken; **make s.o. ~** jdn erschrecken; **~ at** (fig) sofort zugreifen bei (offer); **~ to conclusions** voreilige Schlüsse ziehen ● vt überspringen. **~ up** vi aufspringen

jumper /'dʒʌmpə(r)/ n Pullover m, Pulli m

jumpy /'dʒʌmpɪ/ adj nervös

junction /'dʒʌŋkʃn/ n Kreuzung f; (Rail) Knotenpunkt m

June /dʒu:n/ n Juni m

jungle /'dʒʌŋgl/ n Dschungel m

junior /'dʒu:nɪə(r)/ adj jünger; (in rank) untergeordnet; (Sport) Junioren- ● n Junior m

junk /dʒʌŋk/ n Gerümpel nt, Trödel m

junkie /'dʒʌŋkɪ/ n 🅇 Fixer m

'junk-shop n Trödelladen m

jurisdiction /dʒuərɪs'dɪkʃn/ n Gerichtsbarkeit f

jury /'dʒuərɪ/ n the **~** die Geschworenen pl; (for competition) die Jury

just /dʒʌst/ adj gerecht ● adv gerade; (only) nur; (simply) einfach; (exactly) genau; **~ as tall** ebenso groß; **I'm ~ going** ich gehe schon

justice /'dʒʌstɪs/ n Gerechtigkeit f; **do ~ to** gerecht werden (+ dat)

justifiab|le /'dʒʌstɪfaɪəbl/ adj berechtigt. **~ly** adv berechtigterweise

justi|fication /dʒʌstɪfɪ'keɪʃn/ n Rechtfertigung f. **~fy** vt (pt/pp -ied) rechtfertigen

justly /'dʒʌstlɪ/ adv zu Recht

jut /dʒʌt/ vi (pt/pp jutted) **~ out** vorstehen

juvenile /'dʒu:vənaɪl/ adj jugendlich; (childish) kindisch ● n Jugendliche(r) m/f. **~ delinquency** n Jugendkriminalität f

Kk

kangaroo /kæŋgə'ru:/ n Känguru nt

kebab /kɪ'bæb/ n Spießchen nt

keel /ki:l/ n Kiel m ● vi **~ over** umkippen; (Naut) kentern

keen /ki:n/ adj (-er, -est) (sharp) scharf; (intense) groß; (eager) eifrig, begeistert; **~ on** 🅵 erpicht auf (+ acc); **~ on s.o.** von jdm sehr angetan; **be ~ to do sth** etw gerne machen wollen. **~ly** adv tief. **~ness** n Eifer m, Begeisterung f

keep /ki:p/ n (maintenance) Unterhalt m; (of castle) Bergfried m; **for ~s** für immer ● v (pt/pp kept) ● vt behalten; (store) aufbewahren; (not throw away) aufheben; (support) unterhalten; (detain) aufhalten; freihalten (seat); halten (promise, animals); führen, haben (shop); einhalten (law, rules); **~ s.o. waiting** jdn warten lassen; ~ sth to oneself etw nicht weitersagen • vi (remain) bleiben; (food:) sich halten; ~ **left/right** sich links/rechts halten; ~ **on doing sth** etw weitermachen; (repeatedly) etw dauernd machen; ~ **in** sich stellen mit. ~ **up** vi Schritt halten • vt (continue) weitermachen

keep|er /'ki:pə(r)/ n Wärter(in) m(f). ~**ing** n be in ~**ing with** passen zu

kennel /'kenl/ n Hundehütte f; ~**s** pl (boarding) Hundepension f; (breeding) Zwinger m

Kenya /'kenjə/ n Kenia nt

kept /kept/ see **keep**

kerb /kɜːb/ n Bordstein m

kernel /'kɜːnl/ n Kern m

ketchup /'ketʃʌp/ n Ketschup m

kettle /'ketl/ n [Wasser]kessel m; **put the** ~ **on** Wasser aufsetzen

key /ki:/ n Schlüssel m; (Mus) Tonart f; (of piano, typewriter) Taste f • vt ~ **in** eintasten

key: ~**board** n Tastatur f; (Mus) Klaviatur f. ~**hole** n Schlüsselloch nt. ~**ring** n Schlüsselring m

khaki /'kɑːkɪ/ adj khakifarben • n Khaki nt

kick /kɪk/ n [Fuß]tritt m; **for** ~**s** 🔢 zum Spaß • vt treten; ~ **the bucket** 🔢 abkratzen • vi (animal) ausschlagen

kid /kɪd/ n (🔢: child) Kind nt • vt (pt/pp kidded) (🔢) ~ **s.o.** jdm etwas vormachen

kidnap /'kɪdnæp/ vt (pt/pp -napped) entführen. ~**per** n Entführer m. ~**ping** n Entführung f

kidney /'kɪdnɪ/ n Niere f

kill /kɪl/ vt töten; 🔢 totschlagen (time); ~ **two birds with one stone** zwei Fliegen mit einer Klappe schlagen. ~**er** n Mörder(in) m(f).

~**ing** n Tötung f; (murder) Mord m

'**killjoy** n Spielverderber m

kilo /'ki:ləʊ/ n Kilo nt

kilo: /'kɪlə/: ~**gram** n Kilogramm nt. ~**metre** n Kilometer m. ~**watt** n Kilowatt nt

kilt /kɪlt/ n Schottenrock m

kind¹ /kaɪnd/ n Art f; (brand, type) Sorte f; **what** ~ **of car?** was für ein Auto? ~ **of** 🔢 irgendwie

kind² adj (-er, -est) nett; ~ **to animals** gut zu Tieren

kind|ly /'kaɪndlɪ/ adj nett • adv netterweise; (if you please) gefälligst. ~**ness** n Güte f; (favour) Gefallen m

king /kɪŋ/ n König m; (Draughts) Dame f. ~**dom** n Königreich nt; (fig & Relig) Reich nt

king: ~**fisher** n Eisvogel m. ~**-sized** adj extragroß

kink /kɪŋk/ n Knick m. ~**y** adj 🔢 pervers

kiosk /'ki:ɒsk/ n Kiosk m

kip /kɪp/ n **have a** ~ 🔢 pennen • vi (pt/pp kipped) 🔢 pennen

kipper /'kɪpə(r)/ n Räucherhering m

kiss /kɪs/ n Kuss m • vt/i küssen

kit /kɪt/ n Ausrüstung f; (tools) Werkzeug nt; (construction ~) Bausatz m • vt (pt/pp kitted) ~**out** ausrüsten

kitchen /'kɪtʃɪn/ n Küche f • attrib Küchen-. ~**ette** n Kochnische f

kitchen: ~**garden** n Gemüsegarten m. ~**sink** n Spülbecken nt

kite /kaɪt/ n Drachen m

kitten /'kɪtn/ n Kätzchen nt

kitty /'kɪtɪ/ n (money) [gemeinsame] Kasse f

knack /næk/ n Trick m, Dreh m

knead /ni:d/ vt kneten

knee /ni:/ n Knie nt. ~**cap** n

k

Kniescheibe f

kneel /niːl/ vi (pt/pp **knelt**) knien; ~ **[down]** sich [nieder]knien

knelt /nɛlt/ see **kneel**

knew /njuː/ see **know**

knickers /ˈnɪkəz/ npl Schlüpfer m

knife /naɪf/ n (pl **knives**) Messer nt ● vt einen Messerstich versetzen (+ dat)

knight /naɪt/ n Ritter m; (Chess) Springer m ● vt adeln

knit /nɪt/ vt/i (pt/pp **knitted**) stricken; ~ **one's brow** die Stirn runzeln. ~**ting** n Stricken nt; (work) Strickzeug nt. ~**ting-needle** n Stricknadel f. ~**wear** n Strickwaren pl

knives /naɪvz/ npl see **knife**

knob /nɒb/ n Knopf m; (on door) Knauf m; (small lump) Beule f. ~**bly** adj knorrig; (bony) knochig

knock /nɒk/ n Klopfen nt; (blow) Schlag m; **there was a** ~ es klopfte ● vt anstoßen; (🗅: criticize) heruntermachen; ~ **a hole in sth** ein Loch in etw (acc) schlagen; ~ **one's head** sich (dat) den Kopf stoßen (**on** an + dat) ● vi klopfen. ~ **about** vt schlagen ● vi 🗅 herumkommen. ~ **down** vt herunterwerfen; (with fist) anfahren; (in car) anfahren; (demolish) abreißen; (🗅: reduce) herabsetzen. ~ **off** vt herunterwerfen; (🗅: steal) klauen; (🗅: complete quickly) hinhauen ● vi (🗅: cease work) Feierabend machen. ~ **out** vt ausschlagen; (make unconscious) bewusstlos schlagen; (Boxing) k.o. schlagen. ~ **over** vt umwerfen; (in car) anfahren

knock: ~**down** adj ~**down prices** Schleuderpreise pl. ~**er** n Türklopfer m. ~**out** n (Boxing) K.o. m

knot /nɒt/ n Knoten m ● vt (pt/pp knotted) knoten

know /nəʊ/ vt/i (pt **knew**, pp **known**) wissen; kennen (person); können (language); **get to** ~ kennen lernen ● n **in the** ~ 🗅 im Bild

know: ~**all** n 🗅 Alleswisser m. ~**how** n 🗅 [Sach]kenntnis f. ~**ing** adj wissend. ~**ingly** adv wissend; (intentionally) wissentlich

knowledge /ˈnɒlɪdʒ/ n Kenntnis f (**of** von/gen); (general) Wissen nt; (specialized) Kenntnisse pl. ~**able** adj **be** ~**able** viel wissen

knuckle /ˈnʌkl/ n [Finger]knöchel m; (Culin) Hachse f

kosher /ˈkəʊʃə(r)/ adj koscher

kudos /ˈkjuːdɒs/ n 🗅 Prestige nt

L l

lab /læb/ n 🗅 Labor nt

label /ˈleɪbl/ n Etikett nt ● vt (pt/pp labelled) etikettieren

laboratory /ləˈbɒrətrɪ/ n Labor nt

laborious /ləˈbɔːrɪəs/ adj mühsam

labour /ˈleɪbə(r)/ n Arbeit f; (workers) Arbeitskräfte pl; (Med) Wehen pl; **L**~ (Pol) die Labourpartei ● attrib Labour- ● vi arbeiten ● vt (fig) sich lange auslassen über (+ acc). ~**er** n Arbeiter m

'labour-saving adj arbeitssparend

lace /leɪs/ n Spitze f; (of shoe) Schnürsenkel m ● vt schnüren

lack /læk/ n Mangel m (**of** an + dat) ● vt **I** ~ **the time** mir fehlt die Zeit ● vi **be** ~**ing** fehlen

laconic /ləˈkɒnɪk/ adj, ~**ally** adv lakonisch

445

lacquer | last

lacquer /'lækə(r)/ n Lack m; (for hair) [Haar]spray m

lad /læd/ n Junge m

ladder /'lædə(r)/ n Leiter f; (in fabric) Laufmasche f

ladle /'leɪdl/ n [Schöpf]kelle f ● vt schöpfen

lady /'leɪdɪ/ n Dame f; (title) Lady f

lady: ~**bird** n, (Amer) ~**bug** n Marienkäfer m. ~**like** adj damenhaft

lag[1] /læg/ vi (pt/pp **lagged**) ~ **behind** zurückbleiben; (fig) nachhinken

lag[2] vt (pt/pp **lagged**) umwickeln (pipes)

lager /'lɑːgə(r)/ n Lagerbier nt

laid /leɪd/ see **lay**[1]

lain /leɪn/ see **lie**[2]

lake /leɪk/ n See m

lamb /læm/ n Lamm nt

lame /leɪm/ adj (-r, -st) lahm

lament /lə'ment/ n Klage f; (song) Klagelied nt ● vt beklagen ● vi klagen

laminated /'læmɪneɪtɪd/ adj laminiert

lamp /læmp/ n Lampe f; (in street) Laterne f. ~**post** n Laternenpfahl m. ~**shade** n Lampenschirm m

lance /lɑːns/ vt (Med) aufschneiden

land /lænd/ n Land nt; **plot of** ~ Grundstück nt ● vt/i landen; ~ **s.o. with sth** [1] jdm etw aufhalsen

landing /'lændɪŋ/ n Landung f; (top of stairs) Treppenflur m. ~**stage** n Landesteg m

land: ~**lady** n Wirtin f. ~**lord** n Wirt m; (of land) Grundbesitzer m; (of building) Hausbesitzer m. ~**mark** n Erkennungszeichen nt; (fig) Meilenstein m. ~**owner** n Grundbesitzer m. ~**scape** /-skeɪp/ n Landschaft f. ~**slide** n Erdrutsch m

lane /leɪn/ n kleine Landstraße f; (Auto) Spur f; (Sport) Bahn f; **'get in** ~**'** 'bitte einordnen'

language /'læŋgwɪdʒ/ n Sprache f; (speech, style) Ausdrucksweise f

languid /'læŋgwɪd/ adj träge

languish /'læŋgwɪʃ/ vi schmachten

lanky /'læŋkɪ/ adj schlaksig

lantern /'læntən/ n Laterne f

lap[1] /læp/ n Schoß m

lap[2] n (Sport) Runde f; (of journey) Etappe f ● vi (pt/pp **lapped**) plätschern (against gegen)

lap[3] vt (pt/pp **lapped**) ~ **up** aufschlecken

lapel /lə'pel/ n Revers nt

lapse /læps/ n Fehler m; (moral) Fehltritt m; (of time) Zeitspanne f ● vi (expire) erlöschen; ~ **into** verfallen in (+ acc)

laptop /'læptɒp/ n Laptop m

lard /lɑːd/ n [Schweine]schmalz m

larder /'lɑːdə(r)/ n Speisekammer f

large /lɑːdʒ/ adj (-r, -st) & adv groß; **by and** ~ im Großen und Ganzen; **at** ~ auf freiem Fuß. ~**ly** adv großenteils

lark[1] /lɑːk/ n (bird) Lerche f

lark[2] n (joke) Jux m ● vi ~ **about** herumalbern

laryngitis /lærɪn'dʒaɪtɪs/ n Kehlkopfentzündung f

larynx /'lærɪŋks/ n Kehlkopf m

laser /'leɪzə(r)/ n Laser m

lash /læʃ/ n Peitschenhieb m; (eyelash) Wimper f ● vt peitschen; (tie) festbinden (**to** an + acc). ~ **out** vi um sich schlagen; (spend) viel Geld ausgeben (**on** für)

lass /læs/ n Mädchen nt

lasso /læ'suː/ n Lasso nt

last /lɑːst/ adj & n letzte(r,s); ~ **night** heute od gestern Nacht;

(*evening*) gestern Abend; **at ~** endlich; **for the ~ time** zum letzten Mal; **the ~ but one** der/die/das vorletzte ● *adv* zuletzt; (*last time*) das letzte Mal; **he/she went ~** er-/sie ging als Letzter/Letzte ● *vi* dauern; (*weather:*) sich halten; (*relationship:*) halten. **~ing** *adj* dauerhaft. **~ly** *adv* schließlich, zum Schluss

latch /læʧ/ *n* [einfache] Klinke *f*

late /leɪt/ *adj & adv* (**-r, -st**) spät; (*delayed*) verspätet; (*deceased*) verstorben; **the ~st news** die neuesten Nachrichten; **stay up ~** bis spät aufbleiben; **arrive ~** zu spät ankommen; **I am ~** ich komme zu spät *od* habe mich verspätet; **the train is ~** der Zug hat Verspätung. **~comer** *n* Zuspätkommende(r) *m/f.* **~ly** *adv* in letzter Zeit. **~ness** *n* Zuspätkommen *nt*; (*delay*) Verspätung *f*

later /'leɪtə(r)/ *adj & adv* später; **~ on** nachher

lateral /'lætərəl/ *adj* seitlich

lather /'lɑːðə(r)/ *n* [Seifen]-schaum *m*

Latin /'lætɪn/ *adj* lateinisch ● *n* Latein *nt*. **~ A'merica** *n* Lateinamerika *nt*

latitude /'lætɪtjuːd/ *n* (*Geog*) Breite *f*; (*fig*) Freiheit *f*

latter /'lætə(r)/ *adj & n* **the ~** der/die/das Letztere

Latvia /'lætvɪə/ *n* Lettland *nt*

laudable /'lɔːdəbl/ *adj* lobenswert

laugh /lɑːf/ *n* Lachen *nt*; **with a ~** lachend ● *vi* lachen (**at/about** über + *acc*); **~ at s.o.** (*mock*) jdn auslachen. **~able** *adj* lachhaft, lächerlich

laughter /'lɑːftə(r)/ *n* Gelächter *nt*

launch[1] /lɔːnʧ/ *n* (*boat*) Barkasse *f*

launch[2] *n* Stapellauf *m*; (*of rocket*) Abschuss *m*; (*of product*) Lancierung *f* ● *vt* vom Stapel lassen (*ship*); zu

Wasser lassen (*lifeboat*); abschießen (*rocket*); starten (*attack*); (*Comm*) lancieren (*product*)

laund(e)rette /lɔːn'dret/ *n* Münzwäscherei *f*

laundry /'lɔːndrɪ/ *n* Wäscherei *f*; (*clothes*) Wäsche *f*

laurel /'lɒrl/ *n* Lorbeer *m*

lava /'lɑːvə/ *n* Lava *f*

lavatory /'lævətrɪ/ *n* Toilette *f*

lavender /'lævəndə(r)/ *n* Lavendel *m*

lavish /'lævɪʃ/ *adj* großzügig; (*wasteful*) verschwenderisch ● *vt* **~ sth on s.o.** jdn mit etw überschütten

law /lɔː/ *n* Gesetz *nt*; (*system*) Recht *nt*; **study ~** Jura studieren; **~ and order** Recht und Ordnung

law: ~-abiding *adj* gesetzestreu. **~court** *n* Gerichtshof *m*. **~ful** *adj* rechtmäßig. **~less** *adj* gesetzlos

lawn /lɔːn/ *n* Rasen *m*. **~-mower** *n* Rasenmäher *m*

lawyer /'lɔːjə(r)/ *n* Rechtsanwalt *m* /-anwältin *f*

lax /læks/ *adj* lax, locker

laxative /'læksətɪv/ *n* Abführmittel *nt*

laxity /'læksətɪ/ *n* Laxheit *f*

lay[1] /leɪ/ *see* **lie**[2]

lay[2] *vt* (*pt/pp* **laid**) legen; decken (*table*); **~ a trap** eine Falle stellen. **~ down** *vt* hinlegen; festlegen (*rules, conditions*). **~ off** *vt* entlassen (*workers*) ● *vi* (□: *stop*) aufhören. **~ out** *vt* hinlegen; aufbahren (*corpse*); anlegen (*garden*); (*Typography*) gestalten

lay-by *n* Parkbucht *f*

layer /'leɪə(r)/ *n* Schicht *f*

lay: ~man *n* Laie *m*. **~out** *n* Anordnung *f*; (*design*) Gestaltung *f*; (*Typography*) Layout *nt*

laze /leɪz/ vi ~**[about]** faulenzen

laziness /ˈleɪzɪnɪs/ n Faulheit f

lazy /ˈleɪzɪ/ adj faul. ~**-bones** n Faulenzer m

lead¹ /led/ n Blei nt; (of pencil) [Bleistift]mine f

lead² /liːd/ n Führung f; (leash) Leine f; (flex) Schnur f; (clue) Hinweis m, Spur f; (Theat) Hauptrolle f; (distance ahead) Vorsprung m; **be in the** ~ in Führung liegen ● vt/i (pt/pp **led**) führen; leiten (team); (induce) bringen; (at cards) ausspielen; ~ **the way** vorangehen; ~ **up to sth** (fig) etw (dat) vorangehen

leader /ˈliːdə(r)/ n Führer m; (of expedition, group) Leiter(in m(f); (of orchestra) Konzertmeister m; (in newspaper) Leitartikel m. ~**ship** n Führung f, Leitung f

leading /ˈliːdɪŋ/ adj führend; ~ **lady** Hauptdarstellerin f

leaf /liːf/ n (pl **leaves**) Blatt nt ● vi ~ **through sth** etw durchblättern. ~**let** n Merkblatt nt; (advertising) Reklameblatt nt; (political) Flugblatt nt

league /liːg/ n Liga f

leak /liːk/ n (hole) undichte Stelle f; (Naut) Leck nt; (of gas) Gasausfluss m ● vi undicht sein; (ship) leck sein, lecken; (liquid:) auslaufen; (gas:) ausströmen ● vt auslaufen lassen; ~ **sth to s.o.** (fig) jdm etw zuspielen. ~**y** adj undicht; (Naut) leck

lean¹ /liːn/ adj (-er, -est) mager

lean² v (pt/pp **leaned** or **leant** /lent/) ● vt lehnen (**against/on** an + acc) ● vi (person) sich lehnen (**against/on** an + acc); (not be straight) sich neigen; **be ~ing against** lehnen an (+ dat). ~ **back** vi sich zurücklehnen. ~ **forward** vi sich vorbeugen. ~ **out** vi sich hinauslehnen. ~ **over** vi sich vorbeugen

leaning /ˈliːnɪŋ/ adj schief ● n Neigung f

leap /liːp/ n Sprung m ● vi (pt/pp **leapt** or **leaped**) springen; **he leapt at it** (fig) er griff sofort zu. ~ **year** n Schaltjahr nt

learn /lɜːn/ vt/i (pt/pp **learnt** or **learned**) lernen; (hear) erfahren; ~ **to swim** schwimmen lernen

learn|ed /ˈlɜːnɪd/ adj gelehrt. ~**er** n Anfänger m; ~**er [driver]** Fahrschüler(in) m(f). ~**ing** n Gelehrsamkeit f. ~**ing curve** Lernkurve f

lease /liːs/ n Pacht f; (contract) Mietvertrag m ● vt pachten

leash /liːʃ/ n Leine f

least /liːst/ adj geringste(r,s) ● n **the** ~ das wenigste; **at** ~ wenigstens, mindestens; **not in the** ~ nicht im Geringsten ● adv am wenigsten

leather /ˈleðə(r)/ n Leder nt

leave /liːv/ n Erlaubnis f; (holiday) Urlaub m; **on** ~ auf Urlaub; **take one's** ~ sich verabschieden ● v (pt/pp **left**) ● vt lassen; (go out of, abandon) verlassen; (forget) liegen lassen; (bequeath) vermachen (**to** dat); ~ **it to me!** überlassen Sie es mir! **there is nothing left** es ist nichts mehr übrig ● vi [weg]gehen/-fahren; (train, bus:) abfahren. ~ **behind** vt zurücklassen; (forget) liegen lassen. ~ **out** vt liegen lassen; (leave outside) draußen lassen; (omit) auslassen

leaves /liːvz/ see **leaf**

Lebanon /ˈlebənən/ n Libanon m

lecherous /ˈletʃərəs/ adj lüstern

lecture /ˈlektʃə(r)/ n Vortrag m; (Univ) Vorlesung f; (reproof) Strafpredigt f ● vi einen Vortrag/eine Vorlesung halten (**on** über + acc) ● vt ~ **s.o.** jdm eine Strafpredigt halten. ~**r** n Vortragende(r) m/f;

led | let

(*Univ*) Dozent(in) *m(f)*

led /led/ *see* **lead²**

ledge /ledʒ/ *n* Leiste *f*; (*shelf, of window*) Sims *m*; (*in rock*) Vorsprung *m*

ledger /'ledʒə(r)/ *n* Hauptbuch *nt*

leech /liːtʃ/ *n* Blutegel *m*

leek /liːk/ *n* Stange *f* Porree; **~s** *pl* Porree *m*

left¹ /left/ *see* **leave**

left² *adj* linke(r,s) ● *adv* links; (*go*) nach links ● *n* linke Seite *f*; **on the ~** links; **from/to the ~** von/nach links; **the ~** (*Pol*) die Linke

left: **~-'handed** *adj* linkshändig. **~-'luggage [office]** *n* Gepäckaufbewahrung *f*. **~overs** *npl* Reste *pl*. **~-'wing** *adj* (*Pol*) linke(r,s)

leg /leg/ *n* Bein *nt*; (*Culin*) Keule *f*; (*of journey*) Etappe *f*

legacy /'legəsɪ/ *n* Vermächtnis *nt*, Erbschaft *f*

legal /'liːgl/ *adj* gesetzlich; (*matters*) rechtlich; (*department, position*) Rechts-; **be ~** [gesetzlich] erlaubt sein

legality /lɪ'gælətɪ/ *n* Legalität *f*

legend /'ledʒənd/ *n* Legende *f*. **~ary** *adj* legendär

legi|ble /'ledʒəbl/ *adj*, **-bly** *adv* leserlich

legion /'liːdʒn/ *n* Legion *f*

legislat|e /'ledʒɪsleɪt/ *vi* Gesetze erlassen. **~ion** *n* Gesetzgebung *f*; (*laws*) Gesetze *pl*

legislative /'ledʒɪslətɪv/ *adj* gesetzgebend

legitimate /lɪ'dʒɪtɪmət/ *adj* rechtmäßig; (*justifiable*) berechtigt

leisure /'leʒə(r)/ *n* Freizeit *f*; **at your ~** wenn Sie Zeit haben. **~ly** *adj* gemächlich

lemon /'lemən/ *n* Zitrone *f*. **~ade** *n* Zitronenlimonade *f*

lend /lend/ *vt* (*pt/pp* **lent**) leihen (s.o. sth jdm etw)

length /leŋθ/ *n* Länge *f*; (*piece*) Stück *nt*; (*of wallpaper*) Bahn *f*; (*of time*) Dauer *f*

length|en /'leŋθən/ *vt* länger machen ● *vi* (*lengthen*) länger werden. **~ways** *adv* der Länge nach

lengthy /'leŋθɪ/ *adj* langwierig

lenient /'liːnɪənt/ *adj* nachsichtig

lens /lenz/ *n* Linse *f*; (*Phot*) Objektiv *nt*; (*of spectacles*) Glas *nt*

lent /lent/ *see* **lend**

Lent *n* Fastenzeit *f*

lentil /'lentl/ *n* (*Bot*) Linse *f*

leopard /'lepəd/ *n* Leopard *m*

leotard /'liːətɑːd/ *n* Trikot *nt*

lesbian /'lezbɪən/ *adj* lesbisch ● *n* Lesbierin *f*

less /les/ *a, adv, n & prep* weniger; **~ and ~** immer weniger

lessen /'lesn/ *vt* verringern ● *vi* nachlassen; (*value:*) abnehmen

lesser /'lesə(r)/ *adj* geringere(r,s)

lesson /'lesn/ *n* Stunde *f*; (*in textbook*) Lektion *f*; (*Relig*) Lesung *f*; **teach s.o. a ~** (*fig*) jdm eine Lehre erteilen

lest /lest/ *conj* (*literary*) damit ... nicht

let /let/ *vt* (*pt/pp* **let**, *pres p* **letting**) lassen; (*rent*) vermieten; **~ alone** (*not to mention*) geschweige denn; **~ us go** wir gehen wir; **~ me know** sagen Sie mir Bescheid; **~ oneself in for sth** 🔲 sich (*dat*) etw einbrocken. **~ down** *vt* hinunter-/herunterlassen; (*lengthen*) länger machen; **~ s.o. down** 🔲 jdn im Stich lassen; (*disappoint*) jdn enttäuschen. **~ in** *vt* hereinlassen. **~ off** *vt* abfeuern (*gun*); hochgehen lassen (*firework, bomb*); (*emit*) ausstoßen; (*excuse from*) befreien von; (*not punish*) frei ausgehen lassen. **~ out** *vt* hinaus-/

herauslassen; (make larger) auslassen. ~ **through** vt durchlassen. ~ **up** vi 🔲 nachlassen

'**let-down** n Enttäuschung f. 🔲 Reinfall m

lethal /'liːθl/ adj tödlich

letharg|ic /lɪ'θɑːdʒɪk/ adj lethargisch. ~**y** n Lethargie f

letter /'letə(r)/ n Brief m; (of alphabet) Buchstabe m. ~-**box** n Briefkasten m. ~-**head** n Briefkopf m. ~**ing** n Beschriftung f

lettuce /'letɪs/ n [Kopf]salat m

'**let-up** n 🔲 Nachlassen nt

level /'levl/ adj eben; (horizontal) waagerecht; (in height) auf gleicher Höhe; (spoonful) gestrichen; **one's ~ best** sein Möglichstes ● n Höhe f; (fig) Ebene f, Niveau nt; (stage) Stufe f; **on the ~** 🔲 ehrlich ● vt (pt/pp levelled) einebnen

level 'crossing n Bahnübergang m

lever /'liːvə(r)/ n Hebel m ● vt ~ **up** mit einem Hebel anheben. ~**age** n Hebelkraft f

lewd /ljuːd/ adj (-er, -est) anstößig

liabilit|y /laɪə'bɪlɪti/ n Haftung f. ~**ies** pl Verbindlichkeiten pl

liable /'laɪəbl/ adj haftbar; **be ~ to do sth** etw leicht tun können

liaise /lɪ'eɪz/ vi 🔲 Verbindungsperson sein

liaison /lɪ'eɪzɒn/ n Verbindung f; (affair) Verhältnis nt

liar /'laɪə(r)/ n Lügner(in) m(f)

libel /'laɪbl/ n Verleumdung f ● vt (pt/pp libelled) verleumden. ~**lous** adj verleumderisch

liberal /'lɪbərəl/ adj tolerant; (generous) großzügig. **L~** adj (Pol) liberal ● n Liberale(r) m(f)

liberat|e /'lɪbəreɪt/ vt befreien. ~**ed** adj (woman) emanzipiert. ~**ion** n Befreiung f. ~**or** n Be-

freier m

liberty /'lɪbəti/ n Freiheit f; **take liberties** sich (dat) Freiheiten erlauben

librarian /laɪ'breərɪən/ n Bibliothekar(in) m(f)

library /'laɪbrərɪ/ n Bibliothek f

Libya /'lɪbɪə/ n Libyen nt

lice /laɪs/ see **louse**

licence /'laɪsns/ n Genehmigung f; (Comm) Lizenz f; (for TV) ≈ Fernsehgebühr f; (for driving) Führerschein m; (for alcohol) Schankkonzession f

license /'laɪsns/ vt eine Genehmigung/(Comm) Lizenz erteilen (+ dat); **be ~d** (car:) zugelassen sein; (restaurant:) Schankkonzession haben. ~-**plate** n (Amer) Nummernschild nt

lick /lɪk/ n Lecken nt; **a ~ of paint** ein bisschen Farbe ● vt lecken; (🔲: defeat) schlagen

lid /lɪd/ n Deckel m; (of eye) Lid nt

lie¹ /laɪ/ n Lüge f; **tell a ~** lügen ● vi (pt/pp lied, pres p lying) lügen; ~ **to** belügen

lie² vi (pt lay, pp lain, pres p lying) liegen; **here ~s …** hier ruht … ~ **down** vi sich hinlegen

'**lie-in** n **have a ~** [sich] ausschlafen

lieu /ljuː/ n **in ~ of** statt (+ gen)

lieutenant /lef'tenənt/ n Oberleutnant m

life /laɪf/ n (pl lives) Leben nt; **lose one's ~** ums Leben kommen

life: ~-**boat** n Rettungsboot nt. ~-**coach** n Lebensberater(in) m(f). ~-**guard** n Lebensretter m. ~-**jacket** n Schwimmweste f. ~**less** adj leblos. ~**like** adj naturgetreu. ~**long** adj lebenslang. ~ **preserver** n (Amer) Rettungsring m. ~-**size(d)** adj … in Lebensgröße.

~**time** n Leben nt; **in s.o.'s** ~**time** zu jds Lebzeiten; **the chance of a** ~**time** eine einmalige Gelegenheit

lift /lɪft/ n Aufzug m, Lift m; **give s.o. a** ~ jdn mitnehmen; **get a** ~ mitgenommen werden ● vt heben; aufheben (restrictions) ● vi (fog:) sich lichten. ~ **up** vt hochheben

light¹ /laɪt/ adj (-er, -est) (not dark) hell; ~ **blue** hellblau ● n Licht nt; (lamp) Lampe f; **have you [got] a** ~? haben Sie Feuer? ● vt (pt/pp **lit** oder **lighted**) anzünden (fire, cigarette); (illuminate) beleuchten. ~ **up** vi (face:) sich erhellen

light² adj (-er, -est) (not heavy) leicht; ~ **sentence** milde Strafe f ● adv **travel** ~ mit wenig Gepäck reisen

'light-bulb n Glühbirne f

lighten¹ /laɪtn/ vt heller machen

lighten² vt leichter machen (load)

lighter /ˈlaɪtə(r)/ n Feuerzeug nt

light: ~-**'hearted** adj unbekümmert. ~**house** n Leuchtturm m. ~**ing** n Beleuchtung f. ~**ly** adv leicht; **get off** ~**ly** glimpflich davonkommen

lightning /ˈlaɪtnɪŋ/ n Blitz m

'lightweight adj leicht ● n (Boxing) Leichtgewicht nt

like¹ /laɪk/ adj ähnlich; (same) gleich ● prep wie; (similar to) ähnlich (+ dat); ~ **this** so; **what's he** ~? wie ist er denn? ● conj (🔲: as) wie; (Amer: as if) als ob

like² vt mögen; **I should/would** ~ ich möchte; **I** ~ **the car** das Auto gefällt mir; **I** ~ **dancing/singing** gern tanzen/singen ● n ~**s and dislikes** pl Vorlieben und Abneigungen pl

like|able /ˈlaɪkəbl/ adj sympathisch. ~**lihood** n Wahrscheinlichkeit f. ~**ly** adj & adv wahrscheinlich;

not ~**ly!** 🔲 auf gar keinen Fall!

'like-minded adj gleich gesinnt

liken /ˈlaɪkən/ vt vergleichen (**to** mit)

like|ness /ˈlaɪknɪs/ n Ähnlichkeit f. ~**wise** adv ebenso

liking /ˈlaɪkɪŋ/ n Vorliebe f; **is it to your** ~? gefällt es Ihnen?

lilac /ˈlaɪlək/ n Flieder m

lily /ˈlɪlɪ/ n. Lilie f

limb /lɪm/ n Glied nt

lime /laɪm/ n (fruit) Limone f; (tree) Linde f. ~**light** n **be in the** ~**light** im Rampenlicht stehen

limit /ˈlɪmɪt/ n Grenze f; (limitation) Beschränkung f; **that's the** ~! 🔲 das ist doch die Höhe! ● vt beschränken (**to** auf + acc). ~**ation** n Beschränkung f. ~**ed** adj beschränkt. ~**ed company** Gesellschaft f mit beschränkter Haftung

limousine /ˈlɪməziːn/ n Limousine f

limp¹ /lɪmp/ n Hinken nt ● vi hinken

limp² adj (-er, -est) schlaff

limpid /ˈlɪmpɪd/ adj klar

line¹ /laɪn/ n Linie f; (length of rope, cord) Leine f; (Teleph) Leitung f; (of writing) Zeile f; (row) Reihe f; (wrinkle) Falte f; (of business) f; (Amer: queue) Schlange f; **in** ~ **with** gemäß (+ dat) ● vt säumen (street)

line² vt füttern (garment); (Techn) auskleiden

lined¹ /laɪnd/ adj (wrinkled) faltig; (paper) liniert

lined² adj (garment) gefüttert

'line dancing n Linedance-Tanzen n

linen /ˈlɪnɪn/ n Leinen nt; (articles) Wäsche f

liner /ˈlaɪnə(r)/ n Passagierschiff nt

'linesman n (-men) (Sport)

Linienrichter *m*

linger /'lɪŋɡə(r)/ *vi* [zurück]bleiben

lingerie /'læʒərɪ/ *n* Damenunter-
wäsche *f*

linguist /'lɪŋɡwɪst/ *n* Sprachkundi-
ge(r) *m/f*

linguistic /lɪŋ'ɡwɪstɪk/ *adj*, **-ally**
adv sprachlich

lining /'laɪnɪŋ/ *n* (*of garment*) Futter *nt*; (*Techn*) Auskleidung *f*

link /lɪŋk/ *n* (*of chain*) Glied *nt* (*fig*)
Verbindung *f* ● *vt* verbinden; **~
arms** sich unterhaken

links /lɪŋks/ *n* *or* *npl* Golfplatz *m*

lint /lɪnt/ *n* Verbandstoff *m*

lion /'laɪən/ *n* Löwe *m*; **~'s share**
(*fig*) Löwenanteil *m*. **~ess** *n* Löwin *f*

lip /lɪp/ *n* Lippe *f*; (*edge*) Rand *m*;
(*of jug*) Schnabel *m*

lip: ~-reading *n* Lippenlesen *nt*.
~-service *n* pay ~ Lippenbe-
kenntnis ablegen (**to** zu).
~stick *n* Lippenstift *m*

liqueur /lɪ'kjʊə(r)/ *n* Likör *m*

liquid /'lɪkwɪd/ *n* Flüssigkeit *f* ● *adj*
flüssig

liquidation /lɪkwɪ'deɪʃn/ *n* Liquidation *f*

liquidize /'lɪkwɪdaɪz/ *vt* [im Mixer]
pürieren. **~r** *n* Mixer *m*

liquor /'lɪkə(r)/ *n* Alkohol *m*. **~
store** *n* (*Amer*) Spirituosenge-
schäft *nt*

lisp /lɪsp/ *n* Lispeln *nt* ● *vt/i* lispeln

list¹ /lɪst/ *n* Liste *f* ● *vt* aufführen

list² *vi* (*ship's*) Schlagseite haben

listen /'lɪsn/ *vi* zuhören (**to** dat); **~
to the radio** Radio hören. **~er** *n*
Zuhörer(in) *m(f)*; (*Radio*) Hörer-
(in) *m(f)*

listless /'lɪstlɪs/ *adj* lustlos

lit /lɪt/ *see* light¹

literacy /'lɪtərəsɪ/ *n* Lese- und
Schreibfertigkeit *f*

literal /'lɪtərl/ *adj* wörtlich. **~ly**
adv buchstäblich

literary /'lɪtərərɪ/ *adj* literarisch

literate /'lɪtərət/ *adj* **be ~** lesen
und schreiben können

literature /'lɪtrətʃə(r)/ *n* Literatur
f; 🗓 Informationsmaterial *nt*

lithe /laɪð/ *adj* geschmeidig

Lithuania /lɪθjʊ'eɪnɪə/ *n* Litauen *nt*

litre /'liːtə(r)/ *n* Liter *m* & *nt*

litter /'lɪtə(r)/ *n* Abfall *m*; (*Zool*)
Wurf *m*. **~bin** *n* Abfalleimer *m*

little /'lɪtl/ *adj* klein; (*not much*)
wenig ● *adv* & *n* wenig; **a ~** ein bis-
schen/wenig; **~ by ~** nach
und nach

live¹ /laɪv/ *adj* lebend; (*ammunition*) scharf; **~ broadcast** Live-Sen-
dung *f*; **be ~** (*Electr*) unter Strom
stehen

live² /lɪv/ *vi* leben; (*reside*) wohnen.
~ on *vt* leben von; (*eat*) sich ernähren von ● *vi* weiterleben

livelihood /'laɪvlɪhʊd/ *n* Lebensunterhalt *m*. **~ness** *n* Leben-
digkeit *f*

lively /'laɪvlɪ/ *adj* lebhaft, lebendig

liver /'lɪvə(r)/ *n* Leber *f*

lives /laɪvz/ *see* life

livid /'lɪvɪd/ *adj* 🗓 wütend

living /'lɪvɪŋ/ *adj* lebend ● *n* **earn
one's ~** seinen Lebensunterhalt
verdienen. **~-room** *n* Wohnzimmer *nt*

lizard /'lɪzəd/ *n* Eidechse *f*

load /ləʊd/ *n* Last *f*; (*quantity*) Ladung *f*; (*Electr*) Belastung *f*; **~s of**
🗓 jede Menge ● *vt* laden (*goods,
gun*); beladen (*vehicle*); **~ a camera**
einen Film in eine Kamera einlegen.
~ed *adj* beladen; (🗓: *rich*)
steinreich

loaf /ləʊf/ *n* (*pl* **loaves**) Brot *nt*

loan /ləʊn/ n Leihgabe f; (money) Darlehen nt; **on ~** geliehen ● vt leihen (to dat)

loath /ləʊθ/ adj **be ~ to** do sth etw ungern tun

loath|e /ləʊð/ vt verabscheuen. **~ing** n Abscheu m

loaves /ləʊvz/ see **loaf**[1]

lobby /'lɒbɪ/ n Foyer nt; (anteroom) Vorraum m; (Pol) Lobby f

lobster /'lɒbstə(r)/ n Hummer m

local /'ləʊkl/ adj hiesig; (time, traffic) Orts-; **~ anaesthetic** örtliche Betäubung; **I'm not ~** ich bin nicht von hier ● n Hiesige(r) m/f; (☐: public house) Stammkneipe f. **~ call** n (Teleph) Ortsgespräch nt

locality /ləʊ'kælɪtɪ/ n Gegend f

localization /ləʊkəlaɪ'zeɪʃn/ n Lokalisierung f

locally /'ləʊkəlɪ/ adv am Ort

locat|e /ləʊ'keɪt/ vt ausfindig machen; **be ~ed** sich befinden. **~ion** n Lage f; **filmed on ~ion** als Außenaufnahme gedreht

lock[1] /lɒk/ n (hair) Strähne f

lock[2] n (on door) Schloss nt; (on canal) Schleuse f ● vt abschließen ● vi sich abschließen lassen. **~ in** vt einschließen. **~ out** vt ausschließen. **~ up** vt abschließen; (imprison) einsperren (person)

locker /'lɒkə(r)/ n Schließfach nt; (Mil) Spind m

lock: **~-out** n Aussperrung f. **~smith** n Schlosser m

locomotive /ləʊkə'məʊtɪv/ n Lokomotive f

locum /'ləʊkəm/ n Vertreter(in) m(f)

locust /'ləʊkəst/ n Heuschrecke f

lodge /lɒdʒ/ n (porter's) Pförtnerhaus nt ● vt (submit) einreichen; (deposit) deponieren ● vi zur Untermiete wohnen (with bei); (become

fixed) stecken bleiben. **~r** n Untermieter(in) m(f)

lodging /'lɒdʒɪŋ/ n Unterkunft f; **~s** npl möbliertes Zimmer nt

loft /lɒft/ n Dachboden m

lofty /'lɒftɪ/ adj hoch

log /lɒg/ n Baumstamm m; (for fire) [Holz]scheit nt; **sleep like a ~** ☐ wie ein Murmeltier schlafen ● vi **~ off** sich abmelden; **~ on** sich anmelden

loggerheads /'lɒgə-/ npl **be at ~** ☐ sich in den Haaren liegen

logic /'lɒdʒɪk/ n Logik f. **~al** adj logisch

logo /'ləʊgəʊ/ n Symbol nt, Logo nt

loiter /'lɔɪtə(r)/ vi herumlungern

loll /lɒl/ vi sich lümmeln

loll|ipop /'lɒlɪpɒp/ n Lutscher m. **~y** n Lutscher m; (☐: money) Moneten pl

London /'lʌndən/ n London nt ● attrib Londoner. **~er** n Londoner(in) m(f)

lone /ləʊn/ adj einzeln. **~liness** n Einsamkeit f

lonely /'ləʊnlɪ/ adj einsam

lone|r /'ləʊnə(r)/ n Einzelgänger m. **~some** adj einsam

long[1] /lɒŋ/ adj (-er /'lɒŋgə(r)/, -est /'lɒŋgɪst/) lang; (journey) weit; **a ~ time** lange; **a ~ way** weit; **in the ~ run** auf lange Sicht; (in the end) letzten Endes ● adv lange; **all day ~** den ganzen Tag; **not ~ ago** vor kurzem; **before ~** bald; **no ~er** nicht mehr; **as** or **so ~as** solange; **so ~!** ☐ tschüs!

long[2] vi **~ for** sich sehnen nach

long-'distance adj Fern-; (Sport) Langstrecken-

longing /'lɒŋɪŋ/ adj sehnsüchtig ● n Sehnsucht f

longitude /'lɒŋgɪtjuːd/ n

(*Geog*) Länge *f*

long: ~ **jump** *n* Weitsprung *m*. ~**-lived** /-lɪvd/ *adj* langlebig. ~**-range** *adj* (*Mil, Aviat*) Langstrecken-; (*forecast*) langfristig. ~**-sighted** *adj* weitsichtig. ~**-sleeved** *adj* langärmelig. ~**-suffering** *adj* langmütig. ~**-term** *adj* langfristig. ~ **wave** *n* Langwelle. ~**-winded** /-'wɪndɪd/ *adj* langatmig

loo /luː/ *n* [□] Klo *nt*

look /lʊk/ *n* Blick *m*; (*appearance*) Aussehen *nt*; **[good]** ~s *pl* [gutes] Aussehen *nt*; **have a** ~ **at** sich (*dat*) ansehen; **go and have a** ~ sieh mal nach ● *vi* sehen; (*search*) nachsehen; (*seem*) aussehen; **don't** ~ sieh nicht hin; ~ **here!** hören Sie mal! ~ **at** ansehen; ~ **for** suchen; ~ **forward to** sich freuen auf (+ *acc*); ~ **in** on vorbeischauen bei; ~ **into** (*examine*) nachgehen (+ *dat*); ~ **like** aussehen wie; ~ **on to** (*room:*) gehen auf (+ *acc*). ~ **after** *vt* betreuen. ~ **down** *vi* hinuntersehen; ~ **down on s.o.** (*fig*) auf jdn herabsehen. ~ **out** *vi* hinaus-/heraussehen; (*take care*) aufpassen; ~ **out for** Ausschau halten nach; ~ **out!** Vorsicht! ~ **round** *vi* sich umsehen. ~ **up** *vi* aufblicken; ~ **up to s.o.** (*fig*) zu jdm aufsehen ● *vt* nachschlagen (*word*)

'look-out *n* Wache *f*; (*prospect*) Aussicht *f*; **be on the** ~ **for** Ausschau halten nach

loom[1] /luːm/ *n* Webstuhl *m*

loom[2] *vi* auftauchen

loony /'luːnɪ/ *adj* □ verrückt

loop /luːp/ *n* Schlinge *f*; (*in road*) Schleife *f*. ~**hole** *n* Hintertürchen *nt*; (*in the law*) Lücke *f*

loose /luːs/ *adj* (-r, -st) lose; (*not tight enough*) locker; (*inexact*) frei; **be at a** ~ **end** nichts zu tun haben. ~ **'change** *n* Kleingeld *nt*

loosen /'luːsn/ *vt* lockern

loot /luːt/ *n* Beute *f* ● *vt/i* plündern. ~**er** *n* Plünderer *m*

lop /lɒp/ *vt* (*pt/pp* lopped) stutzen

lop'sided *adj* schief

lord /lɔːd/ *n* Herr *m*; (*title*) Lord *m*; **House of L**~**s** ≈ Oberhaus *nt*; **the L**~**'s Prayer** das Vaterunser

lorry /'lɒrɪ/ *n* Last[kraft]wagen *m*

lose /luːz/ *v* (*pt/pp* lost) ● *vt* verlieren; (*miss*) verpassen ● *vi* verlieren; (*clock:*) nachgehen; **get lost** verloren gehen; (*person*) sich verlaufen. ~**r** *n* Verlierer *m*

loss /lɒs/ *n* Verlust *m*; **be at a** ~ nicht mehr weiter wissen

lost /lɒst/ *see* lose. ~ **'property office** *n* Fundbüro *nt*

lot[1] /lɒt/ *n* Los *nt*; (*at auction*) Posten *m*; **draw** ~s losen (**for** um)

lot[2] *n* **the** ~ alle; (*everything*) alles; **a** ~ **[of]** viel; (*many*) viele; ~**s of** □ eine Menge; **it has changed a** ~ es hat sich sehr verändert

lotion /'ləʊʃn/ *n* Lotion *f*

lottery /'lɒtərɪ/ *n* Lotterie *f*. ~ **ticket** *n* Los *nt*

loud /laʊd/ *adj* (-er, -est) laut; (*colours*) grell ● *adv* [out] ~ laut. ~ **'speaker** *n* Lautsprecher *m*

lounge /laʊndʒ/ *n* Wohnzimmer *nt*; (*in hotel*) Aufenthaltsraum *m*. ● *vi* sich lümmeln

louse /laʊs/ *n* (*pl* lice) Laus *f*

lousy /'laʊzɪ/ *adj* □ lausig

lout /laʊt/ *n* Flegel *m*, Lümmel *m*

lovable /'lʌvəbl/ *adj* liebenswert

love /lʌv/ *n* Liebe *f*; (*Tennis*) null; **in** ~ verliebt ● *vt* lieben; ~**s doing sth** etw sehr gerne machen. ~**-affair** *n* Liebesverhältnis *nt*. ~ **letter** *n* Liebesbrief *m*

lovely /'lʌvlɪ/ *adj* schön

lover /'lʌvə(r)/ *n* Liebhaber *m*

love: ~ **song** n Liebeslied nt. ~ **story** n Liebesgeschichte f

loving /'lʌvɪŋ/ adj liebevoll

low /ləʊ/ adj (-er, -est) niedrig; (cloud, note) tief; (voice) leise; (depressed) niedergeschlagen ● adv niedrig; (fly, sing) tief; (speak) leise ● n (weather) Tief nt; (fig) Tiefstand m

low: ~**brow** adj geistig anspruchslos. ~**-cut** adj (dress) tief ausgeschnitten

lower /'ləʊə(r)/ adj & adv see low ● vt niedriger machen; (let down) herunterlassen; (reduce) senken

low: ~**-fat** adj fettarm. ~**lands** /-ləndz/ npl Tiefland nt. ~ **'tide** n Ebbe f

loyal /'lɔɪəl/ adj treu. ~**ty** n Treue f. ~**ty card** n Treuekarte f

lozenge /'lɒzɪndʒ/ n Pastille f

Ltd abbr (Limited) GmbH

lubricant /'lu:brɪkənt/ n Schmiermittel nt

lubricat|e /'lu:brɪkeɪt/ vt schmieren. ~**ion** n Schmierung f

lucid /'lu:sɪd/ adj klar. ~**ity** n Klarheit f

luck /lʌk/ n Glück nt; bad ~ Pech nt; good ~! viel Glück! ~**ily** adv glücklicherweise, zum Glück

lucky /'lʌkɪ/ adj glücklich; (day, number) Glücks-; be ~ Glück haben; (thing:) Glück bringen

lucrative /'lu:krətɪv/ adj einträglich

ludicrous /'lu:dɪkrəs/ adj lächerlich

lug /lʌg/ vt (pt/pp lugged) 🔲 schleppen

luggage /'lʌgɪdʒ/ n Gepäck nt

luggage: ~**rack** in Gepäckablage f. ~**van** n Gepäckwagen m

lukewarm /'lu:k-/ adj lauwarm

lull /lʌl/ n Pause f ● vt ~ **to sleep** einschläfern

lullaby /'lʌləbaɪ/ n Wiegenlied nt

lumber /'lʌmbə(r)/ n Gerümpel nt; (Amer: timber) Bauholz nt ● vt s.o. with sth jdm etw aufhalsen. ~**jack** n (Amer) Holzfäller m

luminous /'lu:mɪnəs/ adj leuchtend

lump /lʌmp/ n Klumpen m; (of sugar) Stück nt; (swelling) Beule f; (in breast) Knoten m; (tumour) Geschwulst f; a ~ in one's throat 🔲 ein Kloß im Hals

lump: ~ **sugar** n Würfelzucker m. ~ '**sum** n Pauschalsumme f

lumpy /'lʌmpɪ/ adj klumpig

lunacy /'lu:nəsɪ/ n Wahnsinn m

lunar /'lu:nə(r)/ adj Mond-

lunatic /'lu:nətɪk/ n Wahnsinnige(r) m/f

lunch /lʌntʃ/ n Mittagessen nt ● vi zu Mittag essen

luncheon /'lʌntʃn/ n Mittagessen nt. ~ **voucher** n Essensbon m

lunch: ~**-hour** n Mittagspause f. ~**-time** n Mittagszeit f

lung /lʌŋ/ n Lungenflügel m; ~**s** pl Lunge f

lunge /lʌndʒ/ vi sich stürzen (at auf + acc)

lurch[1] /lɜ:tʃ/ n leave in the ~ 🔲 im Stich lassen

lurch[2] vi (person:) torkeln

lure /ljʊə(r)/ vt locken

lurid /'lʊərɪd/ adj grell; (sensational) reißerisch

lurk /lɜ:k/ vi lauern

luscious /'lʌʃəs/ adj lecker, köstlich

lush /lʌʃ/ adj üppig

lust /lʌst/ n Begierde f. ~**ful** adj lüstern

lustre /'lʌstə(r)/ n Glanz m

lusty /ˈlʌstɪ/ adj kräftig
luxuriant /lʌgˈʒʊərɪənt/ adj üppig
luxurious /lʌgˈʒʊərɪəs/ adj luxuriös
luxury /ˈlʌkʃərɪ/ n Luxus m ● attrib Luxus-
lying /ˈlaɪɪŋ/ see lie¹, lie²
lynch /lɪntʃ/ vt lynchen
lyric /ˈlɪrɪk/ adj lyrisch. **~al** adj lyrisch; (enthusiastic) schwärmerisch. **~ poetry** n Lyrik f. **~s** npl [Lied]text m

Mm

mac /mæk/ n 🇬🇧 Regenmantel m
macabre /məˈkɑːbr/ adj makaber
macaroni /mækəˈrəʊnɪ/ n Makkaroni pl
machinations /mækɪˈneɪʃnz/ pl Machenschaften pl
machine /məˈʃiːn/ n Maschine f ● vt (sew) mit der Maschine nähen; (Techn) maschinell bearbeiten. **~-gun** n Maschinengewehr nt
machinery /məˈʃiːnərɪ/ n Maschinerie f
mackerel /ˈmækrl/ n inv Makrele f
mackintosh /ˈmækɪntɒʃ/ n Regenmantel m
mad /mæd/ adj (madder, maddest) verrückt; (dog) tollwütig; (🇬🇧: angry) böse (**at** auf + acc)
madam /ˈmædəm/ n gnädige Frau f
mad 'cow disease n 🇬🇧 Rinderwahnsinn m
madden /ˈmædn/ vt (make angry) wütend machen
made /meɪd/ see make; **~ to**

measure maßgeschneidert
mad|ly /ˈmædlɪ/ adv 🇬🇧 wahnsinnig. **~man** n Irre(r) m. **~ness** n Wahnsinn m
madonna /məˈdɒnə/ n Madonna f
magazine /mægəˈziːn/ n Zeitschrift f; (Mil, Phot) Magazin nt
maggot /ˈmægət/ n Made f
magic /ˈmædʒɪk/ n Zauber m; (tricks) Zauberkunst f ● adj magisch; (word, wand) Zauber-. **~al** adj zauberhaft
magician /məˈdʒɪʃn/ n Zauberer m; (entertainer) Zauberkünstler m
magistrate /ˈmædʒɪstreɪt/ n ≈ Friedensrichter m
magnet /ˈmægnɪt/ n Magnet m. **~ic** adj magnetisch. **~ism** n Magnetismus m
magnification /mægnɪfɪˈkeɪʃn/ n Vergrößerung f
magnificen|ce /mægˈnɪfɪsəns/ n Großartigkeit f. **~t** adj großartig
magnify /ˈmægnɪfaɪ/ vt (pt/pp -ied) vergrößern; (exaggerate) übertreiben. **~ing glass** n Vergrößerungsglas nt
magnitude /ˈmægnɪtjuːd/ n Größe f; (importance) Bedeutung f
magpie /ˈmægpaɪ/ n Elster f
mahogany /məˈhɒgənɪ/ n Mahagoni m
maid /meɪd/ n Dienstmädchen nt; **old ~** (pej) alte Jungfer f
maiden /ˈmeɪdn/ n (liter) (speech, voyage) Jungfern-. **~ name** n Mädchenname m
mail /meɪl/ n Post f ● vt mit der Post schicken
mail: **~bag** n Postsack m. **~box** n (Amer) Briefkasten m. **~ing list** n Postversandliste f. **~man** n (Amer) Briefträger m. **~-order firm** n Versandhaus nt

maim /meɪm/ vt verstümmeln

main /meɪn/ adj Haupt- ● n (water, gas, electricity) Hauptleitung f

main: ~**land** /-lənd/ n Festland nt. ~**ly** adv hauptsächlich. ~**stay** n (fig) Stütze f. ~ **street** n Hauptstraße f

maintain /meɪn'teɪn/ vt aufrechterhalten; (keep in repair) instand halten; (support) unterhalten; (claim) behaupten

maintenance /'meɪntənəns/ n Aufrechterhaltung f; (care) Instandhaltung f; (allowance) Unterhalt m

maize /meɪz/ n Mais m

majestic /mə'dʒestɪk/ adj, -ally adv majestätisch

majesty /'mædʒəstɪ/ n Majestät f

major /'meɪdʒə(r)/ adj größer ● n (Mil) Major m; (Mus) Dur nt ● vi ~ **in** als Hauptfach studieren

majority /mə'dʒɒrətɪ/ n Mehrheit f; **in the** ~ in der Mehrzahl

major road n Hauptverkehrsstraße f

make /meɪk/ n (brand) Marke f ● v (pt/pp made) ● vt machen; (force) zwingen; (earn) verdienen; halten (speech); treffen (decision); erreichen (destination) ● vi ~ **do** vi zurechtkommen (with mit). ~ **for** vi zusteuern auf (+ acc). ~ **off** vi sich davonmachen (with mit). ~ **out** vt (distinguish) ausmachen; (write out) ausstellen; (assert) behaupten. ~ **up** vt (constitute) bilden; (invent) erfinden; (apply cosmetics to) schminken; ~ **up one's mind** sich entschließen ● vi sich versöhnen. ~ **up for sth** etw wieder gutmachen; ~ **up for lost time** verlorene Zeit aufholen

'make-believe n Phantasie f

maker /'meɪkə(r)/ n Hersteller m

make: ~ **shift** adj behelfsmäßig

● n Notbehelf m. ~**-up** n Make-up nt

maladjusted /mælə'dʒʌstɪd/ adj verhaltensgestört

male /meɪl/ adj männlich ● n Mann m; (animal) Männchen nt. ~ **nurse** n Krankenpfleger m. ~ **voice 'choir** n Männerchor m

malice /'mælɪs/ n Bosheit f

malicious /mə'lɪʃəs/ adj böswillig

malign /mə'laɪn/ vt verleumden

malignant /mə'lɪgnənt/ adj bösartig

mallet /'mælɪt/ n Holzhammer m

malnu'trition /mæl-/ n Unterernährung f

mal'practice n Berufsvergehen nt

malt /mɔːlt/ n Malz nt

mal'treat /mæl-/ vt misshandeln. ~**ment** n Misshandlung f

mammal /'mæml/ n Säugetier nt

mammoth /'mæməθ/ adj riesig

man /mæn/ n (pl men) Mann m; (mankind) der Mensch; (chess) Figur f; (draughts) Stein m ● vt (pt/pp manned) bemannen (ship); bedienen (pump); besetzen (counter)

manage /'mænɪdʒ/ vt leiten; verwalten (estate); (cope with) fertig werden mit; ~ **to do sth** es schaffen, etw zu tun ● vi zurechtkommen; ~ **on** auskommen mit. ~**able** adj (tool) handlich; (person) fügsam. ~**ment** n Leitung f; **the** ~**ment** die Geschäftsleitung f

manager /'mænɪdʒə(r)/ n Geschäftsführer m; (of bank) Direktor m; (of estate) Verwalter m; (Sport) [Chef]trainer m. ~**ess** n Geschäftsführerin f. ~**ial** adj ~**ial staff** Führungskräfte pl

managing /'mænɪdʒɪŋ/ adj ~ **director** n Generaldirektor m

mandate /'mændeɪt/ n Mandat nt. ~**ory** adj obligatorisch

mane /meɪn/ n Mähne f

manful /ˈmænfl/ adj mannhaft

man: ~'**handle** vt grob behandeln (person). ~**hole** n Kanalschacht m. ~**hood** n Mannesalter nt; (quality) Männlichkeit f. ~-**hour** n Arbeitsstunde f. ~-**hunt** n Fahndung f

man|ia /ˈmeɪnɪə/ n Manie f. ~**iac** n Wahnsinnige(r) m/f

manicure /ˈmænɪkjʊə(r)/ n Maniküre f ● vt maniküren

manifest /ˈmænɪfest/ adj offensichtlich

manifesto /mænɪˈfestəʊ/ n Manifest nt

manifold /ˈmænɪfəʊld/ adj mannigfaltig

manipulat|e /məˈnɪpjʊleɪt/ vt handhaben; (pej) manipulieren. ~**ion** n Manipulation f

man'kind n die Menschheit

manly /ˈmænlɪ/ adj männlich

'man-made adj künstlich. ~ **fibre** n Kunstfaser f

manner /ˈmænə(r)/ n Weise f; (kind, behaviour) Art f; [good/bad] ~**s** [gute/schlechte] Manieren pl. ~**ism** n Angewohnheit f

manœuvrable /məˈnuːvrəbl/ adj manövrierfähig

manœuvre /məˈnuːvə(r)/ n Manöver nt ● vt/i manövrieren

manor /ˈmænə(r)/ n Gutshof m; (house) Gutshaus nt

'manpower n Arbeitskräfte pl

mansion /ˈmænʃn/ n Villa f

'manslaughter n Totschlag m

mantelpiece /ˈmæntl-/ n Kaminsims m & nt

manual /ˈmænjʊəl/ adj Hand- ● n Handbuch nt

manufacture /mænjʊˈfæktʃə(r)/ vt herstellen ● n Herstellung f. ~**r** n Hersteller m

manure /məˈnjʊə(r)/ n Mist m

manuscript /ˈmænjʊskrɪpt/ n Manuskript nt

many /ˈmenɪ/ adj viele ● n **a good/great** ~ sehr viele

map /mæp/ n Landkarte f; (of town) Stadtplan m

maple /ˈmeɪpl/ n Ahorn m

mar /mɑː(r)/ vt (pt/pp marred) verderben

marathon /ˈmærəθən/ n Marathon m

marble /ˈmɑːbl/ n Marmor m; (for game) Murmel f

March /mɑːtʃ/ n März m

march n Marsch m ● vi marschieren ● vt marschieren lassen; ~ **s.o. off** jdn abführen

mare /meə(r)/ n Stute f

margarine /mɑːdʒəˈriːn/ n Margarine f

margin /ˈmɑːdʒɪn/ n Rand m; (leeway) Spielraum m; (Comm) Spanne f. ~**al** adj geringfügig

marigold /ˈmærɪgəʊld/ n Ringelblume f

marina /məˈriːnə/ n Jachthafen m

marine /məˈriːn/ adj Meeres- ● n Marine f; (sailor) Marineinfanterist m

marital /ˈmærɪtl/ adj ehelich. ~ **status** n Familienstand m

maritime /ˈmærɪtaɪm/ adj See-

mark¹ /mɑːk/ n (former German currency) Mark f

mark² n Fleck m; (sign) Zeichen nt; (trace) Spur f; (target) Ziel nt; (Sch) Note f ● vt markieren; (spoil) beschädigen; (characterize) kennzeichnen; (Sch) korrigieren; (Sport) decken; ~ **time** (Mil) auf der Stelle treten; (fig) abwarten. ~ **out** vt markieren

marked /mɑːkt/ adj. ~**ly** adv deutlich; (pronounced) ausgeprägt

m

market /'mɑ:kɪt/ n Markt m ● vt vertreiben; (launch) auf den Markt bringen. **~ing** n Marketing nt. **~re'search** n Marktforschung f

marking /'mɑ:kɪŋ/ n Markierung f; (on animal) Zeichnung f

marksman /'mɑ:ksmən/ n Scharfschütze m

marmalade /'mɑ:məleɪd/ n Orangenmarmelade f

maroon /mə'ru:n/ adj dunkelrot

marooned /mə'ru:nd/ adj (fig) von der Außenwelt abgeschnitten

marquee /mɑ:'ki:/ n Festzelt nt

marquetry /'mɑ:kɪtrɪ/ n Einlegearbeit f

marriage /'mærɪdʒ/ n Ehe f; (wedding) Hochzeit f. **~able** adj heiratsfähig

married /'mærɪd/ see **marry** ● adj verheiratet. **~ life** n Eheleben nt

marrow /'mærəʊ/ n (Anat) Mark nt; (vegetable) Kürbis m

marr|y /'mærɪ/ vt/i (pt/pp **married**) heiraten; (unite) trauen; **get ~ied** heiraten

marsh /mɑ:ʃ/ n Sumpf m

marshal /'mɑ:ʃl/ n Marschall m; (steward) Ordner m

marshy /'mɑ:ʃɪ/ adj sumpfig

martial /'mɑ:ʃl/ adj kriegerisch. **~ 'law** n Kriegsrecht nt

martyr /'mɑ:tə(r)/ n Märtyrer(in) m(f). **~dom** n Martyrium nt

marvel /'mɑ:vl/ n Wunder nt ● vi (pt/pp **marvelled**) staunen (**at** über + acc). **~lous** a, **-ly** adv wunderbar

Marxis|m /'mɑ:ksɪzm/ n Marxismus m. **~t** adj marxistisch ● n Marxist(in) m(f)

marzipan /'mɑ:zɪpæn/ n Marzipan nt

mascot /'mæskət/ n Maskottchen nt

masculin|e /'mæskjʊlɪn/ adj männlich ● n (Gram) Maskulinum nt. **~ity** n Männlichkeit f

mash /mæʃ/ n [], **~ed potatoes** npl Kartoffelpüree nt

mask /mɑ:sk/ n Maske f ● vt maskieren

masochis|m /'mæsəkɪzm/ n Masochismus m. **~t** n Masochist m

mason /'meɪsn/ n Steinmetz m. **~ry** n Mauerwerk nt

mass[1] /mæs/ n (Relig) Messe f

mass[2] n Masse f ● vi sich sammeln; (Mil) sich massieren

massacre /'mæsəkə(r)/ n Massaker nt ● vt niedermetzeln

massage /'mæsɑ:ʒ/ n Massage f ● vt massieren

masseu|r /mæ'sɜ:(r)/ n Masseur m. **~se** n Masseuse f

massive /'mæsɪv/ adj massiv; (huge) riesig

mass: ~ 'media npl Massenmedien pl. **~pro'duce** vt in Massenproduktion herstellen. **~pro'duction** n Massenproduktion f

mast /mɑ:st/ n Mast m

master /'mɑ:stə(r)/ n Herr m; (teacher) Lehrer m; (craftsman, artist) Meister m; (of ship) Kapitän m ● vt meistern; beherrschen (language)

master: ~ly adj meisterhaft. **~mind** n führender Kopf m ● vt der führende Kopf sein von. **~piece** n Meisterwerk nt. **~y** n (of subject) Beherrschung f

mat /mæt/ n Matte f; (on table) Untersatz m

match[1] /mætʃ/ n Wettkampf m; (in ball games) Spiel nt; (Tennis) Match nt; (marriage) Heirat f; **be a good ~** (colours:) gut zusammenpassen; **be no ~ for s.o.** jdm nicht gewachsen sein ● vt (equal) gleichkommen (+ dat); (be like) passen zu; (find sth similar) etwas Passendes finden zu ● vi zusammenpassen

match² n Streichholz nt. **~box** n Streichholzschachtel f

mate¹ /meɪt/ n Kumpel m; (assistant) Gehilfe m; (Naut) Maat m; (Zool) Männchen nt; (female) Weibchen nt ● vi sich paaren

mate² n (Chess) Matt nt

material /məˈtɪərɪəl/ n Material nt; (fabric) Stoff m; **raw ~s** Rohstoffe pl ● adj materiell

material|ism /məˈtɪərɪəlɪzm/ n Materialismus m. **~istic** adj materialistisch. **~ize** vi sich verwirklichen

maternal /məˈtɜːnl/ adj mütterlich

maternity /məˈtɜːnəti/ n Mutterschaft f. **~ clothes** npl Umstandskleidung f. **~ ward** n Entbindungsstation f

mathematic|al /mæθəˈmætɪkl/ adj mathematisch. **~ian** n Mathematiker(in) m(f)

mathematics /mæθəˈmætɪks/ n Mathematik f

maths /mæθs/ n ① Mathe f

matinée /ˈmætɪneɪ/ n (Theat) Nachmittagsvorstellung f

matrimony /ˈmætrɪmənɪ/ n Ehe f

matron /ˈmeɪtrən/ n (of hospital) Oberin f; (of school) Hausmutter f

matt /mæt/ adj matt

matted /ˈmætɪd/ adj verfilzt

matter /ˈmætə(r)/ n (affair) Sache f; (Phys: substance) Materie f; money **~s** Geldangelegenheiten pl; **what is the ~?** was ist los? ● vi wichtig sein; **~ to s.o.** jdm etwas ausmachen; **it doesn't ~** es macht nichts. **~-of-fact** adj sachlich

mattress /ˈmætrɪs/ n Matratze f

matur|e /məˈtjʊə(r)/ adj reif; (Comm) fällig ● vi reifen; (person:) reifer werden; (Comm) fällig werden

● vt reifen lassen. **~ity** n Reife f; (Comm) Fälligkeit f

mauve /məʊv/ adj lila

maximum /ˈmæksɪməm/ adj maximal ● n (pl **-ima**) Maximum nt. **~ speed** n Höchstgeschwindigkeit f

may /meɪ/

pres may, **pt might**

● modal verb

····▶ (expressing possibility) können. **she may come** es kann sein, dass sie kommt; es ist möglich, dass sie kommt. **she might come** (more distant possibility) sie könnte kommen. **it may/might rain** es könnte regnen. **I may be wrong** vielleicht irre ich mich. **he may have missed his train** vielleicht hat er seinen Zug verpasst

····▶ (expressing permission) dürfen. **may I come in?** darf ich reinkommen? **you may smoke** Sie dürfen rauchen

····▶ (expressing wish) **may the best man win!** auf dass der Beste gewinnt!

····▶ (expressing concession) **he may be slow but he's accurate** mag od kann sein, dass er langsam ist, aber dafür ist er auch genau

····▶ **may/might as well** ebenso gut können. **we may/might as well go** wir könnten eigentlich ebensogut [auch] gehen. **we might as well give up** da können wir uns gleich aufgeben

May n Mai m

maybe /ˈmeɪbɪ/ adv vielleicht

¹May Day n der Erste Mai

mayonnaise /meɪəˈneɪz/ n

Mayonnaise f

mayor /'meə(r)/ n Bürgermeister m. **~ess** n Bürgermeisterin f; (wife of mayor) Frau Bürgermeister f

maze /meɪz/ n Irrgarten m; (fig) Labyrinth nt

me /miː/ pron (acc) mich; (dat) mir; **it's ~** 🔲 ich bin es

meadow /'medəʊ/ n Wiese f

meagre /'miːgə(r)/ adj dürftig

meal /miːl/ n Mahlzeit f; (food) Essen nt; (grain) Schrot m

mean¹ /miːn/ adj (-er, -est) (miserly) geizig; (unkind) gemein; (poor) schäbig

mean² adj mittlere(r,s) ● n (average) Durchschnitt m

mean³ vt (pt/pp meant) heißen; (signify) bedeuten; (intend) beabsichtigen; **I ~ it** das ist mein Ernst; **~ well** es gut meinen; **be meant for** (present:) bestimmt sein für; (remark:) gerichtet sein an (+ acc)

meaning /'miːnɪŋ/ n Bedeutung f. **~ful** adj bedeutungsvoll. **~less** adj bedeutungslos

means /miːnz/ n Möglichkeit f, Mittel nt; **~ of transport** Verkehrsmittel nt; **by ~ of** durch; **by all ~!** aber natürlich! **by no ~** keineswegs ● npl (resources) [Geld]mittel pl

meant /ment/ see **mean**

'meantime n in the ~ in der Zwischenzeit ● adv inzwischen

'meanwhile adv inzwischen

measles /'miːzlz/ n Masern pl

measure /'meʒə(r)/ n Maß nt; (action) Maßnahme f ● vt/i messen; ~ **up to** (fig) herankommen an (+ acc). **~d** adj gemessen. **~ment** n Maß nt

meat /miːt/ n Fleisch nt

mechan|ic /mɪ'kænɪk/ n Mechaniker m. **~ical** adj mechanisch. **~ical engineering** Maschinenbau m

mechan|ism /'mekənɪzm/ n Mechanismus m. **~ize** vt mechanisieren

medal /'medl/ n Orden m; (Sport) Medaille f

medallist /'medəlɪst/ n Medaillengewinner(in) m(f)

meddle /'medl/ vi sich einmischen (in in + acc); (tinker) herumhantieren (with an + acc)

media /'miːdɪə/ see **medium** ● n pl the ~ die Medien pl

mediat|e /'miːdɪeɪt/ vi vermitteln. **~or** n Vermittler(in) m(f)

medical /'medɪkl/ adj medizinisch; (treatment) ärztlich ● n ärztliche Untersuchung f. **~ insurance** n Krankenversicherung f. **~ student** n Medizinstudent m

medicat|ed /'medɪkeɪtɪd/ adj medizinisch. **~ion** n (drugs) Medikamente pl

medicinal /mɪ'dɪsɪnl/ adj medizinisch; (plant) heilkräftig

medicine /'medsən/ n Medizin f; (preparation) Medikament nt

medieval /medɪ'iːvl/ adj mittelalterlich

mediocr|e /miːdɪ'əʊkə(r)/ adj mittelmäßig. **~ity** n Mittelmäßigkeit f

meditat|e /'medɪteɪt/ vi nachdenken (on über + acc). **~ion** n Meditation f

Mediterranean /medɪtə'reɪnɪən/ n Mittelmeer nt ● adj Mittelmeer-

medium /'miːdɪəm/ adj mittlere(r,s); (steak) medium; **of ~ size** von mittlerer Größe ● n (pl media) Medium nt; (means) Mittel nt

medium: **~-sized** adj mittelgroß. **~ wave** n Mittelwelle f

medley /'medlɪ/ n Gemisch nt; (Mus) Potpourri nt

meek /miːk/ adj (-er, -est) sanftmütig; (unprotesting, compliant) widerspruchslos

meet /miːt/ v (pt/pp **met**) ● vt treffen; (by chance) begegnen (+ dat); (at station) abholen; (make the acquaintance of) kennen lernen; stoßen auf (+ acc) (problem); bezahlen (bill); erfüllen (requirements) ● vi sich treffen; (for the first time) sich kennen lernen

meeting /ˈmiːtɪŋ/ n Treffen nt; (by chance) Begegnung f; (discussion) Besprechung f; (of committee) Sitzung f; (large) Versammlung f

megalomania /megələˈmeɪnɪə/ n Größenwahnsinn m

megaphone /ˈmegəfəʊn/ n Megaphon nt

melancholy /ˈmelənkəlɪ/ adj melancholisch ● n Melancholie f

mellow /ˈmeləʊ/ adj (-er, -est) (fruit) ausgereift; (sound, person) sanft ● vi reifer werden

melodious /mɪˈləʊdɪəs/ adj melodiös

melodramatic /melədrəˈmætɪk/ adj, **-ally** adv melodramatisch

melody /ˈmelədɪ/ n Melodie f

melon /ˈmelən/ n Melone f

melt /melt/ vt/i schmelzen

member /ˈmembə(r)/ n Mitglied nt; (of family) Angehörige(r) m/f; **M~ of Parliament** Abgeordnete(r) m/f. **~ship** n Mitgliedschaft f; (members) Mitgliederzahl f

memento /mɪˈmentəʊ/ n Andenken nt

memo /ˈmeməʊ/ n Mitteilung f

memoirs /ˈmemwɑːz/ n pl Memoiren pl

memorable /ˈmemərəbl/ adj denkwürdig

memorial /mɪˈmɔːrɪəl/ n Denkmal nt. **~ service** n Gedenkfeier f

memorize /ˈmeməraɪz/ vt sich (dat) einprägen

memory /ˈmemərɪ/ n Gedächtnis nt; (thing remembered) Erinnerung f; (of computer) Speicher m; **from ~** auswendig; **in ~ of** zur Erinnerung an (+ acc)

men /men/ see **man**

menac|e /ˈmenɪs/ n Drohung f; (nuisance) Plage f ● vt bedrohen. **~ing** adj, **~ly** adv drohend

mend /mend/ vt reparieren; (patch) flicken; ausbessern (clothes)

'menfolk /ˈ/ n pl Männer pl

menial /ˈmiːnɪəl/ adj niedrig

menopause /ˈmenə-/ n Wechseljahre pl

mental /ˈmentl/ adj geistig; (🖭: mad) verrückt. **~ a'rithmetic** n Kopfrechnen nt. **~ 'illness** n Geisteskrankheit f

mentality /menˈtælɪtɪ/ n Mentalität f

mention /ˈmenʃn/ n Erwähnung f ● vt erwähnen; **don't ~ it** keine Ursache; bitte

menu /ˈmenjuː/ n Speisekarte f

merchandise /ˈmɜːtʃəndaɪz/ n Ware f

merchant /ˈmɜːtʃənt/ n Kaufmann m; (dealer) Händler m. **~ 'navy** n Handelsmarine f

merci|ful /ˈmɜːsɪfl/ adj barmherzig. **~fully** adv 🖭 glücklicherweise. **~less** adj erbarmungslos

mercury /ˈmɜːkjʊrɪ/ n Quecksilber nt

mercy /ˈmɜːsɪ/ n Barmherzigkeit f, Gnade f; **be at s.o.'s ~** jdm ausgeliefert sein

mere /mɪə(r)/ adj bloß

merest /ˈmɪərɪst/ adj kleinste(r,s)

merge /mɜːdʒ/ vi zusammenlaufen; (Comm) fusionieren

merger /ˈmɜːdʒə(r)/ n Fusion f

meringue /məˈræŋ/ n Baiser nt

merit /'merɪt/ n Verdienst nt; (advantage) Vorzug m; (worth) Wert m ● vt verdienen

merry /'merɪ/ adj fröhlich

merry-go-round n Karussell nt

mesh /meʃ/ n Masche f

mesmerized /'mezmǝraɪzd/ adj (fig) [wie] gebannt

mess /mes/ n Durcheinander nt; (trouble) Schwierigkeiten pl; (something spilt) Bescherung f ①; (Mil) Messe f; **make a ~ of** (botch) verpfuschen ● vt ~ **up** in Unordnung bringen; (botch) verpfuschen ● vi ~ **about** herumpfuschen; (tinker) herumspielen (**with** mit)

message /'mesɪdʒ/ n Nachricht f; **give s.o. a ~** jdm etwas ausrichten

messenger /'mesɪndʒǝ(r)/ n Bote m

Messrs /'mesǝz/ n pl see **Mr**; (on letter) ~ **Smith** Firma Smith

messy /'mesɪ/ adj schmutzig; (untidy) unordentlich

met /met/ see **meet**

metal /'metl/ n Metall nt ● adj Metall-. ~**lic** adj metallisch

metaphor /'metǝfǝ(r)/ n Metapher f. ~**ical** adj metaphorisch

meteor /'miːtɪǝ(r)/ n Meteor m. ~**ic** adj kometenhaft

meteorological /miːtɪǝrǝ'lɒdʒɪkl/ adj Wetter-

meteorolog|ist /miːtɪǝ'rɒlǝdʒɪst/ n Meteorologe m/ -gin f. ~**y** n Meteorologie f

meter¹ /'miːtǝ(r)/ n Zähler m

meter² n (Amer) = **metre**

method /'meθǝd/ n Methode f; (Culin) Zubereitung f

methodical /mɪ'θɒdɪkl/ adj systematisch, methodisch

methylated /'meθɪleɪtɪd/ adj ~ **spirit[s]** Brennspiritus m

meticulous /mɪ'tɪkjʊlǝs/ adj sehr genau

metre /'miːtǝ(r)/ n Meter m & n; (rhythm) Versmaß nt

metric /'metrɪk/ adj metrisch

metropolis /mɪ'trɒpǝlɪs/ n Metropole f

metropolitan /metrǝ'pɒlɪtǝn/ adj hauptstädtisch; (international) weltstädtisch

mew /mjuː/ n Miau nt ● vi miauen

Mexican /'meksɪkǝn/ adj mexikanisch ● n Mexikaner(in) m(f). '**Mexico** n Mexiko nt

miaow /mɪ'aʊ/ n Miau nt ● vi miauen

mice /maɪs/ see **mouse**

micro: ~**film** n Mikrofilm m. ~**light** (aircraft) n Ultraleichtflugzeug nt. ~**phone** n Mikrofon nt. ~**scope** /-skǝʊp/ n Mikroskop nt. ~**scopic** /-'skɒpɪk/ adj mikroskopisch. ~**wave [oven]** n Mikrowellenherd m

mid /mɪd/ adj ~ **May** Mitte Mai; **in** ~ **air** in der Luft

midday /mɪd'deɪ/ n Mittag m

middle /'mɪdl/ adj mittlere(r,s); **the M~ Ages** das Mittelalter; **the** ~ **class[es]** der Mittelstand; **the M~ East** der Nahe Osten ● n Mitte f; **in the** ~ **of the night** mitten in der Nacht

middle: ~**-aged** adj mittleren Alters. ~**-class** adj bürgerlich

midge /mɪdʒ/ n [kleine] Mücke f

midget /'mɪdʒɪt/ n Liliputaner(in) m(f)

Midlands /'mɪdlǝndz/ npl **the** ~ Mittelengland n

'**midnight** n Mitternacht f

midriff /'mɪdrɪf/ n ① Taille f

midst /mɪdst/ n **in the** ~ **of** mitten in (+ dat); **in our** ~ unter uns

mid: ~**summer** n Hochsommer m. ~**way** adv auf halbem Wege. ~**wife** n Hebamme f. ~'**winter** n Mitte f des Winters

might¹ /maɪt/ modal verb I ~ vielleicht; **it** ~ **be true** es könnte wahr sein; **he asked if he** ~ **go** er fragte, ob er gehen dürfte; **you** ~ **have drowned** du hättest ertrinken können

might² n Macht f

mighty /'maɪtɪ/ adj mächtig

migraine /'miːgreɪn/ n Migräne f

migrat|e /maɪ'greɪt/ vi abwandern; (birds:) ziehen. ~**ion** n Wanderung f; (of birds) Zug m

mike /maɪk/ n ⏏ Mikrofon nt

mild /maɪld/ adj (-er, -est) mild

mild|ly /'maɪldlɪ/ adv leicht; **to put it** ~**ly** gelinde gesagt. ~**ness** n Milde f

mile /maɪl/ n Meile f (= 1,6 km); ~**s too big** ⏏ viel zu groß

mile|age /-ɪdʒ/ n Meilenzahl f; (of car) Meilenstand m

militant /'mɪlɪtənt/ adj militant

military /'mɪlɪtrɪ/ adj militärisch. ~ **service** n Wehrdienst m

milk /mɪlk/ n Milch f ● vt melken

milk: ~**man** n Milchmann m. ~**shake** n Milchmixgetränk nt. ~**tooth** n Milchzahn m

milky /'mɪlkɪ/ adj milchig. **M~Way** n (Astronomy) Milchstraße f

mill /mɪl/ n Mühle f; (factory) Fabrik f

millennium /mɪ'lenɪəm/ n Jahrtausend nt

milli|gram /'mɪlɪ-/ n Milligramm nt. ~**metre** n Millimeter m & nt

million /'mɪljən/ n Million f; **a** ~ **pounds** eine Million Pfund. ~**aire** n Millionär(in) m(f)

mime /maɪm/ n Pantomime f ● vt pantomimisch darstellen

mimic /'mɪmɪk/ n Imitator m ● vt (pt/pp **mimicked**) nachahmen

mince /mɪns/ n Hackfleisch nt ● vt (Culin) durchdrehen; **not** ~ **words** kein Blatt vor den Mund nehmen

mince: ~**meat** n Masse f aus Korinthen, Zitronat usw; **make** ~**meat of** (fig) vernichtend schlagen. ~'**pie** n mit 'mincemeat' gefüllte Pastetchen nt

mincer /'mɪnsə(r)/ n Fleischwolf m

mind /maɪnd/ n Geist m; (sanity) Verstand m; **give s.o. a piece of one's** ~ jdm gehörig die Meinung sagen; **make up one's** ~ sich entschließen; **be out of one's** ~ nicht bei Verstand sein; **have sth in** ~ etw im Sinn haben; **bear sth in** ~ an etw (acc) denken; **have a good** ~ **to** große Lust haben, zu; **I have changed my** ~ ich habe es mir anders überlegt ● vt aufpassen auf (+ acc); **I don't** ~ **the noise** der Lärm stört mich nicht; ~ **the step!** Achtung Stufe! ● vi (care) sich kümmern (about um); **I don't** ~ mir macht es nichts aus; **never** ~! macht nichts! **do you** ~ **if?** haben Sie etwas dagegen, wenn? ~ **out** vi aufpassen

'**minded** adj geistlos

mine¹ /maɪn/ poss pron meine(r), meins; **a friend of** ~ ein Freund von mir; **that is** ~ das gehört mir

mine² n Bergwerk nt; (explosive) Mine f ● vt abbauen; (Mil) verminen

miner /'maɪnə(r)/ n Bergarbeiter m

mineral /'mɪnərl/ n Mineral nt. ~ **water** n Mineralwasser nt

minesweeper /'maɪn-/ n Minenräumboot nt

mingle /'mɪŋgl/ vi ~ **with** sich mischen unter (+ acc)

miniature /'mɪnɪtʃə(r)/ adj Klein-

● n Miniatur f

mini|bus /'mɪnɪ-/ n Kleinbus m. **~cab** n Kleintaxi nt

minim|al /'mɪnɪməl/ adj minimal. **~um** n (pl -ima) Minimum nt ● adj Mindest-

mining /'maɪnɪŋ/ n Bergbau m

miniskirt /'mɪnɪ-/ n Minirock m

minist|er /'mɪnɪstə(r)/ n Minister m; (Relig) Pastor m. **~erial** adj ministeriell

ministry /'mɪnɪstrɪ/ n (Pol) Ministerium nt

mink /mɪŋk/ n Nerz m

minor /'maɪnə(r)/ adj kleiner; (less important) unbedeutend ● n Minderjährige(r) m/f; (Mus) Moll nt

minority /maɪ'nɒrɪtɪ/ n Minderheit f

minor road n Nebenstraße f

mint[1] /mɪnt/ n Münzstätte f ● adj (stamp) postfrisch; **in** ~ **condition** wie neu ● vt prägen

mint[2] n (herb) Minze f; (sweet) Pfefferminzbonbon m & nt

minus /'maɪnəs/ prep minus, weniger; (🔢: without) ohne

minute[1] /'mɪnɪt/ n Minute f; **in a** ~ (shortly) gleich; **~s** pl (of meeting) Protokoll nt

minute[2] /maɪ'njuːt/ adj winzig

miracle /'mɪrəkl/ n Wunder nt. **~ulous** adj wunderbar

mirror /'mɪrə(r)/ n Spiegel m ● vt widerspiegeln

mirth /mɜːθ/ n Heiterkeit f

misad'venture /mɪs-/ n Missgeschick nt

misappre'hension n Missverständnis nt; **be under a** ~ sich irren

misbe'hav|e vi sich schlecht benehmen. **~iour** n schlechtes Benehmen nt

mis'calcu|late vt falsch berechnen ● vi sich verrechnen. **~lation** n Fehlkalkulation f

'miscarriage n Fehlgeburt f

miscellaneous /mɪsə'leɪnɪəs/ adj vermischt

mischief /'mɪstʃɪf/ n Unfug m

mischievous /'mɪstʃɪvəs/ adj schelmisch; (malicious) boshaft

miscon'ception n falsche Vorstellung f

mis'conduct n unkorrektes Verhalten nt; (adultery) Ehebruch m

miser /'maɪzə(r)/ n Geizhals m

miserable /'mɪzrəbl/ adj, **-bly** adv unglücklich; (wretched) elend

miserly /'maɪzəlɪ/ adv geizig

misery /'mɪzərɪ/ n Elend nt; (🔢: person) Miesepeter m

mis'fire vi fehlzünden; (go wrong) fehlschlagen

'misfit n Außenseiter(in) m(f)

mis'fortune n Unglück nt

mis'givings npl Bedenken pl

mis'guided adj töricht

mishap /'mɪshæp/ n Missgeschick nt

misin'form vt falsch unterrichten

misin'terpret vt missdeuten

mis'judge vt falsch beurteilen

mis'lay vt (pt/pp -laid) verlegen

mis'lead vt (pt/pp -led) irreführen. **~ing** adj irreführend

mis'manage vt schlecht verwalten. **~ment** n Misswirtschaft f

misnomer /mɪs'nəʊmə(r)/ n Fehlbezeichnung f

'misprint n Druckfehler m

mis'quote vt falsch zitieren

misrepre'sent vt falsch darstellen

miss /mɪs/ n Fehltreffer m ● vt verpassen; (fail to hit or find) verfehlen; (*fail to attend*) versäumen; (*fail to notice*) übersehen; (*feel the loss of*) vermissen ● *vi* (*fail to hit*) nicht treffen. **~ out** *vt* auslassen

Miss *n* (*pl* **-es**) Fräulein *nt*

missile /'mɪsaɪl/ *n* [Wurf]geschoss *nt*; (*Mil*) Rakete *f*

missing /'mɪsɪŋ/ *adj* fehlend; (*lost*) verschwunden; (*Mil*) vermisst; **be ~ fehlen**

mission /'mɪʃn/ *n* Auftrag *m*; (*Mil*) Einsatz *m*; (*Relig*) Mission *f*

missionary /'mɪʃənrɪ/ *n* Missionar(in) *m* (*f*)

mis'spell *vt* (*pt/pp* **-spelt** or **-spelled**) falsch schreiben

mist /mɪst/ *n* Dunst *m*; (*fog*) Nebel *m*; (*on window*) Beschlag *m* ● *vi* ~ **up** beschlagen

mistake /mɪ'steɪk/ *n* Fehler *m*; **by ~** aus Versehen ● *vt* (*pt* **mistook**, *pp* **mistaken**) ~ **for** verwechseln mit

mistaken /mɪ'steɪkn/ *adj* falsch; **be ~** sich irren. **~ly** *adv* irrtümlicherweise

mistletoe /'mɪsltəʊ/ *n* Mistel *f*

mistress /'mɪstrɪs/ *n* Herrin *f*; (*teacher*) Lehrerin *f*; (*lover*) Geliebte *f*

mis'trust *n* Misstrauen *nt* ● *vt* misstrauen (+ *dat*)

misty /'mɪstɪ/ *adj* dunstig; (*foggy*) neblig; (*fig*) unklar

misunder'stand *vt* (*pt/pp* **-stood**) missverstehen. **~ing** *n* Missverständnis *nt*

misuse[1] /mɪs'juːz/ *vt* missbrauchen

misuse[2] /mɪs'juːs/ *n* Missbrauch *m*

mitigating /'mɪtɪgeɪtɪŋ/ *adj* mildernd

mix /mɪks/ *n* Mischung *f* ● *vt* mischen ● *vi* sich mischen; ~ **with** (*associate with*) verkehren mit. ~ **up** *vt* mischen; (*muddle*) durchein-

ander bringen; (*mistake for*) verwechseln (**with** mit)

mixed /mɪkst/ *adj* gemischt; **be ~ up** durcheinander sein

mixer /'mɪksə(r)/ *n* Mischmaschine *f*; (*Culin*) Küchenmaschine *f*

mixture /'mɪkstʃə(r)/ *n* Mischung *f*; (*medicine*) Mixtur *f*; (*Culin*) Teig *m*

'mix-up *n* Durcheinander *nt*; (*confusion*) Verwirrung *f*; (*mistake*) Verwechslung *f*

moan /məʊn/ *n* Stöhnen *nt* ● *vi* stöhnen; (*complain*) jammern

mob /mɒb/ *n* Horde *f*; (*rabble*) Pöbel *m*; (🔲: *gang*) Bande *f* ● *vt* (*pt/pp* **mobbed**) herfallen über (+ *acc*); belagern (*celebrity*)

mobile /'məʊbaɪl/ *adj* beweglich ● *n* Mobile *f*; (*telephone*) Handy *nt*. ~ **'home** *n* Wohnwagen *m*. ~ **'phone** *n* Handy *nt*

mobility /mə'bɪlətɪ/ *n* Beweglichkeit *f*

mock /mɒk/ *adj* Schein- ● *vt* verspotten. **~ery** *n* Spott *m*

'mock-up *n* Modell *nt*

mode /məʊd/ *n* [Art und] Weise *f*; (*fashion*) Mode *f*

model /'mɒdl/ *n* Modell *nt*; (*example*) Vorbild *nt*; **[fashion] ~** Mannequin *nt* ● *adj* Modell-; (*exemplary*) Muster- ● *v* (*pt/pp* **modelled**) ● *vt* formen, modellieren; vorführen (*clothes*) ● *vi* Mannequin sein; (*for artist*) Modell stehen

moderate[1] /'mɒdəreɪt/ *vt* mäßigen

moderate[2] /'mɒdərət/ *adj* mäßig; (*opinion*) gemäßigt. **~ly** *adv* mäßig; (*fairly*) einigermaßen

moderation /mɒdə'reɪʃn/ *n* Mäßigung *f*; **in ~** mit Maß[en]

modern /'mɒdn/ *adj* modern. **~ize** *vt* modernisieren. ~ **'languages** *npl* neuere Sprachen *pl*

m

modest /'mɒdɪst/ adj bescheiden; (decorous) schamhaft. **~y** n Bescheidenheit f

modif|ication /mɒdɪfɪ'keɪʃn/ n Abänderung f. **~y** vt (pt/pp -fied) abändern

module /'mɒdjuːl/ n Element nt; (of course) Kurseinheit f

moist /mɔɪst/ adj (-er, -est) feucht

moisten /'mɔɪsn/ vt befeuchten

moistur|e /'mɔɪstʃə(r)/ n Feuchtigkeit f. **~izer** n Feuchtigkeitscreme f

molar /'məʊlə(r)/ n Backenzahn m

mole[1] /məʊl/ n Leberfleck m

mole[2] n (Zool) Maulwurf m

molecule /'mɒlɪkjuːl/ n Molekül nt

molest /mə'lest/ vt belästigen

mollify /'mɒlɪfaɪ/ vt (pt/pp -ied) besänftigen

mollycoddle /'mɒlɪkɒdl/ vt verzärteln

molten /'məʊltən/ adj geschmolzen

mom /mɒm/ n (Amer fam) Mutti f

moment /'məʊmənt/ n Moment m, Augenblick m; **at the ~** im Augenblick, augenblicklich. **~ary** adj vorübergehend

momentous /mə'mentəs/ adj bedeutsam

momentum /mə'mentəm/ n Schwung m

monarch /'mɒnək/ n Monarch(in) m(f). **~y** n Monarchie f

monastery /'mɒnəstrɪ/ n Kloster nt

Monday /'mʌndeɪ/ n Montag m

money /'mʌnɪ/ n Geld nt

money: **~-box** n Sparbüchse f. **~-lender** n Geldverleiher m. **~ order** n Zahlungsanweisung f

mongrel /'mʌŋgrəl/ n Promena-

denmischung f

monitor /'mɒnɪtə(r)/ n (Techn) Monitor m ● vt überwachen (progress); abhören (broadcast)

monk /mʌŋk/ n Mönch m

monkey /'mʌŋkɪ/ n Affe m

mono /'mɒnəʊ/ n Mono nt

monogram /'mɒnəgræm/ n Monogramm nt

monologue /'mɒnəlɒg/ n Monolog m

monopol|ize /mə'nɒpəlaɪz/ vt monopolisieren. **~y** n Monopol nt

monosyllable /'mɒnəsɪləbl/ n einsilbiges Wort nt

monotone /'mɒnətəʊn/ n **in a ~** mit monotoner Stimme

monoton|ous /mə'nɒtənəs/ adj eintönig, monoton; (tedious) langweilig. **~y** n Eintönigkeit f, Monotonie f

monster /'mɒnstə(r)/ n Ungeheuer nt; (cruel person) Unmensch m

monstrosity /mɒn'strɒsətɪ/ n Monstrosität f

monstrous /'mɒnstrəs/ adj ungeheuer; (outrageous) ungeheuerlich

month /mʌnθ/ n Monat m. **~ly** adj & adv monatlich ● n (periodical) Monatszeitschrift f

monument /'mɒnjʊmənt/ n Denkmal nt. **~al** adj (fig) monumental

moo /muː/ n Muh nt ● vi (pt/pp mooed) muhen

mood /muːd/ n Laune f; **be in a good/bad ~** gute/schlechte Laune haben

moody /'muːdɪ/ adj launisch

moon /muːn/ n Mond m; **over the ~** 🔲 überglücklich

moon: **~light** n Mondschein m. **~lighting** n 🔲 ≈ Schwarzarbeit f

~**lit** adj mondhell

moor[1] /mʊə(r)/ n Moor nt

moor[2] vt (Naut) festmachen ● vi anlegen

mop /mɒp/ n Mopp m; ~ **of hair** Wuschelkopf m ● vt (pt/pp **mopped**) wischen. ~ **up** vt aufwischen

moped /ˈməʊped/ n Moped nt

moral /ˈmɒrl/ adj moralisch, sittlich; (virtuous) tugendhaft ● n Moral f; ~**s** pl Moral f

morale /məˈrɑːl/ n Moral f

morality /məˈrælətɪ/ n Sittlichkeit f

morbid /ˈmɔːbɪd/ adj krankhaft; (gloomy) trübe

more /mɔː(r)/ a, adv & n mehr; (in addition) noch; **a few** ~ noch ein paar; **any** ~ noch etwas; **once** ~ noch einmal; ~ **or less** mehr oder weniger; **some** ~ **tea?** noch etwas Tee? ~ **interesting** interessanter; ~ **[and** ~**] quickly** [immer] schneller

moreover /mɔːˈrəʊvə(r)/ adv außerdem

morgue /mɔːɡ/ n Leichenschauhaus nt

morning /ˈmɔːnɪŋ/ n Morgen m; **in the** ~ morgens, am Morgen; (tomorrow) morgen früh

Morocco /məˈrɒkəʊ/ n Marokko nt

moron /ˈmɔːrɒn/ n 🄵 Idiot m

morose /məˈrəʊs/ adj mürrisch

morsel /ˈmɔːsl/ n Happen m

mortal /ˈmɔːtl/ adj sterblich; (fatal) tödlich ● n Sterbliche(r) m/f. ~**ity** n Sterblichkeit f. ~**ly** adv tödlich

mortar /ˈmɔːtə(r)/ n Mörtel m

mortgage /ˈmɔːɡɪdʒ/ n Hypothek f ● vt hypothekarisch belasten

mortuary /ˈmɔːtjʊərɪ/ n Leichenhalle f; (public) Leichenschauhaus nt; (Amer: undertaker's) Bestattungsinstitut nt

mosaic /məʊˈzeɪɪk/ n Mosaik nt

Moscow /ˈmɒskəʊ/ n Moskau nt

mosque /mɒsk/ n Moschee f

mosquito /mɒsˈkiːtəʊ/ n (pl **-es**) [Stech]mücke f, Schnake f; (tropical) Moskito m

moss /mɒs/ n Moos nt. ~**y** adj moosig

most /məʊst/ adj der/die/das meiste; (majority) die meisten; **for the** ~ **part** zum größten Teil ● adv am meisten; (very) höchst; **the** ~ **interesting day** der interessanteste Tag; ~ **unlikely** höchst unwahrscheinlich ● n das meiste; ~ **of them** die meisten [von ihnen]; **at [the]** ~ höchstens; ~ **of the time** die meiste Zeit. ~**ly** adv meist

MOT n ≈ TÜV m

motel /məʊˈtel/ n Motel nt

moth /mɒθ/ n Nachtfalter m; [clothes-] ~ Motte f

'**mothball** n Mottenkugel f

mother /ˈmʌðə(r)/ n Mutter f

mother: ~**hood** n Mutterschaft f. ~-**in-law** n (pl ~**s-in-law**) Schwiegermutter f. ~**land** n Mutterland nt. ~**ly** adj mütterlich. ~-**of-pearl** n Perlmutter f. ~-**to-be** n werdende Mutter f

mothproof /ˈmɒθ-/ adj mottenfest

motif /məʊˈtiːf/ n Motiv nt

motion /ˈməʊʃn/ n Bewegung f; (proposal) Antrag m. ~**less** adj bewegungslos

motivat|e /ˈməʊtɪveɪt/ vt motivieren. ~**ion** n Motivation f

motive /ˈməʊtɪv/ n Motiv nt

motor /ˈməʊtə(r)/ n Motor m; (car) Auto nt ● adj Motor-; (Anat) moto-

m

risch ● vi [mit dem Auto] fahren
motor: ~ **bike** n 🔢 Motorrad nt.
~ **boat** n Motorboot nt. ~ **car** n
Auto nt, Wagen m. ~ **cycle** n Motorrad nt. ~**cyclist** n Motorradfah-
rer m. ~**ing** n Autofahren nt. ~**ist**
n Autofahrer(in) m(f). ~ **vehicle** n
Kraftfahrzeug nt. ~**way** n Autobahn f

mottled /'mɒtld/ adj gesprenkelt

motto /'mɒtəʊ/ n (pl -es) Motto nt

mould[1] /məʊld/ n (fungus) Schimmel m

mould[2] n Form f ● vt formen (into
zu). ~**ing** n (decorative) Fries m

mouldy /'məʊldɪ/ adj schimmelig;
(🔢: worthless) schäbig

mound /maʊnd/ n Hügel m; (of
stones) Haufen m

mount /maʊnt/ n (animal) Reittier nt; (of
jewel) Fassung f; (of photo, picture)
Passepartout nt ● vt (get on) steigen auf (+ acc); (on pedestal) montieren auf (+ acc); besteigen (horse);
fassen (jewel); aufziehen (photo,
picture) ● vi aufsteigen; (tension:)
steigen. ~ **up** vi sich häufen; (add
up) sich anhäufen

mountain /'maʊntɪn/ n Berg m

mountaineer /maʊntɪ'nɪə(r)/ n
Bergsteiger(in) m(f). ~**ing** n Berg-
steigen nt

mountainous /'maʊntɪnəs/ adj
bergig, gebirgig

mourn /mɔːn/ vt betrauern ● vi
trauern (for um). ~**er** n Trauern-
de(r) m/f. ~**ful** adj trauervoll. ~**ing**
n Trauer f

mouse /maʊs/ n (pl mice) Maus f.
~**trap** n Mausefalle f

moustache /mə'stɑːʃ/ n Schnurr-
bart m

mouth[1] /maʊð/ vt ~ sth etw laut-
los mit den Lippen sagen

mouth[2] /maʊθ/ n Mund m; (of ani-

mal) Maul nt; (of river) Mündung f

mouth: ~**ful** n Mundvoll m; (bite)
Bissen m. ~**organ** n Mundharmonika f. ~**wash** n Mundwasser nt

movable /'muːvəbl/ adj beweglich

move /muːv/ n Bewegung f; (fig)
Schritt m; (moving house) Umzug m;
(in board game) Zug m; **on the** ~
unterwegs; **get a** ~ **on** 🔢 sich beeilen ● vt bewegen; (emotionally)
rühren; (move along) rücken; (in
board game) ziehen; (take away)
wegnehmen; wegfahren (car); (rearrange) umstellen; (transfer) versetzen (person); verlegen (office); (propose) beantragen; ~ **house**
umziehen ● vi sich bewegen; (move
house) umziehen; **don't** ~! stillhalten! (stop) stillstehen!. ~ **along** vt/i
weiterrücken. ~ **away** vt/i wegrü-
cken; (move house) wegziehen. ~ **in**
vi einziehen. ~ **off** vi (vehicle:) losfahren. ~ **out** vi ausziehen. ~ **over**
vt/i [zur Seite] rücken. ~ **up** vi aufrücken

movement /'muːvmənt/ n Bewegung f; (Mus) Satz m; (of clock) Uhrwerk nt

movie /'muːvɪ/ n (Amer) Film m;
go to the ~**s** ins Kino gehen

moving /'muːvɪŋ/ adj beweglich;
(touching) rührend

mow /məʊ/ vt (pt mowed, pp
mown or mowed) mähen

mower /'məʊə(r)/ n Rasenmäher m

MP abbr Member of Parliament

Mr /'mɪstə(r)/ n (pl Messrs) Herr m

Mrs /'mɪsɪz/ n Frau f

Ms /mɪz/ n Frau f

much /mʌtʃ/ a, adv & n viel; **as** ~
as so viel wie; ~ **loved** sehr geliebt

muck /mʌk/ n Mist m; (🔢: filth)
Dreck m. ~ **about** vi herumlaufen;
(tinker) herumspielen (**with** mit). ~

out vt ausmisten. ~ **up** vt 🔟 vermasseln; (make dirty) schmutzig machen

mucky /'mʌki/ adj dreckig

mud /mʌd/ n Schlamm m

muddle /'mʌdl/ n Durcheinander nt; (confusion) Verwirrung f ● vt ~ [up] durcheinander bringen

muddy /'mʌdɪ/ adj schlammig; (shoes) schmutzig

'mudguard n Kotflügel m; (on bicycle) Schutzblech nt

muffle /'mʌfl/ vt dämpfen

muffler /'mʌflə(r)/ n Schal m; (Amer, Auto) Auspufftopf m

mug[1] /mʌg/ n Becher m; (for beer) Bierkrug m; (🔟: face) Visage f; (🔟: simpleton) Trottel m

mug[2] vt (pt/pp mugged) überfallen. **~ger** n Straßenräuber m. **~ging** n Straßenraub m

muggy /'mʌgɪ/ adj schwül

mule /mjuːl/ n Maultier nt

mulled /mʌld/ adj ~ **wine** Glühwein m

multi /'mʌltɪ/: **~coloured** adj vielfarbig, bunt. **~lingual** adj mehrsprachig. **~'national** adj multinational

multiple /'mʌltɪpl/ adj vielfach; (with pl) mehrere ● n Vielfache(s) nt

multiplication /mʌltɪplɪ'keɪʃn/ n Multiplikation f

multiply /'mʌltɪplaɪ/ v (pt/pp -ied) ● vt multiplizieren (by mit) ● vi sich vermehren

multistorey adj ~ **car park** Parkhaus nt

mum /mʌm/ n 🔟 Mutti f

mumble /'mʌmbl/ vt/i murmeln

mummy[1] /'mʌmɪ/ n 🔟 Mutti f

mummy[2] n (Archaeology) Mumie f

mumps /mʌmps/ n Mumps m

munch /mʌntʃ/ vt/i mampfen

municipal /mju:'nɪsɪpl/ adj städtisch

munitions /mju:'nɪʃnz/ npl Kriegsmaterial nt

mural /'mjʊərəl/ n Wandgemälde nt

murder /'mɜːdə(r)/ n Mord m ● vt ermorden. **~er** n Mörder m. **~ess** n Mörderin f. **~ous** adj mörderisch

murky /'mɜːkɪ/ adj düster

murmur /'mɜːmə(r)/ n Murmeln nt ● vt/i murmeln

muscle /'mʌsl/ n Muskel m

muscular /'mʌskjʊlə(r)/ adj Muskel-; (strong) muskulös

museum /mju:'zɪəm/ n Museum nt

mushroom /'mʌʃrʊm/ n [essbarer] Pilz m, esp Champignon m ● vi (fig) wie Pilze aus dem Boden schießen

mushy /'mʌʃɪ/ adj breiig

music /'mju:zɪk/ n Musik f; (written) Noten pl; **set to ~** vertonen

musical /'mju:zɪkl/ adj musikalisch ● n Musical m. **~ box** n Spieldose f. **~ instrument** n Musikinstrument nt

musician /mju:'zɪʃn/ n Musiker(in) m(f)

'music-stand n Notenständer m

Muslim /'mʊzlɪm/ adj mohammedanisch ● n Mohammedaner(in) m(f)

must /mʌst/ modal verb (nur Präsens) müssen; (with negative) dürfen ● n a ~ 🔟 ein Muss nt

mustard /'mʌstəd/ n Senf m

musty /'mʌstɪ/ adj muffig

mute /mju:t/ adj stumm

mutilat|e /'mju:tɪleɪt/ vt verstümmeln. **~ion** n Verstümmelung f

mutin|ous /'mju:tɪnəs/ adj meuterisch. **~y** n Meuterei f ● vi (pt/pp

-ied) meutern

mutter /ˈmʌtə(r)/ n Murmeln nt
● vt/i murmeln

mutton /ˈmʌtn/ n Hammel-
fleisch nt

mutual /ˈmjuːtʃʊəl/ adj gegenseitig; (ⓘ: *common*) gemeinsam. **~ly**
adv gegenseitig

muzzle /ˈmʌzl/ n (*of animal*)
Schnauze f; (*of firearm*) Mündung f;
(*for dog*) Maulkorb m

my /maɪ/ adj mein

myself /maɪˈself/ pron selbst; (*reflexive*) mich; **by ~** allein; **I thought
to ~** ich habe mir gedacht

mysterious /mɪˈstɪərɪəs/ adj ge-
heimnisvoll; (*puzzling*) mysteriös,
rätselhaft

mystery /ˈmɪstərɪ/ n Geheimnis
nt; (*puzzle*) Rätsel nt; **~ [story]**
Krimi m

mysti|c[al] /ˈmɪstɪk[l]/ adj my-
stisch. **~cism** n Mystik f

mystified /ˈmɪstɪfaɪd/ adj be **~**
vor einem Rätsel stehen

mystique /mɪˈstiːk/ n geheimnis-
voller Zauber m

myth /mɪθ/ n Mythos m; (ⓘ: *untruth*) Märchen nt. **~ical** adj my-
thisch; (*fig*) erfunden

mythology /mɪˈθɒlədʒɪ/ n Mytho-
logie f

. . . .

Nn

. . . .

nab /næb/ vt (*pt/pp* nabbed) ⓘ erwischen

nag¹ /næg/ n (*horse*) Gaul m

nag² vt/i (*pt/pp* nagged) herumnörgeln (s.o. an jdm)

nail /neɪl/ n (*Anat, Techn*) Nagel m;
on the ~ ⓘ sofort ● vt nageln (**to**
an + *acc*)

nail: ~-brush n Nagelbürste f.
~-file n Nagelfeile f. **~ scissors**
npl Nagelschere f. **~ varnish** n Na-
gellack m

naïve /naɪˈiːv/ adj naiv. **~ty** n Nai-
vität f

naked /ˈneɪkɪd/ adj nackt; (*flame*)
offen; **with the ~ eye** mit bloßem
Auge. **~ness** n Nacktheit f

name /neɪm/ n Name m; (*reputation*) Ruf m; **by ~** dem Namen
nach; **by the ~ of** namens; **call s.o.
~s** ⓘ jdn beschimpfen ● vt nennen; (*give a name to*) einen Namen
geben (+ *dat*); (*announce publicly*)
den Namen bekannt geben von.
~less adj namenlos. **~ly** adv
nämlich

name: ~-plate n Namensschild nt.
~sake n Namensvetter
m/Namensschwester f

nanny /ˈnænɪ/ n Kindermädchen nt

nap /næp/ n Nickerchen nt

napkin /ˈnæpkɪn/ n Serviette f

nappy /ˈnæpɪ/ n Windel f

narcotic /nɑːˈkɒtɪk/ n (*drug*)
Rauschgift nt

narrat|e /nəˈreɪt/ vt erzählen.
~ion n Erzählung f

narrative /ˈnærətɪv/ n Erzählung f

narrator /nəˈreɪtə(r)/ n Erzähle-
r(in) m(f)

narrow /ˈnærəʊ/ adj (-er, -est)
schmal; (*restricted*) eng; (*margin,
majority*) knapp; **have a ~ escape**
mit knapper Not davonkommen ● vi
sich verengen. **~-minded** adj engstirnig

nasal /ˈneɪzl/ adj nasal; (*Med &
Anat*) Nasen-

nasty /ˈnɑːstɪ/ adj übel; (*unpleasant*) unangenehm; (*unkind*) boshaft;

(*serious*) schlimm

nation /ˈneɪʃn/ n Nation f; (*people*) Volk nt

national /ˈnæʃənl/ adj national; (*newspaper*) überregional; (*campaign*) landesweit ● n Staatsbürger(in) m(f)

national: ~ **'anthem** n Nationalhymne f. **N~ 'Health Service** n staatlicher Gesundheitsdienst m. **N~ In'surance** n Sozialversicherung f

nationalism /ˈnæʃənəlɪzm/ n Nationalismus m

nationality /næʃəˈnælətɪ/ n Staatsangehörigkeit f

national|ization /næʃənəlaɪˈzeɪʃn/ n Verstaatlichung f. ~**ize** vt verstaatlichen

---

National Trust Eine Stiftung zur Erhaltung und Pflege von Stätten von historischem Interesse oder besonderen Naturschönheiten. Der *National Trust* finanziert sich aus Stiftungsgeldern und privaten Spenden und ist der größte Privateigentümer von Land in Großbritannien. Er hat riesige Landflächen, Dörfer und Häuser gekauft oder erhalten, von denen viele öffentlich zugänglich sind.

---

native /ˈneɪtɪv/ adj einheimisch; (*innate*) angeboren ● n Eingeborene(r) m/f; (*local inhabitant*) Einheimische(r) m/f; **a ~ of Vienna** ein gebürtiger Wiener

native: ~ **land** n Heimatland nt. ~ **language** n Muttersprache f

natter /ˈnætə(r)/ vi 🛈 schwatzen

natural /ˈnætʃrəl/ adj natürlich; ~**[-coloured]** naturfarben

natural: ~ **'gas** n Erdgas nt. ~ **'history** n Naturkunde f

naturalist /ˈnætʃrəlɪst/ n Naturforscher m

natural|ization /nætʃrəlaɪˈzeɪʃn/ n Einbürgerung f. ~**ize** vt einbürgern

nature /ˈneɪtʃə(r)/ n Natur f; (*kind*) Art f; **by** ~ von Natur aus. ~ **reserve** n Naturschutzgebiet nt

naughty /ˈnɔːtɪ/ adj , **-ily** adv unartig; (*slightly indecent*) gewagt

nausea /ˈnɔːzɪə/ n Übelkeit f

nautical /ˈnɔːtɪkl/ adj nautisch. ~ **mile** n Seemeile f

naval /ˈneɪvl/ adj Marine-

nave /neɪv/ n Kirchenschiff nt

navel /ˈneɪvl/ n Nabel m

navigable /ˈnævɪɡəbl/ adj schiffbar

navigat|e /ˈnævɪɡeɪt/ vi navigieren ● vt befahren (*river*). ~**ion** n Navigation f

navy /ˈneɪvɪ/ n [Kriegs]marine f ● adj ~ **[blue]** marineblau

near /nɪə(r)/ adj (-er, -est) nah[e]; **the ~est bank** die nächste Bank ● adv nahe; **draw** ~ sich nähern ● prep nahe an (+ dat/acc); **in der** Nähe von

near: ~**by** adj nahe gelegen, nahe liegend. ~**ly** adv fast, beinahe; **not** ~**ly** bei weitem nicht. ~**ness** n Nähe f. ~ **side** n Beifahrerseite f. ~**sighted** adj (Amer) kurzsichtig

neat /niːt/ adj (-er, -est) adrett; (*tidy*) ordentlich; (*clever*) geschickt; (*undiluted*) pur. ~**ness** n Ordentlichkeit f

necessarily /nesəˈserəlɪ/ adv notwendigerweise; **not** ~ nicht unbedingt

necessary /ˈnesəsərɪ/ adj nötig, notwendig

necessit|ate /nɪˈsesɪteɪt/ vt notwendig machen. ~**y** n Notwendigkeit f; **work from** ~**y** arbeiten, weil

man es nötig hat
neck /nek/ n Hals m; ~ **and** ~
Kopf an Kopf
necklace /'neklɪs/ n Halskette f
necklinen Halsausschnitt m
née /neɪ/ adj ~ **X** geborene X
need /niːd/ n Bedürfnis nt; (misfortune) Not f; **be in** ~ **of** brauchen;
in case of ~ notfalls; **if** ~ **be** wenn
nötig; **there is a** ~ **for** es besteht
ein Bedarf an (+ dat); **there is no**
~ **for that** das ist nicht nötig ● vt
brauchen; **you** ~ **not go** du
brauchst nicht zu gehen; ~ **I**
come? muss ich kommen? **I** ~ **to**
know ich muss es wissen
needle /'niːdl/ n Nadel f
needless /'niːdlɪs/ adj unnötig; ~
to say selbstverständlich, natürlich
'needlework n Nadelarbeit f
needy /'niːdɪ/ adj bedürftig
negation /nɪ'geɪʃn/ n Verneinung f
negative /'negətɪv/ adj negativ
● n Verneinung f; (photo) Negativ nt
neglect /nɪ'glekt/ n Vernachlässi-
gung f ● vt vernachlässigen; (omit)
versäumen (**to** zu). ~**ed** adj verwahrlost. ~**ful** adj nachlässig
negligen|ce /'neglɪdʒəns/ n Nach-
lässigkeit f. ~**t** adj nachlässig
negligible /'neglɪdʒəbl/ adj unbedeutend
negotiat|e /nɪ'gəʊʃɪeɪt/ vt aus-
handeln; (Auto) nehmen (bend) ● vi
verhandeln. ~**ion** n Verhandlung f.
~**or** n Unterhändler(in) m(f)
Negro /'niːgrəʊ/ adj Neger- ● n (pl
-es) Neger m
neigh /neɪ/ vi wiehern
neighbour /'neɪbə(r)/ n Nachba-
r(in) m(f). ~**hood** n Nachbarschaft
f. ~**ing** adj Nachbar-. ~**ly** adj [gut-
]nachbarlich

neither /'naɪðə(r)/ adj & pron kei-
ne(r, s) [von beiden] ● adv ~ **...** nor
weder ... noch ● conj auch nicht

neon /'niːɒn/ n Neon nt
nephew /'nevjuː/ n Neffe m
nepotism /'nepətɪzm/ n Vettern-
wirtschaft f
nerve /nɜːv/ n Nerv m; ([] : courage) Mut m; ([] : impudence) Frechheit f. ~**-racking** adj nervenauf-
reibend
nervous /'nɜːvəs/ adj (afraid)
ängstlich; (highly strung) nervös;
(Anat, Med) Nerven-. ~ '**breakdown** n Nervenzusammenbruch m.
~**ness** Ängstlichkeit f
nervy /'nɜːvɪ/ adj nervös; (Amer:
impudent) frech
nest /nest/ n Nest nt ● vi nisten
nestle /'nesl/ vi sich schmiegen
(against an + acc)
net[1] /net/ n Netz nt; (curtain)
Store m
net[2] adj netto; (salary, weight)
Netto-
'netball n ≈ Korbball m
Netherlands /'neðələndz/ npl **the**
~ die Niederlande pl
nettle /'netl/ n Nessel f
'network n Netz nt
neurolog|ist /njʊə'rɒlədʒɪst/ n
Neurologe m/ -gin f. ~**y** n Neurolo-
gie f
neur|osis /njʊə'rəʊsɪs/ n (pl -oses
/-siːz/) Neurose f. ~**otic** adj neu-
rotisch
neuter /'njuːtə(r)/ adj (Gram) sächlich ● n (Gram) Neutrum nt ● vt kastrieren; (spay) sterilisieren
neutral /'njuːtrl/ adj neutral ● n **in**
~ (Auto) im Leerlauf. ~**ity** n Neu-
tralität f

never /'nevə(r)/ adv nie, niemals;
([] : not) nicht; ~ **mind** macht

nichts; **well I ~!** ja so was! **~end-ing** adj endlos

nevertheless /nevəðə'les/ adv dennoch, trotzdem

new /nju:/ adj (-er, -est) neu

new: **~comer** n Neuankömmling m. **~fangled** /-'fæŋgld/ adj (pej) neumodisch. **~laid** adj frisch gelegt

'**newly** adv frisch. **~weds** npl Jungverheiratete pl

new: **~ 'moon** n Neumond m. **~ness** n Neuheit f

news /nju:z/ n Nachricht f; (Radio, TV) Nachrichten pl; **piece of ~** Neuigkeit f

news: **~agent** n Zeitungshändler m. **~ bulletin** n Nachrichtensendung f. **~letter** n Mitteilungsblatt nt. **~paper** n Zeitung f; (material) Zeitungspapier nt. **~reader** n Nachrichtensprecher(in) m(f)

New: **~ Year's 'Day** n Neujahr nt. **~ Year's 'Eve** n Silvester nt. **~ Zealand** /'zi:lənd/ n Neuseeland nt

next /nekst/ adj & n nächste(r, s); **who's ~?** wer kommt als Nächster dran? **the ~ best** das nächstbeste; **~ door** nebenan; **my ~ of kin** mein nächster Verwandter; **~ to nothing** fast gar nichts; **the week after ~** übernächste Woche ● adv als Nächstes; **~ to** neben

nib /nɪb/ n Feder f

nibble /'nɪbl/ vt/i knabbern (**at** an + dat)

nice /naɪs/ adj (-r, -st) nett; (day, weather) schön; (food) gut; (distinction) fein. **~ly** adv nett; (well) gut

niche /ni:ʃ/ n Nische f; (fig) Platz m

nick /nɪk/ n Kerbe f; (🄵: prison) Knast m; (🄵: police station) Revier nt; **in good ~** in gutem Zustand ● vt einkerben; (steal) klauen; (🄵:

arrest) schnappen

nickel /'nɪkl/ n Nickel nt; (Amer) Fünfcentstück nt

'**nickname** n Spitzname m

nicotine /'nɪkəti:n/ n Nikotin nt

niece /ni:s/ n Nichte f

Nigeria /naɪ'dʒɪərɪə/ n Nigeria nt. **~n** adj nigerianisch ● n Nigerianer(in) m(f)

night /naɪt/ n Nacht f; (evening) Abend m; **at ~** nachts

night: **~club** n Nachtklub m. **~dress** n Nachthemd nt. **~fall** n **at ~fall** bei Einbruch der Dunkelheit. **~gown** n, 🄵 **~ie** /'naɪti/ n Nachthemd nt

nightingale /'naɪtɪŋgeɪl/ n Nachtigall f

night: **~life** n Nachtleben nt. **~ly** adj nächtlich ● adv jede Nacht. **~mare** n Albtraum m. **~time** n **at ~time** bei Nacht

nil /nɪl/ n null

nimble /'nɪmbl/ adj (-r, -st), **~bly** adv flink

nine /naɪn/ adj neun ● n Neun f. **~teen** adj neunzehn. **~'teenth** adj neunzehnte(r, s)

ninetieth /'naɪntɪɪθ/ adj neunzigste(r, s)

ninety /'naɪntɪ/ adj neunzig

ninth /naɪnθ/ adj neunte(r, s)

nip /nɪp/ vt kneifen; (bite) beißen; **~ in the bud** (fig) im Keim ersticken ● vi (🄵: run) laufen

nipple /'nɪpl/ n Brustwarze f; (Amer: on bottle) Sauger m

nitwit /'nɪtwɪt/ n 🄵 Dummkopf m

no /nəʊ/ adv nein ● n (pl noes) Nein nt ● adj kein(e); (pl) keine; **in no time** [sehr] schnell; **no parking/smoking** Parken/Rauchen verboten; **no one = nobody**

nobility /nəʊ'bɪlətɪ/ n Adel m

noble /'nəʊbl/ adj (-r, -st) edel; (aristocratic) adlig. **~man** n Adlige(r) m

nobody /'nəʊbədɪ/ pron niemand, keiner ● n a ~ ein Niemand m

nocturnal /nɒk'tɜːnl/ adj nächtlich; (animal, bird) Nacht-

nod /nɒd/ n Nicken nt ● v (pt/pp **nodded**) ● vi nicken ● vt ~ one's head mit dem Kopf nicken

noise /nɔɪz/ n Geräusch nt; (loud) Lärm m. **~less** adj geräuschlos

noisy /'nɔɪzɪ/ adj , **-ily** adv laut; (eater) geräuschvoll

nomad /'nəʊmæd/ n Nomade m. **~ic** adj nomadisch; (life, tribe) Nomaden-

nominal /'nɒmɪnl/ adj nominell

nominat|e /'nɒmɪneɪt/ vt nominieren, aufstellen; (appoint) ernennen. **~ion** n Nominierung f; Ernennung f

nominative /'nɒmɪnətɪv/ adj & n (Gram) **~[case]** Nominativ m

nonchalant /'nɒnʃələnt/ adj nonchalant; (gesture) lässig

nondescript /'nɒndɪskrɪpt/ adj unbestimmbar; (person) unscheinbar

none /nʌn/ pron keine(r)/keins; ~ of it/this nichts davon ● adv ~ too nicht gerade; ~ too soon [um] keine Minute zu früh; ~ the less dennoch

nonentity /nɒ'nentətɪ/ n Null f

non-ex'istent adj nicht vorhanden

non-'fiction n Sachliteratur f

nonplussed /nɒn'plʌst/ adj verblüfft

nonsens|e /'nɒnsəns/ n Unsinn m. **~ical** adj unsinnig

non-'smoker n Nichtraucher m

non-'stop adv ununterbrochen;

(fly) nonstop

non-'swimmer n Nichtschwimmer m

non-'violent adj gewaltlos

noodles /'nuːdlz/ npl Bandnudeln pl

noon /nuːn/ n Mittag m; **at** ~ um 12 Uhr mittags

noose /nuːs/ n Schlinge f

nor /nɔː(r)/ adv noch ● conj auch nicht

Nordic /'nɔːdɪk/ adj nordisch

norm /nɔːm/ n Norm f

normal /'nɔːml/ adj normal. **~ity** n Normalität f. **~ly** adv normal; (usually) normalerweise

north /nɔːθ/ n Norden m; **to the** ~ **of** nördlich von ● adj Nord-, nord- ● adv nach Norden

north: N~ America n Nordamerika nt. **~-east** adj Nordost- ● n Nordosten m

norther|ly /'nɔːðəlɪ/ adj nördlich. **~n** adj nördlich. **N~n Ireland** n Nordirland nt

north: N~ 'Pole n Nordpol m. **N~ 'Sea** n Nordsee f. **~ward[s]** /-wəd[z]/ adv nach Norden. **~-west** adj Nordwest- ● n Nordwesten m

Nor|way /'nɔːweɪ/ n Norwegen nt. **~wegian** adj norwegisch ● n Norweger(in) m(f)

nose /nəʊz/ n Nase

'nosebleed n Nasenbluten nt

nostalg|ia /nɒ'stældʒɪə/ n Nostalgie f. **~ic** adj nostalgisch

nostril /'nɒstrəl/ n Nasenloch nt

nosy /'nəʊzɪ/ adj ① neugierig

---

not /nɒt/
● adverb
····▸ nicht. **I don't know** ich weiß nicht. **isn't she pretty?** ist sie nicht hübsch?

····▶ not a kein. **he is not a doctor** er ist kein Arzt. **she didn't wear a hat** sie trug keinen Hut. **there was not a person to be seen** es gab keinen Menschen zu sehen. **not a thing** gar nichts. **not a bit** kein bisschen

····▶ (in elliptical phrases) **I hope not** ich hoffe nicht. **of course not** natürlich nicht. **not at all** überhaupt nicht; (in polite reply to thanks) keine Ursache; gern geschehen. **certainly not!** auf keinen Fall! **not I** ich nicht

····▶ not ... but ... nicht ... sondern .... **it was not a small town but a big one** es war keine kleine Stadt, sondern eine große

notab|le /ˈnəʊtəbl/ adj bedeutend; (remarkable) bemerkenswert. **~ly** adv insbesondere

notation /nəʊˈteɪʃn/ n Notation f; (Mus) Notenschrift f

notch /nɒtʃ/ n Kerbe f

note /nəʊt/ n (written comment) Notiz f, Anmerkung f; (short letter) Briefchen nt, Zettel m; (bank ~) Banknote f, Schein m; (Mus) Note f; (sound) Ton m; (on piano) Taste f; **half/whole ~** (Amer) halbe/ganze Note f; **of ~** von Bedeutung; **make a ~ of** notieren ● vt beachten; (notice) bemerken (**that** dass)

'**notebook** n Notizbuch nt

noted /ˈnəʊtɪd/ adj bekannt (**for** für)

note: **~paper** n Briefpapier nt. **~worthy** adj beachtenswert

nothing /ˈnʌθɪŋ/ n, pron & adv nichts; **for ~** umsonst; **~ but** nichts als; **~ much** nicht viel; **~ interesting** nichts Interessantes

notice /ˈnəʊtɪs/ n (on board) An-

schlag m, Bekanntmachung f; (announcement) Anzeige f; (review) Kritik f; (termination of lease, employment) Kündigung f; **give [in one's] ~** kündigen; (person) jdm kündigen; **take no ~I** ignoriere es! ● vt bemerken. **~able** /-əbl/, adj, **-bly** adv merklich. **~-board** n Anschlagbrett nt

noti|fication /nəʊtɪfɪˈkeɪʃn/ n Benachrichtigung f. **~fy** vt (pt/pp **-ied**) benachrichtigen

notion /ˈnəʊʃn/ n Idee f

notorious /nəʊˈtɔːrɪəs/ adj berüchtigt

notwith'standing prep trotz (+ gen) ● adv trotzdem, dennoch

nought /nɔːt/ n Null f

noun /naʊn/ n Substantiv nt

nourish /ˈnʌrɪʃ/ vt nähren. **~ing** adj nahrhaft. **~ment** n Nahrung f

novel /ˈnɒvl/ adj neu[artig] ● n Roman m. **~ist** n Romanschriftsteller(in) m(f). **~ty** n Neuheit f

November /nəʊˈvembə(r)/ n November m

novice /ˈnɒvɪs/ n Neuling m; (Relig) Novize m/Novizin f

now /naʊ/ adv & conj jetzt; **~ [that]** jetzt, wo; **just ~** gerade, eben; **right ~** sofort; **~ and again** hin und wieder; **now, now!** na, na!

'**nowadays** adv heutzutage

nowhere /ˈnəʊ-/ adv nirgendwo, nirgends

nozzle /ˈnɒzl/ n Düse f

nuance /ˈnjuːɑ̃s/ n Nuance f

nuclear /ˈnjuːklɪə(r)/ adj Kern-. **~ de'terrent** n nukleares Abschreckungsmittel nt

nucleus /ˈnjuːklɪəs/ n (pl **-lei** /-lɪaɪ/) Kern m

nude /njuːd/ adj nackt ● n (Art) Akt m; **in the ~** nackt

n

nudge /nʌdʒ/ vt stupsen

nud|ist /'njuːdɪst/ n Nudist m.
~ity n Nacktheit f

nuisance /'njuːsns/ n Ärgernis nt;
(pest) Plage f; **be a ~** ärgerlich sein

null /nʌl/ adj **~ and void** null und
nichtig

numb /nʌm/ adj gefühllos, taub
● vt betäuben

number /'nʌmbə(r)/ n Nummer f;
(amount) Anzahl f; (Math) Zahl f
● vt nummerieren; (include) zählen
(among zu). **~-plate** n Nummernschild nt

numeral /'njuːmərl/ n Ziffer f

numerical /njuːˈmerɪkl/ adj nu-
merisch; **in ~ order** zahlenmäßig
geordnet

numerous /'njuːmərəs/ adj
zahlreich

nun /nʌn/ n Nonne f

nurse /nɜːs/ n [Kranken]schwester
f; (male) Krankenpfleger m. **children's ~** Kindermädchen nt ● vt
pflegen

nursery /'nɜːsərɪ/ n Kinderzimmer
nt; (for plants) Gärtnerei f; **[day] ~**
Kindertagesstätte f. **~ rhyme** n
Kinderreim m. **~ school** n Kindergarten m

nursing /'nɜːsɪŋ/ n Krankenpflege
f. **~ home** n Pflegeheim nt

nut /nʌt/ n Nuss f; (Techn) [Schrau-
ben]mutter f; (🄳: head) Birne f 🄳;
be ~s 🄳 spinnen 🄳. **~crackers**
npl Nussknacker m. **~meg** n Muskat m

nutrient /'njuːtrɪənt/ n Nährstoff m

nutrit|ion /njuːˈtrɪʃn/ n Ernäh-
rung f. **~ious** adj nahrhaft

'nutshell n Nussschale f; **in a ~**
(fig) kurz gesagt

nylon /'naɪlɒn/ n Nylon nt

Oo

O /əʊ/ n (Teleph) null

oak /əʊk/ n Eiche f

OAP abbr (old-age pensioner)
Rentner(in) m(f)

oar /ɔː(r)/ n Ruder nt. **~sman** n Ru-
derer m

oasis /əʊˈeɪsɪs/ n (pl oases /-siːz/)
Oase f

oath /əʊθ/ n Eid m; (swear-word)
Fluch m

oatmeal /'əʊt-/ n Hafermehl nt

oats /əʊts/ npl Hafer m; (Culin)
[rolled] ~ Haferflocken pl

obedien|ce /əˈbiːdɪəns/ n Gehor-
sam m. **~t** adj gehorsam

obey /əˈbeɪ/ vt/i gehorchen (+ dat);
befolgen (instructions, rules)

obituary /əˈbɪtjʊərɪ/ n Nachruf m;
(notice) Todesanzeige f

object¹ /'ɒbdʒɪkt/ n Gegenstand
m; (aim) Zweck m; (intention) Absicht f; (Gram) Objekt nt; **money is
no ~** Geld spielt keine Rolle

object² /əbˈdʒekt/ vi Einspruch erheben (to gegen); (be against)
etwas dagegen haben

objection /əbˈdʒekʃn/ n Einwand
m; **have no ~** nichts dagegen
haben. **~able** adj anstößig; (person) unangenehm

objectiv|e /əbˈdʒektɪv/ adj objek-
tiv ● n Ziel nt. **~ity** n Objektivität f

objector /əbˈdʒektə(r)/ n
Gegner m

obligation /ɒblɪˈgeɪʃn/ n Pflicht f;
without ~ unverbindlich

obligatory /əˈblɪgətrɪ/ adj obligatorisch; **be ~** Vorschrift sein

oblig|e /əˈblaɪdʒ/ vt verpflichten;

(*compel*) zwingen; (*do a small service*) einen Gefallen tun (+ *dat*).
~ing *adj* entgegenkommend

oblique /ə'bliːk/ *adj* schräg; (*angle*) schief; (*fig*) indirekt

obliterate /ə'blɪtəreɪt/ *vt* auslöschen

oblivion /ə'blɪvɪən/ *n* Vergessenheit *f*

oblivious /ə'blɪvɪəs/ *adj* be ~ sich (*dat*) nicht bewusst sein (*of* *gen*)

oblong /'ɒblɒŋ/ *adj* rechteckig ● *n* Rechteck *nt*

obnoxious /əb'nɒkʃəs/ *adj* widerlich

oboe /'əʊbəʊ/ *n* Oboe *f*

obscen|e /əb'siːn/ *adj* obszön. **~ity** *n* Obszönität *f*

obscur|e /əb'skjʊə(r)/ *adj* dunkel; (*unknown*) unbekannt ● *vt* verdecken; (*confuse*) verwischen. **~ity** *n* Dunkelheit *f*; Unbekanntheit *f*

observa|nce /əb'zɜːvns/ *n* (*of custom*) Einhaltung *f*. **~nt** *adj* aufmerksam. **~tion** *n* Beobachtung *f*; (*remark*) Bemerkung *f*

observatory /əb'zɜːvətrɪ/ *n* Sternwarte *f*

observe /əb'zɜːv/ *vt* beobachten; (*say, notice*) bemerken; (*keep, celebrate*) feiern; (*obey*) einhalten. **~r** *n* Beobachter *m*

obsess /əb'ses/ *vt* be **~ed by** besessen sein von. **~ion** *n* Besessenheit *f*; (*persistent idea*) fixe Idee *f*. **~ive** *adj* zwanghaft

obsolete /'ɒbsəliːt/ *adj* veraltet

obstacle /'ɒbstəkl/ *n* Hindernis *nt*

obstina|cy /'ɒbstɪnəsɪ/ *n* Starrsinn *m*. **~te** *adj* starrsinnig; (*refusal*) hartnäckig

obstruct /əb'strʌkt/ *vt* blockieren; (*hinder*) behindern. **~ion** *n* Blockierung *f*; Behinderung *f*; (*obstacle*)

Hindernis *nt*. **~ive** *adj* be **~ive** Schwierigkeiten bereiten

obtain /əb'teɪn/ *vt* erhalten. **~able** *adj* erhältlich

obtrusive /əb'truːsɪv/ *adj* aufdringlich; (*thing*) auffällig

obtuse /əb'tjuːs/ *adj* begriffsstutzig

obvious /'ɒbvɪəs/ *adj* offensichtlich, offenbar

occasion /ə'keɪʒn/ *n* Gelegenheit *f*; (*time*) Mal *nt*; (*event*) Ereignis *nt*; (*cause*) Anlass *m*, Grund *m*; **on the ~ of** anlässlich (+ *gen*)

occasional /ə'keɪʒənl/ *adj* gelegentlich. **~ly** *adv* gelegentlich, hin und wieder

occult /ɒ'kʌlt/ *adj* okkult

occupant /'ɒkjʊpənt/ *n* Bewohner(in) *m(f)*; (*of vehicle*) Insasse *m*

occupation /ɒkjʊ'peɪʃn/ *n* Beschäftigung *f*; (*job*) Beruf *m*; (*Mil*) Besetzung *f*; (*period*) Besatzung *f*. **~al** *adj* Berufs-. **~al therapy** *n* Beschäftigungstherapie *f*

occupier /'ɒkjʊpaɪə(r)/ *n* Bewohner(in) *m(f)*

occupy /'ɒkjʊpaɪ/ *vt* (*pt/pp* **occupied**) besetzen (*seat, Mil country*); einnehmen (*space*); in Anspruch nehmen (*time*); (*live in*) bewohnen; (*fig*) bekleiden (*office*); (*keep busy*) beschäftigen

occur /ə'kɜː(r)/ *vi* (*pt/pp* **occurred**) geschehen; (*exist*) vorkommen, auftreten; **it ~red to me that** es fiel mir ein, dass. **~rence** *n* Auftreten *nt*; (*event*) Ereignis *nt*

ocean /'əʊʃn/ *n* Ozean *m*

o'clock /ə'klɒk/ *adv* **[at] 7 ~ [um]** 7 Uhr

octagonal /ɒk'tægənl/ *adj* achteckig

October /ɒk'təʊbə(r)/ *n* Oktober *m*

octopus /'ɒktəpəs/ *n* (*pl* **-puses**)

Tintenfisch *m*

odd /ɒd/ *adj* (**-er, -est**) seltsam, merkwürdig; (*number*) ungerade; (*not of set*) einzeln; **forty ~ über vierzig**; **~ jobs** Gelegenheitsarbeiten *pl*; **the ~ one out** die Ausnahme; **at ~ moments** zwischendurch

odd|ity /'ɒdɪtɪ/ *n* Kuriosität *f.* **~ly** *adv* merkwürdig; **~ly enough** merkwürdigerweise **~ment** *n* (*of fabric*) Rest *m*

odds /ɒdz/ *npl* (*chances*) Chancen *pl*; **at ~** uneinig; **~ and ends** Kleinkram *m*

ode /əʊd/ *n* Ode *f*

odious /'əʊdɪəs/ *adj* widerlich

odour /'əʊdə(r)/ *n* Geruch *m.* **~less** *adj* geruchlos

---

of /ɒv/, unbetont /əv/
● *preposition*
····▸ (*indicating belonging, origin*) von (+ *dat*); genitive. **the mother of twins** die Mutter von Zwillingen. **the mother of the twins** die Mutter der Zwillinge or von den Zwillingen. **the Queen of England** die Königin von England. **a friend of mine** ein Freund von mir. **a friend of the teacher's** ein Freund des Lehrers. **the brother of her father** der Bruder ihres Vaters. **the works of Shakespeare** Shakespeares Werke. **it was nice of him** es war nett von ihm
····▸ (*made of*) aus (+ *dat*). **a dress of cotton** ein Kleid aus Baumwolle
····▸ (*following number*) **five of us** fünf von uns. **the two of us** wir zwei. **there were four of us waiting** wir waren vier, die warteten

····▸ (*followed by number, description*) von (+ *dat*). **a girl of ten** ein Mädchen von zehn Jahren. **a distance of 50 miles** eine Entfernung von 50 Meilen. **a man of character** ein Mann von Charakter. **a woman of exceptional beauty** eine Frau von außerordentlicher Schönheit. **a person of strong views** ein Mensch mit festen Ansichten

> **!** **of** is not translated after measures and in some other cases: **a pound of apples** ein Pfund Äpfel; **a cup of tea** eine Tasse Tee; **a glass of wine** ein Glas Wein; **the city of Chicago** die Stadt Chicago; **the fourth of January** der vierte Januar

off /ɒf/ *prep* von (+ *dat*); **~ the coast** vor der Küste; **get ~ the ladder/bus** von der Leiter/aus dem Bus steigen ● *adv* weg; (*button, lid, handle*) ab; (*light*) aus; (*brake*) los; (*machine*) abgeschaltet; (*tap*) zu; (*on appliance*) 'off' 'aus'; **2 kilometres ~** 2 Kilometer entfernt; **a long way ~** weit weg; (*time*) noch lange hin; **~ and on** hin und wieder; **with his hat/coat ~** ohne Hut/Mantel; **20% ~** 20% Nachlass; **be ~** (*leave*) [weg]gehen; (*Sport*) starten; (*food:*) schlecht sein; **be well ~** gut dran sein; (*financially*) wohlhabend sein; **have a day ~** einen freien Tag haben

offal /'ɒfl/ *n* (*Culin*) Innereien *pl*

> **off-Broadway** Off-Broadway ist eine Bezeichnung für das nichtkommerzielle amerikanische Theater. Diese experimentelle Gegenrichtung mit kleineren Truppen und Bühnen *i*

gewann nach 1952 an Bedeutung. Viele junge Intendanten sind nicht an kommerziellen Aufführungen interessiert, und ihre Inszenierungen finden in alten Lagerhäusern abseits des *Broadway*, der großen New Yorker Theaterstraße, statt.

offence /əˈfɛns/ n (illegal act) Vergehen nt; **give/take ~** Anstoß erregen/nehmen (**at** + dat)

offend /əˈfɛnd/ vt beleidigen. **~er** n (Jur) Straftäter m

offensive /əˈfɛnsɪv/ adj anstößig; (Mil, Sport) offensiv ● n Offensive f

offer /ˈɒfə(r)/ n Angebot nt; **on (special)** ~ im Sonderangebot ● vt anbieten (**to** dat); leisten (resistance); ~ **to do sth** sich anbieten, etw zu tun. **~ing** n Gabe f

off'hand adj brüsk; (casual) lässig

office /ˈɒfɪs/ n Büro nt; (post) Amt nt

officer /ˈɒfɪsə(r)/ n Offizier m; (official) Beamte(r) m/ Beamtin f; (police) Polizeibeamte(r) m/-beamtin f

official /əˈfɪʃl/ adj offiziell, amtlich ● n Beamte(r) m/ Beamtin f; (Sport) Funktionär m. **~ly** adv offiziell

officious /əˈfɪʃəs/ adj übereifrig

'off-licence n Wein- und Spirituosenhandlung f

off'load vt ausladen

'off-putting adj 🄳 abstoßend

off'set vt (pt/pp -set, pres p -setting) ausgleichen

'offshoot n Schössling m; (fig) Zweig m

'offshore adj (oil field) im Meer; (breeze) vom Land kommend ● adv im/ins Ausland

off'side adj (Sport) abseits

off'stage adv hinter den Kulissen

off-'white adj fast weiß

often /ˈɒfn/ adv oft; **every so ~** von Zeit zu Zeit

oh /əʊ/ int oh! ach! **oh dear!** o weh!

oil /ɔɪl/ n Öl nt; (petroleum) Erdöl nt ● vt ölen

oil: ~field n Ölfeld nt. **~painting** n Ölgemälde nt. **~ refinery** n [Erdöl]raffinerie f. **~tanker** n Öltanker m. **~ well** n Ölquelle f

oily /ˈɔɪli/ adj ölig

ointment /ˈɔɪntmənt/ n Salbe f

OK /əʊˈkeɪ/ adj & int 🄸 in Ordnung; okay ● adv (well) gut ● vt (auch **okay**) (pt/pp okayed) genehmigen

old /əʊld/ adj (-er, -est) alt; (former) ehemalig

old: ~ age n Alter nt. **~-age 'pensioner** n Rentner(in) m(f). ~ **boy** n ehemaliger Schüler. **~-fashioned** adj altmodisch. **~ girl** n ehemalige Schülerin f

olive /ˈɒlɪv/ n Olive f; (colour) Oliv nt ● adj olivgrün. **~ 'oil** n Olivenöl nt

Olympic /əˈlɪmpɪk/ adj olympisch ● n die **~s** die Olympischen Spiele pl

omelette /ˈɒmlɪt/ n Omelett nt

ominous /ˈɒmɪnəs/ adj bedrohlich

omission /əˈmɪʃn/ n Auslassung f; (failure to do) Unterlassung f

omit /əˈmɪt/ vt (pt/pp omitted)

omnipotent | opening

omnipotent | opening   480

auslassen; ~ **to do sth** es unterlassen, etw zu tun

omnipotent /ɒmˈnɪpətənt/ adj allmächtig

on /ɒn/ prep auf (+ dat/(on to) + acc); (on vertical surface) an (+ dat/(on to) + acc); (about) über (+ acc); **on Monday** [am] Montag; **on Mondays** montags; **on the first of May** am ersten Mai; **on arriving** als ich ankam; **on one's finger** am Finger; **on the right/left** rechts/links; **on the Rhine** am Rhein; **on the radio/television** im Radio/Fernsehen; **on the bus/train** im Bus/Zug; **go on the bus/train** mit dem Bus/Zug fahren; **on me** (with me) bei mir; **it's on me** 🅸 das spendiere ich ● adv (further on) weiter; (switched on) an; (brake) angezogen; (machine) angeschaltet; (on appliance) 'on' 'ein'; (light etc) **on** (film:) laufen; (event:) stattfinden; **be on at** 🅸 bedrängen (**zu** to); **it's not on** 🅸 das geht nicht; **on and on** immer weiter; **on and off** hin und wieder; **and so on** und so weiter

once /wʌns/ adv einmal; (formerly) früher; **at** ~ sofort; (at the same time) gleichzeitig; ~ **and for all** ein für alle Mal ● conj wenn; (with past tense) als

oncoming adj ~ **traffic** Gegenverkehr m

one /wʌn/ adj ein(e); (only) einzig; **not** ~ kein(e); ~ **day/evening** eines Tages/Abends ● n Eins f ● pron eine(r)/eins; (impersonal) man; **which** ~ welche(r,s); ~ **another** einander; ~ **by** ~ einzeln; ~ **never knows** man kann nie wissen

one: ~**-parent family** n Einelternfamilie f ● ~**self** pron selbst; (reflexive) sich; **by** ~**self** allein. ~**-sided**

adj einseitig. ~**-way** adj (street) Einbahn-; (ticket) einfach

onion /ˈʌnjən/ n Zwiebel f

on-line adv online

'onlooker n Zuschauer(in) m(f)

only /ˈəʊnlɪ/ adj einzige(r,s); **an** ~ **child** ein Einzelkind nt ● adv & conj nur; ~ **just** gerade erst; (barely) gerade noch

'onset n Beginn m; (of winter) Einsetzen nt

'on-shore adj (oil field) an Land; (breeze) vom Meer kommend

onward[s] /ˈɒnwəd[z]/ adv vorwärts; **from then** ~ von der Zeit an

ooze /uːz/ vi sickern

opaque /əʊˈpeɪk/ adj undurchsichtig

open /ˈəʊpən/ adj offen; **be** ~ (shop:) geöffnet sein; **in the** ~ **air** im Freien ● n **in the** ~ im Freien ● vt öffnen, aufmachen; (start, set up) eröffnen ● vi sich öffnen; (flower:) aufgehen; (shop:) öffnen, aufmachen; (be started) eröffnet werden. ~ **up** vt öffnen, aufmachen

'open day n Tag m der offenen Tür

opener /ˈəʊpənə(r)/ n Öffner m

opening /ˈəʊpənɪŋ/ n Öffnung f; (beginning) Eröffnung f; (job) Einstiegsmöglichkeit f. ~ **hours** npl Öffnungszeiten pl

open: ~**'minded** adj aufgeschlossen. ~ **'sandwich** n belegtes Brot nt

---

Open University - OU   **𝑖**
Eine britische Fernuniversität, die 1969 gegründet wurde und vor allem Berufstätigen im Fernstudium Kurse auf verschiedenem Niveau bietet. Studenten jeder Altersgruppe, selbst

solche ohne die erforderlichen Schulabschlüsse, können das Studium mit dem *Bachelor's degree* und dem *Master's degree* abschließen. Teilnehmer studieren von zu Hause und können auch an Direktunterricht teilnehmen.

opera /'ɒpərə/ n Oper f. ~ **glasses** pl Opernglas n ~**-house** n Opernhaus nt. ~**-singer** n Opernsänger(in) m(f)

operate /'ɒpəreɪt/ vt bedienen (*machine, lift*); betätigen (*lever, brake*); (*fig: run*) betreiben ● vi (*Techn*) funktionieren; (*be in action*) in Betrieb sein; (*Mil & fig*) operieren; ~ **[on]** (*Med*) operieren

operatic /ɒpə'rætɪk/ adj Opern-

operation /ɒpə'reɪʃn/ n (*see operate*) Bedienung f; Betätigung f; Operation f; **in** ~ (*Techn*) in Betrieb; **come into** ~ (*fig*) in Kraft treten; **have an** ~ (*Med*) operiert werden. ~**al** adj einsatzbereit; **be** ~**al** in Betrieb sein; (*law*:) in Kraft sein

operative /'ɒpərətɪv/ adj wirksam

operator /'ɒpəreɪtə(r)/ n (*user*) Bedienungsperson f; (*Teleph*) Vermittlung f

operetta /ɒpə'retə/ n Operette f

opinion /ə'pɪnjən/ n Meinung f; **in my** ~ meiner Meinung nach. ~**ated** adj rechthaberisch

opponent /ə'pəʊnənt/ n Gegner(in) m(f)

opportun|e /'ɒpətjuːn/ adj günstig. ~**ist** n Opportunist m

opportunity /ɒpə'tjuːnətɪ/ n Gelegenheit f

oppos|e /ə'pəʊz/ vt Widerstand leisten (+ dat); (*argue against*) sprechen gegen; **be** ~**ed to** sth gegen etw sein; **as** ~**ed to** im Gegensatz zu. ~**ing** adj gegnerisch

opposite /'ɒpəzɪt/ adj entgegengesetzt; (*house, side*) gegenüberliegend; ~ **number** (*fig*) Gegenstück nt; **the** ~ **sex** das andere Geschlecht ● n Gegenteil nt ● adv gegenüber ● prep gegenüber (+ dat)

opposition /ɒpə'zɪʃn/ n Widerstand m; (*Pol*) Opposition f

oppress /ə'pres/ vt unterdrücken. ~**ion** n Unterdrückung f. ~**ive** adj tyrannisch; (*heat*) drückend

opt /ɒpt/ vi ~ **for** sich entscheiden für

optical /'ɒptɪkl/ adj optisch

optician /ɒp'tɪʃn/ n Optiker m

optimis|m /'ɒptɪmɪzm/ n Optimismus m. ~**t** n Optimist m. ~**tic** adj, -**ally** adv optimistisch

optimum /'ɒptɪməm/ adj optimal

option /'ɒpʃn/ n Wahl f; (*Comm*) Option f. ~**al** adj auf Wunsch erhältlich; (*subject*) wahlfrei

opu|lence /'ɒpjʊləns/ n Prunk m. ~**lent** adj prunkvoll

or /ɔː(r)/ conj oder; (*after negative*) noch; **or [else]** sonst; **in a year or two** in ein bis zwei Jahren

oral /'ɔːrl/ adj mündlich; (*Med*) oral ● n Mündliche(s) nt

orange /'ɒrɪndʒ/ n Apfelsine f, Orange f; (*colour*) Orange nt ● adj orangefarben

oratorio /ɒrə'tɔːrɪəʊ/ n Oratorium nt

oratory /'ɒrətərɪ/ n Redekunst f

orbit /'ɔːbɪt/ n Umlaufbahn f ● vt umkreisen

orchard /'ɔːtʃəd/ n Obstgarten m

orche|stra /'ɔːkɪstrə/ n Orchester nt. ~**stral** adj Orchester-. ~**strate** vt orchestrieren

ordeal /ɔː'diːl/ n (*fig*) Qual f

order /'ɔːdə(r)/ n Ordnung f; (*se-*

quence) Reihenfolge f; *(condition)* Zustand m; *(command)* Befehl m; *(in restaurant)* Bestellung f; *(Comm)* Auftrag m; *(Relig, medal)* Orden m; **out of** ~ *(machine)* außer Betrieb; **in** ~ **that** damit; **in** ~ **to help** um zu helfen ● *vt (put in* ~*)* ordnen; *(command)* befehlen (+ *dat);* *(Comm, in restaurant)* bestellen; *(prescribe)* verordnen

orderly /ˈɔːdəlɪ/ *adj* ordentlich; *(not unruly)* friedlich ● *n (Mil, Med)* Sanitäter m

ordinary /ˈɔːdɪnərɪ/ *adj* gewöhnlich, normal

ore /ɔː(r)/ *n* Erz nt

organ /ˈɔːgən/ *n (Biology)* Organ nt; *(Mus)* Orgel f

organic /ɔːˈgænɪk/ *adj,* **-ally** *adv* organisch; *(without chemicals)* biodynamisch; *(crop)* biologisch angebaut; *(food)* Bio-. ~ **farming** *n* biologischer Anbau m

organism /ˈɔːgənɪzm/ *n* Organismus m

organist /ˈɔːgənɪst/ *n* Organist m

organization /ɔːgənaɪˈzeɪʃn/ *n* Organisation f

organize /ˈɔːgənaɪz/ *vt* organisieren; veranstalten *(event).* ~**r** *n* Organisator m; Veranstalter m

orgy /ˈɔːdʒɪ/ *n* Orgie f

Orient /ˈɔːrɪənt/ *n* Orient m. **o**~**al** *adj* orientalisch ● *n* Orientale m/Orientalin f

orientation /ˈɔːrɪənˈteɪʃn/ *n* Orientierung f

origin /ˈɒrɪdʒɪn/ *n* Ursprung m; *(of person, goods)* Herkunft f

original /əˈrɪdʒənl/ *adj* ursprünglich; *(not copied)* original; *(new)* originell ● *n* Original nt. ~**ity** *n* Originalität f. ~**ly** *adv* ursprünglich

originate /əˈrɪdʒɪneɪt/ *vi* entstehen

ornament /ˈɔːnəmənt/ *n* Ziergegenstand m; *(decoration)* Verzierung f. ~**al** *adj* dekorativ

ornate /ɔːˈneɪt/ *adj* reich verziert

ornithology /ɔːnɪˈθɒlədʒɪ/ *n* Vogelkunde f

orphan /ˈɔːfn/ *n* Waisenkind nt, Waise f. ~**age** *n* Waisenhaus nt

orthodox /ˈɔːθədɒks/ *adj* orthodox

ostensible /ɒˈstensəbl/ *adj,* **-bly** *adv* angeblich

ostentat|ion /ɒstenˈteɪʃn/ *n* Protzerei f ⚠. ~**ious** *adj* protzig ⚠

osteopath /ˈɒstɪəpæθ/ *n* Osteopath m

ostrich /ˈɒstrɪtʃ/ *n* Strauß m

other /ˈʌðə(r)/ *adj, pron* & *n* andere(r,s); **the** ~ **[one]** der/die/das andere; **the** ~ **two** die zwei anderen; **no** ~ sonst keine; **any** ~ **questions?** sonst noch Fragen? **every** ~ **day** jeden zweiten Tag; **the** ~ **day** neulich; **the** ~ **evening** neulich abends; **someone/something or** ~ irgendjemand/-etwas ● *adv* anders; ~ **than him** außer ihm; **somehow/ somewhere or** ~ irgendwie/irgendwo

'otherwise *adv* sonst; *(differently)* anders

ought /ɔːt/ *modal verb* I/we ~ **to stay** ich sollte/wir sollten eigentlich bleiben; **he** ~ **not to have done it** er hätte es nicht machen sollen

ounce /aʊns/ *n* Unze f *(28,35 g)*

our /ˈaʊə(r)/ *adj* unser

ours /ˈaʊəz/ *poss pron* unsere(r,s); **a friend of** ~ ein Freund von uns; **that is** ~ das gehört uns

ourselves /aʊəˈselvz/ *pron* selbst; *(reflexive)* uns; **by** ~ allein

out /aʊt/ *adv (not at home)* weg; *(outside)* draußen; *(not alight)* aus; *(unconscious)* bewusstlos; **be** ~

(sun:) scheinen; (flower) blühen; (workers) streiken; (calculation:) nicht stimmen; (Sport) aus sein; (fig: not feasible) nicht infrage kommen; ~ and about unterwegs; have it ~ with s.o. ⓘ jdn zur Rede stellen; get ~! ⓘ raus! ~ with it! ⓘ heraus damit! ● prep ~ of aus (+ dat); go ~ (of) the door zur Tür hinausgehen; be ~ of bed/ the room nicht im Bett/im Zimmer sein; ~ of breath/danger außer Atem/Gefahr; ~ of work arbeitslos; nine ~ of ten neun von zehn; be ~ of sugar keinen Zucker mehr haben

'outboard adj ~ motor Außenbordmotor m

'outbreak n Ausbruch m

'outbuilding n Nebengebäude nt

'outburst n Ausbruch m

'outcast n Ausgestoßene(r) m/f

'outcome n Ergebnis nt

'outcry n Aufschrei m [der Entrüstung]

out'dated adj überholt

out'do vt (pt -did, pp -done) übertreffen, übertrumpfen

'outdoor adj (life, sports) im Freien; ~ swimming pool Freibad nt

out'doors adv draußen; go ~ nach draußen gehen

'outer adj äußere(r,s)

'outfit n Ausstattung f; (clothes) Ensemble nt; (ⓘ: organization) Laden m

'outgoing adj ausscheidend; (mail) ausgehend; (sociable) kontaktfreudig, ~s npl Ausgaben pl

out'grow vi (pt -grew, pp -grown) herauswachsen aus

outing /'autɪŋ/ n Ausflug m

'outlaw n Geächtete(r) m/f ● vt

ächten

'outlay n Auslagen pl

'outlet n Abzug m; (for water) Abfluss m; (fig) Ventil nt; (Comm) Absatzmöglichkeit f

'outline n Umriss m; (summary) kurze Darstellung f ● vt umreißen

out'live vt überleben

'outlook n Aussicht f; (future prospect) Aussichten pl; (attitude) Einstellung f

out'moded adj überholt

out'number vt zahlenmäßig überlegen sein (+ dat)

'out-patient n ambulanter Patient m

'outpost n Vorposten m

'output n Leistung f; Produktion f

'outrage n Gräueltat f; (fig) Skandal m; (indignation) Empörung f. ~ous adj empörend

'outright¹ adj völlig, total; (refusal) glatt

out'right² adv ganz; (at once) sofort; (frankly) offen

'outset n Anfang m

'outside¹ adj äußere(r,s); ~ wall Außenwand f ● n Außenseite f; from the ~ von außen; at the ~ höchstens

out'side² adv außen; (out of doors) draußen; go ~ nach draußen gehen ● prep außerhalb (+ gen); (in front of) vor (+ dat/acc)

'outsider n Außenseiter m

'outsize adj übergroß

'outskirts npl Rand m

out'spoken adj offen; be ~ kein Blatt vor den Mund nehmen

out'standing adj hervorragend; (conspicuous) bemerkenswert; (Comm) ausstehend

out'stretched adj ausgestreckt

out'vote vt überstimmen

'outward /-wəd/ adj äußerlich; ~ **journey** Hinreise f ● adv nach außen. ~**ly** adv nach außen hin, äußerlich. ~**s** adv nach außen

out'wit vt (pt/pp -**witted**) überlisten

oval /'əʊvl/ adj oval ● n Oval nt

> **Oval Office** Das *Oval Office*
> ist das Büro des amerikanischen Präsidenten. Es befindet sich im westlichen Flügel des Weißen Hauses und sein Name bezieht sich auf die ovale Form des Raumes. George Washington (1. Präsident der USA) bestand auf ein ovales Büro, damit er bei Besprechungen allen Anwesenden in die Augen sehen konnte.

---

ovation /əʊ'veɪʃn/ n Ovation f

oven /'ʌvn/ n Backofen m

over /'əʊvə(r)/ prep über (+ acc/ dat); ~ **dinner** beim Essen; ~ **the phone** am Telefon; ~ **the page** auf der nächsten Seite ● adv (remaining) übrig; (ended) zu Ende; ~ **again** noch einmal; ~ **and** ~ immer wieder; ~ **here/there** hier/da drüben; **all** ~ (everywhere) überall; **it's all** ~ es ist vorbei; **I ache all** ~ mir tut alles weh

overall[1] /'əʊvərɔːl/ n Kittel m; ~**s** pl Overall m

overall[2] /əʊvər'ɔːl/ adj gesamt; (general) allgemein ● adv insgesamt

over'balance vi das Gleichgewicht verlieren

over'bearing adj herrisch

'overboard adv (Naut) über Bord

'overcast adj bedeckt

over'charge vt ~ **s.o.** jdm zu viel berechnen ● vi zu viel verlangen

'overcoat n Mantel m

over'come vt (pt -**came**, pp -**come**) überwinden; **be** ~ **by** überwältigt werden von

over'crowded adj überfüllt

over'do vt (pt -**did**, pp -**done**) übertreiben; (cook too long) zu lange kochen; ~ **it** (![1]: do too much) sich übernehmen

'overdose n Überdosis f

'overdraft n Konto überziehung f; **have an** ~ sein Konto überzogen haben

over'due adj überfällig

over'estimate vt überschätzen

'overflow[1] n Überschuss m; (outlet) Überlauf m; ~ **car park** zusätzlicher Parkplatz m

over'flow[2] vi überlaufen

over'grown adj (garden) überwachsen

'overhang[1] n Überhang m

over'hang[2] vt/i (pt/pp -**hung**) überhängen (über + acc)

'overhaul[1] n Überholung f

over'haul[2] vt (Techn) überholen

over'head[1] adv oben

'overhead[2] adj Ober-; (ceiling) Decken-. ~**s** npl allgemeine Unkosten pl

over'hear vt (pt/pp -**heard**) mit anhören (conversation)

over'heat vi zu heiß werden

over'joyed adj überglücklich

'overland adj & adv /-'-'-/ auf dem Landweg; ~ **route** Landroute f

over'lap vi (pt/pp -**lapped**) sich überschneiden

'overleaf adv umseitig

over'load vt überladen

over'look vt überblicken; (fail to see, ignore) übersehen

485

overnight | oyster

over'night[1] *adv* über Nacht; **stay ~** übernachten

'overnight[2] *adj* Nacht-; **~ stay** Übernachtung *f*

'overpass *n* Überführung *f*

over'pay *vt* (*pt/pp* **-paid**) überbezahlen

over'populated *adj* übervölkert

over'power *vt* überwältigen. **~ing** *adj* überwältigend

over'priced *adj* zu teuer

over'rated *adj* überbewertet

overre'act *vi* überreagieren. **~ion** *n* Überreaktion *f*

over'riding *adj* Haupt-

over'rule *vt* ablehnen; **we were ~d** wir wurden überstimmt

over'run *vt* (*pt* **-ran**, *pp* **-run**, *pres p* **-running**) überrennen; überschreiten (*time*); **be ~ with** überlaufen sein von

over'seas[1] *adv* in Übersee; **go ~** nach Übersee gehen

'overseas[2] *adj* Übersee-

over'see *vt* (*pt* **-saw**, *pp* **-seen**) beaufsichtigen

over'shadow *vt* überschatten

over'shoot *vt* (*pt/pp* **-shot**) hinausschießen über (+ *acc*)

'oversight *n* Versehen *nt*

over'sleep *vi* (*pt/pp* **-slept**) [sich] verschlafen

over'step *vt* (*pt/pp* **-stepped**) überschreiten

overt /əʊˈvɜːt/ *adj* offen

over'take *vt/i* (*pt* **-took**, *pp* **-taken**) überholen

over'throw *vt* (*pt* **-threw**, *pp* **-thrown**) (*Pol*) stürzen

'overtime *n* Überstunden *pl* ● *adv* **work ~** Überstunden machen

over'tired *adj* übermüdet

overture /ˈəʊvətjʊə(r)/ *n* (*Mus*) Ouvertüre *f*; **~s** *pl* (*fig*) Annäherungsversuche *pl*

over'turn *vt* umstoßen ● *vi* umkippen

over'weight *adj* übergewichtig; **be ~** Übergewicht haben

overwhelm /-ˈwelm/ *vt* überwältigen. **~ing** *adj* überwältigend

over'work *n* Überarbeitung *f* ● *vt* überfordern ● *vi* sich überarbeiten

over'wrought *adj* überreizt

ow|e /əʊ/ *vt* schulden/ (*fig*) verdanken ([to] s.o. jdm); **~e s.o. sth** jdm etw schuldig sein. **'~ing to** *prep* wegen (+ *gen*)

owl /aʊl/ *n* Eule *f*

own[1] /əʊn/ *adj* & *pron* eigen; **it's my ~** es gehört mir; **a car of my ~** mein eigenes Auto; **on one's ~** allein; **get one's ~ back** [T] sich revanchieren

own[2] *vt* besitzen; **I don't ~ it** es gehört mir nicht. **~ up** *vi* es zugeben

owner /ˈəʊnə(r)/ *n* Eigentümer(in) *m(f)*, Besitzer(in) *m(f)*; (*of shop*) Inhaber(in) *m(f)*. **~ship** *n* Besitz *m*

> ### Oxbridge *i*
> Eine Wortbildung aus den Namen Oxford und Cambridge. Diese umgangssprachliche Zusammensetzung wird als Sammelbegriff für die zwei Eliteuniversitäten in England verwendet, um sie von anderen Hochschulen zu unterscheiden. Oxford und Cambridge sind die ältesten britischen Universitäten mit dem besten akademischen Ruf. Oxbridge-Absolventen werden häufig von Arbeitgebern bevorzugt.

oxygen /ˈɒksɪdʒən/ *n* Sauerstoff *m*

oyster /ˈɔɪstə(r)/ *n* Auster *f*

Pp

pace /peɪs/ n Schritt m; (speed)
Tempo nt; **keep ~ with** Schritt halten mit ● vi **~ up and down** auf
und ab gehen. **~maker** n (Sport &
Med) Schrittmacher m

Pacific /pə'sɪfɪk/ adj & n **the ~**
[Ocean] der Pazifik

pacifist /'pæsɪfɪst/ n Pazifist m

pacify /'pæsɪfaɪ/ vt (pt/pp -ied) beruhigen

pack /pæk/ n Packung f; (Mil) Tornister m; (of cards) [Karten]spiel nt;
(gang) Bande f; (of hounds) Meute f;
(of wolves) Rudel nt; **a ~ of lies** ein
Haufen Lügen ● vt/i packen, einpacken (article), **be ~ed** (crowded)
[gedrängt] voll sein. **~ up** vt einpacken ● vi ⚠ (machine:) kaputtgehen

package /'pækɪdʒ/ n Paket nt. **~
holiday** n Pauschalreise f

packet /'pækɪt/ n Päckchen n

packing /'pækɪŋ/ n Verpackung f

pact /pækt/ n Pakt m

pad /pæd/ n Polster nt; (for writing)
[Schreib]block m ● vt (pt/pp padded) polstern

padding /'pædɪŋ/ n Polsterung f;
(in written work) Füllwerk nt

paddle[1] /'pædl/ n Paddel nt ● vt
(row) paddeln

paddle[2] vi waten

paddock /'pædək/ n Koppel f

padlock /'pædlɒk/ n Vorhängeschloss nt ● vt mit einem Vorhängeschloss verschließen

paediatrician /piːdɪə'trɪʃn/ n
Kinderarzt m /-ärztin f

pagan /'peɪgən/ adj heidnisch ● n
Heide m/Heidin f

page[1] /peɪdʒ/ n Seite f

page[2] n (boy) Page m ● vt ausrufen
(person)

paid /peɪd/ see pay ● adj bezahlt;
put ~ to ⚠ zunichte machen

pail /peɪl/ n Eimer m

pain /peɪn/ n Schmerz m; **be in ~**
Schmerzen haben; **take ~s** sich
(dat) Mühe geben; **~ in the neck**
⚠ Nervensäge f

pain: **~ful** adj schmerzhaft; (fig)
schmerzlich. **~killer** n schmerzstil-
lendes Mittel nt. **~less** adj
schmerzlos

painstaking /'peɪnzteɪkɪŋ/ adj
sorgfältig

paint /peɪnt/ n Farbe f ● vt/i streichen; (artist:) malen. **~brush** n Pinsel m. **~er** n Maler m; (decorator)
Anstreicher m. **~ing** n Malerei f;
(picture) Gemälde nt

pair /peə/ n Paar nt; **~ of trousers** Hose f ● vi **~ off** Paare bilden

pajamas /pə'dʒɑːməz/ n pl (Amer)
Schlafanzug m

Pakistan /pɑːkɪ'stɑːn/ n Pakistan
nt. **~i** adj pakistanisch ● n Pakista-
ner(in) m(f)

pal /pæl/ n Freund(in) m(f)

palace /'pælɪs/ n Palast m

palatable /'pælətəbl/ adj
schmackhaft

palate /'pælət/ n Gaumen m

palatial /pə'leɪʃl/ adj palastartig

pale adj (-r, -st) blass ● vi blass
werden. **~ness** n Blässe f

Palestin|e /'pælɪstaɪn/ n Palästina
nt. **~ian** adj palästinensisch ● n Pa-
lästinenser(in) m(f)

palette /'pælɪt/ n Palette f

palm /pɑːm/ n Handfläche f; (tree,
symbol) Palme f ● vt **~ sth off on
s.o.** jdm etw andrehen. **P~Sunday**
n Palmsonntag m

palpable /'pælpəbl/ adj tastbar; (*perceptible*) spürbar

palpitations /pælpɪ'teɪʃnz/ npl Herzklopfen nt

paltry /'pɔːltrɪ/ adj armselig

pamper /'pæmpə(r)/ vt verwöhnen

pamphlet /'pæmflɪt/ n Broschüre f

pan /pæn/ n Pfanne f; (*saucepan*) Topf m; (*of scales*) Schale f

panacea /pænə'siːə/ n Allheilmittel nt

'pancake n Pfannkuchen m

panda /'pændə/ n Panda m

pandemonium /pændɪ'məʊnɪəm/ n Höllenlärm m

pane /peɪn/ n [Glas]scheibe f

panel /'pænl/ n Tafel f; ~ **of experts** Expertenrunde f; ~ **of judges** Jury f. **~ling** n Täfelung f

pang /pæŋ/ n ~**s of hunger** Hungergefühl nt; ~**s of conscience** Gewissensbisse pl

panic /'pænɪk/ n Panik f ● vi (pt/pp **panicked**) in Panik geraten. **~-stricken** adj von Panik ergriffen

panoram|a /pænə'rɑːmə/ n Panorama nt. **~ic** adj Panorama-

pansy /'pænzɪ/ n Stiefmütterchen nt

pant /pænt/ vi keuchen; (*dog:*) hecheln

panther /'pænθə(r)/ n Panther m

panties /'pæntɪz/ npl [Damen]slip m

pantomime /'pæntəmaɪm/ n [zu Weihnachten aufgeführte] Märchenvorstellung f

pantry /'pæntrɪ/ n Speisekammer f

pants /pænts/ npl Unterhose f; (*woman's*) Schlüpfer m; (*trousers*) Hose f

'pantyhose n (*Amer*)

Strumpfhose f

paper /'peɪpə(r)/ n Papier nt; (*newspaper*) Zeitung f; (*exam*) Testbogen m; (*exam*) Klausur f; (*treatise*) Referat nt; ~**s** pl (*documents*) Unterlagen pl; (*for identification*) [Ausweis]papiere pl ● vt tapezieren

paper: ~**back** n Taschenbuch nt. ~**-clip** n Büroklammer f. ~**weight** n Briefbeschwerer m. ~**work** n Schreibarbeit f

par /pɑː(r)/ n (*Golf*) Par nt; **on a** ~ gleichwertig (**with** dat)

parable /'pærəbl/ n Gleichnis nt

parachut|e /'pærəʃuːt/ n Fallschirm m ● vi [mit dem Fallschirm] abspringen. ~**ist** n Fallschirmspringer m

parade /pə'reɪd/ n Parade f; (*procession*) Festzug m ● vt (*show off*) zur Schau stellen

paradise /'pærədaɪs/ n Paradies nt

paradox /'pærədɒks/ n Paradox nt. ~**ical** paradox

paraffin /'pærəfɪn/ n Paraffin nt

paragraph /'pærəgrɑːf/ n Absatz m

parallel /'pærəlel/ adj & adv parallel ● n (*Geog*) Breitenkreis m; (*fig*) Parallele f

Paralympics /pærə'lɪmpɪks/ npl **the** ~ die Paralympics pl

paralyse /'pærəlaɪz/ vt lähmen; (*fig*) lahmlegen

paralysis /pə'ræləsɪs/ n (pl **-ses** /-siːz/) Lähmung f

paramedic /pærə'medɪk/ n Rettungssanitäter(in) m(f)

parameter /pə'ræmɪtə(r)/ n Parameter m, Rahmen m

paranoid /'pærənɔɪd/ adj [krankhaft] misstrauisch

parapet /'pærəpɪt/ n Brüstung f

P

paraphernalia /pærəfə'neɪlɪə/ n
Kram m

parasite /'pærəsaɪt/ n Parasit m,
Schmarotzer m

paratrooper /'pærətru:pə(r)/ n
Fallschirmjäger m

parcel /'pɑːsl/ n Paket nt

parch /pɑːtʃ/ vt austrocknen; **be
~ed** (person:) einen furchtbaren
Durst haben

parchment /'pɑːtʃmənt/ n Pergament nt

pardon /'pɑːdn/ n Verzeihung f;
(Jur) Begnadigung f; **~?** 🔢 bitte? I
beg your ~ wie bitte? (sorry) Verzeihung! ● vt verzeihen; (Jur) be-
gnadigen

parent /'peərənt/ n Elternteil m;
~s pl Eltern pl. **~al** adj elterlich

parenthesis /pə'renθəsɪs/ n (pl
-ses /-siːz/) Klammer f

parish /'pærɪʃ/ n Gemeinde f.
~ioner n Gemeindemitglied nt

park /pɑːk/ n Park m ● vt/i parken.
~-and-ride n Park-and-ride-Platz m

parking /'pɑːkɪŋ/ n Parken nt; **'no
~'** 'Parken verboten'. **~-lot** n
(Amer) Parkplatz m. **~-meter** n
Parkuhr f. **~ space** n Parkplatz m

parliament /'pɑːləmənt/ n Parlament nt. **~ary** adj parlamentarisch

> **Parliament** Das britische
> Parlament ist die oberste
> gesetzgebende Gewalt in
> Großbritannien und besteht aus
> dem Souverän (dem König oder
> der Königin), dem House of Lords
> (Oberhaus) und dem House of
> Commons (Unterhaus). Die Partei
> mit der Mehrheit im Unterhaus bil-
> det die Regierung. ▷DÁIL ÉI-
> REANN, ▷SCOTTISH PARLIAMENT,
> ▷WELSH ASSEMBLY.

parochial /pə'rəʊkɪəl/ adj Ge-

meinde-; (fig) beschränkt

parody /'pærədɪ/ n Parodie f ● vt
(pt/pp -ied) parodieren

parole /pə'rəʊl/ n **on ~** auf Bewährung

parquet /'pɑːkeɪ/ n **~ floor** Parkett nt

parrot /'pærət/ n Papagei m

parsley /'pɑːslɪ/ n Petersilie f

parsnip /'pɑːsnɪp/ n Pastinake f

parson /'pɑːsn/ n Pfarrer m

part /pɑːt/ n Teil m; (Techn) Teil nt;
(area) Gegend f; (Theat) Rolle f;
(Mus) Part m; **spare ~** Ersatzteil nt;
for my ~ meinerseits; **on the ~ of**
vonseiten (+ gen); **take s.o.'s ~** für
jdn Partei ergreifen; **take ~ in** teilnehmen an (+ dat) ● adv teils ● vt
trennen; scheiteln (hair) ● vi
(people:) sich trennen; **~ with** sich
trennen von

partial /'pɑːʃl/ adj Teil-; **be ~ to**
mögen. **-ly** adv teilweise

participant /pɑː'tɪsɪpənt/ n Teil-
nehmer(in) m(f). **~ate** vi teilnehmen (**in** an + dat). **~ation** n Teilnahme f

particle /'pɑːtɪkl/ n Körnchen nt;
(Phys) Partikel m; (Gram) Partikel f

particular /pə'tɪkjʊlə(r)/ adj be-
sondere(r,s); (precise) genau; (fastidious) penibel; **in ~** besonders.
-ly adv besonders. **~s** npl nähere
Angaben pl

parting /'pɑːtɪŋ/ n Abschied m; (in
hair) Scheitel m

partition /pɑː'tɪʃn/ n Trennwand
f; (Pol) Teilung f ● vt teilen

partly /'pɑːtlɪ/ adv teilweise

partner /'pɑːtnə(r)/ n Partner(in)
m(f); (Comm) Teilhaber m. **~ship**
n Partnerschaft f; (Comm) Teilhaber-
schaft f

partridge /'pɑːtrɪdʒ/ n Rebhuhn nt

part-'time adj & adv Teilzeit-; **be or work ~** Teilzeitarbeit machen

party /'pɑːtɪ/ n Party f, Fest nt; (group) Gruppe f; (Pol, Jur) Partei f

pass /pɑːs/ n Ausweis m; (Geog, Sport) Pass m; (Sch) ≈ ausreichend; **get a ~** bestehen ● vt vorbeigehen/-fahren an (+ dat); (overtake) überholen; (hand) reichen; (Sport) abgeben, abspielen; (approve) annehmen; (exceed) übersteigen; bestehen (exam); machen (remark); fällen (judgement); (Jur) verhängen (sentence); **~ the time** sich (dat) die Zeit vertreiben; **~ one's hand over sth** mit der Hand über etw (acc) fahren ● vi vorbeigehen/-fahren; (get by) vorbeikommen; (overtake) überholen; (time:) vergehen; (in exam) bestehen; **~ away** vi sterben. **~ down** vt heruntergeben. **~ out** vi ohnmächtig werden. **~ round** vt herumreichen. **~ up** vt heraufreichen; (🗊: miss) vorübergehen lassen

passable /'pɑːsəbl/ adj (road) befahrbar; (satisfactory) passabel

passage /'pæsɪdʒ/ n Durchgang m; (corridor) Gang m; (voyage) Überfahrt f; (in book) Passage f

passenger /'pæsɪndʒə(r)/ n Fahrgast m; (Naut, Aviat) Passagier m; (in car) Mitfahrer m. **~ seat** n Beifahrersitz m

passer-by /pɑːsə'baɪ/ n (pl -s-by) Passant(in) m(f)

passion /'pæʃn/ n Leidenschaft f. **~ate** adj leidenschaftlich

passive /'pæsɪv/ adj passiv ● n Passiv nt

pass: **~port** n [Reise]pass m. **~word** n Kennwort nt; (Mil) Losung f

past /pɑːst/ adj vergangene(r,s); (former) ehemalig; **that's all ~** das

ist jetzt vorbei ● n Vergangenheit f ● prep an (+ dat) ... vorbei; (after) nach; **at ten ~ two** um zehn nach zwei ● adv vorbei; **go ~** vorbeigehen

pasta /'pæstə/ n Nudeln pl

paste /peɪst/ n Brei m; (adhesive) Kleister m; (jewellery) Strass m ● vt kleistern

pastel /'pæstl/ n Pastellfarbe f; (drawing) Pastell nt ● attrib Pastell-

pastime /'pɑːstaɪm/ n Zeitvertreib m

pastr|y /'peɪstrɪ/ n Teig m; **cakes and ~ies** Kuchen und Gebäck

pasture /'pɑːstʃə(r)/ n Weide f

pasty¹ /'pæstɪ/ n Pastete f

pat /pæt/ n Klaps m; (of butter) Stückchen nt ● vt (pt/pp patted) tätscheln; **~ s.o. on the back** jdm auf die Schulter klopfen

patch /pætʃ/ n Flicken m; (spot) Fleck m; **not a ~ on** 🗊 gar nicht zu vergleichen mit ● vt flicken. **~ up** vt [zusammen]flicken; beilegen (quarrel)

patchy /'pætʃɪ/ adj ungleichmäßig

patent /'peɪtnt/ n Patent nt ● vt patentieren. **~ leather** n Lackleder nt

paternal /pə'tɜːnl/ adj väterlich

path /pɑːθ/ n (pl ~s /pɑːðz/) [Fuß]weg m, Pfad m; (orbit, track) Bahn f; (fig) Weg m

pathetic /pə'θetɪk/ adj mitleiderregend; (attempt) erbärmlich

patience /'peɪʃns/ n Geduld f; (game) Patience f

patient /'peɪʃnt/ adj geduldig ● n Patient(in) m(f)

patio /'pætɪəʊ/ n Terrasse f

patriot /'pætrɪət/ n Patriot(in) m(f). **~ic** adj patriotisch. **~ism** n Patriotismus m

patrol /pəˈtrəʊl/ n Patrouille f ● vt/i patrouillieren [in (+ dat)]; (police:) auf Streife gehen/fahren [in (+ dat)]. ~ car n Streifenwagen m

patron /ˈpeɪtrən/ n Gönner m; (of charity) Schirmherr m; (of the arts) Mäzen m; (customer) Kunde m/Kundin f; (Theat) Besucher m. ~age n Schirmherrschaft f

patronize /ˈpætrənaɪz/ vt (fig) herablassend behandeln. ~ing adj gönnerhaft

patter n (speech) Gerede nt

pattern /ˈpætn/ n Muster nt

paunch /pɔːntʃ/ n [Schmer]-bauch m

pause /pɔːz/ n Pause f ● vi innehalten

pave /peɪv/ vt pflastern; ~ the way den Weg bereiten (for dat). ~ment n Bürgersteig m

paw /pɔː/ n Pfote f; (of large animal) Pranke f, Tatze f

pawn¹ /pɔːn/ n (Chess) Bauer m; (fig) Schachfigur f

pawn² vt verpfänden. ~ broker n Pfandleiher m

pay /peɪ/ n Lohn m; (salary) Gehalt nt; **be in the** ~ **of** bezahlt werden von ● v (pt/pp paid) ● vt bezahlen; zahlen (money); ~ **s.o. a visit** jdm einen Besuch abstatten; ~ **s.o. a compliment** jdm ein Kompliment machen ● vi zahlen; (be profitable) sich bezahlt machen; (fig) sich lohnen; ~ **for sth** etw bezahlen. ~ **back** vt zurückzahlen. ~ **in** vt einzahlen. ~ **off** vt abzahlen (debt) ● vi (fig) sich auszahlen

payable /ˈpeɪəbl/ adj zahlbar; **make** ~ **to** ausstellen auf (+ acc)

payment /ˈpeɪmənt/ n Bezahlung f; (amount) Zahlung f

pea /piː/ n Erbse f

peace /piːs/ n Frieden m; **for my** ~ **of mind** zu meiner eigenen Beruhigung

peace|ful adj friedlich. ~maker n Friedensstifter m

peach /piːtʃ/ n Pfirsich m

peacock /ˈpiːkɒk/ n Pfau m

peak /piːk/ n Gipfel m; (fig) Höhepunkt m. ~ed **'cap** n Schirmmütze f. ~ **hours** npl Hauptbelastungszeit f; (for traffic) Hauptverkehrszeit f

peal /piːl/ n (of bells) Glockengeläut nt; ~s **of laughter** schallendes Gelächter nt

'peanut n Erdnuss f

pear /peə(r)/ n Birne f

pearl /pɜːl/ n Perle f

peasant /ˈpeznt/ n Bauer m

peat /piːt/ n Torf m

pebble /ˈpebl/ n Kieselstein m

peck /pek/ n Schnabelhieb m; (kiss) flüchtiger Kuss m ● vt/i picken/(nip) hacken (at an)

peculiar /prˈkjuːlɪə(r)/ adj eigenartig, seltsam; ~ **to** eigentümlich (+ dat). ~ity n Eigenart f

pedal /ˈpedl/ n Pedal nt ● vt fahren (bicycle) ● vi treten

pedantic /prˈdæntɪk/ adj, -ally adv pedantisch

pedestal /ˈpedɪstl/ n Sockel m

pedestrian /prˈdestrɪən/ n Fußgänger(in) m(f) ● adj (fig) prosaisch. ~ **'crossing** n Fußgängerüberweg m. ~ **'precinct** n Fußgängerzone f

pedigree /ˈpedɪgriː/ n Stammbaum m ● attrib (animal) Rasse-

pedlar /ˈpedlə(r)/ n Hausierer m

peek /piːk/ vi 🔟 gucken

peel /piːl/ n Schale f ● vt schälen; ● vi (skin:) sich schälen; (paint:) abblättern. ~ ings npl Schalen pl

peep /piːp/ n kurzer Blick m ● vi gucken. ~ hole n Guckloch nt

peer[1] /pɪə(r)/ vi ~ **at** forschend ansehen

peer[2] n Peer m; **his** ~**s** pl seinesgleichen

peg /peg/ n (hook) Haken m; (for tent) Pflock m, Hering m; (for clothes) [Wäsche]klammer f; **off the** ~ [f] von der Stange

pejorative /prɪˈdʒɒrətɪv/ adj abwertend

pelican /ˈpelɪkən/ n Pelikan m

pellet /ˈpelɪt/ n Kügelchen nt

pelt[1] /pelt/ n (skin) Pelz m, Fell nt

pelt[2] vt bewerfen ● vi ~ [**down**] (rain:) [hernieder]prasseln

pelvis /ˈpelvɪs/ n (Anat) Becken nt

pen[1] /pen/ n (for animals) Hürde f

pen[2] n Federhalter m; (ballpoint) Kugelschreiber m

penal /ˈpiːnl/ adj Straf-. ~**ize** vt bestrafen; (fig) benachteiligen

penalty /ˈpenltɪ/ n Strafe f; (fine) Geldstrafe f; (Sport) Strafstoß m; (Football) Elfmeter m

penance /ˈpenəns/ n Buße f

pence /pens/ see penny

pencil /ˈpensɪl/ n Bleistift m ● vt (pt/pp **pencilled**) mit Bleistift schreiben. ~**-sharpener** n Bleistiftspitzer m

pendulum /ˈpendjʊləm/ n Pendel m

penetrat|e /ˈpenɪtreɪt/ vt durchdringen; ~**e into** eindringen in (+ acc). ~**ing** adj durchdringend. ~**ion** n Durchdringen nt

'penfriend n Brieffreund(in) m(f)

penguin /ˈpeŋgwɪn/ n Pinguin m

penicillin /penɪˈsɪlɪn/ n Penizillin nt

peninsula /pəˈnɪnsjʊlə/ n Halbinsel f

penis /ˈpiːnɪs/ n Penis m

penitentiary /penɪˈtenʃərɪ/ n

(Amer) Gefängnis nt

pen: ~**knife** n Taschenmesser nt. ~**-name** n Pseudonym nt

penniless /ˈpenɪlɪs/ adj mittellos

penny /ˈpenɪ/ n (pl pence; single coins pennies) Penny m; (Amer) Centstück nt; **the** ~**'s dropped** [f] der Groschen ist gefallen

pension /ˈpenʃn/ n Rente f; (of civil servant) Pension f. ~**er** n Rentner(in) m(f); Pensionär(in) m(f)

pensive /ˈpensɪv/ adj nachdenklich

pent-up /ˈpentʌp/ adj angestaut

penultimate /peˈnʌltɪmət/ adj vorletzte(r,s)

people /ˈpiːpl/ npl Leute pl, Menschen pl; (citizens) Bevölkerung f; **the** ~ das Volk; **English** ~ die Engländer; ~ **say** man sagt; **for four** ~ für vier Personen ● vt bevölkern

pepper /ˈpepə(r)/ n Pfeffer m; (vegetable) Paprika m

pepper: ~**mint** n Pfefferminz nt; (Bot) Pfefferminze f. ~**pot** n Pfefferstreuer m

per /pɜː(r)/ prep pro; ~ **cent** Prozent nt

percentage /pəˈsentɪdʒ/ n Prozentsatz m; (part) Teil m

perceptible /pəˈseptəbl/ adj wahrnehmbar

percept|ion /pəˈsepʃn/ n Wahrnehmung f. ~**ive** adj feinsinnig

perch[1] /pɜːtʃ/ n Stange f ● vi (bird:) sich niederlassen

perch[2] n inv (fish) Barsch m

percussion /pəˈkʌʃn/ n Schlagzeug nt. ~ **instrument** n Schlaginstrument nt

perennial /pəˈreniəl/ adj (problem) immer wiederkehrend ● n (Bot) mehrjährige Pflanze f

perfect[1] /ˈpɜːfɪkt/ adj perfekt, vollkommen; ([f]: utter) völlig ● n

(Gram) Perfekt nt

perfect² /pə'fekt/ vt vervollkomm-nen. ~ion n Vollkommenheit f; **to** ~ion perfekt

perfectly /'pɜːfɪktlɪ/ adv perfekt; *(completely)* vollkommen, völlig

perforated /'pɜːfəreɪtɪd/ adj per-foriert

perform /pə'fɔːm/ vt ausführen; erfüllen *(duty)* *(Theat)* aufführen *(play)*; spielen *(role)* ● vi *(Theat)* auf-treten; *(Techn)* laufen. ~ance n Aufführung f; *(at theatre, cinema)* Vorstellung f; *(Techn)* Leistung f. ~er n Künstler(in) m(f)

perfume /'pɜːfjuːm/ n Parfüm nt; *(smell)* Duft m

perhaps /pə'hæps/ adv vielleicht

perilous /'perələs/ adj gefährlich

perimeter /pə'rɪmɪtə(r)/ n [äußere] Grenze f; *(Geometry)* Um-fang m

period /'pɪərɪəd/ n Periode f; *(Sch)* Stunde f; *(full stop)* Punkt m ● attrib *(costume)* zeitgenössisch; *(furniture)* stilecht. ~ic adj, -ally adv periodisch. ~ical n Zeitschrift f

peripheral /pə'rɪfərl/ adj neben-sächlich. ~y n Peripherie f

perish /'perɪʃ/ vi *(rubber:)* verrot-ten; *(food:)* verderben; *(to die)* ums Leben kommen. ~able adj leicht verderblich. ~ing adj (🛈: *cold*) eiskalt

perjur|e /'pɜːdʒə(r)/ vt ~e oneself einen Meineid leisten. ~y n Mein-eid m

perk¹ /pɜːk/ n 🛈 [Sonder]vergün-stigung f

perk² vi ~ up munter werden

perm /pɜːm/ n Dauerwelle f ● vt ~ s.o.'s hair jdm eine Dauerwelle machen

permanent /'pɜːmənənt/ adj ständig; *(job, address)* fest. ~ly adv

ständig; *(work, live)* dauernd, per-manent; *(employed)* fest

permissible /pə'mɪsəbl/ adj erlaubt

permission /pə'mɪʃn/ n Er-laubnis f

permit¹ /pə'mɪt/ vt *(pt/pp -mitted)* erlauben (**s.o.** jdm)

permit² /'pɜːmɪt/ n Geneh-migung f

perpendicular /pɜːpən'dɪkjʊlə(r)/ adj senkrecht ● n Senk-rechte f

perpetual /pə'petjʊəl/ adj stän-dig, dauernd

perpetuate /pə'petjʊeɪt/ vt be-wahren; verewigen *(error)*

perplex /pə'pleks/ vt verblüffen. ~ed adj verblüfft

persecut|e /'pɜːsɪkjuːt/ vt verfol-gen. ~ion n Verfolgung f

perseverance /pɜːsɪ'vɪərəns/ n Ausdauer f

persevere /pɜːsɪ'vɪə(r)/ vi beharr-lich weitermachen

Persia /'pɜːʃə/ n Persien m

Persian /'pɜːʃn/ adj persisch; *(cat, carpet)* Perser-

persist /pə'sɪst/ vi beharrlich wei-termachen; *(continue)* anhalten; *(view:)* weiter bestehen; ~ **in doing sth** dabei bleiben, etw zu tun. ~ence n Beharrlichkeit f. ~ent adj beharrlich; *(continuous)* anhaltend

person /'pɜːsn/ n Person f; **in** ~ persönlich

personal /'pɜːsənl/ adj persönlich. ~ 'hygiene n Körperpflege f

personality /pɜːsə'nælətɪ/ n Per-sönlichkeit f

personify /pə'sɒnɪfaɪ/ vt *(pt/pp -ied)* personifizieren, verkörpern

personnel /pɜːsə'nel/ n Per-sonal nt

perspective /pə'spektɪv/ n Perspektive f

persp|iration /pəːspɪ'reɪʃn/ n Schweiß m. **~ire** vi schwitzen

persua|de /pə'sweɪd/ vt überreden; (convince) überzeugen. **~sion** n Überredung f; (powers of ~sion) Überredungskunst f

persuasive /pə'sweɪsɪv/ adj beredsam; (convincing) überzeugend

pertinent /'pɜːtɪnənt/ adj relevant (to für)

perturb /pə'tɜːb/ vt beunruhigen

peruse /pə'ruːz/ vt lesen

pervers|e /pə'vɜːs/ adj eigensinnig. **~ion** n Perversion f

pervert¹ /pə'vɜːt/ vt verdrehen; verführen (person)

pervert² /'pɜːvɜːt/ n Perverse(r) m

pessimis|m /'pesɪmɪzm/ n Pessimismus m. **~t** n Pessimist m. **~tic** adj, **-ally** adv pessimistisch

pest /pest/ n Schädling m; (□: person) Nervensäge f

pester /'pestə(r)/ vt belästigen

pesticide /'pestɪsaɪd/ n Schädlingsbekämpfungsmittel nt

pet /pet/ n Haustier nt; (favourite) Liebling m ● vt (pt/pp petted) liebkosen

petal /'petl/ n Blütenblatt nt

peter /'piːtə(r)/ vi **~ out** allmählich aufhören

petition /pə'tɪʃn/ n Bittschrift f

pet 'name n Kosename m

petrified /'petrɪfaɪd/ adj vor Angst wie versteinert

petrol /'petrl/ n Benzin nt

petroleum /pɪ'trəʊlɪəm/ n Petroleum nt

petrol: ~-pump n Zapfsäule f. **~ station** n Tankstelle f. **~ tank** n Benzintank m

petticoat /'petɪkəʊt/ n Un-

terrock m

petty /'petɪ/ adj kleinlich. **~ 'cash** n Portokasse f

petulant /'petjʊlənt/ adj gekränkt

pew /pjuː/ n [Kirchen]bank f

pharmaceutical /fɑːmə'sjuːtɪkl/ adj pharmazeutisch

pharmac|ist /'fɑːməsɪst/ n Apotheker(in) m(f). **~y** n Pharmazie f; (shop) Apotheke f

phase /feɪz/ n Phase f ● vt **~ in/out** allmählich einführen/abbauen

Ph.D. (abbr Doctor of Philosophy) Dr. phil.

pheasant /'feznt/ n Fasan m

phenomen|al /fɪ'nɒmɪnl/ adj phänomenal. **~on** n (pl -na) Phänomen nt

philharmonic /fɪlə'mɒnɪk/ n (orchestra) Philharmoniker pl

Philippines /'fɪlɪpiːnz/ npl Philippinen pl

philistine /'fɪlɪstaɪn/ n Banause m

philosoph|er /fɪ'lɒsəfə(r)/ n Philosoph m. **~ical** adj philosophisch. **~y** n Philosophie f

phlegmatic /fleg'mætɪk/ adj phlegmatisch

phobia /'fəʊbɪə/ n Phobie f

phone /fəʊn/ n Telefon nt; be on the **~** Telefon haben; (be phoning) telefonieren ● vt anrufen ● vi telefonieren. **~ back** vt/i zurückrufen. **~ book** n Telefonbuch nt. **~ box** n Telefonzelle f. **~ card** n Telefonkarte f. **~-in** n (Radio) Hörersendung f. **~ number** n Telefonnummer f

phonetic /fə'netɪk/ adj phonetisch. **~s** n Phonetik f

phoney /'fəʊnɪ/ adj falsch; (forged) gefälscht

photo /'fəʊtəʊ/ n Foto nt, Aufnahme f. **~copier** n Fotokopiergerät nt. **~copy** n Fotokopie f ● vt fotokopieren

photogenic /fəʊtəʊ'dʒenɪk/ adj fotogen

photograph /'fəʊtəgrɑːf/ n Fotografie f, Aufnahme f ● vt fotografieren

photograph|er /fə'tɒgrəfə(r)/ n Fotograf(in) m(f). **~ic** adj, **-ally** adv fotografisch. **~y** n Fotografie f

phrase /freɪz/ n Redensart f ● vt formulieren. **~-book** n Sprachführer m

physical /'fɪzɪkl/ adj körperlich

physician /fɪ'zɪʃn/ n Arzt m/ Ärztin f

physic|ist /'fɪzɪsɪst/ n Physiker(in) m(f). **~s** n Physik f

physio'therap|ist /fɪzɪəʊ-/ n Physiotherapeut(in) m(f). **~y** n Physiotherapie f

physique /fɪ'ziːk/ n Körperbau m

pianist /'pɪənɪst/ n Klavierspieler(in) m(f); (professional) Pianist(in) m(f)

piano /pɪ'ænəʊ/ n Klavier nt

pick¹ /pɪk/ n Spitzhacke f

pick² n Auslese f; **take one's ~** sich (dat) aussuchen ● vt/i (pluck) pflücken; (select) wählen, sich (dat) aussuchen; **~ and choose** wählerisch sein; **~ a quarrel** einen Streit anfangen; **~ holes in** □ kritisieren; **~ at one's food** im Essen herumstochern. **~ on** vt wählen; (□: find fault with) herumhacken auf (+ dat). **~ up** vt in die Hand nehmen; (off the ground) aufheben; (learn) lernen; (acquire) erwerben; (buy) kaufen; (Teleph) abnehmen (receiver); auffangen (signal); (collect) abholen; aufnehmen (passengers); (police:) aufgreifen (criminal); sich holen (illness). □

aufgabeln (girl); **~ oneself up** aufstehen ● vi (improve) sich bessern

'pickaxe n Spitzhacke f

picket /'pɪkɪt/ n Streikposten m

pickle /'pɪkl/ n (Amer: gherkin) Essiggurke f; **~s** pl [Mixed] Pickles pl ● vt einlegen

pick: ~pocket n Taschendieb m. **~-up** n (truck) Lieferwagen m

picnic /'pɪknɪk/ n Picknick nt ● vi (pt/pp -nicked) picknicken

picture /'pɪktʃə(r)/ n Bild nt; (film) Film m; **as pretty as a ~** bildhübsch; **put s.o. in the ~** (fig) jdn ins Bild setzen ● vt (imagine) sich (dat) vorstellen

picturesque /pɪktʃə'resk/ adj malerisch

pie /paɪ/ n Pastete f; (fruit) Kuchen m

piece /piːs/ n Stück nt; (of set) Teil nt; (in game) Stein m; (writing) Artikel m; **a ~ of bread/paper** ein Stück Brot/Papier; **a ~ of news/advice** eine Nachricht/ein Rat; **take to ~s** auseinander nehmen ● vt **~ together** zusammensetzen; (fig) zusammenstückeln. **~meal** adv stückweise

pier /pɪə(r)/ n Pier m; (pillar) Pfeiler m

pierc|e /pɪəs/ vt durchstechen. **~ing** adj durchdringend

pig /pɪg/ n Schwein nt

pigeon /'pɪdʒɪn/ n Taube f. **~-hole** n Fach nt

piggy|back /'pɪgɪbæk/ n **give s.o. a ~back** jdn huckepack tragen. **~bank** n Sparschwein nt

pig'headed adj □ starrköpfig

pigment /'pɪgmənt/ n Pigment nt

pig: ~skin n Schweinsleder nt. **~sty** n Schweinestall m. **~tail** n □ Zopf m

pilchard /'pɪltʃəd/ n Sardine f

pile¹ /paɪl/ n (of fabric) Flor m

pile² n Haufen m ● vt ~ sth on to sth etw auf sth (acc) häufen. ~ **up** vt häufen ● vi sich häufen

piles /paɪlz/ npl Hämorrhoiden pl

'pile-up n Massenkarambolage f

pilgrim /'pɪlgrɪm/ n Pilger(in) m(f). ~**age** n Pilgerfahrt f, Wallfahrt f

pill /pɪl/ n Pille f

pillar /'pɪlə(r)/ n Säule f. ~**-box** n Briefkasten m

pillow /'pɪləʊ/ n Kopfkissen nt. ~**case** n Kopfkissenbezug m

pilot /'paɪlət/ n Pilot m; (Naut) Lotse m ● vt fliegen (plane); lotsen (ship). ~**light** n Zündflamme f

pimple /'pɪmpl/ n Pickel m

pin /pɪn/ n Stecknadel f; (Techn) Bolzen m, Stift m; (Med) Nagel m; **I have ~s and needles in my leg** /mein Bein ist eingeschlafen ● vt (pt/pp **pinned**) anstecken (on + acc); (sewing) stecken; (hold down) festhalten

pinafore /'pɪnəfɔ:(r)/ n Schürze f. ~ **dress** n Kleiderrock m

pincers /'pɪnsəz/ npl Kneifzange f; (Zool) Scheren pl

pinch /pɪntʃ/ n Kniff m; (of salt) Prise f; **at a** ~ ☐ zur Not ● vt kneifen, zwicken; (fam: steal) klauen; ~ **one's finger** sich (dat) den Finger klemmen ● vi (shoe:) drücken

pine¹ /paɪn/ n (tree) Kiefer f

pine² vi ~ **for** sich sehnen nach

pineapple /'paɪn-/ n Ananas f

ping-pong n Tischtennis nt

pink /pɪŋk/ adj rosa

pinnacle /'pɪnəkl/ n Gipfel m; (on roof) Turmspitze f

pin: ~**point** vt genau festlegen. ~**stripe** n Nadelstreifen m

pint /paɪnt/ n Pint nt (0,57 l,

Amer: 0,47 l)

pioneer /paɪə'nɪə(r)/ n Pionier m ● vt bahnbrechende Arbeit leisten für

pious /'paɪəs/ adj fromm

pip¹ /pɪp/ n (seed) Kern m

pip² n (sound) Tonsignal nt

pipe /paɪp/ n Pfeife f; (for water, gas) Rohr nt ● vt in Rohren leiten; (Culin) spritzen

pipe: ~**dream** n Luftschloss nt. ~**line** n Pipeline f; **in the** ~**line** ☐ in Vorbereitung

piping /'paɪpɪŋ/ adj ~ **hot** kochend heiß

pirate /'paɪərət/ n Pirat m

piss /pɪs/ vi 🗵 pissen

pistol /'pɪstl/ n Pistole f

piston /'pɪstən/ n (Techn) Kolben m

pit /pɪt/ n Grube f; (for orchestra) Orchestergraben m; (for audience) Parkett nt; (motor racing) Box f

pitch¹ /pɪtʃ/ n (steepness) Schräge f; (of voice) Stimmlage f; (of sound) [Ton]höhe f; (Sport) Feld nt; (of street-trader) Standplatz m; (fig: degree) Grad m ● vt werfen; aufschlagen (tent) ● vi fallen

pitch² n (tar) Pech nt. ~-'**black** adj pechschwarz. ~-'**dark** adj stockdunkel

piteous /'pɪtɪəs/ adj erbärmlich

'pitfall n (fig) Falle f

pith /pɪθ/ n (Bot) Mark nt; (of orange) weiße Haut f

pithy /'pɪθɪ/ adj (fig) prägnant

piti|ful /'pɪtɪfl/ adj bedauernswert. ~**less** adj mitleidslos

'pit stop n Boxenstopp m

pittance /'pɪtns/ n Hungerlohn m

pity /'pɪtɪ/ n Mitleid nt, Erbarmen nt; **[what a]** ~! [wie] schade! **take** ~ **on** sich erbarmen über (+ acc) ● vt bemitleiden

p

pivot /'pɪvət/ n Drehzapfen m ● vi sich drehen (**on** um)

pizza /'pi:tsə/ n Pizza f

placard /'plæka:d/ n Plakat nt

placate /plə'keɪt/ vt beschwichtigen

place /pleɪs/ n Platz m; (spot) Stelle f; (town, village) Ort m; (□: house) Haus nt; **out of** ~ fehl am Platze; **take** ~ stattfinden ● vt setzen; (upright) stellen; (flat) legen; (remember) unterbringen □; ~ **an order** eine Bestellung aufgeben; **be** ~**d** (in race) sich platzieren. ~**mat** n Set nt

placid /'plæsɪd/ adj gelassen

plague /pleɪg/ n Pest f ● vt plagen

plaice /pleɪs/ n inv Scholle f

plain /pleɪn/ adj (-er, -est) klar; (simple) einfach; (not pretty) nicht hübsch; (not patterned) einfarbig; (chocolate) zartbitter; **in** ~ **clothes** in Zivil ● adv (simply) einfach ● n Ebene f. ~**ly** adv klar, deutlich; (simply) einfach; (obviously) offensichtlich

plaintiff /'pleɪntɪf/ n Kläger(in) m(f)

plait /plæt/ n Zopf m ● vt flechten

plan /plæn/ n Plan m ● vt (pt/pp planned) planen; (intend) vorhaben

plane¹ /pleɪn/ n (tree) Platane f

plane² n Flugzeug nt; (Geometry & fig) Ebene f

plane³ n (Techn) Hobel m ● vt hobeln

planet /'plænɪt/ n Planet m

plank /plæŋk/ n Brett nt; (thick) Planke f

planning /'plænɪŋ/ n Planung f

plant /plɑ:nt/ n Pflanze f; (Techn) Anlage f; (factory) Werk nt ● vt pflanzen; (place in position) setzen; ~ **oneself** sich hinstellen. ~**ation** n Plantage f

plaque /plɑ:k/ n (Gedenk)tafel f; (on teeth) Zahnbelag m

plaster /'plɑ:stə(r)/ n Verputz m; (sticking ~) Pflaster nt; ~ **[of Paris]** Gips m ● vt verputzen (wall); (cover) bedecken mit

plastic /'plæstɪk/ n Kunststoff m, Plastik nt ● adj Kunststoff-, Plastik-; (malleable) formbar, plastisch

plastic 'surgery n plastische Chirurgie f

plate /pleɪt/ n Teller m; (flat sheet) Platte f; (with name, number) Schild nt; (gold and silverware) vergoldete/versilberte Ware f; (in book) Tafel f ● vt (with gold) vergolden; (with silver) versilbern

platform /'plætfɔ:m/ n Plattform f; (stage) Podium nt; (Rail) Bahnsteig m; ~ **5** Gleis 5

platinum /'plætɪnəm/ n Platin nt

platitude /'plætɪtju:d/ n Plattitüde f

plausible /'plɔ:zəbl/ adj plausibel

play /pleɪ/ n Spiel nt; (Theater)stück m; (Radio) Hörspiel nt; (TV) Fernsehspiel nt; ~ **on words** Wortspiel nt ● vt/i spielen; ausspielen (card); ~ **safe** sichergehen. ~ **down** vt herunterspielen. ~ **up** vi □ Mätzchen machen

play: ~**er** n Spieler(in) m(f). ~**ful** adj verspielt. ~**ground** n Spielplatz m; (Sch) Schulhof m. ~**group** n Kindergarten m

playing: ~**card** n Spielkarte f. ~**field** n Sportplatz m

play: ~**mate** n Spielkamerad m. ~**thing** n Spielzeug nt. ~**wright** /-raɪt/ n Dramatiker m

plc abbr (public limited company) ≈ GmbH

plea /pli:/ n Bitte f; **make a** ~ **for** bitten um

plead /pli:d/ vi flehen (**for** um); ~

guilty sich schuldig bekennen; ~ with s.o. jdn anflehen

pleasant /'plezənt/ adj angenehm; (person) nett. **~ly** adv angenehm; (say, smile) freundlich

please /pliːz/ adv bitte • vt gefallen (+ dat); ~e s.o. jdm eine Freude machen; ~e oneself tun, was man will. **~ed** adj erfreut; be ~ed with/about sth sich über etw (acc) freuen. **~ing** adj erfreulich

pleasure /'pleʒə(r)/ n Vergnügen nt; (joy) Freude f; with ~ gern[e]

pleat /pliːt/ n Falte f • vt fälteln

pledge /pledʒ/ n Versprechen nt • vt verpfänden; versprechen

plentiful /'plentɪfl/ adj reichlich

plenty /'plenti/ n eine Menge; (enough) reichlich; ~ of money/ people viel Geld/viele Leute

pliable /'plaɪəbl/ adj biegsam

pliers /'plaɪəz/ npl [Flach]zange f

plight /plaɪt/ n [Not]lage f

plinth /plɪnθ/ n Sockel m

plod /plɒd/ vi (pt/pp plodded) trotten; (work) sich abmühen

plonk /plɒŋk/ n 🆒 billiger Wein m

plot /plɒt/ n Komplott nt; (of novel) Handlung f; ~ of land Stück m Land • vt einzeichnen • vi ein Komplott schmieden

plough /plaʊ/ n Pflug m • vt/i pflügen

ploy /plɔɪ/ n 🆒 Trick m

pluck /plʌk/ n Mut m • vt zupfen; rupfen (bird); pflücken (flower); ~ up courage Mut fassen

plucky /'plʌki/ adj tapfer, mutig

plug /plʌg/ n Stöpsel m; (wood) Zapfen m; (cotton wool) Bausch m; (Electr) Stecker m; (Auto) Zündkerze f; (🆒: advertisement) Schleichwerbung f • vt zustopfen; (🆒: advertise) Schleichwerbung machen für. ~ in

vt (Electr) einstecken

plum /plʌm/ n Pflaume f

plumage /'pluːmɪdʒ/ n Gefieder nt

plumb|er /'plʌmə(r)/ n Klempner m. ~ing n Wasserleitungen pl

plume /pluːm/ n Feder f

plump /plʌmp/ adj (-er, -est) mollig, rundlich • vt ~ for wählen

plunge /plʌndʒ/ n Sprung m; take the ~ 🆒 den Schritt wagen • vt/i tauchen

plural /'plʊərl/ adj pluralisch • n Mehrzahl f, Plural m

plus /plʌs/ prep plus (+ dat) • adj Plus- • n Pluszeichen nt; (advantage) Plus nt

plush[y] /'plʌʃ[i]/ adj luxuriös

ply /plaɪ/ vt (pt/pp plied) ausüben (trade); ~ s.o. with drink jdm ein Glas nach dem anderen eingießen. **~wood** n Sperrholz nt

p.m. adv (abbr post meridiem) nachmittags

pneumatic /nju:'mætɪk/ adj pneumatisch. ~ 'drill n Pressluft- hammer m

pneumonia /nju:'məʊnɪə/ n Lun- genentzündung f

poach /pəʊtʃ/ vt (Culin) pochieren; (steal) wildern. ~er n Wilddieb m

pocket /'pɒkɪt/ n Tasche f; be out of ~ (at an einem Geschäft) verlieren • vt einstecken. **~-book** n Notiz- buch nt; (wallet) Brieftasche f. **~-money** n Taschengeld nt

pod /pɒd/ n Hülse f

poem /'pəʊɪm/ n Gedicht nt

poet /'pəʊɪt/ n Dichter(in) m(f). **~ic** adj dichterisch

poetry /'pəʊɪtri/ n Dichtung f

poignant /'pɔɪnjənt/ adj er- greifend

point /pɔɪnt/ n Punkt m; (sharp end) Spitze f; (meaning) Sinn m;

(*purpose*) Zweck *m*; (*Electr*) Steckdose *f*; **~s** *pl* (*Rail*) Weiche *f*; **~ of view** Standpunkt *m*; **good/bad ~s** gute/schlechte Seiten; **what is the ~?** wozu? **the ~ is** es ist darum; **up to a ~** bis zu einem gewissen Grade; **be on the ~ of doing sth** im Begriff sein, etw zu tun ● *vt* richten (**at** auf + *acc*); ausfugen (*brickwork*) ● *vi* deuten (**at/to** auf + *acc*); (*with finger*) mit dem Finger zeigen. **~ out** *vt* zeigen auf (+ *acc*); **~ sth out to s.o.** jdn auf etw (*acc*) hinweisen

point-'blank *adj* aus nächster Entfernung; (*fig*) rundweg

point|ed /'pɔɪntɪd/ *adj* spitz; (*question*) gezielt. **~less** *adj* zwecklos, sinnlos

poise /pɔɪz/ *n* Haltung *f*

poison /'pɔɪzn/ *n* Gift *nt* ● *vt* vergiften. **~ous** *adj* giftig

poke /pəʊk/ *n* Stoß *m* ● *vt* stoßen; schüren (*fire*); (*put*) stecken

poker[1] /'pəʊkə(r)/ *n* Schüreisen *nt*

poker[2] *n* (*Cards*) Poker *nt*

poky /'pəʊkɪ/ *adj* eng

Poland /'pəʊlənd/ *n* Polen *nt*

polar /'pəʊlə(r)/ *adj* Polar-. **~'bear** *n* Eisbär *m*

Pole /pəʊl/ *n* Pole *m*/Polin *f*

pole[1] *n* Stange *f*

pole[2] *n* (*Geog, Electr*) Pol *m*

'pole-vault *n* Stabhochsprung *m*

police /pə'li:s/ *npl* Polizei *f*

police: ~man *n* Polizist *m*. **~ station** *n* Polizeiwache *f*. **~ woman** *n* Polizistin *f*

policy[1] /'pɒlɪsɪ/ *n* Politik *f*

policy[2] *n* (*insurance*) Police *f*

Polish /'pəʊlɪʃ/ *adj* polnisch

polish /'pɒlɪʃ/ *n* (*shine*) Glanz *m*; (*for shoes*) [Schuh]creme *f*; (*for floor*) Bohnerwachs *m*; (*for furni-*

ture) Politur *f*; (*for silver*) Putzmittel *nt*; (*for nails*) Lack *m*; (*fig*) Schliff *m* ● *vt* polieren; bohnern (*floor*). **~ off** *vt* ① verputzen (*food*); erledigen (*task*)

polite /pə'laɪt/ *adj* höflich. **~ness** *n* Höflichkeit *f*

politic|al /pə'lɪtɪkl/ *adj* politisch. **~ian** *n* Politiker(in) *m*(*f*)

politics /'pɒlətɪks/ *n* Politik *f*

poll /pəʊl/ *n* (*election*) Wahl *f*; **[opinion] ~** [Meinungs]umfrage *f*

pollen /'pɒlən/ *n* Blütenstaub *m*, Pollen *m*

polling /'pəʊlɪŋ/: **~-booth** *n* Wahlkabine *f*. **~-station** *n* Wahllokal *nt*

pollut|e /pə'lu:t/ *vt* verschmutzen. **~ion** *n* Verschmutzung *f*

polo /'pəʊləʊ/ *n* Polo *nt*. **~-neck** *n* Rollkragen *m*

polystyrene /pɒlɪ'staɪri:n/ *n* Polystyrol *nt*; (*for packing*) Styropor® *nt*

polythene /'pɒlɪθi:n/ *n* Polyäthylen *nt*. **~ bag** *n* Plastiktüte *f*

pomp /pɒmp/ *n* Pomp *m*

pompous /'pɒmpəs/ *adj* großspurig

pond /pɒnd/ *n* Teich *m*

ponder /'pɒndə(r)/ *vi* nachdenken

ponderous /'pɒndərəs/ *adj* schwerfällig

pony /'pəʊnɪ/ *n* Pony *nt*. **~-tail** *n* Pferdeschwanz *m*

poodle /'pu:dl/ *n* Pudel *m*

pool /pu:l/ *n* [Schwimm]becken *nt*; (*pond*) Teich *m*; (*of blood*) Lache *f*; (*common fund*) [gemeinsame] Kasse *f*; **~s** *pl* [Fußball]toto *nt* ● *vt* zusammenlegen

poor /pʊə(r)/ *adj* (**-er, -est**) arm; (*not good*) schlecht; **in ~ health**

nicht gesund. **~ly** adj be **~ly** krank sein ● adv ärmlich; (badly) schlecht

pop¹ /pɒp/ n Knall m ● v (pt/pp popped) ● vt (🔲: put) stecken (**in** in + acc) ● vi knallen; (burst) platzen. **~ in** vi 🔲 reinschauen. **~ out** vi 🔲 kurz rausgehen

pop² n 🔲 Popmusik f, Pop m ● attrib Pop-

'popcorn n Puffmais m

pope /pəʊp/ n Papst m

poplar /'pɒplə(r)/ n Pappel f

poppy /'pɒpɪ/ n Mohn m

popular /'pɒpjʊlə(r)/ adj beliebt, populär; (belief) volkstümlich. **~ity** n Beliebtheit f, Popularität f

populat|e /'pɒpjʊleɪt/ vt bevölkern. **~ion** n Bevölkerung f

pop-up /'pɒpʌp/ n Pop-up-Werbefenster nt

porcelain /'pɔːsəlɪn/ n Porzellan nt

porch /pɔːtʃ/ n Vorbau m; (Amer) Veranda f

porcupine /'pɔːkjʊpaɪn/ n Stachelschwein nt

pore /pɔː(r)/ n Pore f

pork /pɔːk/ n Schweinefleisch nt

porn /pɔːn/ n 🔲 Porno m

pornograph|ic /pɔːnə'græfɪk/ adj pornographisch. **~y** n Pornographie f

porridge /'pɒrɪdʒ/ n Haferbrei m

port¹ /pɔːt/ n Hafen m; (town) Hafenstadt f

port² n (Naut) Backbord nt

port³ n (wine) Portwein m

portable /'pɔːtəbl/ adj tragbar

porter /'pɔːtə(r)/ n Portier m; (for luggage) Gepäckträger m

'porthole n Bullauge nt

portion /'pɔːʃn/ n Portion f; (part, share) Teil nt

portrait /'pɔːtrɪt/ n Porträt nt

portray /pɔː'treɪ/ vt darstellen. **~al** n Darstellung f

Portugal /'pɔːtjʊgl/ n Portugal nt. **~uese** adj portugiesisch ● n Portugiese m/-giesin f

pose /pəʊz/ n Pose f ● vt aufwerfen (problem); stellen (question) ● vi posieren; (for painter) Modell stehen

posh /pɒʃ/ adj 🔲 feudal

position /pə'zɪʃn/ n Platz m; (posture) Haltung f; (job) Stelle f; (situation) Lage f, Situation f; (status) Stellung f ● vt platzieren; **~ oneself** sich stellen

positive /'pɒzətɪv/ adj positiv; (definite) eindeutig; (real) ausgesprochen ● n Positiv nt

possess /pə'zes/ vt besitzen. **~ion** n Besitz m; **~ions** pl Sachen pl

possess|ive /pə'zesɪv/ adj Possessiv-; be **~ive about s.o.** zu sehr an jdm hängen

possibility /pɒsə'bɪlətɪ/ n Möglichkeit f

possib|le /'pɒsəbl/ adj möglich. **~ly** adv möglicherweise; **not ~ly** unmöglich

post¹ /pəʊst/ n (pole) Pfosten m

post² n (place of duty) Posten m; (job) Stelle f

post³ n (mail) Post f; **by ~** mit der Post ● vt aufgeben (letter); (send by ~) mit der Post schicken; **keep s.o. ~ed** jdn auf dem Laufenden halten

postage /'pəʊstɪdʒ/ n Porto nt

postal /'pəʊstl/ adj Post-. **~ order** n ≈ Geldanweisung f

post: **~box** n Briefkasten m. **~card** n Postkarte f; (picture) Ansichtskarte f. **~code** n Postleitzahl f. **~date** vt vordatieren

poster /'pəʊstə(r)/ n Plakat nt

posterity /pɒ'sterətɪ/ n Nachwelt f

posthumous /'pɒstjʊməs/ adj

p

postum

post: ~**man** n Briefträger m.
~**mark** n Poststempel m

post-mortem /-'mɔːtəm/ n Obduktion f

'**post office** n Post f

postpone /pəʊst'pəʊn/ vt aufschieben; ~ **until** verschieben auf
(+ acc). ~**ment** n Verschiebung f

postscript /'pəʊstskrɪpt/ n Nachschrift f

posture /'pɒstʃə(r)/ n Haltung f

pot /pɒt/ n Topf m; (for tea, coffee)
Kanne f; ~**s of money** 🄳 eine
Menge Geld

potato /pə'teɪtəʊ/ n (pl -es) Kartoffel f

potent /'pəʊtənt/ adj stark

potential /pə'tenʃl/ adj potenziell
● n Potenzial nt

pot: ~**hole** n Höhle f; (in road)
Schlagloch nt. ~**shot** n **take a**
~**shot at** schießen auf (+ acc)

potter /'pɒtə(r)/ n Töpfer(in) m(f).
~**y** n Töpferei f; (articles) Töpferwaren pl

potty /'pɒtɪ/ adj 🄳 verrückt ● n
Töpfchen nt

pouch /paʊtʃ/ n Beutel m

poultry /'pəʊltrɪ/ n Geflügel nt

pounce /paʊns/ vi zuschlagen; ~
on sich stürzen auf (+ acc)

pound[1] /paʊnd/ n (money & 0,454
kg) Pfund nt

pound[2] vi (heart:) hämmern; (run
heavily) stampfen

pour /pɔː(r)/ vt gießen; einschenken (drink) ● vi strömen; (with rain)
gießen. ~ **out** vi ausströmen ● vt
ausschütten; einschenken (drink)

pout /paʊt/ vi einen Schmollmund
machen

poverty /'pɒvətɪ/ n Armut f

powder /'paʊdə(r)/ n Pulver nt;

(cosmetic) Puder m ● vt pudern

power /'paʊə(r)/ n Macht f;
(strength) Kraft f; (Electr) Strom m;
(nuclear) Energie f; (Math) Potenz f.
~ **cut** n Stromsperre f. ~**ed** adj
betrieben (**by** mit); ~**ed by electricity** mit Elektroantrieb. ~**ful** adj
mächtig; (strong) stark. ~**less** adj
machtlos. ~**station** n Kraftwerk nt

practicable /'præktɪkəbl/ adj
durchführbar, praktikabel

practical /'præktɪkl/ adj praktisch.
~ '**joke** n Streich m

practice /'præktɪs/ n Praxis f; (custom) Brauch m; (habit) Gewohnheit
f; (exercise) Übung f; (Sport) Training
nt; **in** ~ (in reality) in der Praxis;
out of ~ außer Übung; **put into** ~
ausführen

practise /'præktɪs/ vt üben; (carry
out) praktizieren; ausüben (profession) ● vi üben; (doctor:) praktizieren. ~**d** adj geübt

praise /preɪz/ n Lob nt ● vt loben.
~**worthy** adj lobenswert

pram /præm/ n Kinderwagen m

prank /præŋk/ n Streich m

prawn /prɔːn/ n Garnele f,
Krabbe f

pray /preɪ/ vi beten. ~**er** n
Gebet nt

preach /priːtʃ/ vt/i predigen. ~**er**
n Prediger m

pre-ar'range /priː-/ vt im Voraus
arrangieren

precarious /prɪ'keərɪəs/ adj unsicher

precaution /prɪ'kɔːʃn/ n Vorsichtsmaßnahme f

precede /prɪ'siːd/ vt vorangehen
(+ dat)

preceden|ce /'presɪdəns/ n Vorrang m. ~**t** n Präzedenzfall m

preceding /prɪ'siːdɪŋ/ adj vorhergehend

precinct /'pri:sɪŋkt/ n Bereich m; (traffic-free) Fußgängerzone f; (Amer: district) Bezirk m

precious /'preʃəs/ adj kostbar; (style) preziös ● adv Ⅰ ~ **little** recht wenig

precipice /'presɪpɪs/ n Steilabfall m

precipitation /prɪsɪpɪ'teɪʃn/ n (rain) Niederschlag m

precis|e /prɪ'saɪs/ adj genau. ~ion n Genauigkeit f

precocious /prɪ'kəʊʃəs/ adj frühreif

pre|con'ceived /pri:-/ adj vorgefasst. ~con'ception n vorgefasste Meinung f

predator /'predətə(r)/ n Raubtier nt

predecessor /'pri:dɪsesə(r)/ n Vorgänger(in) m(f)

predicat|e /'predɪkət/ n (Gram) Prädikat nt. ~ive adj prädikativ

predict /prɪ'dɪkt/ vt voraussagen. ~able adj voraussehbar; (person) berechenbar. ~ion n Voraussage f

pre'dominant /pri:-/ adj vorherrschend. ~antly adv hauptsächlich, überwiegend. ~ate vi vorherrschen

preen /pri:n/ vt putzen

pre|fab /'pri:fæb/ n Ⅰ [einfaches] Fertighaus nt. ~'fabricated adj vorgefertigt

preface /'prefɪs/ n Vorwort nt

prefect /'pri:fekt/ n Präfekt m

prefer /prɪ'fɜ:(r)/ vt (pt/pp preferred) vorziehen; I ~ to walk ich gehe lieber zu Fuß; I ~ wine ich trinke lieber Wein

prefera|ble /'prefərəbl/ adj be ~ble vorzuziehen sein (to dat). ~bly adv vorzugsweise

preferen|ce /'prefərəns/ n Vorzug m. ~tial adj bevorzugt

pregnan|cy /'pregnənsɪ/ n Schwangerschaft f. ~t adj schwanger; (animal) trächtig

prehi'storic /pri:-/ adj prähistorisch

prejudice /'predʒʊdɪs/ n Vorurteil nt; (bias) Voreingenommenheit f ● vt einnehmen (against gegen). ~d adj voreingenommen

preliminary /prɪ'lɪmɪnərɪ/ adj Vor-

prelude /'prelju:d/ n Vorspiel nt

premature /'premətjʊə(r)/ adj vorzeitig; (birth) Früh-. ~ly adv zu früh

pre'meditated /pri:-/ adj vorsätzlich

premier /'premɪə(r)/ adj führend ● n (Pol) Premier[minister] m

première /'premɪeə(r)/ n Premiere f

premise /'premɪs/ n Prämisse f, Voraussetzung f

premises /'premɪsɪz/ npl Räumlichkeiten pl; on the ~ im Haus

premium /'pri:mɪəm/ n Prämie f; be at a ~ hoch im Kurs stehen

premonition /premə'nɪʃn/ n Vorahnung f

preoccupied /prɪ'ɒkjʊpaɪd/ adj [in Gedanken] beschäftigt

preparation /prepə'reɪʃn/ n Vorbereitung f; (substance) Präparat nt

preparatory /prɪ'pærətrɪ/ adj Vor-

prepare /prɪ'peə(r)/ vt vorbereiten; anrichten (meal) ● vi sich vorbereiten (for auf + acc); ~d to bereit zu

preposition /prepə'zɪʃn/ n Präposition f

preposterous /prɪ'pɒstərəs/ adj absurd

prerequisite /pri:'rekwɪzɪt/ n

P

Voraussetzung f

Presbyterian /ˌprezbɪ'tɪərɪən/ adj presbyterianisch ●n Presbyterianer(in) m(f)

prescribe /prɪ'skraɪb/ vt vorschreiben; (Med) verschreiben

prescription /prɪ'skrɪpʃn/ n (Med) Rezept nt

presence /'prezns/ n Anwesenheit f, Gegenwart f; ~ of mind Geistesgegenwart f

present¹ /'preznt/ adj gegenwärtig; be ~ anwesend sein; (occur) vorkommen ●n Gegenwart f; (Gram) Präsens nt; at ~ zurzeit; for the ~ vorläufig

present² n (gift) Geschenk nt

present³ /prɪ'zent/ vt überreichen; (show) zeigen; vorlegen (cheque); (introduce) vorstellen; ~ s.o. with sth jdm etw überreichen. ~able adj be ~able sich zeigen lassen können

presentation /prezn'teɪʃn/ n Überreichung f

presently /'prezntlɪ/ adv nachher; (Amer: now) zurzeit

preservation /prezə'veɪʃn/ n Erhaltung f

preservative /prɪ'zɜːvətɪv/ n Konservierungsmittel nt

preserve /prɪ'zɜːv/ vt erhalten; (Culin) konservieren; (bottle) einmachen ●n (Hunting & fig) Revier nt; (jam) Konfitüre f

preside /prɪ'zaɪd/ vi den Vorsitz haben (over bei)

presidency /'prezɪdənsɪ/ n Präsidentschaft f

president /'prezɪdənt/ n Präsident m; (Amer: chairman) Vorsitzende(r) m/f. ~ial adj Präsidenten-; (election) Präsidentschafts-

press /pres/ n Presse f ●vt/i drü-

cken; drücken auf (+ acc) (button); pressen (flower); (iron) bügeln; (urge) bedrängen; ~ for drängen auf (+ acc); be ~ed for time in Zeitdruck sein. ~ on vi weitergehen/-fahren; (fig) weitermachen

press: ~ cutting n Zeitungsausschnitt m. ~ing adj dringend

pressure /'preʃə(r)/ n Druck m. ~-cooker n Schnellkochtopf m

pressurize /'preʃəraɪz/ vt Druck ausüben auf (+ acc). ~d adj Druck-

prestige /pre'stiːʒ/ n Prestige nt. ~ious adj Prestige-

presumably /prɪ'zjuːməblɪ/ adv vermutlich

presume /prɪ'zjuːm/ vt vermuten

presumptlion /prɪ'zʌmpʃn/ n Vermutung f; (boldness) Anmaßung f. ~uous adj anmaßend

pretence /prɪ'tens/ n Verstellung f; (pretext) Vorwand m

pretend /prɪ'tend/ vt (claim) vorgeben; ~ that so tun, als ob; ~ to be sich ausgeben als

pretentious /prɪ'tenʃəs/ adj protzig

pretext /'priːtekst/ n Vorwand m

prettly /'prɪtɪ/ adj , ~ily adv hübsch ●adv (🄵: fairly) ziemlich

prevail /prɪ'veɪl/ vi siegen; (custom:) vorherrschen; ~ on s.o. to do sth jdn dazu bringen, etw zu tun

prevalence /'prevələns/ n Häufigkeit f. ~t adj vorherrschend

prevent /prɪ'vent/ vt verhindern, verhüten; ~ s.o. [from] doing sth jdn daran hindern, etw zu tun. ~ion n Verhinderung f, Verhütung f. ~ive adj vorbeugend

preview /'priːvjuː/ n Voraufführung f

previous /'priːvɪəs/ adj vorherge-

503

hend; **~ to** vor (+ dat). **~ly** adv vorher, früher

prey /preɪ/ n Beute f; **bird of ~** Raubvogel m

price /praɪs/ n Preis m ● vt (Comm) auszeichnen. **~less** adj unschätzbar; (fig) unbezahlbar

prick /prɪk/ n Stich m ● vt/i stechen

prickl|e /ˈprɪkl/ n Stachel m; (thorn) Dorn m. **~y** adj stachelig; (sensation) stechend

pride /praɪd/ n Stolz m; (arrogance) Hochmut m ● vt **~ oneself on** stolz sein auf (+ acc)

priest /priːst/ n Priester m

prim /prɪm/ adj (primmer, primmest) prüde

primarily /ˈpraɪmərɪlɪ/ adv hauptsächlich, in erster Linie

primary /ˈpraɪmərɪ/ adj Haupt-. **~ school** n Grundschule f

prime[1] /praɪm/ adj Haupt-; (firstrate) erstklassig

prime[2] vt scharf machen (bomb); grundieren (surface)

Prime Minister /praɪ ˈmɪnɪstə(r)/ n Premierminister(in) m(f)

primitive /ˈprɪmɪtɪv/ adj primitiv

primrose /ˈprɪmrəʊz/ n gelbe Schlüsselblume f

prince /prɪns/ n Prinz m

princess /prɪnˈses/ n Prinzessin f

principal /ˈprɪnsəpl/ adj Haupt- ● n (Sch) Rektor(in) m(f)

principally /ˈprɪnsəplɪ/ adv hauptsächlich

principle /ˈprɪnsəpl/ n Prinzip nt, Grundsatz m; **in/on ~** im/aus Prinzip

print /prɪnt/ n Druck m; (Phot) Abzug m; **in ~** gedruckt; (available)

erhältlich; **out of ~** vergriffen ● vt drucken; (write in capitals) in Druckschrift schreiben; (Computing) ausdrucken; (Phot) abziehen. **~ed matter** n Drucksache f

print|er /ˈprɪntə(r)/ n Drucker m. **~ing** n Druck m

'printout n (Computing) Ausdruck m

prior /ˈpraɪə(r)/ adj frühere(r,s); **~ to** vor (+ dat)

priority /praɪˈɒrɪtɪ/ n Priorität f, Vorrang m

prise /praɪz/ vt **~ open/up** aufstemmen/hochstemmen

prison /ˈprɪzn/ n Gefängnis nt. **~er** n Gefangene(r) m/f

privacy /ˈprɪvəsɪ/ n Privatsphäre f; **have no ~** nie für sich sein

private /ˈpraɪvət/ adj privat; (confidential) vertraulich; (car, secretary, school) Privat- ● n (Mil) [einfacher] Soldat m; **in ~** privat; (confidentially) vertraulich

privation /praɪˈveɪʃn/ n Entbehrung f

privilege /ˈprɪvəlɪdʒ/ n Privileg nt. **~d** adj privilegiert

prize /praɪz/ n Preis m ● vt schätzen

pro /prəʊ/ n 🄳 Profi m; **the ~s and cons** das Für und Wider

probability /prɒbəˈbɪlɪtɪ/ n Wahrscheinlichkeit f

proba|ble /ˈprɒbəbl/ adj, **-bly** adv wahrscheinlich

probation /prəˈbeɪʃn/ n (Jur) Bewährung f

probe /prəʊb/ n Sonde f; (fig: investigation) Untersuchung f

problem /ˈprɒbləm/ n Problem nt; (Math) Textaufgabe f. **~atic** adj problematisch

procedure /prəˈsiːdʒə(r)/ n

Verfahren nt

proceed /prə'si:d/ vi gehen; (in vehicle) fahren; (continue) weitergehen/-fahren; (speaking) fortfahren; (act) verfahren

proceedings /prə'si:dɪŋz/ npl Verfahren nt; (Jur) Prozess m

proceeds /'prəʊsi:dz/ npl Erlös m

process /'prəʊses/ n Prozess m; (procedure) Verfahren nt; **in the ∼** dabei ● vt verarbeiten; (Admin) bearbeiten; (Phot) entwickeln

procession /prə'seʃn/ n Umzug m, Prozession f

processor /'prəʊsesə(r)/ n Prozessor m

proclaim /prə'kleɪm/ vt ausrufen

proclamation /prɒklə'meɪʃn/ n Proklamation f

procure /prə'kjʊə(r)/ vt beschaffen

prod /prɒd/ n Stoß m ● vt stoßen

prodigy /'prɒdɪdʒɪ/ n [infant] ∼ Wunderkind nt

produce[1] /'prɒdju:s/ n landwirtschaftliche Erzeugnisse pl

produce[2] /prə'dju:s/ vt erzeugen, produzieren; (manufacture) herstellen; (bring out) hervorholen; (cause) hervorrufen; inszenieren; (play); (Radio, TV) redigieren. **∼r** n Erzeuger m, Produzent m; Hersteller m; (Theat) Regisseur m; (Radio, TV) Redakteur(in) m (f)

product /'prɒdʌkt/ n Erzeugnis nt, Produkt nt. **∼ion** n Produktion f; (Theat) Inszenierung f

productiv|e /prə'dʌktɪv/ adj produktiv; (land, talks) fruchtbar. **∼ity** n Produktivität f

profession /prə'feʃn/ n Beruf m. **∼al** adj beruflich; (not amateur) Berufs-; (expert) fachmännisch; (Sport) professionell ● n Fachmann m;

(Sport) Profi m

professor /prə'fesə(r)/ n Professor m

proficien|cy /prə'fɪʃnsɪ/ n Können nt. **∼t** adj **be ∼t in** beherrschen

profile /'prəʊfaɪl/ n Profil nt; (character study) Porträt nt

profit /'prɒfɪt/ n Gewinn m, Profit m ● vi ∼ **from** profitieren von. **∼able** adj, **-bly** adv gewinnbringend; (fig) nutzbringend

profound /prə'faʊnd/ adj tief

program /'prəʊgræm/ n Programm nt; ● vt (pt/pp **programmed**) programmieren

programme /'prəʊgræm/ n Programm nt; (Radio, TV) Sendung f. **∼r** n (Computing) Programmierer(in) m (f)

progress[1] /'prəʊgres/ n Vorankommen nt; (fig) Fortschritt m; **in ∼** im Gange; **make ∼** (fig) Fortschritte machen

progress[2] /prə'gres/ vi vorankommen; (fig) fortschreiten. **∼ion** n Folge f; (development) Entwicklung f

progressive /prə'gresɪv/ adj fortschrittlich. **∼ly** adv zunehmend

prohibit /prə'hɪbɪt/ vt verbieten (s.o. jdm). **∼ive** adj unerschwinglich

project[1] /'prɒdʒekt/ n Projekt nt; (Sch) Arbeit f

project[2] /prə'dʒekt/ vt projizieren (film); (plan) planen ● vi (jut out) vorstehen

projector /prə'dʒektə(r)/ n Projektor m

prolific /prə'lɪfɪk/ adj fruchtbar; (fig) produktiv

prologue /'prəʊlɒg/ n Prolog m

prolong /prə'lɒŋ/ vt verlängern

promenade /prɒmə'nɑ:d/ n Pro-

505

prominent | prosecute

menade *f* ● *vi* spazieren gehen

prominent /'prɒmɪnənt/ *adj* vorstehend; (*important*) prominent; (*conspicuous*) auffällig

promiscuous /prə'mɪskjʊəs/ *adj* **be ~ous** häufig den Partner wechseln

promis|e /'prɒmɪs/ *n* Versprechen *nt* ● *vt/i* versprechen (**s.o.** jdm). **~ing** *adj* viel versprechend

promot|e /prə'məʊt/ *vt* befördern; (*advance*) fördern; (*publicize*) Reklame machen für; **be ~ed** (*Sport*) aufsteigen. **~ion** *n* Beförderung *f*; (*Sport*) Aufstieg *m*; (*Comm*) Reklame *f*

prompt /prɒmpt/ *adj* prompt, unverzüglich; (*punctual*) pünktlich ● *adv* pünktlich ● *vt/i* veranlassen (**to** zu); (*Theat*) soufflieren (+ *dat*). **~er** *n* Souffleur *m*/Souffleuse *f*. **~ly** *adv* prompt

Proms Die Proms, offiziell *BBC Henry Wood Promenade Concerts*, finden jeden Sommer in der Londoner Royal Albert Hall statt. Bei den Promenadekonzerten steht ein Teil des Publikums vor dem Orchester. In den USA bezeichnet *Prom* einen Ball, den eine ▶HIGH SCHOOL veranstaltet, um das Ende des Schuljahrs zu feiern.

prone /prəʊn/ *adj* **be** or **lie ~** auf dem Bauch liegen; **be ~ to** neigen zu

pronoun /'prəʊnaʊn/ *n* Fürwort *nt*, Pronomen *nt*

pronounce /prə'naʊns/ *vt* aussprechen; (*declare*) erklären. **~d** *adj* ausgeprägt; (*noticeable*) deutlich. **~ment** *n* Erklärung *f*

pronunciation /prənʌnsɪ'eɪʃn/ *n* Aussprache *f*

proof /pruːf/ *n* Beweis *m*; (*Typography*) Korrekturbogen *m*. **~-reader** *n* Korrektor *m*

prop¹ /prɒp/ *n* Stütze *f* ● *vt* (*pt/pp* propped) **~ against** lehnen an (+ *acc*). **~ up** *vt* stützen

prop² *n* (*Theat*, 🄸) Requisit *nt*

propaganda /prɒpə'gændə/ *n* Propaganda *f*

propel /prə'pel/ *vt* (*pt/pp* propelled) [an]treiben. **~ler** *n* Propeller *m*

proper /'prɒpə(r)/ *adj* richtig; (*decent*) anständig

property /'prɒpətɪ/ *n* Eigentum *nt*; (*quality*) Eigenschaft *f*; (*Theat*) Requisit *nt*; (*land*) [Grund]besitz *m*; (*house*) Haus *nt*

prophecy /'prɒfəsɪ/ *n* Prophezeiung *f*

prophesy /'prɒfɪsaɪ/ *vt* (*pt/pp* -ied) prophezeien

prophet /'prɒfɪt/ *n* Prophet *m*. **~ic** *adj* prophetisch

proportion /prə'pɔːʃn/ *n* Verhältnis *nt*; (*share*) Teil *m*; **~s** *pl* Proportionen; (*dimensions*) Maße. **~al** *adj* proportional

proposal /prə'pəʊzl/ *n* Vorschlag *m*; (*of marriage*) [Heirats]antrag *m*

propose /prə'pəʊz/ *vt* vorschlagen; (*intend*) vorhaben; (*motion*) ● *vi* einen Heiratsantrag machen

proposition /prɒpə'zɪʃn/ *n* Vorschlag *m*

proprietor /prə'praɪətə(r)/ *n* Inhaber(in) *m(f)*

propriety /prə'praɪətɪ/ *n* Korrektheit *f*; (*decorum*) Anstand *m*

prose /prəʊz/ *n* Prosa *f*

prosecut|e /'prɒsɪkjuːt/ *vt* strafrechtlich verfolgen. **~ion** *n* strafrechtliche Verfolgung *f*; **the ~ion**

die Anklage. **~or** n [Police] P**~or** Staatsanwalt m

prospect /'prɒspekt/ n Aussicht f

prospect|ive /prə'spektɪv/ adj (future) zukünftig. **~or** n Prospektor m

prospectus /prə'spektəs/ n Prospekt m

prosper /'prɒspə(r)/ vi gedeihen, florieren; (person) Erfolg haben. **~ity** n Wohlstand m

prosperous /'prɒspərəs/ adj wohlhabend

prostitut|e /'prɒstɪtjuːt/ n Prostituierte f. **~ion** n Prostitution f

prostrate /'prɒstreɪt/ adj ausgestreckt

protagonist /prəʊ'tægənɪst/ n Kämpfer m; (fig) Protagonist m

protect /prə'tekt/ vt schützen (from vor + dat); beschützen (person). **~ion** n Schutz m. **~ive** adj Schutz-; (fig) beschützend. **~or** n Beschützer m

protein /'prəʊtiːn/ n Eiweiß nt

protest¹ /'prəʊtest/ n Protest m

protest² /prə'test/ vi protestieren

Protestant /'prɒtɪstənt/ adj protestantisch ● n Protestant(in) m(f)

protester /prə'testə(r)/ n Protestierende(r) m/f

prototype /'prəʊtə-/ n Prototyp m

protrude /prə'truːd/ vi [her]vorstehen

proud /praʊd/ adj stolz (of auf + acc)

prove /pruːv/ vt beweisen ● vi **~to** be sich erweisen als

proverb /'prɒvɜːb/ n Sprichwort nt

provide /prə'vaɪd/ vt für Verfügung stellen; spenden (shade); **~ s.o. with sth** jdn mit etw versorgen

od versehen ● vi **~ for** sorgen für

provided /prə'vaɪdɪd/ conj **~ [that]** vorausgesetzt [dass]

providen|ce /'prɒvɪdəns/ n Vorsehung f. **~tial** adj be **~tial** ein Glück sein

provinc|e /'prɒvɪns/ n Provinz f; (fig) Bereich m. **~ial** adj provinziell

provision /prə'vɪʒn/ n Versorgung f (of mit); **~s** pl Lebensmittel pl. **~al** adj vorläufig

provocat|ion /prɒvə'keɪʃn/ n Provokation f. **~ive** adj provozierend; (sexually) aufreizend

provoke /prə'vəʊk/ vt provozieren; (cause) hervorrufen

prow /praʊ/ n Bug m

prowl /praʊl/ vi herumschleichen

proximity /prɒk'sɪmətɪ/ n Nähe f

pruden|ce /'pruːdns/ n Umsicht f. **~t** adj umsichtig; (wise) klug

prudish /'pruːdɪʃ/ adj prüde

prune¹ /pruːn/ n Backpflaume f

prune² vt beschneiden

pry /praɪ/ vi (pt/pp pried) neugierig sein

psalm /sɑːm/ n Psalm m

psychiatric /saɪkɪ'ætrɪk/ adj psychiatrisch

psychiatr|ist /saɪ'kaɪətrɪst/ n Psychiater(in) m(f). **~y** n Psychiatrie f

psychic /'saɪkɪk/ adj übersinnlich

psycho|a'nalysis /saɪkəʊ-/ n Psychoanalyse f. **~'analyst** Psychoanalytiker(in) m(f)

psychological /saɪkə'lɒdʒɪkl/ adj psychologisch; (illness) psychisch

psycholog|ist /saɪ'kɒlədʒɪst/ n Psychologe m/ -login f. **~y** n Psychologie f

P.T.O. abbr (please turn over) b.w.

pub /pʌb/ n ① Kneipe f

pub Ein *pub*, kurz für *public house*, ist ein englisches Wirtshaus. *Pubs* sind bei allen Schichten der britschen Gesellschaft beliebt und Gäste haben oft eine Stammkneipe, wo sie Bier trinken und Darts oder Pool spielen. Öffnungszeiten sind meist von 11-23 Uhr und in vielen *pubs* kann man auch essen.   *i*

puberty /ˈpjuːbətɪ/ n Pubertät f

public /ˈpʌblɪk/ adj öffentlich; **make ~** publik machen **● the ~** die Öffentlichkeit

publican /ˈpʌblɪkən/ n [Gast]wirt m

publication /pʌblɪˈkeɪʃn/ n Veröffentlichung f

public: **~ 'holiday** n gesetzlicher Feiertag m. **~ 'house** n [Gast]wirtschaft f

publicity /pʌbˈlɪsɪtɪ/ n Publicity f; *(advertising)* Reklame f

publicize /ˈpʌblɪsaɪz/ vt Reklame machen für

public: **~ 'school** n Privatschule f; *(Amer)* staatliche Schule f. **~ 'spirited** adj be **~-spirited** Gemeinsinn haben

public school Eine Privatschule in England und Wales für Schüler im Alter von dreizehn bis achtzehn Jahren. Die meisten *public schools* sind Internate, normalerweise entweder für Jungen oder Mädchen. Die Eltern zahlen Schulgeld für die Ausbildung ihrer Kinder. In Schottland und den USA ist eine *public school* eine staatliche Schule.   *i*

publish /ˈpʌblɪʃ/ vt veröffentlichen. **~er** n Verleger(in) m(f); *(firm)* Verlag m. **~ing** n Verlagswe-

sen nt

pudding /ˈpʊdɪŋ/ n Pudding m; *(course)* Nachtisch m

puddle /ˈpʌdl/ n Pfütze f

puff /pʌf/ n *(of wind)* Hauch m; *(of smoke)* Wölkchen m **●** vt blasen, pusten; **~ out** ausstoßen. **●** vi keuchen; **~ at** paffen an (+ dat) *(pipe)*. **~ed** adj *(out of breath)* aus der Puste. **~ pastry** n Blätterteig m

pull /pʊl/ n Zug m; *(jerk)* Ruck m; *(fig: influence)* Einfluss m **●** vt ziehen; ziehen an (+ dat) *(rope)*; **~ a muscle** sich *(dat)* einen Muskel zerren; **~ oneself together** sich zusammennehmen; **~ one's weight** tüchtig mitarbeiten; **~ s.o.'s leg** *fig* jdn auf den Arm nehmen. **~ down** vt herunterziehen; *(demolish)* abreißen. **~ in** vt hereinziehen **● vi** *(Auto)* einscheren. **~ off** vt abziehen; *fig* schaffen. **~ out** vt herausziehen **● vi** *(Auto)* ausscheren. **~ through** vt durchziehen **● vi** *(recover)* durchkommen. **~ up** vt herausziehen; ausziehen *(plant)* **● vi** *(Auto)* anhalten

pullover /ˈpʊləʊvə(r)/ n Pullover m

pulp /pʌlp/ n Brei m; *(of fruit)* [Frucht]fleisch nt

pulpit /ˈpʊlpɪt/ n Kanzel f

pulse /pʌls/ n Puls m

pulses /ˈpʌlsɪz/ npl Hülsenfrüchte pl

pummel /ˈpʌml/ vt *(pt/pp* **pummelled)** mit den Fäusten bearbeiten

pump /pʌmp/ n Pumpe f **●** vt pumpen; *fig* aushorchen. **~ up** *(inflate)* aufpumpen

pumpkin /ˈpʌmpkɪn/ n Kürbis m

pun /pʌn/ n Wortspiel nt

punch¹ /pʌnʃ/ n Faustschlag m; *(device)* Locher m **●** vt boxen; lochen *(ticket)*; stanzen *(hole)*

p

punch² n (drink) Bowle f

punctual /ˈpʌŋktjʊəl/ adj pünktlich. **~ity** n Pünktlichkeit f

punctuat|e /ˈpʌŋktjʊeɪt/ vt mit Satzzeichen versehen. **~ion** n Interpunktion f

puncture /ˈpʌŋktʃə(r)/ n Loch nt; (tyre) Reifenpanne f ● vt durchstechen

punish /ˈpʌnɪʃ/ vt bestrafen. **~able** adj strafbar. **~ment** n Strafe f

punt /pʌnt/ n (boat) Stechkahn m

puny /ˈpjuːnɪ/ adj mickerig

pup /pʌp/ n = puppy

pupil /ˈpjuːpl/ n Schüler(in) m(f); (of eye) Pupille f

puppet /ˈpʌpɪt/ n Puppe f; (fig) Marionette f

puppy /ˈpʌpɪ/ n junger Hund m

purchase /ˈpɜːtʃəs/ n Kauf m; (leverage) Hebelkraft f ● vt kaufen. **~r** n Käufer m

pure /pjʊə(r)/ adj (-r, -st,) **-ly** adv rein

purge /pɜːdʒ/ n (Pol) Säuberungsaktion f ● vt reinigen

purification /pjʊərɪfɪˈkeɪʃn/ n Reinigung f. **~fy** vt (pt/pp -ied) reinigen

puritanical /pjʊərɪˈtænɪkl/ adj puritanisch

purity /ˈpjʊərɪtɪ/ n Reinheit f

purple /ˈpɜːpl/ adj (dunkel)lila

purpose /ˈpɜːpəs/ n Zweck m; (intention) Absicht f; (determination) Entschlossenheit f; **on ~** absichtlich. **~ful** adj entschlossen. **~ly** adv absichtlich

purr /pɜː(r)/ vi schnurren

purse /pɜːs/ n Portemonnaie nt; (Amer: handbag) Handtasche f

pursue /pəˈsjuː/ vt verfolgen; (fig) nachgehen (+ dat). **~r** n

Verfolger(in) m(f)

pursuit /pəˈsjuːt/ n Verfolgung f; Jagd f; (pastime) Beschäftigung f

pus /pʌs/ n Eiter m

push /pʊʃ/ n Stoß m; **get the ~** 🔲 hinausfliegen vt/i schieben; (press) drücken; (roughly) stoßen. **~ off** vt hinunterstoßen ● vi (🔲: leave) abhauen. **~ on** vi (continue) weitergehen/-fahren; (with activity) weitermachen. **~ up** vt hochschieben; hochtreiben (price)

push: ~-button n Druckknopf m. **~-chair** n [Kinder]sportwagen m

pushy /ˈpʊʃɪ/ adj 🔲 aufdringlich

puss /pʊs/ n, **pussy** n Mieze f

put /pʊt/ vt (pt/pp put, pres p putting) tun; (place) setzen; (upright) stellen; (flat) legen; (express) ausdrücken; (say) sagen; (estimate) schätzen (at auf + acc); **~ aside** or **by** beiseite legen ● vi to sea auslaufen ● adj **stay ~** dableiben. **~ away** vt wegräumen. **~ back** vt wieder hinsetzen/-stellen/-legen; zurückstellen (clock). **~ down** vt hinsetzen/-stellen/-legen; (suppress) niederschlagen; (kill) töten; (write) niederschreiben; (attribute) zuschreiben (to dat). **~ forward** vt vorbringen; vorstellen (clock). **~ in** vt einsetzen/-stellen/-legen; (insert) einstecken; (submit) einreichen ● vi **~ in for** beantragen. **~ off** vt ausmachen (light); (postpone) verschieben; **~ s.o. off** jdn abbestellen; (disconcert) jdn aus der Fassung bringen. **~ on** vt anziehen (clothes, brake); sich (dat) aufsetzen (hat); (Culin) aufsetzen; anmachen (light); aufführen (play); annehmen (accent); **~ on weight** zunehmen. **~ out** vt hinaussetzen/-stellen/-legen; ausmachen (fire, light); ausstrecken (hand); (disconcert) aus der Fassung bringen; **~ s.o./oneself out** jdm/

sich Umstände machen. **~ through** vt durchstecken; (*Teleph*) verbinden (**to** mit). **~ up** vt errichten (*building*); aufschlagen (*tent*); aufspannen (*umbrella*); anschlagen (*notice*); erhöhen (*price*); unterbringen (*guest*) • vi (*at hotel*) absteigen in (+ *dat*); **~ up with sth** sich (*dat*) etw bieten lassen

putrid /'pju:trɪd/ adj faulig

putt /pʌt/ n Putt m

putty /'pʌtɪ/ n Kitt m

puzzl|e /'pʌzl/ n Rätsel nt; (*jigsaw*) Puzzlespiel nt • vt **it ~es me** es ist mir rätselhaft. **~ing** adj rätselhaft

pyjamas /pə'dʒɑːməz/ npl Schlafanzug m

pylon /'paɪlən/ n Mast m

pyramid /'pɪrəmɪd/ n Pyramide f

python /'paɪθn/ n Python-schlange f

Qq

quack /kwæk/ n Quaken nt; (*doctor*) Quacksalber m • vi quaken

quadrangle /'kwɒdræŋgl/ n Viereck nt; (*court*) Hof m

quadruped /'kwɒdruped/ n Vierfüßer m

quadruple /'kwɒdrʊpl/ adj vierfach • vt vervierfachen • vi sich vervierfachen

quaint /kweɪnt/ adj (-er, -est) malerisch; (*odd*) putzig

quake /kweɪk/ n ▣ Erdbeben nt • vi beben; (*with fear*) zittern

qualif|ication /kwɒlɪfɪ'keɪʃn/ n Qualifikation f; (*reservation*) Einschränkung f. **~ied** adj qualifiziert;

(*trained*) ausgebildet; (*limited*) bedingt

qualify /'kwɒlɪfaɪ/ v (*pt/pp* -ied) • vt qualifizieren; (*entitle*) berechtigen; (*limit*) einschränken • vi sich qualifizieren

quality /'kwɒlətɪ/ n Qualität f; (*characteristic*) Eigenschaft f

qualm /kwɑːm/ n Bedenken pl

quantity /'kwɒntɪtɪ/ n Quantität f, Menge f; **in ~** in großen Mengen

quarantine /'kwɒrəntiːn/ n Quarantäne f

quarrel /'kwɒrl/ n Streit m • vi (*pt/pp* quarrelled) sich streiten. **~some** adj streitsüchtig

quarry[1] /'kwɒrɪ/ n (*prey*) Beute f

quarry[2] n Steinbruch m

quart /kwɔːt/ n Quart nt

quarter /'kwɔːtə(r)/ n Viertel nt; (*of year*) Vierteljahr nt; (*Amer*) 25-Cent-Stück nt; **~s** pl Quartier nt; **at [a] ~ to six** um Viertel vor sechs • vt vierteln; (*Mil*) einquartieren (**on** bei). **~'final** n Viertelfinale nt

quarterly /'kwɔːtəlɪ/ adj & adv vierteljährlich

quartet /kwɔː'tet/ n Quartett nt

quartz /kwɔːts/ n Quarz m

quay /kiː/ n Kai m

queasy /'kwiːzɪ/ adj **I feel ~** mir ist übel

queen /kwiːn/ n Königin f; (*Cards, Chess*) Dame f

queer /kwɪə(r)/ adj (-er, -est) eigenartig; (*dubious*) zweifelhaft; (*ill*) unwohl

quell /kwel/ vt unterdrücken

quench /kwentʃ/ vt löschen

query /'kwɪərɪ/ n Frage f; (*question mark*) Fragezeichen nt • vt (*pt/pp* -ied) infrage stellen; reklamieren (*bill*)

p

q

quest /kwɛst/ n Suche f (**for** nach)

question /'kwɛstʃn/ n Frage f; (*for discussion*) Thema nt; **out of the** ~ ausgeschlossen; **the person in** ~ die fragliche Person ●vt infrage stellen; **s.o.** jdn ausfragen; (*police*:) jdn verhören. **~able** adj zweifelhaft. ~ **mark** n Fragezeichen nt

questionnaire /kwɛstʃə'neə(r)/ n Fragebogen m

queue /kjuː/ n Schlange f ● vi ~ [up] Schlange stehen, sich anstellen (**for** nach)

quibble /'kwɪbl/ vi Haarspalterei treiben

quick /kwɪk/ adj (**-er, -est**) schnell; **be** ~! mach schnell! ● adv schnell. **~en** vt beschleunigen ● vi sich beschleunigen

quick: ~**sand** n Treibsand m. ~**-tempered** adj aufbrausend

quid /kwɪd/ n inv 🇬🇧 Pfund nt

quiet /'kwaɪət/ adj (**-er, -est**) still; (*calm*) ruhig; (*soft*) leise; **keep** ~ **about** 🇬🇧 nichts sagen von ●n Stille f; Ruhe f

quiet|en /'kwaɪətn/ vt beruhigen ● vi ~**en down** ruhig werden. ~**ness** n Stille f; Ruhe f

quilt /kwɪlt/ n Steppdecke f. ~**ed** adj Stepp-

quintet /kwɪn'tɛt/ n Quintett nt

quirk /kwɜːk/ n Eigenart f

quit /kwɪt/ v (*pt/pp* quitted or quit) vt verlassen; (*give up*) aufgeben; ~ **doing sth** aufhören, etw zu tun ● vi gehen

quite /kwaɪt/ adv ganz; (*really*) wirklich; ~ [**so**]! genau! ~ **a few** ziemlich viele

quits /kwɪts/ adj quitt

quiver /'kwɪvə(r)/ vi zittern

quiz /kwɪz/ n Quiz nt ● vt (*pt/pp* quizzed) ausfragen. ~**zical** adj fragend

quota /'kwəʊtə/ n Anteil m; (Comm) Kontingent nt

quotation /kwəʊ'teɪʃn/ n Zitat nt; (*price*) Kostenvoranschlag m; (*of shares*) Notierung f. ~ **marks** npl Anführungszeichen pl

quote /kwəʊt/ n 🇬🇧 = quotation; **in** ~**s** in Anführungszeichen ●vt/i zitieren

Rr

rabbi /'ræbaɪ/ n Rabbiner m; (*title*) Rabbi m

rabbit /'ræbɪt/ n Kaninchen nt

rabid /'ræbɪd/ adj fanatisch; (*animal*) tollwütig

rabies /'reɪbiːz/ n Tollwut f

race¹ /reɪs/ n Rasse f

race² /reɪs/ n Rennen nt; (*fig*) Wettlauf m ● vi [am Rennen] teilnehmen; (*athlete, horse*:) laufen; (🇬🇧: *rush*) rasen ● vt um die Wette laufen mit; einem Rennen teilnehmen lassen (*horse*)

race: ~**course** n Rennbahn f. ~**horse** n Rennpferd nt. ~**track** n Rennbahn f

racial /'reɪʃl/ adj rassisch; (*discrimination*) Rassen-

racing /'reɪsɪŋ/ n Rennsport m; (*horse-*) Pferderennen nt. ~ **car** n Rennwagen m. ~ **driver** n Rennfahrer m

racis|m /'reɪsɪzm/ n Rassismus m. ~**t** adj rassistisch ●n Rassist m

rack¹ /ræk/ n Ständer m; (*for plates*) Gestell nt ● vt ~ **one's brains** sich (dat) den Kopf zerbrechen

rack² /n go to ~ and ruin verfallen; (*fig*) herunterkommen

racket /'rækɪt/ n (*Sport*) Schläger m; (*din*) Krach m; (*swindle*) Schwindelgeschäft nt

racy /'reɪsɪ/ adj schwungvoll; (*risqué*) gewagt

radar /'reɪdɑː(r)/ n Radar m

radian|ce /'reɪdɪəns/ n Strahlen nt. ~**t** adj strahlend

radiat|e /'reɪdɪeɪt/ vt ausstrahlen ● vi (*heat:*) ausgestrahlt werden; (*roads:*) strahlenförmig ausgehen. ~**ion** n Strahlung f

radiator /'reɪdɪeɪtə(r)/ n Heizkörper m; (*Auto*) Kühler m

radical /'rædɪkl/ adj radikal ● n Radikale(r) m/f

radio /'reɪdɪəʊ/ n Radio nt; **by ~** über Funk ● vt funken (*message*)

radio|'active adj radioaktiv. ~**ac'tivity** n Radioaktivität f

radish /'rædɪʃ/ n Radieschen nt

radius /'reɪdɪəs/ n (pl **-dii** /-dɪaɪ/) Radius m, Halbmesser m

raffle /'ræfl/ n Tombola f

raft /rɑːft/ n Floß nt

rafter /'rɑːftə(r)/ n Dachsparren m

rag /ræg/ n Lumpen m; (*pej: newspaper*) Käseblatt nt

rage /reɪdʒ/ n Wut f; **all the ~** 🔲 der letzte Schrei ● vi rasen

ragged /'rægɪd/ adj zerlumpt; (*edge*) ausgefranst

raid /reɪd/ n Überfall m; (*Mil*) Angriff m; (*police*) Razzia f ● vt überfallen; (*Mil*) angreifen; (*police*) eine Razzia durchführen in (+ *dat*); (*break in*) eindringen in (+ *acc*); (*of bank*) Bankräuber m

rail /reɪl/ n Schiene f; (*pole*) Stange f; (*hand~*) Handlauf m; (*Naut*) Reling f; **by ~** mit der Bahn

railings /'reɪlɪŋz/ npl Geländer nt

'railroad n (*Amer*) = railway

'railway n [Eisen]bahn f. ~ **station** n Bahnhof m

rain /reɪn/ n Regen m ● vi regnen

rain|~bow n Regenbogen m. ~**coat** n Regenmantel m. ~**fall** n Niederschlag m

rainy /'reɪnɪ/ adj regnerisch

raise /reɪz/ n (*Amer*) Lohnerhöhung f ● vt erheben; (*upright*) aufrichten; (*make higher*) erhöhen; (*lift*) [hoch]heben; aufziehen (*child, animal*); aufwerfen (*question*); aufbringen (*money*)

raisin /'reɪzn/ n Rosine f

rake /reɪk/ n Harke f, Rechen m ● vt harken, rechen

rally /'rælɪ/ n Versammlung f; (*Auto*) Rallye f; (*Tennis*) Ballwechsel m ● vt sammeln

ram /ræm/ n Schafbock m ● vt (pt/pp **rammed**) rammen

rambl|e /'ræmbl/ n Wanderung f ● vi wandern; (*in speech*) irrereden. ~**er** n Wanderer m; (*rose*) Kletterrose f. ~**ing** adj weitschweifig; (*club*) Wander-

ramp /ræmp/ n Rampe f; (*Aviat*) Gangway f

rampage¹ /'ræmpeɪdʒ/ n **be/go on the ~** randalieren

rampage² /ræm'peɪdʒ/ vi randalieren

ramshackle /'ræmʃækl/ adj baufällig

ran /ræn/ see run

ranch /rɑːntʃ/ n Ranch f

random /'rændəm/ adj willkürlich; **a ~ sample** eine Stichprobe ● n **at ~** aufs Geratewohl; (*choose*) willkürlich

rang /ræŋ/ see ring²

range /reɪndʒ/ n Serie f, Reihe f;

(*Comm*) Auswahl *f*; Angebot *nt* (**of** an + *dat*); (*of mountains*) Kette *f*; (*Mus*) Umfang *m*; (*distance*) Reichweite *f*; (*for shooting*) Schießplatz *m*; (*stove*) Kohlenherd *m* ● *vi* reichen; ~ **from ... to** gehen von ... bis. ~**r** *n* Aufseher *m*

rank /ræŋk/ *n* (*row*) Reihe *f*; (*Mil*) Rang *m*; (*social position*) Stand *m*; **the ~ and file** die breite Masse ● *vt/i* einstufen; ~ **among** zählen zu

ransack /ˈrænsæk/ *vt* durchwühlen; (*pillage*) plündern

ransom /ˈrænsəm/ *n* Lösegeld *nt*; **hold s.o. to** ~ Lösegeld für jdn fordern

rape /reɪp/ *n* Vergewaltigung *f* ● *vt* vergewaltigen

rapid /ˈræpɪd/ *adj* schnell. ~**ity** *n* Schnelligkeit *f*

rapist /ˈreɪpɪst/ *n* Vergewaltiger *m*

rapture /ˈræptʃə(r)/ *n* Entzücken *nt*. ~**ous** *adj* begeistert

rare[1] /reə(r)/ *adj* (**-r, -st**) selten

rare[2] *adj* (*Culin*) englisch gebraten

rarefied /ˈreərɪfaɪd/ *adj* dünn

rarity /ˈreərətɪ/ *n* Seltenheit *f*

rascal /ˈrɑːskl/ *n* Schlingel *m*

rash[1] /ræʃ/ *n* (*Med*) Ausschlag *m*

rash[2] *adj* (**-er, -est**) voreilig

rasher /ˈræʃə(r)/ *n* Speckscheibe *f*

raspberry /ˈrɑːzbərɪ/ *n* Himbeere *f*

rat /ræt/ *n* Ratte *f*; (fig: *person*) Schuft *m*; **smell a** ~ fig Lunte riechen

rate /reɪt/ *n* Rate *f*; (*speed*) Tempo *nt*; (*of payment*) Satz *m*; (*of exchange*) Kurs *m*; ~**s** *pl* (*taxes*) ≈ Grundsteuer *f*; **at any** ~ auf jeden Fall; **at this** ~ auf diese Weise ● *vt* einschätzen; ~ **among** zählen zu ● *vi* ~ **as** gelten als

rather /ˈrɑːðə(r)/ *adv* lieber; (*fairly*) ziemlich; ~! und ob!

rating /ˈreɪtɪŋ/ *n* Einschätzung *f*; (*class*) Klasse *f*; (*sailor*) [einfacher] Matrose *m*; ~**s** *pl* (*Radio, TV*) ≈ Einschaltquote *f*

ratio /ˈreɪʃɪəʊ/ *n* Verhältnis *nt*

ration /ˈræʃn/ *n* Ration *f* ● *vt* rationieren

rational /ˈræʃənl/ *adj* rational. ~**ize** *vt/i* rationalisieren

rattle /ˈrætl/ *n* Rasseln *nt*; (*of windows*) Klappern *nt*; (*toy*) Klapper *f* ● *vi* rasseln; klappern ● *vt* rasseln mit

raucous /ˈrɔːkəs/ *adj* rau

rave /reɪv/ *vi* toben; ~ **about** schwärmen von

raven /ˈreɪvn/ *n* Rabe *m*

ravenous /ˈrævənəs/ *adj* heißhungrig

ravine /rəˈviːn/ *n* Schlucht *f*

raving /ˈreɪvɪŋ/ *adj* ~ **mad** fam total verrückt

ravishing /ˈrævɪʃɪŋ/ *adj* hinreißend

raw /rɔː/ *adj* (**-er, -est**) roh; (*not processed*) Roh-; (*skin*) wund; (*weather*) nasskalt; (*inexperienced*) unerfahren; **get a** ~ **deal** fam schlecht wegkommen. ~ **ma'terials** *npl* Rohstoffe *pl*

ray /reɪ/ *n* Strahl *m*

razor /ˈreɪzə(r)/ *n* Rasierapparat *m*. ~ **blade** *n* Rasierklinge *f*

re /riː/ *prep* betreffs (+ *gen*)

reach /riːtʃ/ *n* Reichweite *f*; (*of river*) Strecke *f*; **within/out of** ~ in/ außer Reichweite ● *vt* erreichen; (*arrive at*) ankommen in (+ *dat*); (~ *as far as*) reichen bis zu; kommen zu (*decision, conclusion*); (*pass*) reichen ● *vi* reichen (**to** bis zu); ~ **for** greifen nach

re'act /rɪˈækt/ *vi* reagieren

(to auf + acc)

re'action /rɪ-/ n Reaktion f. **~ary** adj reaktionär

reactor /rɪˈæktə(r)/ n Reaktor m

read /riːd/ vt/i (pt/pp **read** /red/) lesen; (aloud) vorlesen (**to** dat); (Univ) studieren; ablesen (meter). **~ out** vt vorlesen

readable /ˈriːdəbl/ adj lesbar

reader /ˈriːdə(r)/ n Leser(in) m (f); (book) Lesebuch nt

readily /ˈredɪlɪ/ adv bereitwillig; (easily) leicht

reading /ˈriːdɪŋ/ n Lesen nt; (Pol, Relig) Lesung f

rea'djust /riː-/ vt neu einstellen • vi sich umstellen (**to** auf + acc)

ready /ˈredɪ/ adj fertig; (willing) bereit; (quick) schnell; **get ~** sich fertig machen; (prepare to) sich bereitmachen

ready: ~-'made adj fertig. **~-to--'wear** adj Konfektions-

real /rɪəl/ adj wirklich; (genuine) echt; (actual) eigentlich • adv (Amer, 🔟) echt. **~ estate** n Immobilien pl

realis|m /ˈrɪəlɪzm/ n Realismus m. **~t** n Realist m. **~tic** adj, **-ally** adv realistisch

reality /rɪˈælətɪ/ n Wirklichkeit f

realization /rɪəlaɪˈzeɪʃn/ n Erkenntnis f

realize /ˈrɪəlaɪz/ vt einsehen; (become aware) gewahr werden; verwirklichen (hopes, plans); einbringen (price)

really /ˈrɪəlɪ/ adv wirklich; (actually) eigentlich

realm /relm/ n Reich nt

realtor /ˈriːəltə(r)/ n (Amer) Immobilienmakler m

reap /riːp/ vt ernten

reap'pear /riː-/ vi wiederkommen

rear¹ /rɪə(r)/ adj Hinter-; (Auto) Heck-. • **n the ~** der hintere Teil; **from the ~** von hinten

rear² vt aufziehen • vi ~ [up] (horse): sich aufbäumen

rear'range /riː-/ vt umstellen

reason /ˈriːzn/ n Grund m; (good sense) Vernunft f; (ability to think) Verstand m; **within ~** in vernünftigen Grenzen • vi argumentieren; **with ~** vernünftig reden mit. **~able** adj vernünftig; (not expensive) preiswert. **~ably** adv (fairly) ziemlich

reas'sur|ance /riː-/ n Beruhigung f; Versicherung f. **~e** vt beruhigen; **~e s.o. of sth** jdm etw (gen) versichern

rebel¹ /ˈrebl/ n Rebell m

rebel² /rɪˈbel/ vi (pt/pp rebelled) rebellieren. **~lion** n Rebellion f. **~lious** adj rebellisch

re'bound¹ /rɪ-/ vi abprallen

'rebound² /riː-/ n Rückprall m

re'build /riː-/ vt (pt/pp -built) wieder aufbauen

rebuke /rɪˈbjuːk/ n Tadel m • vt tadeln

re'call /rɪ-/ n Erinnerung f • vt zurückrufen; abberufen (diplomat); (remember) sich erinnern an (+ acc)

recant /rɪˈkænt/ vi widerrufen

recap /ˈriːkæp/ vt/i 🔟 = recapitulate

recapitulate /riːkəˈpɪtjʊlət/ vt/i zusammenfassen; rekapitulieren

re'capture /riː-/ vt wieder gefangen nehmen (person); wieder einfangen (animal)

reced|e /rɪˈsiːd/ vi zurückgehen. **~ing** adj (forehead, chin) fliehend

receipt /rɪˈsiːt/ n Quittung f; (receiving) Empfang m; **~s** pl (Comm) Einnahmen pl

receive /rɪˈsiːv/ vt erhalten, bekommen; empfangen (guests). **~r** n

(*Teleph*) Hörer *m*; (*of stolen goods*) Hehler *m*

recent /ˈriːsənt/ *adj* kürzlich erfolgte(r,s). **~ly** *adv* vor kurzem

receptacle /rɪˈseptəkl/ *n* Behälter *m*

reception /rɪˈsepʃn/ *n* Empfang *m*; **~ [desk]** (*in hotel*) Rezeption *f*; **~ist** *n* Empfangsdame *f*

receptive /rɪˈseptɪv/ *adj* aufnahmefähig; **~ to** empfänglich für

recess /rɪˈses/ *n* Nische *f*; (*holiday*) Ferien *pl*

recession /rɪˈseʃn/ *n* Rezession *f*

re'charge /riː-/ *vt* [wieder] aufladen

recipe /ˈresəpɪ/ *n* Rezept *nt*

recipient /rɪˈsɪpɪənt/ *n* Empfänger *m*

recital /rɪˈsaɪtl/ *n* (*of poetry, songs*) Vortrag *m*; (*on piano*) Konzert *nt*

recite /rɪˈsaɪt/ *vt* aufsagen; (*before audience*) vortragen

reckless /ˈreklɪs/ *adj* leichtsinnig; (*careless*) rücksichtslos. **~ness** *n* Leichtsinn *m*; Rücksichtslosigkeit *f*

reckon /ˈrekən/ *vt* rechnen; (*consider*) glauben ● *vi* **~ on/with** rechnen mit

re'claim /riː-/ *vt* zurückfordern; zurückgewinnen (*land*)

recline| /rɪˈklaɪn/ *vi* liegen. **~ing seat** *n* Liegesitz *m*

recluse /rɪˈkluːs/ *n* Einsiedler(in) *m(f)*

recognition /rekəgˈnɪʃn/ *n* Erkennen *nt*; (*acknowledgement*) Anerkennung *f*; **in ~** als Anerkennung (*of gen*)

recognize /ˈrekəgnaɪz/ *vt* erkennen; (*know again*) wieder erkennen; (*acknowledge*) anerkennen

re'coil /rɪ-/ *vi* zurückschnellen; (*in fear*) zurückschrecken

recollect /rekəˈlekt/ *vt* sich erinnern an (+ *acc*). **~ion** *n* Erinnerung *f*

recommend /rekəˈmend/ *vt* empfehlen. **~ation** *n* Empfehlung *f*

recon|cile /ˈrekənsaɪl/ *vt* versöhnen; **~cile oneself to** sich abfinden mit. **~ciliation** *n* Versöhnung *f*

reconnaissance /rɪˈkɒnɪsns/ *n* (*Mil*) Aufklärung *f*

reconnoitre /rekəˈnɔɪtə(r)/ *vi* (*pres p* **-tring**) auf Erkundung ausgehen

recon'sider /riː-/ *vt* sich (*dat*) noch einmal überlegen

recon'struct /riː-/ *vt* wieder aufbauen; rekonstruieren (*crime*)

record¹ /rɪˈkɔːd/ *vt* aufzeichnen; (*register*) registrieren; (*on tape*) aufnehmen

record² /ˈrekɔːd/ *n* Aufzeichnung *f*; (*Jur*) Protokoll *nt*; (*Mus*) [Schall]-platte *f*; (*Sport*) Rekord *m*; **~s** *pl* Unterlagen *pl*; **off the ~** inoffiziell; **have a [criminal] ~** vorbestraft sein

recorder /rɪˈkɔːdə(r)/ *n* (*Mus*) Blockflöte *f*

recording /rɪˈkɔːdɪŋ/ *n* Aufnahme *f*

re-'count¹ /riː-/ *vt* nachzählen

're-count² /riː-/ *n* (*Pol*) Nachzählung *f*

recover /rɪˈkʌvə(r)/ *vt* zurückbekommen ● *vi* sich erholen. **~y** *n* Wiedererlangung *f*; (*of health*) Erholung *f*

recreation /rekrɪˈeɪʃn/ *n* Erholung *f*; (*hobby*) Hobby *nt*. **~al** *adj* Freizeit-; **be ~al** erholsam sein

recruit /rɪˈkruːt/ *n* (*Mil*) Rekrut *m*; **new ~** (*member*) neues Mitglied *nt*; (*worker*) neuer Mitarbeiter *m* ● *vt* rekrutieren; anwerben (*staff*). **~ment** *n* Rekrutierung *f*;

Anwerbung f

rectang|le /'rektæŋgl/ n Rechteck nt. **~ular** adj rechteckig

rectify /'rektɪfaɪ/ v (pt/pp -ied) berichtigen

rector /'rektə(r)/ n Pfarrer m; (Univ) Rektor m. **~y** n Pfarrhaus nt

recur /rɪ'kɜː(r)/ vi (pt/pp recurred) sich wiederholen; (illness:) wiederkehren

recurren|ce /rɪ'kʌrəns/ n Wiederkehr f. **~t** adj wiederkehrend

recycle /riː'saɪkl/ vt wieder verwerten

red /red/ adj (redder, reddest) rot ● n Rot nt

redd|en /'redn/ vt röten ● vi rot werden. **~ish** adj rötlich

re'decorate /riː-/ vt renovieren; (paint) neu streichen; (wallpaper) neu tapezieren

redeem /rɪ'diːm/ vt einlösen; (Relig) erlösen

redemption /rɪ'dempʃn/ n Erlösung f

red: ~-haired adj rothaarig. **~-'handed** adj catch s.o. **~-handed** jdn auf frischer Tat ertappen. **~ 'herring** n falsche Spur f. **~-hot** adj glühend heiß. **~ 'light** n (Auto) rote Ampel f. **~ness** n Röte f

re'do /riː-/ vt (pt -did, pp -done) noch einmal machen

re'double /riː-/ vt verdoppeln

red 'tape n 🗓 Bürokratie f

reduc|e /rɪ'djuːs/ vt verringern, vermindern; (in size) verkleinern; ermäßigen (costs); herabsetzen (price, goods); (Culin) einkochen lassen. **~tion** n Verringerung f; (in price) Ermäßigung f; (in size) Verkleinerung f

redundan|cy /rɪ'dʌndənsɪ/ n Beschäftigungslosigkeit f. **~t** adj über-

flüssig; **make ~t** entlassen; **be made ~t** beschäftigungslos werden

reed /riːd/ n [Schilf]rohr nt; **~s** pl Schilf nt

reef /riːf/ n Riff nt

reek /riːk/ vi riechen (of nach)

reel /riːl/ n Rolle f, Spule f ● vi (stagger) taumeln ● vt **~ off** (fig) herunterrasseln

refectory /rɪ'fektərɪ/ n Refektorium nt; (Univ) Mensa f

refer /rɪ'fɜː(r)/ v (pt/pp referred) ● vt verweisen (to an + acc); übergeben, weiterleiten (matter) (to an + acc) ● vi **~ to** sich beziehen auf (+ acc); (mention) erwähnen; (concern) betreffen; (consult) sich wenden an (+ acc); nachschlagen in (+ dat) (book); **are you ~ring to me?** meinen Sie mich?

referee /refə'riː/ n Schiedsrichter m; (Boxing) Ringrichter m; (for job) Referenz f ● vt/i (pt/pp refereed) Schiedsrichter/Ringrichter sein (bei)

reference /'refərəns/ n Erwähnung f; (in book) Verweis m; (for job) Referenz f; **with ~ to** in Bezug auf (+ acc); **make [a] ~ to** erwähnen. **~ book** n Nachschlagewerk nt

referendum /refə'rendəm/ n Volksabstimmung f

re'fill [1] /riː-/ vt nachfüllen

'refill [2] /riː-/ n (for pen) Ersatzmine f

refine /rɪ'faɪn/ vt raffinieren. **~d** adj fein, vornehm. **~ment** n Vornehmheit f; (Techn) Verfeinerung f. **~ry** n Raffinerie f

reflect /rɪ'flekt/ vt reflektieren; (mirror:) [wider]spiegeln; **be ~ed in** sich spiegeln in (+ dat). **~ on** nachdenken (on über + acc). **~ion** n Reflexion f; (image) Spiegelbild nt; **on ~ion** nach nochmaliger Überlegung. **~or** n Rückstrahler m

r

reflex /ˈriːfleks/ n Reflex m

reflexive /rɪˈfleksɪv/ adj reflexiv

reform /rɪˈfɔːm/ n Reform f ● vt reformieren ● vi sich bessern

refrain[1] /rɪˈfreɪn/ n Refrain m

refrain[2] vi ~ **from doing sth** etw nicht tun

refresh /rɪˈfreʃ/ vt erfrischen. ~**ing** adj erfrischend. ~**ments** npl Erfrischungen pl

refrigerat|e /rɪˈfrɪdʒəreɪt/ vt kühlen. ~**or** n Kühlschrank m

re'fuel /riː-/ vt/i (pt/pp **-fuelled**) auftanken

refuge /ˈrefjuːdʒ/ n Zuflucht f; **take** ~ Zuflucht nehmen

refugee /refjʊˈdʒiː/ n Flüchtling m

'refund[1] /ˈriː-/ **get a** ~ sein Geld zurückbekommen

re'fund[2] /rɪ-/ vt zurückerstatten

refusal /rɪˈfjuːzl/ n (see **refuse**[1]) Ablehnung f; Weigerung f

refuse[1] /rɪˈfjuːz/ vt ablehnen; (not grant) verweigern; ~ **to do sth** sich weigern, etw zu tun ● vi ablehnen; sich weigern

refuse[2] /ˈrefjuːs/ n Müll m

refute /rɪˈfjuːt/ vt widerlegen

re'gain /rɪ-/ vt wiedergewinnen

regal /ˈriːgl/ adj königlich

regard /rɪˈɡɑːd/ n (heed) Rücksicht f; (respect) Achtung f; ~**s** pl Grüße pl; **with** ~ **to** in Bezug auf (+ acc) ● vt ansehen, betrachten (**as** als). ~**ing** prep bezüglich (+ gen). ~**less** adv ohne Rücksicht (**of** auf + acc)

regatta /rɪˈɡætə/ n Regatta f

regime /reɪˈʒiːm/ n Regime nt

regiment /ˈredʒɪmənt/ n Regiment nt. ~**al** adj Regiments-

region /ˈriːdʒən/ n Region f; **in the** ~ **of** (fig) ungefähr. ~**al** adj regional

register /ˈredʒɪstə(r)/ n Register

nt; (Sch) Anwesenheitsliste f ● vt registrieren; (report) anmelden; einschreiben (letter); aufgeben (luggage) ● vi (report) sich anmelden

registrar /redʒɪˈstrɑː(r)/ n Standesbeamte(r) m

registration /redʒɪˈstreɪʃn/ n Registrierung f; Anmeldung f. ~ **number** n Autonummer f

registry office /ˈredʒɪstrɪ-/ n Standesamt m

regret /rɪˈɡret/ n Bedauern nt ● vt (pt/pp **regretted**) bedauern. ~**fully** adv mit Bedauern

regrettab|le /rɪˈɡretəbl/ adj bedauerlich. ~**ly** adv bedauerlicherweise

regular /ˈreɡjʊlə(r)/ adj regelmäßig; (usual) üblich ● n (in pub) Stammgast m; (in shop) Stammkunde m. ~**ity** n Regelmäßigkeit f

regulat|e /ˈreɡjʊleɪt/ vt regulieren. ~**ion** n (rule) Vorschrift f

rehears|al /rɪˈhɜːsl/ n (Theat) Probe f. ~**e** vt proben

reign /reɪn/ n Herrschaft f ● vi herrschen, regieren

rein /reɪn/ n Zügel m

reindeer /ˈreɪndɪə(r)/ n inv Rentier nt

reinforce /riːɪnˈfɔːs/ vt verstärken. ~**ment** n Verstärkung f; **send** ~**ments** Verstärkung schicken

reiterate /riːˈɪtəreɪt/ vt wiederholen

reject /rɪˈdʒekt/ vt ablehnen. ~**ion** n Ablehnung f

rejects /ˈriːdʒekts/ npl (Comm) Ausschussware f

rejoic|e /rɪˈdʒɔɪs/ vi (literary) sich freuen. ~**ing** n Freude f

re'join /rɪ-/ vt sich wieder anschließen (+ dat); wieder beitreten (+ dat) (club, party)

rejuvenate /rɪˈdʒuːvəneɪt/ vt

verjüngen

relapse /rɪˈlæps/ n Rückfall m ● vi einen Rückfall erleiden

relate /rɪˈleɪt/ vt (tell) erzählen; (connect) verbinden

relation /rɪˈleɪʃn/ n Beziehung f; (person) Verwandte(r) m/f. **~ship** n Beziehung f; (link) Verbindung f; (blood tie) Verwandtschaft f; (affair) Verhältnis nt

relative /ˈrelətɪv/ n Verwandte(r) m/f ● adj relativ; (Gram) Relativ-. **~ly** adv relativ, verhältnismäßig

relax /rɪˈlæks/ vt lockern, entspannen ● vi sich lockern, sich entspannen. **~ation** n Entspannung f. **~ing** adj entspannend

relay[1] /riːˈleɪ/ vt (pt/pp **-layed**) weitergeben; (Radio, TV) übertragen

relay[2] /ˈriːleɪ/ n. **~ [race]** n Staffel f

release /rɪˈliːs/ n Freilassung f, Entlassung f; (Techn) Auslöser m ● vt freilassen; (let go of) loslassen; (Techn) auslösen; veröffentlichen (information)

relent /rɪˈlent/ vi nachgeben. **~less** adj erbarmungslos; (unceasing) unaufhörlich

relevan|ce /ˈreləvəns/ n Relevanz f. **~t** adj relevant (to für)

reliab|ility /rɪlaɪəˈbɪlətɪ/ n Zuverlässigkeit f. **~le** adj zuverlässig

relian|ce /rɪˈlaɪəns/ n Abhängigkeit f (on auf). **~t** adj angewiesen (on auf + acc)

relic /ˈrelɪk/ n Überbleibsel nt; (Relig) Reliquie f

relief /rɪˈliːf/ n Erleichterung f; (assistance) Hilfe f; (replacement) Ablösung f; (Art) Relief nt

relieve /rɪˈliːv/ vt erleichtern; (take over from) ablösen; **~ of** entlasten von

religion /rɪˈlɪdʒən/ n Religion f

religious /rɪˈlɪdʒəs/ adj religiös

relinquish /rɪˈlɪŋkwɪʃ/ vt loslassen; (give up) aufgeben

relish /ˈrelɪʃ/ n Genuss m; (Culin) Würze f ● vt genießen

reluctan|ce /rɪˈlʌktəns/ n Widerstreben nt. **~t** adj widerstrebend; **be ~t** zögern (to zu). **~tly** adv ungern, widerstrebend

rely /rɪˈlaɪ/ vi (pt/pp **-ied**) **~ on** sich verlassen auf (+ acc); (be dependent on) angewiesen sein auf (+ acc)

remain /rɪˈmeɪn/ vi bleiben; (be left) übrig bleiben. **~der** n Rest m. **~ing** adj restlich. **~s** npl Reste pl; [mortal] **~s** [sterbliche] Überreste pl

remand /rɪˈmɑːnd/ n **on ~** in Untersuchungshaft ● vt **~ in custody** in Untersuchungshaft schicken

remark /rɪˈmɑːk/ n Bemerkung f ● vt bemerken. **~able** adj, **-bly** adv bemerkenswert

re|marry /riː-/ vi wieder heiraten

remedy /ˈremədɪ/ n [Heil]mittel nt (for gegen); (fig) Abhilfe f ● vt (pt/pp **-ied**) abhelfen (+ dat); beheben (fault)

rememb|er /rɪˈmembə(r)/ vt sich erinnern an (+ acc); **~er** to do sth daran denken, etw zu tun ● vi sich erinnern

remind /rɪˈmaɪnd/ vt erinnern (of an + acc). **~er** n Andenken nt; (letter, warning) Mahnung f

reminisce /remɪˈnɪs/ vi sich seinen Erinnerungen hingeben. **~nces** npl Erinnerungen pl. **~nt** adj be **~nt of** erinnern an (+ acc)

remnant /ˈremnənt/ n Rest m

remorse /rɪˈmɔːs/ n Reue f. **~ful** adj reumütig. **~less** adj unerbittlich

remote /rɪˈməʊt/ adj fern; (isolated) abgelegen; (slight) gering. **~**

con'trol n Fernsteuerung f; (for TV) Fernbedienung f

remotely /rɪ'məʊtlɪ/ adv entfernt; **not ~** nicht im Entferntesten

re'movable /rɪ-/ adj abnehmbar

removal /rɪ'muːvl/ n Entfernung f; (from house) Umzug m. **~ van** n Möbelwagen m

remove /rɪ'muːv/ vt entfernen; (take off) abnehmen; (take out) herausnehmen

render /'rendə(r)/ vt machen; erweisen (service); (translate) wiedergeben; (Mus) vortragen

renegade /'renɪgeɪd/ n Abtrünnige(r) m/f

renew /rɪ'njuː/ vt erneuern; verlängern (contract). **~al** n Erneuerung f; Verlängerung f

renounce /rɪ'naʊns/ vt verzichten auf (+ acc)

renovat|e /'renəveɪt/ vt renovieren. **~ion** n Renovierung f

renown /rɪ'naʊn/ n Ruf m. **~ed** adj berühmt

rent /rent/ n Miete f ● vt mieten; (hire) leihen; **~ [out]** vermieten; verleihen. **~al** n Mietgebühr f; Leihgebühr f

renunciation /rɪnʌnsɪ'eɪʃn/ n Verzicht m

re'open /riː-/ vt/i wieder aufmachen

re'organize /riː-/ vt reorganisieren

rep /rep/ n Ⓕ Vertreter m

repair /rɪ'peə(r)/ n Reparatur f; **in good/bad ~** in gutem/schlechtem Zustand ● vt reparieren

repatriat|e /riː'pætrɪeɪt/ vt repatriieren

re'pay /riː-/ vt (pt/pp -paid) zurückzahlen; **~ s.o. for sth** jdm etw zurückzahlen. **~ment** n Rückzahlung f

repeal /rɪ'piːl/ n Aufhebung f ● vt aufheben

repeat /rɪ'piːt/ n Wiederholung f ● vt/i wiederholen; **~ after me** sprechen Sie mir nach. **~ed** adj wiederholt

repel /rɪ'pel/ vt (pt/pp repelled) abwehren; (fig) abstoßen. **~lent** adj abstoßend

repent /rɪ'pent/ vi Reue zeigen. **~ance** n Reue f. **~ant** adj reuig

repercussions /riːpə'kʌʃnz/ npl Auswirkungen pl

repertoire /'repətwɑː(r)/, **repertory** n Repertoire nt

repetit|ion /repɪ'tɪʃn/ n Wiederholung f. **~ive** adj eintönig

re'place /rɪ-/ vt zurücktun; (take the place of) ersetzen; (exchange) austauschen. **~ment** n Ersatz m

'replay /riː-/ n (Sport) Wiederholungsspiel nt; **[action] ~** Wiederholung f

replenish /rɪ'plenɪʃ/ vt auffüllen (stocks); (refill) nachfüllen

replica /'replɪkə/ n Nachbildung f

reply /rɪ'plaɪ/ n Antwort f (**to** auf + acc) ● vt/i (pt/pp replied) antworten

report /rɪ'pɔːt/ n Bericht m; (Sch) Zeugnis nt; (rumour) Gerücht nt; (of gun) Knall m ● vt berichten; (notify) melden; **~ s.o. to the police** jdn anzeigen ● vi berichten (**on** über + acc); (present oneself) sich melden (**to** bei). **~er** n Reporter(in) m/f

reprehensible /reprɪ'hensəbl/ adj tadelnswert

represent /reprɪ'zent/ vt darstellen; (act for) vertreten, repräsentieren. **~ation** n Darstellung f

representative /reprɪ'zentətɪv/ adj repräsentativ (**of** für) ● n Bevollmächtigte(r) m/f; (Comm) Vertreter(in) m/f; (Amer, Politics)

Abgeordnete(r) m/f

repress /rɪ'pres/ vt unterdrücken.
~ion n Unterdrückung f. **~ive** adj
repressiv

reprieve /rɪ'priːv/ n Begnadigung
f; (fig) Gnadenfrist f ● vt be-
gnadigen

reprimand /'reprɪmɑːnd/ n Tadel
m ● vt tadeln

'reprint¹ /riː-/ n Nachdruck m
re'print² /riː-/ vt neu auflegen

reprisal /rɪ'praɪzl/ n Vergeltungs-
maßnahme f

reproach /rɪ'prəʊtʃ/ n Vorwurf m
● vt Vorwürfe pl machen (+ dat).
~ful adj vorwurfsvoll

repro'duc|e /riː-/ vt wiedergeben,
reproduzieren ● vi sich fortpflanzen.
~tion n Reproduktion f; (Biology)
Fortpflanzung f

reptile /'reptaɪl/ n Reptil nt

republic /rɪ'pʌblɪk/ n Republik f.
~an adj republikanisch ● n Republi-
kaner(in) m(f)

repugnan|ce /rɪ'pʌɡnəns/ n Wi-
derwille m. **~t** adj widerlich

repuls|ion /rɪ'pʌlʃn/ n Widerwille
m. **~ive** adj abstoßend, widerlich

reputable /'repjʊtəbl/ adj (firm)
von gutem Ruf; (respectable) anständig

reputation /repjʊ'teɪʃn/ n Ruf m

request /rɪ'kwest/ n Bitte f ● vt
bitten

require /rɪ'kwaɪə(r)/ vt (need)
brauchen; (demand) erfordern; **be
~d to do sth** etw tun müssen.
~ment n Bedürfnis nt; (condition)
Erfordernis nt

re'sale /riː-/ n Weiterverkauf m

rescue /'reskjuː/ n Rettung f ● vt
retten. **~r** n Retter m

research /rɪ'sɜːtʃ/ n Forschung f
● vt erforschen; (in media) recher-

chieren. **~er** n Forscher m; (for
media) Rechercheur m

resem|blance /rɪ'zembləns/ n
Ähnlichkeit f. **~ble** vt ähneln
(+ dat)

resent /rɪ'zent/ vt übel nehmen;
einen Groll hegen gegen (person).
~ful adj verbittert. **~ment** n
Groll m

reservation /rezə'veɪʃn/ n Reser-
vierung f; (doubt) Vorbehalt m; (enclosure) Reservat nt

reserve /rɪ'zɜːv/ n Reserve f; (for
animals) Reservat nt; (Sport) Reser-
vespieler(in) m(f) ● vt reservieren;
(client:) reservieren lassen; (keep)
aufheben; sich (dat) vorbehalten
(right). **~d** adj reserviert

reservoir /'rezəvwɑː(r)/ n Reservoir nt

re'shuffle /riː-/ n (Pol) Umbildung
f ● vt (Pol) umbilden

residence /'rezɪdəns/ n Wohnsitz
m; (official) Residenz f; (stay) Aufenthalt m

resident /'rezɪdənt/ adj ansässig
(**in** in + dat); (housekeeper, nurse) im
Haus wohnend ● n Bewohner(in)
m(f); (of street) Anwohner m. **~ial**
adj Wohn-

residue /'rezɪdjuː/ n Rest m;
(Chemistry) Rückstand m

resign /rɪ'zaɪn/ vt **~ oneself to**
sich abfinden mit ● vi kündigen;
(from public office) zurücktreten.
~ation n Resignation f; (from job)
Kündigung f; Rücktritt m. **~ed** adj
resigniert

resilient /rɪ'zɪlɪənt/ adj federnd;
(fig) widerstandsfähig

resin /'rezɪn/ n Harz nt

resist /rɪ'zɪst/ vt/i sich widersetzen
(+ dat), (fig) widerstehen (+ dat).
~ance n Widerstand m. **~ant** adj
widerstandsfähig

resolut|e /'rezəlu:t/ adj entschlossen. **~ion** n Entschlossenheit f; (intention) Vorsatz m; (Pol) Resolution f

resolve /rɪ'zɒlv/ n Entschlossenheit f; (decision) Beschluss m ● vt beschließen; (solve) lösen

resort /rɪ'zɔ:t/ n (place) Urlaubsort m; **as a last ~** wenn alles andere fehlschlägt ● vi **~ to** (fig) greifen zu

resound /rɪ'zaʊnd/ vi widerhallen

resource /rɪ'sɔ:s/ n **~s** pl Ressourcen pl. **~ful** adj findig

respect /rɪ'spekt/ n Respekt m, Achtung f (for vor + dat); (aspect) Hinsicht f; **with ~ to** in Bezug auf (+ acc) ● vt respektieren, achten

respect|able /rɪ'spektəbl/ adj, **-bly** adv ehrbar; (decent) anständig; (considerable) ansehnlich. **~ful** adj respektvoll

respective /rɪ'spektɪv/ adj jeweilig. **~ly** adv beziehungsweise

respiration /respə'reɪʃn/ n Atmung f

respite /'respaɪt/ n [Ruhe]pause f; (delay) Aufschub m

respond /rɪ'spɒnd/ vi antworten; (react) reagieren (**to** auf + acc)

response /rɪ'spɒns/ n Antwort f; Reaktion f

responsibility /rɪspɒnsɪ'bɪlətɪ/ n Verantwortung f; (duty) Verpflichtung f

responsib|le /rɪ'spɒnsəbl/ adj verantwortlich; (trustworthy) verantwortungsvoll. **~ly** adv verantwortungsbewusst

rest¹ /rest/ n Ruhe f; (holiday) Erholung f; (interval & Mus) Pause f; **have a ~** eine Pause machen; (rest) sich ausruhen ● vi ausruhen; (lean) lehnen (**on** an/auf + acc) ● vi ruhen; (have a rest) sich ausruhen

rest² n the **~** der Rest; (people) die Übrigen pl ● vi **it ~s with you** es ist an Ihnen (to zu)

restaurant /'rest(ə)rɒnt/ n Restaurant nt, Gaststätte f

restful /'restfl/ adj erholsam

restive /'restɪv/ adj unruhig

restless /'restlɪs/ adj unruhig

restoration /restə'reɪʃn/ n (of building) Restaurierung f

restore /rɪ'stɔ:(r)/ vt wiederherstellen; restaurieren (building)

restrain /rɪ'streɪn/ vt zurückhalten; **~ oneself** sich beherrschen. **~ed** adj zurückhaltend. **~t** n Zurückhaltung f

restrict /rɪ'strɪkt/ vt einschränken; **~ to** beschränken auf (+ acc). **~ion** n Einschränkung f; Beschränkung f. **~ive** adj einschränkend

'rest room n (Amer) Toilette f

result /rɪ'zʌlt/ n Ergebnis nt, Resultat nt; (consequence) Folge f; **as a ~** als Folge (**of** gen) ● vi sich ergeben (**from** aus); **~ in** enden in (+ dat); (lead to) führen zu

resume /rɪ'zju:m/ vt wieder aufnehmen ● vi wieder beginnen

résumé /'rezʊmeɪ/ n Zusammenfassung f

resumption /rɪ'zʌmpʃn/ n Wiederaufnahme f

resurrect /rezə'rekt/ vt (fig) wieder beleben. **~ion** n the R **~ion** (Relig) die Auferstehung

resuscitat|e /rɪ'sʌsɪteɪt/ vt wieder beleben. **~ion** n Wiederbelebung f

retail /'ri:teɪl/ n Einzelhandel m ● adj Einzelhandels- ● adv im Einzelhandel ● vt im Einzelhandel verkaufen ● vi **~ at** im Einzelhandel kosten. **~er** n Einzelhändler m

retain /rɪ'teɪn/ vt behalten

retaliat|e /rɪ'tælɪeɪt/ vi zurückschlagen. **~ion** n Vergeltung f; **in**

~ion als Vergeltung

retarded /rɪˈtɑːdɪd/ adj zurückgeblieben

reticen|ce /ˈretɪsns/ n Zurückhaltung f. ~t adj zurückhaltend

retina /ˈretɪnə/ n Netzhaut f

retinue /ˈretɪnjuː/ n Gefolge nt

retire /rɪˈtaɪə(r)/ vi in den Ruhestand treten; (withdraw) sich zurückziehen. ~d adj im Ruhestand. ~ment n Ruhestand m

retiring /rɪˈtaɪərɪŋ/ adj zurückhaltend

retort /rɪˈtɔːt/ n scharfe Erwiderung f. (Chemistry) Retorte f • vt scharf erwidern

re'trace /riː-/ vt ~ one's steps denselben Weg zurückgehen

re'train /riː-/ vt umschulen • vi umgeschult werden

retreat /rɪˈtriːt/ n Rückzug m; (place) Zufluchtsort m • vi sich zurückziehen

re'trial /riː-/ n Wiederaufnahmeverfahren nt

retrieve /rɪˈtriːv/ vt zurückholen; (from wreckage) bergen; (Computing) wieder auffinden

retrograde /ˈretrəɡreɪd/ adj rückschrittlich

retrospect /ˈretrəspekt/ n in ~ rückblickend. ~ive adj rückwirkend; (looking back) rückblickend

return /rɪˈtɜːn/ n Rückkehr f; (giving back) Rückgabe f; (Comm) Ertrag m; (ticket) Rückfahrkarte f; (Aviat) Rückflugschein m; by ~ [of post] postwendend; in ~ für; in ~ for für; many happy ~s! herzlichen Glückwunsch zum Geburtstag! • vt zurückgehen/-fahren; (come back) zurückkommen • vt zurückgeben; (put back) zurückstellen/-legen; (send back) zurückschicken

return ticket n Rückfahrkarte f;

(Aviat) Rückflugschein m

reunion /riːˈjuːnɪən/ n Wiedervereinigung f; (social gathering) Treffen nt

reunite /riːjuːˈnaɪt/ vt wieder vereinigen

re'use vt wieder verwenden

rev /rev/ n (Auto, Ⓘ) Umdrehung f • vt/i ~ [up] den Motor auf Touren bringen

reveal /rɪˈviːl/ vt zum Vorschein bringen; (fig) enthüllen. ~ing adj (fig) aufschlussreich

revel /ˈrevl/ vi (pt/pp revelled) ~ in sth etw genießen

revelation /revəˈleɪʃn/ n Offenbarung f, Enthüllung f

revenge /rɪˈvendʒ/ n Rache f; (fig & Sport) Revanche f • vt rächen

revenue /ˈrevənjuː/ n [Staats]einnahmen pl

revere /rɪˈvɪə(r)/ vt verehren. ~nce n Ehrfurcht f

Reverend /ˈrevərənd/ adj the ~ X Pfarrer X; (Catholic) Hochwürden X

reverent /ˈrevərənt/ adj ehrfürchtig

reversal /rɪˈvɜːsl/ n Umkehrung f

reverse /rɪˈvɜːs/ adj umgekehrt • n Gegenteil nt; (back) Rückseite f; (Auto) Rückwärtsgang m • vt umkehren; (Auto) zurücksetzen • vi zurücksetzen

revert /rɪˈvɜːt/ vi ~ to zurückfallen an (+ acc)

review /rɪˈvjuː/ n Rückblick m (of auf + acc); (re-examination) Überprüfung f; (Mil) Truppenschau f; (of book, play) Kritik f, Rezension f • vt zurückblicken auf (+ acc); überprüfen (situation); rezensieren (book, play). ~er n Kritiker m, Rezensent m

revis|e /rɪˈvaɪz/ vt revidieren; (for

exam) wiederholen. **~ion** n Revision f; Wiederholung f

revival /rɪ'vaɪvl/ n Wiederbelebung f

revive /rɪ'vaɪv/ vt wieder beleben; (*fig*) wieder aufleben lassen ● vi wieder aufleben

revolt /rɪ'vəʊlt/ n Aufstand m ● vi rebellieren ● vt anwidern. **~ing** adj widerlich, eklig

revolution /revə'lu:ʃn/ n Revolution f; (*Auto*) Umdrehung f. **~ary** adj revolutionär. **~ize** vt revolutionieren

revolve /rɪ'vɒlv/ vi sich drehen; **~ around** kreisen um

revolv|er /rɪ'vɒlvə(r)/ n Revolver m. **~ing** adj Dreh-

revue /rɪ'vju:/ n Revue f; (*satirical*) Kabarett nt

revulsion /rɪ'vʌlʃn/ n Abscheu m

reward /rɪ'wɔ:d/ n Belohnung f ● vt belohnen. **~ing** adj lohnend

re'write /ri:-/ vt (pt rewrote, pp rewritten) noch einmal [neu] schreiben; (*alter*) umschreiben

rhetoric /'retərɪk/ n Rhetorik f. **~al** adj rhetorisch

rheumatism /'ru:mətɪzm/ n Rheumatismus m, Rheuma nt

Rhine /raɪn/ n Rhein m

rhinoceros /raɪ'nɒsərəs/ n Nashorn nt, Rhinozeros nt

rhubarb /'ru:bɑ:b/ n Rhabarber m

rhyme /raɪm/ n Reim m ● vt reimen ● vi sich reimen

rhythm /'rɪðm/ n Rhythmus m. **~ic[al]** adj, **-ally** adv rhythmisch

rib /rɪb/ n Rippe f

ribbon /'rɪbən/ n Band nt; (*for typewriter*) Farbband nt

rice /raɪs/ n Reis m

rich /rɪtʃ/ adj (-er, -est) reich; (*food*) gehaltvoll; (*heavy*) schwer

● **n** the **~** pl die Reichen; **~es** pl Reichtum m

ricochet /'rɪkəʃeɪ/ vi abprallen

rid /rɪd/ vt (pt/pp rid, pres p ridding) befreien (**of** von); **get ~ of** loswerden

riddance /'rɪdns/ n **good ~!** auf Nimmerwiedersehen!

ridden /'rɪdn/ see **ride**

riddle /'rɪdl/ n Rätsel nt

riddled /'rɪdld/ adj **~ with** durchlöchert mit

ride /raɪd/ n Ritt m; (*in vehicle*) Fahrt f; **take s.o. for a ~** [T] jdn reinlegen ● v (pt rode, pp ridden) ● vt reiten (*horse*); fahren mit (*bicycle*) ● vi reiten; (*in vehicle*) fahren. **~r** n Reiter(in) m(f); (*on bicycle*) Fahrer(in) m(f)

ridge /rɪdʒ/ n Erhebung f; (*on roof*) First m; (*of mountain*) Grat m, Kamm m

ridicule /'rɪdɪkju:l/ n Spott m ● vt verspotten, spotten über (+ acc)

ridiculous /rɪ'dɪkjʊləs/ adj lächerlich

riding /'raɪdɪŋ/ n Reiten nt ● attrib Reit-

riff-raff /'rɪfræf/ n Gesindel nt

rifle /'raɪfl/ n Gewehr nt ● vt plündern; **~ through** durchwühlen

rift /rɪft/ n Spalt m; (*fig*) Riss m

rig /rɪg/ n Ölbohrturm m; (*at sea*) Bohrinsel f ● vt (pt/pp **rigged**) **~ out** ausrüsten; **~ up** aufbauen

right /raɪt/ adj richtig; (*not left*) rechte(r,s); **be ~** (*person:*) Recht haben; (*clock:*) richtig gehen; **put ~** wieder in Ordnung bringen; (*fig*) richtig stellen; **that's ~!** das stimmt! ● adv richtig; (*directly*) direkt; (*completely*) ganz; (*not left*) rechts; (*go*) nach rechts; **~ away** sofort ● n Recht nt; (*not left*) Seite f; **on the ~** rechts; **from/to**

the ~ von/nach rechts; **be in the ~** Recht haben; **by ~s** eigentlich; **the R~** (Pol) die Rechte. **~ angle** n rechter Winkel m

rightful /'raɪtfl/ adj rechtmäßig

right-'handed adj rechtshändig

rightly /'raɪtlɪ/ adv mit Recht

right-'wing adj (Pol) rechte(r,s)

rigid /'rɪdʒɪd/ adj starr; (strict) streng. **~ity** n Starrheit f; Strenge f

rigorous /'rɪgərəs/ adj streng

rigour /'rɪgə(r)/ n Strenge f

rim /rɪm/ n Rand m; (of wheel) Felge f

rind /raɪnd/ n (on fruit) Schale f; (on cheese) Rinde f; (on bacon) Schwarte f

ring[1] /rɪŋ/ n Ring m; (for circus) Manege f; **stand in a ~** im Kreis stehen ● vt umringen

ring[2] n Klingeln nt; **give s.o. a ~** (Teleph) jdn anrufen ● v (pt rang, pp rung) ● vt läuten; ~ **[up]** (Teleph) anrufen ● vi (bells:) läuten; (telephone:) klingeln. **~ back** vt/i (Teleph) zurückrufen

ring: ~leader n Rädelsführer m. **~road** n Umgehungsstraße f

rink /rɪŋk/ n Eisbahn f

rinse /rɪns/ n Spülung f; (hair colour) Tönung f ● vt spülen

riot /'raɪət/ n Aufruhr m; **~s** pl Unruhen pl; **run** ~ randalieren ● vi randalieren. **~er** n Randalierer m. **~ous** adj aufrührerisch; (boisterous) wild

rip /rɪp/ n Riss m ● vt/i (pt/pp **ripped**) zerreißen; ~ **open** aufreißen. **~ off** vt 🗉 neppen

ripe /raɪp/ adj (-r, -st) reif

ripen /'raɪpn/ vi reifen ● vt reifen lassen

ripeness /'raɪpnɪs/ n Reife f

'rip-off n 🗉 Nepp m

ripple /'rɪpl/ n kleine Welle f

rise /raɪz/ n Anstieg m; (fig) Aufstieg m; (increase) Zunahme f; (in wages) Lohnerhöhung f; (in salary) Gehaltserhöhung f; Anlass geben zu ● vi (pt rose, pp risen) steigen; (ground:) ansteigen; (sun, dough:) aufgehen; (river:) entspringen; (get up) aufstehen; (fig) aufsteigen (to zu). **~r** n **early ~r** Frühaufsteher m

rising /'raɪzɪŋ/ adj steigend; (sun) aufgehend ● n (revolt) Aufstand m

risk /rɪsk/ n Risiko nt; **at one's own ~** auf eigene Gefahr ● vt riskieren

risky /'rɪskɪ/ adj riskant

rite /raɪt/ n Ritus m

ritual /'rɪtjʊəl/ adj rituell ● n Ritual nt

rival /'raɪvl/ adj rivalisierend ● n Rivale m/Rivalin f. **~ry** n Rivalität f; (Comm) Konkurrenzkampf m

river /'rɪvə(r)/ n Fluss m

rivet /'rɪvɪt/ n Niete f ● vt [ver]nieten; **~ed by** gefesselt von

road /rəʊd/ n Straße f; (fig) Weg m

road: ~-map n Straßenkarte f. **~ safety** n Verkehrssicherheit f. **~side** n Straßenrand m. **~way** n Fahrbahn f. **~works** npl Straßenarbeiten pl. **~worthy** adj verkehrssicher

roam /rəʊm/ vi wandern

roar /rɔː(r)/ n Gebrüll nt; **~s** of laughter schallendes Gelächter nt ● vi brüllen; (with laughter) schallend lachen. **~ing** adj (fire) prasselnd; **do a ~ing trade** 🗉 ein Bombengeschäft machen

roast /rəʊst/ adj gebraten, Brat-; ~ **beef/pork** Rinder-/Schweinebraten m ● n Braten m ● vt/i braten; rösten (coffee, chestnuts)

rob /rɒb/ vt (pt/pp **robbed**) berau-

r

robe | rotten 524

ben (of gen); ausrauben (bank).
~ber n Räuber m. **~bery** n
Raub m

robe /rəʊb/ n Robe f; (Amer: bathrobe) Bademantel m

robin /ˈrɒbɪn/ n Rotkehlchen nt

robot /ˈrəʊbɒt/ n Roboter m

robust /rəʊˈbʌst/ adj robust

rock¹ /rɒk/ n Fels m; **on the ~s**
(ship) aufgelaufen; (marriage) kaputt; (drink) mit Eis

rock² vt/i schaukeln

rock³ n (Mus) Rock m

rockery /ˈrɒkərɪ/ n Steingarten m

rocket /ˈrɒkɪt/ n Rakete f

rocking: ~-chair n Schaukelstuhl
m. **~-horse** n Schaukelpferd nt

rocky /ˈrɒkɪ/ adj felsig; (unsteady)
wackelig

rod /rɒd/ n Stab m; (stick) Rute f;
(for fishing) Angel[rute] f

rode /rəʊd/ see **ride**

rodent /ˈrəʊdnt/ n Nagetier nt

rogue /rəʊg/ n Gauner m

role /rəʊl/ n Rolle f

roll /rəʊl/ n Rolle f; (bread) Brötchen nt; (list) Liste f; (of drum) Wirbel m ● vi rollen; **be ~ing in
money** 🄸 Geld wie Heu haben ● vt
rollen; walzen (lawn); ausrollen
(pastry). **~ over** vi sich auf die andere Seite rollen. **~ up** vt aufrollen;
hochkrempeln (sleeves) ● vi 🄸 auftauchen

roller /ˈrəʊlə(r)/ n Rolle f; (lawn,
road) Walze f; (hair) Lockenwickler
m. **~ blind** n Rollo nt. **R~blades®**
npl Rollerblades® mpl. **~-coaster** n
Berg-und-Talbahn f. **~-skate** n Roll-
schuh m

'rolling-pin n Teigrolle f

Roman /ˈrəʊmən/ adj römisch ● n
Römer(in) m(f)

romance /rəˈmæns/ n Romantik f;

(love-affair) Romanze f; (book) Liebesgeschichte f

Romania /rəʊˈmeɪnɪə/ n Rumä-
nien nt. **~n** adj rumänisch ● n Ru-
mäne m/-nin f

romantic /rəʊˈmæntɪk/ adj, **-ally**
adv romantisch. **~ism** n Romantik f

Rome /rəʊm/ n Rom nt

romp /rɒmp/ vi [herum]tollen

roof /ru:f/ n Dach nt; (of mouth)
Gaumen m ● vt **~ [over]** überda-
chen. **~-top** n Dach nt

rook /rʊk/ n Saatkrähe f; (Chess)
Turm m

room /ru:m/ n Zimmer nt; (for
functions) Saal m; (space) Platz m.
~y adj geräumig

roost /ru:st/ n Hühnerstange f

root¹ /ru:t/ n Wurzel f; **take ~** anwachsen ● vi Wurzeln schlagen. **~
out** vt (fig) ausrotten

root² vi **~ about** wühlen; **~ for**
s.o. 🄸 für jdn sein

rope /rəʊp/ n Seil nt; **know the ~s**
🄸 sich auskennen. **~ in** vt 🄸 einspannen

rose¹ /rəʊz/ n Rose f; (of watering-
can) Brause f

rose² see **rise**

rostrum /ˈrɒstrəm/ n Podium nt

rosy /ˈrəʊzɪ/ adj rosig

rot /rɒt/ n Fäulnis f; (🄸: nonsense)
Quatsch m ● vi (pt/pp rotted) [ver-
]faulen

rota /ˈrəʊtə/ n Dienstplan m

rotary /ˈrəʊtərɪ/ adj Dreh-; (Techn)
Rotations-

rotat|e /rəʊˈteɪt/ vt drehen ● vi
sich drehen; (Techn) rotieren. **~ion**
n Drehung f; **in ~ion** im Wechsel

rote /rəʊt/ n **by ~** auswendig

rotten /ˈrɒtn/ adj faul; 🄸 mies;
(person) fies

rough /rʌf/ adj (**-er, -est**) rau; (uneven) uneben; (coarse, not gentle) grob; (brutal) roh; (turbulent) stürmisch; (approximate) ungefähr ● adj **sleep ~** im Freien übernachten ● vt **~ it** primitiv leben. **~ out** vt im Groben entwerfen

roughage /'rʌfɪdʒ/ n Ballaststoffe pl

rough 'draft n grober Entwurf m

rough|ly /'rʌflɪ/ adv (see rough) rau; grob; roh; ungefähr. **~ness** n Rauheit f

'rough paper n Konzeptpapier nt

round /raʊnd/ adj (**-er, -est**) rund ● n Runde f; (slice) Scheibe f; **do one's ~s** seine Runde machen ● prep um (+ acc); **~ the clock** rund um die Uhr ● adv all **~** ringsherum; **ask s.o. ~** jdn einladen ● vt biegen um (corner). **~ off** vt abrunden. **~ up** vt aufrunden; zusammentreiben (animals); festnehmen (criminals)

roundabout /'raʊndəbaʊt/ adj **~ route** Umweg m ● n Karussell nt; (for traffic) Kreisverkehr m

round 'trip n Rundreise f

rous|e /raʊz/ vt wecken; (fig) erregen. **~ing** adj mitreißend

route /ru:t/ n Route f; (of bus) Linie f

routine /ru:'ti:n/ adj routinemäßig ● n Routine f; (Theat) Nummer f

row¹ /rəʊ/ n (line) Reihe f

row² vt/i rudern

row³ /raʊ/ n 🔲 Krach m ● vi 🔲 sich streiten

rowdy /'raʊdɪ/ adj laut

rowing boat /'rəʊɪŋ-/ n Ruderboot nt

royal /'rɔɪəl/ adj königlich

royal|ty /'rɔɪəltɪ/ n Königtum nt; (persons) Mitglieder pl der königlichen Familie; **-ies** pl (payments) Tantiemen pl

RSI abbr (**repetitive strain injury**) chronisches Überlastungssyndrom nt

rub /rʌb/ vt (pt/pp **rubbed**) reiben; (polish) polieren; **don't ~ it in** 🔲 reib es mir nicht unter die Nase. **~ off** vt abreiben ● vi abgehen. **~ out** vt ausradieren

rubber /'rʌbə(r)/ n Gummi m; (eraser) Radiergummi m. **~ band** n Gummiband nt

rubbish /'rʌbɪʃ/ n Abfall m, Müll m; (🔲: nonsense) Quatsch m; (🔲: junk) Plunder m. **~ bin** n Abfalleimer m. **~ dump** n Abfallhaufen m; (official) Müllhalde f

rubble /'rʌbl/ n Trümmer pl

ruby /'ru:bɪ/ n Rubin m

rudder /'rʌdə(r)/ n [Steuer]ruder nt

rude /ru:d/ adj (**-r, -st**) unhöflich; (improper) unanständig. **~ness** n Unhöflichkeit f

rudimentary /ru:dɪ'mentərɪ/ adj elementar; (Biology) rudimentär

ruffian /'rʌfɪən/ n Rüpel m

ruffle /'rʌfl/ vt zerzausen

rug /rʌg/ n Vorleger m, (kleiner) Teppich m; (blanket) Decke f

rugged /'rʌgɪd/ adj (coastline) zerklüftet

ruin /'ru:ɪn/ n Ruine f; (fig) Ruin m ● vt ruinieren

rule /ru:l/ n Regel f; (control) Herrschaft f; (government) Regierung f; (for measuring) Lineal nt; **as a ~** in der Regel ● vt regieren, herrschen über (+ acc); (fig) beherrschen; (decide) entscheiden; ziehen (line) ● vi regieren, herrschen. **~ out** vt ausschließen

ruled /ru:ld/ adj (paper) liniert

ruler /'ruːlə(r)/ n Herrscher(in) m(f); (measure) Lineal nt

ruling /'ruːlɪŋ/ adj herrschend; (factor) entscheidend; (Pol) regierend ●n Entscheidung f

rum /rʌm/ n Rum m

rumble /'rʌmbl/ n Grollen nt ●vi grollen; (stomach:) knurren

rummage /'rʌmɪdʒ/ vi wühlen; ~ **through** durchwühlen

rumour /'ruːmə(r)/ n Gerücht nt ●vt **it is** ~**ed that** es geht das Gerücht, dass

rump /rʌmp/ n Hinterteil nt. ~ **steak** n Rumpsteak nt

run /rʌn/ n Lauf m; (journey) Fahrt f; (series) Serie f, Reihe f; (Theat) Laufzeit f; (Skiing) Abfahrt f; (enclosure) Auslauf m; (Amer: ladder) Laufmasche f; ~ **of bad luck** Pechsträhne f; **be on the** ~ flüchtig sein; **in the long** ~ auf lange Sicht ●v (pt **ran**, pp **run**, pres p **running**) ●vi laufen; (flow) fließen; (eyes:) tränen; (bus:) verkehren; (butter, ink:) zerfließen; (colours:) abfärben; (in election) kandidieren ●vt laufen lassen; einlaufen lassen (bath); (manage) führen, leiten; (drive) fahren; eingehen (risk); (Journalism) bringen (story); ~ **one's hand over sth** mit der Hand über etw (acc) fahren. ~ **away** vi weglaufen. ~ **down** vi hinunter-/herunterlaufen; (clockwork:) ablaufen; (stocks:) sich verringern ●vt (run over) überfahren; (reduce) verringern; (fig: criticize) heruntermachen. ~ **in** vi hinein-/hereinlaufen. ~ **off** vi weglaufen ●vt abziehen (copies). ~ **out** vi hinaus-/herauslaufen; (supplies, money:) ausgehen; **I've** ~ **out of sugar** ich habe keinen Zucker mehr. ~ **over** vt überfahren. ~ **up** vi hinauf-/herauflaufen; (towards) hinlaufen ●vt machen (debts); auf-

runaway n Ausreißer m

run-'down adj (area) verkommen

rung¹ /rʌŋ/ n (of ladder) Sprosse f

rung² see **ring²**

runner /'rʌnə(r)/ n Läufer m; (Bot) Ausläufer m; (on sledge) Kufe f. ~ **bean** n Stangenbohne f. ~**-up** n Zweite(r) m/f

running /'rʌnɪŋ/ adj laufend; (water) fließend; **four times** ~ viermal nacheinander ●n Laufen nt; (management) Führung f, Leitung f; **be/not be in the** ~ eine/keine Chance haben

runny /'rʌnɪ/ adj flüssig

run: ~**-up** n (Sport) Anlauf m; (to election) Zeit f vor der Wahl. ~**way** n Start- und Landebahn f

rupture /'rʌptʃə(r)/ n Bruch m ●vt/i brechen

rural /'rʊərəl/ adj ländlich

ruse /ruːz/ n List f

rush¹ /rʌʃ/ n (Bot) Binse f

rush² n Hetze f; **in a** ~ in Eile ●vi sich hetzen; (run) rasen; (water:) rauschen ●vt hetzen, drängen. ~**-hour** n Hauptverkehrszeit f, Stoßzeit f

Russia /'rʌʃə/ n Russland nt. ~**n** adj russisch ●n Russe m/Russin f; (Lang) Russisch nt

rust /rʌst/ n Rost m ●vi rosten

rustle /'rʌsl/ vi rascheln ●vt rascheln mit; (Amer) stehlen (cattle). ~ **up** vt 🄸 improvisieren

'rustproof adj rostfrei

rusty /'rʌstɪ/ adj rostig

rut /rʌt/ n Furche f

ruthless /'ruːθlɪs/ adj rücksichtslos. ~**ness** n Rücksichtslosigkeit f

rye /raɪ/ n Roggen m

Ss

sabbath /ˈsæbəθ/ n Sabbat m

sabot|age /ˈsæbətɑːʒ/ n Sabotage f ● vt sabotieren

sachet /ˈsæʃeɪ/ n Beutel m; (scented) Kissen nt

sack n Sack m; **get the ~** 🗓 rausgeschmissen werden ● vt 🗓 rausschmeißen

sacred /ˈseɪkrɪd/ adj heilig

sacrifice /ˈsækrɪfaɪs/ n Opfer nt ● vt opfern

sacrilege /ˈsækrɪlɪdʒ/ n Sakrileg nt

sad /sæd/ adj (sadder, saddest) traurig; (loss, death) schmerzlich. **~den** vt traurig machen

saddle /ˈsædl/ n Sattel m ● vt satteln; **~ s.o. with sth** 🗓 jdm etw aufhalsen

sadist /ˈseɪdɪst/ n Sadist m. **~ic** adj, **-ally** adv sadistisch

sad|ly /ˈsædlɪ/ adv traurig; (unfortunately) leider. **~ness** n Traurigkeit f

safe /seɪf/ adj (-r, -st) sicher; (journey) gut; (not dangerous) ungefährlich; **~ and sound** gesund und wohlbehalten ● n Safe m. **~guard** n Schutz m ● vt schützen. **~ly** adv sicher; (arrive) gut

safety /ˈseɪftɪ/ n Sicherheit f. **~-belt** n Sicherheitsgurt m. **~-pin** n Sicherheitsnadel f. **~-valve** n [Sicherheits]ventil nt

sag /sæg/ vi (pt/pp sagged) durchhängen

saga /ˈsɑːgə/ n Saga f; (fig) Geschichte f

said /sed/ see say

sail /seɪl/ n Segel nt; (trip) Segel-

fahrt f ● vi segeln; (on liner) fahren; (leave) abfahren (for nach) ● vt segeln mit

sailing /ˈseɪlɪŋ/ n Segelsport m. **~-boat** n Segelboot nt. **~-ship** n Segelschiff nt

sailor /ˈseɪlə(r)/ n Seemann m; (in navy) Matrose m

saint /seɪnt/ n Heilige(r) m/f. **~ly** adj heilig

sake /seɪk/ n **for the ~ of ...** um ... (gen) willen; **for my/your ~** um meinet-/deinetwillen

salad /ˈsæləd/ n Salat m. **~-dressing** n Salatsoße f

salary /ˈsælərɪ/ n Gehalt nt

sale /seɪl/ n Verkauf m; (event) Basar m; (at reduced prices) Schlussverkauf m; **for ~** zu verkaufen

sales|man n Verkäufer m. **~woman** n Verkäuferin f

saliva /səˈlaɪvə/ n Speichel m

salmon /ˈsæmən/ n Lachs m

saloon /səˈluːn/ n Salon m; (Auto) Limousine f; (Amer: bar) Wirtschaft f

salt /sɔːlt/ n Salz nt ● adj salzig; (water, meat) Salz- ● vt salzen; (cure) pökeln; streuen (road). **~-cellar** n Salzfass nt. **~-water** n Salzwasser nt. **~y** adj salzig

salute /səˈluːt/ n (Mil) Gruß m ● vt/i (Mil) grüßen

salvage /ˈsælvɪdʒ/ n (Naut) Bergung f ● vt bergen

salvation /sælˈveɪʃn/ n Rettung f; (Relig) Heil nt

same /seɪm/ adj & pron **the ~** der/die/das gleiche; (pl) die gleichen; (identical) der-/die-/dasselbe; (pl) dieselben ● adv **the ~** gleich; **all the ~** trotzdem

sample /ˈsɑːmpl/ n Probe f; (Comm) Muster nt ● vt probieren, kosten (food)

sanatorium /sænəˈtɔːrɪəm/ n

Sanatorium nt

sanction /'sæŋkʃn/ n Sanktion f
● vt sanktionieren

sanctuary /'sæŋktjʊərɪ/ n (Relig)
Heiligtum nt; (refuge) Zuflucht f;
(for wildlife) Tierschutzgebiet nt

sand /sænd/ n Sand m ● vt ~
[down] [ab]schmirgeln

sandal /'sændl/ n Sandale f

sand: ~**bank** n Sandbank f.
~**paper** n Sandpapier nt. ~**-pit** n
Sandkasten m

sandwich /'sænwɪdʒ/ n; Sandwich
m ● vt ~ed between eingeklemmt
zwischen

sandy /'sændɪ/ adj sandig; (beach,
soil) Sand-; (hair) rotblond

sane /seɪn/ adj (r, -st) geistig normal; (sensible) vernünftig

sang /sæŋ/ see sing

sanitary /'sænɪtərɪ/ adj hygienisch; (system) sanitär. ~ napkin n
(Amer), ~ towel n [Damen]binde f

sanitation /sænɪ'teɪʃn/ n Kanalisation und Abfallbeseitigung pl

sanity /'sænɪtɪ/ n [gesunder] Verstand m

sank /sæŋk/ see sink

sap /sæp/ n (Bot) Saft m ● vt (pt/pp
sapped) schwächen

sarcas|m /'sɑːkæzm/ n Sarkasmus
m. ~**tic** adj, -**ally** adv sarkastisch

sardine /sɑː'diːn/ n Sardine f

sash /sæʃ/ n Schärpe f

sat /sæt/ see sit

satchel /'sætʃl/ n Ranzen m

satellite /'sætəlaɪt/ n Satellit m.
~**television** n Satellitenfern-
sehen nt

satin /'sætɪn/ n Satin m

satire /'sætaɪə(r)/ n Satire f

satirical /sə'tɪrɪkl/ adj satirisch

satirist /'sætɪrɪst/ n Satirike-
r(in) m(f)

satisfaction /sætɪs'fækʃn/ n Be-
friedigung f; to **my** ~ zu meiner
Zufriedenheit

satisfactory /sætɪs'fæktərɪ/ adj,
-**ily** adv zufrieden stellend

satisf|y /'sætɪsfaɪ/ vt (pt/pp -fied)
befriedigen; zufrieden stellen (customer); (convince) überzeugen; be
~**ied** zufrieden sein. ~**ying** adj befriedigend; (meal) sättigend

satphone /'sætfəʊn/ n Satelliten-
telefon nt

saturate /'sætʃəreɪt/ vt durchträn-
ken; (Chemistry & fig) sättigen

Saturday /'sætədeɪ/ n Samstag m

sauce /sɔːs/ n Soße f; (cheek)
Frechheit f. ~**pan** n Kochtopf m

saucer /'sɔːsə(r)/ n Untertasse f

saucy /'sɔːsɪ/ adj frech

Saudi Arabia /saʊdɪə'reɪbɪə/ n
Saudi-Arabien n

sauna /'sɔːnə/ n Sauna f

saunter /'sɔːntə(r)/ vi schlendern

sausage /'sɒsɪdʒ/ n Wurst f

savage /'sævɪdʒ/ adj wild; (fierce)
scharf; (brutal) brutal ● n Wilde(r)
m/f. ~**ry** n Brutalität f

save /seɪv/ n (Sport) Abwehr f ● vt
retten (from or + dat); (keep) aufheben; (not waste) sparen; (collect)
sammeln; (avoid) ersparen; (Sport)
verhindern (goal) ● vi ~ [up]
sparen

saver /'seɪvə(r)/ n Sparer m

saving /'seɪvɪŋ/ n (see save) Rettung f; Sparen nt; Ersparnis f. ~**s** pl
(money) Ersparnisse pl

savour /'seɪvə(r)/ n Geschmack m
● vt auskosten. ~**y** adj würzig

saw[1] /sɔː/ see see[1]

saw[2] n Säge f ● vt/i (pt sawed, pp
sawn or sawed) sägen

saxophone /'sæksəfəʊn/ n Saxophon nt

say /seɪ/ n Mitspracherecht nt; **have one's ~** seine Meinung sagen ● vt/i (pt/pp **said**) sagen; sprechen (prayer); **that is to ~** das heißt; **that goes without ~ing** das versteht sich von selbst. **~ing** n Redensart f

scab /skæb/ n Schorf m; (pej) Streikbrecher m

scaffolding /'skæfəldɪŋ/ n Gerüst nt

scald /skɔːld/ vt verbrühen

scale¹ /skeɪl/ n (of fish) Schuppe f

scale² n Skala f; (Mus) Tonleiter f; (ratio) Maßstab m ● vt (climb) erklettern. **~ down** vt verkleinern

scales /skeɪlz/ npl (for weighing) Waage f

scalp /skælp/ n Kopfhaut f

scamper /'skæmpə(r)/ vi huschen

scan /skæn/ n (Med) Szintigramm nt ● v (pt/pp **scanned**) ● vt absuchen; (quickly) flüchtig ansehen; (Med) szintigraphisch untersuchen

scandal /'skændl/ n Skandal m; (gossip) Skandalgeschichten pl. **~ize** vt schockieren. **~ous** adj skandalös

Scandinavia /skændɪ'neɪvɪə/ n Skandinavien nt. **~n** adj skandinavisch ● n Skandinavier(in) m (f)

scanner /'skænə(r)/ n Scanner m

scanty /'skæntɪ/ adj, **-ily** adv spärlich; (clothing) knapp

scapegoat /'skeɪp-/ n Sündenbock m

scar /skɑː(r)/ n Narbe f

scarce /skeəs/ adj (-r, -st) knapp; **make oneself ~e** 🗓 sich aus dem Staub machen. **~ely** adv kaum. **~ity** n Knappheit f

scare /skeə(r)/ n Schreck m; (panic) [allgemeine] Panik f ● vt Angst machen (+ dat); **be ~d** Angst haben (of vor + dat)

scarf /skɑːf/ n (pl **scarves**) Schal m; (square) Tuch nt

scarlet /'skɑːlət/ adj scharlachrot

scary /'skeərɪ/ adj unheimlich

scathing /'skeɪðɪŋ/ adj bissig

scatter /'skætə(r)/ vt verstreuen; (disperse) zerstreuen ● vi sich zerstreuen. **~ed** adj verstreut; (showers) vereinzelt

scatty /'skætɪ/ adj 🗓 verrückt

scene /siːn/ n Szene f; (sight) Anblick m; (place of event) Schauplatz m; **behind the ~s** hinter den Kulissen

scenery /'siːnərɪ/ n Landschaft f; (Theat) Szenerie f

scenic /'siːnɪk/ adj landschaftlich schön

scent /sent/ n Duft m; (trail) Fährte f; (perfume) Parfüm nt. **~ed** adj parfümiert

sceptic|al /'skeptɪkl/ adj skeptisch. **~ism** n Skepsis f

schedule /'ʃedjuːl/ n Programm nt; (of work) Zeitplan m; (timetable) Fahrplan m; **behind ~** im Rückstand; **according to ~** planmäßig ● vt planen

scheme /skiːm/ n Programm nt; (plan) Plan m; (plot) Komplott nt ● vi Ränke schmieden

schizophrenic /skɪtsə'frenɪk/ adj **s** schizophren

scholar /'skɒlə(r)/ n Gelehrte(r) m/f. **~ly** adj gelehrt. **~ship** n Gelehrtheit f; (grant) Stipendium nt

school /skuːl/ n Schule f; (Univ) Fakultät f ● vt schulen

school: **~boy** n Schüler m. **~girl** n Schülerin f. **~ing** n Schulbildung f. **~master** n Lehrer m. **~mistress** n Lehrerin f. **~teacher** n Lehrer(in) m (f)

scien|ce /'saɪəns/ n Wissenschaft f. **~tific** adj wissenschaftlich. **~tist** n

Wissenschaftler(in) *m*(*f*)

scissors /'sɪzəz/ *npl* Schere *f*; **a pair of** ~ eine Schere

scoff¹ /skɒf/ *vi* ~ **at** spotten über (+ *acc*)

scoff² *vt* 🔲 verschlingen

scold /skəʊld/ *vt* ausschimpfen

scoop /sku:p/ *n* Schaufel *f*; (*Culin*) Portionierer *m*; (*story*) Exklusivmeldung *f* ● *vt* ~ **out** aushöhlen; (*remove*) auslöffeln

scooter /'sku:tə(r)/ *n* Roller *m*

scope /skəʊp/ *n* Bereich *m*; (*opportunity*) Möglichkeiten *pl*

scorch /skɔːtʃ/ *vt* versengen. ~**ing** *adj* glühend heiß

score /skɔː(r)/ *n* [Spiel]stand *m*; (*individual*) Punktzahl *f*; (*Mus*) Partitur *f*; (*Cinema*) Filmmusik *f*; **on that** ~ was das betrifft ● *vt* erzielen; schießen (*goal*); (*cut*) einritzen ● *vi* Punkte erzielen; (*Sport*) ein Tor schießen; (*keep score*) Punkte zählen. ~**r** *n* Punktezähler *m*; (*of goals*) Torschütze *m*

scorn /skɔːn/ *n* Verachtung *f* ● *vt* verachten. ~**ful** *adj* verächtlich

Scot /skɒt/ *n* Schotte *m*/Schottin *f*

Scotch /skɒtʃ/ *adj* schottisch ● *n* (*whisky*) Scotch *m*

Scot|land /skɒtlənd/ *n* Schottland *nt*. ~**s**, ~**tish** *adj* schottisch

nach dem Verhältniswahlrecht bestimmt.

scoundrel /'skaʊndrl/ *n* Schurke *m*

scour /'skaʊə(r)/ *vt* (*search*) absuchen; (*clean*) scheuern

scout /skaʊt/ *n* (*Mil*) Kundschafter *m*; **[Boy] S**~ Pfadfinder *m*

scowl /skaʊl/ *n* böser Gesichtsausdruck *m* ● *vi* ein böses Gesicht machen

scram /skræm/ *vi* 🔲 abhauen

scramble /'skræmbl/ *n* Gerangel *nt* ● *vi* klettern; ~ **for** sich drängen nach. ~**d 'egg[s]** *n*[*pl*] Rührei *nt*

scrap¹ /skræp/ *n* (🔲: *fight*) Rauferei *f* ● *vi* sich raufen

scrap² *n* Stückchen *nt*; (*metal*) Schrott *m*; ~**s** *pl* Reste; **not a** ~ kein bisschen ● *vt* (*pt*/*pp* **scrapped**) aufgeben

'scrapbook *n* Sammelalbum *nt*

scrape /skreɪp/ *vt* schaben; (*clean*) abkratzen; (*damage*) [ver]schrammen. ~ **through** *vi* gerade noch durchkommen. ~ **together** *vt* zusammenkriegen

scrappy /'skræpɪ/ *adj* lückenhaft

'scrapyard *n* Schrottplatz *m*

scratch /skrætʃ/ *n* Kratzer *m*; **start from** ~ von vorne anfangen; **not be up to** ~ zu wünschen übrig lassen ● *vt*/*i* kratzen; (*damage*) zerkratzen

scrawl /skrɔːl/ *n* Gekrakel *nt* ● *vt*/*i* krakeln

scream /skri:m/ *n* Schrei *m* ● *vt*/*i* schreien

screech /skri:tʃ/ *n* Kreischen *nt* ● *vt*/*i* kreischen

screen /skri:n/ *n* Schirm *m*; (*Cinema*) Leinwand *f*; (*TV*) Bildschirm *m* ● *vt* schützen; (*conceal*) verdecken; vorführen (*film*); (*examine*) überprüfen; (*Med*) untersuchen

screw /skru:/ *n* Schraube *f* ● *vt* schrauben. **~ up** *vt* festschrauben; (*crumple*) zusammenknüllen; zusammenkneifen (*eyes*); (*sl: bungle*) vermasseln

'screwdriver *n* Schraubenzieher *m*

scribble /'skrɪbl/ *n* Gekritzel *nt* ● *vt/i* kritzeln

script /skrɪpt/ *n* Schrift *f*; (*of speech, play*) Text *m*; (*Radio, TV*) Skript *nt*; (*of film*) Drehbuch *nt*

scroll /skrəʊl/ *n* Rolle *f* ● *vt* **~ up/down** nach oben/unten rollen. **~ bar** *n* Rollbalken *m*

scrounge /skraʊndʒ/ *vt/i* schnorren. **~r** *n* Schnorrer *m*

scrub[1] /skrʌb/ *n* (*land*) Buschland *nt*, Gestrüpp *nt*

scrub[2] *vt/i* (*pt/pp* **scrubbed**) schrubben

scruff /skrʌf/ *n* **by the ~ of the neck** beim Genick

scruffy /'skrʌfɪ/ *adj* vergammelt

scrum /skrʌm/ *n* Gedränge *nt*

scruple /'skru:pl/ *n* Skrupel *m*

scrupulous /'skru:pjʊləs/ *adj* gewissenhaft

scuffle /'skʌfl/ *n* Handgemenge *nt*

sculpt|or /'skʌlptə(r)/ *n* Bildhauer(in) *m*(*f*). **~ure** *n* Bildhauerei *f*; (*piece of work*) Skulptur *f*, Plastik *f*

scum /skʌm/ *n* Schmutzschicht *f*; (*people*) Abschaum *m*

scurry /'skʌrɪ/ *vi* (*pt/pp* **-ied**) huschen

scuttle[1] /'skʌtl/ *vt* versenken (*ship*)

scuttle[2] *vi* schnell krabbeln

sea /si:/ *n* Meer *nt*, See *f*; **at ~** auf See; **by ~** mit dem Schiff. **~food** *n* Meeresfrüchte *pl*. **~gull** *n* Möwe *f*

seal[1] /si:l/ *n* (*Zool*) Seehund *m*

seal[2] *n* Siegel *nt* ● *vt* versiegeln;

(*fig*) besiegeln. **~ off** *vt* abriegeln

'sea-level *n* Meeresspiegel *m*

seam /si:m/ *n* Naht *f*; (*of coal*) Flöz *nt*

'seaman *n* Seemann *m*; (*sailor*) Matrose *m*

séance /'seɪɑ:ns/ *n* spiritistische Sitzung *f*

search /sɜ:tʃ/ *n* Suche *f*; (*official*) Durchsuchung *f* ● *vt* durchsuchen; absuchen (*area*) ● *vi* suchen (**for** nach). **~ engine** *n* Suchmaschine *f*. **~ing** *adj* prüfend, forschend. **~light** *n* [Such]scheinwerfer *m*. **~party** *n* Suchmannschaft *f*

sea: ~sick *adj* seekrank. **~side** *n* **at/to the ~side** am/ans Meer

season /'si:zn/ *n* Jahreszeit *f*; (*social, tourist, sporting*) Saison *f* ● *vt* (*flavour*) würzen. **~al** *adj* Saison-. **~ing** *n* Gewürze *pl*

'season ticket *n* Dauerkarte *f*

seat /si:t/ *n* Sitz *m*; (*place*) Sitzplatz *m*; (*bottom*) Hintern *m*; **take a ~** Platz nehmen ● *vt* setzen; (*have seats for*) Sitzplätze bieten (+ *dat*); **remain ~ed** sitzen bleiben. **~-belt** *n* Sicherheitsgurt *m*; **fasten one's ~-belt** sich anschnallen

sea: ~weed *n* [See]tang *m*. **~worthy** *adj* seetüchtig

seclu|ded /sɪ'klu:dɪd/ *adj* abgelegen. **~sion** *n* Zurückgezogenheit *f*

second /'sekənd/ *adj* zweite(r,s); **on ~ thoughts** nach weiterer Überlegung ● *n* Sekunde *f*; (*Sport*) Sekundant *m*; **~s** *pl* (*goods*) Waren zweiter Wahl ● *adv* (*in race*) an zweiter Stelle *vt* unterstützen (*proposal*)

secondary /'sekəndrɪ/ *adj* zweitrangig; (*Phys*) Sekundär-. **~ school** *n* höhere Schule *f*

second: ~-best *adj* zweitbeste(r,s). **~ 'class** *adv* (*travel, send*)

s

zweiter Klasse. **~-class** adj zweit-klassig

'second hand n (on clock) Sekundenzeiger m

second-'hand adj gebraucht ● adv aus zweiter Hand

secondly /'sekəndlı/ adv zweitens

second-'rate adj zweitklassig

secrecy /'si:krəsı/ n Heimlichkeit f

secret /'si:krɪt/ adj geheim; (agent, police) Geheim-; (drinker, lover) heimlich ● n Geheimnis nt

secretarial /sekrə'teərɪəl/ adj Sekretärinnen-; (work, staff) Sekretariats-

secretary /'sekrətərı/ n Sekretär(in) m(f)

secretive /'si:krətɪv/ adj geheimtuerisch

secretly /'si:krɪtlı/ adv heimlich

sect /sekt/ n Sekte f

section /'sekʃn/ n Teil m; (of text) Abschnitt m; (of firm) Abteilung f; (of organization) Sektion f

sector /'sektə(r)/ n Sektor m

secular /'sekjulə(r)/ adj weltlich

secure /sɪ'kjuə(r)/ adj sicher; (firm) fest; (emotionally) geborgen ● vt sichern; (fasten) festmachen; (obtain) sich (dat) sichern

securit|y /sɪ'kjuərətı/ n Sicherheit f; (emotional) Geborgenheit f; **~ies** pl Wertpapiere pl

sedan /sɪ'dæn/ n (Amer) Limousine f

sedate /sɪ'deɪt/ adj gesetzt

sedative /'sedətɪv/ adj beruhigend ● n Beruhigungsmittel nt

sediment /'sedɪmənt/ n [Boden]-satz m

seduce /sɪ'dju:s/ vt verführen

seduct|ion /sɪ'dʌkʃn/ n Verführung f. **~ive** adj verführerisch

see /si:/ v (pt saw, pp seen) ● vt

sehen; (understand) einsehen; (imagine) sich (dat) vorstellen; (escort) begleiten; **go and ~** nachsehen; (visit) besuchen; **~ you later!** bis nachher! **~ing that** da ● vi sehen; (check) nachsehen; **~ about** sich kümmern um. **~ off** vt verabschieden; (chase away) vertreiben. **~ through** vt (fig) durchschauen (person)

seed /si:d/ n Samen m; (of grape) Kern m; (fig) Saat f; (Tennis) gesetzter Spieler m; **go to ~** Samen bilden; (fig) herunterkommen. **~ed** adj (Tennis) gesetzt

seedy /'si:dı/ adj schäbig; (area) heruntergekommen

seek /si:k/ vt (pt/pp sought) suchen

seem /si:m/ vi scheinen

seen /si:n/ see see[1]

seep /si:p/ vi sickern

seethe /si:ð/ vi **~ with anger** vor Wut schäumen

'see-through adj durchsichtig

segment /'segmənt/ n Teil m; (of worm) Segment nt; (of orange) Spalte f

segregat|e /'segrɪgeɪt/ vt trennen. **~ion** n Trennung f

seize /si:z/ vt ergreifen; (Jur) beschlagnahmen; **~ s.o. by the arm** jdn am Arm packen. **~ up** vi (Techn) sich festfressen

seldom /'seldəm/ adv selten

select /sɪ'lekt/ adj ausgewählt; (exclusive) exklusiv ● vt auswählen; aufstellen (team). **~ion** n Auswahl f

self /self/ n (pl selves) Ich nt

self: **~-as'surance** n Selbstsicherheit f. **~-as'sured** adj selbstsicher. **~-'catering** n Selbstversorgung f. **~-'centred** adj egozentrisch. **~-'confidence** n Selbstbewusstsein nt, Selbstvertrauen nt. **~-'confi-**

dent *adj* selbstbewusst. **~-'con-scious** *adj* befangen. **~-con'trol** *n* Selbstbeherrschung *f*. **~-de'fence** *n* Selbstverteidigung *f*; (*Jur*) Notwehr *f*. **~-em'ployed** selbstständig. **~-e'steem** *n* Selbstachtung *f*. **~-'evident** *adj* offensichtlich. **~-in-'dulgent** *adj* maßlos. **~-'interest** *n* Eigennutz *m*

self|ish /'selfɪʃ/ *adj* egoistisch, selbstsüchtig. **~less** *adj* selbstlos.

self: **~-'pity** *n* Selbstmitleid *nt*. **~-'portrait** *n* Selbstporträt *nt*. **~-re'spect** *n* Selbstachtung *f*. **~-'righteous** *adj* selbstgerecht. **~-'sacrifice** *n* Selbstaufopferung *f*. **~-'satisfied** *adj* selbstgefällig. **~-'service** *n* Selbstbedienung *f* ● *attrib* Selbstbedienungs-. **~-suf-'ficient** *adj* selbstständig

sell /sel/ *v* (*pt/pp* **sold**) ● *vt* verkaufen; **be sold out** ausverkauft sein ● *vi* sich verkaufen. **~ off** *vt* verkaufen

seller /'selə(r)/ *n* Verkäufer *m*

Sellotape® /'seləʊ-/, *n* ≈ Tesafilm® *m*

'sell-out *n* **be a ~** ausverkauft sein; (ⓉⒻ: *betrayal*) Verrat sein

selves /selvz/ *see* **self**

semester /sɪ'mestə(r)/ *n* Semester *nt*

semi|breve /'semɪbriːv/ *n* (*Mus*) ganze Note *f*. **~circle** *n* Halbkreis *m*. **~circular** *adj* halbkreisförmig. **~colon** *n* Semikolon *nt*. **~de-'tached** *adj* & *n* **~detached [house]** Doppelhaushälfte *f*. **~final** *n* Halbfinale *nt*

seminar /'semɪnɑː(r)/ *n* Seminar *nt*

senat|e /'senət/ *n* Senat *m*. **~or** *n* Senator *m*

send /send/ *vt/i* (*pt/pp* **sent**) schi-

cken; **~ for** kommen lassen (*person*); sich (*dat*) schicken lassen (*thing*). **~er** *n* Absender *m*. **~off** *n* Verabschiedung *f*

senil|e /'siːnaɪl/ *adj* senil

senior /'siːnɪə(r)/ *adj* älter; (*in rank*) höher ● *n* Ältere(r) *m/f*; (*in rank*) Vorgesetzte(r) *m/f*. **~ 'citizen** *n* Senior(in) *m(f)*

seniority /siːnɪ'ɒrɪtɪ/ *n* höheres Alter *nt*; (*in rank*) höherer Rang *m*

sensation /sen'seɪʃn/ *n* Sensation *f*; (*feeling*) Gefühl *nt*. **~al** *adj* sensationell

sense /sens/ *n* Sinn *m*; (*feeling*) Gefühl *nt*; (*common*) Verstand *m*; **make ~** Sinn ergeben ● *vt* spüren. **~less** *adj* sinnlos; (*unconscious*) bewusstlos

sensible /'sensəbl/ *adj*, **-bly** *adv* vernünftig; (*suitable*) zweckmäßig

sensitiv|e /'sensɪtɪv/ *adj* empfindlich; (*understanding*) einfühlsam. **~ity** *n* Empfindlichkeit *f*

sensual /'sensjʊəl/ *adj* sinnlich. **-ity** *n* Sinnlichkeit *f*

sensuous /'sensjʊəs/ *adj* sinnlich

sent /sent/ *see* **send**

sentence /'sentəns/ *n* Satz *m*; (*Jur*) Urteil *nt*; (*punishment*) Strafe *f* ● *vt* verurteilen

sentiment /'sentɪmənt/ *n* Gefühl *nt*; (*opinion*) Meinung *f*; (*sentimentality*) Sentimentalität *f* ● **~al** *adj* sentimental. **~ality** *n* Sentimentalität *f*

sentry /'sentrɪ/ *n* Wache *f*

separable /'sepərəbl/ *adj* trennbar

separate[1] /'sepərət/ *adj* getrennt, separat

separate[2] /'sepəreɪt/ *vt* trennen ● *vi* sich trennen. **~ion** *n* Trennung *f*

September /sep'tembə(r)/ *n* September *m*

septic /'septɪk/ *adj* vereitert

sequel /'si:kwl/ n Folge f; (fig) Nachspiel nt

sequence /'si:kwəns/ n Reihenfolge f

serenade /serə'neɪd/ n Ständchen nt ●vt ~ s.o. jdm ein Ständchen bringen

seren|e /sɪ'ri:n/ adj gelassen. ~ity n Gelassenheit f

sergeant /'sɑ:dʒənt/ n (Mil) Feldwebel m; (in police) Polizeimeister m

serial /'sɪərɪəl/ n Fortsetzungsgeschichte f; (Radio, TV) Serie f. ~ize vt in Fortsetzungen veröffentlichen/(Radio, TV) senden

series /'sɪəri:z/ n inv Serie f

serious /'sɪərɪəs/ adj ernst; (illness, error) schwer. ~ness n Ernst m

sermon /'sɜ:mən/ n Predigt f

servant /'sɜ:vənt/ n Diener(in) m(f)

serve /sɜ:v/ n (Tennis) Aufschlag m ●vt dienen (+ dat); bedienen (customer, guest); servieren (food); verbüßen (sentence); **it ~s you right!** das geschieht dir recht! ●vi dienen; (Tennis) aufschlagen. ~r n (Computing) Server m

service /'sɜ:vɪs/ n Dienst m; (Relig) Gottesdienst m; (in shop, restaurant) Bedienung f; (transport) Verbindung f; (maintenance) Wartung f; (set of crockery) Service nt; (Tennis) Aufschlag m; ~s pl Dienstleistungen pl; (on motorway) Tankstelle und Raststätte f; **in the ~s** beim Militär; **out of/in ~** (machine:) außer/in Betrieb ●vt (Techn) warten

service: ~ **area** n Tankstelle und Raststätte f. ~ **charge** n Bedienungszuschlag m. ~**man** n Soldat m. ~ **station** n Tankstelle f

serviette /sɜ:vɪ'et/ n Serviette f

servile /'sɜ:vaɪl/ adj unterwürfig

session /'seʃn/ n Sitzung f

set /set/ n Satz m; (of crockery) Service nt; (of cutlery) Garnitur f; (TV, Radio) Apparat m; (Math) Menge f; (Theat) Bühnenbild nt; (Cinema) Szenenaufbau m; (of people) Kreis m ●adj (ready) fertig, bereit; (rigid) fest; (book) vorgeschrieben; **be ~ on doing sth** entschlossen sein, etw zu tun ●v (pt/pp set, pres p setting) ●vt setzen; (adjust) einstellen; stellen (task, alarm clock); festsetzen, festlegen (date, limit); aufgeben (homework); zusammenstellen (questions); [ein]fassen (gem); einrichten (bone); legen (hair); decken (table) ●vi (sun:) untergehen; (become hard) fest werden. ~ **back** vt zurücksetzen; (hold up) aufhalten; (⊞: cost) kosten. ~ **off** vi losgehen; (in vehicle) losfahren ●vt auslösen (alarm); explodieren lassen (bomb). ~ **out** vi losgehen; (in vehicle) losfahren ●vt auslegen; (state) darlegen. ~ **up** vt aufbauen; (fig) gründen

settee /se'ti:/ n Sofa nt, Couch f

setting /'setɪŋ/ n Rahmen m; (surroundings) Umgebung f

settle /'setl/ vt (decide) entscheiden; (agree) regeln; (fix) festsetzen; (calm) beruhigen; (pay) bezahlen ●vi sich niederlassen; (snow, dust:) liegen bleiben; (subside) sich senken; (sediment:) sich absetzen. ~ **down** vi sich beruhigen; (permanently) sesshaft werden. ~ **up** vi abrechnen

settlement /'setlmənt/ n (see settle) Entscheidung f; Regelung f; Bezahlung f; (Jur) Vergleich m; (colony) Siedlung f

settler /'setlə(r)/ n Siedler m

'set-up n System nt

seven /'sevn/ adj sieben. ~**teen** adj siebzehn. ~'**teenth** adj siebzehnte(r,s)

seventh /'sevnθ/ adj siebte(r,s)

seventieth /'sevntɪɪθ/ adj siebzigste(r,s)

seventy /'sevntɪ/ adj siebzig

several /'sevrl/ adj & pron mehrere, einige

sever|e /sɪ'vɪə(r)/ adj (-r, -st,) **-ly** adv streng; (pain) stark; (illness) schwer. **~ity** n Strenge f; Schwere f

sew /səʊ/ vt/i (pt sewed, pp sewn or sewed) nähen

sewage /'suːɪdʒ/ n Abwasser nt

sewer /'suːə(r)/ n Abwasserkanal m

sewing /'səʊɪŋ/ n Nähen nt; (work) Näharbeit f. **~ machine** n Nähmaschine f

sewn /səʊn/ see **sew**

sex /seks/ n Geschlecht nt; (sexuality, intercourse) Sex m. **~ist** adj sexistisch

sexual /'seksjʊəl/ adj sexuell. **~ 'intercourse** n Geschlechtsverkehr m

sexuality /seksjʊ'ælətɪ/ n Sexualität f

sexy /'seksɪ/ adj sexy

shabby /'ʃæbɪ/ adj, **-ily** adv schäbig

shack /ʃæk/ n Hütte f

shade /ʃeɪd/ n Schatten m; (of colour) [Farb]ton m; (for lamp) [Lampen]schirm m; (Amer: windowblind) Jalousie f ● vt beschatten

shadow /'ʃædəʊ/ n Schatten m ● vt (follow) beschatten

shady /'ʃeɪdɪ/ adj schattig; (🄳: disreputable) zwielichtig

shaft /ʃɑːft/ n Schaft m; (Techn) Welle f; (of light) Strahl m; (of lift) Schacht m

shaggy /'ʃægɪ/ adj zottig

shake /ʃeɪk/ n Schütteln n ● v (pt shook, pp shaken) ● vt schütteln; (shock) erschüttern; **~ hands with**

s.o. jdm die Hand geben ● vi wackeln; (tremble) zittern. **~ off** vt abschütteln

shaky /'ʃeɪkɪ/ adj wackelig; (hand, voice) zittrig

shall /ʃæl/ v aux we **~** see wir werden sehen; what **~** I do? was soll ich machen?

shallow /'ʃæləʊ/ adj (-er, -est) seicht; (dish) flach; (fig) oberflächlich

sham /ʃæm/ adj unecht ● n Heuchelei f ● vt (pt/pp shammed) vortäuschen

shambles /'ʃæmblz/ n Durcheinander nt

shame /ʃeɪm/ n Scham f; (disgrace) Schande f; **be a ~** schade sein; what a **~**! wie schade!

shame|ful /'ʃeɪmfl/ adj schändlich. **~less** adj schamlos

shampoo /ʃæm'puː/ n Shampoo nt ● vt schamponieren

shan't /ʃɑːnt/ = **shall not**

shape /ʃeɪp/ n Form f; (figure) Gestalt f ● vt formen (into zu). **~less** adj formlos; (clothing) unförmig

share /ʃeə(r)/ n [An]teil m; (Comm) Aktie f ● vt/i teilen. **~holder** n Aktionär(in) m(f)

shark /ʃɑːk/ n Hai[fisch] m

sharp /ʃɑːp/ adj (-er, -est) scharf; (pointed) spitz; (severe) heftig; (sudden) steil; (alert) clever; (unscrupulous) gerissen ● adv scharf; (Mus) zu hoch; **at six o'clock ~** Punkt sechs Uhr ● n (Mus) Kreuz nt. **~en** vt schärfen; [an]spitzen (pencil)

shatter /'ʃætə(r)/ vt zertrümmern; (fig) zerstören; **~ed** (person:) erschüttert; (🄳: exhausted) kaputt ● vi zersplittern

shave /ʃeɪv/ n Rasur f; **have a ~** sich rasieren ● vt rasieren ● vi sich rasieren. **~r** n Rasierapparat m

shawl /ʃɔːl/ n Schultertuch nt

she /ʃiː/ pron sie

shears /ʃɪəz/ npl [große] Schere f

shed[1] /ʃed/ n Schuppen m

shed[2] vt (pt/pp shed, pres p shedding) verlieren; vergießen (blood, tears); ~ light on Licht bringen in (+ acc)

sheep /ʃiːp/ n inv Schaf nt. ~-dog n Hütehund m

sheepish /ʃiːpɪʃ/ adj verlegen

sheer /ʃɪə(r)/ adj rein; (steep) steil; (transparent) hauchdünn

sheet /ʃiːt/ n Laken nt, Betttuch nt; (of paper) Blatt nt; (of glass, metal) Platte f

shelf /ʃelf/ n (pl shelves) Brett nt, Bord nt; (set of shelves) Regal nt

shell /ʃel/ n Schale f; (of snail) Haus nt; (of tortoise) Panzer m; (on beach) Muschel f; (Mil) Granate f ● vt pellen; enthülsen (peas); (Mil) [mit Granaten] beschießen. ~ out vi [1] blechen

'shellfish n inv Schalentiere pl; (Culin) Meeresfrüchte pl

shelter /ʃeltə(r)/ n Schutz m; (air-raid ~) Luftschutzraum m ● vt schützen (from vor + dat) ● vi sich unterstellen. ~ed adj geschützt; (life) behütet

shelve /ʃelv/ vt auf Eis legen; (abandon) aufgeben

shelving /ʃelvɪŋ/ n (shelves) Regale pl

shepherd /ʃepəd/ n Schäfer m ● vt führen

sherry /ʃerɪ/ n Sherry m

shield /ʃiːld/ n Schild m; (for eyes) Schirm m; (Techn & fig) Schutz m ● vt schützen (from vor + dat)

shift /ʃɪft/ n Verschiebung f; (at work) Schicht f ● vt rücken; (take away) wegnehmen; (rearrange) umstellen; schieben (blame) (on to auf + acc) ● vi sich verschieben; ([1]: rush) rasen

shifty /ʃɪftɪ/ adj (pej) verschlagen

shimmer /ʃɪmə(r)/ n Schimmer m ● vi schimmern

shin /ʃɪn/ n Schienbein nt

shine /ʃaɪn/ n Glanz m ● v (pt/pp shone) ● vi leuchten; (reflect light) glänzen; (sun:) scheinen ● vt ~ a light on beleuchten

shingle /ʃɪŋgl/ n (pebbles) Kiesel pl

shiny /ʃaɪnɪ/ adj glänzend

ship /ʃɪp/ n Schiff nt ● vt (pt/pp shipped) verschiffen

ship: ~building n Schiffbau m. ~ment n Sendung f. ~per n Spediteur m. ~ping n Versand m; (traffic) Schifffahrt f. ~shape adj & adv in Ordnung. ~wreck n Schiffbruch m. ~wrecked adj schiffbrüchig. ~yard n Werft f

shirt /ʃɜːt/ n [Ober]hemd nt; (for woman) Hemdbluse f

shit /ʃɪt/ n (vulgar) Scheiße f ● vi (pt/pp shit) (vulgar) scheißen

shiver /ʃɪvə(r)/ n Schauder m ● vi zittern

shoal /ʃəʊl/ n (fish) Schwarm m

shock /ʃɒk/ n Schock m; (Electr) Schlag m; (impact) Erschütterung f ● vt einen Schock versetzen (+ dat); (scandalize) schockieren. ~ing adj schockierend; ([1]: bad) fürchterlich

shoddy /ʃɒdɪ/ adj minderwertig

shoe /ʃuː/ n Schuh m; (of horse) Hufeisen nt ● vt (pt/pp shod, pres p shoeing) beschlagen (horse)

shoe: ~horn n Schuhanzieher m. ~-lace n Schnürsenkel m. ~-string n on a ~-string [1] mit ganz wenig Geld

shone /ʃɒn/ see shine

shoo /ʃuː/ vt scheuchen ● int sch!

shook /ʃʊk/ *see* shake

shoot /ʃuːt/ *n* (Bot) Trieb *m*; (hunt) Jagd *f* ● *v* (pt/pp **shot**) *vt* schießen; (kill) erschießen; drehen (film) ● *vi* schießen. **~ down** *vt* abschießen. **~ out** *vi* (rush) herausschießen. **~ up** *vi* (grow) in die Höhe schießen/(prices:) schnellen

shop /ʃɒp/ *n* Laden *m*, Geschäft *nt*; (workshop) Werkstatt *f*; **talk ~** 🔟 fachsimpeln ● *vi* (pt/pp **shopped**, pres p **shopping**) einkaufen; **go ~ping** einkaufen gehen

shop: **~ assistant** *n* Verkäufer(in) *m*(f). **~keeper** *n* Ladenbesitzer(in) *m*(f). **~-lifter** *n* Ladendieb *m*. **~-lifting** *n* Ladendiebstahl *m*

shopping /ʃɒpɪŋ/ *n* Einkaufen *nt*; (articles) Einkäufe *pl*; **do the ~** einkaufen. **~ bag** *n* Einkaufstasche *f*. **~ centre** *n* Einkaufszentrum *nt*. **~ trolley** *n* Einkaufswagen *m*

shop-'window *n* Schaufenster *nt*

shore /ʃɔː(r)/ *n* Strand *m*; (of lake) Ufer *nt*

short /ʃɔːt/ adj (er, -est) kurz; (person) klein; (curt) schroff; **a ~ time ago** vor kurzem; **be ~ of ...** zu wenig ... haben; **be in ~ supply** knapp sein ● adv kurz; (abruptly) plötzlich; (curtly) kurz angebunden; **in ~** kurzum; **~ of** (except) außer; **go ~** Mangel leiden

shortage /ʃɔːtɪdʒ/ *n* Mangel *m* (of an + dat); (scarcity) Knappheit *f*

short: **~bread** *n* ≈ Mürbekekse *pl*. **~ 'circuit** *n* Kurzschluss *m*. **~coming** *n* Fehler *m*. **~ 'cut** *n* Abkürzung *f*

shorten /ʃɔːtn/ *vt* [ab]kürzen; kürzer machen (garment)

short: **~hand** *n* Kurzschrift *f*, Stenographie *f*. **~ list** *n* engere Auswahl *f*

short|ly /ʃɔːtlɪ/ adv in Kürze; **~ly before/after** kurz vorher/danach. **~ness** *n* Kürze *f*; (of person) Kleinheit *f*

shorts /ʃɔːts/ *npl* Shorts *pl*

short: **~-'sighted** adj kurzsichtig. **~-sleeved** adj kurzärmelig. **~ 'story** *n* Kurzgeschichte *f*. **~-'tempered** adj aufbrausend. **~-'term** adj kurzfristig. **~ wave** *n* Kurzwelle *f*

shot /ʃɒt/ *see* shoot ● *n* Schuss *m*; (pellets) Schrot *m*; (person) Schütze *m*; (Phot) Aufnahme *f*; (injection) Spritze *f*; (🔟: attempt) Versuch *m*; **like a ~** 🔟 sofort. **~gun** *n* Schrotflinte *f*. **~-put** *n* (Sport) Kugelstoßen *nt*

should /ʃʊd/ modal verb **you ~ go** du solltest gehen; **I ~ have seen him** ich hätte ihn sehen sollen; **I ~ like** ich möchte; **this ~ be enough** das müsste eigentlich reichen; **if he ~ be there** falls er da sein sollte

shoulder /ʃəʊldə(r)/ *n* Schulter *f* ● *vt* schultern; (fig) auf sich (acc) nehmen. **~-blade** *n* Schulterblatt *nt*

shout /ʃaʊt/ *n* Schrei *m* ● *vt/i* schreien. **~ down** *vt* niederschreien

shouting /ʃaʊtɪŋ/ *n* Geschrei *nt*

shove /ʃʌv/ *n* Stoß *m* ● *vt* stoßen; (🔟: put) tun ● *vi* drängeln. **~ off** *vi* 🔟 abhauen

shovel /ʃʌvl/ *n* Schaufel *f* ● *vt* (pt/pp **shovelled**) schaufeln

show /ʃəʊ/ *n* (display) Pracht *f*; (exhibition) Ausstellung *f*, Schau *f*; (performance) Vorstellung *f*; (Theat, TV) Show *f*; **on ~** ausgestellt ● *v* (pt **showed**, pp **shown**) *vt* zeigen; (put on display) ausstellen; vorführen (film) ● *vi* sichtbar sein; (film:) gezeigt werden. **~ in** *vt* hereinführen. **~ off** *vi* 🔟 angeben ● *vt* vorführen; (flaunt) angeben mit. **~ up** *vi* [deutlich] zu sehen sein; (🔟: ar-

rive) auftauchen ● *vt* deutlich zeigen; (ℹ: *embarrass*) blamieren

shower /'ʃaʊə(r)/ *n* Dusche *f*; (*of rain*) Schauer *m*; **have a ~** duschen ● *vt* **~ with** überschütten mit ● *vi* duschen

'show-jumping *n* Springreiten *nt*

shown /ʃəʊn/ *see* show

show: **~-off** *n* Angeber(in) *m(f)*. **~room** *n* Ausstellungsraum *m*

showy /'ʃəʊɪ/ *adj* protzig

shrank /ʃræŋk/ *see* shrink

shred /ʃred/ *n* Fetzen *m*; (*fig*) Spur *f* ● *vt* (*pt/pp* **shredded**) zerkleinern; (*Culin*) schnitzeln. **~der** *n* Reißwolf *m*; (*Culin*) Schnitzelwerk *nt*

shrewd /ʃruːd/ *adj* (**-er, -est**) klug. **~ness** *n* Klugheit *f*

shriek /ʃriːk/ *n* Schrei *m* ● *vt/i* schreien

shrill /ʃrɪl/ *adj*, **-y** *adv* schrill

shrimp /ʃrɪmp/ *n* Garnele *f*, Krabbe *f*

shrink /ʃrɪŋk/ *vi* (*pt* **shrank**, *pp* **shrunk**) schrumpfen; (*garment:*) einlaufen; (*draw back*) zurückschrecken (**from** vor + *dat*)

shrivel /'ʃrɪvl/ *vi* (*pt/pp* **shrivelled**) verschrumpeln

Shrove /ʃrəʊv/ *n* **~'Tuesday** Fastnachtsdienstag *m*

shrub /ʃrʌb/ *n* Strauch *m*

shrug /ʃrʌg/ *n* Achselzucken *nt* ● *vt/i* (*pt/pp* **shrugged**) **~ [one's shoulders]** die Achseln zucken

shrunk /ʃrʌŋk/ *see* shrink

shudder /'ʃʌdə(r)/ *n* Schauder *m* ● *vi* schaudern; (*tremble*) zittern

shuffle /'ʃʌfl/ *vi* schlurfen ● *vt* mischen (*cards*)

shun /ʃʌn/ *vt* (*pt/pp* **shunned**) meiden

shunt /ʃʌnt/ *vt* rangieren

shut /ʃʌt/ *v* (*pt/pp* **shut**, *pres p* **shutting**) ● *vt* zumachen, schließen ● *vi* sich schließen; (*shop:*) schließen, zumachen. **~ down** *vt* schließen; stilllegen (*factory*) ● *vi* schließen. **~ up** *vt* abschließen; (*lock in*) einsperren ● *vi* ℹ den Mund halten

shutter /'ʃʌtə(r)/ *n* [Fenster]laden *m*; (*Phot*) Verschluss *m*

shuttle /'ʃʌtl/ *n* (*textiles*) Schiffchen *nt*

shuttle service *n* Pendelverkehr *m*

shy /ʃaɪ/ *adj* (**-er, -est**) schüchtern; (*timid*) scheu. **~ness** *n* Schüchternheit *f*

siblings /'sɪblɪŋz/ *npl* Geschwister *pl*

Sicily /'sɪsɪlɪ/ *n* Sizilien *nt*

sick /sɪk/ *adj* krank; (*humour*) makaber; **be ~** (*vomit*) sich übergeben; **be ~ of sth** ℹ etw satt haben; **I feel ~** mir ist schlecht

sick|ly /'sɪklɪ/ *adj* kränklich. **~ness** *n* Krankheit *f*; (*vomiting*) Erbrechen *nt*

side /saɪd/ *n* Seite *f*; **on the ~** (*as sideline*) nebenbei; **~ by ~** nebeneinander; (*fig*) Seite an Seite; **take ~s** Partei ergreifen (**with** für) ● *attrib* Seiten- ● *vi* **~ with** Partei ergreifen für

side: **~board** *n* Anrichte *f*. **~-effect** *n* Nebenwirkung *f*. **~lights** *npl* Standlicht *nt*. **~line** *n* Nebenbeschäftigung *nt*. **~-show** *n* Nebenattraktion *f*. **~step** *vt* ausweichen (+ *dat*). **~walk** *n* (*Amer*) Bürgersteig *m*. **~ways** *adv* seitwärts

siding /'saɪdɪŋ/ *n* Abstellgleis *nt*

siege /siːdʒ/ *n* Belagerung *f*; (*by police*) Umstellung *f*

sieve /sɪv/ *n* Sieb *nt* ● *vt* sieben

sift /sɪft/ *vt* sieben; (*fig*) durchsehen

sigh /saɪ/ n Seufzer m ● vi seufzen

sight /saɪt/ n Sicht f; (faculty) Sehvermögen nt; (spectacle) Anblick m; (on gun) Visier nt; **~s** pl Sehenswürdigkeiten pl; **at first ~** auf den ersten Blick; **lose ~ of** aus dem Auge verlieren; **know by ~** vom Sehen kennen ● vt sichten

'sightseeing n **go ~** die Sehenswürdigkeiten besichtigen

sign /saɪn/ n Zeichen nt; (notice) Schild nt ● vt/i unterschreiben; (author, artist:) signieren; **~ on** (as unemployed) sich arbeitslos melden; (Mil) sich verpflichten

signal /'sɪɡnl/ n Signal nt ● vt/i (pt/pp **signalled**) signalisieren; **~ to** s.o. jdm ein Signal geben

signature /'sɪɡnətʃə(r)/ n Unterschrift f; (of artist) Signatur f

significan|ce /sɪɡ'nɪfɪkəns/ n Bedeutung f. **~t** adj (important) bedeutend

signify /'sɪɡnɪfaɪ/ vt (pt/pp **-ied**) bedeuten

signpost /'saɪn-/ n Wegweiser m

silence /'saɪləns/ n Stille f; (of person) Schweigen nt ● vt zum Schweigen bringen. **~r** n (on gun) Schalldämpfer m; (Auto) Auspufftopf m

silent /'saɪlənt/ adj still; (without speaking) schweigend; **remain ~** schweigen

silhouette /sɪlu:'et/ n Silhouette f; (picture) Schattenriss m ● vt **be ~d** sich als Silhouette abheben

silicon /'sɪlɪkən/ n Silizium nt

silk /sɪlk/ n Seide f ● attrib Seiden-

silky /'sɪlkɪ/ adj seidig

sill /sɪl/ n Sims m & nt

silly /'sɪlɪ/ adj dumm, albern

silver /'sɪlvə(r)/ adj silbern; (coin, paper) Silber- ● n Silber nt

silver: ~-plated adj versilbert. **~ware** n Silber nt

similar /'sɪmɪlə(r)/ adj ähnlich. **~ity** n Ähnlichkeit f

simmer /'sɪmə(r)/ vi leise kochen, ziehen ● vt ziehen lassen

simple /'sɪmpl/ adj (-r, -st) einfach; (person) einfältig. **~-'minded** adj einfältig

simplicity /sɪm'plɪsətɪ/ n Einfachheit f

simpli|fication /sɪmplɪfɪ'keɪʃn/ n Vereinfachung f. **~fy** vt (pt/pp -ied) vereinfachen

simply /'sɪmplɪ/ adv einfach

simulat|e /'sɪmjʊleɪt/ vt vortäuschen; (Techn) simulieren

simultaneous /sɪml'teɪnɪəs/ adj gleichzeitig

sin /sɪn/ n Sünde f ● vi (pt/pp **sinned**) sündigen

---

since /sɪns/

● preposition

····▸ seit (+ dat). **he's been living here since 1991** er wohnt* seit 1991 hier. **I had been waiting since 8 o'clock** ich wartete* [schon] seit 8 Uhr. **since seeing you** seit ich dich gesehen habe. **how long is it since your interview?** wie lange ist es seit deinem Vorstellungsgespräch?

● adverb

····▸ seitdem. **I haven't spoken to her since** seitdem habe ich mit ihr nicht gesprochen. **the house has been empty ever since** das Haus steht seitdem leer. **he has since remarried** er hat danach wieder geheiratet. **long since** vor langer Zeit

● conjunction

····▸ seit. **since she has been living in Germany** seit sie in Deutschland wohnt*. **since they**

s

had been in London **seit sie in London waren***. **how long is it since he left?** wie lange ist es her, dass er weggezogen ist? **it's a year since he left** es ist ein Jahr her, dass er weggezogen ist

···► (*because*) da. **since she was ill, I had to do it** da sie krank war, musste ich es tun

❗ *Note the different tenses in German

sincere /sɪn'sɪə(r)/ adj aufrichtig; (*heartfelt*) herzlich. **~ly** adv aufrichtig; **Yours ~ly** Mit freundlichen Grüßen

sincerity /sɪn'serətɪ/ n Aufrichtigkeit f

sinful /'sɪnfl/ adj sündhaft

sing /sɪŋ/ vt/i (pt **sang**, pp **sung**) singen

singe /sɪndʒ/ vt (pres p **singeing**) versengen

singer /'sɪŋə(r)/ n Sänger(in) m(f)

single /'sɪŋgl/ adj einzeln; (*one only*) einzig; (*unmarried*) ledig; (*ticket*) einfach; (*room, bed*) Einzel- ● n (*ticket*) einfache Fahrkarte f; (*record*) Single f; **~s** pl (*Tennis*) Einzel nt ● vt **~out** auswählen

single: **~handed** adj & adv allein. **~'parent** n Alleinerziehende(r) m/f

singly /'sɪŋglɪ/ adv einzeln

singular /'sɪŋgjʊlə(r)/ adj eigenartig; (*Gram*) im Singular ● n Singular m

sinister /'sɪnɪstə(r)/ adj finster

sink /sɪŋk/ n Spülbecken nt ● v (pt **sank**, pp **sunk**) ● vi sinken ● vt versenken (*ship*); senken (*shaft*). **~ in** vi einsinken; (🔢: *be understood*) kapiert werden

sinner /'sɪnə(r)/ n Sünder(in) m(f)

sip /sɪp/ n Schlückchen nt ● vt (pt/pp **sipped**) in kleinen Schlucken trinken

siphon /'saɪfn/ n (*bottle*) Siphon m. **~ off** vt mit einem Saugheber ablassen

sir /sɜː(r)/ n mein Herr; **S~** (*title*) Sir; **Dear S~s** Sehr geehrte Herren

siren /'saɪrən/ n Sirene f

sister /'sɪstə(r)/ n Schwester f; (*nurse*) Oberschwester f. **~in-law** n Schwägerin f

sit /sɪt/ v (pt/pp **sat**, pres p **sitting**) ● vi sitzen; (*sit down*) sich setzen; (*committee:*) tagen ● vt setzen; machen (*exam*). **~ back** vi sich zurücklehnen. **~ down** vi sich setzen. **~ up** vi [aufrecht] sitzen; (*rise*) sich aufsetzen; (*not slouch*) gerade sitzen

site /saɪt/ n Gelände nt; (*for camping*) Platz m; (*Archaeology*) Stätte f

sitting /'sɪtɪŋ/ n Sitzung f; (*for meals*) Schub m

situat|e /'sɪtjʊeɪt/ vt legen; **be ~ed** liegen. **~ion** /-'eɪʃn/ n Lage f; (*circumstances*) Situation f; (*job*) Stelle f

six /sɪks/ adj sechs. **~teen** adj sechzehn. **~teenth** adj sechzehnte(r,s)

sixth /sɪksθ/ adj sechste(r,s)

sixtieth /'sɪkstɪɪθ/ adj sechzigste(r,s)

sixty /'sɪkstɪ/ adj sechzig

size /saɪz/ n Größe f

sizzle /'sɪzl/ vi brutzeln

skate[1] /skeɪt/ n Schlittschuh m ● vi Schlittschuh laufen. **~board** n Skateboard nt ● vi Skateboard fahren. **~boarding** n Skateboardfahren nt. **~r** n Eisläufer(in) m(f)

skating /'skeɪtɪŋ/ n Eislaufen nt. **~rink** n Eisbahn f

skeleton /'skelɪtn/ n Skelett nt. **~'key** n Dietrich m

sketch /sketʃ/ n Skizze f; (*Theat*) Sketch m ● vt skizzieren

sketchy /'sketʃi/ adj , **-ily** adv skizzenhaft

ski /ski:/ n Ski m ● vi (*pt/pp* **skied**, *pres p* **skiing**) Ski fahren or laufen

skid /skɪd/ n Schleudern nt ● vi (*pt/pp* **skidded**) schleudern

skier /'ski:ə(r)/ n Skiläufer(in) m(f)

skiing /'ski:ɪŋ/ n Skilaufen nt

skilful /'skɪlfl/ adj geschickt

skill /skɪl/ n Geschick nt. **~ed** adj geschickt; (*trained*) ausgebildet

skim /skɪm/ vt (*pt/pp* **skimmed**) entrahmen (*milk*)

skimp /skɪmp/ vt sparen an (+ *dat*)

skimpy /'skɪmpɪ/ adj knapp

skin /skɪn/ n Haut f; (*on fruit*) Schale f ● vt (*pt/pp* **skinned**) häuten; schälen (*fruit*)

skin: **~-deep** adj oberflächlich. **~-diving** n Sporttauchen nt

skinny /'skɪnɪ/ adj dünn

skip[1] n Container m

skip[2] n Hüpfer m ● vi (*pt/pp* **skipped**) vi hüpfen; (*with rope*) seilspringen ● vt überspringen

skipper /'skɪpə(r)/ n Kapitän m

'skipping-rope n Sprungseil nt

skirmish /'skɜ:mɪʃ/ n Gefecht nt

skirt /skɜ:t/ n Rock m ● vt herumgehen um

skittle /'skɪtl/ n Kegel m

skive /skaɪv/ vi [] blaumachen

skull /skʌl/ n Schädel m

sky /skaɪ/ n Himmel m. **~light** n Dachluke f. **~ marshal** n bewaffneter Flugbegleiter m. **~scraper** n Wolkenkratzer m

slab /slæb/ n Platte f; (*slice*) Scheibe f; (*of chocolate*) Tafel f

slack /slæk/ adj (**-er, -est**) schlaff, locker; (*person*) nachlässig; (*Comm*) flau ● vi bummeln

slacken /'slækn/ vi sich lockern; (*diminish*) nachlassen ● vt lockern; (*diminish*) verringern

slain /sleɪn/ *see* **slay**

slam /slæm/ v (*pt/pp* **slammed**) ● vt zuschlagen; (*put*) knallen []; ([]: *criticize*) verreißen ● vi zuschlagen

slander /'slɑ:ndə(r)/ n Verleumdung f ● vt verleumden

slang /slæŋ/ n Slang m. **~y** adj salopp

slant /slɑ:nt/ n Schräge f; **on the ~** schräg ● vt abschrägen; (*fig*) färben (*report*) ● vi sich neigen

slap /slæp/ n Schlag m ● vt (*pt/pp* **slapped**) schlagen; (*put*) knallen [] ● adv direkt

slapdash adj [] schludrig

slash /slæʃ/ n Schlitz m ● vt aufschlitzen; [drastisch] reduzieren (*prices*)

slat /slæt/ n Latte f

slate /sleɪt/ n Schiefer m ● vt [] heruntermachen; verreißen (*performance*)

slaughter /'slɔ:tə(r)/ n Schlachten nt; (*massacre*) Gemetzel nt ● vt schlachten; abschlachten (*men*)

Slav /slɑ:v/ adj slawisch ● n Slawe m/ Slawin f

slave /sleɪv/ n Sklave m/ Sklavin f ● vi **~ [away]** schuften

slavery /'sleɪvərɪ/ n Sklaverei f

slay /sleɪ/ vt (*pt* **slew**, *pp* **slain**) ermorden

sledge /sledʒ/ n Schlitten m

sleek /sli:k/ adj (**-er, -est**) seidig; (*well-fed*) wohlgenährt

sleep /sli:p/ n Schlaf m; **go to ~** einschlafen; **put to ~** einschläfern ● v (*pt/pp* **slept**) ● vi schlafen ● vt (*accommodate*) Unterkunft bieten für. **~er** n Schläfer(in) f; (*Rail*) Schlafwagen m; (*on track*)

Schwelle f

sleeping: ~-**bag** n Schlafsack m.
~-**pill** n Schlaftablette f

sleep: ~**less** adj schlaflos. ~-**wal-king** n Schlafwandeln nt

sleepy /ˈsliːpi/ adj , -**ily** adv schläfrig

sleet /sliːt/ n Schneeregen m

sleeve /sliːv/ n Ärmel m; (for re-cord) Hülle f. ~**less** adj ärmellos

sleigh /sleɪ/ n [Pferde]schlitten m

slender /ˈslendə(r)/ adj schlank; (fig) gering

slept /slept/ see **sleep**

slew see **slay**

slice /slaɪs/ n Scheibe f ● vt in Scheiben schneiden

slick /slɪk/ adj clever

slid|e /slaɪd/ n Rutschbahn f; (for hair) Spange f; (Phot) Dia nt ● v (pt/pp **slid**) ● vi rutschen ● vt schieben. ~**ing** adj gleitend; (door, seat) Schiebe-

slight /slaɪt/ adj (-er, -est) leicht; (importance) gering; (acquaintance) flüchtig; (slender) schlank; **not in the ~est** nicht im Geringsten; ~**ly better** ein bisschen besser ● vt kränken, beleidigen ● n Beleidigung f

slim /slɪm/ adj (slimmer, slim-mest) schlank; (volume) schmal; (fig) gering ● vi eine Schlankheits-kur machen

slim|e /slaɪm/ n Schleim m. ~**y** adj schleimig

sling /slɪŋ/ n (Med) Schlinge f ● vt (pt/pp **slung**) 🔲 schmeißen

slip /slɪp/ n (mistake) Fehler m; 🔲 Patzer m; (petticoat) Unterrock m; (paper) Zettel m; **give s.o. the ~** 🔲 jdm entwischen; ~ **of the tongue** Versprecher m ● v (pt/pp **slipped**) ● vi rutschen; (fall) ausrut-schen; (go quickly) schlüpfen ● vt

schieben; ~ **s.o.'s mind** jdm entfal-len. ~ **away** vi sich fortschleichen. ~ **up** vi 🔲 einen Schnitzer machen

slipper /ˈslɪpə(r)/ n Hausschuh m

slippery /ˈslɪpəri/ adj glitschig; (surface) glatt

slipshod /ˈslɪpʃɒd/ adj schludrig

'slip-up n 🔲 Schnitzer m

slit /slɪt/ n Schlitz m ● vt (pt/pp **slit**) aufschlitzen

slither /ˈslɪðə(r)/ vi rutschen

slog /slɒg/ n [hard] ~ Schinderei f ● vi (pt/pp **slogged**) schuften

slogan /ˈsləʊgən/ n Schlagwort nt; (advertising) Werbespruch m

slop|e /sləʊp/ n Hang m; (inclin-ation) Neigung f ● vi sich neigen. ~**ing** adj schräg

sloppy /ˈslɒpi/ adj schludrig; (senti-mental) sentimental

slosh /slɒʃ/ vi 🔲 schwappen

slot /slɒt/ n Schlitz m; (TV) Sende-zeit f ● v (pt/pp **slotted**) ● vt einfü-gen ● vi sich einfügen (**in** in + acc)

'slot-machine n Münzautomat m; (for gambling) Spielautomat m

slouch /slaʊtʃ/ vi sich schlecht halten

slovenly /ˈslʌvnli/ adj schlampig

slow /sləʊ/ adj (-er, -est) langsam; **be ~** (clock:) nachgehen; **in ~ mo-tion** in Zeitlupe ● adv langsam ● vt verlangsamen ● vi ~ **down**, ~ **up** langsamer werden. ~**ness** n Lang-samkeit f

sludge /slʌdʒ/ n Schlamm m

slug /slʌg/ n Nacktschnecke f

sluggish /ˈslʌgɪʃ/ adj träge

sluice /sluːs/ n Schleuse f

slum /slʌm/ n Elendsviertel nt

slumber /ˈslʌmbə(r)/ n Schlum-mer m ● vi schlummern

slump /slʌmp/ n Sturz m ● vi fal-len; (crumple) zusammensacken;

(*prices:*) stürzen; (*sales:*) zurückgehen

slung /slʌŋ/ *see* sling

slur /slɜː(r)/ *vt* (*pt/pp* slurred) undeutlich sprechen

slurp /slɜːp/ *vt/i* schlürfen

slush /slʌʃ/ *n* [Schnee]matsch *m*; (*fig*) Kitsch *m*

slut /slʌt/ *n* Schlampe *f* ▣

sly /slaɪ/ *adj* (-er, -est) verschlagen ● *n* on the ~ heimlich

smack /smæk/ *n* Schlag *m*, Klaps *m* ● *vt* schlagen ● *adv* ▣ direkt

small /smɔːl/ *adj* (-er, -est) klein ● *adv* chop up ~ klein hacken ● ~ of the back Kreuz *nt*

small: ~ ads *npl* Kleinanzeigen *pl.* ~ 'change *n* Kleingeld *nt.* ~pox *n* Pocken *pl.* ~ talk *n* leichte Konversation *f*

smart /smɑːt/ *adj* (-er, -est) schick; (*clever*) schlau, clever; (*brisk*) flott; (*Amer, fam:* cheeky) frech ● *vi* brennen

smarten /'smɑːtn/ *vt* ~ oneself up mehr auf sein Äußeres achten

smash /smæʃ/ *n* Krach *m*; (*collision*) Zusammenstoß *m*; (*Tennis*) Schmetterball *m* ● *vt* zerschlagen; (*strike*) schlagen; (*Tennis*) schmettern ● *vi* zerschmettern; (*crash*) krachen (**into** gegen). ~**ing** *adj* ▣ toll

smear /smɪə(r)/ *n* verschmierter Fleck *m*; (*Med*) Abstrich *m*; (*fig*) Verleumdung *f* ● *vt* schmieren; (*coat*) beschmieren (**with** mit); (*fig*) verleumden ● *vi* schmieren

smell /smel/ *n* Geruch *m*; (*sense*) Geruchssinn *m* ● *vt/i* (*pt/pp* smelt *or* smelled) ● *vt* riechen; (*sniff*) riechen an (+ *dat*) ● *vi* riechen (**of** nach)

smelly /'smelɪ/ *adj* übel riechend

smelt /smelt/ *see* smell

smile /smaɪl/ *n* Lächeln *nt* ● *vi* lächeln; ~ **at** anlächeln

smirk /smɜːk/ *vi* feixen

smith /smɪθ/ *n* Schmied *m*

smock /smɒk/ *n* Kittel *m*

smog /smɒg/ *n* Smog *m*

smoke /sməʊk/ *n* Rauch *m* ● *vt/i* rauchen; (*Culin*) räuchern. ~**less** *adj* rauchfrei; (*fuel*) rauchlos

smoker /'sməʊkə(r)/ *n* Raucher *m*; (*Rail*) Raucherabteil *nt*

smoking /'sməʊkɪŋ/ *n* Rauchen *nt;* 'no ~' 'Rauchen verboten'

smoky /'sməʊkɪ/ *adj* verraucht; (*taste*) rauchig

smooth /smuːð/ *adj* (-er, -est) glatt ● *vt* glätten. ~ **out** *vt* glatt streichen

smother /'smʌðə(r)/ *vt* ersticken; (*cover*) bedecken; (*suppress*) unterdrücken

smoulder /'sməʊldə(r)/ *vi* schwelen

smudge /smʌdʒ/ *n* Fleck *m* ● *vt* verwischen ● *vi* schmieren

smug /smʌg/ *adj* (smugger, smuggest) selbstgefällig

smuggl|e /'smʌgl/ *vt* schmuggeln. ~**er** *n* Schmuggler *m.* ~**ing** *n* Schmuggel *m*

snack /snæk/ *n* Imbiss *m.* ~**-bar** *n* Imbissstube *f*

snag /snæg/ *n* Schwierigkeit *f,* ▣ Haken *m*

snail /sneɪl/ *n* Schnecke *f;* at a ~'s pace im Schneckentempo

snake /sneɪk/ *n* Schlange *f*

snap /snæp/ *n* Knacken *nt;* (*photo*) Schnappschuss *m* ● *attrib* (*decision*) plötzlich ● *v* (*pt/pp* snapped) ● *vi* [entzwei]brechen; ~ **at** (*bite*) schnappen nach; (*speak sharply*) [scharf] anfahren ● *vt* zerbrechen; (*say*) fauchen; (*Phot*) knipsen. ~ **up** *vt* wegschnappen

snappy /'snæpɪ/ adj (smart) flott; **make it ~!** ein bisschen schnell!

'snapshot n Schnappschuss m

snare /sneə(r)/ n Schlinge f

snarl /snɑːl/ vi [mit gefletschten Zähnen] knurren

snatch /snætʃ/ n (fragment) Fetzen pl ● vt schnappen; (steal) klauen; entführen (child); ~ **sth from s.o.** jdm etw entreißen

sneak /sniːk/ n 🗊 Petze f ● vi schleichen; (🗊: tell tales) petzen ● vt (take) mitgehen lassen ● vi **in/out** sich hinein-/hinausschleichen

sneakers /'sniːkəz/ npl (Amer) Turnschuhe pl

sneer /snɪə(r)/ vi höhnisch lächeln; (mock) spotten

sneeze /sniːz/ n Niesen nt ● vi niesen

snide /snaɪd/ adj 🗊 abfällig

sniff /snɪf/ vi schnüffeln ● vt schnüffeln an (+ dat)

snigger /'snɪgə(r)/ vi [boshaft] kichern

snip /snɪp/ n Schnitt m ● vt/i ~ **[at]** schnippeln an (+ dat)

snippet /'snɪpɪt/ n Schnipsel m; (of information) Bruchstück nt

snivel /'snɪvl/ vi (pt/pp snivelled) flennen

snob /snɒb/ n Snob m. **~bery** n Snobismus m. **~bish** adj snobistisch

snoop /snuːp/ vi 🗊 schnüffeln

snooty /'snuːtɪ/ adj 🗊 hochnäsig

snooze /snuːz/ n Nickerchen nt ● vi dösen

snore /snɔː(r)/ vi schnarchen

snorkel /'snɔːkl/ n Schnorchel m

snort /snɔːt/ vi schnauben

snout /snaʊt/ n Schnauze f

snow /snəʊ/ n Schnee m ● vi schneien; **~ed under with** (fig) überhäuft mit

snow: **~ball** n Schneeball m. **~board** n Snowboard nt. **~drift** n Schneewehe f. **~drop** n Schneeglöckchen nt. **~fall** n Schneefall m. **~flake** n Schneeflocke f. **~man** n Schneemann m. **~plough** n Schneepflug m

snub /snʌb/ n Abfuhr f ● vt (pt/pp snubbed) brüskieren

'snub-nosed adj stupsnasig

snuffle /'snʌfl/ vi schnüffeln

snug /snʌg/ adj (snugger, snuggest) behaglich, gemütlich

snuggle /'snʌgl/ vi sich kuscheln (**up to** an + acc)

so /səʊ/ adv so; **am I** ich auch; **so I see** das sehe ich; **that is so** das stimmt; **so much the better** umso besser; **if so** wenn ja; **so as to** um zu; **so long!** 🗊 tschüs! ● pron **I hope so** hoffentlich; **I think so** ich glaube schon; **I'm afraid so** leider ja; **so saying/doing, he/she ...** indem er/sie das sagte/tat, ... ● conj (therefore) also; **so that** damit; **so what!** na und! **so you see** wie du siehst

soak /səʊk/ vt nass machen; (steep) einweichen; (🗊: fleece) schröpfen ● vi weichen; (liquid:) sickern. **~ up** vt aufsaugen

soaking /'səʊkɪŋ/ adj & adv ~ **[wet]** patschnass 🗊

soap /səʊp/ n Seife f. **~ opera** n Seifenoper f. **~ powder** n Seifenpulver nt

soapy /'səʊpɪ/ adj seifig

soar /sɔː(r)/ vi aufsteigen; (prices:) in die Höhe schnellen

sob /sɒb/ n Schluchzer m ● vi (pt/pp sobbed) schluchzen

sober /'səʊbə(r)/ adj nüchtern; (serious) ernst; (colour) gedeckt. **~ up** vi nüchtern werden

'so-called adj sogenannt

soccer /'sɒkə(r)/ n Ⅰ Fußball m

sociable /'səʊʃəbl/ adj gesellig

social /'səʊʃl/ adj gesellschaftlich;
(Admin, Pol, Zool) sozial

socialis|m /'səʊʃəlɪzm/ n Sozialis-
mus m. **~t** adj sozialistisch ● n So-
zialist m

socialize /'səʊʃəlaɪz/ vi [gesell-
schaftlich] verkehren

socially /'səʊʃəlɪ/ adv gesellschaftlich; **know ~** privat kennen

social: ~ se'curity n Sozialhilfe f.
~ worker n Sozialarbeiter(in) m(f)

society /sə'saɪətɪ/ n Gesellschaft f;
(club) Verein m

sociolog|ist /səʊsɪ'ɒlədʒɪst/ n So-
ziologe m. **~y** n Soziologie f

sock /sɒk/ n Socke f; (kneelength)
Kniestrumpf m

socket /'sɒkɪt/ n (of eye) Augen-
höhle f; (of joint) Gelenkpfanne f;
(wall plug) Steckdose f

soda /'səʊdə/ n Soda nt; (Amer) Li-
monade f. **~ water** n Sodawasser nt

sodden /'sɒdn/ adj durchnässt

sofa /'səʊfə/ n Sofa nt. **~ bed** n
Schlafcouch f

soft /sɒft/ adj (-er, -est) weich;
(quiet) leise; (gentle) sanft; (Ⅰ: silly)
dumm. **~ drink** n alkoholfreies Getränk nt

soften /'sɒfn/ vt weich machen;
(fig) mildern ● vi weich werden

soft: ~ toy n Stofftier nt. **~ware**
n Software f

soggy /'sɒgɪ/ adj aufgeweicht

soil[1] /sɔɪl/ n Erde f, Boden m

soil[2] vt verschmutzen

solar /'səʊlə(r)/ adj Sonnen-

sold /səʊld/ see **sell**

soldier /'səʊldʒə(r)/ n Soldat m
● vi **~ on** [unbeirrbar] weiter-

machen

sole[1] /səʊl/ n Sohle f

sole[2] n (fish) Seezunge f

sole[3] adj einzig. **~ly** adv einzig und
allein

solemn /'sɒləm/ adj feierlich; (serious) ernst

solicitor /sə'lɪsɪtə(r)/ n Rechtsanwalt m/-anwältin f

solid /'sɒlɪd/ adj fest; (sturdy) stabil;
(not hollow, of same substance) massiv; (unanimous) einstimmig; (complete) ganz

solidarity /sɒlɪ'dærətɪ/ n Solidarität f

solidify /sə'lɪdɪfaɪ/ vi (pt/pp -ied)
fest werden

solitary /'sɒlɪtərɪ/ adj einsam;
(sole) einzig

solitude /'sɒlɪtjuːd/ n Einsamkeit f

solo /'səʊləʊ/ n Solo nt ● adj Solo-;
(flight) Allein- ● adv solo. **~ist** n
Solist(in) m(f)

solstice /'sɒlstɪs/ n Sonnenwende f

soluble /'sɒljʊbl/ adj löslich

solution /sə'luːʃn/ n Lösung f

solvable /'sɒlvəbl/ adj lösbar

solve /sɒlv/ vt lösen

solvent /'sɒlvənt/ n Lösungs-
mittel nt

sombre /'sɒmbə(r)/ adj dunkel;
(mood) düster   **s**

some /sʌm/ adj & pron etwas; (a
little) ein bisschen; (with pl noun) einige; (a few) ein paar; (certain) man-
che(r,s); (one or the other) [irgend]-
ein; **~ day** eines Tages; **I want ~**
ich möchte etwas; (pl) welche; **will
you have ~ wine?** möchten Sie
Wein? **do ~ shopping** einkaufen

some: ~body /-bədɪ/ pron & n jemand; (emphatic) irgendjemand.
~how adv irgendwie. **~one** pron &
n = **somebody**

somersault /'sʌməsɔːlt/ n Purzelbaum m 🔟; (Sport) Salto m; **turn a ~** einen Purzelbaum schlagen/einen Salto springen

'something pron & adv etwas; (emphatic) irgendetwas; **~ different** etwas anderes; **~ like this** so etwas [wie das]

some: **~time** adv irgendwann ● adj ehemalig. **~times** adv manchmal. **~what** adv ziemlich. **~where** adv irgendwo; (go) irgendwohin

son /sʌn/ n Sohn m

song /sɒŋ/ n Lied nt. **~bird** n Singvogel m

'son-in-law n (pl **~s-in-law**) Schwiegersohn m

soon /suːn/ adv (-er, -est) bald; (quickly) schnell; **too ~** zu früh; **as ~ as possible** so bald wie möglich; **~er or later** früher oder später; **no ~er had I arrived than ...** kaum war ich angekommen, da ...; **I would ~er stay** ich würde lieber bleiben

soot /sʊt/ n Ruß m

soothe /suːð/ vt beruhigen; lindern (pain). **~ing** adj beruhigend; lindernd

sophisticated /sə'fɪstɪkeɪtɪd/ adj weltgewandt; (complex) hoch entwickelt

sopping /'sɒpɪŋ/ adj & adv **~[wet]** durchnässt

soppy /'sɒpɪ/ adj ☒ rührselig

soprano /sə'prɑːnəʊ/ n Sopran m; (woman) Sopranistin f

sordid /'sɔːdɪd/ adj schmutzig

sore /sɔː(r)/ adj (-r, -st) wund; (painful) schmerzhaft; **have a ~ throat** Halsschmerzen haben ● n wunde Stelle f. **~ly** adv sehr

sorrow /'sɒrəʊ/ n Kummer m

sorry /'sɒrɪ/ adj (sad) traurig;

(wretched) erbärmlich; **I am ~** es tut mir Leid; **she is** or **feels ~ for him** er tut ihr Leid; **I am ~ to say** leider; **~!** Entschuldigung!

sort /sɔːt/ n Art f; (brand) Sorte f; **he's a good ~** 🔟 er ist in Ordnung ● vt sortieren. **~ out** vt sortieren; (fig) klären

sought /sɔːt/ see **seek**

soul /səʊl/ n Seele f

sound¹ /saʊnd/ adj (-er, -est) gesund; (sensible) vernünftig; (secure) solide; (thorough) gehörig ● adv be **~ asleep** fest schlafen

sound² n (strait) Meerenge f

sound³ n Laut m; (noise) Geräusch nt; (Phys) Schall m; (Radio, TV) Ton m; (of bells, music) Klang m; **I don't like the ~ of it** 🔟 das hört sich nicht gut an ● vi [er]tönen; (seem) sich anhören ● vt (pronounce) aussprechen; schlagen (alarm); (Med) abhorchen (chest)

soundly /'saʊndlɪ/ adv solide; (sleep) fest; (defeat) vernichtend

'soundproof adj schalldicht

soup /suːp/ n Suppe f

sour /'saʊə(r)/ adj (-er, -est) sauer; (bad-tempered) griesgrämig, verdrießlich

source /sɔːs/ n Quelle f

south /saʊθ/ n Süden m; **to the ~ of** südlich von ● adj Süd-, süd- ● adv nach Süden

south: **S~ 'Africa** n Südafrika nt. **S~ A'merica** n Südamerika nt. **~-'east** n Südosten m

southerly /'sʌðəlɪ/ adj südlich

southern /'sʌðən/ adj südlich

'southward[s] /-wəd[z]/ adv nach Süden

souvenir /suːvə'nɪə(r)/ n Andenken nt, Souvenir nt

Soviet /'səʊvɪət/ adj (History) sowjetisch; **~ Union** Sowjetunion f

sow¹ /sau/ n Sau f

sow² /sau/ vt (pt **sowed**, pp **sown** or **sowed**) säen

soya /'sɔɪə/ n ~ **bean** Sojabohne f

spa /spɑ:/ n Heilbad nt

space /speɪs/ n Raum m; (Astronomy) Weltraum m ●vt ~ [out] [in Abständen] verteilen

space: ~**craft** n Raumfahrzeug nt. ~**ship** n Raumschiff nt

spacious /'speɪʃəs/ adj geräumig

spade /speɪd/ n Spaten m; (for child) Schaufel f; ~**s** pl (Cards) Pik nt

Spain /speɪn/ n Spanien nt

span¹ /spæn/ n Spanne f; (of arch) Spannweite f ●vt (pt/pp **spanned**) überspannen; umspannen (time)

span² see **spick**

Spaniard /'spænjəd/ n Spanier(in) m(f). ~**ish** adj spanisch ●n (Lang) Spanisch nt; **the** ~**ish** pl die Spanier

spank /spæŋk/ vt verhauen

spanner /'spænə(r)/ n Schraubenschlüssel m

spare /speə(r)/ adj (surplus) übrig; (additional) zusätzlich; (seat, time) frei; (room) Gäste-; (bed, cup) Extra- ●n (part) Ersatzteil nt ●vt ersparen; (not hurt) verschonen; (do without) entbehren; (afford to give) erübrigen. ~ '**wheel** n Reserverad nt

sparing /'speərɪŋ/ adj sparsam

spark /spɑ:k/ n Funke nt. ~[**ing**]-**plug** n (Auto) Zündkerze f

sparkle /'spɑ:kl/ n Funkeln nt ●vi funkeln. ~**ing** adj funkelnd; (wine) Schaum-

sparrow /'spærəʊ/ n Spatz m

sparse /spɑ:s/ adj spärlich. ~**ly** adv spärlich; (populated) dünn

spasm /'spæzm/ n Anfall m;

(cramp) Krampf m. ~**odic** adj, ~**ally** adv sporadisch

spastic /'spæstɪk/ adj spastisch [gelähmt] ●n Spastiker(in) m(f)

spat /spæt/ see **spit²**

spatter /'spætə(r)/ vt spritzen; ~ **with** bespritzen mit

spawn /spɔ:n/ n Laich m ●vt (fig) hervorbringen

speak /spi:k/ v (pt **spoke**, pp **spoken**) ●vi sprechen (**to** mit) ●~**ing!** (Teleph) am Apparat! ~ **up** vi lauter sprechen; ~ **up for oneself** seine Meinung äußern

speaker /'spi:kə(r)/ n Sprecher(in) m(f); (in public) Redner(in) m(f); (loudspeaker) Lautsprecher m

spear /spɪə(r)/ n Speer m ●vt aufspießen

spec /spek/ n **on** ~ ⫶ auf gut Glück

special /'speʃl/ adj besondere(r,s), speziell. ~**ist** n Spezialist m; (Med) Facharzt m/-ärztin f. ~**ity** n Spezialität f

specialize /'speʃəlaɪz/ vi sich spezialisieren (**in** auf + acc). ~**ly** adv speziell; (particularly) besonders

species /'spi:ʃi:z/ n Art f

specific /spə'sɪfɪk/ adj bestimmt; (precise) genau; (Phys) spezifisch. ~**ally** adv ausdrücklich

specification /spesɪfɪ'keɪʃn/ n (also ~**s**) pl genaue Angaben pl

specify /'spesɪfaɪ/ vt (pt/pp -**ied**) [genau] angeben

specimen /'spesɪmən/ n Exemplar nt; (sample) Probe f; (of urine) Urinprobe f

speck /spek/ n Fleck m

speckled /'spekld/ adj gesprenkelt

spectacle /'spektəkl/ n (show) Schauspiel nt; (sight) Anblick m. ~**s** npl Brille f

spectacular /spek'tækjʊlə(r)/ *adj* spektakulär

spectator /spek'teɪtə(r)/ *n* Zuschauer(in) *m(f)*

speculat|e /'spekjʊleɪt/ *vi* spekulieren. **~ion** *n* Spekulation *f*. **~or** *n* Spekulant *m*

sped /sped/ *see* **speed**

speech /spiːtʃ/ *n* Sprache *f*; (*address*) Rede *f*. **~less** *adj* sprachlos

speed /spiːd/ *n* Geschwindigkeit *f*; (*rapidity*) Schnelligkeit *f* ● *vi* (*pt/pp sped*) schnell fahren ● *vi* (*pt/pp speeded*) (*go too fast*) zu schnell fahren. **~ up** (*pt/pp speeded up*) ● *vt/i* beschleunigen

speed: ~boat *n* Rennboot *nt*. **~ camera** *n* Geschwindigkeitsüberwachungskamera *f*. **~ dating** *n* Speeddating *nt*. **~ing** *n* Geschwindigkeitsüberschreitung *f*. **~ limit** *n* Geschwindigkeitsbeschränkung *f*

speedometer /spiː'dɒmɪtə(r)/ *n* Tachometer *m*

speedy /'spiːdɪ/ *adj* , **-ily** *adv* schnell

spell[1] /spel/ *n* Weile *f*; (*of weather*) Periode *f*

spell[2] *v* (*pt/pp spelled or spelt*) ● *vt* schreiben; (*aloud*) buchstabieren; (*fig: mean*) bedeuten ● *vi* richtig schreiben; (*aloud*) buchstabieren. **~ out** *vt* buchstabieren; (*fig*) genau erklären

spell[3] *n* Zauber *m*; (*words*) Zauberspruch *m*. **~bound** *adj* wie verzaubert

'spell checker *n* Rechtschreibprogramm *nt*

spelling /'spelɪŋ/ *n* (*of a word*) Schreibweise *f*; (*orthography*) Rechtschreibung *f*

spelt /spelt/ *see* **spell**

spend /spend/ *vt/i* (*pt/pp spent*) ausgeben; verbringen (*time*)

spent /spent/ *see* **spend**

sperm /spɜːm/ *n* Samen *m*

sphere /sfɪə(r)/ *n* Kugel *f*; (*fig*) Sphäre *f*

spice /spaɪs/ *n* Gewürz *nt*; (*fig*) Würze *f*

spicy /'spaɪsɪ/ *adj* würzig, pikant

spider /'spaɪdə(r)/ *n* Spinne *f*

spik|e /spaɪk/ *n* Spitze *f*; (*Bot, Zool*) Stachel *m*; (*on shoe*) Spike *m*. **~y** *adj* stachelig

spill /spɪl/ *v* (*pt/pp spilt or spilled*) ● *vt* verschütten ● *vi* überlaufen

spin /spɪn/ *v* (*pt/pp spinning*, *pres p spinning*) ● *vt* drehen; spinnen (*wool*); schleudern (*washing*) ● *vi* sich drehen

spinach /'spɪnɪdʒ/ *n* Spinat *m*

spindl|e /'spɪndl/ *n* Spindel *f*. **~y** *adj* spindeldürr

spin-'drier *n* Wäscheschleuder *f*

spine /spaɪn/ *n* Rückgrat *nt*; (*of book*) [Buch]Rücken *m*; (*Bot, Zool*) Stachel *m*. **~less** *adj* (*fig*) rückgratlos

'spin-off *n* Nebenprodukt *nt*

spinster /'spɪnstə(r)/ *n* ledige Frau *f*

spiral /'spaɪrl/ *adj* spiralig ● *n* Spirale *f* ● *vi* (*pt/pp spiralled*) sich hochwinden. **~ 'staircase** *n* Wendeltreppe *f*

spire /spaɪə(r)/ *n* Turmspitze *f*

spirit /'spɪrɪt/ *n* Geist *m*; (*courage*) Mut *m*; **~s** *pl* (*alcohol*) Spirituosen *pl*; **in low ~s** niedergedrückt. **~ away** *vt* verschwinden lassen

spirited /'spɪrɪtɪd/ *adj* lebhaft; (*courageous*) beherzt

spiritual /'spɪrɪtjʊəl/ *adj* geistig; (*Relig*) geistlich

spit[1] /spɪt/ *n* (*for roasting*) [Brat]spieß *m*

spit[2] *n* Spucke *f* ● *vt/i* (*pt/pp spat*,

pres p **spitting**) spucken; (*cat:*) fauchen; (*fat:*) spritzen; **it's ~ting with rain** es tröpfelt

spite /spaɪt/ *n* Boshaftigkeit *f*; **in ~ of** trotz (+ *gen*) ● *vt* ärgern. **~ful** *adj* gehässig

splash /splæʃ/ *n* Platschen *nt*; (⚫: *drop*) Schuss *m*; **~ of colour** Farbfleck *m* ● *vt* spritzen; **~ s.o. with sth** jdn mit etw bespritzen ● *vi* spritzen. **~ about** *vi* planschen

splendid /'splendɪd/ *adj* herrlich, großartig

splendour /'splendə(r)/ *n* Pracht *f*

splint /splɪnt/ *n* (*Med*) Schiene *f*

splinter /'splɪntə(r)/ *n* Splitter *m* ● *vi* zersplittern

split /splɪt/ *n* Spaltung *f*; (*tear*) Riss *m* ● *v* (*pt/pp* **split**, *pres p* **splitting**) ● *vt* spalten; (*share*) teilen; (*tear*) zerreißen ● *vi* sich spalten; (*tear*) zerreißen; **~ on s.o.** ⚫ jdn verpfeifen. **~ up** *vt* aufteilen ● *vi* (*couple:*) sich trennen

splutter /'splʌtə(r)/ *vi* prusten

spoil /spɔɪl/ *n* **~s** *pl* Beute *f* ● *v* (*pt/pp* **spoilt** *or* **spoiled**) ● *vt* verderben; verwöhnen (*person*) ● *vi* verderben. **~sport** *n* Spielverderber *m*

spoke[1] /spəʊk/ *n* Speiche *f*

spoke[2], **spoken** *see* **speak**

'spokesman *n* Sprecher *m*

sponge /spʌndʒ/ *n* Schwamm *m* ● *vt* abwaschen ● *vi* **~ on** schmarotzen bei. **~-bag** *n* Waschbeutel *m*. **~-cake** *n* Biskuitkuchen *m*

sponsor /'spɒnsə(r)/ *n* Sponsor *m*; (*godparent*) Pate *m*/Patin *f* ● *vt* sponsern

spontaneous /spɒn'teɪnɪəs/ *adj* spontan

spoof /spuːf/ *n* ⚫ Parodie *f*

spooky /'spuːkɪ/ *adj* ⚫ gespenstisch

spool /spuːl/ *n* Spule *f*

spoon /spuːn/ *n* Löffel *m* ● *vt* löffeln. **~ful** *n* Löffel *m*

sporadic /spə'rædɪk/ *adj*, **-ally** *adv* sporadisch

sport /spɔːt/ *n* Sport *m* ● *vt* [stolz] tragen. **~ing** *adj* sportlich

sports: **~car** *n* Sportwagen *m*. **~coat** *n*, **~jacket** *n* Sakko *m*. **~man** *n* Sportler *m*. **~woman** *n* Sportlerin *f*

sporty /'spɔːtɪ/ *adj* sportlich

spot /spɒt/ *n* Fleck *m*; (*place*) Stelle *f* (*dot*) Punkt *m*; (*drop*) Tropfen *m*; (*pimple*) Pickel *m*; **~s** *pl* (*rash*) Ausschlag *m*; **on the ~** auf der Stelle ● *vt* (*pt/pp* **spotted**) entdecken

spot: **~'check** *n* Stichprobe *f*. **~less** *adj* makellos; (⚫: *very clean*) blitzsauber. **~light** *n* Scheinwerfer *m*; (*fig*) Rampenlicht *nt*

spotted /'spɒtɪd/ *adj* gepunktet

spouse /spaʊz/ *n* Gatte *m*/Gattin *f*

spout /spaʊt/ *n* Schnabel *m*, Tülle *f* ● *vi* schießen (**from** aus)

sprain /spreɪn/ *n* Verstauchung *f* ● *vt* verstauchen

sprang /spræŋ/ *see* **spring**[2]

sprawl /sprɔːl/ *vi* sich ausstrecken

spray[1] /spreɪ/ *n* (*of flowers*) Strauß *m*

spray[2] /spreɪ/ *n* Sprühnebel *m*; (*from sea*) Gischt *m*; (*device*) Spritze *f*; (*container*) Sprühdose *f*; (*preparation*) Spray *m* ● *vt* spritzen; (**with aerosol**) sprühen

spread /spred/ *n* Verbreitung *f*; (*paste*) Aufstrich *m*; (⚫: *feast*) Festessen *nt* ● *v* (*pt/pp* **spread**) ● *vt* ausbreiten; streichen (*butter, jam*); bestreichen (*bread, surface*); streuen (*sand, manure*); verbreiten (*news, disease*); verteilen (*payments*) ● *vi* sich ausbreiten. **~ out** *vt* ausbreiten; (*space out*) verteilen ● *vi* sich verteilen

spree /spriː/ n 🔟 **go on a shopping** ~ groß einkaufen gehen

sprightly /ˈspraɪtlɪ/ adj rüstig

spring[1] /sprɪŋ/ n Frühling m ● attrib Frühlings-

spring[2] n (jump) Sprung m; (water) Quelle f; (device) Feder f; (elasticity) Elastizität f ● v (pt sprang, pp sprung) ● vi springen; (arise) entspringen (from dat) ● vt ~ sth on s.o. jdn mit etw überfallen

spring: ~-ˈcleaning n Frühjahrsputz m. ~time n Frühling m

sprinkle /ˈsprɪŋkl/ vt sprengen; (scatter) streuen; bestreuen (surface). ~ing n dünne Schicht f

sprint /sprɪnt/ n Sprint m ● vi rennen; (Sport) sprinten. ~er n Kurzstreckenläufer(in) m(f)

sprout /spraʊt/ n Trieb m; [Brussels] ~s pl Rosenkohl m ● vi sprießen

sprung /sprʌŋ/ see spring[2]

spud /spʌd/ n 🔟 Kartoffel f

spun /spʌn/ see spin

spur /spɜː(r)/ n Sporn m; (stimulus) Ansporn m; **on the ~ of the moment** ganz spontan ● vt (pt/pp spurred) ~ [on] (fig) anspornen

spurn /spɜːn/ vt verschmähen

spurt /spɜːt/ n (Sport) Spurt m; **put on a** ~ spurten ● vi spritzen

spy /spaɪ/ n Spion(in) m(f) ● vi spionieren; ~ **on s.o.** jdm nachspionieren. ● vt (🔟: see) sehen

spying /ˈspaɪɪŋ/ n Spionage f

squabble /ˈskwɒbl/ n Zank m ● vi sich zanken

squad /skwɒd/ n Gruppe f; (Sport) Mannschaft f

squadron /ˈskwɒdrən/ n (Mil) Geschwader nt

squalid /ˈskwɒlɪd/ adj schmutzig

squall /skwɔːl/ n Bö f ● vi brüllen

squalor /ˈskwɒlə(r)/ n Schmutz m

squander /ˈskwɒndə(r)/ vt vergeuden

square /skweə(r)/ adj quadratisch; (metre, mile) Quadrat-; (meal) anständig; **all** ~ 🔟 quitt ● n Quadrat nt; (area) Platz m; (on chessboard) Feld n ● vt (settle) klären; (Math) quadrieren

squash /skwɒʃ/ n Gedränge nt; (drink) Fruchtsaftgetränk nt; (Sport) Squash nt ● vt zerquetschen; (suppress) niederschlagen. ~y adj weich

squat /skwɒt/ adj gedrungen ● vi (pt/pp squatted) hocken; ~ **in a house** ein Haus besetzen. ~ter n Hausbesetzer m

squawk /skwɔːk/ vi krächzen

squeak /skwiːk/ n Quieken nt; (of hinge, brakes) Quietschen nt ● vi quieken; quietschen

squeal /skwiːl/ n Kreischen nt ● vi kreischen

squeamish /ˈskwiːmɪʃ/ adj empfindlich

squeeze /skwiːz/ n Druck m; (crush) Gedränge nt ● vt drücken; (to extract juice) ausdrücken; (force) zwängen

squiggle /ˈskwɪgl/ n Schnörkel m

squint /skwɪnt/ n Schielen nt ● vi schielen

squirm /skwɜːm/ vi sich winden

squirrel /ˈskwɪrl/ n Eichhörnchen nt

squirt /skwɜːt/ n Spritzer m ● vt/i spritzen

St abbr (Saint) St.; (Street) Str.

stab /stæb/ n Stich m; (🔟: attempt) Versuch m ● vt (pt/pp stabbed) stechen; (to death) erstechen

stability /stəˈbɪlətɪ/ n Stabilität f

stable¹ /'steɪbl/ adj (-r, -st) stabil

stable² n Stall m; (establishment) Reitstall m

stack /stæk/ n Stapel m; (of chimney) Schornstein m ● vt stapeln

stadium /'steɪdɪəm/ n Stadion nt

staff /stɑːf/ n (stick & Mil) Stab m ●(& pl) (employees) Personal nt; (Sch) Lehrkräfte pl ● vt mit Personal besetzen. **~room** n (Sch) Lehrerzimmer nt

stag /stæg/ n Hirsch m

stage /steɪdʒ/ n Bühne f; (in journey) Etappe f; (in process) Stadium nt; **by** or **in ~s** in Etappen ● vt aufführen; (arrange) veranstalten

stagger /'stægə(r)/ vi taumeln ● vt staffeln (holidays); versetzt anordnen (seats); **I was ~ed** es hat mir die Sprache verschlagen. **~ing** adj unglaublich

stagnant /'stægnənt/ adj stehend; (fig) stagnierend

stagnate /stæg'neɪt/ vi (fig) stagnieren

stain /steɪn/ n Fleck m; (for wood) Beize f ● vt färben; beizen (wood); **~ed glass** farbiges Glas nt. **~less** adj (steel) rostfrei

stair /steə(r)/ n Stufe f; **~s** pl Treppe f. **~case** n Treppe f

stake /steɪk/ n Pfahl m; (wager) Einsatz m; (Comm) Anteil m; **be at ~** auf dem Spiel stehen ● vt **~ a claim to sth** Anspruch auf etw (acc) erheben

stale /steɪl/ adj (-r, -st) alt; (air) verbraucht. **~mate** n Patt nt

stalk¹ /stɔːk/ n Stiel m, Stängel m

stall /stɔːl/ n Stand m; **~s** pl (Theat) Parkett nt ● vi (engine) stehen bleiben; (fig) ausweichen ● vt abwürgen (engine)

stalwart /'stɔːlwət/ adj treu ● n treuer Anhänger m

stamina /'stæmɪnə/ n Ausdauer f

stammer /'stæmə(r)/ n Stottern nt ● vt/i stottern

stamp /stæmp/ n Stempel m; (postage ~) [Brief]marke f ● vt stempeln; (impress) prägen; (put postage on) frankieren ● vi stampfen. **~ out** vt [aus]stanzen; (fig) ausmerzen

stampede /stæm'piːd/ n wilde Flucht f ● vi in Panik fliehen

stance /stɑːns/ n Haltung f

stand /stænd/ n Stand m; (rack) Ständer m; (pedestal) Sockel m; (Sport) Tribüne f; (fig) Einstellung f ● v (pt/pp **stood**) ● vi stehen; (rise) aufstehen; (be candidate) kandidieren; (stay valid) gültig bleiben; **~ still** stillstehen; **~ firm** (fig) festbleiben; **~ to reason** logisch sein; **~ in for** vertreten; **~ for** (mean) bedeuten ● vt stellen; (withstand) standhalten (+ dat); (endure) ertragen; vertragen (climate); (put up with) aushalten; haben (chance); **~ s.o. a beer** jdm ein Bier spendieren; **I can't ~ her** 🔲 ich kann sie nicht ausstehen. **~ by** vi daneben stehen; (be ready) sich bereithalten ● vt **~ by s.o.** (fig) zu jdm stehen. **~ down** vi (retire) zurücktreten. **~ out** vi hervorstehen; (fig) herausragen. **~ up** vi aufstehen; **~ up for** eintreten für; **~ up to** sich wehren gegen

standard /'stændəd/ adj Normal- ● n Maßstab m; (Techn) Norm f; (level) Niveau nt; (flag) Standarte f; **~s** pl (morals) Prinzipien pl. **~ize** vt standardisieren; (Techn) normen

'stand-in n Ersatz m

standing /'stændɪŋ/ adj (erect) stehend; (permanent) ständig ● n Rang m; (duration) Dauer f. **~room** n Stehplätze pl

stand: **~-offish** /stænd'ɒfɪʃ/ adj

s

distanziert. **~point** n Standpunkt m. **~still** n Stillstand m; **come to a ~still** zum Stillstand kommen

stank /stæŋk/ see **stink**

staple¹ /'steɪpl/ adj Grund-

staple² n Heftklammer f • vt heften. **~r** n Heftmaschine f

star /stɑː(r)/ n Stern m; (asterisk) Sternchen nt; (Theat, Sport) Star m • vi (pt/pp starred) die Hauptrolle spielen

starboard /'stɑːbəd/ n Steuerbord nt

starch /stɑːtʃ/ n Stärke f • vt stärken. **~y** adj stärkehaltig; (fig) steif

stare /steə(r)/ n Starren nt • vt starren; **~ at** anstarren

stark /stɑːk/ adj (-er, -est) scharf; (contrast) krass

starling /'stɑːlɪŋ/ n Star m

start /stɑːt/ n Anfang m, Beginn m; (departure) Aufbruch m; (Sport) Start m; **from the ~** von Anfang an; **for a ~** erstens • vi anfangen, beginnen; (set out) aufbrechen; (engine:) anspringen; (Auto, Sport) starten; (jump) aufschrecken; **to ~ with** zuerst • vt anfangen, beginnen; (cause) verursachen; (found) gründen; starten (car, race); in Umlauf setzen (rumour). **~er** n (Culin) Vorspeise f; (Auto, Sport) Starter m. **~ing-point** n Ausgangspunkt m

startle /'stɑːtl/ vt erschrecken

starvation /stɑː'veɪʃn/ n Verhungern nt

starve /stɑːv/ vi hungern; (to death) verhungern • vt verhungern lassen

state /steɪt/ n Zustand m; (Pol) Staat m; **~ of play** Spielstand m; **be in a ~** (person:) aufgeregt sein • attrib Staats-, staatlich • vt erklären; (specify) angeben

stately /'steɪtlɪ/ adj stattlich. **~**

'home n Schloss nt

statement /'steɪtmənt/ n Erklärung f; (Jur) Aussage f; (Banking) Auszug m

> **state school** Eine direkt oder indirekt vom Staat finanzierte Schule in Großbritannien, die keine Schulgebühren verlangt. Der Besuch aller staatlichen Grundschulen und weiterführenden Schulen ist kostenlos. Die meisten Kinder in Großbritannien besuchen solche öffentlichen Schulen. **ⓘ**

'statesman n Staatsmann m

static /'stætɪk/ adj statisch; **remain ~** unverändert bleiben

station /'steɪʃn/ n Bahnhof m; (police) Wache f; (radio) Sender m; (space, weather) Station f; (Mil) Posten m; (status) Rang m • vt stationieren; (post) postieren. **~ary** adj stehend; **be ~ary** stehen

stationery /'steɪʃənrɪ/ n Briefpapier nt; (writing materials) Schreibwaren pl

'station-wagon n (Amer) Kombi[wagen] m

statistic /stə'tɪstɪk/ n statistische Tatsache f. **~al** adj statistisch. **~s** n & pl Statistik f

statue /'stætjuː/ n Statue f

stature /'stætʃə(r)/ n Statur f; (fig) Format nt

status /'steɪtəs/ n Status m, Rang m

statut|e /'stætjuːt/ n Statut nt. **~ory** adj gesetzlich

staunch /stɔːntʃ/ adj (-er, -est) treu

stave /steɪv/ vt **~ off** abwenden

stay /steɪ/ n Aufenthalt m • vi bleiben; (reside) wohnen; **~ the night**

übernachten. ~ **behind** vi zurückbleiben. ~ **in** vi zu Hause bleiben; (Sch) nachsitzen. ~ **up** vi (person:) aufbleiben

steadily /'stedɪlɪ/ adv fest; (continually) stetig

steady /'stedɪ/ adj fest; (not wobbly) stabil; (hand) ruhig; (regular) regelmäßig; (dependable) zuverlässig

steak /steɪk/ n Steak nt

steal /stiːl/ vt/i (pt **stole**, pp **stolen**) stehlen (from dat). ~ **in/out** vi sich hinein-/hinausstehlen

stealthy /stelθɪ/ adj heimlich

steam /stiːm/ n Dampf m ● vt (Culin) dämpfen, dünsten ● vi dampfen. ~ **up** vi beschlagen

'steam engine n Dampfmaschine f; (Rail) Dampflokomotive f

steamer /'stiːmə(r)/ n Dampfer m

steamy /'stiːmɪ/ adj dampfig

steel /stiːl/ n Stahl m

steep /stiːp/ adj steil; (☐: exorbitant) gesalzen

steeple /stiːpl/ n Kirchturm m

steer /stɪə(r)/ vt/i (Auto) lenken; (Naut) steuern; ~ **clear of s.o./sth.** jdm/ etw aus dem Weg gehen. ~**ing** n (Auto) Lenkung f. ~**ing-wheel** n Lenkrad nt

stem[1] /stem/ n Stiel m; (of word) Stamm m

stem[2] vt (pt/pp **stemmed**) eindämmen, stillen (bleeding)

stench /stentʃ/ n Gestank m

stencil /stensl/ n Schablone f

step /step/ n Schritt m; (stair) Stufe f; ~**s** pl (ladder) Trittleiter f. **in** ~ im Schritt; ~ **by** ~ Schritt für Schritt; **take** ~**s** (fig) Schritte unternehmen ● vi (pt/pp **stepped**) treten. ~ **in** (fig) eingreifen. ~ **up** vt (increase) erhöhen, steigen; verstärken (efforts)

~**brother** n Stiefbruder m. ~**child** n Stiefkind nt. ~**daughter** n Stieftochter f. ~**father** n Stiefvater m. ~**ladder** n Trittleiter f. ~**mother** n Stiefmutter f. ~**sister** n Stiefschwester f. ~**son** n Stiefsohn m

stereo /'sterɪəʊ/ n Stereo nt; (equipment) Stereoanlage f. ~**phonic** adj stereophon

stereotype /'sterɪətaɪp/ n Stereotype Figur f

steril|e /'sterarl/ adj steril. ~**ize** vt sterilisieren

sterling /'stɜːlɪŋ/ adj Sterling-; (fig) gediegen ● n Sterling m

stern[1] /stɜːn/ adj (-er, -est) streng

stern[2] n (of boat) Heck nt

stew /stjuː/ n Eintopf m; **in a** ~ ☐ aufgeregt ● vt/i schmoren; ~**ed fruit** Kompott nt

steward /'stjuːəd/ n Ordner m; (on ship, aircraft) Steward m. ~**ess** n Stewardess f

stick[1] /stɪk/ n Stock m; (of chalk) Stück nt; (of rhubarb) Stange f; (Sport) Schläger m

stick[2] v (pt/pp **stuck**) ● vt stecken; (stab) stechen; (glue) kleben; (☐: put) tun; (☐: endure) aushalten ● vi stecken; (adhere) kleben, haften (to an + dat); (jam) klemmen; ~ **at it** ☐ dranbleiben; ~ **up for** ☐ eintreten für; **be stuck** nicht weiterkönnen; (vehicle:) festsitzen, festgefahren sein; (drawer:) klemmen; **be stuck with sth** ☐ etw am Hals haben. ~ **out** vi abstehen; (project) vorstehen ● vt hinausstrecken; heraustrecken (tongue)

sticker /'stɪkə(r)/ n Aufkleber m

'sticking plaster n Heftpflaster nt

sticky /'stɪkɪ/ adj klebrig; (adhesive) Klebe-

stiff /stɪf/ adj (-er, -est) steif; (brush) hart; (dough) fest; (difficult) schwierig; (penalty) schwer; **be bored ~** ☐ sich zu Tode langweilen. **~en** vt steif machen ● vi steif werden. **~ness** n Steifheit f

stifl|e /'staɪfl/ vt ersticken; (fig) unterdrücken. **~ing** adj **be ~ing** zum Ersticken sein

still /stɪl/ adj still; (drink) ohne Kohlensäure; **keep ~** stillhalten; **stand ~** stillstehen ● adv noch; (emphatic) immer noch; (nevertheless) trotzdem; **~ not** immer noch nicht

'stillborn adj tot geboren

still 'life n Stillleben nt

stilted /'stɪltɪd/ adj gestelzt, geschraubt

stimulant /'stɪmjʊlənt/ n Anregungsmittel nt

stimulat|e /'stɪmjʊleɪt/ vt anregen. **~ion** n Anregung f

stimulus /'stɪmjʊləs/ n (pl -li /-laɪ/) Reiz m

sting /stɪŋ/ n Stich m; (from nettle, jellyfish) Brennen nt; (organ) Stachel m ● v (pt/pp stung) ● vt stechen ● vi brennen; (insect:) stechen

stingy /'stɪndʒɪ/ adj geizig, ☐ knauserig

stink /stɪŋk/ n Gestank m ● vi (pt stank, pp stunk) stinken (of nach)

stipulat|e /'stɪpjʊleɪt/ vt vorschreiben. **~ion** n Bedingung f

stir /stɜː(r)/ n (commotion) Aufregung f ● v (pt/pp stirred) vt rühren ● vi sich rühren

stirrup /'stɪrəp/ n Steigbügel m

stitch /stɪtʃ/ n Stich m; (Knitting) Masche f; (pain) Seitenstechen nt; **be in ~es** ☐ sich kaputtlachen ● vt nähen

stock /stɒk/ n Vorrat m (of an + dat); (in shop) [Waren]bestand m; (livestock) Vieh nt; (lineage) Abstam-

mung f; (Finance) Wertpapiere pl; (Culin) Brühe f; (plant) Levkoje f; **in/out of ~** vorrätig/nicht vorrätig; **take ~** (fig) Bilanz ziehen ● adj Standard- ● vt (shop:) führen; auffüllen (shelves). **~ up** vi sich eindecken (with mit)

stock: ~broker n Börsenmakler m. **S~ Exchange** n Börse f

stocking /'stɒkɪŋ/ n Strumpf m

stock: ~market n Börse f. **~-taking** n (Comm) Inventur f

stocky /'stɒkɪ/ adj untersetzt

stodgy /'stɒdʒɪ/ adj pappig [und schwer verdaulich]

stoke /stəʊk/ vt heizen

stole /stəʊl/, **stolen** see steal

stomach /'stʌmək/ n Magen m. **~-ache** n Magenschmerzen pl

stone /stəʊn/ n Stein m; (weight) 6,35kg ● adj steinern; (wall, Age) Stein- ● vt mit Steinen bewerfen; entsteinen (fruit). **~-cold** adj eiskalt. **~-'deaf** adj ☐ stocktaub

stony /'stəʊnɪ/ adj steinig

stood /stʊd/ see stand

stool /stuːl/ n Hocker m

stoop /stuːp/ n **walk with a ~** gebeugt gehen ● vi sich bücken

stop /stɒp/ n Halt m; (break) Pause f; (for bus) Haltestelle f; (for train) Station f; (Gram) Punkt m; (on organ) Register nt; **come to a ~** stehen bleiben; **put a ~ to sth** etw unterbinden ● v (pt/pp stopped) ● vt anhalten, stoppen; (switch off) abstellen; (plug, block) zustopfen; (prevent) verhindern; **~ s.o. doing sth** jdn daran hindern, etw zu tun; **~ doing sth** aufhören, etw zu tun; **~ that!** hör auf damit! ● vi anhalten; (cease) aufhören; (clock:) stehen bleiben ● int halt!

stop: ~gap n Notlösung f. **~over** n (Aviat) Zwischenlandung f

stoppage | street

stoppage /'stɒpɪdʒ/ n Unterbrechung f; (strike) Streik m

stopper /'stɒpə(r)/ n Stöpsel m

stop-watch n Stoppuhr f

storage /'stɔːrɪdʒ/ n Aufbewahrung f; (in warehouse) Lagerung f; (Computing) Speicherung f

store /stɔː(r)/ n (stock) Vorrat m; (shop) Laden m; (department ~) Kaufhaus nt; (depot) Lager nt; **in ~** auf Lager; **be in ~ for s.o.** (fig) jdm bevorstehen ● vt aufbewahren; (in warehouse) lagern; (Computing) speichern. **~-room** n Lagerraum m

storey /'stɔːrɪ/ n Stockwerk nt

stork /stɔːk/ n Storch m

storm /stɔːm/ n Sturm m; (with thunder) Gewitter nt ● vt/i stürmen. **~y** adj stürmisch

story /'stɔːrɪ/ n Geschichte f; (in newspaper) Artikel m; (🔲: lie) Märchen nt

stout /staʊt/ adj (-er, -est) beleibt; (strong) fest

stove /stəʊv/ n Ofen m; (for cooking) Herd m

stow /stəʊ/ vt verstauen. **~away** n blinder Passagier m

straggl|e /'stræɡl/ vi hinterherhinken. **~er** n Nachzügler m. **~y** adj strähnig

straight /streɪt/ adj (-er, -est) gerade; (direct) direkt; (clear) klar; (hair) glatt; (drink); pur; **be ~** (tidy) in Ordnung sein ● adv gerade; (directly) direkt, geradewegs; (clearly) klar; **~ away** sofort; **~ on** or **ahead** geradeaus; **~ out** (fig) geradeheraus; **sit/stand up ~** gerade sitzen/stehen

straighten /'streɪtn/ vt gerade machen; (put straight) gerade richten ● vi gerade werden; **~ [up]** (person:) sich aufrichten. **~ up** gerade biegen

straight'forward adj offen; (simple) einfach

strain /streɪn/ n Belastung f; **~s** pl (of music) Klänge pl ● vt belasten; (overexert) überanstrengen; (injure) zerren (muscle); (Culin) durchseihen; abgießen (vegetables). **~ed** adj (relations) gespannt. **~er** n Sieb nt

strait /streɪt/ n Meerenge f; **in dire ~s** in großen Nöten

strand¹ /strænd/ n (of thread) Faden m; (of hair) Strähne f

strand² vt **be ~ed** festsitzen

strange /streɪndʒ/ adj (-r, -st) fremd; (odd) seltsam, merkwürdig. **~ly** adv seltsam, merkwürdig; **~ enough** seltsamerweise. **~r** n Fremde(r) m/f

strangle /'stræŋɡl/ vt erwürgen; (fig) unterdrücken

strap /stræp/ n Riemen m; (for safety) Gurt m; (to grasp in vehicle) Halteriemen m; (of watch) Armband nt; (shoulder~) Träger m ● vt (pt/pp strapped) schnallen

strapping /'stræpɪŋ/ adj stramm

strategic /strə'tiːdʒɪk/ adj, **-ally** adv strategisch

strategy /'strætədʒɪ/ n Strategie f

straw /strɔː/ n Stroh nt; (single piece, drinking) Strohhalm m; **that's the last ~** jetzt reicht's aber

strawberry /'strɔːbərɪ/ n Erdbeere f

stray /streɪ/ adj streunend ● n streunendes Tier nt ● vi sich verirren; (deviate) abweichen

streak /striːk/ n Streifen m; (in hair) Strähne f; (fig: trait) Zug m

stream /striːm/ n Bach m; (flow) Strom m; (current) Strömung f; (Sch) Parallelzug m ● vi strömen

'streamline vt (fig) rationalisieren. **~d** adj stromlinienförmig

street /striːt/ n Straße f. **~car** n

(*Amer*) Straßenbahn f. ~**lamp** n Straßenlaterne f

strength /streŋθ/ n Stärke f; (*power*) Kraft f; **on the** ~ **of** auf Grund (+ gen). ~**en** vt stärken; (*reinforce*) verstärken

strenuous /'strenjʊəs/ adj anstrengend

stress /stres/ n (*emphasis*) Betonung f; (*strain*) Belastung f; (*mental*) Stress m ● vt betonen; (*put a strain on*) belasten. ~**ful** adj stressig ⚞T⚟

stretch /stretʃ/ n (*of road*) Strecke f; (*elasticity*) Elastizität f; **at a** ~ ohne Unterbrechung; **have a** ~ sich strecken ● vt strecken; (*widen*) dehnen; (*spread*) ausbreiten; fordern (*person*); ~ **one's legs** sich (*dat*) die Beine vertreten ● vt sich erstrecken; (*become wider*) sich dehnen; (*person:*) sich strecken. ~**er** n Tragbahre f

strict /strɪkt/ adj (**-er, -est**) streng; ~**ly speaking** streng genommen

stride /straɪd/ n [großer] Schritt m; **take sth in one's** ~ mit etw gut fertig werden ● vi (*pt* **strode,** *pp* **stridden**) [mit großen Schritten] gehen

strident /'straɪdnt/ adj schrill; (*colour*) grell

strife /straɪf/ n Streit m

strike /straɪk/ n Streik m; (*Mil*) Angriff m; **be on** ~ streiken ● v (*pt/pp* **struck**) ● vt schlagen; (*knock against, collide with*) treffen; anzünden (*match*); stoßen auf (+ *acc*) (*oil, gold*); abbrechen (*camp*); (*impress*) beeindrucken; (*occur to*) einfallen (+ *dat*); ~ **a blow** jdm einen Schlag versetzen ● vi treffen; (*lightning:*) einschlagen; (*clock:*) schlagen; (*attack*) zuschlagen; (*workers:*) streiken

striker /'straɪkə(r)/ n Streikende(r) m/f

striking /'straɪkɪŋ/ adj auffallend

string /strɪŋ/ n Schnur f; (*thin*) Bindfaden m; (*of musical instrument, racket*) Saite f; (*of bow*) Sehne f; (*of pearls*) Kette f; **the** ~**s** (*Mus*) die Streicher pl; **pull** ~**s** ⚞I⚟ seine Beziehungen spielen lassen ● vt (*pt/pp* **strung**) (*thread*) aufziehen (*beads*)

stringent /'strɪndʒnt/ adj streng

strip /strɪp/ n Streifen m ● v (*pt/pp* **stripped**) ● vt ablösen; ausziehen (*person, clothes*); abziehen (*bed*); abbeizen (*wood, furniture*); auseinander nehmen (*machine*); (*deprive*) berauben (*of gen*); ~ **sth off sth** etw von etw entfernen ● vi (*undress*) sich ausziehen

stripe /straɪp/ n Streifen m. ~**d** adj gestreift

stripper /'strɪpə(r)/ n Stripperin f; (*male*) Stripper m

strive /straɪv/ vi (*pt* **strove,** *pp* **striven**) sich bemühen (**to** zu); ~ **for** streben nach

strode /strəʊd/ *see* **stride**

stroke[1] /strəʊk/ n Schlag m; (*of pen*) Strich m; (*Swimming*) Zug m; (*style*) Stil m; (*Med*) Schlaganfall m; ~ **of luck** Glücksfall m

stroke[2] vt streicheln

stroll /strəʊl/ n Bummel m ⚞I⚟ ● vi bummeln ⚞I⚟. ~**er** n (*Amer: pushchair*) [Kinder]sportwagen m

strong /strɒŋ/ adj (**-er** /-gə(r)/, **-est** /- gɪst/) stark; (*powerful, healthy*) kräftig; (*severe*) streng; (*sturdy*) stabil; (*convincing*) gut

strong: ~**hold** n Festung f; (*fig*) Hochburg f. ~**room** n Tresorraum m

strove /strəʊv/ *see* **strive**

struck /strʌk/ *see* **strike**

structural /'strʌktʃərl/ adj baulich

structure /'strʌktʃə(r)/ n Struktur

f; (building) Bau m

struggle /'strʌgl/ n Kampf m; with a ~ mit Mühe • vi kämpfen; ~ to do sth sich abmühen, etw zutun

strum /strʌm/ v (pt/pp strummed) • vt klimpern auf (+ dat) • vi klimpern

strung /strʌŋ/ see **string**

strut¹ /strʌt/ n Strebe f

strut² vi (pt/pp strutted) stolzieren

stub /stʌb/ n Stummel m; (counterfoil) Abschnitt m. ~ **out** vt (pt/pp stubbed) ausdrücken (cigarette)

stubble /'stʌbl/ n Stoppeln pl

stubborn /'stʌbən/ adj starrsinnig; (refusal) hartnäckig

stubby /'stʌbɪ/ adj, (-ier, -iest) kurz und dick

stuck /stʌk/ see **stick²**. ~-**'up** adj 🄸 hochnäsig

stud /stʌd/ n Nagel m; (on clothes) Niete f; (for collar) Kragenknopf m; (for ear) Ohrstecker m

student /'stju:dnt/ n Student(in) m(f); (Sch) Schüler(in) m(f)

studio /'stju:dɪəʊ/ n Studio nt; (for artist) Atelier nt

studious /'stju:dɪəs/ adj lerneifrig; (earnest) ernsthaft

study /'stʌdɪ/ n Studie f; (room) Arbeitszimmer nt; (investigation) Untersuchung f; ~**ies** pl Studium nt • v (pt/pp studied) • vt studieren; (examine) untersuchen • vi lernen; (at university) studieren

stuff /stʌf/ n Stoff m; (🄸: things) Zeug nt • vt vollstopfen; (with padding, Culin) füllen; ausstopfen (animal); (cram) [hinein]stopfen. ~**ing** n Füllung f

stuffy /'stʌfɪ/ adj stickig; (old-fashioned) spießig

stumble /'stʌmbl/ vi stolpern; ~**e across** zufällig stoßen auf (+ acc).

~**ing-block** n Hindernis nt

stump /stʌmp/ n Stumpf m • ~ **up** vt/i 🄸 blechen. ~**ed** adj 🄸 überfragt

stun /stʌn/ vt (pt/pp stunned) betäuben

stung /stʌŋ/ see **sting**

stunk /stʌŋk/ see **stink**

stunning /'stʌnɪŋ/ adj 🄸 toll

stunt /stʌnt/ n 🄸 Kunststück nt

stupendous /stju:'pendəs/ adj enorm

stupid /'stju:pɪd/ adj dumm. ~**ity** n Dummheit f. ~**ly** adv dumm; ~**ly [enough]** dummerweise

sturdy /'stɜ:dɪ/ adj stämmig; (furniture) stabil; (shoes) fest

stutter /'stʌtə(r)/ n Stottern nt • vi stottern

sty /staɪ/ n (pl **sties**) Schweinestall m

style /staɪl/ n Stil m; (fashion) Mode f; (sort) Art f; (hair~) Frisur f; **in** ~ in großem Stil

stylish /'staɪlɪʃ/ adj, -**ly** adv stilvoll

stylist /'staɪlɪst/ n Friseur m/ Friseuse f. ~**ic** adj, -**ally** adv stilistisch

suave /swɑ:v/ adj (pej) gewandt

sub'conscious /sʌb-/ adj unterbewusst • n Unterbewusstsein nt

'subdivi|de vt unterteilen. ~**sion** n Unterteilung f

subdue /səb'dju:/ vt unterwerfen. ~**d** adj gedämpft; (person) still

subject¹ /'sʌbdʒɪkt/ adj **be** ~ **to** sth etw (dat) unterworfen sein • n Staatsbürger(in) m(f); (of ruler) Untertan m; (theme) Thema nt; (of investigation) Gegenstand m; (Sch) Fach nt; (Gram) Subjekt nt

subject² /səb'dʒekt/ vt unterwerfen (to dat); (expose) aussetzen (to dat)

subjective /səb'dʒektɪv/ adj

s

subjektiv

subjunctive /səbˈdʒʌŋktɪv/ n
Konjunktiv m

sublime /səˈblaɪm/ adj erhaben

sub'marine n Unterseeboot nt

submerge /səbˈmɜːdʒ/ vt untertauchen; **be ~d** unter Wasser stehen ● vi tauchen

submission /səbˈmɪʃn/ n Unterwerfung f

submit /səbˈmɪt/ v (pt/pp -mitted,
pres p -mitting) ● vt vorlegen (to
dat); (hand in) einreichen ● vi sich
unterwerfen (to dat)

subordinate[1] /səˈbɔːdɪnət/ adj
untergeordnet ● n Untergebene(r) m/f

subordinate[2] /səˈbɔːdɪneɪt/ vt
unterordnen (to dat)

subscribe /səbˈskraɪb/ vi spenden;
~ to (fig): abonnieren (newspaper).
~r n Spender m; Abonnent m

subscription /səbˈskrɪpʃn/ n (to
club) [Mitglieds]beitrag m; (to newspaper) Abonnement nt; **by ~** mit
Spenden; **(buy)** im Abonnement

subsequent /ˈsʌbsɪkwənt/ adj
folgend; (later) später

subside /səbˈsaɪd/ vi sinken;
(ground:) sich senken; (storm:) nachlassen

subsidiary /səbˈsɪdɪərɪ/ adj untergeordnet ● n Tochtergesellschaft f

subsid|ize /ˈsʌbsɪdaɪz/ vt subventionieren. **~y** n Subvention f

substance /ˈsʌbstəns/ n Substanz f

sub'standard adj unzulänglich;
(goods) minderwertig

substantial /səbˈstænʃl/ adj solide; (meal) reichhaltig; (considerable) beträchtlich. **~ly** adv solide;
(essentially) im Wesentlichen

substitut|e /ˈsʌbstɪtjuːt/ n Ersatz
m; (Sport) Ersatzspieler(in) m(f) ● vt

~e A for B B durch A ersetzen ● vi
~e for s.o. jdn vertreten. **~ion** n
Ersetzung f

subterranean /sʌbtəˈreɪnɪən/ adj
unterirdisch

'subtitle n Untertitel m

subtle /ˈsʌtl/ adj (-r, -st), **-tly** adv
fein; (fig) subtil

subtract /səbˈtrækt/ vt abziehen,
subtrahieren. **~ion** n Subtraktion f

suburb /ˈsʌbɜːb/ n Vorort m. **~an**
adj Vorort-. **~ia** n die Vororte pl

'subway n Unterführung f; (Amer:
railway) U-Bahn f

succeed /səkˈsiːd/ vi Erfolg haben;
(plan:) gelingen; (follow) nachfolgen
(+ dat); **I ~ed** es ist mir gelungen;
he ~ed in escaping es gelang ihm
zu entkommen ● vt folgen (+ dat)

success /səkˈses/ n Erfolg m. **~ful**
adj,**-ly** adv erfolgreich

succession /səkˈseʃn/ n Folge f;
(series) Serie f; (to title, office) Nachfolge f; (to throne) Thronfolge f; **in
~** hintereinander

successive /səkˈsesɪv/ adj aufeinander folgend

successor /səkˈsesə(r)/ n Nachfolger(in) m(f)

succumb /səˈkʌm/ vi erliegen
(to dat)

<hr>

such /sʌtʃ/

● adjective

••••▸ (of that kind) solch. **such a
book** ein solches Buch; so ein
Buch ⑪. **such a person** ein solcher Mensch; so ein Mensch ⑪.
such people solche Leute. **such
a thing** so etwas. **no such example** kein solches Beispiel.
there is no such thing so etwas
gibt es nicht; das gibt es gar
nicht. **there is no such person**

eine solche Person gibt es nicht. **such writers as Goethe and Schiller** Schriftsteller wie Goethe und Schiller

····▸ (*so great*) solch; derartig. **I've got such a headache!** ich habe solche Kopfschmerzen! **it was such fun!** das machte solchen Spaß! **I got such a fright that ...** ich bekam einen derartigen *od* 🗓 so einen Schrecken, dass ...

····▸ (*with adjective*) so. **such a big house** ein so großes Haus. **he has such lovely blue eyes** er hat so schöne blaue Augen. **such a long time** so lange

● *pronoun*

····▸ **as such** als solcher/solche/solches. **the thing as such** die Sache als solche. (*strictly speaking*) **this is not a promotion as such** dies ist im Grunde genommen keine Beförderung

····▸ **such is: such is life** so ist das Leben. **such is not the case** das ist nicht der Fall

····▸ **such as** wie [zum Beispiel]

suchlike /'sʌtʃlaɪk/ *pron* 🗓 dergleichen

suck /sʌk/ *vt/i* saugen; lutschen (*sweet*). ● **~ up** *vt* aufsaugen ● *vi* **~ up to s.o.** 🗓 sich bei jdm einschmeicheln

suction /'sʌkʃn/ *n* Saugwirkung *f*

sudden /'sʌdn/ *adj* plötzlich; (*abrupt*) jäh ● *n* **all of a ~** auf einmal

sue /suː/ *vt* (*pres p* suing) verklagen (**for** auf + *acc*) ● *vi* klagen

suede /sweɪd/ *n* Wildleder *nt*

suet /'suːɪt/ *n* [Nieren]talg *m*

suffice /sə'faɪs/ *vi* genügen

sufficient /sə'fɪʃnt/ *adj* genug, genügend; **be ~** genügen

suffocat|e /'sʌfəkeɪt/ *vt/i* ersticken. **~ion** *n* Ersticken *nt*

sugar /'ʃʊgə(r)/ *n* Zucker *m* ● *vt* zuckern; (*fig*) versüßen. **~ basin, ~-bowl** *n* Zuckerschale *f*. **~y** *adj* süß; (*fig*) süßlich

suggest /sə'dʒest/ *vt* vorschlagen; (*indicate, insinuate*) andeuten. **~ion** *n* Vorschlag *m*; Andeutung *f*; (*trace*) Spur *f*. **~ive** *adj* anzüglich

suicidal /suːɪ'saɪdl/ *adj* selbstmörderisch

suicide /'suːɪsaɪd/ *n* Selbstmord *m*

suit /suːt/ *n* Anzug *m*; (*woman's*) Kostüm *nt*; (*Cards*) Farbe *f*; (*Jur*) Prozess *m* ● *vt* (*adapt*) anpassen (**to** *dat*); (*be convenient for*) passen (+ *dat*); (*go with*) passen (*s.o.* *dat*); (*clothing*): stehen (*s.o.* *jdm*); **be ~ed for** geeignet sein für; **~ yourself!** wie du willst!

suit|able /'suːtəbl/ *adj* geeignet; (*convenient*) passend; (*appropriate*) angemessen; (*for weather, activity*) zweckmäßig. **~ably** *adv* angemessen; zweckmäßig

'suitcase *n* Koffer *m*

suite /swiːt/ *n* Suite *f*; (*of furniture*) Garnitur *f*

sulk /sʌlk/ *vi* schmollen. **~y** *adj* schmollend

sullen /'sʌlən/ *adj* mürrisch

sultry /'sʌltrɪ/ *adj* (*-ier, -iest*) (*weather*) schwül

sum /sʌm/ *n* Summe *f*; (*Sch*) Rechenaufgabe *f* ● *vt/i* (*pt/pp* summed) **~ up** zusammenfassen; (*assess*) einschätzen

summar|ize /'sʌməraɪz/ *vt* zusammenfassen. **~y** *n* Zusammenfassung *f* ● *adj*, **-ily** *adv* summarisch; (*dismissal*) fristlos

S

summer /'sʌmə(r)/ n Sommer m.
~**time** n Sommer m

summer camp Amerikanische Feriencamps haben eine lange Tradition. Sie bieten ein umfassendes Fitnessprogramm, und Schulkinder haben die Möglichkeit, alle erdenklichen Sportarten und Spiele in den Sommerferien auszuprobieren. Hier erhalten die Teilnehmer Survival-Training und lernen außerdem Unabhängigkeit und Führungseigenschaften. Tausende von Studenten arbeiten während der Sommermonate als Betreuer in den Feriencamps.

summery /'sʌmərɪ/ adj sommerlich

summit /'sʌmɪt/ n Gipfel m. ~ **conference** n Gipfelkonferenz f

summon /'sʌmən/ vt rufen; holen (help); (Jur) vorladen

summons /'sʌmənz/ n (Jur) Vorladung f ● vt vorladen

sumptuous /'sʌmptjʊəs/ adj prunkvoll; (meal) üppig

sun /sʌn/ n Sonne f ● vt (pt/pp sunned) ~ oneself sich sonnen

Sunday /'sʌndeɪ/ n Sonntag m

'**sunflower** n Sonnenblume f

sung /sʌŋ/ see sing

'**sunglasses** npl Sonnenbrille f

sunk /sʌŋk/ see sink

sunny /'sʌnɪ/ adj (-ier, -iest) sonnig

sun: ~**rise** n Sonnenaufgang m.
~**roof** n (Auto) Schiebedach nt.
~**set** n Sonnenuntergang m.
~**shade** n Sonnenschirm m.

~**shine** n Sonnenschein m.
~**stroke** n Sonnenstich m. ~**tan** n [Sonnen]bräune f. ~**tanned** adj braun [gebrannt]. ~**tan oil** n Sonnenöl nt

super /'su:pə(r)/ adj 🆃 prima, toll

superb /sʊ'pɜ:b/ adj erstklassig

superficial /su:pə'fɪʃl/ a oberflächlich

superfluous /sʊ'pɜ:flʊəs/ adj überflüssig

superintendent /su:pərɪn'tendənt/ n (of police) Kommissar m

superior /su:'pɪərɪə(r)/ a überlegen; (in rank) höher ● n Vorgesetzte(r) m/f. ~**ity** n Überlegenheit f

superlative /su:'pɜ:lətɪv/ a unübertrefflich ● n Superlativ m

'**supermarket** n Supermarkt m

super'natural adj übernatürlich

supersede /su:pə'si:d/ vt ersetzen

superstiti|on /su:pə'stɪʃn/ n Aberglaube m. ~**ous** adj abergläubisch

supervis|e /'su:pəvaɪz/ vt beaufsichtigen; überwachen (work). ~**ion** n Aufsicht f; Überwachung f. ~**or** n Aufseher(in) m(f)

supper /'sʌpə(r)/ n Abendessen nt

supple /'sʌpl/ adj geschmeidig

supplement /'sʌplɪmənt/ n Ergänzung f; (addition) Zusatz m; (to fare) Zuschlag m; (book) Ergänzungsband m; (to newspaper) Beilage f ● vt ergänzen. ~**ary** a zusätzlich

supplier /sə'plaɪə(r)/ n Lieferant m

supply /sə'plaɪ/ n Vorrat m; **supplies** pl (Mil) Nachschub m ● vt (pt/pp -ied) liefern; ~ **s.o. with sth** jdn mit etw versorgen

support /sə'pɔ:t/ n Stütze f; (fig) Unterstützung f ● vt stützen; (bear weight of) tragen; (keep) ernähren; (give money to) unterstützen; (speak *in favour of*) befürworten; (*Sport*) Fan sein von. **~er** *n* Anhänger(in) *m*(*f*); (*Sport*) Fan *m*

suppose /sə'pəʊz/ *vt* annehmen; (*presume*) vermuten; (*imagine*) sich (*dat*) vorstellen; **be ~d to do sth** etw tun sollen; **not be ~d to** 🗉 nicht dürfen; **I ~ so** vermutlich. **~dly** *adv* angeblich

supposition /sʌpə'zɪʃn/ *n* Vermutung *f*

suppress /sə'pres/ *vt* unterdrücken. **~ion** *n* Unterdrückung *f*

supremacy /su:'preməsɪ/ *n* Vorherrschaft *f*

supreme /su:'pri:m/ *adj* höchste(r,s); (*court*) oberste(r,s)

sure /ʃʊə(r)/ *adj* (**-r, -st**) sicher; **make ~** sich vergewissern of (*gen*); (*check*) nachprüfen ● *adv* (*Amer*, 🗉) klar; **~ enough** tatsächlich. **~ly** *adv* sicher; (*for emphasis*) doch; (*Amer: gladly*) gern

surf /sɜ:f/ *n* Brandung *f* ● *vi* surfen

surface /'sɜ:fɪs/ *n* Oberfläche *f* ● *vi* (*emerge*) auftauchen

'surfboard *n* Surfbrett *nt*

surfing /'sɜ:fɪŋ/ *n* Surfen *nt*

surge /sɜ:dʒ/ *n* (*of sea*) Branden *nt*; (*fig*) Welle *f* ● *vi* branden; **~ forward** nach vorn drängen

surgeon /'sɜ:dʒən/ *n* Chirurg(in) *m*(*f*)

surgery /'sɜ:dʒərɪ/ *n* Chirurgie *f*; (*place*) Praxis *f*; (*room*) Sprechzimmer *nt*; (*hours*) Sprechstunde *f*; **have ~** operiert werden

surgical /'sɜ:dʒɪkl/ *adj* chirurgisch

surly /'sɜ:lɪ/ *adj* mürrisch

surname /'sɜ:neɪm/ *n* Nachname *m*

surpass /sə'pɑ:s/ *vt* übertreffen

surplus /'sɜ:pləs/ *adj* überschüssig ● *n* Überschuss *m* (*of* an + *dat*)

surprise /sə'praɪz/ *n* Überraschung *f* ● *vt* überraschen; **be ~ed** sich wundern (**at** über + *acc*). **~ing** *adj* überraschend

surrender /sə'rendə(r)/ *n* Kapitulation *f* ● *vi* sich ergeben; (*Mil*) kapitulieren ● *vt* aufgeben

surround /sə'raʊnd/ *vt* umgeben; (*encircle*) umzingeln; **~ed by** umgeben von. **~ing** *adj* umliegend. **~ings** *npl* Umgebung *f*

surveillance /sə'veɪləns/ *n* Überwachung *f*; **be under ~** überwacht werden

survey¹ /'sɜ:veɪ/ *n* Überblick *m*; (*poll*) Umfrage *f*; (*investigation*) Untersuchung *f*; (*of land*) Vermessung *f*; (*of house*) Gutachten *nt*

survey² /sə'veɪ/ *vt* betrachten; vermessen (*land*); begutachten (*building*). **~or** *n* Landvermesser *m*; Gutachter *m*

survival /sə'vaɪvl/ *n* Überleben *nt*; (*of tradition*) Fortbestand *m*

survive /sə'vaɪv/ *vt* überleben ● *vi* überleben; (*tradition:*) erhalten bleiben. **~or** *n* Überlebende(r) *m*/*f*; **be a ~or** nicht unterzukriegen sein

susceptible /sə'septəbl/ *adj* empfänglich/ (*Med*) anfällig (**to** für)

suspect¹ /sə'spekt/ *vt* verdächtigen; (*assume*) vermuten; **he ~s nothing** er ahnt nichts

suspect² /'sʌspekt/ *adj* verdächtig ● *n* Verdächtige(r) *m*/*f*

suspend /sə'spend/ *vt* aufhängen; (*stop*) [vorläufig] einstellen; (*from duty*) vorläufig beurlauben. **~ers** *npl* (*Amer:* braces) Hosenträger *pl*

suspense /sə'spens/ *n* Spannung *f*

suspension /sə'spenʃn/ *n* (*Auto*) Federung *f*. **~ bridge** *n* Hängebrücke *f*

suspici|on /sə'spɪʃn/ *n* Verdacht *m*; (*mistrust*) Misstrauen *nt*; (*trace*)

Spur f. **~ous** adj misstrauisch; (arousing suspicion) verdächtig

sustain /sə'steɪn/ vt tragen; (fig) aufrechterhalten; erhalten (life); erleiden (injury)

sustenance /'sʌstɪnəns/ n Nahrung f

swagger /'swægə(r)/ vi stolzieren

swallow[1] /'swɒləʊ/ vt/i schlucken. **~ up** vt verschlucken; verschlingen (resources)

swallow[2] n (bird) Schwalbe f

swam /swæm/ see **swim**

swamp /swɒmp/ n Sumpf m • vt überschwemmen

swan /swɒn/ n Schwan m

swank /swæŋk/ vi (fam) angeben

swap /swɒp/ n [] Tausch m • vt/i (pt/pp swapped) [] tauschen (for gegen)

swarm /swɔːm/ n Schwarm m • vi schwärmen; **be ~ing with** wimmeln von

swat /swɒt/ vt (pt/pp swatted) totschlagen

sway /sweɪ/ vi schwanken; (gently) sich wiegen • vt (influence) beeinflussen

swear /sweə(r)/ v (pt swore, pp sworn) • vt schwören • vi schwören (by auf + acc); (curse) fluchen. **~-word** n Kraftausdruck m

sweat /swet/ n Schweiß m • vi schwitzen

sweater /'swetə(r)/ n Pullover m

Swede|e n Schwede m/Schwedin f. **~en** n Schweden nt. **~ish** adj schwedisch

sweep /swiːp/ n Schornsteinfeger m; (curve) Bogen m; (movement) ausholende Bewegung f • v (pt/pp swept) • vt fegen, kehren • vi (go swiftly) rauschen; (wind:) fegen

sweeping /'swiːpɪŋ/ adj ausholend; (statement) pauschal; (changes) weit reichend

sweet /swiːt/ a (-er, -est) süß; **have a ~ tooth** gern Süßes mögen • n Bonbon m & nt; (dessert) Nachtisch m

sweeten /'swiːtn/ vt süßen

sweet: ~heart n Schatz m. **~ness** n Süße f. **~ 'pea** n Wicke f. **~shop** n Süßwarenladen m

swell /swel/ n Dünung f • v (pt swelled, pp swollen or swelled) • vi [an]schwellen; (wood:) aufquellen • vt anschwellen lassen; (increase) vergrößern. **~ing** n Schwellung f

swelter /'sweltə(r)/ vi schwitzen

swept /swept/ see **sweep**

swerve /swɜːv/ vi einen Bogen machen

swift /swɪft/ adj (-er, -est) schnell

swig /swɪg/ n [] Schluck m

swim /swɪm/ n **have a ~** schwimmen • vi (pt swam, pp swum) schwimmen; **my head is ~ming** mir dreht sich der Kopf. **~mer** n Schwimmer(in) m(f)

swimming /'swɪmɪŋ/ n Schwimmen nt. **~-baths** npl Schwimmbad nt. **~-pool** n Schwimmbecken nt; (private) Swimmingpool m

'swimsuit n Badeanzug m

swindle /'swɪndl/ n Schwindel m, Betrug m • vt betrügen. **~r** n Schwindler m

swine /swaɪn/ n (pej) Schwein nt

swing /swɪŋ/ n Schwung m; (shift) Schwenk m; (seat) Schaukel f; **in full ~** in vollem Gange • v (pt/pp swung) • vi schwingen; (on swing) schaukeln; (dangle) baumeln; (turn) schwenken • vt schwingen; (influence) beeinflussen

swipe /swaɪp/ n [] Schlag m • vt [] knallen; (steal) klauen

swirl /swɜːl/ n Wirbel m ● vt/i
wirbeln

Swiss /swɪs/ adj Schweizer-,
schweizerisch ● n Schweizer(in)
m(f); **the ~** pl die Schweizer. **~
'roll** n Biskuitrolle f

switch /swɪtʃ/ n Schalter m;
(change) Wechsel m; (Amer, Rail)
Weiche f ● vt wechseln; (exchange)
tauschen ● vi wechseln; **~ to** umstellen auf (+ acc). **~ off** vt ausschalten; abschalten (engine). **~ on**
vt einschalten

switchboard n [Telefon]zen-
trale f

Switzerland /'swɪtsələnd/ n die
Schweiz

swivel /'swɪvl/ v (pt/pp **swivelled**)
● vt drehen ● vi sich drehen

swollen /'swəʊlən/ see **swell**

swoop /swuːp/ n (by police) Razzia
f ● vi **~ down** herabstoßen

sword /sɔːd/ n Schwert nt

swore /swɔː(r)/ see **swear**

sworn /swɔːn/ see **swear**

swot /swɒt/ n 🗆 Streber m ● vt
(pt/pp **swotted**) 🗆 büffeln

swum /swʌm/ see **swim**

swung /swʌŋ/ see **swing**

syllable /'sɪləbl/ n Silbe f

syllabus /'sɪləbəs/ n Lehrplan m;
(for exam) Studienplan m

symbol /'sɪmbl/ n Symbol nt (of
für). **~ic** adj, **-ally** adv symbolisch
~ism n Symbolik f. **~ize** vt sym-
bolisieren

symmetr|ical /sɪ'metrɪkl/ adj
symmetrisch. **~y** n Symmetrie f

sympathetic /sɪmpə'θetɪk/ adj,
-ally adv mitfühlend; (likeable) sympathisch

sympathize /'sɪmpəθaɪz/ vi mitfühlen

sympathy /'sɪmpəθɪ/ n Mitgefühl

nt; (condolences) Beileid nt

symphony /'sɪmfənɪ/ n Sinfonie f

symptom /'sɪmptəm/ n Symptom nt

synagogue /'sɪnəgɒg/ n Synagoge f

synchronize /'sɪŋkrənaɪz/ vt synchronisieren

synonym /'sɪnənɪm/ n Synonym
nt. **~ous** adj synonym

synthesis /'sɪnθəsɪs/ n (pl **-ses**
/-siːz/) Synthese f

synthetic /sɪn'θetɪk/ adj syn-
thetisch

Syria /'sɪrɪə/ n Syrien nt

syringe /sɪ'rɪndʒ/ n Spritze f

syrup /'sɪrəp/ n Sirup m

system /'sɪstəm/ n System nt.
~atic adj, **-ally** adv systematisch

Tt

tab /tæb/ n (projecting) Zunge f;
(with name) Namensschild nt; (loop)
Aufhänger m; **pick up the ~** 🗆 bezahlen

table /'teɪbl/ n Tisch m; (list) Tabelle f; **at [the] ~** bei Tisch.
~-cloth n Tischdecke f. **~spoon** n
Servierlöffel m

tablet /'tæblɪt/ n Tablette f; (of
soap) Stück nt

'table tennis n Tischtennis nt

tabloid /'tæblɔɪd/ n kleinformatige
Zeitung f; (pej) Boulevardzeitung f

taciturn /'tæsɪtɜːn/ adj wortkarg

tack /tæk/ n (nail) Stift m; (stitch)
Heftstich m; (Naut & dig) Kurs m
● vt festnageln; (sew) heften ● vi
(Naut) kreuzen

tackle /'tækl/ n Ausrüstung f ● vt angehen (*problem*); (*Sport*) angreifen

tact /tækt/ n Takt m, Taktgefühl nt. **∼ful** adj taktvoll

tactic|al /'tæktɪkl/ adj taktisch. **∼s** npl Taktik f

tactless /'tæktlɪs/ adj taktlos. **∼ness** n Taktlosigkeit f

tag /tæg/ n (*label*) Schild nt ● vi (*pt/pp* tagged) **∼ along** mitkommen

tail /teɪl/ n Schwanz m; **∼s** pl (*tailcoat*) Frack m; **heads or ∼s?** Kopf oder Zahl? ● vt (🔢: *follow*) beschatten ● vi **∼ off** zurückgehen

tail: **∼back** n Rückstau m. **∼ light** n Rücklicht nt

tailor /'teɪlə(r)/ n Schneider m. **∼-made** adj maßgeschneidert

taint /teɪnt/ vt verderben

take /teɪk/ v (*pt* took, *pp* taken) ● vt nehmen: (*with one*) mitnehmen; (*take to a place*) bringen; (*steal*) stehlen; (*win*) gewinnen; (*capture*) einnehmen; (*require*) brauchen; (*last*) dauern; (*teach*) geben; machen (*exam, subject, holiday, photograph*); messen (*pulse, temperature*); **∼ sth to the cleaner's** etw in die Reinigung bringen; be **∼n ill** krank werden; **∼ sth calmly** etw gelassen aufnehmen ● vi (*plant*) angehen; **∼ after s.o.** jdm nachschlagen; (*in looks*) jdm ähnlich sehen; **∼ to** (*like*) mögen; (*as a habit*) sich (*dat*) angewöhnen. **∼ away** vt wegbringen; (*remove*) wegnehmen; (*subtract*) abziehen; **'to ∼ away'** 'zum Mitnehmen'. **∼ back** vt zurücknehmen; (*return*) zurückbringen. **∼ down** vt herunternehmen; (*remove*) abnehmen; (*write down*) aufschreiben. **∼ in** vt hineinbringen; (*bring indoors*) hereinholen; (*to one's home*) aufnehmen; (*understand*) begreifen; (*deceive*) hereinlegen; (*make smaller*) enger machen. **∼ off** vt abnehmen; ablegen (*coat*); sich (*dat*) ausziehen (*clothes*); (*deduct*) abziehen; (*mimic*) nachmachen ● vi (*Aviat*) starten. **∼ on** vt annehmen; (*undertake*) übernehmen; (*engage*) einstellen; (*as opponent*) antreten gegen. **∼ out** vt hinausbringen; (*for pleasure*) ausgehen mit; ausführen (*dog*); (*remove*) herausnehmen; (*withdraw*) abheben (*money*); (*from library*) ausleihen; **∼ it out on s.o.** 🔢 seinen Ärger an jdm auslassen. **∼ over** vt hinüberbringen; übernehmen (*firm, control*) ● vi **∼ over from s.o.** jdn ablösen. **∼ up** vt hinaufbringen; annehmen (*offer*); ergreifen (*profession*); sich (*dat*) zulegen (*hobby*); in Anspruch nehmen (*time*); einnehmen (*space*); aufreißen (*floorboards*); be **∼n up with s.o.** mit jdm über etw (*acc*) sprechen

take: **∼-away** n Essen nt zum Mitnehmen; (*restaurant*) Restaurant nt mit Straßenverkauf. **∼-off** n (*Aviat*) Start m, Abflug m. **∼-over** n Übernahme f

takings /'teɪkɪŋz/ npl Einnahmen pl

talcum /'tælkəm/ n **∼ [powder]** Körperpuder m

tale /teɪl/ n Geschichte f

talent /'tælənt/ n Talent nt

talk /tɔ:k/ n Gespräch nt; (*lecture*) Vortrag m ● vi reden, sprechen (**to**/ **with** mit) ● vt reden; **∼ s.o. into** sth jdn zu etw überreden. **∼ over** vt besprechen

talkative /'tɔ:kətɪv/ adj gesprächig

tall /tɔ:l/ adj (**-er, -est**) groß; (*building, tree*) hoch. **∼ story** n übertriebene Geschichte f

tally /'tælɪ/ vi übereinstimmen

tame /teɪm/ adj (-r, -st) zahm; (dull) lahm [!] ● vt zähmen. **~r** n Dompteur m

tamper /'tæmpə(r)/ vi **~ with** sich (dat) zu schaffen machen an (+ dat)

tampon /'tæmpɒn/ n Tampon m

tan /tæn/ adj gelbbraun ● n Gelbbraun nt; (from sun) Bräune f ● v (pt/pp tanned) ● vt gerben (hide) ● vi braun werden

tang /tæŋ/ n herber Geschmack m; (smell) herber Geruch m

tangible /'tændʒɪbl/ adj greifbar

tangle /'tæŋgl/ n Gewirr nt; (in hair) Verfilzung f ● vt ~ **[up]** verheddern ● vi sich verheddern

tank /tæŋk/ n Tank m; (Mil) Panzer m

tanker /'tæŋkə(r)/ n Tanker m; (lorry) Tank[last]wagen m

tantrum /'tæntrəm/ n Wutanfall m

tap /tæp/ n Hahn m; (knock) Klopfen nt; **on ~** zur Verfügung ● v (pt/pp **tapped**) ● vt klopfen an (+ acc); anzapfen (barrel, tree); erschließen (resources); abhören (telephone) ● vi klopfen. **~-dance** n Stepp[tanz] m ● vi Stepp tanzen, steppen

tape /teɪp/ n Band nt; (adhesive) Klebstreifen m; (for recording) Tonband nt ● vt mit Klebstreifen zukleben; (record) auf Band aufnehmen

'tape-measure n Bandmaß nt

taper /'teɪpə(r)/ vi sich verjüngen

'tape recorder n Tonbandgerät nt

tar /tɑ:(r)/ n Teer m ● vt (pt/pp **tarred**) teeren

target /'tɑ:gɪt/ n Ziel nt; (board) [Ziel]scheibe f

tarnish /'tɑ:nɪʃ/ vi anlaufen

tarpaulin /tɑ:'pɔ:lɪn/ n Plane f

tart¹ /tɑ:t/ adj (-er, -est) sauer

tart² n ≈ Obstkuchen m; (individual) Törtchen nt; (sl: prostitute) Nutte f ● vt ~ **oneself up** [!] sich auftakeln

tartan /'tɑ:tn/ n Schottenmuster nt; (cloth) Schottenstoff m

task /tɑ:sk/ n Aufgabe f; **take s.o. to ~** jdm Vorhaltungen machen. **~ force** n Sonderkommando nt

tassel /'tæsl/ n Quaste f

taste /teɪst/ n Geschmack m; (sample) Kostprobe f ● vt kosten, probieren; schmecken (flavour) ● vi schmecken (of nach). **~ful** adj (fig) geschmackvoll. **~less** adj geschmacklos

tasty /'teɪstɪ/ adj lecker

tat /tæt/ see tit²

tatters /'tætəz/ npl **in ~s** in Fetzen

tattoo /tə'tu:/ n Tätowierung f ● vt tätowieren

tatty /'tætɪ/ adj schäbig; (book) zerfleddert

taught /tɔ:t/ see teach

taunt /tɔ:nt/ n höhnische Bemerkung f ● vt verhöhnen

taut /tɔ:t/ adj straff

tawdry /'tɔ:drɪ/ adj billig und geschmacklos

tax /tæks/ n Steuer f ● vt besteuern; (fig) strapazieren. **~able** adj steuerpflichtig. **~ation** n Besteuerung f

taxi /'tæksɪ/ n Taxi nt ● vi (pt/pp **taxied**, pres p **taxiing**) (aircraft:) rollen. **~ driver** n Taxifahrer m. **~ rank** n Taxistand m

'taxpayer n Steuerzahler m

tea /ti:/ n Tee m. **~-bag** n Teebeutel m. **~-break** n Teepause f

teach /ti:tʃ/ vt/i (pt/pp **taught**) unterrichten; ~ **s.o. sth** jdm etw beibringen. **~er** n Lehrer(in) m(f). **~ing** n Unterrichten nt

tea: **~-cloth** n (for drying) Geschirrtuch nt. **~cup** n Teetasse f

teak /tiːk/ n Teakholz nt

team /tiːm/ n Mannschaft f; (fig) Team nt; (of animals) Gespann nt

'teapot n Teekanne f

tear¹ /teə(r)/ n Riss m ● v (pt tore, pp torn) ● vt reißen; (damage) zerreißen; **~ oneself away** sich losreißen ● vi [zer]reißen; (run) rasen. **~ up** vt zerreißen

tear² /tɪə(r)/ n Träne f. **~ful** adj weinend. **~fully** adv unter Tränen. **~gas** n Tränengas nt

tease /tiːz/ vt necken

tea: **~-set** n Teeservice nt. **~ shop** n Café nt. **~spoon** n Teelöffel m

teat /tiːt/ n Zitze f; (on bottle) Sauger m

'tea-towel n Geschirrtuch nt

technical /'teknɪkl/ adj technisch; (specialized) fachlich. **~ity** n technisches Detail nt; (Jur) Formfehler m. **~ly** adv technisch; (strictly) streng genommen. **~ term** n Fachausdruck m

technician /tek'nɪʃn/ n Techniker m

technique /tek'niːk/ n Technik f

technological /teknə'lɒdʒɪkl/ adj technologisch

technology /tek'nɒlədʒɪ/ n Technik f

teddy /'tedɪ/ n **~ [bear]** Teddybär m

tedious /'tiːdɪəs/ adj langweilig

tedium /'tiːdɪəm/ n Langeweile f

teenage /'tiːneɪdʒ/ adj Teenager-; **~ boy/girl** Junge m/Mädchen nt im Teenageralter. **~r** n Teenager m

teens /tiːnz/ npl **the ~** die Teenagerjahre pl

teeter /'tiːtə(r)/ vi schwanken

teeth /tiːθ/ see tooth

teeth|e /tiːð/ vi zahnen. **~ing**

troubles npl (fig) Anfangsschwierigkeiten pl

teetotal /tiː'təʊtl/ adj abstinent. **~ler** n Abstinenzler m

telebanking /'telɪbæŋkɪŋ/ n Telebanking nt

telecommunications /telɪkəmjuːnɪ'keɪʃnz/ npl Fernmeldewesen nt

telegram /'telɪgræm/ n Telegramm nt

telegraph /'telɪgrɑːf/ **~ pole** n Telegrafenmast m

telephone /'telɪfəʊn/ n Telefon nt; **be on the ~** Telefon haben; (be telephoning) telefonieren ● vt anrufen ● vi telefonieren

telephone: **~ booth** n, **~ box** n Telefonzelle f. **~ directory** n Telefonbuch nt. **~ number** n Telefonnummer f

tele'photo /telɪ-/ adj **~ lens** Teleobjektiv nt

telescop|e /'telɪskəʊp/ n Teleskop nt, Fernrohr nt. **~ic** adj (collapsible) ausziehbar

televise /'telɪvaɪz/ vt im Fernsehen übertragen

television /'telɪvɪʒn/ n Fernsehen nt; **watch ~** fernsehen; **~ [set]** Fernseher m 🔟

teleworking /'telɪwɜːkɪŋ/ n Telearbeit f

tell /tel/ vt/i (pt/pp told) sagen (s.o. jdm); (relate) erzählen; (know) wissen; (distinguish) erkennen; **~ the time** die Uhr lesen; **time will ~** das wird man erst sehen; **his age is beginning to ~** sein Alter macht sich bemerkbar. **~ off** vt ausschimpfen

telly /'telɪ/ n 🔟 = television

temp /temp/ n 🔟 Aushilfssekretärin f

temper /'tempə(r)/ n (disposition)

Naturell nt; (mood) Laune f; (anger)
Wut f; **lose one's ~** wütend werden ● vt (fig) mäßigen

temperament /'tempərəmənt/ n
Temperament nt. **~al** adj temperamentvoll; (moody) launisch

temperate /'tempərət/ adj
gemäßigt

temperature /'temprətʃə(r)/ n
Temperatur f; **have** or **run a ~** Fieber haben

temple¹ /'templ/ n Tempel m

temple² n (Anat) Schläfe f

tempo /'tempəʊ/ n Tempo nt

temporary /'tempərərɪ/ adj, **-ily**
adv vorübergehend; (measure, building) provisorisch

tempt /tempt/ vt verleiten; (Relig)
versuchen; herausfordern a (fate);
(entice) [ver]locken; **be ~ed** versucht sein (**to** zu). **~ation** n Versuchung f. **~ing** adj verlockend

ten /ten/ adj zehn

tenaci|ous /tɪ'neɪʃəs/ adj, **-ly** adv
hartnäckig. **~ty** n Hartnäckigkeit f

tenant /'tenənt/ n Mieter(in) m(f);
(Comm) Pächter(in) m(f)

tend /tend/ vi **~ to do sth** dazu
neigen, etw zu tun

tendency /'tendənsɪ/ n Tendenz f;
(inclination) Neigung f

tender /'tendə(r)/ adj zart; (loving)
zärtlich; (painful) empfindlich. **~ly**
adv zärtlich. **~ness** n Zartheit f;
Zärtlichkeit f

tendon /'tendən/ n Sehne f

tenner /'tenə(r)/ n 🔟 Zehnpfundschein m

tennis /'tenɪs/ n Tennis nt.
~-court n Tennisplatz m

tenor /'tenə(r)/ n Tenor m

tense /tens/ adj (-r, -st) gespannt
● vt anspannen (muscle)

tension /'tenʃn/ n Spannung f

tent /tent/ n Zelt nt

tentative /'tentətɪv/ adj, **-ly** adv
vorläufig; (hesitant) zaghaft

tenterhooks /'tentəhʊks/ npl **be
on ~** wie auf glühenden Kohlen
sitzen

tenth /tenθ/ adj zehnte(r,s) ● n
Zehntel nt

tenuous /'tenjʊəs/ adj schwach

tepid /'tepɪd/ adj lauwarm

term /tɜ:m/ n Zeitraum m; (Sch) ≈
Halbjahr nt; (Univ) ≈ Semester nt;
(expression) Ausdruck m; **~s** pl (conditions) Bedingungen pl; **in the
short/long ~** kurz-/langfristig; **be
on good/bad ~s** gut/nicht gut miteinander auskommen

terminal /'tɜ:mɪnl/ adj End-;
(Med) unheilbar ● n (Aviat) Terminal
m; (of bus) Endstation f; (on battery)
Pol m; (Computing) Terminal nt

terminat|e /'tɜ:mɪnert/ vt beenden; lösen (contract); unterbrechen
(pregnancy) ● vi enden

terminology /tɜ:mɪ'nɒlədʒɪ/ n
Terminologie f

terminus /'tɜ:mɪnəs/ n (pl **-ni**
/-naɪ/) Endstation f

terrace /'terəs/ n Terrasse f;
(houses) Häuserreihe f. **~d house** n
Reihenhaus nt

terrain /te'reɪn/ n Gelände nt

terrible /'terəbl/ adj, **-bly** adv
schrecklich

terrific /tə'rɪfɪk/ adj 🔟 (excellent)
sagenhaft; (huge) riesig

terri|fy /'terɪfaɪ/ vt (pt/pp **-ied**)
Angst machen (+ dat); **be ~fied**
Angst haben. **~fying** adj Furcht erregend

territorial /terɪ'tɔ:rɪəl/ adj Territorial-

territory /'terɪtərɪ/ n Gebiet nt

terror /'terə(r)/ n [panische] Angst
f; (Pol) Terror m. **~ism** n Terrorismus m. **~ist** n Terrorist(in) m(f).

t

~**ize** vt terrorisieren

terse /tɜːs/ adj kurz, knapp

test /test/ n Test m; (Sch) Klassenarbeit f; **put to the** ~ auf die Probe stellen ● vt prüfen; (examine) untersuchen (**for** auf + acc)

testament /ˈtestəmənt/ n Testament nt

testify /ˈtestɪfaɪ/ v (pt/pp -ied) ● vt beweisen; ~ **that** bezeugen, dass ● vi aussagen

testimonial /testɪˈməʊnɪəl/ n Zeugnis nt

testimony /ˈtestɪmənɪ/ n Aussage f

'**test-tube** n Reagenzglas nt

tether /ˈteðə(r)/ n **be at the end of one's** ~ am Ende seiner Kraft sein ● vt anbinden

text /tekst/ n Text m ● vt/i texten. ~**book** n Lehrbuch nt

textile /ˈtekstaɪl/ adj Textil- ● n ~**s** pl Textilien pl

'**text message** n SMS-nachricht f

texture /ˈtekstʃə(r)/ n Beschaffenheit f; (of cloth) Struktur f

Thai /taɪ/ adj thailändisch. ~**land** n Thailand nt

Thames /temz/ n Themse f

than /ðən/, betont /ðæn/ conj als

thank /θæŋk/ vt danken (+ dat); ~ **you [very much]** danke [schön]. ~**ful** adj dankbar. ~**less** adj undankbar

thanks /θæŋks/ npl Dank m; ~! 🔲 danke! ~ **to** dank (+ dat or gen)

<hr>

that /ðæt/

| pl **those** |

● adjective
••••▸ der (m), die (f), das (nt),

die (pl); (just seen or experienced) dieser (m), diese (f), dieses (nt), diese (pl). **I'll never forget that day** den Tag werde ich nie vergessen. **I liked that house** dieses Haus hat mir gut gefallen

● pronoun
••••▸ der (m), die (f), das (nt), die (pl). **that is not true** das ist nicht wahr. **who is that in the garden?** wer ist das [da] im Garten? **I'll take that** ich nehme den/die/das. **I don't like those** die mag ich nicht. **is that you?** bist du es? **that is why** deshalb

••••▸ **like that** so. **don't be like that!** sei doch nicht so! **a man like that** ein solcher Mann; so ein Mann 🔲

••••▸ (after prepositions) da .... **after that** danach. **with that** damit. **apart from that** außerdem

••••▸ (relative pronoun) der (m), die (f), das (nt), die (pl). **the book that I'm reading** das Buch, das ich lese. **the people that you got it from** die Leute, von denen du es bekommen hast. **everyone that I know** jeder, den ich kenne. **that is all that I have** das ist alles, was ich habe

● adverb
••••▸ so. **he's not 'that stupid** so blöd ist er [auch wieder] nicht. **it wasn't 'that bad** so schlecht war es auch nicht. **A nail about 'that long** ein etwa so langer Nagel

••••▸ (relative adverb) der (m), die (f), das (nt), die (pl). **the day that I first met her** der Tag, an dem ich sie zum ersten Mal sah. **at the speed that he was going** bei der Geschwindigkeit, die er hatte

● *conjunction*

····▸ dass. **I don't think that he'll come** ich denke nicht, dass er kommt. **we know that you're right** wir wissen, dass du Recht hast. **I'm so tired that I can hardly walk** ich bin so müde, dass ich kaum gehen kann

····▸ **so that** (*purpose*) damit; (*result*) sodass. **he came earlier so that they would have more time** er kam früher, damit sie mehr Zeit hatten. **it was late, so that I had to catch the bus** es war spät, sodass ich den Bus nehmen musste

thatch /θætʃ/ *n* Strohdach *nt*. **~ed** *adj* strohgedeckt

thaw /θɔː/ *n* Tauwetter *nt* ● *vt/i* auftauen; **it's ~ing** es taut

the /ðə/, vor einem Vokal /ðiː/ *def art* der/die/das; (*pl*) die; **play ~ piano/ violin** Klavier/Geige spielen ● *adv* ~ **more ~ better** je mehr, desto besser; **all ~ better** umso besser

theatre /ˈθɪətə(r)/ *n* Theater *nt*; (*Med*) Operationssaal *m*

theatrical /θɪˈætrɪkl/ *adj* Theater-; (*showy*) theatralisch

theft /θeft/ *n* Diebstahl *m*

their /ðeə(r)/ *adj* ihr

theirs /ðeəz/ *poss pron* ihre(r), ihrs; **a friend of ~** ein Freund von ihnen; **those are ~** die gehören ihnen

them /ðem/ *pron* (*acc*) sie; (*dat*) ihnen

theme /θiːm/ *n* Thema *nt*. **~ park** *n* Themenpark *m*

themˈselves *pron* selbst; (*reflexive*) sich; **by ~** allein

then /ðen/ *adv* dann; (*at that time in past*) damals; **by ~** bis dahin;

since ~ seitdem; **before ~** vorher; **from ~ on** von da an; **now and ~** dann und wann; **there and ~** auf der Stelle ● *adj* damalig

theology /θɪˈɒlədʒɪ/ *n* Theologie *f*

theoretical /θɪəˈretɪkl/ *adj* theoretisch

theory /ˈθɪərɪ/ *n* Theorie *f*; **in ~** theoretisch

therapist /ˈθerəpɪst/ *n* Therapeut(in) *m*(*f*). **~y** *n* Therapie *f*

there /ðeə(r)/ *adv* da; (*with movement*) dahin, dorthin; **down/up ~** da unten/oben; **~ is/are** da ist/ sind; (*in existence*) es gibt ● *int* ~, **~!** nun, nun!

there: **~abouts** *adv* da [in der Nähe]; **or ~abouts** (*roughly*) ungefähr. **~fore** /-fɔː(r)/ *adv* deshalb, also

thermometer /θəˈmɒmɪtə(r)/ *n* Thermometer *nt*

Thermos ® /ˈθɜːməs/ *n* ~ **[flask]** Thermosflasche ® *f*

thermostat /ˈθɜːməstæt/ *n* Thermostat *m*

these /ðiːz/ *see* **this**

thesis /ˈθiːsɪs/ *n* (*pl* **-ses** /-siːz/) Dissertation *f*; (*proposition*) These *f*

they /ðeɪ/ *pron* sie; **~ say** (*generalizing*) man sagt

thick /θɪk/ *adj* (**-er, -est**) dick; (*dense*) dicht; (*liquid*) dickflüssig; (🄘: *stupid*) dumm ● *adv* dick ● *n* **in the ~ of** mitten in (+ *dat*). **~en** *vt* dicker machen; eindicken (*sauce*) ● *vi* dicker werden; (*fog:*) dichter werden; (*plot:*) kompliziert werden. **~ness** *n* Dicke *f*; Dichte *f*; Dickflüssigkeit *f*

thief /θiːf/ *n* (*pl* **thieves**) Dieb(in) *m*(*f*)

thigh /θaɪ/ *n* Oberschenkel *m*

thimble /ˈθɪmbl/ *n* Fingerhut *m*

thin /θɪn/ adj (thinner, thinnest) dünn ● adv dünn ● v (pt/pp thinned) ● vt verdünnen (liquid) ● vi sich lichten

thing /θɪŋ/ n Ding nt; (subject, affair) Sache f; ~s pl (belongings) Sachen pl; **for one** ~ erstens; **just the** ~! genau das Richtige! **how are** ~s? wie geht's? **the latest** ~ ⊤ der letzte Schrei

think /θɪŋk/ vt/i (pt/pp thought) denken (**about/of** an + acc); (believe) meinen; (consider) nachdenken; (regard as) halten für; **I** ~ **so** ich glaube schon; **what do you** ~ **of it?** was halten Sie davon? ~ **over** vt sich (dat) überlegen. ~ **up** vt sich (dat) ausdenken

third /θɜːd/ adj dritte(r,s) ● n Drittel nt. ~**ly** adv drittens. ~-**rate** adj drittrangig

thirst /θɜːst/ n Durst m. ~**y** adj, -**ily** adv durstig; **be** ~**y** Durst haben

thirteen /θɜː'tiːn/ adj dreizehn. ~**th** adj dreizehnte(r,s)

thirtieth /'θɜːtɪɪθ/ adj dreißigste(r,s)

thirty /'θɜːtɪ/ adj dreißig

this /ðɪs/ adj (pl these) diese(r,s); (pl) diese; ~ **one** diese(r,s) da; **I'll take** ~ ich nehme diesen/diese/dieses; ~ **evening/morning** heute Abend/Morgen; **these days** heutzutage ● pron (pl these) das, dies[es]; (pl) die, diese; ~ **and that** dies und das; ~ **or that** dieses oder das da; **like** ~ so; ~ **is Peter** das ist Peter; (Teleph) hier [spricht] Peter; **who is** ~? wer ist das? (Teleph, Amer) wer ist am Apparat?

thistle /'θɪsl/ n Distel f

thorn /θɔːn/ n Dorn m

thorough /'θʌrə/ adj gründlich

thoroughbred n reinrassiges Tier nt; (horse) Rassepferd nt

thorough|ly /'θʌrəlɪ/ adv gründlich; (completely) völlig; (extremely) äußerst. ~**ness** n Gründlichkeit f

those /ðəʊz/ see that

though /ðəʊ/ conj obgleich, obwohl; **as** ~ als ob ● adv ⊤ doch

thought /θɔːt/ see think ● n Gedanke m; (thinking) Denken nt. ~**ful** adj nachdenklich; (considerate) rücksichtsvoll. ~**less** adj gedankenlos

thousand /'θaʊznd/ adj one/a ~ [ein]tausend ● n Tausend nt. ~**th** adj tausendste(r,s) ● n Tausendstel nt

thrash /θræʃ/ vt verprügeln; (defeat) [vernichtend] schlagen

thread /θred/ n Faden m; (of screw) Gewinde nt ● vt einfädeln; auffädeln (beads). ~**bare** adj fadenscheinig

threat /θret/ n Drohung f; (danger) Bedrohung f

threaten /'θretn/ vt drohen (+ dat); (with weapon) bedrohen; ~ **s.o. with sth** jdm etw androhen ● vi drohen. ~**ing** adj drohend; (ominous) bedrohlich

three /θriː/ adj drei. ~**fold** adj & adv dreifach

thresh /θreʃ/ vt dreschen

threshold /'θreʃəʊld/ n Schwelle f

threw /θruː/ see throw

thrift /θrɪft/ n Sparsamkeit f. ~**y** adj sparsam

thrill /θrɪl/ n Erregung f; ⊤ Nervenkitzel m ● vt (excite) erregen; **be** ~**ed** with sich sehr freuen über (+ acc). ~**er** n Thriller m. ~**ing** adj erregend

thrive /θraɪv/ vi (pt thrived or throve, pp thrived or thriven /'θrɪvn/) gedeihen (on bei); (business:) florieren

throat /θrəʊt/ n Hals m; **cut s.o.'s ~** jdm die Kehle durchschneiden

throb /θrɒb/ n Pochen nt ● vi (pt/pp **throbbed**) pochen; (vibrate) vibrieren

throes /θrəʊz/ npl **in the ~ of** (fig) mitten in (+ dat)

throne /θrəʊn/ n Thron m

throttle /'θrɒtl/ vt erdrosseln

through /θruː/ prep durch (+ acc); (during) während (+ gen); (Amer: up to & including) bis einschließlich ● adv durch; **wet ~** durch und durch nass; **read sth ~** etw durchlesen ● adj (train) durchgehend; **be ~** (finished) fertig sein; (Teleph) durch sein

throughout /θruː'aʊt/ prep **~ the country** im ganzen Land; **~ the night** die Nacht durch ● adv ganz; (time) die ganze Zeit

throve /θrəʊv/ see **thrive**

throw /θrəʊ/ n Wurf m ● vt (pt **threw**, pp **thrown**) werfen; schütten (liquid); betätigen (switch); abwerfen (rider); (🄵: disconcert) aus der Fassung bringen; 🄵 geben (party); **~ sth to s.o.** jdm etw zuwerfen. **~ away** vt wegwerfen. **~ out** vt hinauswerfen; (**~ away**) wegwerfen; verwerfen (plan). **~ up** vt hochwerfen ● vi sich übergeben

'throw-away adj Wegwerf-

thrush /θrʌʃ/ n Drossel f

thrust /θrʌst/ n Stoß m; (Phys) Schub m ● vt (pt/pp **thrust**) stoßen; (insert) stecken

thud /θʌd/ n dumpfer Schlag m

thug /θʌg/ n Schläger m

thumb /θʌm/ n Daumen m ● vt **~ a lift** 🄵 per Anhalter fahren. **~tack** n (Amer) Reißzwecke f

thump /θʌmp/ n Schlag m; (noise) dumpfer Schlag m ● vt schlagen

● vi hämmern; (heart:) pochen

thunder /'θʌndə(r)/ n Donner m ● vi donnern. **~clap** n Donnerschlag m. **~storm** n Gewitter nt. **~y** adj gewittrig

Thursday /'θɜːzdeɪ/ n Donnerstag m

thus /ðʌs/ adv so

thwart /θwɔːt/ vt vereiteln; **~ s.o.** jdm einen Strich durch die Rechnung machen

tick[1] /tɪk/ n **on ~** 🄵 auf Pump

tick[2] n (sound) Ticken nt; (mark) Häkchen nt; (🄵: instant) Sekunde f ● vi ticken ● vt abhaken. **~ off** vt abhaken; 🄵 rüffeln

ticket /'tɪkɪt/ n Karte f; (for bus, train) Fahrschein m; (Aviat) Flugschein m; (for lottery) Los nt; (for article deposited) Schein m; (label) Schild nt; (for library) Lesekarte f; (fine) Strafzettel m. **~ collector** n Fahrkartenkontrolleur m. **~ office** n Fahrkartenschalter m; (for entry) Kasse f

tick|le /'tɪkl/ n Kitzeln nt ● vt/i kitzeln. **~lish** adj kitzlig

tidal /'taɪdl/ adj **~ wave** Flutwelle f

tide /taɪd/ n Gezeiten pl; (of events) Strom m; **the ~ is in/out** es ist Flut/Ebbe ● vt **~ s.o. over** jdm über die Runden helfen

tidiness /'taɪdɪnɪs/ n Ordentlichkeit f

tidy /'taɪdɪ/ adj , **-ily** adv ordentlich ● vt **~ [up]** aufräumen

tie /taɪ/ n Krawatte f, Schlips m; (cord) Schnur f; (fig: bond) Band nt; (restriction) Bindung f; (Sport) Unentschieden nt; (in competition) Punktgleichheit f ● v (pres p **tying**) ● vt binden; machen (knot) ● vi (Sport) unentschieden spielen; (have equal scores, votes) punktgleich sein.

t

~ **up** vt festbinden; verschnüren (*parcel*); fesseln (*person*); **be ~d up** (*busy*) beschäftigt sein

tier /tɪə(r)/ n Stufe f; (*of cake*) Etage f; (*in stadium*) Rang m

tiger /'taɪgə(r)/ n Tiger m

tight /taɪt/ adj (**-er, -est**) fest; (*taut*) straff; (*clothes*) eng; (*control*) streng; (🔟: *drunk*) blau ● adv fest

tighten /'taɪtn/ vt fester ziehen; straffen (*rope*); anziehen (*screw*); verschärfen (*control*) ● vi sich spannen

tightrope n Hochseil nt

tights /taɪts/ npl Strumpfhose f

tile /taɪl/ n Fliese f; (*on wall*) Kachel f; (*on roof*) [Dach]ziegel m ● vt mit Fliesen auslegen; kacheln (*wall*); decken (*roof*)

till[1] /tɪl/ prep & conj = **until**

till[2] n Kasse f

tilt /tɪlt/ n Neigung f ● vt kippen; [zur Seite] neigen (*head*) ● vi sich neigen

timber /'tɪmbə(r)/ n [Nutz]holz nt

time /taɪm/ n Zeit f; (*occasion*) Mal nt; (*rhythm*) Takt m; **~s** (*Math*) mal; **at ~s** manchmal; **~ and again** immer wieder; **two at a ~** zwei zur einmal; **on ~** pünktlich; **in ~** rechtzeitig; (*eventually*) mit der Zeit; **in no ~** im Handumdrehen; **in a year's ~** in einem Jahr; **behind ~** verspätet; **behind the ~s** rückständig; **for the ~ being** vorläufig; **what is the ~?** wie spät ist es? **did you have a nice ~?** hat es dir gut gefallen? ● vt stoppen (*race*); **be well ~d** gut abgepaßt sein

time: **~ bomb** n Zeitbombe f. **~less** adj zeitlos. **~ly** adj rechtzeitig. **~-switch** n Zeitschalter m. **~-table** n Fahrplan m; (*Sch*) Stundenplan m

timid /'tɪmɪd/ adj scheu; (*hesitant*) zaghaft

timing /'taɪmɪŋ/ n (*Sport, Techn*) Timing nt

tin /tɪn/ n Zinn nt; (*container*) Dose f ● vt (*pt/pp* **tinned**) in Dosen servieren. **~ foil** n Stanniol nt; (*Culin*) Alufolie f

tinge /tɪndʒ/ n Hauch m

tingle /'tɪŋgl/ vi kribbeln

tinker /'tɪŋkə(r)/ vi herumbasteln (**with** an + *dat*)

tinkle /'tɪŋkl/ n Klingeln nt ● vi klingeln

tinned /tɪnd/ adj Dosen-

'tin opener n Dosenöffner m

tinsel /'tɪnsl/ n Lametta nt

tint /tɪnt/ n Farbton m ● vt tönen

tiny /'taɪnɪ/ adj winzig

tip[1] /tɪp/ n Spitze f

tip[2] n (*money*) Trinkgeld nt; (*advice*) Rat m, 🔟 Tipp m; (*for rubbish*) Müllhalde f ● v (*pt/pp* **tipped**) ● vt (*tilt*) kippen; (*reward*) Trinkgeld geben (**s.o.** jdm) ● vi kippen. **~ out** vt auskippen. **~ over** vt/i umkippen

tipped /tɪpt/ adj Filter-

tipsy /'tɪpsɪ/ adj 🔟 beschwipst

tiptoe /'tɪptəʊ/ n **on ~** auf Zehenspitzen

tiptop /tɪp'tɒp/ adj 🔟 erstklassig

tire /'taɪə(r)/ vt/i ermüden. **~d** adj müde; **be ~d of** etw satt haben; **~d out** [völlig] erschöpft. **~less** adj unermüdlich. **~some** adj lästig

tiring /'taɪrɪŋ/ adj ermüdend

tissue /'tɪʃuː/ n Gewebe nt; (*handkerchief*) Papiertaschentuch nt

tit /tɪt/ n (*bird*) Meise f

'titbit n Leckerbissen m

title /'taɪtl/ n Titel m

to /tuː/, unbetont /tə/
● preposition
⋯▸ (destinations: most cases) zu (+ dat). **go to work/the station** zur Arbeit/zum Bahnhof gehen. **from house to house** von Haus zu Haus. **go/come to s.o.** zu jdm gehen/kommen

⋯▸ (with name of place or points of compass) nach. **to Paris/Germany** nach Paris/Deutschland. **to Switzerland** in die Schweiz. **from East to West** von Osten nach Westen. **I've never been to Berlin** ich war noch nie in Berlin

⋯▸ (to cinema, theatre, bed) in (+ acc). **to bed with you!** ins Bett mit dir!

⋯▸ (to wedding, party, university, the toilet) auf (+ acc).

⋯▸ (up to) bis zu (+ dat). **to the end** bis zum Schluss. **to this day** bis heute. **5 to 6 pounds** 5 bis 6 Pfund

⋯▸ (give, say, write) + dat. **give/ say sth to s.o.** jdm etw geben/ sagen. **she wrote to him/the firm** sie hat ihm/an die Firma geschrieben

⋯▸ (address, send, fasten) an (+ acc). **she sent it to her brother** sie schickte es an ihren Bruder

⋯▸ (in telling the time) vor. **five to eight** fünf vor acht. **a quarter to ten** Viertel vor zehn
● before infinitive
⋯▸ (after modal verb) (not translated). **I want to go** ich will gehen. **he is learning to swim** er lernt schwimmen. **you have to** du musst [es tun]

⋯▸ (after adjective) zu. **it is easy to forget** es ist leicht zu vergessen

⋯▸ (expressing purpose, result) um ... zu. **he did it to annoy me** er tat es, um mich zu ärgern. **she was too tired to go** sie war zu müde um zu gehen. **~er** n Toaster m
● adverb
⋯▸ **be to** (door, window) angelehnt sein. **pull a door to** eine Tür anlehnen

⋯▸ **to and fro** hin und her

toad /təʊd/ n Kröte f

toast /təʊst/ n Toast m ● vt toasten (bread); (drink a ~ to) trinken auf (+ acc). **~er** n Toaster m

tobacco /təˈbækəʊ/ n Tabak m. **~nist's [shop]** n Tabakladen m

toboggan /təˈbɒɡən/ n Schlitten m ● vi Schlitten fahren

today /təˈdeɪ/ n & adv heute; **~ week** heute in einer Woche

toddler /ˈtɒdlə(r)/ n Kleinkind nt

toe /təʊ/ n Zeh m; (of footwear) Spitze f ● vt **~ the line** spuren. **~nail** n Zehennagel m

toffee /ˈtɒfɪ/ n Karamell m & nt

together /təˈɡeðə(r)/ adv zusammen; (at the same time) gleichzeitig

toilet /ˈtɔɪlɪt/ n Toilette f. **~ bag** n Kulturbeutel m. **~ paper** n Toilettenpapier nt

toiletries /ˈtɔɪlɪtrɪz/ npl Toilettenartikel pl

token /ˈtəʊkən/ n Zeichen nt; (counter) Marke f; (voucher) Gutschein m ● attrib symbolisch

told /təʊld/ see **tell** ● adj **all ~** insgesamt

tolerable /ˈtɒlərəbl/ adj, **-bly** adv erträglich; (not bad) leidlich

toleran|ce /ˈtɒlərəns/ n Toleranz f. **~t** adj tolerant

tolerate /ˈtɒləreɪt/ vt dulden, tolerieren; (bear) ertragen

toll /təʊl/ n Gebühr f; (for road)
Maut f (Aust); **death ~** Zahl f der
Todesopfer

tomato /təˈmɑːtəʊ/ n (pl **-es**) Tomate f

tomb /tuːm/ n Grabmal nt

'tombstone n Grabstein m

'tom-cat n Kater m

tomorrow /təˈmɒrəʊ/ n & adv
morgen; **~ morning** morgen früh;
the day after ~ übermorgen; **see
you ~!** bis morgen!

ton /tʌn/ n Tonne f; **~s of** 🄸
jede Menge

tone /təʊn/ n Ton m; (colour) Farbton m • vt **~ down** dämpfen; (fig)
mäßigen. **~ up** vt kräftigen; straffen (muscles)

tongs /tɒŋz/ npl Zange f

tongue /tʌŋ/ n Zunge f; **~ in
cheek** 🄸 nicht ernst

tonic /ˈtɒnɪk/ n Tonikum nt; (for
hair) Haarwasser nt; (fig) Wohltat f;
~ [water] Tonic nt

tonight /təˈnaɪt/ n & adv heute
Nacht; (evening) heute Abend

tonne /tʌn/ n Tonne f

tonsil /ˈtɒnsl/ n (Anat) Mandel f.
~litis n Mandelentzündung f

too /tuː/ adv zu; (also) auch; **~
much/little** zu viel/zu wenig

took /tʊk/ see **take**

tool /tuːl/ n Werkzeug nt; (for gardening) Gerät nt. **~bar** n Werk-
zeugleiste f

tooth /tuːθ/ n (pl **teeth**) Zahn m

tooth: **~ache** n Zahnschmerzen
pl. **~brush** n Zahnbürste f. **~less**
adj zahnlos. **~paste** n Zahnpasta f.
~pick n Zahnstocher m

top[1] /tɒp/ n (toy) Kreisel m

top[2] n oberer Teil m; (upper) Spitze
f; (summit) Gipfel m; (Sch) Erste(r)
m/f; (top part or half) Oberteil nt;

(head) Kopfende nt; (of road) obe-
res Ende nt; (upper surface) Oberfläche f; (lid) Deckel m; (of bottle) Verschluss m; (garment) Top nt; **at
the/on ~** oben; **on ~** oben auf
(+ dat/acc); **on ~ of that** (besides)
obendrein; **from ~ to bottom** von
oben bis unten • adj oberste(r,s);
(highest) höchste(r,s); (best) be-
ste(r,s) • vt (pt/pp **topped**) an erster Stelle stehen auf (+ dat) (list);
(exceed) übersteigen; (remove the
of) die Spitze abschneiden von. **~
up** vt nachfüllen, auffüllen

top: **~ 'hat** n Zylinder[hut] m.
~-heavy adj kopflastig

topic /ˈtɒpɪk/ n Thema nt. **~al** adj
aktuell

topple /ˈtɒpl/ vt/i umstürzen

torch /tɔːtʃ/ n Taschenlampe f;
(flaming) Fackel f

tore /tɔː(r)/ see **tear**[1]

torment[1] /ˈtɔːment/ n Qual f

torment[2] /tɔːˈment/ vt quälen

torn /tɔːn/ see **tear**[1] • adj zerrissen

torpedo /tɔːˈpiːdəʊ/ n (pl **-es**) Torpedo m • vt torpedieren

torrent /ˈtɒrənt/ n reißender
Strom m. **~ial** adj (rain) wolken-
bruchartig

tortoise /ˈtɔːtəs/ n Schildkröte f.
~shell n Schildpatt nt

tortuous /ˈtɔːtjʊəs/ adj verschlun-
gen; (fig) umständlich

torture /ˈtɔːtʃə(r)/ n Folter f; (fig)
Qual f • vt foltern; (fig) quälen

toss /tɒs/ vt werfen; (into the air)
hochwerfen; (shake) schütteln; (un-
seat) abwerfen; mischen (salad);
wenden (pancake); **~ a coin** mit
einer Münze losen • vi **~ and turn**
(in bed) sich [schlaflos] im Bett
wälzen

tot[1] /tɒt/ n kleines Kind nt; (🄸: of
liquor) Gläschen nt

tot² vt (pt/pp **totted**) ~ **up** ⟦T⟧ zusammenzählen

total /'təʊtl/ adj gesamt; (complete) völlig, total ●n Gesamtzahl f; (sum) Gesamtsumme f ●vt (pt/pp **totalled**); (amount to) sich belaufen auf (+ acc)

totalitarian /təʊtælɪˈteərɪən/ adj totalitär

totally /'təʊtəlɪ/ adv völlig, total

totter /'tɒtə(r)/ vi taumeln

touch /tʌtʃ/ n Berührung f; (sense) Tastsinn m; (Mus) Anschlag m; (contact) Kontakt m; (trace) Spur f; (fig) Anflug m; **get/be in** ~ sich in Verbindung setzen/in Verbindung stehen (**with** mit) ●vt berühren; (get hold of) anfassen; (lightly) tippen auf/an (+ acc); (brush against) streifen [gegen]; (fig: move) rühren; anrühren (food, subject); **don't** ~ **that!** fass das nicht an! ●vi sich berühren; ~ **on** (fig) berühren. ~ **down** vi (Aviat) landen. ~ **up** vt ausbessern

touch|ing /'tʌtʃɪŋ/ adj rührend. ~y adj empfindlich

tough /tʌf/ adj (**-er, -est**) zäh; (severe, harsh) hart; (difficult) schwierig; (durable) strapazierfähig

toughen /'tʌfn/ vt härten; ~ **up** abhärten

tour /tʊə(r)/ n Reise f, Tour f; (of building, town) Besichtigung f; (Theat, Sport) Tournee f; (of duty) Dienstzeit f ●vt fahren durch ●vi herumreisen

touris|m /'tʊərɪzm/ n Tourismus m, Fremdenverkehr m. ~t n Tourist(in) m(f) ●attrib Touristen-. ~t **office** n Fremdenverkehrsbüro nt

tournament /'tʊənəmənt/ n Turnier nt

'tour operator n Reiseveranstalter m

tousle /'taʊzl/ vt zerzausen

tow /təʊ/ n **give s.o./a car a** ~ jdn/ein Auto abschleppen ●vt schleppen; ziehen (trailer)

toward[s] /tə'wɔːdz/ prep zu (+ dat); (with time) gegen (+ acc); (with respect to) gegenüber (+ dat)

towel /'taʊəl/ n Handtuch nt. ~**ling** n (cloth) Frottee nt

tower /'taʊə(r)/ n Turm m ●vi ~ **above** überragen. ~**block** n Hochhaus nt. ~**ing** adj hoch aufragend

town /taʊn/ n Stadt f. ~ **'hall** n Rathaus nt

tow-rope n Abschleppseil nt

toxic /'tɒksɪk/ adj giftig

toy /tɔɪ/ n Spielzeug nt ●vi ~ **with** spielen mit; stochern in (+ dat) (food). ~**shop** n Spielwarengeschäft nt

trac|e /treɪs/ n Spur f ●vt folgen (+ dat); (find) finden; (draw) zeichnen; (with tracing-paper) durchpausen

track /træk/ n Spur f; (path) [unbefestigter] Weg m; (Sport) Bahn f; (Rail) Gleis nt; **keep** ~ **of** im Auge behalten ●vt verfolgen. ~ **down** vt aufspüren; (find) finden

'tracksuit n Trainingsanzug m

tractor /'træktə(r)/ n Traktor m

trade /treɪd/ n Handel m; (line of business) Gewerbe nt; (business) Geschäft nt; (craft) Handwerk nt; **by** ~ von Beruf ●vi tauschen; ~ **in** (give in part exchange) in Zahlung geben ●vi handeln (**in** mit)

'trade mark n Warenzeichen nt

trader /'treɪdə(r)/ n Händler m

trade: ~ **'union** n Gewerkschaft f. ~ **'unionist** n Gewerkschaftler(in) m(f)

trading /'treɪdɪŋ/ n Handel m

tradition /trə'dɪʃn/ n Tradition f. ~**al** adj traditionell

t

traffic /'træfɪk/ n Verkehr m; (trading) Handel m

traffic: ~ circle n (Amer) Kreisverkehr m. **~ jam** n [Verkehrs]stau m. **~ lights** npl [Verkehrs]ampel f. **~ warden** n ≈ Hilfspolizist m; (woman) Politesse f

tragedy /'trædʒədɪ/ n Tragödie f

tragic /'trædʒɪk/ adj, **-ally** adv tragisch

trail /treɪl/ n Spur f; (path) Weg m, Pfad m ● vi schleifen; (plant:) sich ranken ● vt verfolgen, folgen (+ dat); (drag) schleifen

trailer /'treɪlə(r)/ n (Auto) Anhänger m; (Amer: caravan) Wohnwagen m; (film) Vorschau f

train /treɪn/ n Zug m; (of dress) Schleppe f ● vt ausbilden; (Sport) trainieren; (aim) richten auf (+ acc); erziehen (child); abrichten/(to do tricks) dressieren (animal); ziehen (plant) ● vi eine Ausbildung machen; (Sport) trainieren. **~ed** adj ausgebildet

trainee /treɪ'niː/ n Auszubildende(r) m/f; (Techn) Praktikant(in) m(f)

train|er /'treɪnə(r)/ n (Sport) Trainer m; (in circus) Dompteur m; **~ers** pl Trainingsschuhe pl. **~ing** n Ausbildung f; (Sport) Training nt; (of animals) Dressur f

trait /treɪt/ n Eigenschaft f

traitor /'treɪtə(r)/ n Verräter m

tram /træm/ n Straßenbahn f

tramp /træmp/ n Landstreicher m ● vi stapfen; (walk) marschieren

trample /'træmpl/ vt/i trampeln

trance /trɑːns/ n Trance f

tranquil /'træŋkwɪl/ adj ruhig. **~lity** n Ruhe f

tranquillizer /'træŋkwɪlaɪzə(r)/ n Beruhigungsmittel nt

transaction /træn'zækʃn/ n Transaktion f

transcend /træn'send/ vt übersteigen

transfer[1] /'trænsfɜː(r)/ n (see transfer[2]) Übertragung f; Verlegung f; Versetzung f; Überweisung f; (Sport) Transfer m; (design) Abziehbild nt

transfer[2] /træns'fɜː(r)/ v (pt/pp transferred) ● vt übertragen; verlegen (firm, prisoners); versetzen (employee); überweisen (money); (Sport) transferieren ● vi [über]wechseln; (when travelling) umsteigen

transform /træns'fɔːm/ vt verwandeln. **~ation** n Verwandlung f. **~er** n Transformator m

transfusion /træns'fjuːʒn/ n Transfusion f

transistor /træn'zɪstə(r)/ n Transistor m

transit /'trænsɪt/ n Transit m; (of goods) Transport m; **in ~** (goods) auf dem Transport

transition /træn'sɪʒn/ n Übergang m. **~al** adj Übergangs-

translat|e /træns'leɪt/ vt übersetzen. **~ion** n Übersetzung f. **~or** n Übersetzer(in) m(f)

transmission /trænz'mɪʃn/ n Übertragung f

transmit /trænz'mɪt/ vt (pt/pp transmitted) übertragen. **~ter** n Sender m

transparen|cy /træns'pærənsɪ/ n (Phot) Dia nt. **~t** adj durchsichtig

transplant[1] /'trænsplɑːnt/ n Verpflanzung f, Transplantation f

transplant[2] /træns'plɑːnt/ vt umpflanzen; (Med) verpflanzen

transport[1] /'trænspɔːt/ n Transport m

transport[2] /træn'spɔːt/ vt transportieren. **~ation** n Transport m

transpose /træns'pəʊz/ vt

umstellen

trap /træp/ n Falle f; (🔲: *mouth*) Klappe f; **pony and** ~ Einspänner m ● vt (pt/pp **trapped**) [mit einer Falle] fangen; (*jam*) einklemmen; **be** ~**ped** festsitzen; (*shut in*) eingeschlossen sein. ~'**door** n Falltür f

trash /træʃ/ n Schund m; (*rubbish*) Abfall m; (*nonsense*) Quatsch m. ~**can** n (*Amer*) Mülleimer m. ~**y** adj Schund-

trauma /'trɔːmə/ n Trauma nt. ~**tic** adj traumatisch

travel /'trævl/ n Reisen nt ● v (pt/pp **travelled**) ● vi reisen; (*go in vehicle*) fahren; (*light, sound:*) sich fortpflanzen; (*Techn*) sich bewegen ● vt bereisen; fahren (*distance*). ~ **agency** n Reisebüro nt. ~ **agent** n Reisebürokaufmann m

traveller /'trævələ(r)/ n Reisende(r) m/f; (*Comm*) Vertreter m; ~**s** pl (*gypsies*) Zigeuner pl. ~**'s cheque** n Reisescheck m

trawler /'trɔːlə(r)/ n Fischdampfer m

tray /treɪ/ n Tablett nt; (*for baking*) [Back]blech nt; (*for documents*) Ablagekorb m

treacherous /'tretʃərəs/ adj treulos; (*dangerous, deceptive*) tückisch. ~**y** n Verrat m

tread /tred/ n Schritt m; (*step*) Stufe f; (*of tyre*) Profil m ● v (pt **trod**, pp **trodden**) ● vi (*walk*) gehen; ~ **on/in** treten auf/in (+ acc) ● vt treten

treason /'triːzn/ n Verrat m

treasure /'treʒə(r)/ n Schatz m ● vt in Ehren halten. ~**r** n Kassenwart m

treasury /'treʒərɪ/ n Schatzkammer f, **the T**~ das Finanzministerium

treat /triːt/ n [besonderes] Vergnü-

gen nt ● vt behandeln; ~ **s.o. to sth** jdm etw spendieren

treatment /'triːtmənt/ n Behandlung f

treaty /'triːtɪ/ n Vertrag m

treble /'trebl/ adj dreifach; ~ **the amount** dreimal so viel ● n (*Mus*) Diskant m; (*voice*) Sopran m ● vt verdreifachen ● vi sich verdreifachen

tree /triː/ n Baum m

trek /trek/ n Marsch m ● vi (pt/pp **trekked**) latschen

trellis /'trelɪs/ n Gitter nt

tremble /'trembl/ vi zittern

tremendous /trɪ'mendəs/ adj gewaltig; (🔲: *excellent*) großartig

tremor /'tremə(r)/ n Zittern nt; [earth] ~ Beben nt

trench /trentʃ/ n Graben m; (*Mil*) Schützengraben m

trend /trend/ n Tendenz f; (*fashion*) Trend m. ~**y** adj 🔲 modisch

trepidation /trepɪ'deɪʃn/ n Beklommenheit f

trespass /'trespəs/ vi ~ **on** unerlaubt betreten

trial /'traɪəl/ n (*Jur*) [Gerichts]verfahren nt, Prozess m; (*test*) Probe f; (*ordeal*) Prüfung f; **be on** ~ auf Probe sein; (*Jur*) angeklagt sein (**for** wegen); **by** ~ **and error** durch Probieren

triang|le /'traɪæŋgl/ n Dreieck nt; (*Mus*) Triangel m. ~**ular** adj dreieckig

tribe /traɪb/ n Stamm m

tribunal /traɪ'bjuːnl/ n Schiedsgericht nt

tributary /'trɪbjʊtərɪ/ n Nebenfluss m

tribute /'trɪbjuːt/ n Tribut m; **pay** ~ Tribut zollen (**to** dat)

trick /trɪk/ n Trick m; (*joke*) Streich m; (*Cards*) Stich m; (*feat of skill*)

Kunststück nt ● vt täuschen, ⊞ hereinlegen

trickle /'trɪkl/ vi rinnen

trick|ster /'trɪkstə(r)/ n Schwindler m. **~y** adj schwierig

tricycle /'traɪsɪkl/ n Dreirad nt

tried /traɪd/ see try

trifl|e /'traɪfl/ n Kleinigkeit f; (Culin) Trifle nt. **~ing** adj unbedeutend

trigger /'trɪgə(r)/ n Abzug m; (fig) Auslöser m ● vt ~ [off] auslösen

trim /trɪm/ adj (trimmer, trimmest) gepflegt ● n (cut) Nachschneiden nt; (decoration) Verzierung f; (condition) Zustand m ● vt schneiden; (decorate) besetzen. **~ming** n Besatz m; **~mings** pl (accessories) Zubehör nt; (decorations) Verzierungen pl

trio /'triːəʊ/ n Trio nt

trip /trɪp/ n Reise f; (excursion) Ausflug m ● v (pt/pp tripped) ● vt ~ s.o. up jdm ein Bein stellen ● vi stolpern (on/over über + acc)

tripe /traɪp/ n Kaldaunen pl; (nonsense) Quatsch m

triple /'trɪpl/ adj dreifach ● vt verdreifachen ● vi sich verdreifachen

triplets /'trɪplɪts/ npl Drillinge pl

triplicate /'trɪplɪkət/ n in dreifacher Ausfertigung

tripod /'traɪpɒd/ n Stativ nt

tripper /'trɪpə(r)/ n Ausflügler m

trite /traɪt/ adj banal

triumph /'traɪʌmf/ n Triumph m ● vi triumphieren (over über + acc). **~ant** adj triumphierend

trivial /'trɪvɪəl/ adj belanglos. **~ity** n Belanglosigkeit f

trod, trodden see tread

trolley /'trɒlɪ/ n (for food) Servierwagen m; (for shopping) Einkaufswagen m; (for luggage) Kofferkuli m; (Amer: tram) Straßenbahn f

trombone /trɒm'bəʊn/ n Posaune f

troop /truːp/ n Schar f; **~s** pl Truppen pl

trophy /'trəʊfɪ/ n Trophäe f; (in competition) ≈ Pokal m

tropics /'trɒpɪks/ npl Tropen pl. **~al** adj tropisch; (fruit) Süd-

trot /trɒt/ n Trab m ● vi (pt/pp trotted) traben

trouble /'trʌbl/ n Ärger m; (difficulties) Schwierigkeiten pl; (inconvenience) Mühe f; (conflict) Unruhe f; (Med) Beschwerden pl; (Techn) Probleme pl; **get into** ~ Ärger bekommen; **take** ~ sich (dat) Mühe geben ● vt (disturb) stören; (worry) beunruhigen ● vi sich bemühen. **~-maker** n Unruhestifter m. **~some** adj schwierig; (flies, cough) lästig

trough /trɒf/ n Trog m

troupe /truːp/ n Truppe f

trousers /'traʊzəz/ npl Hose f

trousseau /'truːsəʊ/ n Aussteuer f

trout /traʊt/ n inv Forelle f

trowel /'traʊəl/ n Kelle f

truant /'truːənt/ n **play** ~ die Schule schwänzen

truce /truːs/ n Waffenstillstand m

truck /trʌk/ n Last[kraft]wagen m; (Rail) Güterwagen m

trudge /trʌdʒ/ vi latschen

true /truː/ adj (-r, -st) wahr; (loyal) treu; (genuine) echt; **come** ~ in Erfüllung gehen; **is that** ~? stimmt das?

truly /'truːlɪ/ adv wirklich; (faithfully) treu; **Yours** ~ mit freundlichen Grüßen

trump /trʌmp/ n (Cards) Trumpf m ● vt übertrumpfen

trumpet /'trʌmpɪt/ n Trompete f. **~er** n Trompeter m

truncheon /'trʌntʃn/ n Schlagstock m

trunk /trʌŋk/ n [Baum]stamm m; (body) Rumpf m; (of elephant) Rüssel m; (for travelling) [Übersee]koffer m; (Amer: of car) Kofferraum m. **~s** pl Badehose f

trust /trʌst/ n Vertrauen nt; (group of companies) Trust m; (organization) Treuhandgesellschaft f; (charitable) Stiftung f ● vt trauen (+ dat), vertrauen (+ dat); (hope) hoffen ● vi vertrauen (in/to auf + acc)

trustee /trʌs'tiː/ n Treuhänder m

'trust|ful /'trʌstfl/ adj, **-ly** adv, **~ing** adj vertrauensvoll. **~worthy** adj vertrauenswürdig

truth /truːθ/ n (pl **-s** /truːðz/) Wahrheit f. **~ful** adj ehrlich

try /traɪ/ n Versuch m ● v (pt/pp **tried**) ● vt versuchen; (sample, taste) probieren; (be a strain on) anstrengen; (Jur) vor Gericht stellen; verhandeln (case) ● vi versuchen; (make an effort) sich bemühen. **~ on** vt anprobieren; aufprobieren (hat). **~ out** vt ausprobieren

trying /'traɪɪŋ/ adj schwierig

T-shirt /'tiː-/ n T-Shirt nt

tub /tʌb/ n Kübel m; (carton) Becher m; (bath) Wanne f

tuba /'tjuːbə/ n (Mus) Tuba f

tubby /'tʌbɪ/ adj rundlich

tube /tjuːb/ n Röhre f; (pipe) Rohr nt; (flexible) Schlauch m; (of toothpaste) Tube f; (Rail, 🔢) U-Bahn f

tuberculosis /tjuːbɜːkjʊ'ləʊsɪs/ n Tuberkulose f

tubular /'tjuːbjʊlə(r)/ adj röhrenförmig

tuck /tʌk/ n Saum m; (decorative) Biese f ● vt (put) stecken. **~ in** vt hineinstecken; **~ s.o. in** vt jdm zudecken ● vi (🔢: eat) zulangen

Tuesday /'tjuːzdeɪ/ n Dienstag m

tuft /tʌft/ n Büschel nt

tug /tʌg/ n Ruck m; (Naut) Schleppdampfer m ● v (pt/pp **tugged**) ● vt ziehen ● vi zerren (**at** an + dat)

tuition /tjuː'ɪʃn/ n Unterricht m

tulip /'tjuːlɪp/ n Tulpe f

tumble /'tʌmbl/ n Sturz m ● vi fallen. **~down** adj verfallen. **~drier** n Wäschetrockner m

tumbler /'tʌmblə(r)/ n Glas nt

tummy /'tʌmɪ/ n 🔢 Bauch m

tumour /'tjuːmə(r)/ n Tumor m

tumult /'tjuːmʌlt/ n Tumult m

tuna /'tjuːnə/ n Thunfisch m

tune /tjuːn/ n Melodie f; **out of ~** (instrument) verstimmt ● vt stimmen; (Techn) einstellen. **~ in** vt einstellen ● vi **~ in to a station** einen Sender einstellen. **~ up** vi (Mus) stimmen

tuneful /'tjuːnfl/ adj melodisch

Tunisia /tjuː'nɪzɪə/ n Tunesien nt

tunnel /'tʌnl/ n Tunnel m ● vi (pt/pp **tunnelled**) einen Tunnel graben

turban /'tɜːbən/ n Turban m

turbine /'tɜːbaɪn/ n Turbine f

turbulen|ce /'tɜːbjʊləns/ n Turbulenz f. **~t** adj stürmisch

turf /tɜːf/ n Rasen m; (segment) Rasenstück nt

Turk /tɜːk/ n Türke m/Türkin f

turkey /'tɜːkɪ/ n Truthahn m

Turk|ey n die Türkei. **~ish** adj türkisch

turmoil /'tɜːmɔɪl/ n Aufruhr m; (confusion) Durcheinander nt

turn /tɜːn/ n (rotation) Drehung f; (bend) Kurve f; (change of direction) Wende f; (Theat) Nummer f; (🔢: attack) Anfall m; **do s.o. a good ~** jdm einen guten Dienst erweisen; **take ~s** sich abwechseln; **in ~** der Reihe nach; **out of ~** außer der Reihe; **it's your ~** du bist an der

Reihe ● vt drehen; (~ over) wenden; (reverse) umdrehen; (Techn) drechseln (wood); ~ **the page** umblättern; ~ **the corner** um die Ecke biegen ● vi sich drehen; (~ round) sich umdrehen; (car:) wenden; (leaves:) sich färben; (weather:) umschlagen; (become) werden; ~ **right/left** nach rechts/links abbiegen; ~ **to s.o.** sich an jdn wenden. ~ **away** vt abweisen ● vi sich abwenden. ~ **down** vt herunterschlagen (collar); herunterdrehen (heat, gas); leiser stellen (sound); (reject) ablehnen; abweisen (person). ~ **in** vt einschlagen (edges) ● vi (car:) einbiegen; (🔲: go to bed) ins Bett gehen. ~ **off** vt zudrehen (tap); ausschalten (light, radio); abstellen (water, gas, engine, machine) ● vi abbiegen. ~ **on** vt aufdrehen (tap); einschalten (light, radio); anstellen (water, gas, engine, machine). ~ **out** vt (expel) vertreiben, (throw out) hinauswerfen; ausschalten (light); hinausdrehen (gas); (produce) produzieren; (empty) ausleeren; [gründlich] aufräumen (room, cupboard) ● vi (go out) hinausgehen; (transpire) sich herausstellen. ~ **over** vt umdrehen. ~ **up** vt hochschlagen (collar); aufdrehen (heat, gas); lauter stellen (sound, radio) ● vi auftauchen

turning /ˈtɜːnɪŋ/ n Abzweigung f. **~-point** n Wendepunkt m

turnip /ˈtɜːnɪp/ n weiße Rübe f

turn: ~**-out** n (of people) Beteiligung f. ~**-over** n (Comm) Umsatz m; (of staff) Personalwechsel m. ~**pike** n (Amer) gebührenpflichtige Autobahn f. ~**table** n Drehscheibe f; (on record player) Plattenteller m. ~**-up** n [Hosen]aufschlag m

turquoise /ˈtɜːkwɔɪz/ adj türkis[farben] ● n (gem) Türkis m

turret /ˈtʌrɪt/ n Türmchen nt

turtle /ˈtɜːtl/ n Seeschildkröte f

tusk /tʌsk/ n Stoßzahn m

tutor /ˈtjuːtə(r)/ n [Privat]lehrer m

tuxedo /tʌkˈsiːdəʊ/ n (Amer) Smoking m

TV /tiːˈviː/ abbr **television**

tweed /twiːd/ n Tweed m

tweezers /ˈtwiːzəz/ npl Pinzette f

twelfth /twelfθ/ adj zwölfter(r,s)

twelve /twelv/ adj zwölf

twentieth /ˈtwentɪɪθ/ adj zwanzigste(r,s)

twenty /ˈtwentɪ/ adj zwanzig

twice /twaɪs/ adv zweimal

twig /twɪg/ n Zweig m

twilight /ˈtwaɪ-/ n Dämmerlicht nt

twin /twɪn/ n Zwilling m ● attrib Zwillings-

twine /twaɪn/ n Bindfaden m

twinge /twɪndʒ/ n Stechen nt; ~ **of conscience** Gewissensbisse pl

twinkle /ˈtwɪŋkl/ n Funkeln nt ● vi funkeln

twin 'town n Partnerstadt f

twirl /twɜːl/ vt/i herumwirbeln

twist /twɪst/ n Drehung f; (curve) Kurve f; (unexpected occurrence) überraschende Wendung f ● vt drehen; (distort) verdrehen; (🔲: swindle) beschummeln; ~ **one's ankle** sich (dat) den Knöchel verrenken ● vi sich drehen; (road:) sich winden. ~**er** n 🔲 Schwindler m

twit /twɪt/ n 🔲 Trottel m

twitch /twɪtʃ/ n Zucken nt ● vi zucken

twitter /ˈtwɪtə(r)/ n Zwitschern nt ● vi zwitschern

two /tuː/ adj zwei

two: ~**-faced** adj falsch. ~**-piece** adj zweiteilig. ~**-way** adj ~**-way traffic** Gegenverkehr m

tycoon /taɪˈkuːn/ n Magnat m

tying /'taɪɪŋ/ *see* tie

type /taɪp/ n Art f, Sorte f; (*person*) Typ m; (*printing*) Type f ● vt mit der Maschine schreiben, 🇩 tippen ● vi Maschine schreiben, 🇩 tippen.
~writer n Schreibmaschine f.
~written adj maschinegeschrieben

typical /'tɪpɪkl/ adj typisch (**of** für)

typify /'tɪpɪfaɪ/ vt (pt/pp **-ied**) typisch sein für

typing /'taɪpɪŋ/ n Maschineschreiben nt

typist /'taɪpɪst/ n Schreibkraft f

tyrannical /tɪ'rænɪkl/ adj tyrannisch

tyranny /'tɪrənɪ/ n Tyrannei f

tyrant /'taɪrənt/ n Tyrann m

tyre /'taɪə(r)/ n Reifen m

· ·

Uu

ugl|iness /'ʌglɪnɪs/ n Hässlichkeit f. **~y** adj hässlich; (*nasty*) übel

UK abbr United Kingdom

ulcer /'ʌlsə(r)/ n Geschwür nt

ultimate /'ʌltɪmət/ adj letzte(r,s); (*final*) endgültig; (*fundamental*) grundlegend, eigentlich. **~ly** adv schließlich

ultimatum /ʌltɪ'meɪtəm/ n Ultimatum nt

ultra'violet adj ultraviolett

umbrella /ʌm'brelə/ n [Regen-]schirm m

umpire /'ʌmpaɪə(r)/ n Schiedsrichter m ● vt/i Schiedsrichter sein (bei)

umpteen /ʌmp'ti:n/ adj 🇩 zig. **~th** adj 🇩 zigste(r,s)

un'able /ʌn-/ adj be **~** to do sth

etw nicht tun können

una'bridged adj ungekürzt

unac'companied adj ohne Begleitung; (*luggage*) unbegleitet

unac'countable adj unerklärlich

unac'customed adj ungewohnt; be **~** to sth etw (acc) nicht gewohnt sein

un'aided adj ohne fremde Hilfe

unanimous /ju:'nænɪməs/ adj einmütig; (*vote, decision*) einstimmig

un'armed adj unbewaffnet

unas'suming adj bescheiden

unat'tended adj unbeaufsichtigt

un'authorized adj unbefugt

una'voidable adj unvermeidlich

una'ware adj be **~** of sth sich (dat) etw (gen) nicht bewusst sein. **~s** adv catch s.o. **~s** jdn überraschen

un'bearable adj, **-bly** adv unerträglich

unbeat|able /ʌn'bi:təbl/ adj unschlagbar. **~en** adj ungeschlagen; (*record*) ungebrochen

unbe'lievable adj unglaublich

un'biased adj unvoreingenommen

un'block vt frei machen

un'bolt vt aufriegeln

un'breakable adj unzerbrechlich

un'button vt aufknöpfen

uncalled-for /ʌn'kɔ:ldfɔ:(r)/ adj unangebracht

un'canny adj unheimlich

un'ceasing adj unaufhörlich

un'certain adj (*doubtful*) ungewiss; (*origins*) unbestimmt; be **~** nicht sicher sein. **~ty** n Ungewissheit f

un'changed adj unverändert

un'charitable adj lieblos

uncle /'ʌŋkl/ n Onkel m

Uncle Sam Eine Bezeichnung für die USA und ihre Einwohner. Meist dargestellt durch einen mit Frack und Zylinder in den Farben und mit den Sternen der Nationalflagge bekleideten hageren Mann mit weißen Haaren und Backenbart. Die Bezeichnung ist besonders durch das Poster von 1917 zur Rekrutierung von Soldaten 'I want you' bekannt geworden.

i

un'comforta|ble *adj*, -bly *adv* unbequem; **feel ~** (*fig*) sich nicht wohl fühlen

un'common *adj* ungewöhnlich

un'compromising *adj* kompromisslos

uncon'ditional *adj*, ~ly *adv* bedingungslos

un'conscious *adj* bewusstlos; (*unintended*) unbewusst; **be ~ of sth** sich (*dat*) etw (*gen*) nicht bewusst sein. **~ly** *adv* unbewusst

uncon'ventional *adj* unkonventionell

unco'operative *adj* nicht hilfsbereit

un'cork *vt* entkorken

un'couth /ʌnˈkuːθ/ *adj* ungehobelt

un'cover *vt* aufdecken

unde'cided *adj* unentschlossen; (*not settled*) nicht entschieden

undeniable /ˌʌndɪˈnaɪəbl/ *adj*, -bly *adv* unbestreitbar

under /ˈʌndə(r)/ *prep* unter (+ *dat/ acc*); **~ it** darunter; **~ there** drunter; **~ repair** in Reparatur; **~ construction** im Bau; **~ age** minderjährig ● *adv* darunter

'undercarriage *n* (*Aviat*) Fahrwerk *nt*, Fahrgestell *nt*

'underclothes *npl* Unterwäsche *f*

under'cover *adj* geheim

'undercurrent *n* Unterströmung *f*; (*fig*) Unterton *m*

'underdog *n* Unterlegene(r) *m*

under'done *adj* nicht gar; (*rare*) nicht durchgebraten

under'estimate *vt* unterschätzen

under'fed *adj* unterernährt

under'foot *adv* am Boden

under'go *vt* (*pt* -went, *pp* -gone) durchmachen; sich unterziehen (+ *dat*) (*operation, treatment*)

under'graduate *n* Student(in) *m* (*f*)

under'ground¹ *adv* unter der Erde; (*mining*) unter Tage

'underground² *adj* unterirdisch; (*secret*) Untergrund- ● *n* (*railway*) U-Bahn *f*. **~ car park** in Tiefgarage *f*

'undergrowth *n* Unterholz *nt*

'underhand *adj* hinterhältig

under'lie *vt* (*pt* -lay, *pp* -lain, *pres p* -lying) zugrunde liegen (+ *dat*)

under'line *vt* unterstreichen

under'lying *adj* eigentlich

under'mine *vt* (*fig*) unterminieren, untergraben

underneath /ˌʌndəˈniːθ/ *prep* unter (+ *dat/acc*) ● *adv* darunter

'underpants *npl* Unterhose *f*

'underpass *n* Unterführung *f*

under'privileged *adj* unterprivilegiert

under'rate *vt* unterschätzen

'undershirt *n* (*Amer*) Unterhemd *nt*

under'stand *vt/i* (*pt/pp* -stood) verstehen; **I ~ that ...** (*have heard*) ich habe gehört, dass ... **~able** *adj* verständlich. **~ably** *adv* verständlicherweise

under'standing *adj* verständnisvoll ● *n* Verständnis *nt*; (*agreement*)

Vereinbarung f; **reach an ~** sich verständigen

'understatement n Untertreibung f

under'take vt (pt -**took**, pp -**taken**) unternehmen; **~ to do sth** sich verpflichten, etw zu tun

'undertaker n Leichenbestatter m; **[firm of] ~s** Bestattungsinstitut n

under'taking n Unternehmen nt; (promise) Versprechen nt

'undertone n (fig) Unterton m; **in an ~** mit gedämpfter Stimme

under'value vt unterbewerten

'underwater[1] adj Unterwasser-

under'water[2] adv unter Wasser

'underwear n Unterwäsche f

'underweight adj untergewichtig; **be ~** Untergewicht haben

'underworld n Unterwelt f

unde'sirable adj unerwünscht

un'dignified adj würdelos

un'do vt (pt -**did**, pp -**done**) aufmachen; (fig) ungeschehen machen

un'done adj offen; (not accomplished) unerledigt

un'doubted adj unzweifelhaft. **~ly** adv zweifellos

un'dress vt ausziehen; **get ~ed** sich ausziehen ● vi sich ausziehen

un'due adj übermäßig

und'uly adv übermäßig

un'earth vt ausgraben; (fig) zutage bringen. **~ly** adj unheimlich; **at an ~ly hour** 🄸 in aller Herrgottsfrühe

un'easy adj unbehaglich

uneco'nomic adj, **-ally** adv unwirtschaftlich

unem'ployed adj arbeitslos ● npl **the ~** die Arbeitslosen

unem'ployment n Arbeitslosigkeit f

un'ending adj endlos

un'equal adj unterschiedlich; (struggle) ungleich. **~ly** adv ungleichmäßig

unequivocal /ʌnɪˈkwɪvəkl/ adj eindeutig

un'ethical adj unmoralisch; **be ~** gegen das Berufsethos verstoßen

un'even adj uneben; (unequal) ungleich; (not regular) ungleichmäßig; (number) ungerade

unex'pected adj unerwartet

un'fair adj ungerecht, unfair. **~ness** n Ungerechtigkeit f

un'faithful adj untreu

unfa'miliar adj ungewohnt; (unknown) unbekannt

un'fasten vt aufmachen; (detach) losmachen

un'favourable adj ungünstig

un'feeling adj gefühllos

un'fit adj ungeeignet; (incompetent) unfähig; (Sport) nicht fit; **~ for work** arbeitsunfähig

un'fold vt auseinander falten, entfalten; (spread out) ausbreiten ● vi sich entfalten

unfore'seen adj unvorhergesehen

unforgettable /ʌnfəˈgetəbl/ adj unvergesslich

unforgivable /ʌnfəˈgɪvəbl/ adj unverzeihlich

un'fortunate adj unglücklich; (unfavourable) ungünstig; (regrettable) bedauerlich; **be ~** (person): Pech haben. **~ly** adv leider

un'founded adj unbegründet

un'furl /ʌnˈfɜːl/ vt entrollen

un'furnished adj unmöbliert

un'gainly /ʌnˈgeɪnlɪ/ adj unbeholfen

un'grateful adj undankbar

un'happiness n Kummer m

un'happy adj unglücklich; (not

u

content) unzufrieden

un'harmed *adj* unverletzt

un'healthy *adj* ungesund

un'hurt *adj* unverletzt

unification /juːnɪfɪ'keɪʃn/ *n* Einigung *f*

uniform /'juːnɪfɔːm/ *adj* einheitlich ● *n* Uniform *f*

unify /'juːnɪfaɪ/ *vt (pt/pp* **-ied)** einigen

uni'lateral /juːnɪ-/ *adj* einseitig

uni'maginable *adj* unvorstellbar

unim'portant *adj* unwichtig

unin'habited *adj* unbewohnt

unin'tentional *adj* unabsichtlich

union /'juːnɪən/ *n* Vereinigung *f*; *(Pol)* Union *f*; *(trade* ∼*)* Gewerkschaft *f*

unique /juː'niːk/ *adj* einzigartig. ∼**ly** *adv* einmalig

unison /'juːnɪsn/ *n* in ∼ einstimmig

unit /'juːnɪt/ *n* Einheit *f*; *(Math)* Einer *m*; *(of furniture)* Teil *nt*, Element *nt*

unite /juː'naɪt/ *vt* vereinigen ● *vi* sich vereinigen

united /juː'naɪtɪd/ *adj* einig. **U**∼ **'Kingdom** *n* Vereinigtes Königreich *nt*. **U**∼ **'Nations** *n* Vereinte Nationen *pl*. **U**∼ **States [of America]** *n* Vereinigte Staaten *pl* [von Amerika]

unity /'juːnɪtɪ/ *n* Einheit *f*; *(harmony)* Einigkeit *f*

universal /juːnɪ'vɜːsl/ *adj* allgemein

universe /'juːnɪvɜːs/ *n* [Welt]all *nt*, Universum *nt*

university /juːnɪ'vɜːsətɪ/ *n* Universität *f* ● *attrib* Universitäts-

un'just *adj* ungerecht

un'kind *adj* unfreundlich; *(harsh)* hässlich

un'known *adj* unbekannt

un'lawful *adj* gesetzwidrig

unleaded /ʌn'ledɪd/ *adj* bleifrei

un'leash *vt (fig)* entfesseln

unless /ən'les/ *conj* wenn ... nicht; ∼ **I am mistaken** wenn ich mich nicht irre

un'like *prep* im Gegensatz zu (+ *dat*)

un'likely *adj* unwahrscheinlich

un'limited *adj* unbegrenzt

un'load *vt* entladen; ausladen *(luggage)*

un'lock *vt* aufschließen

un'lucky *adj* unglücklich; *(day, number)* Unglücks-; **be** ∼ Pech haben; *(thing:)* Unglück bringen

un'married *adj* unverheiratet. ∼ **'mother** *n* ledige Mutter *f*

un'mask *vt (fig)* entlarven

unmistakable /ʌnmɪ'steɪkəbl/ *adj*, **-bly** *adv* unverkennbar

un'natural *adj* unnatürlich; *(not normal)* nicht normal

un'necessary *adj*, **-ily** *adv* unnötig

un'noticed *adj* unbemerkt

unob'tainable *adj* nicht erhältlich

unob'trusive *adj* unaufdringlich; *(thing)* unauffällig

unof'ficial *adj* inoffiziell

un'pack *vt/i* auspacken

un'paid *adj* unbezahlt

un'pleasant *adj* unangenehm

un'plug *vt (pt/pp* **-plugged)** den Stecker herausziehen von

un'popular *adj* unbeliebt

un'precedented *adj* beispiellos

unpre'dictable *adj* unberechenbar

unpre'pared *adj* nicht vorbereitet

unpre'tentious *adj* bescheiden

un'profitable *adj* unrentabel

un'qualified *adj* unqualifiziert; (*fig: absolute*) uneingeschränkt

un'questionable *adj* unbezweifelbar; (*right*) unbestreitbar

unravel /ʌnˈrævl/ *vt* (*pt/pp* **-ravelled**) entwirren; (*Knitting*) aufziehen

un'real *adj* unwirklich

un'reasonable *adj* unvernünftig

unre'lated *adj* unzusammenhängend; **be ~** nicht verwandt sein; (*events:*) nicht miteinander zusammenhängen

unre'liable *adj* unzuverlässig

un'rest *n* Unruhen *pl*

un'rivalled *adj* unübertroffen

un'roll *vt* aufrollen ● *vi* sich aufrollen

unruly /ʌnˈruːlɪ/ *adj* ungebärdig

un'safe *adj* nicht sicher

unsatis'factory *adj* unbefriedigend

un'savoury *adj* unangenehm; (*fig*) unerfreulich

unscathed /ʌnˈskeɪðd/ *adj* unversehrt

un'screw *vt* abschrauben

un'scrupulous *adj* skrupellos

un'seemly *adj* unschicklich

un'selfish *adj* selbstlos

un'settled *adj* ungeklärt; (*weather*) unbeständig; (*bill*) unbezahlt

unshakeable /ʌnˈʃeɪkəbl/ *adj* unerschütterlich

unshaven /ʌnˈʃeɪvn/ *adj* unrasiert

unsightly /ʌnˈsaɪtlɪ/ *adj* unansehnlich

un'skilled *adj* ungelernt; (*work*) unqualifiziert

un'sociable *adj* ungesellig

unso'phisticated *adj* einfach

un'sound *adj* krank, nicht gesund; (*building*) nicht sicher; (*advice*) unzu-

verlässig; (*reasoning*) nicht stichhaltig

un'stable *adj* nicht stabil; (*mentally*) labil

un'steady *adj*, **-ily** *adv* unsicher; (*wobbly*) wackelig

un'stuck *adj* **come ~** sich lösen; (📻: *fail*) scheitern

unsuc'cessful *adj* erfolglos; **be ~** keinen Erfolg haben

un'suitable *adj* ungeeignet; (*inappropriate*) unpassend; (*for weather, activity*) unzweckmäßig

unthinkable /ʌnˈθɪŋkəbl/ *adj* unvorstellbar

un'tidiness *n* Unordentlichkeit *f*

un'tidy *adj*, **-ily** *adv* unordentlich

un'tie *vt* aufbinden; losbinden (*person, boat, horse*)

until /ənˈtɪl/ *prep* bis (+ *acc*); **not ~ erst; ~ the evening** bis zum Abend ● *conj* bis; **not ~ erst wenn;** (*in past*) erst als

un'told *adj* unermesslich

un'true *adj* unwahr; **that's ~** das ist nicht wahr

unused¹ /ʌnˈjuːzd/ *adj* unbenutzt; (*not utilized*) ungenutzt

unused² /ʌnˈjuːst/ *adj* **be ~ to sth** etw nicht gewohnt sein

un'usual *adj* ungewöhnlich

un'veil *vt* enthüllen

un'wanted *adj* unerwünscht

un'welcome *adj* unwillkommen

un'well *adj* **be** or **feel ~** sich nicht wohl fühlen

unwieldy /ʌnˈwiːldɪ/ *adj* sperrig

un'willing *adj* widerwillig; **be ~ to do sth** etw nicht tun wollen

un'wind *v* (*pt/pp* unwound) ● *vt* abwickeln ● *vi* sich abwickeln; (📻: *relax*) sich entspannen

un'wise *adj* unklug

un'worthy *adj* unwürdig

un'wrap *vt* (*pt/pp* **-wrapped**) auswickeln; auspacken (*present*)

un'written *adj* ungeschrieben

up /ʌp/ *adv* oben; (*with movement*) nach oben; (*not in bed*) auf; (*road*) aufgerissen; (*price*) gestiegen; **be up for sale** zu verkaufen sein; **up there** da oben; **up to** (*as far as*) bis; **time's up** die Zeit ist um; **what's up?** Ⓘ was ist los? **what's he up to?** Ⓘ was hat er vor? **I don't feel up to it** ich fühle mich dem nicht gewachsen; **go up** hinaufgehen; **come up** heraufkommen ● *prep* **be up on sth** [oben] auf etw (*dat*) sein; **up the mountain** oben am Berg; (*movement*) den Berg hinauf; **be up the tree** oben im Baum sein; **up the road** die Straße entlang; **up the river** stromaufwärts; **go up the stairs** die Treppe hinaufgehen

'upbringing *n* Erziehung *f*

up'date *vt* auf den neuesten Stand bringen

up'grade *vt* aufstufen

upheaval /ʌp'hiːvl/ *n* Unruhe *f*; (*Pol*) Umbruch *m*

up'hill *adj* (*fig*) mühsam ● *adv* bergauf

up'hold *vt* (*pt/pp* upheld) unterstützen; bestätigen (*verdict*)

upholster /ʌp'həʊlstə(r)/ *vt* polstern. **~y** *n* Polsterung *f*

'upkeep *n* Unterhalt *m*

up'market *adj* anspruchsvoll

upon /ə'pɒn/ *prep* auf (+ *dat/acc*)

upper /'ʌpə(r)/ *adj* obere(r,s); (*deck, jaw, lip*) Ober-; **have the ~ hand** die Oberhand haben ● *n* (*of shoe*) Obermaterial *nt*

upper class *n* Oberschicht *f*

'upright *adj* aufrecht

'uprising *n* Aufstand *m*

'uproar *n* Aufruhr *m*

up'set¹ *vt* (*pt/pp* upset, *pres p* upsetting) umstoßen; (*spill*) verschüt-

ten; durcheinander bringen (*plan*); (*distress*) erschüttern; (*food:*) nicht bekommen (+ *dat*); **get ~ about sth** sich über etw (*acc*) aufregen

'upset² *n* Aufregung *f*; **have a stomach ~** einen verdorbenen Magen haben

'upshot *n* Ergebnis *nt*

upside 'down *adv* verkehrt herum; **turn ~** umdrehen

up'stairs¹ *adv* oben; (*go*) nach oben

'upstairs² *adj* im Obergeschoss

'upstart *n* Emporkömmling *m*

up'stream *adv* stromaufwärts

'uptake *n* slow on the **~** schwer von Begriff; **be quick on the ~** schnell begreifen

'upturn *n* Aufschwung *m*

upward /'ʌpwəd/ *adj* nach oben; (*movement*) Aufwärts-; **~ slope** Steigung *f* ● *adv* **~[s]** aufwärts, nach oben

uranium /jʊ'reɪnɪəm/ *n* Uran *nt*

urban /'ɜːbən/ *adj* städtisch

urge /ɜːdʒ/ *n* Trieb *m*, Drang *m* ● *vt* drängen; **~ on** antreiben

urgen|cy /'ɜːdʒənsɪ/ *n* Dringlichkeit *f*. **~t** *adj* dringend

urine /'jʊərɪn/ *n* Urin *m*, Harn *m*

us /ʌs/ *pron* uns; **it's us** wir sind es

US[A] *abbr* USA *pl*

usable /'juːzəbl/ *adj* brauchbar

usage /'juːsɪdʒ/ *n* Brauch *m*; (*of word*) [Sprach]gebrauch *m*

use¹ /juːs/ *n* (*see* use) Benutzung *f*; Verwendung *f*; Gebrauch *m*; **be (of) no ~** nichts nützen; **it is no ~** es hat keinen Zweck; **what's the ~?** wozu?

use² /juːz/ *vt* benutzen (*implement, room, lift*); verwenden (*ingredient, method, book, money*); gebrauchen (*words, force, brains*); **~ [up]** aufbrauchen

used¹ /juːzd/ *adj* gebraucht; (*towel*) benutzt; (*car*) Gebraucht-

used² /juːst/ *pt* **be ~ to** an etw (*acc*) gewöhnt sein; **get ~ to** sich gewöhnen an (+ *acc*); **he ~ to say** er hat immer gesagt; **he ~ to live here** er hat früher hier gewohnt

useful /ˈjuːsfl/ *adj* nützlich. **~ness** *n* Nützlichkeit *f*

useless /ˈjuːslɪs/ *adj* nutzlos; (*not usable*) unbrauchbar; (*pointless*) zwecklos

user /ˈjuːzə(r)/ *n* Benutzer(in) *m(f)*

usher /ˈʌʃə(r)/ *n* Platzanweiser *m*; (*in court*) Gerichtsdiener *m*

usherette /ʌʃəˈret/ *n* Platzanweiserin *f*

USSR *abbr* (*History*) UdSSR *f*

usual /ˈjuːʒʊəl/ *adj* üblich. **~ly** *adv* gewöhnlich

utensil /juːˈtensl/ *n* Gerät *nt*

utility /juːˈtɪlətɪ/ *adj* Gebrauchs-

utilize /ˈjuːtɪlaɪz/ *vt* nutzen

utmost /ˈʌtməʊst/ *adj* äußerste(r,s), größte(r,s) ● **do one's ~** sein Möglichstes tun

utter¹ /ˈʌtə(r)/ *adj* völlig

utter² *vt* von sich geben (*sigh, sound*); sagen (*word*)

U-turn /ˈjuː-/ *n* (*fig*) Kehrtwendung *f*; **'no ~s'** (*Auto*) 'Wenden verboten'

Vv

vacan|cy /ˈveɪkənsɪ/ *n* (*job*) freie Stelle *f*; (*room*) freies Zimmer *nt*; **'no ~cies'** 'belegt'. **~t** *adj* frei; (*look*) [gedanken]leer

vacate /vəˈkeɪt/ *vt* räumen

vacation /vəˈkeɪʃn/ *n* (*Univ & Amer*) Ferien *pl*

vaccinat|e /ˈvæksɪneɪt/ *vt* impfen. **~ion** *n* Impfung *f*

vaccine /ˈvæksiːn/ *n* Impfstoff *m*

vacuum /ˈvækjʊəm/ *n* Vakuum *nt*, luftleerer Raum *m* ● *vt* saugen. **~ cleaner** *n* Staubsauger *m*

vagina /vəˈdʒaɪnə/ *n* (*Anat*) Scheide *f*

vague /veɪɡ/ *adj* (-r,-st) vage; (*outline*) verschwommen

vain /veɪn/ *adj* (-er,-est) eitel; (*hope, attempt*) vergeblich; **in ~** vergeblich. **~ly** *adv* vergeblich

valiant /ˈvælɪənt/ *adj* tapfer

valid /ˈvælɪd/ *adj* gültig; (*claim*) berechtigt; (*argument*) stichhaltig; (*reason*) triftig. **~ity** *n* Gültigkeit *f*

valley /ˈvælɪ/ *n* Tal *nt*

valour /ˈvælə(r)/ *n* Tapferkeit *f*

valuable /ˈvæljʊəbl/ *adj* wertvoll. **~s** *npl* Wertsachen *pl*

valuation /væljʊˈeɪʃn/ *n* Schätzung *f*

value /ˈvæljuː/ *n* Wert *m*; (*usefulness*) Nutzen *m* ● *vt* schätzen. **~ 'added tax** *n* Mehrwertsteuer *f*

valve /vælv/ *n* Ventil *nt*; (*Anat*) Klappe *f*; (*Electr*) Röhre *f*

van /væn/ *n* Lieferwagen *m*

vandal /ˈvændl/ *n* Rowdy *m*. **~ism** *n* mutwillige Zerstörung *f*. **~ize** *vt* demolieren

vanilla /vəˈnɪlə/ *n* Vanille *f*

vanish /ˈvænɪʃ/ *vi* verschwinden

vanity /ˈvænətɪ/ *n* Eitelkeit *f*

vapour /ˈveɪpə(r)/ *n* Dampf *m*

variable /ˈveərɪəbl/ *adj* unbeständig; (*Math*) variabel; (*adjustable*) regulierbar

variant /ˈveərɪənt/ *n* Variante *f*

variation /veərɪˈeɪʃn/ *n* Variation *f*; (*difference*) Unterschied *m*

u
v

varied /ˈveərɪd/ adj vielseitig; (diet:) abwechslungsreich

variety /vəˈraɪətɪ/ n Abwechslung f; (quantity) Vielfalt f; (Comm) Auswahl f; (type) Art f; (Bot) Abart f; (Theat) Varieté nt

various /ˈveərɪəs/ adj verschieden. ~ly adv unterschiedlich

varnish /ˈvɑːnɪʃ/ n Lack m ● vt lackieren

vary /ˈveərɪ/ v (pt/pp -ied) ● vi sich ändern; (be different) verschieden sein ● vt [ver]ändern; (add variety to) abwechslungsreicher gestalten

vase /vɑːz/ n Vase f

vast /vɑːst/ adj riesig; (expanse) weit. ~ly adv gewaltig

vat /væt/ n Bottich m

VAT /viːeɪˈtiː, væt/ abbr (value added tax) Mehrwertsteuer f, MwSt.

vault¹ /vɔːlt/ n (roof) Gewölbe nt; (in bank) Tresor m; (tomb) Gruft f

vault² n Sprung m ● vt/i ~ [over] springen über (+ acc)

VDU abbr (visual display unit) Bildschirmgerät nt

veal /viːl/ n Kalbfleisch nt ● attrib Kalbs-

veer /vɪə(r)/ vi sich drehen; (Auto) ausscheren

vegetable /ˈvedʒtəbl/ n Gemüse nt; ~s pl Gemüse nt ● attrib Gemüse-; (oil, fat) Pflanzen-

vegetarian /vedʒɪˈteərɪən/ adj vegetarisch ● n Vegetarier(in) m(f)

vegetation /vedʒɪˈteɪʃn/ n Vegetation f

vehement /ˈviːəmənt/ adj heftig

vehicle /ˈviːɪkl/ n Fahrzeug nt

veil /veɪl/ n Schleier m ● vt verschleiern

vein /veɪn/ n Ader f; (mood) Stim-

mung f; (manner) Art f

velocity /vɪˈlɒsətɪ/ n Geschwindigkeit f

velvet /ˈvelvɪt/ n Samt m

vending-machine /ˈvendɪŋ-/ n [Verkaufs]automat m

vendor /ˈvendə(r)/ n Verkäufer(in) m(f)

veneer /vəˈnɪə(r)/ n Furnier nt; (fig) Tünche f. ~ed adj furniert

venerable /ˈvenərəbl/ adj ehrwürdig

Venetian /vəˈniːʃn/ adj venezianisch. v~ blind n Jalousie f

vengeance /ˈvendʒəns/ n Rache f; with a ~ gewaltig

Venice /ˈvenɪs/ n Venedig nt

venison /ˈvenɪsn/ n (Culin) Reh[fleisch] nt

venom /ˈvenəm/ n Gift nt; (fig) Hass m. ~ous adj giftig

vent /vent/ n Öffnung f

ventilat|e /ˈventɪleɪt/ vt belüften. ~ion n Belüftung f; (installation) Lüftung f. ~or n Lüftungsvorrichtung f; (Med) Beatmungsgerät nt

ventriloquist /venˈtrɪləkwɪst/ n Bauchredner m

venture /ˈventʃə(r)/ n Unternehmung f ● vt wagen ● vi sich wagen

venue /ˈvenjuː/ n (for event) Veranstaltungsort m

veranda /vəˈrændə/ n Veranda f

verb /vɜːb/ n Verb nt. ~al adj mündlich; (Gram) verbal

verbose /vɜːˈbəʊs/ adj weitschweifig

verdict /ˈvɜːdɪkt/ n Urteil nt

verge /vɜːdʒ/ n Rand m ● vi ~ on (fig) grenzen an (+ acc)

verify /ˈverɪfaɪ/ vt (pt/pp -ied) überprüfen; (confirm) bestätigen

vermin /ˈvɜːmɪn/ n Ungeziefer nt

vermouth /ˈvɜːməθ/ n Wermut m

versatil|e /ˈvɜːsətaɪl/ adj vielseitig. **~ity** n Vielseitigkeit f

verse /vɜːs/ n Strophe f; (of Bible) Vers m; (poetry) Lyrik f

version /ˈvɜːʃn/ n Version f; (translation) Übersetzung f; (model) Modell nt

versus /ˈvɜːsəs/ prep gegen (+ acc)

vertical /ˈvɜːtɪkl/ adj senkrecht ● n Senkrechte f

vertigo /ˈvɜːtɪgəʊ/ n (Med) Schwindel m

verve /vɜːv/ n Schwung m

very /ˈverɪ/ adv sehr; ~ **much** sehr; (quantity) sehr viel; ~ **probably** höchstwahrscheinlich; at the ~ **most** allerhöchstens ● adj (mere) bloß; the ~ **first** der/die/das allererste; the ~ **thing** genau das Richtige; at the ~ **end/beginning** ganz am Ende/Anfang; only a ~ **little** nur ein ganz kleines bisschen

vessel /ˈvesl/ n Schiff nt; (receptacle & Anat) Gefäß nt

vest /vest/ n [Unter]hemd nt; (Amer: waistcoat) Weste f

vestige /ˈvestɪdʒ/ n Spur f

vestry /ˈvestrɪ/ n Sakristei f

vet /vet/ n Tierarzt m /-ärztin f ● vt (pt/pp vetted) überprüfen

veteran /ˈvetərən/ n Veteran m

veterinary /ˈvetərɪnərɪ/ adj tierärztlich. ~ **surgeon** n Tierarzt m /-ärztin f

veto /ˈviːtəʊ/ n (pl -es) Veto nt

VHF abbr (**very high frequency**) UKW

via /ˈvaɪə/ prep über (+ acc)

viable /ˈvaɪəbl/ adj lebensfähig; (fig) realisierbar; (firm) rentabel

viaduct /ˈvaɪədʌkt/ n Viadukt nt

vibrat|e /vaɪˈbreɪt/ vi vibrieren.

~ion n Vibrieren nt

vicar /ˈvɪkə(r)/ n Pfarrer m. **~age** n Pfarrhaus nt

vice¹ /vaɪs/ n Laster nt

vice² n (Techn) Schraubstock m

vice³ adj Vize-; ~ '**chairman** stellvertretender Vorsitzender m

vice versa /vaɪsɪˈvɜːsə/ adv umgekehrt

vicinity /vɪˈsɪnɪtɪ/ n Umgebung f; **in the ~ of** in der Nähe von

vicious /ˈvɪʃəs/ adj boshaft; (animal) bösartig

victim /ˈvɪktɪm/ n Opfer nt. **~ize** vt schikanieren

victor /ˈvɪktə(r)/ n Sieger m

victor|ious /vɪkˈtɔːrɪəs/ adj siegreich. **~y** n Sieg m

video /ˈvɪdɪəʊ/ n Video nt; (recorder) Videorecorder m ● attrib Video-

video: ~ **cas'sette** n Videokassette f. ~ **game** n Videospiel nt. ~ **recorder** n Videorecorder m

Vienn|a /vɪˈenə/ n Wien nt. **~ese** adj Wiener

view /vjuː/ n Sicht f; (scene) Aussicht f, Blick m; (picture, opinion) Ansicht f; **in my** ~ meiner Ansicht nach; **in** ~ **of** angesichts (+ gen); **be on** ~ besichtigt werden können ● vt (look at) sich (dat) ansehen; besichtigen (house); (consider) betrachten ● vi (TV) fernsehen. **~er** n (TV) Zuschauer(in) m(f)

view: **~finder** n (Phot) Sucher m. **~point** n Standpunkt m

vigilan|ce /ˈvɪdʒɪləns/ n Wachsamkeit f. **~t** adj wachsam

vigorous /ˈvɪgərəs/ adj kräftig; (fig) heftig

vigour /ˈvɪgə(r)/ n Kraft f; (fig) Heftigkeit f

vile /vaɪl/ adj abscheulich

villa /'vɪlə/ n (for holidays) Ferienhaus nt

village /'vɪlɪdʒ/ n Dorf nt. **~r** n Dorfbewohner(in) m(f)

villain /'vɪlən/ n Schurke m; (in story) Bösewicht m

vindicat|e /'vɪndɪkeɪt/ vt rechtfertigen. **~ion** n Rechtfertigung f

vindictive /vɪn'dɪktɪv/ adj nachtragend

vine /vaɪn/ n Weinrebe f

vinegar /'vɪnɪɡə(r)/ n Essig m

vineyard /'vɪnjɑːd/ n Weinberg m

vintage /'vɪntɪdʒ/ adj erlesen ●n (year) Jahrgang m. **~ 'car** n Oldtimer m

viola /vɪ'əʊlə/ n (Mus) Bratsche f

violat|e /'vaɪəleɪt/ vt verletzen; (break) brechen; (disturb) stören; (defile) schänden. **~ion** n Verletzung f; Schändung f

violen|ce /'vaɪələns/ n Gewalt f; (fig) Heftigkeit f. **~t** adj gewalttätig; (fig) heftig. **~tly** adv brutal; (fig) heftig

violet /'vaɪələt/ adj violett ●n (flower) Veilchen nt

violin /vaɪə'lɪn/ n Geige f, Violine f. **~ist** n Geiger(in) m(f)

VIP abbr (very important person) Prominente(r) m/f

viper /'vaɪpə(r)/ n Kreuzotter f

virgin /'vɜːdʒɪn/ adj unberührt ●n Jungfrau f. **~ity** n Unschuld f

viril|e /'vɪraɪl/ adj männlich. **~ity** n Männlichkeit f

virtual /'vɜːtʃʊəl/ adj a **~** ... praktisch ein ... **~ly** adv praktisch

virtue /'vɜːtjuː/ n Tugend f; (advantage) Vorteil m. **by** or **in ~e of** auf Grund (+ gen)

virtuoso /vɜːtjʊ'əʊzəʊ/ n (pl **-si** /-ziː/) Virtuose m

virtuous /'vɜːtjʊəs/ adj tugendhaft

virus /'vaɪərəs/ n Virus nt

visa /'viːzə/ n Visum nt

visibility /vɪzə'bɪlətɪ/ n Sichtbarkeit f; (range) Sichtweite f

visi|ble /'vɪzəbl/ adj, **-bly** adv sichtbar

vision /'vɪʒn/ n Vision f; (sight) Sehkraft f; (foresight) Weitblick m

visit /'vɪzɪt/ n Besuch m ●vt besuchen; besichtigen (town, building). **~or** n Besucher(in) m(f); (in hotel) Gast m; **have ~ors** Besuch haben

visor /'vaɪzə(r)/ n Schirm m; (Auto) [Sonnen]blende f

vista /'vɪstə/ n Aussicht f

visual /'vɪzjʊəl/ adj visuell. **~ dis-'play unit** n Bildschirmgerät nt

visualize /'vɪzjʊəlaɪz/ vt sich (dat) vorstellen

vital /'vaɪtl/ adj unbedingt notwendig; (essential to life) lebenswichtig. **~ity** n Vitalität f. **~ly** adv äußerst

vitamin /'vɪtəmɪn/ n Vitamin nt

vivaci|ous /vɪ'veɪʃəs/ adj lebhaft. **~ty** n Lebhaftigkeit f

vivid /'vɪvɪd/ adj lebhaft; (description) lebendig

vocabulary /və'kæbjʊlərɪ/ n Wortschatz m; (list) Vokabelverzeichnis nt; **learn ~** Vokabeln lernen

vocal /'vəʊkl/ adj stimmlich; (vociferous) lautstark

vocalist /'vəʊkəlɪst/ n Sänger(in) m(f)

vocation /və'keɪʃn/ n Berufung f. **~al** adj Berufs-

vociferous /və'sɪfərəs/ adj lautstark

vodka /'vɒdkə/ n Wodka m

vogue /vəʊɡ/ n Mode f

voice /vɔɪs/ n Stimme f ●vt zum

Ausdruck bringen. **~ mail** n Voicemail f

void /vɔɪd/ adj leer; (not valid) ungültig; **~ of** ohne ● n Leere f

volatile /ˈvɒlətaɪl/ adj flüchtig; (person) sprunghaft

volcanic /vɒlˈkænɪk/ adj vulkanisch

volcano /vɒlˈkeɪnəʊ/ n Vulkan m

volley /ˈvɒlɪ/ n (of gunfire) Salve f; (Tennis) Volley m

volt /vəʊlt/ n Volt nt. **~age** n (Electr) Spannung f

voluble /ˈvɒljʊbl/ adj, **-bly** adv redselig; (protest) wortreich

volume /ˈvɒljuːm/ n (book) Band m; (Geometry) Rauminhalt m; (amount) Ausmaß nt; (Radio, TV) Lautstärke f

voluntary /ˈvɒləntərɪ/ adj, **-ily** adv freiwillig

volunteer /vɒlənˈtɪə(r)/ n Freiwillige(r) m/f ● vt anbieten; geben (information) ● vi sich freiwillig melden

vomit /ˈvɒmɪt/ n Erbrochene(s) nt ● vt erbrechen ● vi sich übergeben

voracious /vəˈreɪʃəs/ adj gefräßig; (appetite) unbändig

vote /vəʊt/ n Stimme f; (ballot) Abstimmung f; (right) Wahlrecht nt ● vi abstimmen; (in election) wählen. **~er** n Wähler(in) m/f

vouch /vaʊtʃ/ vi ~ **for** sich verbürgen für. **~er** n Gutschein m

vowel /ˈvaʊəl/ n Vokal m

voyage /ˈvɔɪdʒ/ n Seereise f; (in space) Reise f, Flug m

vulgar /ˈvʌlɡə(r)/ adj vulgär, ordinär. **~ity** n Vulgarität f

vulnerable /ˈvʌlnərəbl/ adj verwundbar

vulture /ˈvʌltʃə(r)/ n Geier m

Ww

wad /wɒd/ n Bausch m; (bundle) Bündel nt. **~ding** n Wattierung f

waddle /ˈwɒdl/ vi watscheln

wade /weɪd/ vi waten

wafer /ˈweɪfə(r)/ n Waffel f

waffle[1] /ˈwɒfl/ vi 🄴 schwafeln

waffle[2] n (Culin) Waffel f

waft /wɒft/ vt/i wehen

wag /wæɡ/ v (pt/pp wagged) ● vt wedeln mit ● vi wedeln

wage /weɪdʒ/ n (also **~s**) pl Lohn m

wager /ˈweɪdʒə(r)/ n Wette f

wagon /ˈwæɡən/ n Wagen m; (Rail) Waggon m

wail /weɪl/ n [klagender] Schrei m ● vi heulen; (lament) klagen

waist /weɪst/ n Taille f. **~coat** n Weste f. **~line** n Taille f

wait /weɪt/ n Wartezeit f; lie in ~ for auflauern (+ dat) ● vi warten (for auf + acc); (at table) servieren; ~ **on** bedienen (+ acc); ~ **one's turn** warten, bis man an der Reihe ist

waiter /ˈweɪtə(r)/ n Kellner m; ~! Herr Ober!

waiting: **~-list** n Warteliste f. **~-room** n Warteraum m; (doctor's) Wartezimmer nt

waitress /ˈweɪtrɪs/ n Kellnerin f

waive /weɪv/ vt verzichten auf (+ acc)

wake[1] /weɪk/ n Totenwache f ● v (pt woke, pp woken) ~ **[up]** ● vt [auf]wecken ● vi aufwachen

wake[2] n (Naut) Kielwasser nt; in the ~ of im Gefolge (+ gen)

Wales /weɪlz/ n Wales nt

walk /wɔːk/ n Spaziergang m; (gait) Gang m; (path) Weg m; **go for a** ~ spazieren gehen ● vi gehen; (not ride) laufen, zu Fuß gehen; (ramble) wandern; **learn to** ~ laufen lernen ● vt ausführen (dog). ~ **out** vi hinausgehen (; workers:) in den Streik treten; ~ **out on s.o.** jdn verlassen

walker /ˈwɔːkə(r)/ n Spaziergänger(in) m(f); (rambler) Wanderer m/Wanderin f

walking /ˈwɔːkɪŋ/ n Gehen nt; (rambling) Wandern nt. ~**stick** n Spazierstock m

wall /wɔːl/ n Wand f; (external) Mauer f; **drive s.o. up the** ~ 🆃 jdn auf die Palme bringen ● vt ~ **up** zumauern

wallet /ˈwɒlɪt/ n Brieftasche f

'wallflower n Goldlack m

wallop /ˈwɒləp/ vt (pt/pp **walloped**) 🆃 schlagen

wallow /ˈwɒləʊ/ vi sich wälzen; (fig) schwelgen

'wallpaper n Tapete f ● vt tapezieren

walnut /ˈwɔːlnʌt/ n Walnuss f

waltz /wɔːlts/ n Walzer m ● vi Walzer tanzen

wander /ˈwɒndə(r)/ vi umherwandern, 🆃 bummeln; (fig: digress) abschweifen. ~ **about** vi umherwandern

wangle /ˈwæŋɡl/ vt 🆃 organisieren

want /wɒnt/ n Mangel m (of an + dat); (hardship) Not f; (desire) Bedürfnis nt ● vt wollen; (need) brauchen; ~ **[to have] sth** etw haben wollen; ~ **to do sth** etw tun wollen; **I** ~ **you to go** ich will, dass du gehst; **it** ~**s painting** es müsste gestrichen werden ● vi **he doesn't** ~ **for anything** ihm fehlt es an

nichts. ~**ed** adj (criminal) gesucht

war /wɔː(r)/ n Krieg m; **be at** ~ sich im Krieg befinden

ward /wɔːd/ n [Kranken]saal m; (unit) Station f; (of town) Wahlbezirk m; (child) Mündel nt ● vt ~ **off** abwehren

warden /ˈwɔːdn/ n (of hostel) Heimleiter(in) m(f); (of youth hostel) Herbergsvater m; (supervisor) Aufseher(in) m(f)

warder /ˈwɔːdə(r)/ n Wärter(in) m(f)

wardrobe /ˈwɔːdrəʊb/ n Kleiderschrank m; (clothes) Garderobe f

warehouse /ˈweəhaʊs/ n Lager nt; (building) Lagerhaus nt

wares /weəz/ npl Waren pl

war: ~**fare** n Krieg m. ~**like** adj kriegerisch

warm /wɔːm/ adj (-er, -est) warm; (welcome) herzlich; **I am** ~ mir ist warm ● vt wärmen. ~ **up** vt aufwärmen ● vi warm werden; (Sport) sich aufwärmen. ~**hearted** adj warmherzig

warmth /wɔːmθ/ n Wärme f

warn /wɔːn/ vt warnen (of vor + dat). ~**ing** n Warnung f; (advance notice) Vorwarnung f; (caution) Verwarnung f

warp /wɔːp/ vt verbiegen ● vi sich verziehen

warrant /ˈwɒrənt/ n (for arrest) Haftbefehl m; (for search) Durchsuchungsbefehl m ● vt (justify) rechtfertigen; (guarantee) garantieren

warranty /ˈwɒrəntɪ/ n Garantie f

warrior /ˈwɒrɪə(r)/ n Krieger m

'warship n Kriegsschiff nt

wart /wɔːt/ n Warze f

'wartime n Kriegszeit f

war|y /ˈweərɪ/ adj, **-ily** adv vorsichtig; (suspicious) misstrauisch

was /wɒz/ *see* be

wash /wɒʃ/ *n* Wäsche *f*; (*Naut*) Wellen *pl*; **have a ~** sich waschen ● *vt* waschen; spülen (*dishes*); aufwischen (*floor*); **~ one's hands** (*dat*) die Hände waschen ● *vi* sich waschen. **~ out** *vt* auswaschen; ausspülen (*mouth*). **~ up** *vt/i* abwaschen, spülen ● *vi* (*Amer*) sich waschen

washable /'wɒʃəbl/ *adj* waschbar

wash-basin *n* Waschbecken *nt*

washer /'wɒʃə(r)/ *n* (*Techn*) Dichtungsring *m*; (*machine*) Waschmaschine *f*

washing /'wɒʃɪŋ/ *n* Wäsche *f*. **~-machine** *n* Waschmaschine *f*. **~-powder** *n* Waschpulver *nt*. **~-up** *n* Abwasch *m*; **do the ~-up** abwaschen, spülen. **~-up liquid** *n* Spülmittel *nt*

wasp /wɒsp/ *n* Wespe *f*

waste /weɪst/ *n* Verschwendung *f*; (*rubbish*) Abfall *m*; **~s** *pl* Öde *f* ● *adj* (*product*) Abfall- ● *vt* verschwenden ● *vi* **~ away** immer mehr abmagern

waste: **~ful** *adj* verschwenderisch. **~ land** *n* Ödland *nt*. **~ 'paper** *n* Altpapier *nt*. **~-'paper basket** *n* Papierkorb *m*

watch /wɒtʃ/ *n* Wache *f*; (*timepiece*) [Armband]uhr *f* ● *vt* beobachten; sich (*dat*) ansehen (*film, match*); (*keep an eye on*) achten auf (+ *acc*); **~ television** fernsehen ● *vi* zusehen. **~ out** *vi* Ausschau halten (*for nach*); (*be careful*) aufpassen

watch: **~-dog** *n* Wachhund *m*. **~ful** *adj* wachsam. **~man** *n* Wachmann *m*

water /'wɔːtə(r)/ *n* Wasser *nt*; **~s** *pl* Gewässer *nt* ● *vt* gießen (*garden, plant*); (*dilute*) verdünnen ● *vi* (*eyes*) tränen; **my mouth was ~ing** mir lief das Wasser im Munde zusam-

men. **~ down** *vt* verwässern

water: **~-colour** *n* Wasserfarbe *f*; (*painting*) Aquarell *nt*. **~-cress** *n* Brunnenkresse *f*. **~fall** *n* Wasserfall *m*

'watering-can *n* Gießkanne *f*

water: **~-lily** *n* Seerose *f*. **~logged** *adj* **be ~logged** (*ground:*) unter Wasser stehen. **~ polo** *n* Wasserball *m*. **~proof** *adj* wasserdicht. **~-skiing** *n* Wasserskilaufen *nt*. **~tight** *adj* wasserdicht. **~way** *n* Wasserstraße *f*

watery /'wɔːtəri/ *adj* wässrig

watt /wɒt/ *n* Watt *nt*

wave /weɪv/ *n* Welle *f*; (*gesture*) Handbewegung *f*; (*as greeting*) Winken *nt* ● *vt* winken mit; (*brandish*) schwingen; wellen (*hair*); **~ one's hand** winken ● *vi* winken (*to dat*); (*flag:*) wehen. **~length** *n* Wellenlänge *f*

waver /'weɪvə(r)/ *vi* schwanken

wavy /'weɪvɪ/ *adj* wellig

wax /wæks/ *n* Wachs *nt*; (*in ear*) Schmalz *nt* ● *vi* wachsen. **~works** *n* Wachsfigurenkabinett *nt*

way /weɪ/ *n* Weg *m*; (*direction*) Richtung *f*; (*respect*) Hinsicht *f*; (*manner*) Art *f*; (*method*) Art und Weise *f*; **~s** *pl* Gewohnheiten *pl*; **on the ~** auf dem Weg (**to** nach/zu); (*under way*) unterwegs; **a little ~** ein kleines/ganzes Stück; **a long ~ off** weit weg; **this ~** hierher; (*like this*) so; **which ~** in welche Richtung; (*where*) wo; **in some ~s** in gewisser Hinsicht; **either ~** so oder so; **in this ~** auf diese Weise; **in a ~** in gewisser Weise; **lead the ~** vorausgehen; **make ~** Platz machen (**for** dat); **'give ~'** (*Auto*) 'Vorfahrt beachten'; **go out of one's ~** (*fig*) sich (dat) besondere Mühe geben (**to** zu); **get one's [own] ~** seinen Willen durchsetzen ● *adv* weit; ~ **behind** weit zurück. ~ '**in** *n* Eingang *m*

way 'out *n* Ausgang *m*; (*fig*) Ausweg *m*

WC *abbr* WC *nt*

we /wiː/ *pron* wir

weak /wiːk/ *adj* (**-er, -est**) schwach; (*liquid*) dünn. ~**en** *vt* schwächen ● *vi* schwächer werden. ~**ling** *n* Schwächling *m*. ~**ness** *n* Schwäche *f*

wealth /welθ/ *n* Reichtum *m*; (*fig*) Fülle *f* (**of** an + *dat*). ~**y** *adj* reich

weapon /'wepən/ *n* Waffe *f*; ~**s of mass destruction** Massenvernichtungswaffen *pl*

wear /weə(r)/ *n* (*clothing*) Kleidung *f*; ~ **and tear** Abnutzung *f*, Verschleiß *m* ● *v* (*pt* **wore**, *pp* **worn**) ● *vt* tragen; (*damage*) abnutzen; **what shall I ~?** was soll ich anziehen? ● *vi* sich abnutzen; (*last*) halten. ~ **off** *vt* abgehen; (*effect:*) nachlassen. ~ **out** *vt* abnutzen; (*exhaust*) erschöpfen ● *vi* sich abnutzen

weary /'wɪərɪ/ *adj* , **-ily** *adv* müde

weather /'weðə(r)/ *n* Wetter *nt*; **in this** ~ bei diesem Wetter; **under the** ~ 🔟 nicht ganz auf dem Posten ● *vt* abwettern (*storm*); (*fig*) überstehen

weather: ~**-beaten** *adj* verwittert; wettergegerbt (*face*). ~ **forecast** *n* Wettervorhersage *f*

weave[1] /wiːv/ *vi* (*pt/pp* **weaved**) sich schlängeln (**through** durch)

weave[2] *n* (*of cloth*) Bindung *f* ● *vt* (*pt* **wove**, *pp* **woven**) weben. ~**r** *n* Weber *m*

web /web/ *n* Netz *nt*; **the W~** das Web. ~**master** *n* Webmaster *m*. ~ **page** *n* Webseite *f*. ~**site** *n* Website *f*

wed /wed/ *vt/i* (*pt/pp* **wedded**) heiraten. ~**ding** *n* Hochzeit *f*

wedding: ~ **day** *n* Hochzeitstag *m*. ~ **dress** *n* Hochzeitskleid *nt*. ~**-ring** *n* Ehering *m*, Trauring *m*

wedge /wedʒ/ *n* Keil *m* ● *vt* festklemmen

Wednesday /'wenzdeɪ/ *n* Mittwoch *m*

wee /wiː/ *adj* 🔟 klein ● *vi* Pipi machen

weed /wiːd/ *n* Unkraut *nt* ● *vt/i* jäten. ~ **out** *vt* (*fig*) aussieben

'**weedkiller** *n* Unkrautvertilgungsmittel *nt*

weedy /'wiːdɪ/ *adj* 🔟 spillerig

week /wiːk/ *n* Woche *f*. ~**day** *n* Wochentag *m*. ~**end** *n* Wochenende *nt*

weekly /'wiːklɪ/ *adj* & *adv* wöchentlich ● *n* Wochenzeitschrift *f*

weep /wiːp/ *vi* (*pt/pp* **wept**) weinen

weigh /weɪ/ *vt/i* wiegen. ~ **down** *vt* (*fig*) niederdrücken. ~ **up** *vt* (*fig*) abwägen

weight /weɪt/ *n* Gewicht *nt*; **put on/lose** ~ zunehmen/abnehmen

weight-lifting *n* Gewichtheben *nt*

weighty /'weɪtɪ/ *adj* schwer; (*important*) gewichtig

weir /wɪə(r)/ *n* Wehr *nt*.

weird /wɪəd/ *adj* (**-er, -est**) unheimlich; (*bizarre*) bizarr

welcome /'welkəm/ *adj* willkommen; **you're** ~! nichts zu danken! **you're** ~ **to** (**have**) **it** das können Sie gerne haben ● *n* Willkommen *nt* ● *vt* begrüßen

weld /weld/ *vt* schweißen. ~**er** *n* Schweißer *m*

welfare /'welfeə(r)/ *n* Wohl *nt*; (*Admin*) Fürsorge *f*. **W ~ State** *n* Wohlfahrtsstaat *m*

well[1] /wel/ *n* Brunnen *m*;

(oil ~) Quelle f

well² adv (better, best) gut; **as ~**
auch; **as ~ as** (in addition) sowohl
... als auch; **~ done!** gut gemacht!
● adj gesund; **he is not ~** es geht
ihm nicht gut; **get ~ soon!** gute
Besserung! ● int nun, na

well: ~-behaved adj artig.
~-being n Wohl nt

wellingtons /ˈwelɪŋtənz/ npl
Gummistiefel pl

well: ~-known adj bekannt.
~-off adj wohlhabend; **be ~-off**
gut dransein. **~-to-do** adj wohlhabend

Welsh /welʃ/ adj walisisch ● n
(Lang) Walisisch nt; **the ~** pl die
Waliser. **~ man** n Waliser m

> **Welsh Assembly** Das wa-
> lisische Parlament, dessen
> Mitglieder in der Haupt-
> stadt Cardiff zusammentreten. Es
> wurde 1999 (nach einer Volksab-
> stimmung) eröffnet und verleiht
> Wales eine größere Autonomie ge-
> genüber dem britischen Parlament
> in London. Das Parlament setzt
> sich aus 60 Mitgliedern zusam-
> men, 40 sind direkt gewählt, die
> restlichen Abgeordneten von Re-
> gionallisten und nach dem Verhält-
> niswahlrecht.

went /went/ see go

wept /wept/ see weep

were /wɜː(r)/ see be

west /west/ n Westen m; **to the ~
of** westlich von ● adj West-, west-
● adv nach Westen. **~erly** adj
westlich. **~ern** adj westlich ● n Western m

West: ~ 'Germany n West-
deutschland nt. **~ 'Indian** adj west-
indisch ● n Westinder(in) m(f). **~
'Indies** /-ˈɪndɪz/ npl Westindische

Inseln pl

'westward[s] /-wəd[z]/ adv nach
Westen

wet /wet/ adj (wetter, wettest)
nass; (fam: person) weichlich, lasch;
'~ paint' 'frisch gestrichen' ● vt
(pt/pp wet or wetted) nass machen

whack /wæk/ vt 🔘 schlagen. **~ed**
adj 🔘 kaputt

whale /weɪl/ n Wal m

wharf /wɔːf/ n Kai m

> **what** /wɒt/
>
> ● pronoun
>
> ••••> (in questions) was. **what is it?**
> was ist das? **what do you
> want?** was wollen Sie? **what is
> your name?** wie heißen Sie?
> **what?** (🔘: say that again) wie?;
> was? **what is the time?** wie
> spät ist es? (indirect) **I didn't
> know what to do** ich wusste
> nicht, was ich machen sollte
>
> ❗ The equivalent of a preposi-
> tion with **what** in English is a
> special word in German begin-
> ning with wo- (wor- before a
> vowel): **for what? what for?** =
> wofür? wozu? **from what?**
> wovon? **on what?** worauf? wor-
> über? **under what?** worunter?
> **with what?** womit? etc. **what
> do you want the money for?**
> wozu willst du das Geld? **what
> is he talking about?** wovon
> redet er?
>
> ••••> (relative pronoun) was. **do
> what I tell you** tu, was ich dir
> sage. **give me what you can**
> gib mir, so viel du kannst.
> **what little I know** das bis-
> schen, das ich weiß. **I don't
> agree with what you are**

saying ich stimme dem nicht
zu, was Sie sagen
····▸ *(in phrases)* **what about me?**
was ist mit mir? **what about a
cup of coffee?** wie wäre es mit
einer Tasse Kaffee? **what if she
doesn't come?** was ist, wenn
sie nicht kommt? **what of it?**
was ist dabei?
● *adjective*
····▸ *(asking for selection)* welcher
(*m*), welche (*f*), welches (*nt*),
welche (*pl*). **what book do you
want?** welches Buch willst du
haben? **what colour are the
walls?** welche Farbe haben die
Wände? **I asked him what train
to take** ich habe ihn gefragt,
welchen Zug ich nehmen soll
····▸ *(asking how much/many)*
what money does he have?
wie viel Geld hat er? **what time
is it?** wie spät ist es? **what time
does it start?** um wie viel Uhr
fängt es an?
····▸ **what kind of ...?** was für
[ein(e)]? **what kind of man is
he?** was für ein Mensch ist er?
····▸ *(in exclamations)* was für (+
nom). **what a fool you are!** was
für ein Dummkopf du doch bist!
what cheek/luck! was für eine
Frechheit/ein Glück! **what a
huge house!** was für ein riesiges
Haus! **what a lot of people!**
was für viele Leute!

what'ever *adj* [egal] welche(r,s)
● *pron* was ... auch; ~ **is it?** was ist
das bloß?; ~ **he does** was er auch
tut; **nothing** ~ überhaupt nichts
whatso'ever *pron & adj* ≈
whatever

wheat /wiːt/ *n* Weizen *m*

wheel /wiːl/ *n* Rad *nt*; (*pottery*)
Töpferscheibe *f*; (*steering* ~) Lenk-

rad *nt*; **at the** ~ am Steuer ● *vt*
(*push*) schieben ● *vi* kehrtmachen;
(*circle*) kreisen

wheel: ~**barrow** *n* Schubkarre *f*.
~**chair** *n* Rollstuhl *m*. ~**-clamp** *n*
Parkkralle *f*

when /wen/ *adv* wann; **the day** ~
der Tag, an dem ● *conj* wenn; (*in
the past*) als; (*although*) wo ... doch;
~ **swimming/reading** beim
Schwimmen/Lesen

when'ever *conj & adv* [immer]
wenn; (*at whatever time*) wann
immer; ~ **did it happen?** wann ist
das bloß passiert?

where /weə(r)/ *adv & conj* wo; ~
[**to**] wohin; ~ [**from**] woher

whereabouts[1] /weərə'baʊts/
adv wo

'whereabouts[2] *n* Verbleib *m*; (*of
person*) Aufenthaltsort *m*

where'as *conj* während; (*in contrast*) wohingegen

whereu'pon *adv* worauf[hin]

wher'ever *conj & adv* wo immer;
(*to whatever place*) wohin immer;
(*from whatever place*) woher immer;
(*everywhere*) überall wo; ~ **possible**
wenn irgend möglich

whether /'weðə(r)/ *conj* ob

which /wɪtʃ/
● *adjective*
····▸ *(in questions)* welcher (*m*),
welche (*f*), welches (*nt*), welche
(*pl*). **which book do you need?**
welches Buch brauchst du?
which one? welcher/welche/
welches? **which ones?** welche?
which one of you did it? wer
von euch hat es getan? **which
way?** (*which direction*) welche
Richtung?; (*where*) wohin?;
(*how*) wie?
····▸ *(relative)* **he always comes at**

one at which time I'm having lunch/by which time I've finished er kommt immer um ein Uhr; dann esse ich gerade zu Mittag/bis dahin bin ich schon fertig

● *pronoun*

····▸ (*in questions*) welcher (*m*), welche (*f*), welches (*nt*), welche (*pl*). **which is which?** welcher/welche/welches ist welcher/welche/welches? **which of you?** wer von euch?

····▸ (*relative*) der (*m*), die (*f*), das (*nt*), die (*pl*); (*genitive*) dessen (*m*, *nt*), deren (*f*, *pl*); (*dative*) dem (*m*, *nt*), der (*f*), denen (*pl*); (*referring to a clause*) was. **the book which I gave you** das Buch, das ich dir gab. **the trial, the result of which we are expecting** der Prozess, dessen Ergebnis wir erwarten. **the house of which I was speaking** das Haus, von dem *od* wovon ich redete. **after which** wonach; nach dem. **on which** worauf; auf dem. **the shop opposite which we parked** der Laden, gegenüber dem wir parkten. **everything which I tell you** alles, was ich dir sage

which'ever *adj & pron* (egal) welche(r,s); ~ **it is** was es auch ist

while /waɪl/ *n* Weile *f*; **a long** ~ lange; **be worth** ~ sich lohnen; **it's worth my** ~ es lohnt sich für mich ● *conj* während; (*as long as*) solange; (*although*) obgleich ● *vt* ~ **away** sich (*dat*) vertreiben

whilst /waɪlst/ *conj* während

whim /wɪm/ *n* Laune *f*

whimper /'wɪmpə(r)/ *vi* wimmern; (*dog:*) winseln

whine /waɪn/ *vi* winseln

whip /wɪp/ *n* Peitsche *f*; (*Pol*) Einpeitscher *m* ● *vt* (*pt/pp* **whipped**) peitschen; (*Culin*) schlagen. **~ped 'cream** *n* Schlagsahne *f*

whirl /wɜːl/ *vt/i* wirbeln. **~pool** *n* Strudel *m*. **~wind** *n* Wirbelwind *m*

whirr /wɜː(r)/ *vi* surren

whisk /wɪsk/ *n* (*Culin*) Schneebesen *m* ● *vt* (*Culin*) schlagen

whisker /'wɪskə(r)/ *n* Schnurrhaar *nt*

whisky /'wɪskɪ/ *n* Whisky *m*

whisper /'wɪspə(r)/ *n* Flüstern *nt* ● *vt/i* flüstern

whistle /'wɪsl/ *n* Pfiff *m*; (*instrument*) Pfeife *f* ● *vt/i* pfeifen

white /waɪt/ *adj* (**-r**, **-st**) weiß ● *n* Weiß *nt*; (*of egg*) Eiweiß *nt*; (*person*) Weiße(r) *m/f*

white: ~ **'coffee** *n* Kaffee *m* mit Milch. ~**'collar worker** *n* Angestellte(r) *m*. ~ **'lie** *n* Notlüge *f*

whiten /'waɪtn/ *vt* weiß machen ● *vi* weiß werden

whiteness /'waɪtnɪs/ *n* Weiß *nt*

Whitsun /'wɪtsn/ *n* Pfingsten *nt*

whiz[z] /wɪz/ *vi* (*pt/pp* **whizzed**) zischen. ~**-kid** *n* 🄵 Senkrechtstarter *m*

who /huː/ *pron* wer; (*acc*) wen; (*dat*) wem ● *rel pron* der/die/das, (*pl*) die

who'ever *pron* wer [immer]; ~ **he is** wer er auch ist; ~ **is it?** wer ist das bloß?

whole /həʊl/ *adj* ganz; (*truth*) voll ● *n* Ganze(s) *nt*; **as a** ~ als Ganzes; **on the** ~ im Großen und Ganzen; **the** ~ **of Germany** ganz Deutschland

whole: ~**food** *n* Vollwertkost *f*. ~**'hearted** *adj* rückhaltlos. ~**meal** *adj* Vollkorn-

'wholesale *adj* Großhandels- ● *adv* en gros; (*fig*) in Bausch und

w

Bogen. ~r n Großhändler m

wholly /'həʊlɪ/ adv völlig

whom /huːm/ pron wen; to ~ wem ● rel pron den/die/das, (pl) die; (dat) dem/der/dem, (pl) denen

whopping /'wɒpɪŋ/ adj Ⓕ Riesen-

whore /hɔː(r)/ n Hure f

whose /huːz/ pron wessen; ~ is that? wem gehört das? ● rel pron dessen/deren/dessen, (pl) deren

why /waɪ/ adv warum; (for what purpose) wozu; that's ~ darum

wick /wɪk/ n Docht m

wicked /'wɪkɪd/ adj böse; (mischievous) frech, boshaft

wicker /'wɪkə(r)/ n Korbgeflecht nt ● attrib Korb-

wide /waɪd/ adj (-r,-st) weit; (broad) breit; (fig) groß ● adv weit; (off target) daneben; ~ awake hellwach; far and ~ weit und breit. **~ly** adv weit; (known, accepted) weithin; (differ) stark

widen /'waɪdn/ vt verbreitern; (fig) erweitern ● vi sich verbreitern

'widespread adj weit verbreitet

widow /'wɪdəʊ/ n Witwe f. **~ed** adj verwitwet. **~er** n Witwer m

width /wɪdθ/ n Weite f; (breadth) Breite f

wield /wiːld/ vt schwingen; ausüben (power)

wife /waɪf/ n (pl wives) [Ehe]frau f

wig /wɪɡ/ n Perücke f

wiggle /'wɪɡl/ vi wackeln ● vt wackeln mit

wild /waɪld/ adj (-er, -est) wild; (animal) wild lebend; (flower) wild wachsend; (furious) wütend ● adv wild; **run** ~ frei herumlaufen ● n **in the** ~ wild; **the** ~s pl die Wildnis f

wilderness /'wɪldənɪs/ n Wildnis f; (desert) Wüste f

wildlife n Tierwelt f

will¹ /wɪl/
● modal verb

past **would**

····▸ (expressing the future) werden. **she will arrive tomorrow** sie wird morgen ankommen. **he will be there by now** er wird jetzt schon da sein

····▸ (expressing intention) (present tense) **will you go?** gehst du? **I promise I won't do it again** ich verspreche, ich machs nicht noch mal

····▸ (in requests) **will/would you please tidy up?** würdest du bitte aufräumen? **will you be quiet!** willst du ruhig sein!

····▸ (in invitations) **will you have/would you like some wine?** wollen Sie/möchten Sie Wein?

····▸ (negative: refuse to) nicht wollen. **they won't help me** sie wollen mir nicht helfen. **the car won't start** das Auto will nicht anspringen

····▸ (in tag questions) nicht wahr. **you'll be back soon, won't you?** du kommst bald wieder, nicht wahr? **you will help her, won't you?** du hilfst ihr doch, nicht wahr?

····▸ (in short answers) **Will you be there? — Yes I will** Wirst du da sein? — Ja

will² n Wille m; (document) Testament nt

willing /'wɪlɪŋ/ adj willig; (eager) bereitwillig; **be** ~ bereit sein. **~ly** adv bereitwillig; (gladly) gern. **~ness** n Bereitwilligkeit f

willow /'wɪləʊ/ n Weide f

'will-power n Willenskraft f

wilt /wɪlt/ vi welk werden, welken

wily /'waɪlɪ/ adj listig

win /wɪn/ n Sieg m ● v (pt/pp won) (pres p winning) ● vt gewinnen; bekommen (scholarship) ● vi gewinnen; (in battle) siegen. ~ over vt auf seine Seite bringen

wince /wɪns/ vi zusammenzucken

winch /wɪntʃ/ n Winde f ● vt ~ up hochwinden

wind¹ /wɪnd/ n Wind m; (🎗: flatulence) Blähungen pl ● vt ~ s.o. jdm den Atem nehmen

wind² /waɪnd/ v (pt/pp wound) ● vt (wrap) wickeln; (move by turning) kurbeln; aufziehen (clock) vi (road): sich winden. ~ up vt aufziehen (clock); schließen (proceedings)

wind: ~ **farm** n Windpark m. ~ **instrument** n Blasinstrument nt. ~**mill** n Windmühle f

window /'wɪndəʊ/ n Fenster nt; (of shop) Schaufenster nt

window: ~**box** n Blumenkasten m. ~**cleaner** n Fensterputzer m. ~**pane** n Fensterscheibe f. ~**shopping** n Schaufensterbummel m. ~**sill** n Fensterbrett nt

'windpipe n Luftröhre f

'windscreen n, (Amer) **'windshield** n Windschutzscheibe f. ~**wiper** n Scheibenwischer m

wind surfing n Windsurfen nt

windy /'wɪndɪ/ adj windig

wine /waɪn/ n Wein m

wine: ~**bar** n Weinstube f. ~**glass** n Weinglas nt. ~**list** n Weinkarte f

winery /'waɪnərɪ/ n (Amer) Weingut nt

'wine-tasting n Weinprobe f

wing /wɪŋ/ n Flügel m; (Auto) Kot-

flügel m; ~**s** pl (Theat) Kulissen pl

wink /wɪŋk/ n Zwinkern nt; **not sleep a** ~ kein Auge zutun ● vi zwinkern; (light): blinken

winner /'wɪnə(r)/ n Gewinner(in) m(f); (Sport) Sieger(in) m(f)

winning /'wɪnɪŋ/ adj siegreich; (smile) gewinnend. ~**post** n Zielpfosten m. ~**s** npl Gewinn m

wint|er /'wɪntə(r)/ n Winter m. ~**ry** adj winterlich

wipe /waɪp/ n **give sth a** ~ etw abwischen ● vt abwischen; aufwischen (floor); (dry) abtrocknen. ~ **out** vt (cancel) löschen; (destroy) ausrotten. ~ **up** vt aufwischen

wire /'waɪə(r)/ n Draht m

wiring /'waɪərɪŋ/ n [elektrische] Leitungen pl

wisdom /'wɪzdəm/ n Weisheit f; (prudence) Klugheit f. ~ **tooth** n Weisheitszahn m

wise /waɪz/ adj (-r, -st) weise; (prudent) klug

wish /wɪʃ/ n Wunsch m ● vt wünschen; ~ **s.o. well** jdm alles Gute wünschen; **I** ~ **you could stay** ich wünschte, du könntest hier bleiben ● vi sich (dat) etwas wünschen. ~**ful** adj ~**ful thinking** Wunschdenken nt

wistful /'wɪstfl/ adj wehmütig

wit /wɪt/ n Geist m, Witz m; (intelligence) Verstand m; (person) geistreicher Mensch m; **be at one's** ~**s' end** sich (dat) keinen Rat mehr wissen

witch /wɪtʃ/ n Hexe f. ~**craft** n Hexerei f

with /wɪð/ prep mit (+ dat); ~ **fear/cold** vor Angst/Kälte; ~ **it** damit; **I'm going** ~ **you** ich gehe mit; **take it** ~ **you** nimm es mit; **I haven't got it** ~ **me** ich habe es nicht bei mir

with'draw v (pt -**drew**, pp -**drawn**) ● vt zurückziehen; abheben (money) ● vi sich zurückziehen. ~**al** n Zurückziehen nt; (of money) Abhebung f; (from drugs) Entzug m

wither /'wıðə(r)/ vi [ver]welken

with'hold vt (pt/pp -**held**) vorenthalten (**from** s.o. jdm)

with'in prep innerhalb (+ gen) ● adv innen

with'out prep ohne (+ acc); ~ **my noticing it** ohne dass ich es merkte

with'stand vt (pt/pp -**stood**) standhalten (+ dat)

witness /'wıtnıs/ n Zeuge m/ Zeugin f ● vt Zeuge/Zeugin sein (+ gen); bestätigen (signature)

witticism /'wıtısızm/ n geistreicher Ausspruch m

witty /'wıtı/ adj witzig, geistreich

wives /waıvz/ see **wife**

wizard /'wızəd/ n Zauberer m

wizened /'wıznd/ adj verhutzelt

wobb|le /'wɒbl/ vi wackeln. ~**ly** adj wackelig

woke, woken /wəʊk, 'wəʊkn/ see **wake**[1]

wolf /wʊlf/ n (pl **wolves** /wʊlvz/) Wolf m

woman /'wʊmən/ n (pl **women**) Frau f. ~**izer** n Schürzenjäger m

womb /wu:m/ n Gebärmutter f

women /'wımın/ npl see **woman**

won /wʌn/ see **win**

wonder /'wʌndə(r)/ n Wunder nt; (surprise) Staunen nt ● vt/i sich fragen; (be surprised) sich wundern; I ~ **da** frage ich mich; I ~ **whether she is ill** ob sie wohl krank ist? ~**ful** adj wunderbar

won't /wəʊnt/ = **will not**

wood /wʊd/ n Holz nt; (forest) Wald m; **touch** ~! unberufen!

wood: ~**ed** /-ıd/ adj bewaldet.

~**en** adj Holz-; (fig) hölzern. ~**pecker** n Specht m. ~**wind** n Holzbläser pl. ~**work** n (wooden parts) Holzteile pl; (craft) Tischlerei f. ~**worm** n Holzwurm m

wool /wʊl/ n Wolle f ● attrib Woll-. ~**len** adj wollen

woolly /'wʊlı/ adj wollig; (fig) unklar

word /wɜ:d/ n Wort nt; (news) Nachricht f; **by** ~ **of mouth** mündlich; **have a** ~ **with** sprechen mit; **have** ~**s** einen Wortwechsel haben. ~**ing** n Wortlaut m. ~ **processor** n Textverarbeitungssystem nt

wore /wɔ:(r)/ see **wear**

work /wɜ:k/ n Arbeit f; (Art, Literature) Werk nt; ~**s** pl (factory, mechanism) Werk nt ● vi bei der Arbeit; **out of** ~ arbeitslos ● vi arbeiten; (machine, system:) funktionieren; (have effect) wirken; (study) lernen; **it won't** ~ (fig) es klappt nicht ● vt arbeiten lassen; bedienen (machine); betätigen (lever). ~ **off** vt abarbeiten. ~ **out** vt ausrechnen; (solve) lösen ● vi gut gehen, [1] klappen. ~ **up** vt aufbauen; sich (dat) holen (appetite); **get** ~**ed up** sich aufregen

workable /'wɜ:kəbl/ adj (feasible) durchführbar

worker /'wɜ:kə(r)/ n Arbeiter(in) m(f)

working /'wɜ:kıŋ/ adj berufstätig; (day, clothes) Arbeits-; **be in** ~ **order** funktionieren. ~ **class** n Arbeiterklasse f

work: ~**man** n Arbeiter m; (craftsman) Handwerker m. ~**manship** n Arbeit f. ~**shop** n Werkstatt f

world /wɜ:ld/ n Welt f; **in the** ~ auf der Welt; **think the** ~ **of s.o.** große Stücke auf jdn halten. ~**ly** adj weltlich; (person) weltlich gesinnt. **~-wide** adj & adv /-'-/ weltweit

worm /wɜːm/ n Wurm m

worn /wɔːn/ see wear ● adj abgetragen. **~-out** adj abgetragen; (carpet) abgenutzt; (person) erschöpft

worried /'wʌrɪd/ adj besorgt

worry /'wʌrɪ/ n Sorge f ● v (pt/pp worried) ● vt beunruhigen; (bother) stören ● vi sich beunruhigen, sich (dat) Sorgen machen. **~ing** beunruhigend

worse /wɜːs/ adj & adv schlechter; (more serious) schlimmer ● n Schlechtere(s) nt; Schlimmere(s) nt

worsen /'wɜːsn/ vt verschlechtern ● vi sich verschlechtern

worship /'wɜːʃɪp/ n Anbetung f; (service) Gottesdienst m ● vt (pt/pp -shipped) anbeten

worst /wɜːst/ adj schlechteste(r,s); (most serious) schlimmste(r,s) ● adv am schlechtesten; am schlimmsten ● n the ~ das Schlimmste

worth /wɜːθ/ n Wert m; £10's ~ of petrol Benzin für £10 ● adj be ~ £5 £5 wert sein; be ~ it (fig) sich lohnen. **~less** adj wertlos. **~while** adj lohnend

worthy /'wɜːðɪ/ adj würdig

would /wʊd/ modal verb I ~ do it ich würde es tun, ich täte es; ~ you go? würdest du gehen? he said he ~n't er sagte, er würde es nicht tun; what ~ you like? was möchten Sie?

wound¹ /wuːnd/ n Wunde f ● vt verwunden

wound² /waʊnd/ see wind²

wove, woven see weave²

wrangle /'ræŋgl/ n Streit m

wrap /ræp/ n Umhang m ● vt (pt/pp wrapped) ~ [up] wickeln; einpacken (present) ● vi ~ up warmly sich warm einpacken. **~per** n Hülle f. **~ping** n Verpackung f

wrath /rɒθ/ n Zorn m

wreath /riːθ/ n (pl ~s /-ðz/) Kranz m

wreck /rek/ n Wrack nt ● vt zerstören; zunichte machen (plans); zerrütten (marriage). **~age** n Wrackteile pl; (fig) Trümmer pl

wren /ren/ n Zaunkönig m

wrench /rentʃ/ n Ruck m; (tool) Schraubenschlüssel m; **be a ~** (fig) weh tun ● vt reißen; ~ **sth from s.o.** jdm etw entreißen

wrestl|e /'resl/ vi ringen. **~er** n Ringer m. **~ing** n Ringen nt

wretch /retʃ/ n Kreatur f. **~ed** adj elend; (very bad) erbärmlich

wriggle /'rɪgl/ n Zappeln nt ● vi zappeln; (move forward) sich schlängeln; ~ **out of sth** 𝟭 sich vor etw (dat) drücken

wring /rɪŋ/ vt (pt/pp wrung) wringen; (~ out) auswringen; umdrehen (neck); ringen (hands)

wrinkle /'rɪŋkl/ n Falte f; (on skin) Runzel f ● vt kräuseln ● vi sich kräuseln, sich falten. **~d** adj runzlig

wrist /rɪst/ n Handgelenk nt. **~-watch** n Armbanduhr f

write /raɪt/ vt/i (pt wrote, pp written, pres p writing) schreiben. ~ **down** vt aufschreiben. ~ **off** vt abschreiben; zu Schrott fahren (car)

'write-off n ≈ Totalschaden m

writer /'raɪtə(r)/ n Schreiber(in) m(f); (author) Schriftsteller(in) m(f)

writhe /raɪð/ vi sich winden

writing /'raɪtɪŋ/ n Schreiben nt; (handwriting) Schrift f; **in** ~ schriftlich. **~-paper** n Schreibpapier nt

written /'rɪtn/ see write

wrong /rɒŋ/ adj falsch; (morally) unrecht; (not just) ungerecht; **be** ~ nicht stimmen; (person:) Unrecht haben; **what's** ~? was ist los? ● adv falsch; **go** ~ (person:) etwas falsch machen; (machine:) kaputtge-

w

hen; (plan:) schief gehen ● n Unrecht nt ● vt Unrecht tun (+ dat). **~ful** adj ungerechtfertigt. **~fully** adv (accuse) zu Unrecht

wrote /rəut/ see write

wrung /rʌŋ/ see wring

wry /raɪ/ adj (-er, -est) ironisch; (humour) trocken

. . . .

Xx

Xmas /'krɪsməs, 'eksməs/ n Weihnachten nt

X-ray /'eks-/ n (picture) Röntgenaufnahme f; **~s** pl Röntgenstrahlen pl ● vt röntgen; durchleuchten (luggage)

. . . .

Yy

yacht /jɒt/ n Jacht f; (for racing) Segeljacht f. **~ing** n Segeln nt

yank /jæŋk/ vt 🆃 reißen

Yank n 🆃 Ami m 🆃

yap /jæp/ vi (pt/pp yapped) (dog:) kläffen

yard[1] /jɑːd/ n Hof m; (for storage) Lager m

yard[2] n Yard nt (= 0,91 m)

yarn /jɑːn/ n Garn nt; (🆃: tale) Geschichte f

yawn /jɔːn/ n Gähnen nt ● vi gähnen

year /jɪə(r)/ n Jahr nt; (of wine) Jahrgang m; **for ~s** jahrelang. **~ly** adj & adv jährlich

yearn /jɜːn/ vi sich sehnen (for

nach). **~ing** n Sehnsucht f

yeast /jiːst/ n Hefe f

yell /jel/ n Schrei m ● vi schreien

yellow /'jeləʊ/ adj gelb ● n Gelb nt

yelp /jelp/ vi jaulen

yes /jes/ adv ja; (contradicting) doch ● n Ja nt

yesterday /'jestədeɪ/ n & adv gestern; **~'s paper** die gestrige Zeitung; **the day before ~** vorgestern

yet /jet/ adv noch; (in question) schon; (nevertheless) doch; **as ~** bisher; **not ~** noch nicht; **the best ~** das bisher beste ● conj doch

Yiddish /'jɪdɪʃ/ n Jiddisch nt

yield /jiːld/ n Ertrag m ● vt bringen; abwerfen (profit) ● vi nachgeben; (Amer, Auto) die Vorfahrt beachten

yoga /'jəʊgə/ n Yoga m

yoghurt /'jɒgət/ n Joghurt m

yoke /jəʊk/ n Joch nt; (of garment) Passe f

yolk /jəʊk/ n Dotter m, Eigelb nt

you /juː/ pron du; (acc) dich; (dat) dir; (pl) ihr; (acc, dat) euch; (formal) (nom & acc, sg & pl) Sie; (dat, sg & pl) Ihnen; (one) man; (acc) einen; (dat) einem; **all of ~** ihr/Sie alle; **I know ~** ich kenne dich/euch/Sie; **I'll give ~ the money** ich gebe dir/euch/Ihnen das Geld; **it does ~ good** es tut einem gut; **it's bad for ~** es ist ungesund

young /jʌŋ/ adj (-er /-gə(r)/, -est /-gɪst/) jung ● npl (animals) Junge pl; **the ~** die Jugend f. **~ster** n Jugendliche(r) m/f; (child) Kleine(r) m/f

your /jɔː(r)/ adj dein; (pl) euer; (formal) Ihr

yours /jɔːz/ poss pron deine(r), deins; (pl) eure(r), euers; (formal, sg & pl) Ihre(r), Ihr[e]s; **a friend of ~** ein Freund von dir/Ihnen/euch; **that is ~** das gehört dir/

Ihnen/euch

your'self pron (pl **-selves**) selbst; (reflexive) dich; (dat) dir; (pl) euch; (formal) sich; **by** ~ allein

youth /juːθ/ n (pl **youths** /-ðːz/) Jugend f; (boy) Jugendliche(r) m. ~**ful** adj jugendlich. ~ **hostel** n Jugendherberge f

Yugoslavia /juːgəˈslɑːvɪə/ n Jugoslawien nt

....

Zz

....

zeal /ziːl/ n Eifer m

zealous /ˈzeləs/ adj eifrig

zebra /ˈzebrə/ n Zebra nt. ~ **crossing** n Zebrastreifen m

zero /ˈzɪərəʊ/ n Null f

zest /zest/ n Begeisterung f

zigzag /ˈzɪɡzæɡ/ n Zickzack m ● vi (pt/pp **-zagged**) im Zickzack laufen/ (in vehicle) fahren

zinc /zɪŋk/ n Zink nt

zip /zɪp/ n ~ **[fastener]** Reißverschluss m ● vt ~ **[up]** den Reißverschluss zuziehen an (+ dat)

'zip code n (Amer) Postleitzahl f

zipper /ˈzɪpə(r)/ n Reißverschluss m

zodiac /ˈzəʊdɪæk/ n Tierkreis m

zone /zəʊn/ n Zone f

zoo /zuː/ n Zoo m

zoological /zuːəˈlɒdʒɪkl/ adj zoologisch

zoolog|ist /zuːˈɒlədʒɪst/ n Zoologe m/-gin f. ~**y** Zoologie f

zoom /zuːm/ vi sausen. ~ **lens** n Zoomobjektiv nt

y
z

German irregular verbs

1st, 2nd, and 3rd person present are given after the infinitive, and past subjunctive after the past indicative, where there is a change of vowel or any other irregularity.

Compound verbs are only given if they do not take the same forms as the corresponding simple verb, e.g. *befehlen*, or if there is no corresponding simple verb, e.g. *bewegen*.

An asterisk (*) indicates a verb which is also conjugated regularly.

Infinitive	Past tense	Past participle
abwägen	wog (wöge) ab	abgewogen
ausbedingen	bedang (bedänge) aus	ausbedungen
backen (du bäckst, er bäckt)	backte (bäckte)	gebacken
befehlen (du befiehlst, er befiehlt)	befahl (befähle)	befohlen
beginnen	begann (begänne)	begonnen
beißen (du/er beißt)	biss (bisse)	gebissen
bergen (du birgst, er birgt)	barg (bärge)	geborgen
bewegen²	bewog (bewöge)	bewogen
biegen	bog (böge)	gebogen
bieten	bot (böte)	geboten
binden	band (bände)	gebunden
bitten	bat (bäte)	gebeten
blasen (du/er bläst)	blies	geblasen
bleiben	blieb	geblieben
braten (du brätst, er brät)	briet	gebraten
brechen (du brichst, er bricht)	brach (bräche)	gebrochen
brennen	brannte (brennte)	gebrannt
bringen	brachte (brächte)	gebracht
denken	dachte (dächte)	gedacht
dreschen (du drischst, er drischt)	drosch (drösche)	gedroschen
dringen	drang (dränge)	gedrungen
dürfen (ich/er darf, du darfst)	durfte (dürfte)	gedurft
empfehlen (du empfiehlst, er empfiehlt)	empfahl (empföhle)	empfohlen

Infinitive	Past tense	Past participle
erlöschen (du erlischst, er erlischt)	erlosch (erlösche)	erloschen
erschrecken* (du erschrickst, er erschrickt)	erschrak (erschäke)	erschrocken
erwägen	erwog (erwöge)	erwogen
essen (du/er isst)	aß (äße)	gegessen
fahren (du fährst, er fährt)	fuhr (führe)	gefahren
fallen (du fällst, er fällt)	fiel	gefallen
fangen (du fängst, er fängt)	fing	gefangen
fechten (du fichtst, er ficht)	focht (föchte)	gefochten
finden	fand (fände)	gefunden
flechten (du flichtst, er flicht)	flocht (flöchte)	geflochten
fliegen	flog (flöge)	geflogen
fliehen	floh (flöhe)	geflohen
fließen (du/er fließt)	floss (flösse)	geflossen
fressen (du/er frisst)	fraß (fräße)	gefressen
frieren	fror (fröre)	gefroren
gären*	gor (göre)	gegoren
gebären (du gebierst, sie gebiert)	gebar (gebäre)	geboren
geben (du gibst, er gibt)	gab (gäbe)	gegeben
gedeihen	gedieh	gediehen
gehen	ging	gegangen
gelingen	gelang (gelänge)	gelungen
gelten (du giltst, er gilt)	galt (gälte)	gegolten
genesen (du/er genest)	genas (genäse)	genesen
genießen (du/er genießt)	genoss (genösse)	genossen
geschehen (es geschieht)	geschah (geschähe)	geschehen
gewinnen	gewann (gewänne)	gewonnen
gießen (du/er gießt)	goss (gösse)	gegossen
gleichen	glich	geglichen
gleiten	glitt	geglitten
glimmen	glomm (glömme)	geglommen
graben (du gräbst, er gräbt)	grub (grübe)	gegraben
greifen	griff	gegriffen
haben (du hast, er hat)	hatte (hätte)	gehabt
halten (du hältst, er hält)	hielt	gehalten
hängen[2]	hing	gehangen
hauen	haute	gehauen
heben	hob (höbe)	gehoben
heißen (du/er heißt)	hieß	geheißen

Infinitive	Past tense	Past participle
helfen (du hilfst, er hilft)	half (hülfe)	geholfen
kennen	kannte (kennte)	gekannt
klingen	klang (klänge)	geklungen
kneifen	kniff	gekniffen
kommen	kam (käme)	gekommen
können (ich/er kann, du kannst)	konnte (könnte)	gekonnt
kriechen	kroch (kröche)	gekrochen
laden (du lädst, er lädt)	lud (lüde)	geladen
lassen (du/er lässt)	ließ	gelassen
laufen (du läufst, er läuft)	lief	gelaufen
leiden	litt	gelitten
leihen	lieh	geliehen
lesen (du/er liest)	las (läse)	gelesen
liegen	lag (läge)	gelegen
lügen	log (löge)	gelogen
mahlen	mahlte	gemahlen
meiden	mied	gemieden
melken	molk (mölke)	gemolken
messen (du/er misst)	maß (mäße)	gemessen
misslingen	misslang (misslänge)	misslungen
mögen (ich/er mag, du magst)	mochte (möchte)	gemocht
müssen (ich/er muss, du musst)	musste (müsste)	gemusst
nehmen (du nimmst, er nimmt)	nahm (nähme)	genommen
nennen	nannte (nennte)	genannt
pfeifen	pfiff	gepfiffen
preisen (du/er preist)	pries	gepriesen
raten (du rätst, er rät)	riet	geraten
reiben	rieb	gerieben
reißen (du/er reißt)	riss	gerissen
reiten	ritt	geritten
rennen	rannte (rennte)	gerannt
riechen	roch (röche)	gerochen
ringen	rang (ränge)	gerungen
rinnen	rann (ränne)	geronnen
rufen	rief	gerufen
salzen* (du/er salzt)	salzte	gesalzen
saufen (du säufst, er säuft)	soff (söffe)	gesoffen
saugen*	sog (söge)	gesogen
schaffen¹	schuf (schüfe)	geschaffen
scheiden	schied	geschieden
scheinen	schien	geschienen

Infinitive	Past tense	Past participle
scheißen (du/er scheißt)	schiss	geschissen
schelten (du schiltst, er schilt)	schalt (schölte)	gescholten
scheren[1]	schor (schöre)	geschoren
schieben	schob (schöbe)	geschoben
schießen (du/er schießt)	schoss (schösse)	geschossen
schlafen (du schläfst, er schläft)	schlief	geschlafen
schlagen (du schlägst, er schlägt)	schlug (schlüge)	geschlagen
schleichen	schlich	geschlichen
schleifen[2]	schliff	geschliffen
schließen (du/er schießt)	schloss (schlösse)	geschlossen
schlingen	schlang (schlänge)	geschlungen
schmeißen (du/er schmeißt)	schmiss (schmisse)	geschmissen
schmelzen (du/er schmilzt)	schmolz (schmölze)	geschmolzen
schneiden	schnitt	geschnitten
schrecken* (du schrickst, er schrickt)	schrak (schräke)	geschreckt
schreiben	schrieb	geschrieben
schreien	schrie	geschrie[e]n
schreiten	schritt	geschritten
schweigen	schwieg	geschwiegen
schwellen (du schwillst, er schwillt)	schwoll (schwölle)	geschwollen
schwimmen	schwamm (schwömme)	geschwommen
schwinden	schwand (schwände)	geschwunden
schwingen	schwang (schwänge)	geschwungen
schwören	schwor (schwüre)	geschworen
sehen (du siehst, er sieht)	sah (sähe)	gesehen
sein (ich bin, du bist, er ist, wir sind, ihr seid, sie sind)	war (wäre)	gewesen
senden[1]	sandte (sendete)	gesandt
sieden	sott (sötte)	gesotten
singen	sang (sänge)	gesungen
sinken	sank (sänke)	gesunken
sitzen (du/er sitzt)	saß (säße)	gesessen
sollen (ich/er soll, du sollst)	sollte	gesollt
spalten*	spaltete	gespalten
spinnen	spann (spänne)	gesponnen
sprechen (du sprichst, er spricht)	sprach (spräche)	gesprochen
sprießen (du/er sprießt)	spross (sprösse)	gesprossen
springen	sprang (spränge)	gesprungen

Infinitive	Past tense	Past participle
stechen (du stichst, er sticht)	stach (stäche)	gestochen
stehen	stand (stünde, stände)	gestanden
stehlen (du stiehlst, er stiehlt)	stahl (stähle)	gestohlen
steigen	stieg	gestiegen
sterben (du stirbst, er stirbt)	starb (stürbe)	gestorben
stinken	stank (stänke)	gestunken
stoßen (du/er stößt)	stieß	gestoßen
streichen	strich	gestrichen
streiten	stritt	gestritten
tragen (du trägst, er trägt)	trug (trüge)	getragen
treffen (du triffst, er trifft)	traf (träfe)	getroffen
treiben	trieb	getrieben
treten (du trittst, er tritt)	trat (träte)	getreten
triefen[*]	troff (tröffe)	getroffen
trinken	trank (tränke)	getrunken
trügen	trog (tröge)	getrogen
tun (du tust, er tut)	tat (täte)	getan
verderben (du verdirbst, er verdirbt)	verdarb (verdürbe)	verdorben
vergessen (du/er vergisst)	vergaß (vergäße)	vergessen
verlieren	verlor (verlöre)	verloren
verzeihen	verzieh	verziehen
wachsen[1] (du/er wächst)	wuchs (wüchse)	gewachsen
waschen (du wäschst, er wäscht)	wusch (wüsche)	gewaschen
wenden[2][*]	wandte (wendete)	gewandt
werben (du wirbst, er wirbt)	warb (würbe)	geworben
werden (du wirst, er wird)	wurde (würde)	geworden
werfen (du wirfst, er wirft)	warf (würfe)	geworfen
wiegen[1]	wog (wöge)	gewogen
winden	wand (wände)	gewunden
wissen (ich/er weiß, du weißt)	wusste (wüsste)	gewusst
wollen (ich/er will, du willst)	wollte	gewollt
wringen	wrang (wränge)	gewrungen
ziehen	zog (zöge)	gezogen
zwingen	zwang (zwänge)	gezwungen

Englische unregelmäßige Verben

Infinitiv	Präteritum	2. Partizip	Infinitiv	Präteritum	2. Partizip
be	was	been	**drive**	drove	driven
bear	bore	borne	**eat**	ate	eaten
beat	beat	beaten	**fall**	fell	fallen
become	became	become	**feed**	fed	fed
begin	began	begun	**feel**	felt	felt
bend	bent	bent	**fight**	fought	fought
bet	bet,	bet,	**find**	found	found
	betted	betted	**flee**	fled	fled
bid	bade, bid	bidden, bid	**fly**	flew	flown
bind	bound	bound	**freeze**	froze	frozen
bite	bit	bitten	**get**	got	got, gotten *US*
bleed	bled	bled	**give**	gave	given
blow	blew	blown	**go**	went	gone
break	broke	broken	**grow**	grew	grown
breed	bred	bred	**hang**	hung,	hung,
bring	brought	brought		hanged	hanged
build	built	built	**have**	had	had
burn	burnt,	burnt,	**hear**	heard	heard
	burned	burned	**hide**	hid	hidden
burst	burst	burst	**hit**	hit	hit
buy	bought	bought	**hold**	held	held
catch	caught	caught	**hurt**	hurt	hurt
choose	chose	chosen	**keep**	kept	kept
cling	clung	clung	**kneel**	knelt	knelt
come	came	come	**know**	knew	known
cost	cost,	cost,	**lay**	laid	laid
	costed (*vt*)	costed	**lead**	led	led
cut	cut	cut	**lean**	leaned,	leaned,
deal	dealt	dealt		leant	leant
dig	dug	dug	**learn**	learnt,	learnt,
do	did	done		learned	learned
draw	drew	drawn	**leave**	left	left
dream	dreamt,	dreamt,	**lend**	lent	lent
	dreamed	dreamed	**let**	let	let
drink	drank	drunk	**lie**	lay	lain

Englische unregelmäßige Verben

Infinitiv	Präteritum	2. Partizip	Infinitiv	Präteritum	2. Partizip
lose	lost	lost	spend	spent	spent
make	made	made	spit	spat	spat
mean	meant	meant	spoil	spoilt,	spoilt,
meet	met	met		spoiled	spoiled
pay	paid	paid	spread	spread	spread
put	put	put	spring	sprang	sprung
read	read	read	stand	stood	stood
ride	rode	ridden	steal	stole	stolen
ring	rang	rung	stick	stuck	stuck
rise	rose	risen	sting	stung	stung
run	ran	run	stride	strode	stridden
say	said	said	strike	struck	struck
see	saw	seen	swear	swore	sworn
seek	sought	sought	sweep	swept	swept
sell	sold	sold	swell	swelled	swollen,
send	sent	sent			swelled
set	set	set	swim	swam	swum
sew	sewed	sewn, sewed	swing	swung	swung
shake	shook	shaken	take	took	taken
shine	shone	shone	teach	taught	taught
shoe	shod	shod	tear	tore	torn
shoot	shot	shot	tell	told	told
show	showed	shown	think	thought	thought
shut	shut	shut	throw	threw	thrown
sing	sang	sung	thrust	thrust	thrust
sink	sank	sunk	tread	trod	trodden
sit	sat	sat	under-	under-	understood
sleep	slept	slept	stand	stood	
sling	slung	slung	wake	woke	woken
smell	smelt,	smelt,	wear	wore	worn
	smelled	smelled	win	won	won
speak	spoke	spoken	write	wrote	written
spell	spelled,	spelled,			
	spelt	spelt			

Abbreviations/Abkürzungen

adjective	*adj*	Adjektiv
abbreviation	*abbr*	Abkürzung
accusative	*acc*	Akkusativ
Administration	*Admin*	Administration
adverb	*adv*	Adverb
American	*Amer*	amerikanisch
Anatomy	*Anat*	Anatomie
attributive	*attrib*	attributiv
Austrian	*Aust*	österreichisch
Motor vehicles	*Auto*	Automobil
Aviation	*Aviat*	Luftfahrt
Botany	*Bot*	Botanik
collective	*coll*	Kollektivum
Commerce	*Comm*	Handel
conjunction	*conj*	Konjunktion
Cookery	*Culin*	Kochkunst
dative	*dat*	Dativ
definite article	*def art*	bestimmter Artikel
demonstrative	*dem*	Demonstrativ-
Electricity	*Electr*	Elektrizität
something	*etw*	etwas
feminine	*f*	Femininum
figurative	*fig*	figurativ
genitive	*gen*	Genitiv
Geography	*Geog*	Geographie
Grammar	*Gram*	Grammatik
impersonal	*impers*	unpersönlich
inseparable	*insep*	untrennbar
interjection	*int*	Interjektion
invariable	*inv*	unveränderlich
someone	*jd*	jemand
someone (dat)	*jdm*	jemandem
someone (acc)	*jdn*	jemanden
someone's	*jds*	jemandes
Law	*Jur*	Jura
Language	*Lang*	Sprache
masculine	*m*	Maskulinum